A MODERN HISTORY

OF

NEW LONDON COUNTY

CONNECTICUT

EDITOR-IN-CHIEF

BENJAMIN TINKHAM MARSHALL, A.M., D.D.

PRESIDENT OF CONNECTICUT COLLEGE, NEW LONDON

VOLUME III

1922
LEWIS HISTORICAL PUBLISHING COMPANY,
NEW YORK CITY

HISTORY OF
NEW LONDON COUNTY

CHARLES Q. ELDREDGE—Now seventy-six years of age, Mr. Eldredge resides at "Riverview Cottage," Old Mystic, Connecticut, the place of his birth, and on the ground where his parents, Christopher and Nancy Eldredge, passed their lives and left a record of love and helpfulness that will long endure. Mr. Eldredge has seen all sides of life, and had a great variety of experience during his three-quarters of a century. He early broke away from home environment, and in western lumber camps and on western rivers developed a strength of body, mind and character that well fitted him for the place in mercantile life that he was to fill. He started with limited education and without financial backing, but, endowed with common sense, clear vision, courage and willingness to work, he rose from lowly place to the head of large business interests and finally returned to the place of his birth, where he has built a new house, and in beautiful Riverview he has a home which is a model of convenience and comfort, with private workshop, garage, and a private "museum" where over three thousand souvenirs are on exhibition, and where, free of all charge, visitors are welcomed. Christened Charles Eldredge, he at first in mischief but later legally added the middle initial "Q," which he has now used for half a century.

Mr. Eldredge is a descendant of Samuel Eldred, born in England in 1620, died in Kingston, Rhode Island, in 1697. The line of descent to Charles Q. Eldredge, of Old Mystic, is through the founder's son, Captain Daniel Eldredge, of Kingston, Rhode Island, and Stonington, Connecticut, captain of the militia and deputy to the General Court. He died at North Kingston, Rhode Island, August 18, 1726. He added a final "ge" to the name. From him the line continues through his son, James Eldredge, born December 5, 1696, died 1738; his son, Christopher Eldredge, born January 22, 1722, a soldier of the Revolution, wounded during Arnold's attack on New London, September 6, 1781, died in Stonington, Connecticut, 1811; his son, Joshua Eldredge, born in Stonington, August 9, 1769, died there August 17, 1836; his son, Christopher Eldredge, born in Stonington, November 14, 1798, died in Old Mystic, Connecticut, July 26, 1884; his son, Charles Q. Eldredge, born in Old Mystic, New London county, Connecticut, July 15, 1845, and there now residing (May 1, 1921).

Charles Q. Eldredge, eighth and youngest of the children of Christopher and Nancy (Taylor) Eldredge, spent his early youth at the home of his parents in Old Mystic, and obtained his education in the district school. He was employed by various men of his village, at farm, tannery, and quarry, earning meagre wages in accordance with the custom of his day. At the age of seventeen he had the unusual experience of taking a journey to Norfolk, Virginia, where his brother was in the hospital from disabilities received in battles of the Civil War. With his sister-in-law and six months baby, the lad, Charles Q., who had never been more than seven miles from home, started South to visit the sick husband and brother. He made the journey safely, and at Norfolk, after finding his brother much better, he acted for a time as hospital steward at the United States Army Hospital, and later returned home. In December, 1862, he started for Wisconsin with Elisha D. Wightman under contract to work for the latter one year at a salary of one hundred and twenty-five dollars, and on the way to Werner, Wisconsin, narrowly escaped serious injury in a railroad accident that killed or wounded every passenger in the car but Mr. Wightman and Mr. Eldredge.

There he went into a lumber camp; his first winter in the woods was most severe, but he came through, and although he had some trouble with frozen feet, he never lost a day from duty. He was soon given responsibility, he was made time-keeper and had the handling of the payroll, and was a person of influence. He was employed in the woods, on the drive, and at the mills on Yellow river during the first year with E. D. Wightman & Company. Gurdon S. Allen and George F. Langworthy, of Mystic, were interested with Mr. Wightman. At the end of his first year January-December, 1863, he had half a year's wages of the one hundred and twenty-five dollars on hand, and returned to Mystic, where he visited for two weeks, then renewed his contract with E. D. Wightman & Company at a salary of five hundred dollars, and returned to the lumber camp in Wisconsin. During that year he was given still more responsibility and placed in charge of the saw mills after the log drive was over. The next winter he was placed in charge of one of the logging camps, and although under twenty he received a salary of one thousand dollars and capably performed the duty required of him. From logging, driving, sawing, and running a camp, he was advanced to higher position and sent down the river with the rafts, selling the lumber and returning with the money. For eight years the Mississippi river was his home, his business being to find markets for the lumber, subsistence for the raftsmen, and to pay off the men. It was at that time that the old time raftsmen and Mississippi river steamboat men were the roughest, toughest and all around meanest combination that ever existed. In "The Story of a Connecticut Life," Mr. Eldredge says: "My experience would lead me to agree with the classification but I should insist on exceptions."

Each year in camp and mill and on the Wisconsin river was a repetition of its predecessor until finally, in 1869, Mr. Wightman, who had moved from Mystic to Werner, became involved through his bad habits and his partner, Gurdon S. Allen, sold out, and finally the business went into the hands of a receiver, and even under that management paid ninety-five per cent of all claims. Werner, then a place with a post-office, two large hotels, and the largest saw mill on the river, is now obliterated with nothing to mark the place.

With the collapse of E. D. Wightman & Company, in 1869, Mr. Eldredge, with B. F. Miner, bought a farm of one hundred and sixty acres and began raising hops, succeeding however, in "going broke," but paid one hundred cents on the dollar. In the winter of 1870 Mr. Eldredge returned to Mystic to attend his parent's Golden Wedding, and in the spring of 1871 he began running the sloop "Maria" as a freighter, continuing through the season. In 1872 he farmed in Mystic, and in July, 1873, sold out and with the eight thousand and five hundred dollars that he received, he entered into a partnership in M. F. White & Company, in Hoosick Falls, New York, and in September, 1873, was married, and until 1893 resided in Hoosick Falls. In November, 1876, his partner died, and some time later Mr. Eldredge bought his interest together with all real estate formerly owned by the company.

In Hoosick Falls, Mr. Eldredge built and operated a large wood-working factory in connection with his lumber yard, built and conducted the only grist mill for miles around, ran a machine shop, furnished rooms and power to a shirt factory working several hundred girls, rooms and power to a toy factory, and employed a large force of building mechanics, contracting and erecting over two hundred buildings during the years he spent in Hoosick Falls. He was also instrumental in erecting and equipping a knit goods factory, employing two hundred hands, he being superintendent of the mill and treasurer of the corporation for two years. He was one of the two men who secured the incorporation of the First National Bank, of Hoosick Falls, an institution strong and stable and an honor to its promoters.

In 1893 Mr. Eldredge sold his business in Hoosick Falls, he being at that time, next to Walter A. Wood, the largest individual taxpayer of the town. The business, which in 1873 totaled sales of thirteen hundred dollars monthly, had increased in 1893 to thirteen thousand dollars monthly, and the village had increased from twenty-five hundred inhabitants to seventy-five hundred, many of whom were attracted to the village by the opportunity for employment in the many industries established and operated by Mr. Eldredge, and in which he had an interest.

In 1893, he returned to Old Mystic, to the house, "Riverview," which he had built in 1890, and in 1893 he sold his Hoosick Falls real estate, realizing eleven thousand, three hundred dollars for what had cost him in cash one hundred and thirteen thousand dollars, the purchase later making the purchaser the richest man in Hoosick Falls. To make warrantee deeds, no mortgage had to be discharged, as Mr. Eldredge, during his business life, never signed one.

"Riverview," with its thirty-acre park, was its owner's hobby, and during the next decade he built a fine dam, a mile and a half of good roads, trimmed six thousand trees, large and small, that grew wild in the park, dug a well near a log summer house, set out over three thousand catalpa trees, built an observation tower one hundred and twenty-five feet high, and made it an ideal home. In 1904 his youngest son met a tragic death, and as "Riverview" had been planned for him to run, Mr. Eldredge at once advertised it for sale, but not until April, 1913, was a sale effected. In 1904, he made a personal trip to Jamaica, West Indian Islands, and in 1911, having acquired an interest in a citrus fruit plantation in Porto Rico, he visited that island and others of the West Indies, and returned to Connecticut in 1912.

The old homestead, built in 1850, at Old Mystic, in which his parents spent practically their entire sixty years of married life, had been burned down in 1890 and rebuilt by Mr. Eldredge as a tenant house. He moved into that house after the sale of "Riverview" and gradually enlarged it until "Riverview Cottage" has been evolved, a beautiful home fronting on the Mystic river, a model of comfort. In 1917 he built a small building, twenty by twenty feet, the entire construction of that building, excavation, rock foundation, inside finish, tin work, decorating and lettering, all the personal work of Mr. Eldredge. This he fitted up as a private museum, and placed there the many souvenirs he has collected in his many journeys. The museum has proved of interest to the public, and during its first year five hundred visitors registered. He has issued a complete catalogue of the museum's three thousand curios.

A Republican in politics, Mr. Eldredge would never accept office, but in Hoosick Falls, in response to a signed petition, he did consent to serve as village trustee for two years.

Mr. Eldredge married Jennie Waitstill Leavens, in September, 1873, at Lansingburg, New York, and in 1895 his wife, her sister, and mother, all died of typhoid fever at Hoosick Falls, within a period of thirty days. Three children were born to Mr. and Mrs. Charles Q. Eldredge, as follows: 1. Charles Leavens, born at Hoosick Falls, New York, now a Baptist minister at West Bridgewater, Massachusetts; he married May Frink, of old Mystic, and they are the parents of three children: Reginald, deceased; Margarette, and Amethyst. 2. Jennie White, born at Hoosick Falls, New York; she married Frederick Munich, of Bridgeport, Connecticut, and they have two children: Frederick Eldredge and Margaret. 3. Clarence Quincy, born at Hoosick Falls, died at Old Mystic, at eighteen years of age.

Mr. Eldredge married his present wife, Estelle Gilpatrick, at Groton, Massachusetts, January 1, 1891, and in 1893 returned to Mystic and now resides at "Riverview Cottage." In 1919, Mr. Eldredge published "The Story of a Connecticut Life," a record of his long, useful career, which is most interesting. Of this book writes R. W. Shannon, of Albany:

"I have read your book and shall give myself the pleasure of reading it again; yes, several times. I know somewhat of your life, but the details impress me deeply, and your power to master difficult situations and successfully shoulder and carry forward great responsibilities ought to be an incentive to those who will read your book."

The book has had its second printing, and so many kind letters have been received by Mr. Eldredge from its readers, that he has published a pamphlet of forty-nine pages in which he prints many of them under the title, "Kind Words."

ARTHUR GALLUP WHEELER—Since attaining man's estate, Arthur G. Wheeler has cultivated the Cherry Hill farm which his father had previously bought. Later the son purchased the farm from his father, and there he has passed the years which have since intervened, its owner and active manager. Arthur Gallup Wheeler is a son of Nelson H. Wheeler, a "Forty-Niner," and long a New London county farmer, son of Samuel Wheeler, son of Joseph Wheeler, son of Richard (2) Wheeler, son of Richard (1) Wheeler, son of Isaac Wheeler, son of Thomas Wheeler, who came from Lynn, Massachusetts, to Stonington, Connecticut, in 1667, and was made a freeman in 1669, represented Stonington in the General Court in 1673, and in 1674 was one of the nine members forming the organization of the Road Church in Stonington. His wife Mary was one of the first partakers of the communion service in that church. From Thomas and Mary Wheeler, through their only son, Isaac, spring the large and honorable New London Wheeler family.

Samuel Wheeler, of the sixth generation, was born September 14, 1784, and died March 24, 1852. He was a lifelong Democrat, selectman, assessor, liberal supporter of the old Road Church, and all his life a farmer. He married, in 1809, Rebecca Prentice, who died December 9, 1842, the mother of eight children, one of whom was a son, Nelson H. Wheeler, father of Arthur Gallup Wheeler, of Cherry Hill Farm.

Nelson H. Wheeler was born at the homestead in Stonington, March 28, 1827, and there the first eighteen years of his life were passed. He attended district school, and was his father's farm assistant until 1845, when he started out for himself, working as farmer, carpenter and peddler for three years, until he caught a bad case of "gold fever." He took the only way to effect a sure cure, and on January 26, 1849, sailed in the ship "Trescott" for California, rounding the "Horn" and arriving at the Golden Gate in six months and thirteen days. He worked for one year at mining, then engaged in farming and teaming near Sacramento, finally coming home via the Isthmus, in 1853, having been gone more than four years. He farmed the homestead until 1901, when he moved to Mystic, town of Groton, New London county, Connecticut, where he died January 18, 1904.

Nelson H. Wheeler married, April 3, 1853, Melinda Gallup, born in the town of Ledyard, New London county, Connecticut, November 2, 1831, and died August, 1911, daughter of Luke and Melinda (Williams) Gallup. They began their married life at the Wheeler homestead built prior to the Revolution by Nelson H. Wheeler's grandfather, Joseph Wheeler, born January 23, 1747, who occupied it with his wife, Prudence (Palmer) Wheeler, to whom he was married September 18, 1774. Nelson H. and Melinda (Gallup) Wheeler occupied the homestead forty-eight years, 1853 to 1901, then turned it over to their son, George A. Wheeler, who yet owns and cultivates its acres, and moved to Mystic. Three years later, in 1904, Nelson H. Wheeler died, and seven years later, in 1911, Mrs. Wheeler joined her husband in the Spiritland. They were both members of the Baptist church, and were highly esteemed. Nelson H. and Melinda (Gallup) Wheeler were the parents of eight children: 1. Samuel N., born May 20, 1854, a graduate of Boston University, and a school teacher until his death in 1896. 2. Lilla M., born January 4, 1857, died March 30, 1885. 3. Arthur Gallup, of further mention. 4. Mary S., born April 20, 1860, died January 22, 1895; married Rev. O. G. Buddington. 5. Herman E., born April 20, 1862, died April 6, 1885. 6. Agnes M., born May 2, 1864, married Frank L. Lathrop, of Norwich, Connecticut. 7. Fernando, born June 16, 1866 (q.v.). 8. George A., born May 15, 1874, now the owner of the homestead upon which he was born; he married Lucille Billings Thompson.

Arthur Gallup Wheeler, of the eighth generation of his family in New London county, Connecticut, was born at the Wheeler homestead in the town of Stonington, now owned by his brother, October 3, 1858, and there spent the years of his minority. He was educated in the public schools and in Mystic Valley Institute. Upon arriving at legal age, his father purchased the Joseph Davis place, otherwise known as Cherry Hill Farm, in the town of Stonington, and after teaching school for one year, Arthur G. Wheeler took the active management of the farm, which later he bought. He has, with his brother Fernando, handled a great deal of the fruit raised in the district, and has a well cultivated, fertile farm which he has greatly improved since becoming its owner. Mr. Wheeler is a Democrat in his political faith, and has taken an active part in town affairs. For eight years he was collector of taxes, and represented his district in the Connecticut House of Representatives from 1892 to 1893. He is a member of Asylum Lodge, Free and Accepted Masons, and of the Old Mystic Baptist Church.

Mr. Wheeler married, June 7, 1893, Mary Billings, born in North Stonington, May 15, 1877, daughter of Sanford and Emmeline Billings. Mr. and Mrs. Wheeler are the parents of seven children: 1. Nelson Farnsworth, born February 25, 1894. 2. Mary Starr, born September 14, 1895, a graduate of Wellesley College, now in bond department, Guaranty Trust Company, New York City. 3. Arthur Gallup (2), born April 13, 1897. 4. Donald Billings, born

June 28, 1900. 5. Dorothy Billings, twin with Donald Billings. 6. A child who died in infancy. 7. Melinda Williams, born July 23, 1909.

These three sons of Nelson H. Wheeler, Arthur G., Fernando and George A. Wheeler, are all located in the town of Stonington, and near the homestead owned by five generations of their family. More than two and one-half centuries have elapsed since Thomas Wheeler, the American ancestor, settled in Stonington, and the record shows no falling off in the quality of the Wheeler stock. It is one of the strong families of the town, and its twentieth century representatives are worthy.

ERNEST AVERY LATHROP—The Lathrop name is an honored one in New England, and nowhere more so than in New London county, Connecticut, where the family was founded by Samuel Lathrop, who was brought from England by his father, Rev. John Lathrop, in 1634. Rev. John Lathrop come into open conflict with the Archbishop of London, where he was pastor of an Independent church, and with forty-three members of his church was arrested, April 29, 1632, and thrown into prison. While he was in prison, his wife died and finally he was released on the condition that he would leave England. Accordingly he sailed with his children, and in 1634 arrived in New England. He founded a church in Scituate, Massachusetts, and with many of his congregation moved to Barnstable.

Samuel Lathrop was a builder of Boston, and a farmer of Barnstable, finally settling in now New London, Connecticut, where he became one of the judges of the local court organized in 1649. In 1668 he moved to Norwich, Connecticut, where he was chosen constable. He married (first), November 28, 1644, in Barnstable, Elizabeth Scudder. They were the parents of nine children, their eldest, a son, John, baptized December 7, 1645, their youngest a daughter, Anne, born August 7, 1667. Samuel Lathrop married (second), in 1690, Abigail Doane, born January 29, 1632, daughter of Deacon John Doane, of the Plymouth Colony. She survived her husband thirty-four years, living to the great age of one hundred and two. On the centennial anniversary of her birth, her friends assembled at her home and listened to a sermon preached by her pastor, a part of the celebration. She preserved to a remarkable degree her mental powers until her death in 1734, her husband having passed away in 1700. It is from Samuel and Elizabeth (Scudder) Lathrop that Ernest Avery Lathrop, of the town of Montville, descends.

Ernest A. Lathrop is a son of John Lathrop, who was born in Bozrah, New London county, Connecticut, in 1836, and now (1920), at the age of eighty-four years, still farms the old Lathrop homestead in Bozrah. He married (second) Sarah Elizabeth Thomas, born in Colchester, Connecticut, in July, 1840, died in April, 1914. She was a widow with two sons and a daughter when married to John Lathrop, one of these sons, William Brown, now living at the farm of his half-brother, Ernest Avery Lathrop, and assisting in its cultivation.

Ernest A. Lathrop, son of John and Sarah Elizabeth (Thomas) Lathrop, was born in Norwich, Connecticut, January 16, 1873, and there educated in the public schools. In early life he drove a stage between Norwich and Ledyard Center, but after two years in that position entered the employ of Edward Johnson, a farmer of Uncasville. He was engaged in farming and later in teaming until 1901, when he bought the Fred Parker farm in the town of Montville, where he has taken leading rank among the enterprising, successful farmers of his town. His farm is very productive, and his dairy herd contains some very fine Holsteins and all are graded cattle. He uses all modern aids to successful farming, and is very progressive.

Mr. Lathrop was married, October 17, 1894, by Rev. John Avery, at Norwich, to Julia Estell Avery, daughter of Belton Avery, one of the old whaling mariners, born in 1853, died 1901, and Mary Augusta (Reynolds) Avery, who yet survives her husband, and is a resident of Norwich.

CHARLES GILES TURNER—For thirty-four years Mr. Turner has been engaged in carriage and wagon building in Upper Montville and Montville, twenty-three of those years in partnership with his brother-in-law and eleven under his own name. He is one of the best-known men in his town, and hardly a farmer in Montville but at some time has patronized the Turner wheelwright shops. Charles G. Turner is a son of Giles Turner, of Groton, Connecticut, now deceased, and his wife, Hannah (Rathburn) Turner, who with her husband is buried in Comstock Cemetery in the town of Montville, Connecticut. They were the parents of four sons: Irving; Willis; Hazzard, deceased; Charles Turner, of further mention; and a daughter Elizabeth.

Charles Giles Turner was born in Waterford, New London county, Connecticut, November 8, 1852. He was but an infant when his parents moved to the town of Montville in the same county, his home situated on Lake Konomoc. He was educated in the public schools, and until reaching legal age made his home with his parents and helped his father in his farming operations. He spent a few years in the employ of Captain Fitch, then for six years was engaged with Charles Johnson, of Uncasville, Connecticut, in the dye works, in charge of his horses. After a short experience in a general store as clerk, Mr. Turner became associated with his brother-in-law in the carriage building business, and for twenty-three years they operated a plant in Upper Montville. In 1909 Charles G. Turner started business in the same line, under his own name in Montville, and there has since been engaged very successfully. Mr. Turner is a Republican in politics, has served as a member of the town Board of Selectmen, and as an official of the Probate Court. He is a member of Oxoboxo Blue

Lodge, Free and Accepted Masons, and a man highly regarded by his townsmen.

Mr. Turner married Ianthe Browning, of Montville, born May 8, 1856, daughter of Isaac and Martha (Howe) Browning. Mrs. Turner has a brother, Silas, of Montville, and a sister, Martha Brainard. Mr. and Mrs. Turner are members of the Montville Center Congregational church.

CHARLES BURR GRAVES, M.D., was born in the city of Chicago, Illinois, June 10, 1860, a son of Addison and Helen M. (Eaton) Graves. Since early boyhood he has resided in New London, Connecticut, receiving his schooling in the public schools of that city. After preparing for college at Bulkeley High School he entered Yale College and graduated therefrom in 1882 with the degree of Bachelor of Arts. His medical education was obtained at the Harvard Medical School, from which he obtained the degree of M. D. in 1886. His medical course was followed by an interneship in the Boston City Hospital from 1885 to 1887. Soon afterwards he settled in New London, Connecticut, where he has ever since continued to reside and practice medicine.

Besides meeting the many demands of the life of an active general practitioner, Dr. Graves has held several offices of importance. From 1896 to 1907 he served as coroner's physician for the town and city of New London. He was one of the original members of the medical and surgical staff of the New London Memorial Hospital, and secretary from its founding until 1908. He is at present a senior member of the staff of the Lawrence and Memorial Associated Hospitals.

Since entering upon medical practice in 1887 he has been a member of the New London County Medical Association and the Connecticut Medical Society, and was president of the latter in 1920. His address on that occasion was on "Epidemic Diseases in Early Connecticut Times." He is also one of the charter members of the New London (City) Medical Society.

He has held several other public trusts, having been long a member of the board of trustees of Bulkeley School, and having served for many years as trustee of the Manwaring Memorial Hospital and the Public Library of New London. He is also an active member of several botanical and historical societies. In connection with his interest in botanical matters, may be mentioned the fact that he was a member of the committee from the Connecticut Botanical Society which prepared the account of "The Flowering Plants of Connecticut" for the Connecticut Geological and Natural History Society. He also wrote the very exhaustive chapter of Medical History in this work ("History of New London County").

Dr. Graves married, September 10, 1891, Frances M. Miner, of New London, Connecticut. Of their children one daughter, Elizabeth Waterman, born 1898, survives.

BENJAMIN STERRY GALLUP—The old associations which cluster around the homesteads of New London county hold a sacred charm for the student of history, both that history recorded in the printed volume and that spread forth upon the face of nature. For grouped among the wild woods and fields are to be found innumerable records of loving labors performed by hands now forever quiet. In Sprague, Connecticut, the home of the late Benjamin Sterry Gallup still shows the constructive effort of the man now gone, and the careful preservation of the landmarks of a generation long passed out of human ken.

The Gallup family came to New England in the earliest days of its history, some of its members settling in Connecticut but a few years later. Wherever they have settled, members of each generation have been prominent in public affairs, taking part in the Indian wars, in the Revolution and in the civic affairs of community, county, and State. The immigrant ancestor of the family was John Gallup, a native of the parish of Mosterne, Dorsetshire, England, who sailed from Plymouth in 1630, in the ship "Mary and John," arriving at Hull. His wife, Christobel, and children, followed three years later. Mr. Gallup was a son of John Gallup, and a grandson of Thomas and Agnes (Watkins) Gallup, of North Bowood and Strode, whose descendants still own and occupy the manors of Strode. John Gallup, the emigrant, went first to Dorchester, and soon afterward to Boston, where both he and his wife were admitted to the First Church in 1634. He owned Gallup's Island, and was a skillful mariner, achieving distinction by piloting the ship "Griffin," in September, 1633, through a newly found channel when Rev. John Cotton, Rev. Thomas Hooker, and Rev. Mr. Stone were among her 200 passengers. He died in Boston, January 11, 1655, and his wife died there September 27, 1655. Their children were: John, Samuel, and Nathaniel.

Captain John Gallup, born in England, came to this country in 1633. He became a famous Indian fighter and is supposed to have assisted his father in the capture of John Lodham's vessel off Block Island. For distinguished service in the Pequot War, the General Court of Connecticut, in 1671, gave him a grant of 100 acres of land, and in 1650 or 1651 he came to New London. He was also given other tracts of land, and in 1654, he, with his family, removed to the east side of the Mystic river, now Stonington. In 1665 and in 1667 he represented the town in the General Court. Joining the New London county Company, at the head of the Mohegans, under Captain John Mason, of Norwich, he was engaged in the fearful Swamp fight at Narragansett, December 19, 1675, and there, at the head of his men, storming the fort, he, with six other captains, fell in the fight. He married, in 1643, Hannah, daughter of John and Margaret Lake. Their children were: Hannah, John, Esther, Banadam, William, Samuel, Christobel, Elizabeth, Mary, and Margaret.

John Gallup, son of Captain John (2) Gallup, born about 1646, made his home in Stonington where he wedded Elizabeth Harris. Their children were: John, Thomas, Margaret, Samuel, Elizabeth, Nathaniel, William, and Benjamin. Nathaniel Gallup, son of John and Elizabeth (Harris) Gallup, was born July 4, 1682, married June 4, 1717, Margaret Gallup, born May 11, 1698, daughter of Banadam and Hester (Prentiss) Gallup, and resided in Stonington, Connecticut, on the Greenman farm, near the residence of Warren Lewis. They united with the Congregational church, Stonington, July 20, 1718. Their children were: Nathaniel, John, Thomas, Mercy, Margaret, Martha, and Benjamin.

Benjamin (1) Gallup, son of Nathaniel and Margaret (Gallup) Gallup, was born in Stonington, July 26, 1736, and on January 20, 1763, in Voluntown, he was married to Amy Kinne, by the Rev. Levi Hart. Their thirteen children were: Nathaniel, Zeuriah, Thomas, Amy, Mercy, Benjamin, Lucy, Martha, Esther, Margaret, Cynthia, Eunice, and Keturah.

Benjamin (2) Gallup, son of Benjamin and Amy (Kinne) Gallup, was born in Voluntown, May 25, 1774, and was a prosperous farmer and large landholder in his native town. He also engaged in the lumber business for ship building, shipping the timber to Mystic. He died and was buried on the home farm. He was a member of the Baptist church and in politics was a Jacksonian Democrat. On January 30, 1806, by the Elder Peleg Randall, he was married to Huldah Gallup, who also died on the home farm in the faith of the Baptist church, and was buried in the family cemetery there. Their two children were: Amy, born June 13, 1808, married Benjamin Gallup, and resided in Voluntown; and Benjamin, born July 10, 1811.

Benjamin (3) Gallup, son of Benjamin (2) Gallup, and father of Benjamin Sterry Gallup, was born on the old Gallup homestead. He received a substantial education in the schools of his district, and for several terms taught school in Voluntown and vicinity. He early engaged in farming, however, and to his farming interests added the business of shipping lumber for ship building to Mystic, Connecticut, and to Westerly, Rhode Island. He was active in public affairs, serving as selectman for a number of terms; as a member of the board of relief; as school visitor; as justice of the peace; and, for two terms as representative to the state legislature. He gained the high reputation of being one who, in public office, set aside personal interests, devoting the powers of the office and his personal abilities to the public good. He married, October 30, 1831, Caroline Kinne, a descendant of an old and honored family. She died November 15, 1874, aged sixty-one years, a noble, Christian woman, devoted to her home and family. Benjamin (3) Gallup died on the home farm September 2, 1891, at the age of four score, and was also buried in the family cemetery on the farm. The children of Benjamin (3) and Caroline (Kinne) Gallup were: Laura C., who married Avery A. Stanton, of Sterling, Connecticut; Benjamin Sterry, of whom further; Miss Amy, who lives on the homestead; Edwin Byron, who died in infancy; Edwin Byron, born on the homestead, August 13, 1846, married Mary Burdick, and resides in Voluntown; Origen S., born December 31, 1849, deceased, and buried in the family cemetery on the farm; his widow and children still live on the farm; and Albert, who died in Hartford in 1915, and is buried in Scotland, Connecticut. Benjamin (3) Gallup was again married, September 18, 1878, to Fidelia Chapman, who survives him and lives on the homestead.

Benjamin Sterry Gallup, son of Benjamin (3) and Caroline (Kinne) Gallup, was born in Voluntown, April 18, 1840. At an early age he attended school at Connecticut Literary Institute, at Suffield, Connecticut, and also attended the Academy at East Greenwich, Rhode Island, after which he taught in several schools in Voluntown. He was a young man of high ideals, and with fine mental endowment, and was a very successful teacher. Later, for a time, he was a merchant in Voluntown. In April, 1871, Mr. Gallup came to the present family home, in the town of Sprague, near Baltic. This farm was at the time known as the Gordon Place, and after purchasing it, Mr. Gallup made the necessary repairs, carefully preserving the characteristics which clearly distinguished the period of the house, which was one of the first frame houses built in the State of Connecticut. The kitchen of the present home was used in the old days as slave quarters. The farm is a part of a grant of land amounting to one thousand acres, received from Chief Uncas by one Perkins, who built the house.

On this farm Mr. Gallup became a resident of the town of Sprague. During the remainder of his life he conducted the farm and filled a prominent and esteemed position in the daily life of the town. His ability as a man of affairs, and the breadth of his learning were soon recognized by the townspeople and he was called to the public service as second selectman, then as assessor, and was also given important responsibilities on the school committee. His work in these various branches of the town government was always progressive, never self-seeking, and the man was a source of inspiration to his associates. Those who now recall his public life remember Mr. Gallup as a man of great force and decision, yet possessed of the breadth of view that considers every side of a question before committing himself to definite action. Such men are all too few in every branch of human endeavor.

The death of Mr. Gallup, on March 18, 1920, left a gap in the ranks of the public-spirited men of Sprague, and a sense of loss in the hearts of his many friends. His name will be spoken long after his contemporaries have all taken the "path" along which he preceded them, and the work which he laid down will still live, since no worthy effort can die.

Mr. Gallup married Helena Roxa, daughter of Kinney and Harriet (Robbins) Gallup, and they became the parents of eight children: Algernon Sterry, born in Griswold, Connecticut, married Lorena Bell Tyler, of Centerville, Rhode Island, and lives in Centerville; Josephine Kinney, born in Griswold, now the wife of Hubert Allen, of North Agawam, Massachusetts; Caroline Augusta, born in Griswold, a very successful teacher; Oscar Byron, born in Griswold; Harriet Robbins, born in Griswold, died in Sprague, July 10, 1884; Jennie Chapman, born in Sprague, Connecticut, a music teacher of considerable success; Kinney Benjamin, born in Sprague, July 15, 1875, died August 28, 1876; Winfred Cleon, born in Sprague, married Ellen G. Johnson, and is a resident of Norwood, Rhode Island.

Mrs. Benjamin Sterry Gallup, a woman of unbounded hospitality, died May 29, 1914, and the family home is now owned by Oscar B., Caroline A., and Jennie C. Gallup, all of whom live in the homestead made dear to them by life-long association, and by loving memories of those who have passed on, leaving this home as a monument to their industry, their skill and their loving care for their family.

JAMES MITCHELL YOUNG—A successful business man, owner and manager of a large meat market at the corner of Main and Market streets, Norwich, Mr. Young has proved in his life the value of work as a means of developing property in business.

Alexander Young, father of James Mitchell Young, was born in Scotland, and died in Vermont in 1898. He obtained his education in the district school of his native place. When a young man he came with his father, George Young, to the United States, and they settled in Greensboro, Vermont, where they bought a farm which they conducted for a number of years. Alexander Young sold out his interests in the farm to his father, and bought a farm on his own account which he managed until his death. In politics he was a Republican, and was always active in promoting the welfare of the community. In religion he was a Presbyterian, and for many years was deacon of the church there. He married Mary White, and to them were born four children: Jason, a resident of Nashua, New Hampshire; James M., mentioned below; Jennie, now deceased, was formerly the wife of David A. Johnson, of Montville, Connecticut; Hattie, wife of John Findlay, of Greensboro.

James Mitchell Young was born in Greensboro, Vermont, in 1856, the son of Alexander and Mary (White) Young. He received his elementary education in the district schools of his native place, and then entered North Cashbury Academy, from which he was graduated in 1876, after which he went immediately to Norwich, Connecticut, and entered upon his business career, securing a position as clerk in the grocery store of his uncle, Joseph Prentiss, where he remained for three years. In 1880 he became clerk in the transportation office of the New York, New Haven & Hartford railroad and was so employed until 1886, when he returned to his uncle and entered into partnership with him. This partnership continued until his uncle's death in 1894, when James Mitchell Young bought the entire business and continued successively for twenty-two years, finally selling out his interests and travelling to South Dakota, where he bought a half section of land and cultivated it for two years. He then returned to Connecticut, subsequently going to Willimantic, where he bought a market which was owned by Frank Larabee, and managed this for about two years, and then removed to Norwich and bought the grocery business of W. H. Cardwell and also the market of Louis Fraser and moved the two concerns to his present location where he has since this consolidation met with unbounded success. Mr. Young, in connection with this market, owns forty acres of cultivated land, where he raises an enormous supply of vegetables for his trade, also owning a large poultry farm from which he supplies his store with eggs. In politics Mr. Young is a Republican, and has always taken a keen interest in the activities of the party. For nine years he was town clerk and treasurer of Preston county. In religion he is a Baptist.

Mr. Young married, in Norwich, Elizabeth C. Storm, daughter of John and Josephine (Prentiss) Storm, and they are the parents of three children: Marion L., an instructor in Middlebury College, Vermont; John B., served with the hospital unit in the Army of Occupation during the World War, and is now associated with his father in business; James Mitchell, Jr., associated with his father in business, married Ruth Hale, of Willimantic; he also served in the World War.

CHARLES ALLEN CHAPMAN—Held in the highest esteem by his contemporaries, and prominent in every good work of the town, the death, in 1913, of Charles Allen Chapman, of Montville, Connecticut, was regarded as a great loss to the community.

Politically Mr. Chapman had been very active, holding at different times every office connected with public affairs. In the business life of Montville he had for many years been a merchant, for the last forty years of his life conducting a successful grocery establishment. His death occurred when seventy-four years of age, and he was buried in the local cemetery.

Charles Allen Chapman married (first) Mary Edwards, by whom he had one child, Nellie Evelyn, who died in 1918, at the age of forty-eight years. Mr. Chapman married (second) Laura Comstock, of Montville, a daughter of Nathan and Caroline (Whipple) Comstock, the former-named one of the original settlers of Montville. The family of his wife, the Whipples, had been closely identified with the life of New London county since public records had been kept.

The Comstock family is one of the oldest in this

part of the United States, their original ancestor coming to this country in 1620, when the "Mayflower" brought the English refugees from Holland. A sister of Mrs. Laura (Comstock) Chapman is Carrie Comstock, a member of the exclusive organization, "The Daughters of the Mayflower." Their brother was the late Judge Comstock, who during his lifetime was a very able lawyer, prominently known throughout the State.

By his second marriage Charles Allen Chapman and his wife, Laura (Comstock) Chapman, had four children: 1. Charles Everett, born in Montville, February 17, 1878; he is engaged in the grocery business. 2. Mildred May, born May 29, 1886. 3. Florence Caroline, who during the World War was in the service of her country as an ambulance driver in France, in one of the units organized by Mrs. J. Pierpont Morgan; the duty to which Miss Chapman was assigned was the work of following in the wake of battle, assisting in the rescue of the wounded soldiers, and in giving relief to refugees; Florence Caroline Chapman is now postmistress of Palmertown. 4. Laura Comstock, born June 13, 1900; married Mark Furber, and resides in Montville.

The widow of Charles Allen Chapman, Mrs. Laura (Comstock) Chapman, is still residing at her home in Montville, aged sixty-four years. She is a member of the Baptist church of Montville, Connecticut.

DR. ERNEST JAMES JONES has spent fourteen years in Norwich, Connecticut, and these have been years of arduous devotion to the advancement of the dental profession which have placed him in the front rank of the city's practicing dentists.

John S. Jones, father of Dr. Ernest J. Jones, was born in Wales, in 1834, and came to America when a young man, locating in Quebec, where he owns a large farm, and although eighty-six years of age he is still very active and devotes much of his time to agriculture. He married Sarah Davidson, a native of Montreal, Canada, and they are the parents of five children: 1. Charles, born in Quebec, now residing in Williamstown; married Emma Burgess, and they have one child, Sarah. 2. Lillian, wife of George Schuler, of Williamstown. 3. Fred W., a farmer in Quebec; married Elizabeth Cross, of New York City. 4. John, now residing on the farm in Quebec; married Annie Curley, and they have two children, Gordon and Margaret. 5. Ernest James, mentioned below.

Dr. Ernest James Jones was born in Bondville, Province of Quebec, Canada, July 9, 1877. The childhood of Dr. Jones was passed in his native place, and it was there that the preparatory portion of his education was received. After graduating from the high school, he worked on his father's farm for seven years, and then having decided to make the dental profession his career, matriculated in the dental department of the University of Maryland, from which he was graduated in 1904. In 1906 he opened his office in the Shannon block, Norwich, and since that time he has made his headquarters at this place and developed a large and high-class practice, so that he is now regarded among the leaders of his profession here. In politics he is a Republican, and quite unambitious for political preferment. Dr. Jones holds a prominent place in Masonic circles, being a member of Brome Lake Lodge, No. 35, Free and Accepted Masons; Franklin Chapter, Royal Arch Masons; Columbia Commandery, Knights Templar; Sphinx Temple, Ancient Arabic Order Nobles of the Mystic Shrine, and has attained to the thirty-second degree of the Masonic order.

Dr. Jones was united in marriage with Agnes V. McKee, June 27, 1908. Mrs. Jones is the daughter of James and Virginia C. (Humes) McKee; her father was a toolmaker and machinist for the Hopkins & Allen Arms Company for many years. Dr. and Mrs. Jones are the parents of three children: James, born June 9, 1909; Gwendolyn, born July 14, 1910; Pauline, born February 25, 1914.

REV. WILLIAM THOMAS O'BRIEN was born in Portland, Connecticut, September 4, 1882. He is a son of William and Elizabeth (Wall) O'Brien, both natives of County Cork, Ireland, the former having been born there in 1842, the latter, August 11, 1847. His father came to Portland, Connecticut, when a young man, establishing himself in business as a merchant, in which he continued successfully until his death, which occurred July 16, 1897. To Mr. and Mrs. O'Brien were born six children: Michael, Katherine, Mary; William Thomas, of further mention; Delia, and Anna.

The early education of William Thomas O'Brien was obtained in the parochial schools of Portland, St. Johns and New Haven, after which he entered St. Thomas' Seminary at Hartford, Connecticut, where he remained five years. After graduating he went to Paris, France, and there continued his theological studies, where still later he was ordained to the priesthood, on June 29, 1907. Returning to his native land his first assignment was at St. Anne's Church at Waterbury, Connecticut, where he labored eleven years and ten months. Here his work won recognition from his superiors, and appreciation and love from his parishioners. On November 13, 1918, Father O'Brien was appointed pastor of the Catholic church at Baltic where he has since continued with the hearty coöperation of his parishioners and is supported in his work.

Life holds no more beautiful relationship than that which a Catholic priest bears to his people and his people bear to him. From the cradle to the grave he is one whose patience never falters and whose helping hand is never withdrawn. Come what will within the range of human experience, in its midst, you will find the priest toiling, not for himself, but for those he loves. This is the type of priest, this is the manner of friend, this is the kind of pastor Father O'Brien is to all who know him; a noble man full of courage, zeal, and devotion, and abiding religious faith.

Clement L. Perkins

CHARLES HENRY LATHAM, one of the most influential citizens of Griswold, Connecticut, where he has held many positions of responsibility and trust and where he is engaged in the farming business on a large scale, is a member of a family which for many years has resided in New London county, Connecticut.

Henry Brown Latham, father of Charles Henry Latham, was born in Ledyard, Connecticut, and obtained his education in his native place. Later he moved with his parents to North Stonington, Connecticut, and here most of his time was given to aiding his father in the work about the farm, which the latter had purchased upon his arrival in this town. After the father's death Henry Brown Latham continued to cultivate and develop the property until 1914, when he retired from active business life and has since resided at Bean Hill, Norwich, Connecticut. He married Eunice Hewett, and to them were born two children: Emily H., who died at the age of six years; Charles Henry, of further mention. Mrs. Latham died March 19, 1917.

Charles Henry Latham was born July 20, 1870, in North Stonington, Connecticut. His childhood was spent on his father's farm, and his educational advantages were exceedingly meagre. Mr. Latham, however, is one of those characters which are keenly observant and he has learned much in the hard school of experience, especially about that all important subject, his fellow-men. He continued to reside with his parents until he was twenty-four years of age, when he rented a farm in Preston and was there two years. In 1896 he went to Westerly, Rhode Island, where he secured employment in a stone quarry, continuing until 1903 as foreman. He then returned to the home farm in North Stonington, where he continued to remain until 1908, during which time he was continually gaining a wide and extensive knowledge of the subject of farming and becoming well skilled in agricultural methods generally. In the year 1908 he purchased his present farm in the town of Griswold and has here resided up to the present time, the place being formerly known as the Andrew Edmond farm. This property was naturally a fertile one and he has developed and cultivated it to a highly productive state, his place being regarded as one of the well conducted properties in this region.

Charles Henry Latham is one of those who are instinctively interested in the welfare of the communities where they reside, and he has given no little time and energy to the conduct of public affairs. He is a Republican in politics, and has identified himself closely with the local organization of his party which elected him in 1917-1918 to the office of selectman of Griswold. He is a member of Pachaug Grange and the New London County Farm Bureau. He is also affiliated with the Knights of Pythias, Undaunted Lodge, and attends the local Congregational church.

Charles Henry Latham married, June 26, 1894, Susie Champlin, daughter of John M. and Lucy Chesebrough, of North Stonington, Connecticut. Mr. and Mrs. Latham are the parents of two children: 1. Charles Harold, who at the beginning of the World War enlisted in Company F, 26th Division of Hartford, Connecticut, but was later discharged as physically unfit, and subsequently joined the Merchant Marine service, in which he continued as steward during the war. 2. Lewis P., resides at home.

CLEMENT LEROY PERKINS—In the farming circles of Hanover, the name of Perkins is one which is held in high esteem for ability and public spirit. The position won in the community by Clement Leroy Perkins, the result of his own efforts and ability, is at the same time in accordance with the family tradition.

Josiah Perkins, great-grandfather of Mr. Perkins, was a captain in the war of the Revolution, having come to this country in the early part of the Seventeenth Century. He had a son, Charles, who married Betsey Payne. Charles Perkins was a farmer and served as captain in the United States Army during the War of 1812.

Jonathan Perkins, son of Charles and Betsey (Payne) Perkins and father of Clement Leroy Perkins, was born at Hanover, Connecticut, May 15, 1814, in what was known as the Ladd place, which was built by Josiah Perkins upon the latter's arrival in this country. The boy Jonathan, attended the schools of his native place, and after completing his education, adopted teaching as a profession and also became a civil engineer. A man of most engaging personality, true to his friendships, honest, and impeccable in all the relations of life, Mr. Perkins was highly respected and honored by all who knew him. He married (first) Jane Willoughby and had one child. Later he married Mary F. Hebbard, of which marriage there were nine children of whom two are living: William Dwight, born July 23, 1855; Clement Leroy, of further mention. Mr. Perkins died February 4, 1899.

Clement Leroy Perkins, son of Jonathan and Mary F. (Hebbard) Perkins, was born at Canterbury, Connecticut, March 27, 1857. He was educated in the schools of his native place, and at Plainfield Academy, after which he devoted some time to the work upon his father's farm, later moving to Norwich. He there established himself in the jewelry business and for twelve years was travelling salesman for his own enterprise, after which time he sold out this business and returned to agricultural pursuits. He purchased a farm on Scotland road which he later sold, and bought the Kingsley Place on Plain Hill. Here he remained until 1917, when he came to Hanover and purchased his present farm, upon which he has since resided, devoting himself exclusively to the cultivating of his property. During the World War, however, Mr. Perkins worked in the gun shop of Hopkins & Allen, in Norwich, for a time. Although he displays a deep interest in the welfare of the town, which is his home, he remains strictly aloof from public and political life, but is well known and eminently respected throughout the community.

On August 24, 1887, Clement Leroy Perkins was united in marriage with Mary Northup, daughter of William and Emiline Northrup. Mr. and Mrs. Perkins are the parents of one child, Emerson, born September 29, 1890. They are members of the Central Baptist Church, of Norwich.

JAMES THOMAS WILBUR—Having been identified with the American Thread Company at Glasgo, Connecticut, since 1899, James Thomas Wilbur, as agent of this company, prospered financially, and is held in high regard by his business associates. Up to the time of his resignation, he was identified with this particular line of industry, and won his way to the high position of agent of the above company through untiring effort and a fixed determination to succeed.

Thomas Wilbur, father of James Thomas Wilbur, was born in South Kingstown, Rhode Island, the son of William and Mary (Tift) Wilbur. He was educated in the district schools of his native place, and associated with the cotton industry throughout his entire lifetime. About 1854 he moved with his family to Grosvenor Dale, Connecticut, and there entered the employ of the Grosvenor Dale Company. For twenty years previous to his retirement from active business life, he was superintendent of the company, giving faithful, efficient service, fully appreciated by those with whom he was so long associated and held in high esteem as a citizen. He married Sarah Briggs, who died at North Grosvenor Dale, in 1904, at the age of seventy-seven years. To Mr. and Mrs. Wilbur were born three children: 1. Grace, who died in infancy. 2. Leander, who married Oriana Arnold, of Woodstock, Connecticut; he died at North Grosvenor Dale, in 1890. 3. James Thomas, of further mention.

James Thomas Wilbur was born in North Grosvenor Dale, township of Thompson, Connecticut, September 19, 1858, and there received a common school education. At the age of sixteen, business life began for the boy, his first employment being with the Grosvenor Dale Company. Here he served an apprenticeship as a machinist and remained for five years, resigning at the end of that time to enter Bryant & Stratton's Business College at Providence, Rhode Island. One year later he returned to his former employers, this time as bookkeeper, and remained there until 1883, when he came to Glasgo and accepted the position as office manager of the Glasgo Yarn Mill. Seven years later, in 1890, he was promoted to the superintendency of the entire plant, a position he filled until 1899, when the American Thread Company bought this mill, and then Mr. Wilbur was again promoted to his present position of agent. On April 1, 1921, Mr. Wilbur resigned his position as agent for the American Thread Company and bought the drug store known as Soule's Pharmacy, at Jewett City, Connecticut, where he now resides. Mr. Wilbur has been a potent factor in the industrial world, and is one of the strong men of his day upon whose shoulders are laid heavy burdens of development and management.

Mr. Wilbur was identified with several movements for the welfare of Glasgo during his residence there, and was a member of its educational board for many years. A Republican in politics, he has always maintained a deep interest in civic affairs, yet the concerns of his business preclude his taking active part in politics. A Methodist in religion, he attends the church of that denomination at Voluntown.

On September 15, 1880, James Thomas Wilbur was united in marriage with Ida May Robbins, daughter of David N. and Elizabeth (Joslin) Robbins, of East Thompson, Connecticut. Mr. and Mrs. Wilbur are the parents of four children: Edith May, who married H. D. Pollard, assistant cashier of the Windham bank at Willimantic, Connecticut; Sarah Elizabeth, who married Eli G. Lague, of Jewett City, Connecticut; Robert Allen, a mill man of Glasgo, married Grace E. Bicknell; Ralph Carlton, a shipping clerk in the employ of his father.

AZARIE DAYON, one of the most progressive and prosperous business men of Glasgo, Connecticut, where he is owner of a large general store and mercantile business, is a native of Woonsocket, Rhode Island, his birth having occurred there October 24, 1881. He is a son of Edmond and Melina (Langevin) Dayon.

Edmond Dayon was born in the Province of Quebec, and there in the public schools of his native place obtained his education. At the age of eighteen he came to the United States, locating in Woonsocket, Rhode Island, where for several years he was employed in the nearby cotton mills, later removing with his family to Glasgo, Connecticut, since which time he has been an employee of the carding department of the American Thread Company. To Mr. and Mrs. Dayon have been born thirteen children, Azarie, of further mention, being the eldest living child at the present time.

Azarie Dayon was brought by his parents to Glasgo when a young child, and here attended the local public schools. At an early age, however, he terminated his studies and then the business of life began for the lad. His first employment was as clerk in the general store of Dearnley & Clark at Glasgo, where he remained for several years, later resigning in order to accept a clerkship with Oscar Dugas, for whom he worked until 1916, when he bought out the interests of the elder man and has since conducted the business on his own account. Mr. Dayon has been very successful in this venture, his ability as a business man having been fully tested and proven, and under his capable management the business has greatly increased. In politics Mr. Dayon has always been a Republican, and

Chas A. Kuebler

he has been active in public affairs, having served as postmaster of the Glasgo office since 1917, during which time he has proved himself an able and efficient public-spirited citizen. He is a Roman Catholic in religion, and is affiliated with the Foresters of America, Liberty Court, No. 132, of Voluntown, Connecticut.

On January 13, 1905, Azarie Dayon was united in marriage with Amelia La Croix, of Putnam, Connecticut. Mr. and Mrs. Dayon are the parents of six children: Diana, Amelia, Armand, Yvonne, Bella, and Adele.

JOHN FRANCIS FIELDS—Among the pioneer Irish settlers of Lebanon, New London county, Connecticut, was Thomas Fields, born in the parish of Fahram, County Kerry, Ireland, who came to the United States and to Lebanon, Connecticut, when a young man. He settled down to the life of a farmer, and by industry and thrift prospered. He married Catherine Lyons, born in Ireland, who died in Fitchville, Connecticut, the mother of seven children: Elizabeth, married Jeremiah Lynch; Margaret, who since 1886 has been an employee of the Palmer Brothers Mill at Fitchville, she one of the very oldest employees of that corporation in point of years of service; Anna, an employee of the same mill since 1887; Thomas; John Francis, of further mention; Timothy, an employee of Palmer Brothers Mill; and Jeremiah.

John Francis Fields, fifth child of Thomas and Catherine (Lyons) Fields, was born in Lebanon, Connecticut, January 13, 1877. He attended the public schools, and during his youth and early manhood was his father's farm assistant, giving his parents the full benefit of his services until arriving at legal age. In 1898 he entered Palmer Brothers Mill at Fitchville, there becoming a mill overseer, a position he resigned in October, 1918. He then bought the general store in Fitchville, formerly operated by Louis Brand, and there continues to conduct very successfully a general store. He has always taken a deep interest in local politics, and in June, 1919, was appointed postmaster of Fitchville. Mr. Fields is a Democrat in politics, and in 1908 was elected to represent the town of Bozrah in the State Legislature, and during the session he served on committees on woman suffrage and house rules. In 1910 he was reëlected, serving during the session of 1911 on the committee of education. He was a member of the Grand Jury of New London county, 1907-08, and since 1909 has been a member of the school board of the town of Bozrah. He was tax collector for the town of Bozrah, 1912 to 1919. He is a member of St. John's Roman Catholic Church, and White Cross Council, No. 13, Knights of Columbus, of Norwich.

Mr. Fields married, in Fitchville, Connecticut, October 27, 1907, Julia Marie McManus, born in Sprague, New London county, Connecticut, daughter of John and Margaret (Doyle) McManus, her father deceased, her mother living in Norwich. Mr. and Mrs. Fields are the parents of three children, all born in Fitchville: Catherine, Margaret, and Theresa.

CHARLES AUGUSTUS KUEBLER was born in Würtemberg, Germany, September 1, 1852, died in Norwich, Connecticut, May 22, 1912. He was a son of William Frederick Kuebler, a goldsmith, of Würtemberg. The latter became involved in the political turmoil of his times, siding with the Revolutionists, and to escape capture, came to the United States about 1860. He enlisted in the Union army and served during the Civil War, then returned to Germany, where he died about 1895. His wife also died in Germany in 1878, leaving two children: Charles A. and Henrietta, both of whom came to the United States, and both are now deceased, Henrietta dying in Baltimore, Maryland, and Charles A. in Norwich, Connecticut. Other children of William Frederick Kuebler died young.

Charles A. Kuebler was educated in Germany, in the public and high schools, and also attended college in Stuttgart, Germany. He remained in Germany until 1869, then, at the age of seventeen, came to the United States, locating in Washington, D. C., with his sister Henrietta. He soon left that city and was in different localities until finally he located in Norwich, Connecticut. That was in 1871, and his first employer was Michael Rourke, a maker of monuments, and a contractor. Michael Rourke died in 1885, and Mr. Kuebler bought his business from the heirs and conducted a very successful monumental business until his death. In 1888 he bought the property which he had been renting as a business location, and there, on Franklin street, he remained until his death.

Mr. Kuebler was at the head of a very extensive business, which he had practically built up through his own efforts. He was a self-made man, everything which he possessed having been earned by his own labor and business ability. He was highly esteemed and had many friends. He never sought political preferment, but his sole interest outside his business was his home and family. He was an expert designer, and his monuments compare with the best in the many New England cemeteries in which they are found. His masterpiece was the Masonic monument erected in Norwich to the memory of Judge Charles Carter. He was a Democrat in politics, and a thirty-second degree Mason, affiliating with St. James Lodge, Free and Accepted Masons; Franklin Chapter, Royal Arch Masons; Franklin Council, Royal and Select Masters; Columbian Commandery, Knights Templar; King Solomon Lodge of Perfection; Van Rensselaer Council, Princes of Jerusalem; Norwich Chapter of Rose Croix; Connecticut Consistory, Supreme Princes of the Royal Secret, all of Norwich; Sphinx Temple, Ancient Arabic Order Nobles of the Mystic Shrine, of Hartford, Connecticut; Shetucket Lodge, Independent Order of Odd Fellows, of Norwich, and the Norwich Business Men's Association. During his lifetime Mr. Kuebler ran his business under his own name as a private concern, but since his death it has been incorporated as the Charles A. Kuebler Company.

Mr. Kuebler married, in Norwich, April 30, 1874, Kate Elizabeth Metzger, born in Norwich, Connecticut, daughter of Casper and Isabella Metzger, her parents born in Germany. Four children were born to Mr. and Mrs. Kuebler, all born in Norwich: Henrietta Isabella, married Frank R. Smith and resides in Norwich; Isabella Henrietta, married Frank J. Stanley and resides in New Haven, Connecticut; Julia Burnham, married Herbert M. Hitchom, and resides in Norwich; and Mary Elizabeth, who married Daniel J. McCormick, and resides in Norwich.

Mrs. Kuebler and her four daughters survive their husband and father, to whom they were devoted. He was very fond of his home and family and there spent his hours off duty. He is greatly missed, not alone in the home circle where his memory is forever enshrined, but in the city among his business associates.

WILLIAM BRADFORD CASEY, M.D.—Numbered among the professional men of high standing in the city of Norwich, Connecticut, is Dr. William Bradford Casey, son of John and Ellen (Sheridan) Casey.

John Casey, father of Dr. Casey, was born in Cavan, Ireland, and received his education in the National Schools of that country. He came to the United States when a young man, twenty-two years of age, locating in the city of Buffalo, New York. There he worked as a general blacksmith for contractors and builders during the remainder of his life. He died in Illinois, in the year 1905. His wife, who was born in Buffalo, New York, survives him, and is now a resident of Norwich. They were the parents of two children: William Bradford; and Moran, now deceased.

Dr. Casey was born in Buffalo, New York, May 3, 1880. He received his early education in the public schools of that city, then went to the District of Columbia, entering the Georgetown Preparatory College. In 1902 he entered the University of Maryland Medical School, Baltimore, from which institution he was graduated in the year 1906, with the degree of Doctor of Medicine. For one and one-half years thereafter he gained his hospital training at the Columbus Hospital, of New York City, then came to Norwich, Connecticut, where he established himself in private practice. In a short time Dr. Casey won the confidence of the people of Norwich, and has steadily risen in his profession until now he stands among the leaders. He is a member of the Norwich Medical Society, and of the New London County and Connecticut State Medical societies.

Dr. Casey has few interests outside his profession, but keeps abreast of the times in all matters of public interest. Politically he throws his influence on the side of the Democratic party. He is a member of Norwich Lodge, No. 430, Benevolent and Protective Order of Elks. He is a devout member of the Roman Catholic church.

ARTHUR CHESTER BROWN—In 1896, at the age of fifteen, Arthur Chester Brown entered the employ of The Falls Company at the Cotton Mill plant in Norwich, and through all the twenty-three years which have since elapsed he has been true to that first employer, and through a series of merited promotions he has risen to the position of agent and manager. He is a son of Seth Leeds Brown, also a textile mill official until his passing, September 10, 1916.

Seth Leeds Brown was born in Ledyard, Connecticut, March 24, 1850. He there attended the public schools, later being a student in a select school in Preston. At the age of eighteen, with his brother, Aaron A. Brown, he built a woolen mill on the site of the old Ayers factory, later known as Shewville, and for several years the A. A. and S. L. Brown Company conducted a woolen yarn manufacturing business. In 1879, business reverses compelled them to assign, and the plant passed under the control of A. P. Sturtevant, of Norwich, who operated it, with Seth L. Brown as overseer of the carding and spinning departments until 1891. In that year, Mr. Brown transferred his services to the H. B. Porter & Son Company, of Norwich, and was in the employ of that company at the time of his passing. He married Margaret (Cantwell) Brown. Three children were born to Mr. and Mrs. Seth L. Brown: Arthur Chester, of further mention; George Seth, born December 1, 1882, married Henrietta Frances James, now superintendent of the Asland Cotton Company (see sketch appearing elsewhere in this work); Albert Seymour, died in Norwich, June 28, 1908, aged twenty years.

Arthur Chester Brown was born in the town of Ledyard, New London county, Connecticut, May 7, 1881. He was educated in the public schools of Norwich. In 1896 he entered the employ of The Falls Company in their cotton mill in Norwich, and there he has in every department and in practically every position gained a complete knowledge of cotton manufacturing. In 1908 he was appointed assistant superintendent; he was overseer of the finishing department; in 1912 was appointed superintendent of the mill; and in 1914 agent and manager of The Falls Company.

In politics Mr. Brown is a Republican, and has been active in party work as a member of the town committee for several years. He is affiliated with Somerset Lodge, No. 34, Free and Accepted Masons; Franklin Chapter, No. 3, Royal Arch Masons; Franklin Council, No. 4, Royal and Select Masters; Columbian Commandery, Knights Templar; and Connecticut Consistory, Valley of Norwich, thirty-second degree, Ancient Accepted Scottish Rite, all of Norwich; Sphinx Temple, Ancient Arabic Order Nobles of the Mystic Shrine, of Hartford, Connecticut; Loyal Order of Moose; Norwich Lodge, No. 950, Independent Order of Odd Fel-

lows; the Arcanum Club; Chamber of Commerce; and Park Congregational Church.

Mr. Brown married Isabella Yeomans, daughter of George P. and Margaret (MacNichol) Yeomans, of Norwich.

CHARLES I. BARSTOW—A native of Connecticut, as were his parents, Charles I. Barstow is interested in everything connected with his State and town, whether it be in business, politics, religion or organized work. His father, Charles T. Barstow, was born in Bozrah, Connecticut, and in his boyhood was a pupil in the district school in that village. When of suitable age he learned a trade, and some years later became a stationary engineer, so continuing for the remainder of his life, living in different places. He died in Mystic, Connecticut, in 1908. He married Sarah J. Backus, who is yet a resident of Mystic, and to them were born two sons: Charles I., of further mention; and Louis F., who married Lillian Glidhill, of Mystic, where they now reside.

Charles I. Barstow was born in Windham, Connecticut, May 1, 1879. After passing through the primary and grammar schools of South Windham, he completed his education at the Windham High School of Willimantic. In 1901 he located in Mystic, where he obtained employment in the printing shop of A. A. Kidder, there remaining until becoming thoroughly conversant with the art of printing. Later Mr. Barstow established a printing business under his own name, conducting a stationery store in connection with the print shop. He has been very successful in both lines, and is still engaged in the business. Politically, Mr. Barstow is an Independent in thought and action. He is much interested in fraternal societies, and is a member of Stonington Lodge, No. 26, Independent Order of Odd Fellows; Charity and Relief Lodge, No. 72, Free and Accepted Masons; Benevolent Chapter, Royal Arch Masons.

Mr. Barstow married Ella M. Wilcox, of Boston, Massachusetts, and they are the parents of two children: Leander W., and Howard L. The family home is in Mystic, Connecticut.

EDMOND JOSEPH JODOIN—A good example of the successful business man who has risen through his own efforts to a position of prominence in the community is Edmond J. Jodoin, a man honored and respected, whose word is good and whose character is above reproach. He was born in North Grosvenor Dale, Connecticut, February 8, 1887, son of Frederick and Laura (Chartier) Jodoin, the former-named a native of Ware, New Hampshire.

Frederick Jodoin attended the district school, securing a practical education, and in young manhood turned his attention to the meat-cutting business, following this for several years in various localities. He then changed his line of work to something entirely different, accepting a position as agent for the Metropolitan Insurance Company of New York, and so continued until his death, which occurred at his home in Jewett City, Connecticut, March 13, 1906. His wife, Laura (Chartier) Jodoin, a native of Quebec, Province of Quebec, Canada, survives her husband, residing in Jewett City at the present time (1920). They were the parents of nine children of whom Edmond Joseph was the third in order of birth.

Edmond J. Jodoin obtained a practical education in the public schools of Jewett City, and he began his business career as clerk in the employ of George Labonne, Jr., of Jewett City, and he also learned everything connected with meat cutting, which line of work he followed successfully up to the year 1912, when he decided to engage in business on his own account and accordingly purchased the provision market conducted by Driscoll Brothers, located at No. 45 Main street, Jewett City, and this business has since engaged his entire attention, he deriving therefrom a lucrative livelihood. The success he has achieved has been the result of hard and persistent labor, coupled with courtesy to his customers and prompt attention to their needs and wishes, and now ranks among the progressive and enterprising business men of his adopted town, Jewett City. Mr. Jodoin is a member of St. Mary's Catholic Church of Jewett City, that being the religious faith of his forefathers, a member of the Knights of Columbus, White Cross Council, No. 13, of Norwich; Court Griswold, No. 101, Foresters of America, and St. Jean Baptiste Society of Jewett City. He is a Democrat in political affiliation.

Mr. Jodoin married, October 8, 1912, Elizabeth Davan, of Brooklyn, New York, daughter of Edward J. and Catherine (Clair) Davan, and they are the parents of one child, Catherine, born in Jewett City, Connecticut, November 25, 1913.

EDWARD LOUIS BLANCHARD—Among the younger generation of business men in Jewett City, in the township of Griswold, Connecticut, is Edward Louis Blanchard, owner and manager of a grocery store. Public-spirited in the fullest sense of the term, he promotes every suggestion which has for its aim the welfare and advancement of the community which has been his home for so many years.

Edward Louis Blanchard was born at St. Jean Baptiste, Province of Quebec, Canada, July 13, 1896, the son of Clodomir and Olive (Noel) Blanchard. Clodomir Blanchard was born in St. Jean Baptiste, and obtained his education in the parochial schools there, after which he entered upon his business career, becoming a commission merchant until 1896, when he moved with his family to Jewett City, Connecticut, subsequently removing to Taftville, where he secured employment in the mills until 1907, when he returned to Jewett City and established himself as a grocery merchant, where he remained for several years. He then removed to Providence, Rhode Island, this being his place of residence at the present time. To Mr. and Mrs. Blanchard have been born three children: Edna, who married Leon Wheeler, of Jewett City; Edward Louis, of further mention; and Lester, a resident of Jewett City, who married Maud Shippee, of Sterling, Connecticut.

The education of Edward Louis Blanchard was obtained in the public schools of Jewett City, but this terminated at an early date, his business life beginning when he was but a small lad. He made his start in life as a newsboy, then found employment in the cotton mills of Jewett City, which, however, was not to his liking, and he soon left to become clerk in the clothing store of the Desrosier Clothing Company, with whom he remained until 1913, when he resigned this position and accepted another as clerk in the grocery store of Jovite Dugas, the latter selling out his interests in the business the following year to young Mr. Blanchard, who at that time was the youngest business man in the township of Griswold. The wisdom of this venture is proven by the consistent success which has attended his efforts, due entirely to his untiring energy and his firm belief in his power to succeed.

On August 26, 1918, Mr. Blanchard enlisted in the United States army and was assigned to the Ambulance Corps, later being transferred to Motor Company, No. 8, and was stationed at Camp Greenleaf, Georgia. On January 17, 1919, he was sent to Camp Upton and here received his honorable discharge. In religion he is a Catholic, being a member of St. Mary's Roman Catholic Church at Jewett City. He is a member of St. Jean Baptiste Society, of Jewett City; Foresters of America, Court Griswold, No. 2; and Orville La Flamme Post, American Legion, of Jewett City. Mr. Blanchard has purchased several thousand dollars worth of property in Jewett City.

Although Mr. Blanchard has never taken any part in the affairs of the city, no man is more civic-spirited. It is sometimes said of a man whose career is indicative of more than usual promise, "he will be heard from later." Edward Louis Blanchard has already been heard from, and Jewett City thinks that he will be heard from again and again and for many years to come.

CHARLES A. GAGER, JR.—In the business life of his community, in its social and fraternal circles, and to the public generally Charles A. Gager, Jr. is not only well known and highly esteemed, but is regarded with a warmer feeling, for it is in a spirit of genuine helpfulness and sympathy that he does his work as a funeral director and he is a friend in truth.

Mr. Gager is a member of a Connecticut family, his father having been born on the old Gager homestead in the town of Bozrah, near Norwich. Charles A. Gager, Sr. was born June 15, 1837. He grew up in Bozrah, and attended the public schools there; then took charge of the home farm and there spent his entire active life. He retired in 1906 and bought a house in Norwich Town, where he is still living and enjoying excellent health, although an octogenarian. He married Harriet M. Fargo, who was a native of Montville, Connecticut; she died in Norwich, Connecticut, September 24, 1920. They have had five children of whom three are living.

Charles A. Gager, Jr. was born in Bozrah, Connecticut, July 4, 1876. He attended the public schools of the town, and when he had completed the course helped his father on the farm. At the age of twenty-one years he went to Norwich, and entered the employ of the Henry Allen & Son Company, the leading undertakers of that day. Here he remained for a period of six years, and became thoroughly experienced in the undertaking business. He passed the State Board examinations on March 1, 1905, and established himself as a funeral director at No. 70 Franklin street. He has remained in the same location to the present time, and is conceded to be one of the leading men in his line in the county. His establishment is modernly equipped, and he was the first undertaker in the city to own a motor-driven hearse. Courteous and considerate, he combines with his pleasing personality a thorough knowledge of his business and he is very highly esteemed. Mr. Gager finds his relaxation from the cares of a trying business in his fine two-hundred-acre farm in Montville, not far from NorNwich. There he raises thoroughbred cattle, horses, and poultry, taking a great pride in his farm, which is one of the best in that section.

Mr. Gager is a member of Somerset Lodge, No. 34, Free and Accepted Masons; of Franklin Chapter, No. 3, Royal Arch Masons; of Franklin Council, No. 4, Royal and Select Masters; of Columbian Commandery, Knights Templar, of Norwich; and is a thirty-second degree member of the Ancient Accepted Scottish Rite, affiliated with King Solomon Lodge of Perfection; Van Rensselaer Council, Princes of Jerusalem; Norwich Chapter of Rose Croix; Connecticut Consistory, Sovereign Princes of the Royal Secret; Sphinx Temple, Ancient Arabic Order Nobles of the Mystic Shrine, of Hartford; Norwich Lodge, No. 430, Benevolent and Protective Order of Elks; Independent Order of Odd Fellows; Shetucket Lodge, No. 16; and the Arcanum and Rotary clubs, of Norwich; the Order of United American Mechanics, of Norwich; and of the Funeral Directors' Association of Connecticut. In political affairs he will pledge his support in advance to no party, voting for the man he believes best qualified to serve the people.

Mr. Gager married, December 13, 1907, Mira L. Rallion, daughter of Herman and Emma (Crocker) Rallion, of Norwich; they attend the services of the Universalist church.

CLEMENT ANSON FOWLER—In both paternal and maternal lines, Clement A. Fowler, the present-day representative of these families, well known and highly respected in the State of Connecticut, worthily carries on the work laid out by his ancestors, and has also added to its prestige by his conduct and actions, proving himself a worthy follower of the precepts of his forbears, who were among the men to whom more honor should be paid, the pioneers of this great Republic.

On the paternal side the family traces back to William Fowler, a native of England, whence he came to this country in the year 1637, landing at Boston, Massachusetts, later locating in New Haven, Connecticut, being one of the signers of the Constitution of the New Haven Colony. He served as magistrate for that colony from 1643 to 1654. Later he removed to Milford, same State. He died in 1660. The line is traced through his son, Captain William (2) Fowler; through his son, Mark Fowler; Captain Dijah Fowler; through his son, Captain Amos Fowler; through his son, Colonel Anson Fowler, grandfather of Clement A. Fowler.

Colonel Anson Fowler took an active part in the business and political life of the town of Lebanon, Connecticut, his birthplace, being among the men who raised the moral tone of the community, maintained a high and pure standard for the youth of the day, and pointed out the way for honorable, successful living, a worthy record for his time as well as for the present day. He married (first) Sally Robinson, (second) Hannah Peckham, (third) Mehitable Lyon, (fourth) Roxanna Pease. Among the children of the last-named wife was Frank Pease Fowler, grandfather of Clement A. Fowler.

Frank Pease Fowler was born December 23, 1854, in Lebanon Green, Connecticut, in which town he resided during his boyhood and manhood, his active business life being spent as a general merchant, a member of the firm of Fowler & Stark, of Lebanon. He began as clerk in the general store of N. C. Barker at Lebanon, Connecticut, worked for Barker and later formed partnership with Irving W. Stark, and as Fowler & Stark, bought out N. C. Barker. This partnership continued several years, when Fowler bought out Stark and continues alone to date. He was appointed postmaster by President Cleveland during his first administration, was succeeded by his son, Mr. Fowler serving as assistant. During President Cleveland's second administration he reinstated Mr. Fowler as postmaster, in which capacity he served under successive presidents, this fact testifying to his ability and integrity. He also served as selectman and assessor, the duties of these offices being performed to the entire satisfaction of all concerned. He holds membership in the Congregational church, holding the offices of clerk and treasurer; also in Lebanon Lodge, No. 23, Ancient Order of United Workmen, serving as financial secretary for several years. Mr. Fowler married, December 23, 1880, Jessie A. Peckham, daughter of Robert C. and Sarah A. (Segar) Peckham, and they are the parents of Clement Anson, of whom further.

On the maternal side the family traces back to John Peckham, who as early as 1638, was admitted an inhabitant of Newport, Rhode Island; three years later he was made a freeman, and subsequently he removed to what is now Middletown, Rhode Island, where his death occurred in 1681. He married (first) Mary Clarke, (second) Eleanor, and their descendants are now scattered throughout the entire United States, the family still being numerous in that section of Rhode Island, and in Eastern Pennsylvania. One of these descendants who continued his residence in Rhode Island was the great-grandfather of Jessie A. (Peckham) Fowler, who in later life removed to Lebanon, Connecticut, and there spent his remaining years, leaving behind him a reputation, of which any man might be proud. He married, and was the father of six children, five daughters and one son. Robert Peckham, the only son, was born in South Kingston, Rhode Island, removed with his parents to Lebanon, Connecticut, and later made his home in the towns of Goshen, Brooklyn, Pomfret, and then returned to Lebanon. He married Anna Bliss, of Lebanon, and they were the parents of Robert Congdon Peckham, aforementioned, born in Lebanon, Connecticut, May 7, 1811, died April 13, 1898. He resided in Brooklyn, Pomfret, and Windham, finally returning to Lebanon, where he spent his declining years, honored and esteemed by his neighbors and friends. He married, April 8, 1832, Sarah A. Segar, daughter of Thomas and Rebecca (Ward) Segar, and they lived to celebrate their golden wedding. Among their children was Jessie A., aforementioned as the mother of Clement A. Fowler.

Clement A. Fowler was born in Lebanon Centre, Connecticut, September 3, 1889. He attended a select school at Lebanon, completing his studies there at the age of thirteen; for the following three years was a student at Norwich Free Academy, then pursued a course of study at Lansdowne High School, Lansdowne, a suburb of Philadelphia, remaining a student there until the age of eighteen. His business knowledge was gained by attendance at Miller's Business College, New York City, which institution he attended for several years. He added to the theoretical knowledge thus obtained by entering the establishment conducted by his father in Lebanon, and in due course of time became thoroughly familiar with all the details connected with the business, thus proving himself a valuable asset to its success. The firm carries a general line of merchandise, and caters to the best trade in Lebanon and adjoining towns, in which section of the State the family has resided for so many years. Mr. Fowler is a member of the First Congregational Church, as is also his wife, and is a Republican in politics, and serves as postmaster of Lebanon, thus following in his father's footsteps.

Mr. Fowler married, January 1, 1913, Bernice Anzeline Hewitt, born June 8, 1892, in Lebanon, Connecticut, daughter of Erwin Wheeler and Nellie Eliza (Stiles) Hewitt, natives of Lebanon, and a descendant of one of the early settled families of New England, the line being traced through

Thomas Hewitt; his son, Benjamin Hewitt; his son, Major Israel Hewitt; his son, Charles Hewitt; his son, Eli Hewitt; his son, George Hewitt; his son, George Eli Hewitt; his son, Erwin W. Hewitt, father of Mrs. Fowler. Two children have been born to Mr. and Mrs. Fowler: Elois Louise, born February 10, 1914; and Lawrence Clement, born August 5, 1919.

A. FRANK GREENE—In Hunter, New York, a beautiful village of the Catskills, within sight of those peaks named Round Top, High Peak and Pine Orchard, Alfred Edward Greene long lived, there spent many of the later years of his life, and here his son, A. Frank Greene, now a merchant of Norwich, Connecticut, was born. Alfred E. Greene was perhaps the best-known man of the village, for in addition to being a manufacturer in Hunter, he was the village postmaster for sixteen years, holding that office from 1902 until his passing away.

Alfred Edward Greene was born in Jewett, New York, there grew to manhood and became an undertaker, continuing in that business until his removal to Hunter, Greene county, New York, where he was engaged in chair manufacturing. He was appointed postmaster of Hunter, a position he most capably filled for sixteen years, dying in office, in 1918. He married Charlotte Long, born in New York City, who survives him, a resident of New London, Connecticut.

A. Frank Greene, son of Alfred E. and Charlotte (Long) Greene, was born in Hunter, a village and summer resort of Greene county, New York, on the Ulster & Delaware railroad, forty miles south of Albany, December 24, 1887. He spent the first thirteen years of his life in Hunter, there attending the public schools until going to New York City, where for three and one-half years he was employed in the office of a fire insurance company. He later returned to Hunter, where he spent four years in the office of the assistant postmaster. He then spent the years until 1915 in the automobile business in New York City. From 1915 until July, 1917, he was engaged in the automobile business in Hartford, Connecticut. In July, 1917, he located in New London in the same business, there remaining until February, 1920, when he removed to Norwich, Connecticut, where he established the A. F. Greene Company, tires and automobile accessories, located on Main street, where he is building up a good business.

Mr. Greene is a Republican in politics; a member of Lockwood Lodge, Independent Order of Odd Fellows, of Hunter, New York; and is an attendant of the Presbyterian church.

Mr. Greene married, at Jersey City, New Jersey, June 7, 1911, Virginia Brandow, born in Richmond, Virginia, daughter of Justus and Rachael (Johnson) Brandow, her parents later removing to Hunter, New York. Mr. and Mrs. Greene are the parents of a daughter, Virginia Brandow, born in New York City.

Mr. Greene is a young man of energy and fine business qualities, and well liked in Norwich and New London, where his years since 1915 have been passed. He thoroughly understands the business in which he is engaged, and has already established in Norwich a reputation for integrity that is an invaluable asset.

HARRIET ELIZABETH HEWITT—The Hewitt family, of which Harriet E. Hewitt is a present-day representative, is one of the early settled families of New England, the earliest ancestor of the line herein followed, being Thomas Hewitt who, tradition says, was in command of a vessel belonging to Thomas Miner, Sr., on the Mystic river in 1656, and he is supposed to have been lost at sea in 1662. His wife, Hannah (Palmer) Hewitt, bore him a son, Benjamin Hewitt, born in 1662, married Marie Fanning, daughter of Edward and Ellen Fanning, and they were the parents of Israel Hewitt, baptized July 24, 1692, who in later life attained the rank of major. His wife, Anna (Breed) Hewitt, daughter of John and Mercy (Palmer) Breed, bore him a son, Charles Hewitt, born August 16, 1730. He married Hannah Stanton, daughter of Joseph and Anna (Wheeler) Stanton, and they were the parents of Eli Hewitt, born July 31, 1764, a resident of North Stonington, Connecticut, who married Betsey Williams, daughter of Bednam and Hannah (Lathrop) Williams, and among their children was George Hewitt, born in North Stonington, January 26, 1797. He later removed to North Franklin, where he engaged in farming pursuits, and his death occurred at Groton, Connecticut, October 16, 1884. He married Bridget Wheeler, daughter of Nathan and Desire Wheeler, and among their children was George Eli Hewitt, father of Harriet Elizabeth Hewitt, of this review.

George Eli Hewitt was born in North Stonington, Connecticut, May 27, 1820, in the house erected by his grandfather. He received a practical education by attendance at the district school, and the select schools presided over by Major Francis Peabody and Latham Hull. His leisure time was spent in assisting his father in the work of the home farm, and he so continued until the age of thirty-five years, receiving then from his father, as recompense for his labor, five shares of bank stock, a dozen steers and some farming implements. Shortly after his marriage he removed to the farm belonging to his father-in-law, Henry Williams, in Lebanon, and assumed the management of that farm, where he resided until 1869, when he removed to what was known as the Priest Ely Farm, which he had previously purchased. From time to time he added to his purchase, becoming the owner of one hundred and fifty acres of land in the town of Lebanon, also several tenement houses, which he rented advantageously. His own residence was a commodious and comfortable structure, pleasantly located, fitted up with everything needful for the comfort and convenience of its inmates. In addition to general

Geo. G. Brown

farming, he engaged in the buying and selling of live stock, and he made frequent trips to the famous stock market at Brighton, Massachusetts, for the purpose of buying cattle. He was one of the prime movers in the organization of the Lebanon Creamery, was one of its largest stockholders, and served as a director and treasurer for many years. In political affiliation he was a Republican, and in 1873 he was a representative from Lebanon to the State Legislature at the last meeting of that body in the city of New Haven. During his residence in North Stonington he held the commission of a lieutenant in the local militia for three years. He was a consistent member of the Congregational church, active and interested in the work connected therewith. His life was spent in the faithful discharge of his obligations as a son, husband, father, public official, neighbor and friend, and his memory is revered by all who knew him intimately. His death occurred October 5, 1904.

Mr. Hewitt married, October 12, 1854, Anzeline Williams, born in Lebanon, Connecticut, October 28, 1825, died September 3, 1899, daughter of Henry and Harriet (Babcock) Williams. Children: 1. George Henry, born August 9, 1857; married, August 13, 1881, Louise Josephine Noyes, born February 28, 1850; children: Ethel Beatrice and Hazel Adele. 2. Harriet Elizabeth, twin of George Henry, of whom further. 3. Erwin Wheeler, born October 10, 1859; married, November 18, 1880, Nellie Eliza Stiles, born September 19, 1863, in Lebanon, daughter of Edmund A. and Sophia (Sweet) Stiles; children: Arthur Erwin, born June 20, 1881, married Elsie Gardner; Lawrence Alonzo, born May 6, 1883, died April 1, 1885; Charlotte Eliza, born June 5, 1884, married John E. Burgess; Rodney Williams, born August 4, 1889; Bernice Anzeline, born June 8, 1892, married Everett Delos; Gladys Eva Miriam, born December 24, 1894; George Edmund, born February 9, 1898.

Harriet Elizabeth Hewitt, only daughter of George Eli and Anzeline (Williams) Hewitt, was born in Lebanon, Connecticut, August 9, 1857. Her preliminary education was obtained in the school adjacent to her home, and at the early age of eight she became a student in the boarding school of Miss Knotts in New Haven. At the age of twenty-five she went to Boston, Massachusetts, in order to study under Dr. Emerson, a prominent elocutionist, but during the course of study felt it incumbent upon her to return to the old homestead by reason of the condition of health of her parents, which had become greatly impaired. She remained with them until the close of their lives, tenderly and lovingly mnistering to their needs and wants, thus performing a service of love and gratitude in recompense for the many bestowed on her during her entire lifetime by her devoted parents. Thus she fulfilled a part of her mission in life. She inherited the old homestead of her ancestors, wherein she now resides, and of which she is naturally proud. She is a woman of culture and refinement, keenly alive to the questions of the day, and takes an interest in all that concerns the welfare of the town of her birth.

REV. ADELARD ALFRED JALBERT—There is no way by which the value of a life to a community can be estimated, and especially is this true of the life of a Catholic priest. Life holds no more beautiful relationship than that which a Catholic priest bears to his people, and his people bear to him, for his helping hand is never withdrawn, and his patience is without end. A noble man full of courage, zeal and devotion, with deep and abiding faith. Such is the kind of pastor Father Jalbert is to all with whom he comes in contact.

Joseph Jalbert, father of Rev. Adelard Alfred Jalbert, was born at St. Denis on the Richelieu, Canada, February 26, 1863. He came to this country when a young man and settled in Spencer, Massachusetts, and shortly afterwards in New Haven, Connecticut, where for many years previous to his death, which occurred in May, 1919, he was a merchant by trade. He married Virginia Collette, a native of Spencer, Massachusetts, her birth having occurred there April 21, 1867. Mr. and Mrs. Jalbert were the parents of ten children: Delia, Marie, Adelard Alfred, Arthur, Rose, Philip, Alice, Cecilia, Wilfred, and Beatrice.

Father Jalbert was born in New Haven, Connecticut, December 3, 1893. His early education was obtained in the Sacred Heart's School and in the New Haven Hillhouse High School, and in 1911 entered St. Thomas' Seminary at Hartford, Connecticut. Upon completing his studies at this institution, he matriculated at St. Mary's Seminary, Baltimore, Maryland. In 1915 he attended the Grand Seminary at Montreal, where after finishing his course of Sacred Theology he was ordained priest, December 21, 1918, at Hartford, Connecticut, by Bishop Nilan. He was then immediately assigned to St. Mary's Church, at Baltic, where he has since, with hearty co-operation, been supported by his parishioners in his work. Father Jalbert takes a deep and abiding faith in every department of the parish work, and is interested in all that pertains to bettering civic conditions.

GEORGE SETH BROWN, superintendent of the Ashland Cotton Company, Jewett City, Connecticut, is active in the affairs of the community and takes a keen interest in the progress and welfare of the town. He is the son of Seth Leeds and Margaret (Cantwell) Brown, and was born in Ledyard, Connecticut, December 1, 1882.

Seth Leeds Brown was born in Ledyard, March 24, 1850. He attended the district schools there and a select school in Preston until he was eighteen years of age, when, in company with his brother, Aaron A. Brown, he built a woolen mill on the site of the old Ayers factory, later known as Shewville. For a number of years this firm, known as A. A. and S. L. Brown Company, carried on a woolen yarn manufacturing business until business reverses caused an assignment in 1879. A. P. Sturtevant, of Norwich, then secured control of the plant, and Seth L. Brown was retained as overseer of carding and spinning until 1891, when he entered the employ of the H. B. Porter & Son Company, of that place, and remained with them until his death in Norwich, September 10, 1916. To Mr. and Mrs. Brown were born three children: Arthur Chester, agent of the Falls Company in Norwich, Connecticut, married Isabella Yeomans, of Norwich; George Seth, of further mention; Albert Seymour, died at Norwich, June 28, 1908, at the age of twenty years.

George Seth Brown received his education in the public schools of Preston and Norwich, and was a member of the 1900 class of the Norwich Free Academy. He entered the office of the Falls Company upon leaving school and remained there about four years, when he entered the mill proper and learned the cotton carder's trade. After four years' service he left that company and entered the treasurer's office of the Attawaugan and Totokett Manufacturing companies of Norwich, manufacturers of fine cotton goods. Mr. Brown's connection with the Ashland Cotton Company began in March, 1918, when he entered the office department as cost accountant, and shortly afterward was promoted to the position of assistant superintendent. For the period of the World War, he served as a member of the War Industries Board at Washington, D. C., as assistant section chief (cotton manufacturing expert) of the cotton goods section. Late in 1919, Mr. Brown again took up his duties at the Ashland Cotton Company and soon was promoted superintendent, which position he is now filling (1921).

George Seth Brown married, September 20, 1915, Henrietta Frances James, daughter of Charles D. James, born in Voluntown, Connecticut, May 19, 1851, died in Norwich, Connecticut, March 12, 1903, and Catherine L. (Kelley) James, born in Yantic, Connecticut, April 29, 1857. Mr. and Mrs. Brown are the parents of two children: Richard, born in Norwich, Connecticut, died in infancy; and Henrietta Surviah, born in Jewett City, Connecticut.

A man gifted in manner, enterprising and thorough in business, Mr. Brown is personally liked most by those who know him best. He is a man of quiet force, the force that accomplishes large results with but little friction, the force that counts in the upbuilding and maintaining of large industries. A man loyal to his employers and associates which in its own turn secures the full confidence of those under him. He is an enthusiastic devotee of the rod and gun, and has penned many interesting and instructive magazine articles on hunting and fishing.

CHARLES BREWSTER PALMER—The Palmers of New London county, Connecticut, have been connected with the business interests of the county, manufacturing, mercantile and agricultural, for many years. The name was first brought to the county by Walter Palmer, who finally located in Stonington, Connecticut, in 1653. In this present generation Charles B. Palmer married Fannie Ella Brown, a descendant of Joshua Brown, a Revolutionary soldier, and they reside at the old homestead owned by the old patriot. Deacon Simeon Palmer, son of Peleg Palmer, was born in the town of Stonington, Connecticut, in 1800, there spent his life and died in February, 1895. He early learned the carpenter's trade and followed it all his life until old age called a halt, not very many years prior to his death at the age of ninety-five. He was one of the old-time carpenters who went into the woods, selected the trees, and often framed a building right in the woods; then hauled the different parts to the site of the building and put it in position without altering size, mortise or tenon. He built many houses in Stonington and the surrounding country, both for others and himself, building and selling as opportunity offered. He continued his residence in Stonington after his retirement and was one of the best-known men of his town. He married Caroline E. Tiffany, who was born and lived in Salem, Connecticut, until her marriage. She died in Stonington after her husband, but at the same age of ninety-five. They were the parents of nine children, all born in Stonington: Elizabeth, married John Hammond; Mary, married James Lee; Henry, Ebenezer, Susan, William Hyde, all of whom have now passed away; Jerome S. A., a carpenter, of Stonington, married Lucretia Sisson, of Salem, Connecticut; Sarah Amelia, deceased, and Charles Brewster.

Charles Brewster Palmer was born near Stonington, New London county, Connecticut, April 4, 1847, and there spent his first fifteen years. In early life he went to Westerly, Rhode Island, where, at the age of fifteen, he began learning the trade of painter and paper hanger. That was in 1862, and until 1879 he worked in Stonington and several towns in Connecticut and Rhode Island. In 1879 he worked in Jersey City, New Jersey, and then moved to New London, Connecticut, finally returning to Stonington, and there followed his trade until his retirement in 1915. In 1899 he moved to the Randall Brown farm which has since been his home. He conducted the farm in connection with his painting business until 1915, but has since given his full attention to its management.

Mr. Palmer married (first), at Mystic, Connecticut, July 4, 1871, Emma Jane Smith, who was born in Stonington and there died in 1897, leaving two daughters: Mabel B., wife of Edward Ripley, now residing at Ossining, New York; Phoebe W., wife of Thomas Cobb. Mr. Palmer married (second) at Stonington, February 28, 1899, Fannie Ella Brown, born at the Brown homestead in Stonington, daughter of Randall and Mary Ann (Holmes) Brown. Mr. and Mrs. Palmer are members of the Baptist church of Stonington. The home is the old homestead in which Mrs. Palmer was born.

RANDALL BROWN—Randall Brown, father of Mrs. Charles B. Palmer, was born at the Brown homestead on the Stonington road near old Mystic, Connecticut, March 28, 1807, and there died after a life of honorable, upright living, December 13, 1887. The old Brown homestead on which he lived and where his daughter, Mrs. Fannie Ella Palmer, now lives, was first owned in the family in 1786 by Joshua Brown, born in Stonington, April 8, 1740. Joshua Brown, the grandfather of Randall Brown, in 1786 bought the farm in which his great-granddaughter, Mrs. Palmer, lives, pur-

F. C. Mousley.

chasing it from Robert Williams, and moved his family from the northern part of the town to his new home. Joshua Brown was a lieutenant in the Capt. Thomas Holmes company and served in the Revolutionary War in 1776. He married, January 24, 1761, Johanna Rogers, and they were the parents of a son, Randall Brown, who was born at the Brown homestead in Stonington, and there spent his life. He married Sally Palmer, and their son, Randall (2) Brown, was born at the homestead near Old Mystic on the Stonington road, March 28, 1807, and there died December 13, 1887. He attended district schools, and was his father's assistant until the latter's death, then succeeded to the ownership of the homestead, on which his eighty years of life were spent. He was a good farmer and an honorable, upright citizen, scorning to take advantage of any man or to take a cent unlawfully. On the other hand, he would not submit to be defrauded of a cent, but demanded the same justice for himself that he tendered to others. He was one of the most modern and progressive farmers of his day, and as fast as machinery had proved its advantage to the farm, he hastened to adopt it. He bought the first horse-drawn hay rake used in his town, also the first mowing machine. Even-tempered and kindly-hearted, he never spoke but in kindness, and lived a most exemplary life. He was a strong temperance man and used his influence to have others saved from its blight.

Mr. Brown married, January 1, 1833, Mary Ann Holmes, born in Mystic, Connecticut, died at the Brown Homestead in Stonington, February 5, 1894. Randall (2) and Mary Ann (Holmes) Brown were the parents of eight children, all born on home place, three of whom are now living. The children of Randall and Mary Ann (Holmes) Brown: 1. Mary Ann, married Capt. Franklin Hancox, a whaler, deceased. 2. Sarah Palmer, wife of Hon. Elias Williams, of Mystic, both deceased. 3. Helen Elizabeth, died in childhood. 4. Jeremiah Holmes, never married, was in First Rhode Island Cavalry three years during Civil War, lived on home place all his life, died at the age of seventy-four. 5. Susan Almyra, widow of Joseph Smith, of Stonington. 6. Randall, of Mystic, Connecticut. 7. Fannie Ella (Mrs. Charles Palmer). 8. Frederick Henry, was a merchant of Danielson, Connecticut, now deceased.

FRANK CROUSE MOUSLEY—At Warren Paper Mills, in Hunterdon county, New Jersey, Frank Crouse Mousley was born, son of Louis Henry and Jennie (Crouse) Mousley. Louis Henry Mousley was born at a point on historic Brandywine creek, near Wilmington, Delaware, and there spent his boyhood. He was first employed in the Jessup & Moore Paper Mills near Wilmington, going thence to Warren Paper Mills in New Jersey, where he married and remained a paper mill worker for eighteen years. He was next employed with the Piermont Paper Mills in Piermont, New York, and continued in paper manufacturing mills until his retirement, when he moved to New York City, where he yet resides (1921). He was a son of Curtis Mousley, who lived near Wilmington, and his wife, Jennie (Crouse) Mousley, who was born in that same section.

Frank Crouse Mousley was born February 17, 1880, and spent his youth in his native village, Warren Paper Mills, three miles from Bloomsbury post office in Pennsylvania, the village and paper mill, however, in Hunterdon county, New Jersey. As a boy he entered the Warren Paper Mills, first as a cutter boy, and after gaining experience took the next step upward to the job of "back tender." His second job was in the employ of the Bogota Paper Mills, where he remained for two years. He was then promoted to the rank of machine tender in the same mills, but soon afterward the mills were destroyed by fire and he was out of a position. He journeyed to Covington, Virginia, and obtained employment as a machine tender in the West Virginia Pulp and Paper Company, and while there married.

In 1903 he returned North and located in Piermont, New York, obtaining a position as machine tender with the Piermont Paper Company, that company having an association with the Thames River Specialty Company. Mr. Mousley was soon promoted to the rank of boss machine tender, and in all was with the company twelve years. In July, 1914, he was appointed superintendent of the Thames River Specialty Company Mills in Uncasville, town of Montville, New London county, Connecticut, and he is now serving his seventh year in that position. The product of the company is principally folding box boards. The business under his management has shown an increase; there has been an expansion in plant area and buildings, while the general trend in every department has been toward improvement.

At the close of his seven years' service with the Thames River Specialty Company (which had previously passed to the Robert Gair Company) Mr. Mousley became general superintendent of the Federal Paper Board Company, a company with mills located in Versailles, Connecticut, in Massachusetts, in New Jersey, and in Pennsylvania. Mr. Mousley makes his home in Norwich, and divides his time between the four mills under his supervision.

From boyhood, Mr. Mousley has been employed in paper mills, and he thoroughly understands the details of paper manufacture. He is an ideal superintendent, deeply interested in the men and their families, all his concern being toward having a contented, cheerful and prosperous force of employees. He holds the respect and confidence of both the officials of the company and the mill hands, the result being plants run at a high per cent of efficiency with a capable, satisfied working force.

In religion Mr. Mousley is a Presbyterian, and in politics a Republican. He is affiliated with Wawagande Lodge, No. 315, Free and Accepted Masons, of Piermont, New York; Rockland Chapter, Royal Arch Masons, of Nyack, New York; Franklin Council, Royal and Select Masters, of Norwich, Connecticut; Columbia Commandery, Knights Templar, of Norwich; and is a thirty-second degree member of the Ancient Accepted Scottish Rite. He is also a noble of Sphinx Temple, Nobles of the Mystic Shrine, Hartford, Connecticut.

Mr. Mousley married (first) in Covington, Virginia, April 14, 1903, Daisy Brooks, born in Lexington, Virginia, daughter of George and Henrietta Brooks, both of Virginian birth. Mr. and Mrs. Mousley had three children, all students of Norwich Free Academy, namely: Louis Brooks, born March 31, 1904; Harvey Kenneth, born in 1906; Frank Crouse, Jr., born in 1908. Mrs. Mousley died January 29, 1909. Mr. Mousley married (second), August 23, 1910, Hattie Elizabeth Brooks, sister of his first wife.

HERBERT WARREN SWEET—Among the very old families of New England which have become famous for some distinguishing trait, characteristic, or skill, is the Sweet family, widely known as expert bone-setters. As far back as their authentic history can be traced, and from tradition, leading still further, one finds them credited with remarkable skill in this art, and from time to time taking over and successfully performing work which has baffled trained surgeons. James Sweet, of Wales, the recognized ancestor of the family, came to New England in 1630, was a resident of Salem, Massachusetts, in 1631, of Warwick, Rhode Island, in 1638, and later of Kingston, finally settling near North Hill, in North Kingston, Rhode Island, where he married Mary Greene, daughter of John and Joan (Tattersall) Greene, and died in 1695. His children, James, Mary, Benoni, Valentine, Samuel, Jeremiah, Renewed, and Sylvester, were all born in North Kingston between the years 1655 and 1674. From this James Sweet the Lebanon, Connecticut, Sweets are descended through Benoni (2) Sweet, he being a descendant in the fifth generation from James, through Benoni, James (2), and Job Sweet. Three of the above, Benoni, Job, and Benoni (2) Sweet, are on record as having gained wide celebrity as natural bone-setters, Job Sweet having attained such eminence in that line that during the Revolution he was called to Newport to set dislocated bones of the French officers, and after the war, at the urgent request of Colonel Burr, afterward vice-president, went to New York to set a dislocated hip of his daughter's.

Benoni (2) Sweet, who was born October 7, 1760, died August 26, 1840, practiced the family art in South Kingston and vicinity, but, in 1793, when he removed to Lebanon, Connecticut, he resolved to do no more setting of bones, but to give his whole attention to farming. A dislocated shoulder in his neighborhood, however, baffling the surgeons, called him back to the practice of his art, which he never again abandoned. He married Sarah Champlin, and they became the progenitors of the Sweet family in Connecticut, their tenth child being Charles, mentioned below.

Dr. Charles Sweet was born December 3, 1810, and died in Lebanon, December 22, 1896. According to the "History of New London County," published in 1882, "he commenced bone-setting at the early age of sixteen years and for nearly forty years maintained offices in Hartford and New London, Connecticut, and at Springfield, Massaachusetts, each of which he visited one day of each month, successfully treating all kinds of bone dislocation, fractures, and diseases. The greater part of his time was devoted to these things, in which he manifested an intuitive perception truly surprising. In the intervals he carried on farming to some extent, more for a pastime than for pecuniary profit." He married (first) Eliza W. Throop, daughter of Joseph and Polly (Clark) Throop, of Lebanon, and they became the parents of six children, among whom was Charles, Jr., father of Herbert Warren, mentioned below. Dr. Charles Sweet married (second) Sarah Elizabeth Williams, of Mystic, Connecticut, and by this marriage had three children. He married (third) Laura A. Anderson, who died on Thanksgiving Day, 1897.

Charles Sweet, Jr., son of Dr. Charles and Eliza W. (Throop) Sweet, was born at Lebanon, Connecticut, January 1, 1845, and died October 18, 1893. Associated with his father in Lebanon, he also became famous as a bone-setter, and for a time practiced in Hartford, returning later to Lebanon, where most of his life was spent, and where he died. He also did farm work on his father's place. He married (first) Nellie Payne, who died, leaving one child, Arthur P., who married Eudora Spencer and resides in South Windham, Connecticut. Charles Sweet, Jr., married (second) Mary Eva Manning, and they became the parents of nine children: Edith S., now the wife of Dr. Norman Drake, of Little Falls, New York; Herbert Warren, of further mention; Edward P., who died when nine years old; Leon M., of Washington, D. C.; Henry R., of Norfolk, Connecticut; Harold, who died at the age of sixteen; Ruby E., who died aged seven; Wallace Nathaniel, a physician, of Wallingford, Connecticut; and Clifton Worsley, of New Britain, Connecticut. Mrs. Charles Sweet, the mother of Herbert Warren Sweet, survives her husband and resides in Lebanon.

Herbert Warren Sweet, son of Charles, Jr., and Mary Eva (Manning) Sweet, was born January 14, 1876, in Lebanon, Connecticut, where he was reared and where he received his early education. From the schools of Lebanon he entered the State Agricultural College, at Storrs, Connecticut, and then farmed the old Sweet homestead, in Lebanon. Later, he became interested in another line of work, and became a clerk in the general store of F. P. Fowler. After gaining considerable experience in this position he associated himself with the general merchandise business of I. W. Stark, also of Lebanon. Here he was very successful, and in 1916, bought the business of his employer, which he is still (1921) carrying on.

Politically, Mr. Sweet is a Republican, and both he and his family attend the Congregational church. He is a member of Wooster Lodge, No. 10, Free and Accepted Masons, of Colchester; and of the George S. Hull Lodge, Knights of Pythias, Lebanon. Both Mr. and Mrs. Sweet are members of Lebanon Grange, No. 21.

On March 30, 1897, at Tolland, Connecticut, Herbert Warren Sweet married Katherine Hanson, daughter of Lauritz and Emily (Jewell) Hanson, and they are the parents of two children: Ruby, born February 28, 1898, and Charles Herbert, born October 9, 1900. Mrs. Sweet was a very successful teacher before her marriage, and is active in many lines of welfare and community work. One of her most valuable services to her town is her work on the School Board of Lebanon, of which she has been a member since 1915, being reëlected each year.

ARBA BROWNING—"Agriculture is the noblest of all alchemy," says Chatfield, "for it turns earth and even refuse into gold, conferring upon its cultivator the additional reward of health." This oldest of human vocations and noblest of them all has been honored by the successful career of Arba Browning, a lineal descendant of an ancestry that traces back in this country for three centuries, this representative of the family inheriting in large degree the excellent traits and characteristics of his forbears.

Nathaniel Browning, the first of the line herein traced, is of record in Rhode Island as early as 1645, a resident of Warwick and Portsmouth, and was made a freeman in 1655. The descent is traced through his son, William Browning, a resident of Portsmouth and South Kingston. His son, John Browning, a resident of South Kingston. His son, John Browning, Jr., a resident of Exeter. His son, Avery Browning, a native of Exeter, Rhode Island, born February 8, 1786, died in Norwich, Connecticut, May 9, 1865. He removed from his native State to Connecticut in 1834, purchasing a farm in Griswold, from whence he removed to Preston and later to Norwich. He married Mary Arnold, and their third son was Beriah Hopkins Browning, born September 13, 1819, in Exeter, Rhode Island, died in Griswold, Connecticut, May 24, 1890. He accompanied his parents upon their removal to Griswold, Connecticut, and there attended the district schools, also accompanied them upon their removal to Preston, same State, where they resided for several years, removing in 1866 to the Plain Hill District, town of Norwich, Connecticut, and Beriah H. Browning purchased the Morgan place in the town of Griswold, where he engaged in general farming until his death. On November 21, 1843, he married Sarah Elizabeth Campbell, daughter of Bonaparte Campbell, and they were the parents of nine children, the seventh of whom was Arba, of whom further. Beriah H. Browning represented Griswold in the State Legislature in 1873, also served as justice of the peace for over thirty years.

Arba Browning was born in the Plain Hill District, town of Norwich, Connecticut, October 31, 1862. He received a practical education in the district schools of Griswold, and his leisure time was spent in assisting his father in the cultivation of the home place, which became his property by purchase after the death of his father, and whereon he has resided up to the present time (1921). He is engaged in general farming and dairying, to which pursuits he devotes his entire time, and the result of his energy, progressive methods, and tireless application to all details is that he is the possessor of one of the finest farms in that section of the State. Although deeply interested in his chosen line of work, Mr. Browning finds time to devote to public affairs, and has been chosen by his fellow-townsmen to act in public capacity, his tenure of office being noted for efficiency and capability. For three years he served on the Board of Selectmen, for eight years acted as justice of the peace, served as a member of the Committee for the Sale of Land, as a representative for the town of Griswold in the State Legislature in 1905-06, and for the years 1918-19 was a member of the School Board. He is a Democrat in politics, attends the First Congregational Church of Pachaug, and is affiliated with Mount Vernon Lodge, No. 75, Free and Accepted Masons, of Jewett City, and of the Ancient Order of United Workmen, of Jewett City.

Mr. Browning married, September 4, 1890, Harriet Lee Bromley, born in Lisbon, Connecticut, daughter of Charles and Sarah (Thompson) Bromley, of Lisbon. Children: Frank Duane, a sketch of whom follows; Sybil, born August 30, 1898, a teacher in the public schools of Jewett City, Connecticut.

FRANK DUANE BROWNING, D.M.D.—The professional men of New London county form a group of which any locality might be proud. In Jewett City, Dr. Frank D. Browning, the young dentist, is attracting attention as one of the most promising professional men of the day in this section.

Dr. Browning, son of Arba and Harriet L. (Bromley) Browning (q.v.), was born in the town of Griswold, Connecticut, on December 14, 1892. Receiving his early education in the district schools near his home, he continued his studies at Mount Hermon School, Mount Hermon, Massachusetts. There he prepared for Tufts College, and in 1915 entered that institution, in the Dental School, from which he was graduated in 1918, with the degree of D.M.D.

It was just at the time of his graduation that the need of skilled hands in this field in the United States army was most keenly felt, and Dr. Browning enlisted and was called on July 24th of that year. He was commissioned first lieutenant in December, 1918, and stationed at Camp Greenleaf, Georgia, then later was transferred to Camp Seneca, South Carolina. In January, 1919, he was discharged from the service at Camp Jackson, South Carolina. In that same year, Dr. Browning returned to his native town, and began the practice of dentistry in Jewett City. He has already achieved a splendid start in his chosen profession, and is looked upon as one of the coming men of the county.

Dr. Browning is well known and popular in various activities throughout this vicinity. He is a member of Mount Vernon Lodge, No. 75, Free and Accepted Masons, of Jewett City, and of Franklin Chapter, No. 3, Royal Arch Masons, of Norwich. His college fraternity is the Delta Sigma Delta. He attends the Congregational church of Griswold, and supports its social and benevolent organizations. Politically, he reserves the right to personal decision, and votes independently, giving unqualified support to no party.

Dr. Browning married Mildred Louise Akerley, of Reading, Massachusetts, November 15, 1920, she a daughter of Oliver L. and Susan J. Miller. She is a graduate of Abbot Academy at Andover, Massachusetts, class of 1915, and also graduated, in 1916, from the Forsyth Infirmary, at Boston, an infirmary for children.

JOHN CONDON QUINLAN—In the manufacture of marble and granite monuments and memorials of various kinds, John Condon Quinlan is a leader in New London county, Connecticut, and his establishment in Norwich is the largest in the city covering this field.

Mr. Quinlan is a son of Patrick L. Quinlan, who was born in County Limerick, Ireland. He came to this country as soon as he left school, when only fourteen years of age. In 1854 he located in Greenville, Connecticut, one of the suburbs of Norwich, where he was employed in the bleachery, now the United States Finishing Company. After the death of his wife, which occurred in 1864, the young man went to Omaha, Nebraska, and settled there permanently. In 1867 he entered the employ of W. F. Murphy, a very prominent politician of Omaha. Mr. Quinlan was thereafter, for the rest of his life, more or less closely associated with Mr. Murphy, and for twenty-four years held the position of engineer of the Post Office Customs House in that city. He died in Omaha, December 26, 1913. Mr. Quinlan's first wife, Catherine (Condon) Quinlan, was born in Ireland, and died in Norwich, in 1864. Of her three children, John Condon Quinlan, whose name heads this review, is the only one now living. Patrick L. Quinlan married (second) in Omaha, and six children were born of this marriage.

John Condon Quinlan was born in Norwich, Connecticut, on August 18, 1862, and is the third child of Patrick L. and Catherine (Condon) Quinlan. He received his formal education in the public schools of Norwich, and in the Norwich Free Academy. He was a young man of artistic tastes, yet with a natural inclination to the definitely practical, and at the age of seventeen he entered the office of A. G. Cutler, then a prominent architect. He studied the business with Mr. Cutler, and became an expert mechanical draughtsman, remaining there until 1880. In that year he became associated with his uncle, P. R. Condon, who was in the marble and granite business, and the leading monument maker of the day in this section. The young man became very efficient along this line, and worked for his uncle in the capacity of foreman for several years. P. R. Condon died in 1909, and upon his death the business passed into the hands of Mr. Quinlan. The business has continued uninterruptedly ever since, and has grown in volume and importance, until now it is the largest of its kind in the city. Mr. Quinlan's excellent taste, and his talent for fine effects, have placed his work in a class by itself, and many very beautiful memorials have been produced under his eye. He is a member of the National Association of Retail Monument Dealers.

Mr. Quinlan always keeps in touch with public affairs, and is a staunch Democrat, although he has never sought nor accepted public office. He is a member of the Benevolent and Protective Order of Elks, Lodge No. 430, of Norwich, and a member of the Woodmen of the World, Camp No. 90.

Mr. Quinlan married, in Norwich, on June 11, 1905, Nellie M. Corcoran, of that city. She is the daughter of Morris and Ellen (O'Brien) Corcoran, both natives of Cork, Ireland. The family have always been devout members of St. Patrick's Roman Catholic Church.

JOHN PATRICK GORMAN—A prominent figure in the business life of Jewett City is John Patrick Gorman, owner and manager of the Gorman Drug Store, which is located at No. 60 Main street. From the time of his coming to this community he has given his earnest support to all movements calculated to advance the welfare of the place which he has chosen for his residence and field of business activities.

John Patrick Gorman was born in Greenville, town of Norwich, Connecticut, September 14, 1855, the son of Patrick and Beezy (Battle) Gorman. Patrick Gorman was born in Sligo, Ireland, and came to this country in 1848, locating in Norwich, where he secured a position as overseer of one of the departments of the Chelsea Paper Mills, and continued here until his death, which occurred in Norwich. To Mr. and Mrs. Gorman were born three children: Catherine, wife of Anthony J. Murphy, of Norwich, Connecticut; George D., deceased; and John Patrick, of further mention.

After completing his studies in the public schools of Greenville, John Patrick Gorman worked in various places, but in 1884 he entered the employ of Dr. William Soule for the purpose of learning the drug business, and passed the examinations of the Connecticut State Board of Pharmacy in 1904. He then returned to Dr. Soule's drug store as a registered pharmacist and remained there until 1914, when he established himself in the drug business at his present location on Main street. He has been highly successful in his business venture, which is due to his own indefatigable effort and his unfailing belief in his ability to succeed.

In politics he is a Republican, and for ten years has been justice of the peace. He affiliates with Mt. Vernon Lodge, No. 75, Free and Accepted Masons; Franklin Chapter, No. 3, Royal Arch Masons; Franklin Council, No. 4, Royal and Select Masters; Columbian Commandery, Knights Templar; Sphinx Temple, Ancient Arabic Order Nobles of the Mystic Shrine; and Connecticut Consistory, Ancient Accepted Scottish Rite, thirty-second degree. He is also a member of Reliance Lodge, No. 29, Independent Order of Odd Fellows, the Norwich

Alfred H. LaBarre

Nest of Owls, and Undaunted Lodge, No. 34, Knights of Pythias, of Jewett City. He is a member of the Methodist Episcopal Church of Jewett City.

ALFRED HENRY LA BARRE — Born and reared in New London county, and with an honorable record in the great World War, Alfred Henry La Barre, of Taftville, Connecticut, is now his father's assistant in the Rock Water Soda Company plant in Taftville. Mr. La Barre is of French descent, his parents being the first of the family to come to this country.

Albert La Barre was born in the Province of Quebec, Canada, on April 17, 1866, and received his education there in the parochial schools. He came to the United States when sixteen years of age, coming directly to New London county and locating in Jewett City. There he entered the employ of R. R. Church, the leading coal dealer of the Jewett City of that day. The young man soon became manager of the business, and remained with Mr. Church for several years. He then turned his attention to farming, at Griswold, near the village of Pachaug, for eight years, then, in the early nineties, he conducted a bakery in Jewett City, following along this line for a period of two years. Removing at the end of that time to the adjoining town of Plainfield, Mr. La Barre engaged in farming for about one year. After that he lived in several different places until 1910, during all of that time actively engaged in useful endeavor. He then located permanently in Taftville, and established himself in the manufacture of bottled soda. He has been very successful, the product being a popular one throughout an extensive territory. The business was recently incorporated, with Mr. La Barre as president, and is in a most flourishing condition. Mr. La Barre married Mary Le Roux, and they are the parents of thirteen children, all living except one, as follows: Albert, Jr.; Alfred Henry, whose name heads this review; Napoleon, Rose, Albina; George, deceased; Alvia, Diana, Wilfred, Agnes, Theodore, Delina, and Mary. All of these children are still at home (1921).

Alfred Henry La Barre, son of Albert and Mary (Le Roux) La Barre, was born in Jewett City, Connecticut, on December 22, 1890. He received his education in the excellent public schools of that place, and grew up to be a representative American young man. When the call for men overseas came to American manhood, he responded, enlisting on May 19, 1918. He served in Company K, 313th Regiment, 79th Division, American Expeditionary Forces. He was gassed at Montfaucon, France, and suffered severely from the effects of this insidious poison. Discharged at Camp Upton, New York, on May 19, 1919, he returned at once to his home, and is now associated with his father in the prosperous business in Taftville. His business ability and native industry bid fair to make his position in the management one of power and progressive achievement.

Mr. La Barre is well and favorably known in this vicinity, interested in all public activity and community progress. Politically an Independent, he thinks for himself on all subjects of general interest. He is a member of Ponemah Council, Knights of Columbus, of Taftville, Connecticut; Court Wequonnock, No. 88, Foresters of America, of Taftville; Aerie No. 367, Fraternal Order of Eagles, of Norwich; Robert O. Fletcher Post of the American Legion, of Norwich; and Union St. John the Baptiste Society of Taftville. The La Barre family have always been members of the Sacred Heart Roman Catholic Church.

LEWIS ROBERT CHURCH, cashier of the Norwich Water Company, was born in Montville, Connecticut, September 23, 1860, the son of Periz and Jane (Parker) Church. Periz Church was born in Montville, Connecticut, in 1839, and died in 1872. For many years he was a pilot on the steamer "City of Lawrence," which ran from Norwich to New York City. To Mr. and Mrs. Church were born nine children, and four of the number are still living: Louise P., widow of Henry E. Silcox, of Norwich; Frank P., a cigar manufacturer of Norwich, Connecticut, who married Annie E. Pettigrew; John H., a resident of Middletown, Connecticut; and Lewis Robert, mentioned below.

The education of Lewis Robert Church was obtained in the public schools of his native place, after which he worked on his father's farm until 1880, when, together with his brother, Frank P. Church, he engaged in the manufacture of cigars in Norwich, continuing in this line of industry until 1899, when the two brothers bought out the coal business on Thames street from the A. W. Gibbs estate. In 1912 Lewis Robert Church bought out his brother's interest in this business and continued it himself until 1917, when he became manager of the real estate business of A. M. Avery. In 1920 he accepted his present position as cashier and clerk of the water department of the city of Norwich. He is prominent in Masonic circles, being affiliated with St. James Lodge, No. 23, Free and Accepted Masons; Franklin Chapter, No. 3, Royal Arch Masons; Franklin Council, No. 4, Royal and Select Masters; and Columbian Commandery, Knights Templar. In religion he is a Baptist, and attends the Central Baptist Church of Norwich.

Mr. Church married, in Norwich, November 16, 1888, Elizabeth Maynard, daughter of Jedediah and Julia (Rockwell) Maynard. Mr. and Mrs. Church are the parents of two children, both born in Norwich, Connecticut: Lloyd Maynard, sales agent for the Automatic Refrigerating Company of Hartford, Connecticut, married Pauline Huff, of Rochester, New York; Robert Huntington, who served with the United States navy during the World War and was stationed at the submarine base at New London, Connecticut.

ROBERT BOISSON — Although having been identified with Norwich, or in fact the United

States, but a very short time, having come here in 1917, Mr. Boisson has not only identified himself with the business interests of the community which he has chosen for his home, but also as a citizen he is always ready to do all in his power to promote her best welfare and truest progress.

Robert Boisson was born in Lyons, France, October 19, 1890, the son of Felix and Eugenia (Fronbat) Boisson. For a number of years Robert Boisson has been engaged in his present business, that of novelty manufacturer. To Mr. and Mrs. Boisson have been born twelve children, and among the number were Marcel and Rene, who were killed in action during the World War, French army; Felix, an importer in China; Robert, mentioned below.

Robert Boisson, when a young lad, entered the public schools of his native place, and passed through the consecutive grades to his graduation from the Lyons High School, after which he secured a position as clerk in a bank near his native city, remaining there for five years. He then enlisted in the French army, and in 1910 he was called for military duty, for two years served in the Thirtieth Battalion, Chasseurs Alpins, was relieved, and in August, 1914, called back to same regiment and served until July, 1916. He was wounded, July 19, 1916, at the battle of the Somme, was three months in hospital, discharged in March, 1917—lost his left arm. He saw service in the Vosges Mountains, and during this time was in many battles. The Thirtieth Battalion were the Blue Devils. He served as first lieutenant. After his discharge from the war he came to America, landing in New York, accompanied by his wife, Gabrielle (Bietrix) Boisson, whom he had married just previous to sailing; he immediately came to Norwich, Connecticut, subsequently entering into his present position as assistant manager with the J. B. Martin Company, velvet manufacturers.

To Mr. and Mrs. Boisson, who were married in Lyons, France, February 2, 1917, have been born two children: Jeanne, in France, November 16, 1918; Henri, January 5, 1920. The family attend the Sacred Heart Church of Norwich.

HENRY A. MÜLLER—The ancestry of Mr. Müller is German on both the maternal and paternal sides of his family, though Mr. Müller is an American citizen by birth. He is the son of August and Barbara (Scheinlein) Müller, the former a native of Torgua Krais, Daletzsch, Kingdom of Prussia, Germany, where he was born April 19, 1820. August Müller attended the public school in his province until he was seventeen years of age, when he left to become an apprentice in the shop of a cabinet maker at Torgua. After serving his time at this trade he went to Leipzig, Germany, obtaining work in that line and remaining there for six years.

Emigrating to the United States on September 28, 1852, August Müller located in New York City, November 10, 1852, becoming employed at his trade. After remaining there for three years he moved to Stonington, Connecticut, where he went into business as a furniture dealer and also conducted an undertaking establishment in connection with it. He was very successful in both these lines and carried them on until his death, which occurred in Stonington, July 12, 1903. August Müller was quite prominent as a Freemason, being a Master Mason for thirty-five years in Stonington. He was married, in New York City, October 26, 1853, to Barbara Scheinlein, and their son, Henry A., was born there. Mrs. Barbara (Scheinlein) Müller was born in Bavaria, Germany.

While still an infant, Henry A. Müller's parents moved to Stonington and there the lad grew up, attending the public school, and when old enough assisting his father in the furniture store. In 1879 the younger Mr. Müller went out West and, locating in Missouri, became engaged in the furniture and undertaking business, staying there for ten years. Returning to Stonington in 1889, he again joined his father, remaining with him until the death of the elder Mr. Müller, when Henry A. Müller took over the business and has continued it up to the present time (1921).

In politics Mr. Müller is a Democrat, and for the last five years has served on the Board of Burgesses. He is a member of Union No. 50, Ancient Order of United Workmen, of Stonington, and a member of Pequot Council, Royal Arcanum, of the same place.

Mr. Müller married, May 16, 1888, Elizabeth Owens, who was born in Springfield, Ohio. Mr. and Mrs. Müller are the parents of four children: 1. August O., now in business with his father. 2. Grace, who married Albert G. Randell, and resides at New Rochelle, New York. 3. Frank, who resides at Bridgeport, Connecticut; he served in the World War, in the Medical Corps, and was stationed at Fort Oglethorpe, Georgia. 4. Elizabeth, who is a teacher in Westerly, Rhode Island, and resides at home; she graduated from the State Normal School at Willimantic, Connecticut. Mr. and Mrs. Henry A. Müller and their family are members of the Second Congregational Church of Stonington.

BURDETT SILAS DOUBLEDAY—Since 1912, Mr. Doubleday has been a resident of Colchester, Connecticut, and during these few years has already become recognized as a citizen who takes a keen and active interest in all things pertaining to the welfare of the community.

Dwight Doubleday, father of Burdett Silas Doubleday, was born in Columbia, Connecticut, in 1846, and has followed agricultural pursuits throughout his entire lifetime. He married Martha Wheeler, who was also a native of Columbia, and to them were born the following children: Roy, Ida, Amos, Hubert, Hyde, Walter Richard, Martha, and Burdett Silas, of further mention.

Burdett Silas Doubleday was born at Lebanon, Connecticut, May 8, 1880. His childhood was spent on his father's farm, where most of his spare time from school was spent in aiding the elder man with his work about the farm. At the age of eighteen years he terminated

Michael Jacob

his studies and returned to the farm to give his entire time toward gaining a wide knowledge of agricultural methods. In 1912 he came to Colchester, Connecticut, where he purchased his present place, which has been his residence continuously up to the present time. This farm land was naturally fertile, and he continued to cultivate it until he has brought it to its present highly productive state.

Mr. Doubleday has never taken any active part in public affairs, but has always shown particular interest in the welfare of the community, and there is no good work done in the name of charity or religion but finds in him an earnest supporter.

Mr. Doubleday married, September 10, 1906, Emma Baumberger, daughter of Arnold and Emma Baumberger, natives of Hebron, Connecticut. Mr. and Mrs. Doubleday are the parents of seven children: Clara Emma, Alma, Mary, Theodore, John, Helen, and Ernest Silas, deceased. Mr. and Mrs. Doubleday are members of the Congregational church.

WALLACE H. PAYNE—The Paynes of Jewett City, Connecticut, father and son, are well known, the father as a soldier of peace, as taught by the church of which he was long a devoted minister, the son as a militant soldier who fought the "Hun" on his chosen battlefields, inhaled his deadly gasses, and returned to his native United States the victor over his savage foe and his barbarous weapons. Father and son have now joined forces again, and are the editors and publishers of the Jewett City "Press," the elder Mr. Payne having bought that paper in 1907.

Rev. John W. Payne, father of Wallace H. Payne, was born in Cincinnati, Ohio, and there completed a course in public school study. He then was a student at Granville Academy and College, Granville, Ohio, whence he was graduated A. B., becoming later an A. M. He studied divinity at Rochester (New York) Theological Seminary, and was duly ordained a minister of the Baptist church. He accepted calls from various churches of that faith, which he ably administered until 1889, when he was called to the pastorate of the Jewett City Baptist Church. He accepted the call, and for fourteen years was the loved and honored pastor of that congregation. From 1883 until 1889 Rev. John W. Payne was associated with Dr. W. R. Harper, former president of the Chicago University, Chicago, Illinois, as proof reader and specialist in Semitic publications. From 1904 to 1907 he had a small printing business in Jewett City, and in 1907 he purchased the Jewett City "Press," which he has since most ably edited. He married Anna B. Tunison, and they are the parents of three children: Ivah M., wife of Benjamin R. Gardner, of Jewett City; Herbert E., deceased; and Wallace H., of further mention.

Wallace H. Payne was born in New Haven, Connecticut, February 4, 1889. He passed through the public schools of Jewett City, and after finishing his studies, became associated with his father in the publishing of the Jewett City "Press." His newspaper work was interrupted by his service in the United States army, which he entered February 27, 1918, for service in the war against Germany. He was assigned to Company B, 308th Regiment, 77th Division, was sent overseas, and saw hard service in France; was severely burned by mustard gas, but survived every peril of that infernal period in the world's history; returned to the United States, and was honorably discharged and mustered out at Camp Upton, Long Island, April 1, 1919. Since his return, Mr. Payne has resumed newspaper work in Jewett City with his father.

Under its scholarly editor, Rev. John W. Payne, and his son, Wallace H., the Jewett City "Press" has reflected in its pages and in its prosperity the ability of the men who since 1907 have guided its destinies. They have made it a force for good in New London county, and a credit to journalism.

Mr. Payne is a past master of Mount Vernon Lodge, No. 75, Free and Accepted Masons, of Jewett City, and is a member of Jewett City Post of the American Legion, and of the Jewett City Baptist Church.

MICHAEL JACOB—A prosperous farmer and business man, Michael Jacob was one of Taftville's highly respected citizens, and one whose public spirit and co-operation could always be relied upon. He was born in Bavaria, Germany, December 26, 1865, and died at his farm near Taftville, town of Norwich, New London county, Connecticut, February 4, 1918.

He was educated in the schools of his native district, and grew to adult years there. From January 29, 1895, to 1899, he served in the German army, attaining the rank of lieutenant. From 1899 until 1903 he was engaged as a lumber salesman, then came to the United States, joining his father, who had preceded him and was engaged in business in Taftville, Connecticut. Michael Jacob, soon after coming to New London county, bought a farm near Taftville and conducted very profitable farming operations. He also established a meat market in the village, and until his death continued both lines of business. He prospered abundantly, and when death removed him his farm and business affairs were in such good condition that his widow has since conducted both along the same lines. He was a man of industry, and by good judgment and energy won success as a business man, while his virtues as a man insured the respect and esteem of all who knew him. He was a member of Norwich Lodge, No. 430, Benevolent and Protective Order of Elks, and while he met all the demands of citizenship took no active part in political affairs.

Mr. Jacob married, June 14, 1912, Mrs. Lena Krodel, born in Bavaria, Germany, widow of Andrew Krodel, who died in Taftville, September 28, 1911, leaving a daughter Rose, who died November 27, 1913, aged three years. Mrs. Jacob is a good business woman and ably manages the estate committed to her care. She is interested in church and charitable work, and has many friends.

ERASTUS WILLINGTON CARTER—It was not until 1907 that Mr. Carter came to Norwich, Connecticut, but during the fourteen years which have since elapsed he has established and built up a strong general insurance agency. He is of Rhode Island birth and parentage, his parents, Gideon W. and Elizabeth (Freeman) Carter, being residents of North Providence at the time of the birth of their son. Gideon W. Carter was born in Westport, Rhode Island, but when a young man moved to North Providence, where he became a cotton mill worker and finally overseer of the weaving room at the Dyerville mill. When war broke out between the states, he enlisted in Company I, Seventh Regiment, Rhode Island Volunteer Infantry, and served with honor. He returned to Rhode Island after his military service, and being an expert weaver, he continued in the textile mills as overseer until his death, which occurred in February, 1918. His wife died in Danielson, Connecticut, in June, 1905. They were the parents of three children: Erastus W., of further mention; Ida, wife of Benjamin Russell, of Danielson, Connecticut; and George LeMar, who married Elizabeth Whipple, and resides in Providence, Rhode Island.

Erastus W. Carter was born in Providence, Rhode Island, September 2, 1852, and there educated in the public schools. After school years were over he became a cotton mill worker and an expert weaver. He did not confine himself to any particular mill, but, being an expert, could always be sure of a good position wherever he went. He served as overseer of weaving in several New England cotton mills, continuing in the textile business until 1900. He then located in Willimantic, Connecticut, and there established a fire insurance agency, which he successfully conducted until 1907, when he sold his business and located in Norwich, where he yet resides. In Norwich he has conducted a general insurance business, also dealing to a limited extent in real estate. During his earlier years he was always a member of some musical organization, his own specialty being the snare drum. In the various towns in which he lived he belonged to several orchestras and bands, some of them well-known and famous.

In Norwich he is a member of the Fire Underwriters' Association; is a Republican in politics; member of Norwich Lodge, No. 430, Benevolent and Protective Order of Elks; and an attendant of the Episcopal church.

Mr. Carter married, October 4, 1874, Mary A. Gough, daughter of Hugh and Tresia (Newton) Gough, of Plainfield, Connecticut. Mr. and Mrs. Carter are the parents of six children: 1. Geneva, born in Norwich, died at the age of four years. 2. Gertrude L., wife of Arthur A. Thomsette, a civil engineer, of Providence, Rhode Island. 3. Willington H., who married Mary E. Mulholland, a contractor and builder in Miami, Florida. 4. Theresa M., who died at the age of eighteen years. 5. Joseph F., who married (first) Jennie Keon, (second) Lovenia White; an automobile dealer in Pawtucket, Rhode Island. 6. Inez Mae, who lives at home.

JOSEPH FRANCIS LEAHY—In or about 1851 a young emigrant from Ireland landed in the United States, locating in Mystic, Connecticut. He was James Leahy, and he found employment as a stationary engineer in one of the industrial plants in Mystic. He continued there, occupied in various places, until his death in 1888. His wife, Sarah (Carey) Leahy, died four years earlier (1884). They were the parents of twelve children, their son, Joseph Francis, being the eleventh child in this large family.

Joseph Francis Leahy was born in Mystic, New London county, Connecticut, May 22, 1864. He attended the public school in the village and when older went to Stonington, Connecticut, where he became an employee of the Atwood Machine Company. Some time later he was promoted to the position of foreman of the moulding department, holding this position for seventeen years. On March 22, 1915, Joseph Francis Leahy received the appointment of postmaster in the post office at Stonington, where he is located at present.

Always a Democrat in politics, Mr. Leahy has taken a great interest in the village welfare. He has served on the Board of School Commissioners for five years, having been secretary of the board for three years. Joseph Francis Leahy is a prominent member of the Knights of Columbus and is connected with Nina Council, No. 43, in which he is a past grand knight.

In Stonington, on July 3, 1887, Joseph Francis Leahy was married to Ellen Louise Conners, a resident of that town. She is the daughter of Mathew and Bridget (Harvey) Conners, both natives of Ireland. Mr. and Mrs. Leahy have seven children: 1. Sarah L., the wife of Dr. James M. Crowley. 2. Josephine E., living at home. 3. Mathew T., whose wife was Clara Vargas, of Stonington; he is assistant postmaster at Stonington; during the World War he served in the American Expeditionary Forces, in Company B, 177th Regiment, 77th Division, and was in active service in France. 4. James L., a printer in Boston, Massachusetts; during the war he enlisted and was stationed at Camp Devens, Ayer, Massachusetts, in charge of the printing department. 5. Helen, who died in infancy. 6. William J., living at home. 7. Daniel C., also at home. Mr. and Mrs. Leahy and their family are members of St. Mary's Roman Catholic Church of Stonington.

LOUIS IRENCE PRATTE, M.D.—Over a quarter of a century has elapsed since Dr. Pratte began private practice in Taftville, Connecticut, these years, 1887-1920, having returned him richly the honors of his, the oldest of professions. Dr. Pratte is a native of Louisville, Province of Quebec, his parents, Louis and Philomena (Woisard) Pratte, both born in the Province of Quebec. Louis Pratte, his father, lived his entire life in Louisville, and until his death, which occurred in 1900, he owned a large meat market there. His wife died in 1905.

Louis I. Pratte was born in Louisville, Province of Quebec, December 10, 1854. There he attended the parochial schools and then entered Three Rivers Seminary, from which latter institution he was graduated in 1875. Having already decided upon the profession of medicine for his life work, he matriculated in the Medical Department of Victoria College, from which he received his degree of Doctor of Medicine in 1879. Immediately after graduation he went to Baltic, Connecticut, and there entered private practice. Eight years later, in 1887, he came to Taftville, and here he has since been engaged in the practice of his profession. He is a member of the American Medical Association, Connecticut Medical Society, and the New London Medical Society, and holds the high esteem of his professional brethren. In politics he is a Democrat, and served one year as a selectman. In religion he is a Roman Catholic, a member of Sacred Heart Church, and is a member of the Knights of Columbus, Ponemah Council, No. 34, of Taftville, Connecticut.

Dr. Pratte married Mary N. Brophy, a native of Bolton, Connecticut, August 1, 1887, and they are the parents of two children: Louis Edouard, and Marie B. Mrs. Pratte died February 27, 1921, at Taftville, Connecticut.

The success of Louis I. Pratte is a distinct personal triumph, for without the advantage of wealth or influence he has won his way to high position in a profession not lacking in able men, and with that position has come the material reward which accompanies professional success.

LOUIS HALE MAPLES, founder of the Norwich Buick Company, agents for the Buick automobile, is widely known in Norwich, and in addition to his prominence in business is identified with various other features of municipal life.

Louis H. Maples is a son of Judson A. Maples, who was born in Norwich, Connecticut, and there died, in 1895. He was engaged in farming throughout his lifetime, was a Republican in politics, and a prominent member of the Westside Baptist Church, of which he had been deacon for many years. He married Mary E. Birchard, daughter of Asa Hyde Birchard, a butcher, well known throughout his community. To Mr. and Mrs. Maples were born two children: Louis Hale, mentioned below; and Frederick Judson, born in Norwich, Connecticut, July 6, 1884, now a resident of Albany, New York, where he is engaged in the coal and gravel business. He married Mary Rubeck, of Hagaman, New York.

Louis Hale Maples was born in Bozrah, Connecticut, July 31, 1881, and obtained his education in the primary and grammar schools of Norwich. After a year and a half spent on his father's farm, he entered the meat market of A. G. B. Hunt, as clerk, and was there about one year when he decided to learn the silk business. He secured employment at a local mill, but owing to ill health he gave up his position and secured employment on the farm of John M. Moore, of Norwich. At the age of twenty he was appointed janitor of the Backus Hospital, but six months later resigned and for the next few years was engaged in the meat and grocery business. In 1910 he became interested in the automobile business, and for seven years was located in a building at the rear of the Davis Theatre, on Broadway. There he did an excellent business until 1918, when the Buick Company began business in the Majestic building. In 1919 Mr. Maples organized the Norwich Buick Company, for the handling of the Buick car, with salesrooms located at No. 319 Main street, and there is continuing his former success.

In politics he is a Republican, but takes no active part in political affairs. He is affiliated with Somerset Lodge, No. 34, Free and Accepted Masons; Franklin Chapter, No. 4, Royal Arch Masons; Franklin Council, No. 3, Royal and Select Masters; Columbian Commandery, No. 4, Knights Templar; and all bodies of the Connecticut Consistory, Ancient Accepted Scottish Rite, in which he holds the Thirty-second degree. He is also a member of Sphinx Temple, Ancient Arabic Order Nobles of the Mystic Shrine of Hartford, and the Independent Order of Odd Fellows. He attends the Westside Baptist Church of Norwich, the Arcanum Club, and Norwich Grange, Patrons of Husbandry.

On April 30, 1904, Mr. Maples married Josie L. Bailey, daughter of Marvin L. and Lydia (Wilcox) Bailey. Mr. and Mrs. Maples are the parents of one child, Frederick, born December 31, 1907.

WILLIAM EDWARD PECK—During the last two decades of his life William Edward Peck was connected with the Baltic Mills Company, of Baltic, Connecticut, coming to that company in the second year of its existence and continuing in official position until his passing away, filling the position of office manager, director, agent and general manager. There were advantages in the association which contributed to make the connection a mutually profitable one. The Baltic Mills Company was a comparatively new corporation, their plant, erected in 1900, one of the most modern in arrangement and equipment. Their product was a fine grade of cotton cloth, and they needed a modern textile manufacturer to set its equipment in motion and market its product. Mr. Peck was a man in the prime of life, trained in the New England school of experience, who had risen from the ranks of the army of office workers, and was thoroughly capable of filling any position in textile mill management. Thus, the man and his opportunity were brought face to face, and the enterprise which lacked its leader was supplied, and success followed. The relations which existed between the board of directors of the Baltic Mills Company and Mr. Peck were most cordial and helpful, the hearty coöperation of the board giving their agent practically full authority to carry forward the plans and policies he felt were wise and necessary. In this unity there was strength, and the Baltic Mills Company assumed a position among the prosperous textile mills of New England and returned an income most satisfactory.

Mr. Peck, whose memory is herein honored, was the second to bear the name of William Edward Peck, his father bearing it with honor before him. William E. Peck, Sr., was born in East Greenwich, Rhode Island, and died at Napoleonville, Louisiana, August 3, 1865, being stricken with a chill which caused his death two hours later. After completing his education in public schools and East Greenwich

Academy he began the study of law in the office of Richard W. Green, of Providence, Rhode Island, his preceptor later becoming a justice of the Rhode Island Supreme Court. When war broke out between the states of the North and South, Mr. Peck enlisted in a Rhode Island regiment of cavalry as a private, but later attained the rank of first lieutenant. He was on duty in the State of Louisiana when he was appointed judge advocate and transferred to Napoleonville, Louisiana, where he was stricken with a fatal illness. He married Harriet E. Newell, who survived him and later died in Hyde Park, Massachusetts. They were the parents of a daughter, Harriet A., now deceased, and a son, William Edward, Jr., of whom further.

William Edward Peck, Jr., was born in East Greenwich, Rhode Island, March 1, 1857, died in Baltic, Connecticut, April 7, 1921. He was educated in the public schools and East Greenwich Academy, finishing his studies at the last-named institution in 1876. During that same year he became a bookkeeper in New York City, and later returned to East Greenwich, where he was employed for a time in the office of the Union Cotton Mills. He filled office positions in Providence, Rhode Island, and was for several years with the Ladd Watch Case Company, entering that employ as bookkeeper and later becoming general manager. The positions were all preparatory to the great work of his life, his connection with the Baltic Mills Company.

In 1901, Mr. Peck resigned his position with the Ladd Watch Case Company to accept the office management of the Baltic Mills Company. This association, formed in 1901, continued unbroken until 1921, when it was severed by the death of Mr. Peck, who had become agent and general manager of the mills and was also a member of the board of directors. His management had been attended with the greatest success, and so harmonious had been his relations with the directors that his passing was felt not more as a corporation than as a personal loss.

Mr. Peck was appointed a trustee and general manager of the Quidnick-Windham Manufacturing Company, of Willimantic, Connecticut, and Quidnick, Rhode Island, after that company went into the hands of a receiver, and also was a director of the Chelsea Savings Bank of Norwich, Connecticut. He was a member of the National Association of Cotton Manufacturers. In his political views he was an influential Republican; his religious conviction was with the Episcopal faith.

On April 19, 1882, Mr. Peck married, at East Greenwich, Rhode Island, Mary E. Tibbetts, who died without children, in Baltic, April 18, 1914, daughter of Henry A. and Clarinda (Enos) Tibbetts. Such was the life story of William Edward Peck, a story so intimately interwoven with the history of the Baltic Mills Company as to be inseparable. With that company he made his greatest success in life, and under his management the company took place with the prosperous industries of the State. The man has gone, but the corporation lives as a testimonial to his broad vision and wise management.

ARTHUR PETER COTÉ—Providing for the daily needs of the people is the line of business endeavor in which Arthur Peter Côté, of Baltic, Connecticut, is winning substantial success.

Peter S. Côté, Mr. Côté's father, was born in Weedon, Province of Quebec, and educated in the parochial schools of that city. He came to the United States when fourteen years of age, locating in Southbridge, Massachusetts, where he was employed in the machine shops. He came to Baltic, Connecticut, in 1860, and here went into business with his uncle, Treffle Côté, and was associated with him in the general store from that year until 1900, when he died in Baltic. He married Eliza E. Trempe, who was born in Sorel, Province of Quebec, Canada, and who still survives him, being a resident of Baltic at this time. They were the parents of five children, of whom Arthur Peter is the eldest. The other children are: Alby G., one of the leading ice dealers of Baltic, who married Mary Bouchard; Emile L., who married Julia Bouchard, and resides in New York City; Blanche, now the wife of Edward Case, of Norwich; and Melville P., who bore a gallant part in the great struggle of the World War, and now resides in Baltic, and is a traveling salesman, handling a standard line of drugs.

Arthur Peter Côté was born in Baltic, Connecticut, in the town of Sprague, on September 2, 1877. He received his early education in the parochial schools of the town, then completed his studies at the Holy Cross College, in the city of West Farnham, Canada, where he remained for three years. In 1897 he returned to Baltic, and for a short period was associated with his father in the general store. Following this he went to Willimantic, and was employed as clerk in one of the prominent retail stores of that day, conducted by the firm of Mullen & St. Onge. Later on he gained valuable experience in the employ of other merchants, and in 1914 bought the retail meat business theretofore conducted by T. Douville & Company. He found the business congenial, and has thus far made it increasingly profitable. He is considered one of the prominent men of the town, and the outlook for the future is bright.

Mr. Côté takes a deep and constructive interest in the public affairs of his native town. Politically, he is a member of the Republican party, but he is held in such high esteem by the people of the town that his name has repeatedly been placed on both tickets. He is now town clerk and town treasurer of the town of Sprague, having held the former office for sixteen and the latter office for twenty-one years.

Fraternally, Mr. Côté is widely known. He is a member of Lodge No. 430, Benevolent and Protective Order of Elks, of Norwich; of Court Sprague, No. 90, Foresters of America; of the Union St. Jean de Baptiste; and Ponemah Council, No. 34, Knights of Columbus. He is in close touch with the business world of Norwich, being a member of the Norwich Chamber of Commerce. He is a member of the Immaculate Conception Roman Catholic Church.

On January 21, 1909, Mr. Côté married Alma Bibeau,

Arthur P. Côté

of Baltic, daughter of Louis and Milina (Lucien) Bibeau, of this town. Mr. and Mrs. Côté are the parents of five children, three of whom are living: Joseph A., deceased; Wilfred; Henry; Rena, deceased; and Estella, the young people still residing at home.

JAMES HORATIO HYDE—A well-known farmer and cattle dealer of Franklin, New London county, Connecticut, Mr. Hyde tills his acres of the farm upon which he was born, and has won high reputation in his community for energy, integrity and public spirit. He traces lineal descent from William Hyde, one of the original proprietors of Norwich, Connecticut, in 1660, although he is recorded in Hartford, Connecticut, in 1636, his name appearing on the monument erected to the founders of that city. He was a member of the Board of Selectmen of Norwich, and there died, January 6, 1681. He married, and descent in this line is through his son, Samuel.

(II) Samuel Hyde, son of William Hyde, was born in Hartford, Connecticut, about 1637, died at his home, Norwich West Farms, in 1677. He was one of the original proprietors of Norwich in 1660, with his father and others, and had lands assigned to him in that section known as Norwich West Farms. He continued there, a tiller of his own acres until his death. He married, in June, 1659, Jane Lee, of East Saybrook (now Lyme), daughter of Thomas and Phoebe (Brown) Lee, her father sailing from England for New England in 1641, but dying on the passage. Elizabeth Hyde, daughter of Samuel and Jane (Lee) Hyde, born in August, 1660, is said to have been the first white child born in Saybrook.

(III) Jabez Hyde, youngest of the eight children of Samuel and Jane (Lee) Hyde, was born in Norwich, Connecticut, May, 1677, died at Norwich West Farms, September 5, 1762. The part of Norwich West Farms in which he settled, lived and died, is now known as Franklin. He owned a large tract of land and became a wealthy farmer; was a justice of the peace, and representative to the General Court. For many years he was clerk of the Franklin church. He married, December 21, 1709, Elizabeth Bushnell, born January 31, 1686, died August 21, 1768, daughter of Richard and Elizabeth (Adgate) Bushnell, of Norwich. They were the parents of three sons and two daughters.

(IV) Jabez (2) Hyde, eldest son of Jabez (1) and Elizabeth (Bushnell) Hyde, was born in Norwich West Farms, September 16, 1713, died in Franklin, Connecticut, March 6, 1805. He was a large landowner, a magistrate, and a man of considerable importance. He married, December 8, 1736, Lydia Abel, born July 28, 1719, in Norwich, died June 25, 1805, daughter of Benjamin and Lydia (Hazen) Abel. They were the parents of eleven children, born between 1738 and 1762.

(V) Joseph Hyde, eighth child of Jabez (2) and Lydia (Abel) Hyde, was born about 1755, at Norwich West Farms, Connecticut, settled in that part of Norwich now known as Franklin, where he died, March 29, 1809. He married, September 6, 1780, Susannah Waterman, born January 19, 1762, died November 6, 1810, daughter of Nehemiah and Susannah (Isham) Waterman, of Norwich. They were the parents of ten children.

(VI) Horatio Hyde, youngest child of Joseph and Susannah (Waterman) Hyde, was born in Franklin, Connecticut, September 6, 1804, died there February 26, 1889, and is there buried. He learned the stone-mason's trade, but his health would not permit him to follow it, and he turned his attention to farming. He bought a farm in Franklin, which he cultivated with excellent results until his passing away. He was a Republican in politics, and a member of Franklin Congregational Church. He married, January 10, 1847, Laura A. Gager, born in Franklin, May 19, 1822, died April 8, 1895, daughter of Levi and Sybil (Hyde) Gager. Children: 1. Eunice, born January 15, 1848, formerly a school teacher, who died December 1, 1920. 2. Phoebe, born November 10, 1849, a teacher for several years, then resided with her brother at the homestead. 3. Laura Sybil, born February 20, 1852, died March 21, 1893, a teacher. 4. Otis B., born February 25, 1854, died at Norwich, February 9, 1902, a teacher; he married Catherine Kahn, and left a son, Leslie G., now a resident of Jewett City. 5. Arthur G., born February 11, 1856, resides in Franklin. 6. John T., born February 7, 1858, removed to Providence, Rhode Island. 7. Jennie, born January 1, 1860, and always resided at the home farm. 8. James Horatio, of further mention.

(VII) James Horatio Hyde, youngest of the children of Horatio and Laura A. (Gager) Hyde, was born in Franklin, New London county, Connecticut, September 26, 1864, his present home the house in which he was born. He was educated in the public school and early became his father's assistant. He managed the home farm for several years prior to his father's death, and then became its owner through the purchase of the interests of the other heirs. He has continued the operation of his farm until the present time, the area of which has been considerably increased by purchase until it now covers 290 acres, conducting it as a dairy and stock-raising farm. He has followed that line of activity all his life with profitable results, and has also for many years carried on auction sales all over the county, being a remarkably good auctioneer.

In political sentiment, Mr. Hyde is a Republican, and in 1911 represented his district in the Connecticut State Legislature. He was chairman of the Town Committee for twenty years, and has creditably filled a number of town offices. He is a member of Oliver Woodhouse Lodge, Knights of Pythias, of Colchester, Connecticut, and of Bozrah Grange. He has never married, his sisters residing at the homestead with him and making it a most pleasant place to live. Mr. Hyde is well-known, highly esteemed, and a good citizen and neighbor.

DAVID SUSSLER, M.D.—Among the younger professional men of Norwich, Connecticut, who bore a noble share in the recent World War, is Dr. David Sussler, M.D., whose office is in Taftville, a suburb of Norwich.

Dr. Sussler is a son of Frank and Viola (Smernoff) Sussler, both parents having been born in German Poland. Frank Sussler came to the United States about 1885, and located in New York City, where he became a cigar manufacturer. He was very successful in the land of his adoption, and remained in New York City in the same line of business until his death, which occurred in 1899. His wife now resides in Boston, Massachusetts. Of the three children born to Mr. and Mrs Sussler, Dr. Sussler is the second.

David Sussler was born in New York City on November 2, 1892. He received his early education in the public and high schools of New Haven, Connecticut, and was graduated from the latter institution in 1910. Choosing the profession of medicine, he entered the Fordham University Medical School, from which he was graduated in 1916, with the degree of Doctor of Medicine. He went into hospital practice in the Fordham Hospital in 1916, then later to the South Side Hospital, of Pittsburgh, Pennsylvania. This was in 1917, and Dr. Sussler had not yet completed his studies in surgery when the United States entered the war with Germany. He enlisted at once, and was called on October 3, 1917. As a member of the United States Medical Corps he was assigned to the Officers' Training Camp, at Fort Oglethorpe, Georgia, where he remained until December of that year. He was then transferred to Camp Sevier, in South Carolina. He was then assigned to the 30th Division, Ambulance Corps, No. 119, and was sent to France in June, 1918. On arriving there this division was assigned to the British Fourth Army, and was in active service from July to October, 1918, when he was gassed. He was then sent to London, to the Army Base Hospital, where he convalesced, remaining until November 15, of that year. Returning as soon as possible to France, he went back to his same division and company. He arrived home the following March, landing in Charleston, South Carolina. He was mustered out of service at Camp Devens, Massachusetts, on April 3, 1919, with the rank of first lieutenant, and was recommended for the Distinguished Service Cross, for devotion to duty under the most trying conditions at St. Quentin and Ypres.

Dr. Sussler is now established in Taftville, a suburb of Norwich, in the private practice of medicine and surgery, and his friends feel the utmost confidence in his success. He is a member of the Norwich Medical Society; of the New London County Medical Society; of the Connecticut State Medical Society; and of the American Medical Association. The doctor is a Republican by political affiliation, and sincerely loyal to the principles of the party. He is a member of Quinebaug Lodge, Independent Order of Odd Fellows.

CHESTER SANDS MAINE—From early days in Stonington, Connecticut, the name Maine has been a familiar and honored one. Ezekiel Maine, the first permanent settler of that name in Stonington, came in 1670, and in 1672 received a grant of land from the town, and ten years later was again granted lands lying south of Shunnock river. In 1674 he joined the Stonington church, and on June 19, 1714, died. By wife Mary he had children: Ezekiel, Mary, Jeremiah, Thomas, Phoebe, and Hannah. Ezekiel and Mary Maine, through their sons, founded numerous families, and they are the ancestors of those of the name in Eastern Connecticut who trace to early Colonial days. In Stonington and North Stonington the name has always been prominent, the prevailing occupation in this branch having always been agriculture, although many Maines have been successful merchants.

Chester S. Maine of this review, a descendant of the pioneer, Ezekiel Maine, is a son of John S. and Frances Abby (Wheeler) Maine, both father and son born in North Stonington. John S. Maine was a farmer, dealing extensively in cattle, and from his birth, May 9, 1833, until his death, March 25, 1881, he lived in the town of North Stonington. He was buried in the cemetery on the old John Maine homestead, but at the death of his wife the body was removed to the River Bend Cemetery, at Westerly, Rhode Island, where they were buried side by side. His wife, Frances Abby (Wheeler) Maine, was a daughter of Captain Allen Wheeler, and born in the same house as was her son, Chester S., the Maine home being the old Captain Allen Wheeler farm and homestead. Mrs. Frances Abby (Wheeler) Maine died in May, 1915.

Chester Sands Maine was born at the homestead, on the Captain Allen Wheeler farm in North Stonington, New London county, Connecticut, December 16, 1860. He attended the district school, and later was a student at Ashaway Academy in Rhode Island. While yet attending school he opened a little store at Clarks Falls, Connecticut, near his home, serving his customers in the morning and evenings, closing during school hours, Saturdays keeping open all day. After leaving school he engaged in farming and had a milk route, also bought, sold and traded horses and cattle, and was a breeder of light harness horses for the trotting track. In 1880 his father bought the farm upon which Chester S. Maine now lives, and when, ten months later, John S. Maine died, his son, Chester S., assumed the management. In December, 1881, he came of legal age and became the owner of the property and has ever since devoted himself to the cultivation and care of its three hundred acres. All the improvements on the farm, dwelling, barns and other buildings, have been built by Chester S. Maine and are all modern in design and equipment. The farm is conducted as a dairy and stock farm, the grade of cattle and the dairy products ranking very high. The stock and dairy business is conducted under the firm name, Chester S. Maine & Son, Mr. Maine's partner his son, Carroll Chester Maine.

In politics, a Democrat, Mr. Maine, while never seeking office, has frequently been chosen for public duty. In 1909 he represented North Stonington in the State Legislature, was elected member of the Board of Selectmen when twenty-one, and was assessor of taxes many years. He is a member of the New London County Farm Bureau, and of the New England Milk Producers' Association. He is one of New London's best and most progressive farmers, and the foregoing record is but an outline of his activities since boyhood days when he kept a store after school hours. In the younger years he was the personification of energy, and at one time ran a saw-mill and manufactured lumber.

His cattle dealings were extensive, and his connection with the trotting horse market as a breeder and dealer was much more extensive than has herein been indicated. While he has naturally surrendered some of the heavier burdens to his capable son and partner, he is the managing head of one of the largest farms in North Stonington, and that farm, one of the best improved and equipped in the county, reflects the spirit and ambition of its owner. He is a real farmer, practical yet progressive, proud of his estate and full of plans for its still further improvement and development.

Mr. Maine married, in North Stonington, Connecticut, July 7, 1886, Abbie Mary Newton, born in Hartford, Connecticut, daughter of William Augustine and Mary (Manion) Newton, her father born in Hartford, and later a hotel and restaurant proprietor. Mr. Newton is remembered in Hartford as the restaurant keeper who inaugurated the twenty-five cent dinner and proved that it could be made profitable even in a hotel. After retiring from business he bought a farm in Bloomfield, Connecticut, and there died several years later. His wife, Mary (Manion) Newton, born in Providence, Rhode Island, died on Long Island, New York, prior to her husband's death. Mr. Maine has one son, Carroll Chester Maine, born at the home farm in North Stonington, March 23, 1888. There he has always lived, and after his education was finished he was admitted to a partnership with his father, the firm being Chester S. Maine & Son. Mrs. Chester S. Maine was a fine type of the New England woman, much interested in school work and the cause of education, and for three terms of three years each served as a member of the North Stonington School Committee, being one of the first women to serve on a school board in the United States.

JAMES PURTILL DONOVAN, son of Daniel and Kate (Purtill) Donovan, was born in Ashaway, Rhode Island, February 20, 1894. He is numbered among the younger generation of successful business men of Norwich, and takes a keen and active interest in everything pertaining to the welfare and advancement of the community.

Daniel Donovan, father of the subject of this review, was born in Carolina, Rhode Island, and for the greater part of his lifetime has worked as a weaver in worsted and woolen mills. In 1910 he removed his family to Mystic, Connecticut, and here he has since been employed in the weaving department of the Mystic Manufacturing Company. His wife, Kate (Purtill) Donovan, was born in Mystic, Connecticut.

The education of James P. Donovan was obtained in the public schools at Westerly, Rhode Island. After terminating his schooling, he conducted a parcel delivery business at Mystic, Connecticut, being thus engaged until 1917, when he enlisted in the United States army for the period of the World War. He was assigned to Company C, of the 328th Infantry, at Camp Gordon, Atlanta, Georgia. This regiment, part of the 82nd Division, sailed from Boston, Massachusetts, May 1, 1918, and landed in Liverpool, England, May 16th, then proceeded to La Havre, France. Mr. Donovan

saw active service in France for thirteen months, participating in the St. Mihiel drive, Meuse-Argonne offensive, and all fighting incident thereto, at the end of which time he returned to this country and received his honorable discharge at Camp Upton, Long Island, May 28, 1919. That same year he became associated with Orrin F. Lamb, engaging in the motorcycle business, which partnership still continues, and is steadily gaining a large degree of success.

In politics, Mr. Donovan is a Democrat, and in religion he is a Roman Catholic. He is also a member of the Richard William Morgan Post of the American Legion, of Mystic, Connecticut.

Mr. Donovan married, at Mystic, June 4, 1917, Louise Payne, of that town, daughter of Captain Emerson W. and Ella (Mitchell) Payne.

DAVID WOODWORTH PITCHER—Among the substantial citizens of New London county is David Woodworth Pitcher, successful farmer, public-spirited citizen, and highly-esteemed friend among a large circle of associates in Lebanon and vicinity. Mr. Pitcher comes of a family long known in Lebanon and prominent in New England for many generations.

David Pitcher, great-grandfather of David Woodworth Pitcher, was born in Norwich, Connecticut, but removed to Lebanon, where he farmed during the remainder of his life.

Lyman Pitcher, son of David Pitcher, was reared and educated in Norwich, Connecticut, but went to New York City as a young man, learning the grocery business and then engaging in business as a merchant. After many years in New York City, fire brought misfortune, and he removed to Sag Harbor, Long Island, where he engaged in the grocery business until the occurrence of another fire, when he went to Galveston, Texas. After getting his business established, he sent for his wife and family, but died of yellow fever while they were on the way. The widow and children went back to Sag Harbor, she later removing to Bridgeport, Connecticut, where she died. Lyman Pitcher married Betsy Ann Hand, of Sag Harbor, Long Island, and one of their children was Charles Lyman Pitcher, father of David Woodworth Pitcher.

Charles Lyman Pitcher, son of Lyman and Betsy Ann (Hand) Pitcher, was born in New York City, September 26, 1839. When his father died in Galveston, in 1847, he came to Lebanon to live with his grandfather, David Pitcher, and there he remained throughout his life. In 1857 he engaged himself as a farmhand to David S. Woodworth, owner of the old place, the house upon which was built in 1712 by Rev. Samuel Welles, and in which William Williams, one of the signers of the Declaration of Independence, was born. Here Charles Lyman Pitcher remained, and upon the death of David Woodworth, came into possession of the farm, where, although now retired, he still lives, his sons managing the farm. Charles Lyman Pitcher served during the entire period of the Civil War, enlisting, in 1861, for three months' service in Company D, 3rd Regiment, Connecticut Volunteer Infantry, and upon receiving his discharge re-enlisted in Battery D,

1st Heavy Artillery, Connecticut. After serving three years in this regiment, he was discharged, March 1, 1865. On May 18, 1871, he married Augusta Caroline Holbrook, daughter of Charles and Eunice (Bailey) Holbrook, of Lebanon, Connecticut, and they became the parents of two children, both born at Lebanon: Charles Lyman, Jr., born February 14, 1874, who, with his brother, runs the home farm; and David Woodworth, of further mention.

David Woodworth Pitcher, son of Charles Lyman and Augusta C. (Holbrook) Pitcher, was born in Lebanon, Connecticut, December 16, 1877, on the home farm, known as the Welles place. He received his early education in the local school of his district, and then assisted his father on the farm, learning every branch of his chosen occupation and preparing himself to be the successful farmer that he has become. As a man who performs his public duties with unswerving integrity, as a citizen who never forgets local interests, as a friend and intelligent Christian gentleman who recognizes his duties to his fellow-citizens in general, Mr. Pitcher is honored in his native place by all who know him. Politically, he supports the Republican party, and is prominent in the local affairs of his organization. He has served on the board of assessors, and is generally active in promoting the interests of his party.

On March 4, 1904, Mr. Pitcher married Edna Pitcher, daughter of David A. and Lillian (Leisgang) Pitcher, and they are the parents of two children: David Woodworth, Jr., born November 24, 1905; and Stuart Lyman, born February 24, 1907.

EDMUND LATHAM DOUGLASS, M.D.—A graduate M. D., Long Island College Hospital, class of 1916, Dr. Douglass began the practice of medicine in Groton, Connecticut, a community to which he needed no introduction, for he was born there, and his honored father, Dr. Edmund P. Douglass, for over thirty years has been a physician of the borough. Prior, however, to his settling in Groton, he served a year as interne in Harlem Hospital, New York City. During the World War he served in the Medical Corps of the United States army, then followed his location in Groton, as a physician, where he is well established in practice.

Dr. Edmund Latham Douglass, son of Dr. Edmund P. and Mary Hudson (Latham) Douglass, was born in Groton, Connecticut, May 9, 1891. He was educated in Groton and New London public schools, Norwich Free Academy (class of 1909), and Cornell University, receiving his A. B. from the last-named institution with the graduating class of 1913. He studied medicine for three years, 1913-14-15. He then studied one year in the Long Island Hospital Medical College, whence he was graduated M. D., class of 1916. He spent the following year as an interne in Harlem Hospital, New York City, then responded to the government's call for physicians and served in the Medical Corps of the United States army, in New York City, passing his examination in New York Academy of Medicine, and in December, 1917, was commissioned first lieutenant. He was called into service, January 24, 1918, and was sent to Camp McArthur, Waco, Texas, thence to Camp Upton, Long Island, August 1, 1918, and on August 31, 1918, sailed for France on the United States steamship, "Great Northern." He landed with his command in Brest, France, September 6, 1918, and from there was sent to Base Hospital No. 62, Mars-Sur-Allies. He remained there until February 19, 1919, when he was transferred to Base Hospital No. 91, Commercy, France, there being on duty until June 24, 1919, when he left for Brest, there taking passage for New York as a casual on the United States steamship "Leviathan," formerly the German liner "Vaterland." He arrived in New York City and was sent to Camp Dix, New Jersey, where he was honorably discharged and mustered out, July 11, 1919.

With this experience in medicine and surgery, Dr. Douglass returned to Groton and there began practice, and there he is becoming well established as a settled physician and surgeon. He is a member of the staff of the Home Memorial Hospital of New London, member of the American Medical Association, Connecticut State Medical Society, New London County Medical Society, New London City Medical Society, Nu Sigma Nu fraternity, and Warren Coleman Post, American Legion; he is a Republican in politics, and a member of the Congregational Church of Groton.

Dr. Douglass married, in New York City, January 15, 1918, Gladys A. Jolley, daughter of Mr. and Mrs. Charles J. Jolley, of Hamilton, Ontario, Canada, and they are the parents of a son, Edmund J., born April 8, 1919, in Hamilton, Ontario.

ARTHUR NATHAN NASH—A prosperous business man of Westerly, Rhode Island, the State in which he was born, Mr. Nash has long been identified with the State of Connecticut through his residence in Pawcatuck, and his wide connection with the local and grand bodies of the Masonic order of the State, he being a member of both the Grand Lodge, Free and Accepted Masons, and the Grand Chapter, Royal Arch Masons. He is an able, energetic business man, and an intensely public-spirited citizen, interested in the National Guard, spending twenty-five years in active work and retiring as lieutenant-colonel; also interested in fraternal and social organizations, aiding all good causes and holding the sincere regard of a multitude of friends. He is a son of Nathan E. and Ruth R. (Saunders) Nash.

Nathan E. Nash was born at Watch Hill, Rhode Island, and there completed public school courses. He finished his studies at Ashaway Academy, and soon after the outbreak of the war between the North and South he entered the Union army, and throughout the war served in Company B, Ninth Regiment, Rhode Island Volunteer Infantry. After the war he devoted himself to mechanical work, largely inventive, and patented some inventions of great value, one of these being the four-cylinder gas engine, an invention worthy of being classed among the "big" things produced by American inventors. He was a member of Hancock Post, No. 81, Grand Army of the Republic, of Westerly, Rhode Island, and of other organizations, patriotic and professional. He died in Toronto, Canada. Nathan E. Nash married Ruth R. Saunders, born in Bradford, Rhode Island, who survives him, a resident of Pawcatuck, Connecticut, her home with her son, Arthur N. Nash. Mr. and Mrs. Nash were parents of three sons: Irving, deceased; Arthur N., of further mention; and William, deceased.

Arthur N. Nash was born in Bradford, Washington county, Rhode Island, September 27, 1872. He was educated in the public schools of Pawcatuck, Connecticut, finishing with high school. His first employment was as a clerk, but in 1889, at the age of seventeen years, he entered the employ of the C. B. Cottrell Company, of Pawcatuck, as a machinist's apprentice, there remaining twelve years. In 1902 he left the machine shop and bought out the news and tobacco business of George W. Foster in Westerly, Rhode Island, a business founded in 1864. There Mr. Nash still continues under the firm name, Arthur N. Nash, news dealer, one of the substantial, leading business men of Westerly.

In fraternal circles Mr. Nash is affiliated with the Masonic order in both rites, York and Scottish. He is a Master Mason and past master of Pawcatuck Lodge, No. 90, Free and Accepted Masons; a companion and past high priest of Palmer Chapter, No. 28, Royal Arch Masons; a Cryptic Mason of Mystic Council, No. 29, Royal and Select Masters; a Sir Knight and past eminent commander of Narragansett Commandery (Westerly); a thirty-second degree member of Norwich Valley Consistory, Ancient Accepted Scottish Rite; a noble of Palestine Temple, Ancient Arabic Order Nobles of the Mystic Shrine (Providence). He is a member and past president of the Past Masters' Association of the Eighth Masonic District of Connecticut, president in 1916; member of the Order of High Priesthood of Hartford, Connecticut; member of the Massachusetts and Rhode Island Association of Knights Templar Commanders, of Boston, Massachusetts. In the Grand Lodge, Free and Accepted Masons, of the State of Connecticut, he holds the office of grand marshal; and in the Grand Chapter, Royal Arch Masons, of Connecticut, he holds the office of district deputy high priest, and is the grand representative of the Grand Chapter of Delaware near the Grand Chapter of Connecticut. His clubs are the Masonic of Westerly, Rhode Island, of which he is first vice-president; the Westerly Cycle, of which he is a charter life member; and the Colonial of Westerly.

During the Spanish-American War, Mr. Nash served in Company K, First Regiment, Rhode Island Volunteers, as first sergeant, later being promoted sergeant-major. During the War of 1917 he was in command of different forts of the Coast Defenses of Narragansett Bay; he organized the Fifty-eighth Ammunition Train, United States Coast Artillery, of which he was major and commander until mustered out after the signing of the armistice. He is a member of Robert Brucker Camp, No. 6, Spanish War Veterans, of Westerly; member of Harold E. Merrill Post, American Legion, of Westerly; member of Connecticut Commandery of the Military Order of Foreign Wars of Hartford, Connecticut; and in all these bodies takes active part and interest. In church relation he is a member of the Seventh Day Baptist church of Westerly. In politics he is a Republican.

Mr. Nash married, in June, 1901, Nettie Hortense Wilson, daughter of Edgar L. and Anna M. (Farnum) Wilson, of Willimantic, Connecticut. The family home is in Pawcatuck, Mr. Nash doing business just across the river in Westerly, Rhode Island.

Such is the record of a very active, successful, business man, whose versatility is one of his prominent characteristics. He takes a broad view of life, and finds in each department something that interests him and makes him a better citizen.

GEORGE R. McKENNA—Although not a "native son" and barely a citizen, Patrick McKenna, father of George R. McKenna, of Pawcatuck, Connecticut, left his wife and children and enlisted in the Union army, serving his adopted country until wounded in the battle of Fredericksburg, Virginia. But he recovered from his injuries and returned to Pawcatuck, Connecticut, and there spent the remainder of his life. He was born in County Armagh, Ireland, and in 1851 came to the United States, locating in Pawcatuck, where he died in 1876, his wife, Mary (Ward) McKenna, dying in 1894. Patrick McKenna was a granite worker during his years in Pawcatuck. Two of his six children are living: Margaret, residing at the old home in Pawcatuck; and George R., of further mention.

George R. McKenna was born in Pawcatuck, town of Stonington, New London county, Connecticut, August 18, 1865, and there obtained a common school education, finishing at Westerly High School with the graduating class of 1888. From 1888 to 1890 he taught school in Pawtucket. In the year 1890 he entered Yale Law School, whence he was graduated LL. B., class of 1892. He was admitted to the Rhode Island bar in 1892, and established offices in Westerly. His right to practice in Connecticut was already secured through his diploma from Yale Law School, and his practice has been in both states, Connecticut and Rhode Island, although his offices are in Rhode Island, the two states being separated at Westerly by only the Pawcatuck river, which is there spanned by a bridge, many people, the same as in Mr. McKenna's case, living and doing business on opposite sides and in two states. Mr. McKenna's practice is general in character, and he has served his town in legal capacity, being prosecuting attorney for the town of Stonington 1893-1905-1911-1913; also attorney for the town of Stonington two terms. He is a member of the American Bar Association, and the American Law

League. In politics he is a Democrat, and represented the town of Stonington in the Connecticut Legislature for the terms of 1893-1905.

Mr. McKenna married, November 30, 1902, Julia Day, of Pawcatuck, daughter of James and Ellen (Long) Day.

CAPTAIN DAVID CONNER—A veteran of two wars waged by the United States in freedom's cause, and both forced by her enemies, Captain David Conner displayed his valor upon Philippine battlefields and then in a later war, to which only young men were invited overseas. He was commissioned captain, and his experience utilized in the training of the men and in various assignments in which his experience was of inestimable value. To this national service he has added many years of service in the Connecticut National Guard.

Thomas Conner, father of Captain David Conner, was born of Irish parentage and ancestry in Newark, New Jersey, in 1821. He was employed as artist and gilder in New York City. He married Mary Sorce, born in New York City, in 1829, and died in Brooklyn, New York, in her forty-fifth year. Thomas Conner died in New York City in 1886. They were the parents of six children: Mary, Charles, Frank, Roland, Edward; and David, of whom further.

David Conner was born in Brooklyn, New York, in 1862. He was deprived of the care of his parents when in his eighth year, and at that time became an inmate in the home of a friend in Waterford, Connecticut. He remained there several years, and during the summer months assisted in the farm work, attending school in the winter time. In early manhood he left the farm and found employment in New London, Connecticut, with William H. Bentley, truckman and transfer agent. He remained with Mr. Bentley one year, when he injured his hand while loading the saluting battery which was being removed from its accustomed place in the center of the city. That injury was so serious that it kept him idle for a year, then he was able to perform the duties of a caretaker at the State armory. He held that position until the outbreak of war between the United States and Spain. He was commissioned captain of Company D, Third Regiment, Connecticut National Guard, June 27, 1898. This was a local company of the National Guard, and volunteered in a body for service in the Spanish-American War. He was mustered in the United States army as captain of the same Company D on July 3, 1898, after the regiment had entered the United States army as the Third Regiment, Connecticut Volunteer Infantry. He was mustered out with the company at the end of the war with Spain, March 20, 1899.

Captain Conner remained in command of Company D after the muster out, the company again becoming Company D, Third Regiment, Connecticut National Guard. On August 17, 1899, he was commissioned a captain of the Forty-sixth Regiment, United States Volunteer Infantry, and served with his command in the Philippines, taking part in many engagements and skirmishes with the Filipinos in their native jungles and forests. He escaped all injury, was honorably discharged, May 31, 1901, and returned to the United States.

After his return, Captain Conner was again appointed captain in the National Guard of Connecticut, serving until July 25, 1917, when he was again sworn into the service of his country and commissioned captain of the Tenth Company, Coast Artillery Corps, later changed to the Thirtieth Company, Coast Defense, Long Island Sound. He was on active duty at various camps established throughout the country for the training of troops for overseas service against Germany, and at the close of the war, returned to New London. He was largely instrumental in the reorganization of the Connecticut National Guard, and is known as the father of the One Hundred and Ninety-second Artillery (155 mm. guns) and now the adjutant of the Regiment. He has been connected with military affairs, with the exception of a few short periods, ever since eighteen years of age. He is now employed by the New London Water and Sewer Department.

Captain Conner is a Republican in politics; is a Thirty-second degree Mason, a member of Pequot Lodge, No. 85, Free and Accepted Masons; he also is a member of the Independent Order of Odd Fellows, and other local organizations.

Captain Conner married Ruth I. Severn, born in Mystic, Connecticut, in May, 1868, daughter of William Isaac and Mary Severn. Mrs. Conner is a lady of literary culture, and a successful writer of poetry. She traces her ancestry to the Mayflower Pilgrims and is eligible to the patriotic societies. Her grandmother, Sylvia Hopkins, was a lineal descendant of Stephen Hopkins, the signer. Captain and Mrs. Conner are the parents of two children: 1. William Bidwell, who was born in New London, Connecticut, July 30, 1891; married Edith Muldoon, of New York City, daughter of William Muldoon, a former assistant editor of the New York "Times." They are the parents of three children: Creighton, Mary, and Clara Conner. 2. Ida Hopkins, who was born in New London, Connecticut; married Captain Horace Griswold, of New London, now special agent for the United States Shipping Board at Rotterdam, Holland. They are the parents of a daughter, Mary Elizabeth, born April 15, 1920, at New London, Connecticut.

JAMES HENRY HARVEY—Making the motor vehicle the means of his own individual success, James H. Harvey, of Westerly, Rhode Island, is filling a very practical and necessary part in the activities of the town of Stonington, Connecticut.

Mr. Harvey is a son of Isaac and Phebe A. (Hall) Harvey, both of whom are still residents of Westerly. Isaac Harvey has been an iron moulder all his life, and is still actively engaged along this line of endeavor. Mr. and Mrs. Harvey are the parents of seven children, of whom James H. Harvey is the third.

James H. Harvey was born in Westerly, Rhode Island, on February 12, 1893, and received a practical education in the public schools of that city. Being of a mechanical turn of mind, he early took up the machinist's trade, which he followed for a period of eight years, working in various places as opportunity made a change advantageous. In 1919 Mr. Harvey became associated with Elwyn L. Case, of Westerly, and together these young men established a garage in Fort Mill, South Carolina. They were successful in this venture, but they did not, however, remain in the South for a great length of time. Returning North in 1920, they purchased the service department of the C. H. Holdredge garage, on West Broad street, in Pawcatuck. Under the name of Harvey & Case the young men are now conducting this business, which is constantly growing and developing, and undoubtedly faces a brilliant future. The life of Mr. Case is also reviewed in the following sketch.

Mr. Harvey is deeply interested in the public life of the city, and as a public-spirited citizen, makes his own decision in political matters, voting independently.

Mr. Harvey married, at Stonington, Connecticut, August 27, 1920, Alice Elizabeth Harris, of Fort Mill, South Carolina, daughter of Robert Pearson and Daisy Elizabeth (Thomason) Harris, natives of South Carolina. Mr. and Mrs. Harvey are the parents of one child, James H., Jr., born in Westerly, Rhode Island, April 24, 1921. They are members of the First Baptist Church of Westerly, Rhode Island.

ELWYN LLOYD CASE—In the very practical field of automobile service, Elwyn L. Case, of Westerly, Rhode Island, and the town of Stonington, Connecticut, is working out his business success.

Mr. Case is a son of Edmond L. and Lillian B. (Horton) Case, of Patchogue, Long Island, New York. Edmond L. Case has been a lifelong resident of Patchogue, and there received his education in the public schools. He became a carpenter and cabinet-maker, along which lines he is still actively engaged. Edmond L. and Lillian B. (Horton) Case are the parents of four children, of whom Elwyn L. is the third.

Elwyn L. Case was born in Patchogue, Long Island, on December 7, 1893. He received a thorough grounding in the essentials of education in the public schools of Patchogue, after which he became a machinist, and followed this line of activity for some years, going to various different places in pursuit of this trade.

In 1919 Mr. Case became associated with James Henry Harvey, of Westerly, Rhode Island, a sketch of whose life precedes this, in which is reviewed the business life of Mr. Harvey and Mr. Case.

Mr. Case is interested in the various civic and political questions of the day, but votes independently, giving his support wherever he believes it will be for the welfare of the people. He is a member of the Cycle Club, of Westerly.

Mr. Case married, at Fort Mill, South Carolina, December 19, 1919, Cordelia Harris, daughter of Robert Pearson and Daisy Elizabeth (Thomason) Harris, of Fort Mill, South Carolina. Mr. and Mrs. Case are the parents of a son, Lloyd Harris. They are members of the First Christian Church, of Westerly, Rhode Island.

TRYON SMITH—In the field of electrical contracting and supplies in New London, Connecticut, the name of Tryon Smith is a leading one, and stands for the latest developments in the way of practical application of electrical science.

Mr. Smith is a son of Willard F. and Janet A. (Chadwick) Smith. Willard F. Smith was born in Mansfield, Connecticut, and received his education in the public schools of that town. In early life, his health imperatively demanding an out-door life, he followed the sea for three years, engaged on whaling vessels sailing from New London. This rugged life restored him to normal vigor, and he served an apprenticeship as carpenter in New London. Going to Hartford, Connecticut, he entered the contracting and building business, which he followed the rest of his life, his work extending out as far as Andover, Connecticut, his native town. His wife, who still survives him, was born in East Windsor, Connecticut, and now resides at Andover. They were the parents of seven children, of whom Tryon was the sixth. Willard F. Smith died in 1917, at Andover.

Tryon Smith was born in Andover, Tolland county, Connecticut, on May 13, 1885, and received his early education in the public schools of that town. He completed his formal studies at the Windham High School. Thereafter, he went to New Britain, Connecticut, and there entered the business world as a dry goods clerk. The work, however, was distasteful to him, and promised little for the future. Continuing for only one year along this line, he entered the employ of the Connecticut Light and Power Company, at New Britain, serving an apprenticeship as electrician. He then went to New York City and worked for the Bronx Gas and Electric Company, where he had charge of their meter department. Returning to New Britain he was employed by the New England Engineering Company until 1914, when he went into business for himself at Naugatuck, Connecticut, and conducted this business until 1917. In that year he came to New London, as manager of the New London branch of the New England Engineering Company. In October, 1917, he bought out this branch, and entered upon the business as an independent interest, reorganizing and incorporating the concern under the name of the Electric Contracting and Supply Company. The company was capitalized at $10,200, and Mr. Smith was made president of the company. The large, modern central store is located at No. 247 State street, in New London, and the company has a branch store in Mystic. The commercialization of the business, including the selling as well as the installation of all kinds of electrical equipment, was the idea of Mr. Smith himself in mapping out the future of the concern, and the success which is attending the company amply justifies their venture into the mercantile field. Their very advantageous location is, of course, a factor in their success, but the ability which Mr. Smith has displayed in all the branches of the business is a living force for progress and development, and although the beginning was of comparatively recent date, this business is one of the leaders in its line in the city.

In political matters, Mr. Smith takes only the interest of the progressive citizen. He is a member of the New London Chamber of Commerce. Socially, he is widely popular, and is a member of the Harbour Club, the Rotary Club, the Benevolent and Protective Order of Elks, and the Young Men's Christian Association.

Mr. Smith married Marcella Agnes, daughter of John J. and Mary (Grace) Crean, of New Britain. They are the parents of three children: Donald, Janet and Marcella. Mr. and Mrs. Smith reside on Stuart street, at Ocean Beach.

JOHN H. JAMES, JR.—A prominent figure in business life in New London, Connecticut, is John H. James, owner and manager of the James Pharmacy, which is located at No. 318 Bank street. Since establishing himself in business here, Mr. James has always given his earnest support to all movements calculated to advance business development, the welfare and advancement of the community being always uppermost in his mind.

John H. James, Sr., was born in Waterford, Connecticut, and there obtained his education. For many years previous to his retiring from active business life, he followed the sea, but now resides in New London. He married Ellen Sheehan, who died at New London, in 1914. To Mr. and Mrs. James were born three children: Ida M., who married Alfred W. Stoll, of New London; Anna N., who married Harry H. Adams, of New London; and John H., of further mention.

John H. James, Jr., was born at Franklin, Massachusetts, September 29, 1888. Having been brought by his parents to New London when he was a small child, he obtained his education in the local public schools, and after graduating from the Bulkeley High School, in the class of 1905, he entered the Massachusetts College of Pharmacy. Finishing the prescribed course, he became registered in Connecticut, in 1906, and the following year registered as a pharmacist in Massachusetts and subsequently worked in various places until 1914, when he purchased the William Sales Drug Store, changing its name to the James Drug Store. He has been highly successful in this venture and has risen to a place of prominence in business circles in the community. His success is in every sense of the word self-made, and has been won through sheer pluck and that indomitable energy which in its last analysis is the fundamental characteristics of the prosperous business man. In politics, Mr. James is a Democrat, and takes a keen interest in the affairs of the local organization. He affiliates with the Seaside Council, No. 17, Knights of Columbus; in religion he is a Roman Catholic, attending St. Joseph's Church of this denomination.

On October 7, 1916, John H. James, Jr., was united in marriage with Helena M. Dray, daughter of Edward and Mary (O'Meara) Dray. Mr. and Mrs. James are the parents of one child, Elizabeth Ellen, born October 1, 1917, at New London.

WILLIAM MICHAEL REDDEN — After a somewhat varied business career, Mr. Redden, since 1915, has been the head of the Redden Company, Inc., a concern of New London, Connecticut, engaged in construction work, with headquarters at No. 361 Bank street.

William Michael Redden is the son of Michael M. and Hannah (Cokeley) Redden, both natives of Ireland, the former born in County Clare, in 1838. He came to the United States when nineteen years of age, and coming directly to New London, found employment here, but shortly after went to Elizabeth, New Jersey, where he remained for a period of some years, then returned to New London and located on Howard street. At this time Michael M. Redden was in the employ of the New York, New Haven & Hartford Railroad Company, continuing with the company for ten years, leaving it to take up a farmer's life, buying the property known as the Prentice place. This is one of the oldest farms in the county, located in the Jefferson avenue district of New London, a landmark of more than a hundred years' standing. Here Mr. Redden remained for the rest of his life, meeting with great success. Michael M. Redden died at his home January 1, 1910, and was buried in St. Mary's Cemetery, New London. He came to this country with nothing but a determination to succeed, and by perseverance and far-seeing cleverness built up a substantial fortune. His wife, Hannah Copeley, came to the United States from Ireland when sixteen years old, and their marriage took place in New London. They were the parents of nine children, all born in New London: 1. Anna, the wife of William O'Connors. 2. Helen, who married Michael O'Connell, of New London. 3. Katherine, who married James Sullivan. 4. Mary, who died in childhood. 5. Michael, died in infancy. 6. James, died in infancy. 7. Daniel, died in infancy. 8. William Michael, of whom further. 9. Frank Henry, now deceased, who married Mary Doyle, by whom he had two sons, Daniel and Frank.

Spending his early childhood in Elizabeth, New Jersey, William Michael Redden came to New London when his father moved his family to this city and settled in the Howard street house. They lived there eighteen years, then went to their newly-acquired home, the Prentice farm. William M. Redden attended the public schools of New London until old enough to take up some kind of work, then entering the employ of C. D. Bess & Sons, cracker manufacturers, remained with them for three years, leaving to learn the moulder's trade at Brown's cotton gin. Three years later Mr. Redden returned to Elizabeth, New Jersey, working first at the Moore Brothers' Foundry and afterward at the Hydraulic Pump Works, then going into the grocery business with a Mr. Welsch, they carried it on for sixteen years, the firm name being Welsch & Redden.

In 1905 Mr. Redden came back to New London, and becoming interested in commercial life, built the business block known as the Redden building, and engaged in the grocery business again in 1908 after the completion of it. Six years afterward his brother, Frank Henry Redden, dying, William M. Redden bought up his contracting and construction business and has been engaged in it since 1915 under the name of the Redden Company, Inc. Mr. Redden has become very successful as a contractor, building up a large and important business. Mr. Redden had the first contract given out for the construction of the yard of the Groton Iron Works, beginning the work in August, 1917, and completing it in May, 1918.

Not having allied himself with any particular party in politics, Mr. Redden is an independent voter. He is popular among the Knights of Columbus, being a member of Seaside Council, of New London. He attends the Roman Catholic church.

William M. Redden married, at Westerly, Rhode Island, October 12, 1898, Mary C. Coleman. Three children have been born of this union: 1. Coleman, born July 31, 1900. He graduated from St. Mary's School in New London, and later attended the Bulkeley High School for two years, afterward going to the preparatory school of Niagara University for two years, going then to the Catholic University of Washington, D. C., for one year. When this country entered the World War, this boy, though younger than the required age, volunteered and was sent to the Army Training Corps. He died during the epidemic of "flu," and is buried in St. Mary's Cemetery. The young man had gained quite a reputation as an all-round athlete, having won special honors on the football field. 2. Charles, born in May, 1911, now attending a local school. 3. Frank Henry, born June 8, 1913, also at school.

FREDERICK SAMUEL LANGDON—Now a young man, but with a record of energy and professional ability a much older man might envy, Mr. Langdon is pursuing in New London, Connecticut, the profession of architecture as a member of the corporation, Bilderbeck & Langdon. He has followed that profession from boyhood, and before coming to New London county he was for fifteen years in the employ of a firm of architects in New Britain, Connecticut.

Frederick S. Langdon is a son of Wilbur Burton Langdon, who was born in 1847, in Kensington, Connecticut, his birthplace the old Langdon homestead, and died in 1914. Wilbur Burton Langdon married Nellie Wallace, who was born in Bridgeport, Connecticut, and died in February, 1920, aged sixty-two. They were the parents of five sons and one daughter: Frederick S., of further mention; Albert, Leon, Lottie, Harry, and Walter.

Frederick S. Langdon was born in New Britain, Connecticut, September 28, 1886, and there completed public school courses of study. He entered as a student in the architectural course of a leading correspondence school and received therefrom a graduation diploma showing excellence in standing. He supplemented this with practical experience with the firm, Uncklebeck & Perry, architects, of New Britain, Connecticut, then came to the Groton Iron Works, New London, as chief draftsman. During the year he remained with the company he designed several of the buildings comprising the present plant. In 1918 the firm, Bilderbeck & Langdon, architects, of New London, was incorporated, Mr. Langdon, secretary-treasurer. Since the organization of the firm they designed and supervised the Lawrence Hall building on Bank street, a large service station for J. D. Avery, Inc., a four-roomed school building for the Eighth District, borough of Groton, Connecticut, also a large weave shed and power plant for the New England Silk Company at Westerly, Rhode Island, a large amount of engineering work, consisting of 15,000 feet of pipe line for the borough of Groton, and a complete survey of Mason's Island, comprising about 540 acres. He is independent in politics, and a member of the Harbour Club of New London, also affiliated with Brainard Lodge, No. 102, Free and Accepted Masons.

Mr. Langdon married, in March, 1910, Ruth Gladys Rogers, born in Willimantic, Connecticut, daughter of Raymond and Elizabeth (Collins) Rogers, her father a veteran of the Civil War, who died in 1917. Mr. and Mrs. Langdon are the parents of five children: Roger Frederick, Ruth Elizabeth, Wilbur Spencer, Raymond Edward and Richard Collins.

CHARLES HENRY HOLDREDGE—A long and checkered life, including the fortunes of war, and later the satisfaction of substantial and permanent business prosperity, is the story of Charles Henry Holdredge, one of the most prominent citizens of Pawcatuck, New London county, Connecticut, whose storage garage is one of the big business interests of Westerly, Rhode Island.

Mr. Holdredge is a son of Hibbard Henry and Sarah (Rogers) Holdredge, and comes of one of the old families of New London county. Hibbard H. Holdredge was born in the town of Groton, Connecticut, and was educated in the schools of that town. When he was a young man he worked as a salesman for the Bill Publishing Company, then one of the most prominent firms in its line in this part of the State. He also farmed on a small scale. He died in Waterford in 1853, and is buried there. Of the nine children of this union two are now living: Amanda, now Mrs. Greene, who since her husband's death has made her home with her two children in Springfield, Massachusetts; and Charles Henry. Mrs. Holdredge, late in life, married (second) Capt. Benjamin Burrows, both deceased.

Charles Henry Holdredge was born in Waterford, Connecticut, June 27, 1844. He received a limited education in the public schools of his native town, and when only nine years of age was bound out, as was the frequent custom in those days, to Hubbil Loomis, of Salem, Connecticut, a farmer. He remained there for three years, but was treated very cruelly, and when twelve years of age was taken away from the Loomis farm by his parents. Later he went to North Stonington, Connecticut, where he worked on a farm. He returned to Westerly, Rhode Island, and worked as apprentice carriage maker for one year.

At the age of eighteen years, in August, 1862, the young man enlisted in Company A, Seventh Regiment, Rhode Island Volunteer Infantry, for service during the Civil War. He was wounded at Fredericksburg, and Captain Edward Allen, of his own company, took care of him at Captain Allen's headquarters, thus beginning a warm friendship which has continued between the two men through all the years, and is still as cordial as in the time of war.

After the close of the Civil War, Mr. Holdredge returned to Ashaway, Rhode Island, where he was in the employ of Colonel Wells, in the woolen mills, for some time, then later was associated with A. L. Wells, in the wagon shop which the latter conducted there, working also for a short time in various places.

In 1868 Mr. Holdredge made a start in business for himself, buying out the business of Sanders York, of Westerly, theretofore a prominent wagon builder and blacksmith of that town. He developed the business extensively, and became a large carriage manufacturer in Westerly. In 1887 he removed to Mystic, Connecticut, continuing in the same business, but in the following year his plant was destroyed by fire. This setback turned his thoughts to the possibility of a more advantageous permanent location. He decided on a return to his former vicinity, and purchased land on the Connecticut side of the river from Westerly, in the village of Pawcatuck. There he built a shop, and has since continued the manufacture of carriages. When the automobile superseded the horse-drawn vehicles, Mr. Holdredge adapted his energies to the new development, and in 1912 took over the agency of the Munroe automobile, and while he still manufactures carriages, the newer interest has become of greater importance than the old. He also now conducts a very large modern storage garage, the best in the community.

Mr. Holdredge has long been prominent in the public affairs of the town of Stonington, in which the village of Pawcatuck is located. A staunch Republican, he was first selectman of the town of Stonington for two years, and though holding no other offices, has been a leader in the Republican party. For two years he was chief of the Fire Department of Pawcatuck. He has been a member of Hancock Post, Grand Army of the Republic, for many years, and for seven years was commander of the post.

In 1864, Mr. Holdredge married Louise Burdick, of Ashaway, Rhode Island, daughter of William H. and Lucy O. (Gates) Burdick, who died in 1918. They were the parents of six children, of whom four are living: Frederick W., who resides with his father and is associated with him in business; Martha J., who married Frank Howe, and since his death resides at home; Frank L., whose life is also reviewed in following sketch; and Grace B., who resides at home. The family have long been members of the Baptist church.

FRANK L. HOLDREDGE—A member of an old New London county family, and himself holding a prominent position in the business world of this section, Frank L. Holdredge, of Pawcatuck, Connecticut, is broadly representative of the successful man of the day.

Mr. Holdredge is a grandson of Hibbard Henry and Sarah (Rogers) Holdredge, of Groton, New London county, Connecticut, long ago prominent in the county, and a son of Charles Henry and Louise (Burdick) Holdredge (q. v.).

Frank L. Holdredge was born in Pawcatuck, Connecticut, in the town of Stonington, January 21, 1872. He received his education in the public and high schools of Westerly, Rhode Island, just across the Pawcatuck river. Caring little for a higher education or a professional career, he entered at once into the mercantile world as salesman for Edward Smith & Company, of New York City, selling paints, varnishes, etc. Later he became associated with his father, whose carriage factory was one of the leading industrial interests in the town, as foreman of the painting department. Mr. Holdredge still continues in this business, which of recent years has broadened its scope to include the handling and storage, on a large scale, of automobiles. Mr. Holdredge is prominent in various circles outside his business. Politically, he supports the principles and policies of the Republican party. He is a member of Narragansett Lodge, No. 77, Independent Order of Odd Fellows, of Westerly, Rhode Island, and is a member of the Cycle Club, of Westerly.

In 1906 Mr. Holdredge married Gertrude May Ecclestone, daughter of Albert and Ella (Chapman) Ecclestone, of Westerly, and they have had two children: Iris L., who died at the age of seven years; and Charles H., who was born March 4, 1915. The family attend and support the Baptist church.

WILLARD DICKINSON HARRIS—Descended from old New London families, and long active in the mercantile world of New London, Mr. Harris has for the past fourteen years been manager of the local distributing branch of Morris & Company, wholesale dealers in meat.

Christopher Harris, Mr. Harris' father, was born in New London, and after receiving a practical education in the public schools of the city, followed the sea all his life, sailing out of New London. He was one of the early whaling fishermen out of this port, and made one trip that covered a period of thirty-nine months. This is regarded as the longest fishing trip ever made from this port. Christopher Harris died in New London, in 1896. He married Margaret Lyon, also a native of New London, who died here in 1886. They were the parents of five children; Christopher C., who married Annie Chickering, and died in 1912; Ethram, who married Effie Still, and resides in Columbus, Ohio; Henry, who married Beckie Turner, and died in 1904; Willard D., whose name appears at the head of this review; and George C., who married Annie Avery, and resides in New London.

Willard Dickinson Harris was born in New London, June 29, 1862, and received his early education in the public schools of the city, then took the regular course at Bulkeley High School. About 1882 he entered the business world in New York City, where he was employed as assistant bookkeeper by J. Harris & Company, wholesale fish dealers, for a short time. Returning to New London, he became bookkeeper for the Clark S. Stewart Company, wholesale meat dealers.

Later, Mr. Harris became a member of this firm, the name of the concern being changed to Stewart & Harris. Upon the death of Mr. Stewart, which occurred in 1889, Mr. Harris sold out to the National Packing Company, at the same time becoming manager of the business for that concern, and filling this position until 1900, when this company was dissolved per order of the United States Court. In 1907 Morris & Company established a branch in New London, and placed Mr. Harris in charge as manager, which position he still holds.

In the varied interests of the city Mr. Harris has long been interested, and though never a leader in public affairs, has borne a part in the progress of the community. Politically he supports the Republican party, and in the year 1905 served in the City Council. He is a life member of the Niagara Engine Company, of New London, and fraternally, holds membership in Mohican Lodge, No. 55, Independent Order of Odd Fellows, of New London. He attends the Second Congregational Church of New London.

Mr. Harris married, September 1, 1908, Edna Goodwin, daughter of Walter W. and Frances (Benham) Goodwin, of New London. Mr. and Mrs. Harris reside at No. 35 Bellevue place, in this city.

ROBERT MURRAY SMITH—At the age of twenty-one, in 1898, Robert M. Smith entered the service of the railroad, beginning with the New York, New Haven & Hartford Railroad Company as a brakeman, and has remained with this company, having risen through many promotions to his present position, that of assistant superintendent. He is a son of the late John B. and Eliza A. (Sutor) Smith, of Baltimore and Havre de Grace, Maryland.

Robert M. Smith was born in Montgomery, Alabama, January 22, 1877, and when a small child his parents moved to Northumberland, Pennsylvania, where he was educated in the public schools. As a young man he came to New England, and in 1898 entered the service of the New York, New Haven & Hartford Railroad Company, at Norwich, Connecticut, as a yard brakeman, and six months later was promoted to a yard conductor, his next promotion being to that of a freight conductor, in April, 1901, in which position he remained until June, 1914, when he was promoted to a passenger conductor, and until May, 1917, held that position, when he was promoted to assistant trainmaster, with offices at Putnam, Connecticut. In September, 1918, he was promoted to trainmaster, and in November of the same year won the promotion of assistant superintendent, with offices at New London.

Mr. Smith has wide fraternal relations, being affiliated with New London Lodge, No. 360, Benevolent and Protective Order of Elks; Webster Lodge, Free and Accepted Masons, of Webster, Massachusetts; Union Chapter, No. 7, Royal Arch Masons; Cushing Council, Royal and Select Masters; Palestine Commandery, Knights Templar, all of New London; Connecticut Consistory, Valley of Norwich; Ancient Accepted Scottish Rite (thirty-second degree), of Norwich; Pyramid Temple, Ancient Arabic Order Nobles of the Mystic Shrine; Gardner Lodge, No. 46, of Bridgeport; Knights of Pythias of Norwich; and Webster Lodge, Loyal Order of Moose.

Mr. Smith is a member of the Veteran Railroad Men's Association of Boston, Massachusetts; honorary member of Railway Station Agents; member of the Railway Superintendents' Association of St. Louis; Order of Railway Conductors, No. 237, of Worcester, Massachusetts; Cable Club, Round Table Club, of Boston; Boston Athletic Club; New England Railroad Club, of Boston, Massachusetts; and the New Haven Railroad Club, of New Haven, Connecticut. He is ex-vice-president of the Massachusetts Fish and Game Association; an attendant of the Protestant Episcopal church, and in politics is a Republican.

Mr. Smith married, July 2, 1919, Lillian M. Dupre, of Webster, Massachusetts, daughter of John B. and Mary Jane (Veo) Dupre, the father born in St. Jules, Province of Quebec, and the mother born in Enfield, Vermont. The family home is at No. 95 Squire street, New London.

RICHARD C. DAVIDSON—One of the most enterprising citizens of New London, Connecticut, Richard C. Davidson has attained his success within the confines of his native city. He was born in New London, December 27, 1872, son of James and Ellen F. (Somers) Davidson, and grandson of George Davidson, who was the first of the family in New London. George Davidson was born in Scotland, in 1795, and in 1817 removed to Nova Scotia, where he remained until 1853, the year he became a resident of New London. He was a landscape gardener, shipbuilder, and married Ellen McDuffie, who came to America with him.

James Davidson, son of George and Ellen (McDuffie) Davidson, was born in Pictou, Nova Scotia, in April, 1827, and died in New London, April 20, 1896. He attended the public schools and followed the trade of shipbuilder. In his later years he had a marine railway business and employed at times as many as fifty men. Among the ships built by Mr. Davidson are: the "Crescent," "Howard B. Peck," "Charles D. Hall," and the "Elwood H. Smith." These were merchant ships and coastwise vessels. Mr. Davidson married (third), in 1861, Ellen F. Somers, daughter of Daniel Somers, and she died in New London, November 8, 1904. The children of this marriage were: James, Grace, Louisa; Richard C., of further mention; Ellen, Emma, and John.

Richard C. Davidson was educated in the public schools of New London, and as a young man worked with his father in the shipyards for six years. He then became a diver for the Thames Tow Boat Company of New London, following this occupation for three years. In 1908, Mr. Davidson established a Salvaging and Pile Driving Business in New London, under the name of the R. C. Davidson Company, and is now in his thirteenth successful year of business.

Mr. Davidson is a Republican in politics, and actively interested in all public matters. Fraternally, he is a member of Mohican Lodge, No. 54, Independent Order of Odd Fellows.

Mr. Davidson married, in 1899, Mary E. Griffin, of New London, daughter of Patrick H. and Ellen (Gilmore) Griffin, the latter two natives of Ireland. Mr. and Mrs. Davidson are the parents of the following children: Robert F., who served in the World War, 58th Regiment, Second Division, Artillery; Richard, Ellen B., Emma, Charles G., and Louisa.

JOHN H. NEWMAN—Among the men who occupy a leading place in the business life of New London, Connecticut, is John H. Newman. Mr. Newman was born there May 31, 1867, son of Daniel and Margaret (Rhoe) Newman. His parents were of that grand contribution of citizenship which Ireland has often made to this country. The father of Mr. Newman came to America when he was a child, and settled in New London. There he attended the public schools and subsequently served his apprenticeship as plumber and steam-fitter. This was the beginning of the business which has steadily increased to its present size and which is now carried on by Mr. Newman. About 1868, Daniel Newman, in association with J. D. Cronin, established a plumbing and steam-fitting business, under the firm name of Newman & Cronin, and were the largest firm of their kind in New London. Mr. Newman followed this occupation all his life, and died in New London, in 1901. His wife was also a native of Ireland, and married Mr. Newman in New London, where she died. Their children numbered ten, five of whom are now living: 1. Daniel, married Ann Healy, and resides in New London. 2. James P., of New London. 3. John H., of further mention. 4. Ann, deceased. 5. Elizabeth, married Joseph S. Harrigan, and lives in New London. 6. William, deceased. 7. George, deceased. 8. Thomas F., deceased. 9. Mary, deceased. 10. Margaret, married Julian D. Moran, and lives in New London.

John H. Newman attended the public schools of his native city, and in 1884 began to serve his apprenticeship to the plumber's trade with his father. After completing his time he went to work for his father's company, and in 1898 acquired an interest in it by purchase. In 1908 he, with his brothers, purchased the Newman interest in the business and the firm name became Newman Brothers. This arrangement was successfully continued until 1913, when Mr. Newman purchased his brothers' interest and has since continued alone. The business is now the largest of its kind in New London county and under the able management of Mr. Newman is always increasing.

Mr. Newman is an interested citizen in the welfare of New London, and is always willing to aid in any movement which has the general welfare at heart. He is a Republican in politics, and though not a seeker for office is an ardent worker for his party. He is a member of the Chamber of Commerce; the Rotary Club; and the Benevolent and Protective Order of Elks, Lodge No. 360.

Mr. Newman married, August 30, 1893, Margaret A. Carroll, of New London, daughter of John and Johanna (Shea) Carroll, and they are the parents of one daughter, Marian Carroll Newman. Miss Newman is a graduate of the Williams Memorial and of Pratt Institute. With his family Mr. Newman attends St. Mary's Roman Catholic Church and aids in the support of its good works.

ELMER C. HALL—One of the leading grocers of Mystic, Connecticut, Elmer C. Hall, contributes to the general prosperity and well-being of the town in the most practical way—the purveying of food of high quality.

Mr. Hall is a son of Charles and Eugenie A. (Kinney) Hall, the former born in Voluntown, Connecticut, and educated in the district schools there. After completing his studies he became a farmer, following this occupation all his life. He died in Voluntown, his wife surviving him, and residing in Mystic. Mr. Hall was their only child.

Elmer C. Hall was born in Voluntown, Connecticut, on February 7, 1882. Receiving a practical education in the public schools of the town, he thereafter entered the employ of the American Thread Company, at Glasgo, in the town of Griswold. Here he remained for a period of fifteen years, working in the different departments, and for several years holding the position of shipping and receiving clerk.

But Mr. Hall was all this time looking forward to independence, and when opportunity offered, in 1915, he branched out for himself. On February 10, of that year, he purchased the grocery store of Alfred McDonald, in Mystic, Connecticut, and since that time has carried on the business with ever increasing success. Mr. Hall commands an excellent class of trade, and is counted among the leaders in his line of business.

Although his time is largely absorbed by the exacting nature of his business, Mr. Hall is a man of broad interests, and keeps in touch with the progress of events, local, state and national, and is a staunch supporter of the Republican party. Fraternally he is a member of Mount Vernon Lodge, No. 75, Free and Accepted Masons, of Jewett City.

On April 17, 1912, Mr. Hall married Ethel M. Whitman, of Willimantic. She is the daughter of James M. and Elizabeth E. (Loomis) Whitman, of that city. Mr. and Mrs. Hall are members of the Baptist church.

THOMAS TRASK WETMORE, JR., was born in New London, Connecticut, May 5, 1896, and there was educated in the public schools, leaving Bulkeley High School in his junior year. He was in the employ of the Ship and Engine Company until October 30, 1917, when he enlisted in the United States navy for the period of the war between the United States and Germany. He served until honorably discharged, then returned to New London, where he was engaged with the local telephone company until October 1, 1919, when, under the firm name, Wetmore & Beran, he established a real estate and insurance business, now the most important of its kind in the city. This partnership was dissolved in February, 1921, and Mr. Wetmore continues the business alone. Mr. Wetmore is a young man of energy and ability and is succeeding in his business.

Mr. Wetmore is a son of Thomas Trask Wetmore, Sr., born in New London county, now a retired business man, but deeply interested in the subject of antique furniture. His wife, Margaret Ellen (Kaneen) Wetmore, born in New London, died May 10, 1900, leaving a son, Thomas Trask, Jr., of previous mention, and a daughter, Portia Louise, who married Captain Wales A. Benham.

WILLIAM M. JONES—From the time of his entering into the business world, Mr. Jones has been identified with jewelry enterprises, and since 1913 has been established in this particular line in New London, Connecticut.

William M. Jones was born in Springfield, Massachusetts, August 17, 1861, the son of Edwin and Jane (Treverton) Jones. Edwin Jones was a native of Birmingham, England. After obtaining his education he learned the jeweler's trade, and subsequently came to the United States, locating in New York City, where he established himself in the jeweler's business. He died there in 1886. The boy, William M., was educated in the public schools of Jeresy City, New Jersey, after which he went to New York City and served an apprenticeship to the jeweler's business, having, in the meantime, decided to follow in the footsteps of his father. After learning the trade he returned to Jersey City and there established himself in business, remaining here until 1913, when he moved to New London, Connecticut, to his present location, No. 235 State street. Mr. Jones has risen to a place of prominence in business circles and is held in the highest esteem by all who know him.

In politics Mr. Jones is an independent voter, preferring to exercise his own judgment on all public questions and issues rather than identify himself with any formal political party. He affiliates with Bergen Lodge, No. 47, Free and Accepted Masons, of Jersey City, and is a member of the Masonic Club of New London. In religion he is a Methodist.

Mr. Jones married (first), in 1883, Ida Gorry, of Jersey City; she died in 1903. Mr. Jones married (second), in 1906, Mary Matthews, of Monmouth county, New Jersey.

J. WARREN GAY—The electrical contracting firm, the J. Warren Gay Company, was founded in New London, Connecticut, in 1901, by J. Warren Gay, who came to that city from Lynn, Massachusetts, although born in the State of Maine, son of Thomas J. Gay, son of Peter (3) Gay, son of David Gay, who was born January 24, 1743. Thomas J. Gay was a custom shoemaker, but for a number of years previous to his death was station master of Lynn, Massachusetts. He married Harriet E. Hussey, who died in New London, Connecticut. They were the parents of seven children, of whom J. Warren Gay, the principal character in this review, was the second.

J. Warren Gay was born in Augusta, Maine, May 10, 1858, but in his youth Lynn, Massachusetts, became the family home and there he completed public school study. In 1878, Mr. Gay began his work along electrical lines, and for six years was employed in Lynn, becoming well-informed and skilled in the application of electricity to house and mechanical purposes. In 1884 he located in New London, Connecticut, where for seventeen years he was in the employ of W. R. Perry, hardware and electrical supplies. In 1901 he organized the J. Warren Gay Company of New London, electrical contractors, first as a partnership, but later as a corporation, with F. A. Starr, president; J. L. Rush, secretary, and J. Warren Gay, treasurer. The company contracts for all forms of electric installation for home, mill, factory, store or vessel, and deals in all forms of electrical equipment or supplies. The business has developed into one of large proportions, one of the largest of its kind in New London county.

Mr. Gay is a member of Brainard Lodge, Free and Accepted Masons; Union Chapter, Royal Arch Masons; Courtney Council, Royal and Select Masters; Palestine Commandery, Knights Templar, all of New London, and holds the thirty-second degree of the Ancient Accepted Scottish Rite; affiliates with King Solomon Lodge of Perfection; Van Rensselaer Council, Princes of Jerusalem; Norwich Chapter of Rose Croix; and Connecticut Consistory, Sublime Princes of the Royal Secret, all of Norwich, Connecticut. He is also a noble of Pyramid Temple, Ancient Arabic Order Nobles of the Mystic Shrine, of Bridgeport, Connecticut. He belongs to the New London Chamber of Commerce, attends the Methodist Episcopal church, and in politics is a Republican.

On January 1, 1885, Mr. Gay married Elizabeth A. Smith, of Lynn, Massachusetts.

WILLIAM STARK STARR, one of the leading druggists of the city of New London, Connecticut, has for the past thirty-five years been identified with this branch of mercantile endeavor. Mr. Starr is a son of George Edgar and Sarah (Mallory) Starr. George E. Starr was born in Middletown, Connecticut, and there educated in the public schools. Coming to New London as a young man, he became interested in the printing business, which he followed actively in this city for more than fifty years. He became a man of prominence in this city, and a leader in the Democratic party. He was elected mayor of New London and served ably for one term. Later, he was representative to the Connecticut State Legislature. He died in New London. His wife, who was born in New London, also died here. They were the parents of six children, of whom two are now living: William S., whose name heads this review; and Carrie Mallory, the wife of Col. Charles D. Parkhurst, formerly of Providence, Rhode Island, now of New London, Connecticut.

William Stark Starr was born in New London, Connecticut, September 16, 1861. Receiving his early education in the public schools of the city, he attended Bulkeley High School, then later entered the New York College of Pharmacy, from which he was graduated in 1886. Shortly after his graduation, in association with his brother, Charles S. Starr, Mr. Starr purchased the retail drug business theretofore conducted by Henry H. Stoddard, and has continued the business since. Some years ago it was incorporated, Mr. Starr being made treasurer. His brother, Charles S. Starr, died October 27, 1916. This store handles the celebrated Rexall goods, and in all its various departments is doing an extensive and prosperous business.

Mr. Starr is a member of the New London Chamber of Commerce, and has long been prominent in civic matters. Politically, he is an Independent, and has served as councilman for many years. He is a member of Brainard Lodge, No. 102, Free and Accepted Masons; and is a member of the First Congregational Church.

On September 27, 1893, Mr. Starr married Marion Griswold Vail, daughter of Charles and Ann E. (Griswold) Vail, of Long Island. Their two sons are Richard Mallory and Roland Griswold.

WALDO EMERSON CLARKE—Prominent in the public works about New London, Connecticut, and now permanently located in charge of one of the most important engineering achievements of recent years in this county, Waldo Emerson Clarke is a figure of interest to everyone to whom the local records are interesting.

Mr. Clarke is a son of Daniel Wright and Catherine (De Ballard) Clarke. Daniel W. Clarke was born in Westerly, Rhode Island, and there received a practical education. He was a traveling salesman during all his active career, and has resided in many interesting places. He now lives in West Haven, Connecticut.

Waldo Emerson Clarke was born in Ashaway, Rhode Island, on April 17, 1882. Receiving his early education in the public schools of different towns to which his father's business brought the family, he received his high school education in Newark, New Jersey, being graduated in the class of 1902. Having had the advantage of broad opportunities of observation, the young man had by this time a settled purpose in life. Big construction work appealed to him with the greatest force, and his parents seconded his desire to enter this field of endeavor. Accordingly, he entered the New York University, from which he was graduated in 1906, with the two degrees of Civil Engineer and Bachelor of Science. He entered the employ of the New York State Department as civil engineer for the New York water supply. Later, in 1908, he came to New London as city engineer in the highway department, but eventually remained for only a short period. An attractive offer from the United Fruit Company, promising a wealth of valuable experience, was accepted, and carried him to the Panama Canal Zone. Four years later, on November 6, 1912, Mr. Clarke became chief engineer at the State pier, then under construction, and had full charge of the work in progress until its completion, on April 15, 1917. On this date Mr. Clarke was appointed superintendent of the State pier, and still ably fills that responsible position.

In various avenues of interest Mr. Clarke takes an active part. Politically, he supports the Republican party. He is a member of the New London Chamber of Commerce, and influential in the deliberations of that body. Fraternally, he is widely connected. He is a member of Brainard Lodge, No. 102, Free and Accepted Masons; Union Chapter, No. 7, Royal Arch Masons; Cushing Council, Royal and Select Masters; and Palestine Commandery, Knights Templar, all of New London. He is a member of Pequot Lodge, Independent Order of Odd Fellows, and is also a member of the Benevolent and Protective Order of Elks, Lodge No. 360, of New London. He is popular in club circles, and is a member of the Harbour Club, the Thames Club, the Rotary Club, and the Masonic Club, all of New London.

On December 25, 1911, Mr. Clarke married Daisy L. Klinck, daughter of Charles H. Klinck, of New London, and they have two children: Alma D. and Waldo K. The family are members of St. James' Episcopal Church.

EDWARD T. CORCORAN—Holding a responsible position in the public service, Edward T. Corcoran, of New London, is well known in this city as a progressive man. Mr. Corcoran is a son of Edmond and Ellen (Flaherty) Corcoran, natives of Ireland. The elder Mr. Corcoran was educated in the national schools of Ireland, and while still a young man, came to the United States, locating in New London. Here he worked as a mason, following that trade all his life. He died in New London, in 1915, and his wife died July 28, 1921. They were the parents of eight children, of whom four are now living: Hanna, wife of Peter Echenfelder, of New London; Nellie, wife of Lawrence A. Cook, of New London; Edward T., whose name heads this review; and Joseph, also a resident of New London, who married Catherine Fleming.

Edward T. Corcoran was born in New London, Connecticut, April 25, 1883. Receiving his early education in the public schools of this city, he entered Bulkeley High School, and was graduated from that institution in the class of 1901. He then entered the New London post office, in the capacity of clerk, and later became assistant postmaster. This position he has since held continuously, and still ably fulfills its duties.

By political affiliation Mr. Corcoran is a Democrat. He is a member of New London Lodge, No. 360, Benevolent and Protective Order of Elks; is a member of St. John's Literary Association, Rotary Club and of the Nameaug Boat Club, all of this city. His religious faith is that of the Roman Catholic, and he is a member of St. Mary's Church.

A. GRAHAM CREIGHTON—With excellent preparation for his profession, and broad experience in it, A. Graham Creighton, of New London, Connecticut, is placing the stamp of his individuality on the construction work of this vicinity as successor to James Sweeney, the long prominent architect, now deceased.

Mr. Creighton is a son of T. Grassie and Avis Creighton, of Halifax, Nova Scotia, and is the youngest of their five children. He was born in Halifax, on February 18, 1886, and received his early education in the public schols of that city. Following his graduation from the Halifax Academy, in 1903, Mr. Creighton entered the University of Toronto, Canada, in the Department of Architecture, and was graduated from this institution in 1906. Going to Saskatchewan, Mr. Creighton there opened an office, and was identified with much of the development of that region during the next twelve years, his headquarters being at Prince Albert. Disposing of his interests there in 1918, he returned to Halifax, where he practiced his profession for a period of two years. Then, in 1920, he came to New London, and purchased the business of James Sweeney, then recently deceased. Mr. Sweeney established his office here in 1888, and was long a leader in the profession. In taking up his work Mr. Creighton has proved himself able and efficient, the possessor at once of high ideals in his art and practical ideas of its application. He has already won his way to a secure footing.

On December 20, 1911, Mr. Creighton married Jean Mackinnon, of Ottawa, Canada, and they have three children: Allan G., Margaret, and Jane.

JAMES R. COLEMAN—A skilled mechanic, Mr. Coleman found in Groton, Connecticut, a field for his energy and ability when his term of service with the American Army in the World War was completed. He is a contractor of mason work, and his capable wife has conducted a meat market in the village of Groton since 1917, a business she bought prior to her marriage.

James R. Coleman, son of George M. and Laura (Smart) Coleman, was born in Westmoreland county, Pennsylvania, June 9, 1889. His father was also of Westmoreland county birth, a contractor all his adult life. Mr. and Mrs. George M. Coleman were the parents of four children: James R.; Gene E., who was in France for nineteen months with the American Expeditionary Forces, sergeant of the Twentieth Regiment of Engineers, First Division of the First Army; Catherine L.; Mary M.

After completing public school study, James R. Coleman was taught the mason's trade in all its branches, his apprenticeship being served under the direction of his capable father. He worked as a journeyman mason in various places until the United States declared war upon Germany, in 1917, and then he enlisted in Toledo, Ohio, in the United States Marine Corps, Third Ohio Replacement Battalion. He continued in the service until the war was ended, and he was honorably discharged at the Submarine Base in New London, April 15, 1919, ranking as sergeant. After leaving the service he settled in Groton, New London county, Connecticut, where he has ever since been engaged as a contractor of mason work.

Mr. Coleman is a Democrat in politics, member of Wilkinsburg Lodge, No. 315, Benevolent and Protective Order of Elks, of Wilkinsburg, Pennsylvania, and of Latrobe Camp, No. 8688, Modern Woodmen of America, of Latrobe, Pennsylvania.

Mr. Coleman married, January 15, 1919, Sarah Alice Donahue, daughter of John A. and Elizabeth (Keating) Donahue, of New London, Connecticut. Mr. and Mrs. Coleman are the parents of a son, James J., born November 20, 1919.

Mrs. Coleman has three brothers residing in New London, all of whom served in the World War, and has an elder sister who resides with her parents. Her brothers are: George W., was a commissioned officer of the United States Aviation Corps, ranking as second lieutenant; Richard, was a sergeant of the Sixty-eighth Regiment, United States Army; Robert, a sergeant-major of the Fifty-sixth Regiment, United States Army. Sarah Alice (Donahue) Coleman was educated in the public schools of New London, finishing with graduation from Williams Memorial High School, class of 1911. Immediately after graduation she became bookkeeper for the Holton Company, Groton, Connecticut, proprietors of a general market there, remaining until 1917. In that year she bought the business and has operated it very successfully, She is a member of the Sacred Heart Roman Catholic Church of Groton.

GEORGE HAROLD HEMPSTEAD—The hardware business, of which George Harold Hempstead is the virtual executive head, was founded by his father, who early admitted his son to a close relationship therein. Mr. Hempstead, Sr., has seen his business grow from a small beginning to its present large proportions, the growth since 1914 being attributed entirely to the business integrity of his son.

George Robert Warren Hempstead, father of George Harold Hempstead, was born in the town of Preston, but when a small child removed to Groton with his parents. Here he obtained his education, after which he operated a well rig for drilling hydraulic wells and thus continued until 1895, when he established himself in a small way in the hardware business in Groton. The venture proved successful, and when he turned the entire management of the business over to his son, upon his retirement from active business life in 1914, the latter became the executive head of an already well established and steadily increasing business. George R. W. Hempstead married Mary Hazler, who died in 1911. To them were born two children: Dora, deceased; George Harold, of further mention.

George Harold Hempstead was born in Groton, Connecticut, June 24, 1892, and here obtained the preliminary portion of his education. He then entered Norwich Free Academy, and upon graduating from this institution he took a commercial course in New London Business College, after which he became associated with his father in the hardware business. This association continued until 1914 when, as previously stated, the younger man took over the management of the business, and has thus continued up to the present time, 1921.

A Republican in politics, he is an important figure in public affairs, and takes a deep interest in all that pertains to the welfare of the community. Mr. Hempstead is active in Masonic circles, and is a member of Charity and Relief Lodge, No. 72, Free and Accepted Masons; Benevolent Chapter, Royal Arch Masons; Mystic Council, No. 29, Royal and Select Masters; Palestine Commandery, No. 6, Knights Templar, and the Norwich Valley Consistory, and has taken his thirty-second degree in Free Masonry. He is also affiliated with the Independent Order of Odd Fellows, Fairview Lodge, No. 107, of Groton; the Groton Grange, Patrons of Husbandry; and attends the Episcopal church there.

On October 3, 1917, George Harold Hempstead was united in marriage with Beatrice May Coffin, daughter of William H. and Elizabeth (Cooper) Coffin.

WILLIAM CHARLES GREENHALGH—Although not having entered into the business life of Mystic, Connecticut, until 1919, Mr. Greenhalgh has already identified himself with the public affairs of the community, and takes a keen interest in everything pertaining to the development of Mystic.

William Greenhalgh, father of William Charles Greenhalgh, was born in Manchester, England, and there obtained his public school education, after which he served eight years in the British Navy, subsequently coming to the United States with his brother Alfred. Upon arriving in this country both young men entered the United States Army, William enlisting in the Coast Artillery and Alfred enlisting as a musician. Both men served for thirty years. William Greenhalgh died in 1913, and Alfred Greenhalgh passed away in Washington, D. C., in 1920. William Greenhalgh married Barbara Kotovsky, and to them were born four children: William Charles, of further mention; Margaret, who married Captain Charles H. Palmer, a member of the ordnance department of the United States Army; Mary, who married Michael Muller, of Springfield, Massachusetts; John, who married Winifred Richards.

William Charles Greenhalgh was born in Newport, Rhode Island, March 5, 1886. After graduating from the Laredo High School, Texas, in 1904, he went to New London, Connecticut, and there served an apprenticeship to the plumber's trade. This accomplished, he worked as a journeyman plumber until 1919, when he came to Mystic and established himself in this particular line, attaining the success which is due him whose life is one of honesty coupled with intolerance of shams and makeshifts. His innate love of justice and fair-dealing having already won the confidence and esteem of his associates and of all with whom he has business dealings. Mr. Greenhalgh is a Republican in politics, and takes the keen interest in the affairs of the organization which is demanded of every good citizen. He affiliates with the Independent Order of Odd Fellows, Stonington Lodge, No. 26, of Mystic, and in religion is a Roman Catholic, attending St. Patrick's Church.

Mr. Greenhalgh married (first), June 5, 1908, Grace Hawkins, and they were the parents of one child, Harry, who lives with his father. He married (second), Eletha M. Callahan, of St. Peter's Port, Channel Island, England, and to them has been born one child, Eletha, born in Mystic, Connecticut.

CAPTAIN FRANK H. ANDERSON—Since the inception of his business career, Captain Anderson has been interested in boat building. In 1920 he was offered his present position of superintendent of the boat yard at West Mystic of the Boston Sea Sled Company, which he accepted.

Louis Anderson, father of Captain Anderson, was born in Norway, but came to this country when a young man and settled in New London, Connecticut, which has been his home continuously since that time. Boat building and marine railway business has always been his occupation. He married Annah Hogauson, a native of Norway, who bore him two children: Frank H., of further mention; Ailie L., who married William Ritch, a resident of Bridgeport, Connecticut.

Frank H. Anderson was born in New London, Connecticut, December 6, 1884. Upon finishing his studies at the New London grammar school, he entered the Bulkeley High School, from which he was graduated in 1902. He then became interested in boat designing. From 1914 until 1918 he was captain of various yachts, and from 1918 until 1920 was stationed at the Charlestown Navy Yard. In 1920 he was given the position of superintendent of the Boston Sea Sled Company, West Mystic, in which he still continues. The company builds very fast sea sleds, whose speed is fifty miles or more per hour. Captain Anderson's thorough training has fitted him for this position, whose obligations he fulfils to the letter, which is due in no small measure to his unbounded energy, unimpeachable integrity, and perservering industry. He is a Republican party sympathizer, confining his political activity to his vote and influence in favor of just causes and desirable officials. In religion he is a Methodist Episcopal.

On October 29, 1903, Captain Anderson was united in marriage with Margaret D. Osborne, a native of Somerville, Massachusetts. Captain and Mrs. Anderson are the parents of two children: Edger W., born in New London, Connecticut; Robert O., born in Acton, Massachusetts.

ROBERT DWIGHT BRADLEY, station agent of the New York, New Haven & Hartford railroad at West Mystic, holds the distinction of being one of the oldest men in the service. Mr. Bradley has also been postmaster of West Mystic since 1891, the office being located in the station.

Francis H. Bradley, father of Robert Dwight Bradley, was born in Russell, Massachusetts, and obtained his education there in the district schools.

Wm C. Greenhalgh

From the time he was a young man until his death he was connected with the railroad, and helped to build the New Haven road from Stonington to Groton. The railroad which was then known as the New York, Providence & Boston railroad is now known as the New York, New Haven & Hartford railroad. Mr. Bradley held the position of chief road master for many years previous to his death. He married Emiline Parks, and to them were born six children.

Robert Dwight Bradley, fourth child of Francis H. and Emiline (Parks) Bradley, was born in West Mystic, Connecticut, November 16, 1863. After finishing his early education in the schools of West Mystic, he entered East Greenwich Academy, East Greenwich, Rhode Island. In 1879 he returned to his native place, where he accepted his present position as station agent. A Republican in politics, Mr. Bradley has long been an important figure in public affairs, although caring nothing for public office. He is a member of the Veteran Railroad Men's Association of Boston, and of the Order of Railroad Telegraphers, No. 261, of New London. In religion he is a Baptist and attends the Union Baptist Church in West Mystic.

On September 18, 1884, Robert Dwight Bradley was united in marriage with Arlene R. Rathburn, daughter of J. Allen and Hannah (Ashby) Rathburn. Mr. and Mrs. Bradley are the parents of five children: Edith F., who married Wilfred S. Lamb, who is mentioned elsewhere in this work; Bertha R., who married W. C. Collins, and resides in Westfield, New Jersey; Marion, who married Raymond Leonard, both deceased; Carl, who is a resident of Westfield, New Jersey, was an inspector in the United States Army Aviation Corps during the World War with the rank of first lieutenant; F. Harmon, serving in the Merchant Marine.

EDWARD ROWELL GORMAN came to the Groton Water Company as superintendent in 1914, a thoroughly experienced and capable electrical engineer, whose former connections had been with important improvements in the railroad motive power, notably the electrification of the New York, New Haven & Hartford railroad between Stamford, Connecticut, and the Grand Central Station in New York City. He is of a Pennsylvania family, son of Theodore Penn and Annie (Hobbs) Gorman, his father born in Monroe county, Pennsylvania, a wholesale grocer of Harrisburg, Pennsylvania, until his removal to Lancaster, Pennsylvania, where he died in 1902. His wife survives him (1920), residing in Dunlap, Iowa. They had three children: Marvin, now residing in Lincoln, Nebraska; Vera, residing with her mother in Dunlap, Iowa; and Edward Rowell, of whom further.

Edward Rowell Gorman was born in Harrisburg, Pennsylvania, July 18, 1876. He completed the courses of the grade and high schools of Harrisburg, then under the direction of J. G. White & Company devoted three years to the study of electrical engineering. In 1898 he studied under Professor Harris Boardman, of Lancaster, Pennsylvania, remaining with him two years. His study was interrupted by his service in Company K, Sixth Regiment, Pennsylvania Infantry, during the Spanish-American War, 1898, but he finally finished educational preparation and secured his first important position as manager of the electric station of the Baltimore & Ohio railroad in Philadelphia, Pennsylvania. From Philadelphia he went to the Wayne Iron & Steel Company in Pittsburgh, Pennsylvania, coming thence to the New York, New Haven & Hartford railroad as superintendent of their overhead system of wiring between Stamford and New York City. He remained with that company until 1914, then came to Groton, Connecticut, as superintendent of the Groton Water Company in full charge of the water and electric departments of the company. His connection with that company has been mutually pleasant and satisfactory and still continues (1920). Mr. Gorman is a member of the American Institute of Electrical Engineers of New York; Union Lodge, No. 31, Free and Accepted Masons; Union Chapter, No. 7, Royal Arch Masons, all of New London; is an Independent in politics, and an attendant of Groton Baptist Church.

Mr. Gorman married, in June 1902, Hattie B. Russell, of Lancaster, Pennsylvania, daughter of William and Annie (Hull) Russell. Mr. and Mrs. Gorman are the parents of three children: Vera, Helen, and Florence. The family home is in Groton, Connecticut.

JAMES COOPER—Holding a leading position in one of the principal manufacturing plants at Mystic, Connecticut, and also active in the public life of the town, James Cooper is representative of that group of men who have transplanted Old World beginnings to American soil, and are now a vital part of industrial progress in this country.

Mr. Cooper is a son of Thomas and Esther (Styan) Cooper. Thomas Cooper was born in Pontifract, England, this town now being known as Pomfret. He received a thorough education in the National schools of that country, and was a farmer all his life in England. He died in 1880, and his wife died in 1908, both in England. They were the parents of twelve children, of whom four are now living: Elizabeth, who resides in England; Jane, who became the wife of William Crowe, also living in England; John S., who married Martha Hopkinton, and resides in Hartford, Connecticut; and James, of whom further.

James Cooper was born in Huddersfield, England, August 29, 1859. He received his education in the National schools of his native land, thereafter making a thorough study of the manufacture of woolen fabrics. He worked in various famous mills in England, becoming highly efficient in his chosen line, then came to the United States about 1891. Here he located in Rockville, Connecticut, and entered the employ of the Hockanum Mills, Incorporated, having charge of the yarn department. But Mr. Cooper was not to remain long in any subordinate position. He was trained for large interests, and in 1898 the opportunity offered. He became associated with the Mystic Manufacturing Company, Incorporated, as secretary-treasurer and director, and also as superintendent of the production branch of this company's plant. In his work here he has displayed the ability which makes for progress in any line of endeavor, and the business has gone forward constantly. He has been president of the Mystic Real Estate and Building Company, from the time it was incorporated to the present time (1921).

Mr. Cooper was long since sought for public service, and although his time is largely absorbed by his business interests, he has done constructive work on the school committee. He was for eight years a member of the committee, and for four years chairman of the school committee for the town of Stonington, Connecticut. He is serving as chairman of the local Red Cross, and for the past three years has been a member of the board of directors of the Village Nursery Association, also a member of the board of directors of Mystic Community House. Fraternally Mr. Cooper is prominent. He is a member of Charity and Relief Lodge, Free and Accepted Masons, of Mystic, and is a member of Stonington Lodge, No. 26, of Mystic, in which order he holds the office of past noble grand. He has been on the Grand Officers' Staff for four years, now grand marshal.

Mr. Cooper married (first), in England, Lillian McIntagart, of England, and they were the parents of three children: Ethel, who became the wife of Edgar Blinm, and now resides in Middlebury, Vermont; Frank S., who married Mary Kulberg, and resides in Pearl River, New York; and Lillian, now the wife of Hollié Price, of Mystic. The first Mrs. Cooper died in England. On May 1, 1899, Mr. Cooper married (second), in Rockville, Connecticut, Lillian Norris, of that city. They have five children: Marion, Mildred, Norris, Esther, deceased; and Esther; the four living now residing at home. The family are members of the Congregational church.

JOHN WILLIAM McDONALD—The McDonalds of Mystic, Connecticut, descend from William McDonald, a prosperous farmer of Prince Edward Island, a maritime province of Canada, and there Donald McDonald was born and spent his boyhood days. He was a pump maker and a ship carpenter, and spent his youth and early manhood engaged at his trade in his native land. In 1852 he came to the United States, locating in Hoboken, New Jersey, and later lived in Newport, Rhode Island, working at his trade in both cities. Later he moved to Mystic, Connecticut, and was employed in the Greenman Shipyard. After a time he formed a partnership with Samuel Colborn; they worked in the Mallory Yard and took contracts for certain portions of a vessel. In Mystic he married Alice Sutton, of Liverpool, England, who died April 17, 1903. Donald McDonald died in Mystic in 1872. They were the parents of six children: Barbara, married Joseph W. Noble, of Mystic, Connecticut; she is now deceased and left a daughter Jennie; John William, of further mention; Charles Richard, died aged twenty years; Sarah, Alice, and Lizzie, who died young.

John William McDonald, eldest son of Donald and Alice (Sutton) McDonald, was born in Mystic, Connecticut, October 20, 1857. After finishing his public school studies, he worked four years learning the carriage trimmer's trade, and from that time he has been engaged in some form of commercial enterprise. For five years he was in the grocery business with Samuel S. Brown, then for ten years was a partner with J. W. Noble in the meat business, trading as Noble & McDonald. At the end of that period he sold out to his partner, but a year later bought control of the same business and conducted it alone for five years. In all these business enterprises he was successful and prosperous, but it was not until 1903 that he settled down to a permanent business. On April 1, 1903, he bought the Morgan Ice Company from its then owner, Elijah A. Morgan, and conducted the same for three years.

Mr. McDonald married, June 25, 1885, Adelaide A. Hopkins, daughter of George O. Hopkins, who was principal of Mystic public schools for fifteen years. Mr. and Mrs. McDonald are members of the Congregational church, he being church treasurer, and a member of the Knights of Pythias. They are the parents of four children, all born in Mystic, Connecticut: 1. Sarah E., a distinguished nurse of the American Expeditionary Force, who for bravery was awarded the Distinguished Service Cross. In 1916 she was graduated from the Presbyterian Hospital of New York City, a trained nurse. She enlisted, May 14, 1917, with the unit which went out from the Presbyterian Hospital, headed by Dr. Brewer, and went to France as part of the American Expeditionary Force. That unit was stationed at Base Hospital No. 2, and when it was later destroyed by German shell fire, Miss McDonald displayed such heroism under fire that she was personally decorated with the Distinguished Service Cross by General John J. Pershing. The unit to which she belonged was a part of the 42nd Division, and Miss McDonald with the unit was mustered out of the United States service at the Presbyterian Hospital, New York, February 19, 1919. She is a member of William Morgan Post, American Legion, of Mystic. She married, April 21, 1919, Captain Raymond M. Holmes, who during the war period, 1917-1918, was supervisor of gas mask manufacture in Astoria, Long Island. 2. Alice A., resides with her parents in Mystic. 3. Barbara, a teacher in Dr. Taylor's School for the Deaf and Dumb in New York City. 4. Ruth W., a musician, graduate of Connecticut College of Music, New London, now a special student under Professor Frederick Weld, of New York, he professor in the Connecticut College of Music.

WILLIAM SAMUEL WALBRIDGE, a prominent figure in business life in Mystic, where he has resided since 1914, is active also in political and public affairs in the various towns in which he has lived since reaching manhood, and he has always had uppermost in his mind the welfare and advancement of the communities, and since coming to old Mystic has continued to give his earnest support to all measures calculated to advance business development.

William Samuel Walbridge was born April 8, 1868, in Ashford, Connecticut, the son of the late Leander and Emily (Baker) Walbridge, both natives of Ashford. Leander Walbridge attended the district school of Ashford, and upon reaching young manhood turned his attention to agricultural pursuits and followed this vocation throughout his entire lifetime in his native town of Ashford. He eventually retired and moved to Stafford, Tolland county, where he died in 1904. His wife died in Old Mystic in 1915. Mr. and Mrs. Walbridge were the parents of eight children, William Samuel, of further mention, being the sixth child.

William Samuel Walbridge went to school in Ashford, and then entered upon his business career, his first employment being in a grocery store in Staffordville, Connecticut, where he remained for twelve years, subsequently going to Stafford, where he owned and managed a grocery store for eighteen years. In 1914 he came to Old Mystic, Connecticut, and again established himself in the same line of business, in which he has since continued. He was highly successful in this venture, and within a short time rose to a place of prominence in business circles here.

When but a young man, Mr. Walbridge entered the political arena and for sixteen years was registrar of voters in the town of Stafford, Tolland county, where he was also selectman for many years. He has also been registrar of voters, justice of the peace and notary public of the town of Stonington, New London county, Connecticut. In 1912-1913 he represented the town of Stafford in the State Legislature, and since 1917 has been postmaster of Old Mystic. He has always had a genius for politics and for public service, and is a Democrat in National and local issues. Mr. Walbridge fraternizes with the Free and Accepted Masons, being a member of Walcott Lodge, No. 60, of Stafford, and in religion is a Methodist, being an attendant and ardent supporter of the church of this denomination in Mystic.

In Stafford, Connecticut, William Samuel Walbridge married, July 25, 1887, Lenora May Whitney, daughter of James and Mary (Chadwick) Whitney. Mr. and Mrs. Walbridge are the parents of four children: 1. William Earl, who was the first man from the town of Groton, Connecticut, to offer his services to the Government for service in the World War, and served for eighteen months in France with the 20th United States Engineers. 2. Richard Edmund, who served in the World War as a member of the Ordnance Department; married Maud Lacomb; resides in Old Mystic, Connecticut. 3. Florence May. 4. Esther Amy.

HOWARD A. EDGCOMB, senior member of the firm of Edgcomb & Poppe, dealers in men's furnishings in Groton, Connecticut, is a native of this community, his birth having occurred August 14, 1869. His father, Roswell S. Edgcomb, is also a native of Groton, and now lives retired here in his eighty-sixth year, after having served the community well both as a public and private citizen. Mr. Edgcomb, Sr., married Frances Ashby, who died in 1874, and to them were born five children, only two of whom are still living: Howard A., of further mention; Roswell, who married Nellie Richards.

The education of Howard A. Edgcomb was obtained in the public schools of Groton. After completing his education he worked in various stores in the capacity of clerk, but being of an ambitious nature, this was not to his liking, as he had a keen desire to establish himself in business, so with a small capital in 1893 he opened a store of men's furnishings in Groton and thus continued successfully until 1911, when he sold this business and became a partner with Irving H. Poppe under the firm name of Edgcomb & Poppe, which has become highly successful. Mr. Edgcomb is well known in the business world of Groton, highly respected for the fairness of his dealings, and universally recognized as a man whose judgment in matters of business might be readily followed.

In politics Mr. Edgcomb is a Republican, and has always taken an active part in the affairs of the local organization, having been auditor of the town's accounts for several years, and in the year 1920 was elected to the House of Representatives. His Masonic membership is found in Union Lodge, No. 31, Free and Accepted Masons; Union Chapter, No. 7, Royal Arch Masons, of New London; Cushing Council, No. 4, Royal and Select Masters; Palestine Commandery, No. 6, Knights Templar, of which he is a past commander; Pyramid Temple, Nobles of the Mystic Shrine, of Bridgeport, Connecticut; and Norwich Valley Consistory, Ancient Accepted Scottish Rite. He is also affiliated with the Independent Order of Odd Fellows, Fairview Lodge, of Groton, of which he is past noble grand, and in religion is a Baptist.

Mr. Edgcomb married (first), in 1898, Nellie Whiting, a native of Mystic, Connecticut; she died in Groton, in 1903. To them was born one child, Viola, who married Elias Chapman. Mr. Edgcomb married (second), Helen J. Allen, of Groton; she died in 1909, and to them was born one child, Allen A., who was a student at Brown University, and who died June 19, 1921. He married (third) Mathilda Denison, of Groton, in 1912. There is no issue.

FRANCIS ARCHIE LAMBERT, owner and manager of The Sanitary Laundry, Old Mystic, Connecticut, is reckoned among the younger generation of successful business men of this community, for although having been established in business but a comparatively short time he has already attained success which might well be the envy of a much older man.

Augustus Lambert, father of Francis Archie Lambert, was born in Marcelle, Province of Quebec, Canada. At the age of nine years he came to this country with his parents, and located in Slatersville, Rhode Island, where he completed his education. He then secured employment in a woolen mill in Slatersville, where he learned the trade of spinning, and subsequently became overseer of spinning in the woolen mill. In 1903 he retired from active business life, and now lives retired at Old Mystic, Connecticut. Mr. Lambert married Rose Marcelle, a native of Stafford, Connecticut, and to them have been born two children: Francis Archie, of further mention; Raymond H., who was born July 16, 1902.

Francis Archie Lambert was born in Stafford, Connecticut, July 19, 1892. He obtained his education in the public schools of Mystic, Connecticut, where his parents removed when he was very young. After completing his studies he served an apprenticeship to the machinist's trade with J. W. Lathrop Company, of Mystic, Connecticut. In 1917 his ambition having directed him to private enterprise, he organized The Sanitary Laundry in Old Mystic, and still continues in this with consistently increasing success. He attributes his progress in his occupation to the strict attention which he has always given his business and all its numerous details. In the civic affairs of his community and State he holds an intense interest, and is accounted a steadfast member of the Democratic party. In his religious views he is a Roman Catholic, member of St. Patrick's Church, of Mystic.

CAPTAIN CHARLES HERBERT WOLFE—Inheriting from his father a love of the sea, and being brought up from his boyhood to follow it for a livelihood, Charles Herbert Wolfe has sailed all over the world, rounding Cape Horn eight different times, sailing on every ocean known to navigators, and visiting all the leading ports of entry in every country open to commerce.

The father of Charles Herbert Wolfe, Captain Thomas E. Wolfe, was born in Mystic, Connecticut, and after attending the district school there for a time, began to sail the high seas, continuing it until the outbreak of the Civil War. At that time his ship was put into the transport service by the Federal Government, carrying supplies from New York City to New Orleans, Louisiana, he being captain of the vessel. On one of these trips his ship was captured by the Confederate navy, when only a few miles out from New Orleans, and was burned, Captain Wolfe being taken prisoner and later was sent to Libby Prison. After remaining for nearly two years in that dreadful prison, he and five companions made their escape from it; they were Albert D. Richardson, a correspondent of the New York "Tribune"; Junis H. Brown, who was a New York "Herald" newspaper man, and three others. After the war was brought to a close, Captain Wolfe went to Galveston, Texas, and became a State pilot, stationed in Galveston. In 1876, while acting in that capacity on a Mallory Line Steamship, of New York, in Galveston harbor, the ship caught fire and all on board lost their lives. Thomas E. Wolfe married Frances J. Sawyer, who was born in Mason Island, Mystic. Captain and Mrs. Wolfe had six children, as follows: George, who died in infancy; Eugene, who also died in infancy; Charles Herbert, of whom further; Thomas W., who married Mary Fish, and his death occurred in Mystic; T. Emma, the wife of Morris Wells, a resident of Groton, Connecticut; Henry M., who died in infancy.

Charles Herbert Wolfe was born in Mystic, Connecticut, March 19, 1857. He attended the village school for a few years, but when twelve years of age left school to become one of the crew on a fishing smack, "The Gold Hunter," remaining as such for two years. When fourteen years old he became ship's boy on the ship "Bridgewater," of which Charles Sisson was captain. Young Wolfe then made his first trip around Cape Horn on a voyage to California, it requiring in those days six months to make the journey. After this trip, Mr. Wolfe became third mate on the vessel "Jeremiah Thompson," and while on this ship in 1877 had the unpleasant experience of being struck by a tidal wave caused by an earthquake, while at anchor off the coast of Peru, South America. In 1878 Charles Herbert Wolfe became first mate on the "George Moon," the last of the square-rigged ships to be built at Mystic. For ten years he continued on this vessel, the last three years being captain of it. From 1888 until 1893, Captain Wolfe filled the office of first mate on one of the Mallory Steamship Line vessels of New York. Captain Wolfe has never taken an active part in politics, though he is in political faith a Republican. He is a member of Charity and Relief Lodge, No. 72, of Mystic, Ancient Free and Accepted Masons. He is also an attendant of the Baptist church and one of its supporters.

Charles Herbert Wolfe married in Mystic, April 30, 1883, Bessie Heath, daughter of Reuben and Sarah (Benjamin) Heath, of Mystic. Mrs. Wolfe is an active worker and member in the Baptist church, having been superintendent of the Primary Sunday school for the past twenty-five years.

STEPHEN ARTHUR BOYLEN, a native of the Bay State, as were his parents before him, is both by birth and inheritance a son of rugged New England. Born in Boston, Massachusetts, April 3, 1882, he is the son of Alfred F. Boylen, born in Boston, where he was educated in the public schools, and where he learned the trade of a tailor, a business which he followed all his life until a short time ago when he retired from active participation in work and is living quietly in Melrose, Massachusetts. His wife was, before her marriage, Sarah Wigglesworth, born in Newburyport, Massachusetts. Of this union seven children were born, of whom the second is Stephen Arthur Boylen.

Becoming a pupil in the grammar school in Malden, Massachusetts, Stephen A. Boylen acquired a good education there and in the high school of Malden. After leaving school, he became an apprentice in the jewelry shop of W. A. Smith, of Melrose, with whom he remained for four years, from 1900 to 1904, and he then found employment in various jewelry plants in the following seven years, a part of the time being engaged in the extensive works of the Waltham Watch Company, Waltham, Massachusetts. There he gained an unusually thorough training in the manufacture and repair of a watch, becoming an expert in that line. In 1911 Mr. Boylen decided to go into business for himself. He removed to Mystic, Connecticut, and bought out the establishment of Mitchell & Son, where he carried on a very successful business in that line, still continuing it up to date. While Mr. Boylen is a member of the Republican party, he is not greatly interested in political work and has never held any public office. In religion he is a member of the Protestant Episcopal church.

At Waltham, Massachusetts, September 22, 1908, Stephen Arthur Boylen was united in marriage with Florence Stark, a native of that city. She is the daughter of Frank and Frances (Figg) Stark, residents of Waltham. Mr. and Mrs. Stephen Arthur Boylen make their home in Groton township, Connecticut.

JAMES FOLEY—One of the active forces in the growth and development of the town of Mystic, Connecticut, is found in the real estate field. Here James Foley, of this town, is a significant factor, and for the past few years has been identified with many of the real estate transactions which have meant progress in the right direction. Mr. Foley is a son of James and Annie (McMahon) Foley.

James Foley was born at Rosscommon, Ireland, and received his education in the National schools of that country. About 1855, or when the young man was eighteen years of age, he came to the United States, locating in Mystic, Connecticut. He quickly found employment in the woolen mills, and throughout his lifetime followed this line of work. He died in Mystic in 1888, his wife surviving him for twenty-two years thereafter. They were the parents of eight children, of whom five are now living: Charles H., well-known insurance agent of Mystic, married Mary E. Smith; James, whose name heads this review; Margaret, residing at home; George Henry, a sketch of whose life follows; and Mary, who also resides at home.

James Foley was born in Mystic, Connecticut, March 8, 1872. Receiving a thoroughly practical education in the public schools of the town, he entered the business world in 1890, in the employ of Captain J. H. Hoxie, then a prominent real estate dealer of Mystic. This association continued until 1916, the young man gaining a wide and useful experience, and also becoming a power in this field. In that year he severed his connection with the Hoxie office, and went into the real estate business for himself. He also branched out into the insurance field, and has developed an important business along that line. He now stands among the leading business men of Mystic, and is held in the highest esteem by his contemporaries. Politically Mr. Foley affiliates with the Democratic party. He resides at the family home in Mystic, and is a member of St. Patrick's Roman Catholic Church.

GEORGE HENRY FOLEY—Of all the public responsibilities incident to community life and progress, that of postmaster is, perhaps, the most exacting, and in Mystic, New London county, Connecticut, George Henry Foley is filling this office with marked ability. He is a son of James and Annie (McMahon) Foley (q. v.).

George Henry Foley was born in Mystic, Connecticut, February 29, 1876. Receiving a practical education in the public schools of the town, he entered the world of industry in the employ of the Rossie Velvet Mills, where he remained for sixteen years, working in the weaving department. In the course of his long residence in the town of his birth, he became well and favorably known among his townspeople, and in 1915 was appointed postmaster of the town of Mystic, which position he still fills with marked ability. By political affiliation Mr. Foley is a Democrat, and he is interested in every phase of the public welfare. He is a member, and holds the office of trustee, of the Father Murphy Council, Knights of Columbus, Mystic. In 1895 he became an active member of the B. F. Hoxie Engine Company (Fire Company), was made foreman in 1902, being the youngest foreman in the history of the company, served as foreman for two years. He was made an honorary life member in 1914.

On June 26, 1907, Mr. Foley married Mary L. Kinion, of Valley Falls, Rhode Island, daughter of Patrick F. and Catherine (Finnegan) Kinion. Patrick F. Kinion was born in Valley Falls, Rhode Island, and his wife was born in Mystic, Connecticut. They were the parents of six children, Mary L., being the first child. For many years Mr. Kinion was town clerk of the town of Cumberland, Rhode Island. Mr. and Mrs. Foley are the parents of two children: George Henry, Jr., born in Mystic, July 6, 1908; and Helen, born in Mystic, June 10, 1912. The family are members of the Roman Catholic church.

ELMER EDWIN MILLER, a successful farmer of the town of Griswold, Connecticut, is well-known and influential, holding the regard of all men who value integrity and uprightness. He is a son of Oliver S. and Sarah A. (Eccleston) Miller, his father born in Clinton, Connecticut, his mother in North Stonington, both now deceased.

Oliver S. Miller grew up at the home farm in Clinton, which was then a fishing village of some note. Tiring of farm life, he went to sea for a time, but did not long continue a sailor, life on the farm proving to him the more attractive. He returned home, and until 1855 was his father's farm assistant. In that year he bought a farm in the Ashwillett district of the town of North Stonington, and there spent the remainder of his life. His farm was heavily timbered, and this he worked into lumber and ship timber, owning his own saw mill and marketing his product with the ship builders of Noank. As his own timber was cut, he bought other tracts, including the William Bailey and the Dawley farms, both in the Ashwillett district. He prospered in both his farm and lumber activities, and continued in business until his death from a shock, June 6, 1912. His wife, Sarah A. (Eccleston) Miller, survived him for two years, dying at the home of her daughter, Mrs. William Kilroy, in Bozrah, Connecticut, in 1914. They were the parents of twelve children, all of whom were born in North Stonington, except the two eldest, who were born in Clinton, Connecticut: Avery E., deceased; Sarah Almira, married Herbert Stark, whom she survives; Susan, married Daniel Ferguson, who now owns the Oliver S. Miller farm in North Stonington; Everett Oliver, a farmer of Norwich, Connecticut; Lillian, deceased wife of William Hull, of Old Mystic; John, who was drowned when a lad of twelve; Stella, wife of Joseph Wheeler, a farmer of Stonington; Effie, second wife of William Hull, of Old Mystic; Minnie, wife of William Kilroy, of Bozrah; Rose Belle, wife of Warren W. Bentley, of Bozrah; Lydia, died at the age of twenty-two years; Elmer Edwin, of further mention.

Elmer Edwin Miller, twelfth child and youngest son of Oliver Smith and Sarah A. (Eccleston) Miller, was born at the home farm in North Stonington, New London county, Connecticut, April 24, 1873, and obtained his education in the public schools in his district. He remained at home, his father's assistant in his farming and lumbering operations, until 1897, when he moved to a leased farm in North Stonington, where with his wife he spent two years. In 1899 he moved to another leased farm near Glasgow, town of Griswold, and there remained until 1903, when he rented the Albert Ayer farm in Preston, Connecticut. He continued a tenant on that farm until 1908, when he bought the property which became famous as Sunny Hillside Farm. That farm of two hundred and sixty-two acres he cultivated and owned until the last year, 1921, when he sold it and bought the John Hawkins farm of two hundred acres in the town of Griswold, where he is now residing. He devotes his acres to general and dairy farming, is a successful breeder of light harness horses, and since 1914 has had at the head of his stud the stallion, "Peter Agan," 2-13¼, the sire of several fast trotters. Mr. Miller is a well-known county fair exhibitor, his track and draft horses winning many "blue ribbons," prizes and purses. He is a man of high standing in his community, and one of the prosperous and substantial men of the town. In politics Mr. Miller is a Republican, and is at present tax assessor. In religious faith he is a Congregationalist. He is a member of Preston City Grange; New London county Pomona, and the Connecticut State Grange, Patrons of Husbandry.

Mr. Miller married, in North Stonington, January 1, 1895, Sarah Edith Main, born in North Stonington, daughter of Lester and Thankful (Eccleston) Main. Mr. and Mrs. Miller are the parents of three children: 1. Everett Avery, born in North Stonington, Connecticut, July 23, 1897, now engaged in the garage business in Jewett City; he enlisted in the Coast Artillery, Connecticut National Guard, March 16, 1917, his command being reorganized as Battery D, 56th Regiment, United States Artillery, assigned to the 26th (Yankee) Division, and was engaged in the fierce fighting of the Meuse-Argonne drive and other battles with the Germans in France. 2. Ruth Ethel, twin with Everett A., is a teacher, now connected with the Preston public schools. 3. Herbert Lester, born in Preston, Connecticut, May 24, 1906.

SEYMOUR AARON STODDARD—Holding a responsible executive position in Mystic, New London county, Connecticut, Seymour Aaron Stoddard is in one of the constructive branches of business endeavor. He is a son of Ichabod and Eliza (Rogers) Stoddard.

Ichabod Stoddard was born in Montville, and received a practical education in the public schools of that town. He became a carpenter and contractor, following this class of work during all of his active life, then retired, spending his last years in the city of New London, where he died in 1920. His wife, who was born in Montville also, still resides in New London. They were the parents of two children: Myra, who became the wife of Charles Appley, of New London; and Seymour A.

Seymour A. Stoddard was born in Montville, Connecticut, October 15, 1883. Receiving a thoroughly practical education in the public schools of the city of Norwich, he later learned the carpenter's trade with his father, and followed this trade for a period of ten years. Then in the year 1915 he went to Mystic, Connecticut, where he took charge of the hardware department of the Cottrell Lumber Company, of that city. He found his experience along construction lines valuable here, and he was by nature fitted for an executive position. Thus, as time passed, he became a force for progress in the business, and upon the death of the president of this company, Mr. Charles C. Dodge, in 1919, Mr. Stoddard became the manager of the company, in which capacity he is now engaged. In the various interests of public and fraternal life, Mr. Stoddard is well known. He supports the principles and policies of the Republican party, although he consistently declines political preferment. He is a member of the Stonington Lodge, No. 26, of Mystic, Independent Order of Odd Fellows.

On April 11, 1912, Mr. Stoddard married Artis Z. Lamb, of Mystic, daughter of Herbert and Louise (Allen) Lamb, of Mystic. They have one daughter, Emily Louise, born in Mystic, June 4, 1920. The family are members of the Baptist church, and are active in the benevolent and social organizations of the church.

WILLIAM FRANKLIN BITGOOD, wagon manufacturer of Pachaug village, was born in Voluntown, Connecticut, March 10, 1877, the son of William H. and Abby (Lewis) Bitgood. William H. Bitgood was also a native of Voluntown, and there in the district schools obtained his meagre education. After terminating his studies he engaged in farming and continued in this occupation on the old homestead throughout his entire lifetime.

William F. Bitgood attended school until he was eighteen years of age, when he became a woodsman and worked for his uncle, Andrew Jackson Bitgood, for three years, after which he returned to his home and worked on the farm with his father. Still later he apprenticed himself to the carpenter's trade and then removed to Hopeville, Rhode Island, where he engaged in the same business for seven years. In 1911 he came to Pachaug, where he established himself as a wagon manufacturer and blacksmith and has continued thus engaged ever since that time. Mr. Bitgood has always interested himself in everything which pertained to civic welfare, and in politics is a staunch Democrat, taking a keen and active interest in the affairs of the local organization. In religion he is a Congregationalist and attends the church of this denomination in Pachaug.

On June 27, 1896, William Franklin Bitgood was united in marriage with Susan James, the daughter of Ezekiel and Mary E. (Barber) James, both natives of Voluntown. To Mr. and Mrs. Bitgood have been born four children: 1. Harold W., enlisted in August, 1918, in United States army, sent to Camp Greenleaf, Georgia, assigned to the 102nd Sanitary Train to France in November, 1918, and discharged at Camp Upton, Long Island, July 24, 1919; is now associated in business with his father. 2. Herman J. 3. Irving E., deceased. 4. Robert E.

JOHN WILLIAM BIRCHALL—When Mr. Birchall was transferred to Colchester, Connecticut, as manager of the Atlantic & Pacific Corporation's local store he became a resident of the town. This was in March, 1920, and since then Mr. Birchall has identified himself with everything pertaining to civic advancement in Colchester.

John William Birchall was born in Stonington, Connecticut, March 29, 1887, the son of William and Mary (Teevan) Birchall. William Birchall was a native of Manchester, England, and died May 28, 1916, at Stonington, where he had resided since 1884. He was an iron moulder by trade. His wife still resides in Stonington. Eight children were born of this union, John W. Birchall being the second child.

John W. Birchall attended the public schools of New London, Connecticut, and after completing his education at the Bulkeley High School, secured a position as clerk with the Trumbull Grocery Company at Stonington, Connecticut. He remained with this concern for seven years and then resigned to become manager of the New London branch of the Atlantic & Pacific Corporation. Five years later he was transferred to his present position, in which he has continued up to the present time. Active in his business relations and with a ready courtesy for all, he is a man who is a conspicuous figure in the business circles of Colchester. Mr. Birchall is independent in politics, not having identified himself with any particular party, preferring to remain free from all partisan influences in the exercise of his own judgment on public issues. He affiliates with the Knights of Columbus, and in religion is a Roman Catholic.

On June 5, 1912, John William Birchall was united in marriage with Anne Irene Barrett, a native of Queenstown, Rhode Island. To Mr. and Mrs. Birchall have been born five children: John Teevan, born May 15, 1913; Mary, born January 1, 1915, deceased; Joseph, born October 1, 1916; William Francis, born July 5, 1918; and Edward, deceased.

FREDERICK JACKSON APPLEY—In North Stonington, Connecticut, one of the most progressive and up-to-date farmers of New London county is Frederick Jackson Appley, a son of Andrew Jackson and Mary Elizabeth (Armstrong) Appley.

Andrew Jackson Appley was born in Chaplin, Windham county, Connecticut, in the year 1834. He was a farmer in that village, and continued active along this line until the Civil War, when he enlisted in the 18th Regiment, Connecticut Volunteer Infantry, and served all through the period of the war. Returning to his birthplace at the end of the war, he married, and in 1869 he and his wife and infant son, Frederick J., went West, locating in Lee Summit, Lee county, Illinois, then a frontier settlement of the West. It was here that the other three of their four children were born. A few years later the father suffered a sun-stroke, from the effects of which he never fully recovered. He died there on July 3, 1876. Three years later, in 1879, the widowed mother returned East, with two of her remaining children, one having been lost by an accidental death. She went to Summit, Rhode Island, where she purchased a farm. Later she married Warren W. Moone, another veteran of the Civil War, who died April 6, 1915. In 1900 the family removed to North Stonington, Connecticut, and there bought a farm. Later they sold this farm, and bought the present Appley farm, in 1906, where the two brothers, Frederick J. and George H., now conduct a large wholesale and retail dairy business. Mrs. Moone died February 10, 1921. The children of Andrew Jackson and Mary Elizabeth (Armstrong) Appley are: Frederick Jackson, of whom extended mention follows: George Henry, who was born in Lee Center, Lee county, Illinois, married Cora Maine, of North Stonington, and is now associated with his brother on the farm; Bertie, who was born October 13, 1872, in Lee county, Illinois, and was accidentally drowned at the age of two years and a half; and Lillian May, who was born in Lee county, Illinois, January 10, 1875, became the wife of Frank Standley, of Stonington, Connecticut, March 5, 1907, and has two children, Clayton F., born September 5, 1910, and Marian Elizabeth, born September 3, 1915.

Frederick Jackson Appley was born in Chaplin, Windham county, Connecticut, April 15, 1868. Removing with his parents to Illinois, while still a little child, his education was gained in the schools of Lee county, that State. The boy, being eleven years of age when his mother returned East after his father's death, was permitted his own choice, which kept him in the West, with an uncle in Lee county, first in the town of Lee Center, then later in Franklin Grove, in the same county. When the lad was seventeen years of age, his uncle was killed on a hay wagon, and the boy was left to shift for himself. Remaining in Illinois until he was eighteen years of age, he came East and joined his mother in Rhode Island. But the lure of the West was strong, and he soon returned to the State and county where his boyhood had been spent. There he remained until 1895, when he came East permanently. Joining the family in Summit, Rhode Island, he remained with them, and upon their removal to North Stonington,

Connecticut, he allowed nothing to tempt him away from the home place. Now for years he and his brother George H. have carried on the interests of the farm, constantly improving the place, building up a fine herd, and a very large and extensive business. Mr. Appley is now considered by his townspeople one of the most progressive farmers of this section. Mr. Appley is a member of North Stonington Grange, No. 138, Patrons of Husbandry, and in his relationship to the farming community through this organization is a vital force for the upbuilding of the farming interests of the town. Mrs. Appley died February 10, 1901.

EARL STANLEY BAVIER—Ably filling a position of responsibility in the community, prominent in the social and fraternal life of the town, Earl Stanley Bavier is representative of the broadly useful citizens whose interests embrace many branches of activity.

Mr. Bavier is a son of Nelson and Sarah (Curtiss) Bavier. Nelson Bavier was born in Newark, New Jersey, and there received his education in the public schools. Thereafter, he became interested in the manufacture of hardware, and has followed this general line up to the present time. For several years he was superintendent of the New Haven Clock Company at their New Haven plant. He is now located at Chatham, Connecticut, where he is a manufacturer of various kinds of hardware. His wife was born in Waterbury, Connecticut, and is a daughter of Captain Lucius Curtiss, a soldier of the Civil War. Mrs. Bavier's mother, Mary (Cleveland) Curtiss, was a sister of ex-President Grover Cleveland. Mr. and Mrs. Bavier are the parents of four children, three sons and one daughter: Nelson, Jr., now city engineer of Hartford, Connecticut, who married Olive Reeves; Isabelle, who became the wife of Herbert S. Bush, and is a resident of New Haven; George H., now of Boston, who is assistant to the president of the Boston & Maine railroad, and an important figure in New England railway circles, and married Maude White; and Earl Stanley, of whom further.

Earl Stanley Bavier was born in New Haven, Connecticut, on January 28, 1884. He received his early education in the public schools of that city, then completed his studies at the Baypath Institute, of Springfield, Massachusetts. In 1898 he became associated with his father in the office of his factory, remaining until 1901. In that year he entered the employ of the New York, New Haven & Hartford railroad, in their New Haven offices, later becoming inspector of stations, which position carried him to all points on the lines in the control of this company. In 1914 he was sent to Mystic, Connecticut, to reorganize the station management, later becoming agent at this station. He still acts in that capacity, and has become a well-known figure in the life of the town, as well as in his official capacity.

Politically, Mr. Bavier is a supporter of the principles of the Democratic party, although he has never accepted political preferment of any kind. He is a member of the American-Asiatic Society of New York City.

On October 10, 1908, Mr. Bavier married Isabelle Drysdale, of Westerly, Rhode Island, daughter of Robert and Mary (MacCracken) Drysdale, both natives of Scotland. Mr. and Mrs. Bavier attend the Congregational church of Mystic, and are prominent in all its social and benevolent activities.

JOHN JEFFREY HERBERT, the popular and energetic automobile dealer of Norwich, Connecticut, is a native of New London county, and has been well-known in business circles of this vicinity ever since his education was completed.

Mr. Herbert is a son of Jonas L. and Lillian E. (Jeffrey) Herbert, of Voluntown, Connecticut. Jonas L. Herbert was born in Whiting, Vermont, and was educated in the public schools of the city of Quebec, Canada. In 1885 he came to the United States, and located at Voluntown, in New London county, Connecticut. There he bought out the general store, and has continued in this business until the present time, becoming one of the leading men of the town. His wife was born in Westerly, Rhode Island, and they are the parents of four children.

John Jeffrey Herbert was born in Glasgo, New London county, Connecticut, on May 24, 1893. He received his early education in the district schools of Voluntown, then entered the Norwich Free Academy, from which he was graduated in the class of 1912. With this practical preparation for the battle of life he became his father's assistant at the store in Voluntown, where he gained the experience which is now of real benefit to him. He remained with his father until 1919, when he came to Norwich, and bought out the Charles S. Peckham Garage. He has been most successful from the first, and is now considered one of the foremost men in the automobile world of New London county. He handles the Maxwell and Chalmers cars, and has a very complete stock of automobile supplies of every description. Although a comparatively short time has elapsed since his entering this field, he has become a power therein, and is forging ahead to an enviable position in the trade.

Mr. Herbert is alert to every phase of civic and industrial progress, a Republican by political choice, but caring little for the political game. He is a member of the Loyal Order of Moose, of Norwich, and of the Foresters of America.

On August 24, 1916, Mr. Herbert married Eva L. Dawley, daughter of George B. and Anna (Briggs) Dawley, of Plainfield, Connecticut, and they have one son, John Jeffrey, Jr. Mr. and Mrs. Herbert are members of the Methodist Episcopal church.

WILLIAM HENRY BUCKLEY—In the busy manufacturing community of Baltic, Connecticut, William Henry Buckley holds an important executive position, being superintendent of the extensive cotton textile plant of the Baltic Mills Company.

Mr. Buckley is a son of William H. and Mary E. (Newton) Buckley, both of whom were born in England. William H. Buckley was born in Manchester, England, and was educated there. During the greater part of his life he was an exporter of textile machinery, having entered that line of business in 1876. He died in England, in 1914, at the age of seventy-eight years.

His first wife, Mary E. (Newton) Buckley, died in England, in 1875, at the age of twenty-seven years. He married (second) Eliza Ogilvie, also born in England. The children of the first marriage numbered three, and are as follows: James N., now a resident of Manchester, England, and prominent in the insurance business in that city, who married Nellie Tippets, of Manchester; William Henry, of whom further; and Frederick Charles, who married Sarah Fielding, of Manchester, England, both being now deceased.

William Henry Buckley was born in Manchester, England, on September 28, 1868. He received a thorough education in the National schools of that country, then served an apprenticeship in the manufacture of textile machinery, covering a period of seven years. This placed him among the experts in his line, and after working several years in the employ of Platt Brothers, of Oldham, England, he entered the installation field, becoming an erection engineer. This was in 1890, and he set up textile machinery in many different parts of the world. In 1900 Mr. Buckley placed machinery for the same plant of which he is now superintendent, the Baltic Mills Company. Then for two years thereafter he continued along the line of erection engineer. In 1902 he became superintendent of the Coosa Manufacturing Company, of Piedmont, Alabama. Two years later he was induced to accept the position of superintendent for the plant of Thomas Henry & Sons, in Philadelphia, Pennsylvania, then from 1908 until 1911 he acted as superintendent for the Cornwall & York Company, of St. John, New Brunswick. Without exception these plants were cotton mills.

In 1911 Mr. Buckley, with this broad and comprehensive experience behind him, came to Baltic, Connecticut, as superintendent for the Baltic Mills Company. He has been most successful in this connection, and has carried the standard of production to the highest point. For ten years he has held this position, with ever increasing efficiency, and stands among the big men in the textile industry in this county.

Mr. Buckley has few interests outside his business, and is an influential member of the Southern New England Textile Association. Politically, he throws his influence on the side of the Republican party, although he has always declined political honors. He is a regular attendant upon the services of the Baptist church.

On June 8, 1894, Mr. Buckley married Margaret A. Parks, daughter of John and Mary (Wetherell) Parks, of Ireland, and they have one daughter, Mary Ellen, born in Portadown, Ireland. Miss Buckley was graduated from the Connecticut College for Women, of New London, in the class of 1919, with the degree of Bachelor of Science. She is now engaged as an instructor in drawing.

WILLIAM RYAN CROMWELL—Now a general merchant at Poquonock Bridge, town of Groton, New London county, Connecticut, Mr. Cromwell is showing his versatility of talent, for he has given the preceding years of his life to mechanical occupations. He bought the James Fletcher general store at Poquonock Bridge in 1920 and is succeeding in his new field of activity wonderfully well. William R. Cromwell is a son of Ira R. Cromwell, born in Mystic, Connecticut, who has spent his adult life as a carpenter and builder. He married Lillian B. Brown, who was born in Mystic.

William R. Cromwell was born in Mystic, Connecticut, August 23, 1881, and there was educated in the public schools and Mystic Valley Institute. Later he learned the machinist's trade, then went with his father and learned the carpenter's trade, finally becoming his foreman. He continued in that line of activity until 1920, when he bought the general store at Poquonock Bridge, which he now conducts. He is a Republican in politics; a member of Fairview Lodge, No. 101, Independent Order of Odd Fellows, of Groton; Dolgeville Lodge, No. 796, Free and Accepted Masons; and of the Mystic Baptist Church. During the World War, 1917-18, he served with the State Guard.

Mr. Cromwell married, January 2, 1901, at Old Mystic, Connecticut, Julia E. Maine, of Ledyard, Connecticut, daughter of Leeds and Sarah (Holdredge) Maine. Mr. and Mrs. Cromwell are the parents of two children: Lewis Maine, born in Mystic, Connecticut, July 28, 1905; Mae Arline, born in Mystic, July 15, 1912.

CHARLES HENRY SMITH—Success in any chosen line of work is the direct result of perseverance, energy and ability, coupled with a sincere desire to perform all duties in the best manner possible, and these qualities are manifest in large measure in the person of Charles H. Smith, a resident of Noank, Connecticut, his native town.

Oliver R. Smith, father of Charles H. Smith, was born in the town of Eastford, Connecticut, April 15, 1821, and died in Noank, in 1913. He was reared in his native town, educated in the common schools of that day, and upon attaining a suitable age to earn his own livelihood, turned his attention to the pursuits pertaining to the sea, making whaling voyages which covered periods of from two to three years, sailing from the port of Mystic, Connecticut. Although he met with a fair degree of success in this enterprise, he only continued in it up to the year 1850, when twenty-nine years of age, then changing his place of residence to Noank, Connecticut, where he engaged in an entirely different pursuit, that of shoemaking, so continuing for the remainder of his active career. During his long life of ninety-two years he witnessed many changes in the manners and customs of people, in the rapid growth and increase of population in towns and cities, and in various improvements along many lines, all of which added to the comfort and pleasure of humanity. Mr. Smith married Lucy E. Perkins, daughter of Noyes Perkins, who also attained an honorable old age, and who bore him four children: John, died at the age of two years; Charles Henry, of further mention; William Chester, a resident of Noank; and Jennie, who became the wife of John N. Porter, of Noank. Mr. and Mrs. Smith were members of the Baptist church of Noank, in the work of which they took an active interest.

Charles Henry Smith was born in the Moses Ashbey house, near the Cove, Noank, Connecticut, September

10, 1851. He obtained a practical education by attendance at the public schools of Noank, and his first occupation was as clerk in the store conducted by Mr. Fitch, where he remained one year, then entered the employ of W. W. Latham, in whose service he remained for two years. In 1869, deciding to learn the trade of boat building, he served a three years' apprenticeship with Jeremiah Davis, an expert in his line, then began business on his own account in the mold loft at the Palmer yard, where he built all kinds of fishing boats and yachts. In 1875 he erected a shop on land which later became the property of Mr. Palmer, where he successfully plied his trade until the fall of 1898, when he erected a shop and put in a marine railway on the Potter property at Noank; this pulls out fifty-foot boats. His location is excellent for wintering boats, and in addition to building boats he does a general repair business, yachts and other seafaring craft being brought to him for thorough overhaulings. His workmanship is of the best, the materials used being thoroughly inspected, and the success he has achieved is well merited. For many years Mr. Smith has taken an active interest in public life, representing the town of Groton in 1891 and in 1895 in the Legislature, serving on the Fish and Game Committee, and again from 1919 to 1921. From 1911 to 1921 he has served as a county commissioner. He is a Republican in politics.

Mr. Smith married, November 16, 1872, Mary E. Potter, born August 5, 1845, died June 9, 1905, daughter of Joseph and Mary (Fowler) Potter, of Noank, granddaughter of Joseph and Mercy (Burrows) Potter, great-granddaughter of Thomas Potter, and great-great-granddaughter of William Potter, who emigrated to this country in 1784.

ALBERT FORT is the son of English parents, although his father, Hartly Fort, was a native of Glasgow, Scotland, where he grew up to manhood and where he was educated in the public schools. Later he went to Lancaster, England, and became overseer of the spinning department in a cotton mill there, following this calling for the remainder of his life. His wife was Mary (Thompson) Fort, who died in 1877, Mr. Fort dying in 1905. Seven children were born to them, Albert Fort being the youngest.

Born in Lancaster, England, September 4, 1877, Albert Fort acquired his education in the English schools, after which he took up the study of electrical engineering. In 1899 Mr. Fort came to the United States, but after spending a year here he returned to his home in England, remaining there until June, 1908, when he again came to this country, locating in New Bedford, Massachusetts, with his family. Becoming engaged in his profession, Mr. Fort was occupied in various places in electrical engineering and wiring. In 1917 he left Massachusetts, and coming to Stonington, Connecticut, he opened a store for the sale of electrical supplies and entered into general electrical contracting. He has been very successful and is still engaged in that business. Mr. Fort is a member of Asylum Lodge, No. 57, Free and Accepted Masons, of Stonington, and of the Ancient Order of United Workmen of the same town.

On February 8, 1902, Mr. Fort married Ann Frances Fort, of Colne, England. She is the daughter of John and Margaret (Mitchell) Fort, residents of England. Two children have been born of this marriage: Constance M., and Margaret F., both born in England. Mr. and Mrs. Fort are members of the Protestant Episcopal church of Stonington.

JEAN BAPTISTE LE CLAIRE—Among the residents of French-Canadian birth in Jewett City, Connecticut, none is more deserving of mention in a work of this character than the late Jean B. Le Claire, who gave to the country of his adoption a loyalty not to be surpassed by any native-born son, a man of enterprise and public spirit, esteemed by all with whom he was brought in contact, whether in business, fraternal or social life.

Joseph Le Claire, father of Jean B. Le Claire, was born at La Présentation, Province of Quebec, Canada, a descendant of one of the first French settlers of that section. He was reared and educated in the town of his birth, spent his entire life there with the exception of four years spent with his son at Jewett City, gave his attention to agricultural pursuits, becoming the possessor of large holdings of land, and his death occurred there in the year 1896. His wife, Zoe (De Grange) Le Claire, also a native of the Province of Quebec, bore him six children, as follows: Jean Baptiste, of whom further; Napoleon, Adelia, Francis, Hermides, and Jesse, who died in early life.

Jean B. Le Claire was born at La Présentation, Province of Quebec, Canada, February 22, 1856. His boyhood and early youth were spent in attendance at the government schools of his native place and in assisting his father with the labor of the home farm. At the age of sixteen, feeling that the time had come to depend upon his own resources for a livelihood, and realizing that the United States offered more opportunities for advancement than his native land, he accordingly came here, locating at Putnam, Connecticut, where he secured work in a woolen mill. His next position was as driver of a bakery wagon, in which capacity he served until 1886, during which time he accumulated a small amount of capital, the result of prudence and thrift. He then took up his residence at Jewett City, where he engaged in the baking business and he succeeded so well that at the end of two years he was in a position to erect a house for his own use and a bakery, and twelve years later, in 1900, he built the Le Claire block, where he conducted a branch store, and in 1910 he established a meat market in connection with his baking business, deriving a substantial income from both lines of trade, and these enterprises are conducted at the present time (1920) by members of his family. In addition to the property above mentioned, Mr. Le Claire had other parcels of land in different sections of Jewett City, which have increased in value during the passing years. He was interested in all that concerned the welfare of his adopted city, and was chosen by his fellow-citizens to serve in the office of tax collector, the duties of which he performed in an efficient manner for six years, having been elected on the Democratic ticket. He was a member and trustee of St. Mary's Catholic Church at Jewett City, and held membership in the Knights of Columbus, of Taftville, Connecticut, the St. Louis Society, and the St. John Baptiste Society at Putnam.

Mr. Le Claire married, April 20, 1883, Vittline Quiry, daughter of Michael and Adelide Quiry, of Putnam, the ceremony being performed by Father Vygen. Children: Arthur; Albina, who became the wife of Louis Guillotte of Jewett City; Alpheric, Eugene, Eudor, Wilfred, Hector, and Jean Baptiste, Jr. Three children died young.

LOUIS JOSEPH FONTAINE is a familiar figure in the business world of Norwich. He is a descendant of one of the old French families who sought refuge from the horrors of the Revolution by emigrating to Canada.

Henry Fontaine, father of Louis Joseph Fontaine, was born in St. Pie, Province of Quebec. He received his education at the old Convent School in that city. When he was eighteen years of age the United States was in the throes of the Civil War, and the young man left his home and came to this country for the express purpose of taking part in that conflict. He served as a private in Company D, 8th Regiment, New Jersey Volunteer Infantry, with honor and distinction. At the close of the war he came to Connecticut and located at Willimantic, where he was employed in the cotton mills for some years, then removed to Taftville, Connecticut, where he has resided for the past forty-two years. He is now retired from active business, but still hale and hearty. He married Celia Cloutier, also a native of St. Pie, and they were the parents of nine children. They celebrated their golden wedding May 3, 1921.

Louis Joseph Fontaine was born in the town of Baltic, Connecticut, on March 4, 1872, and is the eldest of the family. He received his education in the public schools of the village of Taftville, then at St. Arthabaska College, at Victoriaville, Province of Quebec, where he made a special study of the French language. Then coming to Norwich, he worked for several years as a clerk in the men's furnishing store of Murphy & McGarry, finally rising to buyer. In 1904 Mr. Fontaine bought a drug store in Baltic, and for ten years conducted it under the name of the Fontaine Pharmacy. In 1914 he sold this store, and returning to Norwich, started in business along the line of real estate and insurance. He was successful from the first, and has come to be considered one of the leading men in the city in the line of insurance, having developed this somewhat more extensively than the other branch of the business.

Mr. Fontaine resides in the village of Baltic, and is health officer for the town of Sprague. He is a staunch supporter of the Republican party, and chairman of the Republican Town Committee. He is a charter member of the Benevolent and Protective Order of Elks, Lodge No. 430, of Norwich; a member of the Chamber of Commerce of Norwich; and was postmaster of Baltic, Connecticut, in 1908-12.

Mr. Fontaine married, on June 18, 1901, Rose A. Reeves, of Baltic; they have an adopted daughter, Rhea Despathy. The family are members of the Roman Catholic church.

FREDERICK GEORGE THUMM—Gustave and Rosine (Grauer) Thumm, who were married in their native Wurttemburg, Germany, there resided until 1885, the father a skilled cabinet maker. The family consisted of seven children, all born in Germany. In 1885 Gustave and Rosine Thumm came with their children to the United States, locating in Taftville, New London county, Connecticut, where Gustave Thumm followed his trade until the failure of his health. He then entered the employ of a wholesale tobacco house as traveling cigar salesman, continuing until his death in Taftville, May 6, 1892.

Mrs. Thumm, after being left a widow, removed to Norwich, Connecticut, where in 1900 she bought out a delicatessen store on Franklin street, which her son Gustave had established in 1896. Her son Frederick G. became her assistant, and after conducting the store very successfully for twelve years, Mrs. Thumm sold the business to him and retired. She died in Norwich, February 20, 1916, a woman honored, respected and loved by all who knew her.

Frederick George Thumm, youngest child of Gustave and Rosine (Grauer) Thumm, was born in Wurttemburg, Germany, April 17, 1881, and in 1885 was brought to Taftville, Connecticut, by his parents. He attended Taftville public schools until fourteen years of age, then became a worker in the Ponemah Cotton Mills, there remaining five years, until 1900. His father died in 1892, and in 1896 the eldest son of Gustave Thumm established a delicatessen store in Norwich, which passed under Mrs. Thumm's management and ownership in 1900.

In the latter year Frederick G. Thumm left Taftville and became his mother's store assistant, and in 1912 purchased the business, Mrs. Thumm then retiring. The Thumm delicatessen store has always been a successful business enterprise, and is now the largest of its kind in New London county. The goods sold are of the grade of delicatessen store goods, and most of them are made by Mr. Thumm or under his direction. He thoroughly understands the business, having had the very best of training under an unusually capable housewife, his mother, who was moreover an excellent business woman. Mr. Thumm is a member of the German Lutheran church, and in political faith an Independent. He is affiliated with Somerset Lodge, No. 34, Free and Accepted Masons; Franklin Chapter, No. 4, Royal Arch Masons; Franklin Council, No. 3, Royal and Select Masters; Columbian Commandery, No. 4, Knights Templar; Sphinx Temple, Ancient Arabic Order Nobles of the Mystic Shrine; Gardner Lodge, No. 46, Knights of Pythias, and Norwich Lodge, No. 430, Benevolent and Protective Order of Elks. He is a member of Norwich Chamber of Commerce, and bears his part in making Norwich an attractive place in which to reside.

On June 15, 1905, Frederick G. Thumm married, in Norwich, Bertha Budzeck, born in Prussia, daughter of John and Mary Budzeck. Mr. and Mrs. Thumm are the parents of four children: Emilie Marie, Rudolf Frederick, Gertrude Bertha, Martha Caroline, all residing at the family home, No. 128 Broadway, Norwich. Mr. Thumm's place of business remains at the old stand it has occupied for a quarter of a century (1896-1921), No. 40 Franklin street.

LEONARD EUGENE BILL—Prominent in many activities in Clarks Falls, Connecticut, but best known as a specialist in fine poultry, Leonard Eugene Bill is one of the largest and most successful producers along this line in Eastern Connecticut.

Elisha Bill, grandfather of Leonard E. Bill, was a leading man and extensive farmer in Griswold, Connecticut, in the very early years of the nineteenth century. He married Olivet Geer, also of a prominent family of that day in New London county.

James Leonard Bill, their son, and father of Leonard E. Bill, was born in Griswold, Connecticut, August 16, 1821. He was educated in the district schools near Pachaug village, then upon completing his studies went to Griswold and learned the trade of blacksmith. Later on he went to the ship yards in Mystic, Connecticut, and Westerly, Rhode Island, where for some years he was iron worker. Later still he returned to wagon work and a general line of blacksmithing, and removed to Canterbury, Connecticut, where he followed his trade. At length his health failed, and thus he was obliged to forego heavy work of this nature. He took up farming, and conducted farming operations in various Connecticut towns, spending the last thirty years of his life with his son, Leonard E., in North Stonington. There he died July 18, 1913. He married (first) Lucy A. Maine, daughter of Russell Maine, March 12, 1843. She died January 29, 1845. He married (second) Juliette Chapman, daughter of Prentice Chapman, a member of one of the oldest Pendleton Hill families, August 22, 1848. She died December 23, 1857. He married (third) Addie H. Howland, June 23, 1861. They lived together for more than fifty years, and she now survives him, residing at the home of her step-son at Clark's Falls.

Leonard Eugene Bill is a son of James Leonard and Juliette (Chapman) Bill, and was born in Canterbury, Windham county, Connecticut, August 7, 1852. His first school attendance was on Pendleton Hill, in North Stonington, as his mother had died in his childhood, and he was cared for by his grandparents. Later he went with his father to Chesterfield, Connecticut, and remained there for two years, then still later going to Old Lyme, Connecticut, and Hopkinton, Rhode Island, attending the various schools in these towns, completing his education in the Ashaway, Rhode Island, High School. He then entered the employ of E. P. Chapman, as clerk of the general store at Clarks Falls, and remained with Mr. Chapman for a period of nine years. Developing a good measure of practical business ability, he took up the life insurance business, and for the following fifteen years was successfully engaged along this line in New Jersey, Pennsylvania, and Massachusetts.

During this time Mr. Bill purchased the farm in the town of North Stonington, at Clarks Falls, where he is now located. In 1902, when he was fifty years of age, he retired from all business interests, and coming to this farm permanently established the poultry business which is now one of the largest in this part of the State. He has been most successful, and while constantly working for utility has also some of the finest of show stock. His flock of laying hens regularly numbers over one thousand birds. Mr. Bill finds little time for outside interests, but is always alert to the questions of the day. Politically he holds an independent attitude, making his own decisions and supporting the best man in the field.

On October 25, 1873, Mr. Bill married Ruth Caroline Babcock, in North Stonington, daughter of Hoxie Perry and Elizabeth Perry (White) Babcock. Mrs. Bill's parents were born in North Stonington, and her father was a farmer and carpenter by trade. Mr. and Mrs. Bill are the parents of seven children, three of whom are now living: 1. Herbert Perry, born in North Stonington, January 27, 1875; married Dora Annabelle Brown, of North Stonington, and has two children, Thelma Glendora and Hoxie Babcock, the family now living in Ashaway, Rhode Island. 2. Allison Maillard, born in North Stonington, August 30, 1878; now a resident of Hampton, Virginia, and interested in the hotel and bakery business; married Alfreta Allison, of Yonkers, New York. 3. James Bard, born in North Stonington, April 12, 1888; married Harriet Elizabeth Congdon, also of this town, and is now conducting a farm here; their three children are: Perry Eugene, James Allison, and Edwin Chapman. One other daughter, Grace Deista, who married John Main, of Ledyard, Connecticut, was born in North Stonington, November 3, 1876, and died December 2, 1902, leaving two children: Ruth Elizabeth and Troy Irving.

LEWIS B. BRAND, of the village of Versailles, Connecticut, one of the most delightful suburbs of Norwich, Connecticut, is a New London county man born and bred, and is a son of Lewis and Bridget (Shea) Brand, long residents of Bozrahville.

Mr. Brand's father was born in Bozrah, and educated in the district schools of that town. As a young man he entered the cotton mill which was located there, and worked up to the position of overseer of spinning. He continued along this line until past forty-five years of age, and is still a resident of the town of Bozrah. His wife, who was a native of Ireland, died in Bozrahville, in 1919. They were the parents of six children, of whom four are living.

Lewis B. Brand was born in Bozrahville, Connecticut, on October 22, 1869. He received a practical education in the district schools of the village, then, as a young man, worked in the cotton mill for a short time. This work, however, did not appeal to him for a permanent occupation, and when nineteen years of age he became clerk in the general store at Fitchville, in the town of Bozrah. This store he later bought, and conducted from 1912 to 1918, also being postmaster during the greater part of that time. For the next two years he had charge of a general store at Norwich town. In 1920

Charles Hope.

he bought the general store at Versailles, and is making a success of the venture. Well-known throughout this region, and naturally gifted with business ability, he is recognized as one of the leading men in this branch of mercantilè activity.

Mr. Brand is interested in every line of public endeavor, and politically throws his influence on the side of the Republican party. He is a member of White Cross Council, Knights of Columbus, and of Court City of Norwich, Foresters of America.

Mr. Brand married (first) Annie E. Irwin, of Colchester, Connecticut, who died in 1907. They had three children, of whom two are living: Mary Gertrude, who, in 1921, attended Yale Summer School; and Annie Elizabeth, a student at Willimantic Normal School. He married (second), in 1912, Rose McManus. The family have always been members of the Roman Catholic church.

THOMAS ALPHONSE RIOUX—The success which comes through industry and thrift is that success which makes for the public prosperity as well as for individual gain. It is in such manner that Thomas Alphonse Rioux, the Jewett City, Connecticut, tailor, has placed himself among the most successful men in this progressive and prosperous New London county town.

Mr. Rioux is a native of Canada, and came to this country in 1883. He is a son of Francis and Elionas (Dumont) Rioux, both natives of the town of Trois Pistoles, in the Province of Quebec, Canada. Francis Rioux was an industrious farmer, and spent his entire life in agricultural pursuits in the town of his birth, and died there, in 1893. His wife also was born and died there, she surviving him for two years. They were the parents of nine children, of whom Thomas Alphonse was the seventh.

Thomas Alphonse Rioux was born in Trois Pistoles, Province of Quebec, Canada, on August 9, 1863. He received a thorough education in the parochial schools of the town, then served an apprenticeship as tailor. When he was twenty years of age he came to the United States, locating in Boston. There he worked as a tailor, and from time to time worked in different places, going wherever good opportunities offered, and gaining a wealth of excellent experience. At length, in 1897, fourteen years after his first coming to Boston, Mr. Rioux settled permanently in Jewett City. He opened a men's tailoring shop, thereby establishing the only place of the kind in the town. The lack of competition, however, detracted not one whit from the progressive methods by which Mr. Rioux has conducted this business. He keeps in touch with the latest modes, and the work he turns out is of metropolitan style and workmanship. His shop would do credit to any large city, and the success which has attended his efforts is shown by the fact that he is located in the Rioux block, a structure which is an ornament to the town.

Mr. Rioux is prominent in the social and public life of the town. Politically, he is affiliated with the Republican party, and he is a member of the St. James Club, of Jewett City.

Mr. Rioux married Ellen Gagnon, of Jewett City, daughter of Francis and Mary (Peletier) Gagnon, natives of the Province of Quebec. Both families have always been members of St. Mary's Roman Catholic Church.

CHARLES HOPE—After a varied business experience in different lines of activity, Mr. Hope finally settled in the position which he has now filled for twelve years, 1909-1921, agent for the Central Vermont Railroad in Montville, Connecticut. He is of English parentage, his father, John Charles Hope, a native of Truro in Cornwall, England, and son of Joseph and Elizabeth (Anear) Hope. John Charles Hope came to the United States, settled in Montville, Connecticut, and there for half a century was employed in the woolen mills. He married Elizabeth Arundel Anear, who died in Montville, aged sixty-six; he in 1911, aged seventy-six. One of their sons, Frederick Joseph Hope, a merchant of Montville, married Helen May Skinner. Another son, Charles, is the principal character of this review.

Charles Hope was born in Montville, New London county, Connecticut, October 14, 1867. He there attended the public schools. He completed his studies at New London Business College, and while attending that institution began his business career as a bookkeeper in the C. M. Robertson Paper Mills in Montville. After leaving business college, he entered the office employ of the Central Vermont Railroad in New London, there remaining until entering the employ of C. D. Boss & Son, cracker manufacturers of New London, remaining with that company five years as foreman of the packing department of the factory, a department there employing two hundred and twenty-five girls. For nine years after leaving the Boss Company, Mr. Hope was in the employ of the Metropolitan Life Insurance Company, New London, resigning in 1909 to become station agent in Montville for the Central Vermont Railroad, carrying with it the agency for the American Railway Express Company and other railroad allied businesses. In politics Mr. Hope is a Republican, and in religious preferences a Methodist. He is the third oldest member (in point of years of membership) of Oxoboxo Lodge, No. 116, Free and Accepted Masons, of Montville, a past master of that lodge, and for a quarter of a century past down to the present has been its secretary. He is also a companion of Franklin Chapter, Royal Arch Masons, of Norwich, Connecticut; a Cryptic Mason of Norwich Council, Royal and Select Masters; a Sir Knight of Columbian Commandery, Knights Templar, of Norwich; and a thirty-second degree Mason of the Ancient Accepted Scottish Rite. He is also a Noble of Sphinx Temple, Ancient Arabic Order Nobles of the Mystic Shrine, of Hartford.

Mr. Hope married, in Norwich, Connecticut, September 28, 1896, Charlotte Isabelle Bolles, born in Uncasville, Connecticut, daughter of Jared and Clarissa (Comstock) Bolles, her father, Jared Bolles, for many years a United States mail carrier. Both parents are now deceased. Mr. Hope is one of the progressive, public-spirited men of the village, a good business man, standing high in the regard of his company, and a good citizen, holding the confidence and esteem of his townsmen who have known him from his earliest days.

HENRY ALBERT ADAMS—One of the energetic men of New London county, serving the needs of the motoring public in the line of automobile accessories, is Henry Albert Adams, of Baltic, in the town of Sprague, Connecticut.

Mr. Adams is of English parentage, the son of John and Elizabeth (Lawton) Adams. His father, who is now seventy-three years of age, was born in Devonshire, England. There were two sons, Mr. Adams' brother being John Nelson Adams. He married Dorothy Harrold, and resides in Hanover, Connecticut.

Henry Albert Adams was born in Hanover, Connecticut, April 6, 1882. In the public schools of that town he received a thorough and practical training for the realities of life, and after some years' activity in various industrial fields, came to Norwich, where he opened the present business. He established this business in 1916, and since that time has developed it and broadened its scope, until now, he not only carries on a profitable and prosperous business, but handles everything required by the motorist in the way of accessories. His location outside the city, and on a thoroughfare which is the scene of constant traffic, places him in an ideal position for the convenience of his patrons; and his business ability, and the "quality first" rule of the store are carrying him rapidly forward on the road of success.

Mr. Adams finds little leisure, and his interests outside his business are few. Fraternally he is a member of the Masonic order Ancient Free and Accepted Masons, Mount Vernon Lodge, No. 75, Jewett City, Connecticut; Franklin Chapter, No. 4, Norwich, Connecticut, and in political affiliation he is connected with the Republican party.

He married Edith J. Smith, and they have one daughter, Elizabeth, born June 11, 1918. Mrs. Adams is a daughter of Lester and Imogene (Allen) Smith, of Canterbury, Connecticut.

GEORGE LINTON—For nearly a quarter of a century on the police force of the city of Norwich, Connecticut, George Linton is now chief of the very efficient organization which makes Norwich one of the most desirable residential cities of the State.

Chief Linton was born in the town of Griswold, in New London county, Connecticut, on January 3, 1861. His father, Benjamin Linton, was born in Londonderry, Ireland, and was educated in the National schools of that country. Coming to America when he was a young man, he located in New London county, Connecticut. He worked as a railroad man all his life, and died in Norwich in 1870. He married Martha McClure, who was also a native of Ireland, and she died in Norwich, in 1916. They were the parents of eight children, of whom four are now living.

George Linton, son of Benjamin and Martha (McClure) Linton, was reared in the city of Norwich, and received his education here in the public schools. He grew up with the pride of citizenship in his heart. As a young man he began life as an operative in the cotton mills, but he was not satisfied to live out his life in the factory. On July 1, 1886, he was appointed to a position on the police force of the city. Fully alive to his responsibility to the public as a patrolman, he took pride in keeping his beat the most orderly and quiet in the city. He discharged every duty faithfully, was always punctual, and in every way made himself necessary to the safety and well-being of the public. It was inevitable that he should rise. He was promoted to sergeant, then captain, filling with honor every office in the line, then was made chief in 1912. His long and honorable record is a source of pride to his friends.

Chief Linton is the local vice-president of the State Police Association. He filled the office of health commissioner for one term. He is a member of Uncas Lodge, Independent Order of Odd Fellows; and of Norwich Lodge, No. 430, Benevolent and Protective Order of Elks.

Mr. Linton married, on March 27, 1882, Margaret Phelan, daughter of Thomas and Julia Phelan, of Pownal, Vermont. They are members of the Congregational church.

WILLIAM EDWARD HISCOX, a native son, has spent his years, sixty-six, in New London county, Connecticut, engaged from youth in agriculture. He has since 1908 been the owner of a good farm in the town of Griswold and there he conducts general farming operations. William Edward Hiscox is a son of John Henry Hiscox, who was born in New York City, and there educated in the public schools. Later he moved to Connecticut and was living in North Stonington when his son, William Edward, was born. His business was that of a wholesale fish dealer. John H. Hiscox married Emily Maine, who married a second husband, Henry Palmer, of North Stonington. Their only child, Bertha E., married Manthel Culver, and resides in Stonington.

William Edward Hiscox, son of John Henry and Emily (Maine) Hiscox, was born in North Stonington, New London county, Connecticut, March 17, 1854, and was educated in Stonington public schools. After finishing school years he became a farm worker, employed by others until 1890, when he leased the Billings' farm in North Stonington, and there remained until 1908. He then purchased his present farm of one hundred and seventy-five acres in the town of Griswold, long known as the Smith farm. There he has very successfully conducted a general farming business, and is one of the substantial men of the town. In politics Mr. Hiscox is a Democrat; in religious faith a Methodist.

Mr. Hiscox married Hannah Worden, of Utica, New York.

JOSEPH RIVERS—Since 1912, Joseph Rivers has been connected with Palmer Brothers as engineer at their Fitchville Mills, he having been previously associated with the Keyes Company at their Montville plant. He is a son of Joseph and Marie (La Croix) Rivers, both born in Canada, his father deceased, his mother now residing with him in Fitchville. Joseph Rivers, Sr., was a lumberman and saw mill operator in Canada, but shortly after his marriage came to the United States, locating in Oneco, Windham county, Connecticut, and there continuing in the lumber business; in fact, that was his lifelong business wherever located. From Oneco he went to New Jersey, thence to New London county, Connecticut, here remaining many years, but finally going South. Joseph and Marie (La Croix) Rivers were the parents of eight children, two of whom are deceased. The living are: Joseph, of further mention; William, married Myrtle Duprey, of Colchester, Connecticut; Freemont, married Sarepa Potter, of Groton, Connecticut; Rose, married Allan Maine, of Ledyard, Connecticut; Flora, married John Delosha; Oelina, married John McCain, of Taftville, Connecticut.

Joseph Rivers, third child of Joseph and Marie (La Croix) Rivers, was born in Oneco, Windham county, Connecticut, September 20, 1888. He was quite young when his parents moved to New London county, the family residing on the Thomas farm in Groton. He obtained his education in the public schools of Ledyard and New London. After school years were over, he located in Montville, where he secured employment in the engine room of the Keyes Mills. He there remained for three years, when he was appointed engineer at the Palmer Mill in Fitchville, and has most satisfactorily acted in that capacity during the nine years, 1912-21, which have since intervened.

Mr. Rivers enlisted in the United States army, September 20, 1917, trained at Fort Devens, and for sixteen months was in the service attached to the depot brigade at Camp Devens. He is a member of Robert O. Fletcher Post, of the American Legion, the Fraternal Order of Eagles, Modern Woodmen of America, and of the American Association of Stationary Engineers.

JEROME WILLIAMS HOUSE—Among the old Colonial families of Connecticut not one can claim a straighter line of descent from the founders of New England than the House family of Montville. One of their ancestors came to this country in the "Mayflower" in 1620, and more than a hundred years afterward one of his descendants fought in the Revolutionary War. He was the great-grandfather of Jerome Williams House.

Jerome Williams House is the son of Chauncey and Emma (Stranahan) House. Chauncey House was born in Haddam Neck, Connecticut, where he resided for many years, following the business of a stone cutter, his death occurring in Bristol, Connecticut, in 1888. He is buried in Haddam Neck. Emma (Stranahan) House was born in Bashon, town of Moodus, Connecticut. She was the mother of two sons, Jerome Williams and Albert Silliman. Albert S. was adopted by his aunt. The death of Mrs. House occurred when the former was only three years old. Born in Haddam Neck, Connecticut, February 9, 1867, Jerome Williams House received his name from a friend of the family, an old sea captain, the child being named in his honor. Attending the local school until he reached the age of nine years, the boy then made a trip to California, in those days a much more lengthy journey than it is at the present day. He resided in the city of Los Angeles for eight months, then went to Chicago, Illinois, where he lived for three years, attending school in that city. Coming back to his native State, Jerome Williams House finished his education in Naugatuck, Connecticut, later taking up farming as his occupation in Massapeag, town of Montville, Connecticut. For four years Mr. House remained there. He then returned to Chicago and became interested in the broom corn business, in which he was engaged for three years. Coming to Connecticut again Mr. House entered into the blacksmith business in 1895 in Massapeag, making his home in Uncasville, township of Montville, where he still resides.

Mr. House is one of the foremost citizens in the locality, assisting in all public matters connected with its welfare, and has served on the Board of Selectmen, both third selectman for two terms and as first selectman, which latter office he now holds, 1920-21. In politics he is a Democrat, and was the only one of that party to be elected in the town in 1920. Equally active in fraternal affairs, Mr. House is a charter member of the local lodge of Independent Order of Odd Fellows, Thames Lodge, No. 22, and is a third degree Mason, affiliated with Oxoboxo Blue Lodge, Free and Accepted Masons, of Montville, Connecticut. He is district deputy of that section, and has occupied both chairs in his lodge. He is a past noble grand of the Independent Order of Odd Fellows, also past district deputy and a past master of the Masons.

Jerome Williams House was united in marriage with Lottie Beebe Church, the daughter of Charles and Isabelle (Beebe) Church, of Massapeag. She is a member of an old and highly respected family, the Beebes, who have been prominent in Connecticut for many years. Mr. and Mrs. House had one child, Chauncey Edwin, who died in infancy. They attend and support the Methodist church.

ARTHUR AUSTIN GREENLEAF—The Greenleaf family traces descent through nearly three hundred years of New England life to Edmund Greenleaf, who came to Massachusetts in 1635, and was one of the original settlers of Newbury. Arthur A. Greenleaf, of Groton and New London, Connecticut, is a son of Atherton C. Greenleaf, of Southport, Maine, a descendant of Edmund Greenleaf, the American ancestor of this branch, which prior to the Revolution settled in the State of Maine.

Atherton C. Greenleaf was born in Edgecomb,

Maine, and from boyhood has been connected with the sea food industry, being now a wholesale and retail dealer in fish and lobsters at Southport, Maine. He married Susan P. Chase, and they are the parents of Arthur A. Greenleaf, of Groton, Connecticut.

Arthur A. Greenleaf was born in Edgecomb, Lincoln county, Maine, June 5, 1883, the fifth child of Atherton C. and Susan P. (Chase) Greenleaf. His parents moved to Southport, on a small island of the Maine coast, in Lincoln county, about twelve miles southeast of Bath, and there he attended the public school, finishing his education in business college at Portland, Maine. For twelve years, 1897-1909, he followed the sea and rose to the rank of captain. Upon his retirement from the sea in 1909, he located in New London, Connecticut, where in association with A. L. Young, of Boston, he assumed control of the G. M. Long Company, and still retains the interests in that company, the Young interest having been purchased by N. H. Avery, in 1918. The company deals in fish and sea foods. Mr. Greenleaf is a member of the New London Chamber of Commerce, a Republican in politics, and a member of the Baptist church.

Mr. Greenleaf married, in Southport, Maine, Sadie Alley, daughter of William and Sarah (Nickerson) Alley, of Southport, Maine. Captain and Mrs. Greenleaf are the parents of six children: A. Clayton, Howard P., Susan C., Carl, William A., and Lucy M., all residing at the family home in Groton.

THOMAS J. BURKE—Born in the city of Norwich, and identified always with the business life of New London county, Thomas J. Burke, of Baltic, Connecticut, may well be numbered among the representative men of the section. As a dealer in automobile accessories, he has come to be widely known, both to the people of this vicinity, and to the thousands of tourists who find this highway through Baltic a convenient and delightful motor thoroughfare.

Mr. Burke is a son of John Burke, who was born in Limerick, Ireland, and of Mary Donovan Burke. Mr. Burke was a man of great industry, and followed the occupation of gardening. He and his wife are now deceased.

Thomas J. Burke was born in Norwich, Connecticut, January 30, 1876. He received his education in this city, and in the schools of Baltic, where his family removed when he was ten years of age. He early started out in the world of industry, but, never satisfied to work for others permanently, bent every energy toward the ambition which he realized on March 14, 1911, when he started in business for himself. His early plans had not been decisive in regard to what line he should follow, but they comprehended independence, and this was what he achieved, in his final choice of business. He handles all kinds of automobile accessories, and meets the needs of the stream of motorists which daily sweeps through the little village of Baltic.

Mr. Burke is a man of considerable prominence here, and politically is affiliated with the Democratic party, although thus far he has declined political honors. He is a member of St. Mary's Roman Catholic Church, of Baltic, Connecticut.

GEORGE ALBERT HYDE—A member of one of the old families of Stonington, Connecticut, George Albert Hyde is the son of Theodore Wales and Julia Addie (Lamb) Hyde, of Stonington, and the grandson of Albigence and Nancy (Pulsiver) Hyde. Theodore Wales Hyde was born in Stonington and educated in the public schools there. When a young man he went to New Britain, Connecticut, where he was employed by Landers, Frary & Clark, manufacturers of cutlery, remaining with them for seventeen years as bookkeeper. Resigning from this office, he became a clerk for D. C. Judd, of New Britain, and after a time, in 1896, gave this up and moved his family to Stonington, where he was employed in various occupations. Theodore W. Hyde is now living a retired life in Stonington. He and his wife had but one child, George Albert Hyde, of whom further.

Born in New Britain, January 12, 1882, George Albert Hyde obtained his education in the public school there and afterward became a pupil in the Lincoln Street High School of that town. After graduating from same, he accepted a position with the American Velvet Company of Stonington, having charge of their stock room. In 1904, Mr. Hyde started in business for himself, opening a general merchandise store at Trolley Station, Stonington, where he is still located. In politics, George Albert Hyde is a Republican, though not holding any public office. He is a member of the Second Congregational Church, of Stonington.

THOMAS MELVIN—In Mystic, New London county, Connecticut, Thomas Melvin is engaged in one of the most practical lines of endeavor. As a general blacksmith and wagon builder, he is bearing a very necessary part in the daily activities of the town, and his personal history is of interest to all.

Mr. Melvin is a son of William and Mary (MacKenzie) Melvin. William Melvin was born in England, and educated in the National schools of the country. As a young man he came to the United States, locating in Colchester, Connecticut. Later he went to Nova Scotia, where he conducted a farm during the remainder of his life, and there he died. His wife, who was born in Nova Scotia, died in Mystic, Connecticut, in 1898. Thomas Melvin was their only child.

Thomas Melvin was born in Colchester, Connecticut, on February 24, 1859. Removing with his family to Nova Scotia when he was a little child, it was there that he received his education. However, when he became twenty-three years of age, he returned to the United States, locating in New London, Connecticut. There he worked as wagon builder, and in 1886, four years later, having an opportunity to purchase a prosperous business in this line, he did so. This was the business of Stephen Lamphere, in Mystic, and Mr. Melvin is still carrying on this business in the same location. He has greatly increased its scope, and its growth and development is still a feature of this branch of endeavor in Mystic.

Although always a busy man, Mr. Melvin takes a deep interest in all public matters. Politically, he is affiliated with the Republican party, although he has never been a candidate for public office. He is a member of Stonington Lodge, No. 26, Independent Order of Odd Fellows, of Mystic. He attends the Baptist church, and gives of his means to support the benevolences of the church.

In July, 1888, Mr. Melvin married Blanche C. Newman, of Hartford, Connecticut, and they are the parents of four children: William R., who served in the World War with the American Expeditionary Forces, and is still in the United States army; Erving T., who married Clara Barman, and resides in Stonington, Connecticut; Clarence S., who served in the United States navy during the war, and is now in the Naval Reserves; Stella F., who became the wife of Clifford T. Cornell, and is a resident of Stonington.

SAMUEL STANTON BROWN MacKENZIE—As the name would indicate, the MacKenzie family is of Scotch ancestry, though the father of Samuel Stanton Brown MacKenzie, William MacKenzie, was born in Nova Scotia, Canada, where he was educated in the public schools of his native town. In the early sixties of the last century, William MacKenzie came to the United States, and locating in Mystic, Connecticut, became associated with a man named Haynes in the ship building industry, the firm being known as MacKenzie & Haynes. They built sailing vessels and for many years carried on a very successful business, but as the use of steamships increased, the demand for sailing vessels decreased, so eventually Mr. MacKenzie retired from this line of occupation and entered the employ of the New York, New Haven & Hartford Railroad Company as foreman in the bridge department. He continued with this company until his death, which occurred in Mystic in 1905. William MacKenzie married Isabella Augusta Strang, and of this union ten children were born, of whom eight are now living.

Samuel Stanton Brown MacKenzie was the seventh son of his parents, and was born in Mystic, Connecticut, July 9, 1879. He attended the public school in the village and later the Broadway High School of Mystic. After graduating from this, the young man was employed for several years as an assistant in the market gardening establishment of Ira C. Noyes, of Mystic. Later Mr. MacKenzie became an apprentice in the marble and granite stone cutting business of John Trevena, remaining with him until 1904. For the next seven years he worked at his trade in several different places, and in 1911 formed a partnership with L. F. Barstow, and bought out the business of John Trevena. For six years they conducted a monument works in Mystic, and on July 1, 1917, Mr. MacKenzie bought up his partner's interest in the concern and is now running it in his own name. Active in all affairs of his native place, Mr. MacKenzie is interested in the work of the Republican party, also in the fire department there, being a member of the hook and ladder company; he is connected with the local lodge of Woodmen of the World, and with Stonington Lodge, No. 28, Independent Order of Odd Fellows, of Mystic.

In Mystic, April 19, 1919, Samuel Stanton Brown MacKenzie married Elizabeth Adamson, daughter of Robert and Sarah (Anderson) Adamson, residents of Mystic. Mr. MacKenzie is a member of the Methodist Episcopal church in Mystic, and Mrs. MacKenzie is a member of the Congregational church.

JOHN HURLBURT BUELL, JR., was born in Middletown, Connecticut, January 18, 1886, son of Captain John H. and Lucy M. (Edwards) Buell, his father a master mariner, who, after following the sea all his active years, retired to his birthplace, Clinton, Connecticut, and is now residing there (1921). Captain John H. and Lucy M. (Edwards) Buell were the parents of three sons: 1. John H., Jr., of further mention. 2. Captain Oliver H. Buell, a trans-Atlantic steamship captain, Boston to Hamburg. He enlisted in the United States navy as seaman, and was retired as senior lieutenant in 1919, and is the youngest captain in the service of his present company. 3. George Buell, also a mariner.

John H. Buell, Jr., completed grammar and high school courses of study in Middletown, Connecticut, and finished his studies under the direction of Professor Thomas Emmett. After school years were over, he learned the machinist's trade with the Hubbard Motor Company, and was employed in different shops and places until 1907, when he located in New London. He was engaged at his trade until July 2, 1917, when he enlisted in the United States navy as a first-class machinist for the period of the World War, and served until not longer required, but is still on the reserve list. In 1919 he became manager for C. K. Smith, and in October, 1920, he purchased the business which he is now conducting. He is agent for a number of the principal automobile concerns.

Mr. Buell is a member of Brainard Lodge, No. 102, Free and Accepted Masons, of New London; Trumbull Lodge, Knights of Pythias; the Masonic Club; and the Northwest Fire Company. He attends the Baptist church. In politics he is a Republican. Mr. Buell married, December 22, 1919, Christina H. Rae, of Barrie, Vermont, daughter of James H. and Helen Rae. Mr. and Mrs. Buell are the parents of a son, Charles R. Buell, born September 29, 1920, in New London.

FRANK PALMER WILCOX GEER—Five generations of the Geer family have lived upon the old homestead farm in the town of Griswold, New London county, Connecticut; four generations were actively engaged as farmers, the children in the fifth generation being still too young to assist in its work. This fine old landmark was bought considerably more than one hundred years ago, March 4, 1804, by John Geer, who was born in the town of Preston, New London county, Connecticut. Here he made his home and reared his family, sowing and reaping year after year until his death, which occurred upon the farm, the place then going to the son, John Wheeler Geer, born upon the farm, and who died there. His wife was Mary (Cook) Geer.

Their son was Samuel Leonard Geer, also born on the homestead. He attended the district school in his youth, assisting his father in the care of the farm, and after his father's death he assumed the management of it and continued to live there until his failing health compelled him to give up farming, when he moved into Jewett City in the early part of 1917. He had only lived there a year, when he died February 6, 1918. He married Ella Jane Wilcox, a native of Griswold, where she was born on the Tyler farm, another old family homestead. Since the death of her husband she has continued to reside in Jewett City. Mr. and Mrs. Samuel Leonard Geer were the parents of three children: 1. Samuel Leonard, living in Willimantic, Connecticut, where he is a clerk in a grain establishment; he married Grace Huntington, a resident of Preston, by whom he has one child, Mildred Ella. 2. Frank Palmer Wilcox, of whom further. 3. John Wheeler, who died at the age of fourteen years, having been drowned July 7, 1900.

The second son, Frank Palmer Wilcox Geer, was born on the homestead farm in Griswold, Connecticut, December 5, 1884. He was educated in the district school of Griswold, and was brought up on the farm, assisting his father. Until he reached the age of twenty-one years, he worked for his board and clothing, but after reaching his majority the young man worked out on other farms for a year, then went into Jewett City and obtained employment in the Jewett City Bleachery, where he remained for two years more. It was about this time that his father's health became somewhat impaired and he went back to the home farm, taking charge of it, and in 1910 took over the entire management of it.

On January 15, 1914, Frank Palmer Wilcox Geer married, in Griswold, Ursula Mildred Paten, who was born in Ardsley, New York, the daughter of William Edgar and Sarah Augusta (Ford) Paten, the former a native of Ossining, New York, the latter born in Greenpoint, Long Island, New York. Mr. and Mrs. Frank Palmer Wilcox Geer have three children, all born in Griswold, the eldest on the Thomas Tyler farm, while the other two were born on the homestead farm; they are: Helen Julia, born November 16, 1914; Arthur Frank, born July 10, 1918; Ivy Mildred, born December 14, 1919.

After his marriage, Mr. Geer went to live at the home of his wife's mother, Mrs. Sarah A. (Ford) Paten, who was then living on the Thomas Tyler farm near his own home. Remaining there until 1917, he then returned to Jewett City, becoming an employee in the mill of the Ashland Cotton Company, continuing as such for a year and a half. In the meantime, his father having died, Mr. Geer bought the old place from the other heirs and returned to the home of his ancestors in 1918, where he is still living. The farm consists of one hundred and ninety-six acres, in a fine state of cultivation, and he is engaged in general farming. In politics Mr. Geer is a staunch upholder of the principles of the Republican party, though he is not active in it. He and his family are members of the Congregational church.

ARTHUR ROY, of Baltic, Connecticut, has placed himself high in the business world in one of the constructive lines of industry. As a general blacksmith, and a manufacturer of wagons, he is well and favorably known throughout this vicinity, and is making a profitable and successful career.

Mr. Roy is a son of George and Virginia (Medrou) Roy, natives of the Province of Quebec, Canada. George Roy was educated in his native country, and grew to manhood there, married, and conducted the farm until the year 1879. Then he came to the United States, locating in Baltic, Connecticut, where he found employment in the mills. He followed along this line until his death. His wife was born in White Rock, Rhode Island, and died in Baltic. They were the parents of thirteen children, of whom Arthur is the eleventh.

Arthur Roy was born in Quebec City, Province of Quebec, Canada, on May 22, 1862. He received his education in the schools of that city, then coming to the States with his parents, started out in the world of industry. He first was employed in the plant of the Baltic Mills Company, in the carding department, but continued there for only a short time. He became interested in work of a more directly constructive nature, and served an apprenticeship with Louis St. Onge, of Baltic, one of the most skillful men of that day in the wagon-making and blacksmithing line.

In 1887, Mr. Roy took the step which has led to his permanent and substantial success. He established a blacksmith business of his own in which he has been most successful, and now holds a leading place in this line of work in this part of New London county.

As a public-spirited citizen Mr. Roy is among the first men of the town. Politically a staunch supporter of the Democratic party, he has long been a servant of the people. In 1910 he was elected second selectman, and has been re-elected to that office continually since, having handled the work entrusted to his care with the sound business judgment and common sense that have given him success in his personal endeavors. Socially, Mr. Roy is a member of Union St. Jean de Baptiste of Baltic.

On November 30, 1888, Mr. Roy married Mary Flarety, of Baltic, and they have five children: Mary, now the wife of Virtume P. A. Quinn, of Versailles, Connecticut; George, who resides at home; John, who married Myrtle Morin, of Willimantic, Connecticut; Arthur, who married Emily Gocier; and Irene, who resides at home. The family are members of St. Mary's Roman Catholic Church, of Baltic, Connecticut.

THURSTON BROWNING LILLIBRIDGE—one of the best-known farmers in the town of Norwich, New London county, Connecticut, is also one of the best-loved. Educated and broad-minded, keen of intellect and alive to every opportunity, his life has been a success from whatever angle viewed, and as he now walks amid the greatly lengthened shadows he can review with satisfaction a life lived in one community seventy-six years and not a voice raised but in praise. He is a descendant of ancient English family, herein briefly reviewed.

(I) Thomas Lillibridge, the founder of the fam-

Thurston B Lillibridge

ily of Lillibridge in the United States, was born in England, in 1662. His earliest record in New England is the signing of a petition dated September 26, 1699, to the Earl of Bellomont, there in Newport, Rhode Island, asking that he use his influence with his Majesty, William III., for the establishment of a Church of England at Newport. This church was established, and was the original Trinity Church of which Thomas Lillibridge was a warden, 1709 and 1713, and where he owned pew No. 8 until 1719. He was admitted a freeman at Newport, May 6, 1701, was vestryman in 1718-22-24 in St. Paul's Narragansett Church, built in 1707, moved five miles north of its original site to Wickford; is still occasionally in use, and said to be the oldest Episcopal church north of the Potomac. He settled in old Westerly, in 1715, in that part later set off as Richmond, where he died, August 29, 1724. He married (first) Mary Hobson, (second) Sarah Lewis, who died in Richmond, Rhode Island, January 22, 1761, aged eighty-five. By his first wife, two children were born, by his second wife, nine children. Descent in this branch is traced through Benjamin, the sixth child of the second wife.

(II) Benjamin Lillibridge was born July 11, 1712, died August 11, 1800. He married, December 15, 1743, Annie Sherman, daughter of Jonathan, son of Benjamin, son of Philip, son of Samuel, son of Henry (1) Sherman, of Dedham, England. Benjamin and Annie (Sherman) Lillibridge were the parents of eight children, the seventh child, Gardiner, head of the third generation in this branch.

(III) Gardiner Lillibridge was born September 19, 1758, died in Exeter, Rhode Island, July 23, 1834, a soldier of the Revolution and a pensioner. He married Sarah Dawley, also born and died in Exeter. They were the parents of nine children. This branch of the family descends through Daniel, the third son.

(IV) Daniel Lillibridge, born July 7, 1778, died August 20, 1828, at the homestead in Exeter, Rhode Island, where he was born, lived and died, a farmer. He married, August 18, 1811, Hannah Barber, born in Exeter, August 23, 1793, died October 3, 1878, the daughter of Lillibridge Barber. They were the parents of four children, all sons, descent being traced in this branch through Daniel (2).

(V) Daniel (2) Lillibridge was born in Exeter, Rhode Island, July 27, 1814, died at the Lillibridge homestead on Scotland Road, Norwich, March 26, 1901. He was born in the old homestead and remained at home, his father's assistant, until the latter's death. He was then a lad of fourteen and he continued at home two years more, then in the spring of 1830, he came to the farm owned by his uncle, Captain Leonard Barber, on Plain Hill, Norwich, Connecticut. In 1831 he returned to the home farm in Exeter, where he married in 1834, and remained on the home farm in Exeter until 1845, when he removed to the present Lillibridge farm on Scotland Road, in the town of Norwich, New London county, Connecticut, once owned by his grandfather, Lillibridge Barber. This old farm was once a tavern kept by M. Tracy, the tavern, the present farmhouse, now remodeled and modernized. It is located on Scotland Road, the main road from Norwich North. The last proprietor of the tavern was Gideon Ray, the signboard reading, "G. Ray's Inn." Lillibridge Barber, who became its owner, was a wealthy landowner of Norwich and Exeter, and in his generosity he deeded this farm to his grandson, Daniel (2) Lillibridge, in 1840. Daniel (2) Lillibridge cultivated the farm of two hundred acres until some time prior to his death, when he retired from its active management. He married, May 18, 1834, Hannah Matteson, born in West Greenwich, Rhode Island, April 25, 1815, daughter of Peleg and Mary (James) Matteson, her mother a descendant of Gen. Nathanael Greene, an officer of the Revolution, and a friend of General Washington's. She died on the home farm, February 22, 1901. Mr. and Mrs. Daniel (2) Lillibridge were the parents of five children: Thurston Browning, of whom further; Rhoda B., born February 26, 1838, married, June 2, 1862, Edward Ladd, and died March 6, 1901; Amy, born August 19, 1840, died March 20, 1881, married, November 24, 1862, Henry L. M. Ladd; Alice, born September 13, 1842, died January 25, 1845; Hannah, born July 29, 1845, died April 19, 1879, married, March 5, 1873, Thomas Potter.

(VI) Thurston Browning Lillibridge, eldest child of Daniel (2) and Hannah (Matteson) Lillibridge, was born March 27, 1836, at the Lillibridge homestead, Exeter, Rhode Island, the same in which his father was born, and there spent the first nine years of his life. His parents then moved to the farm on Scotland Road, in the town of Norwich, New London county, Connecticut, where the lad grew to manhood and yet resides. He attended the district public school and private school in Norwich, and later, for several years, taught school in Exeter, Rhode Island, then two terms in Bozrah, Connecticut, and a few terms in Norwich, but always living at home and assisting his father in his farming operations during vacation days. Later, he gave up teaching and remained at home in management of the farm which he inherited from his father, being the only son. The farm which he now owns has been his home for seventy-six years, 1845-1921, he coming to it a lad of nine years, and he is now a veteran of eighty-five, but in remarkably good health. He has now retired from all participation in farm management, that department now being in the hands of his son.

Mr. Lillibridge is a Democrat in politics, and represented the town of Norwich in the State Legislature in 1886-87-88, his first election for one year, his second for two years. For several years he was selectman of the town of Norwich, five of those years, 1888-1893, being first selectman. He was also for years a member of the School Board. He is a member of Somerset Lodge, No. 34, Free and Accepted Masons, one of the oldest members of that lodge, he having been made a Mason therein in 1865. He is a member of the Masonic Veterans' Association, and is held in the highest esteem and veneration by his Masonic brethren and by everybody in his community, one of his neighbors expressing his regard in the sentence which everyone echoes, "a beautiful old man."

Mr. Lillibridge married, November 5, 1865, at Norwich, Lydia Ann Lillibridge, born in North Kingstown, Rhode Island, November 8, 1841, died at the home farm in the town of Norwich, April 10, 1907, daughter of Green and Lucy (Smith) Lillibridge, her father dying in Norwich, Connecticut, February 7, 1892, age eighty-three, son of Benjamin, son of Thomas Lillibridge, the American ancestor. Thurston B. and Lydia A. (Lillibridge) Lillibridge, were the parents of four children: Albert Warren, born January 30, 1867, now in the management of the home farm; Daniel Green, born September 1, 1868, died September 27, 1869; Annie May, born May 20, 1870, married Dwight L. Underwood, of Norwich, Connecticut, and they have a daughter, Bernice; Erroll Courtney, born June 10, 1872, at the home farm, where he now resides, a stone mason, married Mary Sullivan, of Norwich; Charles Frederick, born July 16, 1877, on the home farm, died in Norwich, Connecticut, in 1911, a farmer; he married Susan Austin, who survives him with three children: Thurston Daniel, Charles Gardiner, and Clarence Austin. Mr. Lillibridge retains the ownership of the home farm, which is cultivated by his son, Albert W. He has acquired other farm property, but those farms he has deeded to his sons. He has many friends, and is tenderly cherished by his children.

CAPTAIN JOHN HENRY GURNEY—The great war took its grim toll in lives from every walk of life; every profession, every vocation gave of its best to the end that civilization might survive the menacing onslaught of the "Hun." Previous to our entrance into the war, we had suffered all sorts of humiliations, and even tragedies had occurred in mysterious fashion, the late Captain John Henry Gurney being one of the victims of the Germans.

John Henry Gurney was born in South Rondout, New York, November 7, 1874. He was the son of George and Margaret (Hillsinger) Gurney. George Gurney was for many years captain of the schooner "Sarah Jane," which sailed from New London. He is now identified with the Ship Engine Company, of New London. The boy, John H., remained in his native place until he was sixteen years of age, when he went to Groton, subsequently removing to New London, where for several years he went as cook on his father's vessel, later being promoted to first mate. He later secured employment as a deckhand on a tug boat of the T. A. Scott Company, and for eighteen years was captain of this tug. In fact, it was while he was thus employed that he met his tragic death. In the early part of November, 1916, the German submarine "Deutschland" came into the harbor of New London and the officers of the German boat were entertained by the citizens of the city. After a three days' visit, during which time stores were taken on board for consumption, the craft got under way. It was to have followed the tug boat of which Captain Gurney was in command, but instead the submarine took a sudden dive and rammed the tug which immediately sunk with all on board.

On April 27, 1896, Captain Gurney was united in marriage with Annie May Malone, and to them were born two children: 1. George Maynard, whose birth occurred April 29, 1897; he enlisted in the Medical Corps of the United States army, and was stationed at Fort Monroe; he died May 12, 1918, while in the service. 2. Ralph Henry, who was born September 2, 1900; he is now with the T. A. Scott Company, of New London.

Captain Gurney was a man of strong domestic instincts, who found his chief happiness in his work and the intimate intercourse of family life and with such of his friends as were on terms of close personal friendship with him.

DANIEL PALMER COLLINS—A member of the old Scottish family of Collins, whose ancestry dates back to the romantic days when Mary Stuart was the adored Queen of Scotland, the land of legendary song and story, Daniel Palmer Collins is the son of Daniel and Esther (Bindloss) Collins. Esther Bindloss was an English woman by birth, the daughter of William and Margaret (Palmer) Bindloss, of Kendal, England, the latter a distant relative of the Palmers who are extensively known in connection with their large quilt mills in New London county. The elder Daniel was born in Queenstown, Ireland, March 26, 1821, his father and mother living in Ireland at that time, the father being one of the Scotch Guards stationed in Queenstown when Daniel Palmer Collins was born. Daniel Collins, Sr., early in life, became a cabin boy on board a sailing ship, the "Yorkshire," and for many years followed the call of the sea, rising step by step from cabin boy to the rank of first mate. He crossed the Atlantic ocean one hundred and four times and the finish of the last trip to the United States marked the close of his career as a sea-faring man. It was in 1846 that Daniel Collins, Sr., came to New London, remaining there for the next sixteen years, then, in 1862, moving with his family to Montville, he bought a farm there and for forty-eight years enjoyed his life upon this homestead, dying in 1909, when eighty-nine years old.

Daniel and Esther (Bindloss) Collins were the parents of the following children: 1. Daniel Palmer, of whom further. 2. Joseph Scroggie, a mail carrier, born in New London, in September, 1858; he married Addie Brown, by whom he had one child, which died in infancy. 3. Esther Bindloss, born in New London, now the wife of James Diffley; they have three children: Frank Palmer, James Palmer, and Esther. 4. Ellen Hillier, born in New London; she married James Carver, of Montville, and has two children: Lillian Ellen, and George D. 5. Margaret Palmer, born in New London, the wife of

Charles Crawford Haight, of Torrington, Connecticut; they have one child, Margaret C. 6. Mary Foster, born in Montville; she married Frederick Crocker, who died in 1903; they have no children. 7. Anson Benjamin, a sketch of whom follows.

Daniel Palmer Collins was born in New London, Connecticut, April 7, 1853, on Cedar street, then called Waxer street, one of the first thoroughfares in the county. In his boyhood he attended both public and private schools in the village, going for some time to the old Main Street School, one of the first six schools established in New London. It is now known as the Winthrop School. For three years young Collins also was a pupil at the private school conducted by Mrs. Manning on Post Hill.

After finishing his education, Daniel Palmer Collins obtained employment in a sail loft in Bank street, owned by Carl Barry, and for twenty-eight years remained so engaged. In 1897 he went into business for himself, establishing a sail-making loft on Howard avenue, and taking into partnership James Sterry. This combination continued for five years, then Mr. Collins purchased Mr. Sterry's interest in the business and since that time has carried on the work in his own name, still in the building on Howard street.

In fraternal circles, Mr. Collins is very well known, particularly among the members of the Free and Accepted Masons, he having gone through the Scottish Rite from the Blue Lodge to the thirty-second degree. He is also affiliated with Mohegan Lodge, No. 55, Independent Order of Odd Fellows. Equally popular in other associations, Mr. Collins has been connected with Konomoc Hose Company since 1882, being one of the oldest three men in it. For the past five years he has been a member of the Harbor Club of New London. Actively interested in the work of St. James' Protestant Episcopal Church, Mr. Collins is a vestryman in that body of Christians. In political affairs he is a Republican, generally voting that ticket, but at times choosing the candidate he may regard as the better man, irrespective of party affiliations.

In New London, on December 28, 1885, Daniel Palmer Collins was united in marriage with Grace Evelyn Whiting, born in Waterford, Connecticut, March 31, 1868, the daughter of Noyes Whiting, of Mystic, and his wife, Sarah Nichols, of Waterford, Connecticut. In early manhood Noyes Whiting went to Waterford to reside, being employed as a ship carpenter by the Chappell Company. He died in 1884 and is buried in Cedar Grove Cemetery, New London. Mrs. Sarah (Nichols) Whiting is also deceased. She had one sister, Agnes Nichols, who became the wife of Frederick R. Gould, of Perrysville, Rhode Island. Mr. and Mrs. Daniel Palmer Collins have no children. They reside at No. 104 Montauk avenue, New London.

ANSON BENJAMIN COLLINS, son of Daniel and Esther (Bindloss) Collins (q.v.), was born upon his father's farm in Montville, Connecticut, August 26, 1872. This homestead lies in the district now known as Collins District.

Attending the village school in Montville until he reached the age of twelve years, Anson Benjamin Collins then left home, and going to Mystic, Connecticut, entered the employ of Charles H. Johnson, who was the proprietor of a carriage manufactory there. Remaining there for a year and a half, the boy then came to New London, where he found employment in the wagon works of George A. Richards, being at that time fourteen years old. Continuing in this line for some years, the young man finally bought up the business, owing to the death of Mr. Richards, and has carried it on successfully since that time, and, in addition, conducts a blacksmith establishment.

Interested in the institutions of his town, Mr. Collins is a member of Mohegan Lodge, No. 55, Independent Order of Odd Fellows, and is also connected with the Harbor Club of New London. While a Republican in politics, Mr. Collins frequently exercises the right of selecting the best man for whom to vote.

In New London, Connecticut, in June, 1897, Anson Benjamin Collins was united in marriage with Catherine E. Murray, the ceremony being performed by the Rev. Thomas P. Joint. Mrs. Collins was born in 1872, the daughter of William A. and Mary (Ahern) Murray, of New London. Of this union two children have been born: 1. Benjamin Murray, born in New London, May 1, 1899; he is now a student in Rensselaer Institute of Technology, at Troy, New York. 2. Helen Mary, born February 4, 1902, a student at Wellesley College, Massachusetts. The family home is at No. 84 Montauk avenue, New London.

CASSIUS F. HARRIS—Born in New London and identified with the mercantile interests of this city throughout his career, Mr. Harris is now connected with the Thames River Lumber Company. Mr. Harris is a son of Frederic Hall Harris, who was born and reared in New London, and educated in the schools of the city. Frederic H. Harris, in association with a partner, established a clothing business in New London many years ago, continuing the same, under the name of Shepard & Harris, until his death, which occurred about 1888. Mr. Harris married Frances Burns, and they were the parents of three children, of whom Cassius F. was the youngest.

Cassius F. Harris was born in New London, Connecticut, May 3, 1860, and received his early education in the public schools of his native city, completing his studies at Cheshire Academy, in Cheshire, Connecticut. After finishing his studies, Mr. Harris became associated with his father in the clothing business, but dissolved the partnership not long after his father's death, withdrawing from the firm in 1895. He was later associated with S. R. Wightman, who conducted a thriving business in wholesale and retail tobacco, continuing in this branch of mercantile endeavor until about 1915. He then entered the office of the Thames River Lumber Company, in the capacity of bookkeeper, which position he still holds. By political affiliation, Mr. Harris is a Republican, but takes only the interest of the progressive citizen in public affairs.

On April 30, 1890, Mr. Harris married Marie Elizabeth Payne, daughter of Nehemiah Benjamin and Mary Eunicia (Ransom) Payne, of New London. Mr. and Mrs. Harris have one daughter, Gretchen, born in New London, July 30, 1892, wife of Terence V. O'Brien, who resides in that city.

JAMES SWEENEY—For many years identified with the upbuilding of New London and vicinity as an architect of unusual talent, James Sweeney, whose death has placed his work in other hands, left an enduring record of high achievement in the many fine structures which owe their beauty and stability to his art.

Mr. Sweeney was a son of John and Bridget (Halvey) Sweeney. John Sweeney was born in County Limerick, Ireland, in 1828, and came to the United States in 1843 with his family, locating in Norwich. Receiving a practical education in Ireland and in the public schools of Norwich, he later learned the trade of stone mason, which he followed for many years. During the latter part of his life he did general stevedore work. He died in New London, on April 2, 1881. His wife, who was also born in County Limerick, in 1832, died in New London, November 22, 1900, at the age of sixty-eight years, having survived her husband for nearly twenty years. They were the parents of six children: Hannah, who resides in New London; Thomas R., now retired, a resident of New London; John H., of Waterford, Connecticut, who married Nora Gleason; Timothy W., of New London; James, now deceased, whose name heads this review; and Edward M. Sweeney, who has been engaged in the lumber trade since leaving high school in 1899.

James Sweeney was born in New London, on December 27, 1868, and received his early education in the public schools of the city and Bulkeley High School. Thereafter, he took a special course in architecture at the New York Art School. About 1888 he became connected with Cole & Chandler, of Boston, Massachusetts, and New London, Connecticut, in the capacity of draftsman, and before the end of that year was placed in charge of their New London office. He continued here in their employ until 1893, when he took over the office after the death of George Warren Cole, thereafter continuing the business of constantly increasing importance, as a practicing architect, until his death. He designed many of the prominent buildings in New London and its vicinity. Noteworthy among these are St. Mary's Roman Catholic School, the Municipal building, and the Union Bank and Trust Company's building, all of New London; the Town Hall of Saybrook, Connecticut; the Harbor School of New London, and the Flanders School of East Lynn; Thames Hall, at the Connecticut College for Women, in New London; and hundreds of public buildings, industrial plants and private residences. Mr. Sweeney was reputed one of the best architects in the State, and his work bears the stamp of a competent and creative mind. He died in New London, on July 3, 1919, and among his business and professional associates and personal friends his loss will long be keenly felt. He was a man of thoughtful habit of mind, of pleasing personality, and of unselfish spirit, and numbered the most prominent people of the city among his friends.

Politically, Mr. Sweeney was a Democrat, and was influential in party affairs, although he never accepted nomination for public office. He was a member of the American Institute of Architecture; the Benevolent and Protective Order of Elks, No. 360; and of Seaside Council, No. 17, Knights of Columbus. He was a member of St. Mary's Roman Catholic Church.

BENJAMIN FRANKLIN BAILEY—In the days when the American clipper was winning its way around the world, the defeated opponents asserted that it was neither the ships nor the sailors that outclassed them, but the men that made the sails. In later years, when, having failed again and again to "lift the cup" from American yatchsmen, the famous English sportsman, Sir Thomas W. Lipton, tried to analyze the causes of his failure, he said: "I can equal your yacht builders; my sailors are as good as yours; but I can't beat your sailmakers." There are but few men who have the skill and the technical knowledge necessary for the expert maker of sails in all their various sizes and shapes, and to meet the many needs. Sails that fit and draw, sails light enough to be easily handled, yet staunch enough to hold until the spars are endangered, sails that make the men who depend upon them for life and livelihood want more of them year after year—to be a master maker of such sails means more than the mere possession of knowledge and skill; the sailmaker must be as ruggedly dependable and as staunchly honest as his sails.

To this select class of sailmakers belongs Benjamin Franklin Bailey, of New London, Connecticut. Born in Noank, Connecticut, September 2, 1840, of a father whose whole life was identified with the fisheries of Noank, he early manifested a taste and ability for what later became his profession. Henry Bailey, the father, died about 1861, at the age of sixty-two, having married Susan Franklin, of Block Island, and become the father of ten children: Norris, Rosands, Henry, Charles, William, George, Benjamin Franklin, Diana, and Almira. Associated from earliest life with the sea and with the ships that go out to win a livelihood from the deep, it was natural that the interests of the family should center about ships and that one of them, at least, should give his attention to that important part of the structure upon which so much depends—the sails.

After completing his education in the local schools, Benjamin F. Bailey sought for a place in which he might learn sailmaking and found it in

New London, Connecticut. Four years he spent with Mr. B. Arnold, and, characteristically, when he was ready to enter business for himself it was back to Noank that he went. A few years later, however, came that cataclysm which interrupted and shattered the plans of so many men, the Civil War. He enlisted in 1862, in Company C, 21st Regiment, Connecticut Volunteer Infantry, which formed part of the Army of the Potomac, and took part in no fewer than fifty-two engagements, receiving his honorable discharge in June, 1865. Unlike many of his companions, he was not unsettled by his years of campaigning and soon resumed his business at Noank, where he remained for fifteen years. At the end of that time, in 1880, superior workmanship and business integrity had created the need for a larger field of labor and he moved his business to New London, establishing himself on Bank street. In 1911 he moved further along the same street to his present location, opposite Green street.

Mr. Bailey married (first) Abbey Perry, and to this marriage was born one daughter, Georgina, who is deceased. He married (second) Amanda Franklin, born at Noank, November 25, 1865, daughter of Thomas and Anna Franklin, who died in 1916. To this second marriage were born two children: Frederick, born in Noank, died in 1901, at the age of thirty-four; and John Bennett Bailey, of whom further.

John Bennett Bailey was born at Noank, August 10, 1869. He married Margaret McGowan, of Nova Scotia, New Brunswick, and they are the parents of six children: Gladys Anna, born at Noank, April 20, 1894; Athena Bonita, born at New London, February 7, 1897; Mildred Franklin, born at Noank, August 30, 1901; Eloise Benjamin, born October 27, 1903; Edythe Thelma, born April 9, 1906; and Benjamin Franklin, born August 10, 1909.

BARTHOLOMEW JOSEPH McCARTHY—One of the most loyal and patriotic of New London's citizens is Mr. McCarthy, the subject of this review, an Irishman by birth, with all the love of home and family for which the Irish race is famed. Though he has lived in this country for nearly twenty-five years, he still has a fondness for the land of his boyhood. He comes of purest Irish stock, his ancestors for many generations living in their home section.

The parents of Bartholomew Joseph McCarthy were Jeremiah and Margaret (Hennessey) McCarthy, natives of County Waterford, Ireland, where the former was for many years engaged in farming on a rather more extensive scale than usual. After a long and useful life he died, at the age of ninety-two years, in 1901. His wife, Margaret (Hennessey) McCarthy, survived him for several years, passing away in 1908, when seventy-one years old. Neither she nor her husband had ever left their home in the old country. They had a family of seven children: 1. Jeremiah, born in County Waterford, Ireland, where he was a farmer. He married Catherine Foley; they had no children. 2. John, also born in County Waterford, also a farmer. 3. Patrick, born at the old home in Ireland; he came to the United States in 1892. In his early manhood he spent most of his life in railroad work, but is now employed in a ship and engine company. He married Bridget Corcoran, by whom he has had four sons and one daughter. 4. Thomas, born in Ireland; in his youth he came to this country, but died December 31, 1918, leaving a widow, who before her marriage was Mary Connolly, and six children. 5. Mary, born in Ireland and still living there; she is the wife of Gerald Fitzgerald, and is the mother of four sons and three daughters. 6. Bartholomew Joseph, of whom further. 7. Margaret, who died young.

Bartholomew J. McCarthy was born in County Waterford, Ireland, April 23, 1871. After acquiring a good common school education in the village, the lad assisted his father on the farm for some years, then, in 1896, emigrated to the United States, coming directly to New London to join relatives who had emigrated some time before. Obtaining employment with the New York, New Haven & Hartford Railroad Company in their freight department, Mr. McCarthy remained there for five years and eight months. After leaving the railroad company he was employed in various ways for the next two years, then started at the bottom in the Arnold Rudd Grain Company and by degrees was advanced until he became foreman of that firm, having stayed with them for sixteen years. In September, 1919, Mr. McCarthy established a business of his own, dealing in wholesale quantities of grain and other commodities of like nature, and has been very successful thus far.

A popular man among his associates, Mr. McCarthy is connected with several fraternal orders, being a member of Seaside Council, Knights of Columbus, and also is secretary of the Ancient Order of Hibernians, and is affiliated with the local lodge of the Loyal Order of Moose, No. 304. Though a member of the Democratic party, Mr. McCarthy exercises the right to vote an independent ticket if he so desires. He attends the Roman Catholic church in New London.

Mr. McCarthy married, in New London, June 28, 1911, Annie Reardon, born in County Kerry, Ireland, in September, 1883, the daughter of Michael and Mary (Hussey) Reardon. Mrs. McCarthy is one of an unusually large family, her parents having had twenty children. Mr. and Mrs. McCarthy have two children: Mary Margaret, born June 12, 1912; Margaret Veronica, born July 4, 1913. The family home is at No. 12 Goddard street, New London, Connecticut.

JOHN DEAN AVERY—Many generations of Averys have followed Captain James Avery in New London county, Connecticut, he and his father being contemporaries. Beginning with Christopher Avery, the generations now number ten, John Dean Avery being of the tenth. He is a son of Thomas W. Avery, and grandson of Albert Lay Avery, whose careers are traced in this work under the headings, John Dean Avery, who is the uncle of the present John Dean Avery, and Thomas W. Avery. These Averys, John D. and Thomas W., were born at the homestead at Eastern Point, town of Groton, New London county, and there this second John Dean Avery was born and spent his youth, as did his brother, Albert T. Avery, also of record in this work.

John Dean Avery, son of Thomas W. and Mary Alice (Maine) Avery, was born at the Avery homestead, town of Groton, December 29, 1895, and began his education in the public schools of the town, continuing in Norwich Free Academy, whence he was graduated, class of 1914. He then entered Brown University, there receiving his degree of Ph. D., class of 1917. In that year patriotism was so strong that many of the students hardly waited for the school year to close before offering themselves to the government for army service in the World War. Among these was John Dean Avery, who in 1917 was commissioned first lieutenant in the United States Aviation Corps and assigned to the 316th Aero Squadron. He was flying instructor at Barron Field, Texas, and continued in the service until December, 1918, when he was honorably discharged and mustered out of the service at Camp Dix. He is now retained as an officer in the United States Reserves.

After retiring from the army, Lieutenant Avery, in association with his brother, Albert T. Avery, organized the John D. Avery Company, Inc., and established in the automobile business in New London. They are agents for the Marmon and Nash cars, and in connection with their selling agencies they operate a large garage, modernly equipped with service and supply departments. The business is prosperous, and the company a popular one. Mr. Avery is a member of the New London Auto Dealers' Association; Phi Gamma Delta fraternity; a Republican in politics; and a member of Groton Congregational Church.

Mr. Avery married, June 22, 1917, Irene Woods, of New London, daughter of Howard A. and Lucy (Randolph) Woods, of New London, Connecticut. Mr. and Mrs. Avery are the parents of a daughter, Juliet D., born in October, 1920.

HERBERT AUGUSTUS RICHARDS—In the little village of Occum, in the town of Norwich, Connecticut, is one of the most up-to-date general stores in this section. At the head of this business, and proprietor of it, is Herbert A. Richards, for many years a familiar figure in the industrial and mercantile life of the neighborhood.

Mr. Richards is a son of John Henry and Fannie (Curtis) Richards. The elder Mr. Richards was born in Wakefield, New Hampshire, and educated in the district schools of that State. While still a young man he entered the cotton mills, and after an experience of seven years, became assistant overseer for the Lyman Thread Company, at Holyoke, Massachusetts. There he remained for fourteen years, then went to the Headley Thread Mills, in the same city, as head of their carding department. It was with this practical experience that he came to the plant of the Totoket Cotton Mill at Occum when it was built, and started with that company, at the head of their carding department. Continuing with this company until his retirement from all active work, Mr. Richards still lives in Versailles, and is the oldest resident in the village, having been born in 1843. His wife, who was a native of Ohio, died in 1875. They were the parents of five children: Edith, now the wife of William O. Soule, a dealer in confectionery, doing a prosperous business in Jewett City, Connecticut; Herbert A., whome name heads this review; Mabel, now the wife of Charles Fisk, an iron foundry foreman, in Fairfield, Alabama; Tyler C., bookkeeper for the Hood Rubber Company, at Watertown, Massachusetts, who married Mildren Marr; and Ethel Curtis, deceased.

Herbert A. Richards was born in Holyoke, Massachusetts, on June 27, 1878. His parents coming to New London county when he was only one year old, his education was received in the public schools of the village of Versailles. When he entered the world of industry, it was in the employ of the Totoket Cotton Mill Company, in the carding department, which was under his father's management. He followed this work from 1887 to 1892, then rented the Baldwin Farm, near the village of Occum, going into dairying and general farming. For ten years he handled a large milk route in the adjoining village of Taftville.

In October, 1910, Mr. Richards made the change which has proved substantially and permanently advantageous to him. He bought out the general store of Hall & Hawkins, in Occum, increased the business, and developed its scope, until now he conducts one of the best establishments of this class in New London county. He is held in the highest esteem by his fellow-citizens, and is enjoying the fruits of well-earned success.

Mr. Richards is alive to every phase of public progress, and always interested in the welfare of the people. In political matters he reserves the right to individual decision, and gives unqualified support to no one party. He has never sought nor accepted public office.

Mr. Richards married Iva M. Rathbun, daughter of Isaiah and Emily (Austin) Rathbun, of Hebron, Connecticut, and they have three children: Ethel Julia, born May 4, 1908; Herbert A., Jr., born July 21, 1910; and Iva Emily, born May 11, 1912, who died December 16, 1920. The family are members of the Methodist Episcopal church of Versailles, and interested in all its social and benevolent activities.

HENRY RHODES PALMER—For many years Palmers have inhabited a good farm in the Road district of the town of Stonington, and there Henry Rhodes Palmer of the ninth American generation was born and there resides. He is a descendant of Walter Palmer, who was born in England, and who came to New England probably as early as 1629. He is credited with having built the first dwelling house in Charlestown, Massachusetts, but in 1640 he joined the organizers of the town of Rehoboth and in 1653 located in Stonington, Connecticut, where he died, November 10, 1661. He was twice married, and had sons, descent in this line being through the founder's son, Nehemiah; his son, Nehemiah (2); his son, Thomas; his son, Thomas (2); his son, Thomas; his son, Major Alden Palmer; his son, Eugene Palmer; his son, Henry Rhodes Palmer. Thus, for two hundred and sixty-eight years, 1653-1921, Palmers have been residents of the town of Stonington.

Major Alden Palmer was born July 17, 1802, in Stonington, District No. 7, and earned his rank in the military company of the town. He farmed the old homestead and built the present farm house. He was a Democrat, and a man of influence until his death, March 22, 1876. He married, October 10, 1831, Nancy D. Palmer, born February 20, 1810, died May 13, 1886, daughter of Lemuel and Abigail (Davis) Palmer. Their sixth child was a son, Eugene, father of Henry Rhodes Palmer.

Eugene Palmer was born at the homestead, November 29, 1841, and there died after a life of usefulness and honor, February 11, 1918. With the exception of four years spent in Trenton, New York, his life was spent at the homestead in the town of Stonington, and farming was his lifelong occupation. He married, June 9, 1881, Mary Adelia Chesebrough, born July 30, 1857, daughter of Gideon P. and Anna Adelia (Lasher) Chesebrough, who survives her husband and makes the old farm her home during the summer months. Five children were born to Eugene and Mary Adelia Palmer: Henry Rhodes, of further mention; Daniel Stanton, born September 25, 1884, died May 29, 1903; Mary, born May 2, 1886, died May 5, 1886; Adelia M., born December 2, 1887, married Stanley Clark Johnson, and resides in Providence, Rhode Island; Jean, born August 7, 1900.

Henry Rhodes Palmer, of the ninth American generation and also the ninth in the town of Stonington, Connecticut, only living son of Eugene and Mary Adelia (Chesebrough) Palmer, was born at the homestead upon which he now resides and cultivates, October 26, 1882. He was for years connected with the Narragansett Electric Lighting Company of Providence, Rhode Island, and made his home in that city. He later returned to the homestead, where he continues. He is a director of the New London County Farm Bureau, and a man of modern ideas on all subjects. He is an attendant of the First Congregational Church and a generous supporter of same. In politics he is a Republican.

Henry R. Palmer married, January 1, 1908, Nancy Louise Wheeler, and they are the parents of two children: Sylvia Wheeler, born January 21, 1910; Nancy Wheeler, born September 13, 1920.

THORNTON N. M. LATHROP—Since 1915 Mr. Lathrop has been established in New London in the automobile business, having the agency for the Franklin and Studebaker cars. He is a young man, but since 1906 has been actively employed in some form of construction work, and is a thoroughly capable and efficient young man. He is a son of Edward F. and Nancy (Lane) Lathrop, who at the time of the birth of their son were living in Brooklyn, New York. Edward F. Lathrop was born at South Hadley Falls, Massachusetts, and in early manhood became a contractor of railroad construction, senior member of the Lathrop & Shea Company, whose office headquarters were in New Haven, Connecticut. He was engaged in railroad construction until his death, in Brooklyn, New York, in 1910. His wife, born on Long Island, survives him, and is a resident of Brooklyn, New York.

Thornton N. M. Lathrop, youngest of the five children of Edward F. and Nancy (Lane) Lathrop, was born in Brooklyn, New York, March 8, 1886. He was educated in Brooklyn public schools, finishing with graduation from high school in 1906. The two years following he was employed as salesman for the Brooklyn Edison Company, and for two years next following (1908-1910), he was associated with his father in the Lathrop & Shea Company, engaged in railroad construction. In 1910 he located in New London, Connecticut, and, with R. P. Smith, established a garage and agency for the E. M. F. and Hudson cars. In 1915 he began business under his own name as agent for the Franklin and Studebaker automobiles and has established a garage, salesrooms and service station on Montauk avenue, where he is meeting with merited success.

Mr. Lathrop is a member of the Auto Dealers' Association of New London; member and past president of the Harbor Club; member and director of the Rotary Club; and a member of the Chamber of Commerce, of New London. In Masonry he has attained the thirty-two degrees of Norwich Valley Consistory, Ancient Accepted Scottish Rite, and in the York Rite is affiliated with Brainard Lodge, No. 102, Free and Accepted Masons; Union Chapter, No. 7, Royal Arch Masons; Cushing Chapter, Royal and Select Masters; and Palestine Commandery, Knights Templar. He is also a noble of Pyramid Temple, Ancient Arabic Order Nobles of the Mystic Shrine, of Bridgeport. In politics, he is a Republican, and in religious affiliation, a member of the St. James' Protestant Episcopal Church.

On June 17, 1908, Mr. Lathrop married Clara May Smith, of New London, daughter of William W. Smith. Mr. and Mrs. Lathrop are the parents of two sons: Richard T., and Donald C.

THEODORE N. HANSEN—A practical man in an eminently practical field of endeavor, Mr. Hansen is bearing a significant part in the growth and development of the Mason & Hansen Company, of which he is president.

Mr. Hansen is a son of Hans Peter and Christina

(Ingeberg) Hansen. The elder Mr. Hansen was born in Apenrade, Denmark, and educated in the national schools of his native land. Learning the carpenter's trade there, he followed it throughout his lifetime, first in Denmark and later in this country. He came to the United States in 1880, locating in New Haven, Connecticut, residing there until his death, in 1919. His wife, who was also born in Apenrade, Denmark, survives him, and is a resident of Waterbury, Connecticut. Their three children are as follows: Anna D., who died at the age of ten years; Theodore N., whose name heads this review; and Katie M., the wife of Thomas B. Blaikie, of Waterbury.

Theodore N. Hansen was born in New Haven, Connecticut, March 30, 1888. Receiving his education in the public schools of that city, he early made his start in the business world. Entering the employ of the Peck Brothers Company, wholesale dealers in plumbers' supplies, he continued with this house for eighteen years, for a greater part of the time in the capacity of traveling salesman. In 1920 he became associated with Orion A. Mason, of Medway, Massachusetts, and under the name of the Mason & Hansen Company, founded the present business in the same line for which the experience of both young men had prepared them. The Mason & Hansen Company, located on Sparyard street, New London, is doing a constantly increasing business in the wholesale distribution of plumbers' supplies, and is capitalized at $25,000. The business is at present conducted by Mr. Hansen, president of the company, and E. S. Carpenter, treasurer.

In civic matters Mr. Hansen is interested, and holds a seat in the Chamber of Commerce. Politically, he affiliates with the Republican party. He is a member of Adelphi Lodge, No. 63, Free and Accepted Masons, of Fairhaven, Connecticut; of Palaski Chapter, No. 26, Royal Arch Masons, of Fairhaven; and of Crawford Council, No. 19, Royal and Select Masters, also of Fairhaven. He is a member of the Rotary Club of New London.

Mr. Hansen married Louise Harriet, daughter of Luther E. and Alice (Hewitt) Miller, of Torrington, Connecticut. They have three children: Theodore N., Jr., Henry M., and William P. The family attends the First Congregational Church, of New London.

JOHN B. BEAUVAIS, who is conducting an up-to-date service station in New London, Connecticut, was born in Worcester, Massachusetts, January 27, 1880, and is a son of Albert and Margaret (Germain) Beauvais. The father, who was born and educated in Plattsburg, New York, has been a machinist all his life, and is a resident of Worcester, Massachusetts.

John B. Beauvais was educated in the parochial schools of Worcester, and after leaving school, from 1894 until 1898, he served an apprenticeship with Reed, Prentice & Company, learning the trade of machinist. At the end of his apprenticeship, Mr. Beauvais enlisted in Company I, 2nd Regiment, United States Marine Corps, serving in Cuba and the Philippines during the Spanish-American War. He also served in China during the Boxer uprising, when he was stationed at Pekin. While in China, Mr. Beauvais received a special medal for endurance shown while on a "hike" of two hundred and forty six miles, which was accomplished in a period of ten days. He was discharged from the service on October 12, 1904, and returned to Worcester, Massachusetts, where he filled the position of foreman in the machine shop of Reed, Prentice & Company for ten years. In 1914, Mr. Beauvais came to New London county to accept a position as machinist with the New London Ship and Engine Company, where he continued until December, 1919. At the time he purchased the Willard Service Station, at No. 225 Main street, theretofore conducted by John B. Corbin, and has since conducted a thriving business in this line of endeavor, doing all kinds of battery repairs.

With the veteran organizations in New London, Mr. Beauvais is identified, being a member of the G. M. Cole Camp, No. 7, Spanish War Veterans, and also of the Veterans of Foreign Wars. He is a member of St. Mary's Roman Catholic Church. Politically, he supports the Republican party.

Mr. Beauvais married, June 27, 1906, in Worcester, Massachusetts, Mattie Jarvis, daughter of Augustus and Meciline (Brockway) Jarvis, of New York State. Mr. and Mrs. Beauvais have four children: Lawrence J., Roland J., Bernard J. C., and Margaret M., all born in Worcester.

AUSTIN AVERY MAINE—Among the substantial citizens of New London county was Austin Avery Maine, successful farmer and merchant, who during his entire lifetime lived and worked in various towns and cities of his native county. Born in the town of Griswold, New London county, Connecticut, December 20, 1868, son of Avery Alonzo and Mary Jane (Brown) Maine, he was reared and educated in North Stonington, to which place his parents removed soon after his birth. Griswold was the birthplace of his mother, born September 16, 1847, died, at North Stonington, in 1873.

Austin Avery Maine attended the district schools of North Stonington, Connecticut, and Westerly, Rhode Island, after which he assisted his father upon the home farm until he was twenty-one years of age. He then hired a farm in Stonington, which he worked for one year, and then moved to North Stonington, rented a farm and settled down to the serious business of becoming a successful farmer. For seventeen years he worked steadily and efficiently, then, in 1906, he quit farming, bought out the general store of Calvin Hoxie, in the village of North Stonington, and successfully conducted the business until 1908, at which time, in December, he sold out to Brown & Stone, moved to Voluntown, Connecticut, and took over the management of the farm property and general store of his grandfather, Palmer A. Brown, who was too far along in years to continue the conduct of the business. Under this new arrangement, the grandfather owned the store building, while Austin Avery Maine owned and conducted the business. Here he continued until 1916, when he rtired, continuing to live in Voluntown during the remainder of his life. He died September 26, 1918.

Politically, Mr. Maine supported the Republican party. He served the town of North Stonington as tax assessor, being the candidate of both parties, and filled several public offices of trust, including that of tax collector during a term of several years. A member of the Third Baptist Church of North Stonington, he was active in its work, serving as trustee and as a member of the finance committee, as well as giving of his time and his means for the furtherance of its various lines of work. He was also a member of the North Stonington Grange, No. 138, and of Court Advance, No. 3836, Independent Order of Foresters.

On March 30, 1890, he married, at North Stonington, Connecticut, Eva Angeline Burdick, daughter of Horace Franklin and Mary Frances (Shirley) Burdick, both natives of North Stonington, and both deceased. Since the death of Austin Avery Maine, Mrs. Maine has removed to the village of North Stonington, where, among the friends and scenes of her childhood, she is passing the peaceful evening of her life.

THE PRENTIS FAMILY—Three generations of the Prentis family are herein reviewed, their heads being: Captain Benjamin Prentis, a farmer and seafaring man, sailing his own fishing smack; his son, Eldredge Packer Prentis, undertaker and funeral director of New London; his son, Samuel Mott Prentis, his father's business associate and successor. Two of these three men have passed "to that bourne from which no traveler ever returns," but the third, Samuel M. Prentis, is one of New London's active and respected citizens, successful in business, esteemed in private life, and prominent in city affairs.

Captain Benjamin Prentis was born at the Prentis homestead in Waterford, Connecticut, and was educated in the district public school, attending its sessions during the winter term, and working on the farm during the summer months. The farm lay along the Connecticut coast, and at certain seasons the lad would slip on one of the smacks sailing out of New London harbor. Later he left the farm, and finding fishing a profitable business, adopted it as his regular occupation. He prospered, and finally became the owner of his own vessel, and for many years he was a regular "banks" fisherman, sailing from New London and delivering his fish to New York City buyers. He ran his schooner on her fishing trips from New London to the "banks," thence to New York City, and for many years was very succesful and widely known among the sea-going community as a brave and skillful skipper. He finally retired from the sea and lived a quiet life in New London, free from business cares, until his death. He was for many years custodian of the Light House Department, of New London.

Captain Prentis married Miranda Beckwith, born in East Lyme, Connecticut, who also died in New London, and they were the parents of seven children, two of whom are living: Kate, wife of H. C. Holmes, of New London, Connecticut; and Stephen A., who married Carrie Mason, and resides in New London.

Eldredge Packer Prentis, son of Captain Benjamin and Miranda (Beckwith) Prentis, was born in Waterford, New London county, Connecticut, March 25, 1848, died in New London, February 15, 1921. He was the third child of his parents, and was given a good public school education. After school life was ended he became a clerk in Ralph Smith & Son's general store of New London. He continued in business in New London as an employee until reaching the age of thirty-four, then, in 1882, purchased the undertaking business of Hammond & Caulkins, having been a partner in that firm during the previous year. In 1883 he purchased the entire interest, and from that year until his death conducted the business under his own name. He became widely known as an undertaker, maintained a well-equipped establishment, and was the leading funeral director of the city. He invested largely in New London real estate, and was highly esteemed, his sudden death carrying sorrow to many homes where he was well known and loved.

Eldredge P. Prentis married, in New London, Olive Mott, daughter of Samuel Mott, of Waterford, Connecticut. She died in New London, in 1915, leaving a son, Samuel Mott, of further mention. Mr. Prentis was a Republican in politics, and both he and his wife were members of the Congregational church.

Samuel Mott Prentis, only child of Eldredge Packer and Olive (Mott) Prentis, was born in New London, Connecticut, September 26, 1879, and there yet resides, one of the leading undertakers of the city. He was educated in New London public schools, and in 1896 finished his course with graduation from Bulkeley High School. During the ensuing nine years, 1896-1905, he was an office salesman with F. H. and A. H. Chappell, of New London, his experience with that firm being most valuable and profitable. In 1905 he became associated with his father in the undertaking business, that connection existing for sixteen years, when the hand of death was laid upon the senior member. The son, Samuel M. Prentis, upon the passing of Eldredge P. Prentis, succeeded the latter as head of the business, which, since 1883, has been in the Prentis name, a period of thirty-eight years.

Mr. Prentis is a Republican in politics, and for two terms has represented the Second Ward on the New London Board of Aldermen. He is an ardent and influential party man, and works hard for the triumph of party candidates. He is a member of New London Lodge, No. 360, Benevolent and Protective Order of Elks, of which he is a past exalted ruler; member of Nonanemtuc Tribe, No. 40, Improved Order of Redmen; New London Chamber of Commerce; Konomoc Hose Company, of New London; the Thames Club; and Connecticut State Funeral Directors' Association.

WALTER BODINE SMITH JEFFERS—Engaged in a somewhat varied business career during a life that ended far short of the allotted threescore years and ten, the recent death of Walter Bodine Smith Jeffers removed from Palmertown, Connecticut, a man who had done his work well and whose loss was keenly felt by those with whom he had been associated. He died in Palmertown, August 9, 1920, and was buried in Hanover, Connecticut.

Walter Bodine Smith Jeffers was the son of Josiah Jeffers, a native of Atlantic City, New Jersey, who in his early life had been a seafaring man, but in later years had been employed as a mechanic in Connecticut. His death occurred in 1903, at the age of sixty years. He was buried in the family plot in Jewett City Cemetery. The mother of Walter Bodine Smith Jeffers was Lucy (Yerrington) Jeffers, of Jewett City.

Born in Jewett City, Connecticut, April 18, 1865, Walter Bodine Smith Jeffers was educated in the public schools there, and following this went to his father's old home in Atlantic City, where he remained for a few years. Returning to Jewett City, Mr. Jeffers was employed for a time in flower culture, assisting in the care of a greenhouse, later going into one of the mills in Jewett City. In 1907, accepting the position of superintendent of the Camp Grounds at Willimantic, Mr. Jeffers lived for two years in that city. In April, 1909, he came to Palmertown and entered into mill work again, continuing thus occupied until his death.

During the Spanish-American War, Mr. Jeffers enlisted at Niantic, Connecticut, and was assigned for duty at Savannah, Georgia, where he served as a corporal in Company C, Third Regiment.

Walter Bodine Smith Jeffers is survived by his widow, Mrs. Margaret Louise (Allen) Jeffers, whom he married October 10, 1900, in Hanover, Connecticut. She is the daughter of Alexander Allen, a successful farmer of Hanover, a man who had been prominently connected with affairs in that town, and was for years a deacon in the Congregational church there. He died in 1895. His wife was Caroline Allen, whom he married in Illinois, having met her there during a trip which Mr. Allen made through the West. Their daughter, Margaret Louise Jeffers, was born in Charlton, Massachusetts, March 12, 1872. She had two brothers, Pratt Allen and William Allen who are now deceased.

In addition to his wife, Mr. Jeffers left two sisters, Mrs. Robert Smith, of Phenix, Rhode Island, and Mrs. Fred Gilbert, of Jewett City. Mrs. Margaret Louise (Allen) Jeffers is now librarian of the Community Library, Palmertown.

VIGGO E. BIRD, general manager of the Connecticut Power Company, to which office he was appointed January 1, 1920, is a man whose ever alert public spirit and ready coöperation in all that concerns the general welfare constitute a lasting claim on the regard of the city of New London.

Regnar E. Bird, father of Viggo E. Bird, was born in London, England. When two years old his father moved to Flensburg, Slesvig-Holstein, to look after his shipping interests, and incidently served as British Counsel. The boy secured his primary schooling in Flensburg, but at the age of twelve years was sent to a boarding school near Copenhagen, Denmark. After graduating from this school he matriculated at the University of Copenhagen, in the engineering department, and was subsequently graduated from this institution with the degree of Civil Engineer. He remained in Copenhagen, Denmark, where today he is one of the leading engineering contractors of that country. He married Regina Ewaldsen, and to them have been born four children: Svend, who married Johanna Schmidt, and is an interior decorator in Copenhagen; Tage, who married Jennie Nielsen, and is a civil engineer at Valparaiso, Chili; Uffe, who is a civil engineer, being associated with his father in business, and who married Elizabeth Olsen; Viggo E., of further mention.

Viggo E. Bird, son of Regnar E. and Regina (Ewaldsen) Bird, was born in Copenhagen, Denmark, April 29, 1885. After graduating from the local high school, he entered the engineering department of the University of Copenhagen, winning from this institution, in the class of 1902, the degree of Mechanical Engineer. Two years later he came to the United States and upon landing in New York City, remained there for a while in the employ of the General Electric Company. Some months later, however, he resigned and went to Boston, Massachusetts, where he entered the Massachusetts Institute of Technology, graduating with the degree of Bachelor of Science in 1908, and working for the next ten years for the following companies: Assistant engineer for Harmond V. Hayes, of Boston; engineer for Stone & Webster, of Boston; general superintendent of the Fall River Gas Company; and then to New London, where he secured a position as manager of the New London division of the Connecticut Power Company. In this capacity he proved himself to be an able organizer and executive, keenly alert to every changing phase of the business, and as a man of keen foresight, he was promoted to his present position, general manager of all the divisions for the Connecticut Power Company, January 1, 1920.

The thorough business qualifications of Mr. Bird have always been in great demand on boards of directors of various institutions, and his public spirit has led him to accept many such trusts. He is director of the Lawrence Memorial Associated Hospital of New London; director and

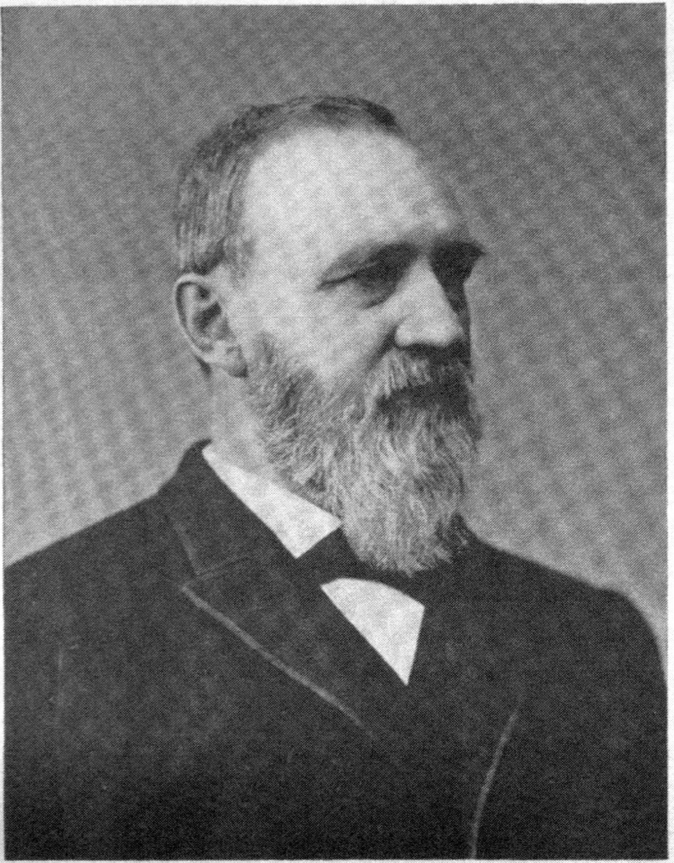

[illegible] Edgar

Janie Leeds Edgar.

Scout commissioner of the Boy Scouts of New London; and is a director of the New London Chamber of Commerce. His political affiliations are with the Republican party, and while he has never consented to be a candidate for office, his advice upon questions of public moment is frequently solicited. A Congregationalist in religion, he attends the First Church of this denomination in New London, and is ever ready to respond to any deserving call made upon him, being widely charitable. His clubs are the Thames and the Shenecossett Country, both of New London.

On April 10, 1911, Viggo E. Bird was united in marriage with Anita Parker, daughter of Thomas G. and Mary (Owens) Parker, of San Francisco, California. Mr. and Mrs. Bird are the parents of four children: Mary P., Elizabeth E., Thora A., and Regnar E. (2).

THOMAS EDGAR—A pioneer of the city of New London, Connecticut, in the insurance business, Thomas Edgar was for many years identified with the progress and growth of the city, and in the business, in which he was one of the first to engage, set a high standard for those who should follow after.

Mr. Edgar came of good old English antecedents. His grandfather, Thomas Edgar, was born at New-Castle-upon-Tyne, England, and was educated there. He came to the United States during the Revolutionary War, and settled at New London, casting his lot with the Colonies.

He lived a retired life, taking no active part in the business affairs of the community. He married Mary Latimer, who was born in New London, and both died there. They were the parents of two children: Mark and Nancy.

Mark Edgar, son of Thomas and Mary (Latimer) Edgar, was born in New London, December 3, 1779, died December 25, 1863. He was educated in the public schools of this city, and when a young man, served an apprenticeship as a carpenter, and later became prominent as a contractor and builder, many of the substantial structures which went up under his hand still being in constant use in the city. He followed this line of activity throughout his lifetime, and died in New London, December 25, 1863. He married Annie Dennis, of Norwich, born March 10, 1788, died June 7, 1873, and they were the parents of four children.

Thomas Edgar, youngest child of Mark and Annie (Dennis) Edgar, was born in New London, Connecticut, January 19, 1829. He received his early education in a private school in Colchester, New London county, Connecticut, then completed his studies in a private school in Farmington, Hartford county, Connecticut. About 1850 he entered the business world in the employ of William Benjamin & Company, of New London, in their dry goods store, which was one of the leading mercantile establishments of that day. Remaining only a few years with this firm, however, he started in business for himself, and for about nine years conducted a thriving dry goods business at No. 104 State street. In 1861 he established himself in the field of insurance, until then scarcely known in this city, and up to that time an undeveloped branch of endeavor. It can truthfully be said that Mr. Edgar was the pioneer in this line, and his activities in the insurance business were beneficial both to himself and to the economic progress of the city during the remainder of his life. He died in New London, on April 2, 1909.

Mr. Edgar married, in 1856, Eliza B. Smith, daughter of Captain Parker and Mary (Potter) Smith, both of New London. His wife died January 8, 1904. They were the parents of two children, both born in New London: George P., a resident of New London, who married Sallie D. Dennis; and Janie L.

Miss Edgar, upon the death of her father, took over the insurance business which he laid down, and added to it a real estate business, in which she has been very successful and is now one of the leading operators in this field in the city of New London.

ROBERT B. KEYES—In New London, Connecticut, his native city and lifelong home, Robert B. Keyes has won high professional standing, and as a musician and teacher of the violin he has no superiors in his city. Keyes Orchestra, which furnishes music for all occasions, is a city institution, and Professor Keyes, one of the best known men of his city. He is a son of Benjamin and Mary (Buckley) Keyes, who were born in Ireland, but spent most of their lives in New London, Connecticut, where Benjamin Keyes, a stationary engineer, died, in 1906. They were the parents of six children: Richard; Jennie; and Robert B., of further mention; all residing in New London, and three deceased.

Robert B. Keyes was born in New London, Connecticut, January 28, 1870, and there was educated in the public schools. From youth he was passionately fond of music, and all through his school years he was a student of the violin, having as his instructor Professor George W. Richards, of New London. After school years were over he continued his lessons in music with Professor Richards, then placed himself under the instruction of Professor Nahan Franko, of New York City. In 1890 he returned to New London, where he has for the past thirty years been a teacher of violin music, his reputation exceedingly high both as performer and teacher.

During those years Mr. Keyes has played with different orchestras in both Connecticut and Rhode Island, and through the medium of Keyes Orchestra, his own organization, has furnished music for many of the great social and public events of New London and vicinity. He has taught and directed many school orchestras both at the Nathan Hale School and at Bulkeley High School in New London. His personal talent as a musical director is not more marked than his natural ability to instruct and really teach others his wonderful mastery of the violin. He is one of the oldest and best vioiln teachers in the State, and for several years has confined his classes to New London. He is not only a musician of note, but a man highly esteemed for his personal qualities. He is a member of the National Association of Musicians, and ranks with the leaders of his profession.

JOHN DOLLBAUM—Since the inception of his business career, John Dollbaum has been identified with the velvet industry, and since 1906 has been assistant superintendent of the American Velvet Company, Stonington, Connecticut. John Dollbaum was born May 1, 1864, in Crefeld-Mischeln, Germany, the son of the late August and Anna (Busch) Dollbaum. August Dollbaum was in the silk and velvet industries throughout his entire lifetime, being overseer in various shops of Germany until his death in 1897.

John Dollbaum obtained his elementary education in the public schools of his native place, after which he entered a trade school in Crefeld, where he devoted himself to the study of the textile industry, and later entered a commercial school. Upon completing the prescribed course at this latter school, he became designer in a velvet mill in Crefeld, subsequently becoming superintendent of this mill. His many efforts toward betterment of the mill equipment led to his inventing and building the Velour Carpet Loom, on which double fancy carpets of any size can be woven. This brought him the "Médaille D'argent" at the World Exhibition in Paris in 1900. Patents were granted in all industrial countries. He remained in Germany until 1906, when he set sail for this country, and in the fall of this same year came to Stonington, Connecticut, and accepted the position of assistant superintendent of the American Velvet Company here, in which he still continues. He is an able organizer, and being keenly alert to every changing phase of the business he is an active factor in its development and growth. In politics Mr. Dollbaum is a Republican, and in his religious views he is a Roman Catholic and attends the church of that denomination in Stonington. He affiliates with Nina Council, No. 43, Knights of Columbus.

On June 30, 1890, John Dollbaum was united in marriage with Adelhaide Isabelle Hymmen. Mr. and Mrs. Dollbaum are the parents of six children: 1. John A., a director in the Compagnie Internationale de Machines Agricoles, of France, who at the outbreak of the World War went to Germany with Frederick J. to settle some business matters for his father, was called to service in the German army, and in 1916 was killed in an airplane accident. 2. Anna A., who married Daniel H. Gleason, a mechanical engineer of New York City. 3. Ernest T., served in the signal corps of the United States Army and was at Camp Devens when the Armistice was signed. 4. Frederick J., who was detained in Germany during the war, and upon his return became a student in Cornell University. 5. Henry J., served with the United States army in France during the World War; since 1920 he is a student at Cornell. 6. Paul M., while a sophomore at the Massachusetts Institute of Technology of Cambridge, and a member of the S. A. T. C. in 1918, died from influenza.

EDWARD B. HOLTON—John Holton, father of Edward B. Holton, of Groton, Connecticut, was born in Ireland, but when a child was brought to Canada where he was educated and learned the ship carpenter's trade. In 1870 he came to the United States, finding employment at this trade in the ship yard in Mystic, Connecticut. Later he moved with his family to Groton, Connecticut, and died December 12, 1916. His widow, Hannah Holton, survives him and is a resident of Groton. They were the parents of twelve children, Edward B. Holton being ninth in order of birth.

Edward B. Holton was born in Groton, Connecticut, August 24, 1882, and there completed public school courses of study. Later he finished a course at New London Business College, and for one year afterward was associated with J. F. Bailey, a meat dealer. In 1913 he bought out a general market in Groton and has since devoted himself to its management. In religious faith Mr. Holton is a Roman Catholic, and in politics a Republican. He married, August 2, 1911, Anna McGill, daughter of Thomas and Ruth (Stanley) McGill, of New York.

CORNELIUS P. BARRY—Robert Barry, father of Cornelius P. Barry, came from his native County Cork, Ireland, to the United States when a young man, and located in New London, Connecticut. There he became a prosperous commission merchant, and for twenty years continued in that business. He then retired to a well-earned life of contentment and ease, and still resides in New London. He married Johanna Collins, and to them ten children were born, Cornelius P. their fifth child.

Cornelius P. Barry was born in New London, Connecticut, March 5, 1888, and there educated in the parochial school, finishing in Bulkeley High School, whence he was graduated, class of 1905. From 1905 until 1913 he was associated with his father's commission business, succeeding his father, Robert Barry, after the latter's retirement. In 1913 he entered the United States postal service as carrier in the New London Post Office, and four years later (1917), was appointed secretary of the Board of Civil Service Commissioners of New London. He served the board until 1919, then was appointed superintendent of the Post Office in Groton, Connecticut, his present position. He is a member of the Roman Catholic Church, and of Seaside Council, Knights of Columbus.

Mr. Barry married, July 6, 1910, Annie Maloney, of New London, daughter of John and Mary (Boggan) Maloney, her parents born in Ireland. Mr. and Mrs. Cornelius P. Barry are the parents of three children: Robert J., Mary A., Lauretta E.

The family home is No. 20 Pleasant street, New London, Connecticut.

RALPH H. KOELB, of Pawcatuck, Connecticut, in the town of Stonington, is one of the fine group of younger men whose business ability and progressive endeavors are carrying this section forward in the march of events. Mr. Koelb was born in the town of Stonington, Connecticut, October 7, 1897, a son of Carl A. Koelb, whose life is reviewed elsewhere in this work.

Gaining his early education in the public schools, he thereafter attended Cushing Academy, then completed his studies at Dartmouth College. Returning to Stonington, he became paymaster for the Ship Construction & Trading Company, one of the principal corporations of Stonington. But he was scarcely settled in the routine of this position before the great call of Humanity reached the young men of America, and he enlisted in the Naval Reserves, serving during the World War. Late in the year 1918 he returned to Stonington, locating in Pawcatuck, where he became associated with the Westerly Grain & Flour Company, in the capacity of manager. He is still with this company, and is ably handling the affairs connected with their wide and important business. Mr. Koelb is broadly interested outside his business connections. He is a member of Asylum Lodge, No. 57, Free and Accepted Masons, and his college fraternity is the Sigma Chi. Politically he is affiliated with the Republican party, and is taking a deep and constructive interest in the public questions of the day.

On July 28, 1919, Mr. Koelb married Gladys C. MacGowan, daughter of Dr. Philip T. and Elizabeth (Collins) MacGowan, of Mystic, Connecticut, and they have an infant son, Clayton T., born May 9, 1920. Mr. and Mrs. Koelb are members of Calvary Baptist Church, of Westerly, Rhode Island.

FRANK COXETER—A well known figure in the business life of Norwich, Connecticut, is Frank Coxeter, one of the leading custom tailors of the city.

George Coxeter, Mr. Coxeter's father, was born in Hampshire, England, and there he received a practical education in the National schools. After leaving school he learned the trade of tailor. In 1870 he came to this country and located in New York City, where he followed his trade for three years, then went to Harrisburg, Pennsylvania, where he still worked at his trade. In 1882 he came to New Haven, Connecticut, and there worked as tailor until his death in 1915. He married Elizabeth Tuson, who was born in Newbury, England, and died in New Haven, in 1900. They were the parents of nine children, of which Mr. Coxeter of Norwich is the fourth.

Frank Coxeter was born on the Isle of Wight, England, on February 18, 1864. When he became of an age to attend school the family resided in Harrisburg, and there the boy's education was begun. Upon the removal of the family to New Haven, he continued his education in the public schools of that city, then served an apprenticeship as tailor. He followed this trade in New Haven until 1907, when he came to Norwich and entered the employ of the N. Johnson Company as cutter. Two years later he bought out the Johnson firm, and continued the business as a merchant tailor under his own name. Mr. Coxeter is remarkably adept in his line, and his success has been definite, and will assuredly be permanent.

Mr. Coxeter keeps in touch with public progress, and may well be called a representative citizen. He is a Republican by political choice, and is a member of the Chamber of Commerce. He is a positive and frankly outspoken disciple of Christian Science. He was one of the organizers of the Christian Science Society of Norwich, and has taken an active interest in this society since its origination and during 1921 served as the First Reader of the society.

Mr. Coxeter married, on June 23, 1908, Ada Crandall, of Norwich.

CHARLES JENNINGS TWIST, agent for the Shetucket Mills, of Norwich, Connecticut, is a young man of Norwich birth, reared in that city, and fitted for his present position by broad experience and special training.

Charles S. Twist, father of Charles J. Twist, was also born in Norwich, and received his education in the public schools of the city. He learned the trade of tinsmith, and for the past fifty-two years has followed the same line of work for the J. P. Barstow Company, of this city, with whom he is still (1921) connected. He married Minnie E. Clark, also of Norwich, and they are the parents of two children: Charles J.; and Elva C., who died in November, 1918.

Charles Jennings Twist was born on June 28, 1881. He received his early education in the public schools of Norwich, then entered the Norwich Commercial School and took a business course. He then entered on his business career and for a time was electrical operator at the Massachusetts Cotton Mills, at Lowell, Massachusetts. He next came to Norwich, as master mechanic for the Shetucket Company, who operate immense cotton mills in this city. The death of Robert A. Smith, former agent of this company, left that office vacant, and Mr. Twist was placed in charge. This was in 1918, and the young man's experience and executive ability made him the right man in the right place. He continues in charge of this important branch of the company's activities.

Mr. Twist is a man of broad interests. He is a Republican by political affiliation. He is a member of the Masonic order, affiliating with Somerset Lodge, No. 34, Ancient Free and Accepted Masons; Franklin Chapter, No. 4, Royal Arch Masons; Franklin Council, No. 3, Royal and Select Masters; Columbian Commandery, No. 4, Knights Templar; all Scottish Rite bodies, of the thirty-second degree; and Sphinx Temple, Ancient Arabic Order Nobles of the Mystic Shrine, of Hartford, Connecticut.

Mr. Twist married, on April 26, 1905, Carrie V. Sherman, daughter of John E. and Sarah E. (McCall) Sherman, of Norwich. They are members of the United Congregational Church.

JAMES HENRY SHEA, Sr. — Well-known among the successful business men of Jewett City, Connecticut, is James H. Shea, owner and manager of a large coal, ice and lumber business here. He was born in Griswold, Connecticut, August 14, 1873, the son of Timothy and Julia (Doyle) Shea, both natives of Ireland. Timothy Shea came to this country when a young man, locating in Plainfield, Connecticut, where he has since been engaged in general farming and dairying. Mrs. Shea, the devoted wife and mother, passed away in February, 1907. To Mr. and Mrs. Shea were born eleven children, James Henry, of further mention, being the sixth child.

After receiving his education in the public schools of Plainfield, Connecticut, James H. Shea worked on his father's farm until 1894, when he came to Jewett City and in company with his brother, Michael E., established, under the name of Shea Brothers, the ice, coal and lumber business in which they have continued to the present time. Mr. Shea is also interested in general farming.

In everything pertaining to the welfare of the community, Mr. Shea's interest is deep and sincere, and no project, which in his judgment tends to further that end, lacks his coöperation and support. He is an active member of the Democratic party, and served as first selectman from 1908 until 1917. He was also constable for many years. He is affiliated with the Knights of Columbus, holding membership in the White Cross Council of Norwich, Connecticut. In religion he is a Roman Catholic, and no good work done in the name of charity or religion appeals to him in vain, for he brings to bear in his work of this character the same discrimination and thoroughness which is manifest in his business life.

On January 2, 1907, James H. Shea was united in marriage with Abbie E. Doyle, daughter of Jeremiah and Mary (Sullivan) Doyle, of Plainfield, Connecticut. Mr. and Mrs. Shea are the parents of eight children: Arthur D., Anna E., Claire J., Margaret M., Abbie E., Doris J., James H., Jr., and Alice M.

THOMAS WILSON REYNOLDS—For more than a quarter of a century Mr. Reynolds has been manager for the Pawcatuck branch of the Standard Oil Company, the first and yet the only manager, his term of service in that capacity at that point beginning February 13, 1893. His previous experience had been in railroad employ, in office and on trains. He is a son of William Franklyn and Clarissa (Wilcox) Reynolds, both of New London ancient and honorable families.

William Franklyn Reynolds was born in Stonington, Connecticut, and after completing public school study, he became a blacksmith's apprentice, serving his full time. Later he became a farmer and truckman, a business which he followed in Stonington until his death, February 26, 1882. His wife, Clarissa (Wilcox) Reynolds, died in 1850, and he married (second) Percy Ann Weaver, of Stonington.

Thomas Wilson Reynolds, son of William Franklyn Reynolds and his first wife, Clarissa (Wilcox) Reynolds, was born in Stonington, Connecticut, August 31, 1854, and there was educated in the public schools. After leaving school he was a farm worker in various places, but in 1875, at the age of twenty-one, he entered the employ of the New York, Boston & Providence Railroad Company as brakeman, and for twelve years he continued in the train of the company. In 1887 he was transferred to the freight department as agent at the Westerly Station, and there continued for six years more, making his railway service a perioa of eighteen years. On February 13, 1893, he was appointed the first manager of the Standard Oil Company in Pawcatuck, Connecticut, a position he has held continuously during the twenty-eight years which have since elapsed. Mr. Reynolds is a Republican in politics, a member of the First Baptist Church, of Westerly, and of the Royal Arcanum, of Stonington.

In Stonington, Connecticut, Mr. Reynolds married, August 24, 1893, Mary Elizabeth Cheseboro, born in Brooklyn, New York, daughter of Enoch and Margaret Cheseboro. Mrs. Reynolds was reared in Stonington, Connecticut. The Cheseboro family is one of the oldest families in Stonington, Connecticut.

WILLIAM CHARLES HARRISON is one of those men who started at the bottom of the ladder, and by means of his own effort has made his way to the position which he now holds in the manufacturing circles of this county.

William Charles Harrison was born in Preston, England, October 9, 1867, the son of Charles and Elizabeth Ellen (Thompson) Harrison. When he was but six years of age his parents brought him to this country, to New Bedford, Massachusetts, where he continued his education, previously started in England. His father died when William was but nine years of age. This necessitated the lad seeking work at an early age, so when he was but fourteen years of age, the business of life began for him. He secured employment in the cotton mills of New Bedford, where he remained for a time, later going to Ware, Massachusetts, as assistant percher in the George Gilbert mills. From this time until 1899 he worked in various mills throughout New England, and then came to Hanover, where he still continued to be identified with manufacturing, and was subsequently given the position of overseer of the Dressing Department, in which position he still continues, fulfilling to the letter every trust committed to him.

Mr. Harrison married Alice Mabel Nickols; she was born in Ware, Massachusetts, the daughter of Edward

Rev. Ulderic O. Bellerose

and Sarah Nickols. Mr. and Mrs. Harrison are the parents of three children: Harlan Mellin, born November 22, 1892; William Charles, Jr., born September 10, 1896; Dorothy May, born October 28, 1901.

The career of William Charles Harrison has been devoted entirely to his work. He has never taken any active part in public affairs but has always interested himself in everything pertaining to the welfare of Hanover which has been his home for so many years. He was a Republican in politics, attended and supported the Congregational Church of Hanover, of which his family are members and of which he is trustee.

REV. ULDERIC OSCAR BELLEROSE—It is peculiarly gratifying to the biographer to record the life history of a man who has devoted his life to the service of the church. Standing, indeed, in the relation of a father to the people under his care, the world is better and the lives of men and women richer for his ministrations. Rev. Ulderic O. Bellerose, pastor of Sacred Heart Church, of Taftville, Connecticut, is deeply beloved and reverenced by the people of the church, and has won the respect of all who know him, regardless of creed.

Father Bellerose is a son of Frederick and Ceserie (Andair) Bellerose, both his parents having been born at St. Cesaire, Province of Quebec, Canada. In 1865 they came to the United States, and located at Grosvenor-Dale, Connecticut, where Mr. Bellerose soon established himself as a general blacksmith, becoming successful in his chosen line, and is still a resident of that town, now retired. Eight children were born of this marriage, Ulderic Oscar the first child.

Father Bellerose was born in North Grosvenor Dale, on December 7, 1873. He received his early education in the parochial schools of that town, then for his classical education went to the College of St. Hyacinthe, at St. Hyacinthe, Province of Quebec, Canada, from which institution he was graduated in January, 1893, with the degree of Bachelor of Letters. He studied philosophy from 1893 to 1895 at St. John's Seminary, in Boston, Massachusetts. Thereafter, he entered St. Mary's Seminary, at Baltimore, Maryland, where he was ordained a priest of the Roman Catholic church, on June 14, 1898, with the degree of S. T. B.

In that same year Father Bellerose was appointed assistant pastor of St. Patrick's Church, in Norwich. He was most devoted in his work in this parish, and won the deepest regard of the people. After four years he was appointed assistant pastor of the Sacred Heart Church in Taftville, again serving most acceptably, and giving great promise of the future. In 1906 he was appointed pastor of the church at Wauregan, where he remained until 1910, and here, in 1908, built a parochial school. In 1910 he was appointed to the Church of St. Mary, in Baltic, where he served for four years, building, in 1912, a new church for that parish.

In 1915, Father Bellerose was appointed pastor of Sacred Heart Church, at Taftville, and the parish is still under his charge. Here he built a new church, and since his appointment to this field, Father Bellerose has built up the church both materially and spiritually. His assiduous and unselfish devotion to duty is a noble example, and the people of the church have learned to love and honor him. He has led the people through the trying period of the World War, comforting, encouraging and succoring, and has been most active in leading the many movements which lent aid to the boys overseas. He is always cognizant of his responsibility to the community-at-large, and his most earnest endeavor is to make his church a living force for progress.

Father Bellerose is an influential member of White Cross Council, No. 39, Knights of Columbus, of Norwich, and is a fourth degree knight in this order. He is also a member of St. Mary's Alumnus, of Baltimore.

ALBERT ANDREW HALEY, owner and manager of an extensive trucking business in Groton, Connecticut, is a native of this place, and since reaching young manhood has identified himself with everything pertaining to the welfare and advancement of the community.

Andrew Haley, father of Albert Andrew Haley, was born in New York City, and when but a child was brought by his parents to Groton, Connecticut. Here he obtained his education, and after finishing his studies, apprenticed himself to the printer's trade, later giving this up to follow agricultural pursuits, in which he continued until his retirement from active business life. He now lives retired with his son, Albert A. Mr. Haley married Josephine P. Eggleston, a native of Groton; she died in 1915. To Mr. and Mrs. Haley was born one child, Albert Andrew, mentioned below.

Albert Andrew Haley was born October 15, 1870, at Groton, Connecticut, and obtained his education in the public schools of his native place. When a young man he secured employment with the Mystic Woolen Company, at Old Mystic, Connecticut, and subsequently became overseer of the spinning department. Here he remained until 1900, when he purchased from Charles Briggs the latter's interest in a trucking business, and has conducted it successfully since that time. Together with this, Mr. Haley became owner and manager in 1910 of a general store at Old Mystic, which he bought from W. D. Beckwith, and also continues his interest in this particular line.

In politics, he is a Republican and is a staunch adherent to the principles and policies of this party. He is affiliated with Stonington Lodge, No. 26, Independent Order of Odd Fellows, of Mystic; and attends the Methodist church of Old Mystic.

On July 6, 1893, Albert Andrew Haley was united in marriage with Kate Mitchell, a native of Groton, and the daughter of William H. and Mary (Edwards) Mitchell.

ERNEST ORVIL RODIER—All honorable success is based upon a definite aim in life and the persistency of purpose which enables one to persevere in a given course regardless of obstacles, difficulties and discouragements. There are many self-made men in this country, and there is full praise here for the man who has started at the bottom and by means of his own efforts made his way to the top. New England has its share of such men, and to this list has been added the name of Ernest Orvil Rodier.

Ernest Orvil Rodier was born in Philadelphia, Pennsylvania, October 3, 1876, the son of Oliver and Anna (Hamilton) Rodier. His father, Oliver Rodier, was born in Montreal, and obtained his education in the public schools there. He was a painter of scenery until his death, which occurred at Philadelphia, in 1877. His mother was a native of Philadelphia, and died there, in 1892.

The education of Ernest Orvil Rodier was obtained in the public schools of Philadelphia, after which he was employed by several different companies, among them the T. W. Clarke, Myers & Taylor Company, and the Otto C. Muller Company. In 1902 he became an agent for the Prudential Life Insurance Company, later being promoted to the position of assistant superintendent of the Philadelphia office. In 1909 he was transferred to Portsmouth, New Hampshire, as superintendent, in the capacity of agency organizer, and was there until 1910, when he came to Norwich, Connecticut, and has continued here to the present time as district superintendent.

In politics, Mr. Rodier is a Republican. He is president of the Building and Loan Association of Norwich, and a member of the Connecticut Underwriters. He is a member of the Chamber of Commerce, a past vice-president of same. He is also prominent in Masonic circles, and is a member of Richard Vaux Lodge, Free and Accepted Masons, of Philadelphia, Pennsylvania; Franklin Chapter, Royal Arch Masons, of Norwich; Franklin Council, Royal and Select Masters, of Norwich; Columbia Commandery, Knights Templar; and is a thirty-second degree member of the Connecticut Consistory, Ancient Accepted Scottish Rite. Mr. Rodier is also a member of Girard Court, Foresters of America, of Philadelphia, Pennsylvania; a member of the Patriotic Sons of America, of Philadelphia; and in religious faith a member of Trinity Methodist Episcopal Church of Norwich, Connecticut.

Mr. Rodier married, October 7, 1903, Emma Raybold, born November 22, 1875, at Philadelphia, Pennsylvania, the daughter of James Raybold, of Philadelphia, and Isabel (Dougherty) Raybold, who was born in England, but whose family moved to Ireland when she was a child. Mr. and Mrs. Rodier are the parents of two children: Isabel H., and Anna P., both children born in Philadelphia.

CHARLES WILBUR GILDERSLEEVE—Prominent in one of the most practical of the mercantile lines in Mystic, Connecticut, Charles Wilbur Gildersleeve is also well known in fraternal circles.

Mr. Gildersleeve is a son of Smith M. and Nina (Hunt) Gildersleeve. Smith M. Gildersleeve was born in Fireplace, Long Island, where he received part of his schooling in the public schools, completing his education in Brooklyn, New York. For many years, as a young man, he worked as traveling salesman, later entering the grocery business in Noank, in the town of Groton, Connecticut. About 1905 he sold the grocery business and worked as a boat builder, but is now living retired at Noank. Smith M. and Nina (Hunt) Gildersleeve were the parents of two children: Charles W., of whom further; and George E., who died about 1910.

Charles Wilbur Gildersleeve was born in Brooklyn, New York, on January 28, 1883. He received his education in Brooklyn, New York, and in Noank, New London county, Connecticut. Upon the completion of his studies, the young man entered the employ of the Brainerd & Armstrong Company, of New London. There he continued as clerk in the offices until the year 1904. He then became connected with the grain business of the Arnold Rudd Grain Company, of which Ernest E. Rogers, of New London, was president. Four years later, in 1908, Mr. Gildersleeve came to Mystic to fill the position of manager of the Mystic Grain Company. His work in this capacity has been most successful, and he is still at the head of this business.

Mr. Gildersleeve is a member of Charity and Relief Lodge, No. 72, Free and Accepted Masons, of Mystic; a member of Stonington Lodge, No. 26, Independent Order of Odd Fellows, in which order he is past noble grand; and a member of Pequot Camp, Modern Woodmen of America, of Mystic. Politically, he upholds the principles of the Republican party.

In April, 1907, Mr. Gildersleeve married Alice Brown, of Noank, daughter of Clarence and Armetta (Moshier) Brown, of Noank. Mr. and Mrs. Gildersleeve have two sons: Ernest W., and Charles E., both born in Mystic, Connecticut. The family are members of the Baptist church.

AGNES (BUTLER) PARK was born in Coos county, Oregon, the daughter of Parker and Mary (Skidmore) Butler. Parker Butler was educated in the public schools of his native place, and upon reaching manhood, became interested in coastwise shipping on the Pacific coast, which occupation he followed throughout his entire lifetime. Captain of a ship for years, he was lost at sea in the Pacific Ocean, in 1872. His wife died in 1901, in Marshfield, Oregon. Mr. and Mrs. Butler were the parents of five children, of which number is Agnes, mentioned below.

The preliminary portion of Mrs. Park's education was obtained in the public schools of East Greenwich, Rhode Island, after which she entered the East Greenwich Academy, subsequently matriculating at Boston University, from which institution she was graduated in 1895 with the degree of Bachelor of Arts. After graduation she became a teacher in Burrillville, Rhode Island, and made her home in Mystic, Connecticut. In 1900 she established herself in business by buying out the Mystic Variety Shop, founded by I. D. Miner in 1897. The venture proved successful, and her business has consistently grown until she has reached her present position, which has placed her among the leading business women of the county. Since coming to this community Mrs. Park has taken a keen interest in public affairs, devoting herself to all measures calculated to benefit the community and promote its rapid and substantial advancement. In politics she is a Republican, and in her religious affiliations she is a Methodist.

On June 15, 1901, she married Amos Park, and to them has been born one child, Ripley B., born in Mystic, Connecticut, January 15, 1903.

SAMUEL EDWARD STEWART, JR.—Among the many young soldiers who returned from serving their country in France during the World War is Samuel Edward Stewart, Jr., who in company with George A. Feeney, a sketch of whom follows, entered into a partnership, opening the Arcade Market, in Stonington, Connecticut, which venture has proved to be a very successful one.

Samuel Edward Stewart, Jr., is the son of Samuel Edward, Sr., and Matilda J. (Mabbitt) Stewart. The elder Mr. Stewart was born in Lancaster, Pennsylvania, where he acquired his education in the public schools and learned the trade of house painter. When twenty-one years of age he came to Mystic, where he has since resided and where he has been employed at his trade. Mrs. Matilda J. Mabbitt) Stewart is a native of Westerly, Rhode Island. She was the mother of four children: May, who died in infancy; Leo, who also died in infancy; Sarah, who is living at home; and Samuel Edward, Jr., of whom further.

Born in Mystic, Connecticut, May 26, 1895, Samuel Edward Stewart, Jr., attended the public school an later the Cushing Academy, and after leaving the latter institution, went into the office of P. F. Cassidy, an attorney of Woonsocket, Rhode Island, where he studied law.

While engaged in this pursuit, the United States entered into the World War, and Mr. Stewart enlisted in the service of his country, January 6, 1917, at Boston, Massachusetts. He was assigned for duty in the Medical Corps, in Ambulance Company No. 28, and was sent with the American Expeditionary Forces to France, where for seventeen months he was engaged in the famous battles of Chateau-Thierry (where he was gassed), St. Mihiel, and also in the various drives on Argonne Forest. He was sergeant of detail, first aid, Company C, of the 47th Infantry, when the great Krupp gun, "Big Bertha," that shelled Paris, was captured. Returning to the United States, he was sent to Camp Dix, New Jersey, where he was honorably discharged, with the rank of sergeant, in August, 1919. In November, 1920, Mr. Stewart, in association with Mr. Feeney, entered into the market business previously referred to.

While not active in politics, Mr. Stewart has joined the ranks of the Republican party. He is also affiliated with Charity and Relief Lodge, No. 72, Free and Accepted Masons, of Mystic; Benevolence Chapter, Royal Arch Masons, of Mystic; Mystic Council, Royal and Select Masters, of Mystic; Palestine Commandery, No. 6, Knights Templar, of New London; and Pyramid Temple, Ancient Arabic Order Nobles of the Mystic Shrine, of Bridgeport, Connecticut. Mr. Stewart is a member of the Protestant Episcopal church of Mystic.

GEORGE A. FEENEY—One of the partners in the Arcade Meat Market of Stonington, Connecticut, is George A. Feeney. Although his business is located there, his residence is in Mystic, where he has lived for most of the years of his life.

The parents of George A. Feeney were both natives of Ireland. His father, Thomas Feeney, was born in County Galway, where he was educated in the National schools. When a young man he came to the United States and located in Pawcatuck, Connecticut, taking up the trade of moulder, working at it all his life. He now resides at Mystic. His wife, Bridget Agnes Casey, was born in Illinois; her death occurred in Mystic, in 1917. They had a family of seven children: 1. Annie, who resides at home. 2. George A., of whom further. 3. Edward, now living at home; he was engaged in active service during the late World War with the American Expeditionary Forces, 68th Regiment, Coast Artillery Corps, having spent eighteen months in France. 4. Francis S., living at home, who also was in the American Expeditionary Forces, serving in Company D, 77th Division. This young soldier was a member of the famous Lost Battalion. 5. Thomas, deceased. 6. Joseph. 7. Mary, both living at home.

The second member of this family, George A. Feeney, was born in Pawcatuck, Connecticut, July 16, 1892. He was educated in the public schools of Mystic, and after leaving school was employed by B. D. Williams, in Mystic, as a clerk, remaining with Mr. Williams for eleven years, when he left, in 1917, to become one of the workers in the shipyard at Groton, Connecticut, and in the Groton Iron Works, where he remained until 1919. At that time, Samuel Edward Stewart, Jr., of Mystic, a sketch of whom precedes this, returned from service in the American army in France, and Mr. Feeney and Mr. Stewart entered into partnership and established a meat market in Stonington, known as the Arcade Market, where they are now located.

In politics, Mr. Feeney is a Democrat; in his religious affiliation he is a member of the Roman Catholic church of Mystic, his people also being attendants there.

PETER HAMMACHER—A prominent figure in the business life of Mystic, Connecticut, is Peter Hammacher, owner of a large general store here. Since coming to this community in 1909, Mr. Hammacher has always taken an interest in everything pertaining to the betterment of civic conditions and the advancement of the business life of the place.

Henry Hammacher, father of Peter Hammacher, was born at Rhyland, Germany, and died in Stonington, Connecticut, in 1902. He obtained his education in the public schools of his native place, and then went to work in the winding department of a velvet mill there until 1892, when he came to this country with his family and located in Astoria, New York, where he became identified with the American Velvet Company. In 1896 this company started a velvet mill at Stonington, and Mr. Hammacher, being a skilled mechanic, helped greatly in the new mill, where he was located until his death. He married Elizabeth Schören, who died in Germany, in 1883.

Peter Hammacher, third child of Henry and Elizabeth (Schören) Hammacher, was born at Rhyland, Germany, June 12, 1877, and attended the public schools of his native place. In 1899 he came to this country and located in Stonington, where he became a weaver with the American Velvet Company. Ten years later he came to Mystic and established himself in business under the name of P. Hammacher & Company, in which he has continued successfully up to the present time.

A Republican in politics, Mr. Hammacher gives to the affairs of the organization the interest demanded of every good citizen, but has never held public office. He affiliates with Mystic Lodge, No. 26, Independent Order of Odd Fellows; he attends the Christian Science church of Mystic.

On February 4, 1901, Peter Hammacher was united in marriage with Elizabeth Muller, a native of Germany. Mr. and Mrs. Hammacher are the parents of one child, Henry P., born at Stonington, Connecticut, January 21, 1902, and now associated in business with his father.

In connection with his general store, Mr. Hammacher operates a large and very complete confectionery store, under the name of the Riverside Ice Cream Parlor.

REV. JAMES EDWARD O'BRIEN—Dedicating his life to the service of the Roman Catholic church, James Edward O'Brien in his early manhood entered the priesthood when twenty-seven years old and has devoted himself to the many demands of his calling.

Born in Branford, Connecticut, October 14, 1870, James Edward OBrien is the son of Daniel OBrien, a native of County Cork, Ireland, and his wife, Catherine (O'Donnell) O'Brien, also born in County Cork. They came to the United States when young and located in Branford, Connecticut, where they have continued to make their home ever since.

The education of their son, James Edward, was acquired in the public school and high school of Branford, graduating from the latter in the class of 1890. During the fall of that same year the young man became a student at St. Mary's Seminary, in Emmitsburg, Maryland, from which he graduated in 1894, with the degree of A. M. Entering upon his preparation for the church, James Edward O'Brien was ordained a priest by Cardinal Gibbons at the Roman Catholic Cathedral of Baltimore, Maryland, in 1898.

Being assigned to the Church of the Immaculate Conception at Waterbury, Connecticut, as assistant priest, Rev. Father O'Brien entered upon his duties there in the same year, continuing as assistant until July, 1914. Upon that date he was advanced to the office of Pastor at Stonington, Connecticut, in St. Mary's Church. Rev. Father O'Brien is still engaged in his work here at the present time (1921).

EDGAR CALVIN STODDARD—During an eventful life of frequent change, Mr. Stoddard spent two years at the Crocker House, New London's hotel landmark, then under the management of A. T. Hale. He has been engaged in many fields of activity, and is a veteran in theatrical work, having been twenty years in the business, a line to which he has recently returned, his present engagement being as assistant manager of the Crown Theatre, in New London. He is a son of James B. and Susan M. (Barnes-Clark) Stoddard, both of Connecticut birth, his father dying in 1900, aged sixty-eight, his mother, daughter of Samuel D. Barnes, who still survives her husband, is in her eightieth year, a resident of Waterford, Connecticut. Mrs. Stoddard was a widow with two children when married to Mr. Stoddard, her first husband being Horatio Clark, a seafaring man, who left two daughters.

Edgar Calvin Stoddard was born in New London, Connecticut, May 5, 1868, and there was educated. He was variously employed until 1886, when he began studying veterinary surgery under a practical teacher, and continued until he was badly injured by a horse he was treating. He then returned to the hotel business, and for seven years was connected with the Crocker House, in New London, during the management of F. E. Parker. He was then for twenty years engaged in theatrical work, but after the death of his wife, in July, 1918, he abandoned the theatre for some time, but since June 20, 1920, he has been manager of the Crown Theatre. He is a musician of great ability, and for seventeen years was president and official of the Musicians' Association.

Mr. Stoddard is a member of Brainard Lodge, No. 102, Free and Accepted Masons; New London Lodge, No. 360, Benevolent and Protective Order of Elks; Jibboom Club, No. 1; and of the Konomoc Hose Company.

Mr. Stoddard married (first), January 1, 1889, Sarah Frances Ashcroft, born in Waterford, in 1874, died in July, 1918, and is buried in Waterford, Connecticut. She was the daughter of John Roe and Mary (Chapman) Ashcroft, of Waterford. Mr. Stoddard married (second) Jessica Stuart McLean, born in England.

WILLIAM FRANCIS BAILEY—Among the comparatively recent additions to the list of automobile dealers in Norwich, Connecticut, the name of William Francis Bailey stands out prominently.

Mr. Bailey is a member of an old Connecticut family, and his father, Jabez H. Bailey, was born in the town of Bozrah. There he conducted a farm until 1893, when he removed his family to Yantic, Connecticut, where he still resides. He is now a mail carrier on a rural free delivery route. He married Fannie E. Spicer, and they have three sons: Albert J., who is married and lives in Yantic; William Francis, of whom more extended mention follows; and Bertram B., who is married and lives in Waterbury, Connecticut.

William Francis Bailey received his primary education in the public schools of Bozrah, where he was born, November 6, 1885. He was eight years of age when his parents removed to Yantic, and his education was continued in the public schools of that town, then completed by a course at the Norwich Free Academy, where he studied for three years. In 1906 he went to Norwich, where he conducted a livery stable. He is still in this line of business, but in 1919 branched out and established a thoroughly up-to-the-minute garage, one of the finest in the city. He handles a complete line of automobile supplies, and the Cole Eight car.

Mr. Bailey is a member of Shetucket Lodge, Independent Order of Odd Fellows, of Norwich, Connecticut; the Benevolent and Protective Order of Elks, No. 430, of the same place, and of the Arcanum Club. He is a member of the Chamber of Commerce, and was a member of the Common Council for a term of two years. His political convictions place him in the ranks of the Republican party.

Mr. Bailey married, on December 19, 1911, Marion R. Parkinson, daughter of John Parkinson, of Norwich; she is a member of the Central Baptist Church, and Mr. Bailey attends and helps to support same.

OSCAR HERBERT MAIN, deputy sheriff of New London county, and county jailer at Norwich, Connecticut, was born in Ledyard, Connecticut, November 19, 1883, the son of Dwight W. and Frances Elizabeth (Johnson) Main. Dwight W. Main was born in Ledyard, and was educated in the district school of his native place. When a young man he worked with his father on the latter's farm, and for the past twenty-five years has owned and managed a large farm of his own in North Stonington, Connecticut, and also owns one at Preston, consisting of three hundred acres. To Mr. and Mrs. Main were born six children: Timothy D., a resident of North Stonington, Connecticut; Mary E., wife of Thomas Conlon; Oscar Herbert, the subject of this review; Alfred E., a resident of Ledyard; Irving B., a resident of Stonington; Edna, wife of Frank Brown, of Stonington, Connecticut, the latter now deceased.

Oscar Herbert Main was educated in the district schools of Preston, Connecticut, and then worked on his father's farm until 1902, when he removed to Hallville, Connecticut, and secured a position as clerk for Wood Brothers, who carry on a general store. Two years later he accepted the position of foreman with the Norwich & Westerly railroad, and one year later was appointed turnkey of the county jail at Norwich. In 1911 he was appointed to his present office, that of deputy jailer of the county jail, and March 15, 1920, was appointed deputy sheriff. In politics he is a Republican, and has always been deeply interested in the welfare of the community, giving his aid in every possible way to the promotion of the public good. He is a member of the Chamber of Commerce, and affiliates with the Benevolent and Protective Order of Elks, Norwich Lodge, No. 430.

On November 29, 1916, Mr. Main was united in marriage with Nettie M. Karoli, daughter of Philip and Isabella (Metzger) Karoli. Mr. and Mrs. Main are the parents of two children, both born in Norwich: Barbara Karoli, born September 17, 1917; Elizabeth Isabella, born February 14, 1920. Mr. and Mrs. Main attend the Episcopal church of Preston, Connecticut.

JOSEPH CHARLES PELOQUINN, one of the progressive and prosperous business men of Occum, where he is the owner of a general store and mercantile business, was born here, June 9, 1883. He is the son of Charles and Melvina (Perreault) Peloquinn. Charles Peloquinn was born in Canada, in 1853, and came to this country when a young man, locating in Occum, where he has continued to reside ever since. To Mr. and Mrs. Peloquinn were born three children: Joseph Charles, of further mention; Charles, a resident of Greenfield, Massachusetts; Fannie, who married Emile Blain, of Baltic, Connecticut.

The education of Joseph Charles Peloquinn was obtained in the schools of his native place, after which the business of life began for the boy. In 1917 he established himself in business, and has since been actively engaged in this enterprise, devoting the greater part of his time to its affairs. Being a good citizen, he has ever by his vote and influence been actively engaged in furthering interests which had for their aim the betterment of civic conditions, and no good work, done in the name of charity or religion, fails to receive his earnest support.

On September 11, 1903, Joseph Charles Peloquinn was united in marriage with Mary Ward, a native of Occum, Connecticut, her birth having occurred there, September 6, 1886. Mr. and Mrs. Peloquinn are the parents of three children: Ward Joseph, born in Waterbury, Connecticut; Marie Elizabeth, born in Sprague; and Irene, born in Sprague.

In politics Mr. Peloquinn is an Independent, and is a member of St. Joseph's Roman Catholic Church, of Occum, Connecticut.

FRANK JOHN FRANER—Having spent the early years of his life in Hungary, Frank John

Franer, when thirty-two years of age, came to the United States, and entering into the business life of the country, has made his home here ever since. His people remained in Hungary, where his father, Frank John Franer, Sr., was the owner of a flour mill. The elder Mr. Franer was born in Central Hungary, and died there, in 1893, at the age of seventy-six years. His wife, Elizabeth Franer, also was a native of Central Hungary, where she died, in 1899, when seventy-six years old. In addition to their son, Frank John, Jr., she and her husband were the parents of two daughters, Caroline Francesca, and Anna, and a son, William.

Frank John Franer, Jr., was born in Central Hungary, January 6, 1862, and in his boyhood was educated in the public schools there. In 1898 he came to America, landing in New York City, remaining there for some years, at first engaged in the hotel business and later holding several other positions for about three years. Crossing the Hudson river to New Jersey, Mr. Franer opened a small moving picture theatre, not far from New York City, being one of the pioneer exhibitors in that line. A few years later he made a trip to his old home in Central Hungary, but returned to the United States after spending a short time there. Buying a home in Brooklyn, New York, Mr. Franer remained in that city for a while. At that time he was the owner of a moving picture house on Jamaica avenue, Richmond Hill. Eventually he went to Waterbury, Connecticut, where he again became interested in the theatre business, buying the Star Theatre. In 1918 he came to New London, Connecticut, and purchased the Orpheum Theatre, changing its name to the Rialto (by which name it is now known) and is engaged in its management.

In Central Hungary, Frank John Franer married Mary Ebenspanger, a native of the same place. They have one child, born in New York City, February 18, 1903. They make their home in New London.

FREDERICK J. OSTMAN—After several years' experience in the wholesale and retail fish market business in connection with his father, Frederick J. Ostman is now sole proprietor of a most successful and up-to-date market in Stonington, Connecticut, supplying the trade for surrounding retail dealers.

The business was started many years ago by Frederick Ostman, a native of Germany, who, with his family, came to the United States when a child of twelve years. The boy had attended the public schools in Germany, and when his people arrived in this country he was sent to the public schools in New York City, where they had located. Having arrived at the age of nineteen years, Frederick Ostman came to Stonington and established the fish market previously referred to. He also entered into the fish catching occupation, which is a very thriving business of the population in the seaboard towns of that locality, Mr. Ostman becoming recognized as one of the big fishermen of his day. After a prosperous and successful life he died at Stonington, January 13, 1912. His wife, Elizabeth (Hammond) Ostman, was born in Stonington; she died in Westerly, Rhode Island, April 26, 1913. Mr. and Mrs. Ostman were the parents of nine children: Annie, deceased; John, who married Gertrude Patterson, and now resides in Stonington; Elizabeth, Jennie, Bessie, Frederick J.; William, who resides in Stonington; Lena, and Etta. The last seven live at home in Stonington.

Frederick J. Ostman, the sixth of this family group, was born in Stonington, February 19, 1883. Attending the public schools of his native town, he acquired a good education, and after graduating from the Stonington High School, in 1900, he became associated with his father in business. For a number of years they continued in this work, then, his father dying, the son took over the management of it and has so continued since 1912.

Interested in every local enterprise, Mr. Ostman is connected with most of the fraternal organizations in the locality; he is a member of Asylum Lodge, No. 57, Free and Accepted Masons, of Stonington; Benevolence Chapter, Mystic Council, Royal and Select Masters; and Palestine Commandery, No. 6, Knights Templar, of New London. He is also affiliated with the local lodge of the Red Men, of Westerly, Rhode Island. Mr. Ostman is interested in the fire department of Stonington, and was foreman for six years, 1911-17. He is a member of the Republican party.

On June 10, 1918, Frederick J. Ostman was united in marriage with Mabel Bates Dias, a resident of Hyde Park, Boston, Massachusetts. She is a daughter of John Q. and Lotty (Jordan) Dias, of Boston, Massachusetts. Mr. and Mrs. Ostman attend the Protestant Episcopal church of Stonington.

EUGENE P. HYDE—The name of Hyde is a familiar one in and around the town of Stonington, Connecticut, where several members of the family have been in business, both in the past and at the present time.

Eugene P. Hyde is the son of Albigence and Nancy L. (Pulcifer) Hyde, the father a native of Canterbury, Connecticut, where he was educated in the district school. As a youth he worked upon his father's farm, but after reaching manhood he went to Norwich and learned the trade of carriage-making and wagon-building. In the early fifties, Albigence Hyde moved to Stonington, where he started a carriage factory, which he conducted until the time of his death, in 1896, his wife surviving him for several years, her death occurring in 1905. They were the parents of five children: Albert, married, and resides in New Britain, Connecticut; Hannah, residing in Stonington; Theodore Wells, retired from business and lives in Stonington; Eugene P.; and Elida, who died in 1910.

The fourth child, Eugene P. Hyde, was born in Stonington, Connecticut, February 28, 1860. In his childhood days he attended the village school, and when older, completed his education with Professor

A. J. Foster, of Stonington. He afterward entered into business with his father, remaining in the carriage-making business with him until the latter's death, when he carried on the business alone, adding automobile repairing and painting to the carriage and wagon works, and has been very successful. He is now retired.

Having been a Democrat in politics all his life and a regular voter, Mr. Hyde has been quite active in the affairs of Stonington, having served on the Board of Burgesses for several years. He and his wife are members of the Baptist church, and are supporters of all its work.

Mr. Hyde has been married twice, his first wife being Hattie B. Taylor, the daughter of John A. Taylor, who died in 1900. Of this marriage two children were born: Frederick E., living at home; and Edmond P., who married Edith Pendleton, of New York City. Eugene P. Hyde married (second), September 26, 1904, Mary Pendleton, of Stonington, daughter of Captain B. F. Pendleton.

JOHN CARLSON, a native of Sweden, came to this country when very young, being only seventeen years old when he arrived in Boston, Massachusetts.

Born in Lurtenburg, Sweden, April 21, 1879, John Carlson was the son of Oscar and Louise (Anderson) Carlson, natives of Sweden. Oscar Carlson was educated in the National schools of Sweden, and learned the trade of carpenter, afterward becoming a contractor, in which business he was occupied during his entire life. He and his wife had four children, John being the third. Oscar Carlson died in 1905, his wife having died in 1891.

Acquiring his education in the National schools of Sweden, John Carlson left his home in 1896 and came to the United States. His first occupation was an instructor in auto driving for the Keith Automobile School of Boston, remaining as such for several years. For some time after leaving there, Mr. Carlson acted as chauffeur in various places, but in 1909 he came to Stonington, Connecticut, as chauffeur for Eugene Atwood, of that borough, by whom he was employed for a long period.

In 1920 Mr. Carlson entered into business for himself, opening a garage under the name of the Stonington Automobile Station, also being the agent for the Lexington automobiles. This is Mr. Carlson's business at the present time.

Since his residence in Stonington, Mr. Carlson has become greatly interested in Masonic matters, having joined Asylum Lodge, No. 57, Free and Accepted Masons, of Stonington; Benevolence Chapter, Royal Arch Masons, of Mystic; and Mystic Council, Royal and Select Masters. In politics Mr. Carlson is a Democrat.

On May 4, 1916, John Carlson was married to Elizabeth Fritz, a resident of Astoria, Long Island, New York. She is the daughter of Theodore and Tillie (Kirchoffer) Fritz. Mr. and Mrs. Carlson are members of and active in the Protestant Episcopal church of Stonington.

FRANK EUGENE ADAMS—The first settler in the town of Colchester, New London county, Connecticut, to bear this old and honored New England name was Benjamin Adams, who settled near Comstock's Bridge. He was a farmer, as his descendants have been in each generation down to the present. Benjamin Adams, the original Adams, in Colchester, had a son, Benjamin Williams Adams, born in Colchester, Connecticut, April 4, 1792, and died here in 1864. He married, August 24, 1824, Hannah Davis Warner, born May 18, 1802, at Chester, Connecticut, who died many years prior to his death. They were the parents of a son, Benjamin Adams, of whom further.

Benjamin Adams was born in Colchester, July 9, 1834, died there, in December, 1911. Benjamin Adams enlisted, in 1861, at Colchester, in Company A, Twenty-first Regiment, Connecticut Volunteer Infantry, and served throughout the entire four years of the Civil War. During the latter part of the war he was a member of the Twenty-first Regimental Band. After the war he returned to his farm and here continued until his final retirement. Mr. Adams was fife major of the famous Moodus Fife and Drum Corps, of Moodus, Connecticut, and during his ten years' membership, travelled with that organization all over the United States, giving concerts and exhibitions. He was also an instructor on the fife. He married Martha Clarissa Bercham, born November 15, 1837, and they were the parents of three children: John W., who died in infancy; Frank Eugene, of whom further; and Carrie Elizabeth, who married Clayton D. Barton, of East Hampton.

Frank Eugene Adams, son of Benjamin and Martha Clarissa (Bercham) Adams, was born at Westchester Center, town of Colchester, New London county, Connecticut, November 29, 1859. After finishing his education in the public schools he became his father's farm assistant and remained at the home farm until the age of thirty-eight. In 1897 he located in East Hampton, Connecticut, where he was employed in the N. N. Hill Brass Company until 1904, when he returned to the town of Colchester and bought the William H. Siems farm at Westchester Center, where he yet resides, a prosperous, general farmer and dairyman. His farm of two hundred acres is well located, modernly improved and equipped, its well-kept appearance indicating thrift and prosperity. He is a Republican in politics, and has served his town as assessor of taxes. He is a member of the Westchester Congregational Church, and of the church committee.

Mr. Adams married (first) in New York City, December 20, 1887, Anna May Bissell, daughter of Hezekiah and Mary J. (Cone) Bissell. Anna May Bissell was born at Hebron, Connecticut, and died in East Hampton, Connecticut, in 1902. Mr. and Mrs. Adams were the parents of three children: Frank Bissell, born October 18, 1888, died September 2, 1889; Clarence Bissell, born December 14,

1890, now station agent at Chestnut Hill for the New York, New Haven & Hartford Railroad; Benjamin Warner, born November 3, 1893, now with the New York, New Haven & Hartford Railroad, at New Haven, Connecticut. Mr. Adams married (second) at New York City, April 26, 1904, Mary Hyde, a native of East Hampton, Connecticut, a daughter of Andrew and Catherine (Wall) Hyde, of East Hampton. Mr. and Mrs. Adams have an adopted daughter, Florence, who was born in New London, Connecticut, September 30, 1910.

THOMAS EDWIN WHEELER—Long active in various branches of individual enterprise and public endeavor, Thomas Edwin Wheeler, of North Stonington, Connecticut, is a representative citizen of New London county.

Mr. Wheeler is a son of Noyes Denison and Susan S. (Wilbur) Wheeler. Noyes D. Wheeler was a native of Rhode Island, and during all his lifetime was a farmer in Hopkinton, in that State, where he died in 1902. His was was born in Richmond, Rhode Island, and died at Mystic, Connecticut. They were the parents of eleven children, of whom Thomas Edwin was the seventh.

Thomas Edwin Wheeler was born in Hopkinton, Rhode Island, August 23, 1858. Educated in the public schools of that town, he began life on the farm, working with his father for several years. For several years he taught school in Hopkinton, Charleston, Exeter, and Richmond, Rhode Island, and also taught in North Stonington and Voluntown, Connecticut. He resigned as school teacher while in North Stonington to accept a position as field manager for King Richardson & Company, publishers, of Springfield, Massachusetts. After three years thus engaged he returned and took up school teaching in Voluntown. Later he again taught in North Stonington and in 1898 he bought a farm on Pendleton Hill, and farmed there till 1918. Then he moved to his present farm at Laurel Glen, a neighboring town of North Stonington, where he still remains, conducting extensive operations in general farming.

In the public life of the town of North Stonington Mr. Wheeler's ability has long since been recognized, and the call of the people has placed responsibility upon his shoulders which closely involved the welfare of the community. In political affiliation a Republican, he was first elected tax collector, and served for a period of six years. He has served on the school committee of North Stonington for a period of three years, having been elected Chairman of the Committee during one year. He is a member of the Loyal Order of Moose, of Westerly, Rhode Island, and is a member of North Stonington Grange, No. 138. He is a devout member of the Baptist chuch.

In the borough of Stonington, on March 15, 1897, Mr. Wheeler married Caroline Hopkins, a native of Council Bluffs, Iowa, daughter of Samuel and —— (Bidmead) Hopkins, of that city, whose parents died when she was a child, and she was raised in Providence, Rhode Island. They have one son, Noyes Denison, who was born on the home farm, Pendleton Hill, North Stonington, was born July 29, 1898.

Noyes Denison Wheeler served during the World War in the Thirty-third Regiment, United States Engineers. He enlisted on March 16, 1918, saw considerable service in France, and was discharged on July 16, 1919.

He married, on September 21, 1920, Mary M. Riley, of Willimantic, Connecticut. They are the parents of a daughter, Katherine Alice, born July 10, 1921.

CHARLES R. STOLL, when twelve years of age, left his native Stuttgart, Germany, and came to the United States, locating in New London, Connecticut, in 1850. There he served an apprenticeship at the stonecutter's trade, finally becoming the owner of a granite quarry at New London, and conducted a profitable business until 1901, when he opened a coal yard in New London, which he conducted until his death in June, 1901. He was one of the leading business men of New London for many years and was highly esteemed. He married Louisa Kopp, who survived him until 1905. Mr. and Mrs. Stoll were the parents of two children: Charles R., of further mention; and Alfred W., who married Ida Jones, and resides in New London.

Charles R. Stoll, eldest son of Charles F. and Louisa (Kopp) Stoll, was born in New London, Connecticut, April 2, 1875, and was educated in the public schools, finishing at Bulkeley High School with the graduating class of 1892. The first years of his business life were spent with Swift & Company, of New London, as accountant, but later he became a salesman. In 1901 he succeeded to the coal business established by his father in New London, and since that year has devoted himself to its management. The business as now conducted embraces in addition to coal and wood a line of building and contractors' materials.

Mr. Stoll is a member of Union Lodge, No. 31, Free and Accepted Masons; Mohegan Lodge, No. 53, Independent Order of Odd Fellows; New London Lodge, No. 360, Benevolent and Protective Order of Elks; Modern Woodmen of America, Camp No. 7523; Komonoc Hose Company, No. 4; and the Chamber of Commerce, of New London. Mr. Stoll is a Democrat in politics. His religious connection is as a member of St. James' Protestant Episcopal Church.

ALBERT C. CARACAUSA—Born in New London, interested in every phase of public progress, and broadly active in welfare work for the Italian-American population, Albert C. Caracausa, of New London, is bearing a constructive part in meeting the public problems of the day.

Mr. Caracausa is a son of Anthony and Vincenza (Poma) Caracausa. Anthony Caracausa was born in Trapani, Italy, June 14, 1848, and received his education in the National schools of his native land.

Thos E Wheeler
Noyes D Wheeler

While still a young man he went to sea as seaman on a sailing vessel, and followed the sea during the greater part of his life. In 1875 he became half-owner and captain of the sailing ship "Emma," and visited many points of interest on his voyages, continuing to follow the sea until he came to the United States in 1891. During his nautical experience he was twice shipwrecked, and once robbed by sea bandits. The robbery occurred off the coast of Africa, Captain Caracausa losing 20,000 lire, and three members of the crew being killed.

Locating in New London with his family in 1891, Captain Caracausa entered the fruit business. But he only continued along this line for one year. His long experience had taught him much of value to others as well as to himself, and he saw a wider field, and his own ability to serve his fellowmen in that field. In 1894 he established a steamship agency, and doing business under his own name, handled foreign exchange, and met the many needs of his fellow countrymen. He carried on this business, which developed to an important interest, until his death, and then left it in the hands of his son. He died in New London, on May 1, 1916, at the age of sixty-eight years, leaving behind him many friends, and a name which all who knew him in his adopted country had learned to honor. His wife, who was also born in Trapani, Italy, survives him and still resides in New London. They were the parents of five children: Albert, who died in infancy; Fillippina, now the wife of Joseph Luppino, and a resident of Brooklyn, New York; Rosaria M., the wife of Prof. Francis Minutollo, of New York City; Emma, the wife of John Belbuno, of New London; and Albert C., whose name heads this review.

Albert C. Caracausa was born in New London, October 19, 1892, and is a son of Anthony and Vincenza (Poma) Caracausa. Receiving his early education in the public schols of this city, he was later graduated from the Bulkeley High School, in the class of 1913, then spent one year at the Rhode Island State College. Thereafter, Mr. Caracausa became associated with his father in business, and upon the death of the elder man, not long afterwards, the son took over the business, which he still carries on. He continues the activities which his father began, and to the steamship agency and foreign exchange he has added an important and constantly growing interest in real estate and insurance, and also has a sub-post office at his place of business at No. 697 Bank street.

Entirely outside of his business, Mr. Caracausa takes a deep interest in all Italians who come to our shores, and actively engages in individual and organized work for their Americanization, always standing ready to be of service to them and help them to their hoped-for success in the new country. He is president of the Italian-American Citizen's Club, of New London, and is an active member of the Chritospher Columbus Lodge of the Sons of Italy, of New London.

When the World War brought the young men of America to take up their responsibility to humanity, Mr. Caracausa enlisted in the United States Naval Reserve Force, and was made chief of the Naval Intelligence Bureau Station, at New London. He enlisted on April 4, 1918, and was discharged December 17, 1918.

Politically, Mr. Caracausa supports the Democratic party. Fraternally, he belongs to Lodge No. 360, Benevolent and Protective Order of Elks, of New London; to Seaside Council, No. 17, Knights of Columbus; and to Lodge No. 654, Improved Order of Red Men. He is a member of the Rotary Club of New London.

On June 2, 1919, Mr. Caracausa married L. Louise Chartier, of Willimantic, Connecticut, daughter of Nicholas and Octave (Bourque) Chartier, formerly of Montreal, Canada, now residents of Willimantic. Mr. and Mrs. Caracausa have one son, Anthony Vincent, born August 9, 1921.

CLARENCE W. THOMPSON—The father of our subject, Eugene W. Thompson, was born in Columbia, Tolland county, Connecticut, and there attended public school, and as a young man worked as a clerk, married, and later became a farmer. He married Hattie A. Post, and they were the parents of ten children, the ninth a son, Clarence W. Thompson, of further mention. Eugene W. Thompson died in New London, Connecticut, in 1891, his widow surviving him twenty-one years.

Clarence W. Thompson was born in Andover, Tolland county, Connecticut, October 21, 1886. He was educated in the public schools of New London, and early in life became interested in automobiles and their construction. He became an expert garage worker, and in different establishments became an expert in his line. In 1915 he started in business under his own name, opening a garage in New London, at No. 289 Bank street. He is agent for the Chevrolet and Columbia cars, and for the Indiana truck. His plant includes a well-equiipped service station and all necessary equipment.

Mr. Thompson is a Republican in politics, and during the years 1915 and 1918 was a member of the New London Board of Aldermen, representing the Fourth Ward. Mr. Thompson is a member of Union Lodge, No. 131, Free and Accepted Masons; New London Lodge, No. 360, Benevolent and Protective Order of Elks; Pequot Lodge, No. 85, Independent Order of Odd Fellows; the Niagara Fire Company; and the New London Auto Dealers' Association. He is also a member of the Chamber of Commerce of New London, a member of the Baptist church, and the Masonic Club, of the same place.

Mr. Thompson married, February 21, 1905, Minnie F. Daly, of New London, daughter of James F. and Christina (Roake) Daly, and they are the parents of two children: Gertrude M., and Helen V.

ALBERT ELI PAQUETTE—Among those men who, by successfully and efficiently carrying on a business necessary to the life of the people serve their community is Albert Eli Paquette, son of Paul and Corrinne (Lamarche) Paquette. Paul Paquette was born in North Adams, Massachusetts, and attended the public schools of that place, and then learned the bakery business. He was first employed by Theophile Perreau at North Adams, Massachusetts, and later began business for himself in Williamstown, Massachusetts, where he remained for sixteen years. He then came to New London and established a business of his own, the Paquette Domestic Bakery; this was in 1907. For the remainder of his life he gave his strength to building up and carrying on his increasingly successful enterprise. He retired in 1916, and died March 4, 1921. His wife, Corrinne (Lamarch) Paquette, survives him, and resides in Fall River, Massachusetts. Paul Paquette and his wife had five children, Albert Eli being the second.

Albert Eli Paquette was born September 8, 1886. He attended the schools of Williamstown, Massachusetts, and then served an apprenticeship in the Paquette Domestic Bakery. Continuing with his father, he acquired a thorough knowledge of the business, and in 1916 formed a partnership with Francis E. Le Blanc. They bought the Paquette Domestic Bakery from Paul Paquette, the father, and have successfully continued the business. The young men have a modern, sanitary plant, and are carrying on an increasingly successful business.

Politically, Mr. Paquette is independent, voting for those candidates who seem to him best fitted to fill the office for which they are nominated. He is a member of the Knights of Columbus, Seaside Council, No. 17, New London, Connecticut; a member of the Chamber of Commerce, of New London; and a member of St. Mary's Roman Catholic Church, of New London.

MORRIS LUBCHANSKEY—A prominent member of the New London county bar, with offices in the city of New London, Connecticut, Morris Lubchanskey is bearing a part in the general progress of the community.

Mr. Lubchanskey is a son of Max and Anna (Wolfe) Lubchanskey. Max Lubchanskey came to the United States from Russia, the land of his birth, in 1892, his family coming later, in 1898. He began life in the new country in the wholesale junk business, and has developed an extensive and important interest in the reclamation of iron and metal waste. He died in 1911.

Morris Lubchanskey, youngest of the six children of Max and Anna (Wolfe) Lubchanskey, was born in Russia, on April 7, 1890, and came to this country in 1898, after the Spanish-American War. Receiving his early education in the public schools of New London, he was graduated from the Bulkeley High School, in the class of 1908. He early determined upon a professional career, and was largely instrumental in working out the financial problems involved. During the four years of his high school course he worked on the New London "Telegraph," one of the city dailies, as city reporter, and in connection with this work, gained much valuable experience as well as funds for his higher education. Entering the University of Michigan, at Ann Arbor, in 1909, he was graduated from that institution in 1912, with the degree of Bachelor of Laws. In the same year he was admitted to the Connecticut bar and the Michigan bar, and began the practice of law in New London. He has won his way to success and a position of influence in his profession.

In various interests, Mr. Lubchanskey is active. He is a member of the Connecticut State Bar Association and of the New London County Bar Association. Politically, he thinks and acts independently. He is a member of Golden Rule Lodge, No. 359, Free and Accepted Masons, of Ann Arbor, Michigan; of the Independent Order of B'nai Brith, of New London, and also of the John Winthrop Club, of New London.

On June 27, 1916, Mr. Lubchanskey married Mildred C. Frankel, of New York City, daughter of Aaron H. and Lillian (Shapiro) Frankel. Mr. and Mrs. Lubchanskey have one son, Harold F., born September 21, 1918. The family attend Ahvat Chesed Synagogue.

CHARLES L. MAXSON—Well known among the business circles of New London, Connecticut, is Charles L. Maxson, owner and proprietor of the "Kosy Korner" Restaurant, which is one of the best in the city, and caters extensively to business men. Being a good citizen, as well as an able business man, Mr. Maxson is ever ready to cooperate with everything pertaining to the welfare and advancement of his home community.

Charles L. Maxson was born at New London, Connecticut, July 7, 1886, the son of the late George W. and Adelaide (Cann) Maxson. George W. Maxson was born in New York City and died at New London, October 11, 1911. At the age of twelve years he came to New London and here in the local public schools continued his education until he entered Amherst College. Following his college career, he early became interested in the laundry business. To Mr. and Mrs. Maxson were born five children, among the number being Charles L., of further mention. Mrs. Maxson survives her husband and resides at New London.

The education of the boy Charles L. was obtained in the public schools of his native city, after which the business of life commenced for him. His first employment was in the G. M. Williams Hardware Store, where he worked as a clerk for eight years, resigning at the end of that time to become a clerk for Palmer Brothers. Here he remained until 1917 when, on March 20th, of that year, he enlisted in the United States navy, was appointed chief commissary steward, and was stationed at Newport, Rhode Island. On May 20, 1919, he was placed on the reserve list, and at this time returned to New London, where he became assistant paymaster of the Groton Iron Works, subsequently resigning to establish himself in the restaurant business, and this he accomplished on September 20, 1920, when he opened the "Kozy Korner" Restaurant. The enterprise has already proven successful, for although it is comparatively but a short time since its inception, business men in large numbers have acquainted themselves with the place, and its popularity is widespread, which is due in no small measure to the capable management of Mr. Maxson.

Mr. Maxson is a member of the Masonic fraternity, being affiliated with Brainard Lodge, No. 102, Free and Accepted Masons; Union Chapter, No. 7, Royal Arch Masons; Cushing Council, No. 7, Royal and Select Masters; Palestine Commandery, Knights Templar; Pyramid Temple, Ancient Arabic Order Nobles of the Mystic Shrine, Bridgeport, Connecticut; Tall Cedars of Lebanon, New London Forest No. 72; and a Thirty-second degree member of Norwich Valley Consistory, Ancient and Accepted Scottish Rite. He is also a member of Mohegan Lodge, No. 55, Independent Order of Odd Fellows, of which he is a past grand master; of Orrin Encampment, No. 4, of which he is past chief patriot; and past commander of Canton Unity, No. 19, Independent Order of Odd Fellows. Mr. Maxson is charter member of the Northwest Hose Company, No. 7; and in religious faith is an Episcopalian, attending the church of this denomination in New London.

On July 14, 1907, at New London, Charles L. Maxson was united in marriage with Mabel Shepard, and to them has been born one child, Dorothy F., born January 1, 1913.

CHARLES B. TINKER, of New London, Connecticut, son of Matthew A. and Carrie (Powers) Tinker, was born in Salem, New London county, Connecticut, June 14, 1888. Matthew A. Tinker was born in the town of East Lyme, New London county, and all his life has been spent as a farmer. He is now a resident of Montville, Connecticut, where he has a farm. He married Carrie Powers, and they were the parents of nine children, Charles B., being the eldest.

Charles B. Tinker was educated in the public schools of Montville. He was first employed by the New York Telephone Company, where he was foreman of construction. He then was employed by the Southern New England Telephone Company, where he filled various offices. From there he went to the Stevens, Duryea Motor Car Company, where he was tester of new chassis, and held other positions. In 1915 he became manager of the Frisbie & McCormick Garage, now W. R. Frisbie, in New London, and still holds that position. He is a Republican in politics; an attendant of the Baptist church; member of Pequot Lodge, No. 85, Independent Order of Odd Fellows, Oxoboxo Lodge, Free and Accepted Masons, of Montville; and New London Lodge, No. 360, Benevolent and Protective Order of Elks. Mr. Tinker married Amy Eva Rip, daughter of Howard A. and Eva (Howard) Rip, of Salem, Connecticut. Children: Elizabeth, Charles B. (2), and Matthew H.

JOHN HENRY WILSON—At "Hillside Farm" in the town of Preston, which has been his home for three decades, Mr. Wilson has proved himself a skillful agriculturist, his farm bearing all the evidences of careful, intelligent cultivation and efficient management in all its branches or departments. He is a man of progressive ideas and spirit, a careful, conservative man, and not afraid to trust his own udgment.

James Wilson was born in Jewett City, Connecticut, and there learned the trade of machinist. He worked as a journeyman machinist in Norwich, Connecticut, for many years, being employed in the old car shops, becoming boss machinist. He later went to the South, where he died. His wife, Lucy (Harvey) Wilson, was born in Jewett City, and is also deceased. They were the parents of John Henry Wilson, of this review.

John Henry Wilson was born in Preston, New London county, Connecticut, May 1, 1863. He was educated in the public schools, and as a young man was employed in farm and mill work. In 1883 he came to the farm in Preston, which is now his home, as an employe of H. H. Hopkins, and there has since conducted general farming, dairy farming, stock and poultry raising operations. He is a Republican in politics, and a member of Preston City Congregational Church. He is a very active member of the old Preston City Grange, Patrons of Husbandry, and has made "Hillside Farm" an attractive and profitable estate.

Mr. Wilson married, September 11, 1888, Jennie Sarah Hopkins, daughter of Henry H. Hopkins, and a descendant of Governor Stephen Hopkins, a signer of the Declaration of Independence.

HENRY HUNT HOPKINS, father of Mrs. John Henry Wilson, was born in the town of Preston, Connecticut, 1808. He was the son of Joseph Olney and Lydia P. (Hazen) Hopkins, grandson of Colonel Silvanus and Mary (Wanton) Hopkins, and the great-grandson of Rufus Hopkins, who filled many positions of trust in the Revolutionary times, such as judge, assemblyman, and one of the owners and builders of Hope Furnace, which cast cannon for the use of the Continental army. Rufus Hopkins was the eldest son of Governor Stephen Hopkins, a signer of the Declaration of Independence, Governor of Rhode Island, chief justice of the Superior Court of Rhode Island, and of the fourth American generation of the family which was founded by Thomas Hopkins, the founder of this very old and distinguished family. The line of descent to Governor Stephen Hopkins is through Major William Hopkins, son of the founder; his son, William Hopkins, is the father of Governor Stephen Hopkins.

From such distinguished ancestry came Henry Hunt Hopkins, whose career is herein traced. He was educated in the public schools of the "Falls" district of Norwich, and at the age of sixteen years became a machinist's apprentice, attracted to that trade through his father's skilled mastery of metal working. The lad remained two years in Allen's machine shop in Greeneville, his father being superintendent of that plant, but the latter becoming superintendent of the Abner Pearce shop in Norwich Falls, he obtained a position there. He completed his years of apprenticeship, became a good machinist, and when his father died the young man was appointed his sucessor as superintendent of the plant, although at that time he had not quite reached the age of twenty-one years. He retained that position one year, then transferred his services to Allen & Thurber, going with that firm to Worcester, but later returned to his native State.

He bought a farm of one hundred and twenty acres in Preston, New London county, Connecticut, after returning from Worcester, and there lived for a year, after which time he began working for Christopher Brand, of Norwich county, who was manufacturing whale guns for the use of the whalers, shooting the harpoon instead of hunting it by hand. He continued at that work eighteen months, then returned to his farm in Preston, and about a year later he purchased a block in the newly formed Hopkins & Allen Company, of Norwich county, of which firm he became superintendent. That company manufactured firearms, and after several years' connection there, Mr. Hopkins sold his stock and returned again to his Preston farm and its management. There he continued his residence until the end of his life, bringing his farm to a high state of cultivation, and conducted almost as successfully a dairy proposition. For more than fifty years he lived upon his Preston farm, and no man in town was more genuinely esteemed. He served the town in official capacities, as selectman, assessor, school committeeman, and was most conscientious in the performance of his duties.

His connection with the inventions leading to the typewriting machine is perhaps not well known. During his connection with the firm of Allen & Thurber, Mr. Thurber invented a machine for the use of blind people, and upon this machine Mr. Hopkins, together with Horace Smith, later senior member of the famous Smith & Wesson Arms Company, worked until it was brought to perfection. That machine formed the nucleus of the typewriting machine later invented.

Mr. Hopkins married, November 20, 1842, Lucy Lathrop Sherman, who died January 5, 1899, in Preston, daughter of Nathaniel Sherman, of that town. They were the parents of the following children: 1. Joseph H., born August 12, 1843, in Norwich, died in Preston in 1914. 2. Henrietta V., born September 7, 1852; married, August 14, 1883, Herbert L. Prentice, and later with her husband moved to Marshalltown, Iowa, where Mr. Prentice engaged in business as a general merchant; Mrs. Prentice died June 7, 1886; no children. 3. William H., born April 2, 1856, died October 28, 1870. 4. Jennie Sarah, born January 21, 1859, married, September 11, 1888, John Henry Wilson, of Preston.

FRANK HORACE BROWN—Long active in mercantile pursuits, and now a leading business man of North Stonington, Connecticut, Frank Horace Brown has for years also taken a progressive and constructive part in the public life of the community.

Mr. Brown is a son of Smith and Rebecca (Miner) Brown, old residents of this vicinity. Smith Brown was born in North Stonington, and there received his education in the district schools near his home. He was a man out of the ordinary, not content always to tread the beaten track. While obviously taking up for his occupation work along agricultural lines, he made his way into a wider field, becoming an extensive dealer in real estate, largely in farm properties. He died in North Stonington in 1892. His wife, who was also born in North Stonington, died about two years previously. They were the parents of six children, of whom four are now living.

Frank Horace Brown, youngest child of Smith and Rebecca (Miner) Brown, was born in Voluntown, Connecticut, September 14, 1851. He also received a practical education in the district schools of the town, then became associated with his father in his farming interests. Continuing along this line until he was twenty-one years of age, the young man then entered the business world. Familiar, as he was, with living conditions in the rural districts, and with the needs of the family under these circumstances, he found the clerkship in the general store in Voluntown the stepping-stone to success. He worked in several different stores in this county, then in 1895 went to Westerly, Rhode Island, and there engaged in business along mercantile lines, remaining there until 1908. In that year he became associated with George H. Stone, whose life is also reviewed in this work, and together they purchased the general store, theretofore conducted by Austin Maine. The partnership still continues Brown & Stone, and this store is the largest and most important in the town of North Stonington.

Mr. Brown has repeatedly been called to the public service. Politically he is a Democrat of the old school, and in 1909 he was elected town representative to the State Legislature, and again in the election in 1913. During his stay at the Capital he was a member of the Railroad Committee, and also of the State Prison Committee. He served as selectman of the town of North Stonington for a period of five years. Mr. Brown is also a member of the North Stonington Grange, No. 138.

In Voluntown, Connecticut, Mr. Brown married Mary Geer, daughter of Henry C. and Mary (Geer) Geer, of North Stonington. Their two children, Mary and Henry, died in infancy.

Frank H Brown

ERNEST DELANO CHAPMAN—In Clark's Falls, Connecticut, in the eastern part of North Stonington, New London county, the general store of the village has for many years been in the hands of the Chapmans, father and son. Ernest Delano Chapman, the present head of the business, is considered one of the leading men of the village, and of the town of North Stonington, of which this village is a part.

Mr. Chapman is a son of Edwin Prentice and Carry L. (Whitford) Chapman. Edwin Prentice Chapman was born on Pendleton Hill, North Stonington, September 26, 1835. He received his education in the district schools of the neighborhood, and for several years taught school here in the winters, working on the farm during the summers. About 1864 he bought out Pelig Clark, of Clark's Falls, for years theretofore the owner of the village store. From that time until the present the store has been in Mr. Chapman's hands. He enlarged the scope of the business, and in 1872 built the large and for that time handsome structure which still accommodates the business. Mr. Chapman's wife was born in Cranston, Rhode Island, and died in 1900. They were the parents of three children: Ernest Delano, whose name heads this review; Arthur E., now deceased, who married Grace Snow, of Providence, Rhode Island; and Addie C., who became the wife of Elbert W. Clark, in Clark's Falls, where they now reside.

Ernest Delano Chapman was born in Clark's Falls, December 10, 1865. Receiving his early education in the district schools of the village, he completed his studies at the Providence, Rhode Island, High School. He then became associated with his father in the general store at Clark's Falls. He is still in this business, now taking the management largely into his own hands on account of his father's advancing years. This store is considered one of the leading establishments of its class in the section. In the public interests of the community Mr. Chapman bears a part, as far as his limited leisure will permit. He is affiliated, politically, with the Republican party. His church membership is with the Baptist denomination. He is postmaster of Clark's Falls, having been appointed March 19, 1894.

REUBEN PALMER SMITH—As one of New London's youngest automobile dealers, Mr. Smith has met with decided success in the business in which he has been engaged since 1910, and since 1915, under his own name. He is a son of William W. and Althea (Whiteman) Smith, his father, born in New London, a grocer in that town, conducting a prosperous business.

Reuben Palmer Smith was born in New London, Connecticut, March 12, 1890, and educated in the public schools of the city. He finished his school work in the New London Vocational Training School, and in 1910 began his connection with the automobile business. In that year, in association with his brother-in-law, Thornton N. M. Lathrop, he established a garage service station and salesrooms for the E. M. F. and Hudson cars. They operated very successfully until 1915, when the firm dissolved, each partner continuing in the same business. Mr. Smith secured the agency for the Dodge Brothers and Overland cars, and has a garage service station and show rooms at No. 555 Bank street, New London. He is a young man of energy and ability, well-liked and widely-acquainted.

Mr. Smith is a Republican in politics. In his church affiliation he is a member of the Second Congregational Church. He is a member of the New London Auto Dealers' Association, the Rotary Club, the Chamber of Commerce, and the Harbour Club.

Mr. Smith married, in January, 1914, Jeannette Franklin Smith, daughter of Frank Smith, of New London. Mr. and Mrs. R. P. Smith are the parents of a son, Laurence P., and a daughter, Virginia.

EDWIN WEST—Three generations of Wests in this branch have tilled the acres they owned in North Stonington and Stonington, New London county, Connecticut. The first of these was William West, who came from Rhode Island to North Stonington and bought a farm which at his death went to his son Edwin, and when the latter was "gathered to his fathers," his son Herbert took charge of it.

William West was born in Westerly, Rhode Island, in 1810, and died in North Stonington, New London county, Connecticut, in 1886. His early life was spent in Rhode Island, but later he became a farmer of North Stonington and there continued a well known and substantial tiller of the soil until his death at the age of seventy-six. He married Demarius Sisson, who survived him until 1891. They were the parents of eleven children, all of whom have joined the "innumerable throng" except Emily, Mrs. John Johnson, of Ashaway, Rhode Island. Two of the sons, Alfred and Robinson, served in the Union Army during the Civil War, Alfred giving up his life for his country. The fourth child was Edwin, to whose memory this review is dedicated.

Edwin West was born in North Stonington, Connecticut, January 24, 1831, and died in the village of Stonington, Connecticut, in 1901. He was educated in the public schools, and early in life became his father's farm assistant. After the death of William West, in 1886, his son, Edwin West, succeeded to the ownership of the home farm, but ill health compelled him to surrender its management to his son in 1891. Edwin West then left the farm and for the following ten years lived in Stonington and there died. He was a man of quiet, industrious life, devoted to his family, and a good citizen.

Edwin West married Sarah Ann Yerington, who died in January, 1912. They were the parents of four children: Edwin Everett, married Elizabeth Chapman, and resides in North Stonington; Jennie, married Charles E. Chapman, of North Stonington;

Ella, resides with her brother Herbert; Herbert, of further mention.

Herbert West was born at the West homestead in North Stonington, Connecticut, February 18, 1866. He was educated in the public schools, and remained at the home farm as his father's assistant until the latter's death in 1901. He continued the operation of the farm until 1905, when he with his sister, Ella West, bought a farm north of the borough of Stonington known as the Hull Farm, part of the Hull Estate, containing one hundred and seventy-five acres, where they reside, both unmarried. The home overlooks Long Island Sound and commands a view of Long Island. They also own the Chase farm adoining, the two farms, forming an estate of three hundred acres. They are members of the First Congregational Church of Stonington, of which Herbert West is trustee, Stonington Grange, Patrons of Husbandry, and highly esteemed residents of their town. Politically, Mr. West is a Republican.

FRANK G. AUBREY—It is often difficult to realize how much of time, thought and executive effort must be expended on the ordinary daily needs of the people. Frank G. Aubrey, general manager of the Mohican Market, Norwich, Connecticut, is a man of fine executive ability, whose foresight and judgment have much to do with the daily well-being of the people.

Mr. Aubrey is descended from New York State and Vermont families. His father, Elias A. Aubrey, was born in Albany, New York, where he was educated in the public schools, later becoming a machinist. He followed the same trade all his life, and now resides in New Haven, Connecticut. He married Josephine Thibodeau, of Vermont birth, and they have had nine children, of whom Frank G. is the eldest.

Frank G. Aubrey was born in Albany, New York, July 24, 1881. His parents removed to Norwich, Connecticut, and he received his education in the public schools of that city. He made his start in life as a clerk for Welcome A. Smith, a local grocer. The young man was ambitious, and it was the farthest from his intentions always to remain in a subordinate position, so he made the most of every opportunity to increase his knowledge of the business, and of business principles in general. He remained in this connection for five years, then became bookkeeper and foreman for R. W. Marshall, remaining for a short period. In 1910 he was offered the opportunity to become a member of the working force of the Mohican Market, which he accepted, acting in the capacity of clerk for a time, then rising to positions of greater responsibility, until now he is general manager of the market. The Mohican Market Company is one of the large corporations operating a wide chain of stores throughout the Eastern States. Mr. Aubrey is a Democrat by political choice; he was a member of the Common Council in 1918 and 1919. He is a member of Norwich Lodge, No. 430, Benevolent and Protective Order of Elks, of which he is past exalted ruler. He is also a member of the Chamber of Commerce.

Mr. Aubrey married, May 15, 1916, Margaret C. Young, daughter of Daniel and Margaret (Donovan) Young, of Norwich. The family were members of the Roman Catholic church.

ALBERT MORGAN BROWN — Nathaniel Brown, grandfather of Albert M. Brown, of the town of Ledyard, New London county, Connecticut, was born on the old Brown farm in the town of Ledyard, as was his son, Albert Brown, and the latter's son, Albert M. Brown. The house in which Nathaniel Brown was born was not the one in which his son and grandson were born, but belonged to an earlier day. Nathaniel Brown married Lottie Wilbur, and both spent their lives on the farm in Ledyard, where he passed away; his wife died in Waterford.

Their son, Albert Brown, was born, lived and died on the same farm, and most of his life was spent in cultivating its acres. He, however, was a skilled wheelwright, and built houses. He was school committeeman, and a man of a good deal of influence in his town. He married Surviah Main, who was born, lived and died in Ledyard. They were the parents of Albert Morgan Brown, of Ledyard, now too passed to his reward.

Albert Morgan Brown was born on the Brown farm in Ledyard, New London county, Connecticut, June 22, 1843, and died at his farm near the Peckham Church, in the town of Ledyard, August 8, 1915. He attended the district schools, and spent his youth after the fashion of the average farmer boy, the old farm his home until he arrived at legal age. He then hired out to others, but continued to assist his father in the latter's saw mill and at such times as he was needed. At the age of twenty-two years he married, and then rented a small farm in Main Town, Ledyard. He continued there nine years, then bought a farm on which he lived for seven years before purchasing the larger farm near the Peckham Church, in the town of Ledyard, upon which he died in 1915.

Albert M. Brown married, at her home in Preston, Connecticut, January 6, 1862, Nancy Amelia Peckham, daughter of John Owen and Margaret (O'Connell) Peckham. After the death of her husband, Mrs. Brown sold the farm in Ledyard and now makes her home with her daughter, Mrs. Emma B. Bennett, in Preston. Mr. and Mrs. Brown attended the Peckham Baptist Church, Mr. Brown, while not a member, being greatly interested in its welfare. They were the parents of four children: 1. Nancy Ella, now the widow of William H. Bennett, a farmer of the town of Preston; Mrs. Bennett continues her residence at the Preston farm; Mrs. Bennett has two children: Albert Philetus and Harriet. 2. Philetus Albert, now a farmer of the town of Stonington, New London county; he married Florence Burris Main, of Ledyard, and they were the parents of a daughter,

Iva Nancy, who died at the age of six years. 3. Emma Betsy, married Earl Bennett, a farmer of the town of Preston. 4. Minnie Agnes, who died at the age of eighteen years.

Albert M. Brown was a man of kindly, generous heart, and universally esteemed. He was a Democrat in his political belief, and served Ledyard as selectman, school committeeman and assessor. He was a quiet, home-loving man and provided well for those depending upon him.

WILLIAM PRENTICE BABCOCK—The Babcock family of North Stonington, Connecticut, is one of the old established families of New London county. For many generations the men of this family have borne a part in every progressive movement of the community, and contributed, through their individual enterprise, to the prosperity of the town. William Prentice Babcock, the present head of one branch of this family, is representative of the citizenship in which his ancestors also took the lead.

Mr. Babcock is a son of John Davis and Eunice Ann (Maine) Babcock. John D. Babcock was born in North Stonington, the son of Stephen and Mercy (Davis) Babcock, natives of North Stonington, and received his education in the district school of the town. Then, like his father, he took up farming, and followed agricultural interests all his life. Except for eleven years of this time, he was a resident of North Stonington. In 1844 John Davis Babcock went to Westerly, Rhode Island, where he conducted a farm until 1855. This was the Morse place, of Westerly, and it was the only time that the family lived outside the town of North Stonington. On returning to this town Mr. Babcock lived on the Martha Stanton place. Later in 1858 he bought the Saxton Maine place, the present home farm of Wm. P. Babcock, his son. He gradually added to his land until he had in all four hundred acres, and did extensive farming until he retired in 1879, renting the farm to his son, William Babcock.

He then moved to Pawcatuck, in the town of Stonington, where he bought a home and lived until 1886. There he made his home with his son, John R., and his daughter, Susan H., at Old Mystic, where he died, January 11, 1887, at the age of seventy years.

He married (first), Harriet Delight Bentley, of North Stonington, and to this union were born two children: Susan H., of Old Mystic; and John Russell, deceased. He married (second), Eunice Ann Maine, a sister of Isaac Maine, of mention elsewhere in this work.| His second wife also was born in North Stonington, and she died there April 30, 1876. They were the parents of four children, all born in North Stonington: Wealthy Ella, who died in 1880, aged twenty-two; Betsy Anna, who died in 1863; Abbie Lathrop, who married Wallace A. Phillips, of North Stonington; and William Prentice.

William Prentice Babcock was born in North Stonington, July 14, 1855. He received a thorough grounding in the essentials of education at the district schools of the town, then followed the long-established precedent of the family, and took up farming as his life work. He has been very successful, and is held in the highest respect in the community. Mr. Babcock now owns the old Babcock homestead, where he has lived since he was nine years old. After the death of his father, he bought out the interest of the other heirs and has owned it for the past thirty-three years or since, 1889. He does general farming and stock raising.

In the public life of the town Mr. Babcock has long been prominent. By political affiliation he is a staunch Democrat, and is one of the leaders of the party here. He has served the public in several different offices, having been elected selectman of the town at three different times, has also been constable, tax collector, and justice of the peace. In all his public duties he is loyal to the highest ideals of responsibility, and carries forward the interests of the town with steadfast integrity. Mr. Babcock is widely interested in the various branches of public endeavor. He is an active member of the New London County Farm Bureau, and gives generously of his time and energies to forward its progress.

On September 24, 1882, Mr. Babcock married Mary Burdick, daughter of Horace Franklin and Mary Frances (Shirley) Burdick, of North Stonington. They are the parents of six children, all born on the Babcock home place, of whom four are now living: 1. Allis May, deceased, who became the wife of George H. Stone, of North Stonington, whose life is reviewed in this work; she died September 21, 1918. 2. Ida Belle, wife of James F. Maine, of Stonington. 3. Anna Louise, who became the wife of Maurice B. Caswell, of Mystic, Connecticut. 4. Bessie Evelyn, now the wife of Thomas McGowan, of North Stonington. 5. Susan Vinnie, deceased, wife of John H. Stedman, of Westerly, Rhode Island, and mother of one son, Orrin Richard. 6. Frances Abbie, wife of Noah Dupont, of Voluntown, Connecticut. The family have always been members of the Baptist church.

HIRAM HENRY AMBURN—In the town of Montville, New London county, Connecticut, Hiram Henry Amburn is considered one of the leading men of the community. Interested quite extensively in general farming, he still follows his trade, that of carpenter, and bears a constructive part in the progress of the town.

Mr. Amburn is a son of George Amburn, who was born in Germany, and received a common school education there, then came to America with his parents at the age of thirteen years. The family located near the village of Poquetannoc, just over into the town of Preston, and the boy took up farm work here. Later they removed to the town of Lebanon, New London county, Connecticut, and there he farmed for many years, and there four of his six children were born. He went to Pennsylvania, remaining for a few years, and there two children were born. He then returned to Lebanon and followed farming there until his death in 1872.

He married Mary Anna Shalk, who was born in Germany, came to America in her youth, and settled in Lebanon, where she died in 1900.

Hiram Henry Amburn was born in Lebanon, Connecticut, September 18, 1870. He was only two years of age when his father died. He attended the district schools of the town of Salem, New London county, Connecticut, then later the public schools of the nearby town of Colchester, where he enjoyed the advantage of the larger schools. From an early age he worked out as farm hand, continuing thus until the age of eighteen years. At that time he went to Norwich and served an apprenticeship as carpenter with his brother, George. This completed, he married, and took up his residence on the Valentine Geer farm, in the northern end of the town of Montville. It was in 1891 that Mr. Amburn came to Montville, and from the first he has carried on important interests in farming, also working, as he found openings along that line, at his trade of carpenter, and doing a considerable amount of blacksmithing. Now outside of his farming activities, he does only carpenter work.

Always a man of tireless industry, and capable in the handling of his many interests, Mr. Amburn soon came to be looked upon as one of the solid citizens of the town of Montville. Five years ago he was made fire warden of the town, and has served most acceptably in that position ever since. Later he was also appointed caretaker of the Norwich City Reservoir. Politically he is affiliated with the Republican party, but always considers the man before he casts his vote. Mr. Amburn is a member of Uncas Lodge, No. 11, Independent Order of Odd Fellows, of Norwich, and of Palmyra Encampment, No. 3, of Norwich, same order. Mr. Amburn attends and aids in the support of the Methodist church of Montville.

On June 18, 1891, Mr. Amburn married, in Montville, Catherine Geer, the adopted daughter of Valentine Geer, and the daughter of Mattis Servis. She was adopted when a little child, and was always considered a member of the Geer family, one of the oldest and most prominent families of this section. Mr. and Mrs. Amburn are the parents of two children: 1. Clarence Henry, born in Montville, September 3, 1892; a mechanic, who was in the utility department of the United States army, at Camp Devens, Massachusetts, during the World War; married Mabel Dexter, of Norwich. 2. Frederick Valentine, born in Montville, July 28, 1894; was in Company E, 307th Supply Train, 82nd Division, American Expeditionary Forces, in France, being captain's orderly; he is also a mechanic. Both young men are members of the Independent Order of Odd Fellows.

COURTLAND BURROWS YORK—One of the fine farms of the town of Stonington is the York farm on the Westerly-Old Mystic road owned by Courtland B. York, who became its owner in the year 1900. It was formerly the Gideon Cheseborough farm, but under Mr. York's modern, progressive management bears little resemblance to the farm of twenty years ago. The farm in its appointments and improvements reflects the nature and spirit of its owner, who is one of the thoroughly modern dairy and general farmers of New London county. His dairy herd is of Guernsey blood, and all modern aids to dairy farming have been given a trial and adopted if found to be a step in advance.

Mr. York is a great-grandson of James York, who owned and cultivated a farm on the Shore road in the town of Westerly, Rhode Island.

He was succeeded by his son, William York, born in the town of Westerly, Rhode Island, and all his life a farmer of Westerly, Rhode Island, Stonington and Groton, Connecticut. He married Mary Barber, and both died in the town of Westerly, where both were born.

William (2) York, son of William (1) and Mary (Barber) York, was born in the town of Westerly, Rhode Island, in 1834, and died at the home of his son, Courtland B. York, in Stonington, Connecticut, December 10, 1915, aged eighty-one years. He lived in Westerly the first twelve years of his life, then his father rented a farm in Stonington, on Togwank Hill, then owned by the Smith family. There the lad finished his school training, and until reaching legal age was his father's farm assistant. From 1855 until 1861, he was employed in the neighborhood as a farm hand, but lived at home. In that year his parents moved to Groton, and soon after the outbreak of the Civil War, William (2) York enlisted from Groton with his brother, Edwin York, in Company K, Twenty-sixth Regiment, Connecticut Volunteer Infantry, for a term of nine months. In that regiment there were sixteen other couples, brothers, who had enlisted together, and the York brothers were the only couple to both escape injury. After the war, William and Edwin York went to the State of California and were employed on farms and cattle ranches. Edwin York remained in California forty-five years, but is now an inmate of a Soldiers' Home in Grand Rapids, Michigan. William York returned to Stonington after two years of California residence, and there made his home, but was engaged in teaming in and around Westerly, Rhode Island. He also learned the blacksmith's trade in Westerly and at the Klondike Stone Quarry in Niantic, Rhode Island. In 1904 he retired from his trade and spent the last eleven years of his life with his son, Courtland B., at the latter's farm in Stonington. William York married Mary S. Wheeler, born in Stonington, Connecticut, and only survived her husband two months, dying at the home of her son, Courtland B., February 12, 1916. William and Mary S. York were the parents of two children: Ellen Fitts, who died December 30, 1915, wife of Abel H. Stanton, a blacksmith of New London, Connecticut; and Courtland Burrows, of further mention.

Courtland Burrows York, only son of William (2) and Mary S. (Wheeler) York, was born in the town of Westerly, Rhode Island, April 19, 1869,

Mr & Mrs C H Norton

and there spent his youth. He attended Westerly district school until fourteen years of age, then became a pupil at the Charleston District School, also attended district school in Niantic, Rhode Island. After school years he was employed as a farm hand for two and a half years, then as a quarry man for six months, going in 1892 as a farm hand for William J. Potter at his Watch Hill farm. A year later he rented the farm and worked it during the years 1893, 1894, and 1895. In 1897 he rented the Sumner Chapman farm on the Shore road in the town of Westerly, there remaining three years. During all these years Mr. York had prospered, and in 1900 bought the Gideon Cheseborough farm of one hundred and thirty acres in the town of Stonington, New London, Connecticut, the farm lying on the Westerly-Old Mystic road in the Anguilla district.

Mr. York has built new houses, barns and outbuildings on the farm, converted the farm house into a modern residence with all conveniences, and transformed the entire property into a beautiful and profitable estate. He is a general farmer, but runs a large dairy and makes the production of milk and dairy products a specialty. He is a believer in the Guernsey breed of cattle for dairy purposes and has a fine herd. He is a member of Stonington Grange, Patrons of Husbandry, and a devoted member of the First Baptist Church, of Westerly, Rhode Island. In politics he is a Republican.

Mr. York married, in Westerly, Rhode Island, April 27, 1899, Lena Sarah Potter, born in Westerly, daughter of William J. and Jennie L. (Mitchell) Potter.

GEORGE HENRY STONE, a progressive citizen and leading merchant of North Stonington, Connecticut. George Henry Stone, of the firm of Brown & Stone, is widely known in New London county.

Mr. Stone is a son of George Washington and Fannie (Geer) Stone, for a considerable period residents of this county. George W. Stone was born in Worcester, Massachusetts. He received a thoroughly practical education in the public schools of that city, then faced the future with dauntless spirit. He was interested in the mercantile world, and at once set foot upon the upward path. He took up the work of travelling salesman, and has been most successful in this line of effort. Now, having reached an age when many men retire from business, he is still actively engaged in selling goods in many states, with the same progressive force which placed him among the successful men of his calling.

George Henry Stone was born in the Clark's Falls district of the town of North Stonington, August 6, 1888. He received his education in the public schools of Westerly, Rhode Island, and became the youngest merchant in Westerly, carrying forward this first business enterprise, a variety store, for four years. At the end of that time, 1908, in association with Frank H. Brown, whose life is also reviewed in this work, he bought out the general store of Austin A. Maine, of North Stonington. This partnership still continues, and in the years which have passed the business has grown and developed, placing this store at the head of the mercantile interests of the vicinity. It is the largest store in the town of North Stonington, and commands a wide trade throughout this section among the best families.

Mr. Stone is prominent in political circles of the town. He is a leader in the Republican party, was a candidate of both parties for legislature, and was elected to represent the town of North Stonington in the State Legislature in the fall of 1916. Contrary to the frequent custom in other New London county towns, he was re-elected, in 1918, serving since his first term on the Committee on Education. Mr. Stone is a prominent member of the North Stonington Grange, No. 138, and he is a member of the Third Baptist Church, of North Stonington.

In North Stonington he married, October 15, 1919, Ruth, daughter of George A. and Grace L. (Pitcher) Thompson, of North Stonington. Mrs. Stone is a native of North Stonington, Connecticut. George Thompson, her father, was a native of Pendleton Hill, in the town of North Stonington, but was reared in North Stonington. Here he was a farmer, owning Sunny Side Farm, north of the village, an extensive farm property, and was engaged in general farming and stock raising, but is now retired. His wife was born in the village of North Stonington. Both the Thompsons and Pitchers are of old New London county families, the Thompsons old settlers of the Pendleton Hill section.

CLARENCE HORATIO NORTON—From boyhood until the present, Clarence H. Norton has been connected with the grain and milling business and with the manufacture of paper board, the former business claiming him until the year 1900, the latter during the last two decades of his life. He is a native of Hebron, Tolland county, Connecticut, his parents, grandparents and great-grandparents also natives of Hebron, but his grandfather, Samuel Summerfield Norton, moved to Colchester, in New London county, that his children might attend Bacon Academy. He did not remain in Colchester, but later in life returned to his native Hebron, where he died. The farm of David Norton, father of Samuel S. Norton, was located in the northeastern part of the town of Hebron, Connecticut, where Samuel S. was born.

Samuel Summerfield Norton was reared at the farm in Hebron, Connecticut, but he was of a mechanical turn of mind and learned the carpenter's trade. In addition to a natural mechanical skill which he developed, he possessed inventive genius and made a superior gauge for the use of carpenters. He lived in Colchester, Connecticut, for many years, and while there was active in the erection of a new Methodist Episcopal church, a denomination with which he was long connected and which he loyally supported. He was an Abolitionist, and when the Republican party was formed, affiliated with that party. He died in Hebron, aged seventy-one years.

Samuel S. Norton married, at Killingworth, Connecticut, Sylvina Chapman, who survived him until April 6, 1888, passing away at the age of eighty-seven. They were the parents of four children: John Summerfield, a graduate of Wesleyan University, who married Josephine Joynes, of Southern birth, settled in Texas, where he engaged as a teacher until the Civil War, when he entered the Confederate army as a musician, serving until Lee's surrender; Daniel Ives, of further mention; Ellen, a graduate of Bacon Academy, married Henry Cook, of North Carolina; Edward H., a merchant of Brenham, Texas, who never married.

Daniel Ives Norton, second son of Samuel S. and Sylvina (Chapman) Norton, was born in Hebron, Connecticut, in 1827, but was young when the family moved to Colchester, New London county, Connecticut. He died in North Westchester, Connecticut, from a stroke of paralysis, October 9, 1880, aged fifty-three years. He was educated in Colchester public schools and Bacon Academy of the same town, then, when school years were over, learned the carpenter's trade under the direction of his father, continuing with him until 1861. He then, in partnership with David Thompson, engaged in the operation of a cotton mill at Hope Valley, in the town of Hebron. In 1876 the mill was destroyed by fire and was not rebuilt. Daniel I. Norton then moved to North Westchester, where he settled on the farm of his father-in-law, Talcott L. Buell. There he repaired the old Buell grain and grist mill, which he put in operation, but in 1877 suffered an attack of paralysis, from which he never recovered. He was a member of the Methodist Episcopal church, and in politics a Democrat. He was buried in North Westchester Cemetery.

Daniel I. Norton married, at North Westchester, Connecticut, Eunice Blish Buell, who died there, aged seventy-nine, daughter of Talcott Loveland and Mary Gates (Carrier) Buell. Talcott L. Buell, a farmer and miller, died in Westchester, in 1885, aged eighty-seven years and nine months. Mr. and Mrs. Norton were the parents of an only child, Clarence Horatio Norton, of whom further.

Clarence Horatio Norton, son of Daniel Ives and Eunice Blish (Buell) Norton, was born in Hebron, Connecticut, October 22, 1853, and educated in the public schools. After the removal to North Westchester, in 1876, poor health incapacitated his father from all but the lightest work, and the work of the mill and farm fell to the lad, Clarence H. When the health of the father utterly failed, and death resulted, in 1880, the son took entire charge of the business of the mill, running both the grist department and the saw mill, purchasing grain, shipping and carrying on a regular county grain and mill business. The saw mill was dropped first, and in 1888 he began the manufacture of straw board in an old building in North Westchester, used by his Grandfather Buell and others. That mill burned in 1893, but was replaced by another much larger, and modernly equipped. In 1900 paper board manufacture became his sole business and he yet operates along that line. A man of remarkable energy, he has won for himself an honored name, and is of the very best type, progressive, upright and thoroughly reliable in all things.

In politics, Mr. Norton is a Democrat, and in 1885 represented his district in the Connecticut State Legislature. He has also served his town as selectman, assessor, and member of the Board of Relief.

Mr. Norton married, in North Westchester, December 24, 1885, Atta Bell Carrier, born in Westchester, in the town of Colchester, New London county, Connecticut, January 2, 1867, daughter of Demas and Roxy Eliza (Staples) Carrier, both her parents born in Westchester, and both deceased. Demas Carrier died December 13, 1893, aged sixty-five years; his wife died at the age of fifty-three. Mr. and Mrs. Carrier also had a son, who died in infancy, and another daughter, Susan Minette Carrier, who married Robert Samuel Brown. Mr. and Mrs. Clarence H. Norton are the parents of four children, all born in North Westchester: 1. Sylvina Chapman, born November 10, 1886. 2. Minette Carrier, born November 1, 1889; married Daniel Wayne Williams, of Wallingford, Connecticut, a purchasing agent, and has two children: Daniel Norton Williams, born December 6, 1917, and Warren Brooks Williams, born March 4, 1921. 3. Marion Eunice, born July 20, 1893; married Edward Forbes Smiley, a minister of the Gospel. 4. Edward Howd, born July 7, 1896, associated with his father in the paper mill. The family are members of the Westchester Congregational Church.

JAMES RICHARDSON ARMSTRONG was born in Rutland, Jefferson county, New York, April 21, 1844, the son of John and Sarah (Porter) Armstrong. John Armstrong was a native of Saratoga county, New York, his birth having occurred at Saratoga, November 7, 1801. He was educated in the district schools of his native place, after which he engaged in farming until his death, March 17, 1887. His wife, Sarah (Porter) Armstrong, was born March 1, 1807, died December 17, 1889. Mr. and Mrs. Armstrong were the parents of seven children, James Richardson, the subject of this review, being the sixth child.

James Richardson Armstrong obtained his education in the district schools of Rutland, and then worked on his father's farm until 1870, when he moved to Westerly, Rhode Island, and there engaged in farming for eight years, removing at the end of that time to Lebanon, Connecticut, where he still followed the same vocation and has continued in agricultural pursuits ever since. In 1895 he purchased what was then the W. A. Browning farm in Griswold, near Jewett City. This estate covers one hundred and eighty acres and here Mr. Armstrong engages in general farming and dairying on a large scale. He also owns thirty-four head of cattle, some of which are registered short-horned cattle, and has built up a large and extremely flourishing business. In his political affiliations he is a staunch Republican, although no office seeker.

Mr. Armstrong married, December 25, 1867, Susan Abby Carpenter, of South Kingston, Rhode Island, and to them have been born seven children: 1. Flora L., a resident of Mount Hermon, Massachusetts. 2. Sarah M., a resident of Foster, Rhode Island. 3. John, married Lillian Carpenter, of Pawtucket, Rhode Island. 4. Hannah M., married Frederick Gregor, and resides in North Attleboro, Massachusetts. 5. Benjamin A., married Bertha Tillinghast, and resides in Balboa Heights, Panama Canal Zone. 6. Charles T., married Nettie A. Geer, of Griswold, Connecticut; he resides on the farm with his father. 7. Susan E., a resident of Mount Hermon, Massachusetts. Mrs. Armstrong passed away May 28, 1916. She was in every sense of the word a helpmate to her husband, and her cheerful disposition and courage in the midst of trials incident to the care of a large family was a considerable factor in making her husband's life the success that it is.

ZOEL GAUCHER—One of the principal industries of the village of Baltic, in the town of Sprague, Connecticut, is the wholesale bakery, conducted by Zoel Gaucher. Mr. Gaucher has been a resident of Baltic for the past twenty-one years, and is widely known thereabouts.

Mr. Gaucher's parents were Canadian born, being natives of St. Damasa, Province of Quebec. They were farming people, and his father died in St. Ceasere, twenty years ago, and is buried there. His mother still survives, at seventy-three years of age, living in St. Ceasere. They were the parents of four sons, of whom Zoel is the eldest. The others are: Jean, thirty-eight years of age; Fred, thirty-five; and Albert, thirty.

Zoel Gaucher was born in Knowlton, Province of Quebec, in the year 1877. He was educated at St. Ceasere, Province of Quebec, Canada, and there learned the trade of baker. He came to this country in August, 1899, coming directly to Baltic, where he has since remained, winning the respect and esteem of the community, and achieving success in his chosen line. He established the big wholesale bakery, which has become a feature of the business life of the town, in the year 1907, and has worked up, until now he controls a very extensive trade, and handles an immense volume of business.

Mr. Gaucher is a leader among his fellow-countrymen in this section, and an influential member of the Societe St. Jean de Baptiste.

He married (first) Evelyn Labunne, who was born in the Province of Quebec, and died, 1913, in Baltic. He married (second) Louise Bles, of Baltic. They have four children: 1. Antoinette. 2. Leo. 3. Randolph. 4. Evelyn.

ORRIN LEONARD SWAIN—In the prosperity of any farming community the hand of the village blacksmith is a vital factor. In North Stonington, New London county, Connecticut, Orrin Leonard Swain meets the need for construction and repairs on the farm, his business covering a wide territory in this section.

Mr. Swain is a son of George W. Swain, who was born in Norwich, Connecticut, and educated in the public schools of that city. After completing the regular course of study, he learned the trade of machinist, which he followed all his active life. He was employed for a period of twenty-two years in C. B. Rogers' machine shop, in Norwich. He is now retired from this work, and lives in the town of North Stonington. He married (first) Maria Rogers, who was born in Montville, Connecticut, and died in Norwich, in the year 1882. They were the parents of two children: George Roberts, who married Addie Holmes, and is now a resident of Old Mystic, Connecticut; and Orrin Leonard. He married (second) Mrs. Eliza (Verguson) Smith.

Orrin Leonard Swain, son of George W. and Maria (Rogers) Swain, was born in Norwich, Connecticut, December 7, 1881. He received his education in the public schools of that city, then served an apprenticeship as a wagon maker and blacksmith with T. H. Peabody, of Norwich, for five years. In 1903 he came to North Stonington, where he established a shop. Here he has built up an extensive business in wagon making and repairing, and general blacksmith work, and is the leading worker along these lines in this part of the county. Mr. Swain is interested in every phase of public progress. Politically he is affiliated with the Democratic party. He is a prominent member of the North Stonington Grange, No. 138.

He married, in North Stonington, in 1902, Frances Melvina Rogers, of Montville, Connecticut, daughter of Frank C. and Kate (Crandall) Rogers, of Montville. They are the parents of ten children: Myrtle F.; Ruby E.; Orrin Leonard, Jr.; Madge P.; Violet T.; Lester M.; Jennie L.; and Beatrice and Barbara, twins; and Donald. The family are members of the Baptist church.

CARL AUGUST KOELB—When the American Velvet Company opened their branch factory in Stonington, Connecticut, they wanted skilled men to fill the important positions connected with its management. Transferring Carl August Koelb from their office in New York City to Stonington, the company made him assistant superintendent under John M. Killars, superintendent and builder of the plant.

Carl August Koelb, Jr., was born a subject of Germany, his parents having lived there all their lives, his father, Carl August Koelb, Sr., following the profession of school teacher for many years. He died in Germany, in 1897, aged sixty-six years. His wife, Maria (Denzer) Koelb, died in 1872. They were the parents of eight children.

Their son, Carl August Koelb, Jr., was born January 15, 1865. Having acquired a good education in the public schools of Germany and also under his father's tuition, young Mr. Koelb, when only eighteen years old, came to the United States, and locating in New York City, in June, 1884, obtained a position with A. Wimpfheimer & Brother, of the American Velvet Company. Remaining with them for eight years, Mr. Koelb was one of those chosen to assist the company in their new enterprise in Stonington. Going there in 1892, he is still in their employ, and is one of the well known residents of the borough, having lived here nearly thirty years.

Becoming greatly interested in Masonic matters, Mr. Koelb joined Asylum Lodge, No. 57, Free and Accepted Masons, of Stonington; also Benevolent Chapter, Royal Arch Masons, of Mystic; and Mystic Council, Royal and Select Masters. In addition to these, Mr. Koelb is affiliated with Stonington Lodge, No. 26, Independent Order of Odd Fellows. He is also a member of the Republican party in that locality.

In Stonington, Connecticut, March 8, 1893, Carl August Koelb was married to Caroline E. Hammond, the daughter of John and Elizabeth (Palmer) Hammond, residents of Stonington. Of this marriage four children have been born: Helen May, living at home; Ralph H., who married Gladys C. MacGowan, and they reside at Westerly, Rhode Island; Howard E., living at home; and Milton C., also at home. Mr. and Mrs. Carl August Koelb and family are members of the Baptist Church of Stonington.

JOHN FRIBANCE—In the manufacturing world of Mystic, Connecticut, one of the skilled workers is John Fribance, who has been master mechanic of the Mystic Manufacturing Company's plant for twenty-three years. He is a son of William and Rose (Payne) Fribance.

William Fribance was born in London, England, where he was also educated, later becoming a mechanic, and following along this line during all his active life. He still lives in London, but is now retired from all active work. Of the twelve children Mr. Fribance, of Mystic, was the eldest.

John Fribance was born in London, England, September 20, 1874. He was educated in the National schools of his native country, but as he approached manhood the lure of the Western Land across the Atlantic reached him with strong appeal, and at eighteen years of age he came to America. Locating in Rockville, Connecticut, he entered the employ of a manufacturing company now the New England Manufacturing Company, in their great woolen mill. He worked there as machinist until 1898, when he came to Mystic, and became master mechanic at the plant of the Mystic Manufacturing Company. This responsible position he still fills.

In the public welfare of the town of Stonington, Connecticut, Mr. Fribance has long borne a part. Always a strong adherent of Republican party principles, he has been a worker in the ranks for many years, and for the past three years has ably filled the office of selectman, his term of office not yet being expired. He is a member of the Mystic Fire District Committee, which numbers three, and is in charge of the fire department, the water department, and the electric lighting department. The other members of the committee are Conrad Kretzer and William L. Main. Mr. Fribance is a member of Charity and Relief Lodge, Free and Accepted Masons, of Mystic, and is a member of Stonington Lodge, No. 26, Independent Order of Odd Fellows, being a member also of the Encampment.

On September 4, 1906, Mr. Fribance married Minnie Austin, of Rockville, Connecticut, daughter of Enoch and Sarah (Bilson) Austin, of that city. Mr. and Mrs. Fribance are the parents of three children: Austin Edward; William Bilson; and Arthur Kenneth. The family are members of the Congregational church of Mystic, and active in the social and benevolent work of the church.

EDWIN FITCH BENJAMIN—One of the honored names which will long live in the memory of the people of Ledyard is that of Edwin Fitch Benjamin, prominent farmer and highly respected citizen of the town of Griswold, Connecticut.

Mr. Benjamin came of an old New London county family, leading people of the community. His father, Levi Benjamin, was born in Preston, Connecticut, July 2, 1830, and lived there during all his lifetime, conducting extensive farming operations, and taking a comprehensive interest in the affairs of the town. He died in Preston, April 4, 1898. He married Anna Webb Hinckley, who was born in Norwich, Connecticut, December 23, 1835, and died in Preston, October 27, 1898. They were the parents of three children: George Hinckley, deceased; Edwin Fitch, deceased; Irving H., resides in Hartford, Connecticut.

Edwin Fitch Benjamin was born in Ledyard, New London county, Connecticut, April 25, 1859, and died in Griswold, Connecticut, February 10, 1920. He received his education in the district schools of Preston, then upon leaving school took up farming. He soon purchased the Kinney farm in Preston, which he conducted for a time, later selling out his interests there and removing to the town of Griswold, where he bought the Leonard farm. Remaining on this place for two years he again sold, and this time bought the Horton farm, in Griswold, which he conducted until his death.

Mr. Benjamin was more or less interested in political matters when living in Preston, and was one of the Democratic party leaders of the town. He served for some time as first selectman of Preston. He was broadly interested in every phase of public progress, and always kept well informed of the affairs of the day, State and National, as well as those of his own community. He was a man of lofty ideals and unselfish spirit, sparing himself no trouble to do a good turn or right a wrong. His influence among those who knew him was always for the betterment of society, and he will long be remembered as a man of upright character and estimable worth.

Mr. Benjamin married (first) Annie Yerington, of Preston, and they were the parents of five children, all born in that town: Clarence E., born December 24, 1893; Elizabeth, born June 14, 1896, who is now a school teacher in Griswold; Daisy, born February 27, 1899; Vernon H., deceased; and Allen H., born February 2, 1907. Mr. Benjamin married (second) Mrs. Amy (Lockwood) McCracken, a native of Brooklyn, New York, widow of Dan C. McCracken. Mr. and Mrs. McCracken were the parents of a son, Dan C., Jr., who is a resident of Preston.

WILLIAM SMIDDY—Recognized by his fellow townsmen as a man of deep thought and broad-minded conclusions, William Smiddy is regarded in Montville, Connecticut, as a progressive citizen who, though entirely a self-made man, has attained a comfortable competence in life.

Of American birth, William Smiddy is the son of Irish parents, who in 1853 came to this country and settled in Montville, Connecticut. His father was Charles Smiddy, born in County Cork, Ireland; he was in the employ of Mr. Hooper, the owner of the Hooper woolen mills of Montville, Connecticut, for a great many years, being his hostler. His death occurred in 1903, at the age of eighty-four years. Charles Smiddy was survived by his wife, Jane (Kelleher) Smiddy, also born in County Cork, Ireland, who died three years later, 1906, when seventy-five years old.

The son of Charles and Jane (Kelleher) Smiddy, William Smiddy, was born in Montville, Connecticut, June 28, 1855. Until thirteen years old he attended the local school, then, starting in the carding room of the Hooper Woolen Mill Company, Montville, Connecticut, he continued in that employment for seventeen years. Having an opportunity to advance in business, Mr. Smiddy became foreman of the Palmer Brothers Mills in Montville, manufacturers of quilts, where he has been engaged for the past thirty-five years as overseer of the carding and filling department.

Having always been a public-spirited man, and active in the affairs of his town, Mr. Smiddy has held several public offices; is now justice of the peace, and was register of voters and judge of local court. He is a Democrat in politics. He is a member of St. John's Roman Catholic Church; Knights of Columbus, Pequot Council, No. 125, of Montville; past grand knight of Independent Order of Odd Fellows, Thames Lodge, No. 22, of Montville.

William Smiddy was twice married, his first wife having been Nellie (Harrington) Smiddy, the daughter of Alding and Lucy (Sweet) Harrington. She died in September, 1915. One child was born of this marriage, William Henry, born December 20, 1884. He died September 28, 1918. Mr. Smiddy's first marriage took place in New London in September, 1872. He married (second) Johana Sopola, a native of Austria, born in 1883, the ceremony taking place in Montville in 1917.

JOSEPH ALBERT MARCOUX—When their son Joseph A. was eleven years of age, John and Mary (Dion) Marcoux left their Canadian home in Eads county, Province of Quebec, and came to the United States, locating in North Grosvenor Dale, Connecticut, and there finding employment in the cotton mills. Six years were spent there, after which John Marcoux moved to Montville, Connecticut, securing a position with the Attawangan Company, they having mills there. He remained in Montville eighteen years, then moved to Willimantic, Connecticut, where he died in 1907. His wife, born in St. Marie, Beauce county, Province of Quebec, Canada, survives her husband, and continues her residence in Willimantic.

Joseph Albert Marcoux was born in Eads county, Quebec, Canada, April 29, 1873, and there spent the years until 1884 attending school, when the family came to the United States. In North Grosvenor Dale, Connecticut, the first home of the family, and later in Montville, New London county, Connecticut, he was employed in the cotton mills, and in Montville he was for twelve years a worker in the weaving room of the Attawangan Mills. He then spent two years in the engine room of the Melcer Mill, then when the C. D. White Company bought the mill he continued with that company for ten years, serving as engineer of the plant. In 1912 the mill was bought by the J. B. Martin Company, and Mr. Marcoux has continued with that corporation during the years which have since intervened. He is now in charge of all outside work around the plant, and is also the general mechanic of the company. He has won high reputation for ability and faithfulness to his duties, and he is an honored and trusted employee. In politics Mr. Marcoux is an Independent, and in religious faith a Roman Catholic. He is a trustee of Montville Camp, Modern Woodmen of America, and takes an active interest in camp affairs.

Mr. Marcoux married, in Montville, March 21, 1894, Josephine Bonville, born in Quebec, Canada, and they are the parents of seven children, as follows: Joseph, born in Windsor Mills, Richmond county, Canada; Adelard, born in Montville, Connecticut, served in the World War with the American Expeditionary Forces; Mary Louise, married Ralph Bugbee, of Montville; Almar, born in Windsor Mills, Canada; William, born in Montville; Agnes, born in Montville; and Rose, also born in Montville.

JAMES DAVID CARVER, numbered among the older generation of residents of Montville, Connecticut, was born in Colchester, July 5, 1844, the son of the late George Nelson and Olive (Shaler) Carver. George Nelson Carver was born in Hebron, and died at Colchester in 1913, at the age of seventy-four years. He was a carpenter by trade.

Mr. and Mrs. Carver were the parents of three children: Frank, Charles, and James David, of further mention.

After receiving his preliminary education in the schools of Colchester, James David Carver entered Bacon Academy. After finishing his studies, he returned home and for the following seven years was employed by the neighboring farmers, so that he gained a thorough knowledge of the subject. He then went to Plano, Illinois, where he was employed by the Marsh Harvester Company for eight years. He resigned at the end of that time and came to Montville, where he purchased a small farm, which he conducted until he purchased his present place, which was the former homestead of his wife's people, and had been in their possession for a great many years. In politics Mr. Carver is an Independent, preferring to remain free and to exercise his own judgment on public issues. He has never held public office, but has always been keenly devoted to the welfare of the community and active in securing the choice of the best men available for the posts. Mr. Carver is a member of the Methodist church of Montville.

Mr. Carver married, in Montville, Ellen Collins, who has been a resident of Montville ever since she was three years of age, her birth having occurred in New London, in 1869. Mr. and Mrs. Carver are the parents of two children: George, who married Macy Coma, of Montville; Lillian, who married Mason Daniels.

WILLIAM WELLES LYMAN, one of the progressive men of Montville, New London county, Connecticut, has from the time of his graduation from college gone steadily forward in the business world, until he now holds the position of superintendent in the Montville Mill of the Palmer Brothers Company.

Born in Brooklyn, New York, May 18, 1888, William Welles Lyman is the son of William Prentice and Octavia (Rudd) Lyman, the former engaged in business with Joseph Wild & Company, Oriental rug importers of New York City. William P. Lyman died in 1890 in New York; his wife resides in New York at the present time. To the marriage were born two children: Virginia, resides at home; and William W., of whom further.

In his boyhood William Welles Lyman attended the public schools in Norwich, Connecticut, graduating in 1903, after which he entered the Norwich Free Academy and graduated from it in 1907. Then going to Ithaca, New York, young Mr. Lyman became a student in the Sibley College of Mechanical Engineering of Cornell University. Graduating from the four-year course in the class of 1911, Mr. Lyman received the degree of Mechanical Engineer. Shortly after leaving college, 1911, Mr. Lyman accepted a position with the Binghamton Gas Works, Binghamton, New York (a subsidiary of the American Light and Traction Company). Holding the position of assistant to the superintendent of the plant for two years, he was promoted to the office of superintendent of works in 1914, remaining as such for one year, when he resigned to become superintendent of the Palmer Brothers Company mill at Montville, where he is located at the present time (1921).

While attending the Norwich Free Academy, Mr. Lyman became a member of a Greek letter fraternity, the Rho Alpha Mu. He is also a member of the Norwich Golf Club and of the Binghamton Tennis Club, out-of-door sports being his special delight. Though not an active worker in the party, Mr. Lyman votes the Republican ticket. Connected with the Connecticut State Guards, he has been for two years lieutenant in the Montville Company.

In Montville, Connecticut, October 1, 1914, William Welles Lyman was united in marriage with Gladys Estelle Latimer, daughter of Joseph Strickland and Arabelle (Palmer) Latimer. Of this union three children have been born: Elizabeth Latimer, born August 3, 1915: William Welles, Jr., born August 31, 1916; Arabelle Palmer, born April 3, 1918. Mr. Lyman is a member of the Protestant Episcopal church of Montville, and Mrs. Lyman is a member of the Union Baptist church of Montville.

HARRY EVERETT CARTER, a young man not yet arrived at man's estate, has proved his ambition and enterprise by establishing in business for himself, and in Montville there is none but wishes him well. He is a son of Edward and Jane (Lesuno) Carter. Edward Carter was born in Canada, and in 1880 came to the United States, settling in Providence, Rhode Island. Later he came to Montville, Connecticut, where he yet resides, a machinist. He married Jane Lesuno, born in Canada, and they have two sons and a daughter: Harry Everett, Edward Gilbert, and Lillian, wife of George McGregor, a merchant of New London, Connecticut. They have two sons, George and Samuel McGregor.

Harry Everett Carter was born in Uncasville, New London county, Connecticut, August 26, 1900, and educated in Palmer Memorial School. He was his father's helper in the machine shop for two years, and in 1919 started a wood-turning and repair shop under his own name, continuing to the present time. He is a young man of energy, well liked and sure to succeed. He is a member of St. John's Roman Catholic church, of Montville, Connecticut. He is a member of the Knights of Columbus, Pequot Council, No. 125, of Montville, and Modern Woodmen of America, of Montville.

GEORGE PETER MADDEN—In the great drama of life Mr. Madden carried his part in a most capable and exemplary manner, and when the final curtain was rung down, he left behind him the record of a well-spent life. He was a man of quiet home-loving tastes, finding his greatest pleasure in ministering to the comfort and pleasure of those he loved. Among business and fraternal associates he was esteemed as a man of high principle, and in his passing all feel a personal loss.

George Peter Madden, son of Hugh and Catherine Madden, was born in Norwich, Connecticut, in December, 1872, and died in the city of his birth, May 18, 1921. He was educated in the public schools and early in life learned the cigarmaker's trade. About 1896 he began business for himself as a cigar manufacturer, having his factory in the Steiner building, later moving to quarters on Bath street and finally to a factory which he built on Cliff street. He built up a large business, his brands of cigars becoming famous through their dependable quality and through Mr. Madden being so well known for his sterling character, his just and upright dealing. He had the distinction of having the largest cigar manufacturing factory between New London, Connecticut, and Worcester, Massachusetts, and was very proud of the fact that his business had grown to such proportions under his own management and solely on merit. For twenty years he maintained a retail tobacco store at No. 243 Main street, that store being a center for baseball and athletic devotees.

Mr. Madden traveled all over Eastern Connecticut and parts of Massachusetts in the interest of his cigar factory, thus becoming widely known. He was enthusiastic in his support of all clean sports and was one of the men that supported the Norwich baseball team in the Trolley League. He was a charter member of Court City of Norwich, Foresters of America, and was initiated a member of Norwich Lodge, Benevolent and Protective Order of Elks, April 1, 1901, being very popular in both orders. He was a member of St. Patrick's Roman Catholic Church and the Holy Name Society. In politics he was a Democrat, and was a member of the Norwich Chamber of Commerce.

Mr. Madden married, in St. Patrick's Church, in Norwich, November 6, 1895, Rev. P. M. Kennedy officiating, Mary Elizabeth Craney, daughter of John and Annie Craney. Five children were born to Mr. and Mrs. Madden. 1. James Joseph, born in Norwich, August 4, 1896; he was his father's business associate until the entrance of the United States in the World War in 1917. He then entered the United States navy at the New London submarine base, June 8, 1917, and was rated a first-class yeoman when honorably discharged from the service, August 30, 1919. He then returned to Norwich, where he again became identified with his father's tobacco business and succeeded his father as manager of the business. 2. Esther Roslyn, born in Norwich, February 22, 1897. 3. George Fullerton, born in Norwich, in January, 1900; he is also associated in the management of the tobacco business. 4. Anna Elizabeth, born in Norwich. 5. Catherine, also born in Norwich. The family home is at No. 40 Otis street, Norwich, Connecticut.

ALBERT TRACEY UTLEY—No list of the long-established business men of Norwich would be complete without the name which stands at the head of this article. As a citizen, Mr. Utley takes a quiet but helpful interest in everything relating to the welfare and prosperity of his community.

John Chapman Utley, father of Albert Tracey Utley, was born in Griswold, Connecticut, and as a boy assisted his father in the labors of the farm. On reaching manhood he obtained a position in the grocery store of D. C. Coon, of Norwich, remaining until he was about thirty years old, when he opened a grocery store of his own on Water street. This he conducted successfully for sixteen years, retaining his active connection with it to the close of his life. A Democrat in politics, he held no office and belonged to no orders. He was an attendant of the Central Baptist Church of Norwich, of which his wife was a member. Mr. Utley married Mary Prentiss Richards, a native of Preston, Connecticut, and they became the parents of the following children, all of whom were born in Norwich: John R., who died in Baltimore, Maryland; George Tyler, who died in Hartford, Connecticut; Frank, who died in Norwich; Mary Ada, also died in Norwich; and Albert Tracey, mentioned below. The death of Mr. Utley occurred in Norwich about 1864, and in 1895 his widow passed away in the same place, having survived her husband more than thirty years.

Albert Tracey Utley, son of John Chapman and Mary Prentiss (Richards) Utley, was born October 29, 1850, in Norwich, Connecticut, and received his education in schools of his native town. When about sixteen years old he began to learn the drug business in the drug store of the Lee & Osgood Company, of Norwich, and after completing his course of preparation, remained with them for a number of years, the entire time of his connection with the firm amounting to a period of thirty-six years.

In 1903, in partnership with R. C. Jones, Mr. Utley opened a drug store at No. 145 Main street, under the firm name of Utley & Jones. Steadily and rapidly the business has increased, the partners acquiring as the years went on what is to-day one of the best trades in its own special line to be found in Norwich.

In politics, Mr. Utley is a Republican, but has never mingled in public life, having neither the time nor the wish to become an office holder. Neither does he affiliate with any orders. The family are members of the Central Baptist Church.

Mr. Utley married, November 4, 1873, in Norwich, Mary Jane Brown, born in that town, daughter of George E. and Elizabeth (Manning) Brown, and they are the parents of two daughters, both of whom were born in Norwich: 1. Ella M., who married Arthur B. Faulkner, of New Brunswick, Canada, and they have three children: Albert, Charlotte, and Marjorie. 2. Laura, who became the wife of William B. Pervis, of Norwich, and has one child, Mary Anne. Like his father before him, Mr. Utley is an active business man, much respected by his townsmen. He has built up, on a basis of unimpeachable integrity, one of the leading drug trades in the State of Connecticut.

GEORGE EDWARD SPARKS—Among the representative citizens of Jewett City, Connecticut, is George Edward Sparks, who holds the distinction of being the oldest employee of the Ashland Cotton Company, having been machinist there since 1886. During the many years of Mr. Sparks' residence in this community, he has ever been a zealous advocate and supporter of its most vital and essential interests.

George Edward Sparks was born in Lisbon, Connecticut, August 25, 1867, the son of Alfred and Alice (Curtis) Sparks. His father, Alfred Sparks, was also a native of Lisbon, and was a mechanic and millwright throughout his entire lifetime. He died in Bozrah, Connecticut, in 1905. To Mr. and Mrs. Sparks were born seven children, George Edward being the second child.

The boy George received his education in the district schools of Bozrah. His inception into business life was made with the Ashland Cotton Company in 1886, where he served an apprenticeship to the machinist's trade. In this machine shop he has continued ever since and has seen many changes throughout these many years, but he himself has continued ever faithfully in the performance of his various duties. His predominating characteristic throughout his career has been his ability, which has been backed by sterling integrity and self-reliance.

In politics he is a Republican, giving to that party the interest demanded of every good citizen, but taking no active part in the affairs of the organization. He is a charter member of Reliance Lodge, No. 29, Independent Order of Odd Fellows, of Jewett City, and attends the Baptist church of Jewett City, of which he is a member.

Mr. Sparks married, at Jewett City, Connecticut, October 8, 1908, Gertrude J. Prior, daughter of Daniel and Anne E. (Phillips) Prior.

JOSEPH PATRICK CUMMINGS, of Cummings & Ring, one of the leading undertaking firms of Norwich, Connecticut, is an up-to-date, progressive man of business, and a man of broad interests and keen sympathies.

His father, Thomas Cummings, was born in the County of Limerick, Ireland, and was educated in the national schools there. He came to America when a young man and located in Norwich, where he lived for the greater part of his life. He was, by trade, a heater in a rolling mill, and this work he followed as long as he lived. He was a thrifty, industrious man, highly respected in the community. He married Bridget Gleason, also born in the County of Limerick, Ireland. He died in Norwich, Connecticut, in May, 1906, his wife, who survives him, now living in Thamesville, Connecticut. They were the parents of seven children, of whom five are now living.

Joseph Patrick Cummings was born in Norwich, Connecticut, October 11, 1881. He received his education in the public schools of the city, growing up in the traditions of the community. As a young man he entered the employ of Charles A. Gager, Jr., as assistant undertaker, remaining with him for eight years. Then, having decided to make this business his life work, Mr. Cummings entered the Massachusetts College of Embalming, taking their regular course, and receiving his diploma in 1906. He also passed the examination of the Connecticut State Board of Embalmers, after which for a time he still continued to work for Norwich undertakers. Then in 1913, in company with John F. Ring, he established an independent undertaking business, under the name of Cummings & Ring. This association has continued to date, the young men having gone forward rapidly to an assured position in their line of business. This is one of the leading undertaking firms in the county. They always have on hand the greatest abundance of fittings and supplies, and have all motor-driven equipment.

Mr. Cummings is deeply interested in all public affairs, keeping in touch with every movement that involves the general welfare. In political affiliation he is a Democrat. He is a member of the Benevolent and Protective Order of Elks, No. 430, of Norwich; of the Knights of Columbus; and of the White Cross Consistory, of the Fourth Degree.

Mr. Cummings married, on September 16, 1916, Annie E. Maher, daughter of Daniel J. and Annie (Devine) Maher, of Norwich, Connecticut, and they have three children: Rosalie, Joseph, and Richard.

The family are members of the Roman Catholic church.

JEREMIAH JEROME SULLIVAN — Nearly three-quarters of a century ago John Paul Sullivan came to Colchester, Connecticut, from his farm in Ireland, and as soon as possible obtained possession of a farm in Colchester, on which he lived in contentment until the end of his useful life, one of the first men of his race to obtain title to lands in this town. He was succeeded in the management of his farm by his youngest son, Jeremiah Jerome Sullivan, who still resides at the home farm, although postmaster of Colchester, an office he has held since 1913. He is a man of enterprise and public spirit, one of the representative men of the community in which he was born and in which his life has been spent. He is well known and is highly esteemed for integrity and ability.

Mr. Sullivan is a son of John Paul and Nellie (Sheehan-Riorden) Sullivan, his parents both born in County Kerry, Ireland. John P. Sullivan was a farmer in Ireland, and there married Mrs. Nellie (Sheehan) Riorden, a widow with a daughter, Mary T. Riorden, who married William T. Irwin, of Lynn, Massachusetts. Immediately after their marriage in 1847, Mr. and Mrs. Sullivan came to the United States, locating in Colchester, Connecticut, where Mrs. Sullivan had a sister living. Mr. Sullivan secured employment in the factory of the Hayward Rubber Company, then a leading industry of Colchester. After a few years his love of the soil asserted itself and he bought the present Sullivan farm, being one of the first Irish landowners of Colchester. He cultivated his farm very successfully and became one of the substantial and prominent men of his community. He was a well educated man and took a deep interest in the schools, serving as school committeeman. He continued at the farm until his passing, October 2, 1899. Mr. and Mrs. John Paul Sullivan were the parents of four children: Daniel John, who died in Indianapolis, Indiana; Nellie Frances, married Timothy P. Sheehan, of New London, Connecticut, who survives her; Nora, died young; Jeremiah Jerome, of further mention.

Jeremiah Jerome Sullivan, youngest son of John Paul and Nellie (Sheehan-Riorden) Sullivan, was born in the town of Colchester, New London county, Connecticut, at the farm he now owns on the Colchester-Norwich State Road, April 16, 1861. He was educated in the public schools near the home farm, Bacon Academy, Colchester, and under the private instruction of Professor George H. Tracy, of Colchester. After completing his own education, he began teaching in Colchester; that period of his career covering the years 1889-1907. During those years he spent his summers at the farm and continued alternately between school and farm until 1907, when he resigned his school to devote all his time to the farm which he owns. From 1907 until August, 1913, he gave himself exclusively to the farm, but in the latter year he was appointed postmaster of Colchester, an office which he yet holds (1921). He continues his home at the farm, his birthplace, but his sons operate the farm with the help of hired labor.

Prior to his appointment as postmaster, Mr. Sullivan had been a member of the Board of Registration for Colchester for twenty-six years. He was a member of the State Central Democratic Committee in 1896, has served on the Board of School Visitors since 1886, and since 1911 has been chairman of the board. He is a strong force in the party locally, and one of the substantial citizens of his town. He is a member of St. Andrew's Roman Catholic Church.

Mr. Sullivan married, April 27, 1888, at New London, Connecticut, Elizabeth McGrath, daughter of Patrick and Catherine (Reddy) McGrath, her parents both born in Ireland. Mr. and Mrs. Sullivan are the parents of six children, all born at the home farm at Colchester, still the family home: Eileen Katherine, now a teacher in Colchester schools; Jerome John, a rural free delivery carrier from the Colchester office; Marion Elizabeth, a graduate nurse; Raymond Joynt, residing at home; Mildred, residing at home; Willard A., residing at home.

Mr. Sullivan has spent his life in the community of which he is now a substantial member, and here he has won public confidence and approval, a man of vision and public spirit, a man to be trusted and relied upon.

HERBERT V. MOXLEY, one of New London's young and successful merchants, is of an old Groton family, founded in that town by Joseph Moxley, who was brought by his parents to Groton in 1736, an infant. All trace seems lost of his parents, but the child grew to manhood, and was the head of a family, when, in 1781, the enemies of his adopted country landed at New London, on pillage and destruction bent. Joseph Moxley volunteered to aid in the defence of Fort Griswold, and there gave up his life. Herbert V. Moxley, of the sixth generation, traces in lineal line through the patriot's third son, Samuel Moxley.

Joseph Moxley, of Scotch ancestry, was born in Glasgow, Scotland, in 1736, but when but six months of age was brought to New England by his parents, they making their home in Groton, Connecticut, now Ledyard. There he lived until the War of the Revolution, a farmer. When Fort Griswold was attacked by the British, he was in the fort as a volunteer, having been, it is said, the last man to enter the fort by the north gate, those troops which came in from Fort Trumbull entering by the south gate of the fort. Joseph Moxley's station was in the southeast bastion, next to Samuel Edgecomb. He was wounded in the abdomen, and was later taken in an ox-cart down the heights, and that night died from his injuries. His son, Joseph (2) Moxley, also a volunteer, was in the fort, and when the massacre began he jumped from the wall, landing on a British bayonet which passed through his body. He was left on the field for dead, but that night he crawled away to a place of succor, and in time his youth (nineteen) asserted itself and he recovered from his wounds and lived until 1815.

Joseph (1) Moxley, at the time of his death in 1781, was forty-five years of age. He married Elizabeth Horsford, of the Royal House of Horsford, and they had six children: 1. Joseph (2), born in 1762; married Prudence Lamb, who survived him; she married (second) Benjamin Daboll, and died aged eighty-five. Joseph (2) Moxley lived in Ledyard, and there died, in 1815. 2. Jonathan, married Sally Woodmansee, and moved to Pennsylvania. 3. Samuel, of whom further. 4 Deborah, married Henry Hallett. 5. Esther, married Moses Jones, who was killed at Fort Griswold; she married (second) a Mr. Colver, of Groton, Connecticut. 6. Elizabeth, married Benjamin Daboll.

Samuel Moxley, third son of Joseph and Elizabeth (Horsford) Moxley, the Revolutionary martyr, was a resident of Groton, New London county, Connecticut, and there married a Miss Woodmansee, and they were the parents of two sons: Samuel (2), and William, descent in this line being through the second son, William.

William Moxley, son of Samuel (1) Moxley, was born in Groton, Connecticut, there passed his life, and died in 1890. He married Lucy Geer, daughter of George and Deidamia (Daboll) Geer, granddaughter of Benjamin and Elizabeth (Moxley) Daboll, and great-granddaughter of Joseph and Elizabeth (Horsford) Moxley. William and Lucy (Geer) Moxley were the parents of a son, George William, head of the next generation in this line, and of a daughter, Mary Abb, born in 1834, died in 1876, wife of Albert Lamb.

George William Moxley, only son of William and Lucy (Geer) Moxley, was born in Groton, Connecticut, in 1831, and there married Amy Green, and they were the parents of two sons: Francis Geer, head of the next generation in this line; and Everett Daboll, born in 1859, married Lucretia Briggs, and had a daughter, Adelaide L.

Francis Geer Moxley, eldest son of George W. and Amy (Green) Moxley, was born in Groton, Connecticut, in 1854, died in New London, Connecticut, in 1913. When a young man he entered mercantile life and became a prosperous New London merchant. He married Mary E. Ayer, born in Preston, Connecticut, who died in 1905. They were the parents of three children: George F., who died young; Herbert V., of further mention; Bessie May, deceased, married Captain George Healy, of New London, a master mariner.

Herbert V. Moxley, second son of Francis Geer and Mary E. (Ayer) Moxley, and of the sixth generation of the family founded by the Scotchman, Joseph Moxley, the Revolutionary martyr, was born in Groton, Connecticut, February 15, 1883. He was educated in Groton and New London public schools, finishing with graduation from Bulkeley High School, New London, class of 1900. He entered the employ of the American Express Company as clerk in their New London office immediately after graduation, and continued with that company for seven years. After the death of his father, Francis Geer Moxley, in 1913, he succeeded him as head of his business, and so continues.

Mr. Moxley is a member of the New London Chamber of Commerce; the Rotary Club; New London Lodge, No. 360, Benevolent and Protective Order of Elks; and the First Baptist Church of Groton. In politics he is a Republican. Mr. Moxley resides in New London.

JOHN PHELPS TAYLOR ARMSTRONG—A native son of New London, and since 1904 connected with one of the city's important corporations, and its general manager, Mr. Armstrong, both by birth and environment, is closely bound to New London, Connecticut, which is also the home of his parents, Benjamin A. and Louisa A. (Smith) Armstrong, his father also of New London birth. Benjamin A. Armstrong was born in 1844, and his wife was born in Franklin, Connecticut, in 1845, both now living in New London. Mr. Armstrong, Sr., a manufacturer of silk, served New London twenty-five years as president of the Board of Water Commissioners. He is a Republican in politics, and a member of the Congregational church.

John P. T. Armstrong was born in New London, Connecticut, July 1, 1882, and there began his education in the public school, finishing the courses of Bulkeley High School with the class of 1899. He then completed courses of preparatory study at Phillips Andover Academy, class of 1900, going thence to Yale University, A. B., class of 1904. He entered the employ of the Brainerd & Armstrong Company as a clerk the same year, and has been with that company during the years which have since intervened, his rank constantly advancing until he is now (1921) general manager, secretary and director. He is a director of the National Bank of Commerce of New London; is a Republican in politics; member of the Second Congregational Church; the Masonic order; Yale Club, of New York City; Thames Club, of New London; Shenecossett Country Club, of New London; and the Norwich Golf Club, of Norwich, Connecticut.

Mr. Armstrong married, at New Rochelle, New York, February 28, 1918, Lillian T. Washburn, born in Owensboro, Kentucky, daughter of Homer T. and Laura Washburn.

JOHN H. W. SCHRÖDER, now and since 1868 superintendent of Elm Grove Cemetery of Stonington, Connecticut, was born in Germany, June 17, 1833, son of Jochiam Schröder. His parents died while he was but a child, but he obtained a good education, studied landscape gardening, and remained in his native Germany until twenty-six years of age. In 1859 he came to the United States, locating in Stonington, Connecticut, where his first position was in caring for and beautifying the Seminary grounds. He came to his present position, superintendent of Elm Grove Cemetery, in 1867, more than half a century ago, and by his skill and artistic talent has developed one of the most beautiful of Connecticut cemeteries. His years, eighty-seven, have been largely spent as a landscape gardener, and if it be true that "he who makes two blades of grass grow where but one grew before is a public benefactor," then John H. W. Schröder is one of the public benefactors, for he has given his life to reclaiming the waste places and causing grass, shrubbery and trees to grow where none grew before, and to making beautiful places more beautiful.

John H. W. Schröder married, in 1861, Maria W. Schröder, who died February 15, 1906. They were the parents of five children: Wilhelmina D., who resides with her father in Stonington, Connecticut; Louisa R., secretary at Teachers' College, Columbia University; Henry C., married Emma Baxter, of Brooklyn, now and since 1885 assistant superintendent of Elm Grove Cemetery, father and son having been associated in its care for thirty-five years; Nettie, married C. W. Crandall, and resides in Groton, Connecticut; Charlotte M., married Charles D. Wolf. Mr. Schröder and family are members of the Congregational church.

EDWIN FITCH COMSTOCK—A list of the very old settlers of Connecticut would be incomplete without mention of the Comstock family, whose members have lived in the State for several hundred years, coming down in a straight unbroken line to the present generation. They were all tillers of the soil, those who have been the backbone of the country, and the present representative of them, Edwin Fitch Comstock, has followed in the footsteps of his forbears, and owns and cultivates his own land in Oakdale, Montville township, Connecticut.

Edwin Fitch Comstock is the son of D. Chester Comstock, and the grandson of David Comstock. D. Chester Comstock was born in Montville, December 15, 1839. He was a farmer, and when the Civil War broke out he left his farm to become a soldier in the Twenty-fourth Regiment, Connecticut Infantry. After the close of the war he returned to Montville, where he married Frances Raymond, born in Montville, December 16, 1839. In addition to their son, Edwin Fitch Comstock, they had two daughters, both now married, one being Mrs. Minnie (Comstock) Rogers and the other Mrs. Julia (Comstock) Beebe. D. Chester Comstock died very suddenly, March 9, 1912, at the age of seventy-three years, his wife having passed away November 2, 1874, when only thirty-five years old.

Born upon his father's farm in Montville, Connecticut, August 21, 1868, Edwin Fitch Comstock attended the district school in his boyhood, and afterward took a course at a business college, then went to California, where he lived in Santa Cruz county until 1893, when he returned to his home in Montville and started upon the life of a farmer. Though a Republican in politics, Mr. Comstock does not always vote for the candidate named on that ticket, preferring to choose the man best fitted for the office under consideration. He has been very active in the public affairs of his township, having held various offices at different times; he was a member of the Board of Selectmen and of the Board of Assessors, also town representative to the State Legislature in 1919, and has served on the Board of Relief. Mr. Comstock and his family are members of and workers in the Congregational church of Montville.

On April 4, 1894, in Montville, Edwin Fitch Comstock married Lena E. Williams, born in Montville, January 12, 1870. She is the daughter of Ephriam and Evelyn (Williams) Williams, of that town. Of this marriage four children have been born: 1. Evelyn, born in Montville, June 1, 1895; she is the wife of Carl Johnson, of Montville, and is the mother of one child, Joice Johnson. 2. Chester Williams, born August 4, 1898; served in the Student Army Training Corps, United States Army, World War. 3. Hope Morgan, born August 19, 1902. 4. Percy Edwin, born January 12, 1905, died aged eighteen months.

ALBERT JOHN FOX—Among the old settlers in or about the town of Montville, the oldest is probably the Fox family, the ancestral members of it having lived here for several generations. The present representative of the name is Albert John Fox, the son of Joel Henry Fox, born in September, 1842, in Montville, where he has been a successful farmer for many years past. He was the son of Robert Fox, also a resident of Montville. Joel Henry Fox married Addie Woodmansee, whose people were residents of Montville, where she was born.

The son of Joel Henry and Addie (Woodmansee) Fox, Albert John Fox, was born in Montville on his father's farm, July 28, 1875, spending his boyhood and youth on the farm and attending the local schools, where he acquired an education. When twenty-two years old Mr. Fox came to the town of Montville, in 1897, and obtaining employment in one of the mills went to work as an ordinary mill hand, beginning at the bottom and working his way upward until now he is foreman of the mill. Not only has Albert John Fox made good in the mill; he has a large farm just outside the town (Oakdale), this being the homestead place of which Mr. Fox is manager, and he has made a great success of it, working early and late to bring it to its present prosperous condition. In the matter of politics, Mr. Fox is not bound to any party, but follows the dictates of his conscience in voting for a candidate for office.

Albert John Fox was united in marriage with Ellen C. Johnson, a native of Hartford, Connecticut, born September 18, 1876. She is the daughter of Bernard and Mary (Anderson) Johnson. Of this union two children have been born: Albert Henry and Charles Raymond, both born on the homestead place in Oakdale, Connecticut. Mr. and Mrs. Fox are members of the First Congregational Church in Montville Center.

THOMAS JOSEPH LYNCH was born in Lebanon, Connecticut, March 26, 1875, the son of Michael and Eleanor (Sullivan) Lynch. Michael Lynch was born in County Cork, Ireland. He came to this country at the age of seventeen years, locating in Lebanon, where he purchased a farm and subsequently became employed by the Haywood Rubber Company factory in Lebanon, in which industry he continued until the factory closed. He then returned to his farm in Lebanon and has conducted it to date, having purchased the farm in 1873. Mrs. Lynch was also a native of Ireland; she died in Lebanon, September 25, 1917, and is buried in Greenville. To Mr. and Mrs. Lynch were born seven children: 1. Katie, born in Lebanon, wife of Thomas Craney, of Norwich. 2. Timothy, born in Lebanon, now lives in Norwich. 3. Thomas Joseph, mentioned below, born on the Lynch farm, Lebanon, as were all later children. 4. Mary, died in infancy. 5. Mary, employed in Palmer Brothers' Mill, Fitchville, Connecticut. 6. Nellie, at home. 7. Anna, died in infancy.

The boyhood of the lad Thomas Joseph was spent on his father's farm, and most of the time was given in aiding the elder man in his work about the place. After terminating his studies in the Lebanon schools, he continued to reside with his parents, and was employed by the neighboring farmers so that he gained a wide and extensive knowledge of the subject, and became well skilled in agricultural methods generally. Thus he continued until 1902, when he came to Fitchville and accepted his present position as head farmer of the Palmer Brothers' Mill farm in the town of Bozrah, which consists of 600 acres, and he also has charge of all outside work, such as teaming, hauling, etc. Upon coming to this community Mr. Lynch purchased an attractive little farm, and together with his sister he has continued to reside here up to the present time. His spare time is devoted to the cultivation of his own property, which he has already brought to a highly productive state. Mr. Lynch is one of those men who take a deep inteerst in the welfare of the community in which they reside, and as such identifies himself with all that makes for the betterment of civic conditions. He is a Democrat in politics, and attends St. John's Roman Catholic Church, Fitchville, Connecticut.

VINCENT MASTRODDI—John Mastroddi, a merchant of Rome, Italy, died there in December, 1910, at the age of seventy-four years, and there was buried. He married Catherine Chicarelli, also born in Rome, who after the death of her husband came to the United States and joined her children. She now resides in New Britain, Connecticut, aged 56 years.

Vincent Mastroddi, son of John and Catherine (Chicarelli) Mastroddi, was born in Rome, Italy, July 4, 1882, and there spent the years of his minority, securing a good education. He came to the United States in 1913, and for ten years was variously employed, his last position prior to coming to New London county being with Armour & Company, of Chicago, in their Hartford, Connecticut, branch. In 1920 he opened a general store near New London, Connecticut, there remaining until recently, when he moved his business to Palmerstown in the town of Montville in the same county, and there is successfully conducting a general store.

Vincent Mastroddi married (first) Rose Filippo, born in Buenos Aires, South America, April 30, 1889, died December 4, 1918, daughter of Dominick Filippo. They were the parents of five children: Catherine, born August 10, 1907; John, born September, 1909; Loquina, born October 28, 1913; Anna, born June 4, 1916; Rose, born November 20, 1918. Mr. Mastroddi married (second) Mrs. Anna (Johnson) Daniel, born in Montville, Connecticut, daughter of Swanty and Ida Johnson, and by her first marriage was the mother of two children, William and Clinton, the first named killed in an automobile accident, October 28, 1920. Mr. Mastroddi is a member of the Woodmen of America, the Catholic church, Pequot Council, No. 125, Knights of Columbus, of Montville, and Norwich Lodge, No. 430, Benevolent and Protective Order of Elks.

ERASTUS DENISON MINER—In 1646 Lieutenant Thomas Miner, an officer of Colonial soldiers, settled in New London, Connecticut, and from that year Miner has been an honored New London county name. Erastus Denison Miner, born in Stonington, Connecticut, December 16, 1830, died April 23, 1907, was of the eighth generation in Connecticut, and son of Elias and Betsey (Brown) Miner, his father a farmer of Stonington all his life. His wife, Betsey (Brown) Miner, was also born in Stonington, and they were the parents of four children, Erastus D., the youngest.

Erastus D. Miner was educated in the district schools of the town of Stonington, and early became a farmer. In 1858 he bought a farm of fifty acres in the Hinckley Hill section in his native township, and there he resided until his death at the age of seventy-seven years. He was a Republican in politics, although he took no part in politics, but he was a devoted member of Broad Street Congregational Church, of Westerly, Rhode Island, and served that church as deacon for forty years. He was a man of upright life and industrious habits, highly esteemed in his town.

Erastus D. Miner married, August 15, 1852, Jane Breed, who died in Stonington, July 1, 1910. On August 15, 1902, they celebrated their Golden Wedding day. Five years later the husband died, his widow surviving him three years. Four children were born to Erastus D. and Jane (Breed) Miner: 1. Herman E., married (first) Fannie Savitte; (second) Fannie Wilcox; (third) Ethel Thorpe, who survives him, a resident of Westerly, Rhode Island. 2. Sarah, married (first) Herman Brown; (second) Henry L. Allen, of North Stonington, Connecticut. 3. Mary E., married Frank E. Wilcox, and resides on the home farm. 4. Annie E., married John Seymour, and resides in Pawcatuck. The home place of fifty acres is run by Frank E. Wilcox.

STAVROS FRANCIS PETERSON—Widely known in New London and Norwich, Connecticut, as owner of the favorite confectionery shops, Stavros F. Peterson is a leading manufacturing confectioner of the State.

Mr. Peterson was born of Greek parents, in Bathy Erdek, Asia Minor, on March 20, 1887. Receiving a limited education in his native land, he came to the United States as a boy of thirteen to work for his uncle, who was also a confectioner.

Thoroughly familiarizing himself with the business, Mr. Peterson established a store in New London in 1907 under the name of Paterson & Peterson. In 1911 he opened a branch store in Norwich, under the title of Peterson & Tyler. Later, under title of Peterson & Nichols, Inc., he engaged in the manufacture of confectionery at Waterbury, Connecticut. This business was subsequently brought to New London and established in the old Boss cracker factory, but was later discontinued. In 1913 he purchased the William Frisbie store in Norwich, which business, combined with the larger and more important store in New London, was incorporated for $50,000, and has come to be a leader in the confectionery business not only in the county, but in the State. Mr. Peterson is president of the company. They make the finest candies and also handle an extensive catering business. In the New London store alone he employs twenty-five people.

Mr. Peterson is a member of the Chamber of Commerce of both New London and Norwich. During the World War he enlisted in the United States navy, and was stationed at the Cloyne School, Newport, Rhode Island, as chief of the Commissary Division. He entered the service on April 20, 1917, and was discharged on December 24, 1918. He is now a member of the John Coleman Prince Post, American Legion.

Politically, Mr. Peterson supports the Republican party. Fraternally, he is a member of Brainard Lodge, No. 102, Free and Accepted Masons; Union Chapter, No. 4, Royal Arch Masons; Cushing Council, Royal and Select Masters; Knights Templar; and the Mystic Shrine. He is a member of Mohican Lodge, No. 85, Independent Order of Odd Fellows; and of New London Lodge, No. 360, Benevolent and Protective Order of Elks. He is a member of the Rotary Club and the John Winthrop Club, both of New London.

On June 16, 1920, Mr. Peterson married Henrietta

L. Costigan, of New York City, and they attend St. James' Episcopal Church, of New London. They reside at the Mohican Hotel.

FREDERICK WILLIAM CHAPEL—The old Hill estate now owned by Frederick W. Chapel and his brother, Charles L. Chapel, has been in the Hill family for over sixty years. Mr. Chapel is a resident of the village of Montville, and there is engaged in milling and farming. He is a son of Leander Davis Chapel, born in Chesterfield Society, town of Montville, New London county, Connecticut, the Chapel family being one of the old families of the county. He married Sibyl Fox Hill, daughter of George Washington Hill, of Montville. They were the parents of two sons: Frederick W., of further mention; Charles Leander, born March 16, 1879.

Frederick W. Chapel was born in the village of Palmerstown, New London county, Connecticut, May 14, 1870. He was educated in the village public schools and Norwich Business College, finishing courses at the latter institution with graduation. His first mercantile position was with Sherman & Larkin as clerk in their grocery store in Montville, but later he went in the same capacity with F. C. Sherman, a merchant of Palmer, Massachusetts. He remained there but seven months, then returned to Palmerstown, where he has since resided, engaged in mill operations and farming. He owns, as stated, in company with his brother, the old Hill homestead, and is a man of high standing in his community. For seven years he has been a member of the Board of Relief for the town of Montville, member of Montville Centre Congregational Church, member of Thames Lodge, No. 22, Independent Order of Odd Fellows, and a Republican in politics.

JACOB DICK is one of those men whose success is in every sense of the word self-made, the result of his own indefatigable belief in his ability to succeed. Coming to this country when but fifteen years of age, he has won his own way to the position which he holds in the community to-day.

Jacob Dick was born in Bavaria, April 1, 1875, the son of the late Frederick and Gertrude (Fuss) Dick, both natives of Bavaria. The boy Jacob went to school in his native place until he was twelve years of age. The business of life then began for the lad, and he apprenticed himself to the bakers' trade. In 1890, at the age of fifteen years, he came to this country and located in Brooklyn, New York, where he secured employment as a baker until 1893, when he went to New London, Connecticut, and worked at his trade in various places until 1918, when he purchased the A. C. Weeks Bakery in Mystic, Connecticut, since which time he has conducted this enterprise under the name of The Mystic Home Bakery. Previous to buying this business, Mr. Dick had been manager of it for Mr. Weeks for seven years, and during this time gained a thorough knowledge of its various branches.

In politics Mr. Dick is a Republican, and while he has never consented to hold office is nevertheless somewhat active in political circles, and always as a good citizen gives loyal support to measures calculated to promote the welfare of Mystic. He is active in church work, and is a member of St. Mark's Episcopal Church of Mystic. Mr. Dick is also affiliated with the Independent Order of Odd Fellows, Stonington Lodge, No. 26.

On June 11, 1897, Jacob Dick was united in marriage with Elizabeth (Muller) Dieter, daughter of William and Elizabeth (Fischer) Muller, widow of the late Emile Dieter, who died in New London, 1894, and the mother of three children: George D., married Nellie Menge, resides in Mystic; Catherine, married to Augustus Dick, resides in Norwich; Augusta, married Otto Hoppe, resides in Montreal, Canada. To the marriage of Jacob and Elizabeth Dick were born six children, as follows: Carrie, who married Francis Brown, of Reading, Massachusetts; Gertrude, who married Charles Phee, of Waterbury, Connecticut; Minnie, who married Harold Fox; Winifred, Jacob F., and Edward J.

CLARENCE A. COOGAN is the youngest child of six children of Edward C. and Lucy E. (Crumb) Coogan, of Mystic, Connecticut. Edward C. Coogan, born in Boston, Massachusetts, came to Putnam, Connecticut, when a boy and there attended public schools. Later he located in Mystic, obtaining employment with the Standard Machine Company and there continues, having been receiving and shipping clerk for the past twenty-one years, 1899-1920.

Clarence A. Coogan was born in Mystic, Connecticut, August 1, 1898. He obtained a good grammar school education in the Mystic public schools. He completed his studies in Stonington High School in 1917, and at once began farming as a business in the town of Stonington, near Mystic. He rented the Walter Morgan farm of one hundred and twenty acres near Mystic, and there has since conducted profitable farming and poultry raising operations. He is a member of Mystic Grange, Patrons of Husbandry, and in politics a Republican.

Mr. Coogan married, March 5, 1919, Clara Avery Morgan, daughter of Walter C. and Martha (Wheeler) Morgan, of Mystic. They are both members of the Congregational church. They are the parents of two children: Clarissa Avery, born in the town of Stonington, October 10, 1920; Edward Carle, born January 27, 1921.

TORRES OLSEN—From Mandal, the southernmost town of Norway, twenty-three miles from Christiansand, on the Skagerrak, came Torres Olsen, now and for twenty-five years engineer with the T. A. Scott Company, of New London, Connecticut. He is a son of Ole and Bergetta Olsen; his father also born in Mandal, where he died at the age of forty-five, in 1897, leaving the following children: Elias, Torres, Olaf, Christian, and Tobine.

Torres Olsen, second son of Ole and Bergetta Olsen, was born in Mandal, Norway, August 15, 1877, and there spent the first eighteen years of his life. He obtained his education in the public schools, and continued his father's helper until 1895, when he came to the United States, finding employment and a home in New London, Connecticut. Soon after coming to New London he entered the employ of the T. A. Scott Company as engineer and there he has continued for a quarter of a century. The T. A. Scott Company are wrecking contractors, and during his service with them Mr. Olsen has had many exciting experiences, for wherever there is a wreck the Scott Company is found, and wherever the Scott Company wrecking outfit is found there will Torres Olsen be found, sometimes in a diver's suit ready for a descent into the dark places beneath the surface, sometimes in the engine room or on other duty, but wherever you find him you will find a man of efficiency, devoted to his employers' interests, and ready for duty. He has worked on many wrecks all along the coast, and made many descents as a diver. He is highly regarded by his employers and by his associates in the often hazardous business in which they are engaged. Men learn to value fidelity and faithfulness in such a business, a business where a man's life hangs on the coöperation of another, and where a slight deviation from the agreed plan may mean disaster to all. So Torres Olsen has gained the reputation he holds, for on his quick action and promptness, his clear head and strong arm, men know they may confidently rely.

Torres Olsen married Hulda Lofholm, born in Finland, July 24, 1875, daughter of Carl Lofholm. Mr. and Mrs. Olsen are the parents of three children: Carl Olaf, born October 7, 1903; Walter William, born October 7, 1905, died April 18, 1920; Edith Johanna, born February 10, 1908. The family home is at No. 53 Sherman street, New London, Connecticut.

LUTHER CLINTON TEFFT—The first position Luther C. Tefft ever held in a mill was with the Palmer Brothers Quilt Mills, and since that time he has filled many positions, now being assistant superintendent of the Bank's Paper Mills in Montville, Connecticut. He is a son of Elmer Tefft, a farmer of the town of Griswold, New London county, Connecticut, but later moved to a farm in Oakdale, Connecticut, where he is now living, aged fifty-four years. He married Jessie McClure, born in Griswold, Connecticut.

Luther Clinton Tefft was born at the home farm in the town of Griswold, Connecticut, August 28, 1891. He attended public schools until fifteen years of age, then secured employment with the Palmer Brothers Quilt Mills in Montville, his parents having previously moved there. He remained three years with Palmer Brothers, going thence to what is now the Keyes Products Company's mill, where he remained until 1915. In that year he came to his present position, assistant superintendent of the Bank's Paper Mills in Montville. Mr. Tefft is a member of Oxoboxo Blue Lodge, Free and Accepted Masons, in Montville, Connecticut, and in politics is extremely independent.

Mr. Tefft married Mabel La Flame, born in Yantic, Connecticut, February 11, 1892, daughter of James and Grace (Windsor) La Flame. Mr. and Mrs. Tefft are the parents of four children: Dorothy T., born February 7, 1912; Ruth, born January 26, 1914; Elsie, born February 16, 1917; Luther, born May 5, 1920. Mr. and Mrs. Tefft are members of the Episcopal church of Norwich, Connecticut.

ROBERT THOMAS BAKER—James Baker, of early Colonial family, was born in Brooklyn, Connecticut, and all his life was a farmer in different Connecticut towns. He died in the year 1900, aged fifty-five years. He married Sophia Fitch, who died in 1890, aged forty years. They were the parents of sons, James Albert and Robert T.; and daughters, Mary, married Luciun Bishop, and Elizabeth, married George Kimball.

Robert Thomas Baker, son of James and Sophia (Fitch) Baker, was born in Woodstock, Connecticut, June 29, 1870. His parents moved to Pomfret, Connecticut, in 1871, and there the boy grew to manhood. He remained at home during his minor years, then was employed in various places until 1892, when he spent three years in Bozrah, Connecticut, engaged as a painter. The next fifteen years were spent in farming in Pomfret, on the Sawyer place, after which Mr. Baker spent two years in farming in the town of Norwich, then spent two years in Bozrah, then bought his present farm in the town of Montville, in the Raymond Hill District, in 1914.

Mr. Baker married, in Bozrah, November 1, 1893, Jessie Sawyer, daughter of Joseph and Mary (Perkins) Sawyer. Joseph Sawyer was of a Lynn, Massachusetts, family of manufacturing people. He died in 1910, and was buried in Hartford, Connecticut. Mary (Perkins) Sawyer, born in Bozrah, August 18, 1850, was a daughter of Samuel Perkins. Mr. and Mrs. Baker have no children. He is an enthusiastic trapper and hunter and very skillful. In politics he is a Republican. They attend and support the Congregational church.

HENRY HASKELL GALLUP—The Norwich of today is the outgrowth of constructive effort on the part of men endowed with breadth of vision and the practical business ability which carries an individual or a community far and high along the "Way of Progress." Henry Haskell Gallup for nearly twenty years president of the Norwich Belt Manufacturing Company, and for more than fifty years active in the mercantile and industrial interests of Norwich, is one of the men who have done most for the development of this city.

In the closing years of the eighteenth century, when the echoes of the Revolutionary guns had scarcely died away in the hearts of New London county citizens, Isaac Gallup, Mr. Gallup's grandfather, was born in that part of Groton which is now called "Ledyard." He grew up to be a youth of courageous bearing, and a man of ambition and resource. Seeing both duty and opportunity in the constructive industries which were to develop the new-fledged nation, he became a carpenter and builder, later broadening the scope of his activity by taking up surveying. In 1828 he came to Norwich, bringing his little family with him, but remained for only a year in the town. The year following, he removed to Preston, bought land, and built a home for his family. This property has ever since been known as the Gallup homestead, and is still in the family. He carried on the farm in connection with his other activities, until his death in May, 1867. He married Prudence Geer, who was born in Ledyard, and died at the Gallup home farm in Preston, in the year 1871.

Isaac (2), son of Isaac (1) and Prudence (Geer) Gallup, was born on the farm in the town of Ledyard, New London county, Connecticut, in 1820. With his parents he removed to Norwich in 1828, and was nine years of age when the farm in Preston was bought and the home built. As a young man he assisted his father on the farm, and upon his father's death inherited the property. He continued to conduct the farm until he was able to retire from active work, but lived there throughout his lifetime. He died there in 1906, at the age of eighty-six years, having spent seventy-seven years on the home farm in Preston. He married Maria Theresa Davis, who was born in Preston, and died at the homestead, December 30, 1910. Isaac and Maria Theresa (Davis) Gallup were the parents of three children, all born on the Gallup homestead in Preston, near Poquetanuck (spelled Poquetannoc in Connecticut State Register and Manual). Henry Haskell, whose name heads this review; Ella Maria, who is now the widow of Avery D. Wheeler, of Norwich, Connecticut; and Charles Davis, who is superintendent and vice-president of the Norwich Belt Manufacturing Company, of which his elder brother is president.

Henry Haskell Gallup was born in Preston, January 2, 1846. He received his early education in the district schools near the farm, then completed his studies in private schools. He then taught school for four winters, in Ledyard, North Stonington, and Norwich, helping on the home place during his vacations.

But the young man was not interested in a professional career, and the future of the city of Norwich appealed to him as full of business possibilities. He came to Norwich in 1868, and secured a position as clerk in a retail clothing store, a little later working as bookkeeper for Barstow & Palmer, in their hardware store. This gave Mr. Gallup practical experience, and a comprehensive grasp of the business situation of the time and the place. In 1871 he made the start which has developed to the important business interest of which he is now the head. He formed a partnership with George S. Smith, and as Smith & Gallup the new firm conducted a business in leather findings, saddle hardware, etc. This arrangement continued until July 10, 1873, and on that date the partners with Frank Ulmer, organized the Norwich Belt Manufacturing Company. They retained the partnership arrangement, which continued for ten years unchanged, and in that first decade the business was placed on a sound basis and developed to become one of the most promising industries of the city. On September 1, 1883, the senior partner, Mr. Smith, retired from the firm, and Mr. Gallup and Mr. Ulmer continued the business jointly. This arrangement continued for ten years, a period of steady growth and development for the firm. The beginning of the twentieth century saw the business developed to such a point that a different form of organization was advisable, and January 1, 1902, the incorporation of the Norwich Belt Manufacturing Company, with a capital of $300,000, became a fact.

In the new concern Mr. Gallup acted as treasurer and general manager of the business. The president of the company was Roswell A. Breed, who held this office until his retirement, in 1911, when Mr. Gallup became president of the company, still retaining the general managership, handling the duties of both offices up to the present time.

The Norwich Belt Manufacturing Company is now one of the oldest as well as one of the most important of the Norwich industries. Their principal product is large and small leather belts for factory and other uses, and they also do an extensive business in tanning leather of many kinds and grades, for all sorts of purposes, their market covering a very wide range of territory. Their office and tannery are on North Main street, in Norwich, and they have a branch office in Providence, Rhode Island.

In both industrial and financial circles of Norwich Mr. Gallup has long been a power for stability and advancement. He has been a director of the Chelsea Savings Bank since 1875, and one of its vice-presidents since 1919. He was a director of the Thames National Bank of Norwich from January, 1888, to November, 1909. He was president of the Norwich Industrial Building Company for twenty-five years. He was president of the Crescent Fire Arms Company, of Norwich, for twenty-six years, up to May, 1919, when he disposed of his interests in this connection. He is president of the Smith Granite Company, of Westerly, Rhode Island, and president of the New London County Mutual Fire Insurance Company. He was president of the Bulletin Company, publishers of the Norwich "Bulletin," for a period of eight years. In all these varied interests Mr. Gallup has displayed the well-balanced judgment and the assured discernment which make for permanent stability in the business world. His fearlessness in every relation is one of his dominant characteristics, but is balanced by a fine conservatism, which nevertheless admits no compromise.

But individual enterprise is not the sum of Mr. Gallup's activities. He has done much for the civic advncement of the city of Norwich. No man who had a worthy object in view has ever found an unwilling listener in Henry Haskell Gallup, when proposing a reform or bringing about a movement which involved the public good, particularly affecting the city of Norwich. He has always been a leader in the promotion of all industrial and manufacturing growth of the city. It has been said of him that he has done more to advance the manufacturing interests of Norwich than any other citizen holding residence here. Of later years he has been obliged to delegate much of the active work along these lines to younger men, but his assistance, in an advisory capacity, is still freely given and highly prized. His long membership on the board of trade was a force for progress, and for two years he was president of that body.

Politically Mr. Gallup has always supported the principles of the Republican party, and it was only in the natural order of sequence that his services were sought for the commonwealth. He was elected State treasurer in 1900, taking office January 1, 1901. He was re-elected in 1902, and served two terms, or until January 1, 1905.

Mr. Gallup has been a member of the Arcanum Club, of Norwich, for twenty-five years. His religious convictions long since placed his membership with Christ Church, of Norwich, of which he has been senior warden for many years.

On September 26, 1871, Mr. Gallup married, at Norwich, Irena Harriot Breed, of this city, daughter of Edward and Harriot (Hebard) Breed. Mr. and Mrs. Gallup are the parents of five children, of whom two are now living: Walter Henry, who was born in Norwich, on April 13, 1873, is also associated with the Norwich Belt Manufacturing Company, and married Maud Anna Morgan, of Norwich, they being the parents of two children, Maria Theresa, and Henrietta Hebard; and a daughter, Susie Irena, who resides at home. Since 1912 Mr. Gallup and his family have made their home at the Mohican Hotel, in New London, Connecticut.

HARRY TODD GRISWOLD, of the J. Warren Gay Electrical Company, electrical contractors, of New London, Connecticut, is of the ninth generation of the family formed in the town of Old Lyme, New London county, Connecticut, by Matthew Griswold, who, with his brother Edward, came to New England in 1639. He first located at Windsor, going thence to Saybrook, and later was the pioneer in the movement from Saybrook to Lyme, where he died in 1698. He was a stone-cutter by trade, and there is registered at Saybrook a receipt for £700, dated April 2, 1679, and signed by Matthew Griswold, in payment of the tombstone of Lady Fenwick. He married Anna Wolcott, who died in 1693, daughter of Henry Wolcott. From Matthew and Anna (Wolcott) Griswold the line of descent to Harry Todd Griswold of New London is through their son, Matthew (2) Griswold, a farmer of Lyme, and a man of great strength; his son, Rev. George Griswold, who was pastor of the Congregational church at Niantic, Connecticut, for thirty-nine years; his son, George (2) Griswold, who lived at Giants Neck, in the town of Lyme; his son, George (3) Griswold, who moved to New York when a young man, and was one of the founders of M. L. & George Griswold, a firm of East India merchants; his son, Richard Sill (1) Griswold, a partner of M. L. & George Griswold, who spent several years in China, and in 1840 built a mansion in Old Lyme; his son, Richard Sill (2) Griswold, merchant and manufacturer; his son, Harry Todd Griswold, of New London.

Richard Sill (1) Griswold was a graduate of Yale College, class of 1829, and immediately after graduation was sent to China as his father's agent, representing M. L. & George Griswold. He spent several years in China, and upon his return to the United States was admitted as a partner. He was a most capable business man and very successful. He occupied the mansion he built in Old Lyme in 1840, although his business interests were in New York City. He married Louisa Griswold Mather, and after her death he married her sister, Frances Augusta Mather, both wives being daughters of James and Caroline (Tinker) Mather, and descendants of Rev. Cotton Mather, the famous Puritan divine.

Richard Sill (2) Griswold was born in Lyme, Connecticut, June 3, 1845, and died June 30, 1904. After completing his education, he entered business life in New York City, and in the course of his business life made about twenty voyages across the Atlantic. He was later in business with Brown & Brother, brass manufacturers, of Waterbury, Connecticut, continuing with them for seven years. He was well-known in business and fraternal circles, and in 1878 and 1879 he represented Lyme in the State Legislature. He was a member of Lodge, Chapter, Council and Commandery of the Masonic order in Waterbury, Connecticut, and held his Scottish Rite degree in Norwich, Connecticut, being affiliated with King Solomon Lodge of Perfection; Van Rensselaer Council, Princes of Jerusalem; Norwich Chapter of Rose Croix; Connecticut Consistory, Sovereign Princes of the Royal Secret; Mecca Temple, Ancient Arabic Order Nobles of the Mystic Shrine, of New York City; and the Veteran Masonic Association. In 1890 the Boxwood School for Girls was established in Lyme, which was under the direction of Mrs. Griswold.

Richard Sill (2) Griswold married, February 9, 1869, in Waterbury, Rosa Elizabeth Brown, born in Aberdeen, Mississippi, November 25, 1849, tracing descent through her father, Dr. James Brown, from Francis Brown, an early settler of Connecticut, one of the seven men who weathered the winter of 1639 in New Haven. Richard S. and Rosa E. (Brown) Griswold were the parents of eight children: 1. Dr. Richard Sill (3) Griswold, born November 15, 1869, a graduate of Bellevue Hospital Medical College; went to the Philippines with the 26th Regiment, United States Volunteer Infantry, as assistant surgeon, ranking as lieutenant, and was killed at Samar, September 28, 1901. 2. Dr. James Brown Griswold, a graduate of Dartmouth Medical College, and the College of Physicians and Surgeons, New York City; married Mary E. Stokes; he was a lieutenant in the Medical Corps during the World War, and died in the fall of 1917. 3. Daniel Eddie Griswold, a graduate of Williams College and Columbia Law School; married Helen Bancroft, daughter of Major Bancroft, of New London. 4. George Griswold, a graduate of the School of Forestry, and of the Bartlett School in Lyme. 5. Harry Todd Griswold, of further mention. 6. Rosa Elizabeth Griswold, a graduate of Miss Porter's School, Farmington, Connecticut. 7. Joseph Perkins Griswold, a graduate of the Bartlett School, as were all his brothers. 8. Woodward Haven Griswold, born July 28, 1885.

W. B. Frink.

From such ancestry came Harry Todd Griswold, born in New Haven, Connecticut, January 22, 1879. He was educated in the Bartlett School in Lyme, whence he was graduated, class of 1896, and for three years was a student of the violin in New York City. Later he pursued courses in civil engineering, and from 1901 until 1904 was with the engineering department of the New York, New Haven & Hartford railroad. In 1904 he became an engineer in the Terminal System of the Pennsylvania railroad in New York City, continuing with that company for three years. During 1907-09 he was engaged in special engineering work for the Lozier Motor Company, at Plattsburg, New York. In 1909, his health having become impaired, he returned to the old home in Old Lyme and engaged in farming.

With health restored, he entered the engineering division of the United States War Department, making special reports on a power development, being stationed at New London, Connecticut. He was so engaged during 1911-13, then, during 1913-17, he was a partner in the electrical contracting firm of J. Warren Gay Electrical Company. Then came the great war period, 1917-18, and, with millions of his young American brethren, Mr. Griswold, whose family had served with distinction in other wars waged by the United States, from the Revolution down, with the memories of Fort Griswold as a part of the family tradition, with the memory of two gallant brothers as a latter day offering on patriotism's altar, volunteered his services and entered the army. Having joined the Connecticut National Guard in 1916, he was commissioned a second lieutenant of the 10th Company, Connecticut Coast Artillery Corps, in April, 1917, that corps of the Connecticut National Guard which later became the 56th Regiment, Coast Artillery Corps, United States army. After training at Fort Wright, New York, at which place he was promoted to a first lieutenant and put in charge of the building and barracks being built at Fort Wright and Fort Terry, he sailed in March, 1918, for France. In August, 1918, he was detached from his regiment, then at the front, and assigned to duty as drilling officer with the Intelligence Section of the First army, being stationed at the headquarters of that army. Lieutenant Griswold was in France until fighting ended. During the spring of 1919 he returned to the United States and was mustered out of service at Fortress Monroe, Virginia.

Upon his return to New London, he formed an association with Major Morris Benham Payne, the firm, Payne & Griswold, resulting. Mr. Keefe being admitted in 1920, the firm name became Payne, Griswold & Keefe, architects and engineers, now successfully operating in New London.

In politics a Republican, Lieutenant Griswold, in 1920, was the successful nominee of his party for the State Legislature, serving on the Railroad Committee. He is a member of Pythagoras Lodge, No. 45, Free and Accepted Masons, of Old Lyme, Connecticut; Burning Bush Chapter, Royal Arch Masons, Essex, Connecticut; Palestine Commandery, Knights Templar, of New London; and is a thirty-second degree Mason of the Ancient Accepted Scottish Rite. He is an associate member of the American Society of Civil Engineers; member of the National Geographic Society of Washington, District of Columbia; American Society for the Advancement of Science; Thames Club of New London; and Old Lyme Post, No. 41, American Legion, of Old Lyme.

Lieutenant Griswold married, at Vergennes, Vermont, September 1, 1907, Florence Van Deusen, daughter of Robert T. and Alys (Bates) Van Deusen, of Kinderhook, New York. Mr. and Mrs. Griswold are the parents of a daughter, Alys E., born in Old Lyme, May 26, 1913.

PLINY LE ROY HARWOOD—At the age of twenty years Mr. Harwood entered the service of the Mariners' Savings Bank of New London, Connecticut, and during the quarter of a century which has since intervened that association has continued.

P. LeRoy Harwood was born at West Stafford, Connecticut, March 25, 1876, and was educated in the schools of New London. He entered the Mariners' Savings Bank in 1896, was elected secretary and treasurer in 1903, and vice-president and treasurer in 1921. He is also vice-president of the New London Morris Plan Bank.

Mr. Harwood is president of the New London Board of Education, and chairman of the Rivers, Harbors and Bridges Commission of the State of Connecticut. His interest is deep in these matters and his service to both city and state is invaluable. In politics he is a Republican. He served in the Connecticut State Guard, attaining the rank of captain. He is affiliated with lodge, chapter and commandery of the Masonic order, and is a past commander of the last-named body, Palestine Commandery, No. 6, Knights Templar. In the Scottish Rite of Masonry he has attained the thirty-second degree. His patriotic and colonial ancestry has gained him admission to the Sons of the American Revolution and to the Society of Mayflower Descendants. He is chairman of the executive committee of the Savings Bank Association of Connecticut, and is highly regarded in financial circles. His clubs are the Thames, of New London, and the Transportation, of New York City. His religious affiliation is with the First Congregational Church of New London.

Mr. Harwood married, at New London, June 6, 1900, Rowena Mosette Lee, and they are the parents of three children: Pliny LeRoy (2), born October 9, 1901; Donald Lee, born April 11, 1905; and Rowena Mosette, born June 23, 1909.

WAYLAND BLACKMAN FRINK—One of the men of Preston now gone to their reward, but whose good deeds live after them, was of the eighth generation of the family founded in New England by John Frink, born in England, who is first of record in Ipswich, Massachusetts, in 1673. John (2) Frink, son of John Frink, the founder, came to Stonington, Connecticut, at an earlier date, being of record there as early as 1666. He served in King Philip's War, and was a landowner. He married Grace Stevens, of Taunton, and they were the parents of four daughters and three sons, the sons all born after the coming to Stonington. Descent from John (2) Frink is traced in direct line through his eldest son ,Samuel Frink, and his wife Hannah (Miner) Frink; their son, Jedediah Frink, who settled in Preston, Connecticut, and his wife, Lucy (Stanton) Frink; their son, Andrew Frink, born in Preston, and his wife, Sarah (Kimball) Frink; their son, Rufus Frink, born in Preston, and his wife, Polly (Smith) Frink; Rufus Frink died in Preston, January 1, 1868, in his ninety-seventh year; their son, George Washington Frink, born in Preston, and his second wife, Cornelia E. (Blackman) Frink; their eldest child, Wayland B. Frink, born in Preston, and his wife, Grace A. (Eccleston) Frink, their children forming the ninth generation in New England.

George Washington Frink, of the seventh generation, was born in Preston, Connecticut, June 17, 1820, and died there May 8, 1892, having spent his life in his native town where three generations of his family had lived before him. His father lived to the age of ninety-seven, and the son resembled him in disposition, being jovial, good-natured, and full of fun, a confirmed optimist and everybody's friend. He was a member of the Preston City Baptist Church, a Whig and later a Republican in politics.

George W. Frink married (first), March 4, 1846, Sally Maria Williams, born in Ledyard, Connecticut, May 13, 1819, died September 14, 1855, daughter of John Anson and Sally (Williams) Williams, of Preston; granddaughter of Amos and Mable (Newton) Williams; great-granddaughter of John Williams, born in 1714, son of Christopher Williams, of Welsh ancestry. Mr. Frink married (second) Cornelia Ellison Blackman, daughter of Benjamin and Caroline Fountain (Chapman) Blackman, her father a farmer of Franklin, Connecticut, until his removal to Norwich, where he died. Four children were born to George W. and Sally M. (Williams) Frink; George Anson, of Preston; Lemuel Williams, an ordained minister of the Baptist church; Charity, married Benjamin F. Bentley; Henry, educated for the ministry, but never ordained, his health failing. Three children were born to George W. and Cornelia E. (Blackman) Frink: Wayland B., of further mention; Charlotte I.; Cornelia Fountain, married William Tarbox, and has two sons, Walter S. and Harold F. Tarbox.

Wayland Blackman Frink was born at the homestead farm in Preston, New London county, Connecticut, November 2, 1860, and died at his farm in Griswold in the same county, November 3, 1916. He was educated in the district public school, private schools at Pachaug and Preston City, finishing his studies in Connecticut Literary Institute, Suffield, Connecticut. He taught school thirteen consecutive winter terms save one, when he sold books in Ohio and Michigan, and was very successful as an instructor of youth. He was popular with both parents and scholars, possessing those pleasing qualities of disposition and those sterling traits of character which made his father and grandfather so popular.

After his marriage in 1888, he resided at the home farm one year, then leased the Butler Chapman farm in Griswold, which he cultivated until 1896. In that year he bought a farm of sixty acres, formerly a part of the Simon Brewster farm, lying one and one-half miles south of Jewett City, and there engaged in general farming and dairying until his death. He was a man of industry and thrift, one of the substantial, influential men of his community, honored and respected by all. A Republican in politics, Mr. Frink never sought public office, but was keenly alive to his obligations as a citizen and shirked no duty. He was a long time member of Preston City and Jewett City Baptist churches, serving the first-named for eight years as superintendent of Sunday school.

Mr. Frink married, February 15, 1888, Grace A. Eccleston, born in Griswold, New London county, Connecticut, June 21, 1865. Mrs. Frink is a daughter of John D. and Susan K. (Chapman) Eccleston, of the town of Griswold, granddaughter of Avery Nelson and Sallie B. (Ray) Eccleston, and great-granddaughter of Benedict Eccleston, a farmer and resident of North Stonington, Connecticut, where he almost reached centenarian distinction, dying at the age of ninety-five years. The family have long been seated in eastern Connecticut, and the name is an honored one in town annals.

Avery Nelson Eccleston was born at the home farm in North Stonington in 1806, and there died in 1891, that town his home all through life except for one year passed in Griswold. He married Sallie B. Ray, born in Griswold, Connecticut, in 1807, died in 1886, daughter of Jabez and Hannah (York) Ray.

One of their ten children was a son, John D. Eccleston, born in North Stonington, August 24, 1844. He was well educated, and for several years was an efficient, popular school teacher. He commenced his first term of school teaching in Rockland, Connecticut, and was boarded around in the district. On returning to Griswold, he taught in the neighboring districts. He was also much interested in church work, belonging to both the Methodist and Baptist societies. He was a violinist and bass singer of unusual ability. Having moved to Iowa, where he resided for three years, he for one year taught school in Manteno. While a resident of Iowa, his son, Hubert Ward Eccleston, was born. He resided in Jewett City, where he served as street commissioner, assistant visitor of schools, and in other capacities served his townsmen. In 1864 Mr. Eccleston married (first) Susan K. Chapman, daughter of Butler Chapman, of Griswold, Connecticut. He married (second) Sarah L. Brown, daughter of Shepard Brown, of Griswold, Connecticut. Five children were born to John D. and Susan K. (Chapman) Eccleston: 1. Lizzie, deceased. 2. Lila, deceased. 3. Annie, deceased. 4. Hubert W., a graduate of Sheffield Scientific Institute, Ph.D., 1896, and a civil engineer of Los Angeles, California; he married Eulalia K. Compton, of California, and has two children, John D., and Doris Huberta. 5. Grace A., married, February 15, 1888, Wayland A. Frink.

Mrs. Frink survives her husband and continues her residence at the home farm, her five children all with her. She was a member of Bethel Methodist Episcopal Church, later joined the Baptist church at Preston City, and later with her husband joined Jewett City Baptist Church, where she continues her membership. Five children were born to Wayland B. and Grace A. (Eccleston) Frink: Arthur A., Marion E., Mabel C., Esther C., and George W.

DUDLEY ST. CLAIR DONNELLY—The career of Mr. Donnelly, of New London, Connecticut, an architect of wide reputation, is one to excite unusual interest. Born at the very threshold of the United States, but under the English flag (Barbadoes, West Indies), he was brought to the United States by his father (who had here been educated) when but a boy of five years, and in Yonkers, New York, took his first lesson in architecture, a profession in which he has gained high and honorable rank, and is a member of Connecticut Chapter, American Institute of Architects. For more than a quarter of a century he has practiced his profession in New London, and there continues a leader.

His father, Henry C. Donnelly, was born in the Barbadoes, West Indies, but was sent to New England to be educated. He then returned to Barbadoes and for several years filled secretarial positions. He married Catherine Barry, and in 1875, with his wife and five-year-old son, Dudley St. Clair, came to the United States and located in Yonkers, New York. He became secretary to Lawrence Brothers, of that city, continuing until his death in 1920. His wife survives him and continues her residence in Yonkers. Henry C. and Catherine (Barry) Donnelly were the parents of eleven children, five of whom survive their father: 1. Dudley St. Clair, of further mention. 2. Mabel, a teacher in a school in Yonkers. 3. James, a contractor of Yonkers, married Frances Percival. 4. Eliza, a musician teaching piano and voice, residing with her mother and sister in Yonkers. 5. George, a deputy sheriff, who married Ethel Wright, and resides in Yonkers.

Dudley St. Clair Donnelly was born in the Barbadoes, West Indies, September 17, 1870, and there passed the first five years of his life. In 1875 he was brought to Yonkers, New York, by his parents, and there finished public school courses, with graduation from high school, class of 1888. He then spent three years in the office of Benjamin Silliman, architect; then, in 1891, continued architectural work in Boston, Massachusetts, under Arthur F. Gray, returning the same year to Yonkers and reëntering the employ of Mr. Silliman. In 1892 he came to New London, Connecticut, with Cole & Chandler, of Boston, the architects of the Winthrop School, which they designed and superintended. Mr. Donnelly was chief draughtsman for Cole & Chandler, and in 1892, shortly after the death of Mr. Cole, opened an office as architect, and designed many buildings. He formed a partnership with Louis R. Hazeltine, of New London, in 1899, the firm being known as Donnelly & Hazeltine. Donnelly & Hazeltine continued successfully until 1906, and during that period they designed several important buildings, including an addition to the Winthrop School in New London (the same building which served as Mr. Donnelly's introduction to New London), the New London Savings Bank building on Main street (which Mr. Donnelly regards with special pride, he having personally designed it), the Congregational church in Groton, the Masonic building in Greenpoint, New York, "Ye Faire Harbour" apartment house in New London, the addition to the Bill Public Library, Groton, and the Mariners' Savings Bank, of New London. On December 1, 1906, Donnelly & Hazeltine dissolved partnership.

In 1907, Mr. Donnelly designed and built the Day and March buildings in New London; in 1908 the Plant Hunting Lodge, in Lyme, and all the buildings pertaining thereto; in 1909, the Walter S. Guard residence, at Neptune Park, and an addition to the New London County Court House; also remodeled the old Rhinelander Mansion at Pequot for Robert Moore; designed and built the Independent Order of Odd Fellows' building on Bank street, New London; and the Fort Griswold Hotel Annex at Groton. His chief building in 1910 was the Percy Coe Eggleston residence at Post Hill, Connecticut; a large garage for Morton F. Plant, and buildings for the Ship and Engine Company, of Groton. In 1911 his contribution to the notable buildings of the Connecticut coast were the Hotel Garde at New Haven, and a high school building at Groton, donated to the town by P. F. Bill; in 1912 the La Pointe factory, the J. N. La Pointe and Mainwaring buildings, and the Polish Society Hall, Norwich, Connecticut. He designed the Natchaug School in Willimantic, Connecticut; the Shennecossett Country Club, at Eastern Point, Groton, in 1913; the Plant building and Monte Cristo garage, New London, in 1914; the Young Men's Christian Association building, New London; and the Plant building in Groton, in 1915; an addition to the Hotel Griswold in 1916, and the Marsh building; a dormitory and gymnasium at Connecticut College for Women at New London; the Sexton building at New London in 1917; the Jewish Synagogue at New London; Belleview Club and winter cottages for Emery Ford and Charles J. Schlotman, of Detroit, at Belleair, Florida, in 1919; and in 1920 the Receiving building at the Connecticut State Farm, Lyme. These complete a list of notable buildings which owe their design to the genius of Mr. Donnelly, and many of these have arisen under his supervision.

Mr. Donnelly is a Republican in politics and has served his city as councilman. He is affiliated with Brainard Lodge, No. 102, Free and Accepted Masons; Union Chapter, No. 4, Royal Arch Masons; and the New London Lodge, No. 360, Benevolent and Protective Order of Elks. He is a member of the Rotary, Thames, and Masonic clubs of New London; Shennecossett Country Club of Groton; Union League Club of New Haven; the Lambs Club of New York, and the American Institute of Architects, of Washington, District of Columbia.

Mr. Donnelly married, at New London, Joanna E.

Hurley, of New London, daughter of Thomas and Elizabeth Hurley. Two children have been born to Mr. and Mrs. Donnelly: Dudley St. Clair (2), and Thomas Henry, both in New London at the outbreak of the World War, 1917-18. Dudley St. Clair (2) Donnely was a student at Dartmouth College, but at once enlisted in the United States Naval Reserves and served as a seaman on a submarine chaser, stationed at New London. He married Mildred Reeves, of New London, and they are the parents of a daughter, Bettie C. Donnelly, born in New London, the home of her parents. Thomas Henry Donnelly also served in the United States Naval Reserve during the World War. He is now engaged in journalism in Hartford, Connecticut, as a reporter.

REUBEN LORD—There was much to admire in the character of Reuben Lord, and little to condemn, although he was a man of strong convictions, and always ready to contend for that which he believed right. He held most decided opinions. His likes and dislikes were very strong, but if he opposed a man he did it openly and fairly; and if you were his friend he never faltered in his friendship, nor would he stand silently by and hear friendship assailed. His opinions were often publicly expressed in the newspapers, but always over his own name, for he never asked a newspaper to use an article signed by an assumed name. He was a man of great energy, and until his health became impaired, was a hard worker. He had a great many sincere friends who deeply mourned his passing. He never hesitated to do a kindness for a friend, and from those unfriendly he asked no favors. As a city official and a pension agent he was much in the public eye, and lawyers always spoke of him as most correct in his conception of proper legal ethics. He was not admitted to the bar, although educated in the law, but this was because he did not wish to practice. Yet he advised his friends in legal matters, and his advice was always in accordance with his genuine belief, as he saw the situation. He died suddenly while in his own office, being about to leave when stricken.

Reuben Lord was a descendant of Thomas Lord, born 1585, who with his wife, Dorothy, came from England to New England in 1635, settling first in Newtown, Massachusetts, but in 1636 moving to Hartford, Connecticut, where his wife died in 1678, aged eighty-seven years. They were the parents of eight children, descent in this line being traced through William Lord, both in 1623; died at Saybrook, Connecticut, May 17, 1768.

William Lord married, and the line continues in this branch through his son, Thomas (2) Lord, of Saybrook, born 1645, died 1730, and his wife, Mary Lee; their son, Joseph (1) Lord, of Lyme, Connecticut, born 1697, died 1736, and his wife, Abigail Comstock; their son, Joseph (2) Lord, of Lyme, born 1730, died 1788, and his wife, Sarah Wade; their son, Reuben (1) Lord, of Lyme, born 1760, died 1804, and his wife, Elizabeth Selden; their son, Joseph (3) Lord, of Lyme, born 1781, died 1836, and his wife, Phoebe Burnham; their son, Reuben (2) Lord, and his wife, Sarah Weaver; their son, Reuben (3) Lord, to whose memory this review is dedicated.

Reuben (2) Lord, of the eighth American generation, was born in Lyme, Connecticut, died in Salem, Connecticut, in 1900. He was a farmer all his life, first as his father's assistant, and later took over the home farm. After his marriage he moved to Ohio, where his son, Reuben (3) Lord, was born. Later the family returned to Connecticut, where he was engaged in farming and fishing, owning fishing rights along the Connecticut river. After his retirement he moved to Salem, Connecticut, where he died. He married Sarah Weaver, born in Lyme, Connecticut, died in the village of Hamburg, town of Lyme, in 1876. They were the parents of six children, one only now living, Walter H. Lord, residing in Terryville, Connecticut.

Reuben (3) Lord was the third child of Reuben (2) and Sarah (Weaver) Lord, was born in Carlisle, Ohio, May 16, 1850; died in New London, Connecticut, September 22, 1908. His parents in 1850 returned to the town of Lyme, Connecticut, where the lad attended the public schools of the village of Hamburg. He was a studious youth, and early showed ambition to become a lawyer. With that end in view, while attending school in New London, in 1871, he became a law student in the office of Thomas M. Waller, of New London, later governor of Connecticut and consul general to London, and soon acquired a remarkable knowledge of law. For some reason, known to himself alone, he would not ask admission to the bar after qualifying, and the only reason he would ever give was that he "did not want to."

But although he never practiced or appeared in court, he did a great deal of legal office work, and was an expert at drawing deeds, contracts and warrants, and for many years was Mr. Waller's valued clerical assistant. As a title searcher it is said that no one excelled him. In July, 1873, he was elected clerk of New London police court, and by reëlection and appointment held that office until September, 1883, when he resigned and also left Governor Waller's office to give his entire time to the pension business, becoming one of the best-known pension attorneys, over 7,000 successful applications for Civil War pensions having been made out by him. Pension office inspectors complimented him many times on his work, and as frequently stated that nothing was ever found to be irregular that came from Mr. Lord's office. In November, 1889, he added real estate and insurance to his pension business, and a few years prior to his death joined in partnership with Wallace R. Johnson, an association dissolved prior to his death. He was in poor health for several years, having heart trouble, but he would not spare himself, and delayed too long before seeking medical aid.

Mr. Lord was a member of Union Lodge, No. 31, Free and Accepted Masons; of Pequot Lodge, No.

85, Independent Order of Odd Fellows; of Trumbull Lodge, No. 48, Knights of Pythias, and was also a member of the Niagara Engine Company, having been affiliated with these orders for many years. In politics he was an ardent Democrat; in religious faith an Episcopalian.

He married, in New London, October 12, 1875, Julia A. Peck, daughter of Palmer and Mary (Caton) Peck. Mrs. Lord did not long survive her husband. She died in New London January 24, 1911.

Associated with Mr. Lord and Wallace R. Johnson prior to the dissolution of the firm was a young lady, Miss Jennie Lester Doyle, daughter of John J. and Sarah (Peck) Doyle, and niece of Mrs. Julia A. (Peck) Lord, and also niece of Mr. Lord by marriage. After the firm dissolved, Miss Doyle remained with Mr. Lord and gave him valuable and deeply appreciated service. Miss Doyle succeeded to the business, real estate and insurance, and, although she is the sole owner, she continues the business under the old firm name, "Reuben Lord & Company." She is an able business woman and a leader among the business women of her city in her line. John J. Doyle died April 19, 1887, and afterward Miss Doyle and her mother resided with Mr. and Mrs. Lord.

GROSVENOR ELY—A man of energy and enterprise, Grosvenor Ely, treasurer of the Ashland Cotton Company of Jewett City, has from the inception of his business career been identified with manufacturing interests, gradually making his way to the position of prominence which he now holds. In everything pertaining to the welfare of the community, he takes a deep interest, as in his undertakings in the business world, and all good causes find in him a friend and ally. He is a son of Edwin S. Ely, paper manufacturer and bank president, and is of the ninth American generation of the family founded in New England by Richard Ely, of Plymouth in Devonshire, England, who came to New England between the years 1660 and 1663. Richard Ely settled, after a brief Boston residence, in Lyme, Connecticut, which in 1660 was a part of Saybrook. Descent in this branch is traced through William Ely, son of Richard, the founder, and his second wife, Mrs. Elizabeth Cullick.

(II) William Ely, born in England in 1647, did not come to New England with his father, but came from the West Indies at his father's invitation in 1670. He married, May 12, 1681, Elizabeth Smith; lived in Lyme, and was for many years judge of New London county court. He died in February, 1717, leaving sons and daughters.

(III) His son, William (2) Ely, married, October 25, 1715, Hannah Thompson, who died in 1733. Mr. Ely died in 1766, and was succeeded in this branch by James Ely.

(IV) James Ely, son of William (2) and Hannah (Thompson) Ely, was born in 1719; died in 1766. He married Dorcas Andrews, and their six sons, James, Jacob, of further mention, Aaron, Andrew, John and Gad, all served in the War of the Revolution.

(V) Jacob Ely, son of James and Dorcas (Andrews) Ely, was of Lyme, Connecticut, born in 1748. He was a Revolutionary soldier, and lived to a good old age, dying in 1836. He married, in 1773, Temperance Tiffany, born in 1747, died in 1781, leaving a son, Eli Ely.

(VI) Eli Ely, son of Jacob and Temperance (Tiffany) Ely, was born in 1780, and married, in 1805, Sarah Sanford, of Plymouth, Connecticut, born in 1784, daughter of Jesse and Sarah (Fenn) Sanford. Mrs. Ely died in 1854; Eli Ely in 1869.

(VII) Jesse Sanford Ely, son of Eli and Sarah (Sanford) Ely, born in 1807, married, in 1835, Harriet Grosvenor, of North Killingly, Connecticut, born in 1813, daughter of Dr. Robert and Mary (Begg) Grosvenor. They moved to Norwich, Connecticut, and were the parents of three sons: General William Grosvenor, a brave officer of the Union, Colonel of the Eighteenth Regiment Connecticut Volunteer Infantry, and was made brigadier general; he married Augusta Elizabeth Greene; Edwin Sanford, of further mention, and Charles Albro Ely, who died young.

(VIII) Edwin Sanford Ely, son of Jesse Sanford and Harriet (Grosvenor) Ely, was born July 17, 1841, died suddenly at his home, May 4, 1898. He was quite young when his parents moved to Norwich, and there he was educated in the public schools and Norwich Free Academy. He studied law under Judge James A. Hovey, but later he engaged in paper manufacture, being owner and manager of the Reade & Obenauer Paper Company, of Versailles. His health broke and he sold his paper mill interest in 1889. From 1882 until 1893, he was president of the Uncas Bank of Norwich, and at the time of his passing was a director of the Broadway Theatre Corporation. He was a member of the Norwich Club, a man of most pleasing personality, and very popular. In politics he was a Republican. Mr. Ely married, May 1, 1873, Mary Brewer Chappell, born November 13, 1845, in Norwich, daughter of Edward and Elizabeth E. (Brewer) Chappell. Mrs. Ely died in Philadelphia, March 19, 1895, the mother of four children: Mary Grosvenor Ely, born May 30, 1875; Augusta Chappell Ely, born April 6, 1878; Edward Chappell Ely, born May 9, 1882, an importer of New York; Grosvenor Ely, of further mention.

(IX) Grosvenor Ely, of the ninth generation, youngest son of Edwin Sanford and Mary Brewer (Chappell) Ely, was born in Norwich, Connecticut, February 21, 1884, and received his education in the public schools of Norwich and at Norwich Free Academy, whence he was graduated in 1900. He took a preparatory course at Hotchkiss School, graduating at the conclusion of his course in 1901. The next few months he spent in travel in France, and then returned to this country and entered Yale College, whence he was graduated, A. B., class of 1906. Immediately after graduation he went again to Europe, remaining there until 1908. Upon his return to this country he decided to make a study of the manufacturer of cotton textiles, and with this end in view spent the year of 1908 in the Falls mills at Norwich, and the Ponemah mills at Taftville. Later he became manager of the Ashland Cotton Company at Jewett City; then agent; and eventually treasurer, which position he now holds. The company has steadily prospered, and today occupies a high position in the industrial world. Mr. Ely is also vice-president and treasurer of the Chadwick Hoskins Company, at Charlotte, North Carolina; treasurer of the Martinsville Cotton Mills, Incorporated, Martinsville, Virginia, and secretary of the Turner Halsey Company, of New York City. In politics Mr. Ely is a Republican, and has served the city of Norwich two years as alderman. His thorough business qualifications are also always in demand, and his public spirit has led him to accept many such trusts. He is a member of the board of governors, and a former vice-president of the National Association of Cotton Manufacturers; trustee of the Norwich Free Academy; trustee of the Young Men's Christian Association; director of the Chamber of Commerce; and formerly vice-president of the Board of Trade; director of the Thames National Bank of Norwich; and director of the Chelsea Savings Bank of Norwich. He was at one time director of the Uncas National Bank, of the Falls Company and of the Shetucket Company of Norwich. He belongs to the Arcanum Club, the Chelsea oBat Club, and the Golf Club of Norwich, of which he has been president for five years, the Yale Club, the University Club, the Merchants' Club of New York City, the Southern Textile Manufacturers' Club, of North Carolina, and the Charlotte Country Club.

Mr. Ely married, September 6, 1906, Mary Learned. Mr. and Mrs. Ely are the parents of two children, Grosvenor (2) and Larned.

LEVI QUINCY RAYMOND—In the city of New London, Connecticut, is located one of the largest concerns in the lumber business in this county—the Raymond & Alexander Lumber Company. Levi Quincy Raymond, as the head of this important corporation, is one of the leading men in this line hereabouts.

Mr. Raymond is a son of Thaddeus K. and Mary (Ayres) Raymond, long ago residents of New London county. Thaddeus K. Raymond was born in Lyme, Connecticut, educated in the district schools of the day, and was a cattle farmer and lumber dealer during his lifetime. He died in 1860, while still a young man. Thaddeus K. and Mary (Ayres) Raymond were the parents of three children: Oliver O., who married Adelaide La Place, and is now a retired cattle dealer, and resides in Wethersfield, Connecticut; Levi Quincy, of whom further; and Helen, who became the wife of William Clifton, moving to Savannah, Georgia, dying shortly thereafter.

Levi Quincy Raymond was born in Lyme, New London county, Connecticut, on March 27, 1857. The family removing to Vineland, New Jersey, when he was a child of seven years, his education was secured in the public schools of that town. His studies completed, the young man entered the world of industry in 1872, choosing his own path in making the start. He went to Taunton, Massachusetts, where he entered the employ of the Mason Locomotive Works, remaining for two years in that connection. In 1874 he went to Springfield, Massachusetts, and there became a machinist for Beames & McCall, remaining for one year. Next he came to New London county, Connecticut, locating in Lyme, where he worked on the farm for his uncle, James L. Raymond, remaining with him for a period of five years. At the end of that time he went to East Haddam, Connecticut, where he took up the business of teaming and lumbering. Among the heavily wooded slopes of that section he gained his start in life. In 1888 he purchased a saw mill, and from that time until the present he has been in the lumber business. At first, and indeed for more than twenty years, he bought standing timber, converting it into the lumber of commerce, and followed along this line until 1901, when he came to New London to make it his home. From that time until 1910 he engaged in real estate and building business, erecting some three hundred houses, and a large block on the corner of Bank street and Montauk avenue, which is now known as the Raymond block. In 1910 he purchased land on Moore avenue and Shaw street, built on it a mill and established a lumber business. This business increased to such an extent that in 1914 he took into partnership F. J. Alexander, whose life is reviewed in the following sketch, the concern taking the title of the Raymond & Alexander Lumber Company, they buying the Hopkins and Chapin plant on Howard street, the site of which was on a part of what was known as Shaw's Cove and at that time mostly under water. They began filling in on the north side of Hamilton street and the east side of Howard street, and built there the plant and office buildings they now occupy. All about them on redeemed land are now new docks, warehouses and railroad yards. This business was capitalized at $60,000, and is now one of the most important concerns in this line in New London county. Besides dressed lumber they handle all kinds of builders' supplies, and kindred stock, and do a very extensive business. Outside of his business Mr. Raymond has few interests, but is a prominent member of the New London Chamber of Commerce. Politically, he supports the Republican party.

Mr. Raymond married (first) Millie Chappell, of Lyme, Connecticut, on February 19, 1880. She was a daughter of Ira Chappell, of that town. She died on December 9, 1903. They were the parents of five children: Thaddeus K., who married, in 1903, Mildred Pearson, and resides in Groton, Connecticut; Charles L., who married, in 1906, Esther Sutton, and is a resident of Lyme; Edward I., who married Mary Robertshaw, and now lives in New London; during the World War he was first sergeant in the Quartermaster's Corps, and was stationed at San Antonio,

L. Q. Raymond

Texas; and twins, Annie and Millie, Annie now being the wife of Arthur Beckman, of Philadelphia, and Millie is deceased. Mr. Raymond married (second) Georgette Burch, of Groton; (third) May E. Walsh, of New London, Connecticut, who is now living. The family are members of the Congregational church of New London.

Mr. Raymond's mother, Mary (Ayres) Raymond, married a second time, becoming the wife of L. Lee Wood, of Lyme, Connecticut, and they were the parents of four children: James R., who married Georgia Tiffany, and resides in Chester, Connecticut; Bell, who became the wife of William Blair, and lives in Hartford; John E., who married Minnie Tiffany, and lives in Hartford; and Mary L., who is also married, and resides in Hartford. The mother died in 1900, and Mr. Wood survived her for five years.

FRANK J. ALEXANDER—For many years interested in extensive agricultural operations in New London county, and now a partner in the important lumber firm of Raymond & Alexander, in the city of New London, Connecticut, Frank J. Alexander has achieved unusual success in life.

Mr. Alexander is a son of Charles P. and Harriet E. (Jerome) Alexander. Charles P. Alexander was born in the town of Groton, Connecticut, in 1832, and there received his education in the public schools. He took up farming in early life, and continued in this line of work until his death, which occurred in 1904. His wife also was born in Waterford, and there died. They were the parents of two children: Charles J., deceased; and Frank J., of whom further.

Frank J. Alexander was born in Waterford, Connecticut, on December 14, 1870. He received a thoroughly practical education in the public schools of the neighborhood, and later attended Snell's Business College, in Norwich, Connecticut, then began business life working on the farm for his father. In 1895 he bought the grocery business of F. P. Robinson, in Waterford, and thereafter conducted the store for a period of six years. In 1901 he took up teaming and contracting, specializing in the building of roads, along which line he did a large amount of work which counted for the permanent improvement of interurban traffic conditions. Later on he purchased a farm of ninety-six acres in Waterford, and still later acquired a farm of one hundred and twelve acres adjoining the first. These farms he stocked, and did a large dairy business. After his mother's death he sold the home place of thirty acres to the Connecticut College for Women for a building site.

In 1914, Mr. Alexander formed his present association with L. Q. Raymond, whose sketch precedes this, in the lumber business which they have developed to such an important interest. The Raymond & Alexander Lumber Company is now one of the principal lumber concerns in New London county, and is capitalized at $60,000. Mr. Alexander is secretary and treasurer of the corporation, and very active in the management of the company's affairs.

In the public life of the city Mr. Alexander is bearing a prominent part. Politically affiliated with the Democratic party, he served for seven years as a member of the Board of Relief of Waterford, and was for years a selectman of the town of Waterford.

Fraternally, Mr. Alexander is well known. He is a member of Oxoboxo Lodge, No. 116, Free and Accepted Masons, of Montville, in this county, and he is a member of Pequot Lodge, No. 85, Independent Order of Odd Fellows, of New London. He is a member of the Harbour Club, of New London.

On October 12, 1897, Mr. Alexander married Alice Lawson, daughter of Otto and Martha (Combs) Lawson, of Waterford. Mr. and Mrs. Alexander have three children: Prentice L., who resides at home; Elizabeth, now the wife of Frederick Schad, of Bellefonte, Pennsylvania; and Alice, at home. The family attend the Baptist church, and are prominent in all its activities.

JOHN G. WHEELER—From a sturdy race of farmers, seafaring men and business men, comes John G. Wheeler, one of the best-known druggists of New London county. Several generations of the Wheeler family have made their home in Mystic, Connecticut, and the name is a well-known one in Stonington township. The first known ancestor in this country was Thomas Wheeler, already a resident of and holding official position in the town of Lynn, Massachusetts, in 1635. He became a freeman in 1642, purchased a large tract of land, and built a saw and grist mill which he operated. He was made a freeman of the Connecticut Colony in 1669, elected to the general court in 1673, and was one of the nine who organized the First Congregational Church in Stonington, June 3, 1674, he and his wife partaking of the first communion service held in that church. Both are buried in the old Whitehall burial place on the east bank of the Mystic river. He died March 6, 1686, aged eighty-four years. Isaac Wheeler, his son, served in the Colonial Indian Wars; married Martha, daughter of Thomas and Dorothy (Thompson) Park; and died June 5, 1712. Richard Wheeler, a grandson, married Prudence, daughter of Deacon John Payson, and granddaughter of Edward Payson and Mary Eliot, sister of Apostle Eliot. Jonathon Wheeler, a great-grandson, born February 7, 1708, married Esther Dennison, and died October 8, 1790. Jonathan (2) Wheeler, born January 20, 1737, married Priscilla Lester, and died January 28, 1807. His son, Lester Wheeler, born July 24, 1757, married Eunice, daughter of David and Eunice (Brown) Bailey, and died May 15, 1835. William Wheeler, son of Lester and Eunice (Bailey) Wheeler, born January 21, 1782, was one of the defenders of Stonington against the attacks of the British. He married Wealthy Turner, in 1800, and they became the parents of two children: Eliza A., born in 1802, married Benjamin F. Williams; and William E., born June 16, 1807. So far the family had won their living from the soil. With the next generation they began to follow the sea.

William E. Wheeler, born at Stonington, went to sea on a sailing vessel, later on whaling vessels, and still later on coasting vessels, sailing from New York to southern United States ports. In 1854, he went into the East India trade, sailing from New York to China for A. A. Lowe & Brothers on the barque "Penguin." In 1865 he ran a steamer from New York to southern ports. He was a member of the State Legislature, and very prominent as a Democrat. He married, in Groton, August 24, 1831, Pedee Heath, of Groton, and they became the parents of four children: Eliza A., who married John J. Godfrey, and died in Groton; William E., Jr.; Charles H.; and Horace N.; the three sons all of further mention.

The son William Edward Wheeler, Jr., went to sea with his father as a cabin boy; then attended the academy at Mystic; served as a shipping clerk; then went to sea again for a year, and upon his return went to work in a sash and blind factory. He then shipped aboard the "Abraham Lincoln," bound for France, and upon his return enlisted for three years in Company C., Connecticut Volunteers. He was wounded at Drury's Bluff, May 16, 1864, and honorably discharged July 1, of the same year. After the War he went to Illinois and to Wisconsin, but returned and went into partnership with his father in the grocery business, later, in 1885, building his own store and handling groceries, dry goods and hardware, until 1902, when he sold out to R. A. Stanton.

He married Sarah Stark, daughter of Albert and Hannah (Wolfe) Stark, of Groton, and to this marriage four children were born: 1. Albert Edward, born February 5, 1871, married Bessie Page, July 22, 1913, and they are the parents of one child, William Edward (3), born August 22, 1915. He was educated in Mystic; went into business with his father; in 1903 was a Democratic representative of his town in the State Legislature, serving on the Committee of Manufactures and Legislative Expenses. 2. Ada, born March 14, 1873; died September 27, 1874. 3. Frank Rowland, born November 4, 1875, a graduate of Connecticut Literary Institute, and of Brown University, from which he received the degree of Bachelor of Arts in 1897, and the degree of Master of Arts in 1898. He later attended Galludet College, and then was a teacher of the deaf at Washington, D. C., and of the deaf and dumb at Jackson, Illinois; and at Fairbault, Minnesota, married Helen M. Rudd, of West Mystic; they have one child, Helen E., born May 25, 1902. 4. Ella Harris, born October 22, 1889; married Palmer Brown, April 8, 1911, and they are the parents of one daughter, Phyllis Wheeler, born July 16, 1911. For many years numbered among the most successful business men, his house ranking among the first of its kind, William Edward Wheeler, Jr., took pride in giving his customers the best articles on the market, at prices as low as was consistent with good quality.

Charles Henry Wheeler, born in Mystic, Connecticut, July 19, 1845, also followed the sea, shipping on the "Penguin," the "B. F. Hoxie," and numerous other vessels. He was captured by the southern privateer, "Florida," and held ten days, then placed on the whaling vessel "Vernon H. Hill," where he remained ten days more, and from which he was landed at Bermuda and placed with the United States consul there. He voyaged to most of the ports of the world, and engaged in almost every kind of seafaring life, finally buying a fish market in New London, which he managed for a while, until he embarked in the grocery business on Pearl street, in Mystic. He married Isabel F. Myers, of Noank, Connecticut, and one child was born to the union, Eliza A., who married George J. Green, and resides in Westport, Connecticut. They are the parents of one child, Estelle Wheeler.

Horace N. Wheeler, born in Mystic, October 8, 1848, did not become a seafaring man. He attended school in Mystic, on the Groton side of the river, and then attended the academy, later studying at Palmer Gallup's Private School, in Connecticut. When he was fourteen years old he began clerking for Francis M. Manning, of Mystic, becoming a druggist in 1873, and in July, 1882, succeeded Mr. Manning in control of the business. He also was interested in the Mystic Distilling Company, manufacturers of witch hazel and witch hazel soap, and controlled the Aceton Medical Company, making a remedy for headache, neuralgia, and grippe. He married, November 30, 1871, at Mystic, Ella E. Giddings, who was born at Mystic, daughter of Gurdon and Louisa (Niles) Giddings, of Groton, and two children were born of the marriage: Margaret Pedee, born May 18, 1873, died February 14, 1874; and John G. Mrs. Ella E. Wheeler is still, 1921, living in Mystic, a very interesting and active woman. She is a charter member of the Fanny Ledyard Chapter of the Daughters of the American Revolution, of Mystic, of which she is past regent, and has been a registrar for many years. Horace N. Wheeler was a very prominent citizen of Mystic, and an active worker in St. Marks' Episcopal Church, where for many years he was junior warden, being succeeded in the office by his son, John G., who held that office until his death.

Throughout his active years he held the unwavering regard of his fellows, for strict adherence to principles of uprightness and rectitude, and he lived always in their regard and esteem. To business problems he brought the same high sense of honor that guided him in personal relations, and he was a substantial, dependable member of the business fraternity of the region. He was representative of a high type of manhood and citizen.

John G. Wheeler, only son of Horace N. and Ella E. (Giddings) Wheeler, was born in Mystic, March 19, 1875, and in his death, May 3, 1921, his community lost a capable, active, helpful member and a public-spirited citizen. He attended the public schools of Mystic, and then continued his studies at the Mystic Academy, after which he entered the Bryant and Stratton Business College at Boston. For two years after finishing his business course, he acted as bookkeeper for the Regal Shoe Company, of Boston, after which he was for a short time associated with the Ivers & Pond Piano Company. Returning to Mystic in March of 1901, he entered the drug store of his father, and after the necessary study became a registered druggist in 1905, continuing with his father until the death of the latter, October 16, 1916. The son then took over the business, which he successfully conducted until his sudden death, May 3, 1921. Mr. Wheeler made a specialty of the Rexall preparations, and conducted a modernly equipped drug store. The business was established by F. M. Manning in 1841, and in the eighty years of its existence has had but three owners, F. M. Manning, Horace Nelson Wheeler, and John G. Wheeler. John G. Wheeler also succeeded his father as proprietor of the Al-ce-ton Medical Company, of Mystic, formerly known as the "Aceton Medical Company," manufacturing in addition to the well-known headache, neuralgia, and grippe remedy, other preparations bearing that name. Politically, Mr. Wheeler was for many years a Democrat, but became a Republican in 1920. He was a member of the Episcopal church, and was active in fraternal work, being affiliated with Stonington Lodge, No. 26, Independent Order of Odd Fellows, located in Mystic.

On October 9, 1901, he married Sadie Balmer, of Cambridge, Massachusetts, and they became the parents of one son, Edwin Reynolds, born at Mystic, Connecticut, April 21, 1905. Death came suddenly to Mr. Wheeler, and his passing leaves a deep sense of loss in the hearts of his many friends and acquaintances. He was highly esteemed by his townsmen, and held a high reputation as a man of integrity and moral worth. Such citizens are the real wealth of their community, and their influence remains long after they have passed from our sight.

HENRY ALFRED RICHMOND—One of the first purchasers of land at Taunton, was John Richmond, born in England, in 1594, the American ancestor of Henry Alfred Richmond, of Preston, Connecticut, a prosperous farmer and business man, now an octogenarian, but well preserved and active, the head of a family of twelve sons and daughters. Teaching has become a favored profession of these children of the ninth American generation, and they are filling or have filled many positions of importance in the educational life of their State.

(II) The line of descent from John Richmond is through his second son, Edward Richmond, born about 1632, probably in England, whose second wife was Amy Bull, daughter of Governor Henry Bull. Edward Richmond, a man of refined and scholarly tastes, was one of the founders of Little Compton, Rhode Island, and the owner of large tracts of virgin soil bought from the Indians.

(III) He was succeeded by his son, John (2) Richmond, born in Newport, Rhode Island, who was a resident of Westerly and Kingstown, Rhode Island, representing the latter town as deputy in 1740. His wife was Elizabeth, her surname unknown.

(IV) Stephen Richmond, son of John (2) and Elizabeth Richmond, was born in Kingstown, Rhode Island, October 3, 1704; died June 26, 1787. He was a member of the Society of Friends, and a minister of that sect. He was deputy, rate maker and moderator president of town council, Richmond, Rhode Island; owned two hundred and fifteen acres in Exeter, also about one-half of Fisher's Island, and the Watch Hill farm in Westerly, Rhode Island. He married Mary Lawton, and among their children was a son, Stephen.

(V) Stephen (2) Richmond, son of Stephen (1) and Mary (Lawton) Richmond, was born in Westerly, Rhode Island, and died at Exeter, December 12, 1797. He was a leather merchant and a member of the Society of Friends. He married Lucy Mowry, of Exeter, Rhode Island, who died February 17, 1825, surviving her husband twenty-eight years.

(VI) John (3) Richmond, son of Stephen (2) and Lucy (Mowry) Richmond, was born in Exeter, Rhode Island, December 25, 1777. He became a farmer and landowner of Exeter, his holdings totaling 157 acres. He served the town for fourteen years as justice of the peace, and for several years was constable. He married, March 22, 1801, Polly Maxson, born in Hopkinton, Rhode Island, February 21, 1783; died January 5, 1857. Their children were: Susannah, born March 22, 1802; Sarah, born February 10, 1804; Stephen H., born December 7, 1805; John M., of further mention; Mary, born January 30, 1811; George W., born April 8, 1813; Robert H., born March 9, 1815; Nancy, born June 15, 1817; Lucy, born November 20, 1819; Almira, born August 20, 1821.

(VII) John Maxson Richmond, head of the seventh generation, and second son of John (3) and Polly (Maxson) Richmond, was born at Exeter, Rhode Island, December 25, 1808, and died in Preston, Connecticut, December 13, 1876. He spent the first quarter of a century of his life in Exeter, where he engaged in farming, after school years were over. In 1835, he located in the town of Preston, Connecticut, leasing a farm in the northern part of the town. A year later he moved to a leased farm on Broad Brook, Preston, which he worked for several years before purchasing its 117 acres. As he prospered he was the owner of four farms, all situated in the town of Preston. He was a man of great energy, frugal and industrious by nature, conscientious and upright, rendering to every man his due. He became one of the substantial men of his town, his wealth all accumulated from his agricultural activities, which included cattle raising and dealing. He continued active and in good health until the closing of his years, at the age of sixty-eight. He was a Democrat in politics, but took no part in public affairs beyond exercising his rights and duties as a citizen.

Mr. Richmond married, in 1832, Emily Frink, who died at the home of her son, George J. Richmond, August 6, 1899, daughter of Rufus and Polly (Smith) Frink. Mrs. Emily Richmond survived her husband twenty-three years and attained the extreme age of ninety-five years. Mr. and Mrs. Richmond were the parents of five children: George John, a farmer of Preston, born January 14, 1833; married May Janette West; Mary Ann, died unmarried at the age of sixty-one; Henry Alfred, of further mention; Albert Ephraim, born July 25, 1841; Harriet Jane, married George O. Malloy, of Preston.

(VIII) Henry Alfred Richmond, of the eighth generation of the family founded in New England by John Richmond, and second son of John Maxson and Emily (Frink) Richmond, was born in Preston, New London county, Connecticut, April 2, 1839, and in that town his eighty-two years have been spent. He attended the Brown district school near the homestead in Preston, and later was a scholar at a private school in Preston City. School years having ended at the age of eighteen, he then became his father's farm assistant. He remained at the home farm until his first marriage, when he bought one of his father's farms in the town of Preston, and from that time until the present has owned and cultivated its 210 acres. There was an interval, from the time of the death of his wife in 1868, to his second marriage in 1871, when he returned to his old home and managed the home farm for his father. Upon taking a second wife he returned to his own farm, and has since known no other home, a full half-century having since elapsed. He conducts a diary business in connection with general farming, and has been very successful in his business undertakings, having learned well the lessons of thrift, industry and economy, taught him by his father through both precept and example.

Mr. Richmond has always enjoyed the confidence and esteem of his townsmen, who have elected him to many of the town offices, and in 1883 sent him to the State Legislature, and he has been assessor and a member of the board of relief, and a grand juror. All these offices he has most creditably filled, and while in the Legislature served with credit on the Agriculture Committee. In politics he is a Democrat, and in religious faith a member of Bethel Methodist Episcopal Church, serving that congregation as steward and trustee for many years.

Mr. Richmond married (first) Juliette Kinney, of Voluntown, Connecticut, who died February 14, 1868, at the home farm in Preston. She was the daughter of Samuel and Lydia (Phillips) Kinney, and the mother of a daughter, Emma, who died in infancy. Mr. Richmond married (second) January 31, 1871, Lucy Ellen Richardson, daughter of William and Lucy Ann (Dawley) Richardson, of North Stonington, Connecticut. To them twelve children were born at the home farm in Preston: (1) Lucy Emily, educated in district and select schools, later becoming a teacher in Griswold and Norwich schools. She married Byron P. Young, a farmer of Sterling, Connecticut, and they are the parents of three sons, Byron Herbert, Raymond Alton, and Richard Milton Young. (2) Juliette, educated in the district school, Norwich Free Academy, and a select school; now a teacher in Jewett City schools, residing at home. (3) Ida Florence, a teacher at the time of her marriage to Albert Saunders, a merchant of Jewett City, Connecticut. Mrs. Saunders died in January, 1919. (4) John Henry, now a contractor and builder of Springfield, Massachusetts. He married Minnie Richardson, of North Stonington, Connecticut, and has three children: John Lloyd, Sylvia Minnie, and Mildred Richmond. (5) Grace Lydia, educated in the district school and Manchester High School, was a teacher in Ellington, Connecticut, prior to her marriage to Merton H. Bartlett, a farmer of the town of Griswold. (6) Bessie May, a teacher in the public schools, who married Albert W. C. Burdick of Jewett City, now in real estate and insurance business, with offices in Norwich and Jewett City. Mr. and Mrs. Burdick have two daughters, Christine and Arline Burdick. (7) William Richardson, now a contractor and builder of Springfield, Massachusetts, married Mamie M. Luther, of Preston, and has five children, Elizabeth M., Luther H., Marguerite, Gertrude E., and Henrietta M. (8) Mary Dawley, educated in Preston schools and a graduate of Willimantic State Normal, and now a teacher in Willimantic schools. (9) Minnie Belle, a teacher in Suffield, Connecticut, prior to her marriage to Raymond Matson, of Windsor, Connecticut. Mrs. Matson died in 1914. (10) Alice Hannah, a teacher in Jewett City, married Lyle C. Gray, a farmer of North Stonington, Connecticut, and they are the parents of four children, Marjorie Flostina, Jeannette, Anita, and Marilyn Gray. (11) Harold A., a graduate of Wesleyan University, A. M. He served nearly two years in the World War, and was captain in the Sanitary Corps. He is now at the head of the sales research division of the Equitable Life Assurance Society of the United States, New York City. He married Marian B. Ireland, of Philadelphia, Pennsylvania. (12) Ernest Albert, a graduate of Norwich Free Academy, who cultivates the homestead farm, the only son to embrace the time-honored calling of his eight generations of great ancestors. All of the daughters of the family became educators, and two of them have made it their life work. Ten of these twelve children are living—a remarkable record.

JOSEPH MATTHEW GANEY, M.D.—A native son, Dr. Ganey has won high standing in the city of his birth, both as a physician of learning and skill and as a citizen of highest motives and loftiest patriotism. He has proved his worth as a physician, as shown by his clientele and his work in the hospitals of New London, and as a patriot, by his volunteer service at home and overseas during the period of war between the United States and Germany, 1917-1918. Dr. Ganey is a son of John Crocker and Mary (Ahearn) Ganey, both born in Ireland,

J. M. Ganey M.D.

but later residents of Portland and New London, Connecticut. John C. Ganey was a skilled worker in metal, and for more than a quarter of a century his trade was that of a blacksmith at the Brown Cotton Mills in New London. Both he and his wife died in New London.

Joseph Matthew Ganey was born in New London, Connecticut, November 8, 1878, and there completed public school study with graduation from Bulkeley High School. Deciding upon the medical profession, he entered the College of Physicians and Surgeons at Baltimore, Maryland, whence he was graduated M. D., class of 1904. He served as interne at the Mercy Hospital, Baltimore, then returned to New London, where in 1905 he began private practice, continuing with satisfactory results until 1909, when he spent a year abroad in special study in the medical department of the University of Vienna, Austria. He returned to New London in 1910, and resumed practice, continuing until June 16, 1917, when at the call of duty he laid aside personal consideration and enlisted in the United States Army and was assigned to duty at Camp Oglethorpe, Georgia, with the rank of first lieutenant. He then was sent to the Coast Defense Artillery Corps, along Long Island Sound, with headquarters at Fort H. G. Wright on Fisher's Island. He was medical officer with the Third Battalion, Fifty-sixth Regiment, Coast Artillery Corps, United States Army, under the command of Major Morris B. Payne, of New London, and with that battalion he went overseas and was in all their battles and experiences in France. His regiment, organized in December, 1917, at Fort Wright, sailed from the United States, March 28, 1918, and arrived in France April 4 following. The 146th Regiment served continuously on the line from August 15 to November 8, 1918. Dr. Ganey was wounded at Chevy-Chartreuse, August 23, 1918. They were engaged in Aisne-Marne, Oise Aisne, Meuse Argonne, in the First Army Sector, and saw war in all its horrible forms until the struggle ended with the overthrow of German power and the flight of the craven Kaiser. Dr. Ganey was awarded the Distinguished Service Cross for his services and exploits, described as follows, in the recommendation for his decoration:

Office of the Surgeon
56th Artillery (C. A. C.), A. E. F.
A. P. O. No. 728, Nov. 21, 1918.

Lt. Ganey with Sgt. Roberts and Privates Gow and Handley of the Sanitary Detachment, 56th Artillery (C. A. C.) arrived at the road between Charpentry and Baulny, France, on the night of Oct. 3, 1918, with the Third Battalion of the 56th Artillery (C. A. C.) under heavy shell fire and concentration of gas which continued all night. On the morning of Oct. 4, 1918, the Infantry attacked at daybreak and a great number of untagged soldiers were brought back to this road from the line just over the hill with their wounds not dressed. Lt. Ganey and his men immediately established an aid station on the side of the road under constant shell and machine gun fire and continued dressing and evacuating wounded from daylight until 11:00 A. M., with utter disregard for their personal safety, the nature of the locality being such as to offer them no protection. During this time they dressed and evacuated several hundred soldiers of the First Division, largely from the 16th and 18th Infantry. The Battalion to which Lt. Ganey and his men were attached was not in action and the improvised aid station was established on his own initiative.

The 56th Artillery sailed from Brest, France, January 5, 1919, still under command of Major Payne, on the United States battleship "South Dakota," and arrived in New York, January 17, 1919. Dr. Ganey was honorably discharged and mustered out, January 29, 1919, at Fort Schuyler, New York, and returned to his home in New London.

After his return from France, Dr. Ganey for the third time began the upbuilding of a practice in New London and as before has met with great encouragement from his acquaintances and friends of a lifetime. He is building up a practice along general lines, including surgery, and makes a specialty of obstetrics, and ranks very high in that department of his profession. He is a member of the New London City, New London County, and Connecticut State Medical societies, and the American Medical Association of Vienna. He served on the staff of the old Memorial Hospital, New London, and the consolidation of that and Lawrence Hospitals under the name of the Lawrence and Memorial Hospital, and from that time until the present, he served as chief obstetrician. He is also assistant surgeon to the United States Public Health at New London. He is a member of the Military Order of the Foreign Wars of Connecticut Commandery, and of John Coleman Prince Post of the American Legion. In politics he is a Democrat, in religion, a Roman Catholic.

On March 22, 1916, Dr. Ganey married, at New London, Anna Williams, born in New London, daughter of John and Mary (Enos) Williams. Dr. and Mrs. Ganey are the parents of three children, Joann, Joseph Matthew (2nd), Jane. The family home is at 205 William street, New London.

WILLIAM MARVIN—When Reynold Marvin, one of the original proprietors of the town of Lyme, Connecticut, settled in that locality, he established a line, which through more than two and a half centuries has continued to furnish valuable citizens to that town, as well as to what is now called, Old Lyme. Elisha Marvin, great-great-grandfather of Judge William Marvin, was born in what is now Old Lyme, and moved from that town to Lyme, where he built the house which has ever since been the family homestead. He married Catherine Mather, and the fourth and last of their children was Joseph Marvin, who, born in the old homestead in Lyme, was a soldier in the Revolutionary War, and died

November 19, 1839. He married, October 16, 1783, Phebe Sterling, and became the father of six children, the third of whom was William Marvin, also born on the old homestead, who served in the War of 1812. He was a deacon in the Congregational church, and was a probate judge. He married, October 21, 1819, Sophia Griffin, of East Haddam, and they became the parents of six children, the fourth of whom was William Joseph, father of Judge William Marvin.

William Joseph Marvin, son of William and Sophia (Griffin) Marvin, was born in the old homestead at Lyme, April 6, 1830, and spent his life in his native place. He attended the Academy at Essex, and then went to work on a farm, in which occupation he continued throughout his life. He was very prominent in the life of the town, and at the time of his death, which occurred April 7, 1878, was treasurer. He married, January 28, 1869, Ann M. Parker, daughter of Marshfield S. Parker, who was born in Lyme, September 30, 1830, and died October 23, 1900. Their two children were: William, mentioned below; and Harry S., born August 8, 1875, who, educated at East Greenwich Academy and at Dow Academy, Franconia, New Hampshire, was a member of the drug firm of Mitchell & Marvin, in Boston for a few years, and is now in the drug business for himself. He married Annie Powell, and is the father of two children, Grace Mary and William Joseph.

Hon. William Marvin, eldest son of William Joseph and Ann M. (Parker) Marvin, was born at the old home in Lyme, March 13, 1873. He attended the local schools, and then went to East Greenwich Academy, in Rhode Island, graduating in 1893. After his graduation, he returned to the home farm, where he has remained. In 1896 he was elected town clerk, although but twenty-three years of age, and has continued to fill that office which, 1921, he still holds. He is also judge of probate, and very active in the political and agricultural affairs of his locality. He is a member of the Lyme Chapter of the Grange, and of the Farm Bureau, in both of which organizations he has given his services to the agricultural interests of the county. He is a Republican in his party affiliation, and was a member of the Connecticut Legislature in 1905 and also in 1907.

Judge Marvin married Julia Niles Ely, daughter of Dr. J. Griffin and Elizabeth (Chadwick) Ely, of Lyme, Connecticut. No children have been born to the union.

JEROME BONAPARTE RATHBUN—Of an ancient Rhode Island family, Mr. Rathbun remained in his native State many years, then located in Groton, Connecticut, coming thence to the village of Niantic, Connecticut, where the past thirty years of his life have been spent. Much of his early life was spent in the saw mills of Summit, Rhode Island, and Groton, Connecticut, and from manufacturing lumber he became a dealer, and until his retirement in 1914 operated a lumber yard in Niantic.

Jerome B. Rathbun was born in Exeter Hill, Rhode Island, December 8, 1858. He was educated in the Exeter Hill public schools and after school years were over, became a saw mill employee, thoroughly learning the business of manufacturing lumber of any dimension from the log. He was employed in different mills, and continued in that line of activity until about 1890, when he located in Niantic, his present home. For ten years he conducted a steam saw mill in Niantic, but in 1914 retired, after a very successful business life. Mr. Rathbun is a member of Fairview Lodge, No. 101, Independent Order of Odd Fellows.

Mr. Rathbun married, in West Greenwich, Rhode Island, May 13, 1881, Harriet Estella Brown, born there October 18, 1866, daughter of Elisha and Louisa Parkis (Capwell) Brown. Twelve children were born to Mr. and Mrs. Brown, six of whom died young. Those who grew to mature years were: 1. Maria Emmeline, born in Exeter, Rhode Island, married George Richmond, of Westerly, Rhode Island, and they are the parents of: George, Frank, Amy and Elizabeth Richmond. 2. Atmore Robinson, who married Nellie Capwell, and they are the parents of: Thomas, Flora and Rose Brown. 3. Henry Elisha, married Adaline Arnold, they the parents of: Lillian, William and Walter Brown. 4. Lois Anna, who married Clarke Greene, of West Greenwich, Rhode Island, and four children were born to them: Laura, Fred, Caliph, Mabel and Anna Greene. 5. Bowen, who married Mary Ann Carr, and they are the parents of: Fanny, Louisa, George, Bertha and Sadie Brown. 6. Harriet E., who married Jerome B. Rathbun, and resides in Niantic. Mr. and Mrs. Rathbun are the parents of six children: Henry Albert, born February 14, 1884, married Agnes Beebe, and resides in Black Hall, Connecticut; Mary Evelyn, born in West Greenwich, Rhode Island, January 23, 1886, married Timothy Maine, of Ledyard, Connecticut, and has two children, Elizabeth and Maurice; Everett Elmer, born in West Greenwich, Rhode Island, September 13, 1888, married Gladys Daniels, and they are the parents of the following children: Lawrence, Earl and Lillian Rathbun; Susan Estelle, born in Groton, Connecticut, September 8, 1891, married Fred Sisson, of Clarks Falls, Connecticut, and has two daughters, Sophia and Evelyn Sisson; Arthur Earl, born at Groton, Connecticut, July 9, 1893, married Julia Beebe, and has a daughter, Pearl; Caribell, born in Center Groton, Connecticut, November 14, 1900, married William Fellows, and has a son, George.

CAPTAIN DAVID CARROLL QUINLEY—The late Captain Quinley was born at North Lyme, Connecticut, August 22, 1848. He was the son of David Tyron and Roxanna (Spencer) Quinley, both deceased. The boy, David C., left the home farm early in life and went to live with his uncle, who was an inland fisherman, plying his trade on the Niantic river. Early in life, David C. Quinley developed a keen interest in the sea, and a familiar sight to the people who lived about here was the lad rowing up

John W. Watson

and down the Niantic. The longing to explore what was beyond the blue horizon finally compelled him when but twelve years old to ship as a deck hand on board a schooner bound for Georges Banks. When he attained manhood he was given command of the schooner "Game Cock," which was used to carry stone from the quarries at Millstone Point to the site upon which was being built the Battery in New York. Later he purchased the schooner "Irving J. Lewis." One day the steps from the deck to the cabin on the "Game Cock" were removed by a member of the crew, who later neglected to replace them. That night Captain Quinley, not knowing of this, fell to the deck below, and in this fall struck his heart against a box. Although he lived for many years after this accident, he never fully recovered from the blow. Selling the "Irving J. Lewis," he subsequently was given command of the yacht "Violet," owned by Mr. Haymes, whose summer estate is at Sandy Point, and it was while engaged in this last capacity that Captain Quinley met with the painful accident which hastened his death; this occurred February 8, 1915.

Captain Quinley was united in marriage with Augusta Anne Wheeler. Mrs. Quinley, who survives her husband, and resides at Niantic, was born at New London, Connecticut, July 27, 1850, the daughter of William and Nancy (Beebe) Wheeler. Mr. and Mrs. Wheeler had six children, three of whom are dead, the others: Augusta Anne, previously mentioned; Isabella, who married Charles Leonard, of Niantic; and Eliza Anna, who married Charles Beckwith, of Hartford.

JOHN WILLETTE WATSON—Perhaps more widely than any others do the records of an ocean-bordered section reach out into the interesting and significant places of the world. In New London county, Connecticut, there are few of the old families who do not count at least one member who has followed the sea, at least for a time. More than eighty years ago, John Willette Watson, as a child, became a resident of this county, and the story of his life closely follows the growth of this section in importance as a mercantile and industrial center, his activities, through the greater part of his life, centering in the agricultural districts of the county, and in the productive pursuits which are the foundation of all prosperity.

Mr. Watson was born in West Greenwich, Rhode Island, January 1, 1833, and died in Gales Ferry, New London county, Connecticut, November 7, 1917, having nearly reached the eighty-fifth anniversary of his birth. He was a son of John and Betsy (Corey) Watson, both of old New England families, and the death of his mother when he was seven years of age brought about changes in the circumstances of the family, and his removal to Westerly. With only the scant opportunities of the district schools of that day for the acquiring of an education, Mr. Watson at a very early age began working on the farm. While still a young lad of impressionable age he came to Mystic, and here the lure of sea reached deep into his soul as he watched the coming and going of the outside fishermen. He soon secured the opportunity of joining them, and for eight years was identified with the fishing trade between here and Florida, taking a man's part in the work of the fleet with which he was connected. At the age of twenty-four years he shipped for a whaling voyage, which eventually covered a period of three years in length and took him all around the world.

A short time after his return to his native land he heard, with the other high-souled young men of the day, the shot which, fired on Fort Sumter, re-echoed to the northernmost boundaries of the nation. He enlisted from the town of Groton, and going to the front, participated in the early battles of the war, including Vicksburg and Port Hudson, serving under General Banks. He was wounded in the latter engagement, and in the year 1863 was honorably discharged from the service. Returning at once to his home in this county, he removed his little family to the community in the southwestern part of Ledyard, known as Gales Ferry. Here he took up the peaceful activities of the little farming village, and throughout the remainder of his lifetime tilled the soil, and occasionally, as the building operations of the neighborhood made occasion, he bore a part as a stone mason. Active almost until the time of his death, Mr. Watson was one of the best known men of the section, and his high integrity and genial disposition gave him the friendship and goodwill of all with whom he came in contact. He was a man of rare good sense, and capable of calm, unbiased judgment, and his influence in his community gave impetus to all good movements and stood as an example in honorable citizenship for the younger men as they followed after him.

Not long after his return from the voyage around the world, Mr. Watson married, in Mystic, Marian Chapman, the ceremony taking place on June 27, 1859. They were the parents of six children: William R.; J. Lewis; Charles H.; Jennie M., who became the wife of Joel H. Davis, a sketch of whom follows: George W., and Augusta E. The mother died at Gales Ferry, in the family home, on October 10, 1904.

As a devoted husband and father, as a citizen loyal not only to the written tenets of his native land but to the ideals which inspire all lofty codes of human conduct, John Willette Watson left a mark on the records of his day, both those records which are written for all men to read, and those records which live in the hearts of men, and which go down to posterity in noble impulses and worthy deeds.

JOEL HARRISON DAVIS, whose life from the age of fourteen had been one of activity on land and sea, closed his earthly career at the age of seventy-three, being at the time of his death a resident of Norwich, Connecticut, and owner of a general store there. At the age of fourteen he made his first voyage at sea, and all through his life he was at times a sailor on country craft, government vessels and private yachts and clipper ships, always, however, on sailing vessels. His life was principally spent at sea, and but for poor health he would never have followed any other occupation. He was a son of Joel Davis, son of Elisha Davis, son of Silas Davis, son of Benjamin Davis (2), son of Benjamin Davis (1), who first settled in Plymouth, Massachusetts, later going to Brookhaven, Suffolk county, Long Island. Benjamin (1) Davis was a land owner, and some of his land remained in the family until 1902, when Joel Harrison Davis sold it.

Elisha Davis, of the fourth generation, was a large landowner in that part of Brookhaven known as Mount Sinai, and there died, in April, 1843. He married Julianna Hulse, their third child a son, Joel, of whom further.

Joel Davis was born in Brookhaven, Long Island, October 13, 1805, spent his entire life at the homestead in Mount Sinai, and there died, April 7, 1883. He was a man of means, owned a large amount of land, and was a prosperous farmer. He was a well-known musician, taught singing school in early life, and for twenty-seven years was chorister of the Congregational church at Mount Sinai, Brookhaven, and later of the church at Port Jefferson, Long Island. He married (first) Sarah Maria Turner, who died December 14, 1846, aged thirty-four, daughter of William Turner, owner of Artist's Lake, Long Island. Five children were born to Joel and Sarah M. (Turner) Davis: Susan M., married Captain Ellsworth Carter, a sea captain; Amelia M., married Erastus Brown, a farmer; Elisha, a sea captain; John, a sea captain and sound pilot; Joel Harrison, of whom further. Joel Davis married (second) Hannah M. Davis, a distant relative, born August 19, 1817, died May 3, 1875. They were the parents of three children: Vincent R., a merchant; Roswell, of Yaphank, Long Island; and Ida Belle.

Joel Harrison Davis, youngest son of Joel Davis and his first wife, Sarah Maria (Turner) Davis, was born, at the homestead at Mount Sinai, Suffolk county, Long Island, November 4, 1845, died at his home in Norwich, Connecticut, December 9, 1918. He attended district school until the age of fourteen, then shipped on the coasting sloop "Guide." He was large for his age and very strong, and was able to perform any work required of him. He again went to sea the following season, and the next became a second mate. In 1862, at the age of seventeen, he was steward of the schooner "Reuben H. Nelson," and on that vessel, commanded by his cousin, Henry G. Davis, he made his first voyage to foreign waters, going to Banacoa, Cuba, returning to New York with the largest cargo of fruit they ever delivered there, 69,000 cocoanuts and 4,600 bunches of bananas.

Shortly after that voyage the lad was taken sick and for three years was not able to do anything, but with the recovery of his health he took a book-selling agency, covering Long Island with splendid success, selling Holland's "Life of Lincoln," and "Sherman's and Grant's Campaigns and Generals." He than was clerk in a Patchogue, Long Island, grocery and restaurant for one year, then took up photography, and for one season owned and traveled with a studio on wheels.

In 1868 his health permitted him to return to his first love, the sea, and he shipped as seaman on the United States revenue cutter "Isaac Tousey," serving on Long Island Sound five months. He then shipped on a coaster, and as steward, made a trip to Tabasco, Mexico. Later he was steward of the schooner "Franken Bell," then steward of the clipper ship "Susan Bergen," sailing to Palermo, Sicily, and in that vessel sailed to Messina and Cuban ports. He was steward on the private "Dreadnaught," then the schooner "Florence Shay," in coasting and foreign trade, sailing as steward and navigator, making a year's voyage to South America. He then sailed as steward on the schooner "Benjamin Jones," the "Jennie Rosaline," the "Hattie B. Kelsey," the "Hattie M. Crowell," the "John Holland," the "Florence Randall," and the "Adalaide Randall." He followed the sea as steward on these different vessels until June, 1891, when he ended his career as a mariner, and thereafter resided in Norwich, a merchant.

In Norwich he bought a general store of E. Walter Phillips and began the work of building up a business. He was very successful and continued active in the business for nearly a quarter of a century, then, in 1915, was compelled by failing health to retire. Mrs. Davis then assumed the management, and until the death of her husband, in 1918, continued the business.

Mr. Davis married, in New London, Connecticut, April 3, 1889, Jennie M. Watson, born at Gales Ferry, Connecticut, daughter of John W. and Marian (Chapman) Watson (see preceding sketch).

After the death of her husband, Mrs. Jennie M. (Watson) Davis rented the store in Norwich, but continues her residence at No. 318 Laurel Hill avenue. She is a member of the Baptist church, and both she and her husband had many friends, all of whom she retains.

HERBERT MORTON SWINNEY, now a prosperous lumber dealer of Niantic, Connecticut, has gone far along the road to success, although only in the prime of his manhood. He is a son of Ethan Edward and Elizabeth (Tillett) Swinney, his father born in Lebanon, Ohio, October 2, 1837. Ethan E. Swinney, a harness maker by trade, died in 1905, aged sixty-eight years, his wife, Elizabeth, in 1897, aged fifty-nine. They were the parents of five children, two of whom survived childhood: Herbert M., the principal character of this review; and Annie G., since deceased.

Herbert Morton Swinney was born in Westerly, Rhode Island, June 14, 1872, and there was educated in the public schools. At the age of seventeen years he began work with Maxson & Company, contractors and builders, of Westerly (and for nineteen years, 1889-1908, he continued in that company's employ. On March 1, 1908, he bought an interest in the firm of Babcock & Wilcox, of Westerly, contractors and builders, and for eight years continued in business as a partner in that firm. He then sold his interest and removed to Niantic, Connecticut, where he, in connection with Louis C. Dimock, bought the lumber yards of Asahei R. DeWolf, an established business of twenty-one years' standing, and at that time was incorporated as the Niantic Lumber Company, Herbert M. Swinney, secretary, treasurer and general manager.

Mr. Swinney is a member of Niantic Lodge, No. 17, Independent Order of Odd Fellows, and the Junior Order United American Mechanics, Hope Council, No. 6, of Westerly, Rhode Island; he is an Independent in politics, and a member of the Seventh Day Baptist church.

Mr. Swinney married, in Stonington, Connecticut, May 16, 1901 Belinda Robinson Southwick, born August 13, 1881, at Wakefield, Rhode Island, daughter of Wanton and Annie Laurie (Holland) Southwick, who were the parents of three daughter: Sarah, Belinda and Annie. To Mr. and Mrs. Swinney four children were born: Morton Remington, born May 5, 1902, in Stonington, Connecticut; Ruth Elizabeth, born March 8, 1918, in Niantic, Connecticut, and two children who died in infancy.

ERNEST CHAMPLIN RUSSELL, clerk of the town of East Lyme, New London county, Connecticut, was born in Niantic, Connecticut, May 6, 1876, and was educated in local schools. Most of his life has been spent in his native village, and since arriving at man's estate he has been engaged in business as a real estate dealer, and to that business has added insurance. Soon after school years were ended he left the village of his birth for a short time, but returned, and for eighteen years, 1903-1921, has been town clerk, an office that he has held continuously, the voters of the town of East Lyme, in which town Niantic is situated, refusing to consider anyone else for the office.

Mr. Russell is a son of Benjamin Franklin Russell, born in Hartford, Connecticut, in 1824, died in Niantic, at the age of seventy-three, and is there buried. He came to Niantic a youth, and became a mariner, following the sea for many years. He married Ellen Lock, of Leeds, England, born in 1834, daughter of Thomas Lock. They were the parents of four children: Marion Clarence; Frank William, of Niantic; Claude Charles, of New Haven, Connecticut; and Ernest C., of previous mention.

CLIFFORD ERWIN CHAPMAN, postmaster of Niantic, Connecticut, to which office he was appointed in 1915, has served his community well in many public capacities, having filled each post with untiring faithfulness and devotion to duty, which are characteristic of the man.

Savalian Edwin Chapman, father of Clifford Erwin Chapman, was born in the Whistle town district of East Lyme, September 16, 1844, and for many years was a farmer and blacksmith. He now lives retired at Niantic. He married Juliet S. Bishop, a native of Stony Creek, Connecticut, and to them have been born three children: John, who was drowned at the age of four years; Clifford Erwin, of further mention; and Perry G., of Hartford, Connecticut, department manager of the Fox & Company store.

Clifford Erwin Chapman was born at Niantic, Connecticut, May 13, 1880, and during his childhood attended the local schools, at the same time devoting his spare time to helping his father in his work about the farm and the blacksmith shop. He was associated with the elder man in business until 1911, when he received his appointment to the Legislature, subsequently returning the following year to his former employment and continuing thus until 1915, when he was made postmaster of Niantic, which office he still holds. He occupies a high place in the opinion of those who know him, a place which he has won by his energy and upright character. The public's interests are well served by servants of this type. In politics he is a Democrat, and in religious faith a Baptist. Mr. Chapman is affiliated with the Masons, and belongs to Bayview Lodge, No. 120, Free and Accepted Masons. It is hard to predict the future of an already sucessful man who is still comparatively young in years, but the past gives promise of an even more brilliant future.

On February 25, 1910, at Niantic, Clifford Erwin Chapman was united in marriage with Minnie A. Beebe, daughter of John and Amanda (Andrea) Beebe, who also have three other children: Arthur, a resident of New London; Chester A., a resident of Niantic; and Almeda Littlefield, who married Dwight Luce, of Niantic. Mr. and Mrs. Chapman are the parents of one child, Andrea Juliette, born February 9, 1911.

ALBERT CLARK FREEMAN, M. D., came to Norwich, Connecticut, in 1913, with his newly-acquired honors bestowed by the University of Vermont. But he did not then begin private practice, for after a year as interne at the M. W. Buckus Hospital, he spent eighteen months in practice in Plainfield, Vermont, his Norwich residence dating from January, 1916. The five years that nave since intervened have brought him a fair share of professional success and he is becoming well established in public esteem.

Dr. Freeman, grandson of George and Mary (Fiske) Freeman, and son of George Freeman, who was born in Brookfield, Vermont, and educated in a Barre, Vermont, school. He was his father's farm assistant until reaching man's estate, when he went West, locating at Rolfe, Pocahontas county, Iowa, thirty miles from Fort Dodge, the center of a farming and stock-raising region. This move was caused by poor health, but in Iowa he bought a farm near Rolfe, and in addition to working his farm, taught in the district school. In 1885 he sold his farm, and in June of that year passed away at Rolfe. He was a Republican in politics, and in religious faith a member of the Methodist Episcopal church, and superintendent of the Sunday school.

George Freeman married Mary Cooley, born in Iowa, died at Rolfe, in 1885, daughter of Henry Cooley, an Iowa pioneer. Mr. and Mrs. Freeman were the parents of three children, all born in Iowa: Kate, married James Mitchell, of Barre, Vermont; Mabel, married George Turner, a contractor of Council Bluffs, Iowa; and Albert Clark, of further mention. After the death of their mother in 1885, the children came East, to Barre, Vermont.

Albert Clark Freeman, son of George and Mary (Cooley) Freeman, was born November 8, 1883, at Rolfe, Iowa, and in 1885 came to Barre, Vermont, an orphan. He attended school in Barre, passing thence to the Montpelier (Vermont) Seminary, whence he was graduated in 1905. Being determined to make his own start in life, Mr. Freeman was employed for about four years at farming, and at the same time taught the district school and sold milk in Barre. His independent spirit and ambition carried him through these formative years. In 1909 he entered the medical department of the University of Vermont, where after a four years' course he was graduated M. D., class of 1913. After one year in the M. W. Buckus Hospital, at Norwich, Connecticut, Dr. Freeman went to Plainfield, Vermont, where he opened an office, remaining about a year and a half. In January, 1916, he returned to Norwich, where he has since been continuously engaged in the successful practice of his profession. He is pathologist of the M. W. Buckus Hospital, of Norwich, and during the World War was post surgeon of that town and also served in the Medical Advisory Board. In politics Dr. Freeman is a Republican, and in 1917 was appointed milk inspector for Norwich, serving until resigning in 1920. Dr. Freeman has been secretary and treasurer of the New London County Medical Association since 1917; is a member of the Norwich Medical Society, the Connecticut State Medical Society, and the American Medical Association. He affiliates with Shetucket Lodge, Independent Order of Odd Fellows, of Norwich; is a member of the Norwich Arcanum Club, and of the United Congregational Church.

Dr. Freeman married, August 11, 1917, in Norwich, Eva Annie Bisbee, born in Waitsfield, Vermont, daughter of Burton and Lucia (Joslin) Bisbee, of that town, her father a prosperous farmer. Dr. and Mrs. Freeman are the parents of two children, both born in Norwich: Alberta, born April 12, 1919; and Emerson Osgood, born December 23, 1920. Progressive in his profession and in his citizenship, genial and friendly in disposition, Dr. Freeman is building up a good practice and forming friendships on a basis which will endure.

PERCY ALPHONSUS WHEELER—One of the enterprising young men of East Lyme, Connecticut, is Percy A. Wheeler, who is achieving success at the attractive shore resort known as Crescent Beach.

Mr. Wheeler is a son of William Ubrick Wheeler, who was born in New Brunswick, New Jersey, lived on a large ranch in the West for a few years, and is now living at Crescent Beach. He married Julia Griffin, of Scotch descent, and their four children are as follows: Harriet, who was born in New Rochelle, New York, and married Lewis Adriene, a New York City banker; Mary G., who was born in New Rochelle, married Vaughn H. Ray, of Hartfort, Connecticut, who is connected with the Travelers' Insurance Company of that city, and has two children: William and Margaret; William A., also born in New Rochelle, who married Mary ——, and has one daughter, Julia; and Percy A., of further mention.

Percy A. Wheeler was born in New Rochelle, New York, December 30, 1894, and came to Crescent Beach, East Lyme, Connecticut, with his family while still a child. He received his early education in the schools of this community, then completed his studies at the vocational school in New London, same State. His first business experience was in the employ of the Buick Motor Car Company, at St. Augustine, Florida, and he continued there during the winter, opening his own garage at Crescent Beach for the summer months. He has been very successful thus far, broadening his operations constantly, and was contemplating opening a large garage of his own in St. Augustine, Florida, for the winter of 1921-22.

On April 4, 1917, Mr. Wheeler enlisted for service in the World War, at New London, in the United States navy. After a short period of training at the Newport Training Station, he was assigned to duty on board the speed boat "Tocksway," a submarine patrol boat, serving for one year. He was discharged from the service in April, 1919, and returned to his interrupted business.

Mr. Wheeler is interested in the affairs of the day, but in political matters holds an independent position, giving his support to the party placing the best man in the field.

On November 10, 1915, Mr. Wheeler married, at Niantic, Connecticut, Florence Luce, of that town, who was born September 25, 1900, and is a daughter of Dwight and Almedia (Beebe) Luce, and their only child. Mr. and Mrs. Wheeler have had three children, the eldest of whom died in infancy. Those living are: Rockwell Augustine, who was born in Niantic, June 13, 1918; and Griffin John, born December 27, 1921, in St. Augustine, Florida.

WILLIAM FRANCIS HILL—The keenest interest attaches to the man of any community who has to do with the development of the city itself. In Norwich, Connecticut, William Francis Hill is one of the leaders in the real estate business.

Mr. Hill comes of a solid old New Hampshire family. His father, Alpheus M. Hill, was a native of Nashua, New Hampshire. Throughout his life he owned a fine stable of horses, and handled the teaming for the granite quarries and lumber mills which form the principal industries of the region around Nashua. He married Elizabeth Dorcas Barker, who was born in New York City in 1834; he died in 1875, and his wife died in 1901, in Lancaster, New Hampshire. They were the parents of four children, of whom William Francis Hill, of Norwich, is the only one now living.

William Francis Hill was born in Nashua, New Hampshire, on February 4, 1860. He received his education in the public schools of the town, then for a time worked in a shoe factory. Later he went to Providence, Rhode Island, where he worked in a gun shop of the Providence Tool Company. In 1879 he came to Norwich, and entered the employ of Hopkins & Allen, gun makers, and here he remained until 1886. In that year he became a railway mail clerk, continuing for one year. At this time his wife had a breakdown, and for the sake of her health, he traveled with her; she died in 1898, in Norwich. In 1899 Mr. Hill established himself in the real estate business, handling also a considerable amount of insurance. He has been very successful, having handled some of the most interesting business in this line in the recent development of Norwich, and is ranked high in the forefront of the real estate business.

Mr. Hill is a Democrat by political affiliation, and for five years, from 1893 to 1898, was city and town tax collector. He belongs to the Masonic order, being a member of Somerset Lodge, No. 34, Free and Accepted Masons; Franklin Chapter, No. 4, Royal Arch Masons; Franklin Council, No. 4, Royal and Select Masters; Columbian Commandery, of Norwich; Sphinx Temple, Ancient Arabic Order Nobles of the Mystic Shrine, of Hartford; and the Connecticut Consistory, thirty-second degree; also of the Knights of Pythias, and the Chamber of Commerce.

Mr. Hill married (first) Nellie H. Crowell, of Norwich, in 1886, and she died in 1898. They had three children: Mary C., who lives at home; Andrew C., who is now associated with his father and is married; and Elmer, who also is associated with his father in business, and is married. Mr. Hill married (second) Mrs. Lucy C. (Coit) Jennings, of Norwich, who died in January, 1912.

MALCOLM MacFARLANE SCOTT was born in New London, Connecticut, July 5, 1877, son of George Hall and Agnes Jane Scott, his father a stock clerk with the Babcock Printing Press Manufacturing Company. He attended the public schools until through grammar school courses, then entered New London Business College, where he completed his studies. He then entered the office employ of the Brown Cotton Gin Company, there continuing for twenty-three years. In 1916 he entered the employ of the Union Bank and Trust Company, of New London, and has continued with that corporation until the present, 1922, holding the position of paying teller.

Mr. Scott, for six years, represented his ward on the Board of Aldermen, and when New London went under the Council manager form of government, became an official and is now serving as councellor. He is a member of the First Church of Christ (Scientist); is a past master of Brainard Lodge, No. 102, Free and Accepted Masons; past high priest of Union Chapter, No. 7, Royal Arch Masons; past thrice illustrious master of Cushing Council No. 4, Royal and Select Masters; member of Palestine Commandery, No. 6, Knights Templar; of New London Lodge, No. 360, Benevolent and Protective Order of Elks; Clan Cameron, No. 154, Order of Scottish Clans; New London Lodge, No. 34, Loyal Order of Moose; and Jibboom Club No. 1.

Mr. Scott married, in New London, Connecticut, October 17, 1898, Abbey Jane Sweet, daughter of Riley and Katherine (Ferguson) Sweet, and they are the parents of a son, Henkle Sweet Scott.

JAMES N. KELLEY, when a boy, came to the city of New London, Connecticut, and there has spent his life, and is now a successful undertaker. He has worked his way upward to an honorable position among business men by his own efforts, and has been from boyhood the architect and builder of his own fortunes. Men respect and honor him for his upright life, and in his business he has no superiors.

James Kelley, father of James N. Kelley, born in Dublin, Ireland, came to the United States when a boy, and early in the decade of 1850-60, located in New London, Connecticut. He was then but a boy, and in New London he obtained his education. After school days were over for the lad he began following the sea, and all his after life he spent as a seaman. He died in New London, July 10, 1903, aged fifty-six. He married Catherine Cronin, born in County Cork, Ireland, died in New London, January 10, 1903, her husband surviving her exactly six months. James and Catherine Kelley were the parents of four children: Mary, married Richard Prendergast, of New London; Catherine, married George Mahoney, of Norwich, Connecticut; James N., of further mention; and Agnes, who died at the age of eleven years.

James N. Kelley, only son of James and Catherine Kelley, was born in Norwich, Connecticut, April 25, 1873, but his education was obtained in New London schools. Upon coming of legal age in 1894, he entered the employ of Keefe & Davis, general merchants, as a clerk, and for ten years continued with that company as such. In 1904 he went with the Stephen Merritt Burial Company, of New London, spending one year in their employ. He liked the business and determined to fit himself to conduct it properly. To that end he pursued a full course at the Massachusetts College of Embalming, Boston, and after receiving his diploma from the college, went before the Connecticut State Board of Examiners and successfully passed all required tests of his ability to conduct the business of an undertaker. He then established undertaking rooms in New London, and has won for himself high reputation and business standing. He is well equipped personally for the business he conducts, and has availed himself of all modern aids used in the care and preservation of the dead.

In politics Mr. Kelley is an Independent; and his religious conviction is as a member of St. Mary's Roman Catholic Church. He is a member of St. John's Literary Society, the Ancient Order of Hibernians, the Benevolent and Protective Order of Elks, the Chamber of Commerce, all these New London bodies, and of the Connecticut State Embalmers' Association.

Mr. Kelley married, at New London, August 6, 1907, Ellen Condon, daughter of John and Ellen (Davis) Condon. Mr. and Mrs. Kelley are the parents of a son, James Davis Kelley, born in New London, Connecticut.

JONATHAN FAIRBANKS LESTER—The life of Jonathan F. Lester was passed in his native county, New London, and in the State of California, where he engaged in farming in the latter place for about seven years. He was a man of energy and enterprise, highly esteemed by all who knew him. He was the son of Isaac A. and Mary (Chapman) Lester, and a descendant in paternal line from Andrew Lester, born in England, who came to New England, settled in Gloucester, Massachusetts, where he was elected constable, January 7, 1646, and licensed to keep an "ordinary" February 6, 1648. His Connecticut residence began in 1651 at Pequot (New London), where he had a home on the "Neck" and had land rights allowed him. He was elected collector of taxes and constable, holding office and being a resident of Pequot until his death, June 7, 1669. The death of his first wife, Barbara, February 2, 1653, is the first death of a woman recorded in Pequot. He married a second wife, Mrs. Joanna Hempstead, widow of Robert Hempstead; and a third, Anna ——. The "Widow Lester" was admitted to the New London church by letter from the church at Concord, Massachusetts, in 1670. By his first wife, Barbara, Andrew Lester had children: Daniel, Andrew, Mary and Anne; by his second wife: Joanna; and by his third wife: Timothy, Joseph and Benjamin, descent being traced through the last-born son.

(II) Benjamin Lester was born in New London, Connecticut, about 1666, and with his half-brother Daniel, and his brother Joseph, settled in the vicinity of the town site. His will was dated May 23, 1737, and it is believed that he died the next day. He married Ann Stedman, and they were the parents of nine sons, also of two daughters. In his will he names his wife, sons—Timothy, John, Benjamin, Isaac, Daniel, and his daughters, Ann and Hannah. Other sons were David, and Jonathan, of further mention; two sons died young. These children were either born in New London or Groton.

(III) Jonathan Lester, son of Benjamin and Ann (Stedman) Lester, was born at New London, Connecticut, July 26, 1706, and was married May 15, 1729, and with his wife owned the covenant at Groton Congregational Church. He had children: Jonathan; Deborah; Thomas; Amos, of further mention; and Wait; these five baptized October 11, 1731; Simeon, baptized August 14, 1734; and David, November 7, 1736.

(IV) Amos Lester, son of Jonathan Lester, was born at Groton about 1730, and baptized with four of his brothers and sisters, October 11, 1731. He was a soldier of the Revolution, engaged at the battle of Groton, and was one of those reported as wounded (Revolution Rolls, p. 578). His wound was in the hip, and he was one of the wagon-load of wounded men that suffered from the careless handling of the wagon which broke loose and coasted down the hill until stopped by a tree. The captain of the company, Samuel Allyn, was killed in the battle, he and Ensign Amos Lester riding to the battlefield together. Amos Lester had a grant of land in 1792 in Pennsylvania, "at the head of Lake Erie," on account of his Revolutionary service. Ensign Amos Lester married Anna Lester, born December 17, 1736, daughter of Peter and Anna (Street) Lester, her mother a daughter of James Street.

(V) Amos (2) Lester, son of Ensign Amos (1) and Anna (Lester) Lester, was born March 25, 1776, and married, January 18, 1800, Sarah Avery, born March 3, 1781, daughter of James Avery, of an ancient New London county family. They were the parents of five children: 1. Anna, who married Oliver S. Tyler. 2. Lydia, married Erastus Kimball. 3. Amos A. 4. Isaac Avery, of further mention. 5. Eliza Maria, who married Asa Lyman Lester.

(VI) Isaac Avery Lester, son of Amos (2) and Sarah (Avery) Lester, was born at Groton, Connecticut, March 4, 1810. He married, October 17, 1838, Mary Chapman, daughter of Ichabod Chapman, they residing in Ledyard, Connecticut. They were the parents of eleven children, the fifth son, Jonathan Fairbanks Lester, to whose memory this review is dedicated. Children: 1. Amos, married Caroline Gallup. 2. Mary Jane, married Courtland Lamb. 3. Nathan Larrabee, married Sarah Elizabeth Spicer. 4. Henry C., died young. 5. Jonathan Fairbanks, of further mention. 6. William Isaac, married Sarah E. Simmons. 7. Frank Larrabee, born April 23, 1850, died November 17, 1876. 8. Samuel Wood, removed to California. 9. Walter C., died in infancy. 10. Sarah E., died in infancy. 11. Edward Everett, married Almyra Chapman.

(VII) Such were the antecedents of Jonathan Fairbanks Lester, who was born in Ledyard, Connecticut, June 11, 1846, died March 14, 1904. He was educated in the public schools, and when his own education was finished he taught school in both Ledyard and Groton. When a young man he went to the State of California and there spent several years engaged in farming. He returned to Connecticut and was for a time engaged in the meat and provision business in Norwich. His California experiences had left a pleasant impression, and later he formed an association with his brothers, Amos, Samuel W. and Frank L., and they all went to California, where for four years they engaged in farm-

J. T. Lester

Cecelia W. Leslie

ing. In 1873 Jonathan F. Lester returned again to Norwich, married the same year, and for a time engaged in the optical manufacturing business. Afterward, and for several years, he was a member of the wholesale produce business of Cook & Lester, and gained high reputation as a man of fine business ability.

Mr. Lester married, May 28, 1873, Cecelia Williams Spicer, born September 30, 1852, daughter of Captain Edmund and Bethiah Williams (Avery) Spicer, of Groton. Captain Edmund Spicer was a son of John and Elizabeth (Latham) Spicer, grandson of Edward, son of John, son of Edward, son of Peter Spicer, who settled in that part of New London county known as Ledyard in 1666. Captain Edmund Spicer, born in North Groton, January 11, 1812, died May 1, 1890. He was one of Groton's most prominent men, selectman seventeen years; clerk and treasurer twelve years; representative to the State Legislature, 1849; candidate for State Senator, 1862; judge of probate twelve years, 1865-77; charter member and for eighteen consecutive years secretary of the Bill Library Association; and from 1867 until his death, postmaster of Ledyard. Captain Spicer married, November 16, 1836, Bethiah W. Avery, daughter of John Sands and Bethiah (Williams) Avery, of Groton. Captain and Mrs. Spicer were the parents of eight children: 1. Mary Affy, who married George Fanning. 2. John Sands, who married Anna Mariah Williams. 3. Joseph Latham, who died in childhood. 4. Sarah Elizabeth, who married Nathan L. Lester. 5. Caroline Gallup, who married Amos Lester. 6. Cecelia Williams, wife of Jonathan F. Lester. 7. Edward Eugene, who married Sarah Adelaide Griswold. 8. George Walter, who married Elizabeth Griswold.

Jonathan F. and Cecelia (Williams) Lester were the parents of five children: 1. Ella Cecelia, born September 12, 1874, a graduate of Mt. Holyoke College, and for several years taught school, now residing at home in Norwich, Connecticut. 2. Jonathan Frank, born November 25, 1876, married (first) Mary Louise Shaw, who bore him a son, Jonathan Forest; he married (second) Nina Grace Skinner, and they have one child, Nina Jean. 3. Fanny Berthia; born May 7, 1880, a trained nurse; married Frederick Osborn Morrill, and resides in Boston; they are the parents of three children: Bethia Cecelia, Olive Marie, and Frederick Lester. 4. Ida May, born March 17, 1882, died September 7, 1891. 5. Mary Carrie, born January 8, 1886, died September 30, 1891.

THOMAS J. HILL—Since 1897 Mr. Hill has been established in the meat and grocery business at Niantic, Connecticut. Beginning in a small way, he has gradually made his way to the position of prominence which he now holds. He has always associated himself earnestly and actively with the life of the community, and is respected and held in the highest esteem by all who know him.

Thomas J. Hill was born at Niantic, Connecticut, May 4, 1874, the son of the late Thomas and Elizabeth (Jose) Hill, the former a stone-cutter by trade.

Thomas J. Hill obtained his early education in the schools of Niantic, after which he entered Wilbraham Academy, where he remained for one term. He then returned to Niantic and worked as a clerk in a grocery store. Three years later he resigned from this position and went to New Haven, Connecticut, where he entered a business college, later going to New York City. In 1897 he again returned to his native town, and established himself in the meat and grocery business. The enterprise proved successful, for since that time Mr. Hill has consistently prospered, being essentially the alert and progressive business man. He affiliates with Bayview Lodge, No. 120, Free and Accepted Masons; Niantic Lodge, No. 17, Independent Order of Odd Fellows; and attends the Methodist church of Niantic. In politics he in an Independent, casting his vote for the man regardless of party label.

Thomas J. Hill married, in 1898, Lillian Merritt, and they are the parents of three children: Grace Elizabeth, who married Leon Mandell Farrin, of Cambridge, Massachusetts; Thomas Merritt, born in February, 1901; and Annie May, born in July, 1902.

HORACE A. ADAMS—A New Hampshire boy and man, a farmer, dairyman and expert buttermaker, Mr. Adams continued along these lines in New Hampshire and Connecticut until early in 1919, when in association with M. Henry Trail, a newly-returned soldier of the World War of 1917-18 (see following sketch), he entered the automobile business as garage proprietor and automobile agent, in Groton, Connecticut, on the Shoreline road between Groton and Mystic. This venture has proved successful, and a good business is being built up.

Horace A. Adams is a son of Hiram Adams, born in Salisbury, New Hampshire, where he spent his youth in obtaining an education and in working on the home farm. Upon reaching manhood he bought a farm at Enfield, New Hampshire, and there engaged in general farming until his death in 1876. He married Harriet Cook, born in Lyme, New Hampshire, who died in Enfield in 1898. They were the parents of six children, three of whom are living: Horace A., of further mention; Mary E., married George E. Amos, and resides in Penacook, New Hampshire; and Charles, a resident of Groton.

Horace A. Adams was born in Enfield, New Hampshire, July 12, 1867, and obtained his education in the public schools of Enfield and Lyme. After leaving school he was engaged in farming until 1887, then left home, and until 1893 was employed by D. W. Wilton & Son, dairymen, of Wilton, New York. There he became thoroughly familiar with modern dairying operations and methods, and an expert in butter manufacture. From the Wilton farm Mr. Adams went, in 1893, to the Peterboro Creamery, at Peterboro, New Hampshire, and there remained as manager of the plant for four years. His next position was as manager of the large estate of Robert P. Bass, a former governor of New Hampshire. This estate was at Peterboro, and there Mr. Adams remained for eight years, until 1905. In that year he came to Connecticut, spending the first two and one-half years in the State at the Norton F. Plant estate in Groton. For the next ten years, 1908-18, he was engaged at the Thomas W. Avery farm in Groton, and then abandoned agriculture for the automobile business.

His partnership with M. Henry Trail began shortly after Mr. Trail's return from the army in January, 1919, they establishing a garage on the Shoreline road between Groton and Mystic, where they have a well-fitted plant, service station and stock of supplies for the automobile. They are also agents for the Atterbury truck, and are fast winning public confidence. In politics Mr. Adams is a Republican; in religious faith a Baptist; and in fraternity, affiliated with Union Lodge, No. 31, Free and Accepted Masons, of New London, and Fairview Lodge, No. 101, Independent Order of Odd Fellows, of Groton.

Mr. Adams married, at Somerville, Massachusetts, September 6, 1892, Isabella Allan, daughter of John D. and Charlotte (Arksen) Allan, of Scotch ancestry. Mr. and Mrs. Adams are the parents of two children: Allan H., who married Bessie Card, of Groton, and resides in Brooklyn, New York; and Leslie E., who married Evelyn Silvia, of Stonington, Connecticut, and resides at Groton, Connecticut.

M. HENRY TRAIL—Upon returning from the service in the United States army in 1919, Mr. Trail, in partnership with Horace A. Adams (see preceding sketch), opened a garage and service station in Groton, Connecticut, and there continues a successful business. He is a young man of forceful character, and is winning many personal business friends through his upright, manly life. He is a son of Marcus and Ann M. (Marquardt) Trail, his father born in the town of Groton, New London county, Connecticut, and is now living retired in Groton, after a busy and useful life as a contractor of road-building. To Mr. and Mrs. Trail six children were born, three of whom are living: Ruth R., a teacher in Kansas State College; M. Henry, of further mention; and Stanley R.

M. Henry Trail was born in Groton, Connecticut, November 15, 1896, and there was educated in the public schools. He was variously employed until August 31, 1917, when he entered the United States army to serve in the war against Germany. He was assigned to duty at Fort Travis, San Antonio, Texas, and served until honorably discharged, January 27, 1919, with the rank of sergeant. Upon leaving the army Sergeant Trail returned to Groton, where, as stated, he is established in the garage business, in association with Horace A. Adams. In politics he is a Republican.

Mr. Trail married, in Groton, June 16, 1917, Esther Spicer, and they are the parents of three children, all born in Groton: Henry S., Esther P., and Ann E.

GEORGE PARKER HILL—Son of a soldier of the Union who gave up his life at Gettysburg, and bereft of a mother's love and care a year later, George P. Hill, of Niantic, Connecticut, had to fight life's battle alone from boyhood. So well has he borne his part that now, although by no means an old man, he has retired from business and is enjoying a well-earned rest. His father, Samuel Hill, was a Philadelphian, and enlisted in the Union army from that city. He was engaged with his regiment at the battle of Gettysburg, July 3, 1863, and was instantly killed, his son, George P., then a boy of five years. In 1864 his mother died, and the boy was alone in the world, his only sister having been burned to death.

George Parker Hill was born in Philadelphia, Pennsylvania, January 30, 1858. He was taken in charge by friendly hands and sent to school until he reached the age of twelve years, when he was sent to South Halifax, Vermont, where he spent a year on a farm. At the age of thirteen he went to Shelburne Falls, Massachusetts, and there found employment with a large stock farmer, with whom he remained until 1878. He was then in his twenty-first year, well-developed, strong, and hearty, his out-of-door life at the farm having developed a strong, self-reliant, resourceful lad. In 1878 he came to the town of Waterford, in New London county, Connecticut, and found work and a home at the Warren Gates & Son's farm, on Durphy Hill. Two years were spent there, then in 1880 he exchanged the farm for the sea, and spent eight years as a Menhaden fisherman, sailing from New London, Connecticut, with factories at Niantic, Connecticut, and Lewes, Delaware. For seven years he was a member of the crew of the fishing steamer "Arizona," of which he was made junior officer in his seventh year. In 1888 he was made first mate of the steamer "Quickstep," and at the close of the season of that year he abandoned the sea and returned to land pursuits.

In 1889 he again made a complete change of business, and in the village of Niantic, opened an ice-cream parlor and confectionery store. He built up a very pretentious establishment, and catered so skillfully to the public taste that he continued in business most successfully for twenty-six years. He then sold his business and retired, but continues his home in Niantic.

Since becoming a landsman again, Mr. Hill has taken an active part in politics, has held about all town offices, and represented his district in the State Legislature, his politics ardently Democratic. He is a member of Niantic Lodge, No. 17, Independent Order of Odd Fellows; the New England Order of Protection; and Niantic Lodge, No. 10, Ancient Order of United Workmen.

Mr. Hill married Emma U. Flint, born in Lyme, Connecticut, August 18, 1864, daughter of William Henry and Catherine Flint, her mother born in England. William H. Flint was born in Greenport, Long Island, and during the Civil War enlisted for

Archie McNicol

Alex McNicol

duty in the Secret Service Department, attached to the Twenty-sixth Regiment, Connecticut Volunteer Infantry, in which he held the rank of sergeant. He was once captured while serving on a secret mission, and evidence of his branch of the service being found upon him, he was sentenced to be shot as a spy. During the night preceding the morning set for the carrying out of the sentence pronounced against him, a Confederate soldier whom Sergeant Flint had befriended, aided him to escape and he lived to a good old age, dying in Lyme, Connecticut, in March, 1914. His wife died in Lyme while her daughter Emma U. was a child. Mr. and Mrs. William Flint were the parents of four children: Lydia Jane; Helen Maria; William Henry (2); and Emma U., wife of George Parker Hill, above mentioned. Mr. and Mrs. Hill have no children.

ARCHIBALD McNICOL—Since 1871, a date now half a century in the past, Archibald McNicol has been an important factor in textile manufacturing in New London county, Connecticut, first, in Norwich, then in Jewett City. The McNicols, Archibald, the father, and Alexander, the son, were contemporary in the business, and when the elder man passed away, at the age of seventy-four, he was succeeded by the son, who from his capable father had received the instruction in manufacturing which made him a worthy successor.

Archibald McNicol was born in Glasgow, Scotland, in 1840, where he spent the first twenty-six years of his life, there obtaining a good education and mastering the details of the machinist's trade in its relation to textile printing machinery. He came from Scotland to the United States in 1866, and for five years was employed in erecting machinery, manufactured by a Scotch firm, and used in the printing of textiles. In 1871 he entered the employ of the Arnold Print Works, and was connected with different mills until 1889, when he came to Greenville, a suburb of Norwich, Connecticut, there associating with the Norwich Bleachery, now the United States Finishing Company, dyers and printers of textiles. In 1893 he was appointed agent and manager of the Aspenook Mills, at Jewett City, Connecticut, a large cotton cloth printing, dyeing and finishing plant. From 1899 until 1902 Mr. McNicol, with his family, visited in Scotland, his old home, and toured Europe, returning in 1902 to Jewett City. There he re-entered business life as founder and principal owner of the Jewett City Textile Novelty Company, of which he was president until his death, in May, 1914, aged seventy-four years. He was one of the strong men of the textile manufacturing business in Eastern Connecticut, and was highly regarded by his business associates and contemporaries.

Mr. McNicol married, in Scotland, Mary Montgomery, born there in 1865, who died in Jewett City, Connecticut, in January, 1919. They were the parents of six children: Archibald (2), who died in Jewett City, aged twenty-one years; Alexander, a sketch of whom follows: Jessie, married Andrew Cossar, and resides in Glasgow, Scotland; Mary, married William Perry, of Norwich, Connecticut, who died in Camp Lee, Virginia, in the service of his country during the World War of 1917-18; William M., married Carol Bliss, of Jewett City; and Andrew, a resident of Jewett City.

ALEXANDER McNICOL—Although one of the youngest textile executives, Alexander McNicol, treasurer and agent of the Jewett City Textile Novelty Company, of Jewett City, Connecticut, has been engaged in the business since leaving school, and in the same plant over which he now has authority he began his training, having the added advantage of being under the direction of a Scotch father, whose motto was "thoroughness," and who made no exemptions on account of relationship. Mr. McNicol is a native son of New London county, educated in Norwich schools, and in his native county his thirty-two years have been spent, his connection with the textile business beginning in 1909.

Alexander McNicol, second son of Archibald and Mary (Montgomery) McNicol (see preceding sketch), was born in the city of Norwich, Connecticut, January 21, 1890. He was educated in Norwich public schools, the free academy and business college, finishing in 1904. He then became associated with his father in the Jewett City Textile Novelty Company at Jewett City, and beginning at the bottom, he worked through the various departments until he arrived at a thorough and complete knowledge of the business of which he is now the head. He was his father's valued and trusted assistant until the latter's passing in 1914, and then succeeded him as agent and manager of the company founded by Archibald McNicol in 1902, and developed by Alexander McNicol, one of the youngest of all New England textile manufacturers, and one of the most able. He has no other business interests of importance, his entire force, energy and business ability being given to the management of the affairs of the Jewett City Textile Novelty Company, a successful corporation from its beginning, nearly two decades ago.

On August 26, 1918, Mr. McNicol entered the United States army, and was sent to Camp Greenleaf, Georgia, for training. On October 25, 1918, he was made corporal, and with his regiment was awaiting marching orders for an embarkation camp when the armistice was signed. His company was ordered to Camp Mills, Long Island, where he was in charge of a sanitary department of the camp, devoted to the reception of home-coming soldiers. He was honorably discharged and mustered out of the service January 26, 1919.

Mr. McNicol is a member of Norwich Chamber of Commerce; the Connecticut Manufacturers' Association; the Rotary Club, of Norwich; Orville La Flamme Post, American Legion, of Jewett City; member, and for years clerk of the Jewett City Congregational Church; member of Reliance Lodge, No.

29, Independent Order of Odd Fellows, of Jewett City; and in politics a Republican.

Mr. McNicol married, August 5, 1917, Bernice Reed, daughter of Alva B. and Mary (James) Reed, of Lynn, Massachusetts. The family home is in Jewett City.

SAMUEL ROGERS—A prominent figure in the business life of Niantic, Connecticut, and the surrounding country is Samuel Rogers. Since 1917 he has been established in the stationery business in Niantic, under the firm name of Rogers & Son, and has also been active in the political and public life of the community. The welfare and advancement of the town is always uppermost in his mind, and he has always given his earnest support to all movements calculated to advance its development.

Samuel Rogers was born at Niantic, Connecticut, August 6, 1871, the son of the late Samuel and Mary B. (Elford) Rogers. Mr. Rogers, Sr., previous to his death, which occurred in 1916, was engaged successfully in the monumental business. Mrs. Rogers was a native of England; she died at Niantic in 1910. To Mr. and Mrs. Rogers were born six children: Lucy Jane, deceased; William, deceased; Ellen, deceased; Samuel, of further mention; Mary, deceased; and Grace, deceased.

The boyhood of Samuel Rogers was spent in his native town, where he attended school, subsequently entering the schools of Clinton, Connecticut, where he remained until the termination of his studies. The business of life then began for the boy and he entered the employ of the New York, New Haven & Hartford railroad, as agent at Millstone, Connecticut. Resigning six years later, he became associated with G. M. Long, of New London, and remained there for eight years, when he returned to Niantic and secured employment with the Humphrey, Cornell Company, wholesale grocers, as a travelling salesman, and thus continued until 1917, when he established himself in his present business. The venture proved successful, and although starting in a small way, he has already built up quite an extensive stationery business. Mr. Rogers is an Independent in politics, preferring to exercise his own judgment on all public questions and issues rather than identify himself with any formal political party. He has been town auditor for ten years. He affiliates with Bay View Lodge, No. 120, Free and Accepted Masons; and Niantic Lodge, No. 17, Independent Order of Odd Fellows.

On June 5, 1895, Samuel Rogers was united in marriage with Minnie Emma Beckwith, daughter of Willard Parker and Stella Beckwith. To Mr. and Mrs. Rogers have been born two children: Elford Parker, mentioned below; Eleanor Hamilton ,who was born December 18, 1904, and is now (1921) attending the William Memorial High School, at New London, Connecticut.

Elford Parker Rogers, son of Samuel and Minnie E. (Beckwith) Rogers, was born at Niantic, Connecticut, March 17, 1896. He was educated in the public schools of his native place and also graduated from the Connecticut Agricultural College, at Storrs, Connecticut. After leaving college he was with the Industrial Bank of Hartford, Connecticut. On April 25, 1917, he enlisted in the United States army, Troop B, of the One Hundred and First Machine Gun Battalion, of Hartford, Connecticut. After a training period at the State military camp he was ordered overseas on October 9, 1917, and arrived at Havre, November 1, 1917, going immediately to the training camp at Neufchateau, where he remained for three months. On February 1, 1918, he went into action, and on July 22, 1918, was desperately wounded in the left leg at Chateau-Thierry. He was honorably discharged October 19, 1920. He is a member of the Veterans of Foreign Wars. Elford Parker Rogers married Sybil Beebe, a daughter of Mr. and Mrs. J. Lee Beebe, of Niantic, and to them one child has been born, Allyn.

Elford P. Rogers is just one more of our brave American lads who was willing to make the supreme sacrifice if necessary. As it happened, he was not called upon to do this, but the wound which he received was so severe that he will never fully recover from its effects. Such a record is certainly worthy of emulation and should certainly have mention in a a work of this nature.

CAPTAIN NELSON J. HUNTLEY—Now an octogenarian, retired from all cares, and living at his comfortable home in Niantic, Connecticut, not far from the place of his birth, Captain Huntley reviews a long life of adventure, during which he sailed the seven seas, faced every form of peril known to those "who go down to the seas in ships," and rose from cabin boy to master. He has travelled to about every port on the Atlantic Ocean, endured every danger and trial that besets the mariner, including shipwreck and all its attendant horrors. Then, too, he recalls the pleasures and the wonders of those voyages, the strange things of the sea and land he saw, of the lights under the Southern Cross, the strange life of the Orient, the wonders of the tropics, and the glory of the Northern Lights as seen from high latitude. Then when the sailing ship gave way to the steamship, he quit the merchant service, but clung to the sea, and for fifteen years was a lightship keeper watching over the destinies of those adventurous souls who trusted him to keep the lights burning that they might make safe entrance to New York Harbor, and he never failed them. Then came a decade at Sandy Hook, and then the quiet, the comfort, the peace of home and loved ones.

Captain Nelson J. Huntley is a son of Elisha Huntley, born in that part of the town of East Lyme, New London county, Connecticut, known locally as Whistletown, and there engaged in farming until his retirement to the village of Niantic, where he died in 1895. Elisha Huntley married Nancy Tinker, born in Whistletown, where she died in the year 1900. They were the parents of six children: Frank:

Nancy; Julia; George;; Mary; and Nelson J., of whom further.

Nelson J. Huntley was born in the Whistletown section of the town of East Lyme, New London county, Connecticut, September 24, 1837, and on his father's farm spent the first fourteen years of his life. He attended the district school at Whistletown until the age of fourteen, when his parents moved to Niantic, and there an inborn love of the sea gained control of his life, and while yet a boy he sailed with the Niantic fishermen. He quickly advanced in rating until he commanded a full share of the vessel's catch, and for ten years he continued a fisherman. He then shipped on deep-sea craft, and from common seaman advanced through every grade of ship life until he trod his own quarter-deck. He commanded ships in the merchant service and sailed to many ports, carrying home products and bringing back the most valuable cargoes from the islands and lands of the far Atlantic. His life was filled with action and adventure for many years, then he engaged in the more peaceful coasting trade, owning his own coal-carrying schooner. Finally he retired from the coasting trade and accepted service with the United States Government in the lighthouse department of the navy. For fifteen years he was in charge of the lightship that marked the entrance to Ambrose Channel, New York Harbor, a life quiet in comparison with his previous one, but filled with adventure and danger when winter storms beset the ship, and lights must be kept burning at any cost. After fifteen years of lightship duty he was transferred to shore duty at Sandy Hook and after ten years there he retired, and has since occupied his home in Niantic. Captain Huntley is a member of the Congregational church; in politics a Republican.

Captain Huntley married, in Saybrook, Connecticut, July 24, 1867, Eleanor Anne Parker, born in Essex, Connecticut, March 26, 1840, daughter of Jonathan and Abigail (Wilcox) Parker. Mrs. Huntley is the last to survive of a large family of children born to her parents. Captain and Mrs. Huntley are the parents of three children, but one of whom survives, Maud Eleanor, born in Niantic, Connecticut, June 8, 1875, married, October 14, 1896, to Gurdon Beckwith Coates, and has two children: Eleanor Irene, born in Niantic, July 29, 1897, married George A. Garrett, of Washington, District of Columbia, and has a son, George Coates (2); and Marjorie Elizabeth, born August 22, 1909. The first child born to Captain and Mrs. Huntley was a son, Walter Nelson Huntley, born in Essex, Connecticut, now deceased; he is buried in Niantic. Their second child died in infancy. Mrs. Coates was their youngest.

While so much of his life has been spent in different places, Captain Huntley's love for the home town has always continued, and his interest is deep in all that concerns the welfare of his town and townsmen. He is now in his eighty-fifth year, but well-preserved for one of his years.

WALTER GIFFORD BARKER, who conducts a popular confectionery store in Niantic, Connecticut, is a son of Captain Walter Harris Barker, who was born in New London, Connecticut, in 1856, and died there in 1911. Captain Barker was captain of the "Mohawk," a coastwise freighter. He married Emma May, who was born in New London in 1864, and still survives him, residing in her native city. They were the parents of three children: 1. Jean, who was born in New London, became the wife of Samuel Mallory, who died, leaving her with two children, Leonard and Viola. 2. Herbert Nelson, also born in New London, who married Arlene Sherman. 3. Walter G. Barker, whose name heads this review.

Walter G. Barker was born in New London, Connecticut, February 18, 1883, and received his early education in the public schools of this city, then, in preparation for the future, went to Washington, District of Columbia, where he attended a physical training school, conducted by Henry S. Curtis. For a number of years following his course at this school, Mr. Barker was identified with physical training work in various parts of the country, for several years serving as physical director of the Young Men's Christian Association at Frederick, Maryland, and for one year holding a similar position with the association at Martinsburg, West Virginia. He then came to Niantic, where he has since been successfully engaged in the confectionery business.

In political affairs Mr. Barker endorses the principles of the Republican party, but holds an independent position, voting with the party only when his judgment coincides. He has for several years served on the school board.

Mr. Barker married Maud Louise Patterson, who was born in Noank in 1886, and is a daughter of William E. Patterson, of that city. They are the parents of two children: Daniel Cleveland, who was born in Bridgeport, Connecticut; and Jane Patterson, born in Niantic, in 1916.

CHARLES BUTSON—Learning the boat-builder's trade from his father, Joseph W. Butson, father and son worked together for some time, the father going to Long Island, where he built boats for twenty-five years, the son going to Mystic, Connecticut, later to Groton, where he has continued a boat-builder for sixteen years, from 1905 to 1921.

Joseph William Butson was born in Fowey, England, and there learned boat-building, which he made his lifelong occupation. In 1889 he came to the United States and located on Long Island, where he died in 1916. He married Mary Hickson, who died in November, 1891. They were the parents of four children, Charles of this review, the second in order of birth.

Charles Butson was born in Fowey, England, May 22, 1872, and there spent the first seventeen years of his life obtaining an education in the public schools. The family came to the United States in

1889, and until 1903 Charles Butson worked with his father in boat-building operations on Long Island. In 1903 he moved to Mystic, Connecticut, and there built boats until 1905, when he moved to his present home in Groton. Here he has continued boat-building, principally small craft, motor and row boats. He is a good workman, and a man highly respected by all who know him. He is a member of the Methodist Episcopal church, the American Order of United Workmen, and in politics he is a Republican.

Mr. Butson married, November 3, 1897, Charlotte Bishop, daughter of Jeremiah and Elizabeth Bishop, and they are the parents of seven children: Charles H., Louis N., Joseph B., Kenneth, Sidney, Frank, and Eugene.

JAMES PATRICK HAYES—Among the representative citizens of Norwich, Connecticut, James P. Hayes, owner and manager of the Dell Hoff Hotel, at No. 26 Broadway, must have mention. A native son of Norwich, he has spent his entire life there, and in everything pertaining to the welfare and advancement of the community he takes a keen and intelligent interest.

John Hayes, father of James P. Hayes, was born in Cork, Ireland, and there was educated and married. When a young man he came to the United States and located in Manchaug, where he was employed in a woolen mill until 1884, then removed to Norwich, Connecticut, where he was with the United States Finishing Company until his death, July 23, 1893. He married Mary Coughlin, also born in Cork, Ireland, who died July 25, 1917. To Mr. and Mrs. Hayes were born five children: Patrick John, associated with his brother, James P., in the hotel business; Mary Theresa, wife of John Driscoll, of Norwich; Dennis Joseph, a partner with his brother, James P., in the ownership and management of the Dell Hoff Hotel, married Nellie Kirby, of Norwich; James P., the subject of this review; and Elizabeth Theresa, principal of the Norwich Falls public school.

James P. Hayes was born in Norwich, Connecticut, March 9, 1886, and there obtained his education in the public and parochial schools. As a young man he served an apprenticeship as a polisher and gunsmith with the Hopkins & Allen Company, continuing until 1904, when he became associated with his brother, Patrick J. Hayes, in the ownership of the Dell Hoff Hotel, one of the leading hotels of Norwich. Hayes Brothers conducted the hotel until 1920, when Patrick J. Hayes retired from the business and was succeeded by his younger brother, Dennis J. Hayes, the new firm, James P. and Dennis J. Hayes, continuing the management of the popular Dell Hoff Hotel.

In politics James P. Hayes is a Democrat, and takes a lively interest in public affairs. Mr. Hayes is past exalted ruler of Norwich Lodge, No. 430, Benevolent and Protective Order of Elks, serving in 1914, and in 1919 was appointed district deputy for the State of Connecticut, representing the grand exalted ruler of the order in the State of Connecticut. As district deputy he visited every Elks' lodge in the State, becoming widely and favorably known to Connecticut Elks, and is likewise well known in the national body of the order, having represented his home lodge in the Supreme Lodge as a delegate and as a member of the Grand Lodge of Connecticut. He has attended several of these national conventions in a private capacity, and is one of the most enthusiastic and loyal Elks in the State of Connecticut. He has been a tireless worker for the good of the order, the purchase of the Osgood homestead in Norwich as a home for the Elks being a project he ardently advocated until the purchase was made. To the homestead a large addition has been made, which is used as a lodge room, the whole forming one of the most complete and beautiful Elks' homes in the State. He labored with all his might to bring about this result, and his work in all Elk activities is bringing him to prominence in Connecticut Elkdom. In religious faith he is a Roman Catholic, a member of St. Patrick's Church, Norwich. He enjoys the respect and confidence of his brethren of the order who nobly second his efforts.

LUCIUS BRIGGS—Although a native-born son of the State of Massachusetts, Lucius Briggs has resided long enough in the State of Connecticut to become identified with its interests, financial, industrial, political and social, contributing his share to the improvement and upbuilding of his adopted city, Norwich, where he is honored and respected, his word there being considered as good as his bond.

The branch of the Briggs family herein followed, traces to John Briggs, who was a resident of Kingston, Rhode Island, in 1671, where he served in public capacity. Among his children was James Briggs, a resident of East Greenwich, Rhode Island, who married, and among his children was Jonathan Briggs, born in East Greenwich, Rhode Island, in 1755; died December 23, 1837. He resided for a time on Block Island, but later removed to Coventry, Rhode Island, where he followed farming as a means of livelihood. He was a Revolutionary soldier, serving for nearly seven years. His wife, Abigail (Greene) Briggs, bore him six children, one of whom was Wanton Briggs, born in Coventry, Rhode Island, October 5, 1788, died, at Phoenix, Rhode Island, March 27, 1849. He served as a soldier in the War of 1812. He married Mary Tift, who bore him twelve children, one of whom was Lucius Briggs, grandfather of the present member of that name, born in Coventry, Rhode Island, December 21, 1825, died at his home in Norwich, Connecticut, January 27, 1901. His boyhood and young manhood were spent in his native town, but in 1849, the year of the gold craze in California, he journeyed West, accompanied by his brother, Wanton Briggs, Jr., and there remained two years. Upon his return East, he located in Masonville, town of Thompson, Connecticut, and entered the employ of the Mason-

James P. Hayes

Lucius Briggs.

ville Manufacturing Company, later acquiring an interest therein, which he disposed of in 1883. He was associated with the Grosvenors and built part of the Grosvenor Dale Mills. He became half-owner and manager of the Glasgo Yarn Mill Company, of Glasgo, Connecticut, where he took up his residence, and in 1898 sold his interest to the American Thread Company. Two years previously he took up his residence in Norwich, where he spent the remainder of his days. He was president of the Thompson Savings Bank; a director in the Thompson National Bank, Thames National Bank, Uncas Paper Company, Manufacturers Insurance Company, and in the Greeneville Bleachery. He was a representative from the town of Thompson in the Lower House of the State Assembly in 1867; served in the State Senate in 1875; and was a presidential elector on the Republican ticket at the time of the second election of General Grant, as president. He married Harriet Taylor Atwood, of Coventry, Rhode Island, and they were the parents of four children, among whom was Charles Wanton, father of Lucius Briggs, of this review. Mrs. Briggs died September 9, 1887.

Charles Wanton Briggs was born in Grosvenor Dale, town of Thompson, Windham county, Connecticut, October 2, 1855, died in Norwich, Connecticut, 1915. After the completion of his studies, which terminated with his graduation from the Highland Military Academy, at Worcester, Massachusetts, in 1874, he accepted a position in the Grosvenor Dale Mills, in due course of time becoming assistant superintendent, which position he filled until 1879. He then was appointed superintendent of a mill at Haydenville, Massachusetts, purchased by his father, and so continued until the latter purchased the mills at Glasgo, Connecticut, and consolidated both mills. Charles W. Briggs then went to Boston, Massachusetts, as special agent of the company, remaining two years, then was sent to New York City, where he filled the same position until 1898, when his father disposed of his interest in the mills. He then engaged in the manufacture of folding box board paper at Bogota, New Jersey, acting as treasurer and general manager of the Bogota Paper Company, and this connection was retained until the year 1902, when the company sold out to the paper trust. Mr. Briggs then returned to his native State, locating in Norwich, and there became interested in several enterprises, serving as director of the Davenport Fire Arms Company. Mr. Briggs married, February, 1880, Sadie Elizabeth Horne, a native of Somersworth, New Hampshire, daughter of Samuel P. and Mary Horne. Her death occurred in Norwich in 1914. Children: Lucius, of whom further; Charles Walter, born October, 1885; Robert Elmer, born June, 1893.

Lucius Briggs was born in Haydenville, Massachusetts, September 30, 1882. The family moved to New York in 1885. He attended the public schools of New York City, and the College of the City of New York, being a student in the latter named institution in 1900, '01, '02. His first employment was in the paper mills at Bogota, New Jersey, in which his father had an interest, he having charge of the selling end of the business. He removed with his parents to Norwich, Connecticut, in 1902, and accepted a position as clerk in the Thames National Bank of that city, serving for two years, and from 1905 to 1908 was assistant bookkeeper in the Uncas Bank of Norwich. From the latter named date to 1911, a period of three years, he served as salesman for the firms of Hornblower & Weeks and Tucker and Anthony Company of Boston, Massachusetts, brokers, selling bonds, etc.. then became connected with the Edward Chappell Company, of Norwich, and in 1913 was chosen to serve as secretary, office manager, and manager of the coal department, and is so serving at the present time, his long incumbency of office being the best testimonial of his efficiency. He is trustee of the Dime Savings Bank of Norwich. He is a Republican in politics, and a member of Arcanum, Norwich Golf, Chelsea Boat, and Rotary clubs, all of Norwich.

Mr. Briggs married, in 1904, Mary Goffe Brewer, of Norwich, Connecticut, daughter of Arthur H. Brewer. Children: Lucius Goffe, born October 8, 1904, and Marion Brewer, born January 11, 1906. Mr. and Mrs. Briggs attend the Episcopal church.

LOUIS PACKER ALLYN—The Allyns of Mystic, Connecticut, now represented by Louis Packer Allyn and his sons, Dr. Louis M. and Dr. Gordon S., trace descent from Robert Allyn, of Allyns Point, from almost the beginning of things in New London county. On the mother's side, these Allyns, mentioned above, descend from Captain James Avery, of Groton.

Robert Allyn, from Salem, Massachusetts, and Captain James Avery were among the company from Gloucester, Cape Ann, who joined John Winthrop and the little colony at New London, Connecticut, in March, 1651, and lots on Cape Ann street, New London, were set off to them. In 1653 Robert Allyn received a grant up the Thames river, and Captain James Avery one on Poquanock Plains. John Allyn, son of Robert Allyn married Elizabeth Gager, daughter of John Gager, who came to Pequot, or London, with John Winthrop, and was also given a grant adjoining and south of Robert Allyn's, at what is now known at Stoddard's Wharf. Before 1670 Robert Allyn and John Gager joined a company in settling Norwich. After his father's death, John Allyn left Norwich and returned to the paternal farm, where he built a house and warehouse near the river, at a place since known as Allyn's Point. (Miss Caulkin's "History of New London"). Robert (2) Allyn, who was the son of John Allyn, married Deborah Avery, daughter of Lieutenant James and Deborah (Stallyon) Avery. His son, Ebenezer Allyn, married Mary Thurber; and Ebenezer's son, Elder Rufus Allyn, married Hannah Billings, daughter of Stephen and Bridget (Grant) Billings. Captain Rufus Allyn, son of Elder Rufus Allyn, married Freelove Morgan, daughter of Deacon Shapley

Morgan, son of John Morgan, who through the Shapleys, his wife's family, and John Pickett, who married Ruth Brewster, was a descendant of Jonathan Brewster, son of Elder William Brewster, of Plymouth.

Gurdon Spicer Allyn, of the sixth American generation, was born at the farm of his parents, Captain Rufus and Freelove (Morgan) Allyn, located just west of Meeting House Hill, in the town of Ledyard, New London county, Connecticut, in 1817, and died in Mystic, Connecticut, in February, 1876, aged fifty-nine. He passed his youth at the home farm, but when young, came to Mystic, where he learned the carpenter's trade under Harry Latham. He worked at that trade as apprentice, journeyman and contractor, but soon abandoned it for quarry and ice interests, but his chief business was menhaden fishing and their conversion of the fish into oil and by-products. He was at one time attracted by the Wisconsin lumber business, but a few years sufficed and he then returned to the fish business, in which he remained engaged until his death. He was a man of tremendous energy, which made it possible for him to conduct his large business interests successfully. He was the leading spirit in any of the enterprises in which he was engaged, and exerted a deep influence in the business affairs of his section of the country. He was the controlling spirit in the building of the old waterworks at Mystic, and in all that pertained to the good of the town he lent a willing and helpful hand. In politics he was a Republican, serving as selectman in 1868 and again in 1874. He represented the town of Groton for two terms in the State Legislature and held many minor town offices. He was a member and trustee of the Union Baptist Church, and affiliated with the Masonic order. Conscientious, upright, and honorable, he won public confidence and esteem to a degree unusual, and the trust reposed in turn was never betrayed. Mr. Allyn married (first) Hannah (Avery) Rathbun, widow of Alden Rathbun, and daughter of Joseph Swan Avery and his wife, Mary (Hudson) Avery, the former a son of Colonel Simeon Avery, who was on the staff of General Washington in the Revolutionary War. Mary (Hudson) Avery was a daughter of Phineas and Margaret (Sabin) Hudson. A number of these Allyns and Averys were killed at Fort Ledyard in 1781. Gurdon S. and Hannah (Avery-Rathbun) Allyn were the parents of four children: Juliette; Louis Packer, of further mention; Francis; and Hannah; all deceased except Louis Packer. Mr. Allyn married (second) Martha Champion, and they were the parents of a son, Gurdon C.

Louis Packer Allyn was born in Mystic, Connecticut, July 22, 1851, and there yet resides (1921). He was educated in the public schools and began business life as a clerk in the Luther A. Morgan & Company general store, in which his father was part owner, remaining there four years. He was then admitted to a partnership with his father and Captain John E. Williams, in the menhaden fishery, and until the death of the senior member, they operated the fishery most successfully as G. S. Allyn & Company. He continued to operate the fishery after his father's death with Captain John E. Williams until 1883, when the company was dissolved and he joined his interests with S. S. Brown & Company. That connection existed for ten years, and after the death of Mr. Brown, he and Captain Lenen formed a new company, known as James Lenen & Company, of Lewes, Delaware, also engaged in the menhaden fishing and manfacturing. Later they merged with the syndicate controlling menhaden fishing on the coast, in which Mr. Allyn was director and the manager of the Lewes, Delaware, plant. When he resigned from the syndicate, he and Captain Lenen formed a new company known as the Menhaden Oil and Guano Company, which they conducted successfully for eighteen years, when they sold out and retired from business.

Athough his business interests led him away from Mystic, he has always maintained his residence there, and retirement from business has given him opportunity for pursuing many interests in his native village. He was active on committees and drives during the World War. He is a director of the Mystic River National Bank; a deacon and trustee of the Union Baptist Church; a member of Charity and Relief Lodge, No. 72, Free and Accepted Masons; and first selectman of the town of Groton, 1920-22. He is on the board of directors of the Community Club.

Mr. Allyn married, October 24, 1876, Emily Fenner Maxson, a descendant of John Maxson, one of the founders of Newport and Westerly, and the daughter of William E. and Sarah Maria (Fenner) Maxson, the former a noted shipbuilder of Mystic, the latter a daughter of Philip A. and Sallie (Potter) Fenner, of Rhode Island. Mrs. Allyn is a member of the Union Baptist Church; of the Fanny Ledyard Chapter, Daughters of the American Revolution, of Mystic; the Daughters of Founders and Patriots of America; of other Colonial societies; and of the Society of 1812, also the Women's Relief Corps; the State Missionary and Promotion boards; and does associational and local church missionary work. Mr. and Mrs. Allyn are the parents of three sons: Louis Maxson; Gurdon Spicer (2); and William Ellery, all of further mention.

Louis Maxson Allyn, after graduation from Mystic High School, prepared at school in Westerly, Rhode Island, and entered Lehigh University. Later he entered the medical department of the University of Pennsylvania, whence he was graduated M.D., class of 1903. He served as a resident physician at St. Joseph's Hospital, Reading, Pennsylvania, until May, 1904, when he located in Mystic, where he has since been in successful practice. He is a member of the local, county, State and national medical societies, and while at the University of Pennsylvania, joined the John Guiteras Medical Society. He was a college athlete, played football at Lehigh, and in 1889 was a member of the "Eight Oar" crew that won the Inter-Class Championship for the University of Pennsylvania. His college fraternity is Delta Upsilon. Dr. Louis M. Allyn was selectman of the town of Groton three years, and highway commissioner ten times. He is chairman of the school committee in his district, and member of the board of school visitors. He is health officer of the town of Groton; chairman of the board of trustees of the Mystic Oral School for the Deaf, a State institution; member of the Union Baptist Church; and of Charity and Relief Lodge, No. 72, Free and Accepted Masons, in which lodge he is the fourth in succession in his line, his great-grandfather, Captain Rufus Allyn, being one of the charter members. Dr. Louis M. Allyn married Laura A. Greenman, of Greenmanville, Mystic, and they are the parents of two daughters: Lucia Greenman; and Emily Maxson.

Dr. Gurdon Spicer (2) Allyn is a graduate of Mystic High School, Bulkeley High School (New London), and took a course in Colgate University, New York. He is a graduate of the medical department of the University of Pennsylvania, receiving his degree of Doctor of Medicine from the last-named institution, class of 1903. He ranked high in college athletics, and rowed on the "Varsity Eight" for four years. In 1900 he was No. 4 in the crew that won the Inter-Collegiate Championship on the Hudson at Poughkeepsie and broke the record for the distance. In 1901 he was No. 6 in the University of Pennsylvania crew which contested at the Henley Regatta in England, and pronounced the best crew the United States ever sent abroad. That crew, while they did not win, had the distinction of being the only foreign crew that ever made the finals for the Grand Challenge Cup at Henley. He rowed No. 6 for three of his four college years, and was made captain of the 1902 crew while in England. In honor of his brilliant career as an oarsman, he was chosen for membership in the senior societies, "Skull and Dagger," and the "Sphinx." He was a member of the John Guiteras Medical Society of the University; of the Alphi Mu Pi Omega, a medical fraternity; and of the Delta Upsilon fraternity. After graduation in 1903, Dr. Allyn was for a year resident physician at St. Joseph's Hospital in Lancaster, Pennsylvania. In October, 1904, he began private professional practice in New London, Connecticut, and was surgeon on the staff of the Memorial Hospital, and also of the Lawrence Hospital. He was a member of New London County and Connecticut State Medical societies. He was selectman for the town of Waterford two years, and is now chairman of the town committee. He is a member of Brainard Lodge, No. 102, Free and Accepted Masons; of the Mayflower Society; and Thames Club, of New London. During the period of war between the United States and Germany, 1917-18, he served as surgeon, ranking as lieutenant, in the United States navy. He is now president of the New London Sand and Stone Company, also president of the Masons Island Company. He is a member of the Union Baptist Church of Mystic. Mr. Allyn married Annie Balfour Hislop, of New London, Connecticut, and they are the parents of two sons: James Hislop, and Gurdon Spicer (3).

William Ellery Allyn, the youngest son of Louis Packer and Emily Fenner (Maxson) Allyn, is a graduate of Bulkeley High School, New London, and had a two years' course at the University of Pennsylvania, class of 1907. His college fraternity is the Delta Upsilon. He began his business career with the Babcock Printing Press Company, of New London, with whom he continued for several years. When he left the company on account of ill health, he was sales manager for the southern territory, from Pennsylvania to the gulf.

During the World War, 1917-18, he served in the United States army, with the rank of captain, in the Department of Ordnance, and was supervisor of inspection of the Railroad and Seacoast Artillery. He is a member of Brainard Lodge (New London), No. 102, Free and Accepted Masons. He was representative from the town of Waterford to the State Legislature in 1920-1922, when he served on the Committee of Finance. He is now chief field deputy of the Internal Revenue Department, District of Connecticut. He is secretary and treasurer of the Masons Island Company; member of the executive committee of the New London County Farm Bureau; secretary and treasurer of the Waterford Farmers' Exchange; director of the Winthrop Trust company, New London; member of the Thames Club, New London; the Hartford Club; Shemacassett Golf Club, New London; and belongs to the Society of Mayflower Descendants. Also is a member of the Baptist church in Waterford. Mr. Allyn married Marguerite Lonard Almy, daughter of Dr. Leonard Almy, of Norwich, Connecticut, and they are the parents of two daughters: Lydia Ballau, and Diana.

JAMES A. BERAN, real estate and insurance broker, was born in Bridgeport, Connecticut, September 19, 1896, son of Andrew and Matilda Beran, both now residing in the town of Waterford, New London county, Connecticut. Andrew Beran, born July 15, 1872, is a farmer, horticulturist, and landscape gardener, very skillful and successful. Matilda, his wife, was born May 18, 1877. Their home in Waterford is on R.F.D. No. 1.

James A. Beran began his education in the Bridgeport schools and continued his studies in Bulkeley High School, New London, after which he spent two years at United States Naval College. From 1919 until 1921, he was a member of the firm of Wetmore & Beran, but since 1921 has conducted the business alone. He is district manager of the Guardian Life Insurance Company of America, 108 State street, New London, and conducts a general insurance and real estate business. He handles a great deal of Ocean Beach property, renting, leasing and selling.

In politics Mr. Beran is a Republican. He served in the Naval Reserves as seaman, yeoman, chief yeoman and assistant paymaster. He is a member of the Harbor Club of New London, and of the Episcopal church, his family belonging to St. Mary's Roman Catholic Church.

WILLIAM TRACY CRANDALL, assistant cashier of the Thames National Bank, of Norwich, is a descendant of John Crandall, who came from Wales to New England in 1635. John Crandall was a Baptist preacher, and one of the persecuted ones of the Massachusetts Colony, who fled to Rhode Island, there finding the freedom of conscience, denied them in Massachusetts. In 1637 he settled in Providence, later was the first elder of the church at Westerly, and died in 1676, in Newport. He was twice married, and had sons: John, Peter, Joseph, Samuel, Jeremiah, and Eber. His son, Joseph, was a minister of the Seventh Day Baptist church, and others of the family have been ministers of the Gospel, including Rev. Phineas Crandall, grandfather of William T. Crandall, of Norwich. Phineas Crandall was a traveling minister of the Gospel in New England, and at the time of the birth of his son, John Newland Crandall, was living in Maine.

John Newland Crandall, son of Rev. Phineas Crandall, was born in the State of Maine, and educated in different schools in the town in which his father was the settled pastor. He was a student at Wilbraham Academy, (Massachusetts), and at Wesleyan Unversity, Middletown, Connecticut, and when his own education was finished he taught school in Norwich, Connecticut, for several years. Later, he was employed in the Norwich Savings Society as clerk, but after a year with that bank he resigned and engaged in the real estate and insurance business. He conducted that business very successfully until 1902, when he retired from active life but continued his residence in Norwich for eight years longer, dying in 1910. He married Frances Emily Tracy, who was born in Franklin, Connecticut, and died in Norwich, April 25, 1898, and they were the parents of four children, William T. being the second.

William Tracy Crandall was born in Norwich, Connecticut, July 28, 1859, and there was educated in the public schools and in the Free Academy, completing his studies in 1878. In that same year he entered the employ of the Norwich National Bank as a clerk. In 1889 he transferred his allegiance to the Thames National Bank of Norwich, of which institution he is now assistant cashier. He has devoted his life to the banking business for more than forty years, and has been with the same institution, the Thames National Bank for more than thirty years. His qualifications are high, his experience wide, and his knowledge of banking, banking laws and procedure, very extensive. He is a member of Park Congregational Church. He holds membership in the Arcanum Club, and politically, gives his support to the Republican party.

Mr. Crandall married, December 19, 1889, Elizabeth A. Gates, of Norwich, daughter of Henry A. and Anna (Albro) Gates. The family home is at No. 161 McKinley avenue, Norwich.

JOHN GILMAN STANTON, M.D.—On November 2, 1877, Dr. John G. Stanton arrived in New London, Connecticut, and began private medical and surgical practice. Forty-four years have since elapsed, and he is now the honored physician and surgeon, with all the professional honors the community can bestow and the intense satisfaction of knowing that he has faithfully and devotedly performed his duty as one of the guardians of the health of that community.

Dr. Stanton is of New Hampshire parentage, a grandson of John Stanton, and a son of John (2) Stanton, the latter born in Brookfield, New Hampshire, December 31, 1810, and died while on a journey to Marseilles, France, in December, 1848. John (2) Stanton went to New Orleans, Louisianna, and organized there an ice company, and later became president of an ice company which bore his name. That company, with headquarters in New Orleans and Mobile, had branches in Savannah, Georgia, Charleston, South Carolina, and Boston, Massachusetts, and was a very large, prosperous concern, Mr. Stanton, its active head until his passing. He married Sophia Cook, born in Wakefield, New Hampshire, died in Amherst, Massachusetts, in 1870.

John Gilman Stanton was born in New Orleans, Louisiana, December 25, 1848, and there resided until the death of his father, when the family came North to Winchester, Massachusetts, where he prepared for and entered Amherst College, whence he was graduated A.B., class of 1870. Deciding upon the medical profession he went abroad and prepared in German institutions, studying in the medical department of the University of Gottingen, a university founded in 1737 and one of the foremost of the German universities. He also spent two years at the University of Berlin, and received his M.D. from the University of Wurzburg, Bavaria, the seat of the famous Julius Hospital founded in 1576.

In the fall of 1874 Dr. Stanton returned to the United States and located in Boston, Massachusetts, where he remained six years. During that period he practiced as an assistant, and as physician to Boston District Hospital eighteen months; for one year surgeon to out patients of the Boston City Hospital; two years as district physician to the Boston Dispensary, and also practiced privately.

He came to New London, Connecticut, November 30, 1877, and there has practiced continuously until the present, 1921. In addition to a private practice, always large, Dr. Stanton has been surgeon to the New London Northern & Central Vermont Railroad for many years, president of the Lawrence and Memorial Associated hospitals of New London, for twenty-five years has been surgeon in the United States Public Health Service, surgeon to the United States Coast Guard Academy at Fort Trumbull, and surgeon, with the rank of major, of the Third Regiment, Connecticut National Guard.

In civic affairs Dr. Stanton has always been the friend of progress, and as the ardent friend of education has been able to do a great deal for the cause, having been for a quarter of a century president of the New London Board of Education and was a member of the Connecticut State Board of Education. He is also president of the New London Public

John G. Stanton. M.D.

Library, president of the board of trustees of the Unitarian church of New London, trustee of the Savings Bank of New London, trustee of New London Vocational Training School. His professional societies are the New London County Medical Society, (past president); Connecticut State Medical Society, and the American Medical Association. He Society, (past president); New London City Medical; is affiliated with Brainard Lodge, Free and Accepted Masons, Brainerd Chapter, Royal Arch Masons, Palestine Commandery, Knights Templar. His college fraternity is Delta Kappa Epsilon. In politics he is Independent Democratic.

Dr. Stanton married in Amherst, Massachusetts, October 13, 1875, Elizabeth Savage Cooper, born in Calais, Maine, daughter of James S. and Abigail (Gerdler) Cooper. Mrs. Stanton died in May, 1920. Dr. and Mrs. Stanton were the parents of a daughter, Alice Cooper, born in New London, Connecticut, married Harrison T. Sheldon, a member of the New Haven, Connecticut, bar, and they have a daughter, Anne.

ANDREW SMITH DEXTER.—After the close of the World War, the little village of Poquonock Bridge, town of Groton, Connecticut, being in need of a new postmaster, the position was tendered Andrew Smith Dexter of the same village, and he has filled the office since July, 1920.

The parents of the young postmaster were Andrew S. and Ida (Anderson) Dexter, the former for many years a resident of Norwich, Connecticut, where he was born, but in the later years of his life residing at Poquonock Bridge, where he died December 30, 1917. In his early youth he was educated at Norwich. After leaving school he took up the study of mechanics and was employed throughout his active life in the mechanical department of the New York, New Haven & Hartford railroad. Mr. and Mrs. Dexter were the parents of seven children: Andrew Smith, of whom further; Marion, George, Merritt, Nellie, Annie, and Arthur, all of whom are living at home.

Andrew Smith Dexter was born in Norwich, Connecticut, April 12, 1897. His parents having moved to Poquonock Bridge shortly after his birth, he grew up there, attending the public school. When the United States became involved in the World War, young Mr. Dexter went into the Groton Iron Works, then greatly in need of men, and remained with them until he received the appointment of postmaster at Poquonock Bridge.

In politics Mr. Dexter is an independent, and his religious interest is with the Baptist church, of Poquonock Bridge, of which he is an attendant. He is also connected with Fairview Lodge, No. 101, Independent Order of Odd Fellows, of Groton, Connecticut; and with Charity and Relief Lodge, No. 72, Free and Accepted Masons, of Mystic.

WILLIAM WHALEY—The life of William Whaley, farmer and merchant, of the town of East Lyme and the village of Niantic, Connecticut, began in the second decade of the nineteenth century, and for sixty-eight years he was numbered among the residents of that town, and there, in the town of his birth, he was laid at rest. He was a man of industry, a good business man, kind-hearted and generous, living a quiet life of usefulness and doing good as he had opportunity. While a quiet, home-loving man, he did not shirk public duty, but served in different capacities, being postmaster for fourteen years, having the office in his store. But one of his three children is now living in the village of Niantic, Miss Emma Baker Whaley, an esteemed lady, who resides in the old home her father built. William Whaley was one of a family of seven. 1. Jonathan, born in Montville, Connecticut, February 5, 1801. 2. Ezra Moore, born February 18, 1808, married (first) Mary Anne ——; and (second) Mary Ann Chapel. 3. James, born June 1, 1811, married Phoebe Harding. 4. Henry, born September 12, 1813, married Mary Brockaw. 5. William, of further mention. 6. Hannah, married Joseph Burton. 7. Waitstill O., born April 25, 1821, married William H. Wheeler.

William Whaley was born in Montville, Connecticut, January 30, 1815, died in the town of East Lyme, New London county, Connecticut, January 3, 1883. He was educated in the district schools and Bacon Academy, Colchester, Connecticut, being a graduate of the last-named institution. After school days were over he became his father's farm assistant, and there remained until 1857, when he moved to the village of Niantic, in East Lyme, where he built a house in which he resided until the erection of the present family home. In Niantic Mr. Whaley conducted a general store with much success until his death. For fourteen years of that period he was postmaster of Niantic, and also held many of the minor town offices. He was a good business man and a good citizen, highly esteemed in his community. He is buried in East Lyme cemetery.

William Whaley married Laura Ransome Turner, born in Montville, Connecticut, February 9, 1815, died August 5, 1905, daughter of James and Mary Turner. Mr. and Mrs. James Turner were the parents of nine children: Nathaniel; David, who was United States Consul at La Paz, Mexico, during President Grant's administration; Mary; Elmira; Laura Ransome, wife of William Whaley; Emmeline; Abby; James Henry; and Pere G.

William and Laura R. (Turner) Whaley were the parents of three children: 1. Laura Turner, born in East Lyme, March 17, 1846, died May 11, 1921; she married George Lester, of Niantic, Connecticut, but they later moved to Brooklyn, New York, where their two children, Edward Whaley and Ursula Hamilton Lester, were born. 2. Emma Baker, born in East Lyme, June 12, 1847; Miss Whaley has resided in Niantic since 1857, when her parents moved from the farm to the village, sixty-four years ago. 3. Sarah Romelia, born in Niantic, Connecticut, married Willis Goddell, of Hartford, Connecticut, and now resides in Newport, Rhode Island; they are the parents of a daughter, Ruth Turner Goddell.

JAMES BERNARD SHANNON—A man of progressive nature and public spirit, James B. Shannon, now gone to his reward, accomplished a great deal for the improvement of the city of Norwich, to which city he came in 1867. For half a century he was engaged in business in the city, continuing it in the same location on Water street for thirty-seven years. It was not until 1892 that he began building operations, but from that year until his death, twenty-five years later, he bought, built, and remodeled countless buildings, made waste places bloom, and the rocks and mighty places become beautiful with homes and improved grounds. He reclaimed many old buildings and made them sightly residences. In fact, the work he did and inspired made a new Norwich, and he set an example in city improvement that is worthy of emulation.

James B. Shannon was of New York City birth, son of Patrick Shannon, born in Ireland, who came to the United States, settled in New York, and in 1849 joined the "gold seekers," and went to California. He died in New York City, in 1870, his wife, Mary (Carroll) Shannon, in 1892. For a time after the return of Patrick Shannon from California, in 1859, the family resided in Worcester, Massachusetts.

James B. Shannon was born in New York City, February 16, 1845, and died in Norwich, Connecticut, June 11, 1917. He was educated in New York City public schools, and there resided until the age of nine years, when he located in Worcester, Massachusetts, there continuing until reaching the age of twenty-one, when he came to Norwich, residing there from 1867 until his death, half a century later. He had been reared to work, and from his early experience came forth a sturdy, self-reliant young man, one not afraid of life, and equipped to resist adverse fortune, a test which fortunately he was not in later life called upon to endure.

Soon after coming to Norwich he established a business on Water street, and continued there until 1904, when he moved to a brick building he had erected at the corner of Market and Commerce streets, there continuing until his retirement. In 1878 he became interested in real estate, and from that year his building operations date, and he became one of the city's largest improvement factors, not, however, as a philanthropist, but as an investor. From the time he began his building operations in 1878 he purchased sites and erected new buildings thereon, bought and remodeled old buildings, many of them difficult to change. For his own use he built a beautiful house on Washington street, with two acres of ground surrounding it, a great addition to the exclusive residential district.

In 1898 he built the first Shannon building, a five-story modern building at the corner of Main and Shetucket streets. That building was destroyed by fire February 9, 1909, but rebuilding on a large scale began as soon as the ruins had cooled enough to allow workmen to enter. The present Shannon building, with one hundred and thirty feet frontage on Main and Shetucket streets, resulted, which is a modern five-story office and store building, rated as a model fire-proof construction. One year after the fire the new building was ready for occupancy.

The Marguerite Block, a modern apartment and store building, was erected in 1901, at the corner of Main and North Main streets, having a forntage of one hundred ninety feet on both streets, and was the first apartment block built in Norwich. The Auditorium Theatre, now The Strand, was built in 1905 on Water street, and the Auditorium Hotel, a modern, five-story, fireproof hotel, in 1915. The same year the Majestic, a modern four-story, fireproof block, with fourteen stores and a roof garden, was erected at the corner of Shetucket and Water streets. This block, the largest in Norwich, covers twenty-two thousand square feet. In all he erected and remodeled more than twenty buildings, the foregoing being the more important, and James B. Shannon is recorded as the largest individual builder and the city's largest individual taxpayer of his time. He owned, in addition to his Norwich properties, a woolen mill at Baltic, Connecticut, and was financially interested in other textile mills. He was a man of genial, friendly nature, very easy to approach, loyal to his friends, and very proud of his city.

Mr. Shannon was a director of the old First National Bank of Norwich. A Democrat in politics, he was very active in party affairs; was State central committeeman for sixteen years, and in 1892 was chairman of the Connecticut delegation to the National Convention held in Chicago, which, for the third time nominated Grover Cleveland for President of the United States. He was a member of the Roman Catholic Church, and very charitable, giving generously to all good causes.

James B. Shannon married (first) at Norwich, in May, 1870, Catherine Frances Cunningham, born in Newton, Massachusetts, who died in Norwich, Connecticut, in July, 1894. Mr. and Mrs. Shannon were the parents of six children, all born in Norwich, Connecticut: 1. James B. (2), a physician of Danielson, Connecticut, who died unmarried, in 1913. 2. Thomas I., a physician, who has made a special study of tuberculosis, and was at one time chief physician in charge of the Loomis Sanitarium at Liberty, New York. He is now proprietor of Falls Village Sanitarium, Falls Village, Connecticut. 3. Mary Gertrude, residing at the Shannon home, Washington street, Norwich. 4. Ella Claire, also residing at home. 5. Margaret Frances, married Charles C. McNamara, a merchant of Norwich, Connecticut. 6. John Henry, a sketch of whom follows. James B. Shannon married (second) in 1895, Katherine Frances Cunningham, who survives him, they the parents of one daughter, Madeleine Valerie, wife of John K. Foran, of New London.

Mr. Shannon found in his home complete relaxation from weighty business cares, and was devoted to his family. He never sought, nor would accept public office, belonged to no secular fraternities, societies or clubs, his only affiliations of that nature

James B. Shannon.

being with organizations of the church. He was emphatically a home man, and there, where best known and loved, he was at his best. Such in brief was the career of one of the solid business men of Norwich, who showed his confidence in the future of his city by his works. He made prosperity, and in every movement which tended to advance the public good he either led the movement or warmly supported it. It is men of like courage, vision and judgment who make communities prosperous.

JOHN HENRY SHANNON—Of the three sons of James Bernard and Catherine Frances (Cunningham) Shannon (q. v.), the youngest, J. Henry Shannon, was the only one to choose a business career, his brothers both having elected the medical profession. The carrying on of the business established and developed by James B. Shannon has fallen upon the shoulders of this capable young man, who was his father's business associate and secretary during the later years of his life. As administrator of the Shannon estate, and as president of the Shannon Building Company, Incorporated, to care for the property interests of the estate he has demonstrated a fine business quality and an executive ability worthy of a veteran. And, indeed, he is a veteran in fact, for he wore the khaki on the battlefields of France during the World War and was overseas until June, 1920.

J. Henry Shannon was born in Norwich, Connecticut, September 12, 1888. After finishing private school study, he entered Norwich Free Academy, whence he was graduated, class of '07. His brothers having both chosen professions, the young man, when academy days were over, took his place with his father, and for ten years bore with him such burdens and responsibilities as the older man would surrender to his son. They were associated in many building and real estate operations, the young man serving his father as secretary in most confidential relation. Those ten years brought to young Mr. Shannon a wide experience, and when on June 11, 1917, the father's strong personality was removed by death, J. Henry Shannon was appointed administrator, and without difficulty or dissention fulfilled this important trust.

The war of 1917 with Germany was on when on February 19, 1918, Mr. Shannon entered the United States army, reporting at Camp Devens, near Lowell, Massachusetts. He was assigned to the Quartermaster's Department at Camp Johnson, Florida, and there spent two months prior to sailing overseas from New York on the transport "Vauban." The transport landed her passengers at St. Nazaire, at the mouth of the River Loire, and three weeks later Mr. Shannon was at Tours, the headquarters of the Quartermaster's Department of the American Expeditionary Forces. From Tours he was sent to the Lorraine front with the American troops engaged in the St. Mihiel sector, and after the armistice he was retained for duty in France until June, 1920, when he returned to the United States and was mustered out with an honorable discharge, June 24, 1920, at Camp Lee, Virginia.

After his return from France, Mr. Shannon resumed business responsibilities as president of the Shannon Building Company, Inc., and so continues. The year of his return he established the Woodstock Dairy, a store for the sale of delicacies and luxuries for the table, and while this business is most successfully run by specialists, Mr. Shannon, as its proprietor, must share in the credit it has brought to its manager.

In politics, Mr. Shannon is a Democrat, and in 1912-13 represented his ward in the Norwich Common Council. In 1913 he officially represented the city of Norwich as one of the delegates to the National Deep Waterways Convention which met that year in Washington, District of Columbia, and at that convention was elected secretary of the Connecticut Deep Waterways Association. He is a member of the Norwich Chamber of Commerce, Norwich Rotary Club, of the executive committee of Robert O. Fletcher Post, American Legion, and is a member of the Roman Catholic Church.

WILLIAM LESLIE FLETCHER—The Norwich postoffice, an institution that comes nearer the lives of the people in the city than any other department of the government, has also been the one great business interest of the life of William L. Fletcher since graduation from Norwich Free Academy in 1880. He is the second eldest man in the employ of the office, being now (January, 1922) superintendent of mails. For forty-two years he has served the government in the Norwich post office, and there has compiled a record of usefulness, efficiency and faithfulness that cannot be excelled. William L. is a son of William Sterry Fletcher, grandson of Joseph Thompson Fletcher, great-grandson of William Fletcher, and great-great-grandson of Thomas Fletcher. This name is found among the earliest comers in New England, but none who came prior to 1630 left descendants. Robert Fletcher who came from Yorkshire, England, in 1630, left sons and established a family.

The family was founded in Norwich, Connecticut, by William Fletcher, born July 26, 1774, who came to that city a man of middle age, and there died in his eighty-fifth year. He married, November 17, 1796, Sarah Young, born February 18, 1776, daughter of James Young, who survived her husband until reaching the great age of ninety-five. One of her sons, the youngest, Sterry Young Fletcher, went West, became a Mississippi river steamboat captain, and resided in Paducah, Kentucky. Another of the sons of William and Sarah (Young) Fletcher was Joseph Thompson, grandfather of William Leslie Fletcher, superintendent of mails, Norwich, Connecticut.

Joseph Thompson Fletcher was born in Warren, Rhode Island, his father at the time of his birth, August 1, 1808, being a mill operative there. At the age of sixteen he went to sea as cabinboy, crossing the Atlantic ocean to Europe, and later was a sailor on vessels trading with the West Indies. At the age of twenty-seven he was made captain of a steamship owned by James L. Day, of Norwich, which ran between New Orleans and Galveston, lower Mississippi river, and other gulf ports. On his first voyage as captain he was taken ill at Mobile, Alabama, there died August 19, 1835, and was buried in the churchyard at Dog River, near Mobile. He married, July 4, 1829, Eliza Lamphere, born in Plainfield, Connecticut, November 1, 1811, daughter of Russell Lamphere. Mrs. Fletcher, left a widow at the age of twenty-four, married a second husband, Ashabel A. Parkerson, whom she survived, dying at the home of her son, William S. Fletcher, in Norwich, in 1896.

William Sterry Fletcher, second son of Joseph Thompson and Eliza (Lamphere) Fletcher, was born in Norwich, January 29, 1833, and died in the city of his birth, in May, 1917. But two years of age when his father died, and there being three children for the young widow to support, the boys at an early age became helpers, the lad William going to live with relatives. He attended the district school of his neighborhood, and remained at the home relatives made for him until 1847, when he left school and home, spending the next two years in the employ of the Falls Company, of Norwich, as a clerk. His pay was fifty dollars annually with board, and for two years he was content. Then his inherited love for the sea won him away and he spent four years as sailor and fisherman. Upon his return to Norwich he entered the employ of Cobb and Bacon, manufacturers of firearms, spending four years with that firm and two with their successor, the Manhattan Arms Company.

In 1858 he returned to his first employer, the Falls Company, and continued in the clerical service of that company for twenty-two years. In 1880 he bought the store, later sold to N. A. Bingham, and in 1884 built the store which he conducted as a dry goods and grocery house very successfully until his last illness. He was a hard worker, a good business man, and a good citizen. In politics he was a Republican and in religious faith a member of the Methodist Episcopal church.

Mr. Fletcher married, in Norwich, Connecticut, September 2, 1860, Sarah Louise Jewett, born in Norwich, October 15, 1842, died May 15, 1899, daughter of Eleazer and Sarah Sherman Jewett. Mr. and Mrs. Fletcher were the parents of three children: William Leslie, of further mention; Cora E.; and Bertha G., who married William G. Browning, a traveling salesman of Providence, Rhode Island.

William Leslie Fletcher, eldest child and only son of William Sterry and Sarah Louise (Jewett) Fletcher, was born in Norwich, Connecticut, March 8, 1862, and there yet resides (January, 1922). He was educated in Norwich Free Academy, whence he was graduated, class of 1880, and the same year admitted to a position in Norwich postoffice as a clerk. Forty years have since intervened and the association remains unbroken. Mr. Fletcher has advanced from post to post until reaching the present position, superintendent of mails. He has seen the office grow from a small affair, has seen administrations and postmasters come and go, but under all administrations and postmasters, and under constantly improving conditions, he has kept on in the even tenor of his way, performing his duties efficiently and to the satisfaction of those he serves. He is a Republican in politics, and a member of the Park Congregational Church.

Mr. Fletcher married, December 11, 1892, Elizabeth Ida Ogden, daughter of John R. and Elizabeth (Stoner) Ogden. Mr. and Mrs. Fletcher are the parents of three children:

1. Robert Ogden Fletcher, born August 8, 1893; sergeant major, 56th Artillery Regiment. The following appeared in one of the local newspapers: "For the second time this week the flag on the City Hall and the flag on Chelsea Parade will fly at half mast, the tribute to Sergeant Robert O. Fletcher, of this city, sergeant major of the 56th Artillery Regiment, who was killed on August 15, 1918, in action, while convoying supplies. Sergeant Fletcher was a native of this city and was twenty-five on the 8th of August. He attended the Falls School, graduated from Norwich Free Academy, class of 1912. He was prominent in athletics in school, and was captain of the baseball team in his graduating year. Immediately after graduation he entered the office of the Hopkins and Allen Arms Company, and from there came to the 'Bulletin' to fill the position of sporting editor, which he did with marked ability for several years, and it was while in this position that he heard the call of his country, and enlisted in the Third Company, Coast Artillery, in the early spring of 1917. He became company clerk, and went to Fort Wright at Fisher's Island, when the company transferred there for training in July, 1917. When the 56th Artillery Regiment was formed from the Connecticut Coast Artillery men, he became regimental supply sergeant, and left with the company for overseas duty on March 20, 1918, and while over there was promoted to sergeant-major. Sergeant Fletcher was one of the thousands of splendid, stalwart, six-foot Americans who swung along the French highways, hailed as saviors of their native country by the aged French men and women. His friends and business associates recall with pride his earnest, manly desire to do his whole part, the interest he took in perfecting himself in soldierly efficiency from the moment of his enlistment, and the eagerness with which he looked forward to the time when he could serve at the front. He was a friend and favorite of all with whom he was associated in business or social relations, and his love is one that will be long felt. He was a member of Park Congregational Church, Norwich Lodge, No. 430, Benevolent and Protective Order of Elks, and Union Lodge, No. 31, Free and Accepted Masons of New London, Connecticut, in which he was raised shortly before leaving Fisher's Island for overseas. As a tribute to him the American Legion Post, No. 4, has named it the Robert O. Fletcher Post. He is survived by a sister, Hazel Louise, and a brother, William L. Fletcher, Jr., who enlisted in the Tank Corps, and was over-

seas from September to March. Mr. Robert served four years as a first baseman with the Norwich Free Academy team. His graduating class of 1912 gave a fund of $200 to the Academy in memory of their classmates, Charles Willey and Robert Fletcher. And the interest from same fund was to be used to provide for future victory on the athletic field each year. There have been memorial trees planted from his church (Park Church), and the manager of the Bulletin Company has planted a memorial tree with a tablet hung to it, showing his birth and how he met his fatal wounds.

2. William Leslie Fletcher, Jr., born October 21, 1897. At the age of twenty years, March 29, 1918, he enlisted in the United States Tank Corps, at New York City, going from there to Fort Slocum, New York. Later he was transferred to Gettysburg, Pennsylvania, for training, being assigned to Company B, 326th Battalion. From Gettysburg he went to Tobyhanna, Pennsylvania, in August, 1918, and in September went overseas, landing first in Liverpool, England, going by rail to Southampton, where his corps went across the channel during the night, touching at Cherbourg, where for two weeks they were in a rest camp. From Cherbourg his battalion headed north for the tank training center at Bourg, five miles west of Langres. He was stationed here until after the armistice. On December 2, 1918, he was transferred to Company C, 303rd Battalion, Tank Corps, at Neuvy-Pailloux. While at the latter place he was taken sick and transferred to Base Hospital No. 63, at Chateauroux, but later assigned back to his company, one day before they left France for home. His company came over on the French liner "Patricia," landing in New York, March 17, 1919. He was discharged at Camp Meade, Maryland, May 1, 1919, as private, first class.

3. Hazel Louise Fletcher, born June 21, 1899; resides with her parents.

FRANK HERBERT MALLOY—With broad experience in his chosen field of activity, Mr. Malloy, of Baltic, New London county, Connecticut, is filling the responsible position of superintendent of the large plant of the Shetucket Worsted Mills.

Mr. Malloy is a son of James and Lillian (Hunt) Malloy. His father was born in Lowell, Massachusetts, and educated in the public schools of that city. About 1875, at the age of seventeen years, he became a fireman on the Boston & Maine railroad. Working up to the position of engineer, he served in that capacity until the time of his death, which occurred in Lowell, in February, 1891. His wife, who was born in Portland, Maine, still resides in Lowell. They were the parents of five children: Lena Maud, born in Lowell, now the wife of Frank Wright; Annie May, the wife of Fred Miller; Alice, the wife of Burton Stockham; Frank H., whose name heads this review; and Mabel, who resides with her sister Alice, in Providence.

Frank Herbert Malloy, fourth child and only son of James and Lillian (Hunt) Malloy, was born in Lowell, Massachusetts, June 9, 1888, and received his early education in the public schools of his native city, then was graduated from the Lowell High School in the class of 1906. During the next three years Mr. Malloy was a student at the Lowell Commercial College, also, during this period, studied nights at the Lowell Textile School, qualifying for a designer of woolen cloth. With this comprehensive preparation Mr. Malloy became assistant designer for the Rhode Island Worsted Company, at Stafford Springs, Connecticut. Taking this position in 1909, he resigned in 1911 to become designer and assistant superintendent for the Faulkner Manufacturing Company, at Stafford Springs, remaining with this concern for one year. In 1912 he went to Atlanta, Georgia, to fill a similar position for the Atlanta Woolen Mills, remaining for three years, returning North in 1915 to become designer and assistant superintendent for the Mohegan Mills at Trading Cove, in the town of Montville, near Norwich, remaining with this concern for a period of two years. Since 1917 until 1920 Mr. Malloy filled the position of superintendent of the Shetucket Worsted Mills, of Baltic, then in January, 1920, went to the Rutland Worsted Mills, of Rutland, Worcester county, Massachusetts, in the capacity of superintendent, remaining for one year. In January, 1921, he returned to Baltic, where he is again filling the office of superintendent of the Shetucket Worsted Mills.

Mr. Malloy is prominent fraternally, being a member of St. James Lodge, No. 23, Free and Accepted Masons; Franklin Chapter, No. 4, Royal Arch Masons; Franklin Council, No. 3, Royal and Select Masters, all of Norwich. Politically he supports the Republican party, and he and his family are members of the Episcopal church.

On December 24, 1910, Mr. Malloy married, in Stafford Springs, Rev. Raymond Dow Adams, minister of the Episcopal church, performing the ceremony, Madeline Lazzerin, daughter of John and Mary (Santin) Lazzerin, natives of Venice, Italy. Mr. and Mrs. Malloy have three daughters: Lillian Marie, born in Stafford Springs, November 11, 1911; Emma Madeline, born in Norwich, September 1, 1917; and Mae Agatha, born in Norwich, January 21, 1922.

JOHN STANTON BLACKMAR, M.D.—Although since 1898 devoted to the healing art as physician and surgeon, Dr. Blackmar has had an active part in two wars, and in the great World War of 1917-18, earned that coveted French decoration, the Croix de Guerre, a decoration pinned upon his breast by the famous French officer, General Petain. His first military experience was in the Spanish-American War, as assistant surgeon, with the rank of lieutenant. In the war of 1917 he went overseas as regimental surgeon, a commissioned captain, and attached to an American regiment brigaded with a French division. That regiment, the 372nd United States Infantry, won honors in France, and received from the French government a regimental decoration. Dr. Blackmar was especially cited and decorated for his service.

CITATION.

At General Headquarters, January 13, 1919.

The Marshal,
Commander-in-Chief of the French Army of the East,

PETAIN.

Order No. 12,833D.

(Extract.)

After approval of the Commander-in-Chief of the American Expeditionary Forces, the Marshal of France, Commander-in-Chief of the French Army of the East, cites a Divisional Order.

Medicine-Major John S. Blackmar, 372nd Infantry Regiment, distinguished himself especially during the period from September 27th to October 6th, 1918, when he showed the greatest zeal in the accomplishment of his duty, working day and night under violent bombardment and taking care of over four hundred wounded, many of whom were in a condition requiring the most difficult operations.

During the interval between the two wars in which he served, Dr. Blackmar practiced surgery and medicine in New York City, and Norwich, Connecticut, returning to the latter city from the army, and is again in private practice.

Dr. Blackmar is a son of George F. Blackmar, born in Killingly, Connecticut, who there obtained a public school education. At a suitable age he learned the machinist's trade and later located at Taftville, where he was employed until his death, which occurred at the age of twenty-six years, becoming a cotton mill master mechanic. He lost his life by drowning in the mill stream at Taftville during a sudden rise in the river in 1876. His widow, Harriet (Stanton) Blackmar, born in Cohoes, New York, yet survives him, her home with her only child, Dr. John S. Blackmar, in Norwich, Connecticut.

John Stanton Blackmar was born in Norwich, Connecticut, March 15, 1875. He was educated in Norwich public schools, Norwich Free Academy, and the College of Physicians and Surgeons, Columbia University, New York City, receiving from the last-named institution the degree of Doctor of Medicine, class of 1898. Soon after returning to Norwich he was commissioned assistant surgeon of the 3rd Regiment, Connecticut Volunteer Infantry, with the rank of lieutenant, and served with that regiment during the war with Spain. He was honorably discharged from the service in March, 1899, and spent the following twenty-seven months as interne at the Harlem Hospital, New York City, then engaged in private practice in New York City until 1912, when he located in Norwich, Connecticut, and there became well established as a skillful physician and surgeon.

On January 15, 1918, Dr. Blackmar was commissioned captain of the United States Army Medical Corps and assigned to Fort Oglethorpe, Georgia, for training in the Army Medical School. Having had former military training, he was only at that camp ten days when he received assignment as regimental surgeon of the 372nd Regiment, United States Infantry, then at Newport News, Virginia. He joined that regiment at once, and on March 30, 1918, sailed for France. The regiment disembarked at St. Nazaire, France, and after a period of training camp duty, the 372nd regiment (colored troops) was attached to the 157th Division of the French army, General Gouraud commanding. The regiment, classed as "shock troops," served on the French front in the following sectors: the Argonne (West) front, Vanquois, Verdun, the Champagne district and Alsace, where they were on duty when the armistice was signed. For meritorious service performed with the regiment during battle, Captain Blackmar was decorated with the Croix de Guerre, as previously mentioned.

After the armistice was signed, the 372nd Regiment was returned to the United States, but Captain Blackmar remained in France, where he was on duty at the American Base Hospital, No. 41, at Is-Sur-Tille. He returned to the United States, July 12, 1919, and was discharged at Camp Devens, Massachusetts, July 30, 1919, with the rank of major in the United States Army Medical Reserve Corps. He at once resumed private practice in Norwich, Connecticut, his present location.

In politics, Dr. Blackmar is a Republican, and in June, 1920, he was elected to represent his ward in the Norwich Common Council. He is a member of the American Medical Association, the Connecticut State Medical and New London Medical societies, and president of the Norwich City Medical Society. He is a member of the staff of William W. Backus Hospital, Norwich; United States public health surgeon in Norwich, and a member of the board of United States Pension Examiners for New London county.

In Masonry, he is affiliated with Bunting Lodge, No. 655, Free and Accepted Masons, of New York City; Franklin Chapter, No. 4, Royal Arch Masons, of Norwich; Franklin Council, No. 3, Royal and Select Masters, of Norwich; Columbian Commandery, No. 4, Knights Templar, of Norwich; King Solomon Lodge of Perfection; Van Rensselaer Council, Princes of Jerusalem; Norwich Chapter of Rose Croix; and Connecticut Consistory, Ancient Accepted Scottish Rite, in which he holds the thirty-second degree. He is a member of Norwich Lodge, No. 30, Benevolent and Protective Order of Elks, and commander of Robert O. Fletcher Post, American Legion. He is a member of the Norwich Chamber of Commerce, and the Norwich Rotary Club, of which he is one of the board of directors (1921).

Dr. Blackmar married, in New York City, October 12, 1910, Mildred Martin, of that city.

CHARLES COTTRELL DODGE—With the untimely passing of Charles Cottrell Dodge, in the prime of his manhood, the town of Mystic, Connecticut, suffered a loss such as no community can afford to sustain. Signally capable as a business executive, a social leader, a patron of all the out-door activities which count so far in the health and well-being of the people, and personally a man of the finest character, he is indeed lamented by all who knew him.

Mr. Dodge was a son of John Lamphere and Fannie A. (Cottrell) Dodge. John L. Dodge was born in Groton, Connecticut, and educated in the public schools of that town. As a young man he made a study of chemistry and medicine, and later became prominent in the field of medicine manufacture. He now resides in the South, and is retired from all active participation in business. Mrs. Dodge was born in Mystic, and their children numbered five, of whom Charles C. was the second.

Charles Cottrell Dodge was born in Mystic, Connecticut, on October 29, 1887. He received his education in the public and high schools of New York City, and thereafter attended the Hotchkiss Preparatory College, from which he was graduated in the class of 1907. In that year he returned to Mystic, where he became associated with the Cottrell Lumber Company. He made a thorough study of the business in all its branches, becoming familiar with every phase of the lumber trade, and in 1910 was elected president of the company, which office he held until his death in 1919.

But this brief industrial career pictures only one side of the man, and that inadequately. He was a living force for all that makes for progress and civic development. Poltically he supported the principles of the Republican party, always working for its interests. Still ahead of the party, as a political organization, he held the ideals of civic and national righteousness.

Mr. Dodge was president of the Country Club, of Mystic. Popular among all the extensive membership of this club, he was an enthusiast in the various branches of sport, particularly those which contribute so materially to the physical health and the upbuilding of the youth of today. In this organization he is sadly missed, and his place will long remain unfilled. Mr. Dodge was a member of Stonington Lodge, No. 26, Independent Order of Odd Fellows.

On August 18, 1910, Mr. Dodge married Jennie Brunson, daughter of William and Bessie (Jones) Brunson, of Perry, Georgia. They were the parents of three children: William Brunson, born on June 21, 1911; John H., born on September 10, 1912; and Hamilton, born October 14, 1917. The family have always been members of the Episcopal church, and prominent in all its activities.

HENRY GAMBER, of Groton, Connecticut, is connected with one of the most important industrial concerns in the county of New London,—the New London Ship and Engine Company, whose plant is located at Groton. With special training for the important position of foreman of the electrical department, he is bearing a significant part in the manufacturing interests of the county.

Mr. Gamber is a son of George and Leah (Van Leer) Gamber. George Gamber was born in Philadelphia, Pennsylvania, and educated in the public schools of that city, Union Academy, and a preparatory school in Pennsylvania. Fortune placed him in such a position in life that he had little to do besides enjoy the money which had been accumulated by other hands. For a time he was employed in the post office department. His wife, a descendant of General Wayne, of Revolutionary fame, was born in Chester county, Pennsylvania, and still resides in Philadelphia, that State. They were the parents of seven children.

Henry Gamber, the fifth child of George and Leah (Van Leer) Gamber, was born in Philadelphia, on April 30, 1876. Receiving his early education in the public schools of that city, he was fired with an ambition to take an active part in the work of the world. He entered the Williamson Free Trade School, taking the electrical-mechanical course, and was graduated from that institution in 1895. As a skilled electrician he entered the world of industry, and was employed in several different places, gaining a breadth of experience which he has since found invaluable. In 1900 he entered the employ of the Electric Boat Company, during the early and experimental stages of the submarine, remaining until 1912, when he came to New London county, and locating in Groton, entered the employ of the New London Ship and Engine Company, as foreman of their electrical department. In this position Mr. Gamber has continued since, ably filling its exacting demands during the trying period of the World War, when production was speeded up to the utmost.

In the public life of the borough, Mr. Gamber takes a deep and constructive interest. Two years ago he was elected warden of the borough, and still holds that office. His political allegiance is given to the Independent-Nonpartisan party. Mr. Gamber is a member of Brainerd Lodge, No. 102, Free and Accepted Masons, of New London, and his church membership is with the Presbyterian denomination.

On September 26, 1901, Mr. Gamber married Lillie McGirr, daughter of Andrew and Mary Elizabeth (Stewart) McGirr, of Philadelphia. Mr. and Mrs. Gamber have three daughters, all at home: Dorothea L.; Grace O.; and Ruth I.

JOSEPH BYERS is the son of John W. Byers, who was born in Massachusetts, but resided in the State of Connecticut, where his son, Joseph Byers, was born, the latter's home later becoming Massachusetts. In 1919 Joseph returned to Connecticut, and in New London is known as one of the enterprising owners of a successful business enterprise, Byers Brothers, Inc., his partner, his brother, John R. Joseph Byers is a veteran of the World War, having enlisted with the first call for volunteers, serving until placed on the reserve list in 1919.

John W. Byers was born in Medford, Massachusetts, and there was educated. He was variously employed until entering the employ of the Southern New England Telephone Company, and still continues with that corporation, being commercial manager of the Newton district, with headquarters at Newton, Massachusetts. He married Fanny L. Rogers, born in Weymouth, Massachusetts, and they are the parents of two children: John R.; and Joseph, of whom further.

Joseph Byers was born in Bridgeport, Connecticut, November 21, 1894, but while young, Newton, Massachusetts, became the family home, and there he was educated, finishing with graduation from the Newton Technical High School, class of 1914. For a year after graduation he was engaged in the printing business in Boston, and in 1915 was appointed to a clerkship in the Webster & Atlas National Bank of Boston, after which he was connected with the Walter B. Snow Advertising Agency. He enlisted in the United States navy during the World War, and was rated a machinist, second class, and advanced to the first class while in the First Division. In 1918 he passed the required examination and was advanced to the rank of ensign, serving in the naval overseas transport service. He was placed upon the naval reserve list in 1919 and retired from active service. In 1919, with his brother, John R. Byers, he established Byers Brothers, Inc., capitalized at $100,000, Joseph Byers, president.

Joseph Byers is a Republican in politics; is a member of the Chamber of Commerce, the John Winthrop Club, of New London, and is an attendant of the Congregational church.

Mr. Byers married, at Newtonville, Massachusetts, January 19, 1918, Louise A. Welch, of Garden City, Long Island, daughter of John I. and Elizabeth (Stedman) Welch, of New York City. Mr. and Mrs. Byers are the parents of two daughters: Edith, born in Brooklyn, New York; and Elizabeth, born in New York City.

LEONE FRANKLIN LA PIERRE, M.D.—Well known as a long-established general practitioner and also as a highly successful specialist, Dr. La Pierre requires no introduction to his friends and neighbors of Norwich, but the simple inscription of his name at the head of this article. It might be added that his name would be greeted with instant and respectful recognition by many of his fellow-citizens far beyond the limits of his home community, by reason of the fact that his work is attracting, with the lapse of each succeeding year, greater attention and more cordial appreciation.

Henry H. La Pierre, father of Leone Franklin La Pierre, was born in Montville, Connecticut, and as a young man learned the mill business, later becoming a farmer in Montville. During the Civil War he enlisted in the Twenty-sixth Regiment, of Norwich, and served nine months. At the end of that time he again enlisted, this time in New Orleans, and was later made orderly to General Canby, a position which he held during the remainder of the war. On returning to Norwich he was engaged for some years in a paper manufacturing mill, and in his later years again became a farmer, this time in Chesterfield, Connecticut. For some years thereafter he served as a watchman for the firm of Porteous & Mitchell, of Norwich. He is now, at the age of eighty years (1921), living in retirement in the home of his son, Dr. La Pierre. In politics he is a Republican. He is a member of the Grand Army of the Republic, and attends the Congregational church. Mr. La Pierre married Fanny A. Rogers, like himself a native of Montville, and they became the parents of the following children: 1. Floyd H., born in Montville, Connecticut, now living in New Haven, Connecticut; married Minnie Maynard, of Norwich, and they have two children. 2. Leone Franklin, mentioned below. 3. Bessie E., born in Norwich, and died there in 1902, at the age of twenty-one. 4. Arnaud Julian, a biography of whom follows in this work.

Leone Franklin La Pierre, son of Henry H. and Fanny A. (Rogers) La Pierre, was born November 6, 1876, in Colchester, Connecticut, and received his early education in Yantic, same State, afterward graduating from the Broadway School of Norwich. For two years thereafter he served as clerk in a drug store in that city, and in the autumn of 1897 entered Yale University, taking the four years' course, and graduating in 1901 with the degree of M.D., *cum laude*. This was followed by a two years' course at the Rhode Island Hospital, Providence, Rhode Island, and he then spent three years as physician of the Hospital for the Insane in Middletown, Connecticut.

In 1906 Dr. La Pierre came to Norwich, opened an office and entered upon a career of independent practice. For about seven years he was steadily engaged in building up a lucrative clientele, and a reputation with the medical fraternity and the general public to which he was justly entitled by reason of talent, knowledge, skill and strict conscientiousness in the performance of his very important duties.

About the year 1913 Dr. La Pierre began to give special attention to the study and treatment of diseases of the eye, ear, nose and throat, and has since, as the years have passed, met with marked success in this field of medical practice.

Politically Dr. La Pierre is a Republican, but has always been too devoted to his profession to have time or inclination for office-holding. He is a member of the City, County and State Medical societies, the American Medical Association, and the Sons of Veterans. He affiliates with St. James Lodge, No. 23, Ancient Free and Accepted Masons, of Norwich, and is a member of the United Congregational church, and the Young Men's Christian Association of that city.

Dr. La Pierre married, October 5, 1906, in Montpelier, Vermont, Ellen Holmes, born in that city, daughter of Rodney and Aletha (Farrar) Holmes. Dr. and Mrs. La Pierre are the parents of the following children: Franklin Holmes, born August 6, 1907; Arnaud Rogers, born August 10, 1910; Bessie Aletha, born April 3, 1912; Warren Winthrop, born September 17, 1914; and Ruth Helen, born December 27, 1915. All these, with the exception of Warren W., whose birthplace was Stonington, Connecticut, were born in Norwich.

The reputation which Dr. La Pierre has already acquired as a specialist gives assurance that greater successes in his chosen department of the profession await him in the years to come.

ARNAUD JULIAN LA PIERRE, son of Henry H. and Fanny A. (Rogers) La Pierre, and brother of Dr. L. F. La Pierre (see preceding sketch), was born in Norwich, Connecticut, June 30, 1885. He completed the courses of Norwich Free Academy, then entered the medical department of the University of Vermont and was graduated from that institution with the degree of Medical Doctor, in the class of 1910. He was for a time physician to Haymarket Square Relief Station, Boston; interne at the Lying-In Hospital, New York City; interne at William W. Backus Hospital, Norwich, after which he engaged in general practice in Norwich for fifteen months. Dr. La Pierre, desiring to specialize, took post-graduate courses at the New York Eye, Ear, Nose and Throat Hospital, then returned to Norwich, where he very successfully specialized in diseases of the eye, ear, nose and throat, his offices with his brother, Dr. L. F. La Pierre, a specialist in the same diseases.

In politics Dr. La Pierre is a Republican, and in religious faith a member of the United Congregational Church. His professional societies are: The Norwich City Medical, New London County Medical, and Connecticut State Medical, and he also is a member of the American Medical Association. He is a member of Burlington Lodge, No. 100, Free and Accepted Masons, of Burlington, Vermont, and of Connecticut Consistory, of Norwich, Ancient Accepted Scottish Rite, in which he holds the thirty-second degree. His college fraternity is Delta Nu.

Dr. A. J. La Pierre married, September 1, 1913, at New Britain, Connecticut, Charlotte Mae Charter, born in Boston, Massachusetts, daughter of George M. and Margaret (Aldose) Charter. Mr. and Mrs. La Pierre are the parents of: Fanny Louise, Charlotte Mae, and Arnaud Julian (2) La Pierre.

CHARLES WILLIAM MILLER—Among the earliest New England colonists the Miller family was represented, and through the nearly three centuries that have passed since the first record of the name appears, members of that family have been steadily contributing to the upbuilding of the life of the nation. Charles D. Miller, the grandfather of Charles William Miller, was a foundryman of Providence, Rhode Island, capable, public-spirited, always ready to serve his community, and the sole founder of the New England Butt Company, of Providence. A man of sturdy independence and of great energy, he left his son, Albert B. Miller, born in October, 1838, in Providence, not only a substantial business interest, but what was of far greater value, an abundant heritage of ideals, ability, and solid worth of character.

Albert B. Miller passed his boyhood days in Providence, and then, wishing to see for himself those western regions which at that time were attracting so much attention, joined one of the westward moving groups and went to California, to Oregon and to other Western States and territories. Unlike most of his fellow-travelers, a tour of the West convinced him that for him opportunity was largest in the East, and he came back to Connecticut, where for several years he was employed in the Scranton Printing Press Works, then located at Norwich. In 1868 he purchased of John T. Trumbull the Joslin Arms Company, an iron and brass foundry, and for several years worked there in association with the Atwood Machine Company. About 1880 he sold the foundry to the Atwoods and built the foundry on Miller street, where he continued in business until his death, which occurred August 7, 1899. He was burgess of the borough of Stonington in 1891, and active in promoting the civic welfare of his community. He married, about 1861, Margaret Gough, a native of Bath, Maine, who spent her early life in Providence, Rhode Island, where she was married. She died in April, 1896. To this marriage four children were born: Charles William, of whom further; Susie M., also born at Norwich, and who married Dr. C. E. Maine, of Stonington; Hattie, teacher of music in the public schools of Providence; and Albert B., of Stonington.

Charles W. Miller, eldest son of Albert B. and Margaret (Gough) Miller, was born in Norwich, Connecticut, July 13, 1863. The family moved to Stonington when he was but four years of age and he attended the public schools of that place, after which he went to Eastman's Business College, at Poughkeepsie, New York, graduating in 1883. Coming back to Stonington, he went into his father's iron and brass foundry, gradually making himself acquainted with all branches of the work, and especially with the executive and administrative departments. From 1892 to 1898, he was engaged in a foundry business at Chicago, Illinois, which he managed successfully, but shortly before his father's death he came back to Stonington and took charge of the foundry there. This plant he has successfully managed since that time. At the foundry work is done for the Consolidated railroad; also for the Robert Palmer & Son Company, ship-builders for nearly forty years; for the Lorraine Manufacturing Company, of Westerly, Rhode Island; for the Thames Towboat Company, of New London; and for the T. A. Scott Company, of New London. Fraternally he is a member of the Benevolent and Protective Order of Elks, and is widely known and greatly respected.

In October, 1882, while in Chicago, Illinois, Mr.

Miller married Margaret Carter, and they are the parents of six children: Albert, Charles E., Chester, Frank, Margaret, and John. Charles E. Miller enlisted for service in the World War, in May, 1917, was stationed at Fort Sam Houston, Texas, commissioned a second lieutenant, and sailed in September, 1918, for France, with the 345th Regiment, 90th Division, being mustered out of service in June, 1919, at Camp Lee, Virginia. Chester Miller served during the World War as a naval reserve, and is now at home. Frank Miller served in the United States army, being stationed at Camp Devens, Massachusetts, during the war.

ALBERT STODDARD CULLEN—Holding a responsible position in the industrial world, and with an honorable record of service in the recent struggle overseas, Albert Stoddard Cullen, of Baltic, Connecticut, is one of those young men who are carrying New London county forward in the march of progress.

Mr. Cullen comes of Scotch ancestry, and his father, James Cullen, was born in Glasgow, Scotland, and educated in the National schools of that country. He came to America when a young man, locating at East Long Meadow, Massachusetts, where he worked as a fancy stone and marble cutter all his active life. He was gifted with artistic talent, and many very beautiful examples of his work have gone out from the yards where he was employed. In 1902 he went to Scotland in the hope of regaining his broken health, but died there in 1903. He married Annie Stoddard, and she still survives him, being a resident of Baltic. They were the parents of four children.

Albert Stoddard Cullen was born in East Long Meadow, Massachusetts, on February 4, 1890. There he attended the public schools, gaining a practical education in preparation for the battle of life. Having completed his education, he entered the West Warren Cotton Mill, in the mechanical department, and continued there from 1906 to 1913. He learned there the machinists' trade, as applied to the cotton industry, and also the trade of stationary engineer. Being naturally of a mechanical bent, he was an adept at this work, and became a valuable hand. In 1913 he came to Baltic, Connecticut, entering the employ of the Baltic Mill Company, in the capacity of engineer. Since 1919 he has been connected with the Shetucket Worsted Mills, Incorporated, in the capacity of master mechanic.

In 1918 Mr. Cullen answered the call of humanity which reached so many thousands of the flower of young American manhood. He was assigned to the 308th Machine Gun Company, of the 77th Division, American Expeditionary Forces, and served with honor in France until the close of the war. He was mustered out of service at Camp Devens, on May 13, 1919, when he returned to his old home in Baltic.

Mr. Cullen is a popular young man of this vicinity, and interested in the various branches of social, fraternal and civic activity. Politically, he is a Republican, and was recently elected selectman of the town of Sprague. He is a member of the Masonic order, belonging to a Warren, Massachusetts, Lodge, Free and Accepted Masons; Franklin Chapter, No. 4, Royal Arch Masons, of Norwich; and Franklin Council, No. 3, Royal and Select Masters, also of Norwich. He is also a member of Quinebaug Lodge, No. 187, Independent Order of Odd Fellows, of Warren. He is a member of the Methodist Episcopal church, and active in the young people's organizations.

ARTHUR DYER TRIPP—Among those who can claim descent from the first families of the State of Rhode Island is the present Tripp family, whose ancestry runs back to the pre-Revolutionary days when good Peregrine Tripp made stout shoes for the people of the village of Exeter, Rhode Island, where he lived, worked and died. His wife, Isabella (Sprague) Tripp, was born August 26, 1768, and died September 26, 1812, leaving a large family behind them. These were: Isabella, born December 22, 1791; John, born November 17, 1793; Sarah, born March 13, 1797, died May 25, 1798; Sarah (2), born August 6, 1799, who married Silas Moore, and died in Richmondtown, Rhode Island, March 19, 1862; Betsey, born October 22, 1802, who married William Northrop, and died in Warwick, Rhode Island; Deborah, born September 29, 1804, who married Mr. Hoxie, of Rhode Island, and died in May, 1846; Lyman, born April 11, 1806, died in March, 1808; and Phoebe, who was born March 28, 1809, and married in Rhode Island.

John Tripp, one of the sons of Peregrine Tripp, carried on farming on the home place until his marriage, when after a few years of working on rented land near Exeter, he came to Plainfield with his wife's parents, all locating in the southern part of the town on a farm which the father-in-law purchased. Until the death of his wife, Mr. Tripp remained on this property and then went to Brooklyn, Connecticut, where he lived with his son until his death, in March, 1852. Through his marriage, in Exeter, to Sarah Bissell, daughter of Samuel and Sarah (Allen) Bissell, John Tripp became connected with one of the leading families of Rhode Island. Samuel Bissell served in the Continental army under General Nathanael Greene, was made a lieutenant, and later became captain of his company. He resigned soon after this last appointment, however, and went on board a privateer, where he assisted in the capture of twenty-seven British vessels. Throughout the Revolutionary War he remained in the navy, and drew a pension until his death. After the war he worked at farming in Plainfield, Connecticut, for many years, and was buried in the private burying ground at Flat Rock in that town, where his wife, who died at the age of forty-nine, had already been buried. The children of John Tripp and his wife were: 1. Lucy Ann, born at Plainfield, in April, 1818, who married Gilbert Robbins, a factory superintendent, and died in Plainfield. 2. Samuel B., born February 23, 1820, who married

Arthur D Tripp

Betsy Keach; he was a shoemaker by trade, entered the army during the Civil War, and was killed at Cold Harbor. 3. Huldah, born October 12, 1821, who married Miner Tucker, and died in Plainfield. 4. Perry G., born October 12, 1823, who married Abbie Pidge; served in the Civil War in the First and (second) Harriet Irene Robbins, of Brooklyn. 5. Stephen H., born in June, 1826, who married Abbie Pidge, served in the Civil War in the First Connecticut Cavalry, later became a farmer, and died in Brooklyn. 6. Henry D., of whom further. 7. Sophia, who died in infancy. 8. Emily, who married Louis Trescott, and died in Providence, Rhode Island. 9. George, born August, 1834, who married Lydia Spicer, and after retiring from seafaring life, engaged in the lumber business at Mystic, Connecticut.

Henry D. Tripp, father of Arthur Dyer Tripp, was born in Plainfield, Connecticut, February 23, 1828, and died in Brooklyn, Connecticut, November 7, 1907, most of his life being spent in Windham county, Connecticut. He worked at farming, principally, but was a tanner by trade and made shoes. He married Adelaide J. Simmons, a native of Providence, Rhode Island, who is now living in East Brooklyn, Connecticut. Mr. and Mrs. Tripp became the parents of twelve children, among whom was Arthur Dyer Tripp, the tenth child.

Arthur Dyer Tripp was born in Thompson, Connecticut, September 25, 1875. He attended the public school at Central Village, in the town of Plainfield, Connecticut, completing his education at Putnam Business College. He chose teaching as a profession, and beginning in 1902, taught sixteen years, half of those years in East Brooklyn, Connecticut, and the other half in different schools. In 1910 he located in Jewett City, and entering into partnership with H. B. Chapman, engaged in the lumber and coal business and the handling of builders' supplies, under the firm name of Chapman & Tripp. The association has been both pleasant and profitable and is continued at the present time, the firm carrying on a large and successful business.

Politically, Mr. Tripp is a Republican. Fraternally, he is affiliated with Mount Vernon Lodge, No. 75, Free and Accepted Masons; Reliance Lodge, No. 29, Independent Order of Odd Fellows, of which order he is a past noble grand; Faith Chapter, No. 82, Order of the Eastern Star, of Jewett City; Undaunted Lodge, No. 34, Knights of Pythias, of Jewett City; and Pachaug Grange, Patrons of Husbandry, of Griswold, Connecticut. He is also secretary of the Slater Library Corporation, of Jewett City. Mr. Tripp attends the Baptist church.

Mr. Tripp married, September 17, 1913, Martha B. Church, daughter of Rollin R. and Lydia (Brown) Church, of Jewett City, and they are the parents of three children: Arthur D., Jr., Rollin Church, and Hermon Brown.

CHARLES ADAMS MARQUARDT, the sixth child of the late George and Martha (Salsman) Marquardt, was born at Groton, Connecticut, September 27, 1869. His father was a native of Germany, and came to this country when a young man, locating in Groton, where he resided the remainder of his lifetime, following agricultural pursuits.

The education of the boy, Charles A., was obtained in the public schools of Groton, after which he served an apprenticeship to the carpenter's trade and it is with this particular line of business that he has ever since been interested in. In 1895 he founded the Marquardt Brothers' Lumber Company, which was incorporated in 1910, and was run under this name until 1917, when it was sold, and is now conducted under the name of the Groton Lumber Company. The success of this organization was due in no small measure to the wonderful business genius and business ability of Charles Adams Marquardt. Since the dissolution of this company, Mr. Marquardt has carried on successfully a large contracting business, and is recognized as one of the most progressive business men of this community.

Mr. Marquardt is an Independent in politics. He affiliates with the Free and Accepted Masons, and with the Independent Odrer of Odd Fellows, Fairview Lodge, No. 101, of which he is a charter member. In religion he is a Baptist, attending the church of this denomination at Groton.

Charles Adams Marquardt was united in marriage with Celia Chapman, of Groton, a daughter of Charles D. and Annie (Morgan) Chapman. Mr. and Mrs. Marquardt are the parents of four children: Alice E.; Gladys A., who married Edward Seaver, of Groton; Percy; and Barbara.

ALBERT LAMATE DUHAIME, proprietor of a moving picture theatre in Mystic, Connecticut, has been in the business here for some years, and conducts a very popular enterprise.

Albert Lamate Duhaime is the son of Joseph L. and Albina (La Montaine) Duhaime, the father being a native of Salix, Iowa, and the mother having been born in Montreal, Canada. Joseph L. Duhaime attended the public school of his birthplace and when quite young became a ranch man, living that life for a year, then, coming back into the business world, he took up the meat market business, continuing it for many years, finally retiring from active work. He now resides in Providence, Rhode Island. He and his wife were the parents of twelve children, of whom their son, Albert Lamate, is the youngest.

Born in Mandeville, Rhode Island, September 8, 1883, Albert Lamate Duhaime acquired an education in the public school of that village, and after leaving it, became employed as manager of one of the large chain of Childs' restaurants, located in Providence, Rhode Island. For the next six years Mr. Duhaime remained in this establishment, but his health becoming somewhat impaired at this time, he gave it up and, coming to Mystic, opened the Lyceum Theatre, in the Gilbert block; some time later the building was destroyed by fire, but this catastrophe did not discourage Mr. Duhaime, for he at once set about opening another theatre in an adjoining building, giving it the name of the Mystic Theatre, though it is devoted entirely to the work of the screen. It has proved itself to be a very successful venture, and Mr. Duhaime is still conducting it.

A member of the Knights of Columbus, Mr. Duhaime is an active worker in Father Murphy Council of Mystic. He also is affiliated with Westerly Lodge, No. 678, of the Benevolent and Protective Order of Elks, of Westerly, Rhode Island. In political faith he is a Republican.

On June 21, 1905, Albert Lamate Duhaime was married to Margaret King, daughter of Patrick King. Three children have been born to them: Ernest L., Margaret L., and Cyril L.; they all live at home. Mr. and Mrs. Duhaime and their children all attend the Roman Catholic church of Mystic.

ALWARD JOHN HUGGARD—Born in the town of Norton, Kings county, New Brunswick, Canada, Mr. Huggard was there educated and spent the first nineteen years of his life. His father, James Huggard, born in Ireland, came to Canada when a lad of twelve, and found a home in Kings county, New Brunswick, and there died in 1876, aged sixty-three years. He married Anne Robinson, born in Queens county, New Brunswick, who died in 1891, aged seventy-one years. She was the daughter of Thomas and Isabella Robinson. James and Anne (Robinson) Huggard were the parents of five sons: Joseph, Thomas, Jacob, James, Alward John, of further mention; and four daughters: Elmira, Isabell, Mary, and Anne.

Alward John Huggard was born March 24, 1868, and attended the public schools in his youth. He remained in New Brunswick until 1887, when he went to Waterville, Maine, there passing eight months as an employee of the Lockwood Cotton Mills. He was next in Lowell, Massachusetts, where for eleven years he was with the Kitson Machine Company. His next employment was with the now Climax Company until 1912, when he went to New Jersey, where he spent the years until May, 1915, as a shipping clerk. On that date he located in Montville, New London county, Connecticut, where as a member of the firm, Chagnon and Huggard Company, he is successfully engaged in the manufacture of paper tubes.

Mr. Huggard married, at Lowell, Massachusetts, in December, 1892, Catherine MacAulay, born in the Province of Quebec, Canada, August 7, 1867, daughter of John and Arabella MacAulay, who had three other daughters who grew to womanhood: Sophia, Annie, and Jane; a daughter, Delina, and a son, Malcolm, are deceased.

RAOUL M. DELAGRANGE—A descendant of an old Huguenot family of France, Raoul M. Delagrange is a native of that country, but since his infancy he has lived in the United States. His father, Adolph A. Delagrange, was born in Fruriner, France, and as a boy attended the public school in his native city. In his young manhood he became a commission merchant and a speculator in all export foods, fruits and such commodities. In 1880, or thereabout, Mr. Delagrange came to this country, bringing his family with him, and located in Long Island City, New York. He only lived a few years there, dying in 1897. By his first wife he had two children: Gaston and Adolph. His second wife, who was a Miss Poulver, also a native of France, died at Long Island City in 1884. They were the parents of two children: Raoul M., and Edgar M., who married Josephine Greiser, a resident of Stonington, where they now reside.

Having acquired an education in the public schools of Long Island City, Raoul M. Delagrange came to Stonington in 1898 and entered the employ of the American Velvet Company, where he learned the velvet weaving business. Continuing in this line for ten years, Mr. Delagrange became interested in marine engines, and in 1908 bought out the business of William F. Broughton, a dealer in marine engines and supplies, adding to this line a machine shop for general jobbing. In 1920 he built a garage, 65x100 feet, which is one of the most up-to-date garages within one hundred miles, equipped with modern machinery, all accessories, welding machines, etc., and the painting of cars is also done here. Mr. Delagrange has inherited from his father a keen desire to speculate and will become interested in anything that promises a money return; to a certain extent that has become somewhat of a hobby.

Mr. Delagrange is what might be called a fraternal man, being connected with several organizations, in which he is quite active. He is a member of Asylum Lodge, No. 67, of Stonington, Free and Accepted Masons, and of Pequot Council, Royal Arcanum. For the past eight years Mr. Delagrange has been foreman of the hook and ladder company of Stonington. He also is a member of the Republican party.

In 1902 Raoul M. Delagrange was married to Josephine Ollweiler, a daughter of George Ollweiler, a native of Germany. To this union four children have been born: Constance M.; Olive; Winona; and Reginald; and they are all living at home with their parents. Mr. and Mrs. Delagrange and their family are all members of the Protestant Episcopal church of Stonington.

CHARLES W. PRENTICE—One of the industries of Taftville and southern Connecticut is the roll covering business, conducted by Charles W. Prentice until his death in 1909, and since then under the ownership of Mrs. Prentice, and managed by their son, Harry E. Prentice, a sketch of whom follows. The roll covering business was introduced into the Prentice family by Ephraim Prentice, father of Charles W., and grandfather of Harry E. Prentice. He was a mechanical genius, a carpenter, millwright and roll coverer, a business he began in one room, with rented power and two assistants. The business continued by his sons is now in the hands of grandsons.

Captain Thomas Prentice, born in England in 1621, married in England, and with his wife, Grace, joined the church in Cambridge, Massachusetts, in

1652. He was captain of a troop of horse fighters in the Indian War, 1675, and died in Newtown, Massachusetts, July 6, 1710. His wife Grace died October 8, 1692, the mother of sons and daughters. The line of descent from Captain Thomas and Grace Prentice is through their eldest son, Thomas Prentice, and his wife, Sarah Stanton; their son, Samuel Prentice, and his wife, Esther Hammond; their son, Joseph Prentice, and his wife, Mary Wheeler; their son, Manasseh Prentice, and his wife, Asenath Benton; their son, Ephraim Prentice, and his wife, Mary Dow; their son, John D. Prentice, and his wife, Abby Gray Gilmore; their son, Ephraim Prentice, and his wife, Rachel S. Wilson; their son, Charles W. Prentice, and his wife, Alice M. Brown; their son, Harry E. Prentice, and his wife, Mary Waterman; their children, Dorothy W., Charles W., and Ruth B. Prentice. In the fourth generation this branch moved from Newtown, Massachusetts, to Preston, Connecticut, and that State has since been the home of this branch of the family. Preston, Plainfield, Moosup, Taftville, and Norwich have all been homes of the family.

Ephraim Prentice, of the eighth generation, was born near Moosup, in the town of Plainfield, Windham county, Connecticut, July 27, 1822, died at his farm in East Brooklyn, then a part of the borough of Danielson, Windham county, Connecticut, November 13, 1899. He learned the carpenter's trade, then was engaged for many years as a millwright, and finally completed a process for covering top rolls used in cotton mills in the making of textiles. He developed a good business in that line at Wauregan, Connecticut, moving in 1883 to East Brooklyn, where he owned the old Stewart property. There he built and prospered, and continued his roll covering plant until his death in 1899, when he was succeeded by his son, George E., in the East Brooklyn plant. In 1871 he established a branch plant at Taftville, New London county, Connecticut, and that was placed under the management of his son, Charles W. Prentice, in 1880.

Ephraim Prentice, after removing to East Brooklyn, devoted a good share of his own time to his sixty-two acres and especially to the breeding of pure-blooded Holstein cattle, having a fine herd. He is a Republican in politics, an attendant and supporter of the Congregational church, and a member of Mount Moriah Lodge, Free and Accepted Masons, of Danielson, Connecticut. He married, in Plainfield, Connecticut, Rachel S. Wilson, born in Plainfield, September 22, 1821, died November 8 1891; both were buried in Westfield Cemetery, Danielson. They were the parents of four children: Charles W., of whom further; Ellen M., who never married but always remained her parents' companion, and after they had passed away she remained at the old home in East Brooklyn; Emma R., who married John Whitaker, of Plainfield; and George E., born June 14, 1860, long associated in the roll covering business with his father, whom he succeeded at the East Brooklyn plant.

Charles W. Prentice, eldest son of Ephraim and Rachel S. (Wilson) Prentice, was born in Greenville, Connecticut, February 13, 1847, died in Taftville, Connecticut, August 25, 1906. His youth was spent in the various Connecticut towns in which his father followed his trade, finally coming to Wauregan, which was the family home for twenty-four years, and there the lad was educated in the public schools. When school years were over he was employed as an assistant bookkeeper in a mill at Wauregan, but soon entered the employ of his father, who had established a shop in Wauregan for the covering of rolls used in textile manufacturing. The branch factory established at Taftville by his father in 1871 was placed under the management of Charles W. Prentice in 1880, and for twenty-nine years he continued its operation, becoming its owner. He became an important figure in cotton manufacturing circles and his business grew to large proportions. He was held in high regard as an able business man, and in his citizenship there was no flaw.

In politics, Mr. Prentice was a Republican, but never active in the party, although keenly alive to his obligations as a good citizen. He was a member of the Masonic order and affiliated with Mount Moriah Lodge, Free and Accepted Masons, of Danielson; the Scottish Rite at Norwich, holding the thirty-second degree; and with Sphinx Temple, Ancient Arabic Order Nobles of the Mystic Shrine. He was very popular in these orders and in his community.

Mr. Prentice married, in Manchester, New Hampshire, Alice M. Brown, who survives him. She succeeded to the ownership of the roll covering business, which she has continued until the present time (1921) under the management of her eldest son, Harry E., of mention below. Leonard Charles Prentice, her youngest son, is also associated with the same business; he married Florence Weller, of Taftville, Connecticut, and has two daughters: Shirley Weller, and Lorraine Elizabeth Prentice.

HARRY EPHRAIM PRENTICE, eldest of the two sons of Charles W. and Alice M. (Brown) Prentice (q. v.), was born at the old home of his mother in Manchester, New Hampshire, November 2, 1888. Norwich, Connecticut, became the family home, and there he was educated in the public schools and Norwich Free Academy (class of 1907), later attending Phillips Exeter, Academy at Exeter, New Hampshire, class of 1909. He then spent two years at the Massachusetts Institute of Technology, returning to Norwich in 1912. In that year he became manager of the business established in Taftville by his grandfather, The Prentice Company, developed by his father, and since the latter's death in 1906, owned and operated by his mother. In politics Mr. Prentice is a Republican, and in religious faith is a Congregationalist.

Mr. Prentice married, at Waterford, Connecticut, July 11, 1911, Mary Waterman, born in Lebanon, Connecticut, April 11, 1889, daughter of Andrew and Julia (Stark) Waterman. Mr. and Mrs. Prentice are the parents of three children: Dorothy Waterman, born April 17, 1912, in Norwich, Connecticut; Charles Wilson, born May 23, 1913, at Taftville, Connecticut; and Ruth Brown, born March 23, 1920, at Norwich, Connecticut. The family home is in Norwich

---

DR. FREDERIC EDMOND RAINVILLE was born in Rouville county, Province of Quebec, January 7, 1861, son of Paul and Sophia (Giroux) Rainville. His father, Paul Rainville, was born in Rouville, and followed agricultural pursuits throughout his entire lifetime. He died in 1871. To Mr. and Mrs. Rainville were born nine children, Frederic Edmond being the third child.

After preliminary education in the public schools of Rouville, Frederic Edmond Rainville entered Feller Institute Preparatory School, whence he was graduated in 1887. In the meantime, having decided to adopt medicine as a profession, he entered the University of Vermont, receiving his M. D. from the Medical Department of that institution in 1891. The same year he was appointed interne at Notre Dame Hospital, Montreal, Canada, where he made a special study of surgery. Later he established in the practice of his profession in Montreal, Canada, where he made a special study of surgery, but later moved to Wauregan, Connecticut, subsequently going to Danielson, where until 1910 he practiced his profession with success. He then came to Jewett City, since which time his practice has been steadily increasing. Dr. Rainville is a Republican in politics.

Dr. Rainville married, December 18, 1910, Elizabeth La Rose, daughter of Simeon and Mary (Closset) La Rose, and to them has been born one child, Frederic F.

JOHN OWEN (2) PECKHAM—Among the eighteen associates of William Coddington, who, under the inspiration of Roger Williams, went out from Massachusetts to found a plantation, was John Peckham, who was of Newport, Rhode Island, in 1638, and there died in 1681, his wife, Mary (Clarke) Peckham, dying in 1648. From John and Mary (Clarke) Peckham the line of descent to John Owen Peckham, farmer and coal dealer of Norwich, Connecticut, is traced through several generations to Benjamin Peckham, who was born in Rhode Island, settled in Ledyard, Connecticut, and married Lucy Wilcox, who also was born in Rhode Island, they the parents of fifteen children. Descent continues through their son, Nathan Peckham, and his wife, Sarah (Perkins) Peckham, both of whom died in Ledyard, Connecticut. They were the parents of five children, one of whom was a son, John Owen (1) Peckham, father of John Owen (2) Peckham, of Norwich, Connecticut.

John Owen (1) Peckham was born in Ledyard, Connecticut, February 22, 1817, and died December 11, 1902, at Preston, Connecticut. He was for several years engaged in farming in New York State, but in 1842, returned to Connecticut, and purchased a farm at Preston, in New London county. He brought his farm of seventy-three acres to a high state of cultivation and prospered abundantly. He was a Democrat in politics, a deacon of the Baptist church, and a man highly esteemed in his community. Mr. Peckham married, in 1840, Margaret Connor, of New York, who died in 1857, in Preston, leaving four children: 1. Mary L., who married Giles H. Bliven. 2. Nancy A., who married Albert M. Brown. 3. Robert M., who married (first) Fannie E. Brown, (second) Hannah Peckham. 4. Clarissa, who married William H. Bennett. Mr. Peckham married (second) November 7, 1858, Sophia Louise Brown, who died May 16, 1908, daughter of Albert and Seviah (Maine) Brown, of Ledyard, Connecticut. They also were the parents of four children: 1. John Owen (2), of this review. 2. Sophia Louise, married Edward Hallowell. 3. Joseph Tyler, married Hannah A. Story. 4. William Hazzard, who married, November 27, 1908, May Ruge. He died August 7, 1919.

John Owen (2) Peckham, eldest son of John Owen (1) and Sophia L. (Brown) Peckham, was born in Preston, Connecticut, August 12, 1859. He obtained his education in district public and select schools, continuing his school years until the age of seventeen, when he became his father's farm assistant, remaining at home until his twenty-third year. For three years following he was in the employ of Mrs. Lyman Randall, of East Great Plain, as her farm foreman. During that period he also ran a milk route in Norwich. He was next foreman on the farm of R. E. Turner, at Laurel Hill, Norwich, and while there, obtained a knowledge of the carpenter's trade.

In 1887 he leased the one hundred acre farm in Ledyard, known as the Theophilus Avery farm, and there brought his bride. In March, 1889, he bought a fine farm in Preston, near the Norwich city line, and cultivated its two hundred acres personally, with the help of a manager, and also conducted a general farm with a dairy department, selling the dairy product in Norwich until he sold out in September, 1913. He has been proprietor of a retail coal business in Norwich since March, 1914, and has prospered in every department of his business. Mr. Peckham is also greatly interested in flowers and makes a specialty of growing dahlias.

Mr. Peckham is a Republican in politics, but beyond grand jury duty has refused all public office. In religious faith he is a Baptist, and for years has served the church at Preston as a member of the Church Committee, assistant superintendent, also superintendent for several years of the Sunday school and librarian of same, his wife also an active worker until her death.

Mr. Peckham married (first) March 13, 1887, Anna Elizabeth Avery, who died August 4, 1913, daughter of Theophilus and Mary Lydia (Corning) Avery, her father a farmer. Two children were born to Mr. and Mrs. Peckham: Florence Belle, and Howard Clifton. Mr. Peckham married (second), October 17, 1914, Ivy Beatrice Otis, daughter of Frederic and Nellie Almira (McClure) Otis. Mr. Peckham is a man highly regarded for his fine business quality and his honorable, upright life.

FRANK CRANSKA—In 1885, Frank Cranska came to the Thames National Bank of Norwich, Connecticut, and has remained with that institution during the thirty-seven and one-half years which have since elapsed. He is the third eldest man in the bank in point of years of service and has won high standing as a business man. He is a son of James and Asenath (Randall) Cranska, his father coming to Connecticut from the State of Maine. He located in Thompson and there established a business and a home. His five sons have all secured honorable position in the business world, Cranska being a name particularly well known in the textile world, and Floyd Cranska among textile manufacturers.

James Cranska was born in Portland, Maine, April 17, 1815, and died in Thompson, Connecticut, in April, 1905. He spent his youth in Maine, coming in youthful manhood to Thompson, where for thirty years he was engaged in the shoe business. He was also for twenty years station agent at Grosvenor Dale on the New York, New Haven & Hartford Railroad in Windham county, Connecticut, thirty-nine miles north of Norwich, and was also postmaster of the village. He was a man of independence and enterprise, a good and useful citizen.

James Cranska married Asenath Randall, daughter of Calvin and Caroline Matilda (Blackmar) Randall, her father owner and manager of the Thompson Mills. Mr. and Mrs. Cranska were the parents of eight children: Helen, a resident of Thompson; Isabel, married George Ballard, of Thompson; Calvin, a factory superintendent of Towanda, Pennsylvania; Caroline Matilda, a resident of Thompson; Floyd, a textile manufacturer, and founder of the Cranska Thread Company of Worcester, Massachusetts, married Evelyn C. Briggs; Frank, of whom further; James, with B. B. & R. Knight, cotton manufacturers; William, deceased.

Frank Cranska was born in Thompson, Connecticut, September 4, 1857, and there was educated in the public schools. At the age of seventeen, in 1874, he entered the office employ of the Grosvenor Dale Company at Grosvenor Dale, Connecticut, that company being manufacturers of cotton goods. He remained with that company ten years and when he resigned, in 1880, he was filling the office of paymaster. In 1883 he entered the employ of the B. B. & R. Knight Company, at Manchaug, Massachusetts, as an accountant, and remained for two years with that largest individual cotton manufacturing concern in the world. In 1885 he located in Norwich, Connecticut, where he entered the clerical service of the Thames National Bank, and for thirty-seven and one-half years has continued with that bank, filling different positions. Mr. Cranska is a Republican in politics, a member of the Chamber of Commerce and of the Central Baptist Church.

He married in New York City, December 25, 1885, Lillian Wythe Leonard, daughter of Dr. Williams Robert and Adelaide Muriel (MacKees) Leonard, of New York. Dr. Williams Robert Leonard, born in Virginia, died in 1892, was a descendant of George Wythe, of Virginia, a signer of the Declaration of Independence. Adelaide Muriel (MacKees) Leonard, who died in Brooklyn, New York, in 1872, was a daughter of George W. and Sarah Louis (Vanderhoof) MacKees, of New Jersey. Mr. and Mrs. Cranska are the parents of five children, all born in Norwich: Marian Asenath, residing at home; Harold Wythe, a veteran of the American Expeditionary Force in France, Company K, 113th Infantry, 29th Division, now teller of the Irving National Bank of New York; Wesley Randall, a veteran of the war with Germany, serving in France with the 304th Engineers, 79th Division, American Expeditionary Force; Wallace Russell (twin of Wesley Randall), died aged two and one-half years; Rosalind Joyce, residing with her parents. The family home is in Norwich, on Laurel Hill avenue.

CLAUDIUS VICTOR PENDLETON, JR.—One of the leading figures of Norwich today is Claudius V. Pendleton, Jr., sporting goods and automobile dealer, and representative to the State Assembly. Mr. Pendleton comes of an old New England family, the name being of Gaelic origin, signifying the summit of a hill, from pendle, the summit, and dun, a hill.

Claudius Victor Pendleton, Sr., was born March 14, 1851. He is a graduate of Yale College, with the degree of Civil Engineer, and while still a young man was the head of an independent business in the building of bridges. For many years he was superintendent of construction with the American Bridge Company, and later was inspector for that concern. At one time he was with the Berlin Iron and Bridge Company, of East Berlin, Connecticut. He married Phebe J. Johnson, who was born in September, 1850.

Claudius Victor Pendleton, Jr., was born in Norwich, Connecticut, June 11, 1885. His education, begun in the public schools of the city, was continued through grammar school and completed in the Norwich Free Academy, which he attended for three and one-half years. His first active interest in life was semi-professional baseball, especially throughout the State of Maine, his position being catcher. In the year 1910 Mr. Pendleton established himself in business in Norwich in the sale of motorcycles and sporting goods, and the interest became very successful. In 1919 he extended his operations to include the sale of Hupmobile cars, and he now handles a large business, continuing all branches as outlined, except motorcycles. Mr. Pendleton's business activities are not, however, the only avenues of usefulness in which he is a familiar figure. A Republican by political affiliation, he has for years been a worker in the party's behalf, always upholding the broader interests of the people in its councils, and some years ago was elected alderman. In the fall of 1920 he was elected town representative to the Legislature of the State. Fraternally, Mr. Pendleton is widely connected, being a member of Somerset Lodge, No. 34, Free and Accepted Masons; Franklin Chapter, No. 4, Royal Arch Masons; Franklin Council, No. 3; Columbian Commandery, No. 4. He is a member of all the Scottish Rite bodies, holding the thirty-second degree in this order, and is a member of Sphinx Temple, Ancient Arabic Order Nobles of the Mystic Shrine. He is also a member of Benevolent and Protective Order of Elks, No. 130, and Uncas Lodge, No. 11, Independent Order of Odd Fellows, and of Palmyra Encampment, No. 3, of the Odd Fellows. He is a member of the Arcanum Club of Norwich, and of Trinity Episcopal Church. His chief recreative interests are hunting and fishing.

Mr. Pendleton married, October 5, 1918, Blanche Hall, daughter of George Everett and Annie B. (Harvey) Hall, her father a prominent woolen manufacturer and business man of this city.

MARTIN E. MULLEN, D.D.S.—Among the younger professional men of New London county, Connecticut, Dr. Mullen is counted among the successful dental surgeons, and with offices in Taftville, he is handling a prosperous and growing practice. Dr. Mullen is a native of Windham county, this State, and prepared for his professional career in the leading institutions of the East. He is a son of Joseph M. and Josephine (Boucher) Mullen, both his parents having been born in Canada. His father, who was for many years active in Willimantic in the grocery business, dealing also in meat, fish and bakery, died in the year 1915. His mother is still living.

Dr. Mullen was born in the city of Willimantic, Connecticut, August 17, 1890. His elementary and intermediate studies were pursued at St. Joseph's and St. Mary's parochial schools in his native place, and he also attended the Windham High School, at Willimantic. For his classical course he attended Niagara University, at Niagara Falls, New York, after which he entered the Baltimore College of Dental Surgery, from which he was graduated in the class of 1917. He has since practiced in Taftville, with the exception of seven months, during which period he served in the United States army, being stationed at Camp Devens, Massachusetts. He was discharged from the service on January 27, 1918, after which he came direct to Taftville, and began his professional career, purchasing the practice of Dr. Raymond Couture. He has thus far been very successful, and is counted among the rising professional men of this section.

In public affairs Dr. Mullen takes only the interest of a progressive citizen. He is a member of the Connecticut State Dental Association, and the Horace Hayden Odontological Society of Baltimore. Fraternally, he is identified with the Benevolent and Protective Order of Elks, and also is a member of the fourth degree, Knights of Columbus. He is a member of the Church of the Sacred Heart.

Dr. Mullen married, in Willimantic, in 1919, Mary Ellen Cheney, a graduate nurse, who was born in Willimantic, and is the daughter of Edward and Anne (Peltier) Cheney. Dr. and Mrs. Mullen have one son, Martin, Jr.; they reside in Taftville, but are widely known in both Willimantic and Norwich.

CARLOS CURTIS PECK—Peck is an honored New England name and has been worthily borne by sons of the family for many generations, in both business and in the professions. Carlos C. Peck, of New London and Norwich, Connecticut, belongs to the Bridgeport branch of the family, his father, Eugene B. Peck, being an eminent member of the New England bar. Carlos C. Peck chose a business career and is one of the successful merchants of New London, Connecticut.

Eugene Benjamin Peck was born in Bridgeport, Connecticut, April 4, 1854, and died in the city of his birth, April 19, 1913. He received his early education in Bridgeport grade and high schools, and then, deciding upon the legal profession, he entered Yale Law School, whence he was graduated Bachelor of Laws, class of 1875. The same year he began the practice of law in Bridgeport and there continued an honorable career until his retirement. He married Mary Curtis, who was born in Bridgeport, October 18, 1856, and died in that city, May 28, 1919; they were the parents of twin sons: Richard Eugene, who married Violet Smith and resides in New York City; and Carlos Curtis, of further and extended note.

Carlos Curtis Peck was born in Bridgeport, Connecticut, July 1, 1877. He passed through the grade and high school courses of Bridgeport public schools, finishing with the high school graduation class of 1897. He then entered Trinity College, Hartford, Connecticut, whence he was graduated, class of 1901. He at once entered business life, locating in Philadelphia, Pennsylvania, in 1901, and there remaining until 1912, as assistant superintendent of the Nelson Valve Company. In 1912 he returned to Bridgeport, where he was appointed assistant superintendent of production for the Bridgeport Brass Company, a promotion he retained for four years. In 1916 he became manager of the Standard Brass & Copper Tube Company, of New London, Connecticut, remaining in that position for two years. In 1918 he organized the Connecticut Machinery & Sales Company, of Norwich, of which he was made president and manager. The company is capitalized at $50,000, deals in mill supplies and farm machinery at both wholesale and retail, and is well established in business. Mr. Peck is a member and former president of the New London Chamber of Commerce, 1918-19; is a member of the American Society of Mechanical Engineers, Trinity College, Chapter of Delta Phi; of the Thames Club of New London; and his religious connection is with St. James Protestant Episcopal Church of New London. He is a Republican in politics.

Mr. Peck married, in New London, Connecticut, November 30, 1918, Mary Palmer, the Rev. J. Romeyn Danforth officiating. The family home is in New London, although Mr. Peck's business is in Norwich.

Jacob Shalitt

Harry M. Shalett

JACOB SHALETT—As president of the Swiss Cleaners and Dyers, Inc., which he established in 1920, at No. 573 Bank street, New London, Connecticut, Mr. Shalett holds a recognized place in the business circles of the city. Since the inception of his business career, Mr. Shalett has been identified with this particular line of industry, and gained a thorough knowledge of it years ago when he was associated with his father, who was a dyer in Russia.

Jacob Shalett was born in Russia, town of Starya, October 30, 1883, the son of Moses and Mary (Kirlick) Shalett. There he was educated and lived until he left Russia. In the fall of 1911, Mr. Shalett came to this country, and after a two months' visit with his brother Nathan at New Haven, Connecticut, he went to New York City, where he secured employment as a cleaner and dyer, and remained in that city working with various prominent firms until the year of 1914. After leaving New York City, Mr. Shalett came to New London and opened a cleaning and dyeing establishment, a year later taking his brother, Harry M. Shalett (see following sketch), in the business with him. In April, 1920, the partnership dissolved, Mr. Shalett selling his share in the firm to his brother, Harry M. The following August a fireproof building was constructed by Jacob Shalett and equipped with the most modern machinery necessary for the various processes of cleaning and dyeing, the plant being known as the Swiss Cleaners and Dyers, Inc. Mr. Shalett has been very successful, and has developed a large and prosperous business.

Mr Shalett married, in 1917, Fannie Rosen, a native of Montville, Connecticut, the daughter of Louis and Sara Rosen, both of Russia. Mr. and Mrs. Shalett are the parents of two children: Marie, born March 12, 1918; Melvin, born March 9, 1920.

HARRY M. SHALETT—One of the busiest men in New London, Connecticut, is Harry M. Shalett, founder of Shalett's Cleaning and Dyeing Company, which is located on Montauk avenue, at Bank street. Since commencing business life in this country, Mr. Shalett has identified himself with local interests, gradually making his way to the position of prominence which he holds at the present time.

Harry M. Shalett was born in Starya, Russia, September 18, 1888, the son of Moses and Mary (Kirlick) Shalett, and brother of Jacob Shalett (see preceding sketch). The boy received his education in public schools and then became associated with his father in the cleaning and dyeing industry. In 1906 he came to this country and located at New Haven, where he attended Yale College, subsequently working with his brother Nathan, who had previously come to America and established a cleaning and dyeing business on his own account. Here Harry M. Shalett remained until 1914, when he removed to New London and, together with his brother Jacob, conducted a cleaning and dyeing establishment. Later, in 1920, he purchased the latter's interest in the business and has since carried it on alone.

We have spoken of Mr. Shalett as one of the busiest men in New London, and he is obliged to be so, for he is the head of a very busy and extensive enterprise, which has branches in Mystic, Norwich, and Westerly. The fact that he is so thoroughly occupied is largely owing to the constant care and consideration which he has bestowed on the upbuilding and maintenance of its interests. He is a member of the Chamber of Commerce, and the Rotary Club, and in the public affairs of the city he manifests the same qualities which characterize him as a business man—steadfast loyalty to principle, and promptness and efficiency in the performance of duty. In politics he is a Republican, and yet, while taking no active part in the affairs of the organization, his opinion is often sought and his word carries weight. Energetic as he is, he is too wise a man to ever sink into a mere business machine, and is never neglectful of the social side of life. He affiliates with the Benevolent and Protective Order of Elks, New London Lodge, No. 360, and is a member of the Harbour Club.

On May 5, 1913, Harry M. Shalett was united in marriage with Haddie Hughes, of Manchester, England, daughter of Gifford and Elizabeth (Berigon) Hughes, of Manchester. Mr. and Mrs. Shalett are the parents of two children: Elizabeth, born May 19, 1914; and Harry, born July 10, 1920.

JOSEPH NAPOLEON LAPOINTE—This is the record of a Canadian lad of eighteen years who came to the United States, and without a false move or mistake found his true vocation in a machine shop, and from apprentice boy passed through the various stages of promotion and development until he was established in a plant of his own, manufacturing for home and foreign use a machine bearing his own name and patentee—the Lapointe Broaching Machine. He has won fame and fortune, and is yet so much the man of action and energy that he has recently embarked in a new line of manufacturing in New London, Connecticut.

Joseph Napoleon Lapointe was born in St. Hyacinthe, a suburb of Montreal, Canada, March 31, 1861, son of Peter and Lucie (Perrault) Lapointe, both born in Canada of French parentage. Joseph N. Lapointe remained in the place of his birth until attaining the age of seventeen, and acquired a fair education there, to which he added to in the schools of Waterbury, Connecticut, his parents moving there in 1878. He entered the Benedict Brass Manufacturing Plant in Waterbury, Connecticut, as an apprentice to the machinist's trade, and proved so apt that his progress was very rapid. He became a skilled workman, and before passing out of his eighteenth year he was foreman of a department of the Waterbury Watch Company, the makers of that one time famous "Waterbury Watch." Mr. Lapointe's department was the making of machine parts, tools, etc., and there he remained seven years, being an important factor in the early development of the Waterbury Watch Company.

He was twenty-five years old when he left the Waterbury Watch Company to go with the Seth Thomas Watch Company, at the request of Mr. Heath, the general master-mechanic of the company. In his new position he was in charge of the "train room" at the Thomaston, Connecticut, plant of the company, a place he capably filled for three years. While with the watch company he invented several devices that were of value and upon which patents were issued, two in particular being most useful, viz.: an automatic rotary pinion and polishing machine. At the age of twenty-eight he left the Seth Thomas Watch Company and opened a small machine shop in Waterbury, Connecticut, a successful enterprise which he later sold to the Pearl Lake Company, Mr. Lapointe then engaging with the Pratt-Whitney Company of Hartford, Connecticut, in charge of experimental work for Mr. Whitney. A year later he was made foreman of a department at the plant. For fourteen years he continued in that position, and during that period his inventive genius was given full rein and he perfected and made many improvements in the manufacturing of both tools and tool making machines. While with Pratt-Whitney Company he devised and inaugurated the broaching system now in general use and known as the Lapointe Broaching System the world over.

From the Pratt-Whitney Company, Mr. Lapointe went to the Becker Milling Machine Company of Hyde Park, Massachusetts, organizing the plant upon a better basis and increasing its rate of production. After three years with that company he again established in business for himself, locating at No. 35 Hartford street, Boston, Massachusetts, where he perfected a broaching machine of his own design. He was short of funds at this period, but he weathered the crisis and in his little shop on Hartford street perfected the Lapointe Broaching Machine and received his first order for a machine. His first order came from the Mason Regulator Works of Milton, Massachusetts, his second from Mr. Clements, connected with an automobile manufacturing company of Paris, France. This machine, which cuts square holes of any size in steel, has been a boon to the automobile trade and has met with a ready sale. In 1902 Mr. Lapointe visited France, and from automobile manufacturers alone took orders for broaching machines totaling $18,000.

In 1906 he built a plant at Hudson, Massachusetts, the Lapointe Machine Tool Company, severing his connection with same in 1911, and then organizing the J. N. Lapointe Company at Marlboro, Massachusetts, for manufacturing broaching machines. In 1913 the company moved to New London, and erected a modern plant, which he operated successfully for six years, employing 200 hands. In 1919 he sold out, and in 1920 bought the Arnold Electric Tool Company, then located in New Haven, Connecticut. He at once removed the plant to New London, and in a new building which he erected is now manufacturing portable electric drills.

Such is the record of an energetic, capable business man, inventive genius and mechanical spirit. From the bottom of the ladder he has risen to a position of influence and has made for himself high reputation as an inventor and manufacturer of tools and machines. But he has not given himself entirely to the pursuit of fame and fortune as a mechanician and business man. He is an accomplished musician, and at Hartford was at the head of a military band bearing his name. He is fond of art, music, and the theatre, and is a man of most social, genial nature. His fortune has been gained through his own ability and genius, and he enjoys its possession. In politics he is a Republican.

Mr. Lapointe married, at Waterbury, Connecticut, June 1, 1880, Malvina Chicoine, and they are the parents of four children: Ralph R., a mechanical engineer of Hudson, Massachusetts; Frank Jerome, owner and manager of the American Broaching Machine Company of Ann Arbor, Michigan; Lionel, a surgeon of the United States navy, assigned to the battle ship "Virginia"; and Liana, wife of Beech Carpenter of New York City. The family home of the Lapointes is in New London, Connecticut, although the children have all founded homes of their own in other localities.

CONRAD KRETZER—A business man of Mystic, Connecticut, who has allied himself with everything pertaining to the welfare and advancement of the community, Conrad Kretzer deserves well of his fellow-townsmen. He was born in New London, Connecticut, August 26, 1864, third child of Conrad and Eva (Rosencranz) Kretzer, both born in Germany. His father, who was a shoemaker by trade, came to the United States as a young man and located at New London, Connecticut, in 1854, and there followed his trade until his death in 1864. To Mr. and Mrs. Kretzer were born three children; the mother died in Mystic.

The education of Conrad Kretzer was obtained in the public schools of Mystic, and after graduation from the high school he worked at various places until 1890, when he purchased the business of George Spink, general merchant of Mystic. The venture proved successful, the business growing consistently, until today Mr. Kretzer owns the large block at the corner of Pearl and Main streets, in which his store is located. He can review his life with satisfaction as he mentally traces his career from a working boy to his present position as a prosperous merchant. He has been the architect of his own fortune, and has won his way through pluck and that indomitable energy which in its last analysis is the fundamental characteristic of the successful business man.

The same qualities that Mr. Kretzer has exhibited

in the conduct of his own business he also has shown in the town business which has been committed to his care. For eleven years he has served as a member of the committee having charge of the town fire, water and light departments, and has proved himself a valuable public official.

Mr. Kretzer is affiliated with Charity and Relief Lodge, No. 72, Free and Accepted Masons; Benevolence Chapter, Royal Arch Masons; Mystic Council, No. 29, Royal and Select Masters; Palestine Commandery, Knights Templar; and is a thirty-second degree Mason of Norwich Consistory. Mr. Kretzer also affiliates with the Independent Order of Odd Fellows, Lodge No. 26, of Stonington, Connecticut, of which he is a past noble grand; and the Ancient Order of United Workmen, of which he is past master. In religion he is an Episcopalian, an attendant of St. Mark's Church of that denomination in Mystic. In politics he is a Democrat and from 1917 to the present (1922) he has been selectman of Groton.

On July 12, 1888, Conrad Kretzer was united in marriage with Lucy J. Bliven, a native of Stonington, Connecticut, daughter of George A. and Ruth A. (Richmond) Bliven. Mr. and Mrs. Kretzer are the parents of one child, Ruth E., who married Leonard J. Hermes, of the same town, and has a daughter, Isabella K., born in Mystic.

REGINALD LESTER LORD—One of the interesting old landmarks of Lyme, Connecticut, is the home of Reginald Lester Lord, the fourth generation born on this homestead, which he now owns. The farm comprises four hundred and some odd acres, the land having been a grant from the Mohican Indians, the original grant being signed by the mark of Chief Chapeto, who was a subordinate chief to Chief Uncas, the head of the Mohican tribe. It is situated in the village of Hamburg, and is still known as Chapeto Farm.

James Lincoln Lord, Mr. Lord's father, was born on this place, March 8, 1869, and for many years carried on an extensive lumber business in connection with the regular farming operations of the place. He is a son of Judah and Mary (Beckwith) Lord, and from childhood was active in the work of the farm until his retirement from business a few years ago. He has long held prominence in the public affairs of the town, having held all minor offices in the gift of the people, also represented the town in the State Legislature of 1897. He has always supported the Republican party, and of recent years has been a leader in its activities. He is still broadly interested in every phase of public progress.

Reginald Lester Lord, son of James Lincoln Lord, was born in the village of Hamburg, October 14, 1895. He received his early education at the district schools near his home, then later attended the Black Hall School, at Black Hall, Connecticut, a well known school for boys. Completing the course at this institution, Mr. Lord then entered Suffield Academy, at Suffield, Connecticut, from which he was graduated in 1915. He thereafter entered Wesleyan University, at Middletown, Connecticut, but left before his graduation to enlist in the United States Naval Reserve, on May 11, 1917, at New London. He was not called to active service until November of that year, and was then sent to the naval station at Newport, Rhode Island. Late in December, 1917, he was transferred to the United States Battleship "Massachusetts," to be trained as a gun captain. Completing his course in gunnery, he was returned to the Newport naval station to await assignment. Later he was placed in charge of a detail of men from New London, and all assigned to the United States steamship "Narragansett," his rating being boatswain, second class. He was at Wilmington, Delaware, until May 30, 1918, on which date he sailed for a naval base to take on supplies, then sailed for France, July 10, 1918, arriving on the twenty-first of the same month. He was returned to the United States the following June, when he was placed on inactive service. After his return, Mr. Lord attended the Massachusetts Agricultural College, at Amherst, in that State, then in March, 1920, returned to Lyme to take charge of his father's farm. He and his father are now (1922) engaged in the general mercantile business in Hamburg, under the name of James L. Lord & Son.

In the public affairs of his home town Mr. Lord, like his father, takes a deep interest, and supports the Republican party. He is a member of the Lyme Grange, Patrons of Husbandry, No. 147, and served as a lecturer of the organization. He is also a member of the New London County Farm Bureau, and is a member of the Lyme Post of the American Legion.

On October 9, 1920, Reginald L. Lord married, in London, England, Marie Florence Shepherd, daughter of Henry and Alice Shepherd, of that city. Mrs. Lord was born in London, England, March 4, 1899. On July 30, 1921, a son, James Lincoln (2) Lord, was born.

JOHN WILLIAM CALLAHAN, M.D., of Norwich, Connecticut, was born in that city on July 19, 1888, and is the son of Thomas F. and Julia (Kelley) Callahan.

His father is a native of Ireland, who came to this country when he was a young man, locating in Norwich, where he still resides, but is now retired from active business. His mother was born in county Kerry, Ireland, and Dr. Callahan is the only son. His sister, Mary E., is principal of the Broad Street School in Norwich. Both Miss Callahan and the doctor reside at home.

Dr. Callahan received his early education in the public schools of Norwich; then attended the Norwich Free Academy, from which he was graduated in 1907. In that same year he entered the College of Physicians and Surgeons, in Baltimore, Maryland, from which he was graduated in 1911 with the degree of Doctor of Medicine. In 1911 and 1912 Dr. Callahan practiced at St. Francis' Hospital, at Hartford, Connecticut. Then in 1912 he came to Norwich, and established himself in private practice in this city, where he has since been successfully engaged.

In 1917 Dr. Callahan offered himself to the Government, and on March 25, 1918, was called for military service. Commissioned as first lieutenant, he entered camp at the Army Medical School, at Washington, District of Columbia, later being assigned to the Medical Examining Board, at Camp Upton, New York, and to various other camps, including Camp Johnson, Florida. He was discharged from the service on May 19, 1919.

Dr. Callahan then returned to Norwich, and took up his practice here. He is now staff doctor of the William Backus Hospital of this city, and is a member of the Norwich Medical Society. He is also a member of the New London County Medical Society, and of the Connecticut State Medical Society. His college fraternity is the Phi Chi, and he is a member of the White Cross Council, No. 13, Knights of Columbus, of Norwich. In political affiliation he is a Democrat.

The doctor's family have always been members of the Roman Catholic church.

NATHANIEL LITTLEFIELD SHEFFIELD, JR.—The first Sheffield of this branch to settle in the town of Old Lyme, New London county, Connecticut, was Nathaniel L. Sheffield, Sr., who came from Block Island, Rhode Island, in early manhood, and there settled on a farm at Hackett's Point. The family trace back in England to William the Conqueror, and in New England to Amos Sheffield, who came from his native England in 1630, being then twenty-eight years of age. His grandson, Amos (2) Sheffield, settled in Newport, Rhode Island, and it was not until the sixth American generation that the family appeared in Connecticut, Rev. John Sheffield, a regularly ordained minister of the Methodist Episcopal church, born in Rhode Island, November 20, 1798, settling in North Stonington while a young man, and before entering the ministry. This branch of the family settled on Block Island, Rhode Island, and there Nathaniel Littlefield Sheffield, Sr., was born, July 14, 1844. He was a young man when he came to Hackett's Point, Old Lyme, Connecticut, and there he long remained on the farm which he purchased there. Later he bought a farm in the Blackhall section of the town, where he now resides (June, 1921). He married Caroline Elizabeth Champion, born in South Lyme, Connecticut; she died when her only son, Nathaniel L. (2), was a child, leaving him to the care of his father and three elder sisters: 1. Caroline Elizabeth, who was born in Old Lyme, married Franklin J. Howard, also born in Old Lyme, and they have four children: Bertha, Daniel, Clarence, and Theodora Howard. 2. Jennie Louise. 3. Lillian Leora. He remembers no other mother than these three sisters, and they have always been devoted to one another.

Nathaniel Littlefield Sheffield, only son of Nathaniel Littlefield and Caroline Elizabeth (Champion) Sheffield, was born in the town of Old Lyme, New London county, Connecticut, January 14, 1878. He was educated in the public schools, and there has spent his life, with the exception of two years passed in Middletown, Connecticut. He began business life as clerk in the general store owned and conducted by James A. Roland, leaving his employ to take a position in Middletown. After two years there he returned to Old Lyme and resumed his old position. In 1910 Mr. Roland retired from active business life, but before doing so, incorporated his business as J. A. Roland & Company, retail general merchants. Mr. Sheffield was given a chance to enter the corporation, which he did, and from its beginning has been treasurer and general manager. He is the managing head and guiding genius of the business, which is an extensive one. His entire business experience has been practically with this one house, he being thoroughly familiar with the minutest detail, and understands the every need of the community and the store he serves.

Mr. Sheffield takes a deep interest in the cause of education as represented by the public schools, and since 1904 has served his town as a member of the school board, for thirteen years being chairman of same.

Mr. Sheffield is a member of Pythagoras Lodge, No. 45, Free and Accepted Masons; Crystal Lodge, No. 88, Independent Order of Odd Fellows; and in politics is a Republican, but very independent.

Mr. Sheffield married Margaret Dickey Rutherford, born in Brooklyn, New York, daughter of James and Fanny Dickey. Mr. and Mrs. Sheffield are the parents of a son, Nathaniel Rutherford Sheffield, born November 29, 1911, at Old Lyme, Connecticut.

KOPLAND K. MARKOFF, M.D., son of Lazar and Sarah (Hurwich) Markoff, was born in Norwich, Connecticut, April 7, 1896. He attended Broadway grammar school, going thence to Norwich Free Academy. He was a student at New York University and the University of Vermont, receiving his degree from the medical department of the last named. He was interne at the Lying-In Hospital, New York City, in 1918; house surgeon at St. Vincent's Hospital, Bridgeport, Connecticut; resident physician at Utica Hospital, Utica, New York; and in 1920-21 was specialist at Manhattan Eye, Ear and Throat Hospital, New York City. In 1921 he was appointed to the visiting staff of Manhattan Eye, Ear and Throat Hospital, and is now practicing in Norwich, Connecticut, as eye, ear, nose and throat specialist, his office suite Nos. 103-104 Thayer building.

On January 17, 1918, Dr. Markoff enlisted in the Enlisted Medical Reserve Corps of the United States army, and served until honorably discharged, December 13, 1919. He is a member of the New London County Medical Society; American Medical Association; Norwich Medical Society; Tau Epsilon Phi fraternity; B'nai B'rith; and Knights of Pythias.

ASAHEL ROWLAND De WOLF—From 1885 until 1916 Mr. De Wolf was an active factor in the business life of the village of Niantic, New London county, Connecticut, and then, after thirty-one years of successful dealing in lumber, retired, and is spending the evening of life in contented ease. He comes from ancient Connecticut family long seated in Old Lyme, coming to that section of New London county from Wetherfield, Connecticut, where Edward De Wolf is first mentioned in 1664. Four years later, in 1668, he is mentioned in the records of Lyme. He was born in 1646, and by his wife, Alice, had a son, Stephen De Wolf, born in 1670, who died in 1702. The line of descent from Edward and Alice De Wolf, the American ancestors, to Asahel R. De Wolf, of Niantic, is through their son, Stephen (1) De Wolf, and his second wife, Hannah; their son, Stephen (2) De Wolf, and his wife, also Hannah; their son, Benjamin De Wolf, born in 1716, and his wife, Lucy Champion; their son, General Stephen De Wolf, and his three wives; his son, Jeremiah Winthrop De Wolf, and his wife, Mary Chadwick; their son, Winthrop Jeremiah De Wolf, and his wife, Hepzibah C. Anderson; their son, John Anderson De Wolf, and his first wife, Mary Abigail Rowland; their son, Asahel Rowland De Wolf, of the ninth American generation now (May, 1921) residing in the village of Niantic, in the town of East Lyme, a section of Connecticut to which his ancestor, Edward De Wolf came more than two and one-half centuries ago.

John Anderson De Wolf, of the eighth generation, was born in the town of Old Lyme, New London county, Connecticut, April 5, 1832, and there died in April, 1913. The death of his father, Winthrop Jeremiah De Wolf, in 1847, threw the burden of managing the home farm upon this boy of then fifteen, the eldest of six children. That burden he capably shouldered, but three years later he entered the mercantile life, and about 1863 he built a store at Black Hall and there conducted a prosperous business for twelve years, then sold his store to his brother, Roger De Wolf. He dealt heavily in cattle and real estate after giving up his store and continued most successfully until his retirement several years prior to his death. He represented Old Lyme in the State Legislature five terms, between 1866-1888, and held about all the leading offices of his town.

Mr. De Wolf married (first) in Old Lyme, November 3, 1855, Mary Abigail Rowland, who died January 12, 1858, daughter of Ashahel Rowland, of Old Lyme. Mrs. De Wolf left a son, Asahel Rowland De Wolf, whose career is hereinafter traced. John A. De Wolf married (second) November 21, 1860, Irene E. Pratt, born March 20, 1840, daughter of Henry Pratt, of Essex, Connecticut. They were the parents of a son, John Anderson (2), born November 30, 1877, who married Annie Rowland.

Asahel Rowland De Wolf, only son of John Anderson De Wolf and his first wife, Mary Abigail (Rowland) De Wolf, was born at Black Hall, in Old Lyme, New London county, Connecticut, June 16, 1857. He spent his early years at the home farm, attended the public school and was also a student at the Morgan School, Clinton, Connecticut. He continued a farmer at the homestead until reaching his twenty-fourth year, when he entered the store of his maternal uncle, J. A. Rowland, in Old Lyme, and there five years were passed in acquiring a thorough mercantile training which prepared him for the business in which his after-life was engaged.

In 1885 the young man, then twenty-eight years of age, formed a partnership with a paternal uncle, George W. De Wolf, and in May of that year established a lumber yard at Niantic, Connecticut, under the firm name of G. W. De Wolf & Company. That business was continued as a partnership until November 7, 1891, when George W. De Wolf retired and A. R. De Wolf succeeded him as head of the business. Mr. De Wolf continued the business in Niantic until January, 1916, when he sold out and retired from the firm with which he had been connected thirty-one years, twenty-five of those years as sole owner.

An Independent in politics, Mr. De Wolf has given much time to the public service. He served the town of East Lyme as first selectmen, a member of the Board of Assessors for three years, and has been road commissioner. He is treasurer of the Congregational church of Niantic, a member of the Ancient Order of United Workmen, the Order of United American Mechanics, and a man highly esteemed in his community.

Mr. De Wolf married, in Old Lyme, November 24, 1885, Mary Elizabeth Moley, born in Old Lyme, September 14, 1858, died February 26, 1919, daughter of Charles L. and Betsey (Ayres) Moley, of Feeding Hills, Massachusetts, later of Old Lyme, Connecticut. Mrs. De Wolf left a daughter, Clara Irene De Wolf, born in Niantic, Connecticut, March 15, 1891, married Milton Whited, of Albany, New York, and has two daughters: Catherine De Wolf, and Elizabeth Moley Whited; and one son, Milton Height Whited. Mr. De Wolf married (second) in February, 1921, at Niantic, Connecticut, Angeline (Rowland) Burns, born in Lyme, daughter of John and Julia (Anderson) Rowland, and widow of Edward Burns. By her first husband Mrs. De Wolf has a son, Edward Rowland Burns.

GEORGE HENRY CLARKE—The name of Clarke is one of great antiquity, and was probably used as early as the eleventh century. It means a learned person, one who could read and write ancient and mediaeval lore, and carried with it special honor in those early ages when even royalty was illiterate. John Clarke, of Shaneford, England, is said to have been a man of extraordinary goodness and fatherly spirit, deeply devoted to all his family, and much beloved by them. His sons were William, Thomas, Joseph and John. William's children were Mrs. Elizabeth Scottan, Ann, and Seth, who came to America. Thomas Clarke was the father of three children: William, of further mention; Mary, and Ann. Mary became the wife of John Adkins, and Ann became the wife of Josiah Shaw, both sisters living and dying in England. Thomas Clarke died in London, England, in 1817. Joseph Clarke, the third son of John Clarke and his wife Hannah, died without issue, and the descendants of Thomas received a small legacy from them in 1845. John, the youngest son of John Clarke, died in his early youth, having never married.

William Clarke, son of Thomas Clarke and great-grandfather of the subject of this sketch, came to America in June of 1800, and after residing in this country for about eighteen years, spent a year in England, then returning to America in 1819, made his home in Exeter, Otsego county, New York, until his death, which occurred in 1842. William Clarke, of Exeter, had a son William, who was the father of Adriel E. Clarke.

Adriel Ely Clarke was born in Otsego county, New York, in 1840. As a young man he enlisted in the Civil War, in Company B, 101st Regiment, New York Volunteer Infantry, and served in the Army of the Potomac, taking part in fifty-two campaigns. Following his honorable discharge he returned home and took up farming, later in life locating at West Winfield, in Herkimer county, New York, near Utica, where he died October 25, 1880. He married Frances Amelia Countryman, who was born in Starkville, New York, and now resides with her son, George H., in Niantic. Adriel Ely and Frances Amelia (Countryman) Clarke were the parents of six children: Frank William; George Henry, of further mention; Florence Mary; Carrie L.; Grace A.; and Charles A.

George Henry Clarke was born in Schenevus Otsego county, New York, August 16, 1868. He was one year old when his parents removed to West Winfield, and there he attended school, securing a broadly practical education along general lines. At the age of twenty-two years he was station agent for the New York Central Railroad at various stations, and was thus engaged for eight years. In February of 1900 he entered the Utica Steam Gauge Company as superintendent, remaining with that company in the same capacity until 1912. The following year he spent in Jersey City, then came to Niantic, Connecticut, and here established a factory under the name of the New England Steam Gauge Company. This was in 1913, and Mr. Clarke has now passed nearly nine successful years, much of his progress being due to his own persistence, thrift and industry. Possessed of business acumen, his upright methods have gained the confidence of the trade, and his personal integrity has placed him high in the respect and esteem of his fellow-citizens.

In politics Mr. Clarke is an Independent voter, and his fraternal affiliations are the following: Member of Baynew Lodge, No. 120, of which he is master; and of Mohawk Lodge, No. 224, Knights of Pythias, of Frankfort, New York.

Mr. Clarke married, on March 28, 1895, Emma L. Kirsh, who was born in Oswego county, New York, February 22, 1878, and is a daughter of John P. and Laura J. (Minckler) Kirsh. They are the parents of one son, Lester George Clarke, born at Harrisville, New York, April 26, 1896, who married Shirley Lamphere, and is the father of two children: Alison and Donald.

JOHN CARL STEVENS—For more than two decades Mr. Stevens has been the proprietor of a mill hotel in Baltic, Connecticut, and is one of the well known men of the town. He is the son of William and Mary (Chamberlain) Stevens, his father born in Topsham, Vermont. William Stevens was employed on a Vermont farm until youthful manhood, then learned the carpenter's trade, which he followed until his death in Newbury, Vermont, in 1890. His wife, Mary (Chamberlain) Stevens, died in June, 1865. They were the parents of three children: John Carl, of further mention; Ellen, who married Guy Granger, and resides in Passumpsic, Vermont; and William, deceased.

John Carl Stevens was born in Barnet, Vermont, June 7, 1861, and there attended public schools. But school years were soon over, and at an early age he became an employee of Baker's Paper Mill, at Bradford, Vermont. For three years he remained in that mill, then spent a year as a farm-hand with the Stater Company, at Webster, Massachusetts. At the end of that period he located with the Valley Falls Company, at Valley Falls, Rhode Island, there remaining fourteen years, becoming their farm manager. He then went to Baltic, Connecticut, where he continues proprietor of the Stevens House, a prosperous hostelry.

Mr. Stevens is a Republican in politics, and is influential in party affairs in the town of Sprague. He has been a delegate to State conventions of his party for the past twelve years, and is influential in his district. He served as assessor from 1908 until 1910, as first selectman of the town of Sprague, 1910-12, and as third selectman, 1912-14. He is a member of Canonchet Tribe, No. 10, Improved Order of Red Men of Valley Falls, Rhode Island; Shetucket Camp, No. 10,464, Modern Woodmen of America, Versailles, Connecticut; Gardner Lodge, No. 46, Knights of Pythias, of Norwich, Connecticut, and also is past chancellor commander of that lodge.

Mr. Stevens married Isabel Morse, born in Canada, and they are the parents of two sons: 1. Roswell C., a veteran of the Spanish-American War, married Minnie Russell, and resides in Moosup. Con-

John C. Stevens

necticut. 2. Clarence E., a soldier of the United States during the war with Germany, 1917-18; he was called for service April 23, 1918, and was honorably discharged July 1, 1919. He was on duty at Camp Upton for fifteen months, his duty the mustering in and out of men sent to that camp. He is now associated with his father in the management of the Stevens House at Baltic.

ROBERT HENRY NOBLE—The grandparents of Robert Henry Noble came to Old Lyme, New London county, Connecticut, when their son, John Henry Noble, was a boy. He was born in Kingston, New York, October 7, 1856, but by far the greater part of his life was spent in Old Lyme. He became a substantial farmer and prominent in the public life of his town, holding most of the offices within the gift of his neighbors, and in 1899 and 1911 represented the district in the Connecticut House of Representatives. He was a member of Pythagoras Lodge, No. 45, Free and Accepted Masons. He died from the effects of an operation, April 12, 1911. He married Josephine Emelie Gibson, born in Brooklyn, New York, April 17, 1859. Mr. and Mrs. Noble were the parents of five children: Mary Louise, Joseph Gibson, Martie Thomas, James Londes, and Robert Henry, of whom further.

Robert Henry Noble, youngest of the children of John Henry and Josephine Emelie (Gibson) Noble, was born in Old Lyme, New London county, Connecticut, December 14, 1880, and was educated in the public schools. Following school days he became his father's farm assistant, remaining at the home farm until reaching legal age, when he entered the employ of J. F. Bugbee in his general store in Old Lyme, and has continued in mercantile life until the present, 1921. In politics Mr. Noble is a Democrat, and has long been prominent in the public life of his town. He has held nearly all town offices, and is now serving as town clerk and judge of probate. In 1919 he represented his district in the Connecticut House of Representatives, as his father had before him, and made an equally good record as an efficient legislator. In religious faith he is a Congregationalist. In fraternal life Mr. Noble is equally prominent, having held the highest honors of both the Masonic and Odd Fellow lodges. He is a past master of Pythagoras Lodge, No. 45, serving in 1915 and in 1919; is a companion of Burning Bush Chapter, No. 29, Royal Arch Masons; was twelve years secretary of Crystal Lodge, No. 88, Independent Order of Odd Fellows; and is a past noble grand of that lodge.

Robert H. Noble married, June 21, 1905, Ruth Bugbee, born in Old Lyme, July 21, 1885, only daughter of James F. and Louise (Swan) Bugbee. Mr. and Mrs. Noble are the parents of two children, both born in Old Lyme: Marjorie, born March 31, 1907; Louise, born March 18, 1909.

CAPTAIN ROBERT I. MACHETT—Widely known in Mystic and vicinity, and highly esteemed as one of the progressive business men of that locality, Captain Robert I. Machett is a representative citizen of New London county. He is descended from various early antecedents who bore their part in the military service of the Colonies and of the young American Republic.

John Machett, Captain Machett's father, was born at Cornwall Landing, on the Hudson, in the State of New York, was educated there, and became an expert potter. He was engaged in the manufacture of pottery until war broke out between the North and South, when he enlisted in defense of the Union and saw hard service with the 127th Regiment, Illinois Volunteer Infantry. He was taken prisoner and was confined in the Andersonville Stockade, but escaped with his life, and after the war ended went with his regimental comrades to Illinois, settling in Pulaski. There he was actively engaged in business as a pottery manufacturer until the time of his death. He married Louisa Parks, who died in Mystic, Connecticut, the home of her family for generations. Through the maternal line Captain Machett is closely connected with the historic period in the War of 1812, when the southern communities of New London county were the center of attention by the young nation and the center of attack by the British Imperial Navy. Captain Machett's mother was a daughter of Isaac and Mary (Billinghurst) Parks, Isaac being the owner of a windmill on Mason's Island. The English landed at the island, and, coming ashore, ordered Isaac Parks to get up in his night clothes and grind corn for them. This accomplished, they further commanded him to accompany them on board and pilot them up the river. It was a very dark and foggy night, but he was thoroughly familiar with the harbor, and ran them aground on Clam Island. They were anxiously looking ahead, and, pushing the tiller hard over as the boat touched bottom, he stepped over the side and began wading ashore. He moved away from her broadside in the fog and darkness, leaving them shooting at him, as they believed, over the stern. He escaped in safety, and the little company of soldiers on duty at Fort Rachel heard the commotion and opened fire on the boat. Isaac Parks was a farmer throughout his lifetime, and lived long to recount to his children and grandchildren the experiences of that exciting time. John and Louisa (Parks) Machett were the parents of two children: Robert I., of further mention; and Augusta L., who became the wife of John Albert Williams, of Waterford, also in this county, and there died.

Robert I. Machett, only son of John and Louisa (Parks) Machett, was born in Mystic, town of Stonington, New London county, Connecticut, May 13, 1856. West Mystic, in the town of Groton, was his mother's home, and there he spent his youth and obtained a broadly practical education in the public schools. In his earlier years he followed the sea, and at the age of thirty-one became captain of a sailing vessel, the "Osprey." Captain Machett sailed the schooner "Osprey" until she was sold to the Pensacola Ice and Fish Company, of Pensacola, Florida, in 1891. At that time he settled in West Mystic, where he has since been engaged in the ice business, developing a largely successful interest, and becoming one of the substantial business men of the community, esteemed by all and taking the part of a progressive citizen in the daily life of the town. Captain Machett also gave to his native State his services in her military organization, enlisting on April 2, 1875, in Company A, 3rd Regiment, Connecticut National Guard, for a period of five years, and received his honorable discharge from the military service of the State on June 25, 1880, by order of the commander-in-chief, on account of the expiration of his enlistment. Captain Machett is prominent fraternally, being a member of Relief Lodge, No. 72, Free and Accepted Masons, of Mystic; Benevolence Chapter, Royal Arch Masons, also of Mystic; Mystic Council, Royal and Select Masters; and Palestine Commandery, Knights Templar, of New London. He is a member of the Union Baptist Church of Mystic.

Captain Machett married, January 10, 1883, Annette V. Burdick, only daughter of Benjamin L. and Jane (Gilroy) Burdick, and granddaughter of Samuel and Vianna (Porter) Burdick, of Norwich, Connecticut, all these names belonging to old New London county families of note and distinction. Mrs. Machett's parents are both now deceased, and her only brother, Robert B. Burdick, is a resident of New London.

JOSEPH ROBINSON—For many years active in the industrial world, and in later life prominent in public matters, Joseph Robinson, of East Lyme, Connecticut, is thoroughly representative of the citizenship which is not only progressive but, in a broad sense, constructive.

Mr. Robinson is a son of George and Mary (Shirt) Robinson. George Robinson was born in England and came to the United States as a young man. He was a painter by trade, and, settling in Woonsocket, Rhode Island, he followed this trade as long as he lived, but was cut down in the prime of his life, and died when Joseph was a child. His wife, who was also born in England, died in 1906, at the age of eighty-eight years, at Woonsocket. They were the parents of three children: Grace Elizabeth, who died in childhood; Ruth, who became the wife of James Farrar; and Joseph, all born in Woonsocket.

Joseph Robinson was born February 28, 1845, and was reared in Woonsocket, receiving his education in the public schools of that city. He began life as a mill worker there, continuing this activity until 1873. On December 23 of that year he came to Taftville, Connecticut, to accept the position of chief engineer of the Ponemah Mills. This plant is said to be the largest textile factory under one roof in the world, and Mr. Robinson ably filled this responsible position until 1909, when he retired from active work. At that time he removed to Flanders, a small community in the town of East Lyme, and has since made his home in this village. He has become very prominent in the political and social life of East Lyme. By political affiliation a Republican, he has taken a keen interest in the progress of the party in this town since his residence here, and with his long experience and ripened judgment, is considered a wise counsellor in all party deliberations. He is a member of the school committee, is justice of the peace, and held the office of town treasurer for a period of eight years. Fraternally Mr. Robinson is well known. He is a member of Woonsocket Lodge, No. 13, Free and Accepted Masons; was a member of Woonsocket Commandery, No. 23, of which he was elected prelate in 1873. On September 17, 1887, he took a demit from that commandery andjoined Columbian Commandery, No. 4, of Norwich. He has been a member of the Norwich Consistory, Ancient Accepted Scottish Rite, since 1906. He is also a member of Niantic Lodge, No. 17, Independent Order of Odd Fellows.

Mr. Robinson married (first) Catherine Virginia Owen, who was born in Salisbury, North Carolina, and they were the parents of three children: George Henry, who was born in Woonsocket, Rhode Island, and died in infancy; Joseph, who was born in Taftville, is a graduate of the medical department of Columbia University, now a successful physician and surgeon of Anaheim, California, married Julia Corcoran, of Cornwall, Connecticut, and has one child, Marjorie Hill Robinson; and Samuel Eli, who was born in Taftville, and died in infancy. Mr. Robinson married (second) Mary Hill Chapman, who was born in Centre Brook, Connecticut, daughter of Frederick William and Adalie Douglas (Beach) Chapman, now residents of East Lyme. Mrs. Robinson died August 30, 1921, and is survived by her husband.

ALBERT JAMES SINAY, D.D.S.—Advancement in any of the learned professions is not so much the result of fortuitous circumstances or of influence as it is the result of individual merit, application and skill. When these are combined with ambition and a fixed determination to achieve success, the desired result is inevitable. Dr. Albert James Sinay, of Norwich, Connecticut, although young to have achieved a reputation in the profession of dentistry, is fairly on his way to acquiring more than local fame. He was born in Linden, New Jersey, July 8, 1888, son of Alexander and Adelia (Kalmary) Sinay. Alexander Sinay was born in Lorraine, Germany, at one time French territory, and came to this country when very young. For many years he has been overseer of the starching department of the United States Finishing Company of Norwich. To Mr. and Mrs. Sinay have been born four children, Albert James, being the second child.

The childhood of Dr. Sinay was passed in his native place, Linden, and it was there that the preparatory portion of his education was obtained. In 1895 he came to Norwich, and it was here that he was prepared for college, subsequently entering the dental department of the University of Maryland, having decided to make that profession his career. He took the usual course and graduated with the class of 1912, taking the degree of Doctor of Dental Surgery. He then returned to Norwich, Connecticut, and opened his office at No. 321 Main street. Since that time he has made his headquarters at this place.

On January 1, 1915, Dr. Sinay married Bessie T. Crary, daughter of Charles K. and Ida (Terry) Crary, and they are the parents of one child, Ralph, born December 1, 1917. The family attend the Broadway Congregational Church of Norwich.

With a vigorous and luminous intellect, Mr. Sinay combines strength of character and a genial disposition. This union of traits explains in a large measure his success and gives promise of even more signal achievements in the future. He is a close student, keeping fully abreast of modern thought in all matters pertaining to his profession and possesses the high esteem and confidence of the general public.

HAROLD MONTAGUE DUNBAR—The founder of the family of which Harold Montague Dunbar is a member was Joseph Dunbar, a native of Scotland, who in 1790 was living in Watertown, Connecticut. His death date is fixed by the pension records as February 2, 1813. The Daughters of the American Revolution Lineage Book, Volume XIV, page 338, gives the following:

"Joseph Dunbar served in Sheldon's Dragoons, and was wounded at the battles of Germantown and Whitemarsh in 1777. His name is found on the invalid pension list of New London county, Connecticut. He was born in Scotland." He married Martha Sutliffe, born June 26, 1755, daughter of Captain John and Martha (Bassett) Sutliffe. Children, from family records, and the Daughters of the American Revolution Lineage Book: Giles, Bassett; Ralph, of whom further; Lola, and Martha.

Ralph Dunbar, son of Joseph and Martha (Sutliffe) Dunbar, was born October 20, 1789, died in Torrington, Connecticut, January 14, 1846. He married Anna Starkweather, who was born August 18, 1791, died November 4, 1856, daughter of Thomas and Sybil (Anderson) Starkweather. Children, the first born in Winchester, the others at Torrington, Connecticut: Hiram, born April 26, 1813; Nelson, born May 20, 1815; Mary Ann, born June 3, 1817; Lyman, born May 2, 1819; Martin, born February 15, 1821; Harriet, born May 29, 1824; Albert, born January 29, 1827; Frederick, born May 15, 1829; Emma (Emeline), born May 1, 1830; Walter, of whom further; and Minerva, born May 7, 1839.

Walter Dunbar, son of Ralph and Anna (Starkweather) Dunbar, was born at Torrington, Connecticut, October 20, 1833. He married, in 1871, Rachel Irene Dunbar (see 2nd Dunbar line) at Bridgeport, Connecticut. Children: Walter L., of whom further; and Howard.

Walter L. Dunbar, son of Walter and Rachel Irene (Dunbar) Dunbar, was born in Bridgeport, Connecticut, died there November 2, 1917. He was reared and educated in this city, completing his education with a special course at Harvard University, and throughout his active years was associated with the Union Metallic Cartridge Company, filling the position of assistant comptroller in that organization. He was a man of strong capabilities and was held in high esteem by his associates. He married, September 23, 1896, Omega Harden Foster, and they were the parents of: Harold Montague, of whom further; Helen Irene, born August 9, 1900; and Walter Beverly, born February 25, 1908. The mother resides at Stratford, Connecticut.

Harold Montague Dunbar, son of Walter L. and Omega Harden (Foster) Dunbar, was born in Bridgeport, Connecticut, January 11, 1898. He attended the public schools of Stratford and upon graduation from high school became a clerk in the Stratford Trust Company, later entering the First National Bank of Bridgeport in the same department and becoming manager of the collection. Subsequently, he received an appointment as assistant National Bank Examiner in the Second Federal Reserve District of New York City, and in August, 1921, he became secretary and treasurer of the Jewett City Trust Company. This office he fills to the present time, bringing to its responsible duties a varied and valuable experience in financial affairs.

Mr. Dunbar is a Republican in political faith and his church is the Methodist. In the Masonic order, he holds membership in St. Johns Lodge, Free and Accepted Masons, Stratford, Connecticut; Jerusalem Chapter, Royal Arch Masons, Bridgeport, Connecticut; and De Witt Clinton Commandery, No. 27, Knights Templar, of Brooklyn, New York. He is also a member of Sphinx Temple, Ancient Arabic Order Nobles of the Mystic Shrine, of Hartford, Connecticut.

(Second Dunbar Line.)

Robert Dunbar, immigrant ancestor of this line, was born in Scotland in 1630. He and his wife, Rose, settled in Hingham, Massachusetts, in 1655. It was the general opinion that he brought with him a considerable sum of money to begin life in the new country, inasmuch as for years there were but two men in the town who paid a higher tax than he. He died October 5, 1693, and his wife, November 10, 1700.

John Dunbar, son of Robert and Rose Dunbar, was born in Hingham, Massachusetts, December 1,

1657. He married (first), July 4, 1679, Mattithiah, daughter of George and Catherine Aldridge, of Dorchester, Massachusetts. He married (second), July 24, 1700, Elizabeth Beecher, of New Haven, Connecticut. In 1697 or 1698 he removed to New Haven.

John (2) Dunbar, son of John and Mattithiah (Aldridge) Dunbar, married, June 14, 1716, Elizabeth Fenn, born April 29, 1692, daughter of Edward and Mary (Thorpe) Fenn, who were married November 15, 1688. She died in 1751. John Dunbar died May 13, 1746.

John (3) Dunbar, son of John (2) and Elizabeth (Fenn) Dunbar, was born September 28, 1724, in Wallingford, Connecticut. He married Temperance Hall, born in Wallingford, April 16, 1727, died May 26, 1770. Her husband died before that date, and both were buried in Plymouth, Connecticut. During the Revolution he was one of three commissaries in Waterbury, chosen to furnish supplies to the Continental army.

Miles Dunbar, son of John (3) and Temperance (Hall) Dunbar, born in Wallingford or Plymouth, removed to Oblong, New York, prior to 1818. He was a fife major during the Revolution; enlisted March 31, 1777, at Waterbury, Connecticut; served until discharged, March 30, 1780, in New York. He became overtaxed at the battle of Monmouth, and on his way home was taken sick at Newtown, New York. His expenses at this time were paid by the State of New York, and the same State afterwards, in 1818, pensioned him. After the war he studied law with Esquire Butler, and followed that vocation during the remainder of his life. In 1776 he joined the Congregational church at Plymouth. He married, May 1, 1779, Tryphose, daughter of Isaac and Rebecca Butler.*

Isaiah Dunbar, son of Miles and Tryphose (Butler) Dunbar, married (first) Rachel Beach; (second) Cloie Fenn. He was the father of six children, four by his first wife, two by his second: Charles, Henry, of whom further, Bertha, Thaddeus, Lucius, Clarissa.

Henry Dunbar, son of Isaiah and Rachel (Beach) Dunbar, married, and had among his children William H. and Rachel Irene, who married Walter Dunbar (see first Dunbar line).

---

*The above, the second line of Dunbar, is from "Genealogical and Family History of the State of Connecticut," Volume II, pages 788-9.

WILLIAM EDWARDS MANNING—In the business, social and public life of Yantic, Connecticut, William Edwards Manning is a prominent figure. Coming of an old New London county family, active, public-spirited, and always abreast of the times, Mr. Manning is one of the leading men of the town.

Edward Manning, Mr. Manning's father, was born in the town of Lebanon, Connecticut, on the old Manning homestead, which had been in the family for many years. He received his early education in district schools of the town, then attended high school at Ellington, Tolland county, Connecticut. After leaving school he became associated with his brother, Dr. J. H. Manning, of Pittsfield, Massachusetts, in the drug business, for which the exacting demands of the doctor's profession left no time. This continued until 1861, thus covering a period of five years. In that year Edward Manning returned to Lebanon, his birthplace, and built a residence on a portion of the old homestead, and conducted farming until his death in 1892. He married Lucy E. Robinson, of Franklin, and she is still living, and in excellent health, at eighty-eight years of age, being now a resident of Yantic. Their four children are all now living: E. Melville, residing in Lebanon on the home place; George, who married Rose Fuller, now resides in Yantic; William Edwards, of whom extended mention follows; and Arad R., now living in Yantic, who married Jennie Ayer, and is now retired.

William Edwards Manning was born in Lebanon, October 1, 1866. He received a practical education in the excellent public schools of that town, then began life on the farm of his uncle. Attracted, however, by a mercantile career, he entered the employ, in 1884, of Peckham & Waterman, who conducted the general store at Bozrahville, Connecticut. Continuing with this firm for a period of seven years, Mr. Manning then bought out this firm in 1890, and continued under his own name. The was successful from the first, and continued the business for eight years and for ten years served as postmaster of Bozrahville. In 1898 he disposed of his interests there and removed to Yantic, where he bought out the general store. Mr. Manning still actively manages this business, and is the leading merchant of the town.

In 1901, Mr. Manning was appointed assistant postmaster of Yantic, then in 1903 became postmaster, which office he has now held for eighteen years to the eminent satisfaction of the people of the town. The postoffice is in the store building, and is the point of departure of several rural free delivery routes which serve a very extensive territory.

Mr. Manning is identified with many branches of public activity. By political choice he is a member of the Republican party, and in response to the insistent demands of the people, he has repeatedly served on the school committee of Bozrah and Yantic. He is secretary of the Volunteer Fire Department of Yantic, and is always a leader in every public movement. He is a member of the Chamber of Commerce of the city of Norwich, and is a member of St. James Lodge, No. 23, Free and Accepted Masons, and Franklin Chapter, No. 4, Royal Arch Masons, of Norwich.

On June 3, 1891, Mr Manning married Grace Fuller, of East Greenwich, Rhode Island, daughter of George H. and Elmira (Millard) Fuller, of that city. Mr. and Mrs. Manning have a son and a daughter: Frederick Fuller; and Lois A., who resides at home. The family are members of Grace Episcopal Church of Yantic, of which Mr. Manning has been vestryman for twenty years.

SIMON (3) BREWSTER—The Brewster farm in Griswold, Connecticut, was first owned in the family by a Simon Brewster, a great-great-grandson of Elder Brewster of "Mayflower" and Plymouth Colony fame. Simon Brewster, of the fourth American generation, bought the farm in the town of Griswold, then Preston, about 1741. Elias Brewster inherited the farm and there resided until his death. He became wealthy through trade and commerce and was the owner of several farms, aggregating 1,100 acres. His son, Simon (2) Brewster, was born on the homestead, May 29, 1801. After the death of his father on March 12, 1834, he purchased the interests of the other heirs in the homestead farm of about four hundred and fifty acres and retained possession of it until his death, August 17, 1867.

There were children by each of the three wives of Simon (2) Brewster, and on account of their varied interests, it was necessary to sell the property. In 1868 the farm was sold and remained out of the family until his son, Simon (3) Brewster, the present owner of the farm, on reaching his majority, bought the old homestead with one hundred and twenty-five acres—all that remained of his father's farm. He lived the first eighteen years of his life at the homestead, was absent three years, returned as owner at the age of twenty-one, and lives there now at the age of seventy. There has been none of those years when he could not have been classed as a worker, for at the age of seven he was helping to drive his father's cattle to Norwich, and the habits of industry, which were so noticeable in his boyhood, are the strong characteristics of the mature man.

Simon (3) Brewster is of the eighth American generation, beginning with Elder William Brewster, the line being traced from the elder's son, Love Brewster, born in England, and also of the "Mayflower," and his wife, Sarah (Collier) Brewster. They were married at Plymouth, March 15, 1634. Their son, William Brewster, married, in 1672, Lydia Partridge, and their son, Benjamin Brewster, born in 1688, and his first wife, Elizabeth (Witter) Brewster, had a son, Simon (1) Brewster, born in 1720, who settled on the farm in now Griswold, Connecticut. Simon (1) Brewster, by his wife, Anne (Andros) Brewster, had a son, Elias Brewster, born in 1759, who inherited and added to the homestead, and had by his first wife, Margery (Morgan) Brewster, a son, Simon (2) Brewster, born May 29, 1801, who bought out the interests of the other heirs and became sole owner of the homestead and its four hundred and fifty acres. He had by his second wife, Abby A. Prentice, a son, Simon (3) Brewster, born May 25, 1850, the present owner of the property, and the principal character of this sketch.

Simon (3) Brewster attended public schools in Jewett City and Preston City, and before his father's death was his valued assistant. He restored the farm to its former condition as a profitable estate, and has added many acres thereto. Half a century has now passed since his return and he has become one of the substantial men of his town, his prosperity equalling that of the generations that preceded him. He has, during his whole life, taken a great interest in agriculture and stock-breeding in his community, and for many years has been a director in, and is now first vice-president of, the New London County Agricultural Society.

Simon (3) Brewster married, April 8, 1873, Sarah Elizabeth Browning, born April 2, 1854, daughter of Beriah Hopkins and Sarah Elizabeth (Campbell) Browning. Mrs. Brewster is the granddaughter of Avery Browning, who married Mary Arnold, daughter of Peleg Arnold, and who died on the Plain Hill farm in Norwich, May 9, 1865.

The Browning family descends from Nathaniel Browning, who is of record in Rhode Island as early as 1645. By his wife, Sarah, he had a son, William, through whom descent is traced. William Browning is of Portsmouth and South Kingston, Rhode Island, and both he and his second wife, Sarah, died in 1730. John Browning, son of William and Rebecca (Wilbur) Browning, was born March 4, 1696, and was head of the third generation. He married Anna Hazard, daughter of Jeremiah and Sarah (Smith) Hazard, of South Kingston, Rhode Island. The head of the fourth generation was their son, John (2) Browning, who by his second wife, Eunice (Williams) Browning, had among other children a son, Avery, the grandfather of Sarah Elizabeth Browning, wife of Simon (3) Brewster.

Simon (3) and Sarah E. (Browning) Brewster are the parents of seven children: 1. Sarah E., born July 17, 1875, died January 15, 1886. 2. Alice Aldrich, born January 19, 1881, died February 24, 1884. 3. Martha Browning, born April 23, 1883, married December 17, 1917, Asahel R. Cook, principal assistant engineer of the Northern Pacific Railroad Company. Mr. and Mrs. Cook reside in Tacoma, Washington. 4. Abby Prentice, born June 22, 1885, a graduate of the Norwich Free Academy, valedictorian of the class of 1903, a successful educator of New York City. 5. Simon (4), born November 5, 1887, now his father's valued assistant. 6. Sarah Elizabeth, born November 12, 1891, married, May 26, 1917, Russell L. Davenport, of Ogden, Utah, attorney-at-law, and now has two children: Mary Brewster, and Eleanor. They reside in Holyoke, Massachusetts. 7. Margery Morgan, born March 12, 1895, a graduate of Connecticut Agricultural College, class of 1914, living with her parents.

These children are of the ninth generation of the Brewster family, one of the oldest families in New England, and one which represents three centuries of American life, 1620-1920. Their Browning lineage is nearly as ancient and equally honorable. The coming of the "Mayflower" in 1620 was the beginning of an epoch memorable in world history, and

Elder William Brewster was one of the men who, through the "covenant," established a new order and built a community upon a religious foundation. Three centuries have proved how well the foundation was laid.

REV. ALBERT EDWARD KINMOUTH, born in Cork, Ireland, May 5, 1846, was educated in the city schools, Villards Academy, and Queen's University, Cork. He studied for the ministry in England, but was not regularly ordained a clergyman until coming to the United States, the ordination ceremonies being held in Pottsdam, New York, in 1874. Later he was ordained an elder at Pottsdam, New York. He was settled pastor over the Congregational church at Seneca Falls, New York, in 1877. That was his first pastorate, and he afterward was called as pastor over several churches, filling every charge with the devoted zeal which marks the true minister of the gospel. At Oswego Falls, New York, he built a new church, and other churches which he served were rescued from a condition of financial distress and restored to a state of usefulness. He served the church at Ledyard, Connecticut, for fifteen years with marked acceptability; then went to Friendship, New York, remaining for four years; then for five years was at Brooklyn, Connecticut, after which time, his health failing, he resigned and retired from the ministry. His life has been a useful one, spent largely in the service of his fellowmen through the medium of the church and its allied forces.

Rev. Albert E. Kinmouth married (first) Elizabeth Roycroft, who died, leaving three children: Catherine, Eva Gertrude, and Richard Ray. Their first-born, Minnie, died in infancy. He married (second) Caroline Henrietta Bellows, born at Seneca Falls, New York, in February, 1860, daughter of William Levin and Caroline P. Catt. They were the parents of four children: Albert William, who will have further mention; George Edward, of Mystic, Connecticut; Raymond Arnold, of further mention; Carrie Fredericka, born in Ledyard, died aged four years, in 1904.

Albert William Kinmouth, son of Rev. Albert Edward Kinmouth and his second wife, Caroline Henrietta Bellows, was born at Stouffville, near Toronto, Canada, July 5, 1881. In 1889 his parents moved to Greenwich, Connecticut, where his father was pastor of the Congregational church, and there the lad attended public school. Later he spent a year in Montville, his father serving the church there one year before going to the Ledyard church in 1893. Albert W., the son, attended the public school until sixteen years of age, then, in 1897, taught school for one term. The next two years he was a student at Mt. Hermon School, then for two years taught in the Lester district, at Gales Ferry. He then abandoned teaching and was employed for several years by different street car companies. In 1916 he returned to the farm in Ledyard, to which his father had retired after leaving the ministry, and there has since been in charge of the farm. Mr. Kinmouth is a member of the Grange, Patrons of Husbandry, and for three years has served his town as second selectman.

Raymond Arnold Kinmouth, a graduate of the Medical Department of the University of Boston, a physician, now at Massachusetts State Hospital for the Insane, and has made a reputation as a surgeon. He enlisted in the United States army during the World War, went overseas with the American Expeditionary Forces, served in the medical corps in France with the 100th Battery of Field Artillery, and was cited for bravery in action. He was a victim of the gas used by the Germans in their reversion to barbarism, and suffered greatly. His parents received a letter from General Edwards commending the bravery of their son and his splendid military record.

CHARLES ORRISON MAINE, M. D.—The family of which Mr. Maine was a member is a very old one in New England. The first one of the family to be known in this country was John Maine, who was a native of York, England. Leaving his home there in 1629, he sailed for the New World, and after a time settled in Maine, at the small village of York. He remained in that locality for forty years, then, in 1669, came to Connecticut and made his home in Stonington, residing there until his death. Many of his descendants are now residing in this same locality. His son, Ezekial Maine, is the forebear of Charles Orrison Maine. Ezekial's wife was named Mary, and they had a son Jeremiah, whose wife was Ruth Brown. Their son, Thomas Maine, became quite prominent as a deacon; he married Anna Brown, by whom he had a son Jonathan. Jonathan's wife was Patience Peckham, who became the mother of Jabis Maine, who married Freelove Edwards. Their son, Sidney O. Maine, was born in North Stonington, where he was educated in the district school and where he afterward became a farmer, following this as a means of livelihood until his death, in North Stonington, in 1897; his wife, Eliza Wentworth, was born in Hillsdale, Massachusetts, dying in North Stonington, in 1899. Mr. and Mrs. Sidney O. Maine had five children, the eldest being Charles Orrison Maine, of further mention.

Charles Orrison Maine was born in New Hartford, Connecticut, June 16, 1845. His education began in the public school of that locality and was finished at Dartmouth College, where he became a student of medicine in 1866, and from which he graduated in 1870, with the degree of Medical Doctor. Going in that same year to Voluntown, Connecticut, he entered into private practice, but after a short period spent there returned to the borough of Stonington, where he carried on his profession for many years, his death occurring at his home March 6, 1916.

Active all his life in the affairs of his borough, Dr. Maine was very prominent in Masonic circles, being a member of Asylum Lodge, No. 57, Free and Accepted Masons, of Stonington, and also

C. A. Maine M.D.

was one of the charter members of the local chapter of the Order of the Eastern Star. He also was connected with the Stonington Grange. Dr. Maine was an active member of several societies relating to his profession, among them being the American Medical Association; the State Medical Association, of Connecticut, and the New London County Medical Society. During the many years that Dr. Maine was a resident of Stonington he was a staunch upholder of the Republican party. In religion he was a member of the Baptist church.

Dr. Maine married, December 18, 1866, Phebe Sarah Maine, the daughter of Robert P. and Phebe E. (Edwards) Maine. To this union one child was born, Charles Everett Maine, D. D. S., practicing in Stonington, Connecticut.

GERTRUDE L. (MAINE) LATHAM—Bereft of both her parents at a very early age, Gertrude L. (Maine) Latham was brought up in the family of Dr. Charles Orrison Maine (see preceding sketch), of Stonington, Connecticut, spending the greater part of her life in his home.

Gertrude L. (Maine) Latham was born in Westerly, Rhode Island, her parents being Crawford R. and Hattie M. (Tucker) Maine. Her father was a native of Voluntown, Connecticut, where he was educated in the district school. Business interests afterward taking his to Westerly, Rhode Island, Mr. Maine died there in 1877, his wife having died in 1875, and Gertrude L. was the only child of their marriage. Going to live at Stonington with Dr. and Mrs. Maine at that time, the young child received a good education in the public schools of the town, and she continued to reside with her relatives until she reached womanhood.

Gertrude L. Maine married, June 29, 1898, Hiram J. Latham, a resident of Mystic, Connecticut. Of this union one child was born, Muriel, born in Pawtucket, town of Stonington, January 6, 1900, who lives at home. Mrs. Latham is the owner of a confectionery store at Stonington, which she personally conducts. During the World War she was appointed assistant postmaster of Stonington. Mrs. Latham is a member of the Baptist church there and active in its work.

JAMES DANA COIT—Filling a position of trust in his native city, and identified with its public and social life, James Dana Coit, of Norwich, Connecticut, is a representative citizen of the day. He is a son of George Douglas Coit, who was born in Norwich, Connecticut, and received his early education in the public schools of the city, Norwich Free Academy and Yale University, receiving from the last named his Bachelor's Degree with the class of 1866. After graduation he returned to Norwich and became associated with the Norwich Fire Insurance Company in the capacity of clerk, remaining in that connection for one year. For a few months he was a part of the executive force of the B. P. Learned Company, of Norwich, then prominent dealers in real estate and insurance. In 1869 he was instrumental in organizing the Dime Savings Bank of Norwich, serving as its first secretary and treasurer. Nine years later, in July, 1878, he transferred his services to the Chelsea Savings Bank, of Norwich, succeeding his brother, Charles M. Coit (who was drowned), as secretary-treasurer of that institution. For twenty-eight years he held that position with the Chelsea Savings Bank, his valuable service terminating with his death, October 3, 1906. He married Frances Henrietta Dana, who was born in New Haven, Connecticut, July 26, 1848, daughter of James D. and Henrietta (Sullivan) Dana, of that city. George Douglas and Frances Henrietta (Dana) Coit were the parents of three children: George D., deceased; Helen, deceased; and James Dana, of further mention.

James Dana Coit was born in Norwich, Connecticut, December 5, 1880. He began his education in the city public schools, passing thence to Norwich Free Academy, where he spent two years. This was supplemented by two years at Holbrook Military School at Sing Sing, New York (Ossining), whence he was graduated, class of 1900. He spent two years at Yale University, but withdrew in his sophomore year, and on December 15, 1902, entered the employ of the Merchants' National Bank of Norwich, where he remained until 1906, when he came to the Chelsea Savings Bank, with which his honored father had so long been connected. He entered as clerk, but the years have brought him promotion, his present position being that of assistant secretary and treasurer. He is well known and highly esteemed in the banking fraternity, and is interested in many of the city's social and philanthropic activities.

Mr. Coit is treasurer of the Norwich Americanization Institute; treasurer of the Norwich Tuberculosis Fund of the American Red Cross; member of the Arcanum Club of Norwich; Norwich Golf Club; Sons of the American Revolution; Society of Colonial Wars; Delta Phi fraternity, and in politics is a Republican.

On May 9, 1906, Mr. Coit married Emily Hurnell Turnbull, daughter of Charles and Gertrude (Tabb) Turnbull, of Baltimore, Maryland. They have one child, Frances Dana Coit. Mr. and Mrs. Coit are members of the Park Congregational Church, and active in all the social and benevolent organizations of the church society.

JAMES WILLIAM BENNETT—Throughout a long and active lifetime James William Bennett traveled through the New England States in the interests of well known manufacturers, catering to the grocery trade, and in his death, in 1921, the friends he had made in every place he had visited, from the great cities down to the most remote hamlets, felt the loss of that genial, warm-hearted nature.

Mr. Bennett was a son of Nathan and Abbie (Manning) Bennett, both from old families of Southern New England. Nathan Bennett was born and educated in Foster, Rhode Island, and as a young man became a manufacturer of woolen fabrics, following the textile industry as a producer for many years. He came to Baltic, in New London county, Connecticut, then known as Lord's Bridge, early in his career, and there operated a small woolen mill. Later he purchased a hotel in the same community, and this he managed personally, with marked success. Eventually retiring from all active business interests, he removed to Hanover, in the town of Sprague, where he spent his declining years in well-earned comfort, and died January 23, 1895. His wife survived him for nearly twenty-two years, and passed away in Canterbury, Connecticut, October 6, 1916, at a good old age.

James William Bennett was born in Franklin, New London county, Connecticut, March 16, 1846, and died in Willimantic, July 19, 1921. As a child he attended the old district schools of Lord's Bridge (now Baltic), later enjoying the privilege of a course at Professor T. K. Peck's school in Hanover. As a young man he began life on the farm, in Canterbury, but after one year of farm life, returned home and was associated with his father in the hotel and livery business in Baltic. Thereafter, Mr. Bennett was employed for seven years by J. S. Ray, of East Haddam, Connecticut, a manufacturer of coffin trimmings. His next step was to become associated with Coles & Weeks, grain dealers, of Middletown, Connecticut, in the capacity of traveling salesman, with whom he remained for four years. Upon severing this connection, Mr. Bennett formed the business tie which endured for a period of thirty years, with the C. D. Boss Company, of New London, the famous cracker manufacturers. For this concern he traveled all over New England until the old company was dissolved, and it was in connection with the "Boss" crackers that he is best remembered in the trade, perhaps. Next, and last, Mr. Bennett was identified with the A. H. Bill Company, of Boston, wholesale tea and coffee merchants, going on the road for them with the establishment of the firm. How largely the success of this concern is due to the ripened experience and wide popularity of Mr. Bennett as a salesman can hardly be estimated, his loyalty to the interests of his house bringing their most scattered customers into close touch with the concern, and immeasurably advancing their mutual good. He was with this concern fifteen years, and died in their service.

The nature of Mr. Bennett's activities as a business man precluded largely those social interests which mean so much. He resided in Middletown in early life, but from his first connection with the Boss concern, resided in Willimantic until 1911, when he removed to Hanover, taking possession of the old Smith homestead, which was inherited by his wife and others, and which had been the home of her people for generations, where she was born and still resides. Through all his travels, however, Mr. Bennett invariably kept in touch with the progress of the times, and his influence, in the many circles which his influence reached, was always for advance, whether in public interests or individual endeavor.

Mr. Bennett was for many years a popular member of the Commercial Travelers' Mutual Benefit Association, and was always broadly active in its interest. Politically, Mr. Bennett was a Republican, but did not always support that ticket, for he was not blind to the faults of his party, as his vote in National and State elections often testified. Fraternally, he held membership in Somerset Lodge, No. 34, Free and Accepted Masons, of Norwich. He attended the Congregational church.

Mr. Bennett married, in Hanover, on November 13, 1872, Ella E. Smith, daughter of Norman and Adeline (Cutler) Smith. Mrs. Bennett survives her husband, also their two children and four grandchildren survive, as follows: Harry Norman, born in East Haddam, Connecticut, September 4, 1873, who is now engaged in the manufacture of chemicals in New York City, married Lillian Louise Bass, of Springfield, Massachusetts, their only child being Harold Bass; and Grace Adeline, born in East Haddam, October 15, 1879, now the wife of Harry L. Andrew, wholesale grocer and provision dealer in New Haven, Connecticut, their three children being Dorothy Cutler, Norma, and Bennett.

It is especially fitting that the life of such a man as James William Bennett should be commemorated in the permanent records of his native county. He lived broadly and fully, and gave to his time the wealth of a rich and generous nature. He will long be remembered by all whose privilege it was to know him.

LOUIS THOMAS CASSIDY, M. D.—Following in the footsteps of his honored father, Dr. Cassidy, of Norwich, has attained a high position in the medical profession in New London county, being a leading physician and surgeon of that city. Dr. Cassidy is a son of Dr. Patrick and Margaret (McCloud) Cassidy, long residents of this city. The father is one of the most prominent medical practitioners of Norwich, with a long record of success behind him. He is still in active practice and widely sought in consultation, a venerable and highly esteemed physician, both among the people to whose needs he has given his life, and to the profession of which he is a noteworthy member. At one time he served as surgeon general of the State of Connecticut.

Louis Thomas Cassidy was born in Norwich, Connecticut, January 12, 1883. His education was begun in the public schools, and he was graduated from the Norwich Free Academy in the class of 1900. His choice of a profession early determined, he entered Georgetown University, at Washington, District of Columbia, and completed his course in arts and letters in 1904, being graduated in that year. He then took up his professional studies at Georgetown Medical School, and was graduated in 1908. He has since practiced in his native city with marked success, and has attained an enviable position among his contemporaries. Standing high in the profession, he is a member of the American Medical Association, the Connecticut State Medical Society, the New London County Medical Society, and the Norwich Medical Society. Widely prominent in fraternal circles, he is a member of the Benevolent and Protective Order of Elks, the Loyal Order of Moose, the Norwich Aerie, Fraternal Order of Eagles, the American Order of Foresters, and the Improved Order of Red Men, all Norwich lodges. His religious affiliation is with the Roman Catholic church.

Dr. Cassidy married, in Washington, District of Columbia, in 1909, Mary Virginia Drury, daughter of John S. and Alice (Mason) Drury.

CLARENCE LOWELL CLARK—In that school which developed some of the greatest business men of their day, the "Yankee peddler wagon," a school now practically closed, but one that filled an important place in New England country life during its heyday, William Frederick Clark gained his training for the honorable place he has since filled in the mercantile life of Old Lyme, Connecticut. William Frederick Clarke is the father of Clarence Lowell Clarke, whose business education began in his father's general store in Old Lyme, but who has since 1903 been in the government postal service as mail carrier and postmaster at Old Lyme.

William F. Clark was born in Chester, Connecticut, and until arriving at manhood was engaged in farming. He left the farm to take up the life of a traveling merchant, and drove over stated territory with his wagon, loaded with tin and other ware, which he sold or exchanged with farmers at their homes. He was a successful merchant of that "old time type," and continued until 1880, when he settled in Old Lyme, New London county, and opened a general store, which he now has successfully conducted for forty years and still manages.

Mr. Clark married Elvira Comstock, born in Old Lyme, of an old New London county family, and among their children was a son, Clarence Lowell Clark, of whom further. Mr. and Mrs. William F. Clark reside in Old Lyme, where so many of their years have been spent. They are highly esteemed in the village, and "Clark's" is a well known and popular trading center.

Clarence Lowell Clark was born in Old Lyme, New London county, Connecticut, June 1, 1885. He was educated in the public schools of Old Lyme, and after finishing high school he was appointed, on July 1, 1903, letter carrier at the Old Lyme post office. He held that office seven years, until July 1, 1910, when he was appointed postmaster of Old Lyme, the appointment being made by Postmaster-General Frank H. Hitchcock. He was reappointed under the Wilson administration by Postmaster-General Burleson, and has held the office continuously under both Republican and Democratic administrations, although by political choice he is a Republican. He has served the village on the school board and before becoming postmaster was village assessor.

Mr. Clark is a member of the Congregational church of Old Lyme. Fraternally he is a member of Crystal Lodge, No. 88, Independent Order of Odd Fellows, of which he is a past noble grand and past district deputy grand master; and Pythagoras Lodge, No. 45, Free and Accepted Masons, both of Old Lyme.

Postmaster Clark married, at Old Lyme, April 23, 1908, May Frances Austin, born in the village, daughter of William Nelson and Susan E. (Chapman) Austin, her father a contractor and builder of Old Lyme.

JAMES BATHGATE—For several centuries the name of Bathgate has been identified in Scotland with the manufacture of woolen fabrics, and a Bathgate, in the early days of the textile industry in America, crossed the ocean and took his place among the pioneers in this field in the United States. With the ingrained ability which is the result of generation after generation following the same line of effort, the accumulated experience of the family went into the development of the industry in America.

James Bathgate was born in Gallashiels, Scotland, and after a few years of successful management of the mills in Scotland, followed the earlier pioneers to Peterborough, Ontario, Canada, and then to this country, and settled in Foxcroft, Piscataquis county, Maine, where he was engaged in the manufacture of textiles for a considerable period. About 1906 Mr. Bathgate came to East Lyme, Connecticut, as treasurer and general manager of the Niantic Manufacturing Company, located in the village of Flanders, now a living monument to the spirit which has lived through the centuries since the first man of this name entered the textile field, and later, with his son, George Hyslop, established a mill in Waterford, Connecticut, known as the Jordan Mill.

James Bathgate married Laura Jane Tanner, who was born in Scottsville, New York. Mr. and Mrs. Bathgate were the parents of one son, George Hyslop (see following sketch), and one daughter, Mabel Agnes, now the wife of Robert E. Hall, of Hartford, Connecticut, who has two daughters: Jane Stuart, and Patricia.

GEORGE HYSLOP BATHGATE, son of James and Laura Jane (Tanner) Bathgate (see preceding sketch, was born in Foxcroft, Maine, December 25, 1889, and received his early education in his native town. As a boy of fifteen he came to East Lyme with his parents, and while residing here, attended

Bulkeley High School, of New London, from which he was graduated in the class of 1908. Thereafter, he attended the Norwich Free Academy for one year. In the fall of 1909 the young man went to Philadelphia, Pennsylvania, where he entered the Philadelphia Textile College, and there learned the most recent developments of the textile art, together with its history, ancient and modern, and the fundamental principles of commercial application. Since his graduation from the textile school in 1911, Mr. Bathgate has been identified with his father's mill in East Lyme, first mastering the practical side of the business, and soon becoming superintendent of the plant; he now holds the positions of secretary and superintendent.

Mr. Bathgate is a member of the Phi Psi fraternity of the Philadelphia Textile College. He takes little leisure for interests outside his business, and politically, while endorsing the principles of the Republican party, reserves the right to individual thought and action.

ROBERT HOOKER BYLES—**Ebenezer Byles**, son of Josias (2), and grandson of Josias (1) Byles, the founder of this family in New England, was of Boston, Massachusetts, birth, but in 1743, at the age of twenty, he removed to the town of Ashford, in Windham county, Connecticut, about thirty miles northeast of Hartford, the village of the same name being known in history as the birthplace of General Nathaniel Lyon. Four generations of the descendants of Ebenezer Byles resided in Ashford: Josias (3), of the fourth; Elisha, of the fifth; Deacon Andrew H., of the sixth; and George Sharpe Byles, of the seventh American generation; all were born at the homestead, located on the turnpike, between Ashford Centre and Warrenville, first owned by Ebenezer Byles, of the third generation, and there lived amid Ashford's familiar scenes, but the last named, George S., who broke the continuity of residence, and in Norwich, New London county, entered business life and there became a prominent merchant, a member of the firm of J. P. Barstow & Company. Robert Hooker Byles, of the eighth generation, continued business activities when he came to a choice of occupation and spent his adult years as a funeral director, and for a decade and a half of years has been located in New London, where he is well settled in a modernly-equipped funeral establishment, at No. 15 Masonic street, where a former residence was purchased, converted into undertaker's uses, and occupied as a mortuary establishment January, 1920. Prosperity has come to Mr. Byles in his New London business, and he is one of the leading men of his profession.

Josias Byles, the founder, came from London, England, to Gravesend, Massachusetts, on the ship "Edward and Mary," arriving in May, 1692. He married, in England, Sarah Hartwell, and there she died, December 16, 1691. He was accompanied from England by his son, Josias (2), and in Massachusetts married a second wife, Sarah Davis, and a third wife, Elizabeth Mather, children being born to each wife. The line of descent from Josias and Sarah (Hartwell) Byles is through their first-born, Josias (2), and his wife, Abigail (Callender) Byles; their youngest child, Ebenezer, and his wife, Anna (Bushnell) Byles; their youngest son, Josias (3), and his wife, Abigail (Clark) Byles; their fourth child, Deacon Elisha, and his wife, Sophia (Huntington) Byles; their youngest son, Deacon Andrew Huntington, and his wife, Martha H. (Sharpe) Byles; their son, George Sharpe, and his wife, Mary Eva (Hooker) Byles; their son, Robert Hooker, of New London, Connecticut, and his wife, M. Hortense (Eagles) Byles.

Elisha Byles, of the fifth generation, was a deacon of the Congregational church, and died at the old farm, at the age of eighty-one. He was succeeded in the ownership of the farm and in the deacon's office by his son, Andrew H. Byles, who left the old farm in 1888 and removed to Willimantic, and there died, May 17, 1894. He was buried in the family burial ground near the old farm in Ashford. He was a man of fine character, with high ideals, possessed rare judgment and tact, and was a power for good in his community. His wife, Martha H. (Sharpe) Byles, was a daughter of Judge George Sharpe, of Pomfret, Connecticut, and granddaughter of Robert Sharpe, a Revolutionary soldier who enlisted from Pomfret.

George Sharpe Byles, son of Andrew H. and Martha H. (Sharpe) Byles, was born at the old farm in Ashford, Windham county, Connecticut, March 1, 1853, and died April 28, 1918. He remained at the farm as his father's assistant until December, 1873, when he came to Norwich, New London county, and entered the employ of his uncle, John P. Barstow, a merchant of Norwich, with whom the young man also made his home. As a clerk he continued for three years, becoming thoroughly familiar with the details of the business, and so valued were his services that in 1876 he was taken in as a partner, as was Frank H. Smith, the firm trading as J. P. Barstow & Company. In 1893 the senior partner died, but the surviving partners continued the business under the old firm name, the house becoming one of the oldest on Water street, its rating high and its business large.

In politics Mr. Byles was a Republican, and in religious faith a Congregationalist, attending the Broadway Church in Norwich. He was a member of Somerset Lodge, No. 34, Free and Accepted Masons; held all degrees of Norwich Consistory of the Ancient Accepted Scottish Rite up to and including the thirty-second; was a noble of Sphinx Temple, Ancient Arabic Order Nobles of the Mystic Shrine; member of the Arcanum Club; and the fraternal orders, New England Order of Protection and the Ancient Order of United Workmen.

George S. Byles married, in Mansfield, Connecticut, Mary Eva Hooker, born in Mansfield, January

James Graham

15, 1854, daughter of Lothrop and Rachel (Sholes) Hooker, her father a manufacturer, of Mt. Hope. Three children were born to Mr. and Mrs. Byles: Robert Hooker, whose career is herein reviewed; Harold H., born March 30, 1883, died April 5, 1893; and Everett Barstow, born February 28, 1890.

Robert Hooker Byles, son of George S. and Mary Eva (Hooker) Byles, was born in Norwich, Connecticut, September 1, 1878. He was educated in the public schools and Norwich Free Academy, entering the latter institution after completing the courses of Broadway Grammar School. After completing school years, he served for seven years as assistant with different undertaking firms of Norwich, then, on October 15, 1903, began business as an undertaker in Lewiston, Maine.

After leaving Lewiston, he located in New London, where he resumed business in July, 1906, as successor to Pendleton & Son, his establishment located at No. 52 Main street. There he conducted business until the completion of the alterations and additions to the dwelling at No. 15 Masonic street, which Mr. Byles had purchased in the fall of 1919. On January 1, 1920, the new establishment was occupied, and there he continues.

Mr. Byles is past master of Union Lodge, No. 31, Free and Accepted Masons, and at present its secretary; member of Union Chapter, No. 7, Royal Arch Masons; Cushing Council, Royal and Select Masters; Palestine Commandery, No. 6, Knights Templar; Pyramid Temple, Ancient Arabic Order Nobles of the Mystic Shrine, of Bridgeport; Hunguent Lodge, No. 499, New England Order of Protection; Mohegan Lodge, No. 55, Independent Order of Odd Fellows; Nonomantuc Tribe, Improved Order of Red Men; New London Lodge, No. 344, Loyal Order of Moose; and the Masonic Club of New London. Mr. Byles is a Republican in politics, and a member of the First Church of Christ (Scientist).

In Norwich, Connecticut, September 26, 1906, Mr. Byles married M. Hortense Eagles, born in Sprague, New London county, Connecticut, September 19, 1886, daughter of William H. and Mary (Rich) Eagles. Three children have been born to Mr. and Mrs. Byles, they of the ninth American generation: George Huntington, born December 10, 1907; Robert Everett, born February 12, 1913; and Mary Lorine, born March 16, 1919.

RICHARD LANE TARRANT is one of the well known business men of Norwich, Connecticut. His father, Nicholas Tarrant, like his son, a prominent realtor, was born in 1846, and died in 1910. His mother, Mary (Coyle) Tarrant, was born in 1866, and died in 1906.

Richard Lane Tarrant was born at Norwich, Connecticut, August 14, 1892. His early school days were spent in the Broadway Grammar and St. Patrick's parochial schools of his native city. He entered the Norwich Free Academy in 1906 and was graduated with the class of 1910. Upon leaving school he went in business with his father as a realtor and insurance agent, and upon his father's death in 1913, took over the office and has built up a large and lucrative business.

During the World War Mr. Tarrant saw service with the American army, being a cadet in the air service. He is an Independent in his political views. His fraternal connections are with the Knights of Columbus, White Cross Council, No. 13; Daniel Mullin Assembly; and the Benevolent and Protective Order of Elks, Norwich Lodge, No. 430. His clubs are the Rotary and Norwich Golf. He is a communicant of the Catholic church.

JAMES GRAHAM—Many and valuable are the contributions which Scotch character has made to the life of this nation. From every station in life and from nearly every Scottish family have come individuals bringing with them the sturdy strength of their native hills. Many of the names long honored in the annals of Scottish history are, and long have been, represented in the United States. Among these there is none that has been more esteemed than that of Graham.

James Graham, father of our subject, was born in Longside, Scotland, in 1822, received his early education in the National School at Longside, and then became a landscape gardener, which work he engaged in until 1872. In that year Edward P. Taft, agent for the Ponemah Mills, manufacturing cotton goods, went to Scotland to secure operators, bringing back two ship loads of Scottish people to work in the mills. James Graham felt that this represented an opportunity to better his condition and that of his family, and joined the group of emigrants, bringing with him his family. He settled in Taftville, Connecticut, and worked in the Ponemah Mills until his death, which occurred August 10, 1900. His wife, Mary (Smith) Graham, was born at Longside, Scotland, in 1824, and died at Taftville in March, 1902. To this union were born four children: Mary, born at Longside, married Thomas Emmerson, who was employed in the Ponemah Mills, but is now retired and lives at Lisbon, Connecticut; Christina, born at Longside, resides in Willimantic, Connecticut; Agnes, deceased, born at Longside, married William Burgess, who is retired and lives at Lisbon; and James (2), of whom further.

James (2) Graham, son of James (1) and Mary (Smith) Graham, was brought to this country by his family when he was seven years of age, received his education in the public schools of Taftville, Connecticut, and then served a three years' apprenticeship as machinist in the Ponemah Mills. His apprenticeship ended, he worked for four years as machinist in that same mill, and then, in 1884, entered Eastman Business College, at Poughkeepsie, New York, where he completed a two years' course. Returning to Taftville, he worked as machinist in the Ponemah Mills for one year more, and then became shipping clerk in the office of that same company, continuing to act in that capacity until 1912. During the period of years between 1896 and 1912, he was also postmaster at Taftville. To energy and ability he added thrift and by 1902 had saved enough to buy a farm of seventeen acres near Taftville, where, in addition to his regular work, he carried on market-gardening on a small scale. In 1912 he gave up his position with the Ponemah Company and bought the two hundred and thirty-two acre farm, known as the Talbut farm, which adjoins the place where he makes his home. Since that time he has devoted his attention to market gardening. He has made a scientific study of the subject, attending lectures at agricultural colleges throughout Southern New England, and keeping closely in touch with experiments and reports sent out by both National and State agricultural bureaus, until at the present time he is regarded as one of the best gardeners in Eastern Connecticut. His two farms, totalling two hundred and fifty acres, are cultivated by thoroughly scientific methods, and the most modern farm machinery is used, including that great labor and time-saving device, the tractor.

In addition to the management of his big farm, Mr. Graham has found time to fill important public offices and to serve his county and his fellow-agriculturists faithfully and well in the State Senate. Since 1915 he has been tax assessor for the town of Lisbon and still (1922) holds that office. In 1916 he was elected representative of Lisbon in the State Legislature, served on the Public Health Commission, and acted as prison coroner; in 1918 he was a member of the Excise Commission; and in 1920 was elected State Senator from New London county, serving on the Agricultural Committee. He is still (1922) State Senator from New London county. Mr. Graham was one of the promoters of the Bankers' Trust Company of Norwich, and when the organization was perfected in 1921, became one of the board of directors.

Mr. Graham married, in Taftville, March 3, 1887, Mary Fulton, daughter of Hugh and Clementine (Martin) Fulton, both of Scottish birth, the latter being a member of a well known family named Copeland. Mr. and Mrs. Graham are the parents of four daughters: Clementine, teacher in Cristobal, C. Z.; Mary, married Fredrick Friswell, and resides in Norwich; Christina, married William Bode, and resides in Norwich; and Agnes, a teacher, residing at home.

MATTHEW A. TINKER—The Tinker homestead, lying in East Lyme, New London county, Connecticut, is very near the Montville town line, and near the village of Chesterfield, the present home of Matthew A. Tinker, one of the prominent men of the town of Montville, although the Tinker homestead lies in East Lyme, and the family history for generations centers around this old home where Matthew A. Tinker was born, as were his parents and grandparents.

Matthew A. Tinker is a great-grandson of William Tinker, who was born in the old Tinker homestead in Lyme, Connecticut, near the Montville line, and there spent his life. He was the father of Matthew Tinker, also born at the Tinker homestead in Lyme, he also farming the old place until his death. He married Mary Miller, who was born in Waterford, New London county, Connecticut, and they were the parents of a son, Matthew (2) Tinker, who was born at the homestead in East Lyme, April 5, 1832, and resided thereon until about 1911, when he retired from farming and moved to Montville, where he died April 7, 1916. He was a good man, public-spirited and helpful, fond of his home and his family, and ready to make any sacrifice for their comfort or happiness. He married Mary Christine Elizabeth Caulkins, born in Montville, and there yet resides (1921).

Matthew A. Tinker, son of Matthew (2) and Mary Christine Elizabeth (Caulkins) Tinker, was born in Montville, New London county, Connecticut, January 24, 1865, and grew to manhood on the old Tinker farm in East Lyme. He attended school in the nearby village of Chesterfield, and was his father's farm assistant until attaining legal age. He then left the farm and went West, and became a fireman on a Great Lakes steamer. After returning East, he was for a time on Long Island Sound boats, and on coastwise steamers, as fireman. Finally he tired of that life and returned to East Lyme, married, and for two years worked a leased farm. He then, in 1898, bought a fine farm property in the town of Montville, near the village of Chesterfield, which he farmed intensively and with great success until 1918, when, on account of ill health, he turned the management of his farm over to his son, William R., and moved into the village of Chesterfield, where he yet resides and conducts a small farm in connection with his auctioneering. Many years ago Mr. Tinker discovered that he had a talent for public selling, and later developed that talent, until he is considered one of the best auctioneers in Eastern Connecticut. For twenty-five years he has been in that business, and each year "cries" many auction sales. He was one of the organizers and a charter member of the Connecticut Auctioneer's Association, and in 1920 was elected vice-president.

Mr. Tinker served on the Board of Selectmen of the town of Montville for six years; also was constable, and in 1915-16 represented the town in the State Legislature. He was excise commissioner; doorkeeper of the House of Assembly, 1919-20, and for twelve years has been a member of the Board of Tax Commissioners for Montville. He is a member of Thames Lodge, No. 22, Independent Order of Odd Fellows; member of Colchester Grange, Patrons of Husbandry; and in religious faith is a Baptist. In politics he is a Republican. He has served the people well in these various offices, and is a man well liked by all who know him.

At New London, on April 5, 1887, Mr. Tinker

married Carrie Jane Powers, born in Stonington, Connecticut, daughter of Frank and Ellen (Coleman) Powers, both parents born in Stonington. Mr. and Mrs. Matthew A. Tinker are the parents of ten children, all born at the farm in the town of Montville: 1. Charles B., married Amy Rix, and is engaged in the automobile business in New London. 2. Christine, married Earl Lathrop, a farmer of Montville. 3. William Raymond, now managing his father's large farm in Montville. 4. Mary, married William Fosberge, engaged as a heating engineer in New London. 5. Stanley, a mechanic of New London. 6. Ruth, a teacher of Lyme, Connecticut. 7. Bertha, a teacher of South Coventry, Connecticut. 8. Carrie. 9. Meredith. 10. Cornelia.

FREDERICK ALLAN BECKWITH—Since 1890 Frederick Allan Beckwith has been a resident of Niantic, and the prominence which he has gained both in business and public life has made him one of the best known and most highly respected citizens of this community. It has been said of Mr. Beckwith that wherever philanthropic work is being done you can always find him ready to give substantial aid to further its progress.

John Tyler Beckwith, father of Frederick Allan Beckwith, was born in New London, Connecticut, July 10, 1838. For many years he was a successful farmer in the section of Waterford known as Town Hill, but later he moved to East Lyme to take charge of his wife's old home, and here resided until his death. He married Annie Turner Beckwith, a native of Golden Spurr, East Lyme, daughter of Horace Beckwith, who was one of the pioneers of East Lyme. To Mr. and Mrs. Beckwith were born two children: Frederick Allan, of whom further; Mary, who married Silas Weaver, of East Lyme.

Frederick Allan Beckwith was born in New London, Connecticut, January 7, 1865, but was brought by his father and mother to the Golden Spurr section of East Lyme, which was the latter's former home and was located one-half mile west on the spurr of the trunk line. The boy was educated in the schools of East Lyme, and after completing his studies taught school, during his spare time assisting his father in his work about the farm. In 1890 he came to Niantic, where he subsequently established himself in the coal business. Starting in a small way his enterprise grew rapidly, due largely to his tireless energy and his unwavering belief in his ability to succeed. The welfare and progress of Niantic have always been the object which has pre-eminently influenced every action of Mr. Beckwith's life, and to the furtherance of which he has given generously of his time, thought and money. In politics he is an Independent, casting his vote for the man, regardless of party label. He has served on the Board of Assessors, and since 1895 has been elected many times to the office of first selectman, which is proof in itself that he has ever fulfilled his duties faithfully as a public servant. Mr. Beckwith is prominent in the local fraternal organizations. He affiliates with Bayview Lodge, Free and Accepted Masons; Niantic Lodge, No. 17, Independent Order of Odd Fellows, of which he is past master; New England Order of Protection, of which he is past warden; Ancient Order of United Workmen, of which he is past warder; The Grange, Flanders Chapter; and the Farm Bureau.

On January 25, 1894, at Waterford, Connecticut, Frederick Allan Beckwith married Marion Standard Mott, daughter of Samuel and Frances (Gilberts) Mott. Mr. and Mrs. Beckwith are the parents of two children: Leslie Mott, born May 17, 1896; and Tracy Tyler, born May 19, 1900.

JUDGE SAMUEL ENEAS HOLDRIDGE is a son of Daniel Holdridge, who was born in Ledyard, in March, 1814, spent his life as a farmer, died in 1880, and is buried in Mystic. He married Eliza Jane Maine, born in North Stonington, in 1847, died in February, 1904, daughter of Samuel Maine. They were the parents of seven children: 1. Eliza, married Samuel Caswell, of Ledyard, and has a son, Wilkes Malcolm Caswell. 2. Charles Daniel, married (first) Etta Yerington, (second) Mary Armstrong. 3. Sarah Hannah, married Leeds Maine, of Ledyard, and they are the parents of eight children: William Leeds, Daniel Holdridge, James Stanton, deceased, Samuel, Cora, Julia, Eliza, and Rose. 4. Susan Burroughs, deceased. 5. Orrin, deceased, married Mary Westcott, and left a daughter, Maude Westcott Holdridge. 6. George Austin, deceased, married Jean Day. 7. Samuel E., of further mention.

Samuel Eneas Holdridge was born in the town of Ledyard, New London county, Connecticut, and educated in the public schools of the district and at Mystic Valley Institute. His father's death compelled him to abandon thoughts of a college education, and at the age of seventeen he began teaching in the district school, continuing four years. He then began farming for others during the summer months and teaching in the winter months. At the age of twenty-three he married, and took his wife to the homestead which they made their home until 1900, when Mr. Holdridge bought the farm upon which he now resides, and there he has developed a large business in strawberries and strawberry plants. His strawberry plants go to every New England State each year, the demand growing greater as the strength of the plants and the superior quality of the fruit they bear have been demonstrated. The business is one that must be done for a time, at least, upon absolute faith, and in a great many cases the results have been very disappointing to the fruit grower, who purchased on faith that the berry would bear some resemblance to the beautiful catalog berry. Mr. Holdridge is one of the growers of plants who does not misrepresent, and duplicate orders invariably follow. He is as well known for his honesty in all his dealings as he is for the excellence of the fruit and plants he produces and sells.

For many years Judge Holdridge has been active in public affairs, and it is no exaggeration to say that he is the strongest political force in his town. Since 1912 he has been judge of probate (nine years), and at the November election he was nominee of his own party (Democratic) and endorsed by the Republican party, a fine compliment to his fitness for the office, and a most striking acknowledgment of his popularity, regardless of party. For nineteen years he was a member of the school board, twelve of those being as secretary of the board. He has served as both first and second selectman, and in every office held, his sterling integrity, sound judgment and public-spirit have been as completely at the service of the public as though the business he was transacting were his own private concern.

Judge Holdridge is a member of Shetucket Lodge, Independent Order of Odd Fellows, having joined that order in 1900. He is a member of Somerset Lodge, Free and Accepted Masons; Franklin Chapter, Royal Arch Masons; and Franklin Council, Royal and Select Masters. He was secretary and active member of Ledyard Grange, No. 167, Patrons of Husbandry, now (1922) master, and was secretary of New London County Farm Bureau, these bodies being two of the strongest and most helpful of all organizations which the farmers of the United States have built up for their mutual benefit.

On March 27, 1888, Judge Holdridge married Phoebe Jane Holmes, born in North Stonington, New London county, August 27, 1873, daughter of Shuabel and Angeline (Gray) Holmes. They are the parents of five sons, two born in the town of Norwich, and the three youngest in Ledyard: Samuel Archibald, born in April, 1898; Roy Daniel, born in July, 1900; Carl Holmes, born May 14, 1904; Lester R., born in September, 1907; Paul Orrin, born in May, 1910. The family home and farm are in the town of Ledyard, Norwich, Connecticut, R. F. D. No. 6.

ELISHA SMITH—The family of Smith is one of the oldest in New London county, and one which has given to the county and State many men of ability who have played well their part in its public life. One of the original proprietors of the town of Norwich was Rev. Nehemiah Smith, who was born in England about 1605. He married Anna Bourne, whose sister Martha was a daughter-in-law of Governor William Bradford, of the Plymouth Colony, and in 1659 he was one of the original proprietors of the town of Norwich, Connecticut, who purchased lands from the Indian Chief Uncas. The descendants of Rev. Nehemiah and Anna (Bourne) Smith are numerous in Eastern Connecticut. This review deals with two men, Elisha Smith, and his son, also Elisha, residents of East Lyme, New London county, Connecticut, whose lives are now a part of that section of the county in which they long resided.

Elisha (1) Smith was born at East Lyme, Connecticut, August 7, 1786, there spent his life, and died September 19, 1860. He was a shoemaker by trade, industrious and upright, a man who held the entire respect of the community in which he so long lived and labored. He married Mary Gorton, born in East Lyme, June 16, 1786, died May 2, 1861, daughter of Collins and Mary G. (Miner) Gorton. They were the parents of seven children, all born in East Lyme, all of whom have passed away after useful lives in the town of their birth, where all are buried: William Augus, born October 8, 1809; John Gorton, born September 24, 1810; Mary Gorton, born March 10, 1812; Edmund, born October 21, 1816; Elisha (2), of further mention; Frances Elizabeth, born March 13, 1824; Charles Henry, born October 27, 1828.

Elisha (2) Smith, fifth child of Elisha (1) and Mary (Gorton) Smith, was born in East Lyme, New London county, Connecticut, February 2, 1820, and died at his home in Niantic, town of East Lyme, May 21, 1889. He attended the public schools of his district. At an early age he was called into service as his father's assistant in the shoe shop, and eventually he became himself a skilled shoemaker. He continued with his father until the years of his minority were about completed, and then he married and with his wife and his brother Edmund journeyed westward to Paw-Paw, Michigan, where the brothers conducted a general store. Four years later they sold their store, contents, fixtures and good will, Elisha Smith and his wife returning to their native State, locating in Hartford. There Mr. Smith turned his trade accomplishments to a good purpose, entering the employ of the Goodman Shoe Company, of Hartford. He prospered in Hartford and while there employed built a modern house in the village of Niantic in his native town, East Lyme. Later, after the death of his wife, when he wished to retire, he came to Niantic and occupied the home he had purchased until his death, which occurred in 1889. Like his father, Elisha (2) Smith was a man of industrious, upright life, a man admired and thoroughly respected wherever known.

Elisha (2) Smith married (first), in East Lyme, about 1840, Sarah Tinker, born in East Lyme, who died in Hartford, Connecticut, without children. He married (second), April 13, 1882, Ella Beckwith, born in Niantic, Connecticut, November 25, 1853, daughter of Captain Elisha and Nancy (Huntley) Beckwith. Captain Beckwith was an off shore fisherman, owning and sailing his own vessel. He had two sons and a daughter, all born in Niantic; the sons were: Calvin Elisha Beckwith; Noble Union Beckwith, married Lottie Curtis, of Meriden, Connecticut, and now engaged in the dry goods business in Meriden. Mr. and Mrs. Smith were the parents of three children: Ella Louise, born in Niantic, Connecticut, June 6, 1885; Edmund Beckwith, born in Niantic, January 20, 1887; Charlotte, born in Niantic, November 17, 1888, died July 15, 1892.

LOUIS H. GODDARD is a native son of New London, was educated in her schools and is one of the successful business and professional men of the city. In association with his father, who was a skilled contractor and builder, he gained his first experience, then turned to architecture and is well established in his profession.

Asa O. Goddard, the father, was born in Waterford, Connecticut, there was educated in the public schools and there learned the carpenter's trade. He later became a contractor and builder, continuing in business until 1908, when he retired. He died in New London, aged sixty-eight years. He married Josephine Benham, born in Waterford, died in New London, Connecticut, and they were the parents of three children: Louis H., of whom further; Royce H., a resident of New London; and Frederick B., of Baltimore, Maryland.

Louis H. Goddard, eldest son of Asa O. and Josephine (Benham) Goddard, was born in New London, Connecticut, and there completed grade and high school courses of study. After leaving school he learned the carpenters' trade with his father, and continued with him from 1888 to 1891. At the age of twenty, he entered the employ of Cole & Chandler, architects of Boston, and had an office in New London. For two years the young man remained with Cole & Chandler, studying architecture, then became a partner with his father and together they conducted a prosperous contracting business for fifteen years, 1893-1908, at the end of which time Mr. Goddard, Senior, retired, Mr. Goddard, Junior, continuing the business until 1911. From 1911 until 1916, Mr. Goddard was draughtsman and estimator in association with H. R. Douglass, of New London, but in 1916 he opened an architect's office in New London, where, under his own name, he has for five years continued in his profession, establishing a prosperous business. During the Spanish-American War, Mr. Goddard enlisted and served as first sergeant in Company I, 3rd Regiment, Connecticut National Guard. He is a member of George M. Cole Post, Spanish War Veterans, and fraternally, is affiliated with New London Lodge, No. 360, Benevolent and Protective Order of Elks.

He married, in New London, June 25, 1902, Lucy A. Avery, daughter of Charles P. and Harriet (Lyman) Avery, of New London. Mr. and Mrs. Goddard are the parents of two sons, both born in New London: Asa Avery, and Robert P.

CHARLES CHILD GILDERSLEEVE, M. D., son of Samuel and Annette Matilda (Child) Gildersleeve, was born at Northport, New York. He is the seventh Charles Child in direct maternal line. His education, begun in the public schools, was continued in New York University for two years, and in Yale Medical School, where he received his M. D., class of 1896. He was interne at Worcester, Massachusetts, City Hospital in 1896 and 1897, then began practice at Woodstock, Connecticut. He was surgeon to the Day-Kimbell Hospital at Putnam, Connecticut, until 1912, when he came to Norwich, Connecticut, where he still remains. He is surgeon to William W. Backus Hospital. Dr. Gildersleeve is a trustee of Connecticut State Hospital, and medical examiner for the towns and cities of Norwich, Bozrah, Franklin and Lebanon, Connecticut. He is a member of the American Medical Association; New London County Medical Society; Norwich City Medical Society; Worcester, Massachusetts, City Hospital Alumni Association; Yale Medical School Alumni Association; the Masonic order, thirty-second degree; Nobles of the Mystic Shrine; Independent Order of Odd Fellows; Loyal Order of Moose; Norwich Chamber of Commerce; the Arcanum Club; Central Baptist Church.

On June 22, 1896, Dr. Gildersleeve married Susan May Corbin, daughter of Frank and Mary (Bradford) Corbin, a direct descendant of Governor William Bradford, of the "Mayflower." Dr. and Mrs. Gildersleeve are the parents of three children: 1. George Harold, born June 28, 1898, a graduate of Brown University, class of 1919; member Yale Medical School, class 1923. 2. Donald Child, born February 22, 1900. 3. Dorothy, born April 14, 1908. The family residence is No. 29 Lincoln avenue, Norwich, Connecticut, his office at No. 310 Main street.

GEORGE VARNUM SHEDD—Rounding out a long and useful life, in which he has figured in many branches of honorable effort, George Varnum Shedd, of Preston, New London county, Connecticut, is spending his declining years on the farm, still taking a constructive part in the public life of the town.

Mr. Shedd is a son of Varnum A. and Phebe (Harrington) Shedd. Varnum A. Shedd was born in Chelmsford, Massachusetts, and there received his education in the public schools. He became a superintendent of the cotton mills of that place, following this line of work throughout his lifetime. For several years he was agent and business manager of the Salmon Falls Cotton Company, of Salmon Falls, New Hampshire. He died in that town in the year 1859. His wife was born in Marlborough, Massachusetts, and died in Waltham, in the same State. They were the parents of seven children, of whom Mr. Shedd, of Preston, is the fourth.

George Varnum Shedd was born in Lowell, Massachusetts, November 14, 1842. Receiving his early education in the public schools of his native city, he later attended the Berwick Academy, in Maine, and then completed his studies at the Gorham Academy, in Maine. After his education was finished the young man became associated with his brother, Albert A. Shedd, in the dry goods business in Boston. At the outbreak of the Civil War they sold out their business, both enlisting, with two other clerks in the store, in defense of the Union. Mr. Shedd served in Company B, 39th Regiment, Massachusetts Volunteer Infantry. He was taken prisoner at Spottsylvania, Virginia, later making his escape. He was transferred to the mustering out department of General Warren, of the Fifth Army Corps.

After the close of the Civil War, Mr. Shedd entered the dry goods business again, conducting a store at Charlestown, Massachusetts, then later was in the same business in Marlborough for five years. Early in the seventies he came to Norwich, Connecticut, where he carried on a store along the same line for a number of years. Then wishing to retire from active business and still hold an interest in some branch of activity, he came to Preston, about 1890, and bought the farm which he now occupies. He is still active about the place, and carrying on an amount of general farming which would do credit to a younger man.

In the public interests of the town Mr. Shedd has been a prominent figure for some years. Politically affiliated with the Republican party, he quickly became a leader of its interests here. He was elected town clerk of Preston in 1908, and was selectman for five years. He has always been deeply interested in the subject of education, and served on the school board of Preston for many years. Mr. Shedd is a member of Sedgwick Post, of Norwich, Sons of the American Revolution. His church membership is with the Congregational church of Preston.

In 1870 Mr. Shedd married (first) Frances Hammond, daughter of Horace Hammond, of Waltham, Massachusetts. Her mother"s family name was Smith. They were the parents of three children: Horace H., now deceased; Arthur E., now a farmer in Preston, who married Carry Morgan, and Ethel F., deceased. The mother of these children died in 1879. Mr. Shedd married (second), in 1887, Abby P. Sears, who died in 1898. He married (third), January 15, 1903, Mary E. Morse, daughter of William and Sarah (Avery) Morse, of Preston. Mr. and Mrs. Shedd are members of the Congregational church, of Preston.

GEORGE ALBERT KEPPLER—Long prominent in the business world of Norwich, and an equally familiar figure in social, theatrical and fraternal circles, George Albert Keppler has for many years borne a significant part in the general progress of this city. Mr. Keppler's family is of German origin, and his father was born there, coming to the United States in his youth.

Sebastian Paul Keppler, Mr. Keppler's father, who was the founder of the oldest tailoring establishment in Norwich, was born in Waldshut, Baden, Germany, January 15, 1833. Coming to America at the age of sixteen years, and although scarcely more than a lad, began life here as a master tailor. He worked at his trade until the breaking out of the Civil War, then enlisted in Company I, 18th Regiment, Connecticut Volunteer Infantry. He saw active service at Gettysburg and Antietam, receiving a severe wound in the latter battle, and he also suffered the horrors of six months' incarceration in Andersonville prison. Returning North, he continued work at his trade until the year 1888, when he founded an independent tailoring business in Norwich. He was actively engaged thus for many years, until his retirement, winning the esteem and cordial good will of all with whom he came in contact. He married Christina Josephine Reiss, who was born December 28, 1843, and they were the parents of two children: George A., whose name heads this review; and Minnie, who is unmarried.

George Albert Keppler was born in Norwich, May 6, 1869. Receiving his early education in the public schools of the city, he was later graduated from the Norwich Free Academy (1887). From childhood interested in his father's work, Mr. Keppler became associated with him after leaving school, and mastering the business, soon took a man's place side by side with his father, the firm name becoming S. P. Keppler & Son. He has spent his entire career with this enterprise, of which he is now the head and owner. His patrons are among the most fastidious people of the city of Norwich, and also of the Thames Valley, and he holds a high position in the business world of this section. It is not only in business circles, however, that Mr. Keppler has won marked prominence. He is an enthusiastic horticulturist, and well known among flower lovers hereabouts. But his chief recreative interest, which has indeed become far more than mere recreation, is his broad activity in theatrical affairs. He has been a leader in amateur theatricals in Norwich for many years, and was director of the pageant which was given on the occasion of the two hundred and fiftieth anniversary of the founding of Norwich. He is esteemed as a theatrical critic of broad vision and discriminating judgment, is the local critic, and is representative of the Dramatic Mirror. Fraternally Mr. Keppler is widely known. He is a member of Somerset Lodge, No. 34, Free and Accepted Masons; Franklin Chapter, No. 4, Royal Arch Masons; Franklin Council, No. 3, Royal and Select Masters; Columbian Commandery, No. 4, Knights Templar; King Solomon Lodge of Perfection; Van Rensselaer Council, Princes of Jerusalem; Norwich Chapter, Rose Croix de Harodim; and Connecticut Consistory, Ancient Accepted Scottish Rite. He received the thirty-third degree in Masonry, in September of 1922, at Cleveland, Ohio. He is also a member of Sphinx Temple, of Hartford, Ancient Arabic Order, Nobles of the Mystic Shrine, and of Uncas Lodge, No. 11, Independent Order of Odd Fellows, of which last named lodge he is past master. He is a member of the Sons of Veterans, and his religious affiliation is with the Universalist Church of the Good Shepherd.

Mr. Keppler married, in Norwich, on March 29, 1892, Ina Francis Ruby, daughter of David Thomas and Annah (Francis) Ruby.

CHARLES HENRY WHEELER—One of the oldest families of New London county, Connecti-

Charles H. Wheeler

cut, is the Wheeler family, which for many generations has been represented in the southeastern part of the county, and has always been familiar in North Stonington. Charles Henry Wheeler, whose death in 1919 removed an upright and honored citizen, was a direct descendant of Thomas Wheeler, the immigrant ancestor of this family, who settled in Stonington early in the seventeenth century. The line follows down through his son, Isaac; Richard, son of Isaac; Jonathan, son of Richard; and Eleazer, son of Jonathan.

Eleazer Wheeler was born in North Stonington, and educated in the district schools of his day. After completing his studies he took up the work of the farm, which he followed throughout his lifetime. He died in North Stonington in 1870. He married Lucinda Morgan, who died in Norwich in 1895, and they were the parents of eleven children.

Charles Henry Wheeler, son of Eleazer and Lucinda (Morgan) Wheeler, was born in North Stonington, December 25, 1836, and was reared in his native town and educated in the district schools. Following the family traditions he also took up farming, working on various farms in North Stonington and Preston, until 1870, when he removed his family to the old Pride Homestead, then owned by his wife's mother. This place is known as Long Rock Farm, a name handed down by the Indians, and now a part of the farm owned and occupied by the Connecticut State Hospital. On this farm Mr. Wheeler carried on extensive farming operations in the old days, and still conducted the farm until the time of his death. He was a man of quiet tastes, always busy about the homely tasks of the farm, the activities upon which the prosperity of the nation is founded. He was devoted to his home and family, his whole life and all his interests centering there. He died February 8, 1919, regretted by all who knew him, and his name is cherished in the little circle of close friends to whom his exemplary life was an inspiration.

Mr. Wheeler married, on January 5, 1865, Emma Louisa Stodder, of Preston, Connecticut, who was born in Sullivan county, New York, September 20, 1846, and is a daughter of Cephas and Clarice (Pride) Stodder. Mrs. Wheeler still survives her husband and resides on the above farm. Their five children are as follows: Frank Stodder, a farmer, who married Annie Gay, and resides on Scotland Road, in the town of Norwich; Minnie Abby, a Norwich school teacher, who resides at home; Charles Henry, a farmer of Scotland, who married Lena Isham; Amos Billings, of Norwich, who married Jennie Browning; and Clara Pride, who resides at home. The family attend the Baptist church, always being interested in Union Chapel, in Preston.

BURTON WINTHROP DEWOLF—With practical experience in various lines of activity, Burton W. DeWolf, of Old Lyme, Connecticut, is bearing a part in the progress of the community in conducting an up-to-date grocery and genera l store.

Mr. DeWolf comes of a very old family in New London county, many members of which have been and still are prominent in the public and mercantile activities of the southwestern part of the county. Mr. DeWolf's grandfather, Roger William DeWolf, was born in Old Lyme, February 11, 1837, and receiving the usual common school education of the day, took up farming with an older brother, then, later in life, entered the grocery business at Black Hall, and for thirty years was identified with this business, placing it in the hands of his son when he retired from the active management of this interest. He has since conducted a small farm directly across the road from this store. Roger W. DeWolf represented the town of Old Lyme in the State Legislature in 1883, and has served the town also as a member of the Board of Relief, being prominent in public affairs, although independent in his political convictions. He married Julia Smith, of Niantic, daughter of William and Eunice Smith, and they were the parents of four children: Winthrop Roger, who took over his store upon his retirement; Claude, who was born April 6, 1869; Roger, who died in childhood; and Agnes Julia, born February 8, 1871, who married (first) James Henry Beebe, of East Lyme, and (second) Henry Rathbun.

Winthrop Roger DeWolf, eldest son of Roger William and Julia (Smith) DeWolf, was born in Old Lyme, Connecticut, in October, 1863, and educated in the schools of his native town. More or less active from boyhood in the interests of the store which his father had founded, when the older man wished to retire, he took over the responsibilities of the business, and carried it forward successfully. He was in full charge of the business from 1891 until 1918, ill health compelling him, in the latter year, to turn the business over into the hands of his son. Winthrop R. DeWolf married Cora Ackerson, and they had one daughter and one son: Caroll Frances; and Burton Winthrop, of whom further.

Burton Winthrop DeWolf was born in the town of Old Lyme, December 27, 1886, and was educated in the district schools of the community. Upon leaving school he was employed at the famous Black Hall greenhouses, and was identified with this work for several years. Later he left his native town, and for some time was engaged in various enterprises. In 1907 Mr. DeWolf was employed by the General Electric Company, of Lynn, Massachusetts. This connection took him through Massachusetts, Connecticut and New York States. When sixteen years old he worked in the Palmer, Bidquitt Mills, at Montville, Connecticut. He later worked as night timekeeper for the New York, New Haven & Hartford Railroad on the Saybrook and Lyme drawbridge. Mr. DeWolf has undergone two very serious operations in the Hartford Hospital. In 1918, on account of his father's broken health, Mr. DeWolf returned to Old Lyme and took charge of the store.

Applying progressive methods and his own enterprising spirit to the business, which has always been prosperous, Mr. DeWolf is carrying it forward to even greater success. For sixty years this business has now been in the DeWolf family, the present owner being the third generation in direct line to hold its management, and friends of the family predict great success for him.

While broadly interested in all progress, Mr. DeWolf has never taken a leading position in the political world. He keeps in touch with political affairs, but votes independently. He is now serving as assistant postmaster.

On October 31, 1918, Mr. DeWolf married Monica Elizabeth Sturges-Jones, of English descent, who was born in New York City in 1897. They have one daughter, Nadine Gale, who was born in Black Hall, October 19, 1919.

CHARLES YOUNG was a successful business man of Norwich, Connecticut, who became wealthy through industry and economy, all his efforts being aided by his capable wife, Phillipena T. F. (Young) Young. Charles Young was born in Bavaria, Germany, his father a farmer. The boy attended school until the age of fourteen, in the meanwhile assisting his father on the farm. Learning the trade of cutler from an elder brother, he was enabled to carry on that trade until he entered the German army, at twenty-two years of age, serving for about six years, until the war broke out between Bavaria and Prussia. He then became an officer in the Bavarian army, but that army being defeated, he was forced to flee from his native land. In 1848 he came to the United States, bringing with him his bride of four weeks. The young couple sailed from Havre, France, and after a voyage of thirty-one days landed in New York City. Two days later they came to Norwich, Connecticut, where he began to learn the trade of a moulder, while his enterprising young wife worked early and late as a seamstress, becoming a very popular dressmaker. During the war the Youngs purchased the building on the corner of Main and Franklin streets, Norwich, Connecticut, (now known as Young's Hotel), and for eighteen years profitably conducted an excellent hotel. Later, they purchased the Stedman property at Norwichtown, Connecticut, formerly the Governor Huntington estate, and there Mr. Young built greenhouses and made other improvements, operating the property as a fruit and flower farm. There Mr. Young made his home until about a year before his death, when he was taken ill and removed to a hospital in Hartford, Connecticut, where he died May 27, 1897, aged seventy-five years. His remains lie in beautiful Yantic Cemetery, Norwich, Connecticut, in a vault which his widow erected a year after his death.

Charles Young married, in Germany, in 1848, Phillipena Theresa Fronica Young, born May 1, 1825, died in Norwichtown, Connecticut, September 13, 1916, in her ninety-first year, daughter of Charles Young, her father and her husband bearing the same name although not related. Mr. and Mrs. Young were the parents of a daughter, who died at birth, only living two days. Mrs. Young was a wonderful business woman, and the Young fortune, which she aided her husband to accumulate, was largely increased during the seventeen years of her windowhood. While she died from old age, she retained her mental faculties until the last and did not need spectacles, having very strong eyes even when numbered with the nonagenarians. She was very active until the last, traveling to the city to transact real estate business until within a very few years of her passing. The beautiful vault she erected for her husband's remains she now shares with him.

Mrs. Young was highly esteemed in Norwich, Connecticut, not alone for her fine business quality, but for her womanly strength of character and for her pleasing personality. By will, Mrs. Young bequeathed her fortune and land estate to her niece, Mrs. Emma M. (Foerstner) Welte, wife of Emil Welte, and mother of Carl M. Welte (see sketch following).

CARL MICHAEL WELTE—The Weltes of Norwich, Connecticut, came to that city in 1867. Their home, at No. 34 East Towne street, formerly the Young homestead, was the former residence of Samuel Huntington, the eighteenth Governor of the State of Connecticut, and a signer of the Declaration of Independence. Upon coming into possession of the estate, real and personal of every kind, Mrs. Emma M. (Foerstner) Welte, the legatee, had the homestead remodelled to conform architecturally with the original Colonial style, and although the house has been remodeled several times, its exterior still retains the appearance it presented in the days when it was the home of Governor Huntington.

Carl M. Welte is a son of Emil and Emma M. (Foerstner) Welte, and grandson of Michael Welte, the latter born on September 29, 1807, in Voernbach, Baden, Germany, and later becoming a freemason and a charter member of "Leopold zu Treue in Oriente" Lodge, in Carlsruhe, Baden, Germany. Emil Welte was born in Voernbach, Schwarzwald, Baden, Germany, April 20, 1841. He attended the elementary school in his native city, and was graduated from the Technical School in Furtwagen, Baden, Germany. At the age of twenty-one years, he was appointed by the Grand Duke Frederick of Baden, to represent the clock and automatic musical instrument industries from the Black Forest section at the London, England, exhibition, 1862. He left his home town, Voernbach, and sailed from Liverpool, England, on January 21, 1866, on the ship "Afrika," one of the first side-wheelers, built about 1841, arriving in Boston, Massachusetts, February 2, 1866, and the following day, Sunday, reached New York City.

Mr. Welte came to America for the purpose of installing a very large and expensive orchestrion in William Kramer's establishment at No. 50 Bowery, New York City. This automatic, self-playing organ attracted favorable comment from critics, and considering it an opportune time to open an establishment here, Mr. Welte wrote to his father in Voernbach to ship him a number of the smaller type of automatic orchestrions. He opened a store on the northeast corner of Fifth avenue and Twenty-second street, New York City, and later opened another on East Fourteenth street, New York City, then the popular shopping district of the city. The business in New York was conducted under the firm name, M. Welte & Son, Branch of M. Welte & Soehne, Voernbach, Germany, and until May 1, 1914, Emil Welte was its active managing head. He then retired to his home, No. 34 East Towne street, Norwichtown, Connecticut, but is still chairman of the executive board of M. Welte & Soehne, now located at Freiburg, Baden, Germany, that house being manufacturers of automatic musical instruments. Mr. Welte is a member of the Masonic order, affiliated with Anchor Lodge, No. 720, Free and Accepted Masons, College Point, Long Island, New York; and a member of Cornucopia Chapter, Royal Arch Masons, Flushing, Long Island, New York. He is now living in retired contentment at Norwichtown, Connecticut, his wife and one son his companions, the latter being his amanuensis and business representative.

Emil Welte married, June 22, 1871, in the Second Congregational Church, Norwich, Connecticut, Emma Marguerite Foerstner, born in Norwich, Connecticut, March 18, 1853, daughter of Joseph and Mary Foerstner, and niece of Mrs. Phillipena T. F. Young.

The Foerstners of this review are of German parentage. Joseph Foerstner, father of Mrs. Emil (Foerstner) Welte, was born March 23, 1825, in Ellwangen, Wurtemberg, Germany. He was a shoemaker by trade and came to the United States on the sailing vessel "Sea Queen," May 20, 1852. While upon this ship he made the acquaintance of Mary Young, and when the ship arrived in New York they were married. From there the young couple went to Norwich, Connecticut, to visit the bride's sister, Mrs. Phillipena T. F. Young, and while there Mr. Foerstner secured employment in the molding room in Vaughn's foundry, and there the Foerstners remained. In 1863 Joseph Foerstner joined the 18th Regiment, Connecticut Volunteers, Company F, under Captain Henry Peale, later Major Peale, and left Norwich on August 22, 1862, at four P. M., with fifty-nine men. While in action near Winchester, Frederick county, Virginia, June 15, 1863, he was captured by the Confederates and thrown into Libby Prison, Richmond, Virginia, and while imprisoned in Libby received such scanty food that starvation undermined his health, and he was placed in camp at Annapolis, Maryland, where he died, August 10, 1863, at the age of thirty-seven years. Mrs. Phillipena T. F. Young traveled from Norwich, Connecticut, to Annapolis, Maryland, to claim the body, which was shipped north, and buried in the old Norwich cemetery, Cliff street, with military honors. Mr. Foerstner had been promoted to the rank of corporal.

Mary (Young) Foerstner was born in Kaiserslantern in the province of Rhenisch, Bavaria, Germany, in June, 1822, died in her home, in Trenton, New Jersey, in November, 1901, and was buried in Trenton. She sailed from Havre, France, May 20, 1852, on the ship "Sea Queen" for the United States, met Joseph Foerstner on board, and upon their arrival in New York City, she became his wife, as above mentioned. Mr. and Mrs. Joseph Foerstner were the parents of four children: Emma Marguerite, born on March 18, 1853, who married Emil Welte, above mentioned; Charles, born in 1855; Pauline, born in 1857; and Josephine Foerstner, born in 1863. All of these children were born in Norwich, Connecticut. Charles and Pauline died while under ten years of age, in Norwich; Josephine Foerstner was married in Norwich, Connecticut, in 1884, to George Noss, and died in Norwich, Connecticut, November 19, 1891, without issue. Of the four children only one is living, Mrs. Emma Marguerite (Foerstner) Welte, of No. 34 East Towne street, Norwichtown, Connecticut.

Emma Marguerite Foerstner, eldest of the above children, was born in Norwich, March 18, 1853, and attended the city public schools until 1867, when she finished the courses of the Broadway school. She pursued musical study at Music Vale Seminary, and at Salem Normal Academy of Music, Salem, Connecticut, and is a graduate of both. As above noted, she married, June 22, 1871, Emil Welte, then of New York City, and on June 22, 1921, Mr. and Mrs. Welte celebrated their fifty-first wedding anniversary in a quiet way, with their immediate family, both being in good health. Mr. and Mrs. Welte are the parents of two sons: Carl Michael, of further mention; and Emil, Jr., born in January, 1874, died November 16, 1881. The family lived in New York City from 1872 until 1914, when they removed to No. 34 East Towne street, Norwich, Connecticut, where they have resided since.

Carl M. Welte was born in Norwich, Connecticut, in the old Governor Huntington Colonial mansion, then the home of his great-aunt, Mrs. Phillipena T. F. Young, August 8, 1872. The same year his parents removed to New York City, where the lad attended public school, finishing primary school at Pleasant avenue and 120th street, New York City, and then passing to Grammar School No. 14, East Twenty-seventh street, New York City, and finally graduating from Packard Commercial College, corner of Fourth avenue and Twenty-third street, New York City. He took a four years' course in the Young Men's Christian Association, at Twenty-third street and Fourth avenue, in mechanical drawing and foreign language, and was a member of that association for eight years. He studied music for seven years under a pianist of professional prominence, that being part of his preparation for his father's musical business. While residing in New York City he attended the Universalist Fourth Divine Paternity Church, then situated at Forty-fifth street and Fifth avenue. In 1889 he entered his father's business, M. Welte & Sons, in New York City, serving as an apprentice and learning the trade of organ builder. In 1893 he was sent to Chicago, Illinois, to the World's Columbian Exposition, to look after the firm's exhibition, in conjunction with his father, Mr. Emil Welte.

In 1901 he became a member of the firm, M. Welte & Soehe, in Freiburg, Baden, Germany, and also of the New York branch, M. Welte & Sons, Inc., sharing in the profits of both firms. On May 1, 1914, he withdrew from active partnership in the New York City firm, M. Welte & Sons, Incorporated, but retained his shares of stock interests, which he sold in September, 1919, after the government sold the alien enemy stock which represented the interests of German citizens, who were shareholders in M. Welte & Sons, Inc. He resides in Norwichtown, Connecticut, where he manages his mother's real estate and his father's financial interests. He is a member of the New London County Historical Society; the Norwichtown Rural Association; a director in the Empire Tin Mining Company, of Tin City, Seward Peninsula, Alaska, acting as an officer of the executive board. He is also a life member of the Luther Burbank Society, of Santa Rosa, California.

Carl M. Welte was married, November 12, 1903, in the rectory of the parish of the Church of the Transfiguration, "The Little Church Around the Corner," No. 1 East Twenty-ninth street, New York City, New York, by the Reverend George Clarke Houghton, D. D., to Annie Easter Morgan, of Norwichtown, Connecticut, and they are the parents of one son, Carl M. Welte, Jr., who was born in 1907, but died July 27, 1908. Mr. and Mrs. Welte are occupying a portion of the homestead at No. 34 East Towne street, Norwichtown, Connecticut, where Mr. Welte was born.

RHODES BURROWS—The Burrows family in New London, Connecticut, descend from Robert Burrows, a Baptist, who came from Manchester, England, to escape persecution, and after residence in Massachusetts, went to Wethersfield, Connecticut, where he was a land owner in 1641. Prior to 1642, he married Mary, widow of Samuel Ireland, and about 1650 moved to New London and was soon numbered among the early settlers of the town of Groton, on the west side of the Mystic river. He was appointed the first ferryman on that stream, and in 1682 died, having survived his wife ten years. Their son, John Burrows, born in 1642, was one of the patentees under the amended Charter of the New London settlement, which at that time included Groton. The first Baptist church in Connecticut was established in New London, and of that church John Burrows was a member. He married Hannah Culver, and they were the parents of five sons, through whom a large family has descended.

Rhodes Burrows, one of these descendants, is a son of Frank S. and Helen (Bromley) Burrows, his father born in Mystic, Connecticut, where he died in 1919; his mother, born in Stonington, is still a resident of Mystic, Connecticut, where all her married life has been spent. Frank S. and Helen (Bromley) Burrows were the parents of three children: Rhodes, of further mention; Nelson, deceased; and Roscoe T., now residing in Boston.

Rhodes Burrows was born in Mystic, Connecticut, June 2, 1877, and there completed public school courses of study; later he prepared under Professor Charles Chapman, of Mystic, and in 1908 entered the dental department of the University of Maryland, whence he was graduated D. D. S., class of 1911. He at once began practice in Mystic, Connecticut, and there continues. He ranks high in professional ability and has built up a large practice. He is a member of the State Dental Association of Connecticut, and is highly esteemed by his professional brethren. He is a Republican in politics; his church membership is with the Baptist church; and he is a member of Stonington Lodge, No. 25, Independent Order of Odd Fellows, of Mystic.

Dr. Burrows married, June 21, 1919, Mrs. Mildred (Denison) O'Neal, of Mystic, Connecticut, widow of Thomas O'Neal.

DEXTER SELLEW CASE—A descendant of one of the oldest and most honored families of Canton, Connecticut, Mr. Case, of Sound View, is successfully conducting a general store at this popular summer resort on Long Island Sound.

Mr. Case's grandfather, Everett Case, was a prominent farmer of Canton, Connecticut, and his son, William Wirt Case, was born in Canton, and followed farming there throughout his lifetime. During the Civil War he enlisted in defense of the Union, and was a member of the Twenty-second Regiment, Connecticut Volunteer Infantry, but after nine months of service was invalided home on account of broken health. He died in Canton, in August, 1910, at the age of seventy-six years, and is buried there. He married Harriet Dexter Sellew, of Coventry, Connecticut, daughter of Nathan and Jerusha Sellew. She died January 31, 1921, and lies buried beside her husband in Canton. They were the parents of two children: Dexter S., of whom further; and Hortense Isabella, who was born in Canton, and is now the wife of Charles French, of Sound View, Connecticut.

Dexter Sellew Case, son of William Wirt and Harriet Dexter (Sellew) Case, was born in Canton, November 20, 1876, and received his early education in his native town, completing his studies at the

Collinsville High School, which is located in the town of Canton. For a number of years after finishing school Mr. Case was engaged in the lumber business and contract work in the northwestern part of Connecticut. Coming to Sound View in 1910, Mr. Case purchased the general store in which he has since gained substantial success. He has carried on this business continuously since establishing himself there.

Mr. Case is well known in the town of Old Lyme, of which Sound View is a part, and is an active worker in the ranks of the Republican party. He fills the office of postmaster at Sound View. He is a member of Collinsville Grange, No. 34, Patrons of Husbandry, and is a member of the Methodist Episcopal church of Old Lyme. In 1907-08 Mr. Case served as lieutenant in the Salvation Army, and labored faithfully in the cause of humanity, but for financial reasons resigned to enter upon his business career.

On August 28, 1913, Mr. Case married Jennie Frances Kimball, who was born December 2, 1884, in New York City, and is a daughter of the late Wilbur and Elizabeth (Chase) Kimball. Mr. and Mrs. Case have four children: Paul Kimball, who was born in Sound View July 28, 1914; David Benjamin, born February 16, 1917; Nathan Dexter, born March 15, 1918; and Ruth Esther, born November 19, 1919; all born in Sound View.

ARTHUR E. ANDREWS—We are very properly full of praise in this country for the man who has started at the bottom of the ladder and made his way by means of his own effort to the top. New England is full of such men, and certainly we are justified in adding to the long list the name of Arthur E. Andrews, born in St. Michael's, Azores, October 9, 1882.

Arthur E. Andrews is the son of Martin and Aurekata (Medeiros) Andrews. Martin Andrews was a sea captain for many years, and during his voyages travelled most of the European coast. To Mr. and Mrs. Andrews were born three children: John, a baker in Norwich; Horace, an attorney; and Arthur E., the subject of this review.

The education of Arthur E. Andrews was obtained in his native place, after which he was a clerk in a grocery store there for about three years. In 1901 he set sail for the United States, and upon landing in this country, remained in Boston, Massachusetts, for eighteen months, where he secured a position as clerk, subsequently going to Melrose and associating himself there with his brother, who was manager of a large bakery. After gaining a thorough knowledge of this trade, he returned to Boston and was placed in charge of the bakery of J. G. & B. S. Ferguson, which position he held for eight years. In 1913 he came to Norwich and opened a small bakery on the present site of his large enterprise of today. He has had two serious fires, through which he has suffered severe losses, the last one occurring in June of the present year (1920). On this site he is erecting a large garage. In 1919 Mr. Andrews opened a retail department on Franklin street, where he has a large and very attractive store.

Mr. Andrews is affiliated with the Loyal Order of Moose, the Knights of the Golden Eagle, and the Portuguese fraternity of the United States. He is also a member of the United Commercial Travelers' Association, St. Michael's Society, and the Norwich Chamber of Commerce. In religion he is an Episcopalian and attends the church of that denomination in Norwich.

On June 10, 1906, Mr. Andrews was united in marriage with Mary George, a native of Norwich, Connecticut. Mr. and Mrs. Andrews have no issue.

Such is the life of Arthur E. Andrews, a self-made man, who started in this country poor in finances, but rich in shrewdness and foresight, traits which go to make up a man among men. He quickly adapted himself to circumstances and readily took advantage of every opportunity which would bring him in contact with the worth-while things in life. Today he stands as one of the most prominent and respected business men of Norwich, a shining example to the youth of America, a product of Democracy's free institutions.

RICHARD SAMUEL PARKER—The name of Parker, in Norwich, Connecticut, is closely identified, so far as business connections are concerned, with the paint trade. In the social, political and religious activities of the community, as in business, it stands for progress all along the line.

Richard Samuel Parker, born June 5, 1853, at South Pettenton, England, a son of William Parker, came to this country with his family when only two years of age. The family located in Brooklyn, New York, and there the boy gained his education in the public schools of the city. As he grew to manhood he was ambitious to go out into the world and make a place for himself among men of business. Accordingly, he became associated with Harrison Brothers & Company, of Philadelphia, Pennsylvania, as a commercial salesman. The firm manufactured an extensive line of paints and painters' supplies, and at that time was high on the list in this industry. Mr. Parker remained with them in the same capacity for thirty years. By this time he had, of necessity, become thoroughly familiar with the ins and outs of the paint business. Never content to know anything superficially, he had also informed himself in detail of the various points involved in the manufacture of paints; and in 1896 he started manufacturing a line of paints in Brooklyn, New York. Beginning in a small way, but with his valuable experience behind him, the business developed rapidly. In 1903, appreciating the advantages of a small city over a large one to any manufacturer, he removed his plant to Norwich, Connecticut. There, with Charles H. Preston, he incorporated under the name, Parker, Preston & Company, with a capital stock of $25,000, of which $15,000 was paid in. Mr. Parker became president and general manager, and Mr. Preston secretary and treasurer of the company, which began the manufacture of a very complete line of shingle stains and paint specialties. After Mr. Preston's decease, a few years later, Mr. Parker became sole owner of the entire concern, and under his management the business has continued to grow and expand, the firm name being a synonym for excellence in both appearance and quality. During the later years of Mr. Parker's life, his son Nelson was associated with him in the business, and has carried it on most successfully since his death. Richard Samuel Parker died in Norwich, June 26, 1918, mourned by a wide circle of friends, as well as by the business associates with whom he had so long been in daily contact. He was a man actuated by the highest principles, and commanded the respect of all with whom he had dealings of any kind. His chief delight, in hours of relaxation, was to enjoy the quiet of his home. He married, November 22, 1877, Mary M. Selsor, of Germantown, Pennsylvania, and they were the parents of eight children, of whom four are living.

Nelson Parker, the seventh child of Richard Samuel and Mary M. (Selsor) Parker, was reared and educated in Brooklyn, New York, receiving his formal training in the public schools. He then learned the paint manufacturing business with his father, and the two worked side by side in carrying on the business, until the elder Parker's death. At that time Mrs. Parker became president of the company, and Mr. Nelson Parker secretary and treasurer, as well as general manager. This arrangement still continues, and the business is now one of the important industries of Norwich. The original name of Parker, Preston & Company is still retained.

Besides being one of the foremost manufacturers of Norwich, Mr. Parker is interested in every phase of public life, and stands for the best in civic development and progress. In political choice he is a Republican. He is a member of Somerset Lodge, No. 34, Free and Accepted Masons, and is a member of the Chamber of Commerce. The family are members of the Central Baptist Church.

On September 17, 1911, Nelson Parker married Mary H. Hurlbutt, of Gales Ferry, Connecticut, daughter of Henry W. and Lydia (Perkins) Hurlbutt. Mr. and Mrs. Parker are the parents of one daughter, Margaret H. Parker.

JOHN WILLIAM CAROLY—For many years the name of the late John William Caroly represented one of Niantic's potent forces in the business circles of the village. Mr. Caroly at the time of his death was proprietor of the National House and was carrying on an extensive ice cream business. He was also active in everything pertaining to the welfare of the community, which always found in him an earnest supporter.

John William Caroly was born in the town of Hosserhumburg-on-the-Rhine, Germany, June 4, 1844, the son of Peter and Mary Caroly. During his early married life Peter came with his family to this country and settled in Preston, Connecticut, later removing to Montville, where he lived until his death. Mr. and Mrs. Caroly were the parents of four children: Philip, who was a farmer in Ledyard, Connecticut, and is now deceased; Joseph, a resident of New London; John William, of further mention; and Elizabeth, who married the late John Goss, of New London.

Having been brought by his parents to Preston, Connecticut, when very young, John William Caroly attended the local schools there and in his spare time helped his father in his work about the farm. Like so many men who were youths at the time of the Civil War, he has a military record. At the age of eighteen he enlisted in Company E, One Hundred and Fifty-eighth Regiment, New York Volunteers, and served throughout the war, taking active part in twenty-two campaigns with the Army of the Potomac, and returning home at the conclusion of the war with an honorable discharge. After spending a short time at the old homestead, Mr. Caroly went abroad and toured the European countries for a number of years. Upon his return to this country he located in California for a short time, but finally returned to Connecticut, where for several years he was engaged in various projects, among them being a freight line, which he operated in the transporting of goods from New London to the surrounding islands. In 1876 he came to Niantic and built the National House, and later, from about 1893, this, together with an extensive ice cream business, occupied the greater part of his time until his death, which occurred May 23, 1913.

In all matters relating to the town's welfare, Mr. Caroly ever manifested a keen and sincere interest, aiding always to the utmost of his power any movement which tended to further public progress. In politics he was an Independent, preferring to vote for the man regardless of party affiliations. He was affiliated with Union Lodge, Free and Accepted Masons, was a charter member of Pequot Lodge, Independent Order of Odd Fellows, and attended the Lutheran church.

On August 12, 1872, at New London, Connecticut, John William Caroly was united in marriage with Susie Estelle Clark, a native of New London, whose birth occurred July 13, 1856. She was the daughter of Horatio and Susan (Barnes) Clark. Mrs. Clark was the daughter of Samuel Barnes, who was a member of one of the oldest and most prominent families in New London county. Samuel Barnes was a spur maker and he built the first town pump and installed it where the monument now stands on State street. Mrs. Clark's mother, Abbie (Fish) Barnes, came from old New London stock and was a sister of Captains James and Coddington Fish, who were among the best known and most success-

Mr & Mrs Nathan Gilman

ful whalers of that time. To Mr. and Mrs. Caroly have been born five children: William Peter, who married Susan Maud Bogart, of Brooklyn, New York, and has two children, William Cornelius and Helen Arline; Bertha Estelle, who married Frank McCarthy, of New Haven; Edna Maude, who married Arthur Lockwood, of Stanford, Connecticut; Mary Josephine, who died in infancy; and James A., who also died in infancy.

NATHAN GILMAN—Among the life stories of successful men of this country there are none that surpass, and few that equal, for inspiring courage in the face of difficulties, for loyalty and devotion to family ties, and for final achievement, the wonder stories of those who have come as immigrants, bringing nothing with them but their ambitions, their faith, their courage and their willingness to work. The story of Nathan Gilman is one of those inspiring wonder stories—the story of a Russian immigrant and of his wife, a good woman, a noble character, and a great helpmate.

There lived in Soroke, Bessarabia, Russia, now Roumania, a poor, struggling tobacco grower, Morris Gilman, and his wife, Rebecca (Partnay) Gilman. Times were hard, and toil as they might there was little chance of making headway. The government took a cruel share of what could be raised, and what the "little white father" and his government left, the church required. But, even though times were hard at home, it takes courage and energy and imagination of a high order to leave the known places and venture out into the great unknown. And so they struggled on. Four children were born to them—and the struggle grew harder. They had once been rich in faith and courage, no doubt, but the cruel hopelessness of their lot wore them down. There was only the long, dusty road ahead, the endless toil with no hope of enjoying the fruits of labor. Others, who toiled not and knew not hunger, ate of the fruits of the struggle.

But nature repeats her miracles, and in the son, born February 22, 1879, had been renewed the faith and courage of their earlier years. As he grew and came to understand the hopeless injustice of the situation his strong young spirit, inured to hardship, rebelled. He had ambitions, he wanted to get ahead. He loved his family and hated the hopelessness of their struggle. Moreover, he had a strong and steady will, so he looked about him and turned his eyes toward America. When one is young, the great unknown may be tried, and so he came to America, arriving in New York City in 1897. He found work in a mattress factory, where for nine months he worked like a slave and hoarded like a miser. At the end of that time he went into business for himself under the firm name, Greater New York Bedding Company. The Fairbanks & Plainfield Mill, located in Bozrahville, Connecticut, supplied much of his cotton mattress materials, and he freely used the products of the mill.

These beginnings of success, however, had not dulled his love for the little struggling family in Russia, and in 1898, one year after his own arrival in the land of opportunity, he welcomed to New York City, Morris and Rebecca (Partnay) Gilman, his parents, Harry and John, his brothers, and his sister, Eva, having sent them money to pay the cost of their coming. They lived in New York City until 1905, the two brothers and the sister finding work. The father having reached an advanced age, did not work, but enjoyed a placid eventide, freed, for the first time in his life, from fear of the wolf which howls at the Russian peasant's door.

In 1905, Mr. Gilman sold his Greater New York Bedding Company and bought the mill in Bozrahville which had been operated by the Fairbanks & Plainfield Company. He bought the entire holding, including the employees' tenement houses, practically every house in the village, much land, and a reservoir located on higher ground in the adjoining town of Lebanon, which supplies water power for the mill. He organized and incorporated the Gilman Brothers Company, which took over all this property, put in new equipment and began the manufacture of shoddy. The village of Bozrahville took on new life, the mill offering employment to all who wished to work, and became once more a thriving village. At this time the father, mother, and children, Harry, John, and Eva, came to Bozrahville, where the father died, May 15, 1919, and the mother is still living, enjoying a peaceful old age. Harry Gilman married Sarah Solomon, and is now a farmer in Colchester county, Connecticut; John Gilman was accidentally drowned at Bozrahville, in July, 1907; Eva Gilman married her cousin, Nathan Gilman, of New York City, thus marrying without change of name.

Nathan Gilman and his wife worked hard, she working in the mill and conducting the mill store. Both practiced strict economy and denied themselves all but the necessities of life. They began to prosper, the new business seemed to have passed its critical time, when along came the financial panic of 1907 which meant hard pulling again for the Gilman Company. In March, 1908, came another blow. The mill was gutted by fire, the loss of machinery, of stock on hand, and of raw and manufactured material amounting to $75,000, and not a cent's worth of insurance on the property. Such was his reputation as a business man, however, that his creditors not only extended the time of payment of bills due, but voluntarily loaned him the money necessary for a new start. He salvaged all he could of the wreckage and, with the encouragement of his wife, went to work again. They soon met with another disaster, a second fire, and while trying to stop the fire by opening a water valve, Mr. Gilman was so badly burned that he was laid up in the hospital for a long time. In seven years, however, he paid every creditor in full, and since then the business has steadily grown and prospered.

In December, 1919, the store building, then rented to a merchant, was destroyed by fire, causing Mr. Gilman a big loss.

Politically, Mr. Gilman is a Republican. He is postmaster of Bozrahville, having taken that position in order to keep the postoffice in the place. Since 1903 he has been a member of Mount Moriah Lodge, No. 27, Free and Accepted Masons, of New York City. He is also a member of Uncas Lodge, Independent Order of Odd Fellows; the Norwich Lodge, Royal Arcanum; and he and his wife are members of the Grange.

Mr. Gilman married, in New York City, February 21, 1904, Clara N. Stern, a native of Moliff, Russia, and daughter of Manuel and Mildred Stern. Mrs. Gilman is an active welfare and community worker, was very active in all the war drives during the World War, and is president of the Bozrahville section of the Council of Jewish Women. Mr. and Mrs. Gilman have seven children: George, born in New York City, December 15, 1904; Lucy Ruth, born at Bozrahville, July 25, 1906; Martin John, born in Bozrahville, November 18, 1907; Lawrence Milton, born in Bozrahville, November 21, 1909; Seymour Irving, born at Norwich, Connecticut, February 9, 1912; Pearl Alice, born at Norwich, Connecticut, August 12, 1914; and Charles Murray, born in Norwich, Connecticut, July 22, 1921.

ANSON RICHMOND GROVER—A decade and a half ago Anson R. Grover, then a young man under thirty years of age, located in Norwich, Connecticut, and became a part of the city's business life. From that day until the present he has been a successful business man, although in 1915 he retired from the wholesale candy business to enter the business founded in 1866 by a Mr. Noyes, the first man to manufacture and place upon the market sugar-coated popcorn. This business, conducted by Mr. Grover and his partner, Noe E. Caron, under the trade name, the Connecticut Pop Corn Company, is known throughout the United States, their product going into many states.

Anson R. Grover is a son of Charles D. and Jennie (Davis) Grover, who at the time of the birth of their son, Anson R., were residents of Hartford, Connecticut. Charles D. Grover, born in South Coventry, Connecticut, spent his active years as a railroad man and contractor, he now living retired in Norwich, his home with his son, Anson R. He married Jennie Davis, who died in Willimantic, Connecticut, in 1889. Two sons were born to Mr. and Mrs. Charles D. Grover: Anson R., the principal character of this review; and Raymond D., a resident of New London, Connecticut.

Anson R. Grover, born in Hartford, Connecticut, December 9, 1876, was educated in the public schools of different towns in which his parents resided during his youth. He was variously employed during the years of his early manhood until 1905, when he located in Norwich and began his very successful mercantile career. In 1905 he established in Norwich a wholesale candy business, which he conducted alone and under his own name until 1908, when it had reached so important a stage that more capital was required to properly conduct it. A partner, William F. Herrick, was admitted in 1908, the firm operating as Grover & Herrick, wholesale confectioners, until 1911, when Mr. Herrick retired, Mr. Grover purchasing his interest and continuing alone until 1915.

In that year he retired from the candy business, as he had been conducting it, substituting therefor the business bought from W. H. Vincent, known as the Connecticut Pop Corn Company. That business had been established in Norwich in 1866, and under Mr. Grover's careful and efficient management had reached a greater degree of prosperity than ever before. The product of the plant, sugar-coated popcorn, is a favorite confection, and is sold everywhere.

In politics Mr. Grover is a Democrat, and is now serving the city of Norwich as alderman, a position to which he was elected in June, 1920. He is affiliated with St. James Lodge, No. 23, Free and Accepted Masons; Franklin Chapter, No. 4, Royal Arch Masons; Franklin Council, No. 3, Royal and Select Masters; Columbian Commandery, Knights Templar; and all Scottish Rite bodies, having attained the thirty-second degree of the Connecticut Consistory of Norwich. He is also a noble of Sphinx Temple, Ancient Arabic Order Nobles of the Mystic Shrine; a member of Norwich Lodge, No. 930, Loyal Order of Moose; the Spanish War Veterans of Norwich; and the Arcanum Club. The family are members of Christ Episcopal Church of Norwich.

During the war with Spain in 1898, Mr. Grover saw ten months' service in various Southern camps, being a private of Company C, Third Regiment, Connecticut National Guard, which was called into the Federal service.

Mr. Grover married, in Norwich, in July, 1900, Mary Elizabeth Butler, daughter of Roswald Butler, of Norwich. Mr. and Mrs. Grover are the parents of a daughter, Viola Mary, born in Norwich, in June, 1901.

ELMER JOHN CARTER—One of the prominent business men of South Lyme, Connecticut, who, after a varied experience, has made this place his home and has located his business here, is Elmer John Carter, successful merchant, active citizen, and loyal supporter of all efforts for civic betterment. Mr. Carter is a son of Charles Emery Carter, who was born December 2, 1846, at Wadhams, New York, on the old home farm, where five generations of Carters have been born. Charles Emery Carter engaged in fárming in various places until 1907, when he moved to South Lyme, Connecticut, and in 1911 went into the general merchandise business in that place, but is now retired and living in South Lyme. His wife, Vinnie (Bowen) Carter, died while Elmer

John was a child, July 27, 1897. They were the parents of two children: Elmer John, an account of whose life appears below; and Laurence Erwin, born at Wadhams, January 28, 1892, who married, in 1916, Isoline O'Brien, of Old Lyme, Connecticut.

Elmer John Carter, son of Charles Emery and Vinnie (Bowen) Carter, was born at Wadhams, New York, May 23, 1887. He attended the local district schools until 1900, when he went to Boston with his parents, where for one term he entered one of the schools of that city, returning in 1901 to Wadhams, where he remained one year and then, his father having sold his farm, moved to Moretown, Vermont, where he completed his education. After leaving school, he went to work for the Central Vermont Railroad Company, at Middlesex, Vermont, passing his final examinations for telegraph operator in 1906, when he became night telegraph operator at Waterbury, Vermont, which position he held until December of that year, when he accepted a more promising position with the Boston & Maine railroad at Belchertown, Massachusetts, where he remained for two months, and then came to South Lyme as telegraph operator and station agent for the New York, New Haven & Hartford Railroad Company, holding that position until the station was closed by the railroad company in March, 1921. He then entered into partnership with George G. Emerson, purchasing the business of his father, Charles E. Carter, dealing in general merchandise, under the firm name of the Carter & Emerson Company. Politically, Mr. Carter is a Republican. He is a member of the school board and a member of the Order of Railroad Telegraphers, New York, New Haven & Hartford railroad, Division No. 29.

Mr. Carter married, June 29, 1910, Lucy Watrous Chapman, daughter of Frederick Way and Marie Louise (Griswold) Chapman, and two children have been born to the union: Grace Chapman, born at South Lyme, July 19, 1911; and Robert Charles, born at South Lyme, January 24, 1914.

PATRICK FRANCIS SWEENEY—Among the broadly successful men of the city of Norwich, Connecticut, is numbered Patrick F. Sweeney, who stands at the head of an important contracting business, and also conducts a thriving planing mill.

Mr. Sweeney is a son of John Joseph Sweeney, who was born in Ireland and educated in the National schools of his native land, coming to the United States in his youth. John J. Sweeney settled in the town of Lebanon, in this county, securing employment in the paper mill, which was some years ago destroyed by fire. He lived on a farm and carried on farming operations on a small scale, working in the mill as long as he lived. His death occurred in Lebanon in 1900. He married Margaret Lynch, who was born in Ireland, and still survives her husband, residing in Fitchville, in the town of Bozrah, in this county.

Patrick Francis Sweeney, third of the nine children of the above couple, was born in Lebanon, January 5, 1886. Reared in his native place, he attended the district school near his home, gaining a practical grounding in the essentials of education. In 1901 Mr. Sweeney went to New Haven, Connecticut, where he served an apprenticeship as carpenter with Allyn & Henderson, general contractors of that city. Remaining with them for four years, he then returned to New London county, and entered the employ of C. M. Williamson, a prominent Norwich contractor, with whom he was associated until 1910. He then became identified with Peck & McWilliams, general contractors of this city, in the capacity of foreman. Remaining with this concern for about three years, Mr. Sweeney then accepted the position of superintendent of construction with Fenton & Chanley, of Norwich. With this extensive practical experience, in 1916 Mr. Sweeney established a contracting business under his own name, which has since grown to be a large and prosperous interest. In 1917, in connection with his contracting business, he opened a large and well equipped planing mill in Norwich, which he still operates, doing considerable custom work as well as filling his own requirements in this line. He now holds a leading position in this field in Norwich, and commands a generous share of the contract work in this vicinity.

In the public life of the city, Mr. Sweeney holds a deep interest, and is a leader in the Democratic party, fearless in his advocacy of its principles. He was elected alderman June 5, 1922, and has for a number of years been a member of the Democratic Town Committee. He is a member of the Norwich Chamber of Commerce, and fraternally holds membership in the Benevolent and Protective Order of Elks, No. 430, and in White Cross Council, No. 13, Knights of Columbus, of Norwich. He is a member of St. Patrick's Roman Catholic Church.

Mr. Sweeney married, in Norwich, on January 29, 1918, Rev. Father John A. Broderick officiating, Julia A. McKay, daughter of Charles McKay, formerly of Meriden, Connecticut, the ceremony taking place in St. Patrick's Church.

CLARENCE GEORGE THOMPSON, M. D.—Dr. Thompson after completing his course in medicine and surgery began private practice in the city of Norwich, Connecticut, and there is building up a general practice. He is the only son of George and Ellen (Harting) Thompson, his father a New York City man and a hotel proprietor until his death there in 1891. Mrs. Thompson survives her husband and still resides in New York City.

Clarence G. Thompson was born in New York City, January 11, 1889. Two years later his father died, and he was reared under the guiding hand of his capable mother. After completing grammar courses he entered Morris High School, New York City, and there was graduated, class of 1911. For four years he was a student in Fordham University, at the end of which period he entered the Medical School of Flower Hospital, New York City, receiving his medical degree at graduation, with the class of 1919. During the period of his preparation for professional practice, he served as interne in Flower Hospital for one year, and then served in the same capacity in the Metropolitan Hospital on Blackwell's Island, New York City Department of Charity, and still later served as an interne in Backus Hospital, in Norwich, beginning his period of service there November 15, 1919. In May, 1920, he began general practice in Norwich, where he is now located.

He is a member of Norwich Medical Society; New London County Medical Society; of the American Medical Association; of Norwich Lodge, No. 430, Benevolent and Protective Order of Elks; and of Norwich Lodge, Loyal Order of Moose. In politics, Dr. Thompson is a Republican; in religious faith an Episcopalian.

WALTER M. BUCKINGHAM—Holding a responsible position in the financial world of New London county, Connecticut, and widely prominent in fraternal circles, Mr. Buckingham is a thoroughly representative citizen of Norwich. He comes of an old Norwich family, and is a son of William Alfred and Mary Day (Reynolds) Buckingham, long residents of this city.

Walter M. Buckingham was born in the city of Norwich, Connecticut, January 25, 1876. His early education was acquired at the Broad street and Broadway public schools, and he was graduated from the latter in June of 1892. Entering the Norwich Free Academy in the fall of the same year, he was a student there until early in the fall of 1895, when he left school to accept a position with the Thames National Bank. Entering the employ of this institution on September 9, 1895. Mr. Buckingham was first active in a subordinate capacity, but advancement from time to time has been the result of his faithful and efficient service, and on November 30, 1918, he was made assistant cashier of the institution with which he has now been connected for nearly twenty-seven years. He has devoted his life to the welfare of the bank and the interests of its patrons, and is looked upon as one of the solid, conservative men of the day in business affairs in this city. In public affairs Mr. Buckingham keeps in touch with the general march of events, but has always declined political honors, although a supporter of the Republican party.

Fraternally, he is a member of St. James Lodge, No. 23, Free and Accepted Masons, in which he has held all offices except treasurer and tyler. He is a member of Franklin Chapter, No. 4, Royal Arch Masons, and has held most of the minor offices in this body, also that of high priest. He also is a member of Franklin Council, No. 3, Royal and Select Masters, which he has served as recorder; and Nemrod Grotto, Mystic Order Veiled Prophets of the Enchanted Realm, of which he is secretary. Mr. Buckingham is a member of the Chelsea Boat Club, of Norwich, of which he has been treasurer for fourteen years, and is a member of the Gales Ferry Country Club, of which he has been treasurer for the past six years. He also is a member and the treasurer of the Village Improvement Association of Gales Ferry, and is affiliated with Christ Episcopal Church of Norwich.

Mr. Buckingham married, on April 24, 1912, in Norwich, Mabel Schofield Clark, of this city, daughter of J. Frank and Isabelle (Schofield) Clark. They reside at Gales Ferry, Connecticut.

FREDERICK NELSON TAYLOR—To follow the occupation of farming successfully a man must be of good physique, must possess the qualities of industry, application, and perseverance, must be of an even temperament, so that he will meet failure of crops and other things which fall to the lot of the farmer philosophically, and yet be of optimistic vision so that he can see the result of his labor long ahead of harvest time. Such a man is Frederick N. Taylor, a well known and highly esteemed resident of Lebanon.

The immigrant ancestor of that branch of the Taylor family of which Frederick Nelson Taylor is a member was one, Daniel Dawson, of English birth, who, being kidnapped and pressed into the service of the British navy, came to this country involuntarily. One day when he was a lad of about twelve years, playing on the English coast with his little sister, a naval officer of one of the English men-of-war lying in the nearby harbor asked him aboard the vessel. Young Daniel accepted the invitation only to find himself pressed into the service of the English navy on board a vessel, which promptly weighed anchor and set sail for America. Arriving in New York, by hiding among the bales of cotton on the wharf, he escaped, and in fear of being recaptured by the British officer, made his way to Long Island and assumed the name of William Taylor. There he hired himself out as a farm boy, and there, too, he met and married Sarah Brayman, soon after, taking up his residence at Mystic, Connecticut, where the remainder of his days were spent. Obsessed by the horror of being retaken by the British, he never left his home in Mystic, and not until shortly before his death, which occurred about 1839, when he was about eighty years of age, did he make public the circumstances of his coming to America. He lived about half-way between Upper and Lower Mystic, and there engaged for many years in fishing and lobstering. He was the father of nine children: Sarah, married a Mr. Eggleston and removed to New York, where she died; William, married Sarah Eldridge, died in Lower Mystic in 1877; John B., mentioned below; George, married Mary Brightman, he supposed to have been lost overboard from a vessel in Charleston, South Carolina, harbor; Frank, married Lucy ———, enlisted during the Revolution, and died during service; Polly, married Jason Brooks, and died in Mystic; Maraby, married Thomas Brooks, and died in Mystic; Abby, died in infancy; Nancy, became the wife of Christopher Eldridge, of Mystic.

John B. Taylor, son of William Taylor, was born in Mystic, Connecticut, in 1797. He farmed in various parts of New London and Windham counties, and then bought a farm in Lebanon, which he operated until he died, June 22, 1874. He married, in Windham county, May 17, 1820, Prudence Avery, daughter of David Avery, who served in the Revolutionary War. She was born in Preston, and died at Lebanon, October 6, 1884. One of their children was Nelson Taylor, of whom further.

Nelson Taylor, son of John B. and Prudence (Avery) Taylor, was born August 13, 1830, in Franklin, Connecticut. His parents removed to Lebanon, Connecticut, when he was about five years of age, and he continued his residence there until his death. He attended the district school, and during his youth assisted his father in the work upon the home farm. With the exception of seven months, when he was employed on the farm owned by Squire Jesse Wright, he was his father's assistant from boyhood, until the year 1869, when he removed to a piece of property which he had purchased the preceding year from L. L. Lyman. This farm, lying on the west of Lebanon Green, was known as the Maxwell place, and to its original acreage he added from time to time until it embraced sixty-five acres of land, which he cultivated with a high degree of success, devoting his attention to general farming and dairying. He was a member of the Congregational church, and a Republican in politics. He married (first) September 12, 1854, Helen A. Topliff, of Willington, Connecticut, who died January 2, 1861. No children were born to this union. He married (second) December 25, 1862, Mary L. Kilbourne, born May 6, 1837, in East Hartford, daughter of Nathan and Lucy (Burt) Kilbourne. Their children were: 1. John Clifton, born March 18, 1869, in Lebanon, graduated with the degree Doctor of Medicine from the Medical School of the University of Michigan in 1891, and practiced his profession in various places in Connecticut, namely, in Scotland, in Manchester, and in New London, where he now resides, a noted specialist in diseases of the eye, ear, nose, and throat. He married (first) Jennie Stofer, of Cleveland, Ohio, (second) Margaret Stevens, of Montgomery's Ferry, Pennsylvania. 2. Frederick Nelson, of whom further mention. Nelson Taylor died at Lebanon, December 2, 1910, and his wife, Mary L. (Kilbourne) Taylor, died October 14, 1913.

The Kilbourne family, of which Mrs. Taylor was a member, is one of the oldest in Connecticut, and she is in the ninth generation from Thomas Kilbourne, who was born in England in 1578, and in 1635 came to America in the ship "Increase," with his wife, Frances, and their children, locating at Wethersfield, Connecticut. The line of descent is through Sergeant John Kilbourne, baptized in Wood Ditton, England, September 29, 1624 (who helped procure the famous Connecticut charter in 1662); Sergeant Thomas Kilbourne, born in Wethersfield, 1651; Thomas Kilbourne (3), born in Hockanum, Connecticut; Thomas Kilbourne (4), born September 8, 1705, at what is now East Hartford; Thomas Kilbourne (5), the great-grandfather of Mrs. Taylor, born August 25, 1729; Ashbel Kilbourne, grandfather of Mrs. Taylor, born in East Hartford, April, 1759, served in Colonel Webb's regiment during the Revolutionary War, was taken prisoner by the British troops in December, 1777, and confined in Philadelphia, from which place he was transferred in a wagon to Hartford, Connecticut. His feet having been frozen while he was in prison, he was a cripple for life, and in the "American Archives," published by order of Congress in 1848, his case is thus cited: "Mr. Kilbourne was disabled while a prisoner in Philadelphia; his feet being frozen, his toes dropped off, and for want of proper care he was totally disabled." Congress granted him a pension and back pay, and the General Assembly of Connecticut, in the May session of 1779, passed the following resolution concerning this patriot: "Resolved, by this Assembly, that the Committee of Pay table, adjust and liquidate the accounts of the memorialist for his sickness, and draw an order on the State for such sums as they shall find due." Nathan Kilbourne, father of Mrs. Taylor, married Lucy Burt, and one of their children was Mary L., who married Nelson Taylor, and became the mother of Frederick N. Taylor.

Frederick N. Taylor was born on the Taylor homestead in Lebanon, Connecticut, May 8, 1878, and lived there until June, 1921. He received his education in the public schools of Lebanon, completing his studies at the age of seventeen, after which he assisted his father in the management of the home farm. Upon the death of his father in 1910, he inherited the farm, which he continued to cultivate until June, 1921, when he sold it and removed to Lebanon Center, where he now resides (1922). Mr. Taylor is now engaged in the insurance business in all its branches.

Mr. Taylor takes a keen interest in all matters pertaining to the welfare of Lebanon, and has been appointed to public offices, serving as registrar of voters for the town of Lebanon since 1905, being re-elected each successive year with the exception of one term of one year, and still serving in that capacity. In 1915 he represented the town of Lebanon in the State Legislature, where he served on the Humane Institutions' Committee. Not only in official capacity does Mr. Taylor serve his community. Whatever project, planned for the good of the town, is launched, he gives of his time, his influence, and his means.

Since he was fourteen years of age, Mr. Taylor has been a member of the Lebanon Grange and has been active in the work of that institution throughout the years that have since passed. He is past master of Lebanon Grange, No. 21, and also of New London county, Pomona Grange, No. 6; he is a member of the Connecticut State Grange and a member of the National Grange, all of these being patrons of husbandry. He serves as State deputy of the Connecticut State Grange, and is deeply interested in all the various phases of the work of the organization in which he has held membership since boyhood, having held all offices in the local grange, including those of lecturer, master, and State deputy. He is also a member of the Eastern Star Lodge, Free and Accepted Masons, of Willimantic, Connecticut. Both Mr. Taylor and his wife are members of the First Congregational Church of Lebanon, where Mr. Taylor serves as deacon and as church clerk.

In Scotland, Connecticut, June 27, 1900, he married Hannah Miranda Kimball, born December 9, 1881, daughter of Eugene and Eva (Moffitt) Kimball. Mrs. Taylor served as assistant steward of the Connecticut State Grange, an office which she held for four years. Mr. and Mrs. Taylor are the parents of two children: Ralph Winslow, born July 12, 1902; and Helen, born December 2 ,1908.

JULIAN LA PIERRE WILLIAMS—The universal popularity of the automobile has brought into existence thousands of business establishments which cater directly to the needs of the motorist. In Norwich, Connecticut, one of the best equipped garages in New London county is that conducted by Julian L. Williams, son of Charles Morgan and Ada (La Pierre) Williams, of Norwich, Connecticut.

Charles Morgan Williams, son of Henry Williams, son of Ephraim Morgan Williams, son of Roger Williams, was a descendant of Robert Williams, born in 1598, in Great Yarmouth, England, who there married Elizabeth Stalham, and came to New England, in the ship "Rose" in 1635. He was a member of the Ancient and Honorable Artillery Company of Boston, in 1644, and died in Roxbury, Massachusetts, September 1, 1693.

Ephraim Morgan Williams was a soldier of the War of 1812, a Democrat in politics, a member of the Methodist Episcopal church, and a farmer of the town of Montville, New London county, Connecticut. He married Mary Ann Spencer, born June 12, 1800, died May 20, 1887, at the Montville homestead, the mother of nine children.

Henry Williams was born in Ledyard, Connecticut, November 23, 1826, lived many years in Montville, and spent the later years of his life in the city of Norwich. He was a contractor and builder for many years, finally passing away in Norwich, February 7, 1886, and was buried in Yantic cemetery. He married (first) Mary Hull, who died March 27, 1871, aged forty-three years, nine months, daughter of Gardner Hull of North Stonington, Connecticut. She was the mother of two sons who came to mature years, Charles Morgan, of further mention; and Henry F.

Charles Morgan Williams was born in Norwich, Connecticut, May 4, 1855. He attended the public school in early life, but while yet a boy he began learning the carpenter's trade under his father, with whom he continued until he reached his majority, becoming a skilled workman. After some years as a journeyman carpenter, he began contracting in Norwich, conducting his business alone until 1898, when he formed a partnership under the firm name of Carpenter & Williams, general building contractors. Six years later, in June, 1904, that firm dissolved, Mr. Williams then continuing alone in his contracting business. A thoroughly reliable builder, he has built up his reputation on that attribute and has never forfeited the reputation he so honestly gained. Mr. Williams is an Independent in politics. He married, October 30, 1878, Ada La Pierre, daughter of Arndud and Sarah A. (Rathbun) La Pierre. Children: Annie Louise, married Frederick M. Holmes, of New Britain, Connecticut, and died June 1, 1904, leaving a daughter, Ada Louise; Julian La Pierre, of further mention.

Julian La Pierre Williams was born in Norwich, Connecticut, on June 11, 1885. He attended the public schools of the city and then entered the Norwich Free Academy, from which he was graduated in 1903. For fourteen years thereafter the young man was associated with his father in business, acting as foreman and taking care of the bookkeeping. In 1917, with so many thousands of American young men, Mr. Williams enlisted in the United States Navy. He booked his enlistment at the United States Naval Station at Newport, Rhode Island, was rated as a first-class machinist, and continued in service until the signing of the Armistice, receiving his discharge on December 13, 1918. Returnng to Norwich, he opened a garage in January, 1919, on Towne street, and is doing a constantly increasing business. He handles the Oldsmobile and the International truck, and conducts one of the best and most thoroughly up-to-date garages in the city.

Mr. Williams is a man of wide social and fraternal connections, and is keenly interested in all affairs of public import. In political choice he is a Republican. He is a member of St. James Lodge, No. 23, Ancient Free and Accepted Masons; of Franklin Chapter, No. 4; of Franklin Council, No. 3; of the Columbian Commandery, of Norwich; and all Scottish Rite bodies, including the thirty-second degree, and a member of the Sphinx Temple, Nobles of the Mystic Shrine, of Hartford. He is also a member of the Chelsea Boat Club, and of the Arcanum Club, of Norwich.

Mr. Williams married Hazel Hewitt, of this city, and they have a little daughter, Louise.

John H Davis

HAROLD H. STARR, treasurer of Starr Brothers, Incorporated, druggists of New London, Connecticut, was born in that city, November 8, 1884.

He was educated in the public schools of New London, and after completing his studies in high school, spent two years at Alfred University, Alfred, New York. Upon his return from the university, he entered business life, his first position being as clerk with the Frank Munsey Company, in the department store at New London. Later, in 1909-11, he was manager of Starr Brothers Drug Stores at Mystic and Stonington, Connecticut. In 1911-13 he was associated with Dr. Bilfinger, of the Carolina Naval Stores Company, Incorporated, carrying on experiments with turpentine and its products. In 1913, Mr. Starr entered the works of the New London Ship and Engine Company, his particular object being to perfect his understanding of the Diessel engine and submarine boat equipment. He became a qualified expert, and during 1914-15 went out as one of a test crew of submarines. In 1915, he was sent to the Russian Government by his company as tester and instructor in submarine operation. In the latter part of 1916, Mr. Starr returned to the United States and bought an interest in Starr Brothers, Incorporated, becoming treasurer of the company as at present (1922). He is a member of all the Masonic bodies up to the thirty-second degree; a member of Pyramid Temple, Ancient Arabic Order, Nobles of the Mystic Shrine, Bridgeport, Connecticut.

JOHN HERBERT DAVIS—Several generations of the Davis family have been residents of the towns of New London county, Connecticut, and men of the name have been successful farmers, merchants and manufacturers. John Herbert Davis, to whose memory this review is inscribed, was a son of Ira Augustus and Lydia (Fenner) Davis, who at the time of the birth of their son were living in Stonington.

John Herbert Davis was born in Stonington, Connecticut, December 14, 1862, and died at his farm in the town of Preston, in the same county, April 30, 1920. He was educated in Stonington public schools and after completing his school years, secured employment in the mills at Old Mystic, becoming a stationary engineer, and for about twenty years was engineer of the Hall Brothers' Mills, at Hillville. In 1886 he bought in the town of Preston a farm of one hundred and sixty-three acres on the Norwich-Westerly State road, upon which he resided until his death, and upon which his widow still resides. He was a member of Company A, Third Regiment, Connecticut National Guard, discharged in 1883; a member of Uncas Lodge, No. 11, Independent Order of Odd Fellows, and of Palmyra Encampment, Lodge No. 3, of the same order. In politics he was a Republican, and in 1902 and again in 1907 represented Preston as a first selectman, and at different times was a member of the Board of Relief and of the Board of Assessors. He also served the State as assistant superintendent of the Capitol building at Hartford for three terms.

Mr. Davis married (first) Nettie Caswell, born in Preston, who died, leaving a son, Ira Augustus Davis, now living in Preston. Mr. Davis married (second) in Preston, March 25, 1881, Frances Harriet Whitmarsh, born in Preston, April 30, 1863, daughter of Edward Dennison and Harriet Barker (Willett) Whitmarsh, her parents now deceased. Four children were born to John H. and Frances H. (Whitmarsh) Davis: 1. John Edwin, born in Old Mystic, Connecticut, June 5, 1884, married Flora Woodmansee, of Norwich, and resides in Massachusetts; they are the parents of a son, Herbert Charles. 2. Flora Ann, born January 17, 1888. 3. Frank, twin with Flora A. 4. Frances Myrtle, born December 14, 1902. Mrs. Davis retained her home for a time at the farm in Preston, where the greater part of her married life was spent, but resides at No. 25 Peck street, Norwich.

BILLINGS FRANCIS STODDARD CRANDALL—The Crandalls came to New London county, Connecticut, from Rhode Island, Billings F. S. Crandall, of Ledyard township, being a great-great-grandson of Jonathan Crandall, of Rhode Island, a farmer, father of Wells Crandall, who was a tanner with his uncle, Paul Woodbridge. They are descendants of Rev. John Woodbridge, who married a daughter of Governor Dudley, of Massachusetts, and also are related to Governor Leet, of Massachusetts. Wells Crandall married Sally Woodbridge, and they were the parents of Stiles Woodbridge Crandall, of whom further.

Stiles Woodbridge Crandall was born in Groton, Connecticut, November 25, 1813, a surveyor and farmer of Groton and Ledyard. He was a Democrat in politics, was assessor of his town for thirty consecutive years, was selectman, and in 1860 was elected representative to the State Legislature by the largest majority ever given in the town up to that time. He died in Ledyard in 1906, at the age of ninety-three. Stiles Woodbridge Crandall married Caroline Boles Green, and they were the parents of three children: Augusta Caroline; Ashbel Woodbridge; and Stiles Ashbel, of whom further. The mother of these children died in Ledyard at the age of eighty-five. Both she and her husband were members of the First Groton Baptist Church at Old Mystic, Connecticut.

Stiles Ashbel Crandall, son of Stiles Woodbridge and Caroline Boles (Green) Crandall, and only surviving child of that family, was born in Ledyard, Connecticut, October 12, 1851, and there spent his youth. He was educated in the public schools, Suffield Academy, and in the law department of Iowa State University. He was admitted to the Connecticut bar, and located in Norwich, Connecticut, where he practiced his profession with success and honor. He was a Democrat in politics until William J.

Bryan infected the party with his heresies, when Mr. Crandall allied with the Republican party. He held numerous city and State offices, including mayor of Norwich, Representative and State Senator. He also was a candidate for lieutenant-governor of the State at one time. He was judge advocate on the staff of General Haven during Governor Coffin's term of office, and was a man high and influential until his retirement. He now resides in Wallingford, Connecticut.

Stiles A. Crandall married Jennie Frances Stoddard, born in Ledyard, Connecticut, daughter of Sanford and Mary Stoddard, of Ledyard, her father a sea captain and farmer of Stoddard's Wharf, Ledyard, Connecticut, who there died in June, 1885, aged thirty-four. Stiles A. and Jennie Frances (Stoddard) Crandall were the parents of two children: Mary Stoddard, who married Philip Stoddard Rigg, of Mystic, Connecticut; and Billings Francis Stoddard, of further mention. Mrs. Crandall died at Ledyard, Connecticut, June 18, 1885. The family are Congregationalists.

Billings Francis Stoddard Crandall, only son of Stiles Ashbel and Jennie Frances (Stoddard) Crandall, was born in Ledyard, Connecticut, June 13, 1885. His early years were spent in Ledyard, near Old Mystic, where he attended public schools. He was a student at Worcester Academy, Worcester, Massachusetts, then, after graduation, he spent three years in New York City, taking an accounting course in New York University and holding positions with the Garfield National Bank and with the Trunk Line Association. He then traveled for a year, covering the United States thoroughly, then settled down to the life of a managing farmer at Stoddard's Wharf, where since 1911 he has cultivated the acres which have been in his mother's family (Stoddard) for over two hundred and twenty-five years. This farm is on the Military Highway in the town of Ledyard, and there Mr. Crandall manages his estate and takes an interest in public affairs. As a business man he is president of the Gales Ferry Cemetery Association, a director of Gales Ferry Free Public Library, and for three years was assessor of the town, and now a member of the Board of Relief. In politics he is a Republican.

Mr. Crandall married, November 4, 1911, Mary Louise Haley, born in Brooklyn, New York, March 14, 1884, educated in Packer Collegiate Institute and Pratt Institute, both in Brooklyn. After completing her education she spent some time in settlement work in New York City. She is a daughter of Irvin and Mary Amelia (Havens) Haley, of Groton, Connecticut, granddaughter of Giles Haley, and great-granddaughter of Hon. Elisha Haley, an enterprising, public-spirited man of his home town, Groton. He represented his town a number of times in the General Assembly, was several times Senator from his district, and served two terms as United States Congressman from Connecticut. Irvin Haley was a wholesale commission merchant of Fulton Market, New York City, he and his wife now residing in Brooklyn. They were the parents of an only child, Mary Louise, who married Billings Francis Stoddard Crandall. Mrs. Crandall is now a member of the Board of Education of the town of Ledyard; also belongs to Anna Warner Bailey Chapter, Daughters of the American Revolution, at Groton. She is a descendant of the "Mayflower."

FRANCIS BEIQUE—In the business world of Taftville, in New London county, Connecticut, Francis Beique is counted among the successful merchants of the day, and conducts his store according to the most modern and approved methods, always keeping in touch with the progress of the times in his line of activity. Mr. Beique comes of a family long well known in the Province of Quebec, and is a son of John B. and Justine (Savariry) Beique. Both his parents were born in Quebec, but lived in Taftville for a number of years, during which time the father was employed in the mills in this vicinity, later returning to his native land, where he died.

Francis Beique was born in St. Paul's Parish (now Abbotsford), Province of Quebec, February 18, 1860. He was educated in the schools of his native place, then in November of 1876, when in his seventeenth year, he came with the family to New London county, stopping for a few weeks in Baltic, then settling permanently in Taftville in November of the same year. He was employed in the mills of Taftville for about seven years, but not finding the work to his liking, he secured a position as a dry goods salesman, and was engaged along this line of effort for about ten years at the Ponemah store for a time, then with Porteous & Mitchell, of Norwich. About nine years ago, Mr. Beique established his present business in Taftville, handling a general line of dry goods. He has gradually expanded the business, introducing other lines of merchandise, and now handles talking machines, records, and many of the varied goods handled in a modern department store. In the social and religious life of the community Mr. Beique is a leader, and has long been prominent. He founded and organized, in 1884, the old Societe St. Jean de Baptiste, of which he was president for seven years; he also organized the St. Louis Society, of which he was president for twelve years. He still holds office in both organizations, and also is a member of the Knights of Columbus. He is a member of the Church of the Sacred Heart.

Mr. Beique married, in Colchester, Connecticut, in 1882, Virginia Roy, who was born in L'Ange Gardien, Canada, and was a daughter of Octave and Priscilla (Lamarine) Roy. Mrs. Beique died June 13, 1919, leaving two children: Denise and Rhea.

EDWARD KIRBY, D. D. S., a graduate of Georgetown University, has, since graduation in 1916, been active in practice, but has only recently established in private practice in his native city, Norwich, Connecticut. He is a son of Edward and Mary A. (Murphy) Kirby, the former born in Ireland, but brought to the United States at the age of eight years. Edward Kirby, Sr., has spent nearly his whole life in Norwich, and is the proprietor of a prosperous barber shop, he an expert in his line.

Dr. Edward Kirby was born in Norwich, Connecticut, September 21, 1894. After completing public school courses he was a student at the Norwich Free Academy until graduation in 1913, and from 1913 until graduation in 1916, was a student in the dental department of Georgetown University, Washington, D. C. He began practice in Waterbury, Connecticut, in 1916, but not long afterward came to Norwich, where he practiced in association with Dr. Comean. Later he opened private dental offices, and practiced under his own name, his office being at No. 32 Thayer building.

Dr. Kirby is an Independent in politics; a member of Norwich Lodge, No. 430, Benevolent and Protective Order of Elks; White Cross Council, No. 13, Knights of Columbus; and of the Roman Catholic church. His fraternity is the Delta Sigma Delta.

JOHN HENRY CHAMPION, who holds a position of responsibility as custodian of the water works at Point o' Woods, is descended from an old family of New London county. His grandfather, Charles Champion, was prominent in this section in the early days of American independence. Charles Champion married Mary Havens, and they were the parents of eight children: Edward, Lodwick, Elisha, Charles Henry, Emily, Harriet, Mary, and Abbey. Harriet is the only surviving member of this family, and is now eighty years of age.

Edward Champion, eldest son of Charles and Mary (Havens) Champion, was born in Old Lyme, Connecticut, in 1830, and resided in this community throughout his lifetime. He was a prominent farmer, highly esteemed among the people of this section, and died in 1906, at the age of seventy-six years. He married Mary Miller Dart, daughter of Gibson and Betsey Dart. They were the parents of eleven children, of whom five died in infancy. Those living are: Fannie, Mercy, Jane, Irofine, John H., and Gilbert.

John Henry Champion was born in South Lyme, Connecticut, September 14, 1856, and was reared and educated in his native town. The sea held his interest from childhood, and as soon as he was old enough to go to work he followed the occupation of fishing. He was identified with the fishing business from boyhood until 1899. In that year he settled in South Lyme permanently, and has since had charge of the water works at Point o' Woods, a large reservation owned by the Sargent Lock Company, of Bridgeport, Connecticut, a beautiful wildwood park. Fraternally, Mr. Champion holds membership in Crystal Lake Lodge, No. 88, Independent Order of Odd Fellows, and has been through all chairs of the order. Politically, he supports the Democratic party, but takes no active part in political affairs.

Mr. Champion married Minnie Grace Stanton, daughter of Thomas and Mary Stanton, and they have one daughter, Ruth Leora, who was born March 11, 1898, in South Lyme.

RALPH HILL MELCER, of Palmer Brothers Company, Fitchville, Connecticut, was born in San Francisco, California, July 4, 1880, son of William and Elizabeth (Hughes) Melcer, his father engaged in the mining and smelting of copper ores.

Ralph H. Melcer attended Thacher School until 1898, then spent a year at Phillips Andover Academy, finishing his studies at Yale University, receiving the degree of Bachelor of Arts, class of 1903. In 1906 he entered business with Palmer Brothers Company, Fitchville, New London county, Connecticut, and there continues, being now treasurer of the company. He is a director of the National Bank of Commerce of New London, Connecticut, and has other business interests of importance. Mr. Melcer serves as chairman of the Montville School Committee. During the years 1917-19 he was sergeant in the Connecticut Home Guard, and bore a helping hand in other activities of the World War period. His clubs are: Yale, of New York; The Thames, of New London; and the Norwich Golf. In religious faith he is connected with Uncasville Methodist Episcopal Church.

Mr. Melcer married, in New York, October 27, 1907, Grace A. Palmer, daughter of Edward A. and Isabel S. (Mitchell) Palmer.

FERNANDO WHEELER — Since Thomas Wheeler settled in the town of Stonington, New London county, Connecticut, in 1667, Wheelers have been among the leading agriculturalists of the county. But in no generation has there been a more enterprising and prosperous farmer of the name than Fernando Wheeler, of Center Farm, a son of the eighth generation of Center Farm, so called because it lies in the exact center of the town of Stonington. When bought by Fernando Wheeler in 1889, it contained 265 acres, but to its area he has added the Latham Miner farm of sixty acres, and the Stanton Brothers farm of ninety-six acres, all of which he cultivates and causes to produce abundantly. His lines are general and dairy farming. He is a son of Nelson Henry and Melinda (Gallup) Wheeler, and the grandson of Samuel, he the son of Joseph, son of Richard (2), son of Richard (1), son of Isaac, son of Thomas Wheeler, the American ancestor.

(I) Thomas Wheeler was elected constable of Lynn, Massachusetts, in 1635. He was admitted freeman in 1642, and owned considerable land. He and his wife, Mary, moved to Stonington county, in 1667, and in 1669 he was made a freeman of Connecticut Colony. He represented Stonington in the General Court in 1673, and in 1674 was one of the nine organizers and charter members of the church in Stonington, his wife, Mary, partaking of the first communion. He died March 6, 1686, aged eighty-four years, leaving one son, Isaac.

(II) Isaac Wheeler, son of Thomas and Mary Wheeler, was born in Massachusetts in 1646. He was a soldier in the Colonial Wars, and died in Stonington county, June 5, 1712. He married Martha Park, daughter of Thomas and Dorothy (Thompson) Park. Descent is traced through their third son, Richard (1).

(III) Richard (1) Wheeler, son of Isaac and Martha (Park) Wheeler, was born in Stonington, March 10, 1677, and died there April 12, 1712. He married December 12, 1702, Prudence Payson, daughter of John and Bathsheba (Tilestone) Payson, of Roxbury, Massachusetts. Their third son, Richard (2), is next in line.

(IV) Richard (2) Wheeler, son of Richard (1) and Prudence (Payson) Wheeler, was born in Stonington, July 23, 1710, and died April 10, 1749. He married August 25, 1734, Anna Pellet, of Canterbury, Connecticut. Descent is traced from this branch from Joseph, their second son.

(V) Joseph Wheeler, son of Richard (2) and Anna (Pellet) Wheeler, was born January 23, 1747. He married, September 18, 1874, Prudence Palmer, who died March 6, 1790, aged thirty-eight years, and the mother of eight children, the sixth, a son, Samuel.

(VI) Samuel Wheeler, son of Joseph and Prudence (Palmer) Wheeler, was born in Stonington, September 14, 1784, died March 24, 1852. Like his ancestors he engaged in farming, beginning as soon as school years were over, and continuing until the end of his useful life. He was active in town affairs, and served as assessor, selectman, member of the Board of Relief, and in all proved himself efficient and zealous. He was an ardent Democrat, and a liberal supporter of the Road Church. He married, in 1809, Rebecca Prentice, who died December 9, 1842, leaving eight children, the youngest a son, Nelson Henry. Samuel Wheeler married (second) Mrs. Hannah Heath Havens.

(VII) Nelson Henry Wheeler, son of Samuel and Rebecca (Prentice) Wheeler, was born March 28, 1827, at the old homestead in Stonington, Connecticut, and there spent the first eighteen years of his life. He attended district school, and after leaving the home farm in 1845, he worked as farmer, carpenter and peddler until sailing on the ship "Trescott" for California, January 26, 1849. The old whaler safely rounded the "Horn" and the young man spent four years in the "land of gold," but only spent one year in mining. He then secured employment near Sacramento, as farmer and teamster, returning to Connecticut via the Isthmus of Panama in 1853. He resumed farming at the homestead in Stonington, and there remained until reaching the age of seventy-three years, when he retired and moved to Mystic, in the town of Groton, and there died January 18, 1904. He was a successful farmer, prominent in his town; a member of the Baptist church, and highly esteemed. He married, April 3, 1853, Melinda Gallup, daughter of Luke and Melinda (Williams) Gallup, of Ledyard, Connecticut. Mrs. Wheeler survived her husband. Nelson Henry and Melinda (Gallup) Wheeler are the parents of the following children: 1. Samuel N., born May 20, 1854, died in 1892. He was a graduate of Boston University, and a teacher. 2. Lilla M., born January 4, 1857, died March 30, 1885. 3. Arthur G., born October 3, 1858. He is a farmer of Cherry Hill Farm, town of Stonington; married Mary Billings. 4. Mary S., born April 20, 1860; married Rev. Osmore D. Buddington; died January, 1895, leaving two sons, Osmore W., and Arthur Francis. 5. Herman E., born April 20, 1862, died April 6, 1885. 6. Agnes M., born May 2, 1864; married Frank L. Lathrop, of Norwich, an official of the New London County Mutual Fire Insurance Company. 7. Fernando, of further mention. 8. George A., born May 15, 1874, who now cultivates the old Samuel Wheeler homestead in Stonington. He married Lucille Billings Thompson.

(VIII) Fernando Wheeler, of the eighth generation of Wheelers in the town of Stonington, New London county, Connecticut, son of Nelson Henry and Melinda (Gallup) Wheeler, was born at the homestead in which his father was born, June 16, 1866, and there spent the first twenty-three years of his life. He obtained a good education in Stonington schools and in the Mystic Valley Institute, and after completing his own studies at the age of seventeen, he began teaching, continuing for five years in Stonington, North Stonington and Preston schools. After representing a New York house dealing in fertilizers, the Mapes Fertilizer Company, for a year or so, Mr. Wheeler bought of Noyes S. Palmer the fine estate and Center Farm, upon which he has now resided thirty-one years, from March, 1890 to March, 1921. This estate with the additions made by purchase has been previously mentioned in this review, but another property not connected, however, and owned by Mr. Wheeler, is the Hinckley Hill Farm of 110 acres, situated on the Westerly road, a highly improved farm, which produces abundantly under the capable care of its owner. This farm has a pretentious modern residence as one of its attractions, and all other improvements are in harmony. Mr. Wheeler has given much attention to fruit growing, and to dairying, blooded Swiss cattle being his choice for a dairy herd, he being one of the few dealers in that grade of cattle in Connecticut. Mr. Wheeler is an independent Democrat in his political opinions; a member of the Old Mystic Baptist Church; Stonington Grange, Patrons of Husbandry; and New London Farm Bureau. He was selectman three terms; tax assessor; and in 1914, '15, '16, '17, '18 he was a member of the Connecticut State Board of Agriculture.

Geo. O. Murphey.

On November 8, 1889, he married (first) Josie Emma Avery, born in Preston, daughter of Ulysses and Lucy A. (Williams) Avery. Mrs. Wheeler died October 7, 1918, without children, and October 4, 1920, Mr. Wheeler married (second) Mrs. Vivian P. (Nichols) Austin, born in Norwich, Connecticut, daughter of William Henry and Sally Brewster Osborne, of Norwich, Connecticut.

WILLIAM H. CASEY was born in Pawcatuck, Connecticut, in the town of Stonington, Connecticut, on August 3, 1867, and was educated in the public schools of Westerly, of which Pawcatuck is a suburb. As a young man he became a patrolman in Pawcatuck, and had the distinction of being the first police officer in the town. His period of service extended over fifteen years, from 1895 to 1910. In the latter year Mr. Casey established an insurance business in Pawcatuck, in which he has been most successful, and continues along this line at present (1922). For the past twenty-five years Mr. Casey has been a deputy sheriff of New London county, serving the public with great ability, and with the most conscientious devotion. He has also been tax collector for the town of Stonington for the past three years. Mr. Casey is a prominent member of Westerly Lodge, No. 678, Benevolent and Protective Order of Elks.

EDWIN HOWARD BAKER, JR., secretary and treasurer of the Shetucket Company, of Norwich, Connecticut, and prominent in civic and club circles in this city, is a son of one of the leaders in the cotton industry in New England.

Edwin Howard Baker, Jr., was born in Ware, Massachusetts, February 23, 1890, and was educated in the Hill School, of Pottstown, Pennsylvania, and Yale University, being graduated from the latter institution in the class of 1913, with the degree of Bachelor of Arts. After completing his course at Yale, Mr. Baker went to New York City, where he was associated with Hallgarten & Company, bond brokers, for four years. With the coming of the World War, he was twice rejected for eyesight disability, but would not brook disappointment, and in May, 1918, sailed for Italy, with the American Red Cross Ambulance Service, as a private in Section 4, attached to the Fifth Army Corps, of the First Army. As ambulance driver he went to the Italian front at once, was under fire at Mont Grappa and the Camballia front. In August he was promoted to first lieutenant and placed in charge of the section. Between October 26 and November 11, 1918, during the final drive, Mr. Baker covered the entire front from Trent to Trieste, meeting with every kind of hardship. He was mustered out of the service in November, 1918, and the following month returned to the United States. In February, 1919, he came to Norwich, to become secretary and treasurer of the Shetucket Company, and still fills this dual office, and is also a director of the concern.

Edwin Howard Baker, Jr., is a member of the Norwich Chamber of Commerce; is a trustee of the Norwich Savings Society; and a corporator of the Dime Savings Bank of Norwich. Politically he supports the Republican party. He is a member of the Psi Upsilon fraternity; of the Elihu Club, of Yale; and of the Yale Club, of New York City; and also is a member of the Rotary Club, of Norwich.

On September 1, 1917, Mr. Baker married, in Greenwich, Connecticut, Lina Grant, of Brookline, Massachusetts, daughter of Lincoln and Sarah (Holmes) Grant, of Brookline. Mr. and Mrs. Baker reside in Norwich, and attend the Congregational church, of which they are members.

GEORGE OSCAR MURPHEY is a son of Oscar F. Murphey, who was born in Westerly, Rhode Island, but early in life came across the river to Pawcatuck, in the town of Stonington, New London county, Connecticut, there attended public schools and learned the carpenter's trade, which he followed all his active life. He married Elizabeth Chapman, who yet survives him, a resident of Pawcatuck. They were the parents of two children, a daughter, Minnie Etta, deceased, and a son, George Oscar, of whom further.

George O. Murphey was born in Pawcatuck, Connecticut, May 8, 1878, and there was educated in the public schools, graduating from Pawcatuck High School in 1895. After finishing his school years he became a machinist's apprentice with the C. B. Cottrell Company, remaining with the corporation from 1898 until 1906, becoming an expert worker in steel and iron. In 1906 he entered the employ of the Standard Machine Company, of Mystic, Connecticut, in charge of the tool making department, remaining in their employ until 1910. In that year he established in business for himself, opening a bicycle sale and general repair shop in Westerly, Rhode Island. Later he added a line of motorcycles and accessories, and finally secured agencies for the Nash and Chevrolet motor cars.

With the new lines, he soon outgrew the establishment in Westerly, and in 1919 he came over into Pawcatuck, purchasing buildings and property for expansion in the heart of the business section, and has developed a prosperous motor sales and service institution founded on the most progressive policies. Upon the organization of the Pawcatuck Bank and Trust Company, of Pawcatuck, Connecticut, in 1922, he was a charter member and one of its board of directors, and now serves in that capacity.

Mr. Murphey is a Republican in politics; a member and past master of Pawcatuck Lodge, No. 90, Free and Accepted Masons; is a companion of Palmer Chapter, No. 7, Royal Arch Masons; member of Mystic Council, No. 4, Royal and Select Masters; a sir knight of Narragansett Commandery, Knights

Templar (Westerly, Rhode Island); a noble of Palestine Temple, Ancient Arabic Order Nobles of the Mystic Shrine (Providence, Rhode Island); member of the Ancient Order of United Workmen (Westerly); Junior Order United American Mechanics; and of the Masonic Club (Westerly). In religious preference he is an Episcopalian.

Mr. Murphey married Lillian G. Pugh, of Westerly, Rhode Island, daughter of Thomas G. Pugh, and they are the parents of two children: Oscar F. (2), and Dorothy. The family home is in Pawcatuck, Connecticut, a village in which Mr. Murphey was born and where all his life has been spent. He is a man of energy and ability, genial and generous, well liked and esteemed by his many acquaintances and friends. Both Mr. and Mrs. Murphey for many years have been accomplished musicians and active in musical affairs of their community.

CALVIN HARRISON FRISBIE—Holding an executive position in the main offices of the Attawaugan Company, in Norwich, Connecticut, Calvin Harrison Frisbie is closely allied with the business interests of the city.

Mr. Frisbie's father, William K. Frisbie, was born in Branford, Connecticut. He received his education in the public schools of that town, and developed such a marked musical talent that he was given an excellent training along that line. He became a professor of music, and taught the piano and organ all his life. He married Harriet Cook, also a native of Branford. He died in 1856, and his wife survived him only three years. They were the parents of four children, of whom one son, Calvin H., is a well known figure in the city of Norwich.

Calvin Harrison Frisbie, son of William K. and Harriet (Cook) Frisbie, was born in Branford, in August, 1852. He was educated in the public schools of Norwich, supplemented by a course at the Norwich Free Academy, which covered two years. He lived in Dayville, and began life in the employ of the Attawaugan Company, manufacturers of cotton fabrics. He was faithful in his work, and always alive to the possibility of progress and advancement; he let nothing connected with his work escape him. He became superintendent of the plant in 1881, then later was made agent of the company and transferred to the main office of the company at Norwich, which is still (1922) under his management.

Calvin Harrison Frisbie married Marian R. Taft, of Smithfield, Rhode Island, on November 4, 1879; she died in November, 1919. They had three children: Harriet, who became the wife of Archibald Mitchell, of Norwich; Henry, who is cashier of the Uncas National Bank, of that city; and William R. Frisbie, of the Frisbie-McCormick Corporation, of Norwich and New London. Mr. Frisbie is associated in this business with Daniel Joseph McCormick, Jr., and their automobile sales room and service station in Norwich are the leading establishments along these lines in this section of the State, while their New London sales room is an important business in itself.

William R. Frisbie is also prominent in social and fraternal circles. He is a member of the City Club, and of the United States Manufacturers' Association; a member of Moriah Lodge, No. 15, Free and Accepted Masons, of Danielson, Connecticut; of Warren Chapter Royal Arch Masons, of Danielson; of Columbian Commandery, No. 4, Knights Templar, of Norwich; and of the Connecticut Consistory, a Scottish Rite Mason of the thirty-second degree. While by no means a politician, Mr. Frisbie is affiliated with the Republican party, and loyal to its principles. He is a member of the United Congregational Church of Norwich.

ALFRED SMITH HOWARD—Among those families of New England which trace their lineage far back into the misty years of the distant past, none can trace a more direct line than that of the Howard family. Back to Thomas Howard, of the ducal house of Norfolk, England, Earl of Arundel and Surrey, the line of descent is clearly established. When Thomas Howard, Earl of Arundel and Surrey, died in 1646, his estate was divided between his eldest son, Sir Henry, and his second son, who was Sir William, viscount of Stafford, the younger son receiving but a small amount of property. This was Thomas Howard (2), and in 1660 he, with other sons of ducal families, came to America, arriving at Saybrook, Connecticut, from Norwich, England, but soon afterward going with Rev. Jonas Fitch, Thomas Bingham, Robert Allyn, John Mason, and others to a nine-mile tract, now the city of Norwich, Connecticut. He married Mary Hollman, and from their children, Mary, Sarah, Martha, Thomas and Benjamin, have descended the numerous branches of the Howard family in America, who have contributed so largely to the building of many communities.

Charles Smith Howard, father of Alfred Smith Howard, was born January 7, 1816, at East Lyme, Connecticut. Reared and educated in East Lyme, he was during most of his life closely identified with the fishing fleets which sailed from Niantic, Connecticut, being a large owner of fishing fleets as well as one of the foremost of the men actively engaged in that industry. Late in life he left the sea and built the beautiful homestead in the present Sound View section, where he devoted himself to the management of the large farm until his death, April 24, 1890. He married Elizabeth Manwaring Hough, born June 14, 1823, and now, at the age of ninety-nine, residing with her daughter, Mrs. Eugene Caulkins, of Old Lyme. She is wonderfully alert and active for a woman of her age. Charles Smith and Elizabeth M. (Hough) Howard were the parents of eleven children: Charles Robert, born August 12, 1842, at Niantic, Connecticut; Mary Eliz-

abeth, born April 22, 1845; Josiah Franklin, born August 28, 1847, deceased; Hannah Jane, born September 1, 1849, married Fred Harding, of Old Lyme; Mary Elizabeth, born April 8, 1852; Daniel Howard, born August 25, 1854, died in 1910; William Palmer, born April 4, 1857; Edwin, born May 16, 1859; J. Franklin, born March 4, 1862; Lucy Howard, born May 17, 1865, wife of Eugene Caulkins, of Old Lyme; and Alfred Smith, of whom further.

Alfred Smith Howard, son of Charles Smith and Elizabeth Manwaring (Hough) Howard, was born May 16, 1867, at Old Lyme, Connecticut. He attended the schools of Old Lyme and then went to Clinton Academy, at Clinton, Connecticut, from which he graduated. After teaching school for three winters in various parts of the county, he went into the grocery business at South Lyme, Connecticut, where he remained for two years, acting as postmaster of South Lyme during that same period. Upon the death of his father in 1890, he sold his business at South Lyme and returned to the old homestead, where he is living at the present time. The farm, a large and beautiful one in the Sound View section, is most efficiently managed, and is one of the show places of the county. Politically, Mr. Howard is a Republican, and has been active in the interests of his community. Always ready to help forward any movement for the betterment of the community, he has not refused to serve in the regular offices which offer large opportunity for faithful performance of civic duty. He has served as third selectman, as second selectman, and as justice of the peace, all in Old Lyme, Connecticut. Fraternally, Mr. Howard is affiliated with Pythagoras Lodge, No. 45, Free and Accepted Masons; and with Crystal Lodge, No. 88, Independent Order of Odd Fellows, in which last he has been through all the chairs. In church membership he is a Baptist.

Alfred Smith Howard married (first) Elizabeth Mary Riddell, daughter of Conrad Riddell, of Old Lyme. Mrs. Howard died October 8, 1909. To this marriage was born one son, Clifford Riddell Howard, May 3, 1897. During the World War he served in the United States navy, from May 28, 1918, to June 28, 1919, on the transports carrying troops to France. Mr. Howard married (second) August 25, 1910, Alma Kristin Peterson, daughter of Johan Peterson, and born in Sweden, July 11, 1875. To this marriage two children have been born: Evelyn Alma, born March 23, 1912; and Charles Smith, born November 30, 1915. Both of these children were born in Old Lyme.

HOWARD E. BECKWITH—Allied with the building trades, and doing a prosperous business in the city of New London, Connecticut, Howard E. Beckwith, of this city, is a prominent man in other lines of public activity. Mr. Beckwith is a descendant of prominent old families of this and neighboring States.

His grandfather was James Beckwith, of Greenport and Sag Harbor, New York, and his grandmother's family name was Brown.

Samuel R. Beckwith, father of Howard E. Beckwith, was a lifelong resident of Sag Harbor, Long Island, New York. He was educated in the public schools of his native town, and learned the trade of mason there, following this trade all his active life. He died in 1892. He married Anna C. Polley, daughter of Samuel M. and Charlotte M. (Edwards) Polley, the Polley line coming from Cotton Mather, of Boston Colonial days, the Edwards line being co-descendants with the celebrated Colonial divine, Rev. Jonathan Edwards. Samuel R. and Anna C. (Polley) Beckwith were the parents of three children: Howard E., whose name heads this review; Russell E., who married Anna R. Gray, and is a resident of New London; and Anna Rose, who is now the wife of Arthur E. Dunmire, residing also in New London.

Howard E. Beckwith was born in Sag Harbor, Long Island, New York, January 26, 1883, and received his education in the public schools of that place. After leaving school he was employed in Southold and Greenport, Long Island, coming to New London, Connecticut, in December, 1903, and in the spring of 1904 entered the employ of Hobron & Root, contracting painters and decorators, as journeyman painter. Mr. Beckwith remained with them until Mr. Root's death in 1917; at that time the business was offered for sale by the Root estate, and Mr. Beckwith, in company with Mr. Curtis F. Gates, who had been employed as bookkeeper, purchased it, using the firm name of Gates & Beckwith. In October, 1918, Mr. Gates died of influenza, and Mr. Beckwith purchased his interest in the business from the heirs, thereafter conducting the business independently, retaining, however, the firm name of Gates & Beckwith as a trade name. He is still thus engaged, and is carrying the business constantly forward, developing it and increasing its scope, and now has an important, wide-reaching interest in this branch of industrial and mercantile endeavor. He does contract painting, paper hanging and decorating, and conducts a well appointed store, selling paints, wall papers, and all kinds of painter's supplies. The store, which is located at the corner of Church and Meridan streets, is large and up-to-date in every way, and Mr. Beckwith is handling an extensive business.

Outside his immediate business interests, Mr. Beckwith is well known about town. He is a member of the New London Chamber of Commerce, the Young Men's Christian Association, Knonomoc Hose Company, No. 4, of the New London Fire Department. Fraternally, he is a member of Brainard Lodge, No. 102, Free and Accepted Masons. Politically, he supports the Republican party.

On January 20, 1910, at New London, Mr. Beckwith married Ethel E. Harris, daughter of Nelson E. and Ella M. (Carpenter) Harris, of this city, her father a native of New London, her mother born in

Mystic, Connecticut. Mr. and Mrs. Beckwith are the parents of three children: Harold Edwards, born January 31, 1913, died February 28, 1913; Lois Alma, born November 22, 1916; Russell Howard, born January 8, 1920. The family are members of St. James' Episcopal Church.

LYMAN BUCKINGHAM SMITH—A conspicuous figure in the life of this community, and one who has taken a keen and active interest in its affairs, is Lyman Buckingham Smith. Until his farming operations grew so extensive that he was unable to give his attention to other things than his own business affairs, he was always a prominent figure in the life of Montville and an active promoter of its interests.

The Smith families are numerous in this country, and the name is perhaps the most frequent one in New England. It has furnished the country with many statesmen and members of the various professions, and during the year 1825 there were two hundred and fourteen graduates from the various colleges of New England and New Jersey bearing the name of Smith, one-fourth of whom became clergymen. James Smith, of Groton, Connecticut, was the ancestor of Lyman B. Smith, the line being traced through five generations from James Smith to Henry A. Smith, father of Lyman B. Smith.

Henry Austin Smith, son of Lyman and Emeline (Fanning) Smith, was born at Massapeag, Connecticut, June 27, 1837. He attended the Montville local school, and then entered Poquetanuck Academy, where he studied for three terms, and then went to Colchester, where he studied for two years at Bacon Academy. At the age of twenty-one years he began teaching, and for some twenty or thirty terms taught in various schools, working on the farm in the summer time. In August, 1862, he enlisted in Company A, 26th Connecticut Volunteer Infantry, was made first lieutenant at Camp Russel, Norwich, and when the captain of his company was wounded, took command, being thus in command at Port Hudson. Prior to this he had been in command of Fort Banks on the Mississippi river, where the explosion of a shell had destroyed the hearing of his right ear. On May 27, 1863, Captain Smith was wounded in the right shoulder and in the right leg, and because of these injuries was honorably discharged, August 17, 1863, at Norwich. Upon his return home he engaged in farming, with short intervals of teaching, until finally, in 1880, he purchased the homestead and devoted his entire attention to general farming. His farm was an exceedingly well kept one and very prosperous. He married Harriet Eliza Mitchell, daughter of David and Eliza (Grant) Mitchell, of Salem, Connecticut. She died in 1909, and he was killed by a train, September 15, 1913. They were the parents of one child, Lyman Buckingham.

Lyman Buckingham Smith, son of Henry A. and Harriet Eliza (Mitchell) Smith, was born in the historic Stoddard homestead, October 15, 1865. This property was formerly owned by a sea captain whose name was Church, and of whom was written the story "Before the Mast." The childhood of Lyman B. Smith was spent on his father's farm, and most of his time was spent in helping the older man with the work about the place. His opportunities for attending school were meagre, and after his brief terms in the local school he remained at home. Upon the death of his father, the son succeeded to the management of this property, and in 1913 purchased the farm of eighty-five acres, which he now owns in Montville, and which is considered one of the finest and most productive farms in the community—due in no small measure to the tireless energy of Mr. Smith. He is a Democrat, and has identified himself closely with the local organization of his party, which, until his business cares necessitated his declining more honors, elected him to numerous important offices. He has been a member of the Board of Relief, of the Board of Assessors, and justice of the peace. In religion, he is a Congregationalist and attends the First Congregational Church, of Montville.

Mr. Smith married, September 13, 1893, at Montville, Connecticut, Harriet Champlin, daughter of Captain Azel Fitch and Harriett (Smith) Champlin. Azel Fitch Champlin, who was a sea captain for forty years in the coasting fleet, was the son of Samuel Champlin, who was one of seven sons, all sea captains. Mrs. Champlin was the daughter of Asa and Miranda Smith. Mr. and Mrs. Smith are the parents of one son, Lyman Earl.

Lyman Earl Smith was born January 4, 1896. During the World War he enlisted in the United States Army and went to Camp Upton, New York, from which place he was transferred to Camp Meade, and from there ordered across seas, attached to Company M, 79th Division, 313th Infantry. He was wounded in the Argonne Forest, September 26, 1918, and sent to the hospital at Chaumont, where he remained until sent home on the hospital ship "La France," landing in New York December 24, 1918, and being mustered out January 3, 1919. Lyman Earl Smith married Bessie Agnes Bushnell, daughter of Irving Henry and Agnes Jane (Gillney) Bushnell, and they are the parents of one child, Elsie Mae, born March 20, 1921.

MERITT ELY TOOKER, for twenty-two years has been postmaster of Uncasville, a village in the town of Montville, New London county, Connecticut, on the Thames river, six miles north of New London. The village and villagers have greatly changed since 1898, when Mr. Tooker first assumed the duties of custodian of the village mail, and administrations have come and gone, but the village postmaster has survived all changes, and no postmaster-general of whatever faith has ever interfered with the veteran postmaster of Uncasville.

Mr. Tooker is a son of William B. and Mary Jane

(Capron) Tooker, his father an engineer, running on boats of the Norwich Line, New London to New York, his home in Montville. He served his town as selectman, town clerk, and in other capacities until his death in Montville in 1912. His wife, Mary Jane Capron, born in Sharon, New York, died in Montville, Connecticut. Mr. Tooker is a member of Thames Lodge, Independent Order of Odd Fellows; Loyal Order of Moose; and Oxotoxo Lodge, Free and Accepted Masons. He was born in the town of Montville, June 8, 1872, and here he has spent his life.

GEORGE ALEXANDER CHAGNON—Many hardy Canadians have crossed the borderline and come into the United States, where they have engaged in agriculture, or in some other line of business connected with the wood pulp and paper industry. Among these was Alexander Chagnon, born in the Province of Canada, but brought to the State of Massachusetts when a child. He is now a man of sixty-two, and engaged as an operator in a cotton mill in the city of Lowell. He married Nellie Blanchette, born in Quebec, Canada, daughter of Eli Blanchette, and they became the parents of six children, George A. being the eldest.

George A. Chagnon was born in West Boylston, Massachusetts, June 10, 1880, and attended the public schools of West Boylston. After leaving school he went on a farm and for twelve years was a tiller of the soil. At the end of that time, feeling that there was greater opportunity in other directions, he went into the Climax Paper Tube Company's employ, and worked there for another twelve years, from 1903 to 1915, when he formed a partnership with A. J. Huggard, under the name, Chagnon, Huggard Company, and established a paper tube business in Montville, Connecticut. This business has steadily prospered and increased, and at the present time is doing a flourishing business, which gives steady employment to a number of people of the village. Mr. Chagnon is a Grand Knight of the Knights of Columbus, and a member of St. John's Roman Catholic Church. Politically, he supports the Republican party.

Mr. Chagnon married Bella Levesque, who was born in Quebec, Canada, December 7, 1888, and they are the parents of seven children: George A.; Irene, who died in infancy; Roland; Paul; Lucien; Robert; and Joseph, who died in infancy. The family home is in Montville, Connecticut.

FREDERIC A. BARNES—Among the representative citizens of Old Mystic, Connecticut, no name stands out more prominently than that of Frederic A. Barnes, a native of this place, his birth having occurred here January 6, 1866. Mr. Barnes was the son of Amos T. and Mary A. (Browning) Barnes, who had, beside Frederic A., a daughter, Ida, who married Dr. W. H. Gray, of Mystic.

The education of Frederic A. Barnes was obtained in the public schools of Old Mystic, where he acquired the fundamentals that have enabled him, from observation and experience, to attain a general knowledge of men and things, especially fitting him for the management and successful carrying on of the large enterprises he has been at the head of. After leaving school he assisted his father for several years in the lumbering business, which was carried on in a small way. In 1903 he purchased the farm upon which he now lives, and a little later built the large house he now lives in, which is a model home and equipped with all known modern conveniences. The farm is considered in many ways the "banner farm" of the town of Stonington. It is bounded on the west by the Mystic river, which has a channel at this place twelve feet deep. Every acre of it can be worked by machinery and is very fertile. Inheriting from his father a love of lumbering, Mr. Barnes has for the past fifteen years made this his main business, and no man in the town of Stonington has run as many sawmills or furnished as much material for the government and for private construction as he has.

In politics he is a Republican, but he has never been an office seeker. His Masonic membership is found in Charity and Relief Lodge, No. 72, Free and Accepted Masons; Benevolent Chapter, No. 21, Royal Arch Masons; Mystic Council, No. 29, Royal and Select Masters; Palestine Commandery, No. 6, Knights Templar; Pyramid Temple, Ancient Arabic Order Nobles of the Mystic Shrine, of Bridgeport, Connecticut. He is a member of King Solomon Lodge of Perfection, fourteenth degree; Van Rensselaer Council, Princes of Jerusalem, sixteenth degree; Norwich Chapter of Rose Croix, eighteenth degree; and Connecticut Consistory of Supreme Princes of the Royal Secret, thirty-second degree, Valley of Norwich, Connecticut. He also is past master of Charity and Relief Lodge, No. 72, and of Stonington Grange, Patrons of Husbandry, No. 68, and fraternizes with the Independent Order of Odd Fellows, Stonington Lodge, No. 26, of Mystic.

In 1893 Mr. Barnes was united in marriage with Eliza H. Chapman, and to them have been born eight children, namely: Clark A., Esther B., Charles F., Mary E. (deceased), Henry T., Amos A., Ruth A., and Lucy H. Mr. Barnes and family affiliate with the Old Mystic Methodist Episcopal Church.

HUGH R. WHITMAN—A leader in agricultural affairs, not only of a local nature but of general interest throughout the county, Mr. Whitman, of Waterford, New London county, Connecticut, is a noteworthy figure. Mr. Whitman comes of old Vermont ancestry, and is a native of that State. He is a son of Clarence D. and Sarah J. (Redway) Whitman, and his father, reared on the farm and experienced in various branches of farm endeavor, came from Vermont in 1902, bringing his family and locating on Fisher's Island. He later came to Waterford, but eventually returned to Fisher's Island, where he still resides. The mother, who also is a native of Vermont, resides on Fisher's Island.

Hugh R. Whitman was born in Brattleboro, Vermont, in 1881. When the family removed to Fisher's Island he was old enough to be deeply interested in the farming business, which formed the chief activity of the place, later becoming manager of the poultry farm. Coming to Waterford with the family in 1912, he became his father's associate in the purchase of the Newbury farm, in this town, of which he is now the owner and manager. This farm consists of 225 acres, and carries fifty head of cattle, the milk being disposed of entirely in the city of New London. Mr. Whitman also has an extensive poultry plant here, and carries on some diversified farming. His interest in farm progress throughout the county has long been well known, and with the organized endeavors of recent years in county farm affairs he has been brought into prominence. He has for the past year been president of the New London County Farm Bureau, and for the past three years has been president of the Waterford Farmers' Exchange, which is doing a splendid work for the agricutural interests of this community. He is also a member of Konomoc Grange, No. 91, Patrons of Husbandry, of Waterford. Politically, Mr. Whitman supports the Republican party, and is a worker for civic advance, but has never sought political honors.

Mr. Whitman married, on Fisher's Island, in 1907, Bessie May Webber, of New York State, and they have one daughter, Margaret Sarah.

JAMES OTIS SWEET—During the years, eighty-two, granted James O. Sweet on earth, he compiled a record of usefulness and success as a business man and public-spirited citizen that will long linger in the memory of his many friends. "In his business life he gave unto every one his just measure, and often more, and he did not seek his own but in a temperate way."

> Formed on the good old plan,
> A true, a brave, and downright honest man.
>
> * * *
>
> Loathing pretense, he did with cheerful will
> What others talked of while their hands were still.

Mr. Sweet was a wise counsellor, a fatherly guide and friend, who kept in touch with progressive ideas in his many business activities. In his private business, and in public affairs, his business ability was strongly manifested. He became treasurer of the town of Griswold when the town was burdened with debt, and for fourteen years held that office, leaving to his successor a town free from all indebtedness. In his private business he prospered abundantly, but his wealth was fairly earned and when he was called away he took with him the respect and esteem of the community in which the greater part of his life was passed. Benevolent and sympathetic, he aided all good causes; was an ardent lover of his home, and with kindly word and pleasant smile, greeted his friends and acquaintances, his disposition so sunny that seldom, indeed, was he moved to anger. He was deeply interested in young people, and was happiest with his children and grandchildren about him. He was of honored New England ancestry, and the life record of this descendant was a tribute to their sterling virtues reflected in him.

James Otis Sweet, son of Constant and Eliza (Greene) Sweet, was born in Kingston, Rhode Island, May 7, 1831, died at his home in Sylvandale, in the town of Lisbon, New London, Connecticut, March 27, 1913. He attended the public schools of the district and finished school years at Wickford Academy. He taught school for a short time at Wickford Academy, also at Newport, Rhode Island, but at the age of sixteen entered business life as a clerk with W. H. Allen. Later he started in business for himself in Lafayette, Rhode Island, but in 1858 he moved to Jewett City, in the town of Griswold, New London county, Connecticut, there purchasing from George H. Howard the store formerly belonging to the old Ashland Cotton Company. He operated this store until 1864, then entered the employ of the Ashland Cotton Company as bookkeeper, still, however, continuing his store business. He continued in the employ of the company in the recording department for twelve years, becoming thoroughly familiar with the business details of textile manufacturing. In 1876 he was appointed agent for the company, and five years later, in 1881, was made treasurer and general manager. Until January 8, 1909, he filled this dual post, and during that more than quarter of a century he controlled manufacture and company finances so well that two mills owned by the company were kept in continuous operation save for a short time when the hard times compelled their closing. He retained control as treasurer and general manager until January 8, 1909, when weight of years (he was then seventy-eight) and ill health caused his resignation. But he did not sever his connection with the company, retaining his place on the board of directors until his death, four years later. The company prospered under his management of the departments, and his business ability was fully tested during the period 1876-1909, when as agent, treasurer and general manager he was salesman, financier and in general charge of the business.

While this period of forty-five years with the Ashland Cotton Company was the chief business interest of Mr. Sweet's life, there was another interest of equal importance covering nearly the same period. He was one of the organizers of the Jewett City Savings Bank, and upon its incorporation, June 11, 1873, Mr. Sweet was chosen director and vice-president of the company, and until July 11, 1901, held that office, only giving it up to accept the presidency, an office he held eight years until his passing.

A Republican in politics, Mr. Sweet, during his

residence in Jewett City, was elected to all the offices he could be prevailed upon to accept. He was township treasurer for fourteen years; a member of the Board of Education for several years; warden of the borough of Jewett City, 1900-1902; and representative from the township of Griswold to the State Legislature in 1876. He was chairman of the Ecclesiastical Committee of the Second Congregational Church of Jewett City, during which time the church now standing was built; was a member of Mt. Vernon Lodge, No. 75, Free and Accepted Masons; charter member of Reliance Lodge, No. 29, Independent Order of Odd Fellows; and member of the National Manufacturers' Association.

Mr. Sweet married, January 1, 1862, Ellen M. Cole, of Jewett City, who died August 8, 1905, and they were the parents of seven children, four daughters surviving their father, as follows: 1. Rena Ellen, who married A. N. H. Vaughn, of Norwich. 2. Clara Agusta, who married John J. Crawford, born in Boston, and who died in New York; they were the parents of a son, James Sweet, who was drowned at the age of seven years. 3. Maud May, who married Edward A. Faust, a sketch of whom follows. 4. Ruth Clementine, who married Frederick D. Ballou, of Providence, Rhode Island, they the parents of two children: David Sweet, and Ruth Aldrich. Mr. Sweet was laid to rest in Jewett City Cemetery with his wife and three children. Children: Otis Greene, who died at the age of ten years; Willard Anthony, who died at the age of two years; and Alice, who died in infancy.

EDWARD ANDREW FAUST came to Jewett City in 1896 as clerk in the office of The Aspinook Company, and there for a quarter of a century has been employed, being now the capable superintendent of the plant. He is a son of Andrew and Louisa (Eimer) Faust, his father born in Germany, June 10, 1843. Andrew Faust remained in his native land until seventeen years of age, and in 1860 came to the United States, landing in New York City, where he remained three years. In 1863 he came to Norwich, Connecticut, where he died May 23, 1917, having for half a century been engaged in market gardening. He married, in 1863, Louisa Eimer, born in Germany, in January, 1843. She came to the United States in 1860, and died in Norwich, May 24, 1911. They were the parents of five children, all born in Norwich: Elizabeth Willimena, now residing in Norwich; Louisa Caroline, married Lucius A. Fenton, of Norwich; Edward Andrew, of further mention; May Nellie, married John H. Hoffman, of Norwich; Natalie Orene, deceased.

Edward Andrew Faust was born in Norwich, Connecticut, June 20, 1872. He attended the Norwich public schools until 1889, when he became a clerk in the office of the New York Transportation Company, New York City. He remained in that position for seven years, when he removed to Jewett City, Connecticut, there entering the employ of The Aspinook Company. He displayed an aptness and ability which won him promotion to the position of paymaster, and in 1905 he was made superintendent of the mills. The Aspinook Company have large mills in Jewett City, where they bleach, finish and print fine quality cotton goods. Mr. Faust has made a close study of his business and ably fills the important position which he holds. He is a director of The Aspinook Company and has other interests.

Mr. Faust is a member of Mount Vernon Lodge, No. 75, Free and Accepted Masons, of Jewett City; Franklin Chapter, Royal Arch Masons; and is affiliated with all bodies of the Ancient Accepted Scottish Rite, in which he holds the thirty-second degree. He is a member of Sphinx Temple, Ancient Arabic Order Nobles of the Mystic Shrine, of Hartford. He is a Republican in politics, and for five years, 1910-15, he was a member of the Electric Light Commission of the borough of Jewett City. He is a trustee of the Slater Library Corporation of Jewett City, elected in 1914. In religious faith he is a member of the Second Congregational Church of Jewett City.

Mr. Faust married, in Jewett City, Connecticut, October 11, 1899, Maud May Sweet, daughter of James O. and Ellen M. (Cole) Sweet, of the town of Griswold, New London county (see preceding sketch). Mr. and Mrs. Faust are the parents of three children, all born in Jewett City: Edward Andrew, Jr., born December 14, 1903, now a student in Loomis Institute, Windsor, Connecticut; Harold Eimer, born February 11, 1905, also a student in Loomis Institute; and Ellen Clementine, born September 14, 1907.

WALTER ALLEN OLDREAD—The Oldread family of Norwich, Connecticut, came to that city from Saco, Maine, where Robert Oldread has long been a cotton mill official, and where his son, Walter Allen Oldread, was born and spent the first thirty-five years of his life. They are of English blood, Robert Oldread being born in that country. Both father and son are expert textile workers and both capable of filling high positions in textile manufacturing.

Robert Oldread, born in England, came to the United States in 1862, and located in Lewiston, Maine. He secured employment in the "slasher" room of a cotton mill as a "back tender," the business of that mill being the making of cotton warp and yarn. He became foreman of the "slasher" room of the York Manufacturing Company, Saco, Maine, and for thirty years remained with that company in Saco. He married Frances Harnett, born in Saco, and there they yet reside. They are the parents of twelve children, their eighth child a son, Walter Allen Oldread, of further mention.

Walter Allen Oldread was born in Saco, Maine, August 28, 1880, and there was educated in the public schools and Thornton Academy, graduating from the latter institution in 1905. The year following, he pursued post-graduate courses at Thornton Academy, going thence in 1906 to the University of Maine, there completing the freshman year. That closed his school work, and in the latter part of 1907 he entered the employ of the York Manufacturing Company at Saco, in the designing room, and there remained eight years, becoming assistant designer. He resigned that position in 1915, and in 1916 came to Norwich, Connecticut, there entering the employ of the Falls Company cotton mills as overseer of the beaming and slashing departments. In June, 1920, Mr. Oldread was appointed assistant superintendent of the same plant and is now (1922) holding that position.

In politics, Mr. Oldread is a Republican, and is a communicant of St. James' Protestant Episcopal Church, Norwich. He is affiliated with Unity Lodge, No. 15, Knights of Pythias, of Saco, Maine; and with Osgood Lodge, No. 39, Independent Order of Odd Fellows, of Norwich.

Mr. Oldread married, October 18, 1910, Ethel Hearn, of Saco, Maine, daughter of Luther and Elizabeth Phillips Hearn. Mr. and Mrs. Oldread are the parents of four children, all born in Saco: Ethel May; Elizabeth Martha; Robert Luther; and William Roland Oldread.

JOHN R. STERLING, automobile liveryman of the village of Old Lyme, is of an old family of the town of Lyme, son of John R. Sterling, a steamboat man, and grandson of James A. Bill, a farmer, both of these men now deceased, John R. Sterling dying when his son was but a child. John R. Sterling married Elizabeth Bill, who was born in Lyme and died in January, 1918, aged seventy-eight. She was of ancient New England family, long seated in Connecticut. They were the parents of four sons, all born in Lyme: John Randall, James Alexander, Gilbert Bill, and Simon Smith. James Alexander married, in October, 1893, Mendana Merice Reynolds, daughter of Ephriam Reynolds, her mother a Brockway. They had one son, Merice Reynolds, born October 20, 1895. Gilbert Bill married, in December, 1897, Florence Mather Ely, daughter of Dr. Josiah and Elizabeth (Chadwick) Ely, and they have one daughter, Elizabeth, born in December, 1901, and one son, Esmond, born in July, 1909. Simon Smith married, in May, 1908, Ruth Leavenworth, daughter of Esti and Jennie (Dolph) Leavenworth, and they had one son, Herbert Bill, born in July, 1920, died March, 1921, and one daughter, Violet May, born in August, 1921.

John Randall Sterling was born in the town of Lyme, New London county, Connecticut, August 23, 1868, and there was educated in the district school. He was left fatherless when young and most of his boyhood and manhood was spent at the farm of his grandfather, James A. Bill, in the town of Lyme. He was a young man of thirty when he left his grandfather's employ and forsook the farm, locating in the village of Old Lyme, there establishing a business which he now conducts, an automobile livery. He keeps six cars in daily use, and has gained high reputation for the quality of service he renders. He has prospered in his business which he has so conducted, and is one of the substantial men of the community. Mr. Sterling is a member of the village Board of Relief, is affiliated with Crystal Lodge, No. 48, Independent Order of Odd Fellows.

He married, at Lyme, March 14, 1894, Minnie Amanda Marvin, born in Lyme, June 24, 1868, daughter of Augustus and Emma (Hall) Marvin, who were also the parents of Bertha Elizabeth Marvin, now deceased. Mr. and Mrs. Sterling were the parents of three children: Myrtle Marvin, born in Lyme, January 20, 1895; their second child died in infancy; Myra Elizabeth, born in Lyme, December 23, 1899, died September 25, 1900. The family home is in the village of Old Lyme, which has now been Mr. Sterling's residence since 1905. He is highly regarded in his community and has a host of friends.

CHARLES W. BURTON, superintendent of the Norwich Water Works, was born in Norwich, Connecticut, March 8, 1872, the son of William and Margaret (McFarland) Burton. William Burton was born in England, and came to this country when a young man, locating in Norwich. He was a contractor and builder for many years, and died in Norwich, in 1895. He was prominent in politics, and was the first Republican member of the Assembly from the town of Preston, Connecticut. To Mr. and Mrs. Burton were born six children, among them Charles W., of further mention.

Charles W. Burton was educated in the public schools of Norwich, and at Snell Business College. Upon completing his education, he learned the trade of bricklayer and later became a contractor and builder, which occupation he followed for twenty-eight years. In 1915 he was made cashier of the Norwich Water Works, and five years later, in June, 1920, was appointed to his present position, superintendent of the department. Mr. Burton also deals largely in residential real estate properties.

In politics Mr. Burton is a Republican. Fraternally, he is a member of St. James' Lodge, No. 23, Free and Accepted Masons; Franklin Chapter, Royal Arch Masons; Franklin Council, Royal and Select Masters; Columbian Commandery, No. 4, Knights Templar; Connecticut Consistory, Ancient Accepted Scottish Rite, a thirty-second degree Mason; and Sphinx Temple, Ancient Arabic Order Nobles of the Mystic Shrine, of Hartford, Connecticut. He also affiliates with the Benevolent and Protective Order of Elks, Hartford Lodge, No. 19. He also served five years as a member of Company C, Connecticut National Guard, and has been a member of the Greeneville Hook and Ladder Company, No. 2, for thirty-two years, and is an ex-foreman of the company.

On March 8, 1910, Mr. Burton was united in marriage with Rosa E. Pierce, a native of Norwich, Connecticut. Mr. and Mrs. Burton have no children; they reside at "Bideawee," located at No. 744 North Main street, Norwich, Connecticut.

LAWRENCE WESTPHALL PERRY—A native of New London, Connecticut, where his birth occurred August 15, 1891, Lawrence Westphall Perry, son of Charles Ellsworth and Augusta (Westphall) Perry, was brought by his parents to Uncasville when he was but an infant, and here he has since resided. After obtaining his education in the schools of Montville, Connecticut, he served an apprenticeship to the carpenter's trade and subsequently became engaged in this particular line until the latter part of 1920, when he established himself in the automobile supply business in the town of Waterford. Together with his brother, Allen, they conduct an extensive garage, their enterprise already having attained great success, due in no small way to the untiring devotion and energy which Mr. Perry has given to it.

Mr. Perry married, October 19, 1913, Katherine Rogers, a native of Montville, Connecticut, and the daughter of A. Fitch and Mary (Jerome) Rogers. Mr. and Mrs. Perry are the parents of two children: Dorothy Helen, born December 18, 1914; and Catherine Augusta, born April 19, 1916.

Although never having taken any active part in the public life of the community, Lawrence Westphall Perry is ever ready to give his earnest support to all measures calculated to promote civic betterment, and is held in the highest esteem by all who know him.

PERLIN WILLIAM CALKINS—This branch of the Calkins family came to Norwich from Willimantic, Connecticut, but prior to their coming here in 1890, Blanford, Massachusetts, was the family home. Perlin W. Calkins, of Norwich, came to the city as yard man with the Edward Chappell Company, and has continued with that company until the present, 1922.

William Edgar Calkins was born in Berkshire county, Massachusetts, and there spent his youth. Later he became a farmer of Blanford, Massachusetts, but in 1891 sold his farm there and moved with his family to Willimantic, Connecticut, where he secured employment with the New York, New Haven & Hartford Railroad Company, in the bridge-building department. He is still with the company (1922) and resides in Norwich, Connecticut. He married Carrie Bell Nye, born in Blanford, Massachusetts, and they are the parents of eight children: 1. Perlin William, of further mention. 2. Abbey Elizabeth, married Percy M. Alden. 3. James Eugene, married Helena Wilbur; a sailor of the United States navy during the war period between the United States and Germany. 4-5. Bertha, and a twin, now deceased. 6. Hazel Bell, married Ernest Taylor, whom she survives, a resident of Norwich. 7. Annie, married William Buckley, and resides in Norwich. 8. Theodore Getchel, residing at home.

Perlin William Calkins, eldest of the children of William E. and Carrie Bell (Nye) Calkins, was born in Blanford, Massachusetts, December 27, 1886, but was educated in Willimantic (Connecticut) public schools, the family moving there in 1890. After leaving school he was variously employed as a clerk until 1908, when he entered the employ of the Edward Chappell Company, in Norwich, as a yard man, continuing in that capacity until 1917, when he was advanced to his present position, yard foreman.

Mr. Calkins is a member of Norwich Lodge, No. 34, Free and Accepted Masons; Franklin Chapter, No. 4, Royal Arch Masons; Franklin Council, No. 3, Royal and Select Masters; Columbian Commandery, No. 7, Knights Templar; Sphinx Temple, Ancient Arabic Order Nobles of the Mystic Shrine (Hartford); Nimrod Grotto, Tall Cedars of Lebanon; Uncas Lodge, No. 11, Independent Order of Odd Fellows; Palmer Encampment, No. 3, of the same order; Chamber of Commerce; is a Republican in politics; and an attendant in the services of the Congregational church.

Mr. Calkins married (first) Catherine Levitsky, who died in Norwich, September 6, 1918, leaving three children: Perlin Frederick; Donald Eugene; and Catherine Alma Calkins, all born in Norwich. Mr. Calkins married (second) in Norwich, November 23, 1921, Helen E. Gleason.

JOHN JORDAN, a long time groceryman of Norwich, Connecticut, was born in New London, Connecticut, in 1864, son of James Jordan, a railroad and seafaring man. After school years were over, he entered business life, and in the year 1882 became a clerk in the store of O. C. Dimock, grocer, finally becoming one of the members of the firm, when he and his brother, Alexander Jordan, bought an interest in the business. This was conducted as O. C. Dimock & Company until 1885, when the Jordan brothers bought O. C. Dimock's interest in the business, and conducted it until 1888 under the same name, Alexander Jordan then selling his interest in the business back to O. C. Dimock, John Jordan still holding his interest in the business, run under the firm name of Dimock & Jordan. In 1889 Dimock & Jordan sold to Appley & Prentice, who did business until 1892, when John Jordan bought out the interest of C. Prentice in the business and formed a partnership with Chester Appley, which continued under the firm name of Appley & Jordan until 1907, when he bought Chester Appley's interest and has continued the business since under the name of John Jordan, No. 88 West Main street.

John Jordan married Dora Henken, and they have a daughter, Irene, wife of Theodore Robinson. Mr. Jordan is a member of the Royal Arcanum Club, an able business man and a good citizen.

JOHN MINOR GRAY—In the town of Groton, New London county, Connecticut, Austin Gray, father of John M. Gray, was born, February 12, 1805. He learned the wheelwright's trade, located in the town of Ledyard in the same county, and there died, February 21, 1875. He married Betsey Frances Smith, born in North Groton, Connecticut, November 5, 1810, and died November 7, 1875. They were the parents of five children: John Minor, of further mention; Austin, Elizabeth, Julia Frances, Sarah Jane.

John Minor Gray, son of Austin and Betsey Frances (Smith) Gray, was born in Ledyard, New London county, Connecticut, October 6, 1850. He attended the district school until seventeen years of age, then was employed by different farmers until taking a farm for himself. In 1876 he began keeping a store in connection with his farm labors, and for several years was postmaster. In 1901 he bought his present farm in Ledyard and continues its management until the present, and also operates a store.

Mr. Gray is a member of Ledyard Grange, No. 167, Patrons of Husbandry; is a Democrat in politics; a Congregationalist in religious faith, having been a deacon of the church for many years and superintendent of the Sunday school for thirty-five years; and has served his town as register of voters, postmaster, and assessor of taxes; he also is a trustee of the library.

Mr. Gray married Flora Peckham, born in New London county, in 1856, daughter of Benjamin B. and Hannah Elizabeth (Reynolds) Peckham. They are the parents of the following children: Marion Ida, John Reynolds, and Leslie P. The home farm and store is in the town of Ledyard, Norwich, R. F. D. No. 6.

BRYAN FRANCIS MAHAN—While always a prominent business man, it is for his strong personality and his record in public affairs that the name of Bryan Francis Mahan is most usually mentioned.

During the nearly nine years of his former service as Mayor, and under his vigorous leadership, New London, Connecticut, carried out the largest and most swiftly developed program of municipal improvements in recent Connecticut history. Of these works, nearly all of them of a permanent character for the community betterment, Mayor Mahan was not only in every instance a prime mover, but often the originator. Taken together, it is fair to say that they constitute a characteristic monument to his career.

The city's many miles of uniform granolithic sidewalks, its well paved streets, its enlarged park system, its splendid, new municipal building, its great State pier, its growing woman's college, its many new industrial plants, beautiful residential districts, and the network of magnificent highways connecting it with the surrounding country, are physical objects with which the people are daily familiar.

But these advantages did not come of their own accord. They were plotted, labored for, and sacrificed for, in the beginning, by a few against the prejudice and reluctant conservatism of many. Mayor Mahan championed this fight. It could not have been won without him. His identification with it, in connection with a rare genius for organization and tireless devotion to detail, was the secret of Mayor Mahan's political success, crowned, so far as popular recognition is concerned, by election in 1912 to the Federal Congress as the first Democratic Representative from his district in seventy-five years.

In partisan politics Mr. Mahan has been conspicuous for decades, at the front of all local battles, and prominently known in Democratic circles throughout the State. From time to time he held office. In 1881, and the year following, he was elected Representative to the State Legislature. In 1884 he became a member of the New London Board of Education, and was also the candidate of his party for Secretary of State, but, although receiving a plurality of 2,000 votes, he did not have a majority of all ballots cast, and from a peculiarity of the Connecticut law was declared not elected. The choice was thrown into the House, where Republican control prevailed.

Later on, Mr. Mahan was city attorney, and a member of the Board of Water Commissioners. In 1904 he became Mayor, retaining this honor in repeated contests until 1912. While so incumbent, he was also, in 1911, a State Senator, serving upon the important Committee on the Judiciary, and acting as minority leader. It was at this time, and while entertaining a legislative committee in connection with the State pier project, that Mr. Mahan took what was in those days justly considered an imminent risk of his life and rode to the height of more than 1,500 feet over the Thames river in an aeroplane. He "got the appropriation."

Since 1904 Mr. Mahan was four times a delegate to Democratic National conventions, including that at Baltimore, Maryland, in which Woodrow Wilson was finally nominated. He was made Postmaster in 1915, and is at present upon his third term, having enjoyed an earlier appointment under President Cleveland.

The Mahan ancestry is Irish. Born in 1856, at New London, one of seven other children, Mary, Kate, Elizabeth, John, Ellen, Owen and James, Bryan Francis was the son of Andrew and Mary Dougherty Mahan. After completing the public school courses at Bartlett High School, he studied law and was graduated from the Albany Law School, LL.B., class of 1880. He at once opened a law office at home and established a good practice. He has built up a large private business in investments, connected chiefly with real estate, and has financed many of the enterprises which have materially added to New London's area and prestige.

Mr. Mahan married in October, 1884, at Baltic,

Bryan F. Mahan.

Connecticut, Nora Shahan, who died in January, 1887, daughter of Dennis Shahan, of that town. He married the second time in January, 1907, Margaret Whittlesey, of New London, born in this city, and daughter of Ezra Chappell Whittlesey. Seven children have followed this marriage: Margaret W., formerly secretary to the Dean of Amherst, and now in Mt. Holyoke College; Alfred W., a graduate of Williams College, class of 1921; Norman W., Elizabeth Chappell; Bryan Francis, Jr.; Gordon, and Charles.

These brief recitals furnish only a skeleton outline of a life which has been as remarkable for its influence in innumerable private acquaintanceships and what are often mistakenly called small concerns, as for public significance.

A volume would not suffice to tell all that New London has received through the personal contributions of this native son, for long the most aggressive and picturesque figure in the community. It is noticeable that he never failed to receive hearty endorsement at the polls whenever his reputation was put to test by the votes of his townsmen.

ANTHONY DIXON, since the inception of his business career, has been identified with the woolen industry, and as superintendent of the Jordan Woolen Mills at Waterford, Connecticut, which position he accepted in December, 1919, Mr. Dixon entered upon his duties as one fully equipped with both a theoretical and practical knowledge of the business, and the success he has attained is conclusive evidence of the experience he had acquired and the use he had made of it.

It is interesting to note here that the progenitor of the Dixon family in this country, who came from the disputed lands of Great Britain lying between England and Scotland, was named Anthony, and this name has been carried on down through the many generations. Anthony Dixon, the father of the subject of this review, was born at Newport, Rhode Island, April 27, 1825, and here obtained his education. Going to South Kingston as a young man, he subsequently became superintendent of S. Rodman & Sons Woolen Mills, and here continued until his death, which occurred July 31, 1893. He married Hannah C. Knowles, a native of South Kingston, where her birth occurred, March 19, 1832, and to them were born eight children: Patience Taylor; James; Anne; Anthony, mentioned below; Lewis Lincoln; Hannah C.; George Peckham; and Marion.

Anthony Dixon, son of Anthony and Hannah C. (Knowles) Dixon, was born at South Kingston, Rhode Island, May 8, 1863. He spent his boyhood in his native place, and graduated from the local high school in the class of 1880. The following year, having in the meantime decided to engage in the woolen industry, he went to East Lyme, Connecticut, and here secured employment in the extensive mills of A. P. Sturbesant, subsequently, until 1901, working for various woolen companies and gaining a thorough knowledge of the industry. At this time, 1901, Mr. Dixon went to Millbury, and was with the National Crash Manufacturing Company for seventeen years, where he finally rose to the position of general manager of the company. On December 15, 1919, he came to Waterford, Connecticut, and accepted his present position as superintendent of the Jordan Woolen Mills, and as such occupies a prominent position in industrial circles. In politics he is a Progressive Republican. He affiliates with Millbury Lodge, Improved Order of Red Men.

On November 22, 1884, Anthony Dixon was united in marriage with Aimee Parkhurst, a native of Lisbon, Connecticut, where her birth occurred, June 23, 1868. To Mr. and Mrs. Dixon have been born eleven children: 1. Maude Ethel, born June 6, 1886, married George Somerscols; children, George and Harold. 2. James Anthony, who married Clare Dyke, and has one child, Vernon. 3. Anna Pearl, born at Middletown, Connecticut, May 20, 1893; she is the wife of Thomas Kidd, and has one child, June Elizabeth. 4. Carrie, born July 13, 1894, deceased. 5. Louis Elmer, born December 28, 1896; he is in the United States navy on the ship "Ramapo." 6. Amy Allen, who married Everett Draper, of Millbury, Massachusetts, and has one child, Evelyn Hunter. 7. Chauncy Tracy, born December 16, 1900, who is at Cherry Valley, Massachusetts. 8. Harold R., born March 15, 1903, died May 1, 1915. 9. Ruth Marion, born June 26, 1905. 10. Theodore, born September 19, 1906. 11. Florence May, born May 12, 1909.

GEORGE DENISON PALMER—The Palmer name is an old one in New England, the "old Palmer homestead," now occupied by Charles Benjamin Palmer, having been built by William Palmer in 1720. Three times since that early date it has been rebuilt, but all through the years it has been the home of some branch of the Palmer family. George Denison Palmer, the grandfather of the present owner, inherited the homestead farm upon which he was born and where he spent his entire life. He married Harriet Benjamin, and their son, George Benjamin Palmer, grew up on the farm, assisting his father with the work, developing strength and endurance, and gaining a thorough knowledge of the farming of his day. He later left the farm and went to Jewett City, but upon the death of his father returned to the old farm, which he cultivated until his death, April 9, 1907. He married Mary Ada Bennett, of Plainfield, Connecticut, daughter of Durien and Mary (Hayes) Bennett, and they became the parents of Charles B. and George Denison.

George Denison Palmer, son of George Benjamin and Mary Ada (Bennett) Palmer, was born July 6, 1899, on the homestead farm. He attended the schools of Griswold, and worked on the farm outside of school hours. Both George Denison and his brother,

Charles B., were from earliest years interested in scientific, up-to-date methods of farming, and when the father died in 1907, the two brothers took over the management of the farm. The old farm is a beautiful place of some three hundred acres, located in the southern end of the town, and the brothers have equipped it with modern machinery, making it in every way a thoroughly modern agricultural establishment. During the World War, Charles B. enlisted in the navy, leaving his young brother to manage the farm. Young George Denison abundantly demonstrated his ability as a manager, and fully justified the confidence reposed in him.

Politically, Mr. Palmer is a Democrat. He is a member of Pachaug Grange, of Griswold, and of the New London county Pomona Grange; and his religious affiliation is with the Baptist church, also located in Griswold.

ERVIN JAMES LUCE—In the year 1839, Cathcart Luce, his wife, Mary Ann (Butler) Luce, and their seven children settled in that part of the town of East Lyme, New London county, Connecticut, known as "Little Boston," and in partnership with his brother, Arvin Luce, bought a farm, Cathcart owning a two-thirds interest. The farm was operated by the brothers jointly, and there Cathcart Luce died March 18, 1854. He was born on the Island of Martha's Vineyard, Massachusetts, December 1, 1792, and spent many years of his life a mariner, going "a whaling," and also a seaman on coastwise vessels. On October 21, 1819, he married Mary Ann Butler, born March 15, 1801, at Tisbury, Massachusetts, died at the home farm in East Lyme, Connecticut, in 1858. In the spring of 1838, they moved to Holland county, Connecticut, from Martha's Vineyard, and in the spring of the next year to the town of East Lyme. Cathcart Luce was a man of high standing in his community, and reared a large family, all of whom fill honorable places in town life. They were the parents of nine children. These children were: 1. Caroline M., married Charles D. Allen. 2. Charles C., a "forty-niner," who died on the south fork of the Yuba river, California, July 27, 1850, aged twenty-six years. 3. Eliza W., married (first) Edward Luce, (second) Ansel Reed. 4. Edward, a captain of fishing vessels, a member of the Connecticut Legislature, and a leading Methodist; married Julia E. Beckwith. 5. Francis C., a smack fisherman and fertilizer manufacturer; married Mary Ann Mainwaring. 6. John W., a smack fisherman, later, with his brother, manager of a fish mill at Rocky Point owned by the Luce Brothers, Edward, Francis C., John W., and James V.; they were manufacturers of fish oil and fertilizers; married Mary Elizabeth Beckwith. 7. James Valentine, of further mention. 8. Mary A., married Nelson Monroe Havens. 9. Tamson A., married Ansel Reed, whose first wife was her sister, Eliza W. Luce.

James Valentine Luce, seventh child of Cathcart and Mary Ann (Butler) Luce, was born at Martha's Vineyard, Massachusetts, May 14, 1838, died at the "Cathcart Luce farm," in "Little Boston," East Lyme, Connecticut, September 14, 1914. He was but one year old when his parents moved on the farm in East Lyme, and there his life was spent with the exception of five years during which he was engaged in quartz gold mining in Virginia. He was interested with his brothers in the fish mill at Rocky Point, a business they operated for twenty-eight years. The original mill was conducted at Rocky Point for three years, then was established at Napeogue, Long Island, and operated for six years. The firm then bought the ferry boat, "Union," erected a fish mill upon it and operated wherever most profitable and convenient. Later they built a fish mill at Giants Neck. At one time the brothers were operating four steamers in their business of manufacturing fish oil and fertilizers. The business was entirely wholesale and under the management of John W. Luce. The brothers owned a mill at Lewes, Delaware, but that was sold to the American Fishing Company in 1899.

Aside from his interest in the fish oil mill, James V. Luce owned and operated a quarry at Rocky Neck for many years, shipping rock to the New Jersey coast for building sea walls and for other purposes to different places. He became the owner of the home farm in East Lyme, and all his after life made its cultivation his personal business. He built the present house on the farm, and made his home there until his death at the age of seventy-seven. He was a member of the Methodist Episcopal church, and a man of fine character.

James V. Luce married (first) Sophia A. Havens, who died May 23, 1882, daughter of Silas Havens. He married (second) Terrie F. Havens, born in 1849, sister of his first wife. Mrs. Luce survives her husband, her home with her only son, Ervin J. Luce, who is of further mention. She also has a daughter, Laura Sophia, born at the old homestead in East Lyme, now the wife of Frank Gorton, and the mother of two sons, Wayne Luce and James Robert Gorton.

Ervin James Luce, only son of James Valentine and Terrie F. (Havens) Luce, was born at the homestead in "Little Boston," town of East Lyme, New London county, Connecticut, July 3, 1886. He was educated in the public schools of Niantic, and has passed his life at the farm, as did his father, but like him he spent some time with his father at the stamp mill at the quartz gold mine in Virginia. He owns the old farm that has always been his home, and is one of the prosperous, substantial men of his town. He is independent in politics, and a member of Niantic Lodge, No. 17, Independent Order of Odd Fellows.

Mr. Luce married Myrtle Bogue, of Lyme, Connecticut, daughter of George and Alice Bogue. Mr. and Mrs. Luce are the parents of two children: Daphne Faye, born December 21, 1909; Rodney James, born January 19, 1918.

EDWIN C. FORD—Of an old Connecticut family, Mr. Ford has spent his life within the borders of his native State, and since 1886 within the limits of New London county, being manager-in-charge of the New London office of the Southern New England Telephone Company. He is a son of Dwight and Caroline (Cooper) Ford.

Dwight Ford was born in New Haven, Connecticut, and there lived and died, a paper-maker. He married Caroline Cooper, and they were the parents of two children: Caroline, deceased; and Edwin C., of whom further.

Edwin C. Ford, only son of Dwight and Caroline (Cooper) Ford, was born in New Haven, Connecticut, July 3, 1861, and there was educated in the public schools. He was variously employed during the years of his minority, but in 1882 he entered the employ of the Southern New England Telephone Company as night operator in the Waterbury office of that company, where he remained for four years. In 1886 he was transferred to the New London office of the company, as manager, and there remains as head of the commercial department.

In politics, Mr. Ford is a Republican, and in religious faith is connected with the Second Presbyterian Church of New London. He is affilated with Brainard Lodge, No. 102, Free and Accepted Masons, of New London; Townsend Lodge, No. 89, Independent Order of Odd Fellows, of Waterbury, Connecticut; and New London Lodge, No. 360, Benevolent and Protective Order of Elks.

Mr. Ford married, in February, 1886, in Waterbury, Connecticut, Mary Morse, and they are the parents of two children: 1. Myra Gladys, who married Robert W. Clark, a contractor of Waterbury, and they have three children: Robert, Edwin, and Lewis. 2. Sarah Priscilla, a graduate of Connecticut College, B. A., class of 1919.

NATHAN HOLDRIDGE—The name of Holdridge is an old one in New London county, Connecticut, and members of this family have been prominent in many ways in every generation. Nathan Holdridge, the subject of this review, and now a leading resident of Ledyard, this county, is a highly esteemed member of that farming community, which is not far distant from the city of New London.

Phineas Holdridge, grandfather of Mr. Holdridge, was a resident of Ledyard, probably born there in the early days of American Independence.

Randall Holdridge, son of Phineas Holdridge, was born in Ledyard, on August 25, 1808, just below the farm now occupied by his son. He was a lifelong farmer, and prominent in the community. He accumulated considerable property, and purchased the Holdridge homestead about a century ago. He died on January 15, 1885, in his seventy-seventh year. He married (first) on March 1, 1832, Emeline Frances Reed, and they were the parents of ten children. He married (second), on July 9, 1854, Nancy Maine, a member of another old family in this county, and they lived in the old homestead for many years, and were socially prominent. Randall and Nancy (Maine) Holdridge were the parents of six children: Joseph, James, Anne, Mary, Fannie, and Nathan, of whom further.

Nathan Holdridge was born in Ledyard on March 11, 1865, in the old homestead, where he still resides. He received a practical education in the district schools near his home, and at the age of fourteen years began regular work on the farm for his father. On his father's death Mr. Holdridge inherited the farm, and he has continued to conduct extensive farming operations there ever since.

Thus holding a prominent position in the community, Mr. Holdridge has always been more or less active in public affairs, although with one exception he has declined public office. For a considerable period he served on the Board of Relief. By political affiliation he is a Democrat, but does not blindly follow the dictates of party leaders, and usually supports the best man in the field.

STANLEY JORDAN, superintendent of the Harkness estate at Waterford, Connecticut, was born in Hungerford, England, April 14, 1874. He is the son of Joseph and Emily (Jarrold) Jordan, who reside at Wiltshire, England, at the present time. The lad was educated in the eastern part of England, where his parents moved when Stanley was a small child, and there he obtained his education. In 1894 having in the meantime decided to adopt horticulture as a profession, he went to London, and there studied and prepared himself for his chosen career. Having perfected himself in his art, he secured positions in and about London and thus continued until 1910, when he resigned his position, which was in one of the largest nurseries in London, and came to the United States. Upon landing in this country he went to Seabright, New Jersey, where for a time he was employed on the Selma Hess estate, subsequently becoming assistant horticulturist for Mrs. Willis James. While here he met Mr. Edward Harkness, who was very much impressed with the former's success in his work, and consequently engaged him as superintendent of the Harkness estate. Mr. Jordan has continued in this capacity ever since 1910, and the estate, which covers two hundred acres, comprises large greenhouses, separate buildings for the servants, a large home for the superintendent, and the pretentious mansion where the Harkness family resides during the summer months. To be competent to superintendent an estate of this kind is sufficient proof of Mr. Jordan's ability in his particular line, his early training having fitted him for successfully holding a position such as this. In politics Mr. Jordan is an Independent, preferring to exercise his own judgment on all public questions and issues, rather than identify himself with any political party.

In November, 1912, Stanley Jordan was united in

marriage with Elsie Hodges, of Somerset, England. They have no issue.

WILLIAM FINLEY SCOTT—One of the most highly respected citizens of the town of Waterford, Connecticut, was the late William Finley Scott, whose genial presence and wholesome outlook upon life is remembered in many cricles.

Mr. Scott was born in Glasgow, Scotland, in 1841, of ancestors possessing all the sterling qualities of that race. He came to the United States as a young man, and was one of the pioneer paper-makers of this region. Locating at once in Waterford, he entered the employ of the Robertson Paper Company, one of the earliest paper manufacturing concerns in this part of the State, and remained with them through all his active life. With his natural thrift he was soon able to buy an attractive little farm home, and this he improved constantly, dividing his time between the mill and the farm. He gradually added to the little farm, until it now contains twenty-nine acres of land, and his constant care left it in such excellent condition that his son now makes a comfortable living on the place.

Mr. Scott was a man of more than ordinary prominence in the community. He was a leader of the Democratic party, and at one time or another held all the minor town offices. He also was a member of the Independent Order of Odd Fellows. He died in January, 1919, leaving many friends to mourn with his family the passing of a worthy spirit.

Mr. Scott married (first) Margaret Robinson, who was born in Scotland, was a member of the Robinson family which was famous in the paper industry, and died many years ago. She left three children: William Robinson, Jeannette R., and James, the eldest son having long ago bought a large ranch in the far West, and dropped out of sight of his friends here. Mr. Scott married (secand) Margaret Pillman, daughter of John and Margaret Pillman, born on Prince Edward Island, who died in 1914. They were the parents of six children: Agnes Finlay, Thomas Hamilton, Walter S., Winifred Hancock, Nina Florence, and Frank Pillman. The latter is single and now owns the farm.

WILLIAM L. BEEBE—The descendants of the immigrant ancestor, John Beebe, were early settled in New London, Connecticut, and undoubtedly the members of the family of William Lyman Beebe are of this line. The surname of Beebe is a very old one, and is found in many different forms, among them being: Bebi, Beeby and Beby.

William Beebe, father of William Lyman Beebe, was born in Waterford, Connecticut, January 1, 1820, died in Toledo, Ohio, August 8, 1863. He enlisted in Company C, 26th Regiment, Connecticut Volunteers, in the Civil War. His entire lifetime was spent in East Lyme, where he was a quarryman. He married Maria N. Harding, born February 1, 1823, died June 16, 1891, and their children were: 1. Mary D., born December 22, 1845, died November 4, 1916. 2. Abbie A., born February 23, 1850, died January 25, 1917. 3. Fannie E., born April 8, 1852, died May 14, 1914. 4. William L., of further mention. 5. Jane, born May 7, 1854, died September 23, 1902. 6. Madora Anna Powers, born December 3, 1856. 7. Sarah A., born April 18, 1859, died June 14, 1921.

William Lyman Beebe was born September 7, 1853, the youngest son of his family. He was educated in the local schools of East Lyme, and at the age of twenty-three years went to sea with a fishing fleet.

For the subsequent twenty years Mr. Beebe was identified with the Menhaden fishing industry, after which time he returned to the old homestead, where he has since followed farming. Mr. Beebe is one of the most prominent citizens of East Lyme. He is held in the highest respect by all who know him, and is always to be found willing to perform his share as a citizen. For forty years he has been a member of Niantic Lodge, No. 17, Independent Order of Odd Fellows, and has passed through all the chairs.

Mr. Beebe married, January 19, 1888, at Essex, Connecticut, Emma Mack, born June 18, 1866, at Glastonbury, daughter of Benjamin and Martha Jane Mack. Their children are: 1. Emma A., born November 14, 1888, wife of Ernest Decker, of New London. 2. William Orrimal, born January 21, 1891, married Ruth Marion Beebe, and is the father of four children: Oliver, Westley, Ira and Norris. 3. Benjamin Mack, born August 21, 1895, served in the World War; he married Blanche Brown. 4. Louis, born February 15, 1897, served in the United States Coast Artillery, and spent six months in France. 5. Thelma A., born September 3, 1898.

HENRY GALLUP PECK—A leading figure in financial, civic and fraternal circles in his native city of Norwich, Connecticut, Henry Gallup Peck is a man of more than local note. He comes of early New England pioneer stock, and is a son of Seth Lee and Eunice (Gallup) Peck, residents of the Norwich of a day now gone by. In direct line he is descended from the Peck family, which settled the city of New Haven, Connecticut. His maternal line traces back to Captain John Gallup, who came to America with Governor Winthrop in 1630. He is also a descendant, on the maternal side, of Major John Mason, military leader of the founders of the city of Norwich.

Henry Gallup Peck was born in Norwich, Connecticut, January 27, 1863. His early education was acquired in the public schools of his native place, and he was later graduated from the Norwich Free Academy. Shortly after completing his education, the young man became associated with his father in business, but a few years later formed the firm of Peck, McWilliams & Company. As one of the

Henry G. Peck.

early concerns in the field of building contracting, and dealers in building materials, this company bore broad significance to the growing city of Norwich in the closing decade of the nineteenth century, and its continually widening activities have made it one of the foremost organizations of its kind in Eastern Connecticut. The associates of this company have always been alert to the movement of the times, and have handled many contracts in Norwich, including some of the finest buildings in the city, and also in surrounding towns. But Mr. Peck's activities have not been limited to the construction world. As early as 1895 he became a member of the board of trustees of the Chelsea Savings Bank, and two years later was made a director. He has served continuously since, in one capacity or another, and is now active in the responsible office of first vice-president. He was a member of the building committee which brought into being the present Chelsea Savings Bank building, one of the finest and most stately bank structures in all New England.

In public life Mr. Peck was many years ago brought forward. Elected as a member of the Board of Education of the West Chelsea School District, he served eighteen years on the same board, filling the office of president of the board for six years of that period. His more personal interests include membership in the Masonic order. He is a member of Somerset Lodge, No. 34, Free and Accepted Masons, and he holds membership in all the Scottish Rite bodies up to and inclusive of the thirty-second degree. For thirty-seven years Mr. Peck has been a member of the Chelsea Boat Club, of Norwich, and for four years served the club as commodore. He is also a member of the Arcanum Club, and a director of the same. He has not declined to lend his influence to religious advance, and was formerly a member of the Broadway Congregational Church, serving on the board of trustees for nine years. With the consolidation of the Broadway and Second Congregational churches he was elected chairman of the board of trustees of the new ecclesiastical body, since known as the United Congregational Church, and this office he now holds.

Mr. Peck married (first) Lizzie M. Wanser, of Brooklyn, New York, in 1891. Mrs. Peck died in Norwich in 1912, leaving one daughter, Vilette M., who now resides in Norwich. Mr. Peck married (second), in 1915, Mabel L. Kies, daughter of George A. Kies, grand secretary of the Grand Masonic Lodge of Connecticut. They are the parents of one son, George Kies, born in Norwich in 1919. The family home is on Sachem terrace, one of the most beautiful streets of Norwich.

GEORGE AUGUSTUS FORSYTH—To the cause of freedom, Latham Forsyth, grandfather of George A. Forsyth, offered his services during the Revolution, and in every war fought by this country, from King Philip's War, 1675, to the World War of 1917, Forsyths have taken a part. Two sons of George A. Forsyth enlisted in the Motor Transport Service in 1917, and one of them, Sergeant Leon A. Forsyth, slept in a soldier's grave in France until the spring of 1921, when he was brought home.

The members of the Forsyth family were among the early settlers of Hartford, Connecticut, in 1637, and about 1750 descendants settled in Salem, Connecticut. Through intermarriage, they are connected with the early Latham and Brown families, Julia A. (Latham) Forsyth, wife of George Forsyth, being a descendant of Carey Latham, who in 1654, was granted a lease and monopoly of the ferry over Pequot river (now Thames) for fifty years, from March 25, 1655. Captain William Latham was in the massacre at Fort Griswold during the Revolution, and was wounded there.

George Forsyth, of Waterford, New London county, Connecticut, is a grandson of Latham Forsyth, a soldier of the Revolution and son of George Forsyth, born in Salem, Connecticut, January 20, 1820, died in Waterford, Connecticut, March 2, 1903. George Forsyth, a farmer of Salem all his active life, married Julia Abbey Latham, born in Lebanon, Connecticut, December 1, 1833, died at Salem, May 24, 1902. They are the parents of five children: Harriet Elizabeth; John Latham; George A., of further mention; Fannie Elizabeth; and Jennie Maria.

George A. Forsyth, son of George and Julia A. (Latham) Forsyth, was born in Norwich, Connecticut, April 28, 1864. Shortly after his birth the family moved to Salem, Connecticut, where he was educated in the public school and spent the years of his minority on the Salem farm as his father's assistant. In 1889 he located in Waterford, Connecticut, where he farmed summers and taught school winters for fourteen years. In 1913 he bought the farm upon which he has since resided. He is now first selectman of his town, and a member of the Patrons of Husbandry.

Mr. Forsyth married, in Salem, Connecticut, May 2, 1888, Sarah Rhoda Hanney, born in Stonington, Connecticut, April 2, 1869, daughter of Samuel and Catherine (Daly) Hanney. Mr. and Mrs. Forsyth are the parents of five children, their first dying in infancy. The others are: 1. Leroy Ernest, born September 23, 1890, at Waterford, now in the employ of the New Haven railroad; he served in the Motor Truck Transport Service during the World War, 1917-18; he married, in 1919, Nina La Rue Elliott, of Arlington, Texas, and they are the parents of one child, Leon Ernest. 2. Leon Augustus, of further mention. 3. George Earl, born September 4, 1896, died June 25, 1913. 4. Richard Hanney, born July 22, 1898, also in the employ of the New Haven railroad; he married, February 17, 1920, Anna Elizabeth Campbell, of Noank, Connecticut, and they are the parents of one child, Richard H., Jr.

Leon A. Forsyth was born in Waterford, Connecticut, June 28, 1892. He was the first man to enlist in a motor truck company formed in New London at the beginning of the World War of 1917, and was called into active service in September, 1917, being assigned to 303rd Company, 401st Motor Supply Train, at Fort Strong, Boston Harbor, there remaining until December 1, 1917, when with his company he sailed overseas.

After arriving in France, he was assigned to Company F, First Division Motor Supply Train, and was on duty in the Toul sector from January to April, 1918. His division was then transferred to the Montdidier sector, where they were used in the defence of Paris. He was sergeant of his company and from the time of his arrival in France until stricken with a fatal illness, June 25, 1918, he was never on a rest area, his unit being kept continuously at its work. On the night of June 27, Sergeant Forsyth was operated upon for appendicitis, recovered from the operation, and all apparently was well when on July 5th there was a sudden change, and on July 6, 1918, at Field Hospital No. 12, at Bonvilliers, France, his brave spirit took its flight. He was buried in Cemetery No. 170, the same in which were buried many of his comrades who fought at the battle of Cantigney, but in April, 1921, his body was returned to his native land, and buried with his kindred in the family burial ground in Waterford.

Sergeant Leon A. Forsyth was well known in New London and Waterford. He was a graduate of Bulkeley High School and New London Business College, and prior to his enlistment was local agent for the Velie automobile. He was master of Konomoc Grange, No. 41, Patrons of Husbandry, and was most highly esteemed in his community.

ERNEST ELSWORTH BULLARD was born in Pomfret, Connecticut, February 20, 1887, the son of Olin B. and Mary (Griggs) Bullard. Olin B. Bullard was born in Eastford, Connecticut, and obtained his education in the district school there, after which he worked on his father's farm for a short time and then, at the age of fourteen years, went to Willimantic, Connecticut, where he learned the trade of woodworker with Hillhouse & Taylor. He remained with this concern for a number of years finally being promoted to the position of foreman. When about twenty-eight years of age he came to Norwich, Connecticut, and secured a position as foreman for H. B. Porter, with whom he continued for twenty years. It was during this time that he became interested in violin making and for several years he has been devoting his whole time to making these instruments, which have become very popular throughout the country. In 1914 he removed to Bridgeport and there he has since manufactured and repaired violins. In politics, he is a Republican, and in religion he is a Methodist. To Mr. and Mrs. Bullard have been born two children: Ernest Elsworth, mentioned below; and Annie Edna, who married Edward S. Beebe, and has two children: Mae D., and Olive B.

Ernest Elsworth Bullard received his formal education in the public schools of Norwich, graduating from the local high school in 1905. Along with his school studies, from the time he was seven years of age, he had been studying the violin, and after graduation he immediately started upon his career as a violin teacher, though continuing his violin studies for a period of two years longer. This profession he has continued to follow to the present time (1922), and although he is a young man his career has been one of good work and satisfactory results. There can be no reasonable doubt that the years which lie before him will be filled with greater effort and more signal achievement.

During the World War he enlisted in the United States army, leaving Norwich, August 5, 1917, and going first to Fort Slocum, later to Camp McClellan, Alabama, where he remained until he received his honorable discharge, February 3, 1918, having been all this time with the 27th Regiment, Field Artillery. In politics he is a Republican.

On December 14, 1916, Mr. Bullard was united in marriage with Elmire Sevigny, and they are the parents of one child, Elmire, born January 1, 1920.

JAMES A. QUINN—On April 21, 1921, James A. Quinn and Jeremiah A. Desmond, trading as Quinn & Desmond, opened at No. 283 Main street, Norwich, Connecticut, a gentleman's furnishings and clothing store. Both these young men were former clerks with the Porteous & Mitchell Company, of Norwich, Mr. Quinn for eleven years and Mr. Desmond for seventeen years, both having wide experience along the lines they are now doing business.

J. A. Quinn is a son of Michael Quinn, born in Ireland, who came to the United States in 1859, settling in Norwich, where he was employed as stationary engineer in a Norwich mill until his passing in 1900. He married, in Norwich, in 1869, Margaret Slattery, born in Ireland, and they were the parents of ten children, six of whom are living: Louise Quinn; Mary, wife of John Shea; Rose, who married Irving Forbes; Nellie, who married Clarence Rathburn; John J., of Norwich; and James A., of further mention.

Mr. Quinn was born in Norwich, December 25, 1882, was educated in the public schools, and practically his entire life has been spent in the same business. He is a member of the Benevolent and Protective Order of Elks; the Knights of Columbus; Foresters of America; and the Chamber of Commerce. His church membership is with St. Mary's Roman Catholic Church.

Mr. Quinn married, in New London, in 1903, Annie Manning, of that city, daughter of James H. and Catherine Manning, her father with the F. H. &

A. N. Chappel Company, coal and lumber. Mr. and Mrs. Quinn are the parents of two children: James A. (2), and Borgia Marie.

WILLIAM THOMAS CURRY — Prominent among those who occupy highly-respected positions in the estimation of the public in Lebanon township, Connecticut, may be mentioned William Thomas Curry, he having rendered service to his State and town as legislator and town official upon numerous occasions.

The family of which Mr. Curry is a descendant claims Great Britain as its ancestral home. His father, William Wilcox Curry, was born in Wales in 1836, and died August 15, 1909, while William Thomas Curry was born in Holmn, England, May 24, 1866. The latter's early education was acquired in the common schools of Montreal, Canada, after which he entered the Canadian Active Militia, June 10, 1884, receiving an honorable discharge February 10, 1887.

After leaving the service Mr. Curry came to the United States, locating in Chicopee Falls, Massachusetts, thirty-two years ago. Entering the employ of the Victor Bicycle Company there, he continued with them for eleven years, when he decided to make Lebanon, Connecticut, his home, and purchasing his present delightful residence at Goshen in that township, has remained there nineteen years. Mr. Curry, having taken up farming, devotes his time now to that occupation and to his numerous township interests. He has at one time or another held many public offices in the gift of the people of Lebanon, having been, or is at the present time, justice of the peace, town auditor, and official of the Board of Health. In 1917 Mr. Curry was elected to the State Legislature. At that time the Niantic bridge matter was up for discussion, it being an issue of some importance, and Mr. Curry, who evinced intelligent interest in and understanding of the subject, was asked to serve on the committee appointed to wait upon the governor of the State in regard to its adjustment. During the progress of the World War, at the time when conflicting opinions were rife as to the advisability of the United States entering into it, Mr. Curry made a motion in the Legislature that the President of the United States be supported and upheld during the crisis at that time; the motion was unanimously carried (Page 1015, "House Journal," 1917). During his term in office, Mr. Curry always took a leading part in all discussions having the public welfare for their object. Another work in which he beeame prominent was the organization of the "home guards" during the war; he was a corporal in the Tenth Separate Company of Colchester, from 1917 to 1919. It may be truly said of him that he is always deeply interested in promoting every movement pertaining to the betterment of his town and State.

In the affairs of the community of a nature not political, Mr. Curry is equally active. He is the secretary and treasurer of the church which he and his family attend, and in fraternal matters, Mr. Curry also occupies a prominent position, being a past master of the Freemasons, and is now secretary of Wooster Lodge, No. 10, of Colchester; a past regent of the Royal Arcanum; a member of the United American Men, and of the local Grange; also various other societies.

William Thomas Curry married, at Chicopee Falls, November 6, 1888, Sarah B. Grant, daughter of Nathaniel and Anna (Brown) Grant. Mrs. Curry, was born in the North of Ireland, January 10, 1860, her death occurring October 15, 1918. Of this marriage four children were born: 1. William George, born March 16, 1890. 2. Archie Robert, born November 7, 1891. 3. Ruth Eveline, born October 19, 1893, who married W. C. Thomas, of Lebanon; she is now deceased. 4. Eva Grant, born January 18, 1897. The second son, Archie Robert, has an excellent war record. When the United States became involved in the World War he enlisted in New London and was sent to Boston for two months' training, soon after being sent to France, where he saw active service in Headquarters Detachment of Provision Train, No. 115, of the 90th Division. He remained in France until after the signing of the armistice, serving in the army of Occupation in Germany. In this case, father and son have both served their respective countries when the call to arms came, as their grandfathers did before them.

JAMES BUCHANAN CHAPMAN—From boyhood Mr. Chapman has been connected with farm life, first as a boy on his father's farm, and since on the farms in different localities which he has owned and sold. He came to his present position, superintendent of the Town Farm belonging to the town of Norwich, New London county, Connecticut, in 1910, and has made a fine record during the eleven years he has been in control. He is a son of George A. and Martha (Bromley) Chapman, his father, born at the Chapman homestead in the town of Griswold, New London county, in 1819, died in 1888, his mother dying in 1863. George A. and Martha (Bromley) Chapman were the parents of five children: George A. (2), who married Sivia Main, and died in 1912; Betsey, who married Amasa Main, a farmer of the town of North Stonington, New London county; Sarah, who married William Oston, a farmer of Hope Valley, Rhode Island; Nellie, who married Henry Stickling, of New London county; and James B., of further mention.

James Buchanan Chapman was born at the home farm in the town of Griswold, New London county, Connecticut, January 22, 1857. He was educated in the public schools of the district and at Griswold Select School in North Stonington. After leaving school he became his father's farm assistant, continuing as such until 1877, when he sought other employment. In 1879, at the age of twenty-two, he bought his first farm, a tract lying in the town of Griswold. A little later he sold that farm and bought another one located in North Stonington, where he remained two years, when he sold out and bought again in the town of Franklin, New London county, and there remained five years. He sold that farm in 1905, but immediately bought another in the town of Bozrah, New London county, which he sold in 1910. The same year he accepted appointment as superintendent of the Norwich Town Farm, where he has since been in charge, eleven years. His many changes in farm ownership were not indicative of a vascillating nature, but in pursuance of a fixed business plan to always sell when a good profit was offered. He improved the farms he bought and made them desirable to buyers, who were always glad to get a Chapman farm. Under his management the Norwich Town Farm has acquired high reputation for the character and quality of its products, and the superintendent has gained equal reputation as a farm manager. He is a property owner of the cities of Norwich and Willimantic, Connecticut, and does some dealing in real estate besides his own holdings. In politics he is a Republican and has served the town of Franklin as constable and grand juror. In religious faith he is a member of the Methodist Episcopal church.

Mr. Chapman married, in June, 1879, Jennie E. Rathbun, daughter of John and Anna (Stetcher) Rathbun, of Norwich, Connecticut. Mr. and Mrs. Chapman are the parents of three children: Frederick R., an electrician of New London, Connecticut, married Carrie Guile; Sadie, married John Hanna, and died in 1916; and Amanda, married Everett Gallup, of Howard, Rhode Island.

CALVIN WILCOX—In New London county, Connecticut, one of the well known names is that of Wilcox, and Calvin Wilcox, who resides in Ledyard at the time of his death, was long an esteemed representative of this family. Always active along agricultural lines, he was identified with the general prosperity of the community, and in achieving his remarkable success, had also contributed materially to the progress of this county.

Mr. Wilcox was a son of Thomas and Bessie (Sweet) Wilcox, old residents of this vicinity, both long since deceased. Thomas Wilcox was a lifelong farmer, and a successful man, being a large grower of cattle; also conducted extensive farming operations.

Calvin Wilcox was born on Stone Hill, on September 15, 1845, and there received his education in the schools near his home. He was ambitious to succeed in life, and knowing farming, put all his energies into this line of work. As time passed he purchased large tracts of land, first wood land, and later improved land, and was, without doubt, at the time of his death one of the leading owners of farm property in Eastern Connecticut. He began acquiring land before he was twenty-one years of age, and at one time owned two thousand five hundred acres in this neighborhood.

Mr. Wilcox married, on September 11, 1895, in Jefferson county, Mississippi, Mattie Rosa Wilcox, daughter of Lieutenant David and Rosa (Emanuel) Wilcox. Lieutenant David Wilcox was a veteran of the Civil War. Calvin and Mattie Rosa (Wilcox) Wilcox were the parents of five children: 1. Rosa Salome, born on August 11, 1896, at Griswold, Connecticut, and now a teacher of ancient history at the Norwich Free Academy. 2. Calvin Eugene, born on January 20, 1898, who is now a shipwright employed in Groton; he married Helen Anne Starkweather, granddaughter of Senator H. H. Starkweather, a very prominent man, and they are the parents of one daughter, Helen Anne. 3. Jesse Randall, born on October 17, 1899. 4. Raymond Gustavus, born on January 25, 1902, and now a student at the Worcester Polytechnic Institute. 5. Kirk Hammond, born on February 23, 1905. Mr. Wilcox died in Ledyard, July 16, 1921, following a year of failing health.

HARRY HERBERT HILL, who occupies a conspicuous position among most successful merchants and business men of Norwich, Connecticut, and who is universally recognized as one of the most public-spirited citizens of the community, is the son of the late Charles W. and Jennie (Briggs) Hill. Charles W. Hill was a native of Killingly, Connecticut, and died in Norwich, December 27, 1912. As a boy he worked on a farm in his native town, later becoming a clerk in a grocery store at Danielson, where he remained for several years or until 1871, when he came to Norwich and formed a partnership with H. T. Phillips, buying out the interests of the former partner, Mr. Fitch, and the firm became known as the C. W. Hill Company. At the end of five years, Mr. Hill bought Mr. Phillips' interest and conducted it alone for eighteen years. In 1904 he removed to No. 147 Franklin street, and here met with unbounded success. He always took a keen interest in the affairs of the community, and Norwich lost a valued citizen when his death occurred. He was a member of St. James Lodge, Free and Accepted Masons, and was affiliated with the Central Baptist Church of Norwich for many years. He was also treasurer of the New London County Agricultural Society for eighteen years. To Mr. and Mrs. Hill were born two children: Harry Herbert, of further mention; Charles, born June 4, 1884, now associated in the grocery business with his brother, Harry H., and married to Inez Briggs, who has one child, Muriel.

Harry Herbert Hill was born in Danielson, Connecticut, January 3, 1871, and obtained his education in the public schools of Norwich and the Free Academy there, but remained at the latter institution only a short time, owing to ill health. In 1885 he entered his father's grocery store as a clerk and was thus employed for ten years, at the end of which time he became a partner with his father and took over the business when the latter died. In politics he is a Republican, but no office seeker, and in religion he is a Baptist.

On November 5, 1890, Mr. Hill was united in marriage with Edna B. Nash, who was born in Ware, Massachusetts, the daughter of George W. and Nancy (Braman) Nash. Mr. Nash was in the mill business in Norwich for many years, and died in 1905. Mr. and Mrs. Harry Herbert Hill are the parents of two children: Herbert Nash, born in Norwich, January 11, 1894, and married to Nellie C. Tibbets; Floyd B., born in Norwich, July 17, 1904, a graduate of Norwich Free Academy, and will attend Hobart College this fall (1922).

SAMUEL PRESCOTT ALLEN—Well known among the business men of Norwich, Connecticut, is Samuel Prescott Allen, who has, since the inception of his business career, been closely identified with the particular line in which he is engaged at the present time, which is the grocery business.

Samuel Prescott Allen was born in Pomfret, Connecticut, September 1, 1876, the son of Samuel and Ellen (Smith) Allen. Mr. Allen, Sr., was born in Pomfret, and died there in 1905. For many years he raised and sold stock on a large scale, and owned a large farm. To Mr. and Mrs. Allen were born five children: 1. Mary R., born in Chaplin, Connecticut, and now resides in Montville, same State; she married George A. Bullard, and they have four children: Donald G., Roger A., Doris E., and Lorna I. 2. G. Clifton, born in Pomfret, where he died in 1893; he married Annie Danford, of Waterbury, Connecticut, and they have one child, Charles Burton. 3. Newell, born in Pomfret, and died there in youth. 4. Pearl, born in Pomfret, also died there in youth. 5. Samuel Prescott, mentioned below.

Samuel P. Allen obtained his education in the district school of Pomfret, and the high school of Danielson. In the fall of 1897 he came to Norwich as manager in a grocery store owned by A. H. Armington, which was located where Gilbert's furniture store is at the present time, and here he remained one year, at the end of which time Mr. Armington sold out his business to R. F. Smith, and Mr. Allen became chief clerk for him, which position he held for thirteen years. In 1913 he removed to Leominster, Massachusetts, owing to ill health, but remained there only one year, and then returned to Norwich and was clerk in the market and grocery store of James M. Young, on Main street, for two years. In 1916 he established himself in the grocery business at his present location, No. 113 Franklin street. A staunch Republican, he is ever ready to lend his influence and aid to any good cause. He affiliates with the Independent Order of Odd Fellows, and the Brotherhood of the United Congregational Church of Norwich.

Mr. Allen married, September 1, 1906, Catherine McEwen, daughter of Wilbur F. and Wilhelmina (Bell) McEwen, of New Haven, Connecticut. Mr. and Mrs. Allen are the parents of four children: Faith, born January 23, 1909; Marion B., born July 12, 1912; Lois M., born February 21, 1917; and Wallace W., born September 22, 1919.

While assiduous in business, Mr. Allen is moved by a generous interest in his fellow-citizens, and promotes every suggestion for the welfare of Norwich. His devotion to his friends and his strict probity in all his business relations so well known to his associates, have met only that return of warm personal regard and financial success such distinguishing qualities merit.

WILLIAM WARREN PALMER—The subject of this review is known and honored as one of the representative citizens of the community and has been a resident of Lebanon all his life. He has always taken a practical interest in all that concerns the welfare of the place in which he resides, and for a greater number of his mature years has been prominently in the public eye as the holder of public position.

William Warren Palmer was born at Lebanon, Connecticut, February 15, 1859, the son of Warren William and Hannah (Eldridge) Palmer. He attended the local public schools until he was seventeen years of age, when he went to work on his father's farm and in the grist mill. Upon the latter's death, William Warren Palmer took the farm and grain business, and has continued in these pursuits ever since.

For many years Mr. Palmer has served on the Board of Assessors, and is at present (1922) a member of the Relief Board. He fraternizes with the Ancient Order of United Workmen. He has been active in carrying on the work instituted by his father, and is adopting it in a practical and progressive manner to the changing needs of the present time. While his ideas are conservative to a certain extent, he keeps well in touch with the trend of times, and incorporates in his plans for the development of his property the best ideas to be gathered from agricultural developments of a similar kind in various other sections.

Mr. Palmer married (first) February 1, 1883, Cora H. Storrs, adopted daughter of Artimus and Lydia (Harding) Storrs, of Lebanon. Mrs. Palmer died November 1, 1895. To Mr. and Mrs. Palmer were born two children: Wallace Warren, who died June 27, 1919; Helena Inez, born January 5, 1884, married Gurdon Tracy Chappell, from which union three children have been born: Cora Inez, Elinor Margaret, and Mary Palmer. Mr. Palmer married (second) Sophia Thompson, a native of Andover, Connecticut, and they are the parents of one son, Robert Addison Palmer, born April 19, 1898, and died July 31, 1916.

GEORGE THOMPSON, M. D.—There are numerous branches of the Thompson family in Maine, and this State has given liberally of her sons of that name in every crisis of the country from Colonial times to the present. Dr. Thompson, of this record, is a descendant of John Thompson, a Revolutionary soldier who enlisted from Bristol, Lincoln county, Maine. This John Thompson was the father of James, who was living at Union, Maine, in 1797. He married, in 1804, Lucretia Brown, and died March 22, 1825. Issue: Hannah Walker, born August 31, 1805; James B., born March 7, 1807; Marlborough M., born August 1, 1808; Isaac, born April 22, 1810, died 1811; Charles, born November 23, 1811; Milton, of whom further; Isaac, born February 23, 1815; Seldom, born June 29, 1816, died 1816; Anna Booth, born July 29, 1817; Fanny Walker, born November 26, 1819.

Lucretia (Brown) Thompson was born January 24, 1782, daughter of James Brown. He was born in Georgetown, July 11, 1755, resided in South Thomaston, and died July 6, 1803. He married (first) probably November 14, 1778, Ruth Weed; (second) July 30, 1789, Nancy Braison or Brison. He died July 6, 1803. Issue (by first wife): Lydia, born October 5, 1779, died 1800; Lucretia, mentioned above; John, born April 27, 1784; William, born February 24, 1786; Nancy, born May 27, 1788; (by second wife): Isaac, born May 24, 1790; Ruth, born March 9, 1792; Nancy, born April 14, 1794; Bethiah, born June 16, 1796; Hannah, born March 26, 1798; Amos, born November 30, 1800.

Milton Thompson, son of James and Lucretia (Brown) Thompson, was born October 3, 1813. He married Amanda Adams, born in Gardiner, Maine, March 23, 1814, died in 1906, daughter of Peter and Betsey (Stone) Adams. Peter Adams was born in Franklin, Maine, January 19, 1783, son of John (3) Adams, born 1748, died 1836, and Naomi (Pratt) Adams. John (3) Adams was a son of John (2) Adams, born in Wrentham, Massachusetts, June 18, 1715, died 1793, and Rachel (Adams) Adams. The Franklin Vital Records name Ensign John Adams, and give his date of death as May 30, 1793. John (2) Adams was a son of John (1) Adams, born in England in 1685, and Sarah (Fairbanks) Adams. John (1) Adams, the founder of this line of the family, was married in America, in 1713, and settled in that part of Wrentham, Massachusetts, now known as South Franklin.

Edwin L. Thompson, son of Milton and Amanda (Adams) Thompson, was born in 1838, died in 1897. He was a painter by trade and was associated for many years with Wingate & Simmonds, having charge of all their painting and ornamental work. He married Margaret Sullivan, and they were the parents of four children, of whom George was the second.

George Thompson was born in Union, Maine, March 21, 1861, and attended the public schools of Union for his elementary education; subsequently was a student in Reedfield Seminary of Maine, whence he was graduated in 1886. Having determined upon a medical career he matriculated at the medical school of Bowdoin College, Brunswick, Maine, and after completing the usual course of three years received his degree, Doctor of Medicine, in 1889. In the same year he began to practice at Taftville, Connecticut, and from that time to the present has continued with a high degree of success. He is a physician of wide accomplishments and has earned a well-deserved reputation for knowledge and skill. He is a member of the American Medical Association, the Connecticut State Medical Association and the New London County Medical Society.

In politics he affiliates with the Republican party, taking a lively interest in all public matters, and especially in that phase of administration which safeguards the health of the community and commonwealth. In 1920 Dr. Thompson was elected to represent his district in the State Legislature, serving on the public health and safety committees as clerk. He has been local health officer for the past fifteen years. Dr. Thompson is a member of Somerset Lodge, No. 34, Free and Accepted Masons; Franklin Chapter, No. 4, Royal Arch Masons; Franklin Council, No. 3, Royal and Select Masters; and Columbian Commandery, Knights Templar. He is also a member of the Benevolent and Protective Order of Elks, Norwich Lodge, No. 430.

Dr. Thompson married, September 9, 1890, Mary Greene, daughter of Frederick S. and Jane (Hight) Greene, of Athens, Maine. Dr. and Mrs. Thompson are the parents of two children: Hartwell Greene, a physician of Hartford, Connecticut, who served in the World War as surgeon in the tank corps, with the rank of first lieutenant, and married Seigrid Johnson; Helen Greene, secretary of the Girls' Club at Boston, Massachusetts.

AMOS THATCHER OTIS—One of the most successful business men of Norwich, Connecticut, where he is the owner of a large grocery store, is Amos Thatcher Otis, who in addition to his prominent connection with the business life of his city, is influentially associated with the various other elements of her life as a municipality.

Amos T. Otis, father of the subject of this review, was born in Colchester, Connecticut. When a young man he went to Norwich, Connecticut, and became a clerk in the grocery store of D. B. Miner, on Main street. In 1865 he bought the business from Mr. Miner and continued there successfully until 1904, when he died. In 1901 he took two of his sons, A. Thatcher and Robert, into the business. Mr. Otis was a Republican in politics, but no office seeker. In religion he was a Baptist, and for many years was deacon of the Central Baptist Church of Norwich. He married Mary Cowan, and they were the parents of four children: A. Thatcher, mentioned below; Lucy, wife of B. H. Palmer, of

Geo Thompson

Norwich; Marion, wife of George Ashley, who is associated with the J. V. Martin Company; Robert, who is in the grocery business, and who married Bessie Beckley, a native of Meriden, Connecticut. The death of Amos T. Otis was felt as a severe loss throughout the entire community where he had lived for so many years and occupied so firm a place in the esteem of his fellow-citizens.

A. Thatcher Otis, son of Amos T. and Mary (Cowan) Otis, was born in Norwich, Connecticut, August 25, 1865, and attended the public schools of his native place until he was seventeen years of age, when he accepted a position as clerk with Allen, Blanchard & Latimer, wholesale grocers. He was with this concern for ten years, during the latter years acting as traveling salesman. In 1891 he left and entered his father's employ, and in 1900 was made a partner; he continued in the management of this store on Main street until 1915, when the property was sold, he then removing to his present location on Franklin street, where a prosperous business has rewarded the energy and ability which he has put into its development.

In politics Mr. Otis is a Republican, but he has never sought public office, as his tastes are quite opposed to this. In his religious belief, Mr. Otis is a Baptist, and is trustee of the Central Baptist Church of Norwich, having been one of its leading and most active members for many years.

On October 15, 1889, Mr. Otis was united in marriage with Josephine Peters, a native of Colchester, Connecticut. To Mr. and Mrs. A. Thatcher Otis have been born one child, Helene Chester, July 3, 1898; she married Oliver F. Horeck, who is connected with the telephone company at Hartford, Connecticut.

ALBERT LESTER WHEELER, a well known business man of Mystic, Connecticut, where he is manager of a market for Munger Brothers, of East River, is a native of Stonington, Connecticut, his birth having occurred here June 28, 1876. His father, William F. Wheeler, was also a native of Stonington, where he spent his entire life; he died in 1889. He married Theresa Brown, who died in 1910. Mr. and Mrs. Wheeler were the parents of four children, Albert Lester, of further mention, being the youngest.

Albert Lester Wheeler attended the schools of his native place and then worked in the capacity of clerk in various places. In 1913 he was offered his present position, in which he has continued up to the present time. In his business career, capable management and unfaltering enterprise are well-balanced factors. Since coming to this community in 1913, Mr. Wheeler has given much time and energy to the furtherance of the welfare and progress of Mystic. In politics he is a Republican, and as a vigilant and attentive observer of men and measures, holding sound opinons and taking liberal views, his ideas are highly-regarded in the community. A Baptist in his religious affiliation, he attends the church of this denomination at Old Mystic.

In February, 1899, Albert Lester Wheeler was united in marriage with Mary H. Brown, daughter of Aaron and Deborah (Perkins) Brown, of Ledyard. To Mr. and Mrs. Wheeler have been born three children: Clara Belle, who died in infancy; Lester B.; and Elizabeth P.

FRED ALFRED BURNAP—Prominent in the practical activities of Crescent Beach, one of the most popular summer resorts of the Connecticut coast, Mr. Burnap is carrying on a very successful business. He is a son of Frank Alfred and Jennie (Sherman) Burnap, his father a civil engineer by profession, who was employed by the Winstead-Tuttle Company, of Springfield, Massachusetts, but died when Mr. Burnap was a boy, and is buried in Norwich, his native city. The mother, who was also born in Norwich, is a daughter of Rufus Sherman, and now resides in New London, Connecticut. They were the parents of one son and two daughters: Fred Alfred, of whom further; Mildred Sherman, born in Springfield, Massachusetts, now the wife of Howard Littlefield, of Niantic; and Marian Edith, also born in Springfield, who now resides with her mother in New London.

Mr. Burnap was born in Springfield, Massachusetts, April 7, 1883, and received his education largely in the schools of that city. He was fifteen years of age when his father died, and the family returned to Norwich, where they remained for one year, thereafter removing to Niantic. Attending school in the latter place for a time, he then started in business, doing trucking and teaming in connection with his regular farm work. The trucking business has grown to large proportions, and Mr. Burnap is one of the successful men of the town.

On political questions, Mr. Burnap thinks and acts independently, taking only the interest of the progressive citizen. He is a member of Niantic Lodge, No. 17, Independent Order of Odd Fellows.

Mr. Burnap married Nellie Lynch, who was born in Ireland, in August, 1882, and is a daughter of Michael Lynch. Mr. and Mrs. Burnap have had two children, both born in Norwich, and both died in infancy. The elder was named Elizabeth Jennie.

SAMUEL JEFFREY COIT—A native son of Norwich, Mr. Coit has always remained within her borders and is entirely a "Norwich boy" in birth, education, business training, and business interests. Indeed, so was his father and grandfather, and further back into the past, Coits have made New London county their home.

The ancestor of the New London county Coits was John Coit, who is thought to have come from Glamorganshire, Wales, between the years 1630 and 1638. He remained in Massachusetts until 1651, then came to New London, Connecticut, and settled on land granted him in 1650. The family has ever been prominent in the city and county, and in Norwich, a branch early settling there. Samuel J. Coit, of this review, is a son of John W. L. Coit, born in Norwich, Connecticut, a plumbing contractor and prominent business man of Norwich, who died there in 1909. John W. L. Coit married Adelaide G. Jeffrey, who yet resides in Norwich, and they were the parents of nine children, two of whom are living, Samuel J. being the eldest.

Samuel Jeffrey Coit was born in Norwich, May 10, 1871, and was there educated in the public schools. After school years were over he entered the employ of the Hopkins & Allen Company, manufacturers of fire arms, and for twelve years remained with that company, becoming master machinist. In 1897 he engaged in business for himself, opening a bicycle repair shop in Norwich, which he successfully conducted until 1902. In that year he opened a general repair shop and garage in Norwich, modernly equipped, and there he continues the machine shop, having sold the garage to Sidney S. P. Smith. He is a master of his business, a man of fine business quality, and commands the best class of patronage. He conducts a general machine business. In politics, Mr. Coit is independent, suiting his ballot to his opinion of the man and the measures submitted for his action. He attends the Park Congregational Church, and is interested in all forward movements. He is affiliated with Norwich Lodge, No. 430, Benevolent and Protective Order of Elks; and the Norwich Nest of Owls.

Mr. Coit married, December 11, 1896, Lena H. Vetter, of Norwich, daughter of Jacob and Emma (Hildebrand) Vetter. Mr. and Mrs. Coit are the parents of two children: Sadie A., wife of Howard Page Benjamin, of Norwich; and Jeffrey V.

Jeffrey V. Coit enlisted in the United States navy April 3, 1917, at New London, and served at State Pier, New London, for a short period. In May he was sent to the training station at Newport, Rhode Island, and on June 1, to the United States Warship Class, and later in the same month to City Park Barracks, New York City. On January 1, 1918, he was consigned to the battleship South Dakota as a seaman, and was on convoy duty until honorably discharged in November, 1918. He reenlisted, April 5, 1920, at New Haven, Connecticut, was assigned to the United States destroyer "Parrott," as a seaman, and on that ship cruised through the Panama Canal to San Diego, California. He received an extended furlough, March 1, 1921, and is now on the reserve list.

ABIAL TRIPP BROWNING—The ranks of the former generations of representative citizens of Lebanon are thinning fast, but seldom is the town called to mourn the loss of one whose personality and career formed so strong a link with the welfare of the community as did those of the late Abial T. Browning, a successful farmer of this locality.

Abial T. Browning was born in Lebanon, Connecticut, October 3, 1865. He moved to Rhode Island when a small boy and obtained his education there, after which he moved to the town of Norwich, Connecticut, where he lived for eight years. In 1889 he came to Franklin and here followed agricultural pursuits until his death. A Democrat in politics, he always took an active part in the affairs of the organization, and for many years was a member of the local school board. He was also a selectman of the town and representative of the district, and to the promotion of the interests of the place which he chose to make his home he was always enthusiastically devoted. He affiliated with the Ancient Order of United Workmen, and in religion was a Congregationalist. But no description of Mr. Browning would be complete without emphatic mention of those endearing personal qualities which made him beloved in private life, even as he was admired and honored in the world of affairs.

On May 1, 1889, Mr. Browning was united in marriage with Lillian Mowry Larkin. Mrs. Browning was born in the town of Lebanon, July 20, 1865, and received her education in the schools of Lebanon. At the age of sixteen she went to Onarga, Illinois, where she resided for a short period, subsequently going to South Windham, where she remained for a year, and then came to Franklin, her father having bought the farm at that time. To Mr. and Mrs. Browning have been born three children: Lucius A., born February 28, 1890, married Reba Rockwell Race, and now resides in Norwich; Mary Ethel, married Harold W. Riley, of Norwich, an automobile mechanic; Myrtice Lillian, born October 1, 1904.

The death of Abial T. Browning, which occurred May 17, 1918, was felt as a severe loss throughout the entire community, where he lived for so many years and occupied so firm a place in the esteem of his fellow-citizens. Mrs. Browning was a devoted wife and helper to her husband, who ever found at his hearthstone a refuge from the cares of business.

CHARLES THOMPSON CRANDALL, JR.—Since 1890 Charles Thompson Crandall has been a resident of West Mystic, Connecticut, and his name is one held in high esteem for ability, integrity and public spirit. The position won in the community by Mr. Crandall is in accordance with the family tradition, and is at the same time the result of his own efforts and ability, and in no way owing to the prestige of the family name or the influence of another man's achievement.

Benjamin Potter Crandall, grandfather of Charles Thompson Crandall, was born in Westerly, Rhode Island. When a young man he went to New York City, where he engaged in the manufacture of toys and baby carriages, and it is interesting to note here that he was the first manufacturer of the latter article in this country. He married Mary Brown, who was also a native of Westerly, and to them was born a son, Charles Thompson.

Charles Thompson Crandall, son of Benjamin

Potter and Mary (Brown) Crandall, was born in New York City, and died in Mystic, Connecticut. After finishing his education in the schools of his native place, he became associated with his father in business and continued in the manufacture of toys and baby carriages throughout his entire active life. He married Martha Ackley, and they were the parents of a son, Charles Thompson, Jr.

The boyhood of Charles Thompson Crandall, Jr., was spent in his native city, where he attended school. After reaching young manhood, he became associated with his father, continuing until 1890, when he came to West Mystic, where he has since continued to reside. He was first employed by the Atwood Machine Company and here became skilled as a mechanic. He resigned from this position, and with C. H. Denison purchased the service department of the business of Mystic Auto Station of John F. Noyes. The venture proved successful, and in the time which has since intervened the business has made rapid strides.

Mr. Crandall is a Republican in politics, and takes a keen and active part in the affairs of the organization. He served on the finance committee, representing the town of Groton in the Legislature from 1915 to 1917, was vice-president of the Firemen's Association, and was secretary of the Mystic Hook and Ladder Company for twenty-five years. In religion he is a Baptist, and attends the church of this denomination.

On June 6, 1904, Mr. Crandall was united in marriage with Anna Louise Gallup, daughter of Charles H. and Ella (Edison) Gallup, residents of Mystic.

FRANK SEARPH JOSEPH—Holding a responsible position of trust in the financial world of New London, Mr. Joseph is bearing a part in the general progress. He is a son of Emanuel and Mary (Searph) Joseph. The father was born in Lisbon, Portugal, in 1848, and educated in the national schools of his native land, coming to the United States at the age of twenty-four years, in 1872. He founded his home in Groton, this county, but followed the sea throughout his lifetime. He died in Groton, February 17, 1911, but his wife, who was born in Stonington, still survives him, residing in New London. They were the parents of two children: William E., now deceased, who was a prominent attorney of New London, and married Lillian Whipple, of Groton; and Frank Searph, whose name heads this review.

Frank S. Joseph was born in Groton, Connecticut, April 21, 1886. He received his early education in the public schools of his native town, and is a graduate of Bulkeley High School, of New London, class of 1905. During the winter of 1905-06, Mr. Joseph took a special commercial course in the New London Business College, in the Manwaring building, at the close of this school year entering the Mariners' Savings Bank, of New London, in the capacity of clerk. He is still in the employ of this institution, and has risen to the position of paying teller. Still a young man, the future opens broadly before him, and he is facing in the right direction.

By political affiliation Mr. Joseph is a Republican, but takes only a citizen's interest in public affairs. Fraternally he is well known, being a member of New London Lodge, No. 360, Benevolent and Protective Order of Elks, and of Fairview Lodge, No. 101, Independent Order of Odd Fellows, of Groton. He is a member of St. Mary's Roman Catholic Church, of New London.

FREDERICK RATHBUN—The Rathbuns, of Noank, in the town of Stonington, New London county, Connecticut, are descendants of John Rathbone, who was one of the sixteen purchasers of Block Island from Governor Endicott and three others who, two years before, had received it from Massachusetts as a grant for public services. John Rathbone settled on Block Island and became one of its leading men, representing Block Island in the Rhode Island General Assembly in 1648. He married Margaret Dodge, and both died in the year 1702, leaving five sons. Many years before his death he settled his sons on farms on Block Island and there they settled, but their grandchildren scattered until only the descendants of Samuel Rathbone, a son of the founder, remained on the island. One of the family, John, moved before 1715 to Colchester (now Salem), Connecticut, bought land from the Indians, which in part is yet in the family name. Joshua Rathbun, another grandson of the settler, located in Stonington, Connecticut, as descendants of Samuel Rathbone.

In the Noank branch, the name Rathbun seems to have come in with Elijah Rathbun, of the fourth generation, whose father spelled the name Rathbone. Captain Samuel Rathbun, of Noank, of the fifth generation, was a seafaring man, as were so many of his name, and he left a large family. His title captain was gained through his commanding fishing smacks which made Noank their harbor. Fishing was an important business activity with the Noank branch, and was followed by Frederick Rathbun, of this review, until he had reached middle age, abandoned the sea, and became a successful general merchant of Noank. He is a son of James Winthrop Rathbun, born in Noank, Connecticut, and his wife, Charlotte (Boose) Rathbun, born in New York City. They were the parents of two sons and two daughters: Frederick, of further mention; William Henry, now engaged in the fishing industry; Charlotte; Harriet Elizabeth, wife of Frank Freeman, chief of the water works department of the city of Springfield, Missouri.

Frederick Rathbun was born in Mystic, Connecticut, March 17, 1871. He obtained his education in the public schools. After school days were over he was variously engaged, but principally his years until 1901 were spent in the fishing industry and in business. In the year 1910 he succeeded his father in the coal business. Later he built the general store in Noank which he now (1921) conducts, and has been very successful as a merchant. He is a Democrat in his political faith, but very independent in his action, supporting men and measures in which he believes, regardless of party label. He has served on the school committee, but he gives his time to his business and neither seeks nor desires office. In religious faith he is a Baptist.

Mr. Rathbun married (first) Carlotta Andrews, born in Center Groton, Connecticut, died May 13, 1896, daughter of Frank and Jane (Potter) Andrews. The only child of this marriage, a son, died in infancy. Mr. Rathbun married (second) Stella Potter, born in Noank, Connecticut, daughter of Elihu and Augusta (Tuthill) Potter. Mr. and Mrs. Rathbun are the parents of three children: Elbert Potter, born May 31, 1904; Grace Harriet, born May, 1909; Elihu, born September 8, 1917. The family home is in Noank, Connecticut, where the Rathbuns and Potters have resided for many generations. They are both members of the Baptist church, and the Rathbun's home is the abode of hospitality and good fellowship.

CHARLES IRA FITCH—For many years holding a position of trust with the leading railroad in New England, Charles Ira Fitch, of Noank, Connecticut, holds a prominent position in the community.

Mr. Fitch is a son of Elisha and Muriel (Wilbur) Fitch. Elisha Fitch was born in Noank in the year 1826. He received a limited education in the public schools of the town, then followed the sea all his life, visiting many parts of the world in his younger days, then making shorter trips as a fisherman. He died in Noank in 1908. His wife, who was born in Noank in 1830, died there in 1900. They were the parents of six children, three now living: Alfred, who married Lida Lathrop, of Noank, and resides here still; Charles Ira, whose name heads this review; Ida, who became the wife of Ernest Palmer, and also resides in Noank.

Charles Ira Fitch was born in Noank, Connecticut, March 27, 1859. Receiving his early education in the public schols of the town, he thereafter attended the Mystic Valley Institute. After completing his studies he became assistant agent at the Noank station of the New York, New Haven & Hartford railroad. This was in 1875, and five years later he became agent at this station, which position he still occupies. Thus briefly is a record of forty-one years of service outlined, more than four decades of the most exacting service, entailing great responsibility. This places Mr. Fitch among the oldest employees of the New York, New Haven & Hartford railroad, and even in this interesting group few have served for such a long period at one certain point.

A lifelong resident of Noank, Mr. Fitch is well and favorably known throughout the town. The nature of his work has been such that he has been unable to serve the public in political office, but he is a staunch supporter of the Republican party. He is a member of Stonington Lodge, No. 26, Independent Order of Odd Fellows, and his church membership is with the Baptist denomination.

In 1881 Mr. Fitch married Lucy Perkins, daughter of Albert Warren and Julia Avery (Barrows) Perkins, of Noank, the life of her brother, Warren C. Perkins, also being published in this work. Her father was an old sea captain, famed throughout the county. Mr. and Mrs. Fitch have four children: Marian, who became the wife of Jerome Anderson, Jr., of Stonington, Connecticut; Herbert, who married Isabelle Henry, and resides at Jacksonville, Florida; Julia, who became the wife of Frank Banning, superintendent of the Connecticut State Fish Hatchery, at Noank; and Maria, who became the wife of George W. Brown, of Noank.

ROBERT SAMUEL BROWN, at the age of eighteen, began his business career as an employee of Norton's Grist Mill in Colchester, Connecticut. From that time he has been connected with that plant, although the former grist mill is now a paper mill, and the boy helper has long been the superintendent. The success of Norton's Paper Mill is due in no small degree to the able manner in which Mr. Brown has fulfilled the important duties of his position. He is a son of Samuel and Mary (Flint) Brown, now both deceased, but who were living at Hebron, Connecticut, at the time of the birth of their son, Robert S., in 1867. Mr. and Mrs. Samuel Brown were the parents of six children: Alvin, Fred, Lafayette, Harriet, Isabel; and Robert S., of further mention.

Robert S. Brown, youngest of the children of Samuel and Mary (Flint) Brown, was born in Hebron, Connecticut, November 10, 1867. He was educated in the public schools of Westchester, Connecticut, and was variously employed until 1885, when he secured a position in Norton's Grist Mill in Colchester, Connecticut, which village has since been his home. The boy of eighteen is now the veteran of fifty-four, and his record of continuous service with the two industries which have occupied the mill since his coming in 1885 is highly creditable to him.

Mr. Brown is a Republican in politics, but he has given his entire time to his business, and has never sought nor held public office. He is a member of the Congregational church, and fraternally a member of Wooster Lodge, No. 10, Free and Accepted Masons, of Colchester, Connecticut.

Mr. Brown married, December 2, 1890, Susan Carrier, born in Westchester, Connecticut, daughter of Demas and Roxanna (Staples) Carrier, of Westchester. Mr. and Mrs. Brown are the parents of five children, all born in Westchester, Connecticut: LeRoy Carrier, Atta Margaret, Harriet Belle, Burton Robert, and Helen Almina. This brief review of the career of Robert S. Brown reveals a man of industry and enterprise, self-reliant and resourceful, who has worked his way to honorable position and public esteem.

R S Brown

SIDNEY BRYANT WILCOX—Since the early part of the eighteenth century the little village of Noank has been one of the chief fishing ports along the Connecticut coast. From here the fishermen ship their catch direct to New York City, and their constant coming and going forms the picturesque and characteristic life of this port.

One of the most genial of the whole-souled men of the village is Sidney Bryant Wilcox, who was born in Noank, August 14, 1865, a son of James Grumley and Amanda (Bryant) Wilcox. His father was always a seafaring man, carrying on an independent fishing business, and died in Noank, at the age of seventy years, in 1906. The mother was born in Stevenson, Connecticut, and was a daughter of Harvey and Annette Bryant, of that place.

Mr. Wilcox was reared in Noank, and received a practical education in the public schools of this community. He entered the fishing industry in early life, and has followed this line of effort continuously since, being still actively engaged thus. He has been successful in this calling, and has also become one of the leading men of the village, active in its public life.

Mr. Wilcox married Nellie Brown, who was born in Hartford, Connecticut, January 4, 1869. They are the parents of three children, all born in Noank, Connecticut, namely: 1. Florence Emeline, born March 17, 1890; married, September 12, 1918, Howard E. Tracy. 2. Archibald Arthur, born August 6, 1894; he has had a remarkable experience on the deep seas; on July 22, 1912, he shipped as a cadet on the bridge for the American Line on the "New York"; on May 15, 1914, he went with the American Hawaiian Company, and while in their service he received his second officer's license at the age of twenty-one; he also received his chief officer's license; at the age of twenty-four he received his captain's license, and was the youngest man in his company to receive such an honor; on November 28, 1912, he shipped as captain on the "Lansdowne." His training for this position was secured from nautical schools in England and New York and on the high seas. At the age of twenty-seven he has completed his fiftieth round trip between here and Europe, touching mainly the countrys of England, Scotland, Ireland, Germany, France, Italy and Algeria. During the World War he was a lieutenant-commander on the "Ohioan." He married, September 12, 1918, Marie Luc, of St. Nazaire, France. 3. Lynton Gibson, born January 16, 1902; he has made several trips with his brother on the "Lansdowne."

JEREMIAH JOHN DRISCOLL, a successful farmer of Franklin, where he has resided since 1895, has always been recognized as a public-spirited citizen, giving readily, sound judgment and substantial aid to whatever in his judgment tended toward public progress. He was born in County Cork, Ireland, April 15, 1861, the son of John and Ellen (O'Brien) Driscoll, both natives of County Cork.

The education of Jeremiah John Driscoll was obtained in the schools of his native place. He remained in his native country for many years, where he devoted himself entirely to agricultural pursuits, and here gained a wide and extensive knowledge of the subject. In 1882, with little else than ambition and a stout heart, he set sail for this country, and upon landing secured work on various farms until 1895, when he came to Franklin and purchased his present place, where he has continued to reside ever since. Being a tireless worker, he has devoted these past twenty-five years to the cultivation of his farm, and today it stands in its highly productive state as a monument to his labors. Mr. Driscoll has never cared for public office, preferring to give his entire attention to his particular field of activity. He is a man of energy, has prospered through his own efforts and enterprise, and fairly won his way to success.

Jeremiah John Driscoll married, April 19, 1892, at Franklin, Hannah Ohearn, a native of Franklin, daughter of Michael and Jane (Hannafort) Ohearn. To Mr. and Mrs. Driscoll have been born three children: Ellen Mary, May 13, 1893; John Michael, born September 25, 1895; Anna Louise, born February 11, 1901, died July 29, 1920.

TIMOTHY C. MURPHY—In Southwestern Ireland, in the Province of Munster, lies the County of Kerry, the birthplace of Timothy C. Murphy, now a prosperous merchant of Norwich, Connecticut. He was only four years of age when his widowed mother came with her children to the United States, Timothy C. being the ninth of the eleven children of Cornelius and Mary (Downing) Murphy. Cornelius Murphy died in Kerry, the county of his birth, in 1861, and in 1863 Mrs. Murphy came with some of her children to Norwich, Connecticut, where she died in old age.

Timothy C. Murphy was born in County Kerry, Ireland, March 23, 1859, and there obtained a public school education. When school years were finished, he became a grocer's clerk, but soon gave that up and began an apprenticeship to the moulder's trade. In 1883, at the age of twenty-four, he was appointed to the Norwich police force as patrolman, and for seven years trod the "beat" in that city. In 1890 he formed a partnership with William P. McGarry and opened a men's clothing and furnishing store in Norwich, trading as Murphy & McGarry. The firm is a prosperous and substantial one and conducts their large business most ably.

When a young man, Mr. Murphy was a noted oarsman, excelling with the single sculls. He spent a great deal of his time "off duty" on the Thames river, in practice, and during that period saved thirteen persons who but for him would have been drowned. In recognition of his bravery and humanity he was awarded a governmental Medal of Honor, which was presented to him by John Sherman, then Secretary of the Treasury.

In politics Mr. Murphy is a Democrat, and from

1912 to 1916 was mayor of Norwich. He is a member of the Chamber of Commerce of Norwich; is affiliated with Norwich Lodge, No. 430, Benevolent and Protective Order of Elks; White Cross Council, Knights of Pythias; and is first vice-president of the Bankers Trust Company of Norwich. His religious affiliation is with the Roman Catholic Church.

Mr. Murphy married (first) Elizabeth N. Flood, of Norwich, who died, the mother of four children, two of whom are living: Catherine, wife of Henry D. Busley, of Norwich; and William P., associated with his father in the clothing business. Mr. Murphy married (second) Isabelle A. Flood, of Worcester, Massachusetts, and they are the parents of three children, two of whom are living: Isabelle A., wife of Dr. William T. Driscoll, of Norwich; and Alice M., residing with her parents.

WARREN WEBSTER CHURCH—The Church family is one long known in New London county in the Montville, Preston, and Norwich sections, Colonel Benjamin Church being one of the military men of the town who drove the Indians from Mount Hope in Montville. Jonathan Church, the American ancestor, was an early settler in North Parish, New London, and the family have always been of prominence in their communities.

Elisha R. Church, a descendant of Jonathan Church, was born in the town of Montville, New London county, Connecticut, and there passed his boyhood and youth. His father, a farmer, claimed his services during his minority, but later the young man located in Norwich, and there established a fish and oyster market, a business that is yet continued by his son, Theodore Nelson Church. Elisha Church conducted this business in Norwich most successfully until his death in 1891, but he ever continued his residence in Preston, then a part of Norwich, and there his death occurred. He married Melissa Williams, born in Montville, died in Norwich, Connecticut.

Warren Webster Church, son of Elisha R. and Melissa (Williams) Church, was born in the town of Preston, New London county, Connecticut, February 14, 1871. He was educated in the public school of Preston, and when school years were over he entered business life as clerk in Norwich business houses. He was later employed by his brother, Theodore N. Church, in his fish market at Norwich, remaining with him until the year 1900, when Warren Church entered the clerical employ of the Edward Chappell Lumber Company, of Norwich. In October, 1901, he was appointed foreman of the coal department of the company's business, a position he has now most acceptably filled for twenty years, being the oldest employe of the Edward Chappell Company in point of years of service. Mr. Church is a Republican in politics; member of the Norwich Chamber of Commerce; the Colonial Club, and an attendant of the Baptist church.

He married (first) Minnie Gray, deceased; (second) Nettie Gray, divorced; (third) Elva Twist, deceased.

JAMES MARION OSTEN, one of the prominent automobile dealers of Norwich, Connecticut, was born in Passaic, New Jersey, April 19, 1892, and is a son of Frank and Wanda Osten, both of his parents being born in New Jersey. Mr. Osten's father was for many years a real estate dealer in Yonkers, New York. He died in 1908, and his wife in 1902. They were the parents of four children, of whom three are living.

James Marion Osten received his education in the public schools of Passaic, New Jersey. It was at about the time he completed the course that the automobile was reaching the height of popularity, and he started life as an automobile mechanic. He worked in several places in this capacity; then, on March 21, 1918, he laid down the work of enlistment in the United States navy. He was rated a second class mechanic's mate, and served for nearly a year, being discharged in February, 1919. He then came to Willimantic, where he entered the employ of Learned Brothers, as automobile mechanician. In the same year he came to Norwich, where he became associated with Ernest White, a dealer in automobiles. Mr. Osten took charge of the service station which was operated in connection with the salesrooms. In 1920 he became equal partner with Mr. White, and this association still continues. They handle the Hudson and the Essex cars, besides doing a general line of repairing. Besides his business and home life, Mr. Osten is active in political and fraternal circles. He is a staunch Republican.

Mr. Osten married, June 17, 1918, Sarah Jackson, of Willimantic. They are members of the Episcopal church.

ERASTUS W. YERRINGTON, superintendent of construction for the Ponemah Mills Company, settled in Taftville, Connecticut, when a young man of twenty, and during the thirty years (1891-1921) which have since intervened has been continuously in the employ of that company and a resident of Taftville. He is a son of Edwin Franklyn and Happy (Eggleston) Yerrington, his parents both deceased. Edwin F. Yerrington was born in North Stonington, January 1, 1841, died July 20, 1916, a farmer and cattle dealer. Mrs. Yerrington died in 1889, the mother of seven children: 1. Charles Edward, married Carrie Summers, and resides in Norwich, Connecticut. 2. Elizabeth, deceased. 3. John Franklyn, married Alice Summers, and resides in Norwich. 4. Erastus William, of further mention. 5. Edgar Elmer, married Jennie Williams, and resides in Norwich. 6. George Ransom, married Alice Bogue, and resides in Columbia, Connecticut. 7. James Byron, married M. Washburn, and resides in Franklin, Connecticut.

Erastus William Yerrington was born in North Stonington, New London, Connecticut, June 5, 1871, and was educated in the public schools of that district and of New London, Connecticut. He began his wage earning career in Robinson Bros.' paper mills, his next position being with an ice making company in Norwich. In 1891 he located in Taftville, securing employment as a teamster with the Ponemah Mills Company. He continued with that company in that capacity until 1905, when he was promoted to his present position, superintendent of all company construction, a position he has most satisfactorily filled for sixteen years. He has built up a high reputation for ability and integrity and has the perfect confidence of his employers as well as the good will and respect of his fellow workers.

Mr. Yerrington married, April 26, 1898, Catherine Brown, born in Scotland, and they are the parents of four children, all born in Taftville: 1. Estella Janet, born November 20, 1900. 2. Nyra Arline, born March 20, 1904. 3. Raymond Everett, born July 21, 1906. 4. Mildred Lucille, born July 8, 1911.

JAMES ALLYN STODDARD—The farm, cultivated by Stephen Morgan Stoddard after his retirement from the sea, was the scene of his death and also the birthplace of his son, James Allyn Stoddard, who was its owner until about 1919. The farm lies in the town of Ledyard, New London county, and when sold in 1919 had been in the Stoddard family for about a century and a quarter. James A. Stoddard is a son of Stephen Morgan Stoddard, also born at the homestead in Ledyard, New London county, who, as a young man, "went a whaling" after the fashion of the young men of the New England coast, and after tiring of the adventurous life of a whaler, became a farmer, tilling the old homestead acres until his death in 1879, at the age of sixty-eight. He married Henrietta Allyn, who died in 1885, daughter of Roswell Allyn, and they were the parents of four sons and a daughter: Stephen Dennison, born April 17, 1841; Orrin Edward, born July 9, 1843; James Allyn, of further mention; Albert Morgan, born April 11, 1850; Henrietta Adelaide, born October 20, 1857.

James Allyn Stoddard, son of Stephen Morgan and Henrietta (Allyn) Stoddard, was born in the town of Ledyard, New London county, Connecticut, October 18, 1848. He was educated in the public schools of the district and early became his father's farm assistant. He continued at the farm, its virtual manager, until the death of his father in 1879, when he became its owner. He continued the cultivation of the old homestead for forty years longer and then sold the farm and retired.

Since retiring from the farm, Mr. Stoddard has given much of his time to the public service. For eighteen years he has been health officer of the town and has also served as tax collector and as a member of the board of assessors. He is secretary-treasurer of the Ledyard Cemetery Association and interested in other town activities.

He married, September 10, 1873, Anna Davidson, born in West Goshen, Connecticut, who died March 10, 1892, leaving three children: Henrietta, born November 19, 1874; Stephen Davidson, born December 31, 1878; Albert, born January 19, 1881. Mr. Stoddard married (second), December 28, 1893, Amy Jane Hopkins, born July 1, 1865, died June 8, 1905, daughter of James Milton and Ruth (Harvey) Hopkins. He married (third), March 18, 1908, Bessie Anna Williams, daughter of Olive Chamberlain Williams. No children.

HOMER FRASER, who has had thorough training and wide experience in his line of activity, is becoming widely known in Norwich and vicinity, as one of the successful restauranteurs of the day in this section.

Mr. Fraser is a son of Moise and Pomelo (St. Pierre) Fraser. Moise Fraser was born in St. Moise, Province of Quebec, Canada, and was educated in the parochial schools of his native town. After finishing school, he took up farm work, and was engaged actively along this line for several years, eventually, in 1880, purchasing a farm in St. Moise, where he is still successfully engaged in general farming and dairying. Of the twelve children of this union, Mr. Fraser, of Norwich, is the ninth.

Homer Fraser was born in St. Moise, Province of Quebec, May 3, 1893, and was educated in the Jusenat d'Outremont College, in Montreal. After completing his education he served an apprenticeship of three years as chef at the Sacret Heart College, Central Falls, Rhode Island. In 1913 he came to the United States and located in Central Falls, Rhode Island, where he worked at his profession of chef in one of the leading restaurants of that city, remaining for two years. In 1915 he came to Norwich as chef for the City Lunch, which is connected with the Martin House. With the exception of the months during which he was in the service of the United States army, Mr. Fraser continued with this restaurant, as chef, until May 3, 1920. On that date, in association with Ex. Ravenell, Jr., of Norwich, he purchased the City Lunch from the former proprietor, C. A. Chamberlain, of Norwich. This restaurant is one of the most popular and attractive eating houses in the city of Norwich, has all modern equipment, and is conducted in a thoroughly up-to-date manner. Under Mr. Fraser's management it has grown steadily, and he is doing a very large business.

On April 30, 1917, Mr. Fraser enlisted in the 5th Company, Coast Artillery Corps, Connecticut National Guard, this company being stationed in Norwich. Called to Federal service, it became the 56th Regiment, American Expeditionary Forces, at For. Ferry, New York, and Mr. Fraser was later transferred to the 17th Anti-Aircraft Battery, of whic he was made mess sergeant. Sailing for France with this battalion, he was stationed at Fort d Stein, France, and in February, 1919, was returned to the United States and at once mustered out of the service at Fort Wadsworth, New York.

Fraternally Mr. Fraser holds membership with the Veterans of Foreign Wars, of Norwich, and is a member of Robert O. Fletcher Post, American Legion, of Norwich. He is a member of the Benevolent and Protective Order of Elks, Lodge No. 430; and of the Loyal Order of Moose, Lodge No. 950, both of Norwich; also of the St. John the Baptist Society of America. Politically he supports no party unqualifiedly, and votes an independent ticket.

In October, 1917, Mr. Fraser married Lillian Landry, daughter of Joseph and Phebe (St. Amant) Landry, both natives of the Province of Quebec. Mr. and Mrs. Fraser have two sons: Homer Woodrow, born April 19, 1919; and Paul Joseph, born March 19, 1922.

HERBERT CLINTON WATSON—Among the representative citizens of Potopaug Hill, where he has resided continuously since 1888, is Herbert Clinton Watson, a prominent farmer of this district. Mr. Watson takes a keen interest in the history of this locality, and it is interesting to note here that on the summit of Potopaug Hill stands a little red school house, which was standing at the time of the reign of George V. of England, and here in this little house of learning many famous men have received the foundation of their educational training.

Herbert Clinton Watson was born December 9, 1850, at Quidnick, Rhode Island, the son of Jeffery Watson, who was a native of East Greenwich, Rhode Island, and died in Sprague, Connecticut, in December, 1910. The education of the boy, Herbert C., was obtained at the "little red schoolhouse" on Potopaug Hill, to which place he removed with his parents when he was very young. At the age of ten years, however, he went with his parents to Scotland and attended school there until their return to the old homestead in 1863, then resumed his studies at Sprague until he was fifteen years of age, when the business of life began for the boy. His first employment was with the Sprague Manufacturing Company, where he was bookkeeper for three years, subsequently being changed to their plant at Cranston, Rhode Island, and still later, in recognition of his ability as an accountant, he was made auditor, and was also employed by the other branches of the concern at Natick, and Arctic. But he did not remain in this position for very long, resigning later to accept the office of assistant postmaster to his father, who was at that time postmaster of the Baltic postoffice. All this was accomplished before the young man had reached the age of twenty-one, which is ample proof of the exceptional ability of Mr. Watson even at that time. The three years he spent as assistant postmaster were also years active in the affairs of the community, where he was leader of the local band, assistant foreman of the local fire company, town clerk and tax collector. At the end of this time he returned to the old homestead and remained on the farm four years, going thence to Andover, Massachusetts, and later to Centredale, Rhode Island, where he followed the occupation of farmer, finally returning to Potopaug Hill in 1888, which has since been his home. Since that time he has taken an active interest in the affairs of the town, serving on the Board of Selectman, Board of Assessors, and the School Board, also as justice of the peace.

Mr. Watson married, July 26, 1872, Mary Esther Wilcox, a native of Griswold, Connecticut, and the daughter of Abram and Rebecca (Selden) Wilcox. To Mr. and Mrs. Watson were born four children: Maude, Walter, Herbert, and Niola.

ELIJAH STARK ABEL—Descended from early settlers of New London county, Connecticut, spending his lifetime in agricultural activity, and also devoting a large share of his time and energy to the advancement of the public welfare along many avenues of progress, Elijah Stark Abel has won his way to a high position in his native town of Bozrah, New London county, Connecticut.

Mr. Abel is a son of Elijah Hosford Abel, who was born in Bozrah, July 19, 1815, and died there January 22, 1882. Elijah Hosford Abel was reared on the farm in his native town, and his educational opportunities were limited to the district schools of the day in this community. As a young man he assisted his father on the farm, but was ambitious to make his way in the world, and in addition to the farm work, which he followed throughout his lifetime, he took up the nursery business, making a study of tree grafting, etc. He followed this for fourteen years and did quite an extensive business in nursery stock, many of the beautiful shade trees in Bozrah and Norwich being set out by him. From early life the responsibilities of the family fortunes lay upon his shoulders, as he was still only a young man when his father died. In connection with the homestead farm he rented two other farms, and later on, in 1869, he bought the present Abel farm on Bashan Hill, Bashan, in the town of Bozrah. This farm comprised one hundred and thirty-five acres of improved land, with excellent buildings, but he made further improvements and built the present horse barn. Elijah Hosford Abel married, on November 15, 1865, Mary Stark, who was born in Bozrah, June 23, 1840, and is still (1922) living. They were the parents of three children: 1. Elijah Stark, whose name heads this review. 2. Edward Everett, who was born in the present Abel home, May 20, 1870, and died in January, 1918, having been a farmer all his life in the town of Norwich, this county, in the section known as East Great Plain; he married, on January 7, 1891, Carrie A. Gager, of Bozrah, who, with their daughter Frances, survives him. 3. Louis Hosford, born in the present Abel home on November 21, 1874, a graduate of the New York Dental College, and now practicing his profession in New York City, residing in White Plains, New York. Mrs. Abel married (second), March 25, 1891, in Norwich, Quincy M. Bosworth, a minister from Ohio. He died in January, 1900.

Elijah Stark Abel, eldest son of Elijah Hosford and Mary (Stark) Abel, was born in Bozrah, December 2, 1868. Receiving his early education in the

Mary Abel Bosworth

district schools near his home, he later gained a broadly practical preparation for his career through a course at the Connecticut Agricultural College, at Storrs. Only thirteen years of age at the time of his father's death, he took over the entire management of the farm as soon as he returned home from college. He has always carried on large operations in general farming and stock raising, also has a large flock of poultry, making a specialty of turkeys. He has bought much additional property, and the home farm now is increased to three hundred acres, and a part of its equipment is an up-to-date blacksmith shop, where general blacksmith work is done for the public. Mr. Abel has resided in his present home for fifty-two years.

In public life Mr. Abel was long since placed in a leading position. Always a Republican, his party early recognized his ability and his fearlessness in matters involving a moral issue of the public welfare, and has placed him in public office repeatedly. He has served as registrar of voters, as selectman, still holding the former office, and is also now health officer and tax assessor of the town of Bozrah. He served as town constable of Bozrah for a period of twenty-one years. At the November election of 1920 Mr. Abel was elected town representative to the State Legislature, and during his stay at the State House, served on the Agricultural, New Towns, and Probate committees. Outside the realm of politics, and still in the nature of a public service, was the reform which he brought about in the matter of telephone tolls. The Norwich exchange, in which Bozrah is located, serves a very wide territory, covering many little towns in the northern part of New London county, and formerly an extra charge was made for a call between Bozrah and other towns in the same exchange. Mr. Abel recognized the injustice of this custom, and secured a ruling from the Connecticut Public Utilities Commission permitting telephone connection without extra charge between all subscribers of any given exchange. This ruling benefited not only the subscribers of the Norwich exchange, Mr. Abel's immediate interest, but of every telephone exchange in the State of Connecticut. Mr. Abel is an active member of the New London County Farm Bureau, and of the Bozrahville Congregational Church.

On October 10, 1889, Mr. Abel married, at Lebanon, Amorette Eliza Avery, who was born in Lebanon, and is a daughter of Isaac Gallup and Eliza Maria (Williams) Avery, both members of old Lebanon families, and both now deceased. Mr. and Mrs. Abel are the parents of six children, all born at the Abel homestead: 1. Ethel Louise, born January 21, 1891, now the wife of Jabez G. Lathrop, a prominent farmer of Bozrah, and has one child, Louise. 2. Amorette Mildred, born May 4, 1893, who is now the wife of George W. Maples, a machinist of Fitchville, and has one child, Ruth Louisa. 3-4. Lawrence Isaac, and Lloyd Elijah, twins, born February 18, 1895, both farmers of Bozrah; Lawrence I. married Robye Boynton, of Montville, and Lloyd E. married Alice Rodman, of Lebanon, and has two children: Lloyd, and Mary Alice. 5. Alfred Louis, born October 30, 1898. 6. Theodore Stark, born August 8, 1902. Both the younger sons still reside at home, being associated with their father in the conduct of the farm.

HENRY THOMAS GORMAN holds the responsible position of supervisor of repairs for State Highway Department for New London county, Connecticut. Mr. Gorman's father was born in Ireland, and received his education in the National schools of that country. He came to America when still a young man and located in New London county, Connecticut, where he engaged in farming and gardening, and continued in that line of work as long as he lived. He married Catherine Mulligan, who was born in Sligo, Ireland, and both are now deceased. They were the parents of nine children, of whom four are now living, Henry Thomas Gorman being the youngest.

Mr. Gorman was born in Norwichtown, Connecticut, on August 8, 1872. He received his education in the public schools of Norwichtown; then, for a short period, worked in a cotton mill. But the young man was not of the indoor sort; he liked free space, green fields, and the animal life that goes with the out-of-door world, so took up the livery business, which he followed for eighteen years. Until recently he owned a livery and coal and wood business in Versailles, a small town in this county. In the year 1913, Mr. Gorman became foreman for the State Highway Department, and his excellent management of the work placed in his charge brought him further advancement in this line. As before stated, he is now supervisor of repairs for New London county, in the State Highway Department. This position carries with it a full measure of responsibility, as well as the honor attached to any office in the gift of the State. He has sold out all other business in which he was interested, and devotes his full time to the highway work, giving his personal oversight to a very large amount of repair work in progress, and keeping in touch with the latest methods and materials.

For one term, Mr. Gorman was selectman for the town of Sprague, and was on the school board for nine years. He is independent in politics, giving his support to the party having the best candidates in the field.

Mr. Gorman married Ellen V. Donahue, of Nanticook, Pennsylvania, in 1901. They are the parents of six children, of whom five are living, the eldest, Henry, being deceased; those living: Alice, Katherine, Mary, Helene and Marguerite. The family are members of the Roman Catholic church.

WILLIAM SPICER GRISWOLD—In the town of Griswold, Connecticut, the Town Farm, where the poor of the community are cared for, might well be termed a model farm. William Spicer Griswold, who has charge of this department of the town's affairs, is one of the most progressive men in this up-to-date farming community, and to his energy and excellent management is due the success of this branch of public endeavor.

Mr. Griswold is a son of Samuel L. and Mary L. (Averill) Griswold, old family names in this section. Samuel L. Griswold was born on Plain Hill, in the town of Norwich, Connecticut. He received his education in the district schools of that vicinity, then followed farming all his life, the greater part of which he spent on the Dr. Gay place, in the town of Ledyard, in the same county. In his old age he retired to a small place at Pachaug, in the town of Griswold, where he died in 1892. His wife, who was born in the town of Lisbon, Connecticut, died in Griswold in 1908. They were the parents of ten children.

William Spicer Griswold, the seventh child of Samuel L. and Mary L. (Averill) Griswold, was born in Ledyard on August 1, 1866. In the district schools of the town he received a practical education, then, as a young man, worked on the farm for his father. Later on, he removed to the Smith farm, in Plainfield, Connecticut, which he conducted for a period of thirteen years. In April, 1919, Mr. Griswold took charge of the Town Farm, for the town of Griswold, where he is still located. From the first, Mr. Griswold's ability as a farm manager was clearly evident, and he made many improvements, bringing the buildings and their stock and equipment fully and completely up to latest approved standards of agricultural progress.

While Mr. Griswold's attention is centered upon this branch of the public welfare, he is interested in every phase of public progress, and politically is affiliated with the Democratic party.

Mr. Griswold married, on November 25, 1896, Rose Mohan, of Plainfield, Connecticut, daughter of James and Elizabeth (Vallely) Mohan, of that town, and they are the parents of one son, Joseph Kenneth Griswold. The family are members of the Roman Catholic church.

EDWARD EVERETT CLARKE—There is a satisfaction which Mr. Clarke may enjoy as in retrospect he reviews the years since he first entered the textile industry, at an early age, in the spinning room, for, since that day, he has been continuously with the same firm and has advanced through every grade of promotion up to his present position—superintendent of the four mills of the Briggs Manufacturing Company, of Voluntown, Connecticut, a position he has most ably filled for twenty years, since 1902.

Edward Everett Clarke was born in Hopkinton, Rhode Island, October 27, 1880, one of six children of Henry and Emily (Greene) Clarke. His father, also a native of Hopkinton, where he was for many years a farmer, is now (1921) living retired in the village of Rockville, Rhode Island. His mother, who was born in Voluntown, died in Hopkinton, November 10, 1882, when he was but two years old. He attended the village school of Rockville, Washington county, Rhode Island, and spent his youth at the home farm in that place.

It was at Rockville that Mr. Clarke first found connection with textile work at the Briggs Manufacturing Company, then located there, but later located in Voluntown, Connecticut. He stayed at the Rockville mill until he had learned the details of the business in every department, and in July, 1900, when he was nineteen years of age, he was advanced to "second hand" in the carding room of the plant in Voluntown, and a short while later was made overseer in the same department. He proved himself worthy and competent, and promotions came along rapidly, for in 1902, after but two years' service in Voluntown, and at the age of twenty-one, he was promoted to the responsible position of superintendent of the four mills of the company. This is the only manufacturing plant in Voluntown, and employs about three hundred hands in the manufacture of cotton cloth, yarns, thread and tire fabric. Over the entire plant, Mr. Clarke is the general superintendent, and is considered by the company as thoroughly competent, having not only managed the business successfully, but as having built it up to larger proportions, giving his entire time and energy in the effort, to the great satisfaction of the company.

With the prime of life still ahead of him, Mr. Clarke has much to look forward to, and with past successful experience to aid him, he will go far in the textile world. He is thoroughly practical, farseeing, understands the business to it's finest detail, and possesses the qualities that win for him the confidence and friendship of his employees, and the trust and appreciation of his associates in the company, all of which proves that he has the ability to make any enterprise a success, and that he has the tact and keen judgment in help management, which is essential. He has won his way in the world entirely through his own ability and endeavor, having none of the aid of wealthy, influential friends to make his way easier. It has been his life ambition to be upright in character, above reproach, and to make the most of his opportunities, and having accomplished this, he is a worthy example for others to follow. He is known as a man of excellent character, exceptional ability and energy, and in Voluntown and vicinity he is regarded as one of the best of men from whom to obtain advice and help, which is always willingly given. He keeps in close touch with his employees, and their interests are given his consideration.

Being one of the leading business men of Eastern Connecticut, he is influential and very popular, and he has a host of friends not only in his home town, but throughout the states of Connecticut and Rhode Island.

In politics, Mr. Clarke is a Republican, and for thirteen years, 1908-1921, has been a valued member of the Voluntown School Board. He is affiliated with Jewett City Lodge, Free and Accepted Masons; Franklin Chapter, Royal Arch Masons; Columbian Commandery, Knights Templar, and in Scottish Rite Masonry has attained the thirty-second degree. He is a noble of Sphinx Temple, Ancient Arabic Order Nobles of the Mystic Shrine, of Hartford, Connecticut.

Mr. Clarke was married, at New Britain, Connecticut, November 23, 1910, to Cora Kilbourn, who was born at Lansdowne, Ontario, Canada, in 1887, the only daughter of William Russell Kilbourn, also born in Canada (but of American parentage), and Isadore Alden (Wooster) Kilbourn, a native of Connecticut. Mrs. Clarke and both of her parents are of Revolutionary ancestry, and are members of the Alden Kindred of America.

FRANK EMERSON PALMER—In 1897, after attendance at Worcester Institute of Technology, Frank E. Palmer entered Palmer Brothers' Mills at Fitchville, Connecticut, and there has steadily risen through different positions and departments to his present position, that of mechanical engineer of the mills, winning his promotion solely upon his own merits. He is a son of William Henry and Adelaide Randall (Wood) Palmer, his father a previous mechanical engineer at the Palmer Brothers' Mills.

Frank Emerson Palmer was born in Middletown, Connecticut, December 23, 1874. In 1884 his parents moved to Norwich, where the lad continued public school study, later being a student at Norwich Free Academy. He then spent two years at Worcester Institute of Technology, at Worcester, Massachusetts, leaving that institution in 1897. The same year he entered the employ of Palmer Brothers' at their mills at Fitchville as carpenter's apprentice. He was in due season advanced to a carpenter's duty and pay, continuing until his transfer to the drafting room of the machine shop department of the mills and later going into the machine shops. As he became qualified he was advanced to the position of foreman in charge of the machine shop. His next promotion was to his present position as master mechanic of the mills.

Mr. Palmer was elected a member of the School Board for the town of Bozrah, in 1910, and has now held that office for eleven consecutive years. He served in the 3rd Regiment, Hospital Corps, Connecticut National Guard, 1895. In politics he is a Republican; in church affiliation an Episcopalian.

He married, in Waterford, Connecticut, July 6, 1897, Helen Gay Dawley, daughter of Joseph and Frances (Gay) Dawley, both natives of Griswold, Connecticut, her father a farmer, now deceased. Mrs. Dawley now resides in Bozrah.

JOHN MARVIN HUNTLEY—One of the old families of the southwestern part of New London county, Connecticut, is the Huntley family. Always identified with the progress of the community, but in an unostentatious way, they have borne a part in the general advance.

John Marvin Huntley, who was born in Lyme in 1803, spent his early life on steamboats, and later settled down on the farm in his native town, where he spent his remaining days. He married Delia Caulkins, a member of the pioneer Caulkin's family, of Lyme, and they were the parents of twelve children: Sarah; Abbey; Florence; Frank; John Marvin, of whom further; Delia; Cora; Charles; David; Ervin; Jennie; and Gertrude.

John Marvin Huntley, son of John Marvin and Delia (Caulkins) Huntley, was born in Old Lyme, in October, 1859, and educated in the district schools of his native place. After completing his studies, he took up the work of the farm with his father, and has followed farm work all his life. He has always been interested in the welfare of the community, and is highly esteemed as a friend and neighbor, but though he now stands among the prominent men of the town, he has never been a candidate for public office, and votes independently. He is a member of Old Lyme Chapter, Patrons of Husbandry (Grange).

On January 3, 1880, Mr. Huntley married Emma Irman, who was born in Norwich, and died in Lyme, in December, 1918, at the age of sixty-one years. She was a daughter of Adelphus Irman, and the marriage was solemnized in Canterbury, Connecticut. Mr. and Mrs. Huntley were the parents of two children: Louis, born July 3, 1883; and Nettie M., born September 12, 1889, who is now the wife of Thomas Burke, and has three children: Everett, Florence, and Doris.

AUBREY WILSON JARVIS—Being now in the tenth year of his service as superintendent of cemeteries of Norwich, Mr. Jarvis is thoroughly identified in the minds of his fellow-citizens with the punctilious discharge of the important duties of that reasonable office. He is, however, more conspicuously and widely known as a musician of local prominence, having made a reputation both as a cornetist and a musical director not only in Norwich, but also in different parts of the states of Connecticut and Massachusetts.

Edward Jarvis, grandfather of Aubrey Wilson Jarvis, was a native of England, formerly an officer in the English army, who from London emigrated to Nova Scotia, becoming a farmer in Kings county, where land was granted him by the English governor, and where the remainder of his life was passed.

Nelson Jarvis, son of Edward Jarvis, was born in Kings county, Nova Scotia, and he and his brother were both children when death deprived them of their father. They were, in consequence, bound out until they reached the age of twenty-one. Nelson, as a young man, purchased a farm in Kings county, and as long as he lived led the life of a farmer. He was a man of some prominence in the community, serving at one time on the school committee. His religious membership was in the Methodist Episcopal church. He married Mary Eagles, also a native of Kings county, and their children were: Charles, deceased; Eliza, now living in Nova Scotia; Anne, also living in Nova Scotia; Thomas, deceased; Margaret, living in Groveton, New Hampshire; Louise, deceased; Alice, living in Fitchburg, Massachusetts; Aubrey Wilson, mentioned below; Delia, living in Lancaster, New Hampshire; and Henry, of Fitchburg, Massachusetts. Mrs. Nelson Jarvis passed away when about forty years of age, in Kings county, and her husband died in the same place, being then, in 1895, about seventy-two years old.

Aubrey Wilson Jarvis, son of Nelson and Mary (Eagles) Jarvis, was born May 27, 1857, in Greenwich, Kings county, Nova Scotia, and received his education in the district school of his native town. Until his sixteenth year he was engaged in farming, but at that age, moved by the spirit of adventure, he set out for Sacramento, California. He got no further than Grafton, Massachusetts, where, for a time, he was employed on the farm of a Mr. Crosby, and also on farms belonging to Mr. Warren and Mr. Clarke. He was then, from 1878 to 1881, occupied in learning the currier's trade with S. W. Dodge and Son, of Grafton, and during his sojourn in that town became interested in music, an event which has exercised a lasting influence on his life from that day to this.

Eager for the development of the gift which he now, for the first time, estimated at its true value, Mr. Jarvis went to Boston and took a course of instruction at the New England Conservatory of Music. In July, 1881, he moved to Norwich, where he associated himself with the Hood Fire Arms Company for the purpose of learning the art of gun-making. Remaining until January, 1882, he then entered the service of the Hopkins Arms Company, maintaining this connection for sixteen years, and during twelve years of that time filling the position of foreman.

While thus prospering as a business man, Mr. Jarvis found his talent for music a source of both profit and pleasure, and while serving as conductor of the Jarvis Military Band composed several pieces of music for that body. About 1896 he moved to Leominster, Massachusetts, where, for about two years, he was director of the Leominster Military Band.

At the end of that time Mr. Jarvis returned to Norwich and for several years was director of the orchestra of the Broadway Theatre. He was also, during that time, foreman for the Crescent Arms Company of Norwich, and for several seasons was granted leave of absence in order that he might be free to direct the orchestra at Watch Hill, one of the popular summer resorts of that part of the State. He also took a course in piano tuning with the Niles Bryant Correspondence School of Michigan, and after leaving the Crescent Arms Company carried on the business of a piano tuner in Norwich for about two years.

As a good citizen, always ready to "lend a hand" in any movement having for its object the betterment of community conditions, the qualifications of Mr. Jarvis for public office were recognized by his friends and neighbors by his election as superintendent of cemeteries of Norwich. That was in 1910 and the fact that he is still the incumbent of that office furnishes the most convincing proof of the satisfaction which his competence and fidelity have afforded to his fellow-citizens.

The fraternal associations of Mr. Jarvis include affiliation with St. James' Blue Lodge, No. 53, Free and Accepted Masons; Hartford Shrine; Columbian Commandery, of Norwich; and all Scottish Rite bodies of that city, including the thirty-second degree. He also affiliates with Uncas Lodge, No. 11, Independent Order of Odd Fellows, of Norwich, and belongs to the Arcanum Club. He is a member of the United Church of Norwich. Both as business man and musician, Mr. Jarvis has been the architect of his fortune and the result is such as he is entitled to contemplate with reasonable pride and heartfelt satisfaction.

Mr. Jarvis married, May 2, 1881, in Grafton, Carrie Ella Balcom, born in that place, daughter of Marcus and Sarah (Prentiss) Balcom, both of whom were natives of Grafton, and both of whom are deceased. Mr. Balcom, who was a Civil War veteran, was a shoemaker for the Gibbs Shoe Manufacturing Company of Grafton. Mrs. Jarvis died, in Norwich, Connecticut, in 1916.

WILLIAM ORRIN RATHBUN—The sea has lured many Rathbuns from land pursuits, but they have been equally attracted by the profits of mercantile enterprises, and William O. Rathbun has been able to divide his life between the two, following the sea from the age of thirteen until about forty, and during the last two decades engaging in business as a grocer in Noank. He is a son of Captain Samuel Orrin Rathbun, a sea captain, grandson of Samuel (4) Rathbun, a mariner and Civil War soldier, dying in the service, great-grandson of Captain Samuel (3) Rathbun, a captain of fishing smacks running out of Noank. Captain Samuel (3) Rathbun was a son of Elijah Rathbun, the first of this branch to change the spelling of the name from Rathbone to Rathbun. This Elijah Rathbun was born in Guilford, Vermont, but after his first marriage settled in Groton, Connecticut, where he died, February 4, 1825, at the home of his son, Deacon Elijah Rathbun. The father of Elijah Rathbun was Samuel (2) Rathbone, born on Block Island, April 6, 1705, who in 1755 was a member of the Rhode Island General Assembly. He was a son of Samuel (1) Rathbone, born on Block Island, August 3, 1672, son of John Rathbone, who was one of the original sixteen purchasers of Block Island, which two years earlier (1658) had been granted Governor Endicott and two others by the Massachusetts Colony for services rendered. (Later the Island was attached to the State of Rhode Island.)

John Rathbone, the American ancestor, son of

Richard and Marion (Whipple) Rathbone, settled on Block Island, and on May 4, 1664, he was accorded full political rights. He held many local offices and in 1681-82-83-84 was a member of the Rhode Island General Assembly, representing Block Island. He married Margaret Dodge, and both passed away in 1702. He was a man of property, and long before his death had settled each of his five sons on Block Island farms.

The line of descent from John and Margaret Rathbone to William O. Rathbun is through their son, Samuel Rathbone, and his wife, Patience Rathbone; their son, Samuel (2) Rathbone, and his wife, Elizabeth (Dodge) Rathbone; their son, Elijah Rathbun, and his wife, Betsey (Burrows) Rathbun; their son, Captain Samuel (3) Rathbun, and his wife, Nabby (Burrows) Rathbun; their son, Samuel (4) Rathbun, and his wife, Phoebe A. (Packer) Rathbun; their son, Samuel Orrin Rathbun, and his wife, Mary Ellen (Fitch) Rathbun; their son, William Orrin Rathbun, of Noank, Connecticut. All of these from and including Captain Samuel Rathbun, of the fifth generation, were seafaring men, captains, sailors, fishermen, but all followed the sea. Samuel (4) Rathbun, of the sixth generation, enlisted February 16, 1863, in Company C, Twenty-first Regiment, Connecticut Volunteer Infantry, and died in Satterlee Hospital, Philadelphia, September 25, 1864. He married Phoebe A. Packer, and their eldest son was Samuel Orrin Rathbun, father of William Orrin Rathbun.

Captain Samuel Orrin Rathbun was born in the town of Groton, New London county, Connecticut, in 1836, died in 1870. He early began following the sea and became a master of coasting vessels. His father died in the service of this country in 1864, and a brother, Charles H. Rathbun, was enlisted in the same regiment as his father, serving from July 28, 1862, in Company C, Twenty-first Regiment, Connecticut Volunteer Infantry, until honorably discharged and mustered out, June 16, 1865. Captain Samuel O. Rathbun built the schooner "William O. Irish," during the war, and was her captain in the work of carrying supplies to the armies South. He was a member of the Masonic order, and a man of strong character, well liked by all. His death at the early age of thirty-four was deeply regretted. He contracted swamp fever in Florida and died from its effects. He is buried in the cemetery at Noank. He married Mary Ellen Fitch, born in the town of Groton, in 1834, and still survives her husband, having been a widow half a century. Her home is in Noank with her son, William O. Rathbun, her only living child, her children, Dora and Ira, having passed away, and a son died in infancy.

William Orrin Rathbun, of the eighth generation, son of Captain Samuel Orrin and Mary Ellen (Fitch) Rathbun, was born in the town of Groton, New London county, Connecticut, September 24, 1858. He attended Noank public schools until thirteen years of age, then having lost his father, and being the eldest of the children, he became a wage earner, adopting the family calling and shipping on a fishing smack. He continued a fisherman and sailor many years, alternating service on fishing smacks with voyages on coasting vessels as best suited his interest. In November, 1899, he quit the sea and began clerking in a Noank grocery. Three years later he bought the business, taking possession in April, 1902. He has greatly enlarged and improved the store since becoming its owner, and has made this enterprise a prosperous and profitable one. He is a member of the Junior Order of United American Mechanics, of the Baptist church, and is church librarian. He also belongs to the fraternal order, Sons and Daughters of Liberty. Mr. Rathbun is unmarried. His home in Noank has long been presided over by his widowed mother, now in her eighty-eighth year and a widow since 1870.

FRANKLIN WILLIAMS STEWARD—Spending his lifetime in the tilling of the soil and carrying on a productive business which supplies the daily needs of the people, Franklin W. Steward, of Waterford, Connecticut, one of the best dairy sections of New London county, represents the modern New England farmer of the twentieth century.

Mr. Steward is a son of Livy Steward, who was born in New London, Connecticut, and in early life worked as a butcher in that city. Later he came to Waterford, and purchasing land, built the substantial house which is now the residence of his son, and which has come to be known as the Steward homestead. He followed farming until his death, which occurred on January 22, 1898, when he was fifty-four years of age. Livy Steward married Eliza Clarke, who was born in Ledyard, May 12, 1845, and is still living, at seventy-seven years of age. They were the parents of the following children: Willis Grant, born in New London, who married Frances Chappell, and has had three children, of whom two died in infancy; Anna, who was born in New London, and is the wife of Gideon Huntley, and has four children: Earl, Ida, Livy, and Spicer; Eleanor, the wife of George Adelbert Sharp, of East Lyme, and they have had four children: one died in infancy, Adelbert, Clinton, Beatrice, and Ellwood; and Franklin William, of whom further.

Franklin William Steward was born in New London, October 26, 1879, and the family removing to Waterford when he was one year old, it was in the schools of this town that he received his education. As soon as his studies were completed, he joined his father in carrying on the work of the farm, taking more and more responsibility as the years passed, and since his father's death he has carried on the farm alone. The farm is situated in the Gilead district of Waterford, where he conducts a very extensive dairy business. He has always been a hard-working man, taking little time for relaxation, and is one of the successful men of the community.

Mr. Steward married, at Saybrook, Connecticut, on June 4, 1910, Mary Dennis, daughter of Frederick Latimer and Mary (Sharp) Dennis. Mr. and Mrs. Steward are the parents of five children: Dorothy Latimer, born in Waterford, March 2, 1911; Adelaide Eliza, born November 19, 1914; Francis Eugenia, born December 14, 1916; Franklin William, Jr., born June 8, 1918; and Denise Churchill, born January 25, 1922.

EXEVERIE J. RAVENELL, JR.—A well known resident of Norwich, and successful business man of the town, Exeverie J. Ravenell is one of the genial proprietors of the City Lunch, one of the most widely patronized restaurants in Norwich.

Mr. Ravenell is a son of Joseph and Helen (Carroll) Ravenell. Joseph Ravenell was born in the Province of Quebec, Canada, and worked there as a farm hand. He died, when still a young man in the prime of life, at Angel Garden, Province of Quebec, in 1887, leaving his young wife and four little children, of whom Mr. Ravenell of Norwich is the second. Helen (Carroll) Ravenell later married Charles A. Chamberlain, of Norwich, and they are now residents of this city, also owners and managers of the Martin House, at No. 16 Broadway, one of the most popular hotels of the Thames valley.

Exeverie J. Ravenell was born in Taftville, in the town of Norwich, October 23, 1881, and received his early education in the public schools of Jewett City, also in this county, thereafter completing his studies at the Holy Cross College, at Farnham, Province of Quebec. Returning to the United States after his college course, Mr. Ravenell was employed for a short time in the plant of the Ashland Cotton Company, of Jewett City. In 1902 he came to Norwich, where he served an apprenticeship as a barber, which business he followed here until 1907. At that time he went to Providence, Rhode Island, where he established a barber shop on a large scale, conducting a very high class place, with gratifying success. In 1918, however, being induced to locate once more in Norwich, he accepted the position of counter man and chef at the City Lunch, while awaiting a desirable opportunity to establish himself permanently. This lunch room, which is one of the most attractive in the city, and was founded in 1913, was at this time under the management of Chamberlain & Company. In May, 1920, Mr. Ravenell, in association with Homer Fraser, whose life is reviewed elsewhere in this work, purchased the City Lunch from Mr. and Mrs. Charles A. Chamberlain, and since that time Messrs. Ravenell and Fraser have conducted the restaurant with constantly increasing success. The place is equipped in the most modern way, is a model eating house in every way, and is very widely patronized.

Mr. Ravenell is a member of the Norwich Chamber of Commerce, and in political affairs reserves the right of independent thought and action. He served an enlistment in Company C, Third Infantry, Connecticut National Guard, as a private, from 1905 to 1908. Fraternally, he is a member of Norwich Lodge, No. 430, Benevolent and Protective Order of Elks, and of Norwich Lodge, No. 490, Loyal Order of Moose. He and his family are members of St. Mary's Roman Catholic Church.

On October 18, 1905, Mr. Ravenell married, at Taftville, Connecticut, Anna Caron, daughter of Joseph and Caroline (Dubee) Caron, of Norwich. Mr. and Mrs. Ravenell are the parents of three children: Helen Anna, who was born in Norwich; Alfred Leon, born in Providence, Rhode Island; and Edwin Alousious, also born in Providence. The family now resides in Norwich.

ROMAIN BEAUREGARD—A native son of Taftville, Connecticut, Mr. Beauregard is now one of the enterprising and successful merchants of that village. Energetic and public-spirited, he has compelled success, and his future is secure. His business is that of a meat dealer, and prior to his becoming its head, his father, Wilford Beauregard, had conducted the same business in the same village for about a quarter of a century, retiring in 1915. Wilford Beauregard was born in St. Rosalie, Province of Quebec, Canada, and there spent the first fourteen years of his life in attendance at the parish school. He was a sturdy adventurous lad, and at the age of fourteen came to the United States, finding employment in a Massachusetts chair factory. That was in 1877, and until about 1890 he was variously employed. He then came to Taftville, New London county, Connecticut, where he was employed in a meat market, conducted by Napoleon LeBlanc, whose daughter, Rosanna, he married in 1894. About 1894 Mr. LeBlanc sold out to his son-in-law. Wilford Beauregard, who conducted the market until 1915, when he sold the business to his son, Romain, and retired. Wilford and Rosanna (LeBlanc) Beauregard are the parents of seven children: Romain, of whom further; Constance, born in 1899; Armand, born in 1901; Leo, born in 1902; Albert, born in 1905; Anthony and Antoinette, twins, born in 1907. The family reside in Taftvill·

Romain Beauregard, eldest son of Wilford and Rosanna (LeBlanc) Beauregard, was born in Taftville, New London county, Connecticut, August 9, 1896, and since 1915 has been one of the prosperous merchants of that village. He attended village schools until ten years of age, then a private school in Granby, Quebec, Canada, returning to Taftville in 1909. He was then a lad of thirteen, and for the next six years he was in his father's employ in his meat market, and there he gained his business education and laid his plans for the future. On September 1, 1915, he bought the meat market in which for six years he had been an employee, and has now been its owner and manager for seven years. While a man cannot be judged by seven years of his life, a fair estimate can be made of his methods and character. Mr. Beauregard has developed the traits which make success sure, and he is succeeding.

Romain Beauregard.

A feature of his business is his "store on wheels," the first of its kind in Connecticut. This is a five-ton truck fitted up and stocked as a combined grocery and meat market, with a sold storage department, and in miniature is a modern store. This truck he sends over given routes on given days, and is building up a profitable business in addition to his meat market in the village. Mr. Beauregard, just fairly started along life's pathway, has improved his years, twenty six, wondrously well, and has gained with his business success the respect and esteem of his community. Mr. Beauregard is a member of Sacred Heart Roman Catholic Church of Taftville, and a fourth degree member of Ponemah Council, Knights of Columbus. In politics he is a Republican.

Mr. Beauregard married, January 11, 1917, at the age of twenty-one, Mary Bois Clair, and they are the parents of two children: Arthur Joseph, born December 13, 1918; and Reathea Mary, born January 11, 1920. The family home is in Taftville.

YOUNGS MORGAN—The Morgans are an old Colonial family, long seated in New London county, Connecticut, James Morgan, immigrant ancestor, having settled in New London in 1650. He was born in Wales in 1607, arrived in Boston in April, 1636, settled in Roxbury, and there married Margery Hill, April 6, 1640. In 1650 his home was in New London, near the present town burial grounds in the western suburb of the city of New London. He sold his homestead, December 25, 1656, and removed to what is now the town of Groton, New London county, where he became an extensive land owner and an influential citizen. He was selectman, deputy to the General Court in 1657 and for nine terms thereafter, and was prominent in the church. His son, Captain James Morgan, was one of the first two deacons of the first church of Groton, as well as the principal town magistrate, and for years transacted the greater portion of the civil business of that community. He was moderator of the first town meeting, first selectman of the town, and captain of the first brass band in 1692. The same year he was a deputy to the General Court and for years he was a commissioner to "advise and direct the Pequot Indians" in the management of their affairs. Deacon James Morgan, son of Captain James Morgan, throughout his lifetime was active and useful in church and civic affairs, drawing wills, deeds and legal papers, his name generally appearing as moderator of the town and society meetings. He was the father of a fourth James Morgan, who occupied the old original homestead in Groton, being the fourth in lineal line, and the fourth James Morgan to occupy it. The Morgan and Avery families have intermarried and Avery has been frequently used as a middle Morgan name. From this James Morgan of Groton comes Youngs Morgan, also of Groton, son of Captain John A. Morgan, grandson of Youngs Morgan, and great-grandson of Nicholas Morgan, a farmer and owner of the old family property at the foot of Old Fort Hill.

At that homestead Youngs Morgan was born February 5, 1814, and there he lived until 1845, when he moved to a farm on Poquonock Plains, owned by Morgans, where he spent the remainder of his life. During his younger days, he, like many young men of the neighborhood, went to sea, three successful whaling voyages being made by him before the thirst for adventure was satisfied.

Captain John A. Morgan, son of Youngs and Elizabeth Morgan, was born at the homestead, foot of Fort Hill, which was later destroyed by fire, and died in the village of Groton. In 1845 the Poquonock Plains farm became the family home, the lad securing his education in the school at Poquonock Bridge and at Mystic Academy. He early began following the sea, making several deep sea voyages and visiting many foreign ports. He was also engaged in menhaden fishing, and in 1864 shipped as able seaman on the brig "William Edwards," engaged in the coastwise trade. In 1865 the vessel was run down by a steamer off Little Egg Harbor, the crew being rescued and taken to New York. In 1866 he returned to menhaden fishing and became captain of a vessel and engaged in that business extensively.

In 1867 Captain Morgan obtained an interest in a fish oil factory at East Boothbay, Maine, and for twenty-one years he continued in the fishing business and in the manufacture of fish-oil and other fish products. In 1881 he retired and in 1895 removed to Groton Village, where he resided until his death.

Captain Morgan was a man of strong character, fearless, strictly honorable and public-spirited. He served as selectman and as assessor and gave much of his time to the Volunteer Fire Department. He was active in the movement which resulted in the forming of Groton Fire District, No. 1, and was elected chairman of the first fire district committee, an office he held continuously until 1903, when failing health compelled his retirement. He, however, held the office of fire chief from the organization of the department until his death. He was a member of Thames Lodge, No. 13, Ancient Order United Workmen; of Fairview Lodge, No. 101, Independent Order of Odd Fellows; of Charity and Relief Lodge, No. 72, Free and Accepted Masons. He was a Democrat in politics and for five years, under President Cleveland, captain of a government launch at the Navy Yard on the Thames. Captain John A. Morgan married, February 21, 1877, at East Boothbay, Maine, Ann Mary Gould, daughter of John Gould, of East Boothbay, and they were the parents of three children: Mary A., who married William G. Stebbins and resides in Groton; Youngs (2), of further mention; and Edward G., who married Jennie Maynard, and resides in Groton.

Youngs (2) Morgan was born in Groton, Connecticut, October 6, 1879, and was educated in the public schools. Arriving at a suitable age, he learned the plumbing trade under Neuman & Cronin, of New London, continuing with that firm until 1912. He then engaged in business under his own name and for the past ten years has successfully conducted a plumbing and steam fitting establishment in Groton. He is a skilled worker himself and an energetic progressive business man. He is a Democrat in politics; member of Fairview Lodge, No. 101, Independent Order of Odd Fellows, and an attendant of the Baptist church.

Mr. Morgan married, June 10, 1914, Sarah Browning, of Pictou county, Nova Scotia, daughter of Joseph Browning. Mr. and Mrs. Morgan are the parents of a son, William S. Morgan, born December 5, 1916. The family home is in Groton, not far from the locality in which James Morgan, the American ancestor, settled in 1650.

VINE WILLARD STARR—Among the successful farmers of Waterford, Connecticut, where he carries on an extensive milk business, is Vine Willard Starr. He was born at Lakewood, New Jersey, November 19, 1870, the son of Lafayette Waldo and Harriett (Saddleman) Starr. Lafayette W. Starr was born in Stonington, Connecticut, and for many years previous to his retirement from active business life was a carriage blacksmith. He now makes his home at Norwich. To Mr. and Mrs. Starr have been born five children: Agnes Elizabeth, who married William Stanton, of New London, and by this union has one child, Ellwood; Henry Lucius, who married Maude Davis, of New London; Lafayette Herbert, who married Mary Champlin, of Torrington, Connecticut; Vine Willard, mentioned below; and Jennie Louise, who married Ernest Newbury, of New London.

Vine Willard Starr was brought by his parents to Middletown, Connecticut, where he attended the local public schools, subsequently removing to Hopkinton, Rhode Island, and thence to New London. Here the greater part of his life was spent until he was thirty years of age. He worked in various capacities as follows: Chore boy for Dr. Tobey; grocery clerk for Joseph Kopp; coachman for H. M. Knapp; New London street railway; and then secured a position as foreman for the East Lyme street railway, which position he held for ten years, when he subsequently resigned and purchased his present farm. This enterprise has already proven successful, for although Mr. Starr has been thus engaged but a comparatively short time, having bought this place in 1917, he has developed a large trade and is recognized as one of the largest milk producers in the community. He holds membership in the Farm Bureau, and is affiliated with the Republican party. He is a deacon and trustee of the First Baptist Church, and a bass singer of rare ability.

On September 20, 1889, Vine Willard Starr was united in marriage with Rose Halloway, a native of Waterford, born August 12, 1869. Mr. and Mrs. Starr are the parents of three children: Harriett O., who married Leonard Anderson; Willard Waldo, married Lillian McGourty, and has one child, Willard; and Charles Henry.

ARTHUR JAMES BEEBE—Holding a position of broad responsibility as assistant superintendent of the Connecticut State Farm for Women, Mr. Beebe is prominent in the public life of East Lyme. He is a son of James Henry Beebe, who was born in Niantic, in 1872, and for many years conducted a farm in the town of East Lyme, where he died in 1914. James Henry Beebe married Agnes Julia DeWolf, who was born in Black Hall, February 8, 1871, and was a daughter of Roger William DeWolf, a member of one of the old families of this part of New London county.

Roger William DeWolf, Mr. Beebe's maternal grandfather, was a man of more than usual prominence. He was born in Old Lyme, February 11, 1837, and educated in the schools of the day in this community. In early life he was associated with an older brother in farming operations, later entering the grocery business in Black Hall, in which he was engaged for more than thirty years. In 1891 he retired from this business, which he passed down to his son, and has since farmed, in a modest way, residing directly across the road from his old store. He was very prominent until quite recent years in the public life of the town, and represented Old Lyme at the State Legislature in 1883, also served at one time on the Board of Relief. He is independent in his political views, and supports the best man in the field. Mr. DeWolf married Julia Smith, daughter of William and Eunice Smith, of Niantic, and they were the parents of four children: Winthrop Roger, who was born in Old Lyme in October, 1864, married Cora Ackerson, and had two children: Caroll, deceased, and Burton Winthrop, whose life is also reviewed in this work; Claude, who was born in Old Lyme, April 6, 1869; Roger, who died in childhood; and Agnes Julia, who became the wife of James Henry Beebe, as above noted. James H. and Agnes J. (DeWolf) Beebe were the parents of two children: Arthur James, of whom further; and Julia Agnes, now the wife of Arthur Rathbun, of Groton, Connecticut, they being the parents of one child, Pearl. After the death of Mr. Beebe, Mrs. Beebe married Henry Rathbun.

Arthur James Beebe, son of James Henry and Agnes Julia (DeWolf) Beebe, was born in East Lyme, June 18, 1894, and educated in the district schools of the town. After leaving school he took up farming, in which he has always been deeply interested, and gained valuable experience. In 1917 he came to the State Farm for Women, in the capacity of assistant superintendent, and still ably fills this position. In political matters, Mr. Beebe acts independently, reserving the right to individual decision, and supports the side he believes to be right. He is a member of Niantic Lodge, No. 17, Independent Order of Odd Fellows, and of Pequot Lodge, No. 45, of the same order.

On June 15, 1920, at Philadelphia, Pennsylvania, Mr. Beebe married Jeannette Covenant Strahn, of that city.

WALTER PATRICK MORAN—A skilled electrician, holding a responsible position, Walter P. Moran left his position and offered himself to his country to do with as was thought best. That he went to France, saw active service, was badly wounded, and lay ten months in a hospital, are only details; the great fact is that he gave all he had to give and was willing even to make the supreme sacrifice, that he might serve his country's cause. Walter P. Moran is a son of John A. and Mary E. (O'Mahoney) Moran, the former of whom came to Norwich, Connecticut, in 1885, from Milwaukee, Wisconsin. John A. Moran established a real estate and insurance business in Norwich, and at the present time has a large and profitable insurance agency, and is one of the leading real estate dealers of Norwich. Walter P. Moran is the seventh child of John A. and Mary E. (O'Mahoney) Moran.

Walter P. Moran was born in Norwich, Connecticut, June 20, 1891, and there educated in the public schools. In 1906 he located in Schenectady, New York, in the employ of the General Electric Company, and there remained eight years, becoming an expert electrician. He returned to Norwich in 1914, and was appointed chief engineer to the Norwich Gas & Electric Company. He capably filled that position until September 1, 1917, when he resigned and entered the United States military service, his country then being at war with Germany.

Mr. Moran enlisted in the United States army, September 1, 1917, and was assigned to Company G, 102nd Regiment, and on February 16, 1918, was sent overseas. He was severely wounded in action in France, and sent to a base hospital, the first soldier to be treated there for wounds. For ten months he was under treatment at the hospital, then was returned to the United States as a "casual." He was honorably discharged, April 1, 1919, and returned to Norwich.

In his native city he again took up the battle of life, but not as before—an employee—but as proprietor of an electric automobile battery station, and as agent for the Willard Battery. His prospects are good and the broken threads of his life have been gathered again most satisfactorily.

In politics Mr. Moran is a Democrat, and in religious faith Roman Catholic. He is a member of the American Legion, and of Norwich Lodge, No. 430, Benevolent and Protective Order of Elks. He is highly esteemed in his community and has a wealth of friends.

GEORGE DAVIS JOHNSON—Of English ancestry, by birth a Canadian, George Davis Johnson is by adoption and residence a citizen of the United States, coming to this country more than thirty-five years ago.

George Davis Johnson is a native of Liverpool, Nova Scotia, where he was born December 15, 1862. He is the son of John H. and Verisinde L. Johnson, both born in London, England. Their son acquired an education in the public schools of Liverpool, and after leaving school remained in Canada for a few years, but in this twenty-third year Mr. Johnson came to the United States, locating in Boston, Massachusetts, where he entered the employ of the Western Union Telegraph Company, in the plant department. Continuing with them from 1885 until 1891, he then came to Connecticut and was engaged in the South New England Telephone Company, also in the plant department, later being placed in the commercial and traffic department. In 1899 Mr. Johnson was transferred to their telegraph exchange in Norwich, Connecticut, remaining there until he was again transferred, this time to Mystic, where he was appointed, in 1899, to the position of manager of that exchange, an office he has held for the past twenty-two years. While living in Norwich, Connecticut, Mr. Johnson joined the Volunteer Fire Department of the town, and for three years was foreman of the Blackstone Hose Company.

After taking up his residence in Mystic, Mr. Johnson very soon became interested in the various enterprises and associations of the town, joining the fire department there, and for one year held the position of chief of that department. He is an honorary member of the hook and ladder company of Mystic.

As a lodge man, Mr. Johnson is quite prominent; he is a member of Stonington Lodge, No. 26, Independent Order of Odd Fellows, being a past noble grand of the lodge, and also a trustee. In Masonic matters he is equally to the fore, being a member of Charity and Relief Lodge, No. 76, Free and Accepted Masons; Benevolent Chapter, Royal Arch Masons; and Mystic Council, Royal and Select Masters. He is vice-president of the Masonic Corporation of Mystic, and is a past chief patriot of Mystic Encampment, and belongs to the Order of the Eastern Star.

Though a member of the Republican party, Mr. Johnson is not active in political affairs. In religion he is an Episcopalian, he and his wife both attending the Protestant Episcopal Church of Mystic.

George Davis Johnson was united in marriage with Annie Friswell, a resident of Norwich, Connecticut, she a daughter of William and Annie (Dowell) Friswell, the former for many years a prominent jeweler of Norwich. Since Mr. Friswell's death the business has been carried on under the same name, and is managed by his children. Mr. and Mrs. Johnson have one child, Ethel L., born in Norwich; she attended the public school and is a graduate of the Westerly High School, class of 1913. For the past seven years she has been employed in the Mystic Telephone Exchange as cashier.

ALMON RATHBUN MEISTER, one of the prominent business men of Noank, Connecticut, is a lifelong resident of New London county. He is a son of John and Abbie (Rathbun) Meister. John Meister was born at Pigeon Cove, Cape Ann, Massachusetts, where he received a limited education, then followed the sea all his life. He came to Noank, New London county, Connecticut, many years ago, and was a fisherman and also a marine engineer. He died in Noank in 1904. His wife died three years earlier. They were the parents of one son, Almon Rathbun.

Almon Rathbun Meister was born in Noank, in the town of Groton, Connecticut, March 20, 1888. He received his education in the public schools of the town, and the New London Business College, later taking a special course with the International Correspondence School, Scranton, Pennsylvania, for the study of electrical engineering. This profession he followed very successfully for a number of years. In 1916 Mr. Meister established the business in which he is now engaged, and in which he has won gratifying success, a garage, where he does a large amount of work outside of the province of the usual garage limits, along the line of marine and railway repair work. In public affairs Mr. Meister is always interested, and supports the principles of the Republican party. He is prominent in fraternal circles, being a member of Charity and Relief Lodge, No. 72, Free and Accepted Masons, of Mystic, and also of Stonington Lodge, No. 26, Independent Order of Odd Fellows.

Mr. Meister married, April 2, 1908, Charlotte Ackley, of Perth Amboy, New Jersey, and they have three children: Delma, Vivian, and Doris, all residing at home. The family are members of the Baptist church of Noank.

GEORGE FRED HELMBOLDT—From the beginning of his business career, George Fred Helmboldt has been interested in the dyeing industry, and since 1910 has been identified with the book cloth department of the United States Finishing Company, textile manufacturers. Not only is he intimately associated with the manufacturing interests of this community, but his ever alert mind and ready co-operation is always exerted in whatever concerns its advancement and general welfare.

George Fred Helmboldt was born at Boston, Massachusetts, November 2, 1881, the son of Albert and Louise (Enders) Helmboldt, his father, a native of Saxony, Germany, who came to this country in 1870 and located in Boston, where he now lives retired after many years connection with the baking business. The lad, George F., was educated in the public schools of Boston, after which he became interested in dyeing, serving as assistant chemist and colorist in Boston laboratories and at the Holliston Mills, Norwood, Massachusetts, going thence to Lanett, Alabama, but later returning to Massachusetts, where for the following ten years he was engaged as a dyer and chemist in the textile mills in Boston and Norwood. In 1910 he came to Norwich, Connecticut, as overseer of the book cloth department of the United States Finishing Company, a position he has now held for twelve years.

A Republican in politics, Mr. Helmboldt, since coming to this community, has identified himself closely with the local organization of his party, which has elected him to a number of important offices on its ticket. He is a member of the Board of Relief, and is secretary and treasurer of the Republican Town Committee. Mr. Helmboldt is also warrant officer of the town. He is a member of Somerset Lodge, No. 34, Free and Accepted Masons; Frankln Chapter, No. 4, Royal Arch Masons; Franklin Council, No. 3, Royal and Select Masters; Columbian Commandery, No. 4, Knights Templar; Sphinx Temple, Ancient Arabic Order Nobles of the Mystic Shrine; and Connecticut Consistory, Ancient and Accepted Scottish Rite.

George Fred Helmboldt was united in marriage with Clara Kaempffe, who was born in Germany, January 18, 1886, her parents first coming to Norwich, Connecticut, in 1872. George F. and Clara (Kaempffe) Helmboldt are the parents of three sons, as follows: Charles Frederick, Harold George, and Raymond. Mr. Helmboldt is interested in farming, and what time he can spare from his business cares he devotes in part to his property, which he has under cultivation.

Mr. Helmboldt is an accomplished musician, a member of musical organizations, a past president of Local Lodge, No. 235, American Federation of Musicians, and a frequent delegate to musical conventions and gatherings. He plays the cello, bass viol, and brass bass, is a member of the Grotto, Tall Cedars and Shrine bands, in which he plays the tuba, 2 B flat. Upon coming to Norwich he resided in the Greenville section of the city until 1917, when Lisbon became the family home.

NATHAN STANTON BUSHNELL—In the daily interests of the community, in the pressing activities of his own large farming operations, and in the unostentatious support of every good word and work, Nathan Stanton Bushnell, of Norwichtown, is a man whose influence is always for progress. Seeking nothing of public responsibility or distinction, he nevertheless carries forward the principles which make for the general good.

Mr. Bushnell is a member of the old and widely known New London county family of that name. His grandfather, James Bushnell, was born and reared on the old family homestead, which is located in the community known as Occum, in Norwichtown, and spent his entire lifetime on this farm, where he was always extensively engaged in farming operations. James Bushnell was a man of lofty spirit, respected and honored in the vicinity in which he lived. His wife was born in Hanover, a part of the town of Sprague, also in New London county, and was a member of the Smith family of that place, noted as the owners of the mills which made this village a prosperous industrial center of two or three generations ago.

William Henry Bushnell, father of Nathan S. Bushnell, was born on the family homestead in Norwichtown, and educated in the district schools near his home. He removed to Canterbury, Windham county, Connecticut, where he rented the Dr. Baldwin farm, shortly after his marriage, and continued there for a period of three years. He then became associated with the Shetucket Mills, of Norwich, taking charge of the mill farm as outside foreman, and remaining for three years here. In 1855 he purchased the farm, which has since been known as the Bushnell farm, and here his sons were born. It was previously owned by Charles Allen, and is located in Norwichtown, on the Canterbury turnpike. Mr. Bushnell carried on this place, which contained forty-five acres, until 1872, then bought the old Eben Lathrop farm, adjoining, and removed his family to the house on the Lathrop farm, continuing, however, to conduct farming operations on both places. In 1884 he retired from active work, and turned over the management of the entire property to his sons, who worked it together until his death, which occurred on August 4, 1908. William Henry Bushnell is remembered in Norwichtown as a man of kindly manner and the highest personal integrity. Although considered one of the most prominent men of the community, he never would allow his name to be brought forward in the race for public honors. He married Jane Gray Prentice, a native of Griswold, this county, who died on the Bushnell farm, May 28, 1912. They were the parents of four children: William Henry, Jr., who lived only to the age of twenty-nine months; Mary Jane, who died at the age of three years; Charles Prentice, also a prominent farmer of Norwichtown, whose sketch appears elsewhere; and Nathan Stanton, whose name heads this review.

Nathan Stanton Bushnell was born August 30, 1863, on the old homestead in Norwichtown. He received a practical education in the public schools of Taftville, Connecticut, then returned to the home farm and assisted his father in the activities about the place. After his father's retirement he bore a more responsible part, sharing in the management of the farm, then, a year after the death of the father, the property was divided between the two sons, Mr. Charles P. Bushnell receiving the home farm and certain lands adjoining, and Nathan S. Bushnell receiving the lands and buildings which were formerly the Eben Lathrop farm. He has been very successful, and is still actively engaged in general farming and stock raising.

In the public life of the town Mr. Bushnell takes the interest of the progressive citizen, but beyond lending his cordial co-operation to the advancement of every forward movement, he has taken little part in the town government, preferring to leave the honors of public office for others. Fraternally, he is a member of the Fraternal Order of Foresters.

Mr. Bushnell married, in Brooklyn, Connecticut, April 29, 1889, Anne Mary Gilleney, daughter of Patrick and Abby (Burdick) Gilleney.

GODFREY ANDREW GEISTHARDT, of Preston City, New London county, Connecticut, an aged and esteemed farmer of the town, is a noteworthy example of the pioneer spirit, which leaves tradition behind, comes to a new country, and there achieves success, and sets the feet of the next generation upon the paths of higher achievement. Mr. Geisthardt is a son of Paul and Elizabeth Barbara (Frickman) Geisthardt. Paul Geisthardt was born in Eistfeldt Saxe-Meiningen, Germany, where he spent his entire lifetime. He was educated in the public schools of that town, then learned the trade of weaver of cotton and linen cloth. He made the finest linen cloth on hand looms at his home, working at this trade all his life. He died in the town of his birth in 1852. His wife was born in the same town, and survived her husband, later coming to the United States with her son, locating in Norwich, where she died in 1867, having made her home with her son while she lived.

Godfrey Andrew Geisthardt was born in Eisfeldt, Saxee-Miningen, Germany, in the same house in which his father was born, on August 26, 1834. He received a thorough education in the public schools of his native town, attending regularly for nine years. After he had completed his education he learned the trade of weaver from his father, then at the age of nineteen years, went to Berlin to gain more knowledge of the art of weaving, especially of delicate silk and the finest wool weaving, and the making of ladies' fine shawls. After two years in Berlin the young man was obliged to report for military duty. He served his training period, and after six months in the army he secured a release on account of his mother's widowhood. He returned to Berlin to complete his training along the line of fine silk and wool weaving, after which he purchased a loom, and going back to his native town, began making fine shawls at home. After taking a wife, and becoming the father of a son, Godfrey Geisthardt looked into the future for the sake of the boy that was to come up after him, and turned his face to the land of opportunity. Bringing his mother and his little family, he came to the United States, and looked up an uncle who had previously located in Worcester, Massachusetts. There he worked in the Crompton Loom Works for a short time, then removed to Norwich, Connecticut, where he was employed in a gun factory on Franklin street, making bayonets for guns for the use of the Union army in the Civil War. After the close of the war he worked out as a farm hand in Montville, Connecticut, for one year. Then in 1866 Mr. Geisthardt came to Preston.

At first he rented a small farm, then a large one. A tireless worker, and thrifty in his habits and tastes, he saved his money, and in 1898 bought a fine farm of one hundred and seventy acres near

Preston City, where he still lives. For many years he bore the brunt of the farm work, constantly enlarging his operations and improving the property, but now for some years past he has been obliged to leave the heavy work to his son, to whom he has given charge of the farm. He is remarkably well preserved for a man of his years, and is still keenly interested in every phase of the world's progress, his excellent education and his lifelong habit of always keeping abreast of the times, giving him a comprehensive grasp of affairs in every realm of human interest. In the public interests of the town of Preston, Mr. Geisthardt was long since called to bear a part. By political choice a Republican, he served as first selectman of the town for three years, and was the incumbent of this office when the Preston-Norwich State road was in process of construction. He has served as tax collector, has served on the Board of Relief, and in other offices to which the vote of the people has called him. He is a devout member of the Lutheran church.

Godfrey Andrew Geisthardt married, at Eisefeldt, Germany, on August 30, 1864, Rosalie Tower, who was also born in Eisefeldt, and was a milliner by trade. She is still living at the home farm in Preston. They are the parents of four children: Stephen Leonhardt; Emma; Charles Moritz; and Julia Augusta.

Stephen Leonhardt Geisthardt, the eldest child of Godfrey Andrew Geisthardt, was born in Eisefeldt, Germany. He came to this country with his parents, and received his early education in the district schools of Preston, New London county, Connecticut. Going thereafter to the Norwich Free Academy, he was the second in his class on his graduation. Later he entered Yale College, and although he worked his way through the University through his own efforts as private instructor to the grandchildren of Henry Ward Beecher, he stood second in his class upon his graduation from Yale. He then went to the New York University Law School, working his way through this institution also, in the capacity of French interpreter for a Wall street firm. He completed the course here, and was graduated from the New York Law school, then was advised by Henry Ward Beecher to go West. Acting upon this advice, he went to Lincoln, Nebraska, where he entered the University of Nebraska, as instructor in the law department. After two years he resigned to engage in the private practice of law, and is now one of the most noted attorneys of the State. Before the World War Mr. Geisthardt was appointed vice-consul for Nebraska, and while holding that office made five trips to Germany in connection with his duties.

Emma, elder daughter of Godfrey and Rosalie (Tower) Geisthardt, was born in Norwich, and now resides at the home farm in Preston.

Charles Moritz, the younger son, was born in Preston, and now has considerable interests there in a saw mill, and assists on the home farm.

Julia Augusta, the younger daughter, was born in Preston, and is now the wife of Guy Dawsey, a civil engineer, of Omaha, Nebraska, and they have one child, Stephen L.

GEORGE ANDREW MILLS—There is now and then a man, who after he has passed away lives in the minds of many not only by reason of results accomplished, but also in consequence of a singularly forceful personality. So survives the memory of the late George Andrew Mills, for many years a successful farmer in the town of Lebanon.

George Andrew Mills was a native of Colchester, his birth having occurred there, February 3, 1853. He received his education at the Bacon Academy, from which institution he was graduated in 1866, at the age of thirteen years, and then secured a position as a clerk in the Hubert Aborn grocery store at Norwich, where he continued for four years. In the meantime having chosen to devote himself to agricultural pursuits, he came to Lebanon to the farm known as "Haynes Corners," and as the years went on took his place among the leading farmers of the community. In politics he was a Republican, and ever manifested that lively interest in everything relating to the public welfare which is demanded of every good citizen. In 1897 he was elected a member of the school board; represented his town in the Legislature, and was one of the assessors for a long period of years; for five years was first selectment of the town; for three years was second selectman and at the time of his death was constable and health officer. The unaffected dignity of his manner was combined with a cordiality and a consideration for others which gave to his personality a singular attractiveness.

Mr. Mills married, May 23, 1872, Annah M. Porter, and they became the parents of six children: George A., died in infancy; Mary Louise, who became the wife of Clifford King, of Lebanon; Charles A., deceased; Anna B., who married J. A. Thomas, of Lebanon; Olive H., who married George Judd; and Bertha B., deceased.

So strong were Mr. Mills domestic affections that they might be said to constitute the governing motive of his entire life and the mainspring of his actions. The crowning blessing of his years was his union with a woman who was his helper, and the presiding genius of his fireside. On May 1, 1920, this truly good and useful man passed away, mourned by many and followed by the blessings of many to whom he had been a friend in time of need. The name of Mills is inscribed with honor in the local records.

FRANK GAUDREAU—Meeting the daily needs of the motorist, whether the casual tourist who stops in passing through the village, or the resident whose car must receive daily care, Frank Gaudreau has developed in a few years in Taftville a very prosperous and steadily growing business interest.

Mr. Gaudreau was born in Manatee, Canada, in the year 1881, and received his education in the public schools of the Dominion. Learning the business of electrician in Pawtucket, Rhode Island, he was active in that field of endeavor for a number of years before coming to New London county. In 1908 he came to Taft's Junction, where he was employed by the J. B. Martin Company as electrician until 1918, then he established the present business under the firm name of the Taftville Public Garage. Although he anticipated a struggle to gain a foothold in the business, his success was definite from the start, and in April of the same year he built the present structure, a two-story building, 45 x 45 feet in area, and he occupies the entire building, requiring the full space for handling the various branches of work included in his activities. He does a general garage business, and carries extras and supplies of all kinds. He handles a great deal of business in the regular care of cars for mercantile and industrial concerns, also for residents of this section, and handles gas and the various lubricating oils in general demand. He is highly esteemed as a citizen, and is counted among the enterprising and progressive men of the community.

Mr. Gaudreau married, in Pawtucket, Rhode Island, Theresa Collette, of that city, and they are members of the Roman Catholic church.

WILLIAM HENRY STEBBINS—The J. B. Martin Company, of Norwich, Connecticut, succeeded to the plant of Hopkins & Allen, after that plant had been used for making machine gun parts during the World War. The J. B. Martin Company purchased the mill after it had ceased making munitions of war and converted it into a more peaceful purpose, the manufacture of velvet. It is with this company that William H. Stebbins is connected as plant engineer and purchasing agent of supplies, having been with the J. B. Martin Company in Taftville, Connecticut, in the same capacity since 1913. He is a son of Henry D. and Mercy (Wheeler) Stebbins, his father of Western birth, and a member of a large family. Henry D. Stebbins located in Lebanon, Connecticut, and was a successful business man, the owner of an establishment combining blacksmithing in all its branches, wagon-making, and dealings in all makes of vehicles. He retired from active life in 1891. His wife, Mercy Wheeler, born in North Stonington, Connecticut, was one of a family of twelve children. Mr. and Mrs. Stebbins were the parents of two sons: William H., of further mention; and Alfred L., of Jewett City, Connecticut, assistant superintendent of the Ashland Cotton Company.

William H. Stebbins was born at Lebanon, Connecticut, September 22, 1881, and was educated in the public schools of Lebanon and Norwich. After school years were over he learned the machinist's trade with the company with which he is now associated, and followed this until 1906, at which time he accepted a position as motorman with The Connecticut Company in Norwich. A short time thereafter he was chosen for the duties of dispatcher and remained with the company until 1913. In this year he was appointed master mechanic at the J. B. Martin Company mill in Taftville, and when this company widened its operations, obtaining control of the previously mentioned Hopkins and Allen plant on Franklin street, Norwich, and the Pequot Mills at Montville, Mr. Stebbins became plant engineer. His duties include supervision of power, equipment, and mechanical repairs, and the purchasing of all mill supplies for the three plants mentioned, with headquarters at the Franklin street plant.

Mr. Stebbins is a member of Somerset Lodge, Free and Accepted Masons; Franklin Chapter, No. 4, Royal Arch Masons; Franklin Council, No. 3, Royal and Select Masters; Columbian Commandery, Knights Templar, all of Norwich, and Sphinx Temple, Ancient Arabic Order Nobles of the Mystic Shrine, of Hartford. He is a regular attendant of the Greenville Congregational Church, and a member of Norwich Grange. Mr. Stebbins is a staunch Republican and interested in the affairs of the community, supporting all progressive movements.

He married Mabel A. Murray, of Norwich, September 15, 1914, daughter of Peter and Eliza (Mathews) Murray.

ANDERSON OLIVER MARTIN—Among the older generation of representative citizens of Lebanon, Connecticut, is Anderson Oliver Martin, a native of this place, where he was born on the old homestead, December 27, 1850, the son of William and Mary (Champlain) Martin.

Anderson Oliver Martin was educated in the select schools until he had reached the age of sixteen years, when he terminated his studies and entered upon his business career, securing employment in the pharmacy of Lanmau & Sevens, at Norwich, Connecticut, where he remained for six months, subsequently returning to the home farm, where he remained for one year on account of his father's death, which occurred at this time. He then returned to Norwich, this time accepting a position with Staples & Pressey, acting in the capacity of manager of the firm for two years, after which he bought out the enterprise and established himself in the wholesale fruit business. He afterwards sold this business in order to enter the employ of Austin & Nichols, wholesale grocers of New York City, subsequently entering the employ of Dunn's Mercantile Rating Agency, where he remained for a short period, at the end of which time he removed to Staten Island, where he improved the estate of his uncle, John M. Martin, who was a lawyer in New York. He remained here twenty-three years. In 1902 he again returned to his native place in order to buy the old homestead and an adjoining farm upon which he now resides.

It is with the Republicans that Mr. Martin casts his vote, and no man has more at heart the welfare and true progress of his home community, but office-seeking is something for which he has no inclination. Mr. Martin was first selectman of the town of Lebanon for a short period, and also chairman of the school board, but resigned because of the serious sickness of his wife. In religion he is an Episcopalian and attends the church of that denomination in Windham.

In 1873 Mr. Martin married (first) Emma House, daughter of John C. and Almeda (Bidwell) House, natives of Salem, Connecticut. Mrs. Martin died December 26, 1907. To them were born four children: John William, a resident of Wyoming; Anderson O., a resident of New York City; Haywood Champlin, resides on the old homestead; Ralph E., a resident of New Jersey. Mr. Martin married (second) Annie Louise King, on February 27, 1911, daughter of John S. and Susan (Cross) King. Mrs. Martin is a teacher of the piano and organ, and has played in the local churches for many years.

GEORGE GEER, one of the most influential citizens of Sprague township, where he has held many positions of responsibility and trust, and where he is engaged in farming on an extensive scale, is a native of the town of Franklin, where his birth occurred, May 7, 1858. He is the son of Nathan and Mary Geer. Nathan Geer was born in Griswold, April 7, 1825. At the age of eighteen he came to Franklin, where he purchased the home in which his son George was born. He was engaged in agricultural pursuits throughout his entire lifetime, and died October 30, 1905. Mrs. Geer was born at Preston, August 24, 1821, and died Augst 31, 1904. To Mr. and Mrs. Geer were born two children: George, of further mention; and Mary Abbie, deceased.

George Geer obtained his education in the public schools of Sprague and Norwich. After terminating his studies he returned to Sprague, and later purchased his present farm and has here resided continuously ever since. This property was a fertile one and he developed and cultivated it until he has brought it to its present highly productive state. The home on the farm is large and extremely attractive, being among the very best in the township. Mr. Geer is one of those men who are instinctively interested in the welfare of the communities where they reside, and he has given no little time and energy to the conduct of public affairs. He has served as third selectman of the town, and as justice of the peace. But it is to the religious affairs that Mr. Geer gives the greater part of his time and interest, and is very prominent in the affairs of the Methodist Episcopal church, of which he is a member, holding the offices of treasurer, trustee, and steward, and secretary and treasurer of its Sunday school.

Mr. Geer married Grace Elizabeth Parker, daughter of Daniel and Josephine (Rice) Parker, of Pawtucket, Rhode Island. Mr. and Mrs. Geer have no children.

OZRO DEWEY FULLER—Ozro Dewey Fuller, one of the prominent citizens of Lebanon, Connecticut, where he has resided since 1876, is a member of an old New England family, his maternal ancestor, ——— Dewey, having come over on the "Mayflower." To this same branch of the family belonged Admiral Dewey, of Manila Bay fame.

Ozro Dewey Fuller was born August 4, 1850, at Columbia, Connecticut, the son of Lawson Hill and Mary Little (Dewey) Fuller. The boy received his education in the schools of his native place and on terminating his studies at the age of fourteen, began immediately to work on his father's farm. At the age of twenty-six he came to Lebanon, bought a farm and has continued in agricultural pursuits ever since. As a true citizen, Mr. Fuller willingly gives his support and influence to the furtherance of all good measures that conserve the interest of good government. He has always taken an active interest in educational matters, and for many years served as a member of the school committee.

Mr. Fuller married Mercy Cobb, a native of Willimantic, where she was born, September 1845, the daughter of Charles H. and Elizabeth (Tilden) Cobb. Mrs. Fuller died at Lebanon in 1915, at the age of seventy years. To Mr. and Mrs. Fuller were born four children: Harley Tilden, deceased; Willis Ozro, married, and has three children: Charles D., Lena, and Allen; Hortense Elizabeth, married Otto Pultz, superintendent of the Lebanon Creamery, and has one son, Laverne; Gertrude A., married Monroe Pultz, and has two children: Florence, and Merton Pultz.

LOUIS S. DOYLE—Now proprietor of a garage and service station at Mystic, Connecticut, Mr. Doyle is well established after a life of considerable change in occupation and residence. Born on Prince Edward Island, a maritime province of Canada, his mother a native of that island, his father born in the State of Maine, the lad was early brought to the United States, and in Maine, Rhode Island, and Connecticut, he gained the experience which well fits him for his present business. His father, David E. Doyle, was a shipyard worker and contractor of the State of Maine, but not long after the birth of his youngest son, Louis S., moved to Noank, Connecticut, where he yet resides and conducts a trucking business. He married Alice C. Breem, and they are the parents of six children, Louis S. the sixth in order of birth.

Louis S. Doyle was born September 9, 1880, and began his education in the schools of Bath, Maine. In 1890 the family moved to Noank, Connecticut, where the lad completed his studies in the public schools. After he left school he spent several years in Providence, Rhode Island, becoming a thoroughly capable stationary engineer and machinist. He continued in Rhode Island until 1909, then moved to Mystic, Connecticut, where he built a garage and service station, 46 by 60 feet, and is well established in business as proprietor of same.

Mr. Doyle is a member of Stonington Lodge, No. 26, Independent Order of Odd Fellows, and is past chief of Mystic Encampment of the same order. He also is a member of Oriental Lodge, Independent Order of Odd Fellows, of Providence, and Canton Arane Patriarchs Militant, of Mystic. He is a member of the Mystic Hook and Ladder Company. In his religious belief he is a Baptist, and in politics a Republican.

Mr. Doyle married, March 22, 1909, Louise J. Davis, of Westport, Massachusetts. Mr. and Mrs. Doyle are the parents of three children: Clarence, associated in business with his father; Louis, and Chester, both deceased.

WILLIAM WEAVER was born in Fitchville, Connecticut, December 17, 1856, the son of Melger and Marion (Uprest) Weaver. Melger Weaver, or Weber, as it was known in Switzerland, where he was born March 4, 1814, came to this country when a young man, bringing with him his wife, who was also a native of Switzerland. To Mr. and Mrs. Weaver were born ten children: Harriett, deceased; Mary; Harriett; Catherine; Rosina; Godfrey; John; William, deceased; Pauline; and William, the subject of this review.

The boy William obtained his education in the public schools of Columbia, Connecticut, after which he entered the employ of the firm of Terry & Brown, cabinet makers at Willimantic, with whom he remained for many years. In 1913 he came to this community as caretaker of an estate. Mr. Weaver is a man of industry and good judgment. In politics he is a Republican, and, always public-spirited, he has consented at the solicitation of his fellow-citizens to serve them on the school board and as tax collector while residing in Columbia, Connecticut.

William Weaver married, February 25, 1890, Ella Brown, a native of Baltic, Connecticut, and the daughter of Isaac Newton and Harriett (Reynolds) Brown. Mr. and Mrs. Weaver were the parents of one child, William Raymond, who died in infancy.

NATHANIEL H. AVERY—The Averys of New London county descend from Captain James Avery, who came from England with his father, Christopher Avery, and, after living for a period in Massachusetts, came, in 1650, to the Pequot Plantation (New London, Connecticut), where he acquired large tracts of land in what is now Poquonock Bridge, Groton, east of New London. About 1656 he built the home of the Averys at the head of Poquonock Plain. Some additions were made to this house in 1684, and it was occupied for more than two centuries until destroyed by fire in 1894. On the spot now stands a monument to the memory of Captain James Avery, who, in 1676, was captain of one of the four companies which protected the frontier, and for twenty-six years was an officer of the town. Twelve times, from 1656 to 1680, he was deputy to the General Court; also assistant judge in the Perogative Court, and prominent in the church. From Captain James Avery came Latham Avery, born in Groton, Connecticut, now retired, after an active life as a banker and broker of New York City. He now resides in Groton. He married Mary Jane Hillyer and they are the parents of four children, Nathaniel H. being the youngest of the family.

Nathaniel H. Avery was born in Groton, Connecticut, November 10, 1887. He was educated in the public schools of Groton and New London, finishing with the 1906 graduating class of Bulkeley High School, New London. After leaving school, he became a clerk in the National Whaling Bank and rose through a series of promotions to the assistant-cashier's position. He continued with the bank until March 1, 1919, when he resigned, and the same year, in association with Arthur A. Greenleaf, bought the business of the G. M. Long Company, of New London, wholesale and retail fish dealers, and has continued the business under the same name with success during the year which has since elapsed. In politics Mr. Avery is a Democrat. He is also a member of the Thames Club and of the Chamber of Commerce, of New London, and his religious affiliation is with the Congregational Church of Groton.

Mr. Avery married Martha H. Beckwith, and they are the parents of one child, Grace.

JOHN HENRY ECCLESTON—Always a resident of New London county, John Henry Eccleston has, for the past twenty-one years, conducted his own farm in Waterford, and carried on an extensive and important milk business.

Mr. Eccleston is a son of George Eccleston, who was born in the year 1836, in North Stonington, and died in Waterford, December 7, 1900, aged sixty-three years. George Eccleston received his education in the schools of North Stonington, and was identified with farming interests there until the breaking out of the Civil War, when he enlisted in Company E, 21st Regiment, Connecticut Volunteer Infantry. He served in the army of the Potomac, taking part in fifty-two battles, and upon his discharge returned to his native town, where he was employed as a carpenter for a few years. Removing to New London, he went to sea from that port on fishing schooners, and followed the sea for several years. Thereafter, he removed his family to Waterford, where he carried on farming operations in various sections of the town, renting the places he worked, and was thus engaged until his death. He married Eleanor Simons, and they were the parents of seven children: Nellie, George, Elizabeth, John Henry, Harriet Noyse, Leander Wilcox, and Albert Warren, of whom the last three mentioned died in infancy.

John Henry Eccleston was born in Mystic, Connecticut, and came to Waterford at the age of twelve years, the family becoming residents of this town at that time. He received his education in the district schools of Mystic and Waterford, and after he had finished his studies worked with his father on the farm, which was located in the Cohanzie district of Waterford. Later he worked on other farms in different parts of New London county, then in 1900 took over his present place. He has developed the farm into a high state of cultivation, produces milk on a large scale, and is considered one of the leading farmers in this section.

In public affairs Mr. Eccleston takes a deep interest, and although he has never sought public office, has served on the school committee of the town for a number of years. He supports no political party unreservedly, voting independently as he thinks best for the good of the community. He is a member of Waterford Grange, Patrons of Husbandry.

On November 13, 1885, Mr. Eccleston married Ruth Dana, who was born in Charlestown, Washington county, Rhode Island, the only child of Henry and Susan Dana. Mr. and Mrs. Eccleston are the parents of four children: Clarence Henry, born in Waterford, January 7, 1889; Helen Christine, born September 15, 1900; Eleanor Kenyon, who died in childhood; and Dana Lester, born July 15, 1907. The family are prominent in the social life of Waterford.

SAMUEL JAMES BOTTOMLEY, the genial proprietor of the Majestic Garage, of Norwich, Connecticut, was born in St. John, New Brunswick, on May 31, 1868, the son of Joseph A. Bottomley, who was born in England, and came to this country when but twelve years of age. Joseph A. Bottomley located in Norwich, Connecticut, and was employed in the Hopkins & Allen gun shop, then one of the leading industries of the city. He remained with them for several years, then was employed by the United States Finishing Company for a number of years. At length he bought a farm in Plainfield, Connecticut, and spent the remainder of his life there. He died in Norwich, on April 7, 1915, at the age of seventy-five years. He married Margaret Duncan, who was a native of St. John, New Brunswick, and still survives him, being now a resident of Hartford, Connecticut. They had ten children, of whom nine are living, Samuel James being the fourth.

Mr. Bottomley received his education in the public schools of Greenville, Connecticut, then served an apprenticeship as millwright. He followed this trade in the employ of the Aspinook Company, of Jewett City, Connecticut, until the year 1908. He then opened a general repair shop there, doing business under his own name. A skilled workman, and industrious, always attending promptly to the requirements of his patrons, he was very successful. But as time passed he concluded that he would be more advantageously placed in a larger community, so, in 1916, he removed to Norwich, where he opened a garage in the Majestic building. This is an excellent location, and with Mr. Bottomley's business qualifications, his future was assured. He still remains at this location, and is doing a constantly increasing business, in fact, is one of the leading men of his line in the city. Mr. Bottomley is a member of the Chamber of Commerce, and while never seeking nor accepting office, is a staunch supporter of the Republican party.

Mr. Bottomley married Anna A. Card, of Auburn, Rhode Island, the daughter of Samuel and Amy (Austin) Card, and they have two sons: Joseph S., who is married, and is associated with his father in business; and Henry H., who is employed by the United States Finishing Company, of Norwich.

ROWLAND STANTON BROWNING has lived "near to nature's heart" for as many years as his life numbers. Born on his father's farm at Babcock Hill, Lebanon township, Connecticut, July 20, 1883, he grew up accustomed to the constantly recurring tasks of the farmer, the yearly sowing and reaping, and the many pleasant incidents which go to make up the life of the average "man with the hoe."

The parents of Rowland Stanton Browning were both New Englanders, the father, Ezekial Howard Browning, having been born in South Kingston, Rhode Island, in 1825, and the mother, Mary Elizabeth (Gould) Browning, was born in Wofield, Rhode Island, the daughter of Daniel and Penelope (Rodman) Gould. Both father and mother are dead; the death of Ezekial Howard Browning occurring at Lebanon in February, 1914, and that of his wife in April, 1919. During his boyhood Rowland Stanton Browning attended the public schools of Lebanon until he had finished the course of study, then started a man's work on his father's farm. Here he continued until he purchased, three years ago (1919), a farm in North Franklin township, where he and his family are now living.

Mr. Browning married Alice Bessie Meech, born in Griswold, July 11, 1882, the daughter of Charles and Emily K. (Kegwin) Meech. Mr. and Mrs. Browning became the parents of seven children: Robert Stanton, born in 1904; Ruth, born December 15, 1905, died June 17, 1922, at the age of sixteen years; Rowland, born May 24, 1907; Marion, born December 25, 1911; William H., born January 24, 1915; Alton Monroe, born March 15, 1916; and Alice Bessie, born in July, 1919.

In the matter of politics Mr. Browning follows the dictates of his conscience when voting and is not bound to any political party whatever. He is interested in several of the village societies, being a member of the Grange, and of the local lodge of the Junior Order, United American Mechanics.

GEORGE HENRY TETREAULT, who conducts a prosperous grocery and general merchandise business in the village of Occum, in the town of Sprague,

Connecticut, should be numbered among the progressive men of New London county.

Mr. Tetreault's father, Joseph Tetreault, was born in Canada, and as long as he remained in that country was a mill worker. He came to the United States when he was a young man and located in Moosup, Connecticut. He is now a resident of Danielson, Connecticut, a capable, active man at the age of sixty-five years, regularly employed in the mills of that town. He married Margaret Lusnow, who was born in Canada, and died at White Rock, Rhode Island, in 1889.

George Henry Tetreault was born in Moosup, Connecticut, July 27, 1883. The family removing to Montville, in this county, it was there that he attended the public schools, receiving a practical preparation for the battle of life. This education was supplemented by one year at high school in Westerly, Rhode Island, then the boy entered the cotton mill at Montville, and made his start in the world of industry. Not long afterwards, when fifteen years of age, he went to Versailles, near where he is now located, and entered the employ of the Brown Bake Shop. He remained in this connection for fourteen years, then nine years ago established the present business, in which he has made more than ordinary success. He is now counted among the solid business men of this section. Mr. Tetreault is interested in all public progress, his political convictions leading him to support the Democratic party. He is a member of the Loyal Order of Moose, Norwich, Connecticut, and of the Modern Woodmen of the World.

He married, May 6, 1902, Marie Lucier, daughter of Joseph and Selinger Lucier, and they have six children, one son and five daughters, all at home: 1. Nancy Mary, born April 1, 1903. 2. Stella Margaret, born October 7, 1906. 3. Aldea Alma, born November 29, 1908. 4. Leo Harry, born February 4, 1910. 5. Alice Grace, born May 25, 1915. 6. Rita Medora, born June 14, 1919.

OLIVER RUDD TRACY—Among the families of note in this section of the country, none are more highly regarded than that of Tracy. This family was represented in the colonies by one John Tracy, who married Mary Winslow, the daughter of the first woman to land from the "Mayflower." The Tracy farm was a grant from Chief Uncas and originally comprised one thousand acres, a portion of which, including the homestead, has descended through the eldest son to the present owner. New England has remained the home of various branches of the Tracy family to the present time. Almond Tracy, father of the subject of this review, was born upon the farm in 1800, and died here in August, 1861. He married Abby Jane Huntington, a native of Franklin; she died April 1, 1904. To Mr. and Mrs. Tracy was born one son, Oliver Rudd, of further mention.

Oliver Rudd Tracy, son of Almond and Abby Jane (Huntington) Tracy, was born October 23, 1848, upon the old homestead at Yantic, where nine of his forebears had been born. The lad acquired his education at the Franklin Hill School, and later went to work upon his father's farm, following agricultural pursuits throughout his entire lifetime. As a public-spirited citizen, Mr. Tracy has always readily given practical aid to any movement which in his judgment would advance the public welfare. In politics he is a Republican, and has served on the school board for many years. He is also a justice of the peace. In religion he is a Methodist and attends the local church of that denomination.

On May 30, 1877, Mr. Tracy was united in marriage with Ada R. Mott, daughter of Albert Morgan and Clarissa C. (Graves) Mott, of Lebanon. To Mr. and Mrs. Tracy have been born one child, Mabel A., who resides with her parents.

ALFRED HUNT—Since 1890 Alfred Hunt has been identified with the business cricles of Norwich, Connecticut, as a landscape gardener. His ability is widely recognized and the success which he enjoys is well deserved.

Edward Hunt, father of Alfred Hunt, was born in Hampshire, England, and died in Newark, New Jersey, in 1895. He obtained his education in his native town, after which he studied landscape gardening, working on some of the largest estates in that locality until he was thirty years old, when he set sail for America. Upon landing in New York he went first to Fishkill, New York, where he remained for a short time only, subsequently removing to Long Island, and thence to Newark, New Jersey, where for a number of years he was superintendent of a large estate. He then established himself in business as a landscape gardener and continued in that line successfully until his death. In religion he was an Episcopalian and was an active worker in the Episcopal church at Newark. Mr. Hunt married Jane Gould, and to them were born six children, three of whom are still living: Alfred, mentioned below; Lena E., married A. M. Peaves, of Newark, New Jersey; Ida S.

Alfred Hunt was born in Southhampton, England, March 4, 1858, the son of Edward and Jane (Gould) Hunt, and was brought by his parents to Newark, New Jersey, when he was two years of age. Here he attended the public schools until he was twelve years of age and then started to work with his father, they being partners in business for many years previous to Mr. Hunt senior's death. In 1890, Alfred Hunt removed to Norwich, Connecticut, and established himself in his present florist's business at No. 110 Lafayette street. The flourishing condition of the business and its continued prosperity during the many years that it has been in existence testifies to the sound judgment and untiring energy which Mr. Hunt has brought to the discharge of the duties of this enterprise.

In politics, Mr. Hunt is a Republican, but the influence which he exerts as a citizen is of the quietest and most unobstrusive description, for publicity in all forms, has always been distasteful to him. He affiliates with the Benevolent and Protective Order of Elks, having been its past exalted ruler and secretary for three years; and is also a member of the Loyal Order of Moose; and of the Foresters of America. In religion he is an Episcopalian, and attends Christ's Episcopal Church of Norwich.

On October 23, 1888, Mr. Hunt was united in marriage with Martha A. Prest, daughter of John and Elizabeth (Armitage) Prest, formerly of Newark, New Jersey, but now deceased. Mr. and Mrs. Hunt are the parents of four children: 1. Jane E., born in Newark, New Jersey, February 3, 1890, died in Norwich, March 19, 1913. 2. Alfred G., born in Norwich, November 11, 1892, and died in Norwich, February 14, 1920; married Isabelle May Douglas, of Colchester, Connecticut. 3. Child, died in infancy. 4. Homer F., born in Norwich, October 9, 1902, is now engaged with the Telephone Company of Norwich.

ALVIN LEO DARGATZ was born in Chicago, Illinois, June 5, 1891, son of Rudolph and Frederica Dargatz. He was educated in Chicago schools, and took courses at Crane Technical School and Armour Institute, and completed a course at Chicago Business College. He was variously employed until 1908, then enlisted in the United States Navy, serving eleven years, until honorably discharged, December 17, 1919, being then a warrant officer. In 1920 he was appointed assistant superintendent of the State Pier at New London, and is still serving in that capacity. During his life in the United States Navy, Mr. Dargatz was "made a Mason" in Naval Lodge, No. 24, of Florida. He is a thirty-second degree Mason of the Ancient Accepted Scottish Rite at Norwich, Connecticut; a noble of the Mystic Shrine (Palestine Temple), Providence, Rhode Island; a member of the Independent Order of Odd Fellows, Philadelphia, Pennsylvania; and the Masonic Club of New London. In politics, he is a Republican; in religious preference a Lutheran.

Mr. Dargatz married, November 5, 1911, Dorothy M. Barrie, of Newport, Rhode Island. The family home is at No. 6 Oneco avenue, New London.

MICHAEL ANGELO BARBER, proprietor of a machine and engineering shop on Chestnut street, Norwich, was born in New London, Connecticut, June 19, 1854. Mr. Barber's father, John Elliot Barber, was for many years a resident of Norwich. He was an expert machinist, having learned the trade in his youth, and being by nature of a mechanical turn of mind. He conducted a machine shop in Norwich for many years, but is now deceased. In 1843 John Elliot Barber built the first typewriter, known as the Therbur typewriter. He married Elizabeth D. Sherman, a descendant of Roger Sherman, of Rhode Island; she still survives him, residing in Norwich at the age of ninety. They had two children: Michael Angelo, and Elliot B. The latter married Minnie Brennan, of North Orange, New Jersey, where they reside.

Michael A. Barber received his education in the public schools of New London. He was always deeply interested, as a boy, in his father's work, and when he had completed the school course he served an apprenticeship with his father, learning the trade of machinist. His father had opened a shop in Norwich in 1857, and when the older man died, his son took over the shop. Up to that time the business had been under the name of J. E. Barber, but when the son became sole proprietor he continued the business under his own name. This business has endured well the test of time, and has continued to prosper, until now it is one of the foremost establishments of its kind, doing all manner of machine work and handling extensive interests in the engineering line. Mr. Barber is a member of the Chamber of Commerce, and of the Arcanum Club. He is a staunch supporter of the Republican party.

He married (first), in 1880, Fannie Burnett, of Norwich, who died in 1892. They had one son, Clarence E., a sketch of whose life appears elsewhere in this work. He married (second) in 1894, Theodora A. Hill, of Norwich. The family are members of the Universalist church.

WILKES MALCOLM CASWELL—A lifetime resident of New London county, Connecticut, Wilkes Malcolm Caswell is a well known member of that large group of successful agriculturalists who comprise the very foundation of the prosperity of this section. Mr. Caswell is a son of Samuel John Caswell, who was born in North Stonington, in this county, on July 26, 1841. He brought his little family to Ledyard, when the son was a child of four years, purchasing the farm which has been in the family ever since. He is now retired from all active participation in the management of the farm, and was recently very ill, but is still interested in all the vital questions of the day. He married Eliza Jane Holdrige, of the prominent Holdrige family of Ledyard, who was born on September 23, 1847. She is a daughter of Daniel and Eliza (Maine) Holdridge, of North Stonington. Samuel J. Caswell was a son of David Caswell.

Wilkes Malcolm Caswell, only son of Samuel John and Eliza Jane (Holdrige) Caswell, was born in North Stonington, New London county, Connecticut, on June 15, 1869. Being only four years of age when the family moved to Ledyard, it was here that he received the practical education of the district schools, completing his studies at the age of sixteen years. He immediately, thereafter, took up the farm work with his father, and while at various times he has worked out on different farms, his lifetime has been spent at the homestead. As his father became advanced in years he took over the management of the farm, and for some years has conducted it himself.

Mr. Caswell married Harriet Ingram, who was born in North Stonington on August 13, 1879, and is a daughter of Henry and Eliza (Donnelly) Ingram. Her father was born in Preston, Connecticut, and her mother in New York City. Mrs. Caswell's sister, Mabel, who is the widow of William Clark, resides in North Stonington. She had four brothers, who are all now deceased: Charles, John, Frank, and William.

FRANK ALBERT VINING—With long experience in various branches of endeavor, Frank Albert Vining, of Sound View, Connecticut, is now successfully conducting a grocery business in this community.

Mr. Vining was born in Springfield, Massachusetts, October 27, 1865, and the family removing to New Haven, Connecticut, in his childhood, it was in that city that he acquired his education. After he had completed his studies the young man entered the employ of the Whitney Arms Company, where he learned the gun business, and was employed there for some years. Later he conducted an extensive dairy business in New Haven, Connecticut, being engaged thus for a period of seventeen years. In 1911 he sold out his interests here, and for two years thereafter devoted his time to rest and travel. In 1915 he came to Sound View, a popular summer resort in the town of Old Lyme, purchasing a grocery business, later also leasing a small farm near the store, where he carries on farming in a modest way, as he has opportunity to do so in connection with his constantly growing business.

In public affairs Mr. Vining is broadly interested, and politically, supports no party unqualifiedly, thinking and acting for himself. During the World War he was employed, for the winter of 1918-19, by the General Motors Corporation, of Bristol, Connecticut, making airplane parts for the United States Government. Fraternally, Mr. Vining holds membership with Day Spring Lodge, No. 30, Free and Accepted Masons, and he is a member of the Congregational church.

On May 27, 1889, Mr. Vining married Jennie Eliza Hopcroft, who was born in New Haven, August 30, 1872, and is of English extraction. They are the parents of seven sons: 1. Albert L., who was born in Hamden, Connecticut, in 1891, and is now chief clerk of the Great Northern railroad; he married, and has one son, Albert. 2. Frank Latham. 3. Pearly Howell, who is married, and has two children. 4. Robert Bruce, born May 25, 1902. 5. Thomas Clifford, born May 27, 1907. 6. A child, who died in infancy. 7. Walter Clifford, who was born in 1914.

HUGH MAC KENZIE, one of the most successful farmers of this community, was born in Perthshire, Scotland, April 7, 1884. He was the son of Donald and Margaret (Buchanan) Mac Kenzie. Donald Mac Kenzie was a native of Argyleshire, Scotland. For many years previous to his death, which occurred in 1907, he managed an extensive sheep farm in Perthshire. He married (first) Margaret Buchanan, who bore him three children: Peter, William, and Hugh. She died in 1886. He married (second) Mary Drummond, a native of Buchlyrie, Scotland, and to them have been born five children: Donald, Isabella, Mary, Jessie, and John.

Hugh MacKenzie spent his childhood on his father's farm, and most of his time was given to aiding the elder man in his work about the place. He came to this country in 1906, and later revisited Scotland, and while there was married, as hereinafter noted. Upon his return to this country, Mr. Mac Kenzie went to Rockland county, where he secured employment on the William Pierson Hamilton estate, and later became foreman of the farm. He was there for five years, then resigned and came to the town of Waterford, to the Stillman place, starting a dairy business, subsequently going to Groton. While at this last place he purchased the Sound View Farm, one of the best farms in New London county, on Durfey Hill, at Waterford, and lives there at the present time. This property was naturally a fertile one, and he developed and cultivated it until he has brought it to a highly productive state. He is a member of the Grange and the Farm Bureau. In politics he is a Republican, and in religion a Congregationalist.

On November 2, 1907, at Aberfoyle, Scotland, Hugh Mac Kenzie married (first) Jean Gilfillan McArthur, a daughter of John and Helen (Edmund) McArthur, of Stirlingshire, Scotland. Mrs. MacKenzie died January 5, 1921. On June 25, 1922, Hugh Mac Kenzie married (second) Nettie Viola Edwards, a resident of Waterford, Connecticut, and principal of the Jordan School.

GEORGE ROBERT DEAN—Widely known in the farming section which comprises the southwestern part of New London county, Connecticut, George Robert Dean, the blacksmith, conducts a thriving business in the little village of Niantic. Mr. Dean is a son of Robert and Elizabeth (Beckwith) Dean, old residents of that part of Lyme known as Niantic Hill.

Robert Dean was born in Hamburg, Connecticut, September 16, 1854, and has resided in this part of New London county throughout his lifetime. He is one of the leading farmers of this community, and is still actively engaged in general farming. His wife was born in 1856, and they are the parents of seven children.

George Robert Dean was born in Hamburg, July 5, 1883, and received his education in the public schools of the community. As a boy he became interested in the work of the farm, and assisted his father for several years. He then struck out for himself and learned the trade of blacksmith, eventually becoming the owner of his present shop in Niantic, which is well equipped and advantageously located. He has won not only the patronage of the people in a business way, but their sincere esteem. Of fine physique and remarkable strength, he is also a man of fearless spirit and broad sympathies. He looks upon every phase of life and progress through his own eyes, and brings to bear his individual convictions on all matters of public responsibility, political or otherwise.

On April 10, 1905, Mr. Dean married Mia Lena Daniels, and they have six children: Olive Mazel, born in Lyme, April 8, 1906; George Robert, Jr., born in New London, June 14, 1908; Hazel May, born in Lyme, May 8, 1911; Laurence Brackett, born in Groton, December 9, 1918; Chelsea Roberta, born in East Lyme, June 5, 1920; and Clarence Edward, born June 4, 1922.

CHRISTIE HASKIN FOSTER was born in New London county, Connecticut, June 8, 1887, the son of George H. and Sarah (Gardner) Foster. George H. Foster was born in Hopkinton, Rhode Island, and received his elementary education in the district school of his native place, after which he entered Eastman Business College at Poughkeepsie, New York, and upon completing his studies at this institution, kept books for several years, then took up the carpentry business, and later moved to Lebanon, where he became a successful dairy farmer, and followed this occupation until his death, which occurred August 19, 1918. To Mr. and Mrs. Foster were born five children: Ada L., wife of Myron C. Peckham, of Manchester, Connecticut; John R., married Fannie Tucker, of Lebanon; Christie Haskin, of further mention; Edith; Edwin D.

Christie Haskin Foster obtained his education in the district schools of Lebanon and the high school at Willimantic, and upon graduating from the latter institution he taught school for a year in the Babcock Hill district of Lebanon, after which he became associated with his father on the latter's farm. In 1914 Mr. Foster bought the Elmwood farm, which was owned by Dr. Henry Sweet, and this, together with his own farm, covers territory which comprises 285 acres, which he devotes to general farming and dairy products. In everything pertaining to the community's welfare, Mr. Foster's interest is deep and sincere, and no project which in his judgment tends to further that end, lacks his co-operation and support. He is an active member of the Republican party, and is now serving on the Board of Relief. He affiliates with Wooster Lodge, No. 10, Free and Accepted Masons; with the Order of United American Men, No. 72, of Lebanon; with the Knights of Pythias, No. 74; and with Lebanon Grange, No. 61, Patrons of Husbandry.

On August 18, 1914, Mr. Foster was united in marriage with Eva Brown, daughter of William B. and Harriett (Dunbar) Brown, of Mansfield, Massachusetts. Mr. and Mrs. Foster are the parents of two children: Ruth H. and George Bradford. The family are Congregationalists, and attend the church of that denomination at Lebanon.

HENRY FRANCIS BAMBER, of Norwich, Connecticut, was born in Pawtucket, Rhode Island, November 12, 1891, a son of Joseph B. and Julia (O'Rourke) Bamber.

Both Mr. Bamber's parents were born in Lancashire, England. His father was educated in the National schools of that country, and came to America when he was seventeen years of age. He located in Pawtucket, Rhode Island, where he still resides, and where he is a prominent figure in the building industry of the section, having been a contractor and builder for many years, and having handled many important pieces of construction work. His wife died in 1901. They were the parents of two children, of whom Henry Francis is the younger.

Henry Francis Bamber received his education in the public and high schools of Pawtucket, Rhode Island, and then entered the employ of the Providence Autogenous Welding Company, of Providence, as an apprentice. He served an apprenticeship of three years, after which he was employed by the Capitol Welding Company in that city for seven years. In 1917 he came to Norwich, Connecticut, and became associated with the Norwich Welding Company. This firm handles all kinds of welding and brazing, and Mr. Bamber is still with them. Mr. Bamber is a man of public spirit, interested in all movements tending to advance the welfare of the people. He is a member of Lodge No. 401, Benevolent and Protective Order of Elks.

He married, on June 12, 1912, Rachael McDade, of Saylesville, Rhode Island, and they have three children: Henry F., Jr., Rita, and Elizabeth R. The family are members of the Roman Catholic church.

GEORGE ALBERT KIEBURG, proprietor of a modern laundry in Mystic, Connecticut, is a son of Adolph and Augusta (Berthol) Kieburg, both born in Germany and educated in the State schools. They came to the United States when comparatively young and located in New Jersey, where Adolph Kieburg was for a number of years employed in a textile mill. Later, he located in Stonington, Connecticut, where he was in the mill employ of the American Velvet Company for several years. He then returned to New Jersey and is now residing at Union Hill in that State. Mr. and Mrs. Kieburg are the parents of eleven children, George Albert Kieburg, of Mystic, Connecticut, being the tenth in order of birth.

George Albert Kieburg was born in Hudson county, New Jersey, December 7, 1893. He was educated in the public schools of Mystic, Connecticut, and after leaving school became a textile weaver of velvet, employed in the mills of the Rossie Velvet Company in Mystic. He continued a weaver of velvet until 1915, when he bought the laundry business of Herman Stoetzel, of Mystic, which he has since conducted very successfully. He is a member of Stonington Lodge, No. 26, Independent Order of Odd Fellows, of Mystic; and of the Sons of Herman, New London, Connecticut. In politics he is a Republican; in religious preference a Congregationalist.

Mr. Kieburg married Phoebe Josephs, of Stonington, Connecticut, daughter of Manuel E. Josephs.

Mr. and Mrs. Kieburg are the parents of a son, George Albert (2).

EUGENE D. CAULKINS—In Old Lyme, New London county, Connecticut, the Caulkins family have long been prominent, the name being spelled both Caulkins and Calkins. The American ancestor, Hugh Calkins, born in England, came to Gloucester, Massachusetts, in 1640, with wife and children. He was a man of importance in Gloucester and in New London, Connecticut, coming to the latter place about 1651. About 1660 he moved to Norwich, where he was one of the thirty-five proprietors of the town. He was a deputy to the General Court of New London and served several terms from Norwich in the same body. He died in 1690, aged ninety. He left two sons, John and David, and five daughters: Rebecca, Sarah, Mary, Susan, and Deborah.

Elisha Caulkins, of the sixth American generation, was a farmer of East Lyme, Connecticut, and prominent in its public life. His son, Lemuel Caulkins, was born on the Caulkins homestead and later inherited it from his father. He farmed the homestead all his life until his death in 1896, aged seventy-two. He held about every town office, and like his father, was prominent and popular. Lemuel Caulkins married Maria Calkins, born in Wilbraham, Massachusetts, daughter of Luke Calkins. Mrs. Maria (Calkins) Caulkins died in 1906, aged seventy-four years, the mother of five children, all born in Old Lyme: 1. Herbert, formerly probate judge of his native town. 2. Frederick L. 3. Frank L. 4. Eugene D., of further mention. 5. Emma Avery, who married William Searle, of New London.

Eugene D. Caulkins, youngest son of Lemuel and Maria (Calkins) Caulkins, was born in the town of Old Lyme, New London county, Connecticut, April 17, 1863, his birthplace the old Caulkins homestead in which his father was born. He was educated in the district public school, and from boyhood was his father's helper, becoming later his trusted assistant, and upon the latter's death inherited his homestead, upon which he yet resides, never having known any other home.

For twenty years Mr. Caulkins has been a member of the town Board of Selectmen, being third selectman for some time, then second, and now is first selectman; in 1907 he represented Old Lyme in the Connecticut House of Representatives; and is a trustee of the library. In religious faith he is a Baptist, in politics a Democrat. As a farmer, Mr. Caulkins has been very successful and is one of the prosperous men of his town. He is a member of Old Lyme Grange, Patrons of Husbandry, and is a strong friend of the order.

Mr. Caulkins married, April 9, 1891, Lucy E. Howard, born May 17, 1863, daughter of Captain Charles Howard, of Old Lyme. They have no children. Mr. Caulkins is a man of high standing in his community, and is one of the progressive men of the town who uphold the good name the town has always borne for substantial improvement and reliable men.

FREDERICK ELISHA BAKER, whose life has been one of frequent change, is quietly ending it in Colchester, Connecticut, which place has been his home since 1883. He is a son of Daniel and Cornelia (Simmonds) Baker, both born in New York City, his father receiving fatal injuries while hunting in the woods around Colchester, where he had relatives living. He died in 1868, and that same year his son, Frederick Elisha Baker, began his life in Colchester, although for several years later he resided elsewhere.

Frederick Elisha Baker was born in New York City, March 4, 1861, and there spent the first seven years of his life. When his father was accidentally killed, the lad, Frederick E., was brought to live in Colchester, Connecticut, with Mrs. George B. Avery, his aunt. He attended Bacon Academy until finishing with graduation, after which he became a clerk in the William B. Otis store in Colchester, and there remained until 1880, when he went to Woodbury, Connecticut, and was for a time employed in the store of A. A. Root. That same year he married, and in January, 1882, moved to New Britain, Connecticut, where he entered the employ of the P. & F. Corbin Company as a polisher. In the fall of 1882 he moved to Middletown, Connecticut, and was employed as a polisher by the Victor Sewing Machine Company. In May, 1883, the family moved to Colchester, Connecticut, where Mr. Baker entered the employ of the Hayward Rubber Company as a bootmaker, remaining until the mill closed in March, 1894. In 1896 the new leather factory was built in Colchester and when it opened for business Mr. Baker was employed as engineer, a position he held for two and a half years, when the plant closed. In 1901, when the Turner Silk Throwing Company started business in the shoe company plant, Mr. Baker was employed as engineer during the stay of the company in Colchester. After the closing of the silk mill he was employed in various capacities until entering the employ of C. W. Blakeslee & Sons, contractors of the new State road to Colchester, as clerk, and remained with that company until the completion of their contract.

In politics, Mr. Baker is a Republican, and in 1913 was elected warden of the borough of Colchester, a position he held for eight years. He was elected registrar of voters in 1921. He is an attendant of the First Congregational Church of Colchester, and a member of Colchester Lodge, No. 30, Ancient Order of United Workmen; Norwich Lodge, No. 430, Benevolent and Protective Order of Elks; and Oliver Woodhouse Lodge, No. 51, Knights of Pythias.

Mr. Baker married, in Roxbury, November 5, 1880, Maria Alice Dooley, daughter of John and Margaret Dooley, and to them two sons were born: William Elisha, born in Roxbury, September 14,

1881, now assistant secretary of the Landers, Frary & Clark Company, of New Britain, Connecticut. He married, in 1910, Margaret Sanderson, and has a son, William A., and a daughter, Alyson. 2. George B. A., who was born in Middletown, Connecticut, March 14, 1883; he was manager of the Alling Rubber Company's store in New Britain, Connecticut, until 1921, when he was transferred to the company store at Meriden, Connecticut, in the same capacity. He married, in 1913, Emily Huck, and they are the parents of a son, Robert A., and daughters, Georgine, and Dorothy.

FRANK B. WALKER was born at Woolwich, Maine, in 1874, and after graduating from Gray's Business College at Portland, Maine, soon became a hotel employee, spending seven years in the steward's department at Young's Hotel in Boston. He then spent a year with George W. Armstrong & Company, at North Union Station, Boston, that experience being followed by two years in managerial position at Congress Square Hotel, Portland, Maine. In 1904 he came to the Mohican at New London, where he has been manager for nearly nineteen years. Mr. Walker is vice-president of the Winthrop Trust Company, of New London; member of the Thames Club, and of the Benevolent and Protective Order of Elks.

Mr. Walker married, in 1904, in Boston, Massachusetts, Anna Jane Straight.

GEORGE WILLIAM PEABODY—In the rich farming community of Gilead, in the town of Waterford, Connecticut, is the farm home of George William Peabody, who has spent his lifetime in this county, and has always followed farming. Mr. Peabody is a son of Thomas Peabody, who was born in Salem, in this county, January 25, 1834, and died in 1879, in the prime of life, having always been a farmer. He married Lucy Jane Herrick, born in Salem, Connecticut, and a daughter of Elijah and Lucy (Baker) Herrick. She is still living, at the age of eighty-seven years. They were the parents of ten children: Alonzo, George William, of whom further; Catherine, Abbey, Thomas, Alice, Jennie, Lula, Frank, and an infant, who lived for only a short time.

George William Peabody was born in the city of New London, July 8, 1860, but as a child removed with the family to Montville, also in this county, where he was reared and educated. Following school days, he worked on the farm, continuing until his marriage, then went to Waterford, in the Great Neck section, where he was engaged in farming for two years. He then went to New London, there locating on the old homestead farm where he was born, on Pequot avenue, which he conducted for one year. Thereafter returning to Montville, he remained for two years, then bought a farm home in Waterford, where he lived for twenty years or more. The present farm was bought fifteen years ago, and he has continued here since, his farm now being considered one of the show places of the town. He has won a secure position in the esteem of his fellow-townspeople, and served on the Board of Assessors for a period of thirteen years.

On March 25, 1885, Mr. Peabody married Annie Mitchell, who was born in Salem, Connecticut, and is a daughter of Levi and Nancy Mitchell. Mr. and Mrs. Peabody have three children: Laura, born June 13, 1886, now the wife of Clarence Douglass, of Milford, Connecticut; Hadley L., born April 27, 1888; and Leslie L., born May 28, 1903.

FRED EVERETT CRANDALL was born in Montville, Connecticut, November 24, 1887, son of Francis C. and Harriet Ella (Green) Crandall, and grandson of John and Annie (Delmere) Crandall, John Crandall, a seaman. Francis C. Crandall was born in Middletown, Connecticut, April 9, 1854, and is now a resident of Montville, Connecticut.

Fred E. Crandall attended the public schools and was for several years stock clerk at Palm Brothers Mill in Montville. In 1914 he started a taxicab business, which he has since continued.

Mr. Crandall is a member of the Masonic order, thirty-second degree; a noble of Sphinx Temple, Ancient Arabic Order Nobles of the Mystic Shrine; member of the Independent Order of Odd Fellows; the Order of United American Mechanics; and of the Methodist Episcopal church. He is unmarried.

CLAYTON GEORGE MILLER—The Miller farm in the Unionville school district, town of Colchester, Connecticut, has been the birthplace of several generations of the family, and has descended in ownership from father to son. The present occupant is Clayton George Miller, who resides at the farm with his father, George Bulkley Miller, to whom it came from his father, George Miller, each of these men being born on the farm, as well as spending their lives thereon. The property comprises two hundred and seventy-five acres, and is both well situated and efficiently managed, dairy farming being conducted in connection with general farming.

George Bulkley Miller, son of George and Abby (Bulkley) Miller, was born at the Miller homestead in Colchester, March 30, 1859, and there yet resides. His father, George Miller, was also born on the farm and there spent his life, cultivating its acres with his brother Henry until his death. George Miller married Abby Bulkley, who was born in Salem, Connecticut, who after the death of her husband went to live with her daughter in New York City, where she died.

George B. Miller attended the public school of the district and early became his father's farm assistant and finally his successor. After the death of his father the ownership of the farm passed to George B., who continued its operation until 1911, when he in turn retired in favor of his son, Clayton G. Miller, in whom the management has since been vested (1921). George B. Miller is a Republican in politics; member, senior warden and active worker in Calvary Protestant Episcopal Church of Colchester; member of the Order of United Workmen, and Woodmen of the World, of Colchester, and a man most highly esteemed. His years, sixty-two, have all been spent at the old homestead farm, which in truth is the old Miller place. Mr. Miller married, at Colchester, December 14, 1887, Annie Foote, born in the same town, daughter of Albert and Mary Ann (Chase) Foote. Mr. and Mrs. George B. Miller are the parents of four children: Florence Adelia, who married Captain Chester B. McCoid, of the United States army; Clayton George, of further mention; Mary Abby, who married Clarence Chittenden, of Killingworth, Connecticut; and Amy Foote, who died in childhood.

Clayton George Miller, only son of George Bulkley and Annie (Foote) Miller, was born at the Miller homestead in the Unionville school district of the town of Colchester, New London county, Connecticut, November 16, 1890, and there has spent the years which have since intervened. He was educated in the public schools of the district, and at Bacon Academy, in Colchester, and after school years were ended he became his father's farm assistant, so continuing until the latter's retirement, when the son succeeded him in the management, so continuing until the present time (1921). The Miller farm, under his supervision, is kept up to the high standard of former years and is one of the well cultivated and profitable farms of the town.

Clayton G. Miller, like his father, holds to the Republican party in political faith, and to the Protestant Episcopal church in matters of religious faith, being a member of Calvary Parish, Colchester. He is a member and past master of Wooster Lodge, No. 10, Free and Accepted Masons, of Colchester; also member and past master of Colchester Grange, Patrons of Husbandry. He served his town as constable for a term, and is one of Colchester's highly esteemed young men.

Mr. Miller married, October 28, 1915, at Ivoryton, Connecticut, Hannah Serena Antonson, born in that village, daughter of Carl and Augusta (Olson) Antonson. Mr. and Mrs. Clayton G. Miller are the parents of two children: Clayton George (2), born July 15, 1916; and Marion Elizabeth, born June 30, 1919; both born at the homestead, and at the old home three generations of Millers are living, children, father and grandfather, all born in the homestead. These children are great-grandchildren of George Miller, who was also born at the farm in Colchester.

AUGUSTIN LE MOINE—For a number of years active as a blacksmith, Augustin LeMoine has for the past nine years conducted a constantly increasing business in general trucking, with an office in Taftville.

Mr. LeMoine is a son of Alfred and Julia (Pelouquin) LeMoine, the former born in Sorel, Province of Quebec, and came to the United States about 1875, locating in Baltic, where he was employed in the cotton mill for a number of years. He later removed his family to Taftville, where he died in 1897. His wife, Julia (Pelouquin) LeMoine, who was also born in Sorel, still survives him, and is a resident of Taftville. They were the parents of ten children, of whom Augustin is the fifth.

Augustin LeMoine was born in Baltic, in the town of Sprague, New London county, Connecticut, and was educated in the parochial schools of Taftville. After completing his studies he served an apprenticeship at the trade of blacksmith, with a Mr. Roy, of Baltic, eventually remaining in his employ until 1908. Thereafter, for about five years, Mr. LeMoine worked at his trade in various places, then, in 1913, established an express business in Taftville. He has since developed a very large and prosperous business, and now keeps several motor trucks busy handling long distance transportation, in addition to his local work. He is counted one of the successful men of this community.

In the interests of the town and in all general progress Mr. LeMoine is always ready to endorse a forward movement, and politically holds independent views, supporting the individual or party which his judgment dictates. He is a member of the Society of St. John the Baptist, of Taftville; a member of the Sacred Heart Roman Catholic Church, of this place; also of Ponemah Council, No. 34, Knights of Columbus.

Mr. LeMoine married, in Taftville, June 10, 1906, Amelia Caron, and they are the parents of one child, Augustin Raymond, who was born in Taftville, December 17, 1913.

ANDREW MEECH AVERY—The Averys of New London county, Connecticut, descend from Captain James Avery, who was born in England about 1620 and came to New England with his father, Christopher Avery, and resided with him in Gloucester, Massachusetts, for several years. James Avery married, November 10, 1642, Joanna Greenslade, who in 1644 received a letter of dismissal from the church in Boston commending her to the church in Gloucester. The name of James Avery appears with those men from Gloucester, Massachusetts, who were granted land in New London county in October, 1650. About 1652 James Avery was granted a farm in South Groton, but he continued in New London for several years, although in 1653 he secured another farm farther up the river in what is now the town of Ledyard. About 1656 he built the "Hive of the Averys" at the head of Poquonock plain, in the present town of Groton, one and one-half miles from the river Thames. James Avery seems to have taken an active part in town affairs as well as becoming an active business man. He is variously referred to as ensign, lieutenant, captain, and in the great fight with the Narragansetts, December 19, 1675, commanded the Indian allies. He was selectman for twenty years; was twelve times elected to the General Court, and was active in the church.

All but the first three of the children of Captain James and Joanna (Greenslade) Avery were born in New London, those three in Gloucester, Massachusetts. Captain Avery died April 18, 1700.

Andrew M. Avery, a descendant of Christopher and Captain James Avery, is a grandson of John Avery, and a son of Andrew Avery, born in Preston, Connecticut, July 19, 1822, and died March 15, 1903, a man of prominence and influence. Andrew Avery married (first) Asenath Williams Geer, who died leaving a daughter, Delia, wife of Louis Southworth, now deceased. Andrew Avery married (second) Jane Hewitt, born in Preston county, who died leaving two sons: Dr. Amos Avery, a graduate of Long Island Hospital Medical College; and Rev. Oliver Perry Avery. Andrew Avery married (third) Mary Leonard Meech, born in Griswold county, March 7, 1843, daughter of Edwin Butler and Sarah (Geer) Meech, a descendant of Stephen Meech, who located in what is now North Stonington, who married and founded a family well known and influential in the town of Preston. They were the parents of an only son, Andrew Meech Avery, of further mention.

Andrew Meech Avery was born in North Stonington, Connecticut, June 19, 1884, only child of Andrew Avery and his third wife, Mary Leonard (Meech) Avery. He was educated in the district school near his home; Norwich Free Academy, from which institution he graduated with the class of 1905, and Yale University, whence he graduated A. B., class of 1909. For eighteen months after graduation he was in the West, engaged in the lumber business, but coming East on the death of his half-sister, Mrs. Delia Southworth, he decided to remain. He engaged in the insurance business in Norwich until the United States declared war against Germany, when he enlisted in the Norwich company of the Connecticut National Guard, January 15, 1915, and rose from private to second lieutenant. He entered the United States army and went to France with the 56th Artillery, March 27, 1918. He was at the front in the Argonne for two months, and until the fighting was over was in active service, and after the Armistice he was transferred to the Government Claim Service, and on July 13, 1919, arrived in New York, soon afterward being honorably discharged. After his return from France, he settled on a farm in the town of Ledyard, and in October, 1919, bought his present farm. He is a member of Ledyard Grange, No. 167, Patrons of Husbandry; and in politics a Republican.

Mr. Avery married, August 1, 1919, Goldie Bell Davis, born in Norwich county, daughter of John and Adelaide (Spiegel) Davis, and they are the parents of a daughter, Dorothy Crary Avery, born July 12, 1920.

JOHN CALVIN CRANDALL—The Crandall family is one of the best known in New London county, Connecticut, where the name has been familiar for generations. Rev. John Crandall, the American ancestor of the Crandalls, came from Wales to Boston, Massachusetts, in 1634-35. He was a Baptist minister, and to escape persecution, fled to Rhode Island, where he found the religious freedom denied him in Massachusetts. From Rev. John Crandall, who had sons, John, Peter, Joseph, Samuel, Jeremiah and Eber, come all the early families of the name in Rhode Island and Connecticut, as well as many of those who settled in New York.

John Calvin Crandall, of Waterford, Connecticut, son of Russell and Lydia Crandall, was born in that section of the town of Waterford, New London county, known as "Great Neck," August 10, 1874. When a child, his parents moved to New London, where the father soon afterward died and was buried in Jordan Cemetery. In New London the lad, John C. Crandall, was educated, but he has always lived in the section in which he was born. In 1886 he entered the employ of the Palmer Brothers' Mills and there continued under the direct supervision of Fred Mercer. Later, when Mr. Mercer left the Palmer Brothers' Mills to engage in business for himself as the New England Carpet Lining Company, Mr. Crandall went with him and is now foreman of a department of the New England Carpet Lining Company, an extensive plant. He is a member of Pequot Lodge, No. 85, Independent Order of Odd Fellows, and a man of good repute in his community.

Mr. Crandall married, in October, 1899, Etta Crocker, of New London, daughter of Captain Alvin Melville and Ada Crocker. Mr. and Mrs. Crandall are the parents of a son, Harold Herrick, born in New London, July 30, 1900.

ISAAC GALLUP GEER—The Geer family is one of the oldest in New London county, Connecticut, George Geer settling in New London about 1651, his home yet known as the Geer homestead, located in that part of the town which has since been set off as the North Society of Groton, and is now the town of Ledyard. The homestead has been in the possession of descendants of George Geer during all the years which have intervened since his death. George Geer arrived in New England from England in 1635, with a younger brother Thomas, the record from that date until 1651 being unreliable. In that year George Geer settled in New London county, and Thomas Geer in Enfield, Connecticut, in 1682. George Geer appears on the records of New London, February 17, 1658, the date of his marriage to Sarah Allyn. Right after his marriage he was granted fifty acres by the town of New London, and the same year an additional one hundred acres. He also owned lands in the town of Preston, a part of which was granted him by Owaneco, son of the Indian Sachem, Uncas, under date of December 11, 1691. In 1705 he was selectman of the town of Groton, where he died in 1726. His wife, Sarah (Allyn) Geer, died a short time before him. The name Allyn has been retained through all the generations, sometimes as a given name, sometimes as a middle name, as in the case of Jacob Allyn Geer, father of Isaac Gallup Geer, of Ledyard, a prosperous, substantial farmer and public-spirited citizen. The farm on which Isaac G. Greer lives was the property of his great-great-grandfather, Amos (1) Geer, a graduate of Yale College about 1760, and his grandfather, Amos (2) Geer, a descendant of George and Sarah (Allyn) Geer, and where Amos Geer and his wife, Prudence (Allyn) Geer passed their adult lives. Amos and Prudence (Allyn) Geer were the parents of Jacob Allyn Geer, who married Julia Gallup, and they were the parents of Isaac Gallup Geer of this review. Jacob A. Geer taught school for several years when a young man, but finally settled down on the home farm, and there died, in 1857, at the age of forty. Julia (Gallup) Geer, his widow, survived him nearly forty years, dying December 20, 1896, aged seventy-two. They were the parents of three children: Isaac Gallup, of further mention; Prudence Emma, who married Nathan Gallup, both deceased; and Nellie Wight, residing at home.

Isaac Gallup Geer, only son of Jacob Allyn and Julia (Gallup) Geer, was born in Ledyard, New London county, Connecticut, July 24, 1848. He was educated in the public schools and has spent his life at the homestead, early succeeding to its management, his father dying when his son was but nine years of age. Mrs. Geer rented out the farm until her son was able to lift the burden from her shoulders. In addition to the home farm, Mr. Geer owns a tract of one hundred and twenty-five acres, bought from the Thomas estate, and other parcels of land in Ledyard. He is a man of energy and character, having the confidence of his community and their respect.

A Republican in political faith, Mr. Geer represented his town in the Connecticut Legislature in 1913-1915, serving on the committee on shell fish. For years he has served as selectman of Ledyard, also assessor, and member of the town Board of Visitors. He is a member of the Patrons of Husbandry, and of the County Farm Bureau. In religious faith he is a Congregationalist.

Mr. Geer married, January 4, 1888, Amanda Chase Belden, of Ledyard, daughter of James H. and Augusta (Allyn) Belden. Mr. and Mrs. Geer are the parents of two children: 1. Earl Belden, who married Anna Blatherwick, and resides in Ledyard; they are parents of one child, Isaac Gallup (2). 2. Florence A., married Ernest E. Smith, and resides in Franklin, Connecticut; two children were born to them: Elizabeth Chase, and Isabelle Goodwin.

THOMAS JOSEPH HEALY, who conducts an up-to-date tire shop at No. 372 Main street, Norwich, is a native of New London county, Connecticut.

Mr. Healy's father, Thomas J. Healy, was born in Ireland, and educated in the National schools of that country. He came to the United States in 1868, locating in Colchester, Connecticut, where he was engaged in the grocery business for many years. He is now retired, and lives in Naugatuck, Connecticut. He married Ellen Campbell, and they are the parents of seven children, five now living, of whom Thomas Joseph is the second.

Thomas Joseph Healy was born in Colchester, Connecticut, on January 16, 1874. He received his early education in the public schools of that town, and then took a course at the Bacon Academy, of Colchester. In 1890 the young man entered the employ of the Colchester Rubber Company, a large factory which has since been destroyed by fire. He remained in this connection until 1894, when he went to Bristol, Rhode Island, where he was also employed in the rubber industry. Following his stay there Mr. Healy worked in various places for short periods and then, in 1916, came to Norwich, where he opened a tire repair shop, at No. 372 Main street, doing business under his own name. He was very successful, making good from the start. He handles a full line of new tires and tubes, and also does all kinds of rubber repairing. Mr. Healy takes a keen interest in public and political affairs, but declines to support any party unreservedly, and votes independently.

He married, on November 20, 1917, Lena C., daughter of Julian and Margaret (Bray) Boudreau, and they have one daughter, Mary I. Mrs. Healy was organist of St. Mary's Roman Catholic Church, of Norwich, from 1899 to 1919. The family are members of this church.

ERASTUS CRANDALL BEEBE—For a century or more Beebes have resided in the town of Waterford, New London county, Connecticut, John C. Beebe, whose life covered a span of but fifty-two years, having been born there in 1821. He was a farmer of Waterford all his life, and there married Susan Boynton, also born in Waterford, who died in 1907, aged eighty-two. Five children were born to John C. and Susan (Boynton) Beebe: Marvin, deceased; Pickett L., deceased; Anne, deceased; Lydia, deceased; and Erastus C., of whom further.

Erastus C. Beebe was born at the home farm in Waterford, March 15, 1855. He attended the district school, but losing his father in boyhood, he early became a farm worker. After reaching an age when he could choose for himself, he quit the farm and went to New London, where he engaged in business as a meat dealer. He continued in that business until 1908, when he sold out, returned to the farm and there continues. He is a member of the Baptist church, a Democrat in politics, and has served his town as a member of the Board of Assessors and Board of Relief. He is a prosperous, progressive farmer, a member of the Connecticut Farm Bureau, and modern in all his farming methods.

Mr. Beebe married Martha Tinker, born in Waterford, Connecticut, April 7, 1860, died August 22, 1899, daughter of Richard and Martha Tinker. Mr. and Mrs. Beebe are the parents of four children, all born at the farm in Waterford: 1. Beulah, born in

1876, married Fred Comstock, of Quaker Hill, Connecticut, and has a daughter, Millicent, who married W. Victor Washabaugh, they the parents of a daughter Jane. 2. Richardetta, born in 1877, married Hugh Kenyon. 3. Hayward Earl, born in 1880, married Fannie Gallup, and they have three children: Carol, born in 1909; Allen, born in 1910; and Barbara, born in 1921. 4. Pearl, born in 1889, married Henry Schlink, and has a son, Norman, born in 1916.

HUBERT GEORGE DART—To have four generations of a family living at the same time in the same town is rather an unusual occurrence, but to have each one bear the same name is still more rare. This is the case of the Dart family of Montville, Connecticut. The great-grandfather is Ezra Fitzland Dart, a native of Ledyard, Connecticut, who is now residing in Montville, where he celebrated his ninety-fourth birthday anniversary in 1920. His son, George William Dart, born in North Waterford, Connecticut, is now a merchant of Montville. He married Hattie Allen, also born in Montville, and their son, Hubert George Dart, is the third in this family line, the fourth generation being represented by his two sons, Lester Crandall and Dana Dart, both of whom were born in Montville.

Hubert George Dart was born in Montville, April 18, 1882. In his boyhood he attended the public school there, and after graduating became a clerk for his father in the grocery store of which George William Dart is the owner. After some time spent in this employ, the young man went to Westerly, Rhode Island, and obtained a position as a machinist there in the machine shop of The C. B. Cottrell Company. Two years later, Hubert George Dart returned to Montville and opened a commission business and bakery of his own. After carrying on this establishment for two years, Mr. Dart gave it up to go West, becoming a salesman for Armour & Company, in Minneapolis, Minnesota. For two years Mr. Dart remained with the Armour people, and at the end of that time returned to Montville to take charge of his father's store, as manager. In this capacity he continued for eight years, when, having the opportunity of becoming superintendent of the Massasoit Mills, Mr. Dart gave up the grocery business and accepted the latter position in 1918. The Massasoit works are located at Oakdale, a suburb of Montville, and Mr. Dart still resides in Montville.

Having taken an active interest in the politics of his home town, Mr. Dart has always voted the Republican ticket. He has held public office for some years, being on the Board of Selectmen, having been first, second, and third in rank, and at the present time serving as third selectman. Equally interested in the Masonic fraternity, Mr. Dart is a member of Franklin Council, Free and Accepted Masons.

Hubert George Dart married Pansy Crandall, born in East Haddam, Connecticut, daughter of Lodowick Crandall. They have three children: Lester Crandall Dart, Elace Faye Dart, and Dana Hubert Dart.

JOHN POTTER—The home of John Potter since his sixth year, 1875, has been upon the farm to which Captain James, a whaling captain, retired after leaving the sea, which was bought by Elisha Potter in 1875. The old homestead was the boyhood home of Henry B. Brown, of the United States Supreme Court, and the house was built by Samuel Tyler in 1798. The old chimney stone in the old mansion bore the inscription, "S. T., 1798," and when John Potter, the present owner, built a new mansion on the site of the old one in 1904, this old stone was laid in the foundation wall, along with a new one marked, J. P. 1904." The old farm upon which all but six of John Potter's fifty-one years have been passed, is one of the finest estates in the town of Griswold, the mansion, modern and beautiful in its surroundings, handsomely fitted with all city conveniences. John Potter is a descendant in the ninth American generation of the family, founded in New England by Nathaniel Potter, born in England, who was admitted an inhabitant of Rhode Island, in 1638. The line of descent from Nathaniel and Dorothy Potter to John Potter is traced through the founder's son, Nathaniel (2) Potter, and his wife, Elizabeth Stokes; their son, Nathaniel (3) Potter, and his wife, Joan Wilbur; their son, William Potter, and his wife, Mary Browning; their son, David Potter, and his wife, Susanna Barber; their son, Incom Potter, and his wife, Elizabeth Arnold; their son, Caleb Potter, and his wife, Sally Green; their son, Elisha Potter, and his third wife, Angeline (Whitford) Douglass; their son, John Potter, the principal figure in this review.

Elisha Potter, of the eighth generation, was born in Voluntown, Connecticut, February 23, 1801, died in the town of Griswold, New London county, Connecticut, April 2, 1888. After securing his own education he began teaching, and for several years taught during winter terms in the district schools and farmed during the summer months. His farm was in Voluntown, and much of the timber on his place he converted into charcoal, which he sold in Norwich. He resided in Voluntown until 1871, then moved to the town of Griswold, and in 1875 to the Captain James farm, now the home of his son John. For thirty-seven years Elisha Potter was town clerk of Voluntown, and for seven terms represented that district in the Lower House of the Connecticut Legislature, 1834, '36, '41, '42, '44, '51, and '54. He was also elected State Senator and was one of the leading Democrats of his county. He died in Griswold April 2, 1888. Elisha Potter married Tacy Newton, November 28, 1822, and had a son, Caleb P. Potter, of Norwich, now deceased. He married (second) Mrs. Crary, a widow. He married (third) Mrs. Angeline (Whitford) Douglass. She was born in Coventry, Rhode Island, and died at the farm in Griswold, Connecticut, October 2, 1898, surviving her husband ten years, and leaving a son, John, of further mention.

John Potter was born in Voluntown, Connecticut, November 2, 1869, where the first two years of his life were spent. In 1871 his father moved to Griswold, and in 1875 the Captain James farm became the family home. John Potter, then six years of age, grew up on the old farm with its old Colonial mansion, and but few of his after years have been spent elsewhere. They were years of educational training for a profession he was fated never to follow. He attended the district school in Griswold, then pursued a four years' course at New Hampton Literary Institute, at New Hampton, New Hampshire, then entered Yale Law School. There his health failed, and he was obliged to abandon his studies and returned to the farm to recuperate. But the death of his father in 1888 demanded that the son succeed him in the farm management. He was then nineteen years of age, and from that time until the present, the old farm has been under his management. In 1904 he built his present residence, and there he is enjoying all the comforts and pleasures that accrue to the successful American farmer.

Mr. Potter is a Democrat, and for fifteen years at various times served the town of Griswold as selectman and has taken great interest in the town schools, serving as official visitor. In 1895 and in 1916 he represented the district in the State Legislature. He is a member of Mt. Vernon Lodge, No. 73, Free and Accepted Masons, of Jewett City.

He married, October 6, 1897, Bertha I. Barber, born in Killingly, Connecticut, daughter of William J. Barber. Mrs. Potter died July 18, 1910, leaving a son, Paul Barber Potter, born August 6, 1898. He enlisted in the student army during the War with Germany, and is now a student at Bates College, Lewiston, Maine.

CHARLES GEORGE JACOBSON was born in Taftville, Connecticut, June 5, 1887, the son of Fred F. and Sophia (Oleson) Jacobson, both natives of Sweden. Fred F. Jacobson was educated in his native town, Gutenburg, and in 1880 came to this country, settling in Taftville, where he has resided ever since, being engaged in the carpenter's trade. To Mr. and Mrs. Jacobson were born four children, Charles George, the subject of this review, being the youngest.

After graduating from the Norwich Grammar School in 1905, Charles George Jacobson entered upon his business career, his first employment being with Hopkins & Allen, where he worked as a machinist for two years, subsequently becoming machinist for S. J. Coit, with whom he worked for the following seven years. In 1914 he opened his repair service station on Bath street, Norwich, and has been successfully engaged in business here ever since. In politics Mr. Jacobson is a Republican, keenly alive to his responsibilities as a citizen, and taking an active interest in public affairs.

Mr. Jacobson married, April 28, 1916, Esther Rudburg, a native of Sweden, and they are the parents of one child, Richard, born March 28, 1917.

Such is the life of Charles George Jacobson, a self-made man, starting in business poor in finances but rich in shrewdness and foresight, traits which distinguish a man among men. He has adapted himself to circumstances and taken advantage of every opportunity and today stands as one of the respected and prominent citizens of Norwich. Such a man gives promise of still greater achievements.

RANDALL WOOD PALMER—For many generations, Palmers were leading spirits in the town of Montville, a section of that town bearing the name of "Palmertown," and in that section William Henry (2) Palmer, of the eighth generation of the family founded in New England by Walter Palmer, was born, October 1, 1843. William Henry (2) Palmer was the son of William Henry (1) Palmer, son of Gideon, son of Elder Reuben, son of Gershom, son of George, son of Deacon Gershom, son of Walter Palmer, the American ancestor, who came to New England as early as 1629, but did not locate in Connecticut until 1653. These were the ancestors of Randall Wood Palmer, of the ninth American generation, son of William Henry (2), and Adelaide R. (Wood) Palmer, of Fitchville, Connecticut.

William Henry (2) Palmer, son of William Henry (1) and Clarissa (Stanton) Palmer, was born in the town of Montville, New London county, Connecticut, October 1, 1843. He was educated in the public schools, and when seventeen years of age attempted to enlist in the Union army. He was rejected, but later was allowed to enlist, and for three years he served his country as a soldier. After the war he returned home and later became superintendent of the Arawanna Mills at Middletown, Connecticut. He continued with that and other Middletown companies for a time, finally, in 1886, becoming associated with Palmer Brothers, of Montville, Connecticut, manufacturers of bed quilts and comfortables. William H. Palmer became superintendent of construction and machinery, and several valuable patents owned by the company were the product of his inventive genius.

A Republican in politics, Mr. Palmer gave a great deal of time to the public service, being for four years a member of the Middletown Common Council, and for three years a member of the School Board. After moving to Norwich, in 1882, he served as alderman; member of the Lower House of the Connecticut Assembly; and in 1895 was elected State Senator. He was also secretary of the Norwich Industrial Building Company, and a director of the Norwich Savings Society. He was formerly a commander of Sedgwick Post, Grand Army of the Republic; member of the Republican State Central Committee for eight years; member of the State Board of Education; and affiliated with lodge, chapter and council of the Masonic order. He served his community well in whatever position called to, and never sought an office nor declined a public duty.

Mr. Palmer married (first) Adelaide R. Wood, born in Rhode Island, who died in Middletown, Connecticut, leaving two sons: Frank E., and Randall W., both of mention in this work. Mr. Palmer married (second) June 15, 1898, Ellen Reynolds, of Washington, D. C.

Randall Wood Palmer, youngest of the two sons of William Henry (2) Palmer and his first wife, Adelaide R. (Wood) Palmer, was born in Middletown, Connecticut, August 12, 1878. Four years later the family moved to Norwich, Connecticut, and there the lad was educated in the public schools. He was variously employed until September 1, 1902, when he entered the office employ of Palmer Brothers, at Fitchville, Connecticut, and still continues with that company. He began as a clerk in the mill office and advanced in position until 1915, when he was promoted to his present position, assistant superintendent of the mill. In politics, Mr. Palmer is a Republican, and in religious faith an Episcopalian.

HENRY J. SPENCER—Having a model market in every way, Henry J. Spencer, of Mystic, Connecticut, takes great pride in keeping it up to the standard that he maintained when, in 1898, he became proprietor of it. Mr. Spencer deals in everything that is good to eat, including meat, fish, vegetables, and other provisions.

Most of Mr. Spencer's life has been spent in Mystic, where he was born September 16, 1871. His parents were Henry and Emily F. (Denison) Spencer, the former being a native of New York State. Henry Spencer began his education in the district school in the section of the State in which he lived, but coming to Stonington, Connecticut, when a young boy, he attended the public school there for a time. His father was a farmer, and after leaving school, Henry Spencer worked upon the farm for a few years, after which he became a fisherman, a calling he followed for many years. In the latter part of his life he gave up deep-sea fishing and took up shipbuilding, working in various shipyards about Mystic. His death occurred in Mystic in 1898, his wife surviving him until 1917. They had a family of six children, the youngest of them being Henry J. Spencer, of whom further.

Spending his boyhood in Mystic, attending the public and high school there, Henry J. Spencer finished his education at Snell's Business College in Norwich, Connecticut. Returning to his native town in 1889, he received the appointment of assistant postmaster of Mystic, holding the office for six years. Going in 1895 to Westerly, Rhode Island, Mr. Spencer obtained a position as clerk there, continuing it until 1898, when he came back to Mystic and bought out the market of A. C. Hayes, a well established business of sixty years' standing. It was and always had been a high-grade food market, and Mr. Spencer has not only continued along the original lines, but has added to its first-class reputation, having introduced new and up-to-date improvements.

In politics, Mr. Spencer is a Republican; in religion, a member of the Methodist Episcopal church of Mystic. In organization work he is affiliated with the Independent Order of Odd Fellows, being a member of Stonington Lodge, No. 26, of Mystic.

Henry J. Spencer married, in April, 1896, Lena C. Babcock, a daughter of Francis Babcock, of Mystic. To this union three children have been born: Edith L.; Clifford W.; and Henry R.; all are living at home. Mrs. Spencer is a member of the Women's Christian Temperance Union of Mystic, and is also a worker in the Methodist church. She is a member of the First Baptist Church of Westerly, Rhode Island, which was her church home while a resident of that town.

JOHN ABBOT ACKLEY—One of the substantial citizens of the town of Groton, this county, is Mr. Ackley, who has for years conducted extensive farming operations in this vicinity, and for the past fourteen years has carried on what is known as the Miniere place, now being its owner. He also operates and leases the Winthrop place.

Mr. Ackley is a son of Augustus and Sarah (Whipple) Ackley. The elder Mr. Ackley was born in Milton, Maine, and educated in the district schools of that neighborhood, after which he worked as a farmer in his native State until 1870, when he came to New London county, Connecticut, bringing his family, and located in Ledyard. Here he purchased a farm, where he still resides, at the age of eighty-three years. His first wife, Sarah (Whipple) Ackley, who was the mother of two children, died, and he later married her sister, Josephine M. Whipple, seven children being born to the second union. The sisters were both born in Groton.

John A. Ackley, now the only surviving child of the first marriage, was born in Ledyard, this county, June 2, 1880. He received a practical education in the district schools of that community. As a young man he took up the work which his father had always followed, and was employed on different farms until 1901, when he rented the Barnes place, in Ledyard, and engaged in general farming for himself. He was very successful, and continued along this line, and in 1907 removed to Poquonnock, in the town of Groton, where he rented the Winthrop farm, conducting it for nine years on a rental basis, then in 1916 purchased the farm, and has since gone forward to even greater success. Politically, Mr. Ackley supports the Republican party, and with his family attends and supports the Congregational church. He is a busy man, taking little leisure from the multitudinous duties which large agricultural operations entail.

On December 15, 1903, Mr. Ackley married Mabel Gottschalk, of Groton, daughter of Henry and Nellie (Bingle) Gottschalk. Mr. and Mrs. Ackley are the parents of eight children: Henry and Augustus, both of whom died in infancy, and the youngest died in infancy, the others being as follows: Winifred J., John Edward, Theodore Roosevelt, Ralph William, Edith Mabel. The living children all reside at home.

JACOB MUNZ—In Amriswil, a town of Switzerland, in the canton of Thurgau, ten miles from Constance, Jacob Munz, of Norwich, Connecticut, was born. He is a son of John Jacob and Caroline (Hungerbuehler) Munz, both natives of the mountain republic, the father a manufacturer of cotton yarn until his passing.

Jacob Munz, born August 23, 1866, remained in his native Switzerland until 1889, during that period of twenty-three years acquiring a good education and becoming skilled in the detail of cotton manufacture, having had the privilege of association with his honored father. In 1889 the young man came to the United States, where he became a student at the Philadelphia Textile School, specializing in the detail of silk manufacture. He passed four years at the school, completing full regular and post-graduate courses, and then went out into the actual manufacturing world, beginning in the silk mills of Paterson, New Jersey. He remained in the "Silk City" six years, being employed in different mills, widening his knowledge of his business and adding greatly to his fund of experience. In 1899, ten years after coming to the United States, he came to Norwich, Connecticut, as superintendent of J. B. Martin & Company, Inc., manufacturers of high quality silk velvets. For nineteen years, 1899-1918, he continued as superintendent, then was advanced to his present position of manager. His qualifications are high, and the position he holds is one that calls for the best that is in him, for Martin velvets are standard and must maintain the highest standard of excellence.

Mr. Munz married, at Paterson, New Jersey, October 23, 1899, Charlotte Adelaide Symonds, born in Chicago, Illinois. Mr. and Mrs. Munz are the parents of a daughter, Helen Jeanette, born in Paterson, New Jersey. They are members of the Congregational church.

GEORGE LACROX—Of Canadian birth and parentage, George Lacrox was born January 2, 1872, on a farm in West Farnam, Province of Quebec, where his father, Joseph Lacrox, was born in 1840. The elder Mr. Lacrox was a farmer, and in addition was employed in one of the local mills. He came to the United States about 1880, and settled in Baltic, Connecticut, where he lived until his death in 1892. He worked as a mill man. He was a member of St. Joseph Society. He married Esther Lamoureux, also a native of West Farnam, Canada, the daughter of Joseph Lamoureux.

George Lacrox was a boy of eight years when his people came to live in Baltic, Connecticut. He attended the parochial school there until sixteen years old, when he went to work in one of the Baltic mills in that section. Later, the mill burning down, the young man went to several different towns, obtaining employment in the mills, and finally returned to Baltic, where he became interested in farming, and has been engaged in that line more than twenty years. In 1898 he bought the Beaver Brook farm of 178 acres.

Mr. Lacrox bought a large farm in Sprague township and has become very successful, keeping an orderly, up-to-date farm, of which he is justly proud. He has become a good American citizen, taking an interest in the affairs of his neighborhood, and has joined the Republican party. He served for six years as a member of the Board of Selectmen.

George Lacrox married Eliza Trudeau, the daughter of Ouessine and Adelaide (Aubin) Trudeau. Mrs. Lacrox was born in Lacadie, Dominion of Canada, July 10, 1872. Seven children were born of this marriage: 1. George Joseph, born in Natick, Rhode Island, May 1, 1894. 2. Leodore Ouessine, born October 3, 1897, in Moosup, Connecticut. 3. Doloria Beatrice, born in Baltic, April 11, 1900. 4. Fluerdina Virginia, born February 7, 1902, in Baltic. 5. Gilbert Stanislaw, born September 2, 1904, in Baltic. 6. Romeo Hermenegile, born September 13, 1907. 7. Aime Blaise, born in August, 1909. The eldest son, George Joseph, is married, his wife being Leona Eva (Bourque) Lacrox, born in Moosup, Connecticut, Ajril 1, 1896. She is the daughter of Neol and Eliza Bourque. The Lacrox family are all members of the St. Mary's Roman Catholic Church.

ROY DUMAS GARDNER—The earilest authentic knowledge of the Gardner family is the fact that the original paternal progenitor left the Roger Williams Colony, and coming to New London county, Connecticut, bought a section of land there from the Indians. It is the country of which Gardner's Lake is a part, and there Mr. Gardner now makes his home.

At the time of his birth, the parents of Mr. Gardner were residents of Uncasville, Connecticut, where his father, Ulysses Selden Gardner, was occupied in farming, a calling he followed during his entire life. He was born in Bozrah, Connecticut, and his death occurred in 1914. The mother of Roy Dumas Gardner was Cleta (Dumas) Gardner, the daughter of a seafaring man, Captain Pierre Dumas, whose ship was stationed in South American waters when his daughter was born on board the vessel.

Roy Dumas Gardner was born in Uncasville, October 17, 1884, and his early life was spent in Bozrah, he attending the local school there. When older the young man attended Norwich Academy for a time, then obtained employment in the Norwich Bleachery, where he remained until 1907, when he came to Montville and entered the mills of the C. M. Robinson Company as a general hand at the plant. At the end of six months he was made the estimator, and continued in this position for some years. In 1917 Mr. Gardner made another change in business, going to New Haven and becoming an employee of the Winchester Company in that city. His health breaking down, Mr. Gardner was forced to resign from this occupation and to return to Norwich, six months later accepting a position with the Marlin, Rockwell Corporation, of Norwich. Giving this up and coming to Montville, he finally re-entered the C. M. Robinson Company mill, now known as the Robinson Paper Company, where he fills the office of superintendent of the plant at the present time.

Mr. Gardner is interested in fraternal matters, being a third degree Mason, a member of Oxoboxo Blue Lodge, Free and Accepted Masons, of Montville. In politics, he is a Republican. He attends and supports the Baptist church.

FREDERICK MARVIN RODMAN—Since coming to Franklin in 1895, Frederick Marvin Rodman has devoted his entire time to farming, and his place is regarded as one of the well conducted properties of the place. In the course of these years Mr. Rodman has won for himself a place high in the esteem of his fellowmen.

Fred Alphonso Rodman, father of Frederick Marvin Rodman, was born at Chatham. He married Harriett Maria Lucas, who was also born in Chatham. To Mr. and Mrs. Rodman were born two children: Frederick Marvin, of further mention; and Theresa, who married L. B. Armstrong, of Franklin.

Frederick Marvin Rodman was born at Haddam Neck, Connecticut, October 17, 1876. He attended the public schools of Chatham until he was fourteen years of age, when he came to Franklin, and here has been engaged in agricultural pursuits ever since. That he chose wisely is amply proven by the success which has attended his efforts. His career from its beginning is characterized by much hard and persistent expenditure of labor, and the substantial position that he has come to occupy in the community is the obvious and appropriate reward of application of the unstinted order.

On October 17, 1901, Frederick Marvin Rodman was united in marriage with Mary Elizabeth Armstrong, daughter of Durkee and Julia Ann (Porter) Armstrong. Mrs. Rodman is a native of Franklin, born June 2, 1881. To Mr. and Mrs. Rodman have been born two children: Julia Anna, born May 21, 1906; and William Frederick, born July 15, 1911.

ROBERT PATON, though a native of Scotland, came to the United States at such an early age that he has only a vague knowledge of any other home. His parents came from Scotland to this country in the autumn of 1893, George Paton, the father (of Scottish birth), having come to Montville for the benefit of his health, obtained employment at his trade. He died two years after his arrival here, and was buried in Montville in 1895. His wife, Jane (Smith) Paton, a native of Scotland, is still living in Montiville. They had a family of seven children: George, Mary, Anne, Ellison, Robert, of further mention, and two who died in infancy.

Robert Paton was born in Glasgow, Scotland, November 19, 1884. His education was begun there in the local schools, and after his arrival in America, in 1893, he finished his school days in Montville. After leaving school the youth engaged in mill work in one of the local mills, and has continued along that line ever since, now being overseer of the packing department in the Palmer Brothers' Company Montville mills. A man who is interested in all things connected with his town's progress, Mr. Paton has engaged somewhat in political matters, and for some time past has held the office of register of voters. He is also active in several fraternal socities, being a third degree Mason, a member of Oxoboxo Blue Lodge, Free and Accepted Masons, and Union Chapter, No. 7, New London, and also is affiliated with the local lodge of the Independent Order of Odd Fellows.

In Montville, June 14, 1911, Robert Paton was married to Mary Bell Johnson, daughter of David and Jennie (Young) Johnson, residents of Montville, where their daughter was born. Mr. and Mrs. Paton have two daughters: Edna May, born in 1914, and Doris Jennie, born in 1917. The family reside in the Palmertown section of Montville. They are members of the Montville Center Congregational Church of Montville.

HENRY JOHN KENDALL—One of the prominent farms of Lisbon, New London county, Connecticut, is that of Henry John Kendall, whose residence in this town has been marked by personal prosperity and a large degree of public usefulness.

Mr. Kendall is a son of John Martin and Julia (Oben) Kendall. John M. Kendall was a native of Keene, New Hampshire, but is now deceased. His wife was born in Toronton, Canada, and still survives him.

Henry John Kendall was born in Ontario, Canada, on December 12, 1862. He received his education in Taftville, Connecticut, where he came in the fall of 1876. Here he worked in the cotton mill for many years, then came to Lisbon, where he bought a farm. This was seventeen years ago, and he still continues active in agricultural lines here. He has been very successful, and has not only established himself here in a financial way, but has become a vital part of the public life of the town of Lisbon.

Mr. Kendall was long since called to the public service, and has held the offices of assessor and first selectman, being the incumbent of the latter office at the present time. He has also served on the Board of Relief, and on the School Board. In 1920 he was elected town representative to the Legislature for the State of Connecticut, and is now (1922) serving.

Mr. Kendall married Fannie Maria Holmes, daughter of John and Lucretia Holmes, who was born in Columbia, Connecticut. Mr. and Mrs. Kendall have eleven children: William, John, Theodore, George, Ralph, Etta, Laura, Rita, Vesta, Edna, and Eva. Mr. Kendall has one brother, William Charles, and a sister, Elsie.

JAMES RAYMOND BOLGER—In the Province of Ontario, Canada, August 10, 1854, James Raymond Bolger was born and there spent his youth. He is a son of John Bolger, also born in Canada, who died in the year 1900, aged sixty-six years. He was a shoemaker by trade, and in early manhood came to the United States. Later in life he was employed at the Natural Bridge in Jefferson county, New York, by the New York Central railroad. He married Mary Anne McDonald, who died in 1916, at the age of seventy-four years, and is buried at Natural Bridge, New York.

James Raymond Bolger was brought to the United States by his parents in 1874, and later became a skilled worker in wood. For sixteen years he was superintendent of the Composite Board Company of Niagara Falls, New York, that firm making the fine material used in automobile tops, interior work on steamships, and for various purposes where a light lining or finishing material is necessary. In 1903 Mr. Bolger located in Montville, Connecticut, where he is superintendent of the Keyes Products Company, also manufacturing composite board similar to that made at Niagara.

Mr. Bolger married Elizabeth Kelly, and they are the parents of one child, James, deceased.

OTIS AUSTIN JENCKS—In the farming community of Preston the name of Otis A. Jencks stands for the most up-to-date developments in dairying, in which branch of practical farming Mr. Jencks is meeting with unusual success.

Mr. Jencks is a son of George Albert Jencks, who was born in Norwich and spent the early years of his life there. In later life, after his marriage, he became a resident of the old family homestead of his wife's family, in Preston, for many years known as the Bentley place, a large and handsome farm, which has always been noted for its extensive and well handled dairy business. In the course of time the farm fell to his wife, and he carried it on until his death, in 1920, at the age of sixty-four years. During the latter part of his life, however, owing to a long period of ill health, he kept only a general oversight of the affairs of the farm. He married Ella Bentley, daughter of Oliver H. and Mary M. Bentley, and they were the parents of two sons: Harrison, who was born in Preston, June 12, 1882; and Otis Austin, whose name appears at the head of this review.

Otis A. Jencks was born at the Bentley homestead in Preston, June 15, 1886. He received a practical education in the public schools of his native place, and assisted his father about the farm work until he was twenty-one years of age. At that time he entered the employ of the Shore Line Electric Company, in the capacity of motor-man, following this work for a period of eight years. Thereafter, his father's ill health imperatively demanded his retirement from active work, so Mr. Jencks returned to the Preston home, and has since conducted the farm, assuming full responsibility upon his father's death. Mr. Jencks has kept pace with every development of modern science as applied to milk production, and has a model dairy, equipped with every facility for the work in hand. Politically, he supports the principles and policies of the Republican party, and his religious affiliation is with the Baptist church.

On March 1, 1910, Mr. Jencks married Inez Elizabeth Brown, who was born in North Stonington, this county, January 15, 1888, daughter of John and Sarah Brown, farming people, now residents of North Stonington. Mr. and Mrs. Jencks have three children: Howard Bentley, born in Preston, April 24, 1915; and Dorothy May and Donald Lester, twins, born in Preston, July 24, 1916. Donald Lester Jencks died March 6, 1922.

CLARENCE SEYMOUR BEEBE—Farming has always been the occupation of Clarence Seymour Beebe, beginning same when a boy on his father's farm and continuing in his manhod. He is indeed a "son of the soil" of Connecticut, for he is a native of that State and has lived in it all his life.

Born in East Haddam, June 6, 1864, Clarence Seymour Beebe was the son of Sherman Beebe, a resident of East Haddam, and Mary Jane (Hulbert) Beebe, of Portland, Connecticut. The elder Mr. Beebe has always been a farmer also, father and son loving their occupation equally. Sherman Beebe and his wife were the parents of nine children.

The early education of Clarence Seymour Beebe was acquired at the select school of East Haddam, but he was still in his boyhood when he ceased attending this institution and devoted his time and energies to the tilling of the land at East Haddam. Seven years ago Mr. Beebe chose Colchester as his future home, and purchasing the farm known as the "Taintor Place," in that township, he and his family moved to this new location, where they continued to reside until April 21, 1921, when Mr. Beebe purchased a small place, situated on Main street, in Flanders village, town of East Lyme, to which he and his family removed. He continues farming, only on a much smaller scale.

Clarence Seymour Beebe married Ada Champlin, born in East Haddam, the daughter of John and Marion (Smith) Champlin, residents of that town. Of this union two children were born: 1. Florence, now living in Vermont, the wife of Dennis Bigelow. 2. Grace Seymour, who now resides at home with her parents in Flanders. Mr. Beebe has never become interested in town politics, and never having sought a public office, has not held any.

SANDS WILLIAM THROOP, for more than fifty years has been a resident of Lebanon, Connecticut, following farming as an occupation and leading a quiet life in a delightfully situated region.

To Mr. Throop the soil of Connecticut is his "native heath," for he was born in Mystic, June 14, 1860, spending the early years of his life there, and acquiring an elementary education in its primary school. When seven years old he, with his family, moved to Lebanon, where he has lived ever since.

Mr. Throop is the son of Henry H. Throop, a native of Lebanon, born October 5, 1816, and Matilda A. (Williams) Throop, of Ledyard. She was born June 4, 1835. Henry H. Throop was twice married, his first wife being Eliza Ann (Bissell) Throop, by whom he had one child, Mary Bissell, who died in infancy. The second wife, Matilda A. (Williams) Throop, was the mother of four children: 1. John James, born in Lebanon, July 5, 1856. 2. Sands William, of further mention. 3. Mary Welch, born in Lebanon, May 17, 1869, who died as a girl. 4. Sarah Elizabeth, married C. W. Allen, of Groton, born November 1, 1873, and they were the parents of five children: Wilson T., Matilda W., Richard, Robert, and Elizabeth. Henry H. Throop purchased, in 1867, the homestead which is located in the western part of the town and where his children grew to maturity. He also owned the old Troupf farm in the eastern part of town.

Though holding to the principles of the Republican party, Sands W. Throop is not a politician and has neither sought nor held any public office. He is, however, actively interested in the work of the Grange.

Sands William Throop married Mary S. Williams, of Lebanon, who was born May 3, 1856, the daughter of Nathaniel B. and Jane Elizabeth (Parker) Williams, the former a native of Lebanon, where he lived all his life, a farmer and landowner, and where he died, September 5, 1918, in his ninety-seventh year. Jane Elizabeth (Parker) Williams was a native of Pittsfield, Massachusetts; she died April 29, 1903, at the age of eighty years. Mr. and Mrs. Williams were the parents of two children: 1. Ellen C., who married Rev. Leander Elliott Livermore, a native of Independence, New York, who lives in Lebanon in the summer months and in Florida in winter. 2. Mary S. (Mrs. Sands William Throop). Mr. and Mrs. Throop have no children.

CHARLES HENRY PEABODY was born September 3, 1840, the son of Joseph and Catherine (Baker) Peabody. His early childhood was spent on his father's farm, which lies at the corner where the towns of Salem, Montville and East Lyme unite. When he was eleven years of age he removed with his parents to Waterford and here he has resided continuously up to the present time. A young man at the outbreak of the Civil War, heartily in sympathy with the cause of the Union, and fired with the patriotism which swept the North at the firing on Fort Sumter, he enlisted in November, 1861, as a private in the Volunteer Infantry of the 12th Connecticut Regiment, going almost immediately to the fighting line. With his regiment he participated in the following stirring engagements of the war: Georgia Landing, October 27, 1862; Pattersonville, March 27, 1863; B——, April 18, 1863; the Siege of Port Hudson, May 25, July 9, 1863; Winchester, September 19, 1864; Fisher's Hill, September 22, 1864; and Cedar Creek, October 19, 1864. He was twice promoted on the field, and was honorably discharged from the United States service as a commissary sergeant, August 22, 1865. On his return to the North he again took up his residence at the old homestead and here he has since been engaged in farming on a large scale.

Mr. Peabody is a Republican in politics, and has identified himself closely with the affairs of the local organization which has elected him to many important offices. He is a member of Perkins Post, Grand Army of the Republic, and in religion is a Baptist.

In 1870, at Waterford, Connecticut, Charles Henry Peabody was united in marriage with Josephine Douglas, and to them have been born six children: Charles Douglas, who died at the age of fourteen, and is buried at Waterford; Myra, who married the late J. Frank Rogers, of Stony Creek, and has one child, Douglas Francis; Joseph, an engineer; Raymond Avery, born June 29, 1889, and married Mildred Lord; Josephine; and Lucy D.

JOHN EDWIN BURGESS—Since becoming fifteen years of age, John Edwin Burgess has devoted himself to farming and today his property, which he bought in 1899, is regarded as one of the well-conducted places in this region, due in no small part to the tireless energy with which he has devoted himself towards its cultivation.

Philo Burgess, father of John Edwin Burgess, was born in Franklin, Connecticut, and has devoted his entire lifetime to farming. He married Emily Bliven, and to them was born a son, John Edwin, of further mention.

John Edwin Burgess was born at Lebanon, Connecticut, November 4, 1880. He attended the local district school until he was fifteen years of age, when he terminated his studies and went to work upon his father's farm. Here he continued to aid the elder man, in the meantime gaing a wide and extensive knowledge on the subject of farming, and in the short space of four years he had become so well skilled in agricultural methods generally that he rented the George Hewitt farm at Kick Hill, upon which he resided for twenty years. He later purchased his present place, upon which he has continued to reside ever since, and today is reckoned among the most successful farmers of the community. Mr. Burgess has never taken any active part in public affairs, although he displays always a deep interest in the welfare of the town which has been his home for so many years.

Mr. Burgess married (first) Charlotte Hewitt, a native of Lebanon; she died in 1909. To this union were born two children: Maurice, born February 20, 1903; and Edna, born January 11, 1904. Mr. Burgess married (second) Iva Bogue, a native of Montville, and the daughter of Charles and Nellie (Brown) Bogue. Mr. and Mrs. Burgess are the parents of one child, Donald, born May 10, 1912.

JAMES BYRON BRIGHAM is a member of one of the oldest families of Vermont, his great-grandfather, Paul Brigham, having emigrated to that State in his early manhood, making the trip on foot from North Coventry, Connecticut, his wife making the trip on horseback, he driving a number of pigs and other cattle. They settled on what has since been known as Brigham Hill. Paul Brigham served in the Revolutionary War, and for twenty years was governor of the State of Vermont.

James Monroe Brigham, son of Paul Worcester Brigham, and father of James Byron Brigham, was born at Norwich, Vermont, and for many years previous to his death, which occurred in February, 1920, carried on successful farming operations there. He married Harriett Partridge, and to them was born a son, James Byron, of further mention.

James Byron Brigham was born on the old homestead at Norwich, Vermont, June 6, 1883. His childhood was spent on his father's farm, and his spare time was given to aiding the elder man in his work about the place. He continued to reside with his parents until he was twenty years of age, then went to work for Swift & Company. Through these many years he has continued with this organization, and is now, 1921, manager of the New London Tallow Company, at Waterford, Connecticut. Mr. Brigham also owns a place called Whitehall Farm at Waterford, and here he specializes in graded cattle on an extensive scale. Although he has never taken an active part in politics, Mr. Brigham has always taken a keen interest in the Republican party, in which members of his family have been prominent for many generations. He is a member of the Grange and the County Farm Bureau, and gives most generously of his substance to everything which he believes will further civic progress.

Mr. Brigham married (first) Mattie Hutchison, of Hanover, New Hampshire, and to them were born five children: Chester Hutchison, who, during the World War, was stationed at the experimental station at New London, and is now a resident of Waterford; Holland Worcester; Eva Belle; Nina; and James Byron. Mr. Brigham married (second) Minnie Greenhagen, a native of New York City, and they are the parents of one child, Mildred Catherine, born February 15, 1916.

THOMAS ALVIN LYMAN—The entire life of Thomas Alvin Lyman has been spent in the following of agricultural pursuits, his entire interests having been interwoven with the interests of his native place, and to the maintenance and advancement of those interests he has been steadfastly loyal.

Albert G. Lyman, father of Thomas A. Lyman, was born in Lebanon, in 1838, and died there, April 12, 1900. He was a farmer throughout his entire lifetime. He married Lucinda Segar, and to them were born two children: Thomas Alvin, of further mention; and Eugene.

Thomas Alvin Lyman was born in Lebanon, in the part known as "The Hollow," January 29, 1851. He attended the schools of his native place until he was eighteen years of age, when he secured work on a farm in the northern part of the township. At the age of twenty-one he went to South Winsor, continuing his agricultural pursuits, later removing to Lebanon, where he still pursues the same vocation on what is known as "Mariners Corner." In politics he is a staunch Republican, entering with public-spirited interest into the advancement of any cause which promises betterment of municipal government, but studiously refraining from taking any active part in political affairs. In religion he is a Baptist and attends the church of that denomination in Lebanon.

On March 1, 1876, Mr. Lyman was united in marriage with Julia Ely Adams, the daughter of Samuel and Mary (Bailey) Adams, of Willimantic, Connecticut. Mrs. Lyman passed away April 10, 1917. To Mr. and Mrs. Lyman was born one child, Grace, who died at the age of twenty-one years, and is buried in Lebanon Cemetery.

EDWARD ALBERT HOXIE—Among the prominent residents of Lebanon, Connecticut, is Edward Albert Hoxie, who takes a public-spirited interest in every good cause and worthy enterprise, and whose entire life has been devoted to the advancement and maintenance of those interests to which he has always been steadfastly loyal.

Albert Thomas Hoxie, father of the subject of this review, was born in Kingston, Rhode Island, and obtained his education in the schools of his native place, after which he went to work upon his father's farm. His parents came to Lebanon, when he was a boy in school, and bought a farm. Here he continued to follow his agricultural pursuits until his death, which occurred October 13, 1916. He married Mary Elizabeth Tucker, a native of Lebanon, and they were the parents of eight children: Edward Albert, of whom further; Samuel, deceased; Clarence, deceased; Myron, deceased; Frederick; Herbert; Minnie, deceased; and Clarence.

Edward Albert Hoxie was born in Lebanon in 1868. The boy was educated in the schools of his native place, after which he followed in his father's footsteps by continuing in agricultural pursuits. In 1895 he purchased the farm on which he now lives.

In politics, Mr. Hoxie is a staunch Republican, and as a vigilant and attentive observer of men and measures, holding sound opinions and taking liberal views, his ideas carry weight among those with whom he discusses public problems. During the year of 1917 he was elected representative from this district, and in 1919 was assistant superintendent of the House. His people attended the Baptist church of this district.

On February 26, 1890, Edward Albert Hoxie was united in marriage with Lena Maria Peck, a native of Franklin. Mr. and Mrs. Hoxie are the parents of four children: 1. Albert Clifton, born January 24, 1892; he married Dorothy I. Gould, of Woburn, Massachusetts, on April 19, 1916; they have one daughter, Phyllis, born March 4, 1917. 2. Myron Joseph, born December 5, 1893; he married Gladys Mae Clarke, of Liberty Hill, on December 8, 1915, and they have one son, Hermon Clarke, born October 26, 1919. 3. Vera Hulda, born September 20, 1895; she married Frederick F. Manning, of Yantic, on September 20, 1916, and they have two sons, Edward Hoxie Manning, born July 20, 1917, and Harold William Manning, born August 12, 1919. 4. Earle Edward, born March 21, 1901; he married Mary Elizabeth Standish, of Lebanon, June 27, 1922.

JAMES PATRICK DUFFY was born February 13, 1888, at Lebanon, Connecticut, the son of Patrick and Elizabeth (Trainor) Duffy, both natives of Ireland. Patrick Duffy was born March 12, 1841, and came to this country when a young man, locating in Lebanon, where he followed agricultural pursuits throughout his entire lifetime. Mrs. Duffy was born in Monahan county, Ireland, in January, 1861, and now resides with her son, James Patrick Duffy, To Mr. and Mrs. Duffy were born three children: Francis John, December 8, 1884; James Patrick, of further mention; and Elizabeth Ferdinand, deceasd.

James P. Duffy attended the schools of his native place until he was fifteen years of age, when he went to work on his father's farm in Lebanon, and has continued in this particular line of occupation ever since, being numbered among the successful farmers of the community. He has served the town as constable and registrar of voters, and is now (1922) one of its auditors, and aids to his utmost every movement which has for its aim the betterment of civic affairs. A Democrat in politics, he takes an active part in the affairs of the local organization. During the World War he was prominently identified with the various campaigns whose purpose it was to raise necessary funds for carrying on the great work, which illustrates his ever-ready response to any deserving call made upon him. Mr. Duffy is unmarried.

PALMER WILLIAM MINER, son of George W. and Mary A. (Chapman) Miner, was born at the home farm in North Stonington, Connecticut, February 1, 1894. George W. Miner died June 26, 1913. His wife, Mary A. Miner, soon followed, her death occurring March 1, 1916.

Palmer W. Miner was educated in the public schools, finishing in Wheeler High School. With his brother, Herbert Allen Miner, born August 20, 1898, he bought out the other brothers' shares in the home farm. Since then they have added buildings and modern improvements to same. They carry on an extensive farming and dairy business under the well known title, Miner Brothers.

EDWARD H. McCALL.—In the town of Lebanon, Connecticut, there are several attractive looking residences and in one of them dwells Edward H. McCall with his family, he engaging in farming and sometimes taking part in the political affairs of that portion of the State.

The McCall family have every right to be proud of their ancestry, for they belong to the same Revolutionary stock of which the youthful patriot, Nathan Hale, was a member. Though not a lineal descendant of this nobly hanged hero, the McCall family came from a lateral branch, Nathan Hale being the great-uncle of Edward H. McCall's father.

The parents of Edward H. McCall were David Hale McCall, born in Lebanon, and Caroline (Foote) McCall, of Colchester, Connecticut, and their son, Edward H., was born in Lebanon, March 10, 1868. All of his childhood was spent in Lebanon, Connecticut, he attending Norwich Free Academy, and later graduated from Eastman Business College. For two years he taught school. At the expiration of this time, upon the death of his mother, his father having died during his boyhood, he became by inheritance the owner of the old homestead. Mr. McCall has always taken a great interest in the political situation of Lebanon township, and in 1889 he was chosen to represent his district in the State Legislature; also has served on the Board of Assessors. At the present time Mr. McCall has the honor of being one of the selectmen of the village.

Mr. McCall holds membership in two fraternal bodies; he is a third degree Mason, and also is connected with the Norwich Lodge, of Woodmen of the World.

Mr. McCall married Cornelia Louise Brown, of Colchester. She was born March 18, 1867, daughter of John Fred and Nancy (Lombard) Brown. The Brown family for many years were residents of Lebanon township, settling in Lebanon when their children were quite young. Mr. and Mrs. McCall are the parents of four children: 1. Royce Fred, born in 1895. 2. Calvin Hale, born in 1897. 3. Edwin Hobart, born in 1898. 4. Dorothy, born in 1903. The two older sons "did their bit" in the World War, Royce F. in the navy, serving on the United States steamship "Leelandia," and Calvin H. was a member of the Marine Corps in the 6th Regiment, 2nd Division, serving with the Army of Occupation.

JEREMIAH JOSEPH MAHONEY, numbered among the successful farmers of this district, was born at Franklin, August 22, 1880, the son of Cornelius and Catherine (Haley) Mahoney. The boy received his preliminary education in the schools of his native place, after which he entered the Norwich High School, and following graduation went to work upon his fathers farm, being thus employed until he himself inherited the farm in 1913, since which time he has been actively engaged in the management of it. Success has attended his efforts from the first, and his progress is being marked not only by the acquisition of material gains, but also by the formation of many warm friendships. All movements tending toward civic betterment have received from Mr. Mahoney's active interest and energetic co-operation. He was a member of the School Board.

At Norwich, Connecticut, April 19, 1911, Jeremiah Joseph Mahoney was united in marriage with Carrie Ladd, a daughter of Charles Hazen and Rebecca (Steere) Ladd, of Norwich. Mr. and Mrs. Mahoney are the parents of five children: Mary Rebecca, born April 29, 1912; Francis Harold, born December 17, 1914; Jeremiah Joseph, Jr., born November 11, 1915; Catherine, born July 3, 1917; and Sadie Theresa, born September 1, 1919.

JOHN WILLIAM FINEGAN—Left fatherless when an infant of four months, and motherless at the age of nine years, and his school years cut short by the necessity of earning his living, John W. Finegan found himself finally the owner of the Brewster farm, where, for about four years, he had worked as a hired hand. That proud record shows the quality of the man, who for fifty years has been known by the people of the town of Ledyard, Connecticut, and who regard him as one of the leading men of their town. He is the second of the name, his father also being John William Finegan, born in Cork, Ireland, who died in Ledyard in 1870, a farmer, but before coming to Ledyard had been in the paint business in New York City. John W. (1) Finegan married Phoebe Esther (Maine) Harrington, of Ledyard, and they were the parents of a daughter, Sarah Esther Finegan, who died at the age of thirty-four years, and a son, John W. (2), of further mention. The father died in 1870, the mother in 1879. Both John W. and Phoebe Esther (Maine-Harrington) Finegan had been married before, and John W. (2) Finegan has a half-brother, Dr. James Leon Harrington, born in Ledyard, in 1879.

John W. (2) Finegan was born in the town of Ledyard, New London county, Connecticut, September 1, 1869, and there has spent the fifty years of his life which have passed. He attended the public district school, but being early orphaned, his first problem was not an education, but an existence. He began life as a farmer boy, in the employ of James Holdridge, and was employed by several farmers of the town, until finally he entered the employ of William F. Brewster, a farmer. He remained with Mr. Brewster four years, then, in 1892, purchased the farm from his employer, and there yet resides, honored and respected, and one of the substantial men of his town. He is a Republican in politics, and has been collector of taxes for four years. His family are members of Ledyard Grange, No. 167, Patrons of Husbandry; in religious faith the members of the family are Congregationalists.

Mr. Finegan married, December 5, 1892, Henrietta A. Stoddard, born in Groton, Connecticut, November 9, 1874, daughter of James and Anna (Davidson) Stoddard. Mr. and Mrs. Finegan are the parents of four children, all born in the town of Ledyard, New London county: 1. Anna Alice, born October 24, 1893, married Ellsworth Gray, of Ledyard and North Stonington, and they have two children: Anna Alice, and Harold Ellsworth Gray. 2. Grace Lillian, born January 4, 1896, a teacher in the public schools of New London county; she married Frank L. Barlow, April 14, 1921. 3. John William (3), born November 29, 1897, married, November 6, 1920, Catherine Page, of Groton. 4. Carrie Eldora, born July 14, 1900, a stenographer and teacher; she married, June 26, 1922, Harold Mansfield.

WILLIAM A. JOHNSON—Since the inception of his business career, William A. Johnson has been connected with the New York, New Haven & Hartford railroad. Starting as a fireman he has worked his way up to his present position, general yard master at Midway, by means of his own efforts, achieved through sheer dint of American pluck.

Dexter A. Johnson, father of William A. Johnson, was born in Norwich, Connecticut, and there in the public schools obtained his education. He became a painter and followed this trade throughout his entire lifetime. He died in Preston, Connecticut, in 1918, at the age of seventy-six years. During the Civil War he served with the Twenty-sixth Connecticut Infantry, and was honorably discharged as sergeant at the end of the war. Mr. Johnson married Mary E. Van Wagner, who now resides in Preston.

William A. Johnson, fifth child of Dexter A. and Mary E. (Van Wagner) Johnson, was born in Brooklyn, New York, May 2, 1884. He received his education in the public schools of Preston, Connecticut, having been brought there by his parents when he was very young. In 1900 he became a fireman for the New York, New Haven & Hartford railroad, later becoming a brakeman, in which capacity he worked until 1907, when he entered the Midway yard, subsequently being appointed assistant yard master, and in 1914 night yard master. In 1917 he was made general yard master, his present position. He can review his life with satisfaction, having won his way through sheer pluck and that indomitable energy which is the fundamental characteristic of the successful man of today. In politics, Mr. Johnson is a Republican. He affiliates with

Union Lodge, No. 31, Free and Accepted Masons; the Independent Order of Odd Fellows, Fairview Lodge, of New London; and the Yard Masters of America. In religion he is a Methodist and attends the church of this denomination at Preston, Connecticut.

On June 3, 1909, in New London, Connecticut, William A. Johnson was united in marriage with Lula May Oliver. Mr. and Mrs. Johnson are the parents of three children: Samuel T., Gertrude E., and William D.

HENRY PHILIP KAROLI—A lifelong resident of New London county, Connecticut, and now an unusually successful man along agricultural lines, Henry Philip Karoli is a prominent and representative citizen of Ledyard. Mr. Karoli is of German ancestry, his parental grandparents, Peter and Mary Karoli, having spent their lifetime in Germany, their native land.

Philip Karoli, Mr. Karoli's father, was born in Germany, on August 4, 1836, and came to this country when he was a boy of fourteen. He engaged in farming in New London county, and was very successful. He bought the farm now occupied by his son on March 4, 1870. He was a hard-working man and devoted to his family. He married Isabelle Metzger, daughter of Caspar and Elizabeth Metzger, who was born in Greenville, New London county, Connecticut, on December 25, 1841, and now (1922) resides with her son. Philip and Isabelle (Metzger) Karoli were the parents of four children: Elizabeth, deceased; Henry Philip, whose name heads this review; Christie Isabelle, who is now the wife of Arthur E. Robinson, of Gardner, Massachusetts; and Nettie May, who became the wife of Oscar Maine, and has two children: Barbara Karoli, and Elizabeth Isabelle. Philip Karoli died January 1, 1915.

Henry Philip Karoli was born in Greenville, Connecticut, on February 5, 1868. The family removing to Ledyard when he was two and one-half years of age, it was there that he received his education in the public schools of the town. Leaving school at an early age, he helped his father on the farm, the broad acres of which are now his own. In his early manhood, Henry P. Karoli purchased a farm in another part of the town, and leaving the home place, conducted extensive operations there, but after his father's death he sold that place and took over the homestead. He has since bought the old Standish place, near by, and conducts the two farms together.

Mr. Karoli is a man of broad interests and progressive individuality. He is interested in the public welfare, and although caring little for the honors of public office, at one time served on the school committee of the town of Ledyard.

DONAT BOURQUE—Although a native of Canada, Donat Bourque has resided in Baltic, Connecticut, for many years, and since 1906 has been recognized as one of the successful farmers of the region, for since taking up his residence in this community, he has instinctively interested himself in the affairs of the town.

Julian Bourque, father of Donat Bourque, was born in St. Charles, Canada, in 1833. At the age of twenty-six years he came to Baltic, where he continued to reside until his death in 1867. He married Miss A. Jefferson, who was also a native of Canada, and to them were born eleven children, of whom were: Julian, Henry, Virginia, Octavia, Delia, Louise, Josephine, and Donat, of further mention.

Donat Bourque was born at St. Charles, Province of Quebec, Canada, March 10, 1851, and was brought by his parents to Baltic when he was eight years of age. He commenced his education in the schools of his native place and upon reaching Baltic he entered the local schools, which he continued to attend until he was fourteen years of age. After finishing his studies he secured employment in various mills, working in different capacities until 1906, when he purchased his present farm, the Silas Frink farm of 235 acres, upon which he has continued to reside up to the present time, devoting himself entirely to the cultivation of his property, which he has brought to a highly productive state.

Mr. Bourque married Euphenia Chartier, a Canadian by birth, and to them have been born six children: Delsie, deceased; Leorge, deceased; Adolph, deceased; Eugene J.; Albert; and Joseph. The family are members of St. Mary's Roman Catholic Church of Baltic, Connecticut.

DESIRE CHARRON was born in the Province of Quebec, Canada, February 28, 1858. He was the son of Desire and Adele (Shepard) Charron, the former a native of Canada, died August 15, 1913, at Baltic, Connecticut, the latter, also a native of Canada, died in 1905, at the age of sixty-seven years. Desire Charron was their first son.

When but six years of age the lad was brought by his parents to Baltic, where he attended school for a very short time. He then went to Brandon, Vermont, later returning to Baltic, where he secured work in the mills. For twenty-two years he was foreman for the Baltic Mills Company, which position he resigned one year ago, 1921. Two years earlier, in 1919, he had established a variety store, and this he is successfully conducting at the present time. In politics, Mr. Charron is a Republican, and takes a keen interest in the affairs of the local organization, although he has never sought public office.

Mr. Charron married Cornelia Richard, a native of the Province of Quebec, Canada, her birth having occurred there January 10, 1858. Mr. and Mrs. Charron are the parents of the following children: Delia, Delena, Desire, Theodore, Thomas, Cornelia, Sophia, Alphonso, Rose, Charles, Arthur, Elizabeth, Eli A., Walter A., Clifford, and two who died when very young.

Mr. Charron is in truth a self-made man, the architect of his own fortune, the position which he holds today being the result of his own tireless energy. As a private citizen he has ever taken his share in the burdens of the community, serving it with faithfulness and unsparing zeal, and he is held in the highest esteem by his fellow-men.

ORIN FULLER LAMB was born in Mystic, Connecticut, October 10, 1895, the son of Denison and Alice (Fuller) Lamb, both natives of Mystic, Connecticut. Denison Lamb obtained his education in the district school of his native place. For thirty years of his lifetime he was a fisherman, but the latter part of his life, and until his death in January, 1916, he was a carpenter. He died in Mystic. To Mr. and Mrs. Lamb were born five children, Orin Fuller Lamb, of further mention, being the eldest child.

The education of Orin F. Lamb was received in the public schools of Mystic. After graduating from the Mystic High School in 1913, the business of life began for the boy and he went to work for Samuel Girven, of Westerly, Rhode Island, where he gained a thorough knowledge of the repairing of motorcycles, and in 1917 became a tester at the New London Ship and Engine Company, New London, Connecticut. Here he continued until August 5, 1918, when he was drafted into the service of the United States army, being assigned to the 102nd Replacement Regiment at Camp Upton, Long Island, later being transferred to the 80th Division overseas, leaving for France in September, 1918, and from the latter part of September until December 8, 1918, was in training. On December 8, 1918, he was appointed a motorcycle despatch carrier in France. He returned to this country in July, 1919, and received his honorable discharge from the service at Camp Mills, Long Island, July 26, 1919. After his discharge he came to Norwich, and on October 1, 1919, became associated with James P. Donovan, of whom mention is made elsewhere in this work, and opened a motorcycle shop at No. 48 Water street, which is their present location. The concern has the agency for the Harley Davidson motorcycles. The enterprise is proving to be a highly successful venture, and is rapidly and consistently developing until it is now one of the largest of its kind in the city.

In politics, Mr. Lamb is an Independent, and has not identified himself with any political party, preferring to remain free from all partisan influences in the exercise of his own judgment on public issues. He is an attendant of the First Baptist Church of Mystic, and is unmarried.

ELON RAY MANNING was born in Lebanon, Connecticut, January 30, 1877, the son of Nathaniel and Harriet (Pember) Manning. Nathaniel Manning was born in the old homestead at Lebanon, and died there August 12, 1920. The Manning family have resided in this locality for many years, Nathaniel Manning being the fourth generation to reside in the old home.

The education of Elon Ray Manning was obtained in the select school at Lebanon and the grammar school at Norwich, Connecticut. After terminating his studies, he decided to follow agricultural pursuits and went to work upon his father's farm. In politics, Mr. Manning affiliates with the Republican party, but is no office seeker, preferring to devote his entire time to his business cares.

Mr. Manning was united in marriage, January 31, 1898, with Lillian E. Stark, and they are the parents of five children: Alma Harriet, born February 12, 1900, associated with C. A. C. at Storrs, Connecticut; Edmund Nathaniel, born March 3, 1902, and is now in the United States navy; John, born October 6, 1903; Raymond, born September 18, 1909; and Cora, born June 18, 1913.

FRANK ARTHUR SISK—Since the inception of his business career, Mr. Sisk has been identified with the drug business, and since 1916 has been owner and manager of the drug store on Franklin street, Norwich, Connecticut, where he has built up a large and prosperous drug business.

Thomas Sisk, father of Frank Arthur Sisk, was born in New London, Connecticut, and has spent his entire life in that city. He is a painter by trade, and after having been associated with his father, John Sisk, for many years, he established himself in the paint business, being thus engaged ever since. He is a Democrat in politics, and a Roman Catholic in religion. He married Mary Keating, a native of England; she died in New London, in 1895. To Mr. and Mrs. Sisk were born six children, three of whom are still living: Mary, wife of Frederick W. Golden, of New London, Connecticut; Thomas H., a druggist, of New London, who married Elizabeth Denning, a resident of Brattleboro, Vermont; and Frank Arthur, of further mention.

Frank Arthur Sisk obtained his education in the public schools of New London, and after spending two years in the high school there, entered upon his business career at the age of sixteen years, in the capacity of clerk, with the druggist, E. A. Small, on Broad street. Two years later he secured a position with Starr Brothers, druggists, at New London, and remained there for six years, after which he passed examinations as a regesitered pharmacist, and in the spring of 1913 removed to Norwich, Connecticut, where he became associated with the Lee Osgood drug store on Main street, acting in the capacity of registered pharmacist for three years. In 1916 he opened his present drug store on Franklin street, and a successful druggist has been his record ever since. Mr. Sisk has held all the offices in the Connecticut State Board of Pharmacy, and on June 1, 1920, was elected first vice-president of the Norwich Druggists' Association. In politics, he is a Democrat, but is no office seeker. He is affiliated with the Knights of Columbus, holding the office of faithful pilot, and is past faithful controller for the district of Norwich. He is also a member of the Benevolent and Protective Order of Elks, Lodge No. 430.

Mr. Sisk was united in marriage on October 7, 1914, with Julia Anthier, dughter of Albert and Julia (Brand) Anthier, her father a prominent grocer in Sprague, Connecticut, for many years, where he died. Mr. and Mrs. Sisk are the parents of three children: Frank A., Jr., born October 6, 1915; William Brand, born July 28, 1917; and Julia Alberta, born January 24, 1920.

JOSEPH PEABODY—Among the progressive and successful farmers of Waterford, New London county, Connecticut, is Joseph Peabody, owner and manager of a seven hundred acre farm in the Gilead district, near Waterford. The family is of English origin, Joseph Peabody, grandfather of Mr. Peabody, having lived and died in England, where he married a daughter of the Burton family and became the father of seven sons and one daughter. Of these, Joseph and Thomas came to America together, the latter settling in Canada, where a number of his descendants still reside.

Joseph Peabody was born at Waterford, England, in February, 1808, and died at the age of eighty-seven years. He came to the United States at the age of twenty-one, and engaged for some time in the old whaling trade, but at the time of his marriage left the adventurous life of the sea and bought a farm at Salem, Connecticut, later removing to Waterford, where he farmed for years, and where he finally died. He married Katherine Baker, daughter of Colonel Baker, of Revolutionary War fame, and they became the parents of six children: Thomas, who died in East Lyme, where he was engaged in farming, married Lucy Jane Herrick; Joseph, of further mention; Elizabeth, married Alonzo Chappell, of Waterford; Charles H., married Josephine Douglas, of Waterford, where he is engaged in farming; Sophia, married Thomas Crandell, but is now a widow residing in East Lyme; and Jane A., married David H. Geer.

Joseph Peabody, son of Joseph and Katherine (Baker) Peabody, was born at Salem, Connecticut, March 16, 1835, where, until he was about fifteen years of age, he attended the public schools of his native town. He then went with his family to Waterford, Connecticut, and until he was twenty-one worked on his father's farm in the Gilead district. At this time his father hired for one year the farm which Mr. Peabody now owns, and young Joseph began farming for Squire Nathaniel Chapman, working one season for eighteen dollars a month, which was two dollars a month more than any other farmer was receiving in the town of Waterford. At the end of the season he, with Samuel Williams, operated the Jordan grist mill for a year, and then for two years and a half hired the mill and ran it on his own account. He went back to farming, however, and was so engaged when the Civil War began. Answering to the call of the Federal Government, he enlisted in Company A, Twenty-sixth Regiment, Connecticut Volunteers, and served in the New Orleans area and around the Gulf, being commissioned second lieutenant. He served through the bloody campaign of Port Hudson, the siege of which began May 27, and ended July 8, in the second year of the war. During the battles associated with the siege of Port Hudson, the captain and first lieutenant of Mr. Peabody's company were seriously wounded and Mr. Peabody took charge, leading his company to victory. The most desperate fighting of the siege occurred May 27, and June 14, 1863, and on August 15, 1863, Mr. Peabody was honorably discharged. Returning to the Gilead section of Waterford, he worked out on neighboring farms for the remainder of the summer and then went up into the copper mines around Lake Wisconsin, where he remained for eight months and then returned to the Great Neck section of Waterford, where his father was farming. Two years later he bought the place which he now owns and works, and which he has gradually enlarged until it has absorbed three farms besides the original one and now comprises some seven hundred acres. The farm is a thoroughly modern one and splendidly equipped for large-scale scientific farming. One of the finest herds of graded cattle in the county is owned by Mr. Peabody, and he takes great interest in the live stock and dairying part of his modern plant.

With so large an establishment to claim his time and attention, he still finds time for other interests. Always interested in the welfare of his community, he has served as second selectman in the town of Waterford for twenty-one terms, and was sent as a representative to the State Legislature in 1890.

Mr. Peabody married, February 8, 1866, Marietta Austin, daughter of David and Elizabeth (Beebe) Austin, born April 6, 1843, and they became the parents of four children: Mary Elizabeth, born at Waterford, Connecticut, married, and has three children: Marietta, Grace, and Ralph; Austin, born in December, 1869, at Waterford; Elmer, born in December, 1872, married Jane Oger, of New London; and Charles William, born August 10, 1882, married Clara Oger, and has four children: Lois, Erma, Joseph, and Wendell.

ROBERT LEWIS FRENCH—The business which now supplies Mr. French with occupation and livelihood, photography, was a fad of his boyhood days, the little outfit which he had for his own pleasure and to which he added a small room for developing films for his friends having grown into a modern plant, where he specializes in commercial photography. He is a son of Rev. Charles Leonard French, who was born in Plainfield, Connecticut, and died in Montville, New London county, Connecticut. When young he went West, and after graduation from Lawrence University taught school for seven years. He then studied for the ministry at the Chicago Theological Seminary, and after ordination to the ministry of the Congregational church, was seated over a church in Providence, Illinois. In 1907 he returned to his native State as pastor of the First Church of Griswold. Later he was pastor of the church at Montville, and there died.

Robert Lewis French, son of Rev. Charles Leonard and Harriet French, was born at Whitewater, Wisconsin, July 26, 1900, and there spent his first seven years. In 1907 the family moved to Jewett City, town of Griswold, New London county, and there resided four years, moving to Montville, Connecticut, in 1911. The lad, Robert L., attended public schools in all these places, also pursued a course at business college and attended Cushing Academy. While at the academy he became very much interested in amateur photography, although he was preparing for a musical career, but the illness, and later death, of his father changed his plans and he left school, returned home and began preparing for a business career. Photography naturally attracted him and he opened a small studio for developing and printing the kodak pictures of amateurs. This grew into a permanent photographic business, and he is well located in Uncasville, Connecticut, doing a good business in commercial photography. He has won high commendation for his splendid work and is well patronized.

SIDNEY ASHBEY BROWN is one of the best known men of New London county, Connecticut. He has given many years of his life to the public service and is now the high sheriff of his native county—New London. He is a son of Thomas and Mary Abby (Clark) Brown, his father born in the town of Stonington, but later residing in Mystic, Connecticut, where he died in 1862. Mary A. (Clark) Brown was born in Groton, and died in Mystic, Connecticut, in 1874.

Sidney A. Brown was born in Mystic, town of Groton, New London county, Connecticut, June 24, 1858, and there was educated in the public schools. He was employed as grocer's clerk, and in various positions until 1881, when he was appointed turnkey at the New London county jail, at Norwich. In 1882 he left Mystic for Norwich, and in 1883 was turnkey at the New London jail, continuing until 1895. He was out of the public service two years, returning in 1897 as deputy United States internal revenue collector for the New London district, serving two years. He then served the city of New London as tax collector until 1905, when he resigned to accept appointment to the office of high sheriff of New London county. This appointment was made February 2, 1905, by the Connecticut Legislature, to fill out the unexpired term of George O. Jackson, who died in office. In 1907 Mr. Brown was elected sheriff by the people, and every four years since that date they have honored their fellow-townsman in a similar manner, he having now filled the sheriff's office most ably and satisfactorily for sixteen years, 1905-1921.

Sheriff Brown is a Republican in politics; member of the Second Congregational Church, the Thames Club, the Benevolent and Protective Order of Elks, the Knights of Pythias, and in Masonry holds the thirty-second degree of the Ancient Accepted Scottish Rite. He is very popular, both as official and citizen, and when in 1911 the Republican ticket was engulfed in a sea of adverse ballots, Sheriff Brown was the only Republican on this ticket who survived, and he was carried through by his many Democratic friends.

Mr. Brown married, at New London county, October 13, 1894, Ella E. Hawkins, born in Griswold, Connecticut, daughter of Frank and Susan (Rood) Hawkins, her father born in Plainfield, Connecticut, and was, for sixteen years, sheriff of New London county. Susan (Rood) Hawkins was born in the town of Griswold, New London county, and after their marriage they resided in Jewett City, Connecticut.

JAMES ELIJAH LATHROP—The American ancestor of the Lathrops of New London county was Rev. John Lathrop, who came from England in 1634, a victim of religious persecution. His wife died in England, but his children came with their father, and through his son, Samuel, descent is traced in this branch. Samuel Lathrop was the first of his family to settle in Connecticut, he coming in 1648 to New London, but going thence to Norwich, where he died in 1700, leaving a widow, the second Mrs. Samuel Lathrop, who survived her husband thirty-four years, dying in 1734, aged one hundred and two. Samuel Lathrop was a man of importance in the colony, a housebuilder, farmer and landowner, magistrate and constable. His first wife was Elizabeth Scudder, and they were the parents of nine children. Descent in this branch is traced through Israel, the sixth child.

Israel Lathrop was born in October, 1659, died in Norwich, Connecticut, March 28, 1733, a man of thrift and substance. He married, April 8, 1686, Rebecca Bliss, daughter of Thomas Bliss, of Saybrook and Norwich. They were the parents of ten children, Samuel, the fourth child being head of the fourth generation.

Samuel Lathrop was born in Norwich, July 12, 1692, and after his marriage, June 26, 1712, to Elizabeth Waterman, located in the town of Bozrah, New London county.

Captain Elisha Lathrop, eldest son of Samuel and Elizabeth (Waterman) Lathrop, was born July 13, 1713, was killed by a falling tree at Lebanon, New Hampshire, July 2, 1787. He lived in Bozrah prior to his removal to Lebanon. He married (first), January 31, 1732, Margaret Sluman, who died October 10, 1742, leaving sons: Elias, Elijah, and Lebbeus.

He married (second) Hannah Hough, who died in Hanover, New Hampshire, January 16, 1807. This branch descends through Lebbeus, third son of Captain Elisha Lathrop and his first wife, Margaret Sluman.

Lebbeus Lathrop was born in Norwich, New London county, Connecticut, January 3, 1739, but did not go to New Hampshire with his father, settling in the town of Bozrah, where he married, lived his entire life, and died, leaving a daughter, Polly, and a son, Lebbeus (2). Lebbeus (2) was born in Bozrah, in 1780, and died in Lebanon, New London county, Connecticut, January 25, 1866. He was a prosperous farmer in the southern part of the town of Bozrah, but late in life moved to Lebanon in the same county. He married Lucretia Maples, born April 29, 1781, daughter of William and Joanna (Stebbins) Maples. They were the parents of eight children, descent in this line being traced through their eldest son and third child.

Elisha Lathrop was born in the town of Bozrah, New London county, Connecticut, in October, 1808, and settled in the town of Lebanon in the same county. He married Caroline Avery, and they were the parents of Elijah Willard Lathrop, of the ninth, and grandparents of James Elijah Lathrop, of the tenth generation of Lathrops in New England, and the ninth generation in New London county, Conecticut.

Elijah Willard Lathrop was born in the town of Bozrah, New London county, Connecticut, and educated in the public schools. He was a cripple, but has always led an active life, following farming in his home town and elsewhere, ran a tin peddlers wagon through the county, and in 1874 bought the farm in the town of Montville upon which he still resides. There all his children were born, and there he has prospered abundantly. He married Eliza Gifford Pierce, born in Montville, New London county, and they are the parents of five children: James Elijah, of further mention; Charlotte Hannah, married Captain William Denison, of Norwich, and has two son: Grant, and Gilbert Denison; Earl Chapell, now a farmer, married Christine Tinker, and has two sons: Melvin, and Merril Lathrop; Grace Seigfried, married William Sanders, of Norwich, Connecticut, and has two sons: William Russell, and Kenneth Lathrop Sanders; Lawrence Nelson, residing at home.

James Elijah Lathrop, of the tenth generation of the family founded in New England by Rev. John Lathrop, was born in the town of Montville, New London county, Connecticut, March 12, 1876. He attended public schools and remained his father's farm assistant until of age, and thereafter, until his marriage in 1900. He then rented a farm in Bozrah which he cultivated until March, 1908, when he bought the James Allen farm in the Raymond Hill district of the town of Montville, and there has since engaged in general farming and stock breeding with most satisfactory results. His farm contains one hundred and fifty acres, is well improved, and shows in its thrifty appearance the careful progressive character of the owner.

Mr. Lathrop married, in Montville, September 20, 1900, Belle Williams Austin, born in Montville, daughter of Frank Ezekiel and Susan Williams (Swan) Austin, of ancient Colonial family. Mr. and Mrs. Lathrop are the parents of four children, and they are the eleventh American generation: Austin Douglass, born in Bozrah, Connecticut, August 18, 1906; Agnes Mary, born in Montville, Connecticut, August 6, 1908; Tryon Avery, born in Montville, August 9, 1911; Theron Merril, born in Montville, August 1, 1917. Mr. Lathrop is a member of the Baptist church of Salem, and in politics, Republican. Mr. Lathrop is one of the largest breeders of Jersey cattle in New London county, his stock all registered thoroughbreds. His Jersey bull, Laddie, won the grand championship at the New London County Fair in 1920. He also exhibited two herds, one in the young Jersey herd class, and one in the old herd class, winning first prize in both classes. At the same fair, he took first prize with his champion Berkshire boar. He is a member of New London County Farm Bureau; is thoroughly modern and progressive in his business and in his citizenship.

THE AUSTIN FAMILY—Mrs. Belle Williams (Austin) Lathrop is a descendant of Robert Austin, of England, whose name appears in a list of sixty-five persons who in 1661 were residents of Newport, Portsmouth, and Kingstown, and were to have lots in the new settlement of Westerly, Rhode Island. Robert Austin did not settle in Westerly, however, but in 1687 was an inhabitant of Kingstown. The genealogist of the Austin family says, "Many facts seem to warrant the assumption that he was the father of Jeremiah Austin, of Kingston and Exeter, Edward and Joseph Austin, of Kingstown, and John Austin, of Kingstown." East Greenwich and West Greenwich from Jeremiah Austin descended the Exeter family of that name. The line of descent to Mrs. Lathrop is thus traced from Robert Austin, the founder, through his son, Jeremiah, of Kingstown, North Kingstown, and Exeter, Rhode Island, and his wife, Elizabeth; their son, Robert Austin, a shoemaker and farmer, probably the first Austin to settle permanently in Westerly, Rhode Island, and his wife, Hannah Crandall; their son, Jeremiah Austin, born 1730, died December 20, 1815, a member of the Society of Friends, and his wife, Margaret Congdon; their son, Ezekiel Austin, of North Kingstown, and his wife, ——— Champlain; their son, Champlain Austin, a farmer of Hope Valley, Rhode Island, and his wife, ——— Hall; their son, Ezekiel Austin, born in the town of Foster, Rhode Island, and lived in Montville, Connecticut, and his wife, Suzanna Douglass; their son, Frank Ezekiel, born in Waterford, Connecticut, and his wife, Susan Williams

Swan; their daughter, Belle Williams Austin, wife of James E. Lathrop.

Ezekiel Austin of the seventh generation was a stone mason by trade, and finally settled in the town of Montville, New London county, Connecticut, where he died. His wife, Suzanna Douglass, born in Waterford, Connecticut, was a daughter of Elisha Avery and Margaret (Dart) Douglass, and of ancient New England county family, of Scotch descent.

Their son, Frank Ezekiel Austin, was born in Waterford, New London county, Connecticut, but when nine years of age was brought by his parents to the town of Montville, and there he has since lived. He became a farmer and followed that occupation for several years, but is now a retired star route mail carrier. He married Susan Williams Swan, born in Montville, and they are the parents of Belle Williams (Austin) Lathrop.

HARRY EDGAR VAN HOFF—Inheriting from both parents fine characteristics and pride of family, Harry Edgar Van Hoff is the descendent of ancestors whose lines were cast within the charmed and sheltered circle which marks the class of those born to ease and culture.

The paternal grandfather of Harry Edgar Van Hoff was Frink Van Hoff, one of a long succession of coal barons in Germany. The family of Van Hoff had held coal concessions from the reigning house of Germany for generations, and were held in great esteem by those in high position.

Frink Van Hoff, Jr., father of Harry Edgar Van Hoff, was the son of Frink Van Hoff, and was born in Cologne, Germany, in 1849. In early manhood he left the Fatherland to come to the United States in order that he might carve out for himself a future in a new environment. Landing in New York City, the young man entered into business there, making his home in Union Hill, New Jersey. He took up the work of interior decorating along the lines of frescoing and art plastering, being a pioneer in that form of wall and ceiling finishing. For three years Frink Van Hoff lived at Union Hill, then went to New York City to reside, continuing his business for twenty years, then, becoming interested in foreign imports, he carried on that line of business for the next ten years. His health breaking down at that time, Mr. Van Hoff returned to Europe, touring the Continent and seeking out specialists in the cure of cancer in the hope of regaining his health, but finally, coming back to New York, he died there in 1908, at the age of fifty-nine years.

While on his way homeward from Europe, Mr. Van Hoff, with his wife and three eldest children, took passage in a sailing vessel named "Amsterdam," and were wrecked off the coast of the Sable Islands, he and his family being among the few survivors. The wife of Frink Van Hoff, Johanna Albertdina Plogue, was born in Amsterdam, Holland, in November, 1853, the daughter of General William Albert Plogue, of the army of Holland, who died in 1911, at the advanced age of one hundred and one years, in Holland. His wife survived him for nine months, then died at her home there, aged ninety-six years. She and her husband were married in Holland and lived there all their lives.

Mr. and Mrs. Frink Van Hoff had a family of eight children: 1. Frink George, born in Union Hill, New Jersey, a business man in New York City. 2. William Albert, born in Union Hill; he is married and has two children: Allan and Elmer. 3. Johanna Albertdina, born in New York City, the wife of Louis Frederick Rockwell, of Redlands, California; they have two children: Stanton Edgar and Harold Albert. 4. Harriet Ellinore, born in New York City; she married Kerwin Holmes Fulton, of Nova Scotia. 5. Charles, died in childhood. 6. Henrietta, also died in childhood. 7. Harry Edgar, of whom further. 8. Virginia Dimmock, now the wife of Major Arthur H. Miller, in the regular army of the United States, stationed at Washington, District of Columbia; they have one child, Harriet Miller.

Harry Edgar Van Hoff was born in New York City, August 28, 1882. He is now located in New London, Connecticut, where he is a merchant, having his place of business on State street, his home being at No. 317 William street. He is greatly interested in the public affairs of New London, and is one of the board of directors of the Rotary Club, of which he is a member. He is not active in politics, is not connected with any party, but votes an independent ticket.

Harry Edgar Van Hoff married Leonora Beatrice Van Sickler, born October 22, 1888, in Canada, in the Province of Quebec. She is the daughter of William A. and Mary (Holland) Van Sickler, of Johnstown, New York, and is one of a family of six children: 1. Clara, born in Johnstown, New York, the wife of Charles A. Ball, of that city; they had one child, who died in infancy. 2. William, born in Johnstown; he is married and has one child. 3. Ellinore, also born in Johnstown, and is the wife of Edward E. Hammond, of Albany, New York. 4. A child who died in infancy. 5. Another child who died in boyhood. 6. Leonora Beatrice, wife of Harry Edgar Van Hoff. Mr. and Mrs. Van Hoff have two children: Kerwin Harry, born September 20, 1912, at Johnstown; Carroll Johnson, born in Johnstown, New York, January 22, 1917; and Mrs. Van Hoff's family, the Van Sicklers, are of very ancient ancestry both in the United States and in Europe, their lineage being traced back to some of the oldest families in the Old World. Quite some time and money have been expended in a quest to unearth their coat-of-arms, but to date it has been of no avail. The city of Johnstown, New York, was named after Sir William Johnson, the closest associate and friend of the great-great-grandfather of the wife of Harry Edgar Van Hoff, Mrs. Leonora Beatrice (Van Sickler) Van Hoff.

EARL ERNEST GILBERT is numbered among the representative citizens of Jewett City, Connecticut. In addition to his prominent connection with the business life of the community, he is influentially associated with the various other elements pertaining to her welfare and advancement.

Seth C. Gilbert, father of Earl Ernest Gilbert, was born in the township of Killingly, Connecticut, and obtained his education in the district school there, after which he served an apprenticeship as a millwright and worked at that trade throughout his lifetime. He died in Danielson, Connecticut, August 16, 1911. He married Harriett F. Cook. Mrs. Gilbert is still living and resides with her son, Earl Ernest. To Mr. and Mrs. Gilbert were born six children: Walter C., who resides at Derby, Connecticut; Frederick H., married Grace Jeffery; Bertha O., married Frank Spalding, of Brooklyn, Connecticut; Martha O., married Allen White, of Norwich, Connecticut; Earl Ernest, of further mention; and Maud A., who married Edward Beebe, of New London, Connecticut.

Earl Ernest Gilbert was born in Danielson, Connecticut, April 10, 1884, and received his education in the public schools of his native place and the high school at Killingly. After completing his studies he became associated with his brother, Frederick H., a general contractor of Jewett City, and was thus engaged until 1915, when he bought the undertaking business of F. H. and F. W. Tillinghast, and established himself in this particular line, in which he has continued ever since. Together, with this enterprise, he bought his brother's contracting business in April, 1919, in which he also is meeting with great success, being recognized as a representative of one of the largest contracting organizations in eastern Connecticut.

The political allegiance of Mr. Gilbert is given to the Republican party, and at present he is secretary of the Board of Education of Griswold township. In religious faith he is a Baptist and attends the church of that denomination at Jewett City. He affiliates with Mt. Vernon Lodge, No. 95, Free and Accepted Masons; and with Reliance Lodge, No. 29, Independent Order of Odd Fellows, of which he is past noble grand.

On December 6, 1912, Mr. Gilbert was united in marriage with Emma Babcock, of Jewett City, daughter of Albert H. and Ellen (Durr) Babcock. Mr. and Mrs. Gilbert are the parents of two children: Mildred O., and Earl Ernest, Jr.

Happily gifted in disposition and taste, enterprising and original in business methods, personally liked most by those who know him best, and as frank in declaring his principles as he is sincere in maintaining them, Earl Ernest Gilbert's career is marked by the appreciation of men whose good opinion is best worth having.

DR. CALVIN RAWSON MAIN—This branch of the Main family is known as the Ledyard branch, Thomas (4) Main, great-grandfather of Calvin Rawson Main, and of the sixth generation of the family founded in Stonington by Ezekiel Main, having settled in the town of Ledyard, where his son, William Leeds Main, was rated as the largest landowner and the wealthiest man in Ledyard. He was the father of John L. Main, farmer, Civil War veteran, and father of Calvin Rawson Main, a farmer of Ledyard and extensive fruit grower.

(I) Ezekiel Main, of the first generation, made permanent residence in Stonington, Connecticut, in 1670, receiving a land grant from the town in 1672. He bought land, and in 1680 received another grant, his property then lying along the Shunoc river, on the south of what is now North Stonington. He was admitted to the Stonington church, September 3, 1676, and died June 19, 1714. By his wife, Mary, he had born to him three sons: Ezekiel, Jeremiah, of whom further; and Thomas; and three daughters: Mary, Phoebe, and Hannah.

(II) Jeremiah Main married, October 11, 1692, a widow, Ruth Brown, who with her daughter, Ruth, were admitted to the First Church of Stonington, and were baptized July 16, 1699. Descent follows through their eldest son, Deacon Thomas.

(III) Deacon Thomas Main was born July 19, 1700, and died in 1771. He married, April 20, 1720, Ann Brown, daughter of Eleazer and Ann (Pendleton) Brown. She died March 1, 1766, the mother of nine children, including a son, Thomas (2).

(IV) Thomas (2) Main was born in Stonington, February 12, 1721, and there spent his entire life. He married Mary Pendleton, February 3, 1742, and they were the parents of four children, including a son, Thomas (3).

(V) Thomas (3) Main was born in Stonington, August 8, 1747, and resided there, a prosperous farmer, until his death. He married Dolly Woodward, and they had eight children, among them a son, Thomas (4).

(VI) Thomas (4) Main was born at the old home in Stonington, but when a young man settled in the town of Ledyard in the same county, where he died, aged eighty-seven years. He was a man of powerful physique, a hard worker, and a prosperous farmer. He was a Democrat and held several town offices, his genial manners rendering him very popular. He married Lois Brown, and they were the parents of sixteen children, all of whom grew to mature years and married, except Nathaniel, the eleventh child, who remained on the old homestead in Ledyard all his life, and died unmarried. All were the parents of children (one having a family of ten) except Thomas B., the eldest, who married Lydia Hall, and died without children. The fourth child and son was William Leeds Main, head of the seventh generation in the branch, father of John L. Main and grandfather of Calvin R. Main.

(VII) William Leeds Main was born in the town of Ledyard, New London county, Connecticut, July 4, 1812, and died there June 22, 1890. During his active years he operated a general store in Ledyard, a grist mill, a saw mill and was a large landowner. Energetic, conscientious, and upright, he prospered abundantly, but always in honorable undertakings, for he held his word sacred, and rendered and demanded strict justice. He was a loyal friend, and freely extended a helping hand to others less fortunate than himself. He held several town offices, and at one time represented the Ledyard district in the State Legislature. He married, February 26, 1837, Sarah A. Frink, born April 11, 1818, and died October 30, 1859, daughter of Zachariah and Phoebe E. (Holmes) Frink. William L. and Sarah A. (Frink) Main were the parents of eleven children: 1. Sarah Maria, married David Boss. 2. John L., of further mention. 3. Leeds, married Sarah Holdridge. 4. Phoebe E., married (first) John Finnegan, and (second) William Harrington. 5. Laura H., who never left the homestead. married Sarah Holdridge. 4. Phoebe E., married William Richmond. 8. Alonzo, married Ethel Main. 9. Melissa, twin with Alonzo; married Joseph E. Holdridge. 10. Horace H., married Phoebe Partelo. 11. Amos, married Lucy Madison.

(VIII) John L. Main, eldest son of William Leeds and Sarah A. (Frink) Main, was born in Ledyard, New London county, Connecticut, August 25, 1841. He spent his entire life as a farmer, and died in February, 1916, and is buried in the town of Preston. He served with the Second Regiment, Connecticut Volunteer Infantry, and was with the Army of the Potomac in its campaigns until injured by a falling tent pole. He married Phoebe Frink, born in North Stonington, in March, 1845, died in October, 1918, and is buried in Preston county. She was the daughter of Thomas and Sarah (Hopkins) Frink, her father being a Union soldier, who died from his hardship and experience endured while in the service. John L. and Phoebe E. (Frink) Main were the parents of seven children: William O., deceased; John I.; Sadie E.; Calvin R., of further mention; Nellie M.; Melissa A.; and Grace E.

(IX) Calvin Rawson Main, of the ninth generation of the family in New London county, Connecticut, was born in the town of Ledyard, June 15, 1872, his birthplace being about one mile from his present farm and residence. He was educated in the public schools and after completing his own study, taught the winter terms in the district school. He continued this until 1899, when at the age of twenty-seven he entered the Plute Homeopathic Medical School at Cincinnati, Ohio, whence he was graduated M. D., class of 1902. He practiced for two years after graduation in Warren county, Ohio, but his own health breaking, he withdrew from practice and spent two months at Hot Springs, Arkansas, then, in 1905, returned to the old farm in Ledyard. Outdoor work and exercise quickly built him up and he later purchased his present farm, not far from his birthplace.

Dr. Main has never returned to active practice, but is well known for his extensive orchards and his high-grade cattle. He is at present a member of the Board of Selectmen, and has served his town as assessor, member of the School Board and Board of Relief.

Dr. Main married Gertrude Kenneth, born in New York City, daughter of Rev. Albert and Elizabeth (Roycroft) Kenneth. Dr. and Mrs. Main are the parents of four children: 1. Kenneth Walton, born October 3, 1900. 2. Calvin Rawson (2), born July 6, 1903. 3. Caroline Elizabeth, born April 19, 1905. 4. Robert Winston, born October 21, 1908.

OLIVER M. BELLEFLEUR—Among the younger men of Norwich who are placing the city in the front line of business progress is Oliver M. Bellefleur, whose up-to-date drug store at No. 40 Spaulding street, is one of the dependable establishments of this nature. Mr. Bellefleur's personal history is of interest to every one who knows him in a business way.

Of French descent, as is indicated by the name, Mr. Bellefleur's father, Oliver L. Bellefleur, was born in Manchester, New Hampshire, on August 3, 1857. He has for many years been a resident of Taftville, where he has carried on the drug business in which he is now assisted by his son. He married Telouise Goulet, who was born in 1856.

Oliver M. Bellefleur was born in Taftville, in the suburbs of Norwich, on November 13, 1892. He received his early education in the public schools of the vicinity, following which he continued his studies at the Norwich Free Academy. For his technical study he went to the Massachusetts College of Pharmacy, and there prepared for the career in which he has made such a promising beginning.

The urgent call of humanity, to which so many thousands of our young men responded, reached Mr. Bellefleur at the outset of his career. He enlisted during the World War in the Medical Corps at Boston, Massachusetts, was assigned to General Hospital No. 14, Oglethorpe, Georgia, was later transferred to the Hook-Worm Survey Corps, and still later was detailed to the Officers' Training School of the United States Infantry. He was discharged on November 30, 1918, and returned to Norwich, where he again took up his interrupted work, and has since been associated with his father in the drug business. Mr. Bellefleur is interested in every phase of public progress, civic, State, and National. He has aligned himself with the Republican party, and bears a part in every movement for the public good.

HARRY JOSEPH MORSE, proprietor of the extensive electrical engineering business of Olsen & Morse since the withdrawal of his partner, was born in Waterbury, Connecticut, on August 6, 1882, and is a son of George and Mary (Bowden) Morse.

As one of the representative men of Norwich, Connecticut, his life story is of interest to the people of New London county.

George Morse, father of Harry J. Morse, was born in Waterbury, Connecticut, and received his education in the public schools of that city. He then served an apprenticeship as a carpenter, and later became a prominent contractor and builder in Waterbury. It was in 1888 that he established himself in this business, and he continued along the same line until 1895, when his untimely death, in the very prime of life, cut short a most promising career. He died in the town of Prospect, one of the hill suburbs of Waterbury. His wife, who was born in Snow Hill, Maryland, still survives him, residing in Bristol, Connecticut. They were the parents of four children, three of whom are living: Florence, who became the wife of Edward Drake, superintendent of the casting department of one of the large Bristol foundries; Sarah, who became the wife of Ernest Gilford, an architect and draftsman, of Waterbury, and who is now deceased, her death occurring in 1915; Harriet, twin sister of Harry Joseph, the Norwich engineer, now the wife of Ernest Hubbell, a caster in a brass foundry, formerly of Waterbury, but now a resident of Bristol; and Harry Joseph, whose name heads this review.

Harry Joseph Morse received a thoroughly practical education in the public and high schools of Waterbury, Connecticut, being graduated from the latter institution in the class of 1900. Directly thereafter he entered the employ of the New England Engineering Company, of Waterbury, remaining with this company for five years. During that entire period Mr. Morse occupied every possible moment in the study of electrical engineering, becoming thoroughly expert in this line of work. He then became associated with the New England Engineering Company, of New York City, as traveling electrical engineer, installing all kinds of electrical equipment in various parts of the country. He remained with them for fifteen years, then, in 1918, in company with Louis Olsen, founded the business which is now a prominent interest in the electrical world of New London county. They established themselves as electrical contractors, covering from the first a very wide field, and achieving remarkable success. Mr. Morse bought out Mr. Olsen in 1900, and has since carried on the business alone, handling the extensive operations of his employees with the same efficiency which built up the reputation of the firm.

Mr. Morse is an influential member of the Norwich Chamber of Commerce, a man of broad views and sound judgment. Politically, he supports the principles of the Republican party, but has never been a candidate for political office.

Mr. Morse married, in June, 1902, May Maude Dooley, of Waterbury, Connecticut. Mrs. Morse is a daughter of Hartley W. and Elizabeth (Bissell) Dooley, of that city. Their children are: George B.; Hartley B.; Harry Joseph, Jr.; Leon L., deceased; and Lucille M. The family are members of the United Congregational Church of Norwich, and interested in all the social and benevolent activities of the church.

ALBERT ELLSWORTH FIELDING is a direct descendant of Uncas, first chief of the Mohegans. The Indian Chief Uncas, born about 1588, was a Pequot, but for heading a revolt against Sassacus, chief of his tribe, he was cast out in 1635. He had many followers, whom he organized into an independent tribe, to whom he gave the ancient name of the Pequots-Mohegan, and became their chief. His territory lay to the East and North of Lyme. He signed a treaty of peace with the whites, and in 1637 was with Mason's Expedition against the Pequots, which completely destroyed their power. After the war he evinced such friendliness for his former tribe that the English grew suspicious of him. In 1643 a feud, long smoldering, broke out between the Narragansetts and the Mohegans, and in a battle between one thousand Narragansetts, led by their chief, Miantonomo, and six hundred Mohegans, led by Uncas, Miantonomo was taken prisoner. Uncas had proposed to Miantonomo before the battle that to save the lives of many of their warriors the two met, saying: "Come like a man and we will fight it out." Miantonomo replied: "My men came to fight and they shall fight." They did fight, and although outnumbered, the Mohegans won.

Miantonomo was captured and confined in jail at Hartford, but the English condemned him to death, having decided at a meeting of the commissioners that "Uncas cannot be safe while Miantonomo lives." He was accordingly put to death by the Mohegans, the English approving. Later, in 1656, when sore pressed and surrounded by their foes, the Narragansetts, Mohawks, and Pocomatocks, Uncas got word through to an English captain whom he knew, Thomas Leffingwell, who came to his relief with a canoe loaded with food. Thus heartened, Uncas drove off his foes and regained his power. His gratitude to Thomas Leffingwell knew no bounds, and he deeded him all the lands now included within the borders of the city of Norwich. Leffingwell failed to record the deed to this land, but not for other gifts made him by Uncas, and that land is yet in the Leffingwell name.

Uncas kept faith with the English and shielded the colonists from the attacks of other tribes. In one of his eloquent speeches, he said: "This heart is not mine, but yours. I have no men, they are all yours. Command, I will do it. I will not believe Indians against the English. If any kills an Englishman, I will kill him." He was too old to fight in King Philip's War, but his son, Oneco, aided in the defeat of seven hundred of King Philip's men at Hadley. In 1825 a granite obelisk was erected to the memory of Uncas at Norwich, Connecticut,

the corner stone being laid by General Andrew Jackson. Uncas died at his capital in 1682.

There are now but forty full-blooded Indians of the Mohegan tribe living, but the tribal relation is continued, Lemuel Miller Occum Fielding being the present chief consul, he five generations removed from the first chief, the great Uncas. When the photoplay, "The Last of the Mohegans," was being filmed, this remnant of the once powerful tribe; led by their chief, aided in several of the scenes. Albert Ellsworth Fielding is a son of the present chief, and can claim the proud title of "American," for he is of pure Indian blood, six generations from Uncas.

Lemuel Miller Occum Fielding, chief consul of the Mohegan tribe of Indians, derived the name Occum from Sampson Occum, who married a daughter of Uncas, the first Mohegan chief. For thirty-three years he has been engaged in the wholesale drug house of Lee & Osgood, of Norwich. He married Alice Betsey Casey, born in Plainfield, Connecticut, February 12, 1864, and they have a daughter, Mystice, wife of James Otis Germaine, and four sons: Albert Ellsworth, of further mention; Everett Miller, Elmer Morrison, and Lemuel Osgood Fielding.

Albert Ellsworth Fielding was born in the town of Norwich, New London county, Connecticut, January 30, 1890, and was educated in the public schools. In 1909 he sailed on a whaling voyage to the Antarctic Ocean, a voyage which consumed many months. He sailed on the schooner "Margaret," the object being to capture seals as well as whales. Upon his return from his successful voyage to the frozen seas, he entered Washington College, in Tennessee. After his return to his home he accepted a position in the Connecticut State Hospital at Norwich, and there continues.

During the period of war between the United States and Germany, Mr. Fielding served in the United States navy, on the U. S. S. "Munplace," entering the service June 23, 1918, and receiving honorable discharge in June, 1919. During his service he made two voyages overseas to France.

Mr. Fielding married Isabella Mary McGee, born in Brooklyn, New York, October 6, 1894, daughter of Charles McGee. Mr. and Mrs. Fielding are the parents of a son, Albert Ellsworth (2), born in Norwich, January 20, 1920.

ALBERT HARRISON FOOTE—The town of Colchester, New London county, Connecticut, has long been the home of members of the Foote family found in Connecticut, Nathaniel Foote being first of New England record at Watertown, Massachusetts, where he took the oath of allegiance in 1633. Later, he became of the first settlers of Wethersfield, Connecticut, where he died in 1644, "an intelligent, pious, and industrious farmer," and one of the magistrates of the colony of Connecticut. He was succeeded by his son, Nathaniel (2) Foote, and he by his son, Nathaniel (3) Foote, whose widow, Margaret Bliss Foote, died in Colchester, Connecticut, April 3, 1745, aged ninety-five years. Although there is no record that Nathaniel (3) Foote lived in Colchester (dying in Wethersfield), some of his children settled there, and the town has never since been without a goodly Foote representation.

This Nathaniel (3) Foote and his wife Margaret (Bliss) Foote, had born to them a son, Joseph Foote, December 28, 1690, who married (first) Ann Clothier, and lived in Colchester, where their son, Jeremiah Foote, was born, October 11, 1725. Jeremiah Foote married Ruhama Northam, of Colchester, and there he died May 15, 1784, his widow surviving him until February 8, 1809, passing away aged eighty-two years Their son, Stephen Foote, born in 1755, married April 29, 1779, Esther Clark, of Colchester, and there lived on the old homestead.

Erastus Foote, son of Stephen and Esther (Clark) Foote, was born at the homestead in Colchester, May 9, 1790, and there resided all his life. He married Betsey Crouch, and one of their children was a son, Albert, also born on the same farm in Colchester, as his father.

Albert Foote, of the eighth American generation, a descendant of the original Nathaniel Foote and his wife, Elizabeth Deming, was born in the town of Colchester, New London county, Connecticut, July 22, 1821, and here spent his life, a farmer, being buried in a private burial plot on the farm on which he was born. He died September 30, 1869, aged forty-eight. He married Mary Ann Chase, born in Amherst, Massachusetts, who long survived him, dying at the age of seventy-five. Albert Foote was school committeeman and held other local offices.

Albert Harrison Foote, son of Albert and Mary Ann (Chase) Foote, was born at the old Foote farm in Colchester, New London county, Connecticut, January 1, 1853, and has passed his entire life at the homestead which he now owns (1921). He was educated in the public schools, and early became his father's farm assistant. He was sixteen years of age when his father died, and he continued at the homestead, managing the farm for his mother. Later, he purchased the interest of the heirs of Albert Foote, and became sole owner of the Foote homestead now embracing one hundred and thirty-nine acres, which he devotes to general farming and dairying. He is one of the prosperous, substantial farmers of his town, and he has fully maintained the honor of the Foote name, one that dates back so far into the past history of Colchester.

Mr. Foote is a Republican in politics, and had held several local offices: Assessor of taxes, school committeeman, and member of the Board of Relief, his service in public office covering a long period of years. In November, 1920, he was elected to represent Colchester in the Connecticut House of Representatives, serving during the session of 1921 on the committees of labor, and sale of lands. He is a member of Colchester Methodist Episcopal church, and was formerly a member of the board of trustees. He is affiliated with the American Order United Workmen, and with the Patrons of Husbandry, the family all being members of Colchester Grange. He also belongs to the fraternal and beneficial order, Woodmen of the World, and is interested in these various organizations for mutual benefit.

Mr. Foote married, April 6, 1881, at Colchester, Ella Louise Payson, born in Andover, Connecticut, daughter of E. Ferdinand and Emma (Wilbur) Payson, and they are the parents of three sons: Allison Albert Foote, born January 31, 1882, died December 29, 1891; Frank Edward Foote, born May 20, 1891, now with the New Haven Dairy Company, at New Haven, Connecticut; and Elmer Harrison Foote, born November 11, 1893, now associated with his father in the management of the home farm, which has known no owner but a Foote for so many years. Elmer H. Foote is a member of Wooster Lodge, Free and Accepted Masons, Colchester Grange, Patrons of Husbandry, and a chapter of the order of the Eastern Star.

GEORGE BYRON DIMON—The pleasant farm on Chestnut Hill in Lebanon township, New London county, Connecticut, is owned and occupied by George Byron Dimon, who in addition to his agricultural activities is extensively engaged in chicken-raising and breeding Cocker Spaniel dogs. He is also manager of the Columbia Co-Operative Association, Incorporated, which does a business of from $60,000 to $70,000 a year.

John Dimon, father of George Byron Dimon, was born in Bristol, Rhode Island, July 18, 1828. In his early manhood he was bookkeeper and general manager for the Store Peacedale Manufacturing Company in Rhode Island, and after severing his connection with that concern was for several years engaged in operating a large farm on Prudence Island. In 1865 he purchased a farm in Pomfret, Connecticut, a large tract containing 255 acres and generally known as the Dimon Stock Farm. Here he bred fancy stock of various kinds, including Ayrshires, Devons, Guernseys, and Jersey cattle, trotting, running, and general purpose horses, fancy poultry of leading varieties, sheep, swine, etc., continuing in this line for nineteen years, at the end of which time, in 1884, he sold out and went to Detroit, Michigan. There he purchased a livery and boarding stable business, which he conducted until 1888. He then purchased a large stock, grain, and dairy farm at Fort Wayne, Indiana, where, with his son, George B. Dimon, as assistant, he remained for a period of seven years. He then went back to New England, settling in Hartford, Connecticut, where his long years of study and practical experience in the breeding and raising of horses were gathered together in a book which he published, entitled, "American Horses and Horse Breeding." He died in East Hartford, Connecticut, in 1898, at the age of seventy years. He married Hanna Barney, and they were the parents of George Byron Dimon, the subject of this sketch.

George Byron Dimon was born in Pomfret, Connecticut, July 20, 1868, and received his earliest education in the village school at Pomfret, later attending the district school in Putnam. When fourteen years of age he became a pupil of the Brighton Academy in Boston, where he continued his studies for several years. When his education was completed he realized a long cherished desire to visit the great Northwest, of which he had heard much since his father's westward migration in 1884. Young George B. Dimon visited many cities and towns, both in Canada and in the United States, working for two years in Detroit, Michigan, where his father was then located, and for seven years at Fort Wayne, Indiana, where he was associated with his father in the milk business, his share of the work being the retail delivery of milk over an extensive route. When this business was sold both father and son returned to New England, settling in Hartford, Connecticut, where the son became associated with the creamery business of J. J. and Rev. Francis Goodwin, on Woodland street. There he remained for eight years, having charge of the private creamery of the above mentioned gentlemen and caring for a herd of Jersey stock. This connection he maintained until 1903, when he returned to New London county and settled in Lebanon. He purchased a farm on Chestnut Hill, which is his present home. Here he does not confine himself to the raising of the usual farm crops. He has a flock of from 600 to 800 laying hens, is an extensive breeder of Cocker Spaniels, which he ships to all parts of the country, this breed being extensively used for hunting, and in addition to all these activities and interests is the efficient manager of the Columbia Co-Operative Association, Incorporated, which handles from three to six cars of grain a month and does a yearly business of from $60,000 to $70,000. The association unloads at Chestnut Hill, Andover, and Bolton Notch, and handles the products of a large number of farms.

Mr. Dimon takes an active interest in the welfare of the district in which he lives, and serves the public interests in various ways. He is a member of the School Board, and in 1920 was elected a member of the High School Committee, appointed for the purpose of building a suitable plant for the high school. The committee has met its responsibilities with marked ability and success, and has completed the George Lyman High School at Lebanon, situated on South Green, opposite the Congregational church. Mr. Dimon is also a member and chairman of the board of trustees of the Liberty Hill Congregational Church.

In 1893, at Decatur, Indiana, George Byron Dimon married Eva Wagner, who was born January 7,

1868, daughter of James and Lydia (Martz) Wagner, residents of Indiana. One son was born of this marriage, George Richard, his birth occurring June 13, 1904.

ALBERT BOARDMAN—One of the well known names in the business and political circles of Norwich is that of Albert Boardman, the head of the Household Store on Franklin street, and one of the foremost leaders of the Socialist party in this part of the State.

The Boardman family originated in England, and Peter Boardman, Mr. Boardman's father, was born in Blackburn, Lancashire, England, bringing his family to the United States in 1870. Being by trade a weaver of cotton cloth, he settled in Fall River, Massachusetts, later removing to New Bedford, where he died in 1901. He married Sarah Ann Pettinger, who was born in Yorkshire, England, and who died in Philadelphia, Pennsylvania, in 1911. They were the parents of five children, of whom three are living, as follows: Albert, whose name heads this review; Horace Peter, a sketch of whom follows; and Alice Elizabeth, wife of Samuel Rhoades, of Philadelphia.

Albert Boardman was born in Lowell, Massachusetts, December 8, 1870, and was educated in the public schools of his native State and the New Britain (Connecticut) State Normal School, from which he was graduated in the class of 1895. Having completed his education, Mr. Boardman taught school in New Britain and other places for about ten years, entering the business world at the end of that period. Coming to Norwich he established, in association with his brother, Horace P. Boardman, what has since been known as the Household Store, in Norwich, this being a general hardware store, carrying a very complete and comprehensive stock of such goods as are ordinarily included within the scope of this general term. This has become one of the successful business interests of the city, and is still going forward. Holding advanced ideas regarding the imminence and the practicability of a mutually benevolent social order, and possessing the courage of his convictions, Mr. Boardman has long been one of the most fearless and outspoken advocates of Socialism in this county. He has suffered prosecution several times in Norwich for dissemination of the principles of his party in public speeches, but in no way have his convictions been shaken, and he speaks with pride of his vicissitudes in defence of his principles.

Mr. Boardman married, in Waterville, Connecticut, Grace Lillie Melville, daughter of George H. and May (Dilworth) Melville, both natives of this country. Mr. and Mrs. Boardman are the parents of four children, of whom all are living: Bessie Alice, born in Westerly, Rhode Island; Gladys Lillian, born in Windsor, Connecticut; Grace Alberta, and Mary Dilworth, born in Westerly, Rhode Island. Mrs. Boardman and children are members of the Methodist Episcopal church of Norwich, and active in all the social and benevolent organizations of the church.

HORACE PETER BOARDMAN—From his first residence in Norwich, Connecticut, some twenty-seven years ago, through his activities in the industrial and business world since that time, Horace Peter Boardman, junior partner of the Household Store, in Norwich, has always borne a definite share in the general progress, working for the good of the people at all times and in all places.

Mr. Boardman is a son of Peter and Sarah Ann (Pettinger) Boardman, and brother of Albert Boardman (see preceding sketch). Horace P. Boardman was born in Newburyport, Massachusetts, January 2, 1872, and received a practical public school education. About 1895 Mr. Boardman came to Norwich, and here entered the employ of the Vaughan Foundry Company, as an apprentice iron moulder, serving four years in learning this trade. For the next six years he worked as a moulder in various places, then, in association with his brother, Albert Boardman, established the present business, which is located at No. 74 Franklin street. With a complete stock of hardware and the various merchandise usually handled by a store of this class, the concern has achieved a marked success, and is one of the substantial and widely known business enterprises of this city.

As an individual Mr. Boardman is deeply interested in every phase of public advance, and politically endorses the principles of the Socialist party, being one of the most ardent advocates of that doctrine in this section, and a staunch supporter of the party. He is a member of the Congregational church, his family also holding membership in that church.

Mr. Boardman married, in Taftville, Connecticut, Melissa Crosby, of Norwich, daughter of John Crosby. Mr. and Mrs. Boardman have two children: Ruth, born in New Bedford, Massachusetts, now the wife of Fred Gabeille, of Norwich; and Viola, born in Valley Field, Province of Quebec, Canada. The family residence is at No. 17 Arnold street, Norwich.

HORACE PALMER LANPHEAR and his father, Captain Horace Clark Lanphear, both made high reputation in the service of the public, the father as a captain of sound steamboats, the son as a locomotive engineer, and when a change of occupation seemed desirable, both retired to a farm, the father long gone to his reward, the son yet tilling the fertile fields of "Pleasant View" farm, overlooking Long Island sound.

Lanphear is an ancient Rhode Island family name, this branch tracing to George Lanphear, who was of Westerly, Rhode Island, in 1669. He bought land in that year, took the oath of allegiance in 1671, was baptized in 1678, and had two hundred acres laid out to him in 1704. He died October 6, 1731. The name of his wife is unknown.

From George Lanphear the line of descent is through his son, John Lanphear, who was a resident of Westerly, Rhode Island, and there died in 1757. His wife, Ruth, died in 1730, the next in line being their son, Nathan.

Nathan Lanphear married, June 22, 1739, Mary Langworthy, and reared a large family, all born in Westerly. Descent is traced through their son, Nathan (2).

Nathan (2) Lanphear was born February 18, 1742. His second wife, Sarah (Landers) Lanphear, whom he married October 31, 1771, bore him a son, Enoch.

Enoch Lanphear, born January 14, 1782, married Susanna Berry. He followed the water most of his life, but also was a farmer and a shoemaker. He died at the age of seventy, his wife at the age of sixty.

Captain Horace Clark Lanphear, youngest son of Enoch and Susanna (Berry) Lanphear, was born in Westerly, Rhode Island, June 24, 1826, died in Waterford, Connecticut, July 16, 1902. At the age of ten he made his first voyage, going as cook for Captain Brand, who for nine months paid the boy two dollars monthly wages. Five dollars per month was his next pay, then seven, and as second mate with Captain Berry he was raised to ten dollars. He was mate of the smack "Herald," for three years, then bought the smack "Commerce," and was his own captain. He sold the "Commerce" in October, 1844, and went on a whaling voyage on the "Robin Hood," the first vessel to enter the Ochotsk Sea in quest of whales. The ship was thirty-four months on this voyage, but brought back oil and whale bone in large quantities. In October, 1849, he engaged as pilot and sailing master of the sloop "Catherine Hale," running between Westerly, Stonington, and New York City. In 1852 he became captain of the sloop "Leader," and in 1853-54-55 was captain and part owner of the sloop "E. W. Babcock." In 1856-57 he was captain and part owner of the schooner "Orlando Smith," running between Boston and Philadelphia, touching at New York.

In 1858 he changed to steam and was captain of the "Richard Law;" in 1859 was first pilot of the steamer "Commodore," running from Stonington to New York. He was with the Stonington Line until January 1, 1865, serving as first pilot on the "Commodore," "Vanderbilt," Commonwealth," "Plymouth Rock," and "State of Maine." His first position with the Norwich Line, January 1, 1865, was as first pilot of the "City of Boston" (two and one-half years). He was then made captain of the "City of New London" (six years), captain of the "City of Lawrence" (two and one-half years), "City of New York," which he commanded until assigned as captain of the "City of Worcester," which, at the time of her building, was considered the finest and handsomest of all sound steamboats. He was then senior captain of the line, and it was a reward for long and faithful service that he was given the new and handsome "City of Worcester." He retired from the service of the Norwich line, having never had an accident in all his many years in command of sound steamboats. During his term, there was one service he rendered which should always be credited to his memory. This was the rescue of the passengers of the "Narragansett," after her collision with the "Stonington" on a foggy night in June, 1879. Captain Lanphear heard signals of distress and quickly brought his boat, the "City of New York," to the scene of the collision, the "Narragansett's passengers then being in the water clinging to boxes, planks or anything that would float. For three and one-half hours the boats of the "City of New York" were engaged in their work of rescue, taking two hundred and forty out of the water and placing them on the "City of New York." How many lives were lost was never known, but the world rang with the praises of the gallant captain and his men. Captain Lanphear received testimonials from all over the country, and a handsomely engraved set of resolutions from the directors of the Norwich Line.

Captain Lanphear served as captain of every steamer of the Norwich line except the "City of Lowell," which was built after his retirement. He was a man of rugged constitution and a thorough sportsman. In 1882 he entered a race off Ocean Beach in the sound, the craft being half hogsheads propelled by an oar. Captain Lanphear enjoyed the sport all the more as he won the race and received a silver ice pitcher as a prize. When captain of the "City of Boston" he broke all speed records between New London and New York, making the run in six hours and five minutes. That record stood until the "Greyhound of the Sound," the "City of Lowell," lowered it.

After his retirement, Captain Lanphear resided at his farm overlooking Long Island sound, "Pleasant View," an ideal home for a retired mariner.

Captain Lanphear married, January 28, 1850, Abby M. Owen, who died February 25, 1903, in Waterford, daughter of Josiah and Rhoda M. Owen, of Coventry, Rhode Island. They celebrated their golden wedding, January 28, 1900, but two years later the gallant captain passed away, his widow surviving until 1903. They were the parents of three children, only one of whom survived childhood, Horace Palmer.

Horace Palmer Lanphear was born in Westerly, Rhode Island, November 17, 1851, and until the age of fifteen attended public schools in Westerly, Groton, and New London, finishing in Bartlett High School, Groton being for a time the family home. At the age of sixteen he entered railroad employ, beginning as fireman on the Providence & Stonington, going thence two and one-half years later to the New London & Northern railroad as fireman. He now became a qualified engineer, and for about two months ran a train on the New Jersey Southern railroad from the boat junction at Sandy Hook. While there he had the honor of running the special train which carried President Grant from Sandy Hook to Long Branch, New Jersey, then known as the "Summer Capitol." After leaving the New Jersey Southern railroad, he became an engineer on the Pennsylvania railroad, and for three years ran a freight and passenger train between New York and Philadelphia. In 1876 he married, and in 1877 he settled on the farm in Waterford, which was the home of his father after his retirement and the home of Horace P. Lanphear from 1877 until the present, 1921. The original house burned down and has been replaced by a splendid modern residence built near the site of the old house. The fifty acres comprising the farm are principally devoted to dairy farming, the place being near Pleasure Beach, near the sound, and is widely known as "Pleasant View" farm. Mr. Lanphear is a Republican in politics; a member of the First Baptist Church of Waterford; Union Lodge No. 31, Free and Accepted Masons; Pequot Lodge, No. 85, and Orion Encampment, No. 4, Independent Order of Odd Fellows; Waterford Lodge, Ancient Order of United Workmen; and Fraternal Benefit Lodge, of Waterford.

Mr. Lanphear married, December 20, 1876, Ursula Judson Potter, born April 27, 1855, daughter of John S. and Mahala (Crandall) Potter, of Westerly, Rhode Island. Mr. and Mrs. Lanphear are the parents of three children: 1. Mabel Clark, born September 25, 1880; married, June 8, 1904, Leonard F. Williams, of Waterford, now his father-in-law's assistant; he is a son of William and Jessie (Moses) Williams, who had two other sons, Leslie and Frederick. Mr. and Mrs. Williams have three children: Clara Ursula, born December 2, 1906; Leonard Horace, born October 4, 1909; Flora Lanphear, born August 17, 1916, all born in Waterford. 2. Everett Potter, born November 19, 1885, in Westerly, Rhode Island, died July, 1918. 3. Alice Judson, born May 20, 1887, residing at home.

CHARLES NATHAN BROWN—Identified for many years with the business interests of New London county, Connecticut, then after his retirement residing in North Stonington, Charles Nathan Brown has long been a leading factor in the progress and prosperity of this vicinity.

Mr. Brown is a son of Jedediah and Eunice (Bailey) Brown, of North Stonington, Connecticut. Jedediah Brown was born in this town, and received his education in the district schools near his home. After completing his studies, he took up the work of the farm homestead, and all his life lived upon this place, which he inherited from his father. He died there in 1891. His wife, who was also born in North Stonington, died at the homestead in 1881. They were the parents of ten children, of whom five are now living, Charles N. being the seventh child.

Charles Nathan Brown was born in North Stonington on March 30, 1856. With the practical education of the district schools his only preparation for life, he worked on the farm with his father until he became twenty-one years of age, then rented a farm in Voluntown, Connecticut, also in this county, which he conducted for one year. At the end of this time he made a radical change in his line of effort, and this change was amply justified by his later success. He removed with his family to New London, and in that city established a livery and sales stable. This business he found profitable, and for twenty years continued along this same line. The advent of the automobile found him, at the height of a satisfactory success, ready to retire to the less active interests of country life. He returned to North Stonington, where he conducted a general store, establishing this business in 1903, and continuing same until 1920. During all this time he was widely interested in real estate, largely in this county, amounting to a business of considerable importance. Mr. Brown is now retired from all active participation in business interests of any kind, and still resides in North Stonington.

Mr. Brown has responded more than once to the call to public service. He has thrice been selectman of the town of North Stonington, and was also elected tax assessor at one time. He has long been an active member of the North Stonington Grange, No. 138, and for four successive years was president of the Grange Fair, of North Stonington. Politically, he is a Democrat.

Mr. Brown married (first) Lydia Ann Dougherty, of Rhode Island. He married (second) Iphogenia Whitford, of Mankato, Minnesota. They attend and support the Congregational church.

GEORGE EVERETT MARTIN—The Martin family is found in New England from the coming of the "Mayflower," although Christopher Martin, who came on that ship, left no descendants, the entire family being carried away by the "first sickness." A dozen of the name came before 1650, and in this branch, Massachusetts was the family State until the coming of Anderson O. Martin to Colchester, in New London county, Connecticut, he the father of William C. Martin and grandfather of George Everett Martin, of Lebanon, Connecticut, the principal character of this review. The surname Martin is derived from the baptismal name Martin and is traced to ancient origin. In England the family is a large and important one, thirty-nine families by the name of Martin having coats of arms; fifty Martin families may be added to the list in the United Kingdom.

Anderson Oliver Martin, the first comer of this branch in Connecticut, was a son of Anderson Oliver Martin, of Massachusetts, in which State Anderson O. (2) was born. Upon coming to Connecticut, he settled in Colchester, New London county, Connecticut, and became an extensive dealer in horses. In that business he was later assisted by his father and his fame as a horse dealer spread through all New England. He married Elizabeth Stanton, a sister of Joseph Stanton, a Revolutionary hero. Among their children was a son, William Charles Martin, of further mention.

William Charles Martin was born in Lebanon,

Connecticut, and there educated in the public schools. After completing his own education he became a school teacher, so continuing for several years. He then engaged in the real estate business, dealing in New England farms and building up an extensive business. He also owned a farm which he cultivated until his passing at Lebanon. He married Mary C. Champlain, who died in Lebanon, Connecticut, March 29, 1897. Mr. and Mrs. Martin were the parents of six children, all born in Lebanon: 1. Anderson Oliver (3), married (first) Emma House, who died in Lebanon, leaving four children; he married (second) Annie S. King, and resides at Lebanon, a farmer. 2. Charles William, married Alice Wood, and resides in Lebanon, retired. 3. John Milton, deceased, married Mary Hurley. 4. Frank Stanton, deceased, married Anna Ford. 5. George Everett, of further mention. 6. Ernest Linoln, now residing in Williamantic, Connecticut.

George Everett Martin, fifth child of William Charles and Mary C. (Champlain) Martin, was born in Lebanon, Connecticut, April 22, 1858. He was educated in the public schools of Lebanon, finishing in high school. After leaving school he learned the painter's trade, serving an apprenticeship as painter and paperhanger with Hull & Beckwith, in Newark, New Jersey. He then read law under his uncle, John M. Martin, an eminent member of the New York bar, his office at No. 10 Wall street, where he specialized in the law of real estate. In 1877 George E. Martin returned to Lebanon, Connecticut, where he spent four years in the employ of the Norwich Lock Manufacturing Company, then for two years was in Willimantic, employed by the Willimantic Linen Company. He was on the road as a traveling salesman for different firms between 1883 and 1890, retiring to engage in the manufacture of a cough syrup known as The Gem Cough Remedy, in Lebanon. He continued in that business for five years, returning in 1895 to his original trade, painter and paper hanger, and there continues (1921). In 1915 he opened a confectionery store at his home on Lebanon Green, which he still owns. He has built up a good business and is one of the highly esteemed men of his community. He is a Republican in politics, a member of George S. Hull Lodge, No. 72, Knights of Pythias, the Junior Order of United American Mechanics, and attends the Baptist Church.

Mr. Martin married, June 28, 1892, in New Haven, Connecticut, Anna S. Santry, daughter of John and Anna Santry, of New Haven, Connecticut.

ALFRED OBEN COLBY—It is not often that one man is the possessor of three different means of earning a livelihood, but Alfred Oben Colby is particularly fortunate in that respect, having studied art and pharmacy in addition to having been engaged in mercantile life and in clerical work.

Alfred Oben Colby is the son of Amos George and Alice Pierce (Oben) Colby, the former a native of Harrington, Maine, where he lived as a boy and where he acquired an education in the district school. In his early manhood he led a sea-faring life and became captain of a vessel engaged in coastwise shipping. Amos G. Colby was among those who volunteered for service when the Civil War broke out and was assigned for duty in the First Battery, Field Artillery, Maine Volunteers. He was engaged in twenty-one different battles, some of them the most famous of the rebellion, among them being Gettysburg, Pennsylvania, Petersburg, Virginia, and Bull Run. After the close of the war, Amos G. Colby was discharged from duty, his rank being duty sergeant. Locating in Boston, Massachusetts, he became an interior decorator, an occupation in which he was very successful, following it until his death in 1914 at the age of seventy-two years. His wife, Alice Pierce (Oben) Colby, was born in Stonington, Connecticut, in 1841. She survived her husband by one year, dying in 1915, aged seventy-four years. Alfred Oben Colby was their only child.

Born in Boston, Massachusetts, August 7, 1869, Alfred Oben Colby was educated in the grammar schools there and later in the Boston High School, graduating from this in 1887. The young man then took up the study of art, taking a course in the private school of Charles H. Haden, of Boston, continuing it for two years. In 1889 Mr. Colby became interested in the drug business and for the next three years was employed in a store in Boston. From 1892 until 1895 he was engaged in the hardware trade, giving it up to become associated with his father in interior decorating work, continuing it until 1900. At that time Mr. Colby entered the employ of the Wilcox Fertilizer Company, located in Mystic, Connecticut, as their assistant secretary, remaining with them to date. Making his home in Mystic, Mr. Colby became greatly interested in the affairs of the town, joining the Baptist church there and becoming a member of Charity and Relief Lodge, Free and Accepted Masons, of Mystic. He is an upholder of the principles of the Republican party, though not active in its work.

In November, 1902, at Mystic, Connecticut, Alfred Oben Colby was married to Edna Elizabeth Burrows. She is the daughter of Benjamin F. Burrows, a resident of Mystic, whose wife was Miss Greene, also of that town. Two children have been born to Mr. and Mrs. Colby: 1. Elizabeth, born in October, 1903; and Alice P., born in January, 1907.

FRED WHALEN HOXIE, numbered among the successful farmers and prominent residents of this locality, is a native of Lebanon, Connecticut, his birth having occurred December 5, 1871. He is the son of Albert and Mary E. (Tinker) Hoxie. Albert Hoxie was born in South Kingston, Rhode Island, in 1838, and died at Lebanon in 1918, having been engaged in farming throughout his entire lifetime. His wife was born in Lebanon in 1839.

Fred Whalen Hoxie obtained his education in the schools of his native place, after which he went to work on his father's farm and here continued until he was twenty-one years of age, when he bought what was then known as the Mason place. In 1915 he sold this farm and bought his present place, erecting buildings which have been fully equipped with every modern device used by successful farmers of the present day. That this venture has proven profitable is readily seen by the large material gains which he has acquired in the past five years, as well as by the beauty of his estate, which is recognized as one of the most beautiful in this community. Seldom is it that a man as successful in business as Mr. Hoxie takes the keen and helpful interest in civic affairs to which his record bears testimony. A man of action rather than words, he demonstrates his public spirit by actual achievement, which advance the prestige and wealth of the community, and is ever ready to respond to any deserving call made upon him. He served in the Legislature as representative from this district in 1912, and has also been a member of the Board of Relief, during the tenure of both offices aiding to the utmost of his power all movements and measures which in his judgment tended to further the community's welfare and promote the cause of good government.

Mr. Hoxie married Fannie Faith Mason, born in Lebanon, August 12, 1872, daughter of James Fitch and Fannie Mason. Mr. and Mrs. Hoxie are the parents of two children: Herbert Mason, born August 19, 1897; Mabel Gladys, born November 4, 1900. Mr. Hoxie is essentially a home-lover, devoted to the ties of family and friendship.

ROBERT WEIR GOODFELLOW—Tracing descent from the founders of the Highland Clan Cameron through his mother, and of Scotch parentage and birth, Robert Weir Goodfellow possesses the sturdy brains of his honored race, and in his adopted city has gained the respect and esteem of all who knew him. He came to the United States via Canada, where his parents long resided, and in New London, Connecticut, his own home, he is now superintendent of the marine department of the United States Electric Heater Corporation, a position he assumed recently after selling his boat building plant in the Pequot avenue section of New London, to the above named corporation. He is a son of Joseph and Henrietta (Weir) Goodfellow, both of ancient Scottish lineage, and a grandson and namesake of a sturdy highlander, Robert Weir.

Joseph Goodfellow was born in Glasgow, Scotland, and there became a ship caulker. He remained in Glasgow until after his marriage to Henrietta Weir, and the birth of their eldest son, Robert W., in 1867, then came to the United States with his family, settling in Adams, Massachusetts. From Adams he removed to Canada, thence in 1877 retracing his steps to his old home in Glasgow. About a decade later, Joseph Goodfellow with his family again crossed the Atlantic, ascended the St. Lawrence and found a desirable location in Kingston, Ontario, Canada. He and his son, Robert W., were both expert ship builders, and in Kingston found ample employment. In 1892 the family separated, but Joseph and his wife remained in Canada where they prospered. But old age came on and they sold their home in Kingston and joined their sons in the United States. Mrs. Goodfellow, aged eighty-four, is now sojourning with their son Robert in New London; Joseph, the father, with their son James at Hanover, New Hampshire. Joseph and Henrietta (Weir) Goodfellow are the parents of four sons and a daughter: Robert Weir, of further mention; Joseph, James, Mary and Alexander.

Robert Weir Goodfellow was born in Glasgow, Scotland, August 4, 1867, but soon afterward was brought to the United States, to Adams, Massachusetts. As stated, the family journeyed from Adams to Canada, thence in 1877 to the old home in Glasgow, Scotland, where the lad Robert was educated. He grew up in the shadow of the great ship building yards and as his father was a ship caulker, he naturally embraced the ship building trade. He accompanied the family to Kingston, Canada, where he engaged in building lake vessels and there remained until 1892, when he married and brought his wife to reside in New York City. There he was engaged with a boat building company, specializing in electrically propelled boats and, as superintendent of the Electric Launch Company, he continued six years, making New York City his home.

Every Scotchman inherits a love for the soil, and in 1898 Mr. Goodfellow bought a farm in Lebanon, New London county, Connecticut, the Lyon Huntington farm situated on Goshen Hill, one of the best farms in the town. For two years Mr. Goodfellow cultivated his farm and made it his home, then went to the peach raising section of the town of Montville, buying a farm at Kittenomang; but after moving to that section, he devoted most of his time in the boat building industry along the coast, and in 1919 he bought a modern residence near Connecticut College, and in the Pequot avenue district of New London, built an extensive boat building shop. He ran the shop until the spring of 1912, then was bought out by his neighbor, the United States Electric Heater Corporation, Mr. Goodfellow then accepting a position with the corporation as superintendent of their marine department. He is a member of Clan Cameron, New London Post, Order of Scottish Clans; is a Republican in politics, and in church affiliation a member of the Second Congregational Church.

Mr. Goodfellow married Maude Tarrant, born at Wolf Island, Province of Ontario, Canada, April 9, 1872, daughter of John and Henrietta (Bennett) Tarrant, both of English birth, and the parents of eight children. Mr. and Mrs. Goodfellow are the parents of four children: Agnes Maude, born in Kingston, Canada, June 22, 1896, now a teacher in the town of Groton, New London county; Mildred Muretta, born April 26, 1898, married a boatswain of the first class in the United States navy; they are the parents of two daughters: Eleanor and Helen; Robert Alexander, born in Perth, Ontario,

Canada, March 6, 1900; and Jessie Weir, born in Kingston, Ontario, July 28, 1903, married John Monte of Norwich, Connecticut, and has two children: John Weir and Maria Monte.

WILLIAM AVERY COOKE—The name of Cooke is a very old one and may be found in the Doomesday book of "William the Conqueror," Gislebertus Cocus, also Captain James Cook. In 1462 a Cooke was lord mayor of London. Sir Thomas Cook, of Middlesex, was governor of the East India company. Sir Thomas Cook, of Worcestershire, founded the Worcester College at Oxford. Sir Anthony Cooke was tutor of King Edward in 1543. In 1612 a Cooke was chancellor of the Irish Exchequer. In 1504-08 Edward Cooke was mayor of Doncaster. Sir Edward Cook was secretary of foreign affairs in the cabinet of Charles I in 1635. The name can be traced in America for nearly three hundred years through three historians: Jackson, in his "History of Newton;" Dr. Band, in his "History of Watertown;" and Savage, in his "Genealogical Dictionary of New England," down to 1700, copies of which can be found in many large libraries. A copy of the Cooke coat-of-arms is in the family of the present generation.

William Avery Cooke, of Fort Hill farm in the town of Montville, New London county, Connecticut, is of the ninth generation of the family founded in New England, by (I) Gregory Cooke, born in England, and died in Watertown, Massachusetts, in 1690. The line of descent from Gregory Cooke, is through (II) his son Stephen, born in England in 1647, died at Cambridgeville, Massachusetts in 1738, (III) his son Stephen (2), born in Newton, Massachusetts in 1683, died in 1760; (IV) his son John, born at Newton, Massachusetts, settled in 1710 in Preston, Connecticut, died in 1762; (V) his son James, born in 1717; (VI) his son Isaiah, born in 1741, died in 1803; (VII) his son Captain James, born in 1768, died in 1850; (VIII) his son Colonel Dwight W.; (IX) his son William Avery. The following matter relates to Isaiah Cooke (VI) and to Captain James Cooke of the seventh generation, also some of his children, this being of especial interest as it is historical in its relation to the woolen industries of the United States.

(VI) Isaiah Cooke, great-grandfather of William Avery Cooke, was the pioneer in the woolen industry of Eastern Connecticut. He was not in sympathy with the revolutionary movements of the colonies in the beginning, but experienced a change of heart and became so intense in his devotion to the cause, that he gave almost the entire product of his mill to be made into clothing for the soldiers of the Colonial army. He was a warm friend of Governor Trumbull, the war governor of Connecticut. The three historical cases of clothing sent to General Washington at Valley Forge were largely carded, spun and reeled in his mill in Preston, and woven on hand looms in Windham and New London counties.

(VII) Captain James Cooke, born in 1768, died in 1850, was bred a woolen manufacturer and worked with his father until 1823, when he located with his brother Chester in Northfield, Massachusetts. He sold out in 1828, and in 1830 removed to Lowell, Massachusetts, as agent of The Middlesex Mills, remaining with that company until 1845. Up to 1840 all figured woolen cloth had been woven on hand looms, and it was thought it always would be. But under Mr. Cooke's direction the Crompton loom for weaving cotton was altered and changed to weave wool, which proved a great success, and there fancy cassimeres were woven on a power loom, the first in the United States. Mr. Cooke for many years had a cutting from the original piece of cloth, the first ever woven on a power loom in the world. In 1846, Mr. Cooke went as agent to the Winooski Mills at Burlington, Vermont, and remained six years. During this period he took the gold medal of the American Institute, and the Massachusetts Mechanic's Fair, for goods manufactured at the Winooski Mills. Samples of various fabrics in assorted colors were sent to the World's Fair of all nations, held at London in 1851, for which Mr. Cooke received a diploma signed by Prince Albert, consort of Victoria, Queen of England, a bronze medal and a large printed volume of the history, catalogue and awards of the great exhibition. In 1853 Mr. Cooke was mayor of Lowell.

(VIII) Chester Cooke, born in 1798, died in 1880, was also bred a woolen manufacturer, which business he followed in Poquetanuck, Connecticut, Northfield, Massachusetts, and Skaneatles and Rochester, New York.

(VIII) Calvin Worthington Cooke, born in 1800, died in 1873, was superintendent of Middlesex Mills of Lowell, Massachusetts, 1830 to 1845. While there he made a study of dyeing, and was during his lifetime one of the most expert originators and producers of fancy colors for shawls in this country. He also designed and produced a wonderful number of the finest and most expensive patterns known to the trade during his lifetime. During his business life, and as manager of the Waterloo Shawl Manufacturing Company, he designed over six hundred shawl patterns, of which he kept a working copy, and could duplicate any that might be called for. Although he was not the inventor of the drop shuttle, now so indispensable to all manufacturers of woolens, it was through his adaptation of and improvements, that it was first brought into actual, successful and practical use in the manufacture of unique and beautiful designs of ladies' shawls. He attended the World's Fair in London, 1857-58, and exhibited his shawls in the Crystal Palace, where he was specially honored by the Queen, and received medals and diplomas for designs, and merit for colors. Queen Victoria was very much interested in the display of beautiful shawls, and had several private consultations with him, and selected the designs and gave him an order for a large number of shawls which she wished to distribute as marks of her esteem to her maids in waiting and personal friends. She also consulted him as to designs and special workmanship, as to superior quality and colors, and selected two patterns which he specially designed for her with the understanding that, as they were for her personal use, the patterns should be destroyed and no duplicates ever made. Mr. Cooke was more than a mechanical expert, he was religious, moral, and an ornament to society, a pillar as well as a warden of the church. At St. Paul's Church, Waterloo, New York, he was prominent in the Sunday school work, and was remarkably successful in managing that special branch of church work. At one time in Waterloo he had a school of over six hundred attendants. As soon as he perceived an outlying district beyond the convenience of his school in Waterloo, he organized another school and conducted them all to the great benefit of the community and to the growth of the church. Since Mr. Cooke's death, St. Paul's Church has erected a beautiful chapel in memory of his devout life, and labors among them. The triple chancel window bears the following inscription:

"TO THE GLORY OF GOD AND IN MEMORY OF CALVIN W. COOKE," and the text, "That they may rest from their labors, and their works do follow them."

(VIII) Isaac H. Cooke, born in 1804, with his brother, Dwight W. Cooke, continued in the manufacturing of woolen goods under the firm name of I. H. & D. W. Cooke, 1832 to 1857, succeeding to the business and conducting its development with the advance of the time.

(VIII) Colonel Dwight W. Cooke, father of William Avery Cooke, and son of Captain James Cooke, was born February 6, 1813, and died in 1877. He removed to Norwich in 1861, and for many years conducted a brokerage business in Connecticut, fleece wools, also washed wools, and wool waste. He was colonel of the Eighteenth Regiment, the organization that took the place of the "minute men" of the earlier period.

The last meeting of this organization, before being disbanded, was held on Canterbury Plain, Connecticut. Colonel Dwight W. Cooke married Abby Amelia Avery, of ancient and honorable family, born June 20, 1819, daughter of Isaac Avery, of Preston, Connecticut, granddaughter of Isaac Avery, who, with his brother Jonas, was a member of Captain Frederick Witter's Company, General Israel Putnam commanding, and fought at Bunker Hill, Long Island, and at White Plains, New York, where Jonas was severely wounded. Sergeant Isaac Avery took his brother home to Preston, and there he died from his wounds and was buried. His gravestone bears this inscription:

Stop Curious Mortals
As you pass this way,
A debt to Nature pay,
For Life and Liberty and all
on earth you prize
I and ten thousand were a
sacrifice

(IX) William Avery Cooke, son of Colonel Dwight W. and Abby Amelia (Avery) Cooke, was born in Preston, New London county, Connecticut, August 15, 1847. He was educated in the public schools of Preston and Norwich, finishing with graduation from Norwich Free Academy, class of 1866. After leaving school, he engaged in mercantile life, and until 1888 was in the wholesale produce business in Norwich. In that year he purchased the Fort Hill farm in the town of Montville, and there has since resided and managed the cultivation of its four hundred and fifty fertile, productive acres. Mr. Cooke married Celia Rosaline White, born in Norwich, November 27, 1846, daughter of Francis and Belinda (Shaw) White, her mother of the prominent Weymouth, Massachusetts, Shaw family of shoe manufacturers. Mr. and Mrs. Cooke are the parents of three children: William Dwight, Amelia Avery, and Francis Edward, the latter an officer of the United States navy during the War with Germany, 1917-18. Mr. Cooke's sister, Ida Amelia, was the wife of George S. Palmer, a prominent manufacturer of New London, Connecticut. Mr. Cooke was a successful merchant in Norwich, and since taking the Fort Hill farm thirty-three years ago, has taken equally high rank as an agriculturist. He is a public-spirited, progressive man, modern in his methods and highly esteemed by his townsmen.

The present estate of William Avery Cooke is Fort Hill farm, containing four hundred and fifty acres, once a part of the three thousand acres owned by the State of Connecticut, and the old house, built two and a half centuries ago, was the home of the overseer of the Mohegan Indians. The old place is pregnant with memories of the past, and in review seem to pass the old settlers, the overseer, who was a father to the tribe, the young Indians who came to the house to be instructed from books, and the men to learn to till the three thousand acres of productive land which comprised the reservation. The place was reached by a bridle path in the olden days. The path was later laid out as a turnpike and post road, and was built from the proceeds being, it is said, the first toll gate erected, that being, it is said, the first toll turnpike in the United States. The State of Connecticut sold the farm in 1872 by authority of the State Legislature, the purchaser being Theodore Raymond, from which William A. Cooke in 1888 bought the four hundred and fifty acres which he now owns.

MRS. ROSE (MULLEN) SULLIVAN—As the head of a progressive and growing interest in Niantic, Mrs. Sullivan is taking a very practical part in the welfare and advance of the community. The Bay View House, of which she has been the proprietor for four years, and the owner for three years, is one of the most attractive of the smaller summer hotels which are scattered along the coast of Connecticut.

Rose (Mullen) Sullivan was born in Sunbury, in

the Province of New Brunswick, Canada, and came to the United States in 1888, taking up her residence in the city of Norwich. Coming to Niantic from that city in 1918, she leased the Bay View House, which she operated for one year under the lease, thereafter purchasing the property. Mrs. Sullivan personally manages the business, and since taking over the hotel has made many important improvements, including a new water system of a design which has received the approval of noted health authorities. The house contains twenty-five rooms, and is much sought by those desiring a quiet and refined atmosphere, somelike and comfortable, while still among the popular resorts of the summer season, and close to some of the most fashionable localities on the New England coast. Mrs. Sullivan is well known in the community and is a member of the Methodist Episcopal church.

Rose Mullen married (first) in 1890, Mr. E. E. Fensley, of Norwich, who died in 1897, leaving three sons, two of whom are now living: Robert W., a marine engineer, whose home is in New London; and Adam Lindsay, a millwright by trade, who is married and resides in Niantic. She married (second) Daniel Sullivan, of Versailles, Connecticut, in 1902. Mrs. Sullivan has one adopted daughter, Elsie May Sullivan.

JOHN LATHAM MAIN—An honored citizen throughout his lifetime of Ledyard, New London county, Connecticut, John Latham Main was also one of those men whom this State delights to count among her heroes—the men who helped preserve the Union when the question of slavery threatened to disrupt the country.

Mr. Main was one of the eleven children of William L. Main and Sarah A. (Frink) Main, of Ledyard. William Leeds was born in Ledyard, lived there throughout his lifetime, always actively engaged in farming. His wife was a native of North Stonington. Both are long since deceased, and are buried in Ledyard.

John L. Main was born August 25, 1841, and was educated in the schools of the neighborhood. Just as he reached an age to feel the interest of sturdy manhood in the affairs of the Nation, the Civil War broke out, and he enlisted in Company G, Twenty-first Regiment, Connecticut Volunteer Infantry. He served with honor throughout the war, and returned to his native place after his discharge, following agricultural interests during the remainder of his life. He was repeatedly offered the honors of public office, which he always declined. His home was his all, and he took no interest in public life beyond that of the progressive private citizen.

John Latham Main married Phebe A. Frink, of North Stonington, who was born April 13, 1845, and died October 10, 1918. The ceremony was performed on March 12, 1864, by the Rev. Nehemiah Cook, of Ledyard. Mr. and Mrs. Main were the parents of following children: 1. William Oscar, died in infancy. 2. John Orrin, born in Ledyard, died September 22, 1909, at the age of forty-one years. 3. Sadie Elizabeth, born March 13, 1870; became the wife of Herbert Richardson, of Preston, and has three children: Fern Lenora, Calvin Main, and Hazel Hopkins. 4. Calvin Roson, born January 15, 1872; married Gertrude Elizabeth Kinmouth, of Ledyard, and has four children, Kenneth Walton, Calvin Roson, Carrie Elizabeth, and Robert Winsted. 5. Nellie Maude, born January 7, 1874; became the wife of Albert William Kinmouth, the wedding taking place at Grace Church, New York City, January 16, 1908, Rev. Carl Reiland, rector, officiating, and they had four children: Carl Albert and Caroline Fredrika, twins; of whom the daughter is deceased; Dona Catherine, born April 21, 1910; Earl Mortimer, born July 20, 1913.

LEEDS MAIN—There are men in every community who live on, in spirit, long after they are gathered to their fathers. The work which they have done, as citizens and as individuals, is carried forward by those whom they leave behind, but it is the name of him who has gone that still inspires effort and accomplishes progress. Such a man was Leeds Main, of Ledyard, New London county, Connecticut. Mr. Main was a son of William Leeds and Sarah A. (Frink) Main, of Ledyard.

Leeds Main was born in Ledyard, in September, 1845. He received a thorough and practical education in the schools of the vicinity, then when he had completed his studies, took up the work of the farm in association with his father. Continuing thus until twenty-three years of age, the young man then hired the farm from his father, and conducted it for himself. This arrangement held for about ten years, then in the late seventies Mr. Main bought the farm, which is now the family home. For about fifteen years he lived to enjoy the satisfaction of success and the development of the farm, which with the passing of the years grew ever dearer to him, as the scene of his prosperity and the home which was brightened by his children. Before he had reached the half-century mark, while still in the prime of life, Leeds Main was cut down, and the friends with whom he had walked saw him no more.

Mr. Main was a man of sterling integrity, always standing on the side of right. A member of one of the oldest New London county families, he bore himself with the dignity that reflected only honor on the name. He died November 9, 1894, and was buried in Ledyard, but later the remains were removed to Mystic, to rest in the family plot.

The Holdridge family is another of the old families of New London county, and with this family Mr. Main united, in his marriage with Sarah Hannah Holdridge, who was born in Ledyard, June 21, 1852. She is a daughter of Daniel and Eliza (Main) Holdridge, of North Stonington. Leeds and Sarah Hannah (Holdridge) Main were the parents of eight children: 1. William Leeds, born in Ledyard, March

6, 1870; married Elizabeth Benjamin, of Preston, and has one daughter, Hazel. 2. Daniel Holdridge, born in Ledyard, February 25, 1872; married Olive Stimpson, and has four children: Clarence, Arthur, Mildred, Elsie. 3. James Stanton, born August 6, 1874; married Elizabeth Brown; died December 25, 1905, leaving three children: Harold, James, and Leeds. 4. Samuel Lewis, born February 14, 1877; married Mary Chapman, and has seven children, five of whom are as follows: Marshall, Myrtle, Sarah, Gladys, Chester. 5. Cora Ida, born August 16, 1881; now the wife of George Appley, of North Stonington. 6. Julia Etta, born August 5, 1884; now the wife of William Cromwell, and has two children: Lewis, and Mary. 7. Eliza Jane, now the wife of Clarence Davis, and has two children. 8. Rose Lee, born March 19, 1887; now the wife of Frank Mansfield, and has two children, Edna Mary, and Charles Holdridge.

GEORGE RAYMOND GRAY—The life of George R. Gray was one of increasing effort, and in his battle of life he was largely dependent upon his own efforts. That he won so successfully but proves the strength of his character and the extent of his natural ability. He left behind him an honored name.

George Raymond Gray was born at Chaplin, Connecticut, January 18, 1868, son of John Shapley and Delia (Baldwin) Gray. John Shapley Gray taught school in his younger days, engaged in various enterprises, and later became a farmer in Groton, Connecticut. He was a son of Benjamin and Sarah Janet (Lewis) Gray, also of the vicinity of Groton.

George R. Gray attended various schools in Connecticut, finishing at Sheffield High School, Massachusetts, whence he was graduated, March 17, 1887. On leaving school he at first worked as a clerk in a general merchandise store, then went to North Wilton, Connecticut, and was there in a general store, remaining there so long that he was appointed a notary public, and also held other town offices. From North Wilton he moved to New London and there was employed for a few months by the United Express Company. When this company retired from business, Mr. Gray went to Willimantic and entered into partnership with his uncle, Jerome Baldwin, in the clothing business. A year later this partnership was dissolved on account of the ill health of Mr. Baldwin, and then Mr. Gray became head clerk for a Mr. Larrabee in a grocery store. He next went to Turnerville, took charge of the mill store and operated it for several years. On the death of his father-in-law, Jared Reid Avery, he came with his family to New London and took over the grocery business of the former, buying the business from the Avery estate. This business he conducted very successfully up to the time of his death, November 4, 1909. He was succeeded in business by his wife, who still continues it with a marked degree of success.

Mr. Gray was first and last a business man; he gave his whole time and energy to whatever line of work he was engaged in, and won his way from the bottom of the ladder to the position of a successful and substantial merchant. Though always interested in the welfare of the community in which he resided, his close application to business gave him but little time for politics and civic affairs. He was a lover of books, and spent most of his leisure time by the home fireside reading his favorite authors. In politics he was a Republican, and in church matters was a consistent member of the Second Congregational Church, of New London. His hobby was bees and chickens, and wherever located he usually had a number of beehives and a small run for chickens.

On October 17, 1894, Mr. Gray married Josephine Lamb Avery, daughter of Jared Reid and Josephine Alice (Lamb) Avery. Jared Reid Avery was a son of Jared Reid and Sarah (Agnew) Avery. James Reid Avery, Sr., was a son of Ebenezer (2) Avery, who was a son of Ebenezer (1) Avery, a soldier in the Revolutionary War, and descended from James Avery. Eight children were born to Mr. and Mrs. Gray, as follows: 1. Willard Avery, born May 16, 1896, at North Wilton, Connecticut. 2. Dorothy Baldwin, born November 23, 1897, at New London, Connecticut. 3. Eunice Cutler, born December 9, 1898, at Willimantic, Connecticut. 4. Jared Reid Avery, born December 9, 1900, at Willimantic, Connecticut. 5. Helen Delia, born September 9, 1902, at Willimantic. 6. John Shapley, born January 4, 1905, at New London, Connecticut. 7. Allyn Baldwin, born July 25, 1906, at New London, Connecticut. 8. Josephine Avery, born October 27, 1907, at New London.

WILLIAM AVERY WILCOX—The Wilcox family traces descent in Stonington, Connecticut, to Captain Jesse Wilcox, a sea captain, who, with his son Jesse, was drowned in Long Island Sound, July 5, 1828, during a heavy squall which overtook them and capsized their small boat. His son, Elias Wilcox, of the seventh American generation, was the founder of the first oil and fertilizer business, later known as the Wilcox Fertilizer Company. The family in this branch have remained in Stonington.

William A. Wilcox and his father, Horace G. Wilcox, were both born in Stonington, but Horace G. Wilcox removed to the State of Maine in later life, and died in the city of Portland in 1895. He was a blacksmith by trade, but for years was associated with the Smith Granite Company at their quarry in Westerly, Rhode Island, later establishing a quarry business of his own at Stonington, Maine, which he continued to conduct to the time of his death. He married Mary C. Barber, of Carolina, Rhode Island, who died in Pawcatuck, Connecticut, in 1873. They were the parents of two sons: George S., now a resident of Boston, Massachusetts; and William A., of further mention.

William A. Wilcox was born in the town of Stonington, New London county, Connecticut, February 17, 1873, and received his education in the public school of that town and in the Pawcatuck High School, from which he was graduated with the class of 1892. He began teaching in the same year and until 1907 taught in various Southern New England towns. Meantime, in 1900, he began, in his spare hours and during vacation times, to deal in real estate. His judgment of real estate values proved to be excellent, and by 1907 the business begun as a side issue had grown to such proportions that he felt justified in giving up his school work and devoting his entire time to the real estate business. He opened an office at Pawcatuck, and the business continued to grow and prosper until by 1914 the development was ready for another long step forward. In that year Mr. Wilcox formed an association with Wayland B. Batson, of New York City, opening an office on Fifth avenue, of which Mr. Batson became manager. This venture, too, has been successful.

Mr. Wilcox specializes in farm property, and throughout New England is known as the "farm specialist." He is widely known personally, and his catalogues are distributed over a very wide extent of territory. Business men in New York City who tire of cobblestones and pavements and long for the charms of country life and the farm find in Mr Wilcox a resourceful and expert aid in finding the right place. Those who seek a home within commuting distance, and yet far enough away to be free from the noise and confusion of the city, may also go to Mr. Wilcox, or to his partner on Fifth avenue, in New York City, and there receive expert advice and help. Mr. Wilcox himself still conducts the office in Pawcatuck, and is a resident of that town. In politics, he is a Republican, as assistant prosecuting attorney of the town of Stonington, and takes an active interest in the welfare of the community. He has served as chairman of the Stonington School Board since 1914. Fraternally, he is a member of Pawcatuck Lodge, No. 90, Free and Accepted Masons; and Palmer Chapter, No. 28, Royal Arch Masons. He is also a member of Westerly Lodge, Ancient Order of United Workmen, of Pawcatuck. Pawcatuck is on the Pawcatuck river, directly opposite Westerly, Rhode Island, two places being practically one community, although in different States, and many residents of Pawcatuck give their address as Westerly, Rhode Island.

In Pawcatuck, Connecticut, William Avery Wilcox married, on February 5, 1897, Augusta L. Sweet, daughter of Leonard and Anna (Baird) Sweet, of Stonington. Mr. and Mrs. Wilcox are the parents of two children: 1. Byron Edward, born May 15, 1898, who is an inspector for the Western Electric Manufacturing Company, stationed in Chicago, Illinois. He served in the Students' Army Training Corps during the World War in the aviation branch. 2. Ruth Gertrude, born March 12, 1900, in Stonington; she is a graduate of Bryant & Stratton's Business College, of Providence, Rhode Island, and of Miss McClintock's School for Girls, of Boston (1922), and is now holding a position as private stenographer in Boston, Massachusetts.

HENRY A. BECKWITH—The Beckwiths of New London county trace their descent to Matthew Beckwith, born in England, in 1610, who came in 1635 to Saybrook Point, Connecticut, thence to Branford in 1638, Hartford in 1642, and is recorded among the first settlers of Lyme in 1651. He became the owner by purchase of large tracts of land lying in both Lyme and New London, and the bark "Endeavor," the first vessel launched at New London, was built for and owned by him. He died December 18, 1681. From Matthew and Elizabeth Beckwith sprang numerous families, the branch of which Henry A. Beckwith, of New London, is representative, settling in Waterford, New London county, Connecticut, where Daniel A. Beckwith was born and spent his youth. Daniel A. Beckwith was for twenty-six years clerk and bookkeeper with the New York, New Haven & Hartford railroad at New London, and is now (May, 1921) cashier at the Municipal docks in New London. He married Hannah N. Perkins, and they were the parents of three children of whom the third was a son, Henry A.

Henry A. Beckwith was born in New London, Connecticut, December 29, 1888, and there was educated in the public schools. He began business life as shipping clerk for the R. & J. Warte Company, of New London, but later became manager of a storage battery company, a position he retained for three years. In 1919 he formed the partnership of Beckwith & Tooker, and opened an electrical shop for doing all kinds of electrical work along storage battery and kindred lines, automobile wiring and battery, and is also agent for the Indian motorcycle.

Mr. Beckwith married Etta M. Williams, of Colchester, Connecticut, and they are the parents of a daughter, Doris S., born January 23, 1912. The family are members of the Third Baptist Church, of New London.

CHARLES HAWLEY PHILLIPS—During his lifetime Charles Hawley Phillips occupied a prominent position in the town of Baltic, and when death removed him in his middle age, his passing out was felt to be a great loss to the community, not only because of his extensive business affairs, but of his ever ready willingness to assist in all things pertaining to the welfare and advancement of his home town.

Born in Griswold, Connecticut, October 21, 1864, Charles Hawley Phillips was the second son of Ralph and Jane (Burdick) Phillips. Early in life he gave evidence of fine business abilities, conducting for years a prosperous lumber and grain trade, and in addition to this, carrying on a large trucking business. Mr. Phillips was also one of the most progressive farmers in the locality, taking much pride in keeping his farm in every way abreast of the times. He was what might be called a self-made man, and his success in life was entirely due to his own perseverance and good judgment. Though keenly interested in public affairs and in general politics, Mr. Phillips several times declined to accept political office, though frequently urged to do so by his townspeople, even when nominated for it, always giving as his reason that he would be unable to do justice to his friends and to his many other interests as well. Mr. Phillips was a member of the fraternal organization, the Modern Woodmen.

Charles Hawley Phillips married (first) Evelyn James, of Canterbury, Connecticut, from whom he was afterwards separated. Two children were born of this union: Charles Elmer, who married Edith Rouse, of Preston, Connecticut; Bertha, now the wife of Augustus Condon. Mr. Phillips married (second) Mabel Helen Ferrell, born in Wilbraham, Massachusetts, February 16, 1886. She was the daughter of George Henry and Mira (Stewart) Ferrell. One daughter was born of this marriage, Mildred Alma, born June 18, 1910.

When Charles Hawley Phillips died he left an exceedingly prosperous and well paying establishment, which has been carried on by his widow, now Mrs. Mabel Helen Cole, she having married again quite recently into the Cole family.

WALLIN T. MURPHY was born in New London, Connecticut, April 21, 1887, son of John H. and Mary A. (McGarry) Murphy, his father one of the first minstrels in the show business.

Wallin T. Murphy attended grade and high public schools, finishing his school years at New London Business College. He began business life as clerk in the New London Savings Bank, but soon resigned his position to accept appointment as treasurer of the Lyceum Theatre, at that time under the managerial control of Mr. Jackson. That was in 1905, and later he became acting manager, Mr. Jackson going to Bridgeport, Connecticut, where he died in 1907, Mr. Murphy then succeeding him as manager of the Lyceum Theatre in New London.

In 1912 the Wallin T. Murphy Amusement Company was organized, which co-leased the Lyceum Theatre, and in 1914, when the Crown Theatre was built in New London by the New England Amusement Company, it was leased by the Wallin T. Murphy Amusement Company. That company built the New Capitol Theatre in New London, which opened to the public, November 21, 1921, these three playhouses, Lyceum, Crown, and Capitol, being under the direct management of the Wallin T. Murphy Amusement Company.

Mr. Murphy is a man of friendly, genial nature, a good business man with a host of friends. He is an honorary life member of New London Lodge, Benevolent and Protective Order of Elks, a fourth degree member of the Knights of Columbus, and chairman of the New London Athletic Commission.

ALBERT BASSETT—Public responsibility, business endeavor, and the tilling of the soil—all these have helped to fill the busy life of Albert Bassett, now retired, of Voluntown, Connecticut.

Mr. Bassett is a son of Ralph and Sarah M. (Hill) Bassett. Ralph Bassett was born in Voluntown, Connecticut, in the early years of the nineteenth century. His education was limited to the opportunities of the district schools of the day, and as a young man he took up farming in the vicinity of his home. Later the lure of the precious metal beckoned him Westward, and in 1858 he went to California, as a prospector. The gold rush of history was still at that time a living force in the development of the West, but while the young man met with more than a little success, he returned East in 1862, locating in Voluntown. Again, in 1872, Mr. Bassett went to California, this time taking his entire family with him. In 1882 he returned permanently to Voluntown, retiring from active work, and making his home with his son Albert, who had preceded him some years earlier. He died in February, 1912. His wife, who was born in New London, Connecticut, died in 1884. They were the parents of seven children, among them Albert, of whom further.

Albert Bassett, fourth child of Ralph and Sarah M. (Hill) Bassett, was born in Voluntown, New London county, Connecticut, on June 26, 1848. Receiving his education in the district schools of the neighborhood, he assisted his father on the farm until he was twenty-one years of age, then went to Providence, Rhode Island, where he worked as guard at the State Prison, remaining in that capacity for a period of four years. He then accompanied his father to California, but remained only for two years, then returned to Rhode Island, and located at Cranston, where he again became a guard in the State Prison, this time remaining in the work for eight years. At the end of that time Mr. Bassett purchased a farm in Coventry, Rhode Island, which he conducted for fifteen years. He then bought a farm in Voluntown, where he still resides.

A number of years ago Mr. Bassett retired from the active work of the farm, turning over to younger hands the care of his interests along this line. For a considerable time, however, he has been dealing in farm real estate, and this business he continues to conduct with appreciable success and profit. His activities along this line are not only of personal benefit to him, but they tend to forward the progress of the community and the general prosperity.

Mr. Bassett is interested in every matter which involves the public welfare, and while always declining public office, is a staunch supporter of the Democratic party. He is a member of Providence Lodge, No. 3, Ancient Order of United Workmen. He is a member of the Baptist church.

Mr. Bassett married, on September 17, 1875, Dolly Burdick, of Voluntown, a daughter of Jowell and Caroline Burdick, and they have five children, all living: Lillian, who became the wife of Simon Corp, now residing in Washington, Rhode Island; Ralph, who married Dorothy Crandall, and now lives in Boston, Massachusetts; Grace, who became the wife of Alfred I. Bennett, of Rockland, Rhode Island; William, who married Bessie Gulisipy, and now resides at Coventry, Rhode Island; and George H., a resident of Providence.

JEREMIAH A. DESMOND—The family of which Jeremiah A. Desmond is a member is of Irish descent, Ireland having been the birthplace of his father, Jeremiah H. Desmond, born in 1864. His mother, Bridget (Healy) Desmond, was born in Boston, also in 1864, and they were the parents of two daughters, Mary and Katherine, and three sons, Joseph, Harold and Jeremiah A. In Norwich, his birthplace, Mr. Desmond has been identified with mercantile operations since boyhood, and is now a partner in an enterprise established in 1921, Quinn & Desmond, which has made substantial progress in its special field, men's clothing and furnishings.

Jeremiah A. Desmond was born January 29, 1889. He obtained his education in the public schools and Norwich Free Academy, entering business life as a cash boy in the employ of Porteous & Mitchell, leading merchants of Norwich. Successive promotions put him through various grades of service to the position of manager of the men's furnishings department, and his association with this well known firm extended over a total of seventeen years. Mr. Desmond resigned from this employ early in 1921, and on April 21, 1921, he formed a partnership with James A. Quinn, who had been with the same firm for eleven years, under the firm name of Quinn & Desmond. They opened a gentlemen's clothing and furnishings store at No. 283 Main street, Norwich, and the long experience of both partners in this line of work has formed the basis of a successful and flourishing undertaking.

Mr. Desmond has a wide acquaintance in civic and social affairs, is secretary of the Democratic town committee, and in 1917-1919 filled the office of city clerk. He is a member of St. Mary's Roman Catholic Church, St. Joseph's Sodality, the Knights of Columbus, and the Norwich Chamber of Commerce.

Mr. Desmond married, in Norwich, in 1917, Helen Gertrude Hinchey, of this city. They are the parents of Jeremiah A., Jr., born in May, 1918; John, born in November, 1919; and Helen, born in October, 1921.

DWIGHT BAILEY RICHMOND—The Richmonds of this review came to East Lyme, New London county, Connecticut, from Wyoming county, New York, but the family originally were of Glastonbury, Connecticut, from whence Edmund Richmond took his departure for Wyoming county. They resided in that county about fifteen years, Dwight B. Richmond being then a lad of thirteen. It was in 1868 that the family returned to Connecticut and settled in East Lyme.

Edmund Richmond was born in Glastonbury, Connecticut, in April, 1833, died in East Lyme, New London county, Connecticut, in 1901. He spent his boyhood in Glastonbury and there attended the public schools. Later he resided in Meriden, Connecticut, where he was employed in the silver manufactories. He next moved to Wyoming county, New York, and there remained until his son Dwight B. was thirteen years of age, when the family returned to Connecticut, locating at Niantic Hill in the town of East Lyme, New London county. There Edmund Richmond engaged in farming until his passing in 1901. He married Phoebe Elizabeth Bailey, born April 6, 1833, daughter of Dwight and Annis Electa (Cook) Bailey, her father passing away May 6, 1879, her mother born May, 1811, dying July 26, 1847. Dwight Bailey and Annis Electa Cook were married January 23, 1831. Mrs. Phoebe (Bailey) Richmond still survives her husband now aged eighty-eight years, and makes her home with her eldest daughter, Mrs. Olive Isabella Donals. Mr. and Mrs. Edmund Richmond were the parents of four children, their first born dying in infancy. The second child was their only son, Dwight B. Richmond, of further mention. Their eldest daughter, Olive Isabella, married Albert Donals, of Groton, Connecticut. The youngest daughter, Nellie Christine, married Walter Watrons, of Willimantic, Connecticut.

Dwight Bailey Richmond, only son of Edmund and Phoebe E. (Bailey) Richmond, was born in Wyoming county, New York, August 11, 1855, and there spent the first thirteen years of his life. In 1868 the family returned to their native Connecticut, locating at Niantic Hill, in the town of East Lyme, New London county, on a farm, and there Dwight Richmond continued a farmer until after his marriage. He then spent some time in Munson, Massachusetts, engaged as a housepainter, but not long afterward he returned to Niantic Hill, where he bought a farm, near the farm of his parents. This farm was known as the "Elisha Miller Place," and a great deal of local history attaches to it. Soon after his return to Niantic Hill, Edmund Richmond fell ill, and in 1901, Dwight sold his Niantic Hill farm and purchased the Norman Rogue farm of ninety-four acres, located near the village of Flanders, where he still continues a prosperous farmer. He is a member and chairman of the Board of Relief, and formerly served on the school committee. In politics he is independent, in religious faith a Baptist.

Mr. Richmond married at Waterford, Connecticut, November 11, 1881, Rose Holland, born in Bridgewater, Vermont, August 22, 1862, only child of Thomas Holland. Dwight B. and Rose (Holland)

Richmond are the parents of five children: Harry Barton born January, 1883, deceased; Grace Chapman, born February 29, 1885, at Munson, Massachusetts, married Percy Hart, of Bristol Connecticut, when a widow with three children, Clayton, Gordon, and Elizabeth; Roy Bailey, born in Munson, Massachusetts, June 17, 1887, married Helen Harold, of Munson, Connecticut, and has a daughter, Doris; Myrtle Frances, born in 1889, married William Andrews, of Willimantic, Connecticut, and has two children: Kenneth and Evelyn Andrews; Helen Elizabeth, born at the farm at Flanders, Connecticut, June 29, 1905.

ANTHONY SILVA, born in New London, Connecticut, September 11, 1872, has in the near half century which has since intervened resided continuously in his native city, where he has since 1912 been successfully engaged in the real estate and fire insurance business. His parents, John C. and Isabella Silva, were of Portugese ancestry, the father born in Lisbon, Portugal, the mother in the Azores, but now living in New London, a widow, aged sixty-eight.

Anthony Silva attended New London public schools, but at the age of eight years began selling papers on the streets after or before school hours. He literally grew up, developing a prosperous newspaper business, and for eighteen years was a wholesale dealer, supplying a great part of New London county with his papers and periodicals. He continued the wholesale business until 1912, when he engaged in his present business, real estate and fire insurance. He is a member of the Loyal Order of Moose; Benevolent and Protective Order of Elks; and the Niagara Fire Department.

Mr. Silva married Hattie Maria Ayres, born in Westfield, Massachusetts, daughter of Henry and Emma Ayres.

MICHAEL B. RING—Although Michael B. Ring's death occurred but half a decade ago, he belonged to a business which was of an early pioneer period, a business in which half a century of his life was spent—carriage building. He founded carriage works and a blacksmith shop in Norwich, and continued both until the automobile came, then transferred his energy to the latter, and established a business now continued in Norwich by his sons.

Michael B. Ring, son of David and Margaret (Killiker) Ring, was born in Norwich, Connecticut, March 31, 1852. After completing public school courses, he learned the carriage maker's trade at the corner of Willard and Chestnut streets, Norwich, having as a partner Lyman L. Whipple, they doing business as Whipple & Ring, carriage builders. Mr. Ring acquired the property, Nos. 11-17 Chestnut street, and about 1898 bought the land at Nos. 19-31 Chestnut street, which included the Converse property. He continued in business as a carriage builder and blacksmith until 1908, when, seeing that a new mode of transportation had come to stay, he entered the automobile business, being one of the first men in that activity. He continued active in that business until his death in Norwich, May 21, 1917. But the Ring name was not to disappear from the roll of Norwich business men, for the veteran builder of vehicles left two sons, M. Bernard, and Joseph F., who succeeded their father and continue the business under the firm name, Ring Brothers.

Mr. Ring was a member of the Catholic Benevolent League, life member of the New London Agricultural Society, Norwich Chamber of Commerce, a member and one of the promoters of the Gentleman's Driving Club of Norwich, a one time organization of lovers of the light-harness horse. At one time Mr. Ring was president of the Connecticut Horse Shoers' Association, and vice-president of the national organization.

Michael B. Ring married, May 31, 1876, Mary Terry, of Norwich, born December 15, 1859. They were the parents of five sons and a daughter, namely: 1. Charles B., born January 17, 1879, a manufacturer of automobile bodies, of Springfield, Massachusetts, with branches at Cambridge, Massachusetts, and Portland, Maine. 2. M. Bernard, born September 31, 1884, his father's successor in business; member of the Knights of Columbus, and the Benevolent and Protective Order of Elks. 3. James T., born May 6, 1886, deceased; was a pharmacist of Norwich until his decease. 4. John F., born April 22, 1888; deceased; until his death he was engaged as an undertaker, a member of the firm of Ring & Cummings, of Norwich. 5. Joseph F., born March 31, 1891; his father's successor in business, he and his brother, M. Bernard, conducting the automobile business in Norwich under the name of Ring Brothers; he served in the United States Army during the World War, 1917-18; he is a member of the Knights of Columbus and of other organizations in Norwich. 6. Mary B. P., born November 6, 1896.

CHESTER LEON HUSSEY—As a mechanical draughtsman, Mr. Hussey has been employed in different places, his residence in Norwich, Connecticut, beginning in 1915 with the Hopkins & Allen Company, manufacturers of firearms. He is a son of George A. and Ora (Harrison) Hussey, his father born in Chicago, Illinois, his mother in Buffalo, New York. George A. Hussey, after completing his education in Chicago public schools, learned the carpenter's trade, which he followed all his life. He and his wife now reside in Belchertown, Massachusetts.

Chester Leon Hussey, eldest of the five children of George A. and Ora (Harrison) Hussey, was born in Spencer, Massachusetts, August 7, 1895, and there was educated in the public schools. He then studied mechanical drawing in Bridgeport, Connecticut, for one year under a capable instructor and made such progress that at the end of a year he was able to fill a draughtsman's position. He was so employed in several places until 1915, when he located in Norwich and entered the employ of the Hopkins & Allen Company. During the period of war between the United States and Germany, 1917-18, the Hopkins & Allen plant was turned over to the Martin & Rockwell Company, manufacturers of machine-gun parts, and was utilized for that purpose during the entire war period, Mr. Hussey continuing with the operating company. Later the Hopkins & Allen plant was sold to the J. B. Martin Company, manufacturers of velvets, Mr. Hussey still remaining with that company as mechanical draughtsman.

In his political faith Mr. Hussey is a strong supporter of the Henry George theory of the single tax. He is affiliated with Somerset Lodge, No. 34, Free and Accepted Masons, of Norwich, and with the United Congregational Church of the same place.

Mr. Hussey married, in March, 1918, Alice M. Jackson, daughter of George and —— (Crocker) Jackson.

ADELARD GADUE—Although of Rhode Island birth, Adelard Gadue came to Connecticut from Canada, his father, Anthony Gadue, moving to Canada in 1874 and remaining there, later returning to the United States, locating in Baltic, New London county, Connecticut, there securing employment as a mill worker.

Adelard Gadue, son of Anthony Gadue, was born in Rhode Island, in 1873, and there spent the first year of his life. The next few years were spent in Montreal, Canada, then the family returned to the United States. He was for a time employed as a mill boy; at the age of twelve he became an employee of a lumber yard at Versailles, and later became clerk in a general store at Occum, Connecticut. He has since become proprietor of his own store in Occum, and conducts a grocery and provision store in his own building. He is a member of the Loyal Order of Moose, and of St. Joseph's Roman Catholic Church.

Adelard Gadue married (first) Mrs. Josephine Desmanes, who died about 1902, the mother of two children: Hilda, now Mrs. A. Roundau, and Irene, now Mrs. Paul Touchette. Mr. Gadue married (second) Alfonsine Savagau, and they are the parents of six children: Leona, Agnes, Mary, Adelard, Almira, and Margaret.

JOHN DEAN AVERY—Nine generations of Averys have lived in New England, tracing from Christopher Avery down to John Dean Avery, of North Stonington, New London county, Connecticut. Christopher Avery came from England at a date unknown, but he was a selectman of Gloucester, Massachusetts, in 1645, 1652, and 1654, and took the oath of fidelity, June 29, 1653. In 1658 he sold land in Gloucester, and in the same year he moved to Boston, buying real estate in what is now the center of the city, and on which the Boston Post Office building is now located. For that land (the deed acknowledged before Governor Endicott) he paid forty pounds. He moved, with his son James, to New London, Connecticut, and there died, March 12, 1678.

(II) Captain James Avery, the only son of Christopher Avery, was born in England in 1620, and came to New England with his father, his death occurring in New London, Connecticut, April 18, 1700. He was granted, in New London, October 19, 1650, a town lot on Cape Ann Lane, and in addition "Little Owle Meadow." In 1652 he obtained a grant of land in South Groton county, and in 1653 became the owner of a farm on "Pocketannock Grants" on the River Thames. In 1684 he bought the "Unadorned Church and watchtower of the Wilderness," and from the timber he constructed a dwelling which stood until destroyed by fire in 1902. In the Indian wars of his period he bore an active and foremost part, ranking as captain. He was in charge of the three towns, New London, Stonington, and Lyme, during King Philip's War, and in the stubborn fight at South Kingston, Rhode Island, Sunday, December 19, 1695, against the Narragansetts, he commanded the friendly Pequot Indians. He was equally prominent in civil life, serving as selectman twenty years, was commissioner of the peace, twelve times elected member of the General Court, and filled many temporary positions on committees and commissions. He was active in the church and was one of the strong men of his day, eminent in all the relations of life, a man of whom his descendants may be proud. Captain James Avery married, November 10, 1643, Joana Greenshade, of Boston, who died in 1714, the mother of six sons, this branch descending through the eldest son, James (2), who is also Captain James Avery.

(III) Captain James (2) Avery was a man of affairs in his section, serving as deputy to the General Court for New London six terms, was commissioner of the peace, captain of the train band, and counselor to the Pequot Indians. He appeared before the General Court in 1695, in behalf of the inhabitants of the east side of the river, who wished to establish a church, and that was the beginning of the church in Groton. He married Deborah Stallyon, and their tombstones, in a fair state of preservation, may be seen near the center of the burying ground at Poquonock. He died in Groton country, August 22, 1748, in his one hundredth year. His wife died March 27, 1729. The line of descent from these wonderful old pioneers is traced thus: (IV) James (3) Avery; (V) John Avery; (VI) Elijah Avery; (VII) John J. Avery; (VIII) Albert Lay Avery; (IX) John Dean Avery; head of the present generation.

(VIII) Albert Lay Avery was born at Eastern Point in the town of Groton, New London county, Connecticut, and died in the village of Groton, in 1885. At one time Mr. Avery's farm included the entire area of Eastern Point, some five hundred acres, and until the day of his death he was one of the leading influential men of his town. He married Johanna B. Wheeler, born in North Stonington, Connecticut, who died in 1867, and they were the parents of nine children: 1. Albert, married Mary A. Maine, and died in 1893. 2. Rebecca Williams, died January 6, 1900. 3. Maria Lay, married Judson Avery, both deceased. 4. Martha Wheeler, died aged seven years. 5. Augustus Pomeroy, married Clara Weed, and resides in Brooklyn, New York. 6. John Dean, of further mention. 7. Jerusha Pomeroy, married William A. Farran, and resides in Providence, Rhode Island. 8. Thomas Wheeler, a sketch of whom follows. 9. Annie Hine, a resident of New London county.

(IX) John Dean Avery, sixth child of Albert Lay and Johanna B. (Wheeler) Avery, was born at the homestead in the town of Groton, New London county, Connecticut, June 6, 1852. After completing the courses of study available in the district school, he entered the State Normal School at New Britain, Connecticut, whence he was graduated a qualified teacher. In 1875 he leased the William Pilts farm in North Stonington, and for fifteen years tilled the acres very profitably. In 1890 he bought the Alfred Miner farm of two hundred and eighty-eight acres near the village of North Stonington, and for thirty-three years he has devoted his energies to its cultivation and improvement. He has brought the farm to a high state of productiveness, has made many improvements of a modern and substantial nature, and has made the farm one of the best in the town.

Mr. Avery is a member of the New London County Farm Bureau, for three years its vice-president, for one year president, and for seven years has been a member of the board of directors. He is a member and for two years was master of North Stonington Grange, No. 138, Patrons of Husbandry. He was superintendent of the Sunday school of the North Stonington Congregational Church for thirty-three years. He united with the Groton Congregational Church when fourteen years of age, and when he settled in North Stonington took a letter from the Groton church to the North Stonington church. He is a Republican in politics, and for two terms served as selectman.

Mr. Avery married, December 2, 1885, Mary A. Rice, of Meriden, Connecticut, daughter of Benjamin F. and Abbie (Harvey) Rice. They have an adopted daughter, Alice E., wife of Samuel L. Root, of Farmington, Connecticut.

THOMAS WHEELER AVERY—On the old Eastern Point homestead of Albert Lay Avery, his son, Thomas Wheeler Avery, was born, and when the father laid down life's burdens in 1885, the son assumed the management, and there resides, never having known any other home. He is a descendant of Christopher and Captain James Avery, and the son of Albert Lay and Johanna B. (Wheeler) Avery, their eighth child and youngest son (see preceding sketch).

Thomas Wheeler Avery was born in the town of Groton, New London county, Connecticut. He was educated in the public schools of Groton and early became his father's farm assistant. He is a member of the Congregational church of Groton, a Republican in politics, and influential in his town.

Mr. Avery married, March 6, 1884, Mary Alice Maine, daughter of Charles Henry and Louisa (Miner) Maine, granddaughter of Richard H. and Abby (Stanton) Maine, and great-granddaughter of Simeon T. and Martha (York) Maine, all these generations residents of North Stonington, and farmers. Mr. and Mrs. Thomas Wheeler Avery are the parents of two sons: Albert Thomas Avery, a sketch of whom follows; and John Dean (2) Avery, who during the World War, 1917-18, enlisted in the United States Aviation Corps, and was in training at the Aviation Officers' Training School at Dallas, Texas, afterward flying instructor. He is now a partner with his brother in the firm, John D. Avery & Company, Incorporated, automobile dealers of New London county. He married, at New London, Irene Wood.

ALBERT THOMAS AVERY—On June 25, 1890, on the old Wheeler homestead at Eastern Point, town of Groton, New London county, Connecticut, Albert Thomas Avery was born, his father, Thomas Wheeler Avery, having also been born there, the son of Albert Lay and Johanna B. (Wheeler) Avery, (see two preceding sketches).

Albert Thomas Avery grew up at the homestead at Eastern Point, and after attendance at the public school of the district, he entered at the Norwich Free Academy and finished preparatory study there with the class of 1909. He entered Cornell University, whence he was graduated mechanical engineer, class of 1914. During the four years of the World War, 1914-1918, he was in the employ of the Electric Boat Company, at Fore River, Massachusetts, and Montreal, as engineer in submarine construction, and in 1919, in association with his brother, John D. Avery, he formed the firm, John D. Avery & Company, Incorporated, and established an automobile business in New London, Albert T. Avery as manager. The company is agent for the Marmon and Nash cars, and operates one of the largest garages in the State, with well-equipped service, supply, and repair departments. Mr. Avery is a Republican in politics, a member of Groton Congregational Church, and of the Harbor Club of New London. In his business relations with the public, he has established high reputation as a man of ability and integrity.

Mr. Avery married, September 11, 1916, Rachel White, daughter of Charles E. and Mary (Wheeler) White, of Groton, Connecticut. Mr. and Mrs. Avery are the parents of a daughter, Patricia, born March 16, 1918.

LEWIS ANTHONY ANDREWS—Among the successful merchants of Norwich, Connecticut, is Lewis Anthony Andrews, a member of the firm of

Charbennean & Andrews, shoe dealers at No. 159 Main street. A native of this city, he gives his support to all measures calculated to advance business development.

Lewis Anthony Andrews was born in Norwich, Connecticut, May 2, 1891, the son of Lewis and —— (Lucier) Andrews. Lewis Andrews, Sr., was born in Vermont, and obtained his education in the district schools there, after which he became a moulder and has followed this trade up to the present time. To Mr. and Mrs. Andrews have been born four children: Flora, deceased; Lewis Anthony, of this review; Arthur J., a resident of Pawtucket, Rhode Island; and Lena, died in infancy. The education of Lewis Anthony Andrews was obtained in the public schools of Norwich and Norwich Free Academy. After graduation in 1904 he entered upon his business career as a clerk for the J. F. Cosgrove Company, at Norwich, and here he remained until 1914, when he became associated with Mr. Charbennean, which partnership has continued up to the present time.

In politics, Mr. Andrews is a Republican, giving to the affairs of the organization the interest demanded of every good citizen. He is prominent in the local fraternal organizations, being affiliated with the Benevolent and Protective Order of Elks, Lodge No. 430; the Knights of Columbus, White Cross Council, No. 13; Loyal Order of Moose, Lodge No. 950, of which he is the secretary; Fraternal Order of Eagles, No. 67; and past chief ranger of the Foresters of America.

On March 31, 1913, Mr. Andrews was united in marriage with Viola M. Lanoie, of Franklin, Massachusetts, the daughter of Napolean and Mary (Crepeau) Lanoie. Mrs. Andrews passed away in February, 1920. To Mr. and Mrs. Andrews were born four children: Hazel V.; Lewis A.; Lena L.; and Richard N.

ALFRED GREENE LILLIBRIDGE—Norwich has no more aggressive representative of the automobile industry than she possesses in the man whose name stands at the head of this article. Mr. Lillibridge is a useful citizen, always ready to do his utmost toward the furtherance of any project which promises improvement of municipal conditions.

Christopher Lillibridge, father of Alfred Greene Lillibridge, was a carpenter and builder, and all his life followed his trade in Norwich. He was a Republican, and at one time served on the district school committee. He affiliated with the Independent Order of Odd Fellows, of Norwich, holding the office of clerk of his lodge. His religious membership was in the Congregational church. Mr. Lillibridge married Abbie McCullen, a native of Norwich ,and their children were: Georgie, married Thomas Young, of Norwich; Ida, now living in Norwich, where she was born, as was her sister; and Alfred Greene, mentioned below. Mr. Lillibridge died in Norwich in 1913, and his widow now resides there.

Alfred Greene Lillibridge, son of Christopher and Abbie (McCullen) Lillibridge, was born in December, 1884, in Norwich, and attended the public schools of his native city, graduating from the Norwich High School. He then spent three years with the Ponema Company, of Norwich, acquiring a thorough knowledge of the machinist's trade. Having finished his apprenticeship, Mr. Lillibridge entered the service of the Stevens-Duryea Company, of Chicopee Falls, Massachusetts, for the purpose of learning the automobile business. After remaining with the company for the space of a year, he felt competent, in all respects, to go into business for himself, at least, before very long. Returning to Norwich, he was employed as a driver in the town until 1913, when he associated himself with the automobile business of Amos C. Swan, of Norwich. Almost from the first he proved himself of value to the concern, and after the death of Mr. Swan he was advanced to the position of general manager, which he has since retained. By his able fulfillment of the duties of this responsible post, Mr. Lillibridge has done much for the upbuilding of the business on a sure and substantial basis and for the extension of its transactions in different directions and along various lines.

In politics, Mr. Lillibridge is a Republican, but has never had either time or inclination for office-holding. He affiliates with Somerset Lodge, No. 34, Free and Accepted Masons, of Norwich, and attends the Congregational church.

Mr. Lillibridge married, in Norwich, Bonnielyon Corey, born in that place, daughter of Eli Corey. Mr. Corey is now deceased, but his wife resides in Norwich. Mr. and Mrs. Lillibridge are the parents of two children, both of whom were born in Norwich: Alfred, Jr., born June 23, 1911; and Donald, born September 16, 1914. A fine type of the self-made man is Alfred Greene Lillibridge. He is one of the men who are helping to build up the industrial future of the city of Norwich.

DAVID AUSTIN RICE—In the prosperous farming community of Waterford, one of the most attractive environs of the city of New London, Connecticut, the name of Rice is well and favorably known, and David Austin Rice is one of the successful citizens of the town.

Mr. Rice is a son of James Rice, who was born May 2, 1818. Coming to the United States in his childhood, James Rice was reared and educated in the northwestern part of New York State, where the family settled. As a young man he engaged, with an elder brother, in the manufacture of brick, their yards having been located at Albany, New York. This business became very successful, and was carried on for some years, under the name of Rice Brothers. Later in life James Rice came to

New London, and here he married Amy Copron Whipple, the ceremony taking place on April 6, 1858. Mrs. Rice was a daughter of Anthony and Hannah (Fargoe) Whipple, a member of an old pioneer family of New London county. Upon their marriage, Mr. Rice became a resident of the old Whipple homestead, in the Gilead section of Waterford, one of the very old houses in this section, built by one Anthony Whipple, in 1642. They were the parents of four children, all born at Waterford, Connecticut: John, born December 17, 1861; Mary Jane, born February 20, 1863; William, born March 20, 1865; and Thomas, born August 29, 1868. The mother died on the day that the youngest child was born. James Rice married (second) Mary Delia Hawkins, who was born in England, and was a daughter of the eminent English surgeon, Dr. Edwin Hawkins, and his wife, Nancy (McDonald) Hawkins. There were six children born to the second union: Amy Jane, born May 16, 1870, who became the wife of Charles Griswold; David Austin, of whom further; Austin David, twin brother of David Austin; James H., of whom further; Josephine, born December 24, 1881; and Lillian Ada. Mary Delia (Hawkins) Rice died in Waterford, December 13, 1917, in her ninetieth year.

David Austin Rice, son of James and Mary Delia (Hawkins) Rice, was born December 25, 1872, in Waterford, Connecticut, and is a twin brother of Austin David Rice, widely famous in pugilistic circles, and one-time holder of the lightweight belt. Mr. Rice was reared in his native town, and received a practical education in the public schools of Waterford. After completing his studies he took up the work of the farm in association with his father, and bore the burden of farm operations during his father's declining years. He had lived on the home farm all his life, and since his father's death has owned the property, which is one of the finest farms in this part of the county, taking great pride in keeping abreast of the times in all matters of agricultural progress. He has never married, and lives very quietly, taking only the interest of the citizen in public affairs.

James H. Rice, son of James and Mary Delia (Hawkins) Rice, was born June 11, 1876. He married Flora Daton, of Waterford, Connecticut, and five children were born of this union: Alice, Edna May, Nelson Daton, Kenneth, and Cora Valentine.

JOSEPH MARION was born at Joliette, Province of Quebec, Canada, April 19, 1882. He is the son of Isaac Marion, who received his education in the parochial schools of the Province of Quebec, after which he came to the United States, locating in Putnam, Connecticut, where he has since been actively employed in mills. To Mr. and Mrs. Isaac Marion were born the following children: Joseph, of further mention; F. O., owner and manager of a store at Putnam; and Leon P., who married Helen E. Dawley, of Voluntown, Connecticut, May 30, 1920, and is associated with Joseph in business.

The education of Joseph Marion was obtained in the public schools of Putnam. At an early age he completed his studies and then worked as a clerk in the store of his brother, F. O. Marion, at Putnam. In 1918, together with his brother, Leon P., Joseph bought the store of J. L. Herbert & Son, of Voluntown, Connecticut. The venture proved successful, the business consistently growing to its present-day extensive proportions. The local postoffice is situated in this store, Joseph Marion having been installed as postmaster. In politics, Mr. Marion has always been a Democrat and active in civic affairs. He affiliates with the Putnam Nest of Eagles, and in religion is a Roman Catholic.

Joseph Marion married, on April 8, 1906, Delia Paquett, of Putnam. Mr. and Mrs. Marion are the parents of three children: Gertrude D., Mary Louise and Gerald P.

HOWARD JAMES WIGHT—After being engaged in the cabinet business for some time, Howard James Wight gave it up to become a farmer, locating in Baltic, Sprague township, where he is still interested in farming.

Born in West Greenwich, Rhode Island, August 2, 1889, Howard James Wight afterward came to Connecticut to live, attending the public schools of Jewett City in his boyhood. After his school days were over the young man learned the trade of a cabinet maker, and for several years was employed in Hartford, Connecticut, in that line of work. In 1916, abandoning his trade, Mr. Wight came to Sprague township where he has been ever since. The father of Howard James Wight is Howard Myron Wight, born in Natick, Massachusetts, in May, 1852. He now resides in Taftville, Connecticut. His wife is Sarah Jane Wight, a native of Preston, Connecticut, where she was born on December 3, 1860. They had a family of ten children, four sons and six daughters: Howard James, whose name heads this review; Otis Harmond, born in May, 1895; George Lester; Royal, born in 1903. Of these sons, two were engaged in the World War, Otis Harmond serving in the 137th Engineers overseas, where he was slightly wounded. George Lester served with the Marines, and died of "Flu" while in service. The daughters are: Mary, deceased; Emilie, also deceased; Annie; Olive; Etta; and Ethel, deceased.

Howard James Wight married Clara Louise Wullkay, who was born in Norwich, June 7, 1892. She is the daughter of Julius and Mary Wullkay. Two children have been born of this union: Ruth Marie, born in Norwich, July 9, 1916; and Myron Julius, born September 13, 1920.

DAVID JOSEPH TURNBULL—With experience on both sides of the Atlantic in the textile industry, David J. Turnbull is now filling an important position as manager of the Thames Dyeing & Bleaching Company, of Niantic, Connecticut.

Mr. Turnbull is a son of William and Isabella (Stokes) Turnbull. His father was born in Newcastle-upon-Tyne, England, in 1836, has been a mill worker all his life, and now at the age of eighty-five years, is still actively engaged in the textile industry. The mother, who was also born in England, died in the year 1897. They were the parents of five children: David J., William, Mary, Anna, and Isabella.

David Joseph Turnbull was born at Newcastle-upon-Tyne, England, September 22, 1867, and received his education in the schools of that city. After leaving school he became interested in the bleaching, dyeing, and printing of cotton fabrics, and spent ten years of his early manhood in this industry, in the famous mills of Yorkshire, England. In 1891 he came to the United States, locating in Rhode Island. For some years he was identified with the cotton mills of that State, at various localities, then became associated with the Aspinook Mills, of Jewett City, Connecticut, where he was employed for a period of twenty-five years. At the end of that time, in the year 1919, Mr. Turnbull came to Niantic, to accept the position of manager of the Thames Dyeing & Bleaching Company, one of the leading plants of the day in this field. Mr. Turnbull is prominent in fraternal circles, being a member of Reliance Lodge, Woodmen of America, of Jewett City, and of Norwich Lodge, No. 430, Benevolent and Protective Order of Elks.

In April, 1894, Mr. Turnbull married Anna Gorman, who was born in Providence, Rhode Island, and is a daughter of Thomas and Mary Gorman. Mr. and Mrs. Turnbull had the following children: William, born in East Greenwich, now deceased; Alice Mary, born in Jewett City; and George Joseph, also born in Jewett City.

CLARENCE ORVILLE REYNOLDS—Among the prominent business executives of Mystic is Clarence O. Reynolds, who has for upwards of two years been manager of the Holmes Coal Company. Mr. Reynolds is a son of Orville Augustus and Emma A. (Bissell) Reynolds. The father was born at Cross Rivers, Westchester county, New York, February 17, 1848, and was educated in the district schools near his home, thereafter working with his father on the farm. About 1868 he came to Waterbury, Connecticut, where he was employed in a rubber shop for a time, in the capacity of shipping clerk, then went to Danbury, to enter the mechanical department of the "Danbury News." In 1894 he again removed, this time to New Haven, where he acted as manager for the Babcock Oil Company, continuing in that capacity until 1910, when he retired from active business. His wife, who was born in Waterbury, February 22, 1853, died in New Haven, June 22, 1915. They were the parents of four children: Leita E., who married Eugene Clark, of New Haven, and died in 1908, in that city; Leila B., who married William R. Bailey, of New Haven, and died in 1915; Clarence Orville, whose name heads this review; and Chares H., who married ——— Verseconer, and resides in New Haven. The youngest son served for seventeen months in France, during the World War, in the ordnance department of the First Division.

Clarence Orville Reynolds was born in Mount Kisco, Westchester county, New York, October 25, 1886. The family removing to New Haven, it was there that he received his education in the public and high schools. In 1901 he became associated with his father, but two years later chose a different field of endeavor, entering the employ of S. H. Moore, one of the leading florists of New Haven, and thoroughly mastering the business. He remained at the Moore plant for a period of seventeen years. On August 12, 1918, Mr. Reynolds joined the United States army, and was stationed at Camp Greenleaf, in Georgia, rated as a wagoner. He was later transferred to the Motor Ambulance Corps (No. 4), which was a part of Field Hospital No. 65. They had just been assigned to duty overseas when the armistice was signed, and Mr. Reynolds was discharged from the service at Camp Upton, New York, January 27, 1919. Returning to New Haven, he continued with the Moores until January 12, 1920, when he came to Mystic, on that date entering upon the duties of his present position as general manager of the interests of the Holmes Coal Company. He has since held a prominent place in the business world of this community. Both Mr. Reynolds and his father now reside in Mystic. Politically, Mr. Reynolds supports the Republican party, although he has thus far taken no active part in political affairs. He is a member of the American Legion, and of the First Congregational Church, both of New Haven.

FREDERICK VAN REED KNOUSE—Holding a responsible position in the business world of Norwich, of which city he has been a resident for more than a decade, Mr. Knouse has been definitely instrumental in keeping this city in the lead commercially, through his influence in the establishing of the present steamship line between Norwich and New York City.

Descended from a line of prominent men, Mr. Knouse is a son of the late Rev. William Henry Knouse, widely known in Middlesex county, this State, as a Congregational clergyman. Rev. Mr. Knouse was born in New York City, and prepared for his career in the educational institutions of that city, his course in letters having been at the New York University, and his course in theology at the Union Theological Seminary, also of that city. After his ordination he entered upon the duties of his first charge, at Greenwich, Connecticut, and later served in Cutchogue, Suffolk county (Long Island), New York. Remaining there, however, but a short period, Rev. Mr. Knouse accepted a call to Deep River, Connecticut, where he served for a period of thirty-three years, or until his death. He was deeply and sincerely devoted to the welfare of the people, and was greatly beloved by them, his death causing wide regret throughout the section in which he was so well known. He married Frances Odelia Carpenter, who was also born in New York City, and died in Deep River, and they were the parents of five children, of whom Mr. Knouse of Norwich was the fourth.

Frederick Van Reed Knouse was born in Cutchogue, Long Island, December 29, 1869. Attending first the public schools of his native place, he completed his education at Wesleyan College, then for one year served as a clerk in the Deep River National Bank. Next going to New Haven, he acted as clerk at the Yale National Bank of that city for about one year, then about 1891 went to New York City. He was there engaged in the offices of the Cromwell Steamship Company, until the outbreak of the Spanish-American War. Enlisting early, he served during the period of the war as private, in the 14th Regiment, New York Volunteer Infantry, at various camps, but saw no active service. Returning to New York City at the close of hostilities, he became connected with the Clyde Steamship Company, in the capacity of clerk, continuing for several years, then for three years thereafter, acted as manager of a hotel at Fire Island, New York. In 1903 Mr. Knouse entered the employ of the Mallory Steamship Company, of New York, taking charge of the clerical department, and remaining with this concern until 1911. At that time he came to Norwich to accept the office of agent and manager of the Norwich office for the Chelsea Steamboat Company. The bankruptcy of this concern in 1917 placed Mr. Knouse at liberty, and despite the abnormal conditions he was able to interest the Cape Cod Steamship Company in water transportation from this point, and they established the present line from Norwich to New York, placing Mr. Knouse in the office of agent and manager, in full charge of their affairs here. This position he still holds, successfully carrying forward the interests of the line.

A member of the Norwich Chamber of Commerce, Mr. Knouse serves on the transportation committee of that body. Politically, he supports the Republican party, and fraternally holds membership in Somerset Lodge, No. 34, Free and Accepted Masons, of Norwich, also being a member of Norwich Post, Spanish War Veterans. He and his family attend and support the Congregational church.

Mr .Knouse married, in Norwich, in December, 1915, Catherine Birraecree, of this city, and they have three children, all born in Norwich: Miriam Frances, Catherine Grace, and Dorothy Winifred. The family reside at No. 52 Church street, Norwich.

NATHANIEL BOYNTON ROYALL—There is now and then a man who, after he has passed away, lives in the minds of many, not only by reason of results accomplished, but also in consequence of a singularly vivid personality. So survives the memory of the late Nathaniel Boynton Royall. He was born in Elmira, New York, in 1844, and acquired his education in the public schools of his native place. For a number of years he was in the government employ at the New York City Post Office, after which he established himself in the manufacture of wagons at Hughville, Pennsylvania, later removing to Glenhazel, where his business was destroyed by fire. Mr. Royall then returned to New York City, and after remaining there for a short period came to Lebanon, where he passed the last twenty-three years of his life.

Always dignified in bearing, Mr. Royall was also singularly approachable, and his loyalty in friendship inspired a like sentiment in all who were brought into close relations with him. Actuated in public and private by one high motive, the welfare of all whom he served and of all with whom he served, he was a genial, kindly gentleman, and by his death, which occurred in November, 1917, Lebanon was deprived of one of her representative citizens.

Mr. Royall married, May 5, 1869. Mrs. Royall was born in Liberty, Sullivan county, New York, November 30, 1846. She obtained her education in the Hancock public schools and the Liberty Normal School, after which she removed with her father's family to Newark Valley, where her father was a sole leather manufacturer. Here she remained until her marriage in 1869. To Mr. and Mrs. Royall were born three children: Ralph, born July 8, 1871, in Brooklyn, New York, is now practicing law in New York City, with the law firm of Sullivan & Cromwell; Edson D., born December 1, 1875, was graduated from the College of Physicians and Surgeons, and died in Lebanon in 1907; and Eunice Natalie, who died at the age of eleven years, at Hughville. Mrs. Royall survived her husband, but is now deceased.

CLINTON ELLIOTT LANE—Henry Clinton Lane, father of Clinton E. Lane, of Norwich, Connecticut, was born in Clinton, a banking town of Huron county, Ontario, Canada, on the Grand Trunk railroad, and there spent the first fourteen years of his life. He was also of Springfield, Massachusetts, later of Canada, and eventually settled in Dodgeville, Wisconsin, where he conducted his blacksmithing business in his own shop after a term of journeyman blacksmith with Stratman Brothers. He married in Dodgeville, and in 1890 came East, locating in Norwich, Connecticut, where he bought the Charles Scolt blacksmith shop at No. 17 Chestnut street. For twenty-five years he continued in business, then moved in 1915 to his present well known shop in Durke lane. He married Mary Louise Elliott, born in Dodgeville, Wisconsin, now residing in Norwich.

Clinton Elliott Lane was born in the town of Cobb, Iowa county, Wisconsin, March 25, 1886, and in 1890 was brought to Norwich, Connecticut, by his parents. He was educated in Norwich schools, and after completing school years began a regular apprenticeship at the blacksmith trade under his capable father, and seven years later, when that apprentiveship ended, he was a skilled worked in metals. He established a shop for vulcanizing automobile tires and tubes in the rear of his father's blacksmith shop at No. 17 Chestnut street, which was the first tire repair shop to be opened in Norwich. This was in 1909, and six years later, in 1915, he moved to No. 60 Franklin street, adding tires and auto accessories, etc. He opened another store at No. 59 Franklin street, and continued the management of both until July 1, 1918, when he sold both to the Todd Rubber Company, of New Haven, Connecticut, and became the Norwich resident manager for the company, moving the business to No. 324 Main street. This arrangement continued one year, then on August 1, 1919, he repurchased his business from the Todd Rubber Company and has since conducted it under the name of the Lane Rubber Company, at the same address. Mr. Lane is a dealer in tires and automobile accessories, and has a modernly equipped plant for the vulcanizing of tires and tubes, the recharging of batteries and work of a similar nature. This is the pioneer shop of its class in Norwich, and one that is well patronized.

Mr. Lane is a successful business man, and is highly regarded in the city to which he came as a boy. He is master of his business, and of such genial friendly nature that he makes many friends. He is a member of the Norwich Rotary Club; Chamber of Commerce; Somerset Lodge, No. 34, Free and Accepted Masons; Franklin Chapter, Royal Arch Masons; Franklin Council, Royal and select Masters; Columbian Commandery, Knights Templar; King Solomon Lodge of Perfection; Van Rensselaer Council, Princes of Jerusalem; Norwich Chapter of Rose Croix; Connecticut Consistory, Sovereign Princes of the Royal Secrét; Sphinx Temple, Ancient Arabic Order Nobles of the Mystic Shrine (Hartford); and Norwich Lodge, No. 430, Benevolent and Protective Order of Elks. In politics he is a Republican, and in religious preference an Episcopalian.

Mr. Lane married, April 15, 1915, at Norwich, Ella Frances Brooks, born in Providence, Rhode Island, daughter of Crawford A. Brooks. Mr. and Mrs. Lane are the parents of two children: Mary Frances and Elliott Clinton.

BYRON JOSEPH BLAKESLEE—Though his residence in Lebanon township has been of only a limited time, and his early years spent in various business ways, yet Byron Joseph Blakeslee has made a success of his recent venture, that of farming.

Byron Joseph Blakeslee is the son of Albert Taylor Blakeslee, who was born in Northfield, Connecticut, February 28, 1843, and his wife Marion (Abbott) Blakeslee, born in Watertown, Connecticut, October 24, 1842. They were the parents of four children: Byron Joseph, of further mention; Anna Nettleton, Harry Seeley, and Ida Marion.

Their son, Byron Joseph Blakeslee, was born in Watertown, Connecticut, November 23, 1868. Attending the public schools in his native town, he acquired an education, then finding employment in the clock shop of Seth Thomas, in Thomaston, Connecticut, remaining there for some time. He was later employed by the Waterbury Brass Company, Waterbury, Connecticut, where he continued for twelve years as toolmaker. After leaving this plant, Mr. Blakeslee was connected for eight years with the Blake & Johnson Manufacturing Company of Waterville, Connecticut, as foreman. Wishing to make a change in his business affairs, he came to Lebanon, Connecticut, and engaged in farming. Mr. Blakeslee has not taken any active part in political affairs of the locality, but is a member of the Republican party.

On June 13, 1894, Byron Joseph Blakeslee was united in marriage to Lillian Wellman Peckham, only daughter of Asa Coggeshall Peckham, who was born in Lebanon, Connecticut, July 5, 1842, and his wife Nancy (Wellman) Peckham, born in Townsend, Vermont, November 23, 1841. To this union two children have been born: Edith Lillian, born in Waterbury, Connecticut, and Wallace Peckham, born in Waterbury, Connecticut.

THOMAS F. DORSEY, JR.—Among the enterprising and progressive young men of New London, Mr. Dorsey is well known, his chosen line of activity identifying him constantly with the growth of the new city which is gradually replacing the old. Mr. Dorsey is a son of Thomas F. and Charlotte (Whalen) Dorsey. His father is one of the most prominent figures in the professional world of New London, having been active in the practice in this city for the past thirty years.

Thomas F. Dorsey, Jr., was born in New London, October 18, 1897. After covering the elementary and high school courses in the New London schools, in 1919, he entered the business world with offices in the Harris building. He has since handled real estate and insurance brokerage, and has been identified with many important transactions. He is now taking a leading place in this field. In civic affairs Mr. Dorsey takes a general interest, and politically holds independent convictions. During the World War he served from March 1, 1918, to July 1, 1918, with the Construction Division, Quartermaster Corps, stationed at Fort Wright, New York, From July 1, 1918, to January 18, 1919, he was a member of the 44th Headquarters Brigade, stationed at Fortress Monroe, Virginia.

Fraternally he is well known, being a member of the Benevolent and Protective Order of Elks, No. 360, of New London. He is a member of the Rotary Club of New London, of the Knights of Columbus, Sea Side Council No. 17, and is also prominent in social affairs. His favorite recreative interests take him into the great out-of-doors, fishing being his chief sport. He is a member of the Roman Catholic church.

THOMAS FRANCIS KELLY—Since 1899, Thomas Francis Kelly has been a resident of Baltic, Connecticut, and in everything pertaining to the welfare and advancement of the town, Mr. Kelly has taken an active interest, being recognized today as one of her foremost citizens.

John Kelly, father of Thomas Francis Kelly, was born in Ireland, in 1827, and came to this country when a young man, settling finally in Uxbridge, Massachusetts. He married Katherine Kearns born in 1830, a native of Dublin, Ireland, and to them were born three children: Thomas Francis, of further mention; Mary Anne, and Anne Elizabeth.

Thomas Francis Kelly was born in Uxbridge, Massachusetts, September 15, 1862, and attended the public schools of his native place until he was thirteen years of age, when the business of life commenced for the boy. His first employment was with the Woonsocket Lumber Company, where he continued until 1899, when he came to Baltic, Connecticut, and found a position with the Shetucket Mills, where he is located at the present time. In politics Mr. Kelly is a Democrat, a firm believer in the principles of his party, and a loyal supporter of its welfare. He is a member of the local school board, and the board of assessors, and for twelve years he has been justice of the peace. He has always been industrious and zealous in the performance of his public duties, and curteous and honorable in all his dealings.

Mr. Kelly married Katherine Agnes Brown, daughter of John and Katherine Brown, of Uxbridge, Massachusetts. Mr. and Mrs. Kelly are the parents of three children: Edward Joseph, who is employed as a railway mail clerk; Thomas Francis Jr.; Katherine, who is employed in the income tax office at Washington, D. C.

JAMES HYDE HAZEN—In the town of Franklin, New London county, Connecticut, James Hyde Hazen was born, and there, after a lifetime of usefulness, died. He was a son of Charles Thomas and Mary (Armstrong) Hazen; grandson of Simeon and Temperance (Sabin) Hazen; great-grandson of Moses and Joanna (Sampson) Hazen; great-great-grandson of Thomas (2) Hazen; son of Thomas (1) Hazen, son of Edward Hazen, the American ancestor, who is recorded in Rowley in 1649, in connection with the burial of his wife, Elizabeth. They came from Northampton, England. His second wife was Hannah Grant, daughter of Thomas and Hannah Grant. Edward Hazen was selectman several times, and a man of means and influence. His son Thomas Hazen, born February 29, 1657, was the first of this branch to settle in Connecticut, his home being in latter years in the town of Norwich, not the town of Franklin, New London county. Moses Hazen of the fourth American generation owned the farm in Franklin, which was later owned by his grandson, Charles Thomas Hazen, and later by his son, James Hyde Hazen.

Simeon Hazen of the fifth generation was born at the home farm in Franklin, New London county, June 10, 1769, and there died July 22, 1864, having spent his entire life on the farm. He was a successful farmer and became quite wealthy. He was a Democrat in politics, was selectman several terms, and a man of a good deal of influence. He is buried in Portipang Cemetery. Simeon Hazen married (first) December 16, 1790, Nabby Sampson; February 28, 1810, he married (second) Temperance Sabin, of New Hampshire, and had children by both marriages.

Charles Thompon Hazen of the sixth generation was born at the old homestead in the town of Franklin, New London county, Connecticut, July 13, 1818, and there lived to a very old age. He attended the district schools each year until the age of seventeen, and at the age of nineteen began to teach, and continued in different localities until he had taught eight terms. He then married and rented a farm in Franklin (later owned by D. W. Grant), and there he remained seven years. He then returned to the home farm and managed it for his father, and when the latter passed away in 1864, he became the owner of its one hundred and forty acres. He continued its operation until old age overtook him, when he retired and was succeeded by his son, James Hyde Hazen. In 1866-1867 he erected a new house on his farm, and during his years of ownership, made many improvements. He was a Democrat in politics and for twenty-five years served as justice of the peace. He was selectman many years, a member of the State Legislature in 1860, and held about every other town office.

He married, January 9, 1842, in Franklin, Mary Armstrong, born January 29, 1817, and died January 24, 1903, after a happy married life of sixty-one years. Mr. and Mrs. Hazen were the parents of three children: May Elizabeth, married Daniel G. Tucker, and moved to Columbia, Connecticut; Phoebe E., married Adelbert R. Young, and moved to Jewett City, Connecticut, their children are: Mabel and Irene Young; James Hyde, of further mention.

James Hyde Hazen, only son of Charles Thomas and Mary (Armstrong) Hazen, was born in the town of Franklin, New London county, Connecticut, May 10, 1848, his parents at that time renting the D. W. Grant farm. He died at the farm inherited from his father in the same town. He grew up on the home farm to which his parents moved, that property lying on Portipang Hill. He was well educated in private schools, but at the age of eighteen became his father's farm assistant. He resided in Syracuse, New York, for several years, then returned to the farm succeeding his father in the management when the years grew heavy. He continued at the farm until his death, operating it very successfully.

James Hyde Hazen married Emma Barlow, born in Meriden, Connecticut, who died leaving two children: (1) Mary Westerly, born July 10, 1876, in Meriden, Connecticut, wife of Joseph W. Wellington, born December 5, 1879, in Bridgeport, Connecticut, son of George Wellington, of Bridgeport, born

March 6, 1852. Mr. and Mrs. Wellington reside on their farm at Portipang Hill in the town of Sprague, and have a son, Joseph Hazen Wellington, born in New Haven, Connecticut, September 26, 1903. Mr. Wellington was a member of the town school boaro, and is affiliated with the Independent Order of Odd Fellows. (2) Florence Edna, born December 15, 1880, mrried Leroy Moulthrop and has a son. They reside in Shetton, Connecticut.

J. FRANK COREY—In the public life of Norwich, an interesting figure is J. Frank Corey, at present clerk of the Court of Common Pleas. Mr. Corey's father, John Fenner Corey, was born in Southbridge, Massachusetts, and received his education in the public schools of that town. When a young man he came to Westerly, Rhode Island, where he worked as a machinist for various plants in that city for a time. He then came to Norwich, where he followed the machinist's trade the greater part of his life. At the time of the great Boston fire of 1872, he was stoker of the Wauregan steamer, of the Norwich Fire Department. Mr. Corey went to Boston with this steamer, the transportation being accomplished by rail. At this fire he contracted small pox, and falling ill after arriving home, he died on December 5, 1872. He married Jeannette H. Crandall, who was born in Voluntown, Connecticut. She died in Norwich in December, 1915. They were the parents of two children: J. Frank, and Emma, who died in infancy, of the dread disease which her father contracted in the course of performing his duty, costing the life of both.

J. Frank Corey was born in Norwich, on February 11, 1865, and received his education in the public schools of the city. Left fatherless at an early age, he started out in life to make his own way as soon as he had finished school. He worked in various plants as a shipping clerk, continuing along this line until 1885, when he became a clerk for the Norwich & Worcester railroad. In 1893 he was station master at Norwich for a short period. All this time the young man was improving his spare time to increase his efficiency along the line of his chosen work, and now an opportunity offered to take a step forward. He accepted a position with John C. Averill, clerk of the Common and Superior courts, as private secretary, and filled this position from 1894 to 1915. In 1909 he was appointed assistant clerk of the Court of Common Pleas, which office he still ably fills.

Mr. Corey is a Republican by political choice and a staunch supporter of its principles. He is a member of the Ancient Free and Accepted Masons, Somerset Lodge, No. 34, and has been musical director of the order for the past thirty-one years. He is a member of Franklyn Chapter, No. 3, and Franklyn Council, No. 4; was past commander of the Council in 1900 and 1901. He is secretary of the four Scottish Rite bodies, and secretary of the Connecticut Consistory, of which he is a thirty-second degree member. He was clerk of the parish of Christ Episcopal Church from 1897 to 1920.

Mr. Corey married, on October 15, 1899, Sarah E. Hilton, daughter of Charles O. and Lydia S. (Northrop) Hilton, of Norwich. They have two children: Herbert H. and Grace M.

J. HYMAN LONDON—Rabbi Fabyan London, father of J. Hyman London, of Colchester, Connecticut, was a learned and devout exponent of the Jewish faith, living at the time of the birth of his son (1867) in his Russian Poland. In 1875 Rabbi London migrated to London, England, where his wife, Jennie C. Goldberg London died. He remained in London until 1895, then came to the United States where he is now living (1921).

J. Hyman London, son of Rabbi Fabyan and Jennie C. (Goldberg) London, was born in Russian Poland, February 3, 1867, and there he spent the years until 1875, when the family moved to London, England. He was instructed by his father in the letter of the law, and all this education was preparatory to his filling a rabbi's place in the synagogue. His education continued in Jewish institutions until 1889, when the young man went to South Africa, where he remained until 1904, engaged in various kinds of business in different cities. In 1904 he came to the United States to the Colchester colony, where he engaged as a farmer and later bought his own farm. In 1919 he bought out a garage and service station in the village of Colchester. In 1920 he sold his farm and now devotes himself entirely to his garage. In politics Mr. London is an Independent, and has served his town as constable. He is a member of the Jewish church, and a man greatly esteemed.

Mr. London married, in London, England, March 10, 1890, Sarah Lando, born in Russian Poland, and they are the parents of a son, Joseph, born in London, England, February 4, 1891, who has traveled over a great part of the world. He married Lena Turner, born in Austria, Europe, and they have two children: Leon and Charles, both born in Colchester, Connecticut.

WILLIAM EDWARD BABBITT—Having spent the early years of his life engaged in one or another of the many mills in Connecticut, William Edward Babbitt has, for the past several years, been a tiller of the soil. The youngest of a family of six children, William Edward Babbitt is the son of James Monroe and Sarah Babbitt; the former was born in Danielson, Connecticut, and for most of his life has been employed in various parts of New London county as a worker in the mills. He and his wife are the parents of four sons and two daughters: Albert Zachariah, Julia, James Monroe, Welcome Barnes, Captola, and William Edward.

William Edward Babbitt was born in Montville, Connecticut, growing to manhood there. His education was acquired in the public school of his native town, and there he became a mill operative, continuing as such until 1912, when he left Montville, and coming to Baltic, Sprague township, became interested in farming. Mr. Babbitt has continued in this line of work ever since he came to Baltic.

While living in Montville, William Edward Babbitt was married to Louise Beckwith, a native of Montville, the daughter of Allan and Mary (Hyland) Beckwith. Mr. and Mrs. Babbitt have one child, Lottie May, born in Montville, February 2, 1908.

CLAYTON HUNTINGTON LATHROP was born at Franklin, Connecticut, November 11, 1892, son of Clayton Hyde and Estelle J. (Smith) Lathrop. Clayton Hyde Lathrop was born in Colchester, Connecticut, and died in Franklin, in 1900, at the age of forty-three. He taught school for many years, and also engaged in farming on a large scale. Mrs. Lathrop, who now resides with her son, Clayton H. Lathrop, was born in Franklin, August 30, 1856.

The early education of Clayton Huntington Lathrop was received in the schools of his native place, after which he attended Natchave Grammar School, in Willimantic, and later entered Windham High School, from which he graduated. He then engaged in farming for two years, after which he went into the automobile business, working in the capacity of mechanic for several concerns, filling the position of head mechanic at the Griswold Hotel. In 1915, Mr. Lathrop was chosen representative from the town of Franklin, and held the distinction of being the youngest member of that body, being at that time but twenty-three years old. He has also served as grand juror, auditor, and registrar of voters. He is affiliated with Uncas Lodge, No. 11, Independent Order of Odd Fellows, and is also a member of Franklin Grange, No. 184. In politics he is a staunch Republican.

Clayton Huntington Lathrop married, October 31, 1917, Anna Harriet Mosher, of Willimantic, born in Moodus, Connecticut, June 1, 1896, daughter of Charles H. and Ella (Rogers) Mosher. Mr. and Mrs. Lathrop are the parents of one child, Clayton Elliot, born November 21, 1918.

HARRISON HUBERTA WARD—Since 1914, when he joined the rank of farmer, Mr. Ward has devoted his entire time to this occupation, and the success which he has already attained within these comparatively few years is ample proof of the wise choice which he made in his life work.

Thomas Henry Ward, father of Harrison Huberta Ward, was born July 14, 1859, at Lebanon. Here he has resided continuously up to the present time, and has been engaged in agricultural pursuits. He married Edith Frances Manning. Mrs. Ward is also a native of Lebanon, and the daughter of Benjamin and Senith (Robinson) Manning. To Mr. and Mrs. Ward have been born eight children: Harrison Huberta, of further mention; Albert A., born November 25, 1885; Millicent Huntington, born July 26, 1888; Helen Louise, born November 24, 1890; John Philip, born June 8, 1896; Paul Arthur; Annette Stella, born June 23, 1900; and Edith Frances, born June 6, 1906.

Harrison Huberta Ward was born at Franklin, Connecticut, January 21, 1884, the eldest child of Thomas Henry and Edith Frances (Manning) Word. He attended the select school of Lebanon until he was twelve years of age, when without the usual time allotted to the growing youth for play, he left school and went to work on his father's farm. Some years later, desirous of trying other lines of employment, he secured work with the electric road, and also spent six months in the study of telegraphy. In 1914, however, he purchased his present place and has continued to reside here ever since, devoting his entire time to his farm. Having previously gained a wide and extensive knowledge of agricultural methods, which has stood him in good stead, he now carries on successful farming operations which are the outcome of these years of tireless devotion which he has given to his work. Mr. Ward has never taken any active part in public affairs, but in a quiet and unassuming way gives his best influence to whatever he deems is worthy of consideration.

CLARENCE EUGENE BARBER, of Norwich, Connecticut, is one of the younger men in mechanical lines of work in the city, but is making his shop on North Main street a genuine force for industrial progress. Mr. Barber is a son of Michael Angelo and Fannie (Burnett) Barber. Elsewhere in this work is found a sketch of the life of Michael A. Barber, who has always followed the same line of work; and whose father, Julius E. Barber, spent his entire life in mechanical work. Thus three generations of this family have been and are identified with the manufacturing industries of the city.

Clarence Eugene Barber was born in Norwich, on September 28, 1881. He received his education in the public schools of the city, and the Norwich Free Academy, the institution from which he graduated, in 1901. From boyhood he planned to follow the same line of work in which his father and grandfather had always been actively engaged; but was resolved to gain special training to fit him for distinctive branches of the work. So in the fall of 1901 he entered the Massachusetts Institute of Technology, for a three years' course. He graduated in 1904, and returned to Norwich, where he went into his father's shop and worked with him. Then in 1907 he entered the employ of the Fore River Ship Yard, to gain experience on marine engines and that class of work. He remained for one year, then went to the William A. Harrison Company, of Providence, Rhode Island, working as road engineer. Here he remained until 1911, when he returned to Norwich, and became foreman in his father's shop. Later he worked for others in various places for a short time, then in 1913 he went into the automobile business, handling the Dodge and Hudson cars, and the Stewart trucks, also a general line of accessories. He followed this until

1918, then opened a machine shop on North Main street, under his own name. He has been very successful thus far, and the future looks most promising. He handles a fine grade of work, and is equipped for every branch of machine work, and for engineering covering a broad scope.

Mr. Barber is a Republican by political choice, and was elected councilman in 1919; his term of office not yet being expired. He is connected with many fraternal and social organizations; is a member of Somerset Lodge, No. 34, Ancient Free and Accepted Masons; Franklin Chapter, No. 4; Franklin Council, No. 3; Columbian Commandery, of Norwich; and Sphinx Temple, Nobles of the Mystic Shrine, of Hartford. He is a member of all Scottish Rite bodies, of the thirty-seocnd degree; and a member of the Eastern Star, No. 57, of Norwich. He is also a member of the Arcanum Club.

He married, on November 20, 1907, Ella Halt, of Norwich, daughter of Thomas J. and Lucy (Stocking) Halt, both natives of Providence, Rhode Island. Mr. and Mrs. Barber have one son, Sherman H. They are members of the Universalist church.

OWEN LINCOLN STEWART—In the affairs of Sprague, Owen Lincoln Stewart has always taken a keen interest and has ever given substantial aid as well as influence toward the advancement of civic welfare, being recognized as a leader among the progressive men of the town.

Owen Lincoln Stewart was born December 14, 1864, in the town of East Lyme. He was the son of Lyman and Mary Alice (Maynard) Stewart, the latter a daughter of Gordon Maynard, of East Lynne. The boy attended the public schools of his native place until he was seventeen years of age, when he chose to follow in the footsteps of his father, to become a farmer. Having gained a thorough practical knowledge of this occupation when a boy upon his father's farm, he followed this particular line with considerable success, and when the elder man died in 1910, the son purchased the home farm. The ground was naturally very fertile, and its continued cultivation has brought Mr. Stewart much remuneration.

Mr. Stewart has always been active in the political life of Sprague. He is a member of the Republican party, and for several years served on the local public school board. He holds membership in the Grange, and affiliates with the Ancient Order of United Workmen.

Owen Lincoln Stewart married (first) Maud Watson, who bore him five children: Ethel, Hugh Miller, Herbert, Bernice and Allan. He married (second) Mary Alice Stocz, a native of New London, Connecticut, the daughter of Ludwig and Estelle Stocz. Mr. and Mrs. Stewart are the parents of one child, Doris Estelle, born in June, 1911.

LOUIS RAYMOND ABEL—The World War that engulfed Europe in 1914, and swept over all our land ere its course was run, took its grim toll of lives from every walk of life, every profession, every vocation, every science, and every art gave of its all, that civilization might conquer its deadliest foe. One of the brave spirits that went out over a battle field of France was Louis Raymond Abel, to whose memory this review is dedicated. He was a grandson of Edwin Leroy and Jane (Carpenter) Abel (the former born in Lebanon, Connecticut, the latter in Brooklyn, New York), and son of Joseph Payson and Ida M. (Peckham) Abel.

Joseph Payson Abel was born in Brooklyn, New York, December 3, 1853, died in Lebanon, Connecticut, November 11, 1908. He attended the public schools until sixteen years of age, then entered upon his business career, his first employment being with the Western Union Telegraph Company in New York City. He became prominent in the business world and in Freemasonry, holding the thirty-second degree of the Ancient Accepted Scottish Rite, and eminent in the northern jurisdiction of the United States, supervising that rite. He married Ida M. Peckham, daughter of Benjamin and Alice (Spink) Peckham, and to them were born three children: Louis Raymond, of further mention; William Hurlbert, and Eugene Peckham.

Louis Raymond Abel was born in Brooklyn, New York, August 11, 1881, and obtained his education in the public schools. Terminating his studies at an early age, he entered upon his business career in New York City, subsequently becoming associated with the Westinghouse Company, by whom he was sent to South America in the employ of the Electric Engineering Corporation, later going to Chicago. While there he enlisted in the United States army, subsequently being sent in May, 1917, to the officers' training camp at Madison barracks, remaining there for one year, training at Camp Hancock. On May 1, 1918, he embarked on the transport "Aquatania," going overseas as first lieutenant with the 112th Regular Infantry, with the Twenty-eighth Division. Upon landing in France, he took active part in some of the important engagements down to the Argonne, where he was killed in action on the first day of the offensive, on the plains of Montdidier, September 27, 1918. He was buried in the Argonne Cemetery in France. It is interesting to note here, that a thirty-second degree Mason's ring, which was taken from the finger of a dead German on the Argonne front October 4, 1918, had inscribed the name of Joseph P. Abel; a Masonic brother, in turn taking the stolen ring and returning it to Lieutenant Abel's widow.

On November 7, 1902, Louis Raymond Abel was united in marriage with Anna M. Hallen, of Lebanon, Connecticut, and to them was born a son, Edwin Leroy, June 16, 1904. The death of Lieutenant Abel at the beginning of a promising career is one of the tragedies of war, but he died a hero on the field of battle, and his death was mourned as a personal loss by the officers of the American forces, who paid eloquent tribute to his services.

CHARLES A. PERKINS—Descended from a family of ancient lineage, tracing back in this country to the year 1630, Charles A. Perkins, prominent in the affairs of Lebanon, Connecticut, agricultural, political and social, demonstrates in his career the value of heredity, displaying the characteristics which make for success in any line of work.

John Perkins, the first American ancester of whom we have record, was born at Newent, England, in 1590, and died in Ipswich, Massachusetts, in 1654. He embarked for the New World in the ship "Lyon," his destination being Boston, Massachusetts, where he arrived in February, 1631. He was accompanied on the journey by his wife, Judith Perkins, and their five children. Two years later he removed to Ipswich, Massachusetts, and there spent the remainder of his days. He served several times as deputy to the General Court. One of his children was Sergeant Jacob Perkins, born in England in 1624, and died in 1699-1700. He married (first) Elizabeth ———, and (second) Mrs. Demaris Robinson. The three sons of Sergeant Perkins: Joseph, Jabez, and Mathew Perkins, were the progenitors of the family in the State of Connecticut, removing in 1695 to that part of Norwich which later became Lisbon.

Samuel Perkins, a descendant of one of the above, and father of Charles A. Perkins, of this review, was a resident of Lisbon, New London county, Connecticut. He spent his boyhood and young manhood there, then changed his place of residence to Bozrah, same State, where he engaged in the lumber business until 1876, then removed to Lebanon, and there engaged in agricultural pursuits, continuing the same until his death, April 11, 1878, his remains being interred in the Dr. Johnson Cemetery at Bozrah. He was a Democrat in politics, and was a member of the old military company at Bozrah until it was disorganized. His wife, Philura H. (Miner) Perkins, a native of Bozrah, daughter of Thomas and Freelove Miner, survived her husband until March 30, 1892. She bore him thirteen children, as follows: Alfred, Horace C., Mary, Frank S., Ellen, John G., George L., Nancy M., Hattie, Charles A., Jared, James B., Byron.

Charles A. Perkins, sixth son of Samuel and Philura H. (Miner) Perkins, was born in Bozrah, Connecticut, October 25, 1863. He attended local schools at Bozrah and Lebanon until fourteen years of age, at which time his parents took up their residence in Lebanon, and after the death of his father, when the lad was fifteen years of age, he assumed the management of the home farm, so continuing for four years, when his mother disposed of the property. He then secured employment in the Yantic Paper Company as fireman, rising to the position of engineer, and remained an employee of that company until 1885, resigning then on account of impaired health. Feeling that out-door employment would prove of benefit to him, he rented a farm in Lebanon, which he worked for one year, then removed to another farm, where he remained for four years. He then turned his attention to the trade of carpenter, at which he worked until the year 1897, when he purchased his present farm, consisting of fifty acres, and in the interval has improved his property considerably, deriving therefrom a lucrative livelihood, to which he adds by working at the trade of carpenter, for which he has a special liking and aptitude.

He has taken a prominent part in the social and political life of the community, and in 1907 his associates chose him as their representative in the Legislature, where he served the usual term; he has also served as a member of the Board of Relief, and for five years as tax collector, the duties of these offices being performed in a most satisfactory manner. His political affiliations are with the Republican party, and fraternally he is connected with the Knights of Pythias, William Williams Council, No. 72, Order of United American Mechanics, passing all the chairs in the latter order, also representing the council at State convention several times, and a member of the Ancient Order of United Workmen.

Mr. Perkins married, September 10, 1884, Julia A. Sisson, of North Stonington, Connecticut, who was born there, September 10, 1863, daughter of Albert B. and Amelia (Dunbar) Sisson. The family of Sisson originated in North Stonington, and its history is full of interesting tales. William Sisson, uncle of Mrs. Perkins, was lost while serving as ice pilot on the ship "Genetta," while exploring in the Arctic region, and Gurdon Dunbar was lost on Desolation Island, remaining there for three years before he was rescued. Two children were born to Mr. and Mrs. Perkins: 1. Frank Charles, born November 22, 1888; is located in Springfield, serving as foreman for the Westinghouse Company, manufacturers of the Browning machine guns. 2. Fannie Clara, born February 12, 1891, resides at home. The family are members of the Congregational church, Mr. Perkins having served at one time as assistant superintendent of the Sunday School connected therewith.

JOHN HENRY ROSE—Descended from grandparents who were born in different kingdoms in Europe, John Henry Rose has inherited from his father's family the characteristics of the Holland Dutch people and of the Germans.

His grandfather was Adam Rose, born in Holland, who emigrated to the United States in the early part of the last century and, settling in New London, Connecticut, bought property and built the old Rose homestead there, he and his wife and children being one of the pioneer families of that section of Connecticut. His wife was a native of Germany, but came to this country when quite young. They had several children, one of whom was Charles Henry, of whom further.

Charles Henry Rose was born upon the homestead, February 19, 1845. He was educated in the local schools, and some years afterward became engaged in the trucking and transfer business, which he carried on extensively for a number of years, but for the past few years he has retired from active business and lives quietly at his home on Rosemary street, New London. He is assistant chief of the New London Fire Department, and is also fire marshall. He is a member of the Order of Eagles, and of Nonawantick Tribe, Improved Order of Red Men. The wife of Charles Henry Rose, Sarah Rose, was born in Jersey City, New Jersey, about fifty-five years ago, and is a member of the well known Nieve family of that city. Their children were as follows: 1. Maude, born in Jersey City; she is the wife of Frank Howard, of New London, and has two children: Ella May and Edgar Howard. 2. John Henry, of whom further. 3. Goldie Elizabeth, born in New London; married James O'Connor, and resides in New York City; she is the mother of two daughter: May and Vera. 4. Earl Nieve, born in New London; he married Doris Fournier, of New London, by whom he had one child, Charles Earl. 5. Sadie Iola, born in New London, where she now lives, at home, and is a teacher in one of the schools there. 6. Ruth Estelle, born in New London; living at home.

John Henry Rose, son of Charles Henry and Sarah Rose, was born at the home of his grandfather in Jersey City, New Jersey, February 23, 1884, while his mother was on a visit to her former home. As soon as practicable the young mother returned to her husband's home in New London, Connecticut, where her son grew up.

Having acquired an education in the public schools of New London, John Henry Rose learned the trade of a carpenter, working at it for a number of years, then, joining his father in the trucking and transfer business, he assisted him for some time, and when thirty-two years old bought out the business from his father and has been conducting it himself for the last five years, having made a great success of it.

John Henry Rose married, in New London, September 7, 1909, Bessie Ray Morey, born in Williston, Vermont, April 21, 1888. She is the daughter of John Irwin and Adelaide (Goodrich) Morey, the former in his youth a farmer in Vermont, but in later manhood he became engaged in railroad business, continuing for several years, and is now retired from active service, living at his home in New London. John Irwin Morey's great-great-grandmother was an Indian princess before her marriage to John Morey, the great-great-grandfather of John Irwin Morey.

Mr. and Mrs. John Irwin Morey had five children: 1. Earl Ralph, born in November, 1886, at Williston, Vermont, and died June 16, 1914; he is buried in Jordan Cemetery, New London. 2. Bessie Ray, wife of John Henry Rose. 3. Mary Teresa, born in Williston, Vermont, August 3, 1890; she married (first) William Valley, by whom she had two children: Muriel and Irwin; married (second) Albert Dunster, a native of England; they have two children: Dorothy and Pershing Albert. 4. Cecil Irene, born at St. Albans, Vermont; she married (first) John MacLaughlin, of New London; married (second) Joseph Towen. 5. John Timothy, born in St. Albans, Vermont; married Anna Quinn, and has one child, Earl Ralph.

After the marriage of John Henry Rose and Bessie Ray Morey, in 1909, they went to California to live, remaining there for several years. While there two of their children were born. They have three daughters and one son: 1. Dulcie Emmeline Adelaide, born February 2, 1912, in Los Angeles, California. 2. Keil Emmerson, born February 10, 1914, in Los Angeles, California. 3. Winifred Arabella, born March 21, 1916, in New London, Connecticut. 4. Gwendolyn Elizabeth, born August 4, 1918. Mr. and Mrs. Rose, with their children, reside at No. 96 Raymond street (extension), while Mr. Rose has his trucking business located at the corner of State and Bradley streets.

FRANK WASHBURN SPENCER—A conspicuous figure in the life of South Windham, where he resided for many years, was the late Frank Washburn Spencer. He never took an active part in public affairs, but in his quiet and unassuming way could always be counted upon to give his earnest support to everything pertaining to the welfare of the community.

Frank Washburn Spencer was born at Lebanon, Connecticut, January 11, 1869, son of Charles Edward and Harriet (Haskell) Spencer. He attended the schools of his native place for several years, and then engaged in the occupation of farming, which he followed throughout his entire lifetime, and to which he devoted his entire time. His place was regarded as one of the well conducted places of the region, and no expense was spared in the cultivation of the propery, which was brought to a highly productive state long before he passed away.

Frank Washburn Spencer married Edna Woodmansee. She was born at North Franklin, Connecticut, May 20, 1879, the daughter of Sylvester and Lucy Anne Woodmansee. Mrs. Spencer survives her husband and resides on the farm. She, like her husband, is ardently devoted to the place, and readily gives substantial aid to all things pertaining to the advancement of civic betterment.

FREDERICK ROHMELING—To the many guests who have patronized the Morton House at Niantic, Connecticut, during the past seven years, the name Rohmeling recalls a delightful experience, for as owner and proprietor of that well known summer hotel he has not only made it a most desirable stopping place for those who delight in beautiful surroundings and a good cuisine, but also for those who value that intangible thing which is sometimes called "atmosphere" and "homelike." The Morton House has become popular under his management, and its fine location on the Shore road, its well decorated rooms, and a famous chef and cook in the person of Mrs. Rohmeling, insures it a permanent patronage.

Frederick Rohmeling was born in Brooklyn, New York, May 30, 1877, a son of Frederick Rohmeling, born in Denmark, a builder, who came to the United States, working in Brooklyn for a number of years. Later he returned to Denmark, where his death occurred. Frederick and Wilhelmina Rohmeling are the parents of four children: Ernest William, born in the old country; Amelia, born in the old country; Frederick, born in Brooklyn, New York; Bertha, born in Brooklyn, New York. Mrs. Rohmeling did not return to Denmark with her husband, but still occupies the old home in Brooklyn.

Frederick Rohmeling was educated in the schools of Brooklyn, and after school years were over, he learned the painter's trade with especial reference to interior decoration. For several years he was employed as a decorator in Brooklyn, New York, Philadelphia, Baltimore, and Washington, then having capital at his command he opened a restaurant in Brooklyn, New York, at the corner of Lafayette and Franklin avenues. In 1916, he sold his restaurant and came to Niantic, Connecticut, purchasing the Morton House, which he completely renovated and beautifully decorated. It is a large commodious house, well situated on the Shore road in Niantic, and there he has been very successful.

Mr. Rohmeling married, March 30, 1910, Jeanette Stenzel, born in St. Louis, Missouri, December 12, 1888, daughter of Herman and Clara Stenzel, who were also the parents of Oscar, William, Otto, and Herman Albert Stenzel. Mrs. Rohmeling is a famous cook and has a great deal to do with the popularity of the Morton House.

JOHN FRANK YERRINGTON—The Yerringtons, of Norwich, are of English descent, Edwin Frank Yerrington having come from his native England to the United States in boyhood. He found a home in New London county, Connecticut, and during his lifetime was employed in farming in various parts of the county. He died in 1915, aged sixty-eight years, and is buried in the town of Ledyard. He married Happy Eccleston, born in North Stonington, Connecticut, of an old and honored county family, who died July 10, 1884. They were the parents of six sons: John Frank, Charles Edward, Erastus Williams, Edgar Elmer, George Ransom, and James Byron Yerrington.

John Frank Yerrington, of this family of sons, was born at the home farm in the town of Ledyard, New London county, Connecticut, May 17, 1872. He attended the public schools of his district, but at the age of twelve left home and began life for himself as an employe of James Allan, of New London. He was variously employed until the year 1904, one of his positions being on a Sound steamer. In 1904 he became engineer at the State Hospital in Norwich, and there has served continuously during the seventeen years which have since intervened, now being the chief engineer of the plant. Mr. Yerrington married Alice Summers, born in Norwich.

JACOB ALFRED PAHLBERG—Since 1873 Jacob Alfred Pahlberg has been engaged in deep-sea diving, and as such holds the record of having been under water for a longer period than any other person living. Although having passed the three score years and ten mark, Mr. Pahlberg is still hale and hearty, this being justly proven by the fact that he is still active as a diver.

John Eric Pahlberg, father of Jacob Alfred Pahlberg, was born in Sunndswell, Sweden, in 1839, and there died in 1901. He was a glass-blower by trade. He married Johanna Strandsel, who was also a native of Sweden, born in 1841, died in 1903, at the age of sixty-two years. Mr. and Mrs. Pahlberg were the parents of eight children: John, who is engaged in business in New York City; Christine, who married, and to whom has been born four children, Theodore, Hannah, Albert, and Anna; Charlotte, who was twice married; Uldrick; Jacob Alfred, of further mention; Frederick, died in 1921 in Sweden; Gustave, died in Sweden; Theodore, died in Sweden.

Jacob Alfred Pahlberg was born in Sunndswell, Sweden, July 15, 1847. At the age of ten he moved from his native place, and for a time he worked as a glass-blower. In 1861 he secured passage as a cabin boy on a full-rigged brigg called the "Framoat." One year later he shipped as an able-bodied seaman on the ship "Rosa," but subsequently transferred to the German ship, "Vera," which was later wrecked. In 1871 Mr. Pahlberg came to New York, where he became on of the crew of the schooner "Pearl," which was sunk in New York harbor, November 24, 1872, while carrying stone for the building of the Brooklyn bridge. The T. A. Scott Company wreckers came to raise the schooner "Pearl," and it was at this time Mr. Pahlberg secured a position with Captain Scott, who moved his business from New York to New London, Connecticut. The former became interested in deep-sea diving at this time, and his first experience along this line for the Scott Company was at Race Rock, outside of Fisher Island, at the time of the building of the lighthouse there. Since that time Mr. Pahlberg has devoted his entire time to diving, and has travelled from Key West to New Brunswick, making a total of forty-seven years as a diver. He affiliates with the Mohegan Lodge, No. 55, Independent Order of Odd Fellows, and the Rebecca Lodge of Odd Fellows (Orient). He is also a member of the Golden Cross Society. In politics, Mr. Pahlberg is a Republican.

Jacob Alfred Pahlberg was united in marriage with Mary Louise Larson, a native of Carlstad, Sweden, her birth having occurred August 26, 1853. Her father died when she was a child, and her mother came to this country, dying in New York City. Mrs. Pahlberg had two sisters: Annie (Mrs. Russell), of Brooklyn, New York; and Josephine. Mr. and Mrs. Pahlberg are the parents of three children: Alfred Theodore, who was born in New London, 1879, unmarried, follows the sea for a livelihood; Carrie Ethel, born in New London, married Nelson Weymouth, of Soco, Maine, who is in charge of the telephone station at Norwich, Connecticut, and has one child, Nelson, Jr., born in 1916; Charlotte Ethel, born in New London, and is employed by the T. A. Scott Company.

EUGENE HULBERT CHAPMAN, one of the successful farmers of this locality, in which occupation he has been engaged since 1916, was born in Sterling City, January 25, 1865, the son of the late Lyman Griswold and Nancy (Brown) Chapman. Lyman G. Chapman was a native of Lebanon, and died at Moosup in 1911, at the age of seventy-three years. He married Nancy Brown, who died in 1908, at the age of sixty-four years. Mr. and Mrs. Chapman were the parents of seven children: Sarah, Minnie, Lavinia, Adelbert, Fred; Ernest, deceased; and Eugene Hulbert, of further mention.

Eugene Hulbert Chapman attended the schools of his native place where his opportunities for education were very meager. He then went to work in the cotton mills of Moosup and worked in this capacity until he was eighteen years of age, when he moved to Plainfield and engaged in farming until 1888, when he made another change and went to Norwich, Connecticut. Here he secured employment with the railroad, working in various capacities until he had attained the position of yard conductor. In 1916, desirous of returning to agricultural pursuits, he purchased his present farm at Montville and has resided here continuously up to the present time. In politics, Mr. Chapman is a Democrat, and while he has never sought public office he has always taken a keen interest in the affairs of his chosen party.

Eugene Hulbert Chapman married (first) Celia Marcy. To them was born a child, Therox. Mr. Chapman married (second) Augusta Tolland. There have been no children from this union.

FRED H. CROSS was born in Adamsville, Quebec, Canada, April 27, 1881, son of Jerome L. and Clarcy (Beauregard) Cross. Jerome L. Cross was born in Burlington, Vermont, June 18, 1852. He married in Chicopee, Massachusetts, June 21, 1872, Clarcy Beauregard, born in Fairfield, Vermont, a niece of General Pierre G. T. Beauregard, a general of the Confederate army during the Civil War. Mr. and Mrs. Cross were living in Quebec, Canada, at the time of the birth of their son, Fred H., where Mr. Cross followed his trade, that of a bricklayer.

In 1886 Fred H. Cross was brought to the United States by his parents, who settled in Springfield, Massachusetts. He attended school until ten years of age, then became errand boy in a meat market, holding that place three years. At the age of thirteen he went to Adams, Massachusetts, where he attended school for two years, then, at the age of fifteen, he began learning carriage painting, becoming an expert. When twenty-one years of age he returned to Springfield, where he was employed by the Birney-Berry Skate Company for two years, then spent two years in the baking business. His next work was at his trade, that of a painter, working with Thomas O'Brien in Springfield for two years, and since then has traveled and worked at his trade in many parts of the United States.

At Trenton, New Jersey, he enlisted in the United States army as a cavalry man, entering the service May 29, 1917, and serving principally at Fort Meyer, near Washington, District of Columbia, until honorably discharged, June 14, 1919. Soon after his discharge he entered the employ of the Blue Ribbon Auto Body Company, in the painting and finishing department, remaining until May 9, 1920, when he located in New London, Connecticut, opening a shop on Bank street, on May 11th, and there continuing for a year as a painter, having a partner. The next year that partnership was dissolved, Mr. Cross then establishing in the same business at No. 6 Raymond street, under the firm name of the Blue Ribbon Auto Paint Shop, and there has developed a prosperous business.

Fred H. Cross married, July 5, 1920, Sarah Girard, daughter of Emory and Ermine (Susprenant) Girard, of Adams, Massachusetts. Mr. and Mrs. Cross are the parents of a daughter, Enid, born May 10, 1921.

FRANK O. BARBER—The Barbers are of an ancient New England family, settled in 1635 by Thomas Barber, who was the first of his name in the Colonies, and an early settler of Windsor, Connecticut. Descendants settled in Massachusetts, Connecticut, and Rhode Island, and the name has been borne by some very eminent men. The branch of the family of which Frank O. Barber is representative is of the Washington county, Rhode Island branch, Leander, father of Frank O. Barber, settling in Mystic, Connecticut.

Leander Barber was born in Ashaway, Washington county, Rhode Island, and there attended the public schools. Later he entered Mystic Valley Institute, whence he was graduated, class of 1860. In the business world he was head of the Mystic River Twine Company, an enterprise with which he was connected until his death in Mystic, Connecticut. He married Mary Burdick, who also died in Mystic. They were the parents of three children: Helen, wife of Major Lloyd P. Horsfall, of the United States army, now stationed at Pekin, China; Frank O., of further mention; and Abbie E., wife of John Noyes, who resides in Mystic, Connecticut.

Frank O. Barber, only son of Leander and Mary (Burdick) Barber, was born in Mystic, Connecticut, January 1, 1883, and attended the public school, going thence to Norwich Free Academy and there finishing with the class of 1903. The same year he entered Rhode Island State College, completing his studies there in 1908, having pursued full courses in electrical engineering. For a time he was engaged with the General Electric Company, as engineer, then became interested in the automobile business, opening a garage at Mystic, which he successfully conducted until 1918, when he opened another garage, service station, and selling agency for the Hudson and Essex cars at No. 392 William street, New London.

Mr. Barber is a Republican in politics; a member of Charity and Relief Lodge, No. 72, Free and Accepted Masons, of Mystic; Mystic Chapter, Royal Arch Masons; Mystic Council, Royal and Select Masters; Narragansett Commandery, Knights Templar; Providence Consistory, Ancient Accepted Scottish Rite (thirty-second degree); Pyramid Temple, Ancient Arabic Order Nobles of the Mystic Shrine; Westerly Lodge, No. 678, Benevolent and Protective Order of Elks; and of the Charity and Relief Club of Mystic. In his religious belief he is a Baptist, a member of the church of that denomination of Mystic.

Mr. Barber married, October 14, 1911, Anna N. Wood Knight, of New York, daughter of Rufus M. and Ladora (Bank) Knight. Mr. and Mrs. Barber are the parents of two children: Helen L., and Robert F. Barber.

HALLECK LEECH GILLETTE—Prominent among the progressive farmers of the town of Waterford, New London county, Connecticut, is Halleck L. Gillette, whose place lies in the Gilead section of the town. Mr. Gillette is of old New London county family, and is a son of Pascal and Ellen Clarissa Chapman. His father was for many years a farmer of Lyme, and his mother, who was born in East Lyme, was a daughter of Solomon Chapman. Both are now deceased. They were the parents of four children, of whom Halleck L. was the eldest, the others being May Ellen, Everett C., and Gertrude.

Halleck Leech Gillette was born in the town of Lyme, December 19, 1874, and was reared and educated in his native place. He helped about the farm out of school hours, until about thirteen years of age. He then struck out for himself and worked in various places for a time, after which he returned to Lyme. In the fall of 1917 he came to Waterford, where he now has a large farm which he operates successfully.

During his stay in Lyme, Mr. Gillette served the town for some years in the capacity of first selectman, and also served on the Board of Relief. He was master of Lyme Grange, No. 147, Patrons of Husbandry, for a period of two years, and long active in the interests of that order. He is also a member of Crystal Lodge, No. 88, Independent Order of Odd Fellows. Politically, he supports the Republican party, and he is a member of the Methodist Episcopal church.

Mr. Gillette married Alma Whiting, who was born in East Lyme, July 8, 1876, and is a daughter of James Whiting. Mr. and Mrs. Gillette have five children: Rose Irene, Ralph, Norman, Robert, and Winship.

FRANCIS EDWARD LE BLANC, son of Francis A. and Eliza (Herbert) Le Blanc, was born at Williamstown, Massachusetts, October 21, 1886. Francis A. Le Blanc was born in Napierville, Province of Quebec, Canada, and educated in the parochial schools of that place. About 1874 he came to the United States and located in Williamstown, Massachusetts, where he has worked as a farmer and gardener for the remainder of his life. His wife was also born in Napierville. They had seven children, the first being Francis Edward, of whom further.

Francis Edward Le Blanc attended the public schools of Williamstown, Massachusetts, and in 1900, at the age of fourteen, became a clerk in the grocery store of Herbert & Son, of Williamstown. Five years later he associated himself with Neeland & Quinn, of Williamstown, and worked as clerk in their general store until 1916, when he formed a partnership with young Albert Eli Paquette. The young men bought the Paquette Domestic Bakery in New London, which is one of the oldest-established bakeries there, and was founded by Paul P. Paquette, the father of Albert Eli Paquette, in 1907. Politically, Mr. Le Blanc is a Republican. He is a member of the Foresters of America, Lodge No. 176, of Williamstown, Massachusetts; and a member of St. Mary's Roman Catholic Church, of New London.

Mr. Le Blanc married Margaret Victoria Paquette, daughter of Paul P. Paquette, of North Adams, Massachusetts, November 7, 1905, at Williamstown, Massachusetts. To the union were born four children: Norbert E., Roland H., Bernard A., and Marie A.; all born at Williamstown except Marie A., who was born at New London.

EDWIN WALLACE ELY, who is a lifelong resident of Old Lyme, comes of an old family of New London county. He is a son of Enoch Ely, who was born at Ely's Ferry, in the town of Old Lyme, and later removed to Baltimore, Maryland, there engaging extensively in the lumber business. He spent the greater part of his life in Baltimore, and died in that city in the year 1913.

Joseph C. Ely, son of Enoch Ely, and Mr. Ely's father, was born in Baltimore, September 27, 1855, and was reared and educated in his native city. Coming to Old Lyme as a youth of sixteen, he has since been engaged in farming on a large scale, his place in this town being now one of the finest farms in the county. He has long been a staunch Republican, and a leader in party councils, and served the community for many years as justice of the peace. He married Elizabeth Tooker, of Lyme, daughter of William and Mary Elizabeth (Marrin) Tooker. The Tooker family is also an old one in this county. Mr. Tooker was a prominent farmer of a generation or two ago; he died in 1878 at the age of fifty-five years. William and Mary E. (Marrin) Tooker were the parents of five children: William Nathan, William B., Albert, Laura, and Elizabeth. Joseph C. and Elizabeth (Tooker) Ely are the parents of the following children: Edwin Wallace, whose name appears at the head of this review; Lila Cortright, born December 12, 1878, in Old Lyme, who died at the age of twenty years; John Christopher, born May 9, 1880; Mabel Gladwin, born May 20, 1882; William Beckwith, born June 28, 1883; Samuel, born in the year 1885; Pearl Jennie, born March 10, 1891; Earl, born March 10, 1893; and Blanch, born April 17, 1899. The other children died in infancy, and all were born in Old Lyme.

Edwin Wallace Ely was born in Old Lyme, August 15, 1877, and received a thoroughly practical education in the district schools of the town. From boyhood interested in the work of the farm, he chose farming as his life-work, and has thus far followed it most successfully. He stands among the prominent and highly respected men of the community, and politically, has always supported the Democratic party, but has been too busy to accept political preferment, although broadly interested in all progress. He is a member of Crystal Lodge, No. 88, Independent Order of Odd Fellows.

Mr. Ely married Mary Nobel, who was born in Old Lyme, and is a daughter of John and Josephine (Gibson) Nobel. Mr. Nobel died in 1911, and his wife, who is a native of New Jersey, survives him. Edwin W. and Mary (Nobel) Ely were the parents of three children: Laurence, born August 15, 1898; Harry, born in November, 1900; and Leslie, born April 23, 1902. The family are members of the Congregational church.

CHARLES STEPHEN PECKHAM—Prominently identified with the automobile business, with which he has been actively associated for the past five years, Charles Stephen Peckham occupies a place of importance in the business circles of Norwich, Connecticut. He is a son of Stephen and Phoebe E. (Williams) Peckham, and was born in Ledyard, Connecticut, January 2, 1869. Stephen Peckham was born in Ledyard, and there received his education in the district school. He then assisted his father with farm work, later becoming the owner of a farm in the north end of the town, where he resided until his death in 1908. Phoebe E. (Williams) Peckham also was born in Ledyard, where she still resides. Two children were born of this union: Mary E., who became the wife of Charles A. Gray, a farmer of Ledyard; and Charles Stephen, of further mention.

Charles Stephen Peckham attended the district school of his native place, and Snell Business College at Norwich, Connecticut. While still a youth he entered upon his business career, securing a position as clerk in the grocery store of J. M. Young, at Norwich, subsequently, in 1892, becoming a clerk in the New London office of the New York, New Haven & Hartford railroad, where he remained for two years, at the end of which time he was employed by Allen Beeman, as clerk and travelling salesman. In 1911, while travelling, he met with a severe accident, which necessitated his giving up work for three years. In 1915 he established himself in the automobile business, and it is with this business that he is occupied at the present time (1920), holding the agency for the Studebaker cars.

In politics, Mr. Peckham is an Independent, holding to an independent course where the most important consideration is the capability of the candidate for the performance of business connected with his office. He is a member of Trinity Methodist Episcopal Church.

Mr. Peckham married, in 1895, Mary Hagberg, of Norwich, Connecticut, and they are the parents of two children: Everett S., a resident of Norwich, who married Eva Atwood, of Waterbury, Connecticut; and Charlotte E. Mrs. Peckham passed away in 1911.

THEOPHILUS HYDE HANNEY was born in San Francisco, California, January 25, 1863, the son of Samuel and Katherine (Doley) Hanney. Samuel Hanney was born at Trowbridge, England, September 21, 1837, and came to this country at the age of seventeen years, locating in Connecticut. Here he married Katherine Doley, born in New York, 1835, and shortly afterwards moved to California, later in life returning to Salem, Connecticut, where he died. Mrs. Hanney survives her husband and resides at Quaker Hill, Connecticut. To Mr. and Mrs. Hanney were born five children: Theophilus Hyde, of further mention; Samuel David; Sarah Rhoda; Mary Katherine; Isabella Agnes.

Theophilus H. Hanney returned with his parents to Connecticut when he was but a child. The family lived in various places in the eastern part of the State until 1876, when they finally located at Salem, where the elder man purchased a farm. Theophilus H. continued to reside with his parents until 1887. At this time he married and removed to Montville, where he rented a small farm, but subsequently returned to his father's home. In 1901 he went to Waterford and purchased his present place, which is located on Durfee Hill. Having throughout the preceding years gained a wide and extensive knowledge of farming, he had become well skilled in agricultural methods generally, and the property which he purchased, being naturally a fertile one, he developed and cultivated it, bringing it to a highly productive state, and from the beginning has carried on successful farming operations here. The house itself is an old Colonial structure, having been built in the style of a century previous, the entire place being regarded as one of the well conducted properties in this region.

Mr. Hanney is one of those men who are instinctively interested in the welfare of the community where they reside, and he has given no little time and energy to the conduct of public affairs. He has served the town as auditor and also as assessor, and has always taken a keen and active interest in everything pertaining to its welfare. He is a member of the Farm Bureau and the Konomoc Grange, No. 41, and affiliates with the Independent Order of Odd Fellows, Mohegan Lodge, No. 55.

On March 16, 1887, Mr. Hanney was united in marriage with Jennie Marie Forsyth, a native of Norwich, Connecticut, born July 16, 1860, daughter of George and Julia Forsyth. To Mr. and Mrs. Hanney were born five children: Theophilus Forsyth, May 22, 1888; Harriet Grace, October 24, 1889; Floyd Latham, August 28, 1892; Ernest John, July 14, 1899; Harold Edwin, February 23, 1903. Mrs. Hanney passed away December 29, 1917. She was a woman whose kindness and thoughtfulness endeared her to all who were brought within the sphere of her fine influence. She was an ideal wife and mother, making her husband's fireside the place where he passed his happiest hours, devoted as he was to the ties of home and family.

HENRY ALBERT GAUCHER, the well known merchant of Baltic, Connecticut, was born in Milton, Province of Quebec, Canada, and there received his education in the public schools. His father, who was born at Saint Damase, Province of Quebec, died at Milton, and is buried there. He followed farming during all his active lifetime. He married Philomene Lagain, and they were the parents of ten children, five boys and five girls, among them Henry A., of further mention.

Beginning his career on the farm at the age of fifteen years, Henry A. Gaucher soon became interested in the great world of industry outside, and came to this country, locating in the village of Occum, one of the suburbs of the city of Norwich, Connecticut. Here he became interested in the manufacture of textiles, and was employed in the mills for a time. When sixteen years of age he returned to Canada, going to Montreal to supplement his early education with two terms of study at the Royal College there. He was graduated from that institution at the age of twenty-two years, and thereafter returned to Taftville, where he was once more employed in the mills, this time in the spinning room. In 1899 Mr. Gaucher went into business "on the Hill," continuing for thirteen years in that location, then, in 1912, he came to Baltic, and established himself here, where he has been located ever since.

Mr. Gaucher married, and is the father of ten children, five sons and five daughters, among them a son, Joseph, who was a graduate of the University of Maryland Medical School, at Baltimore; he died on December 17, 1917. Another son, Lorenzo, an interne at the Bridgeport Hospital, will also take up the practice of medicine.

ETIENNE RIEL—In the village of Baltic, Sprague township, Connecticut, many prosperous, pleasant farms are to be found, showing the care and thrift of the owners. Among them is one which gives evidence of the energy and perseverance necessary to develop a successful farm. It is owned and managed by Etienne Riel.

Etienne Riel is a native of Canada, as his father and mother were before him; the former, Neol Riel, was born at St. Patrick, Sherrington, Canada, November 2, 1839, and is still living there, having celebrated his eighty-first birthday anniversary in 1920. The wife of Neol Riel was Messelin (Bordeau) Riel, who died in 1889, at the age of forty-eight years. She was the mother of fifteen children, her son Etienne being the third child in this family.

Born at St. Patrick, Sherrington, June 11, 1864, Etienne Riel grew to early youth in Canada, and when seventeen years old came to the United States. He was employed as a mill worker in various places for many years, among them being North Adams, Massachusetts, where he was located for quite a long period. In 1913 Mr. Riel came to New London county, Connecticut, and buying a farm in Baltic, Sprague township, has enjoyed the life of a farmer, and has improved his property considerably during the past year.

Etienne Riel married Mary Leaclerc, also born in St. Patrick, Sherrington, Canada, November 4, 1866. They have had thirteen children, of whom eleven are now living: Margaret, deceased; Leonore, deceased; Clara; Anthony; Anne Goss; Benedict; Mary; Etienne, Jr.; Patrick; Ambrose; Joseph; Leo; Marceline.

RAYMOND J. JODOIN—The career of Mr. Jodoin has been one of industry and at no time has he ever been discouraged to the point of surrender. He has been a worker since the age of nine, having had to work both for a living and an education at the same time. He acquired both, then went forward to a business success which has placed him among the sunbstantial men of his county. He has earned it all, and richly deserves that often misused title, "a self-made man."

Raymond J. Jodoin was born in St. Hyacinthe, Province of Quebec, Canada, September 15, 1865, one of eleven children born to his parents, his father a factory worker. The family moved to Baltic, Connecticut, in November, 1865, and there Raymond J. yet resides, a man of prosperity, established in business, and high in the esteem of his townsmen. He began as a mill worker at the age of nine, and each week carried home three dollars, his weekly wage. As the other children of the family became wage earners, the lad Raymond J. was able to save a part of his earnings, and soon he was operating a livery stable in Baltic, in a small way. He was not satisfied with that business, sold it, went to Providence, Rhode Island, and secured a position as a travelling salesman with the wholesale grocery house, Waldron, Wightman & Company. He built up a good trade in a territory that an experienced salesman had been covering for years, and remained with the firm ten years, receiving frequent salary increases. After leaving Waldron, Wightman & Company, Mr. Jodoin formed a connection with Daniels & Cornell (later Humphreys & Cornell), wholesale grocers of Providence, they allowing him as his territory, Eastern Connecticut, Southern Massachusetts, and Western Rhode Island. He has been very successful in business, turning in a large volume of business from his territory, and winning friends wherever he goes. He has built up his trade on confidence, never betraying the men who trust him.

Mr. Jodoin, as he began having a balance of income over expense, decided that Baltic real estate was a good investment and he has never changed his opinion. He has seen his investments increase in value, and he is known as the largest individual real estate owner in the village of Baltic. He built the Sprague House, a modern hotel in Baltic, also a large theatre, and prior to this had, in 1898, built the Roderick Block in Baltic. The same year he built his own residence in Baltic, and at Pleasure Beach, built a summer home.

A Democrat in politics, Mr. Jodoin, in 1899 and 1900, served as chairman of the Board of Selectmen, and in 1903 was again elected. He has served as first selectman and also represented his town in the State Legislature. In the Legislature he was instrumental in securing the passage of an act allowing the motorman to sit, and compelling the car companies to furnish them with suitable seats. He is a member of the Benevolent and Protective Order of Elks, and a man thoroughly esteemed.

Mr. Jodoin married Azilda Bourque, born in Baltic, Connecticut, daughter of Julian Bourque. They have two adopted children: Antonia and Roderick. Antonia was educated in the Convent of Saint Marie in Canada, spending five years there, finishing at the Convent of the Holy Family, at Baltic. Roderick, the son, was well educated in Baltic schools, and during the World War period, 1917-18, served in the United States army.

ARTHUR EDWIN HEWITT was the fourth generation of this branch of the Hewitt family to be born in the old homestead at Lebanon, his birth occurring June 20, 1881. He is the son of Erwin and Nellie Elizabeth (Styles) Hewitt, both natives of Lebanon, the former having been born October 10, 1858, the latter in 1864. To Mr. and Mrs. Hewitt were born seven children: Arthur Edwin, of further mention; Rodney; Everett; George; Bernice; Gladys; Charlotte, deceased.

Arthur E. Hewitt obtained his early education in the schools of Lebanon, and then went to Morse's Business College. After terminating his studies at this latter institution, he returned to his father's farm and has since been actively engaged in following this particular line of occupation. As a boy he gained a wide experience in agricultural subjects while at work with his father, and then with the training which he acquired at school he became well skilled in business management, thus this combination has well fitted him to conduct affairs with excellent results, and as well may be imagined he has met with unbounded success. In politics, Mr. Hewitt is a Republican, and while he is no office seeker, he has ever by his vote and influence aided the community in whatever has seemed in his judgment best for its welfare.

Arthur Edwin Hewitt was united in marriage with Elsie Louise Gardener, born in Colchester, May 12, 1879, daughter of William and Mary Jane (Whipple) Gardener, of Colchester, Connecticut. Mr. and Mrs. Hewitt are the parents of one child, Dorothy Gardener, born July 17, 1904.

JOSEPH FRED ENOS—After a number of years spent in other practical branches of business activity, Joseph F. Enos has for the past two years carried on a successful garage at Quaker Hill.

He is a son of Richard Enos, who was born in New London, in the year 1851, and died there in 1915. He married Nellie Briggs, of New London, and they were the parents of six children: Richard; Nellie, now the wife of Arthur Beckwith, of Waterford, this county; Joseph F., of whom further; Fannie, Arthur, Gertrude.

Joseph F. Enos was born in New London, Connecticut, December 27, 1876. He received his education in the public schools of his native city, after which he assisted his father in the trucking business. When he was twenty-three years of age he began to learn the carpenter's trade, and as an apprentice and journeyman spent about fourteen years in this occupation. On December 16, 1919, Mr. Enos came to Quaker Hill, Connecticut, and established a garage and by so doing met a very acute need of the community. He has been very successful, and his garage is one of the most popular in a large section. In fraternal circles, Mr. Enos is well known, being a member of Fairview Lodge, Independent Order of Odd Fellows, and of New London Lodge, Loyal Order of Moose.

Mr. Enos married Cassie May Nagel, who was born in Greenport, Long Island, in 1878, a daughter of Jacob Nagel.

DANIEL MARKHAM PECK, one of the representative citizens of Baltic, Connecticut, where he is engaged in the farming business on a large scale, is a member of a family which for generations has been identified with the State of Connecticut, and has been represented here by many men who have stood high in the esteem of the community. It was founded in this country at a very early date in Colonial history, the progenitor being among the first settlers of Connecticut.

George Peck, father of Daniel M. Peck, was born at East Haddam, Connecticut, December 25, 1843, and died there March 26, 1905. Mr. Peck married Harriett Emeline Markham, born at Chatham, Connecticut, September 15, 1848, the daughter of Daniel Niles and Mary (Skinner) Markham. Mr. and Mrs. Peck were the parents of two children: Daniel

Markham, of further mention; and Olmstead, born June 6, 1884.

Daniel Markham Peck was born June 6, 1883, at Colchester, Connecticut, and here received the preliminary portion of his education, later supplementing this with a course at Bacon Academy. After completing his studies he engaged in farming, gain- a wide and extensive knowledge of this subject and becoming well skilled in agricultural methods generally. With his brother Olmstead, he purchased the property known as the Plain Hill Farm, and here he has resided continuously up to the present time. This property was naturally a fertile one, and they have developed and cultivated it until it is now in a highly productive state. This homestead was the original Peck home and is two hundred years old, fifty years of this time, however, it passed out of the family, only to be bought back again by Daniel Markham Peck and his brother, Olmstead Peck. The house contains various articles of interest, and many antiques, some two hundred years old, among them many pieces of mahogany, all of beautiful design. Many relics of rare interest have also been picked up around the farm, such as ancient Indian implements of war and peace. Mrs. Peck, the mother, guards and cherishes these valuables, but with a rare hospitality is ever ready to show her treasures to the interested visitor. Unlike his father, who was a staunch Republican, Mr. Peck is a Democrat, and gives to the affairs of the community the interest and attention demanded of every good citizen. Mr. Peck is unmarried.

JAMES E. F. BROWN—Born on his father's farm and brought up on it, James E. F. Brown early in life became an expert in the care and training of horses, and especially in judging horses, their valuation, etc. Therefore, it was quite a natural thing that he should, in manhood, become a dealer in horseflesh.

James E. F. Brown was born in the town of Groton, Connecticut, November 19, 1861. His parents were Roswell and Catherine (Chesbro) Brown, of Groton, the former a native of North Stonington, the latter born in Groton. Roswell Brown attended the district school for some years, then took up farming, in which he was engaged nearly all his life. He was a very prominent worker in the politics of his borough on the Republican ticket, and at different times held public offices. For thirteen years he was deputy sheriff under Sheriff Richard A. Wheeler, also served as a member of the Board of Selectmen. At another time Mr. Brown was chosen tax collector, and filled various other offices. In his later life he retired from active work, and moved, with his family, into the town of Mystic, his death occurring there at the age of seventy-four years. His wife died in Mystic, aged seventy-six years. They had a family of five children: 1. Roswell, who died in early childhood. 2. Charles, also died when very young. 3. Daniel C., a farmer living in Groton; his wife, Sybil Halstead, was a native of Cuba, New York. 4. James E. F., of whom further. 5. Rosie E., deceased.

Having attended the district school of Mystic for some years, James E. F. Brown completed his education at the Mystic Valley Institute. Following this he became interested in dealing in horses and has continued in this line ever since, now owning large sales stables and also conducting an extensive livery business. Many of his horses he buys in Boston, Massachusetts, and Providence, Rhode Island, shipping them to Mystic for sale.

Like his father, James E. F. Brown has been much engaged in local politics and is well known in the Republican ranks. He was at one time appointed deputy sheriff under Sheriff Sidney A. Brown, and afterward elected for a second term; he held the office for eight years. Mr. Brown is also interested in fraternal matters, and is a member of Stonington Lodge, No. 26, of Mystic, Independent Order of Odd Fellows.

James E. F. Brown married, on October 26, 1888, Mary S. Togee, at Danielson, Connecticut. She is the daughter of Mr. and Mrs. James R. Togee, residents of Danielson. Two children have been born of this marriage: 1. Frank Harris, who died in 1916. 2. Albertus Bruce, who is an electrical engineer at Meridan, Connecticut. Mr. Brown and his wife are members of the Protestant Episcopal church.

CHARLES BUTTOLPH DAVIS—Among the representative citizens of Franklin, Connecticut, is Charles B. Davis. Since coming to this community in 1890, he has taken a keen and active interest in the welfare of the place, and has ever by his vote and influence furthered whatever pertained to civic betterment.

Charles Crandall Davis, father of Charles B. Davis, was born in Rhode Island, and died in 1917. He followed agricultural pursuits throughout his entire lifetime. He married Harriett Frances Barnes, a native of Preston, her birth having occurred there September 1, 1832; she died May 1, 1920. Mr. and Mrs. Davis were the parents of ten children: Joseph Elmer, Edwin Gardner, Nancy G., A. Barnes, Gilbert Smith, George Warren, Chauncy Crandall, Harriett Isabel, John Mason, deceased; Charles B., of further mention.

Charles B. Davis was born at Preston, Connecticut, December 20, 1853. His childhood was spent on his father's farm, but his educational advantages were exceptionally good and after obtaining his preliminary schooling in the district schools of his native place he entered a literary institution from which he graduated in 1875, at the age of twenty-two years. Having already gained a wide and extensive knowledge of farming while at work with his father on the farm, he decided to continue in this line. In 1890 he came to Franklin, where he purchased his present place, and has here resided continuously up to the present time. He has developed and cultivated it until he has brought it to its highly productive state, and has since carried on successful farming operations. Mr. Davis is one of those who are instinctively interested in the welfare of the communities where they reside, and has given no little time and energy to the conducting of public affairs. He is justice of the peace, chairman of the town school committee, and for twenty-one years was selectman of the town. Mr. Davis is also master of Bozrah Grange.

On January 21, 1883, Charles B. Davis was united in marriage with Sarah Emma Palmer, a native of Perryville, Rhode Island, her birth having occurred there January 9, 1862. To Mr. and Mrs. Davis have been born four children: Carrie, married Clifford Lathrop; Benjamin P., mentioned elsewhere in this work; Charles Emerson, and Clarence Howard.

STANTON LEROY BRIGGS was born at Lebanon, Connecticut, May 9, 1892. His early education was obtained in the schools of his native place, after which he supplemented this with a course at a business college in Norwich, Connecticut. Upon terminating his studies at last named institution, he became engaged in farming, which he has continued up to the present time. Mr. Briggs has also devoted much of his time to auctioneering, and is credited with having attained much success in this particular line at North Franklin, which is his place of residence.

On April 26, 1918, Stanton Leroy Briggs enlisted in the United States army and was ordered to Camp Devens, where he was assigned to the Twenty-sixth Division of the 101st Massachusetts Regiment. Three months later, on July 4, 1918, he sailed for France on the transport "Burma Glasgow." While overseas he took an active part in many of the important engagements, and after the signing of the armistice returned to this country upon the transport "America."

Mr. Briggs has always been active in public affairs in Lebanon, and has been identified with several movements for the advancement of the community's welfare. He is a Republican in politics, and at the time of the writing of this article was nominated on the ticket of his party for representative from this district. He was constable, but is now deputy sheriff. Although comparatively young in years, Mr. Briggs has won for himself a place in the community which might well be the envy of a much older man. He has given liberally to every undertaking, the aim of which is the good of the community, having ever shared his fortunes with his fellow-men. Mr. Briggs is unmarried.

VICTOR MARC AURELE—Victor Aurele, born in Quebec, Canada, came to Taftville, New London county, Connecticut, and there was employed in the cotton mills. He married Virginia Sury, born in Quebec, and they were the parents of fifteen children, the eldest a son, Victor Marc, now a retired farmer of Taftville, Connecticut.

Victor M. Aurele was born in Quebec, Canada, in 1854, and there spent the first fifteen years of his life. He then came to the United States, finding a home in Northampton, Massachusetts, where he learned the carpenter's trade and remained eleven years. In 1880 he came to Taftville, Connecticut, where his father and family were living, and there he became carpenter with the Pomona Mill Company, and for nine years remained in the employ of that company. He then bought a farm on School street from the Pomona Mill Company, which he cultivated very profitably until 1921, when he retired. He is a member of the Roman Catholic church, of Taftville, and a Republican in politics.

Mr. Aurele married, in Canada, Mary Dapot, of Quebec, and they are the parents of nineteen children, nine of whom are living, namely: Joseph and Henry, living in Greenville; Frederick and Tusant, of Taftville; Alexsena, married Louis Pouta, of Taftville; Albertine, residing at home; Cora, married John Michon, of Taftville; Bernodett, married L. De Bouve; Beatrice, married Clifford Crary.

JAMES WILLIAM HUNTINGTON was born at Bozrah, Connecticut, December 15, 1877, in the old homestead which is directly across the road from his present farm. The road which divides these two homes runs directly in front of each and is the dividing line between the towns of Bozrah and Franklin. He is the son of Benjamin Franklin and Henrietta (Ladd) Huntington. Benjamin Franklin Huntington was born in Columbus, Ohio, August 28, 1839, and was brought by his parents to Bozrah in March, 1840, when he was but one year old. It is interesting to note here that his father drove a three-horse prairie schooner from Ohio to Bozrah, Connecticut.

The childhood of James William Huntington was spent on his father's farm and most of the time was given to aiding the elder man in his work on the farm. The lad attended the district school until he was fourteen years of age, when he terminated his studies and devoted his entire time to farming. Having in the meantime gained an extensive knowledge of the subject, he soon became well skilled in agricultural methods generally, and his present farm which he purchased has proven highly successful. In politics Mr. Huntington is an Independent, and has not identified himself with any political party, preferring to remain free from all partisan influences in the exercise of his own judgment on public issues. Mr. Huntington is unmarried.

NOE ISIDORE CARON—Especial interest attaches to the business enterprise which follows out-of-the-ordinary channels, and such is the confectionery business in Norwich, in which Mr. Caron is interested, and in which he has been a partner for upwards of seven years.

Mr. Caron is a son of Noe I. Caron, Sr., who was born in St. Aisne, Quebec, and educated in the parochial schools of that community. At the age of seventeen years he came to the United States and settled in Baltic, Connecticut. This was in

1873, and the young man learned the carpenter's trade here, afterwards becoming a successful contractor and builder in this county. He retired from business in 1916, and is now a resident of Baltic. He married Rosana Bouget, daughter of Benjamin and Rosalie (Cartier) Bouget, Benjamin Bouget being a brother of Bishop Ignace Bouget, who at the time of his death, which occurred in Montreal, was bishop of the diocese of the Province of Quebec. A beautiful monument to the memory of Bishop Bouget stands on the grounds of the cathedral in Montreal.

Noe Isidore Caron, third in order of birth of the thirteen children of Noe I. and Rosana (Bouget) Caron, was born in Baltic, in the town of Sprague, in this county, October 18, 1886. Educated in the parochial schools of this community, Mr. Caron's first employment was in the capacity of clerk in the grocery store of H. F. Frink, of Norwich, and here he remained until 1911. At that time he formed his first connection with Mr. Anson R. Grover, his present partner, whose life is also reviewed in this work, and who was then prominent in the wholesale confectionery business. Mr. Caron acted as salesman for Mr. Grover for about four years, then in 1915, uniting in a partnership, they purchased the present business, Mr. Grover coincidentally retiring from the wholesale confectionery business he had theretofore conducted. The Connecticut Pop Corn Company, which they then absorbed, was established in Norwich in 1866, and prior to 1911 was for many years carried on by W. H. Vincent. The present concern has been most successful, broadening the scope of the business until their popcorn confections are familiar practically all over the United States.

In the public affairs of the city Mr. Caron is deeply interested, and supports the Democratic party, but takes no leading part in political matters. He is a member of Norwich Lodge, No. 430, Benevolent and Protective Order of Elks, and of the Union of St. John the Baptist, of Taftville. He is a member of St. Mary's Church, of Baltic, where he resides.

On September 7, 1920, Mr. Caron married, in Taftville, Josephine Molleur, daughter of Joseph and Argellia (Gregory) Molleur, of Taftville.

WALTER EATHEL BURGESS—The American surname of Burgess is a variation of the ancient English name Burgh, and the family was originally settled in Salem, Massachusetts, in 1620, the American progenitor, Thomas Burgess, having served the town of Salem in every public office. He died February 13, 1685, at the age of eighty-two years, highly respected and honored by his fellow-citizens.

Philo Burgess, father of Walter Eathel Burgess, was born in Franklin, Connecticut, March 6, 1843. At the age of seven he was brought by his parents to Lebanon, where he followed agricultural pursuits until his death, which occurred February 12, 1914. He always took an active interest in the public affairs of the community, and for fifteen years was farm auditor, and eight years served as a member of the local school board. He married Emily F. Poilen, a native of Windham, her birth having occurred there, November 8, 1842. Mr. and Mrs. Burgess were the parents of four children: Walter E., of further mention; Grace, born March 21, 1874; Fred, born July 14, 1876; John Edward, born November 4, 1880.

Walter Eathel Burgess was born in Windham, Connecticut, December 28, 1872, and obtained his education in the schools of Lebanon, after which he entered upon his business career, securing a position at the Lebanon Creamery, where he remained until 1902, when he bought his present farm, and is recognized as one of the most successful farmers of the community. As a citizen Mr. Burgess manifests the same qualities which characterize him as a businessman, steadfast loyalty to principle, and promptness and efficiency in the performance of duty. Taking no active part in politics, he is quietly influential in the affairs of the community, and he is emphatically a man whose opinion carries weight. Mr. Burgess is unmarried.

REXFORD EDWARD CUMMINGS, one of the most prosperous farmers of this district, comes from a family who have long resided in this town, his ancestors being among the first settlers of Lebanon. He was born in the old homestead July 17, 1893, the son of Edwin and Ida (Lathrop) Cummings. Edwin Cummings spent his entire lifetime in his native town and devoted himself exclusively to farming. To Mr. and Mrs. Cummings were born nine children: Charles, Claude, Hazel, Kenneth, Burnett, Harold, Leo, Carlton and Rexford.

The education of Rexford Edward Cummings was obtained in the schools of his native place, and after leaving school he turned his entire attention to agricultural methods, having in the meantime, while a lad, helped his father with his work until he had acquired considerable knowledge of the various branches of this subject. He has continued in this particular line up to the present time, and the highly productive state of the land upon which the old homestead stands is due in no small measure to the labors of Rexford Cummings. Mr. Cummings has never taken any active part in the public affairs of the town, but nevertheless he is public-spirited to a large degree, and no good work which has for its aim the welfare of the community ever fails to find in him an earnest supporter.

Mr. Cummings married Ruth Pulse, daughter of Elmer Pulse, a prominent farmer of this region. Mr. and Mrs. Cummings are the parents of two children: Shirley and Hazel.

THEODORE NELSON CHURCH—From boyhood Theodore N. Church has been engaged in the fish and oyster business in Norwich, Connecticut, his father before him engaging in the same business from youthful manhood until his death. He taught his sons his business, and in 1880 Theodore N. and Henry E. Church established their own business, Theodore N. later becoming sole owner of that business and also of the business formerly owned by his father.

Elisha P. Church was born in the town of Montville, New London county, Connecticut, and there passed his youth and early manhood, obtaining his education in the district school and assisting his father in the farm management. While still a young man he settled in Norwich, and there established a fish and oyster business which he conducted until his death in 1891. He made his home in the town of Preston, then a part of the town of Norwich, and there died. He married Melissa Williams, born in Montville, died in Norwich, Connecticut. They were the parents of six children, Theodore N., the eldest.

Theodore Nelson Church, son of Elisha P. and Melissa (Williams) Church, was born September 14, 1859, and attended the district school near his Preston home. At the age of twelve he became his father's helper in his fish and oyster market in Norwich, and has continued in the fish business until the present. He continued with his father's business until reaching legal age in 1880, then with his younger brother, Henry E. Church, established a fish business in Norwich. For twenty-two years the brothers continued their independent fish business, then in 1902 Henry Church sold his interest to his brother Theodore, the latter continuing the same until the present (1922), also being the owner of the old fish and oyster business founded by his father. For more than half a century Mr. Church has been connected with the fish business in Norwhich, and for the greater part of that time as proprietor. In politics he is a Democrat, and has served the city officially two years as a member of the board of relief; one year as councilman. In religious faith he is a Baptist, a member of Central Church, Norwich.

Mr. Church married in August, 1880, Adelaide Josephine Souer, of Preston, Connecticut, daughter of Peter and Julia Souer. Mr. and Mrs. Church are the parents of two children: Ruby Souer, born in Preston, now Mrs. Richards, resides in Norwich; Theodore Paul, born in Preston, now associated in business with his father. In 1885 the family moved from Preston to Norwich, which city is still the family home.

DWIGHT ELIOT SMITH, son of William and Charlotte Smith (Hammond) Smith, was born in the town of Bozrah, October 28, 1887. His childhood was spent on his father's farm, and most of the time was given to aiding the elder man in his work about the place. His educational advantages were meager, but Mr. Smith is one of those men who are keenly observant, and he has learned much in the hard school of experience, especially about that all important subject, his fellow-men. He continued to reside with his parents until he was sixteen years of age, when he left the farm and sought employment in the Palmer Brothers' Mills, where he worked for several years, finally resigning in 1920, when he purchased his present farm, which he has under extensive cultivation at the present time. He now gives his entire time to farming, and his place is regarded as one of the well conducted properties in this region.

Mr. Smith married (first) Edith Iva Gardner, a native of Colchester, Connecticut. To Mr. and Mrs. Smith were born two children: Bertram Gardner, born in 1897; and Leslie Ely, born in 1898. Mr. Smith married (second) Olive Alice Jackson, a native of Sweden, her birth having occurred there November 8, 1872. Mr. and Mrs. Smith are the parents of one child, Louisa Olive, born November 1, 1915.

CHARLES HARRISON FITCH, born at Lisbon, Connecticut, March 4, 1878, is the son of Charles and Esther (Wilcox) Fitch, the former a native of Preston, the latter of Griswold, Connecticut.

The boy Charles H. attended the schools of his native place until he was sixteen years of age, when he terminated his studies and devoted his entire time to his father's farm, the elder man having passed away at this time. From childhood, the son had spent most of his spare time in aiding his father in the work about the place, so when the time came for him to take entire charge he had already acquired considerable knowledge of the subject, and was well skilled in agricultural methods generally. Today his place is recognized as one of the well conducted properties of this region, due in no small measure to the tireless energy Mr. Fitch has given to his labors.

Besides being ardently devoted to farming, Charles Harrison Fitch is one of those men who have always interested themselves in everything pertaining to the welfare of the community in which they have chosen to reside, and he has given no little time and energy to the conduct of its affairs. He is selectman of the town, and has been a member of the local school board for many years.

Mr. Fitch was united in marriage with Nora Geist, a native of Lisbon, Connecticut, and the daughter of Paul and Annie Geist. To Mr. and Mrs. Fitch have been born five children: Clarence Palmer, Ralph Harrison, Tyler Theodore, Doris Geist, and Charles Ernest.

LOUIS JOSEPH JARRY—In the village of Taftville, New London county, Connecticut, Louis J. Jarry began his existence and there continues an enterprising merchant, who by his energy and public spirit has contributed to the prosperity of the community in which his lot has been cast. He is a son of Damase and Melinda Jarry, his father born in Montpelier, Vermont, his mother of Canadian birth. Damase Jarry was educated in the public schools and grew to manhood a Vermont farmer. About 1875 he came to Taftville, Connecticut, securing employment in the weaving department of the Ponemah Cotton Mill. He married Melinda ———, born in St. Caisare, Province of Quebec,

Canada, and they were the parents of nine children, three of whom are living in Taftville: Louis Joseph, of further mention; Yvonne Emma, born in Taftville, in 1899; Andrew, born in Taftville, in 1902.

Louis Joseph Jarry was born in Taftville, New London county, Connecticut, April 20, 1894. He attended Sacred Heart Parochial School, Taftville, until fourteen years of age, then left school to enter the weaving department of the Ponemah Cotton Mill, there continuing until his sixteenth year. He began his apprenticeship under Henry Morris, a baker of Taftville, in 1910, serving three years. From 1913 until 1916 he worked in different localities, then bought out a confectionery store and lunch room in Taftville, which he conducted for about four years, until 1921, when he bought the Bausoliel bakery in Taftville, which he is conducting very successfully, it being the only bakery in the village. He is a member of Sacred Heart Roman Catholic Church, Taftville; member of the Society of St. John the Baptist, and of the Society of St. Louis, both of Taftville. In politics he is an Independent, voting for the men and measures he believes best for the public welfare.

Mr. Jarry married, in 1915, Grace Anna Robellaird, daughter of Eli and Apoline (Carron) Robellaird, of Norwich, Connecticut. Mr. and Mrs. Jarry are the parents of two children: Gerard Louis, born in Taftville, May 28, 1917, and Lucille Grace, born in Taftville, October 19, 1920.

ALBERT ALLEN RIST—The farming communities of New London county, Connecticut, are always abreast of the times, always taking front rank in every movement for the public good, and keeping pace with the cities in the line of progress. In Lisbon, Connecticut, Albert Allen Rist is one of those men whose activities are making this true.

Mr. Rist is the only son of Isaac Swan Rist, who was born in the village of Leffingwelltown, town of Bozrah, Connecticut, in 1849, and died in 1901.

Albert Allen Rist was born in Norwich, Connecticut, January 22, 1883. He attended the educational institutions that are the pride of this city, gaining a practical preparation for the battle of life. His father's last illness ended his education, and he went into the industrial world to provide for himself. He entered the employ of the Norwich Nickel-Brass Company, where he continued for a period of eleven years. At the end of that time he made a radical change in his line of effort, fulfilling thereby a long-cherished dream. He came to Lisbon, and purchased the farm which is now his home, and upon which he has achieved unusual success. He has now been a resident of this town for nine years, and in that time has won the cordial regard and respect of the townspeople, and has become one of the leading farmers of this vicinity.

In the public service Mr. Rist has borne a part almost since his coming to this town. Although acknowledging the domination of no party, so far as his individual action is concerned, he was elected town clerk eight years ago, and has been re-elected ever since, now (1922) holding that office to the satisfaction of all concerned. Mr. Rist is a hard-working man, carrying on extensive farm interests, but his duties as a public servant are performed with the utmost precision and thoroughness. Aside from the duties of office, Mr. Rist is taking a constructive part in the matter of education. He is agitating various improvements in the schools of the town, the practicability of which is unquestionable.

Mr. Rist married Ella May Bennett, daughter of Charles Sterry and Nellie Bennett. Mr. and Mrs. Rist have three children: Helen Mae, Newell Palmer, and William Allen.

CHRISTIAN NIELSON—Living a quiet, well-ordered life, much respected by his neighbors and fellow-townsmen, Christian Nielson works his farm and harvests his crops, enjoying the fruits of his labor with his family.

By birth Mr. Nielson is a Dane, his forbears for many generations having been good and loyal citizens of Denmark. His parents were Frederick and Maria (Olsen) Nielson, both born there, the latter having died while her son was an infant.

Christian Nielson was born July 16, 1870. At the age of six his education began, he attending the common schools until he was fourteen years old; from that time until his manhood he was employed in farming and, when twenty-three years old, he determined to come to America. He arrived in the United States in 1893, locating at first in Mansfield, Connecticut, but after a time removing to Willimantic. Here he obtained employment with the Buck Grain Company, remaining with this firm for seven years. Mr. Nielson's love of farming led him to make a change in his occupation and, deciding upon Lebanon as his future home, he bought the farm where he is now living, in 1908. It is situated upon the road to Chestnut Hill, one of the many villages in Lebanon township.

Christian Nielson married Helma G. Johnson, a native of Sweden, having been born there September 17, 1868. Two children were born of this union: Ernest Hulbert, born in 1901 in Willimantic; Ellen Matilda, born in 1904, also in Willimantic.

Having no political aspirations, Mr. Nielson has neither sought nor held any public position, nor is he interested in fraternal societies.

PETER SELLAS—Among the public-spirited citizens of Norwich the earnest work of Peter Sellas for the general advance is widely recognized. Mr. Sellas is the son of John K. and Alexandra (Batis) Sellas, both natives of Greece, and still residents of that country. John K. Sellas is a large land owner and successful farmer, and they are the parents of eight children, of whom Peter is the eldest.

Peter Sellas was born in Peloponnesus, Greece, June 21, 1886, and came to the United States in 1902. First locating in Stamford, Connecticut, he was employed as clerk in a confectionery store for about five years, then came to Norwich. Here he at once became associated as a partner with Peter Maniaty and Peter Bimbicos, who owned and operated a confectionery store. This business was established about 1902, and had become a thriving interest. In 1910 Mr. Sellas purchased the interest of Mr. Maniaty, then two years later bought out Mr. Bimbicos, thus becoming sole owner of the business. Since that time he has carried it forward under the name of the Sellas Spa, with marked success. Broadening his activities in 1912, Mr. Sellas opened a modern restaurant adjoining the confectionery store, under the name of Sellas Lunch. Two years later he received a brother into partnership and this association of interest still continues. Mr. Sellas has also, personally, branched out into other lines of activity, purchasing the Strand building on Main street from William Lust, of New York City, in 1919. Still further, he purchased in 1921, the Majestic Garage in Norwich, now controlling that enterprise He is also vice-president of the American Cotton Company of Norwich. His rise from obscurity in his adopted country has been a noteworthy instance of the possibilities in store for a young man who is willing to devote himself wholeheartedly to a business career, and win his way by industry and fair dealing, returning to the public full measure of value for their patronage and support. He is a member of the Norwich Chamber of Commerce.

But Mr. Sellas has not gained success by slighting his responsibilities to society. Early becoming an American citizen he has long taken a deep interest in Americanization work among newcomers from his native land, and his influence in this regard can hardly be overestimated. Whether assistance, encouragement or advice is needed, he lends a helping hand to his fellow-countrymen. During the World War he served on all drives and was a member of the Liberty Loan committees. Politically, he supports the Republican party. Fraternally, Mr. Sellas is a member of St. James Lodge, No. 4, Free and Accepted Masons; of Franklin Chapter, No. 4, Royal Arch Masons; Franklin Council, No. 3, Royal and Select Masters; Columbian Commandery, Knights Templar; and the consistory, Ancient Accepted Scottish Rite, all of Norwich, and is also a member of Sphinx Temple, Ancient Arabic Order Nobles of the Mystic Shrine, of Hartford, Connecticut. He is a member of Norwich Lodge, No. 430, Benevolent and Protective Order of Elks.

Mr. Sellas was married in New York City, on November 23, 1910. Mr. and Mrs. Sellas have two children: John Peter, born May 1, 1919, and Helen P., born in 1921.

JAMES SELLAS—Prominent in the business life of Norwich, and there associated with his brother, Peter Sellas, James Sellas is representative of the progressive young men who have come from Greece and have taken a constructive part in twentieth century American civilization. Mr. Sellas is a son of John K. and Alexandra (Batis) Sellas, both natives of Peloponnesus, Greece, his father a successful farmer and landowner in his native country.

James Sellas was born in Peloponnesus, Greece, and educated in the national schools of that country. Coming to the United States in 1910, Mr. Sellas located in Norwich, where he was employed for four years with his brother, then, in 1914, he became his partner in the confectionery and lunch business, which they still carry on here. The confectionery business was founded in 1902 by Peter Maniaty and Peter Bimbicos, and purchased from them by Peter Sellas in 1910. The lunch room was founded by Peter Sellas in 1912, and is known as the Sellas Lunch. James Sellas is active in the management of these enterprises and is widely known as a young man of high integrity and progressive spirit.

During the World War Mr. Sellas served with the American Expeditionary Forces as a private. Sent first to Camp Devens, Massachusetts, he was assigned to Company 8, 301st Machine Gun Battalion, 76th Division. Sailing for France in June, 1918, he was there transferred to Company 8, 3rd Machine Gun Battalion, 1st Division, and was under fire at St. Mihiel, Soissons, and the Argonne Forest. In the Argonne he was gassed, and was returned home with the 145th Machine Gun Battalion, 37th Division, reaching this side on April 1, 1919. He was mustered out of the service at Camp Devens, on May 1, 1919, and returned to Norwich to take up the interrupted interests of citizenship. James Sellas is a member of Robert O. Fletcher Post, American Legion, of Norwich, and of the Veterans of Foreign Wars.

FREDERICK WAY CHAPMAN—One of the prominent men of East Lyme, a resident of this community since childhood, and now a successful farmer, although practically retired from active work, Frederick Way Chapman is a representative man of New London county.

Mr. Chapman is a son of Robert Fairbanks Chapman, who was born in the Chesterfield district of Old Lyme, in the year 1821. Robert Fairbanks Chapman was educated in the local district schools, and after completing his studies took up the work of the farm, which he followed throughout his lifetime in his native town until he was about thirty years of age, then in Lyme. He became a prominent and influential man in the community, was always a Democrat by political affiliation, and in 1869-70 represented his town in the State Legislature. He also served on the school board, and was instrumental in advancing the progress of education in this section. He died in Old Lyme in the year 1875, at the age of fifty-four years, scarcely past the prime of life. He married Laurel Anne Watrous, who was born in Lyme, October 15, 1824, and died in Lyme. She was a daughter of Daniel Watrous, a farmer of Lyme, who was born in 1791, and died in 1880.

Laurel Anne (Watrous) Chapman was the eldest of seven children, the others being Harriett, Mary Anne, Caroline, David, Daniel, and Allen Watrous. Robert Fairbanks and Laurel Anne (Watrous) Chapman were the parents of four children: Mary Anne, born in Waterford, Connecticut, November 12, 1846; Frederick Way, whose name heads this review; Lucy Grace, born in Lyme, February 25, 1859; and Laura Watrous, born in Lyme, March 13, 1861. The mother died in Waterford, and the son is now the only surviving member of this family.

Frederick Way Chapman was born in Waterford, Connecticut, March 3, 1848. Coming to the town of Lyme with the family at the age of three years, it was here that he received his education in the district schools of the day. After finishing the common school course, he became associated with his father in the work of the farm, eventually carrying on the place for himself. He has worked hard all his life, and has been very successful, having made the farm one of the finest in the county, and has won the respect and esteem of his fellow-townsmen. He has always held the public interests of the community at heart, and has encouraged every worthy movement, but while a staunch Democrat by political faith, he has consistently declined political honors, as his life has been too busy to permit his doing justice to public responsibilities.

Mr. Chapman married (first), May 9, 1877, Mary Louise Griswold, who was born in New York City, and was a daughter of John Griswold, deceased. Ten children were born to this union: Robert Fairbanks, born March 22, 1878; Lucy Watrous, born April 4, 1880; John G., born March 4, 1882; Eliza M., born December 31, 1885; May L., born March 10, 1891; Frank H., born March 11, 1892; Emma, born May 15, 1893. Three children died in infancy, and all were born in Lyme. Mr. Chapman married (second) Clara Beebe Medcalf, who was born in Niantic, in the town of Lyme, September 26, 1849, and is a daughter of Samuel A. and Louisa F. Medcalf. She was the fourth of their eight children: Samuel, Charles Willard, Josephine Louise, Clara B., John A., George W., Mary E., and Jessie F.

ENOS MORGAN GRAY, JR.—Enos Morgan Gray, Sr., was born in the town of Ledyard, New London county, Connecticut, May 21, 1851, died at his farm in the same town, July 29, 1919. He was educated in the public schools, and after completing his studies began farming, an occupation he followed until his death. The farm in the town of Ledyard is now owned by his widow, and managed by his son, Enos Morgan Gray, Jr., his mother's business representative.

Mr. Gray married Pamella McKenzie, born in St. John, New Brunswick, Canada, daughter of William McKenzie. They were the parents of six children: 1. Enos M., Jr., of whom further. 2. Mason, married Elizabeth Clegg, of Providence, Rhode Island, and has a son, Benjamin. 3. Benjamin. 4. Nathan, married Jeannette Bennett. 5. Mattice, married Daniel Gray, of Ledyard, and they have five children: Ellsworth, Philip, Hadley, Sarah, Alton. 6. Mamie.

Enos Morgan Gray, Jr., was born in the town of Ledyard, New London county, Connecticut, March 10, 1898, and was educated in the local public school. He was his father's assistant until his death in 1919, then became its manager, his mother inheriting the property. Mr. Gray married, February 4, 1919, Bessie Clark, born in Mystic, Connecticut, April 19, 1900, daughter of Elisha and Luella (Strickland) Clark. They have a daughter, Ruth Clark Gray, born July 4, 1920.

LEON BRODER—In Ekaterinoslav or Yekaterinoslav (meaning the "fame of Catherine"), a town of South Russia, capital of a province of the same name, situated about two hundred and fifty miles northeast of the city of Odessa, on the right bank of the Dnieper river, Leon Broder was born, as were his parents, Joseph and Rachel Broder. Ekaterinoslav, the province, abounds in minerals, and the soil is fertile, yielding large crops of grain. The city is a modern town of about 12,500 population, founded during the reign of Queen Catherine II, of Russia. It is the seat of a large iron and steel industry and has large flour mills.

Joseph Broder was a farmer, spent his life in his native Russia, and died in Kiememchug, a town on the Dnieper, in 1902. His wife died in Ekaterinoslav in 1904. They were the parents of four children, the youngest a son, Leon.

Leon Broder was born in 1874, and there spent the first twenty-six years of his life. He obtained an education in the State schools, finishing the courses equivalent to those of an American grammar school. He prospered as a farmer and conducted also a grain business, for Ekaterinoslav had large flouring mills, and grain dealing was a sure and usually profitable business. In 1900 he closed out his business affairs in Russia and sailed from Asthonia, Russia, via Hamburg, for New York City, arriving in April, 1900, after a voyage of fourteen days, coming as a steerage passenger, and very happy to be able to come under any conditions. From New York he went to Philadelphia, Pennsylvania, but in May, 1900, he moved to Colchester, Connecticut, where he secured farm employment with P. Cutter, his pay three dollars ($3.00) monthly. He remained eighteen months, and used his earnings to gain a knowledge of the English language, studying nights to accomplish his aims. After leaving the Cutter farm, Mr. Broder was employed for two years at farming, then in 1903 conducted a meat market in Colchester, to which he devoted his own time, but continued to send his meat wagon over his old routes in charge of a competent man. To the meat market a general store has been added, and in 1912 a retail grain business was established, the three departments all being owned and under the management of Leon Broder. He is an alert, capable business man, and has won his way to a secure place in public esteem.

Having thoroughly absorbed American ideals and principles, Mr. Broder has completed naturalization and is an American citizen in all that the word implies. He affiliates with the Democratic party, has served his county as a grand juror and his town as assessor and as a justice of the peace. He is true to the traditional faith of his fathers, and worships with his co-religionists.

Mr. Broder married, in Colchester, December 24, 1906, Fannie Super, born in Beluto, Russia, who came to the United States in 1899. Mr. and Mrs. Broder are the parents of three children, all born in Colchester, Connecticut: Maurice, born November, 1907; Jacob, October 5, 1909; and Anna Lelia, August 15, 1917.

During the World War period, 1917-18, Mr. Broder took an active part in local war work and the Red Cross Society, also being chairman of the Liberty Loan Campaign. Mrs. Broder was equally to the fore in women's war work measures, winning a prize for an unusually large sale of Liberty Loan Bonds. Mr. Broder is a member of the Woodmen of the World, the Knights of Pythias, and the Independent Order of B'rith Abraham.

JAMES NELSON HOLDRIDGE—From the time he was fifteen years of age, James N. Holdridge has been connected with farming, either with his father at the home farm, with other farmers of his district, or on his own farm, formerly known as the "Gallup Farm," which he bought in 1902. The dwelling thereon had formerly been used as a meeting house for the Congregationalists of that part of the town of Ledyard, but later they built a church. Since 1902 Mr. Holdridge has cultivated the acres of the old farm and has caused them to yield plentifully.

He is a son of Randall Holdridge, born in Ledyard, New London county, Connecticut, where he died about 1890, aged seventy-seven, a farmer all his life. He married Nancy Barnes, born in Ledyard, and with her husband is buried in the local cemetery. They were the parents of three sons: James Nelson, of further mention; Joseph, now a farmer of Ledyard, aged sixty-five; Nathan, the youngest, also a farmer of Ledyard. Their only daughter, Fannie, married Thorpe Brown, of Norwich, where she died in 1919.

James Nelson Holdridge was born in the town of Ledyard, New London county, Connecticut, August 16, 1859. He attended local select schools until fifteen years of age, then became his father's farm helper, so continuing until reaching legal age, when he began working for other farmers and was so employed in different parts of New London county. He did not become a land owner until 1902, although he continued working on a farm all the years between 1880 and 1902. He then bought the "Gallup Farm" in Ledyard, which has ever since been under his management and ownership.

Mr. Holdridge married Sarah Finnigan, born in Ledyard, in September, 1856, and died in November, 1895; she was the daughter of John and Phoebe (Maine) Finnigan. They are the parents of the following children: 1. Phoebe Esther, married Fred Clarke, of Noank, and they are the parents of seven children: Fred, Jr., Edith, Helen, Ruth, Robert, Esther, Pauline. 2. Harry, born January 5, 1891; he attended the district school until the age of seventeen, then bought a farm in North Stonington, which he cultivated for seven years, then returned to the homestead which he bought; he married Marguerite Blanche Williams, born in Ledyard in September, 1896, daughter of Joseph and Wildy (Crouch) Williams; they have two children, Harry Jr., born March 2, 1915, and Blanche Arline, born May 3, 1918. 3. Morris, born in Ledyard, October 5, 1893; enlisted in the United States army in May, 1917, and went overseas with the American Expeditionary Forces, and for a year was with the 29th Division of Infantry in all the important battles in which that division took a part; he was "gassed" in one of the fierce contests of the closing period of the war, and in May, 1919, returned to the United States. 4. Sarah, born in Ledyard, November 3, 1895; she married Cecil Williams, of Ledyard, and they are the parents of three children: Cecil, Margaret, and Elizabeth Williams.

FRED ALFRED CARON—The C. and C. Paint Shop was established in New London, in 1919, by Fred A. Caron and Fred Cross, both expert painters and finishers of automobile bodies. Mr. Caron is a native son of New London, and learned his trade in Bridgeport, Connecticut; he was called for service and in the aviation department "did his bit" in the war with Germany, 1917-18. He is a son of Christopher and Matilda Caron, his father born in Baltic, a town of Sprague, New London county, Connecticut. Christopher Caron attended the public school and for several years worked as a farm hand in the town of Sprague. Later he moved with his family to Taftville, and there, for many years, was foreman of the large farm owned and cultivated by the Ponemah Mills Company. He also lived in New London before moving to Taftville, where he died in 1915, and there his widow, Matilda still resides (1921). Mr. and Mrs. Caron were the parents of eight children, the seventh a son, Fred Alfred, of further mention.

Fred Alfred Caron was born in New London, Connecticut, October 10, 1891. He was educated in the public schools of Taftville, Connecticut, and at Norwich Free Academy, whence he graduated, class of 1906. From 1906 to 1908 he was in the employ of the Pope-Hartford Automobile Company at Hartford, Connecticut, but returned to Norwich in 1908, and was engaged as chauffeur in various places until 1914, when he went to Bridgeport, Connecticut, and served an apprenticeship with the Bridgeport Body Company, there learning high class painting and finishing of automobile bodies. He had spent three years there when called for service in the United States army. Entering the army in November, 1917, he was assigned to the aviation service, becoming crew captain on the De Auerland Airplane stationed at Kelly Field, San Antonio, Texas. Later he was transferred to Dayton, Ohio, continuing in the service until honorably discharged January 17, 1919. He then located in New London, where in partnership with Fred Cross, he established the C. & C. Paint Shop for auto painting. Mr. Caron is a member of John Coleman Prince Post of the American Legion; is independent in politics, and is a member of St. Mary's Roman Catholic Church.

He married in Norwich, in 1913, Yvonne Marcille, and they have two children: Jeanne A. and Eva, the last named dying in infancy.

NORMAN CHURCH LATHROP—Two generations of the Lathrops have lived in New England, the family tracing their descent from Rev. John Lathrop, a minister of the Church of England, who for failure to conform to ecclesiastical authority was imprisoned, but was released on condition that he should leave England. He arrived in New England with his family in 1634, and was admitted a freeman of Plymouth Colony in 1636-37, and two years later with a greater part of the congregation of the church he had founded at Scituate, moved to Barnstable, Massachusetts. He is described as a man of "deep piety, great zeal and large ability." The line of descent from Rev. John Lathrop to his descendant of the tenth American generation, Norman Church Lathrop, of Uncasville, Connecticut, is thus outlined: Rev. John Lathrop and his first wife, who died in England while her husband was in prison; their son, Samuel Lathrop, who came from England with his father, and in 1648 moved to now New London, Connecticut, moving to Norwich twenty years later, and there died in 1700, and his first wife, Elizabeth Scudder; their son, Israel Lathrop, of Norwich, Connecticut, and his wife Rebecca Bliss; their son, Samuel Lathrop, of Bozrah, Connecticut, and his wife, Elizabeth Waterman; their son Captain Elisha Lathrop, of Borah, Connecticut, and Lebanon, New Hampshire, and his first wife, Margaret Sluman; their son, Lebbeus Lathrop, of Norwich, and Borah, Connecticut; their son, Lebbeus (2) Lathrop, of Bozrah and Lebanon, Connecticut, and his wife, Lucretia Maples; their son, Harvey Lathrop, of Lebanon and Norwich, Connecticut, and his wife, Octavia Woodworth; their son, John Baldwin Lathrop, and his first wife, Alice M. Church; their son, Norman Church Lathrop, to whom this review is inscribed.

John Baldwin Lathrop was born in the town of Lebanon, New London county, Connecticut, March 24, 1848, and died in 1909. He was educated in the public schools, then learned the carpenter trade in Norwich, but later purchased the Norman E. Church interest in a general trucking business in Montville, and continued that business in partnership with his brother, Arthur D. Lathrop, until October, 1873, when he bought full control and continued its successful operation of the business until his death. But this was only one of his activities. He conducted an extensive coal business with the Montville Mills, and was president of the Uncas Dyewood and Extract Company, founded on the business of the Johnson Dye Works. Mr. Lathrop was a member of Oxoboxo Lodge, No. 116, Free and Accepted Masons, of Montville; a member of the Methodist Episcopal church; a Republican, and a useful, influential citizen of Montville, very popular and highly esteemed.

Mr. Lathrop married (first), January 1, 1873, Alice M. Church, who died in Montville, December 22, 1885, daughter of Norman E. Church, of Montville. They were the parents of two children: Norman Church, of further mention; and one who died in infancy. Mr. Lathrop married (second), October 14, 1887, Mary B. Robertson, daughter of Carmichael Robertson,, who died in December, 1888. He married (third), April 29, 1891, Addie L. Church, a sister of his first wife, who yet survives her husband, a resident of Montville (1921).

Norman Church Lathrop, only son of John Baldwin Lathrop and his first wife, Alice M. (Church) Lathrop, was born October 8, 1874, his birthplace just across the road from his present residence, four generations of his ancestors having occupied the homestead. He was educated in the public schools of the district (Norwich), and Mt. Hermon, finishing at Eastman's Business College, Poughkeepsie, New York. He then returned home and after farming for a time was associated with his father in the trucking and coal business in Montville. He is now a farmer in the village of Uncasville, in the town of Montville.

Mr. Lathrop married, May 23, 1897, in Waterford, Lulu Perry, born in Waterford, Connecticut, May 3, 1875, daughter of Alvin and Louisa (Hewitt) Perry, her mother of the old New London county Hewitt family founded by Thomas Hewitt, who is first of mention as the captain of a vessel which came down the Mystic river in 1656 to trade with the farmers. There he met and on April 26, 1659, married Hannah, daughter of Walter Palmer. He then bought land on the east side of the Mystic river, at what is now Elm Grove Cemetery, in Stonington, and there built a residence in primitive style. He continued his voyages to points along the coast and to the West Indies, and in 1662 sailed with a full cargo for the West Indies, and from the date of sailing was never again heard from. He left two children, Thomas and Benjamin, and from these sons sprang the two branches of the Hewitts in New London county, the Lebanon and Waterford branches. Eight years after Captain Hewitt's sailing, his wife, Hannah (Palmer) Hewitt, was given permission by the General Court to marry again, and on December 27, 1671, married Roger Sterry, who died in 1680. She married (third), August 25, 1681, John Fish. Mrs. Louisa (Hewitt) Perry, mother of Lulu (Perry) Lathrop is of the Waterford branch of the descendants of Captain Thomas Hewitt. Norman C. and Lulu (Perry) Lathrop are the parents of a son, Frederick Baldwin Lathrop, born January 9, 1899.

JAMES SANTACROCE—A leader in his own field, that of custom tailor, James Santacroce, of New London, Connecticut, is broadly interested in every branch of public activity.

Mr. Santacroce is a son of Frank and Nicholette (De Matteo) Santacroce. The elder Mr. Santacroce was born in Lettomanoppello, Italy, and came to the United States in early manhood, locating in the city of New London. Throughout his lifetime he followed the tailor's trade, and died in 1913, at the age of forty-eight years. His wife also was a native of Italy. They were the parents of seven children, of whom five are now living: Mary, deceased; Mary (2), deceased; David; Camillo; Raphael; James, of whom further; and Anna.

James Santacroce was born in Lettomanoppello, Italy, May 30, 1891, and came to the United States in his childhood. He was reared and educated here, and early decided to enter the same business in which his father was engaged. Having learned much of his father's business he left home and went to New York City, where he was engaged for a year or more in that business. With this experience and his natural ability for designing, Mr. Santacroce is especially well fitted to meet the requirements of particular and tasteful customers, and upon his return to New London he found an extensive clientele, appreciative of the service he was prepared to render. Establishing his own shop in this city, it was a success from the start, and he is now considered one of the leading tailors not only of the city of New London, but of the entire county as well.

Mr. Santacroce is a member of the New York Costume Cutters' Association; the Merchant Tailors' and Designers' Association; and of the New London Chamber of Commerce. He is a cordial supporter of every movement for the public welfare, and holds a medal for splendid co-operation in the building of the Connecticut State pier at New London. His personal tastes include a fondness for literature, and he is a member of St. John's Literary Association, and a finished writer on many topics.

On December 27, 1917, Mr. Santacroce married Mary Piro, who was born in Italy, and is a daughter of Anthony and Teresa Piro. Mr. and Mrs. Santacroce have one son, Frank, who was born November 8, 1918.

LEONARD FRANKLIN LOVETT—Now a farmer of the town of Preston, Connecticut, Mr. Lovett reviews a business career of great activity which began when he left the home farm in Canterbury, Windham county, Connecticut, at the age of nineteen. Twenty years have since elapsed, but they have been busy years and full of reward.

Leonard Franklin Lovett is a son of Donald Leonard Lovett, a carpenter by trade, now living on a farm in Westminster, Connecticut, and his second wife, Mary Jane (Franklin) Lovett, who was born in 1848, and died November 6, 1918; she was of the Benjamin Franklin family. By his first wife Mr. Lovett has a son, Charles Edward Lovett, of Willimantic, Connecticut. By his second marriage he has two sons: Dwight and Leonard F., and a daughter, Annie Laura, who married Judge John Read, and died in September, 1918.

Leonard Franklin Lovett was born in Canterbury, Windham county, Connecticut, April 23, 1881. He was educated at Westminster School in Miller Hill, a local school of note, from which many men later famous have been graduated. After he left school he was his father's assistant at the farm until the year 1900, when he left home and secured employment with the A. T. Gardiner Company in their sawmill. He continued in that line of work for about three years, being employed in different parts of the State in the manufacture of lumber. In 1903 he came to New London county as agent for the Adams Express Company at Groton, later becoming assistant station agent. He was for a time a traveling salesman, and during the World War period, 1917-18, he was on guard duty at the Martin & Rockwell Corporation plant. Later he came to his present farm in the town of Preston. Mr. Lovett is an Independent in politics; and is a member of the Ancient Order of United Workmen.

Mr. Lovett married Lucy Etta Yerrington, born January 12, 1892, daughter of Edwin and Alma (Slocum) Yerrington. Mr. and Mrs. Lovett are the parents of a daughter, Madelyn Lenore, born March 6, 1916. The family are members of the Baptist church.

LLOYD PENDLETON AYERS, a prominent farmer at Franklin, Connecticut, is a member of one of the oldest Colonial families in New England. John Ayers, immigrant ancestor and founder, was born in Ipswich, England, and is first on record in the American Colonies at Haverhill, Massachusetts. In 1663 he came to Franklin, where he was the first white man to settle in this region, the home which he built still being occupied by his descendants.

Edward Eugene Ayers, direct lineal descendant of John Ayers, and father of Lloyd Pendleton Ayers, was born on the old homestead at Franklin, Connecticut, November 12, 1833. He obtained a common school education, and later became a teacher, which profession he followed for many years. He married Adelaide Pendleton, a native of Norwich, Connecticut, and to them were born two children: Jennie Osgood, who married Aaron Manning; and Lloyd Pendleton, of further mention. It is interesting to note here that John Hyde Pendleton, brother of Mrs. Ayers, ran the first train over the Norwich & Worcester railroad.

Lloyd Pendleton Ayers was born December 26, 1864, at Norwich, Connecticut. At the age of two weeks he was brought by his parents to the old homestead at Franklin, Connecticut, and here he has resided continuously up to the present time. After completing his education in the public schools of Franklin and Willimantic, he became well skilled in agricultural methods generally. The farm on which he resides is naturally a fertile one, and he has continued in the cultivating and developing of it until he has brought it to its present high productive state.

Mr. Ayers takes a keen interest in the welfare of the community where he resides, and has given no litle time and energy to the conduct of public affairs. He is a Republican in politics, yet he has been nominated and elected to office three times by both parties for second selectman of the town. He has also served on the Board of Assessors.

Lloyd Pendleton Ayers was united in marriage with Alberta Vallert, daughter of James Park Vallert, of Voluntown, Connecticut. Mr. and Mrs. Ayers are the parents of one child, Joseph Eugene, born June 11, 1898.

FREDERICK FULLER MANNING, one of the prominent men of the automobile world of Norwich, Connecticut, comes of the old Manning family of Lebanon, Connecticut, and is a son of William E. Manning, of Yantic, Connecticut, postmaster and merchant in that town, a sketch of whose life appears elsewhere in this work. William E. Manning married Grace H. Fuller, of East Greenwich, Rhode Island, and they had two children, Frederick F., being their only son.

Frederick Fuller Manning was born in Bozrahville, Connecticut, on November 27, 1893. He received his early education in the public schools of Yantic, and completed his studies at the Norwich Free Academy, from which he was graduated in the class of 1912. For two years, thereafter, Mr. Manning assisted his father in his store, then later, from 1914 to 1918, acted as mail carrier on one of the rural free delivery routes centering in the Yantic Post Office.

On May 5, 1919, Mr. Manning became associated with the Jordan Garage, of Norwich, one of the most efficient service stations in the city. Mr. Manning entered this business as manager, and still continues in that capacity. He has become well known in automobile circles, and is carrying the business forward to even greater success. Outside his business Mr. Manning is interested in all civic and national progress. He is a Republican by political affiliation, but is not an office seeker. He is a member of the Yantic Fire Department, residing at No. 39 Fanning avenue, in that town.

Mr. Manning married, on September 20, 1916, Vera H. Hoxie, daughter of Edward A. and Lena M. (Peck) Hoxie, of Lebanon, Connecticut, and they have two children: Edward H., and Harold W. Mr. and Mrs. Manning are members of Grace Episcopal Church, of Yantic.

FREDERICK MATTERN—Born in Darmstadt, Germany, Daniel Mattern, father of Frederick Mattern, there became a journalist of high reputation, and a well known writer on current topics. He died in 1857, when his son Frederick was two years old. His wife, Margaret, died in Poquetanuck, New London county, Connecticut, in 1907. She left two sons: Frederick, of whom further; and Henry.

Frederick Mattern was born in Darmstadt, Germany, November 10, 1855, where he was educated and there spent the first twenty-five years of his life. He came to the United States in July, 1880, with his wife and two children, and until 1882 was employed in an upholstery establishment in New York City In that year Mr. Mattern left New York and settled on a rented farm in New London county, Connecticut, and there has since resided. He continued a tenant farmer until 1898, then bought the Holdredge farm of ninety acres on the State road in the town of Preston, and there has spent the years which have since intervened. He has made farming a profitable business, and his farm shows the hand of a careful, thrifty and progressive owner.

Mr. Mattern married, in Darmstadt, Germany, in August, 1876, Katherine Kraft, daughter of Jacob and Katherine (Spesier) Kraft. Six children have been born to Mr. and Mrs. Mattern, two in Germany, and four in the United States. 1. John, at home. 2. Freda, married Adolph Heinrich, and has five children; her son, Edward, served in the United States navy, 1917-18, during the World War. 3. James, died at the age of twenty-three. 4. Julius, residing at home. 5. August Martin, married Mabel Spooner, and they are the parents of: Florence, Harold, Olive and Kenneth Mattern. 6. Elsie, married Richard Sneider. The family are German Lutherans in religious faith.

EDWARD WRIGHT JONES—Among the men active and prominent in the affairs of Lebanon, Connecticut, is Edward Wright Jones, a native of New Haven, Connecticut, his birth having occurred there August 19, 1877.

Theodore Jones, father of Edward Wright Jones, was born in New Haven, Connecticut, and obtained his education in the local public schools. For many years previous to his death, which occurred in New Haven, he was a sea captain. He married Lillian Patterson, who was born in New Haven, and died there. Mr. and Mrs. Jones were the parents of four children: Frank, deceased; Edward Wright, of further mention; Edwin (twin of Edward W.), a resident of Buffalo, New York, married Ella Thomas, of Lebanon; Erwin M., a farmer, at Lebanon, Connecticut.

Edward Wright Jones was educated in the public schools of New Haven and Lebanon, and then went to work on the farm of James W. Thomas, whose daughter he later married. Mr. Thomas has retired from active business and now lives retired upon the farm which is conducted by Mr. Jones. This estate has been in the Thomas family for two hundred years.

Always a good citizen, entering with public-spirited interest into any cause which promises betterment of business methods and municipal government, Mr. Jones takes an active part in political affairs. In 1919 he was elected representative from the town of Lebanon. He has also served on the Humane Institution Committee, and was tax collector of the town for one year. He is a member of Lebanon Lodge, Free and Accepted Masons, and also holds membership in the Lebanon Grange, and the New London Farm Bureau. In religion he is a Congregationalist, and attends the church of that denomination at Lebanon.

Mr. Jones, married, on November 21, 1906, Eunice Thomas, daughter of James W. and Ella (Avery) Thomas, and they are the parents of three children: Bradford, Edith, and Donald. By long identification with the life of Lebanon, which has been his home for so many years, and by his fair-mindedness and goodwill as a representative citizen, Mr. Jones has won for himself a permanent place in the hearts of the people of the community.

ARTHUR HOUGH GAGER—The Gagers of New London county, trace descent from Dr. William Gager, who came to New England in 1630 with Governor Winthrop, but died the same year. He left a son John Gager, who settled in New London county, receiving a grant of two hundred acres from the town of New London, east of the river, now in the town of Ledyard. There he settled about 1650, remaining until joining in the settlement of Norwich, his home and lot there being recorded under the date of the earliest survey, November, 1659. In 1674 and 1688, he was constable of Norwich. He died extremely old, December 10, 1703.

Arthur Hough Gager, a descendant of Dr. William and John Gager, is a son of John J. and Mary (Hough) Gager. His father was born in the town of Bozrah, New London county, Connecticut, and spent his life on the homestead farm which he bought from his father. He died in December, 1911. Mary (Hough) Gager was born in Bozrah, and died there April 1, 1917. John J. and Mary (Hough) Gager were the parents of three children: Arthur Hough, of further mention; Samuel A., twin with Arthur H., died in Bozrah, in 1917; Lillie E., now residing at the home farm in Bozrah.

Arthur Hough Gager was born at the homestead, in the town of Bozrah, New London county, Connecticut, October 22, 1871, was there educated in the public schools, and until twenty years of age was his father's home assistant. In 1891 he left the farm and entered the silk mill of the Brainard, Armstrong Company, of New London, and there continued for twenty-one years. In 1912 he formed a partnership with Thomas M. Crawford, and established the Gager, Crawford Company, a corporation capitalized at $20,000, of which Mr. Gager is president. The company operates a fine modern market at the corner of State and Main streets, New London, and has met with most gratifying success from the public. He is a member of the New London Chamber of Commerce, Namaug Boat Club, and of the First Congregational Church of New London. In politics he is a Republican.

Mr. Gager married, in 1915, Ruth Glassburner, of Waterford, Connecticut, daughter of John and Mary Glassburner. Mr. and Mrs. Gager are the parents of three children, all born in the town of Waterford, the family home: John J., Mary Hough and Francis Fox.

EDGAR JOHNSON TUCKER was born in Lebanon, Connecticut, in September, 1859, the son of Ezekiel Johnson and Mary (Brown) Tucker, of Middletown. Ezekiel J. Tucker was a native of Kingston, Rhode Island, and when a young man came to Lebanon, where he engaged in farming, following this vocation throughout his entire lifetime.

The education of Edgar Johnson Tucker was obtained in the schools of his native place which he attended until he was seventeen years of age. He then chose to devote himself to agricultural pursuits, and with this end in view followed in the footsteps of his father, now taking his place among the leading farmers of the county.

Mr. Tucker has ever manifested that lively interest in everything pertaining to the public welfare, which has always been a characteristic of his family. In politics, he is an Independent, not having identified himself with any political party, preferring to remain free from all partisan influences in the exercise of his own judgment on public issues.

Mr. Tucker married (first) Louise Manning, a native of Lebanon. She died on the home farm at the age of fifty years. Two children were born of this union: Leroy, a resident of Bridgeport; and Edith, wife of Frank Burroughs, a plumber of New London, Connecticut. Mr. Tucker married (second) in December, 1915, Laura V. White, a native of Hartford, Connecticut. They have no children.

HERBERT ROWLAND GARDNER—One of the most progressive citizens in Norwich township, a section of Norwich, Connecticut, is Herbert Rowland Gardner, who has been instrumental in improving many otherwise neglected portions of the township. His hobby has been to buy up unproductive farms and, developing them into prosperous, paying properties, has made the land yield him a good return in addition to making it a credit to the section in which he is located. The farm upon which Mr. Gardner makes his home has been in his possession for many years, and he also maintains and manages another one on the Canterbury road.

Herbert Rowland Gardner was born April 22, 1877, in Hampton, Connecticut, where his parents resided at that time. While still in his infancy they moved to Norwich township and he has lived here ever since. His father was Edward Lawton Gardner, a farmer, who died in Norwichtown, about 1890, at the age of eighty-six years. The mother of Herbert Rowland Gardner was before her marriage Mary Davis, of Norwich township, where she was born in 1857. She was the mother of five children, of whom Herbert Rowland Gardner is the eldest. She resides with him and looks after his home, as he has never married. Though interested in the welfare of his township and in the politics of the country-at-large, Mr. Gardner is not connected with any political party, preferring to vote as his conscience dictates.

ADELARD MORIN—One of the most important executive positions in Norwich, Connecticut, is ably filled by Adelard Morin, vice-president and general manager of the Plaut-Cadden Company. This house is probably the largest distributor of furniture and musical instruments in Eastern Connecticut.

Pierre Morin, Mr. Morin's father, was born in St. Jude, Province of Quebec, Canada. He was educated at the parochial school in that town, and later conducted a farm, following general farming until he came to the United States in 1883. He located in Woonsocket, Rhode Island, where he worked as a carpenter. He became an expert in this line of work, and after a time handled general contracting. He died in 1900. Mr. Morin married Mary La Frenaye, who was born in Lyons, France, and died in Norwich, Connecticut, in 1917. They were the parents of ten children, of whom four are living: Henry, married Mira Michon, and is now a baker in Woonsocket; Adelard, of whom further; Olivine, who married William Lambert, now deceased, and since his death resides in Taftville, Connecticut; and Anna, also a resident of Taftville.

Adelard Morin was born in St. Jude, Province of Quebec, on February 24, 1880. He received his education in the parochial school of Taftville, then, upon leaving school, worked for Hirch & Company, as clerk in their clothing store, remaining for ten years in their employ. He then became associated with the Plaut-Cadden Company, as piano salesman. This was in 1905, and Mr. Morin continued with this company, rising step by step, until now he is general manager of the business and vice-president of the company. This is the largest mercantile concern in the city of Norwich handling immense stocks of furniture, pianos, mechanical music and jewelry, and draws trade from the entire western part of the State, and from large districts in Rhode Island and Massachusetts. Mr. Morin is a member of the Chamber of Commerce; is a staunch supporter of the principles of the Republican party, and is a member of the Rotary Club, of Norwich.

Mr. Morin married, on November 22, 1910, Alma Bousquet, of Norwich, daughter of Victor and Melvina (Messier) Bousquet. Mr. and Mrs. Morin have three children: Aline, Alma and Rutherford. The family are devout members of the Roman Catholic church.

JOSEPH ALFRED CLARK—Alfred Clark, born in Norwich, New London county, Connecticut, spent most of his life as a farmer of Ledyard, where he died in March, 1916. He was selectman of the town and always took an active interest in town affairs. He married Mary Cooley, born in Groton, Connecticut, and they are the parents of three children: Joseph Alfred, Fred, and Albert.

Joseph Alfred Clark was born at the home farm in the town of Ledyard in 1883. He attended the public schools of the district and has from youth been engaged in farming. Upon the death of his father in 1916, he assumed the management of the home farm of one hundred and sixty acres, and conducts general farming operations. He is a charter member of Ledyard Grange, Patrons of Husbandry, Pomona Grange of New London county, and of the State and National granges. He has served his local grange as master in 1920-21, and has always been deeply interested in its growth and prosperity. He is also a member of Uncas Lodge, Independent Order of Odd Fellows, of Norwich. He is a Democrat in politics, and served his town as collector of taxes.

Mr. Clark married in Ledyard, August 15, 1909, Fannie Laub, daughter of Daniel and Fanny (Chapman) Laub. Mr. and Mrs. Clark are the parents of three children: Louise, Joseph Alfred, Jr., and George Pendleton.

ELMER WATSON RUSSELL—In the village of Somers, Tolland county, Connecticut, Lester Watson and Salome (Pease) Russell were living at the time of the birth of their son, Elmer Watson Russell, in 1874. Lester W. Russell was born in the same village as his son, March 10, 1842, and spent his adult life a farmer. He died in Somers, November 25, 1918, and is buried there. Salome (Pease) Russell was born in Somers, May 24, 1843, died in her native town, March 23, 1919, and is buried beside her husband. They were the parents of seven children, all born in Somers: Albert Everett, married Clara Hulburt, of Somers, and has two children: Harris and Edith; Clara Pease; Elmer Watson, of further mention; Mahlon Lester; Elsie May; Lena Jane; and Alice Amanda.

Elmer Watson Russell was born February 27, 1874, and attended Somers public schools, supplementing the instruction there licensed by a full course in the Springfield Business College. After graduation from business college, he was for a half year employed in a furniture store in Springfield, Massachusetts. Then his early training averted itself and he returned to the business he had been taught by his father—agriculture. In 1902 he located on his present farm at Crescent Beach, in the town of East Lyme, New London county, Connecticut, and there he very successfully engaged in that highly profitable form of agricultural truck-growing. He is a member of Bay View Lodge, No. 120, Free and Accepted Masons, and politically an Independent Republican.

Mr. Russell married, November 26, 1916, Mattie Buddington, born in Ashaway, Rhode Island, July 21, 1875, only child of Oliver Russell and Laura (Chapman) Buddington. By a former marriage Mrs. Russell has two daughters: Sarah Louise and Ruth Mabel. Mr. and Mrs. Elmer W. Russell are the parents of a daughter, Phyllis, born October 16,

1917, and two sons: Philip Buddington, born February 24, 1919, and Elmer Watson, Jr., born October 14, 1922. Mr. Russell is a man of industry and energy, devoted to his home and family, and highly esteemed in his community as a man of upright, honorable life.

THOMAS NEWMAN—The forebears of Thomas Newman were farmer folk in Ireland for many generations, the first of this branch of the family to be known in this country being John Newman, born in County Meade, Ireland, in 1831. Emigrating to America when a very young man, he located in Franklin, Connecticut, and took up farming as a means of livelihood, later buying the property on which stands the family homestead. His wife was Margaret Thornton who came from the same part of Ireland as her husband, County Meade, where she was born in 1848. Their son, Thomas, was born in Irvington, New York, and when the child was three years old the family moved to Franklin.

The education of Thomas Newman was acquired at the local school which he attended during the sessions, working on his father's farm as his schooling would permit. When he attained early youth his school days were brought to a close, and he devoted himself to farming on the homestead which he inherited at his father's death, which occurred twenty-nine years ago.

Thomas Newman married Leona Genard, at Woonsocket, Rhode Island. Of this union two children were born: Doris Irene, born August 4, 1916; and Margaret, born in January, 1918. The public affairs of Franklin township, form another interest in Mr. Newman's life, occupying much of his time when not engaged with farming. He holds the office of justice of the peace at the present time, and has served on the local school board for the past ten years; the farm bureau, of which he is a member, is also one of the village matters in which he is greatly interested. Mr. Newman is regarded by his fellow-citizens as a popular man in that section, well thought of and respected.

JOHN DREW (2) NOYES—The Noyes family of New London county, Connecticut, spring from Rev. Moses Noyes, the first pastor of the Congregational church at Lyme, where he preached in a rude log cabin. John Drew (1) Noyes, of Uncasville, is a son of John Drew (1) Noyes, born at the old homestead at Noyes Beach, son of William Noyes. John Drew (1) Noyes was a landowner and a man of good standing in his community. He married Jane Houston McNaught, born in Scotland. They were the parents of four sons: John Drew (2) of further mention: William Parker, George, and Byron.

John Drew (2) Noyes was born in Greenville, Connecticut, October 16, 1859, and until nine years of age attended the public school at Blissville, Connecticut. At the age of nine he began working in the mills at Taftville, Connecticut. continuing one year, when he was taken to Clark's Falls, Rhode Island, where for the next three years he attended school. He was then employed in various mills until 1916 when he came to the Uncasville Manufacturing Company at Uncasville, and is now engineer in charge of the stationary engines used at the plant.

Mr. Noyes married Elsie Bayel, born in North Adams, Massachusetts, and they are the parents of seven children: Harold, who died in infancy; Bessie Jane, John Drew (3), Byron Harriman, Frank, Morton, and Elsie. Mr. Noyes has a sister, Jeannette, wife of Frank Mitchell, of Mystic, Connecticut, and another, Elizabeth, who died in youthful womanhood.

BENJAMIN PALMER DAVIS—Among the younger generation of farmers in this vicinity is Benjamin Palmer Davis. His interest in all that concerns the town's welfare is deep and sincere, being ever a zealous advocate and supporter of her most vital interests.

Benjamin Palmer Davis was born in Preston, Connecticut, November 14, 1888, the son of Charles B. and Emma (Palmer) Davis. Charles B. Davis was born in North Stonington, Connecticut, December 20, 1853. He is now engaged in farming in Franklin. The boy received his preliminary education in the local public schools after which, having decided upon an agricultural career, he matriculated at Connecticut Agricultural College from which he was graduated in 1913. He then came immediately to Franklin, and in 1919 bought his present farm which he has proceeded to develop with remarkable success. Having been endowed with much natural ability, and with a training fitting him with the most modern methods for pursuing his work, his progress has already been marked by the acquisition of large material gains. Foresight is one of Mr. Davis' dominant characteristics. Quick to think, he is quick to act, and is in the habit of accomplishing whatever he undertakes. As a rule, however, he brings it about without antagonizing his opponents. In politics he is a staunch supporter of the Democratic party. He is now, 1920, serving the town as clerk and treasurer. Mr. Davis is affiliated with the Free and Accepted Masons, and with the Ancient Arabic Order Nobles of the Mystic Shrine.

Benjamin Palmer Davis was united in marriage with Charlotte E. Franklin, daughter of Charles E. and Etta (Chappell) Franklin. Mr. and Mrs. Davis are the parents of one child, born October 14, 1917. The business transactions of Mr. Davis are conducted in accordance with the highest principles, and in his official capacities he fulfills to the letter, every trust committed to him, being generous in his feelings and conduct toward all. We have not said that he is a good citizen for that fact is self-evident, and his record is worthy of emulation.

HERMAN AROD GAGER was born October 16, 1859, at Franklin, Connecticut, the son of Samuel Hawkins and Miranda (Robinson) Gager. Samuel

Hawkins Gager was born in Franklin in 1819, and died there in 1871, having been engaged in farming throughout his entire lifetime. Mrs. Gager was born in Franklin, December 16, 1823, daughter of Arod Robinson, who was a direct descendant of Rev. John Robinson who came over on the "Mayflower."

The boy Herman A. attended the schools of his native place until he was eighteen years of age, when the business of life began for him. His first employment was with the Emerson Hydraulic Corporation of Boston, for which concern he traveled through thirty-six states. In 1910 he returned to the old homestead at Franklin, but a little later left to accept a position with the Shore Line Trolley Company, with whom he remained for six years, subsequently returning again to Franklin, where he has since been engaged in farming. He has always taken a keen interest in civic affairs, serving his town as second selectman in 1894, and now, 1920, is representative from this district. For many years Mr. Gager was constable.

Mr. Gager was united in marriage with Ella Esther Parker, a native of Franklin, born April 1, 1861. Mr. and Mrs. Gager are the parents of two children: Harry Dwight, and Faith Natalie. The duties of Herman Arod Gager have always been weighed by the consideration for all whom he serves, and commands the highest respect of all classes of people in his community, being recognized as one of her representative citizens for betterment of living conditions.

GEORGE HENRY HOXIE was born at Lebanon, December 31, 1859, and obtained his education in the schools of his native place, the schools of Norwich, Connecticut, and also at Wilburham Academy, Massachusetts. After finishing his studies he worked in a market at Lebanon for a short time, and then followed his vocation as a farmer on his father's farm, at the latter's death. Mr. Hoxie has the most modern equipped farm in the township, is enterprising, progressive and broadminded, and in his careful, capable management, unfaltering enterprise, and a spirit of justice, are all well balanced factors.

Seldom is it that a man actively successful in business as Mr. Hoxie, takes the keen and helpful interest in civic affairs which he ever manifests, his name being associated with various projects of the utmost municipal concern. In politics he affiliates with the Republican party; was a representative from this district in 1911, and is now a member of the local school board.

On November 20, 1884, Mr. Hoxie was united in marriage with Lucie Allan Williams, a daughter of William Allan and Jane (Stoddard) Williams. Mr. and Mrs. Hoxie are the parents of three children: George Hammond, born February 22, 1892, is now a justice of the peace at Lebanon; Allan Williams, born April 3, 1893, is now with the United States navy in Alaska; Wilton Henry, born February 16, 1897.

AMOS JELSON LILLIE—In 1910 Amos J. Lillie bought the farm upon which he now resides, in New London county, Connecticut, causing his acres to return him fair recompense for his labor. He is a son of William Perry Lillie, born in the town of Lebanon, Connecticut, in 1853, who married Mary Briggs, born in the same town in 1856, of one of the pioneer families of Lebanon. William P. and Mary (Briggs) Lillie were the parents of eight children: Amos Jelson, of further mention; W. LeRoy, Charles Phelps, Walter Perry, Robert, Fred Briggs, Amy Adelaide, and Alice Elizabeth.

Amos J. Lillie was born February 11, 1887, and until fifteen years of age attended the district school. He then began working for the farmers of the neighborhood, and other parts of New London county. He carefully conserved his earnings and at the age of twenty-three was able to purchase the farm upon which he now resides. He is a member of Patrons of Husbandry, and Knights of Pythias. In politics he is a Republican.

Mr. Lillie married Mary Adler Pultz, born in New York State, June 29, 1892, daughter of Elmer and Florence Pultz.

EDWARD NELSON O'BRIEN, who was born in New York, December 19, 1879, came at the age of three years to Montville, to reside with his adopted parents, John Turner and Mary Julia (Smith) O'Brien. John Turner O'Brien was born at Preston, Connecticut, May 30, 1828, and died at Montville, July 4, 1919. At the age of seventeen he went to Ledyard, where he engaged in farming for a year, going subsequently, to California. Later, he returned only to go again to California, where he remained for seven years, and while there was interested in mining and ranching. Upon his return East he purchased a farm at Montville, and married Julia Smith, who was the daughter of Lyman and Emmeline (Fanning) Smith. She died September 7, 1920.

Edward Nelson O'Brien attended school at Montville, after which he returned to the farm and has since devoted himself entirely to agricultural pursuits. Since the death of Mr. O'Brien, Sr., he has taken complete charge of the management of the property upon which he continues to reside. In politics Edward N. O'Brien is an independent, and has not identified himself with any political party, preferring to remain free from all partisan influences in the exercise of his own judgment on public issues. He has always maintained through life the reputation of an energetic business man, and in his social relations is benevolent and kind.

JOSEPH THOMAS CHURCH has been a resident of Connecticut all his life, as his father and grandfather were, his ancestors, both on the paternal and maternal sides of his family, claiming Connecticut as their native State. For several generations back they have all been farmers in New London county.

The father of Joseph Thomas is Thomas Church,

born in Poquonock, May 19, 1853, but since 1882 a resident of Montville, where he now resides, engaged in farming and other occupations, taking an active part in the affairs of the locality, being regarded as one of the foremost citizens of his time. The mother of Joseph Thomas Church was Henrietta Coswell, daughter of Warren Coswell, of Ledyard. She died in 1903 at the age of thirty-one years, and is buried in Montville. She and her husband had six children: 1. Joseph Thomas. 2. Harold, aged twenty-four. 3. Earl, who died in infancy. 4. Leroy, also died in infancy. 5. Ethel, now the wife of Henry Chapman, of Montville. 6. Grace, who married Charles Chapman, of Norwich, Connecticut, has two children.

Born in Ledyard, Connecticut, February 2, 1878, Joseph Thomas Church went with his parents to Montville when four years old, where he attended the local school and learned to be a farmer. Later, joining with Richard Davis, of Montville, they took a farm to work, but after a time Mr. Church went to Preston, and was employed in the Shoals farm. Buying a farm in Montville, he conducted it for fourteen years, then, selling it to Jonathan Hill, Mr. Church remained as manager of it, and is so engaged at the present time (1921), having lived on the same place for twenty years. A member of the Republican party, Mr. Church has been quite prominent in political affairs in Montville, and though on the opposite side was elected by the Democrats to the office of constable. He has been assessor for the town since 1916, still retaining the office. Active in lodge work, Mr. Church is a member of the local lodge of Free and Accepted Masons, and of the Independent Order of Odd Fellows of Montville.

Joseph Thomas Church married, in Montville, Grace Beaulack, born in North Adams, Massachusetts, March 27, 1873. She is the daughter of Joseph Beaulack, of Howell Point. Mr. and Mrs. Church had four children, all of them now deceased. They were: Lawrence Joseph and Gertrude Nellie, twins, who died at the age of seven years; Elsie Elizabeth, who died when sixteen years of age; Marian Eleanor, died at the age of seventeen years.

FREDERICK HENRY RACE was born in Farmington, Connecticut, August 8, 1860, the son of Henry A. and Hadassah (Rockwell) Race. Henry A. Race was born and died in Franklin. To Mr. and Mrs. Race were born two children: Frederick Henry, of further mention; and A. Rockwell Race, a merchant at Lebanon.

Frederick Henry Race attended the district school at Lebanon until he was fourteen years of age, when the business of life began for the boy, and he went to work for the Lebanon Creamery, which was run at that time by O. W. Stark. After five years he went to Westfield, Massachusetts, and worked there as a carpenter, subsequently going to Lebanon where he became interested in agriculture, later removing to Franklin where he bought the old Robinson farm. The Robinson house was the first house built in Westfarm, which was the original name of Norwich, and was built in 1685 by one Robinson, whose wife was an Indian squaw. Frederick Henry Race and his family still reside in the original house. Mr. Race is a Republican in politics and since taking up his residence in Franklin, nearly forty years ago, he has always taken a keen and active interest in civic affairs, and in every movement which has for its object the betterment of social conditions.

On June 26, 1890, Mr. Race was united in marriage with Jeannette T. Hoffman, a native of Bloomfield, New Jersey, her birth having occurred there, August 16, 1857. Mr. and Mrs. Race are the parents of one child, Frederick H., born August 26, 1894, and now with the Travellers Insurance company of Pittsfield, Massachusetts.

GEORGE ALFRED ASHBEY—As cashier and office manager of the J. B. Martin Company, George Alfred Ashbey holds a recognized place in the industrial life of New London county, Connecticut, and as such his record is worthy of mention in a work of this sort.

George Alfred Ashbey was born in Mystic, Connecticut, June 1, 1869, the son of Captain George B. and Catherine B. (Holdredge) Ashbey. George B. Ashbey was also born in Mystic where he attended the public schools. He was a sea captain for many years, retiring just previous to his death, which occurred in 1883. Mrs. Ashbey survived her husband for a number of years, passing away in Norwich in 1910. To Mr. and Mrs. Ashbey was born but one child, George Alfred, of further mention.

After receiving his education in the public schools of his native place, George Alfred Ashbey entered into business life at the age of seventeen as clerk in the office of the Norwich & New York Transportation Company, at Norwich, Connecticut, and was thus employed until 1900, when he resigned to become clerk for the J. B. Martin Company, at Taftville, subsequently advancing to the position of cashier and office manager, which position he still holds. The flourishing condition of this branch of the organization testifies to the sound judgment and untiring energy which he has brought to the discharge of the duties of his responsible office.

In politics, Mr. Ashbey is a Republican, but the influence which he exerts as a citizen is of the quietest and most unobtrusive description. He is a Baptist in his religious views and attends the Central Church of that denomination. In the charitable and benevolent institutions of his community, he takes an active interest, assisting to the extent of his ability any cause which commends itself to his standards of justice and philanthropy. Mr. Ashbey also holds membership in the Arcanum Club of Norwich.

George Alfred Ashbey married, on October 23, 1895, Marion Cowen Otis, daughter of Amos T. and Mary G. (Cowen) Otis, of Norwich. Mr. and Mrs.

Ashbey are the parents of one child, George R., a student at Brown University, Providence, Rhode Island.

FRANK BENAJAH TERRY—One of the well known names in the town of Griswold, Connecticut, is Terry, and Frank Benajah Terry is prominent in the various activities of the town. David Terry, Mr. Terry's grandfather, was born in Exeter, Rhode Island, and was the first of this family to come to Griswold. He acquired a large amount of farm property in the southern end of the town, comprising several different farms, and followed agricultural pursuits all his life. His wife's family name was Kenyon.

David Kenyon Terry, their son, was born in Exeter, Rhode Island, and came to New London county with his parents while quite a child. His school attendance was at Voluntown, and later at Jewett City, then as a young man he assisted his father in his extensive farming operations, continuing thus until he married. He then bought a farm from his father, this was one of the old Lester farms, and he conducted it for three years, thereafter, trading it for the old Lester homestead, in Griswold. He conducted this farm until his death, in December, 1875. After the father's death five sons conducted the place for their mother, and for the estate. David Kenyon Terry married Susan Amelia Thompson, who was born in Voluntown, Connecticut, and died at the Terry farm home in 1910. They had a large family, six sons and five daughters, of whom six are still living, three sons and three daughters.

Frank Benajah Terry, fourth child of David Kenyon and Susan Amelia (Thompson) Terry, was born in the Terry homestead, in the southern part of the town of Griswold, on September 29, 1854, and has always lived within half a mile of the present home farm. He received a practical education in the district schools of the neighborhood, then helped his father on the farm, later working out among the neighboring farms. After the death of his father, he was one of the boys who carried on the home farm. In 1905 he and his brother, Willis C. Terry, bought out the various heirs interested in the property, and they conducted the home farm together until 1910. At that time Mr. Terry sold his interest in the old place to his brother Willis, and a year later bought his present home, a farm of one hundred and five acres. He carries on diversified farming and stock raising, and is one of the successful men of the town. Mr. Terry is a prominent member of the Griswold Grange, and takes an active part in the work of that organization. He is interested in every phase of public progress, and politically affiliates with the Democratic party. He has never married.

FRED BRIGGS LILLIE—Among the younger generation of successful farmers of this community is Fred Briggs Lillie. He was born at Lebanon, September 1, 1884, the son of William Perry and Mary (Briggs) Lillie. William Perry Lillie was born on the old homestead at Lebanon, which had been purchased by his father. To Mr. and Mrs. Lillie were born eight children: Amos J., W. Leroy, Charles Phelps, Walter Perry, Robert, Fred Briggs, of further mention; Amy Adelaide and Alice Elizabeth.

The education of Fred Briggs Lillie was obtained in the district school of his native place, where he continued until he was fourteen years of age, during which time he helped his father on the latter's farm. Here he became thoroughly acquainted with the subject, and in a short time had gained a thorough knowledge of farming. In 1905 he purchased his present farm where he has resided continuously up to the present time, and has met with great success in his farming operations. Mr. Lillie has never held public office, but has always taken an active interest in the affairs of the town, and no good work done in the name of civic welfare but finds him eager to do his part toward the furtherance of the cause. Mr. Lillie is unmarried.

JAMES LEIL WADE—Having been engaged in farming for many years upon land belonging to others, James Leil Wade bought a farm for himself in 1909, and since that time, he and his family have lived upon it. It is located in Baltic, Sprague township, Connecticut.

A native of Montville, Connecticut, James Leil Wade, was born September 12, 1871. He was the son of Jared Wade, born in 1843, also in Montville, and Mary (Perkins) Wade, born in Lyme, Connecticut. Mr. and Mrs. Jared Wade had, in addition to their son James Leil, two other children: a daughter, Jeannette, and a son, Willis Wade. James Leil Wade acquired his education in the public school of Montville, and after his boyhood days were over, he became engaged in farming, though he did not buy his own farm for some years afterward. Mr. Wade has proved to be a very successful farmer and has greatly improved the property since purchasing it.

James Leil Wade married Abby Baker, a resident of Eastford, Connecticut, the daughter of Henry and Ellen (Snow) Baker. To this marriage seven children have been born: Viola, Leon, Earl, Everett, Sylvester, Russell, and Charles.

RENIE (2) GAUVIN—In the year 1900 Renie (2) Gauvin, a young Canadian farmer, came to New London county, Connecticut, and for three years worked in and around the village of Baltic. He then bought his preesnt farm in the town of Sprague, and since 1903 has cultivated its acres. He is a son of Renie (1) and Sophia (Broden) Gauvin, both born in Canada, the father, born in the Province of Quebec, Canada, in 1826, died there in 1865. They were the parents of thirteen children, Renie (2) the third son.

Renie (2) Gauvin was born in the province of Quebec, Canada, April 15, 1854. He there obtained his education. He worked in Canadian mills and on Canadian farms until his coming to the United

States, and in the year 1900 his life in New London county began. His farm, bought in 1903, is situated in the town of Sprague in the extreme northern part of New London county, and there he leads a contented, prosperous life.

Mr. Gauvin married Heleda Rox, born in Canada, daughter of William Rox. They are the parents of six children: Melvina, Frank, Emma, Ernest, Mary Jane and Albert.

EVERETT C. THOMPSON was born in Ledyard, New London county, Connecticut, in 1895, son of Charles Avery and Eveline (Chapman) Thompson. Charles A. Thompson was born in Ledyard, Connecticut, in 1859, and is yet an active farmer of the town in which his life has been spent. He married Eveline Chapman, born in Groton, Connecticut, and they are the parents of six children, five of whom are living: Jeannette, Lawrence, Everett C., Carl and Helen.

Everett C. Thompson has spent his life as a farmer in Ledyard, where he continues. He is a member of the Patrons of Husbandry and of other town organizations.

He married, in 1915, in Ledyard, Laura A. Clark, daughter of Alfred and Mary (Cooley) Clark. Mr. and Mrs. Thompson are the parents of a daughter, Elaine Frances.

CHRISTOPHER GREENE NEWBURY, who is one of the leading dairy farmers of the town of Waterford, in this county, is a son of Horace Manchester Newbury, an old sea-captain who sailed from New London with whaling fleets in the old days, then later in life bought a large farm in the Gilead section of Waterford, which he conducted for a number of years, finally retiring from all active work and residing in Groton. He died in Groton in 1906, at the age of sixty-five years. He married Mary Elizabeth (Newbury) Gard, who is still living, and is over eighty years old. They had two sons: Daniel, who was born in Groton, and Christopher Greene.

Christopher G. Newbury was born in Groton, and received his education in the schools of his native town. The family removing to Gilead when he was fourteen years of age, he took up the work of the farm with his father, and until the retirement of the latter worked side by side with him, eventually taking over the farm. Later he removed to the Town Hill section of Waterford, after selling the homestead, and there has since carried on a very extensive dairy business, becoming one of the most successful men of the town. In the public activities of the community Mr. Newbury is prominent, and by political conviction is an independent Democrat.

Mr. Newbury married (first) Adelaide I. Rogers, of Waterford, January 15, 1873, daughter of Christopher Rogers. Mrs. Newbury was one of the very prominent women of the town, especially as a church worker, having been a member of the Baptist church and serving as superintendent of the Sunday school for a period of five years. She was killed on March 4, 1912, by an automobile striking the carriage in which she was driving to prayer meeting, and is now buried in Joran Cemetery, in Waterford. She was a woman of broad sympathies and beautiful Christian character, and is mourned by a large circle of friends. She left no children. It was shortly after this accident that Mr. Newbury sold the old homestead and removed to Town Hill. Mr. Newbury married (second) Edwina D. Morgan, who was born in New York City, and is a daughter of Edwin D. Morgan. They have three children: Morgan Christopher, born in August, 1915; Mary Elizabeth, born in February, 1917; and Henry Alexander, born in July, 1919.

HYMAN RUBIN—In the farming districts of New London county, Connecticut, there is no more delightful section than the town of Preston, and in the town of Preston there is no more up-to-date and progressive farmer and poultryman than Hyman Rubin, who came to America from the Old World a dozen years ago.

Mr. Rubin is a son of Esaak and Rishe (Ledvitch) Rubin, of Bobruisk, Minsk, Russia. Esaak Rubin was born there, and during his lifetime was engaged as a city official, having charge of the city lighting, and also being sealer of weights and measures. He died in Russia, in 1919. His wife was also born in Bobruisk, and died there in the same year. They were the parents of four children, all born in Bobruisk: 1. Rose, who married Borris O. Jafe, of the same city, and had five children; Borris O. Jafe and his wife both died in Russia, and their five children still live in their native city, Bobruisk, Russia. 2. Annie, wife of Esaak Marron, of Bobruisk, since 1901 residents of New York City, the parents of six children, three born in Russia and three in New York City: Rose H., William, Ida, Mary, Sarah, and George. 3. Rebecca, wife of Harry Ledwitz, residents of Brooklyn, New York, and the parents of two children: Lillian and Samuel. 4. Hyman, of whom further.

Hyman Rubin was born in Bobruisk, Minsk, Russia, May 16, 1888. He received his education in the city of his birth, attending school up to the age of fourteen years. When thirteen years of age he began learning the trade of lithographer, and as soon as he completed his studies at school went to Odessa, Russia, where he worked at this trade for two years. At the end of that time he went to Nicholaef, Russia, and there remained for one year, then went to Eckaterinoslov, Russia, where he still worked at his trade. Stories of success in America reached the young man as he worked in his native land, and he decided to come here to build his own success. Returning to his native city for final farewells, he left from there and sailed for the United States via Hamburg, Germany, reaching New York City, June 7, 1907. In a very short time he found employment in designing ladies' waists and dresses, and followed along this line in New York until 1918. At that time he decided to go on the farm. Coming to Preston, Connecticut, he purchased the Woodmansee farm, near Preston City, a fine place of ninety-three acres, taking possession in February, 1918. He took up general farming, but is specializing in poultry. He grows Rhode Island Reds and White Leghorns, and particularly in this specialty is doing a very large and successful business. He is making an all round success on his place here, and is commanding the respect and admiration of the people of this vicinity. In becoming a citizen of this country he has become thoroughly American. Mr. Rubin takes a deep interest in all the public affairs of the time, State and National as well as local, and in political matters holds an independent position, and throws his influence on the side which he believes stands for the best interests of the people.

On December 20, 1909, in New York City, Mr. Rubin married Esther Cohen, who was born in Bobruisk, Russia, and was betrothed to him there, coming to America to marry him. She is a daughter of Mitchel and Hodee (Rubinchick) Cohen, also natives of Bobruisk. Mr. and Mrs. Rubin have two children: Hilda, born in New York City, October 18, 1911; and Ruth, also born in New York City, November 16, 1913.

EDWARD CAROLINE—On a farm near the town of Slonim, in far-away Russia, the parents of Edward Caroline—Isaac and Rita (Brodo) Caroline—were living at the time their son was born. The parents were both born in the same neighborhood, the father a farmer, his mother an able assistant. When Edward was six years old, in 1893, the father came to the United States, and for seventeen years New York City was the family home, the father a shirt manufacturer. He was alone in New York City four years, then in 1897 was able to send for his family. Three children came before the mother, she following with four children. In 1919 Isaac Caroline moved to Montville, Connecticut, with his wife, where he joined his son, Edward, and this town is still the home of father and son, the capable mother having gone to her rest in 1917.

Edward Caroline was born in Russia, June 20, 1887, and at the home farm near Slonim spent the first ten years of his life. He attended school there for a time, but in 1897 was brought to New York by his mother, there joining his father, who had come over in 1893. The lad completed public school courses in New York City, finishing in De Witt Clinton High School. For a few years he was engaged in office work in New York, moving in 1908 to the town of Montville, New London county, Connecticut, where he bought a farm of one hundred and fifty acres, and began farming, although he knew very little about agriculture as a business. He was joined by his father and mother, who were experienced, and the farm has been made a profitable enterprise. While general farming is carried on, dairying is the specialty, a route in Norwich being supplied with milk and other products from the Caroline farm. He is one of the leading Jewish farmers of Montville, and is highly regarded by his townsmen. A success in his own business, he is interested in the success of others and keeps in touch with all local affairs. He holds to the highest principles of sanitation in the care of his cattle, his herd being graded stock, and he fully realizes the importance of keeping the milk supply pure as a measure of public health.

Mr. Caroline married, in Montville, Connecticut, May 28, 1911, Celia Tepper, born in New York City, daughter of Jacob and Sarah (Nemirof) Tepper, her parents both born in Russia. Mr. and Mrs. Caroline are the parents of three children: Milton, born May 13, 1912; Ephraim Gilbert, born April 9, 1915; Solomon William, born June 24, 1919.

ABRAHAM MILLER was born in Krovo, Russia, December 16, 1873, son of Israel Miller. His parents both died in Russia, his father in 1906. The lad, Abraham, obtained his education in Russian schools and became a butcher by trade. He remained in Russia until 1904, then came to the United States, locating in New York City during the first two years of his American residence. In 1906 he located in the town of Montville, New London county, Connecticut, where he has since been engaged in business as a cattle dealer and butcher. He is a man of an industrious, quiet life, and a successful business man.

Mr. Miller married, May 1, 1897, Rose Robinson, born in Krovo, Russia, and there their first seven years of married life were spent prior to their coming to the United States. They are the parents of seven children: Bessie, Rebecca, Jennie, Fannie, Sylvia, Lillian and Irving. The family are members of St. Joseph's Synagogue, of Chesterfield. Mr. Miller is a Republican in politics.

JOHN DE PINTO, an Italian by birth, is one of those men who started at the bottom of the ladder, and by means of his own effort has worked his way up to his present successful position in the community which has been his home since 1915. Mr. De Pinto was born in Italy, September 13, 1887, the son of Joseph and Annette De Pinto. Joseph De Pinto still resides in Italy, where he is a successful farmer. Mrs. De Pinto died in 1907, at the age of thirty-five years.

John De Pinto early gained a knowledge of farming by aiding his father at home, and at the age of twenty-three years, with an extensive knowledge of this subject, he came to this country, locating in Norwich, Connecticut, where he remained until 1915, when he purchased his present farm, which is considered one of the best conducted properties in Messapeak, and is undoubtedly one of the most picturesquely located. Mr. De Pinto has erected many buildings and has a large and commodious dwelling. Ever ready to do his bit for the community which he has chosen for his home, he is instinctively interested in whatever pertains to the welfare of the place, and is ever willing to give substantial aid to the furtherance of a worthwhile project.

On January 10, 1916, John De Pinto married Mary Pagona, who came to this country in 1910. She is a daughter of Felix and Isabella Pagona. Mr. and Mrs. De Pinto are the parents of two children: Joseph, born March 25, 1917; Annette, born March 10, 1920. Quick to grasp the necessity of choosing the things of value, Mr. De Pinto has already realized the necessity of education and in this is most anxious for his children to make use of the many opportunities which are offered to the growing child. Progression is the chief characteristic of Mr. De Pinto, and today he stands by means of his own untiring efforts as one of the successful and respected citizens of this community.

JOHN ROBERT KAPLAN—In far away Russia, that land of mystery, John Robert Kaplan was born in 1865. He there grew to manhood, and married, his wife Sarah coming with him to the United States not long after their marriage. They settled in Chesterfield, Connecticut, after a short sojourn in New York City, and there Mr. Kaplan is a prosperous general merchant and owner of a fine farm. Mr. and Mrs. Kaplan are the parents of seven children: 1. Rose, who married Louis Saul, of New York City, and they have three children: Violet, Arthur, and Bernard Saul. 2. Ida, who married Maurice Solomon, of Norwich, and has three children: Mildred, Elizabeth, and Ruth Lea. 3. Molly, married George Meisner, of New York City, and has a son, Alfred Meisner. 4. Goldie, who married Fred Herman, of Norwich. 5. Benjamin, now on a ranch in Oklahoma. 6. Helen, the store manager, representing her father. 7. Jacob, aged twenty-three, who assists his sister Helen and his father. Mr. Kaplan is a member of the Order B'rith Sholon.

MARTIN ROZYCKI—Martin Rozycki, a wholesale grocer of Norwich, Connecticut, was born in Russian Poland, on October 30, 1877. His father, Joseph Rozycki, was also a native of Russian Poland, and still lives in that country. He was educated there, and learned the baker's trade, which he has always followed, and now owns a bakery. He married Anna Sidwinski, and they have had eight children, of whom seven are living, Martin being the eldest child of the family.

Martin Rozycki received his education in the public and high schools of his native town; then, at the age of seventeen years, came to America. He went first to a little mining town in Pennsylvania, and went to work in the coal mines. He remained there for a year; then, in 1895, went to Jersey City, New Jersey, where he was employed as clerk in a meat market, having had experience enough in that line to be familiar with meat cutting. In 1897 he went to Scranton, Pennsylvania, and worked there for two years, again as meat cutter. Then the lure of the West reached him and he took the long journey overland to the State of Washington, locating in Carbonado, where he worked in the coal mines for three years. During the next nine years Mr. Rozycki spent a short time in each of several different places in the far West, then, in 1911, came to Norwich, Connecticut, and established himself in the grocery and meat business. He was very successful, and continued along this line until 1918, when he had an opportunity to sell the business to advantage, which he did. Early in 1919 he went into the wholesale grocery business, under the name of the Norwich Wholesale Grocery, Inc., he being treasurer and general manager of the business. He was successful from the beginning, and has increased the business until he is now handling a good share of the wholesale trade in this line.

Mr. Rozycki is an up-to-date American, interested in all the public affairs of his adopted country. He is a loyal adherent of the Republican party, and in 1918 was elected city councilman on the Republican ticket, which office he continues to hold. He is a member of the Chamber of Commerce; also a member of White Cross Council, No. 13, Knights of Columbus; of the Society of St. George, of Norwich; and of the Polish National Alliance of the United States of North America, of Chicago, Illinois.

Mr. Rozycki married Anna Skowrcki, of Jersey City, on November 11, 1900, and their five children are: Lottie, Celia, Stella, Phylis, and Marcel. They are members of the Roman Catholic church.

PETER JOSEPH SHANDEOR—Frank Shandeor, born in Italy, came early to the United States, settling in New London, Connecticut, which is yet his home, although nearly half a century has since elapsed. He married Sarah Caracausa, and they were the parents of three children, one of whom was Peter Joseph Shandeor, born in New London, Connecticut, July 19, 1891. He attended New London public schools, including the vocational school. After he left that institution, he entered the employ of H. Yale & Company, of New London, continuing with them for nine years, until 1917, when he bought out a grocery and meat market at Noank, Connecticut, and there conducts a very successful business. He is a wide-awake, energetic young man, his store well kept and attractive. He is a member of the New London Benevolent and Protective Order of Elks, is Independent in politics, and a Roman Catholic in religious faith.

INDEXES

HISTORICAL--BIOGRAPHICAL

HISTORICAL INDEX

Note—In this work the History proper ends at page 619. The Biographical section follows immediately after, and is paged to itself.

Abell, Caleb, early settler, Norwich, 162
Academy, Norwich Free—Dr. Gulliver's remarks, 253; Dr. Robert Porter Keep, 252; First principal, Elbridge Smith, 251; Henry A. Tirrell, 252; Original building, 250; Prof. William Hutchison, 250.
(Plainfield), 288
(Tisdale's), 288
Acourt, Dr. Charles, early physician, Saybrook, 388
Adams Express Co., beginnings of, 81
John (President) visitor at Lebanon, 192, 533; at Norwich, 147
John (1st Prin. Bacon Academy), 255
J. Hunt, officer Thames Nat. Bank, Norwich, 434
Pygan, early goldsmith, 555
Rev. Eliphalet, pastor, New London, 290, 292
Richard, officer Norwich Savings Society, 432
Samuel, visitor at Lebanon, 192
William J., owner of New London "Day," 401
Addenda—Benedict Arnold, The Groton Massacre, Mrs. Mary Branch, Fire Insurance in New London County, 617
Additional Church History—Church of Christ (Scientist), at Mystic, 321, 322; at New London, 322; Universalist Society, 321
Adgate, Thomas, original proprietor, Norwich, 127, 160
William, early goldsmith, Norwich, 556
Adventists, 273
Agents N. L. Co. Mut. Fire Ins. Co., 467
of various companies in N. L. Co., 469
Algonquin race, 3
Allen's "Hist. of Battle of Groton Heights," 24
Point, 214
Allen, Peter, early teacher, Norwich, 36
Samuel, tavern keeper, 542
William H., Pres. Uncas Nat. Bank, Norwich, 444
William H., Pres. Mariners' Savings Bank, New London, 448
Allis, Wallace S., Pres. Uncas Nat. Bank, Norwich, 444
Allyn, Robert (Allyn's Pt.), 160; early settler, Ledyard, 200
Andre, Major, conviction of, 87; arrest, 138
Andros, Sir Edmond, and Connecticut Charter, 8, 9, 10
Anne, Queen, cases of Indians in time of, 205
Anniversary, 250th of New London, 223; 250th of Norwich, 224; 200th of Norwich, 29
Apprentices—Of William Cleveland, David Greenleaf, Thomas Harland, Nathaniel Shipman, Eli Terry, 558

N.L.—2.32.

Archbishop of Canterbury, Commissions Notaries Public before Revolution, 325
Arms, Rev. Hiram P., pastor First Congregational Church, 294, 297; distinguished resident Norwich, 170
Armstrong, Benjamin L., banker, 428, 443, 493
Armstrong, Peleg, early potter, 548, 549
Arnold, Benedict—At Groton Heights, 63, 64, 71, 76, 106; his report of expedition against New London, 107; Hurd's account of his career, 137, 163, 617; John, witness of deed, 126
Art Gallery, Old Lyme, 212
Articles of Confederation, 137
Asbury, Bishop, visits New London, 271, 272, 310
Atha, Rev., George R., Baptist pastor, 302
Attawanhood, Sachem, 124
Atwood, James S., Treas. Ponemah Mills Co., 502
Austin, John, original house lot holder, New London, 102
Samuel, principal early school, Norwich, 35
Averill, John C., Pres. Chelsea Savings Bank, 445
Avery, Caleb, narrative of Groton Heights, 75
Christopher, early settler, Ledyard, 200
Ebenezer, house of, 74
Ira S., New London City Nat. Bank, 430
John, early goldsmith, 567, 568
N. H., cashier Nat. Whaling Bank, 439
Robert, goldsmith, 568
Rufus, in battle of Groton Heights, 65
Ayer, James Cook (patent medicine), 86
Rev. Joseph, pastor, 206, 282
Ayres, Col., at battle of Groton Heights, 65, 71, 76

Backus, Eber, incorporator Norwich Savings Society, 432
Isaac, Baptist clergyman, 86
Joseph, Pres. N. L. County Mutual Fire Ins. Co., 466
William, one of founders of Norwich, 160
William, Jr., Lieut., founder of Norwich, 160
Bacon Academy (Colchester), foundation of, 180; charter, 253; trustees, 254; donors to, 255; eminent alumni, 255
Bacon, Pierpont, benefactor of Bacon Academy, 253
Rev. Edward Woolsey, pastor, New London, 297
Rev. Leonard W., article of, 196
Rev. Leonard Woolsey, pastor Park Church, 296
Bailey, Anna Warner (wife of Capt. Elijah Bailey), 86, 87
Dr. Alfred, physician, 398
Family, 205
Baker, Milton M., cashier, New London, 443

Baldwin, John, founder, Norwich, 160
Banks, New London County—Bank of Maryland, 425; Bank of New Haven, 426; Bank of New York, 425; Bank of North America, 425; Bankers Trust Co., 453; Chelsea Savings Bank, 445; Dime Savings, 450; First National, Stonington, 440; Groton Savings, 444; Hartford, 426; Jewett City Savings Bank, 452; Trust Co., 453; Mariners Savings Bank, 447; Mass. Bank, 425; Merchants Nat. Bank, Norwich, 431; Mystic River National, 439; National Bank of Commerce, New London, 441; National Whaling Bank, New London, 436; New London City National, 428; Norwich Savings Society, 432; Pawcatuck Bank & Trust Co., 454; Providence, 425; Savings Bank of New London, 436; Thames National, Norwich, 434; Uncas National, 443; Union Trust, 425; Winthrop Trust Co., 454
Baptist (Young People's Union), 276
Baptist Churches—Beginnings of, 299; Bozrah, 301; Central Baptist, Norwich, 302; Chesterfield, 301; Colchester Borough, 301; East Lyme, 300; First Baptist, Groton, 299; First Baptist, New London, 301; First Baptist, Norwich, 301; Fitchville, 302; Grace Memorial, 302; Groton Heights, 302; Jewett City, 301; Lakes Pond, 302; Laurel Glen, 302; Lebanon, 301; Ledyard, 302; Montauk Baptist, New London, 302; Montville Union, 302; Moodus, 301; Mt. Calvary, 302; Mystic Union, 302; Niantic, 302; Noank, 302; North Lyme, 301; North Stonington, 301; North Stonington First, 300; North Stonington Second, 300; Old Lyme, 302; Packerville, 301; Poquonnock, 302; Preston City, 301; "Quaker Hill," 300; Salem, 300; Scott Hill, 300; Second Baptist, Waterford, 300; Shiloh, 302; Stonington, 300; Stonington Third, 302; Voluntown, 301
Baptists, "first day," 208; seventh day, 208;
Bar, New London County Members, 430
Bard, Charles, banker, 416, 433, 435
Barker, Dr. Benjamin Fordyce, physician, Norwich, 382
  Dr. John, physician, Franklin, 373, 378
  Frank E., cashier, 430
Barnes, John H., lawyer, 342
  William H., banker, 448
Barns, Acors, banker, 443
  William H., banker, 443
Barral, Louis, early resident, Norwich, 579
  Theodore, builder of famous house, 575
Barry, Carlos, banker, 428, 442
  Secretary, N. London School Committee, 260
Bartholomew, Edward Sheffield, sculptor, 87
Bartlett, William, house lot holder, New London, 102; donor of school funds, 38
Bath, Rev. William H., presiding elder, 314
Bathgate, James, banker, 428
Beardsley, Rev. John, pastor, 307
Beckwith, Col., commander at Groton Heights, 72, 75
Bedeel, Robert, house lot holder, New London, 102
Bedquilt industry, 218
Beebe, Nathaniel, early settler, Stonington, 207
Beecher, Henry Ward, visits Norwich, 88; article on Norwich, 172
Beesbran, Peter, house lot holder, New London, 102
Belcher, Nathan, trustee, Bulkeley School, 257
  William, banker, 430, 437
Belden, Richard N., banker, 430
Bell, Dr. Robert, physician, 383
  Phillip, early settler, 200
  Thomas, early settler, Stonington, 207
Bemis, James, house lot holder, New London, 102
Bennett, Henry L., bank officer, 436
Bentley, Dr. Edwin, early physician, 398
Berkeley, Bishop, gift to Yale College, 304
Bibliography for medical chapter, 399
Bigelow, Asa, trustee Bacon Academy, 254
Bill, Elijah A., insurance actuary, 466
  Henry, incorporator Chelsea Savings Bank, 445; Memorial Library, 213
Bingham, Capt. Elisha, first victim of yellow fever, 371
  Deacon Thomas, founder, Norwich, 161
Birchard, John, founder, Norwich, 161
  John, recorder, Norwich, 127
Birge, Maj. Gen. Henry W., 170
Bishop, Lieut. Samuel, early landowner, 201
Bissell, Clark, Governor, 197
Bixler, Rev. James Wilson, 298
Black Hall, 213
"Black Point," 213
Blackstone, Lorenzo, banker, 416, 436, 445
  William N., banker, 444
Blake, Rev. S. Leroy, pastor "Old First," 297
Blakeslee, Rev. Solomon, Rector, 307
Blinman, Rev. Mr., original lot holder, New London, 102
  Rev. Richard, first pastor, New London, 278
Bliss, J. Homer, Norwich Bulletin, 415, 420
  John, builder "Old Torrent" Engine, 475
  Thomas, founder, Norwich, 161
Bloomfield, Capt., British officer, Groton Heights, 69
Bodenwein, Theodore, of New London "Day," 401
Bolles, Albert S., of Norwich Bulletin Co., 416
  John C., early physician, 386
  John G., author of "The Edelwiss," 97
Bonaparte, in war of 1812, 77
Bond, Henry R., banker, 443, 448
Bordman, William, lot holder, New London, 102
Boroughs (N. L. Co.), 222
Boss, Charles D., Jr., banker, 442
Boston Fire (Norwich dept. aided), 480
Boswell, Dr. Lemuel, early physician, 381
Boteler, Lady Alice, 203
Bowers, Morgan, lot holder, Norwich, 161
Boylston, Dr. Zadiel, introduced inoculation of smallpox, Boston, 368
Bozrah, District probate court, 325; town of, 205, 228
Bradford, John, lot holder, Norwich, 161
Bradstreet, Rev. Simon, First Church, New London, 285, 366

Brady, Rev. John, pastor R. C., Norwich, 319
Brainard, Jeremiah Gate, judge of County Court, 326
John Gardiner Calkins, 95
M. G., 121
Brainerd & Armstrong, silk manufacturers, 493
Brainerd, Dyer T., physician, 375, 394
James P., silk manufacturer, 493
Branch, Mary Lydia, author, 95
Mrs. Mary, 617
Brandagee, Augustus, life of, 345
Dr. Frank D., physician, 397
Frank B., lawyer, 337
Breed, John, early goldsmith, 432, 562
Brewer, Arthur H., banker, 433, 435
Lyman, incorporator Norwich Savings Society, 432
Brewster, Abel, early goldsmith, 564
John, banker, 431
Jonathan (Brewster's Neck), 130
Jonathan, early settler, Ledyard, 200
Lucretia, wife of Jonathan, 200
Bride Brook, 100, 101, 102
(Marriage, poem by Miss Caulkins), 180, 213
Story of, 278
Bridges, Hon. Samuel A., 256
Briscoe, Willis A., banker, 435
Brockway, Dr. John C. M., physician, 399
Broderick, Rev. Thomas, pastor, Roman Catholic, 318
Bromfield, Major, officer at Groton Heights, 75
Bromley, Isaac H., editor Bulletin, 88, 170, 415, 419
Brook, Lord, a proprietor at Saybrook, 203, 283
Brooks, Dr. Jona. W., early physician, 383
Brotherhood of St. Andrews, 276
"Brother Jonathan" (Trumbull) at Lebanon, 59
Brothertown tribe (of Six Nations), 57
Brown, Arthur M., lawyer, 339
Dr. Henry C., physician, 398
Dr. Samuel, early physician, 389
John H., Fire Chief, 490
John Newton, author of note, 95
Lucius, banker, 433; judge, 431; lawyer, 338
Rev. J. Eldred, Archdeacon, 309
Brunner, Frank J., editor New London "Day," 408
Buckingham, Deacon Samuel, early settler, 188
Hon. William A., War Governor, 170, 196, 197
Rev. Dr. Samuel, remarks at Lebanon, 196
Rev. Thomas, early connected with Yale, 277
Walter M., bank officer, 436
William A., 85, 90, 180
Buell, Colin S., Prin. Williams' Memorial Institute, 258
Bulkeley, Hon. Morgan G., descendant of Rev. Gershom, 281
Leonard Hallam, founder of Bulkeley School, 257, 281
Maj. Roger, trustee Bacon Academy, 254
Rev. Gershom, pastor Old First Church, 286, 289, 387
Bulkeley School—Building, 257; graduates, 258; trustees, 257; Eugene Collister, principal, 257
Bulkley, Dr. John, son of Rev. Gershom, 385
Bull, Edward, Jr., bank, 428
Bulletin (Norwich), description of it's growth, 409
Burgess, Dr. Chauncey, physician, 383
Dr. Reuben, physician, 383
Burial Ground, oldest in county, 85
Burnette, Principal Bacon Academy, 255
Burnham, W. R., shareholder Norwich Bulletin, 416
Burr, Rev. E. F., author, 204
Burrell, Theophilus, early goldsmith, 556
Burrows, Daniel, friend of Bishop Seabury, 310
Burton, Rev. Asa, author, 95
Bushnell, Dr. Caleb, early physician, 377
Ebenezer, early editor, 411
Rev. Horace, at Norwich, 94
Richard, early settler, 162
Buswell, John L., banker, 432
Butler, Charles W., lawyer, 447
Deacon Charles, banker, 443
Dr. Benjamin, early physician, 382
Butts, Charles R., bank officer, 433
Byles, Rev. Mather, Jr., pastor, 293

Cabot, Sebastian C., early instructor, 35
Cambridge, Nathan Hale at, 60
"Cambridge Platform," (1648), 273
Camp Fire Girls, 276
Canonicus, Indian Chief, 4, 7
Captains, of Whalers, 79
Carew, Capt., veteran of Civil War, 142
Carpenter, Joseph, early goldsmith, 562
Carrier, Andrew, grist mill owner, 181
Joseph B., Fire Chief, 480
Carroll, Lucius W., banker, 434
Cashiers, Uncas National Bank, 444
Caulkins, Deacon Hugh, founder, Norwich, 161
Caulkins' "History of Norwich," 34, 39; of New London, 39
Caulkins, John, founder, Norwich, 161
Chace, B. C., early potter, 551
Chadwick, Daniel, lawyer, 335
Chamberlain, George B., early potter, 551
Joseph, selectman, 178
Rev. L. T., pastor, 296
Champion, Gen. Epaphroditus, trustee, Bacon Academy, 254
Champlin, John, early goldsmith, 559
Channing, Rev. Henry—Account of yellow fever epidemic, 372; pastor, 293; trustee of Bacon Academy, 254
Chapman, Lieut. Richard, at Groton Heights, 73
Robert, ancestor of William Henry, 259
Sir John, ancestor of William Henry, 259
William, early settler, 200
William H., banker, 428
William Henry, founder of New London Vocational School, 259
Chappell, Edward, 430, 495
Ezra, 430, 437
Frank H., 404, 496
Frank H., Jr., 496
Frank V., 430
George, 102
Lawrence A., 428, 496

Charles I., sends Uncas Bible, 52
Charles II. and Connecticut Charter, 8, 45
Charter, Story of Connecticut, 8, 10
Charter Oak, Story of, 8, 10
Charter of 1662, Connecticut, 45
Chastellux, Marquis de, visitor at Lebanon, 553
Chauncey, Sarah, wife of Rev. Gershom Bulkeley, 281
Chelsea Grammar School, 37
Chesebrough, Elisha, settler, 207
Ephraim, banker, 437
Mrs. Anna, settler, 207
Nathaniel, settler, 207
William, leader Stonington settlers, 206
Chester, Capt. John, early settler, 177
Joseph Lemuel, antiquarian, 94
Chew, J. Lawrence, banker, 428
Chief Justices of Supreme Court, Connecticut, 326—Matthew Griswold, 1769-84; Samuel Huntington, 1784-85; John D. Park, 1874-89; Samuel Oscar Prentice, 1913-20; Gurdon Saltonstall, 1711-12; Jonathan Trumbull, 1766-69; Henry M. Waite, 1854-57
Child, Rev. Willard, 296
Cholera, epidemic of, 372
Christian Endeavor, 276
Christophers, Christopher, 556
Christophus, Robert, early settler, 177
Church, Frederick Stuart, eminent painter, 87
Leonard P., bank officer, 436
Church History — Bozrah, 294, 301; Canterbury, 288; Central Baptist (Norwich), 302; Chesterfield, 301; Christ Church (Norwich), 306; Church of St. James, 292; Colchester Borough, 301; East Lyme, 300; Episcopal Churches with pastors in New London Co., 303; Exeter, 288; First Baptist, (Groton), 286, 299; First Baptist (New London), 301; First Baptist (Norwich), 301; First Baptist (Waterford), 300; First Church of Christ (Lebanon), 288; First Church of Christ (New London), 272; First Church of Christ (Norwichtown), 287; First Church of Colchester, 289; First Ecclesiastical Society of New London, 290; Fitchville, 302; Franklin, 289; Goshen, 288; Grace Memorial, 302; Grassy Hill, 284; Greenville Congregational, 297; Groton Heights, 302; Hamburg, 284; Hanover, 294; Jewett City, 294; Jewett City, 301; Lake's Pond, 302; Laurel Glen, 302; Lebanon, 301; Ledyard, 302; Liberty Hill, 288; Lisbon (Newent), 290; Long Society of Christ, 288; Lyme, 284; Methodist Churches, 310; Mohegan, 294; Montauk Baptist (New London), 302; Montville Union Baptist, 302; Moodus, 301; Mt. Calvary, 302; Mystic Union, 302; Niantic, 284; Niantic, 302; Noank, 302; North Lyme, 301; North Parish (Montville), 290; No. Stonington First, 300; No. Stonington Second, 300; No. Stonington Third, 301; Old Lyme, 283; Old Lyme, 302; Old Saybrook, 283; Onconk or "Line" Church, 283; Packerville, 301; Park Congregational, 296; Poquonnock Bridge, 302; Preston City, 301; "Quaker Hill" Church, 300; Roman Catholic Churches (names, with pastors), 317, 321; Salem, 284; Salem Baptist, 300; Scott Hill, 300; Second Congregational of New London, 295; Second Ecclesiastical Society of Lyme (Niantic), 290; Shiloh, 302; Stonington First, 300; Stonington Third, 302; Voluntown, 301
Circulation of "The Day," 407
City Court, New London, 324
Civil War Records (N. L. Co. representatives in various Connecticut regiments), 581
Clark, Col. James, Bunker Hill veteran, 188, 193
Edward F., agent Thames Tow Boat Co., 496
Cleaveland, William P., banker, 427, 437
William P., Jr., banker, 437
Cleveland, Aaron, native of Norwich, 163
Grover, descended from William Hyde, 170
Moses, settler of Cleveland, Ohio, 289
President, eminent son of New London County, 85
William, goldsmith, 163, 548, 558, 564
Cleworth, Allan, owner Norwich Record 422
Cleworth & Pullen (Record) 422
Clift, William, banker, 439, 445
Clinton, Sir Henry, despatches from Groton Heights, 76
Coates, Dr. A. W., physician, 398
Dr. Elias F., physician, 398
Coit, Alfred, corporator New London Vocational School, 260; banker, 428
Charles, banker, 431, 446
Daniel L., director, banker, 426
Daniel Wadsworth, extracts from life of, 79, 80
Dr. Thomas, Jr., physician, 369, 374, 391
Dr. Thomas, Sr., outline of life, 389, 391
Joshua, lawyer, 326
Joshua, life of, 327
Rev. Joseph, 288
Robert, banker, 428, 437; stockholder "The Day," 404
Thomas Chester, silversmith, 566
Thomas Winthrop, clergyman, 95
William H., banker, 428
"Coit Elms" (Norwich), mentioned by Oliver W. Holmes, 91
Coke's Commentaries upon Littleton, 2
Colchester, borough, 182; boundaries, 182; probate court, 325; in Revolutionary War, 180; population, 181; list of voters, 1725, 181
Colchester, town of, 1, 8; Bacon Academy, 180; boundaries, 178; early industries, 181; early settlement, 177; eminent men, 180; first church, 178; Hayward Rubber Co., 181; population, 181; religions, worship and instruction, 179
Collegiate School of Conn., later Yale College, 276
Collester, Eugene B., of Bulkeley School, 257
Collier, Thomas S., author, 194
Colony of Connecticut, eastern boundary, 27; western boundary, 27

Commissioners' Court, 99
Comstock, A., grist mill of, 181
Christopher C., banker, 442, 448
John, witness to deed, 203
John Lee, scientist, author, 95
Cone, Dr. Charles C., physician, 397
Rev. Salmon, 254
Congregational Churches—Bozrah, 294, 301; Broadway, 296; Canterbury, 288; Colchester, 289; Exeter, 288; First Church of Christ (Lebanon), 388; Fitchville, 302; Franklin, 289; Goshen, 288; Greenville, 297; Groton, 293; Hamburg, 284; Hanover, 294; Jewett City, 294; Liberty Hill, 288; Lisbon (Newent), 290; Long Society, 288; Lyme, 284; Mohegan 294; Niantic, 284; North Parish (Montville), 290; North Society of Stonington, 282; Norwichtown, 287; New London, 272; Old Lyme, 283; Park Congregational (Norwich), 296; Plainfield, 288; Salem, 284; Second (New London), 298; Second Church (Norwich), 295; Second Congregational (New London), 295; Second Ecclesiastical Society (Lyme), 290; "Separates" movement, 292
Connecticut, College aims, courses, 245; foundation of, 244; ideals of, 246; status of, 247; record of graduation, 247; first endowment campaign, 264
Connecticut Medical Society, 392
River, 2, 212
River Toll Bridge, 212
State of, 8
Constitution of Connecticut, of 1818, 33
Cooley, John G., founder of "Cooley's Weekly," 422
John G., Jr., son of former, 422
Copp, Bolton A., bank officer, 437
Bolton A., Jr., banker, 439
Corning, Erastus, banker, railroad builder, 95
Cotton Industry, 218
Council of Safety, Revolutionary War, 192
Court, City of New London, 324; for prominent members of Bar see "Lawyers"
Court of Common Pleas, Norwich and New London, 324
Courts—Probate, 324; Supreme, 324; Superior, 324
"Covenant," Seven Articles of, 29, 30
Coventry, birthplace of Nathan Hale, 59
Cragin, Dr. Edwin B., 180
Cragin Memorial Library, 180
Crandall, Herbert L., banker, 430
William T., bank officer, 436
Crescent Beach, part of Niantic, 213, 233
Cricket, played in early days, 148
Crump, John G., editor, 406
William C., trustee Bulkeley School, 257
Culver, Edward, early settler, 200
Cunningham, British provost marshal, 62
Dr. Cornelius, physician, 390
Cutler, James F., benefactor Bacon Academy, 255
Timothy, President of Yale College, 292

Daboll, Celadon Leeds, inventor, 96
Charles Miner, inventor of steam fog-horn, 96
Nathan, almanac of, 36, 186; author of Arithmetic, 95, 118
Nathan, (son of Nathan), almanac publisher, 96, 186
Daggett, Rev. Oliver Ellsworth, 298
Dakota, 33,000 tons, built at New London, 81
Dalrymple, Lord, at Groton Heights, 76
Dana, Rev. Malcolm McG., founder of Park Church, 296
Danforth, Rev., J. Romeyn, Pastor Old First, New London, 297
Darrow, Elder Zadok, pastor, Waterford, 301
Francis, grandson and successor of, 302
William M., banker, 430
Dartmouth College, foundation at Columbia, then Lebanon, 54, 197
Dartmouth, Earl of, benefactor of Dartmouth College, 55
Davenport, John, Separatist preacher, 292
Davie, John, early resident of Groton, 185, 304
Davis, Charles Harold, 88
Day, Hon. Erastus Sheldon, trustee Bacon Academy, 356
"Day," New London paper, 238
"Day," New London newspaper, forty years of, 401
Dean, Benjamin D., early physician, 383
Deane, James, Indian missionary, 96
Silas, commissioner sent to England, 86
Silas, early settler, Ledyard, 200
Decatur Hill, 214
Decatur, Stephen, at "Decatur Hill," War of 1812, 89, 115, 186
Deed of Norwich, signed by Mohegan chiefs, 125
Delancy, Daniel A., Fire Chief, 280
Delaware race, 3
Deming, David, donor to Bacon Academy, 182
Denison, Capt. George, early settler, 206
Charles Wheeler, newspaper editor, 96
Elisha, bank officer, 430
John, early inhabitant, Stonington, 207
John (3d), early inhabitant, Stonington, 208
John (4th), early inhabitant, Stonington, 207
Joseph (2d), early inhabitant, Stonington, 207, 208
Deshon, Daniel, goldsmith, 555
George, Catholic missioner, 95
Desmond, Jeremiah A., lawyer, 342
Dickinson, Rev. James T., 296
"District System," Schools in Connecticut, 47
Doane, Joseph H., bank officer, 431
Dodge, Ezra, silversmith, 560
Jonathan, physician, 386
Douglas, Dr. Archibald T., physician, 397
Dr. Charles, physician, 392
Dr. Luke, physician, 392
Robert, silversmith, 559
Dow, Dr., teacher, 38
Ulysses, teacher, 39
Dr. James R., physician, 386
Downer, Dr. Avery, physician, 383
Dr. Joshua, physician, 383
Downing, Dr. Eleazer Burler, physician, 384

Dunham, John, proprietor of newspaper, 411, 445
Durfee, Dr. Joseph, physician, 398
Durkee, Col. John, early resident, Norwich, 165
Dutch, in Connecticut, 9
Dutton, Elijah F., banker, 430
Mary E., occupant of Lebanon War Office, 534
Dwight, Dr. Timothy, President of Yale, 87
Theodore, in Hartford Convention, 77
Timothy, President of Yale, 87
Dyer, Elisha Jr., physician, 375, 383

East Haddam, 59
East Lyme, Description of, 213; District probate court, 325; poem, Miss Caulkins' "Bride Brook Marriage," 182; town of, 1, 182
Eaton, William P., physician, 383
"Edelwiss," poem, description of historic New London, 97
Edgcomb, Samuel Jr., in battle of Groton Heights, 68
Edgerton, Richard, early settler, 161
Education, a definition of, 31, 32
Edwards, Jonathan, in early religious life of New England, 273
Eells, Cushing, bank officer, 430
Rev. Nathaniel, pastor, 282
Elder, Rev. Joseph A., pastor, 302
Elderkin, John, early settler, Norwich, 162, 570
Eldridge, Ensign Charles, in battle of Groton Heights, 68
Eliot, Dr. Jared, physician, 364
Ellis, Dr. Benjamin, physician, 378
Ely, Edwin S., banker, 444
Jesse S., banker, 444
Rev. Zebulon, pastor, 288
Richard, husband of Col. Fenwick's sister, 204
Endicott, Captain, and Indians, 3
Engine Companies—Blackstone Hose, No. 1, 479; Greenville Hook and Ladder, No. 2, 480; Groton Company, 491; Independent Hose Co., No. 6, 479; Independent Nameaug Fire Co., 489; Konomac Co., 490; Neptune No. 5, 477; New London Department, 490, 491; Niagara No. 2, 478; Niagara Engine Co., 489; No. 2, 476; No. 3, 476; Volunteer Companies, 482; Wauregan Hook and Ladder Co., 478; Wauregan Steam Fire Engine Co. No. 1, 477
Epidemic Diseases, 366
Episcopal Churches—303
Black Hall, St. Ann's Mission; Colchester, Calvary Church; Groton, Bishop Seabury Memorial; Jewett City, Episcopal Mission; Mystic, St. Mark's Church; New London, Pequot Chapel; New London, St. James'; Niantic, St. John's Chapel; Noank, Grace Chapel; Norwich, Christ Church; Norwich, Trinity Church; Poquetanuck, St. James' Church; South Lyme, St. Michael's Church; Stonington, Calvary Church; Yantic, Grace Church, 303
Epworth League, 276
Errata, for "3300 Tons read "33000 Tons," 81
Evans, Evan D., banker, 439
Everest, Rev. Mr., pastor, 294

Fairfax, Lord, John Mason served under, 4
Fairfield, 6, 29
Fanning, Edmund, early settler, 200, 207
Thomas, early resident, 170
Farnsworth, H. P., early principal, 39
Federal Reserve Act, 424
Federalist Party, 77
Federation of Churches, 277
Fenwick, Col., leader at Saybrook, 130
Col. George, original patentee, Saybrook, 203
Lady, wife of above leader, 204
Fermin, Giles, physician, 363
Field, Rev. Thomas P., pastor, 297
Fillmore, Millard, descended from Capt. John Fillmore, 169
Fillmore, President, 85
Filton, pastor, Worcester, 318
Fire Department, Norwich, 475; New London, 389
Fire Insurance, 457
First American Companies, 458; in Eighteenth Century, 462; Mutual Assurance Co., Norwich, 459; Norwich Fire Insurance Company, 463; Other early companies, 464; Thames Insurance Company, 464
Fire Insurance Companies, 464
Hartford County Mutual, 464; Litchfield, 464; Middlesex, 464; New London, 464; Thames Fire Insurance Company, 468; Tolland County Mutual, 464; Windham, 464
Fire Insurance in New London County, 617
Firemen's Pension Fund, 487
Fires, disastrous in Norwich, early days, 476
Fish, John, early settler, 207
Nathan G., banker, 445
Rev. Joseph, pastor, 282
Fisher's Island, residence of John Winthrop, younger, 8
Fitch, Ebenezer, tavern keeper, 543
Elizabeth, letter to, 11
family, 205
James, pastor, 129
James, assistant, 126
James, Jr., record of lands, 126, 201
Lieut. Andrew, at Bunker Hill, 193
Major James, early resident, 53, 163
N. K., banker, 431
Rev. James, early settler, pastor, 11, 29, 53, 161, 278, 280
Stephen, banker, 431
Fitzmaurice, Walter, newspaper publisher, 406, 408
Fleming, Robert, original settler, 207
Foote, Nathaniel, emigrant, 177
Nathaniel (3rd), original settler, 177
Forbes, William, lot holder, New London, 102
Ford, John D., physician, 383
Paul Leicester, visitor at "Pinehurst," 579
Fort Point, Preston, 219
Fosdick, Capt. Samuel, settler of Colchester, 177

Samuel, house on Niantic river, 38
Fossecar, John, settler, 102
Foster, Hon. Lafayette S., career of,170, 330, 433, 435
Founders of Norwich, 160, 161, 162
Francis, Dr. David P., physician, 397
Franklin, settlement of, 1, 58, 184, 185, 205
Franklin, Benjamin, visitor at Lebanon, 192, 458
Franklin, Honor Roll, 185
Franklin, "West Farms," 184
Fraternal Bodies—Eagles, Elks, Foresters, Junior Order United American Mechanics, Knights of Columbus, Knights of Pythias, Maccabees, Moose, Owls, Red Men, 518
Fraternal Orders, Women's—Eastern Star, D. A. R., Daughters of Pocahontas, Daughters of Rebekah, Pythian Sisters, 518
Freeman, Richard Patrick, lawyer, 337
French, officers and regiments at Lebanon, 196
Fuller, John P., physician, 383
"Fundamental Orders," of Connecticut, 33
Furlong, Father, pastor, 318

Gager, John, settler, 102
John, early resident, 161
Othniel, banker, 446
Gale, Charles W., banker, 435
Gale's Ferry, part of Ledyard, 200
Gallup, Andrew, in battle of Groton Heights, 75
Benadam, early settler, 200
Capt. John, early settler, 206
Charles A., banker, 430
Henry H., banker, 447
John, Jr., early settler, 207, 466
Gardiner, John, early goldsmith, 559
Lieut., dealt with Uncas, 4
Lion, engineer under Gov. Winthrop, 128
Garfield, James A., (descended from Major John Mason and also from Rev. James Fitch), 170
Garrett, Harmon, Pequot chief, 281
Geer, George, early settler, 200
General Assembly of Connecticut, 2
General Court of Connecticut, 10
"Giant's Neck," on Long Island Sound, 213
Gibbs, E. N., banker, 416, 435
Nathan A., author chapter on Banks, 423, 435, 436
Gibson, Rev. James R. L., pastor, 318
Gifford, Stephen, witness of Indian deed, 126, 163
Gifts to Yale, by Norwich citizens, 86
Gilbert, S. Alphaeus, banker, 433
Gillett, Samuel, owned saw-mill, 181
Gillette, S. Lewis, benefactor of Bacon Academy, 255
Gilman, Daniel Coit, President Johns Hopkins, 170
Dr. Daniel Coit, historian, 28, 53, 87, 571
William C., eminent resident, owner of historic home, 171, 432, 577
William C., editor 250th anniversary quarter Millennial, 225
William C., editor, 79
Goddard, Calvin, member Conn. Supreme Court, 327
Dr. Giles, physician, 388
George Willard, lawyer, 334
Hon. Calvin, eminent resident, 171
Mrs. Calvin, gave collation to Indians, 572
Goldsmith, Samuel A., banker, 430
Gould, Lyman, banker, 444
Grace, Rev. P., pastor, 318
Graham, Rev. Richard R., pastor, 308, 309
Dr. William, early physician, 392
Grange, Norwich, 229
Grant, Ulysses S., descended from Christopher Huntington, 169
Ulysses S., (President) Norwich descent, 85
Graves, Dr. Charles B., physician, 363
Rev. Matthew, pastor, 306
Gray, Dr. Alvah, physician, 398
Dr. Jonathan, physician, 398
John, early goldsmith, 554
Samuel, early goldsmith, 554
"Great Awakening," religious revival, 273
Great Plain, Norwich, 7
Great River, of Pequot country, 99
Greenberg, Louis W., Fire Chief, 481
Greene, Dr. Ralph E., physician, 384
Gardiner, jurist, 338, 416, 450
James Lloyd, banker, 416, 436
William P., banker, 171, 435
Greenfield, James, stockholder, the "Day," 404
Greenleaf, David, goldsmith, 556, 558
Grignon, Rene, donor of bell, 552
Griswold, town of New London county, 1, 185, 228
(Fort), battle of Groton Heights, 63, 65, 66, 71
Gov. Roger, trustee Bacon Academy, 1, 254
Griswold Home, (Old Lyme), 212
Griswold, Lieut. Francis, early settler, Norwich, 161
Matthew, Chief Justice, 204, 213, 326
Mrs. Anna Walcott, resident, 204
Nathan, resident, 203
Rev. George, pastor, 290
Roger, eminent lawyer, 327
Groton—Boundaries, 185; battle of Groton Heights, 186; in War of 1812, 186; John Davie, 185; today, 231; town of, 1, 27, 187
Groton Banks Temperance Society, 275
Groton, birthplace of Bishop Seabury, 187
Groton District Probate Court, 325
Groton Heights, battle of, 63-76, 186
Groton Massacre, comments on, 617
Groton Monument, 187, 213, 275
Groton, War of 1812, 186
Gulliver, Daniel F., physician, 171, 383
Rev. John P., founder of Norwich Free Academy, 249
Rev. John Putnam, pastor, 296
Gurley, Jacob B., banker, 39, 430, 437

Haile, Dr. Ashland Bradford, physician, 382
Hale, Nathan, patriot, 39, 59, 63
"Half-way Covenant," footnote on 279, spread of, 286
"Halifax," ship of British, 61
Hall, Ely R., of Bulkeley School, 258
Joseph, banker, 431
Hallam, Edward, banker, 426, 430
George, banker, 427

John, banker, 428
Rev. Isaac W., rector, 308
Rev. Robert A., rector, 308
Robert, banker, 428
Hallett, William, settler, 102
Halsey, Capt. Elias H., in battle of Groton Heights, 66
Hon. Jeremiah, bequest to Norwich Free Academy, 253
Jeremiah, eminent lawyer, 328, 331, 349
Hamilton, Alexander, and National Banks, 423
Hamburg Cove, 212
Hamlin, Capt. John, settler, 177
Hancox, Edward, settler, 207
Harding, President, descendant of New London, 85
Harland, Gen. Edward, banker, 445
Thomas, silversmith, 475, 557
Harlem Heights, battle of, 60
Harris, in battle of Groton Heights, 75
Jeremiah, public house of, 543
J. N., banker, 429
Jonathan, banker, 430
Mary, will of, 103
Hart, Dr. David, physician, Groton, 398
Judah, goldsmith, 564
Rev. Mr., pastor, 294
Hartford, 4, 9
Convention, and War of 1812, 77 . .
Hartshorne, Dr. David, early physician, 377
Dr. Elijah, early physician, 378
Haskell, Daniel, President Vermont University, 36
Hassam, Childe, resident at Lyme, 204
Haughton's Cove, 544
Tavern, 544
Haven, Henry P., banker, 429
Henry P., trustee Bulkeley School, 257
"Hawks Nest," 213
Hayes, President, of Norwich ancestry, 85
Rutherford B., descendant from John Birchard, 169, 170
Haynes, Governor, early settler, 206
Hayward Rubber Co., at Colchester, 181
Hedding, Rev. Elijah, pastor, 310
Hempstead, Joshua, diary of, 367
Stephen, narrative of Groton Heights, 71
Henderson, James C., banker, 431
Hibbard, Oliver, settler, 207
Hide, Dr. Phineas, physician, 398
Higbie, Edward, settler, 102
Higgins, Edwin Werter, lawyer, 338
Hill, George, early teacher, 36
Hillhouse, William, manager of lottery, 209
Rev. James, pastor, 290
Hinckley, Dyar T., early teacher, 36
Hine, Rev. Orlo D., pastor, 187
Hislop, James, trustee N. L. Vocational School, 260
Hitchcock, Mr. F. S., Principal Vocational High School, 259, 261
Mrs. E. L. Cheney, wife of above, 262
Hobron, Dr. Albert, physician, 397
Holbrook, S. T., lawyer, judge, 334
Holloway, Charlotte M., author, 120
Charlotte Molyneux, author, 223
Miss Charlotte M. (Ct. Quarterly), 77
Holmes, George H., trustee N. L. Vocational School, 260
Oliver Wendell, descendant of Newent resident, 91
Robert, settler, Stonington, 207
Holt, Charles, publisher, 371
Honor Roll, World War—Bozrah, 591; Groton, 613; Ledyard, 609, 611; Lisbon, 611, 612; Lyme, 612; Montville, 612; New London, 613; Norwich, 600, 609; No. Stonington, 591, 600; Old Lyme, 614; Preston, 612; Sprague (Baltic), 613; Stonington (Pawtucket), 614. (For others, see towns).
Hooker, Dr. Worthington, physician, 382
Rev. Asahel, pastor, 295
Hopkins, Dr. Lemuel, physician, 364
Hosmer, Capt. Joseph, pottery, 548
Hospital, Backus (Norwich), 216
Householders, New London, original lots, 102
Norwich, original lots, 127
Hovey, James Albert, lawyer, judge, 333, 444
Howard, Nathan, pastor, 300
Thomas, early settler, 161
Howard's Ledge, fishing grounds, 301
Howe, General, British commander, 62
Rev. Chester H., pastor, 301
Rev. Samuel S., pastor, 297
Howland, Joseph, banker, 426
Hubbard, Amos H., banker, 432
Charles L., banker, 435
James L., banker, 436
Rev., pastor, editor, chapter on religion, 271, 322
Russell, First President Norwich Free Academy, 171, 432
Hull, Hadlai A., lawyer, 342
Hunt Family of Bozrah, 205
Hunt, Thomas S., eminent son of Norwich, 171
Huntington, Benjamin, early resident, 163
Benjamin, appointed to look into lottery, 209
Benjamin, judge, 327, 433
Capt. Simeon, resident Norwich, 142
Charles P., banker, 432
Christopher, early settler, 161
Christopher, early settler, 127, 161, 163
Col. Joshua, early resident, 165
Deacon Simon, early settler, 161
Dr. Asher, physician, 398
Dr. Christopher, physician, 385
Ebenezer, famous resident, 164
Family, of Norwich, 205
General, of Norwich, 38
General Andrew, resident of Norwich, 164
Gen. Jabez, early resident, Norwich, 165
Gen. Jedidiah, Norwich and New London, 138, 139
Gov. Samuel, signer of Declaration of Independence, 326
Hon. Jabez W., eminent son of Norwich, 164, 171
Isaac, signer of deed, 202
Jabez, banker, 432
Jedidiah, banker, 109, 164, 426, 533
Jedidiah, son of Jabez Huntington, 87
John P., bank officer, 433
Jonathan G., president Fire Insurance Company, 466

(Long Island), 61
Phillip, goldsmith, 563
Rev. Daniel, principal Female Academy, 39
Roswell, goldsmith, 563
Simon, Jr., early resident, 164
Huntting, Dr. Samuel, early physician, 393
Hurlbut, Joseph, donor of school, 38
Hurlbutt, John, settler, 200
Hutchison, Prof. William, principal Norwich Free Academy, 252
Hyde, Dr. Nathaniel, physician, 378
Dr. William, Sr., physician, 397
Dr. William, Jr., physician, 397
Elisha, attorney, 326, 548
Elizabeth, early settler, 163
Family of Lisbon, 205
John, early teacher, 36
Lewis, banker, 431, 434
Samuel, early settler, 161
William, early settler, 161, 375

Income Taxes, New London County, 236
Indian School (missionary), 55
Inland City, poem by E. C. Stedman, 123
Isham, Jirah, bank officer, 328, 437
Joseph, trustee Bacon Acedemy, 254
Ralph, benefactor Bacon Academy, 182

Jackson Andrew, present at dedication Uncas Monument, 77, 86
James II. and Conn. Charter, 9
Jay, John, visitor at Lebanon, 192, 533
"Jefferson" name for North Stonington, 206
Jefferson, Thomas, Declaration of Independence, 197; policy of, 77; visitor at Lebanon, 192, 533
Jennings, Charles B., Supt. of New London Schools, 260
"Jeremiah's Farm," original name of Colchester, 177
Jerome Family of Montville, 205
Jewett City, in Griswold, 214
Dr. David H., early physician, 368, 386
Eleazer, first settler, 185
Rev. David., pastor, 290
Jewish Settlers, in Colchester and Montville, 218
Johnson, Charles, banker, 433
Dr. Samuel, physician, 385
Home, in famous house, 543
John M., banker, 444
Joseph, Mohegan, educated in Wheelock's School, 57
Oliver L., banker, 436
Rev. James Gibson, pastor, 298
William, visit of Nathan Hale at house of, 61
Johnston, James P,. banker, 448
Jones, Charles E., benefactor Bacon Academy, 255
John Paul, Capt. Charter Bulkeley served with, 257
Josiah, son of Owaneco, 126
Judd, Rev. Bethel, rector, 307
Judges of Probate, when elected, 324
Judson, Rev. Ephraim, pastor, 295
Justices of Peace, number of, 325

Keefe, Arthur, lawyer, 430
Keep, Prof. Robert Porter, principal Norwich Free Academy, 252
Keith, Rev. John, visited New London, 271
Kelley, Oliver Hudson, Grange organizer, 521
Kellogg, Nathaniel, settler, Colchester, 181
Samuel, bank officer, 431
Kelly, Rev. Father, pastor, 319
Kerredge, Rev. Philip M., pastor, 308
Kibby, Epaphras, traveling preacher, 310
King George, statue at New London, 60
Jeremiah, physician, 383
Rev. Walter, pastor, 36, 295
King Philip's War, 28, 29
Kingsbury, Dr. Obadiah, physician, 378
Kingsley, Dr. Oliver, physician, 399
Family, Franklin, 205
Kinne, H. C., publisher, 414
Kinney, Newcomb, bank officer, 35, 432
Kirkland, Rev. Daniel, pastor, 290
Kitemaug, on Thames river, 215
Klinck, Charles H., banker, 428
Knight, Dr. Earl, early physician, 385
Madame Sarah, resident of New London and Norwich, 13, 164
Knight's, Madame Sarah, Journal, 13, 28
Knights of King Arthur, institution of, 276
Knowlton, Col., on Washington's staff, 61
Knox, General, visitor at Lebanon, 192, 533

LaFayette, house visited by, 535
Marquis de, visitor at Lebanon, 71, 192, 533
Street (once "Mill-lane"), 573
Lake, Hon. Everett J., Governor, 270
Mrs., sister of Mrs. Winthrop, 203
Lalor, Rev. P. P., R. C. pastor, 318
Lamb, Isaac, settler, 200
Martha, author, 203
"Landing," part of Norwich, 573
Lanman, Charles J., famous resident Norwich, 171
James, famous resident Norwich, 171
James, Judge, 327
"Lantern Hill," part of North Stonington, 214
Larrabee, Greenfield, early settler, 204
Latham, C., in battle of Groton Heights, 67
Capt. Edward, in battle of Groton Heights, 67
Cary, early settler, 102
Daniel, banker, 448
Daniel D., banker, 448
John R., banker, 430
William, in battle of Groton Heights, 65
Lathrop, Arthur D., banker, 444
Charles, potter, 546
Daniel, famous resident, 171, 172
Dr. Daniel, eminent resident, 171; gift to Norwich School, 35, 171; gift to Yale, 54
Dr. Joshua, early resident Norwich, 172
Elijah, smallpox patient, 368
Elisha, manager of lottery, 209
Harriet, wife of Rev. Mr. Winslow, missionary, 294
John, bank officer, 431
Joshua, bank officer, 426
Samuel, early settler, 102

Samuel, early settler, 162
Lauzun, Marquis of, at Lebanon, 196
Law, Richard, famous son, judge, 327
Lawrence, Leonard C., banker, 428
Lawyers—Augustus Brandagee, Frank B. Brandagee, Jeremiah G. Brainard, William E. Brainard, Allen H. Brown, Arthur M. Brown, Frank T. Brown, Franklin H. Brown, Lucius Brown, Daniel Chadwick, Joshua Coit, William B. Coit, Erastus S. Day, Jeremiah A. Desmond, Joseph T. Fanning, Lafayette S. Foster, Richard P. Freeman, Calvin Goddard, George W. Goddard, Gardiner Greene, Matthew Griswold, Roger Griswold, Jeremiah Halsey, Edwin W. Higgins, S. T. Holbrook, James A. Hover, Hadlai Hull, Benjamin Huntington, Samuel Huntington, Elisha Hyde, Jirah Isham, James Lanman, Richard Law, Solomon Lucas, Bryan F. Mahan, Charles J. McCurdy, Walter C. Noyes, John D. Park, Elvin Perkins, William H. Potter, George Pratt, Samuel O. Prentice, George B. Ripley, Gurdon Saltonstall, William H. Shields, Henry H. Starkweather, James Stedman, Elisha Sterling, Abel P. Tanner, John M. Thayer, Seneca S. Thresher, Jonathan Trumbull, John T. Waite, Henry M. Waite, Marvin Waite, Morrison R. Waite, Charles B. Waller, Thomas M. Waller, Joseph Williams. (For other names see lists on pp. 326, 340, 341).
Learned, Ebenezer, bank officer, 32, 39, 437
Edward, banker, 437
Francis C., banker, 437
Horace C., bank officer, 437
Joshua C., banker, 437
Walter, corporator, New London Vocational School, 260, 437
Leavens, Francis J., bank officer, 450; visit of Lincoln to Norwich, 158
Lebanon Crank (Columbia), 288; District Probate Court, 325; Proprietors—Mason, Stanton, Brewster, Birchard, 187; in Revolutionary War, 190; poem delivered at Lebanon, 195; six governors of Connecticut and other facts, 193; statistics, 189; town of, 1, 54, 187, 201
Ledyard, Capt. Youngs, 68
Col. William, slain at battle of Groton Heights, 2, 65, 67, 72, 75, 76, 201
Description of, 233
District Probate Court, 325
Early Settlers, 200
Ebenezer, in battle of Groton Heights, 69, 74
Fannie, aid to wounded, Groton Heights, 74
John, famous traveler, 87
Settlement of town, 200
Lee, Capt. Ezra, of Revolutionary fame, 390
Dr. James, physician, 372, 391
Dr. Joseph Woodbridge, physician, 392
Dr. Samuel H. P., physician, 369, 375, 390
Gen. Charles, tried by court-martial, 87
Jesse, early preacher, 271, 309
Rev. J. Beveredge, pastor, 298
Leffingwell, Capt. Christopher, house of, 535
Col. Christopher, owner of pottery, 535, 546
Lieut. Thomas, settler, 161
Thomas, early settler, 127
William, famous in Norwich, 534
Lester, Charles E., bank officer, 431
Walter, bank director, 431
Walter F., officer Fire Insurance Co., 457
Lethrop, Dr. Gurdon, physician, 391
Lexington, and Nathan Hale, 60
Library, Bill Memorial, Groton, 213
Otis, Norwich, 216
Peck, part of Norwich Free Academy, 250
Lincoln, President, in Norwich, 158
Lippitt, Costello, bank officer, 431, 433, 436
Lisbon, early settlement, 202, 205, 228; deed of "Newent," 201
Livingston, Madam, daughter of Gov. Winthrop, 27
Logan, Rev. William, R. C. pastor, 319
Longdon, Andrew, early settler, 102
Long Point, (Stonington), 207
"Looking Back at Boyhood" (Ik Marvel), 82
Loomis, Jonathan, physician, 368
Samuel, early settler, 178
Lord's Cove, 212
Lord, Dr. Daniel, physician, 398
Dr. Elisha, physician, signer of memorial, 381
Dr. Robert McCurdy, physician, 397
Dr. William, physician, 398
Family, near Lord's Bridge, 206
John, afterward president of Dartmouth, 36
Rev. Benjamin, pastor, 58, 126
Rev. Benjamin, pastor, 290
Rev. Hezekiah, pastor, 287
Lottery, Stonington, 208; Groton Monument, 275
Lowell, Sherman J., 527
Lucas, Solomon, eminent lawyer, 342
Lusk, Dr. William Thompson, famous son of Norwich, 89
Luze, John and Robert, signers of Lyme deed, 203
Lyme, Town of, 1, 8, 202; District Probate Court, 325; "Mother of Lawyers," 204; Regis, 1
Lynch, John G., Journalist, 408, 422

McCurdy, Charles Johnson, lawyer, 330
McEwen, Rev. Abel, pastor, 294
McGinley, John, reporter, 401
McGuigan, Clara M. H., principal Mystic Oral School, 265
McNally, Rev. Charles R., pastor, 301
Machinery in New London, 219
Mahan, Bryan Francis, lawyer, congressman, 339
Hon. B. F., prominent citizen, mayor, 260
Main, Ezekiel, settler, 207
Mallory, Charles, banker, 439
Mann, Horace, eminent educator, 58
Manning, Diah, drum major, Washington's body-guard, 164
Dr. Luther, physician, 384
Dr. Mason, physician, 398
Francis M., banker, 439

Mason, physician, 375
William D., proprietor Norwich Bulletin, 415, 420
Mansfield, Dorcas, first depositor Norwich Savings Society, 433
Elisha Hyde, silversmith, 566
Richard, resident of New London, 93
Manufactures in New London County—Ashland, 502; Aspinook, 502; Babcock Printing Press Company, 500, 501; Brainerd & Armstrong, 493, 494, 495; T. P. Cleary, 500; Falls Company, 502; Makane Company, 499; J. B. Martin Company, 502; New London Ship and Engine Company, 497, 498; Palmer Bros., 502; W. R. Perry Ice Corporation, 500; Ponemah Mills, 502; 505; Shetucket Company, 502; Thames Tow Boat Company, 495; Totoket Mills, 502; U. S. Finishing Company, 502; D. Whiton Company, 496
Manufacturing concerns of New London County—Among the largest are:
Admore Woolen Mills Co., Airlee Mills, American Thermos Bottle Co., American Thread Co., American Velvet Co., Ashland Cotton Co., Aspinook Co., Auto Radiator & Lamp Co., Babcock Printing Press M'f'g Co., Baltic Mills, Blissville Mills, Brainerd & Armstrong, Climax Tube Co., Connecticut Power Co., H. F. & A. J. Dawley, Eastern Connecticut Power Co., Electric Boat Co., Federal Paper Board Co., General Machine and Electric Co., Glengarry Mills, Glen Woolen Mills, Groton Iron Works, Hallville Mills, J. B. Martin Co., Jewett City Textile Novelty Co., Millstone Granite Quarries, Mystic Lace Mills Co., Mystic Woolen Co., N. L. Ship & Engine Co., Norwich Belt M'f'g Co., Norwich Woolen Co., Packer M'f'g Co., Paluser Bros., Pequot Mills, Ponemah Mills, Richmond Radiator Co., Robertson Co., Saxton Woolen Co., Shetucket Worsted Mills, Slater Mills, Standard Brass & Copper Tube Co., Submarine Boat Co., Thames River Specialties Co., Thames Tow Boat Co., Totoket M'f'g Co., Ulmer Leather Co., Uncasville M'f'g Co., United States Finishing Co., D. Whiton Machine Co., Winchester Woolen Co., Yantic Mills, 220
Manwaring, Dr. R. A., early physician, 375, 395
Marie Antoinette, and French Revolution, 146
Marsh, Dr. Jonathan, physician, 380
Marshall, Dr. Benjamin Tinker, president Connecticut College, 243
Marvin, Dr. Elihu, hospital for inoculation, 368, 372
Dr. Elihu, physician, 378
Renald, signer of deeds, 203
Mason, Capt. John, life of, 131, 132, 133, 161
Capt. John, military leader, 4, 5, 6, 7, 8, 28, 129
Capt. Samuel, Colchester, 177
John, (Stonington), and the Indians, 205
Samuel, early settler, 207
Mason's Island, 235
Masonic Temple Corporation, Norwich, 514
Masons in New London County—Asylum, No. 57, Stonington; Bay View, No. 120, Niantic; Brainard, No. 102, New London; Charity and Relief, No. 75, Mystic; Oxoboxo, No. 116, Montville; Pawcatuck, No. 90, Pawcatuck; Pythagoras, No. 45, Old Lyme; Somerset, No. 34, Norwich; St. James, No. 23, Norwich; Union, No. 31, New London; Wooster, No. 10, Colchester, 587
Massachusetts (claims Pequot), 99
Massapeag, pest house at, 146
Mather, Dr. Eleazer, physician, 398
Dr. Samuel, physician, 398
John P. C., trustee Bulkeley School, 257
Matthews, A. S., bank officer, 441
"May Day," picture by W. L. Metcalf, 212
"Mayflower Compact," of 1619, 33
Maynard, William, early settler, 200
Mayors of New London, 238
Mayors of Norwich, 237
Medicine, in early days, 363
Meech, Stephen B., cashier, 435
Meeting Houses and Burying Grounds (Norwich), 165
Memorial petition for incorporation of physicians of State, 373
Mercer, Archibald, physician, 437
Merriman, Rev. Daniel, pastor, 296
Metcalf, W. L., artist, 212
Methodism in New London County—Beginnings of; under Jesse Lee, 309; Bethel (Griswold), 312; East Main Street, Methodist, 311; First Church in New London, 310; First Church in Norwichtown, 311; First Methodist Church in New England, 310; Gales Ferry, 312; New London, 313; Niantic, 313; Old Mystic, 312; Uncasville, 312
Miantonomoh and Uncas, 140
Miantonomoh, leader of Narragansetts, 5, 7, 8
Mifflin, Gen., British officer at Groton Heights, 71
Millard, Rev. Nelson, pastor, 296
Miller, Jeremiah, New London settler, 388
"Millstone" Quarry, at Waterford, 213
Miner, Dr. John Owen, physician, 398
Dr. Orrin E., physician, 398
Dr. Reuben L., physician, 399
Dr. Thomas, physician, 399
Dr. William W., physician, 397
Ephraim, settler, 207
Hon. Charles, (letter on 200th Anniversary of Norwich), 141, 142
Joseph, settler, 207
Sidney H., bank officer, 439
Thomas, settler, physician, 206, 375
Minnesota, 33,000 tons, built at New London, 81
Minor, Manasseh, diary of, 366
Nathaniel, settler, 208
Thomas, diary of, 369
Mitchell, author, see below, 39
Donald G., "Ik Marvel," 82, 91, 172, 547
John, bank officer, 433, 436
Mrs. E. V., and Connecticut College, 264

Rev. Alfred, pastor, 295
Model Schools for Normal Courses, 50
Moffatt, Dr. Thomas, physician, 389
"Moheagan," early name for Norwich, 570
Mohegan Hill, Indian reservation, 215
Mohegans, admitted to citizenship, 105
Mohegans, Indians near Norwich, 5, 6, 7
"Mohegin," another form of "Mohegan," 129
Montgomery, Major, in battle of Groton Heights, 65, 66, 67, 72, 75
Montville, town of, 1, 205, 232; District Probate Court, 325
Monuments, Cap. John Mason, at Norwich, 215; Groton landmark, 213; Miantonomoh, at Norwich, 215; Soldiers and Sailors, New London, 214; Uncas, at Norwich, 215
Moore, Capt. N., killed at Groton Heights, 68
"Moor's Charity School" (Dartmouth), q.v., 197, 288
Morgan, Dr. Frederick C., physician, 386
Dr. James, physician, 395
James, early settler, 200
William, early settler, 207
Morris, Robert, and Bank of North America, 423
Morrison, Dr. Norman, physician, 364
Morrow, Rev. Cornelius W., pastor, 296
Morton, William, early settler, 102
Moses, Paul, slayer of Moses Clark, Indian, 56
Moss, A. S., organizer of Fredonia Grange, 523
Mott, Col. Samuel, entertained Washington, 534
Mowry, James D., banker, 434; shareholder Norwich Bulletin, 416
Mudge, Jarvis, settler, 102
Mullen, Rev. Father, pastor, 319
Mumford, Abigail, wife of Samuel Seabury, 305
Murdock, J. Bates, 36
Murray, John, universalist preacher, 321
Music Vale Seminary, 205
Music Vale Seminary, in Salem, 58
Muster roll, Spanish-American War service, 586
Mystic, partly in Groton, 207; partly in Stonington, 2, 231; Fort, 7
Oral School for the Deaf, 265
River, 2, 213
Valley Institute, 268

Nameaug (name of New London), 182
"Nameaugs" (survivors of Pequot tribe), 105
Naming of streets, city of Norwich, 578
Narragansett, Indian tribes, 4, 7, 8
Natal Day in New London, "Caulkins' History," 98
National Bank System, beginning of, 424
Naval Base, New London, 211
Naval Expedition, first sent out by Continental Congress, 86
Nehantic, name for "Niantic," 5
Nelson, Dr. A. W., physician, 395
Nevins, Capt., resident, Norwich, 142
Newcomb, Frederick S., trustee Vocational School, 260
"New Connecticut" of Vermont, Pennsylvania and Ohio, 197
Newent, now Lisbon, 201
New London—Arnold's attack on, 107; boundaries of, 99; Bride Brook, 101; burning of, 63; chronology for forty years, 238; City National Bank, 428; controversy with Lyme, 100; county (as first constituted), 271; County Medical Society, 373; Decatur at, 115; development later days, 107; District, 324; early enterprise, 4, 116; early schools, 37; early settlers, 102; estate of Gov. Winthrop, 104; ferry, 19; fire department, 489; founding of, 18; historic houses of, 120; historic landmarks and memorials, 120; in Revolution, 106; Mad. Knight's Journal, 18; mayors, 238, 243; "Nameaug," 183; natal day, 98; patent of, 102; poem, "The Old Mill," 121; population of, 106; press at, 117; Ship & Engine Co., 497; town of New London County, 2, 97, 122, 229; Uncas in conflict with settlers of, 105; Vocational High School, 259; whale fisheries of, 109; will of May Harris, 103
New Orleans, 77
Newspapers (early press of New London), 117, 118, 119, 120
(Norwich), 155, 156
Niantic, town of, 2, 233; "Nahantic," early name, 100
Lake, 233
River, 2
Nichols, Francis, bank officer, 433
Noank, village in Groton, 2, 213
Normal Schools in Connecticut, 51
"Norredge" (Norwich), a legal township, 162, 280
North, Dr. Elisha, physician, 369, 375, 392
Dr. John, professor of physics, 387
Northam, Samuel, settler of Colchester, 177
North Groton, now Ledyard, 201
Northrop, Rev. M., 250th anniversary sermon, Norwich, 30
"North Society" of Stonington, now North Stonington, 206
North Stonington, 1, 205; probate court at, 325;
Norton, H. B. and T. P., shareholders Bulletin, 416, 436
Norwich—Boundaries of, 124; deed of, 124; description of, by H. W. Beecher, 172, 175; District Probate Court, 325; early commerce, 133; early industries described by Miss Caulkins, 148, 149, 150, 167, 168; early occupations, 146, 147; early physicians, 156, 157, 158; early settlement, 216, 217; early settlers, 162; Female Seminary, 37; Fire Department, 375; founders, 160; 161; Free Academy, 248, 253; historic homes, 570; in Civil War, 139; in Revolutionary days, 134, 135, 136, 137; "Jubilee," 39; "Landing,"28; largest town of New London County, 18, 40, 79; mayors, 237; original proprietors, 126, 127; "Rose of New England," 229, 570; "Texts," 40, 44; town of New London County, 1, 7, 8, 28, 29; town plot, 128
Norwich-Worcester Railroad, 81
Notaries Public, 325

Nott, Rev. Dr., pastor, 58
Rev. Samuel, remarkable service of, 184
Noyes, Charles D., bank officer, 433
Dr. James, physician, 398
Dr. John, physician, 399
Dr. Richard, physician, 399
Franklin B., banker, 441
George W., banker, 439, 440, 445
Henry B., bank officer, 440
Henry B., Jr., bank officer, 440, 445
Ira C., bank officer, 445
James, early settler, 207
Judge Walter C., eminent resident of Lyme, 212
Rev. James, pastor, 282
Rev. Moses, pastor, 282
Rev. Moses, brother of Rev. James, 212, 284
Richard, physician, 375
Samuel, goldsmith, 557
Walter C., lawyer, 337
William, bank officer, 430

Occum, Samson, Indian preacher, 54, 89
Occum, village named for Samson Occum, 214
Ocean Beach, 229
Ockford, Charles L., Fire Chief, 490
Odd Fellows (Independent Order)—Lodges: Crystal, Lyme; Fairview, Groton; Mohegan and Pequot, New London; Niantic, Niantic; Reliance, Jewett City; Shetucket, Norwich; Stonington, Mystic; Uncas, Norwich, 516
Old Lyme, District Probate Court, 325; Old Lyme Street Art Gallery, 212; town of New London County, 1, 212
Old Paths, later roadways, 537
Old Signs, 540
"Old Torrent,' fire engine, 475
Olmstead, Dr. John, early physician, 376
Dr. John, early resident, 161
Onkos (Uncas), friend of settlers, Mohegan chief, 124
"Ordinary" (taverns), 538
Organizations—Connecticut Veterans of Foreign Wars of the United States, Daughters of the American Revolution, Military Order of Foreign Wars; Naval and Military Order of Spanish American War, Society of the Cincinnati, Society of the Colonial Wars, Society of War of 1812, Sons of the American Revolution, 594
Osgood, Charles, bank officer, 434
Charles Henry, bank officer, 433
Dr. Erastus, physician, 384
Henry Hugh, banker, 415, 436, 459
William C., bank officer, 450
Otis, Asa, benefactor of Bacon Academy, 255, 429
Mr. Asa, donor of over a million dollars to Foreign Missions, 294
Owaneco (Sachem), 124; and Colchester, 177, 187, 201
Owen, John ("Master Owen"), early teacher, 38

Pachaug, village in Voluntown, 209
Paddock, Dr. L. S., physician, 395
Palmer, Benjamin, settler, 207
Dr. George E., physician, 397
Elijah, early settler, 209
family (Montville), 205
Frank L., shareholder New London "Day," 404
Frank L., banker, 437
Gershom, early settler, 207
Henry R., journalist, 234
Moses, early settler, 207
Mrs. Rebecca, early settler, 207
Rev. William S., pastor, 296
Walter, early settler, Stonington, 206
Palmes, Dr. Guy, physician, 388
Park, John D., lawyer, Supreme Court judge, 326, 333
Mohegan, Norwich, 215
Robert, early settler, 200, 206
Robert ("Meeting House Hill"), 279
William, early settler, 207
Parker, Ebenezer F., president fire insurance company, 466
William, signer of deed to Lyme, 203
Parsons, Dr. Ezekial W., physician, 386
Rev. Jonathan, pastor, 284
Partridge, Mary, one of founders of Connecticut College, 264
Patent of New London, 102, 103
Patrons of Husbandry—List of Granges, 521-528
Paukataug River (Madame Knight's Journal), 17, 214
Pawcatuck River, 2, 5, 207
Peabody, Dr. Joseph, physician, 386
Pease, John, early settler, 161
Peck, Capt. Bela, Revolutionary soldier, 142, 432
Peckham, Elder, connected with first church, 300
Pendleton, M. A., grandson of first settler, 441
Moses, bank officer, 441
Pentz, M. A., author of Article on Architecture, 235
"Pequod" River, now Thames, 99
Pequot, early name for New London, 1, 8, 750
Pequot Hill, 5
Pequot Indians, defeated and scattered, 200
Pequot plantation of John Winthrop, the younger, 98
Pequot War, fully described, 3, 4, 5, 6, 7, 8
Perkins, Capt. Jabez, settler, 201
Col. George L., centenarian, 172
Dr. Alfred E., gift to Yale College, 54
Dr. Austin F., physician, 399
Dr. Joseph, physician, 377
Elias, bank officer, 430
Elvin, lawyer, 326
F. A., bank director, 431
Francis A., bank officer, 432
George L., bank officer, 432
Joseph, settler, 201
Joseph, bank officer, 426
Joshua Newton, owner of famous house, Norwich, 578
Maj. Joseph, early resident, Norwich, 172
N. Shaw, trustee, Bulkeley School, 257
Nathaniel I., incorporator Savings Bank, 437
Nathaniel S., physician, 375, 394
Perry, Christopher, father of Oliver and Matthew, 89

Fred S., and death of "Day" manager, 406
James N., publisher, 415, 419
Oliver and Matthew, naval heroes, 85
Peters, Major Nathan, lawyer, 326
Thomas, associate of John Winthrop, Jr., 99, 100, 278
Phelps, Charles H., bank officer, 431
Dr. Charles, physician, 397
Rev. Benjamin C., pastor, 312
Phillips, George, bank officer, 426
Physicians who came with first immigrants, 363
Pierce, Moses, founder Aspinook Co., 543
Pierpont, Rev. James, host of Mme. Sarah Knight, 27
Pierson, Rev. Abraham, parsonage of, 276
Pilgrim, first settlers, 3
Pinehurst, historic mansion, 569
Pitkin, William, founder, Colchester, 177
Plant, Morton F., remarkable estate of, 213
Platt, Charles B., partner Norwich Bulletin, 416
Policy Holders, early, 461
Pollard, William J. H., banker, 441
Pond, Harold G., bank officer, 439
Rev. Alvan, pastor, 296
Ponemah Mills, full account of, 502-505
Population, 220, 222
Population of New London County, 1860, 81
Poquetanuck, in Preston, 214
Poquonock River, 2
Porteous, John, bank officer, 433
Porter, Dr. Ezekiel, physician, 364
Dr. I. G., early physician, 375, 396
Epaphras, bank director, 431
Porter's Rocks, 5
Post, John, early settler, 127, 162
Samuel, 556
Thomas, early settler, 162
William, early settler, 102
Potter, Dr. Henry, physician, 397
Rev. James, pastor, 311
William H., lawyer, 335
Potteries in New London County, 544
Powell, Elizabeth, married Rev. Samuel Seabury, 305
Pratt, George, lawyer, 334
Rev. Dr. Llewellyn, historic address by, at Academy exercises, 128; pastor Broadway Church, 248, 296
William, signer of deed to Lyme, 203
Prentice, A. W., owner of shares, Bulletin, 416, 468
Judge Samuel O., address, 250th anniversary; Chief Justice Supreme Court from New London County, addenda, 216
Prentis, John, house of, 426
Prentiss, Dr. Amos, Jr., early physician, 398
Dr. Amos, Sr., early physician, 398
Presidents whose ancestors came from New London County—Cleveland, Fillmore, Garfield, Grant, Harding, Hayes, 85
Prest, George B., bank officer, 442
Preston, town of, 1, 8, 204, 228
Preston City, part of Preston, 214
Proprietors, Norwich, 127
Public buildings, Norwich, 166
Pullen, Frank H., editor Norwich "Record," 422
Punderson, Rev. Ebenezer, pastor, 306
Puritan, 2
Putnam, Gen., visits Lebanon, 533

Quakers (Friends) in New London County, 208
Quincy, President of Harvard, quoted, 292
Quinn, Rev. James, R. C. pastor, 320
Quinnebaug River, 2

Ramsdell, Albert N., banker, 430
Ranger, Henry, artist, 204
Rawson, Dr. Thomas H., physician, 392
Raymond, Sherwood, banker, 431
Read, Josiah, early settler, 162
Record, Norwich Evening, 422
Red Cross, New London County, 529-531
"Red Jackets," early fire fighters, Norwich, 475
Reed, F. Dana, connected with "Day," 406
Reeves, William H., bank officer, 443
Reid, Capt. Samuel Chester, naval hero, 92
"Relief" law, exempting Church of England members, 290
Remington, Rev. B. D., Baptist clergyman, 302
Representatives from New London County, 239
Reynolds, John, early settler, 162
John, early settler, 207
Rhodes, James, manager of lottery, 209
Richards, Capt. Peter, in battle of Groton Heights, 72
Guy, early officer Union Bank, 426
Peter, incorporator Savings Bank, 437
Richardson, Amos, early settler, 207
Ricketson, Frank B., corporation official, 433
Ricketts, Rev. Charles H., pastor, 297
Riley, Thomas, Fire Chief, 490
Ripley, Alice Adams, fiancée, Nathan Hale, 62
Dr. Dwight, resident, Norwich, 172
Dwight, bank officer, 432
George Burbank, lawyer, 327
George Coit, lawyer, 336
James L., bank officer, 431
Risley, Sidney, potter, 550
Roath, Benjamin F., physician, 383
Roswell Walstem, silversmith, 567
Roberts, George, Methodist preacher, 310
Robertson family, Montville, 205
Robinson, Dr. Horatio, physician, Groton, 398
Dr. William, early physician, Groton, 397
Faith, wife of Governor Trumbull, 533
John, early settler, New London, 102
Thomas, of Norwich Female Academy, 37
Rochambeau, Count, visits Lebanon, 533
Rock Nook Home, historic spot in Norwich, 543
Rockwell, Charles W., eminent citizen, Norwich incorporator, Norwich Savings Society, 172, 432
Gen. Alfred P., eminent citizen, 172
Rockwell's Tower, on "Jail Hill," Norwich, 37
"Rogerenes," account of beliefs, 272, 284
Rogers Brothers, officers of "Savannah," 81
Rogers, Dr. George, physician, 386
Dr. James, physician, 395

Dr. Jeremiah, physician, 368
Dr. John D., physician, 399
Dr. Theophilus, signer Medical Memorial, 374, 377, 378
Dr. Theophilus, Jr., physician, 378
Moses, commander of "Savannah," 116
Mrs. Elisha E., historian, 375
Samuel, 27
Stevens, sailing master of "Savannah," 116
Rolfe, William H., original member of "Day," 402
Roman Catholic Churches—Immaculate Conception (Baltic), Rev. William T. O'Brien, pastor; Our Lady of Perpetual Help, Rev. Paul Kosczyk; Our Lady of the Rosary (Jewett City), Rev. John McCabe, pastor; Sacred Heart (Groton), Rev. William Fox, pastor; Sacred Heart (Norwichtown), Rev. C. W. Brennan, pastor; Sacred Heart (Taftville), Rev. W. O. Bellerose, pastor; parochial school; St. Andrew's (Colchester), Rev. Philip J. Morney, pastor; St. Joseph's (New London), Rev. William G. Fitzsimmons, pastor; St. Joseph's (Norwich), Rev. Ignatius Maciejewski, pastor; St. Joseph's (Occum), Rev. Frederick Dessureault, pastor; St. Mary's (Norwich), Rev. W. A. Keefe, pastor; parochial school; St. Mary's Star of the Sea (New London), Rev. Timothy M. Crowley, pastor; St. Mary's (Stonington), Rev. James E. O'Brien, pastor; St. Patrick's (Mystic), Rev. W. J. Fitzgerald, pastor; St. Patrick's (Norwich), Rev. M. H. May, pastor; parochial school, 317, 321
Roosevelt, Mrs. Theodore, descended from Gen. Daniel Tyler, 170
"Rose of New England" (Norwich), 215
Rosseter, Rev. Ebenezer, pastor, 282
Rousseau, Jean Jacques, "Contrat Social" of, 199
Rowe, William H., bank cashier, 430
Royce, Jonathan, early resident, 162
Ruskin, quotation from, 32
Russell, Rev. Ebenezer, North Society, 282

Sabin, Dr. John, physician, 377
Sachems Plain, Norwich, Indian battle ground, 7
Saco, flight of Pequots to, 6
Safford, John, settler (Newent), Lisbon, 201
Salem, town of, 1, 58, 204, 205, 232
Salem District probate courts, 325
Saltonstall, Dr. Winthrop, physician, 392
Gurdon, Chief Justice, 326
Nathaniel, banker, 437
Rev. Gurdon, pastor, 19, 27, 277, 286
Sanford, Zachariah, signer of deed to Lyme, 203
Sassacus, leader of Pequot Indians, 5
Savannah, first steamship to cross Atlantic, 84; voyage described, 116
Saxton, L. Henry, bank officer, 431
Say and Seal, Lord, leader Saybrook Colony, 203, 283
Saybrook Fort, 4, 128, 203
"Saybrook Platform," religious beliefs, 273
Sayles, Sabin N., shareholder Bulletin, 416
homas D., bank officer, 436
Scarborough, Mr., early schoolmaster, 36
"School Fund," from sale of "Western Reserve," 33
School History, early, 33
Schools of Norwich, 34
Scott, Capt., in battle of Groton Heights, 70
Dr. John, physician, 385
Ella, principal Mystic Oral School, 269
Scouts, Boy and Girl, part of general religious work, 276
"Seabrook," Mme. Knight's Journal, 19
Seabury, Bishop Samuel, first American bishop, 187
Charles, rector, 307
Inscription on gravestone, 187
John, father of Samuel, 305
Samuel, born July 8, 1706, 305, 391
Samuel, Jr., consecration in Aberdeen, 307
Samuel, Jr., physician, 391
Searls, John, settler, 207
Selden, Col. Richard, resident of Lyme, 330
Maria, wife of Judge Henry M. Waite, 330
Senators, State, from New London County, 237
"Separatism" in the County, 272, 273
"Sessions House" of First Church, New London, 294
Seymour, Capt. William, in battle of Groton Heights, 73
Shapley, Capt. Adam, battle of Groton Heights, 66, 71, 72, 73, 390
Shaw, Capt. Nathaniel, bearer of message, 70
Mansion, Acadian Builders, 215
Mansion, New London, 85
Thomas, settler, 207
Sheffield, L. T., bank officer, 430
W. Kyle, bank officer, 428
Shephard, C. I., part owner "Day," 406
Julius T., Jr., news editor "Day," 406
Shetucket River, 2, 7
Shields, Judge William H., lawyer, 356
Shipman, Judge Nathaniel, eminent son of Norwich, 225; incorporator Norwich Savings Society, 432
Nathaniel, silversmith, 564
Shipping of New London, statistics of, 114
Sholes, Alonzo W., Fire Chief, 490
Showtucket (Shetucket River), 201
Sigourney, Lydia H., famous poetess, 92, 144; poem at opening of Norwich Free Academy, 249
Silk Industry of county, 218
Silversmiths of New London County, 552
Simmons, Abel H., banker, 445
Sistare, Charles C., bank cashier, 428
Ebenezer, bank cashier, 428
Joseph, banker, 437
Sizer, Dr. Abel T., physician, 397
Skinner, Dr. Thomas, early physician, 386
Ichabod Lord, trustee Bacon Academy, 254
John, settler, Colchester, 178
Slater, John Fox, shareholder Bulletin, 94, 416
Memorial Hall, gift of William A. Slater, 215, 253
William A., benefactor Norwich Free Academy, 215, 253
Smallpox, epidemics of, 146

Smith, Dr. John, physician, 398
Dr. John L., physician, 396, 399
Dr. Marvin, physician, 399
Dr. Rufus, physician, 384
Dr. Seth, physician, 396
Dr. Vine, physician, 384
Francis Hopkinson, 93
George B., publisher, 413
J. Hunt, bank officer, 431
Oliver, settler, 207
Prof. Elbridge, first principal Norwich Free Academy, 251
Rev. C. Harley, pastor, 313
Rev. Nehemiah, early resident, 162
Richard, signer of deed to Lyme, 203
Sons of American Revolution, 194
"Southertown" (Stonington,) 281
"Southerntown" (Mystic), 207
Spalding, Asa, eminent lawyer, 326
Dr. Asa, physician, 398
Dr. Rufus, Norwich, 326
Judge Luther, Norwich, 326
Spanish War Records, from Conn. Roster, 582
Spaulding, Daniel B., bank president, 444
Spicer, Peter, early settler, 200
Sprague, town of, 1, 206, 228
Stage Coach and Tavern Days, 536
Stanford, Mrs. Leland, descendant of Norwich ancestors, 93
Stanners, John, Fire Chief, 490
Joseph A., bank officer, 428
Stanton, Dr. John G., 260
Howard L., Fire Chief, 481
John, settler, 207
Joseph, settler, 207
Lewis E., benefactor Bacon Academy, 255
Stiles, bank officer, 441
Thomas, settler, 206, 207
"Star Papers," Henry Ward Beecher, 172
Starkweather, Henry Howard, congressman, 332, 420
Starr, Jonathan, bank president, 427
Statistics, manufacturing, 493, 505
Staunton, Lieut. Enoch, in battle of Groton Heights, 68
Stearns, Raymond, bank officer, 439
Stebbins, John, early settler, 102
Stedman, Edmund Clarence, eminent author, 92, 123
James, lawyer, 327
Sterling, Gen. Elisha, lawyer, 326
Sterry, Consider, early teacher, 35
Robert, early settler, 207
Stevens, Henry, early settler, 207
Stewart, William, early bank officer, 426
Stinson, Jesse B., officer, Groton Savings Bank, 445
Stockholders, National Whaling Bank, 438
Stockman, Charles I., bank incorporator, 437
Stoddard, Dr. Benjamin F., early physician, 398
Ralph, early settler, 200
Stoddard's Wharf, Ledyard, 214
Stonington—Boundaries of, 207; danger from King Philip, 207; District Probate Court, 207; early settlement, names of settlers, 206, 231; house lot holders, 207; in Revolution, 207; largest town of New London County in 1800, 77; local historian, Richard Wheeler, 207; Long Point settlement, 207; lottery for church, 208; Mme. Knight's Journal, 18, 27; mark where three States meet, 213; town of New London County, 1, 8
Storey, Arthur E., bank officer, 431
Storrs, Dr. Melanchthon, physician, 386
Story, Isaac, bank officer, 432
Strahan, Rev. P. P., pastor, 320
Strong, David O., bank cashier, 434
George C., bank president, 448
Henry, lawyer, 329; president Norwich Savings Society, 433
Mary (Huntington), mother of Henry Strong, 329
Rev. Dr., pastor at Norwichtown, 58, 144, 145, 272, 294, 533
Rev. Joseph, pastor First Church, Norwichtown, 329
Sturdy, George A., connected with "Day," 408
Submarine Base, 589
Sullivan, Gen., visits Lebanon, 533
Superior Court at New London, 324
Support of Public Schools, 44
Supreme Court at New London, 324
Surrenderers, Indians settled in Lisbon, 201
Swift, Hon. Zephamiah, trustee Bacon Academy, 254
Sykes, Rev. Dorson Ebenezer, publisher, 412

Taft, Cyril, founder Ponemah Mills Co., 502
E. P., and the Ponemah Mills Co., 502
Taftville (named for E. P. Taft), 502
Taintor, Charles N., benefactor Bacon Academy, 255
Judah Lord, benefactor Bacon Academy, 255
Michael, early settler, 177
Talbot, Rev. John, preached at New London, 271
Talcott, John, coach driver, 181
Tanner, Abel P., lawyer, New London, 340; speech at rededication of New London County Court House, 352
Taverns, list of, 539
Taverns, Norwich, 168
Taylor, Rev. Edward, letter to Miss Fitch, 11
Rev. John Phelps, Second Church, New London, 298
Terry, Eli, clock maker, 558
Thames River, 2, 211, 212
Thames Towboat Company, 495
Thatcher, Anthony, bank cashier, 430
Thayer, John M., attorney, 445
Rev. John, Roman Catholic missionary, 272, 319
Thomas, Capt., in battle of Groton Heights, 70
William B., Fire Chief, 490
Thompson, Edward R., bank trustee, 450
Isaac, bank officer, 430, 437
Rev. William, early pastor, 207
Rev. William, missionary to Indians, 281
"Thornuary," a game played in early days, 143

Thresher, Seneca S., lawyer, 344
Thurston, Horace, physician, 383
Tibbetts, Rev. C. C., pastor, 312
Tibbitts, Dr. John C., physician, 384
Major John A., lawyer, 401
Tiernay, Admiral, visitor at Ledyard, 533
Tinker, George F., bank president, 258, 428
Tirrell, Henry A., bank director, 433
Presiding Elder Eben, Norwich district, 311
Tisdale, George, physician, 375
Nathan, physician, 190, 375
Touzain, Dr. Dominie, French surgeon, 381
"Town Deposit Fund," schools of Connecticut, 46
Towne, Walter A., principal Bulkeley School, 257
Tozer, Dr. Richard, pupil of Dr. Benjamin Wheat, 380
Tracy, Andrew, holder of land, Norwich, 548
Daniel W., foreman Bulletin, 421
Dr. Philemon, physician, 364, 375, 379
Dr. Solomon, physician, 164, 377
Elisha, bank officer, 379; physician, Norwich, 368, 431
Erastus, brother of Gurdon Tracy, 560
Gurdon, silversmith, 560
Henry B., bank president, 431
Isaac, owner of mill, Norwich, 548
Lieut. Thomas, early settler, 162, 377, 571
Phineas L., early teacher, 36
Richard P., physician, 375, 381
Sergeant John, early settler, 162
Trade Schools, 49
Trading Cove, near Norwich, 215
Trankla, John, first pressman Bulletin, 421
Treat, Governor, of Connecticut, 9, 10
Governor Robert, early settler, 102, 103
"Trinitarian," religious controversy regarding, 274
Trott, Jonathan, silversmith, 558
Trumbull, Col. John, historical painter, 89
Faith, wife of Gov. Trumbull, 533
Fort, New London, 65, 66
Governor ("Brother Jonathan"), 57
Governor, famous son of Lebanon, 190, 196, 533
Gov. Jonathan (Proclamation of 1776), 197
Gurdon, Norwich resident, 145
Jonathan, Chief Justice Supreme Court, 326; trustee Bacon Academy, 254
Jonathan, Jr., Governor of City, 197
Jonathan, Norwich historian, 193
Jonathan, Sr., Governor of City, 197
Joseph, Capt., early resident, 164, 189
Joseph, Governor of City, 197
Lyman, Senator, famous graduate of Bacon Academy, 180
Tully, Rev. Bernard, R. C. pastor, 319
Tunnel, first railroad tunnel in U. S., 81
Turner, Dr. John, son of Philip Turner, 381
Dr. Philip, physician, Norwich, 164, 364, 374, 380; signer of memorial, 373
Ezekiel, early settler, 200
Guy, bank incorporator, 437
John C., connected with New London "Day," 401
Turnpike, first in United States, 81
Tyler, Dr. Bishop, physician, 384
Dr. Lucius, physician, 384
Rev. John, rector, 308, 533

Uncas; Onkos, Sachem (same as Uncas), 4, 5, 6, 7, 8, 52, 53, 105, 124, 187
Benjamin, ward of Rev. Eliphalet Adams, 292
Betty, Mohegan Queen, 148
Uncas Monument, Norwich, 86, 571
Uncasville, named for Chief Uncas, 215
Underhill, 5
Union School, New London, 39
Union Trust and Bank Company, 425
Unitarian belief spreading in New England, 274
United Colonies, 7
Universalist Society, 321
Utley, Dr. Vine, physician, 369, 375, 399

Various religious bodies in county, 314
Versailles, 214
Viets, Carl J., publisher, 223
Vocational High School (New London), 259; act of incorporation, 260; article by Mr. F. S. Hitchcock, principal, 259; courses of instruction, 262; helped in edowment drive for Connecticut College, 264; miscellaneous facts about, 265; modeled after various famous institutions, 260; origin of, 259
Voluntown, 1, 209; "Volunteers' Town," 229
Von Humboldt, Alexander, remarks on county, 85

Wade, Robert, early settler, 162
Wadsworth Athenaeum (Hartford) relics of Groton Heights, 75
Wadsworth, Capt. Joseph, 10
Wait, John Turner, lawyer, 331
Waite, George P., lawyer, 330
Henry M., lawyer, 326, 329
Marvin, eminent lawyer, 328, 426
Morrison R., Chief Justice, 89, 180, 213, 328, 331
Richard, lawyer, 330
Waitstill, Avery, (Mecklenburg, Conn.), 86
Waldo, John, signer of deed to Lyme, 203
Waller, Charles B., attorney, Mariners' Savings Bank, New London, 448; lawyer, 336, 340
Hon. Thomas M., Governor of Connecticut, 222, 447
Thomas M., eminent lawyer, 336
Thomas M., mentioned in "Day," 404
William, signer of deed to Lyme, 203
Wallis, Hamilton, benefactor Bacon Academy, 255
War of 1812, as it affected the county, 115
Ward, Benjamin, small-pox inoculation, 368
John E., bank officer, 450
Warner, Dr. Andrew T., physician, 398
Dr. Richard, physician, 399
Warren, Dr. William W. J., physician, 399
Washington, General, visitor at Lebanon, New London, and Norwich, 57, 59, 61, 533
Waterford, town of, 1, 209
Water power, use of, 218
Waterman, Sergeant Thomas, early settler, 162

Watrous, Daniel, trustee Bacon Academy, 254
Dr. John R., physician, 369
John, early physician, 374
John R., trustee Bacon Academy, 254
John R., benefactor Bacon Academy, 182
John R., early physician, 374, 385
Watson, Nathaniel, early settler, 102
Wattles, Dr. Thomas R., physician, 389
Waweequa, Indian local name, 8
Webb, Julius, bank trustee, 450
Webster, Major Durkee, 543
Welch, Rev. George H., Universalist, 322
Wellington, and Napoleon, 77
Wells, David Ames, eminent resident Norwich, 93
Dr. John P., physician, 398
Dr. Thomas J., physician, 398
Wentworth, Erastus, owner of pottery, 549
Lucy, wife of Erastus, 549
Mary, second wife of Erastus, 549
Rev. Erastus, missionary to China, 139, 140, 141
Wesleyan and Connecticut College, 244
West, Thomas, bank incorporator, 437
Westchester, part of Colchester, 178
Western Reserve and School Fund, 33, 45
West Point Academy and General Huntington, 139
Wetheral, Capt. Daniel, early settler, 177
Wethersfield, 9
Whaling from New London, statistics of, 78, 79, 109, 110, 111, 112, 113 114
Wheat, Dr. Benjamin, Norwich, 370
Samuel, bank officer, 426
Wheeler, Isaac, early settler, 207
Judge Ralph, address of, 348
Richard A., historian, 206, 235
School and Library, 214
Thomas, early settler, 207
Wheelock, Deacon Ralph, father of Eleazar, 288
John, 56, 193
Rev. Eleazor, founder Wheelock School, 54, 55 273
Whipple, Enoch and Mystic Oral School, 266
Home School, Mystic Oral School, 266
Jonathan, 266
Terah Colburn, 266
Samuel, 266
Whistler, James Abbott McNeil, artist, 209
Whitaker, Horace, bank officer, 450
Rev. Nathaniel, went to England with Sampson Occum, 55, 295
White, Charles E., bank officer, 428, 437
Joel W., bank officer, 431
Whitfield, George, evangelist, 273
Whiting, Edward, bank president, 435
James W., physician, 368
Maj. Ebenezer, owner of historic house, Norwich, 574
Whitney, Asa, and first Pacific railroad, 201
Stephen, railroad builder, 86
Whiton, D. E., manufacturer, New London, 496
Lucius E., mayor New London, 260, 428; bank officer, 496
Whittlesey, Ezra C., manager "Day," 406
George, incorporator Vocational School, 260; officer Savings Bank, New London, 438
Oramel, founder Salem School of Music, 58
Wight, Rev. Jabez, pastor Long Society, 288
Wightmans, father and son, Babtist clergymen, 299
Wilcox, Alvan, silversmith, 565
Rev. G. B., pastor, 298
Willey, Isaac, early settler, 102
Williams, Augustus C., part owner of "Day," 402
Charles P., bank president, 441
Hon. N. B., speech at Lebanon, 193
Joseph, lawyer, bank officer, 328, 426, 431, 432
Mansion, New London, 38
Memorial Institute, 258
Mrs. Harriet Peck, founder of Williams Memorial Institute, 258
Rev. Joshua L., early teacher, 36
Rev. Solomon, pastor, 288
Rev. Thomas, early teacher, 36
Thomas, bank incorporator, 437
Thomas, 546
William, bank officer, patriot and helper of Gov. Trumbull, signer Declaration of Independence, 430, 431, 191, 433, 200, 193
William M., fire chief, Norwich, 480
Willis, Rev. Henry, pastor, 289
Williston, Seth, 39
Wilson, Increase, bank incorporator, 437
Windsor, 9
Winslow, Rev., missionary to Ceylon, 294
Winters, Charles J., president Fire Insurance Company, 466
Winthrop, Deane, early settler, 102
Deane, brother of John, Jr., 100
Fitz John and Waitstill, sons of John W., younger, 104
Gov. Fitz John, parishioner of Rev. G. Saltonstall, 287
Gov. John, younger, son of Mass. Governor, 2, 8, 9, 22, 27
John, estate of, 104
John, Governor of Massachusetts, 97
John, the younger, 97, 203, 376
John, younger, and Saybrook, 128
Mrs. John, on Fisher's Island, 203
Withey, William E., bank officer, 430
Witter, Ebenezer, early schoolmaster, 36
Josiah, early settler, 207
Wolcott, Dr. Simon, physician, 374, 390
Wolves, in New London, bounty on, 85, 105, 186, 188
Wood, Consider, settler, 102
W. R., shareholder, Bulletin, 416
Woodard, Frank L., Dime Savings Bank, 431
Woodbridge, Dr. Dudley, physician, 397
Rev. Ephraim, father of Dr. Dudley, 397
Rev. Ephraim, First Church of Christ, 286, 293
Samuel, bank officer, 426
William, principal of School, Norwich, 36
Woodward, Ashbel, physician, historian, 375, 382
Rev. John, pastor, "Nine-Mile Tract, 281, 289
Wooster, Dr. Sylvester, physician, 399
Worden, Dr. Thomas, physician, 377
World War Records, various towns, 584
Worthington, Asa, signer of deed to Newent, 202

Wright, Elizabeth, one of founders of Connecticut College, 264
Wyllys, Samuel, home of, Hartford, 10

Yale College, gifts from Norwich, 53
Yantic River, 2
Yellow Fever in New London County, 86, 371
York, Dr. Edward, physician, 398
James, early settler, 207
Young, Alfred A., bank director, 436
Mason, shareholder New London "Day," 404
Y. M. C. A., 314, 315

BIOGRAPHICAL INDEX

ADDENDA AND ERRATA

Crandall, page 365; Billings F. S. Crandall was elected judge of probate for the District of Ledyard in 1922.

Abel, Alfred L., 397
Amorette E., 397
Anna M., 46
Edwin L., 466
Elijah H., 396
Elijah S., 396
Eugene P., 466
Ida M., 466
Joseph P., 466
Lawrence I., 397
Lloyd E., 397
Louis R., 466
Theodore S., 397
William H., 466
Abell, Charles H., 35
Charles J., 34, 35
Clara L., 35
Frederick M., 35
James M., 34
John W., 35
Lucy W., 35
Sarah L., 35
Silas, 34
Thomas C., 34
Ackley, Augustus, 424
John A., 424
Mabel, 424
Adams, Allan H., 306
Anna M., 261
Benjamin, 261
Benjamin W., 261, 262
Charles, 305
Clarence B., 261
Edith J., 236
Frank E., 261
Henry A., 236
Hiram, 305
Horace A., 305
Isabella, 306
John, 236
Leslie E., 306
Mary, 262
Agnew, Ellen E., 144
Robert R., Dr., 143
William B., 143
Alexander, Alice, 293
Charles P., 293
Frank J., 293
Prentice L., 293
Allen, Catherine, 387
Samuel, 387
Samuel P., 387
Allyn, Annie B., 313
Carlos W., 128, 129
Ebenezer, 311
Emily F., 312
Gurdon S., 312
Gurdon S., Dr., 313
James, 129
John, 128, 311
Laura A., 313
Louis M., Dr., 312
Louis P., 311, 312
Marguerite L., 313
Matilda W., 129
Robert, 128, 311
Rufus, 311
Sarah E., 129
William E., 313
Wilson, 129
Wilson T., 129
Amburn, Catherine, 270
Clarence H., 270
Frederick V., 270
George, 269
Hiram H., 269, 270
Anderson, Frank H., Capt., 222
Louis, 222
Margaret D., 222
Andrews, Arthur E., 357
Horace, 357
John, 357
Lewis, 458
Lewis A., 457, 458
Martin, 357
Mary, 357
Viola M., 458
Anthony, Abby G., 100
Albert, 100
Alice M., 100
Daniel S., 100
Edward M., Rev., 100
Appley, Andrew J., 229
Frederick J., 229
Mary E., 229
Armstrong, Benjamin A., 273, 280
Charles T., 273
James R., 272
John, 272, 273
John P. T., 280
Lillian T., 280
Susan A., 273
Ashbey, George A., 490
George B., Capt., 490
Marion C., 490
Aubrey, Elias A., 268
Frank G., 268
Margaret C., 268
Aurele, Mary, 476
Victor, 476
Victor M., 476
Austin, Champlain, 436
David, 85
Ezekiel, 436, 437
Frank E., 436, 437
Jeremiah, 436
John, 85
John P., 86
Louisa, 86
Robert, 436
Susan W., 437
Willis R., 85, 86
Avery, Albert L., 245, 456
Albert T., 457
Andrew, 420
Andrew M., 419, 420
Annie H., 457
Augustus P., 457
Christopher, 245, 411, 419, 456
Goldie B., 420
Irene, 246
James, Capt., 411, 419, 456
John, 420
John D., 245, 246, 456, 457
John D. (2), 457
Latham, 411
Martha H., 411
Mary A., 457
Nathaniel H., 411
Rachel, 457
Thomas W., 245, 457
Ayers, Alberta, 485
Edward E., 484
John, 484
Joseph E., 485
Lloyd P., 484
Ayling, Henry M., 14
John, 14
Mildred, 15
Nelson J., 14

Babbitt, James M., 464
Louise, 465
William E., 464
Babcock, John D., 269
Mary, 269
William P., 269
Bailey, Abbey, 245
Amanda, 245
Benjamin F., 244
Casper K., 153, 154
Cassie W., 171
Elijah W., 170
Faith, 154
Gurdon, 170
Henry, 244
Henry L., 170
Henry L., Jr., 171
Jabez H., 259
John B., 245
Jonathan, 170
Lewis P., 171
Louisa S., 171
Margaret, 245
Marion R., 259
Perry L., 153
William F., 259
Baker, Daniel, 417
Edwin H., Jr., 369
Frederick E., 417
George B. A., 418
James, 284
Jessie, 284
Lina, 369
Maria A., 417
Robert T., 284
William E., 417
Bamber, Henry F., 416
Joseph B., 416
Rachel, 416
Barber, Anna N., 471
Clarence E., 414, 465
Ella, 466
Elliot B., 414
Fannie, 414
Frank O., 470
John E., 414
Julius E., 465
Leander, 470
Michael A., 414, 465
Theodora A., 414
Barker, Herbert N., 309
Maud L., 309
Walter G., 309
Walter H., Capt., 309
Barnes, Amos T., 373
Avery, 22
Chester M., 23
Eliza H., 373
Erva L., 23
Evangeline, 23
Everett P., 22, 23
Ezra, 22
Frederic A., 373
Mary B., 23
Susie B., 23
Barry, Annie, 252
Cornelius P., 252
Robert, 252
Barstow, Charles I., 191
Charles T., 191
Ella M., 191
Bassett, Albert, 453
Dolly, 454
George H., 454
Ralph, 453, 454
William, 454
Bathgate, George H., 345
James, 345
Laura J., 345
Bavier, Earl S., 230
Isabelle, 230
Nelson, 230
Beauregard, Mary B., 403
Romain, 402
Wilford, 402
Beauvais, Albert, 248
John B., 248
Mattie, 248
Beckwith, Daniel A., 452
Ethel E., 371
Etta M., 452
Frederick A., 349
Henry A., 452
Howard E., 371
James, 371
John T., 349
Leslie M., 349
Marion S., 349
Matthew, 452
Samuel R., 371
Tracy T., 349
Beebe, Ada, 427
Arthur J., 404
Benjamin M., 382
Clarence S., 427
Emma, 382
Erastus C., 421
Grace S., 427
Hayward E., 422
James H., 404
Jeannette C., 405
John, 382
John C., 421
Louis, 382
Martha, 421
Sherman, 427
Thelma A., 382
William, 382
William L., 382
William O., 382
Beique, Francis, 366
John B., 366
Virginia, 366
Bellefleur, Oliver L., 439
Oliver M., 439
Telouise, 439
Bellerose, Ceserie, 255
Frederick, 255
Ulderic O., Rev., 255
Benjamin, Amy, 275
Annie, 275
Clarence E., 275
Edwin F., 274
Elizabeth, 275
Levi, 274
Bennett, Ella E., 344
Harry N., 344
James W., 343, 344
Laura C., 162
Nathan, 344
William A., 162
Bentley, Benjamin F., 161
Benjamin F. (2), 161, 162
Charity, 162
George, 161
Robert, 161
William, 161
Beran, Andrew, 313
James A., 313
Matilda, 313
Bilderbeck, George L., 118
Bill, Allison M., 234
Elisha, 234
Herbert P., 234
James B., 234
James L., 234
Leonard E., 234
Ruth C., 234
Billings, Byron, 111
Ebenezer, 110
Gilbert, Capt., 110
Horatio N., 110
Lucy E., 111
Sanford, 110
Sanford N., 110
Sanford N., Jr., 111
William, 110
William W., 111
Bindloss, Christopher, 126
Christopher, Sir, 125
Elizabeth E., 126
Frank M., 127
Helen S., 127
John B., 127
Peter, 126
Philip, 126
Robert, 125, 126
William, 126
William P., 125
Birchall, Anne I., 229
John W., 229
William, 229
Bird, Anita, 251
Regnar E., 250
Viggo E., 250
Bishop, Edward A., 148

James, 148
Lena, 148

Bitgood, Frank S., 55
George E., Dr., 55
Harold W., 229
Herman J., 229
Lucy A., 56
Robert E., 229
Susan, 229
William F., 228
William H., 228
Black, Jacob H., 115
Laura E., 116
Ross E., Dr., 115
Blackmar, George F., 320
John S., Dr., 319, 320
Mildred, 320
Blakeslee, Albert T., 462
Byron J., 462
Harry S., 462
Lillian W., 462
Blanchard, Clodomir, 191
Daniel, 144
Edward L., 191, 192
Ella M., 144
Olive, 191
William C., 144
Boardman, Albert, 443
Daniel, 146
George, 146
Grace L., 443
Hezekiah, 146
Horace P., 443
Joseph, Capt., 146
Melissa, 443
Peter, 443
Phebe E., 147
Thomas, 146
Wait J., 146
Bodenwein, Theodore, 117
Bogue, Elizabeth J., 176
Elsie R., 176
Harlow L., 176
Irving E., 176
John W., 175
Russell, 175
Ruth, 176
William F., 175, 176
Boisson, Felix, 202
Gabrielle, 202
Robert, 201, 202
Bolger, Elizabeth, 427
James R., 427
John, 427
Bosworth, Mary, 396
Quincy M., 396
Bottomley, Anna A., 412
Henry H., 412
Joseph A., 412
Joseph S., 412
Samuel J., 412
Bourdeau, Flora, 172
Jeremie, 172
Jeremie (2), 172
Joseph J., 173
Mary, 173
Moses, 172
Bourque, Donat, 432
Eugene J., 432
Euphemia, 432
Julian, 432
Boylen, Alfred F., 226
Florence, 227
Stephen A., 226
Bradley, Arlene R., 223
Carl, 223
F. Harmon, 223
Francis H., 222
Robert D., 222, 223
Brainard, Daniel, 142
Martha M., 143
Martin Van B., 142, 143
Zeno, 142
Brand, Annie E., 235
Charlotte, 117
Dudley, Capt., 117
Dudley A., Capt., 116, 117
Harold E., 117
Jennie F., 117
Lewis, 234
Lewis B., 234
Rose, 235
Breed, Allen, 59
Isaac S., 59
John, 59
Lucy A., 60
Samuel, 59
Sarah A., 60
William S., 59
Brewer, Arthur H., 41, 42
Charles H., 42
Daniel, 42
Daniel, Rev., 42
Frank C., 42
Isaac, 42
Lyman, 42
Mary P., 43
Brewster, Abby P., 341
Margery M., 341
Sarah E., 341
Simon, 341
Simon (2), 341
Simon (3) 341
Simon (4), 341
Briggs, Charles H., 55
Charles S., 54
Charles W., 54, 311
Elizabeth P., 55
George E., 55
James, 310
John, 310
Jonathan, 310
Leroy S., 55
Lucius, 310, 311
Mary G., 311
Palmer, 54
Robert E., 311
Stanton L., 476
Wanton, 310
Brigham, Chester H., 429
James B., 429
James M., 429
Mattie, 429
Minnie, 429
Paul, 429
Paul W., 429
Briscoe, Charles, 53
Charles H., 53
Edward, 53
Isaac, 53
James, 53
Margaret C., 54
Nathaniel, 53, 54
Traver, 53, 54
Willis A., 53
Broder, Fannie, 482
Joseph, 481
Leon, 481
Brooks, Clarence G., Dr., 19
Ethel L., 20
George O., 19
Brown, Albert, 268
Albert M., 268
Albertus B., 475
Arthur C. (A. Chester), 190
Charles N., 445
Daniel C., 475
Ella E., 435
Frank H., 266
Frederick J., Hon., 16
Frederick O., 17
George S., 195, 196
Grace W., 18
Henrietta F., 196
Iphogenia, 445
Isabella, 191
James E. F., 475
Jedediah, 445
John M., 16
Joshua, 196
Lydia A., 445
Mary, 266
Mary A., 197
Mary S., 475
Nancy, 17
Nancy A., 268
Nathaniel, 268
Philetus A., 268
Randall, 197
Randall (2), 197
Robert S., 392
Roswell, 475
Samuel, 392
Seth L., 190, 195
Sidney A., 435
Smith, 266

Susan, 392
Thomas, 435
Browne, Daniel M., 36
Gertrude, 36
Tyler, 36
W. Tyler, Dr., 36
Browning, Abial T., 390
Alice B., 412
Arba, 199
Avery, 199, 341
Beriah H., 199
Ezekial H., 412
Frank D., Dr., 199
Harriet L., 199
Howland S., 412
John, 199, 341
Lillian M., 390
Lucius A., 390
Mildred L., 200
Nathaniel, 199, 341
Rowland S., 412
William, 199, 341
Buckingham, Eliza, 68
Mabel S., 362
Samuel, 67
Thomas, Rev., 67
Walter M., 362
William A., 362
William A., Hon., 67, 68
Buckley, Margaret A., 231
Mary E., 231
William H., 230
William H., Jr., 230, 231
Bucklyn, John K., Capt., 52
John K., Dr., 52
Mary E., 53
Mary McK., 52
Buell, Christina H., 239
John H., Capt., 239
John H., Jr., 239
Bullard, Elmire, 384
Ernest E., 384
Olin B., 384
Burgess, Charlotte, 429
Emily F., 477
Iva, 429
John E., 428
Philo, 428, 477
Thomas, 477
Walter E., 477
Burke, John, 238
Mary, 238
Thomas J., 238
Burnap, Frank A., 389
Fred A., 389
Nellie, 389
Burrows, Frank S., 356
John, 356
Mildred, 356
Rhodes, Dr., 356
Robert, 356
Burton, Charles W., 376
Rosa E., 377
William, 376
Bushnell, Anne M., 407
Charles E., 153
Charles P., 152, 153, 407
Helen E., 153
James, 152, 406
Nathan S., 406, 407
William H., 152, 407
Butler, Mary, 256
Parker, Capt., 256
Butson Charles, 309
Charlotte, 310
Joseph W., 309
Byers, John R., 322
John W., 321, 322
Joseph, 321, 322
Louise A., 322
Byles, Andrew H., 346
Ebenezer, 346
Elisha, 346
George S., 346
Josias, 346
M. Hortense, 346, 347
Robert H., 346, 347

Calkins, Alfa, 104
Amas, 103
Arthur B., 103
Catherine, 377
Clara I., 104
Daniel, Dr., 103
David, 103
Elisha C., 103
Helen E., 377
Hugh, 103
James E., 377
Jonathan, Lieut., 103
Perlin W., 377
Theodore G., 377
William E., 377
Callahan, John M., 117
John W., Dr., 333
Mary E., 333
Nellie A., 118
Patrick J., 117
Thomas F., 333
Caracausa, Albert C., 262, 263
Anthony, 262
L. Louise, 262
Carlson, Elizabeth, 261
John, 261
Oscar, 261
Caroline, Celia, 493
Edward, 493
Isaac, 493
Caroly, John W., 358
Joseph, 358
Peter, 358
Susie E., 358
William P., 359
Caron, Adelia, 158
Christopher, 482
Fred, 482
Fred A., 482
John B., 157, 158
Josephine, 477
Louis, 157
Noe I., 476
Noe I., Jr., 476, 477
Yvonne, 483
Carpenter, Agnes R., 142
Joseph E., 141
Lewis M., 141
Carroll, Adams P., 49, 50
Amos, 49
Catherine V., 60
Charlotte L., 50
Emma F., 50
George W., 50
George W., Jr., 50
John F., 60
Lucius W., 49, 50
Martin, 60
Nathaniel, 49
Wyman, 49
Carter, Charles E., 360
Edward, 276
Elmer J., 360, 361
Erastus W., 203, 204
Gideon W., 204
Harry E., 276
Jane, 276
Joseph F., 204
Laurence E., 361
Lucy W., 361
Mary A., 204
Willington H., 204
Carver, Ellen, 276
George, 276
George N., 275
James D., 275, 276
Case, Cordelia, 213
Dexter S., 356
Edmond L., 213
Elwyn L., 213
Everett, 356
Jennie F., 357
William W., 356
Casey, Ellen, 190
John, 190
William B., Dr., 190
William H., 369
Cassidy, Louis T., Dr., 344
Mary V., 345
Patrick, Dr., 344
Caswell, David, 414
Harriet, 414
Samuel J., 414
Wilkes M., 414
Caulkins, Elisha, 417
Eugene D., 417
Frank L., 417
Frederick L., 417

Herbert, 417
Hugh, 417
Lemuel, 417
Lucy E., 417
Chagnon, Alexander, 373
Bella, 373
George A., 373
Champion, Calvin B., 12, 13
Charles, 367
Clifford V., 12, 14
Edgar R., 12, 13
Edgar W., 12, 14
Edith J., 14
Edward, 367
Frederick, 12, 13
Henry, 12, 13
Henry, Capt., 12, 13
John H., 367
Minnie G., 367
Wallace R., 12, 13
Chapel, Charles L., 283
Frederick W., 283
Leander D., 283
Sibyl F., 283
Chapman, Augusta, 470
Carry L., 267
Celia, 470
Charles A., 46
Charles E., 47
Clara B., 481
Clifford E., 301
Edwin P., 267
Ernest D., 267
Eugene H., 470
Florence C., 47
Frank H., 481
Frederick R., 386
Frederick W., 480, 481
George A., 385
James B., 385
Jennie E., 386
Laura, 46
Lyman G., 470
Mary, 46
Mary L., 481
Mildred M., 47
Minnie A., 301
Perry G., 301
Robert F., 480
Savalian E., 301
Chappell, Adelaide, 105
Alfred H., 104, 105
Alfred H., Jr., 105
Comfort, 104
Edward, Capt., 104
Ezra, 104
Frank V., 104, 105
Franklin, 104
George, 104
George S., 105
Henry C., 105
Charron, Cornelia, 432
Desire, 432
Desire, Jr., 432
Chipman, Charles, 107
Clifford E., 107
Edwin C., Dr., 106, 107
Eunice C., 107
John, 106
Nathan F., 107
Nathan T., 107
Samuel, 107
Truman F., 108
Church, Adelaide J., 478
Elisha P., 478
Elisha R., 41, 394
Elizabeth, 201
Elva, 394
Erastus, 41
Grace, 490
Harold, 490
Harriet C., 41
Henry E., 477
John, 39, 40
Jonathan, 40, 394
Joseph T., 489, 490
Kenneth B., 41
Leonard P., 41
Lewis R., 201
Lloyd M., 201
Melissa S., 41
Minnie, 394
Nettie, 394
Peleg, 41
Perix, 201
Reynold, 39
Richard, 40
Robert, 39
Robert H., 201
Theodore N., 477, 478
Theodore P., 478
Thomas, 489
Warren W., 394
Clark, Albert, 487
Alfred, 487
Clarence L., 345
Fannie, 487
Fred, 487
Joseph A., 487
May F., 345
William F., 345
Clarke, Adriele, 336
Amelia, 37
Cora, 399
Daisy L., 220
Daniel W., 220
Edward E., 398
Emma L., 336
George H., 335, 336
Henry, 398
James M., 37
John, 36, 37, 336
Joseph, 37
Lester G., 336
Thomas, 336
Waldo E., 220
William, 336
Coats, Allen A., 124
Ansel, 123
Fannie W., 124
George D., 123
George F., 123
Nellie H., 124
Coggeshall, Freeborn, Rev., 28
Henry J., Hon., 28
John, 28
John A., 28, 29
John C., 28
Katherine, 29
Mason F., 28, 29
Mason J., 28
Samuel W., Rev., 28
Coit, Charles, Col., 93
Charles M., Col., 93, 94
Emily H., 343
George D., 343
James D., 343
Jeffrey V., 390
John, 73, 74, 93, 389
John W. L., 390
Joseph, 73, 74, 93
Joseph, Rev., 93
Joshua, Hon., 74
Lena H., 390
Lucretia, 75
Mary B., 95
Nathaniel, 93
Robert, 73, 74
Samuel, Col., 93
Samuel J., 389, 390
Colby, Alfred O., 446
Amos G., 446
Edna E., 446
Coleman, George M., 221
James R., 221
Sarah A., 221
Collins, Anson B., 243
Benjamin M., 243
Blanche, 7
Catherine E., 243
Daniel, 6, 7, 242
Daniel P., 7, 242, 243
Gilbert, 6
Grace E., 243
Harriet K., 7
John, Capt., 60
Margaret L., 61
Marjorie, 7
Robert J., Dr., 60, 61
Colver, Amos, 25
Bertha E., 26
Coddington, 25
Courtland E., 25
Jonathan, 25
Louisa J., 26
Moses J., 25

Comeau, Anthony, 57
Joseph G., Dr., 57, 58
Laudia E., 58
Comstock, Ada, 169
Amos, Capt., 168
Andrew F., 169
Catherine, 169
Chester W., 281
D. Chester, 280
Edwin F., 280, 281
Frances A., 169
James H., 168, 169
Lena E., 281
Mary C., 169
Conner, David, Capt., 212
Ruth I., 212
Thomas, 212
William B., 212
Coogan, Clara A., 283
Clarence A., 283
Edward C., 283
Cooke, Calvin W., 448
Celia R., 449
Chester, 448
Dwight W., Col., 448
Francis E., 449
Gregory, 448
Isaac H., 449
Isaiah, 448
James, 448
James, Capt., 448
John, 448
Stephen, 448
William A., 448, 449
William D., 449
Cooper, Frank S., 224
James, 223
Lillian, 224
Thomas, 223
Corcoran, Edmond, 220
Edward T., 220
Ellen, 220
Corey, J. Frank, 464
John F., 464
Sarah E., 464
Costello, Cornelius C., 6
Mary C., 6
Michael E., 6
Coté, Alma, 206
Arthur P., 206
Peter S., 206
Coxeter, Ada, 253
Frank, 253
George, 253
Crandall, Anna L., 391
Benjamin P., 390
Billings F. S., 365, 366
Charles T., 390
Charles T., Jr., 390, 391
Elizabeth A., 314
Etta, 420
Francis C., 418
Fred E., 418
Harold H., 420
Harriet E., 418
John, 314
John C., 420
John N., 314
Jonathan, 365
Joseph, 314
Mary L., 366
Phineas, Rev., 314
Russell, 420
Sailes A., 365
Stiles W., 365
Wells, 365
William T., 314
Cranska, Frank, 329
Harold W., 329
James, 329
Lillian W., 329
Marian A., 329
Rosalind J., 329
Wesley R., 329
Cranston, Benjamin, 26
Benjamin T., Jr., 26
Julia A., 27
William B. L., 26
Creighton, A. Graham, 220, 221
Jean, 221
T. Grassie, 221
Crocicchia, Anthony, Dr., 135
Emma, 135
George J., 135
Isabella A., 135
Stephen, 135
Cromwell, Ira R., 231
Julia E., 231
William R., 231
Cross, Fred H., 470
Jerome L., 470
Sarah, 470
Crowell, Adelaide, 178
Annie M., 178
Frederick C., 178
Frederick S., 178
Zadoc C., 178
Cullen, Albert S., 324
Annie, 324
James, 324
Cummings, Annie E., 278
Edwin, 477
Joseph P., 278
Rexford E., 477
Ruth, 477
Thomas, 278
Curry, Archie R., 385
Sarah B., 385
William G., 385
William T., 385
William W., 385

Danielson, Edwin L., Dr., 38, 39
Elisha, Capt., 39
Emma F., 39
James, 39
James, Serg., 39
Samuel, 39
William, 39
Dargatz, Alvin L., 414
Dorothy M., 414
Rudolph, 414
Dart, Ezra F., 422
George W., 422
Hubert G., 422
Pansy, 422
Davidson, George, 217
James, 217
Mary E., 218
Richard C., 217
Robert F., 218
Davis, Benjamin, 300
Benjamin P., 476, 488
Charles B., 475, 488
Charles C., 475
Charles E., 476
Charlotte E., 488
Clarence H., 476
Elisha, 300
Frances H., 365
Frank, 365
Ira A., 365
Jennie M., 300
Joel, 300
Joel H., 299, 300
John E., 365
John H., 365
Nettie, 365
Sarah E., 476
Silas, 300
Dayon, Amelia, 189
Azarie, 188
Edmond, 188
Dean, George R., 415
Mia L., 416
Robert, 415
Delagrange, Adolph, 326
Adolph A., 326
Edgar M., 326
Gaston, 326
Josephine, 326
Raoul M., 326
De Pinto, John, 493
Joseph, 493
Mary, 494
Desmond, Catherine C., 99
Helen G., 454
Jeremiah A., 454
Jeremiah H., 454
Jeremiah J., Hon., 98
Marguerite A., 99
Thomas G., 99
Timothy, 98
De Wolf, Angeline, 335
Asahel R., 335
Benjamin, 335

Burton W., 353
Edward, 335
Jeremiah W., 335
John A., 335
Mary E., 335
Monica E., 354
Roger W., 353
Stephen, 335
Winthrop J., 335
Winthrop R., 353
Dexter, Andrew S., 315
Andrew S., Jr., 315
Ida, 315
Dick, Elizabeth, 283
Frederick, 283
Jacob, 283
Dimon, Annie L., 113
Eva, 442
George B., 442
John, 442
John N., Dr., 112
May K., 113
Theodore D., 112
Dixon, Aimee, 379
Anthony, 379
Anthony, Jr., 379
Chauncy T., 379
James A., 379
Louis E., 379
Dodge, Charles C., 320, 321
Jennie, 321
John L., 321
Dollbaum, Adelhaide I., 252
August, 252
Ernest T., 252
Frederick J., 252
Henry J., 252
John, 252
John A., 252
Paul M., 252
Donahue, Elizabeth, 221
George W., 221
John A., 221
Richard, 221
Robert, 221
Donnelly, Dudley St. C., 289
Dudley St. C., Jr., 290
Henry C., 289
Joanna E., 289
Thomas H., 290
Donovan, Daniel, 209
James P., 209
Louise, 209
Dorsey, Charlotte, 462
Thomas F., 462
Thomas F., Jr., 462
Doubleday, Burdett S., 202
Dwight, 202
Emma, 203
Douglass, Edmund L., Dr., 210
Edmund P., Dr., 210
Gladys A., 210
Downey, Mary, 130
Roger, 129
Stephen J., 129
Doyle, Clarence, 411
David E., 410
Jennie L., 291
John J., 291
Louis S., 410
Louise J., 411
Sarah, 291
Driscoll, Hannah, 393
Isabel M., 150
Jeremiah J., 393
John, 393
John M., 393
Timothy, 150
William T., Dr., 150
Duffy, Elizabeth, 430
Francis J., 430
James P., 430
Patrick, 430
Duhaime, Albert L., 325
Joseph L., 325
Margaret, 326
Dunbar, Harold M., 339
Henry, 340
Isaiah, 340
John, 339, 340
Joseph, 339
Miles, 340
Omega H., 339
Ralph, 339
Robert, 339
Walter, 339
Walter L., 339

Eccleston, Avery N., 288
Benedict, 288
Clarence H., 412
George, 411
Hubert W., 288
John D., 288
John H., 411, 412
Ruth, 412
Sarah L., 288
Susan K., 288
Edgar, Eliza B., 251
George P., 251
Janie L., 251
Mark, 251
Thomas, 251
Edgecomb, Helen J., 225
Howard A., 225
Mathilda, 225
Nellie, 225
Roswell S., 225
Eldredge, (Eldred),
Charles L., 180
Charles Q., 179
Christopher, 179
Daniel, Capt., 179
Estelle, 180
James, 179
Jennie W., 180
Joshua, 179
Samuel, 179
Ely, Earl, 472
Edwin S., 291
Edwin W., 471, 472
Eli, 291
Enoch, 471
Grosvenor, 291
Harry, 472
Jacob, 291
James, 291
Jesse S., 291
John C., 472
Joseph C., 471
Laurence, 472
Leslie, 472
Mary, 292, 472
Richard, 291
Samuel, 472
William, 291
William B., 472
Enos, Cassie M., 474
Joseph F., 474
Richard, 474

Farnsworth, Amos, 91
Amos, Maj., 91
Benjamin, 91
Charles, Col., 90, 92
Harriet P., 92
Matthias, 90
Ralph, Dr., 91
Faust, Andrew, 375
Edward A., 375
Maud M., 375
Feeney, Bridget A., 257
Edward, 257
Francis S., 257
George A., 257
Joseph, 257
Thomas, 257
Fellows, George E., 33, 34
George R., 34
Joshua E., 34
Lila E., 34
Fenner, Annie C., 121
Arthur, Capt., 48, 120
George P., 120
Stephen, 48
Thomas, Maj., 48, 120
Ferrin, Blanche, 16
Carlisle F., Dr., 15
Chester M., Dr., 15
Fielding, Albert E., 440, 441
Isabella M., 441
Lemuel M. O., 441
Fields, John F., 189
Julia M., 189
Thomas, 189
Finegan, Henrietta A., 431

John W., 431
John W. (2), 431
John W., (3), 431
Fitch, Alfred, 392
Asa, 87, 89
Asa, Col., 88
Charles, 478
Charles H., 478
Charles I., 392
Douglass W., 89
Elisha, 392
Herbert, 392
James, Rev., 87
Louise C., 90
Lucy, 392
Nora, 478
Stephen, 88
William, 89
William H., 87, 90
Fletcher, Elizabeth I., 318
Hazel L., 319
Joseph T., 317
Robert O., 318
Thomas, 317
William, 317
William L., 317, 318
William L., Jr., 319
William S., 317, 318
Foerster, Joseph, 355
Mary, 355
Foley, Annie, 227
James, 227
James, Jr., 227
Mary L., 227
Fones, Abbie E., 137
Byron A., 137
John, Capt., 136
Joseph, 136
William A., 135, 136
William H., 136
Fontaine, Henry, 233
Louis J., 233
Rose A., 233
Foote, Albert, 441
Albert H., 441
Ella L., 442
Elmer H., 442
Erastus, 441
Frank E., 442
Jeremiah, 441
Joseph, 441
Nathaniel, 441
Stephen, 441
Ford, Dwight, 381
Edwin C., 381
Mary, 381
Forsyth, George, 383
George A., 383
Latham, 383
Leon A., 383
Leroy E., 383
Richard H., 383
Sarah R., 383
Fort, Albert, 232
Ann F., 232
Hartly, 232
Foster, Christie H., 416
Edwin D., 416
Eva, 416
George H., 416
John R., 416
Fowler, Amos, Capt., 193
Anson, Col., 193
Benjamin, 31
Bernice A., 193
Charles A., 31
Charles S., 31
Clement A., 192, 193
Dijah, Capt. 193
Esther E., 31
Frank P., 193
Frederick E., 31
James, 31
Mark, 193
Samuel, 31
Wells R., 30, 31
William, 193
William, Capt., 193
Fox, Albert J., 281
Ellen C., 281
Joel H., 281
Franer, Frank J., 260
Frank J., Jr., 259, 260
Mary, 260
Fraser, Homer, 395
Lillian, 396
Moise, 395
Freeman, Albert C., Dr., 301, 302
Eva A., 302
George, 301
French, Charles L., Rev., 434
Harriet, 435
Robert L., 434, 435
Fribance, John, 274
Minnie, 274
William, 274
Frink, Andrew, 288
Arthur A., 289
Esther C., 289
George W., 288, 289
Grace A., 288
Jedidiah, 288
John, 287
Mabel C., 289
Marion E., 289
Rufus, 288
Samuel, 288
Wayland B., 287, 288
Frisbie, Calvin H., 370
Henry, 370
Marian R., 370
William K., 370
William R., 370
Fuller, Lawson H., 410
Mercy, 410
Ozro D., 410
Willis O., 410

Gadbois, Catherine, 132
Lewis C., 131, 132
Peter, 132
Washington I., 132
Gadle, Joseph P., 157
Margaret, 157
Paul F., Dr., 157
Gadue, Adelard, 456
Alfonsine, 456
Anthony, 456
Josephine, 456
Gager, Arthur H., 486
Charles A., 192
Charles A., Jr., 192
Ella E., 489
Herman A., 488, 489
John, 486
John J., 486
Mira L., 192
Ruth, 486
Samuel H., 488
William, Dr., 486
Gallup, Algernon S., 185
Benjamin, 184
Benjamin S., 183, 184
Caroline A., 185
Helena R., 184
Henry H., 284, 285
Irena H., 286
Isaac, 284
Isaac, Jr., 285
Jennie C., 185
John, 183, 184
John, Capt. 183
Oscar B., 185
Susie I., 286
Thomas, 183
Walter H., 286
Winfred C., 185
Gamber, George, 321
Henry, 321
Lillie, 321
Ganey, Anna, 297
John C., 296
Joseph M., Dr., 296, 297
Gardner, Cleta, 425
Edward L., 486
Herbert R., 486
Mary, 486
Roy D., 425
Ulysses S., 425
Gaucher, Evelyn, 273
Henry A., 473
Joseph, 473
Lorenzo, 473
Louise, 273
Philomene, 473
Zoel, 273

Gaudreau, Frank, 408, 409
Theresa, 409
Gauvin, Heleda, 492
Renie, 491
Renie (2), 491
Gay, David, 219
Elizabeth A., 219
J. Warren, 219
Peter, 219
Thomas J., 219
Geer, Amanda C., 421
Amos, 421
Bertha L., 166
David A., 166
Earl B., 421
Ebenezer, 166
Edward A., 165, 166
Elijah D., 166
Frank P. W., 239, 240
George, 166, 410, 420
Grace E., 410
Harold F., 166
Isaac G., 420, 421
Jacob A., 421
John, 239
John W., 166
Margaret G., 166
Nathan, 410
Robert, 166
Samuel L., 240
Ursula M., 240
Geisthardt, Charles M., 408
Emma, 408
Godfrey A., 407
Paul, 407
Rosalie, 408
Stephen L., 408
Gibbs, Emily R., 19
Matthew, 18
Natalie K., 19
Nathan A., 18
Nathan P., 18
Thomas, 18
William, 18
Gilbert, Earl E., 438
Emma, 438
Frederick H., 438
Seth C., 438
Walter C., 438
Gildersleeve, Alice, 256
Charles C., Dr., 351
Charles W., 256
Donald C., 351
George H., 351
Samuel, 351
Smith M., 256
Susan M., 351
Gillette, Alma, 471
Everette C., 471
Halleck L., 471
Pascal, 471
Gilman, Clara N., 360
Harry, 359
Morris, 359
Nathan, 359
Gledhill, Agnes, 110
Eli, 109
Ingham, 109
Martha, 110
Goddard, Asa O., 351
Louis H., 351
Lucy A., 351
Goodfellow, Agnes M., 447
Joseph, 447
Maude, 447
Robert A., 447
Robert W., 447
Gorman, Beezy, 200
Edward R., 223
Ellen V., 397
Hattie B., 223
Henry T., 397
John P., 200
Patrick, 200
Theodore P., 223
Graham, Agnes, 348
Clementine, 348
James, 347
James, Jr., 347
Mary, 348
Grant, Charles H., 24
Charles W., 24
George G., 24
Mathew, 24
May C., 25
Walter S., 24
Graves, Addison, 183
Charles B., Dr., 183
Frances M., 183
Gray, Amandan, 62
Austin, 378
Benjamin, 481
Bessie, 481
Charles C., 138
Charles E., 138
Cressingham, LaF., 138
Dorothy B., 63
Emma R., 138
Enos M., 481
Enos M., Jr., 481
Flora, 378
George R., 62, 63, 451
Helene M., 62
James B., 62
Jared R. A., 451
Jerrod R., 63
John, 138
John C., 63
John M., 378
John R., 378
John S., 451
Josephine L., 63, 451
La Fayette, 138
Leslie P., 378
Lyle C., 138
Marian, 62
Mason, 481
Nathan, 481
Thomas B., 62
Willard A., 63, 451
Greene, A. Frank, 194
Alfred E., 194
Virginia, 194
Greenhalgh, Eletha M., 222
Grace, 222
William, 222
William C., 222
Greenleaf, Arthur A., 237, 238
Atherton C., 237
Sadie, 238
Greenman, Charles R., 163
Griswold, Florence, 287
George, 286
George, Rev., 286
Harry T., 286, 287
Joseph K., 398
Matthew, 286
Richard S., 286
Richard S., Jr., 286
Rose, 398
Samuel L., 398
William S., 397, 398
Grover, Anson, R., 360
Charles D., 360
Mary E., 360
Raymond D., 360
Guild, Frank W., 171
Mabel, 172
William, 171
Guile, Daniel S., 162
Daniel S., Col., 163
Frank E., 163
Harry, 162
Henry D., 163
Lydia A., 163
Gurney, Annie M., 242
George, 242
George M., 242
John H., Capt., 242
Ralph H., 242

Haley, Albert A., 255
Andrew, 255
Kate, 255
Hall, Alice D., 141
Charles, 218
Elmer C., 218
Ethel M., 218
Ezra, 140
George, 140
Isaac, 140
Jonathan, 140
Judah S., 140
Nathan H., 140, 141
Samuel, 140
Ursula R., 141

Halsey, Elizabeth, 76
Jeremiah, Col., 76
Jeremiah, Hon., 75, 76
Jeremiah S., 76
Hammacher, Elizabeth, 258
Henry, 258
Henry P., 258
Peter, 257, 258
Hammond, Charles W., 124
Isaac, 124
Josiah, 124
Margaret, 125
Ruth M., 125
Thomas, 124
Hankey, Charlotte J., 113
Jacob C., 113
Philip Z., 113
Hanney, Ernest J., 473
Floyd L., 473
Harold E., 473
Jennie M., 473
Samuel, 472
Samuel D., 472
Theophilus F., 473
Theophilus H., 472
Hansen, Hans P., 247
Louise H., 248
Theodore N., 247, 248
Harper, Francis J., Dr., 23, 24
Matilda F., 24
Richard, 23
Harriman, Bertha E., 30
James, 29
Mary T., 30
Patrick H., Dr., 29
Harris, Cassius F., 243
Christopher, 216
Edna, 217
Frederic H., 243
Marie E., 244
Willard D., 216
Harrison, Alice M., 254
Charles, 254
Harlan M., 255
William C., 254
William C., Jr., 255
Harvey, Alice E., 213
Isaac, 212
James H., 212, 213
Harwood, Pliny LeR., 287
Rowena M., 287
Havens, Carleton H., 145
Carrie A., 145
Edwin, 145
George R., 145
Mabel A., 145
Hayes, Dennis J. ,310
Elizabeth T., 310
James P., 310
John, 310
Mary, 310
Patrick J,. 310
Hazard, Amey A., 106
Beulah I., 106
Harriet S., 106
James O., 106
Jeffrey, Lieut.-Gov., 106
John R., 106
Martha J., 106
Natalie S., 106
Natt, 106
Robert, 106
Hazen, Charles T., 463
Edward, 463
Emma, 463
James H., 463
Moses, 463
Simeon, 463
Thomas, 463
Healy, Lena C., 421
Thomas J., 421
Thomas J., Jr., 421
Helmboldt, Albert, 406
Clara, 406
George F., 406
Hempstead, Beatrice M., 222
George H., 221
George R. W., 221
Henkle, Alexander, 133
Emanuel A., Dr., 133
Sophia, 134
Herbert, Eva L., 230
John J., 230
Jonas L., 230
Hewitt, Ann M., 167
Anzeline, 195
Arthur E., 474
Benjamin, 194
Benjamin H., Hon., 167
Benjamin P., 167
Charles, 194
Eli, 194
Elsie L., 474
Erwin, 474
Erwin W., 195
George, 194
George E., 194
George H., 195
Harriet E., 194, 195
Israel, 194
Thomas, 194
Heyer, Harold H., Dr., 118
Levi, 118
Margaret, 118
Hickey, James, 160
Joseph L., 161
Mary, 161
Michael J., 160
Hill, Alpheus M., 302
Andrew C., 302
Charles W., 386
Edna B., 387
Elmer, 303
Emma U., 306
George P., 306
Harry H., 386
Herbert N., 387
Lillian, 305
Lucy C., 302
Nellie H., 302
Samuel, 306
Thomas, 305
Thomas J., 305
Thomas M., 305
William F., 302, 303
Hiscox, Hannah, 236
John H., 236
William E., 236
Hislop, Frances E., 103
Graham S., 102, 103
James, 102
Holbrook, Charles S., 20
Ella P., 21
Frank W., 20
Joseph, 20, 72
Mary, 73
Peter, 20, 72
Sabin, 20, 72, 73
Seth, 20, 72
Supply T., Hon., 20, 72, 73
Thomas, 20, 72
Holdredge, Charles H., 215
Gertrude M., 216
Grace B., 215
Frank L., 216
Frederick W., 216
Hibbard H., 215
Louise, 216
Holdridge, Charles D., 349
Daniel, 349
Harry, 482
James N., 482
Joseph, 482
Morris, 482
Nancy, 381
Nathan, 381, 482
Phineas, 381
Phoebe J., 350
Randall, 381, 482
Samuel E., 349
Sarah, 482
Holmes, Bartlett, 150
Flora A., 151
George N., 151
Harry F., 151
Raymond M., Capt., 224
Rose C., 151
Sarah E., 224
William P., 150, 151
Holton, Anna, 252
Edward B., 252
John, 252
Hooper, Hellen B., 157
Hope, Charles, 235
Charlotte I., 235
Fred J., 178

Helen M., 178
John C., 178, 235
Joseph, 235
Hopkins, Henry H., 265
Joseph O., 265
Lucy L., 266
Rufus, 265
Silvanus, Col., 265
House, Chauncey, 237
Jerome W., 237
Lottie B., 237
Howard, Alfred S., 370, 371
Alma K., 371
Charles R., 370
Charles S., 370
Clifford R., 371
Edwin, 371
Elizabeth M., 371
J. Franklin, 371
Thomas, 370
William P., 371
Hoxie, Albert, 446
Albert C., 430
Albert T., 429
Allan W., 489
Earle E., 430
Edward A., 429
Fannie F., 447
Fred W., 446
George H., 489
George H. (2), 489
Herbert M., 447
Lena M., 430
Lucie A., 489
Myron J., 430
Wilton H., 489
Huggard, Alward J., 326
Catherine, 326
James, 326
Hulbert, Annie E., 45
Calvin B., Rev., 45
Chauncey P., 45
Eliza L., 45
Henry W., Rev., 45
Woodward D., 45
Hunt, Alfred, 413
Edward, 413
Homer F., 414
Martha A., 414
Huntington, Benjamin F., 476
Henrietta, 476
James W., 476
Huntley, Eleanor A., 309
Elisha, 308
Emma, 399
John M., 399
John M., Jr., 399
Louis, 399
Nelson J., Capt., 308, 309
Hussey, Alice M., 456
Chester L., 455
George A., 455
Hyde, Albigence, 238, 260
Edmond P., 261
Eugene P., 260
Frederick E., 261
George A., 238
Hattie B., 261
Horatio, 207
Jabez, 207
James H., 207
Joseph, 207
Julia A., 238
Laura A., 207
Mary, 261
Samuel, 207
Theodore W., 238
William, 207

Jacob, Lena, 203
Michael, 203
Jacobson, Charles G., 423
Esther, 423
Fred F., 423
Jalbert, Adelard A., Rev., 195
Joseph, 195
Virginia, 195
James, Helena M., 214
John H., Jr., 214
John H., Sr., 214
Jarry, Damase, 478
Grace A., 479
Louis J., 478, 479
Jarvis, Aubrey W., 399, 400
Carrie E., 400
Edward, 399
Henry, 400
Nelson, 399
Jeffers, Caroline, 250
Josiah, 250
Margaret L., 250
Walter B. S., 250
Jencks, George A., 427
Harrison, 427
Inez E., 427
Otis A., 427
Jennings, Annie, 102
Carl W., 102
George G., 102
George H., Dr., 101, 102
James, 101
John G., Dr., 102
Jewett, Edward W., 97
Hazel G., 97
William R, 97
Jodoin, Azilda, 474
Edmond J., 191
Elizabeth, 191
Frederick, 191
Raymond J., 473
Roderick, 474
Johnson, Annie, 405
Dexter A., 431
Ethel L., 405
George D., 405
John H., 405
Lula M., 432
William A., 431
Jones, Agnes V., 186
Edward W., 485
Edwin, 219, 485
Ernest J., Dr., 186
Erwin M., 485
Eunice, 486
Ida, 219
John S., 186
Mary, 219
Theodore, 485
William M., 219
Jordan, Alexander, 151
Clementine E., 152
Dora, 377
Elsie, 382
Harold A., 152
James, 151, 377
John, 377
Joseph, 381
Louise A., 152
Stanley, 381
Joseph, Emanuel, 391
Frank S., 391
Mary, 391

Kaplan, Benjamin, 494
Helen, 494
Jacob, 494
John R., 494
Sarah, 494
Karoli, Henry P., 432
Isabella, 432
Peter, 432
Philip, 432
Kelley, Ellen, 304
James, 303
James N., 303
Kelly, Edward J., 463
John, 463
Katherine, 463
Katherine A., 463
Thomas F., 463
Thomas F., Jr., 463
Kendall, Fannie M., 426
Henry J., 426
John M., 426
Keppler, George A., 352
Ina F., 352
Sebastian P., 352
Keyes, Benjamin, 251
Mary, 251
Robert B., 251
Kieburg, Adolph, 416
George A., 416
Phoebe, 416
Kilbourne, Ashbel, 363
John, Serg., 363
Lucy, 363
Nathan, 363
Thomas, 363
Thomas, Serg., 363

Kimball, David, 112
Harriet, 112
Irving W., 112
Janet L., 112
John, 111
Nathan, 112
Nathan P., 112
Prosper, 112
Richard, 111
Kinmouth, Albert E., Rev., 342
Albert W., 342
Caroline H., 342
Elizabeth, 342
George E., 342
Raymond A., 342
Kinney, Andrew E., 174
Elijah C., Dr., 33
Harriet, 33, 174
Jacob W., 33
Llewellyn E., 174
Newcomb, 33
Kirby, Edward, 367
Edward, Dr., 366, 367
Mary A., 367
Kneeland, Albert G., 30
Harriet J., 30
Warren M., 30
William, 30
William A., 30
Knouse, Catherine, 461
Frederick Van R., 460, 461
William H., Rev., 460
Knowles, Catherine, 165
Charles E., 165
Edwin H., Dr., 164, 165
Isaac C., Dr., 165
James R., Dr., 165
John H., Dr., 165
Mary, 165
Mary E., 165
William C., Dr., 165
William H., 165
Koelb, Carl A., 253, 273
Carl A., Jr., 273
Caroline E., 274
Gladys C., 253
Howard E., 274
Milton C., 274
Ralph H., 253, 274
Kretzer, Conrad, 332
Conrad, Jr., 332
Lucy J., 333
Kuebler, Charles A., 189
Kate E., 190
William F., 189

LaBarre, Albert, 201
Alfred H., 201
Mary 201
Lacrox, Eliza, 425
George, 425
George J., 425
Joseph, 425
Ladd, Allison B., 60
Allison B., Jr., 60
Katherine A., 60
Lamb, Alice, 433
Denison, 433
Edith, 173
Orin F., 433
Prentice, 173
Wilfred S., 173
Lambert, Augustus, 226
Francis A., 225, 226
Rose, 226
Lane, Clinton E., 461
Ella F., 462
Henry C., 461
Langdon, Frederick S., 215
Ruth G., 215
Wilbur B., 215
Lanphear, Alice J., 445
Enoch, 444
George, 443
Horace C., Capt., 444
Horace P., 443, 444
John, 444
Nathan, 444
Ursula J., 445
LaPierre, Arnaud J., 323
Charlotte M., 323
Ellen, 323
Floyd H., 322
Henry H., 322
Leone F., Dr., 322
Lapointe, Frank J., 332
Joseph N., 331
Lionel, 332
Malvina, 332
Peter, 331
Ralph R., 332
Larkin, Alfred A., 63
Edward, 63
Ellen A., 63
Helen B., 64
Isaac G., 63
Roger, 63
Samuel, 63
William, 63
Latham, Charles H., 187
Charles H. (2), 187
Gertrude L., 343
Henry B., 187
Hiram J., 343
Lewis P., 187
Susie, 187
Lathrop, Anna H., 465
Arthur D., 139
Arthur H., 138, 139
Belle W., 436
Clara M., 247
Clayton H., 465
Clayton H. (2), 465
Earl C., 436
Edward F., 247
Elijah W., 436
Elisha, 436
Elisha, Capt., 139, 435, 483
Elizabeth Mac L., 140
Ernest A., 182
Frederick B., 484
Harvey, 139, 483
Israel, 139, 435, 483
James E., 435, 436
John, 139, 182
John, Rev., 182, 435, 483
John B., 483
Julia E., 182
Lawrence N., 436
Lebbeus, 139, 436, 483
Lulu, 483
Norman C., 483
Samuel, 139, 182, 435, 483
Thornton N. M., 247
Lawless, Alice W., 116
John J., Maj., 116
William, 116
Leahy, Daniel C., 204
Ellen L., 204
James, 204
James L., 204
Joseph F., 204
Mathew T., 204
William J., 204
LeBlanc, Francis A. 471
Francis E., 471
Margaret V., 471
LeClaire, Arthur, 233
Jean B., 232
Joseph, 232
Vittline, 232
Lee, James B., Rev., 61, 62
Madlyn L., 62
Meredith, 61, 62
Schuyler, 62
Leffingwell, Addie E., 57
Andrew, 56
Clarence F., 57
Daniel C., 56
Edith A., 57
Forrest C., 56, 57
Frederick A., 57
Gladys M., 57
Gurdon, 56
Marvin, 56
Samuel, 56
Thomas, 56
LeMoine, Alfred, 419
Amelia, 419
Augustin, 419
Lena, Helen F., 65
Hugh F., Dr., 64
Patrick H., 64
Leonard, Esther, 174
Marian E., 174
William, 173
William R., 173, 174

Lerou, Bertha B., 156
Evans M., 155
Herbert M., 155
Mary S., 156
Lester, Amos, 304
Andrew, 304
Benjamin, 304
Cecelia W., 305
Charles D., 61
Ella C., 305
Isaac A., 304
Jonathan, 304
Jonathan F., 304
Jonathan F., Jr., 305
Mary A., 61
Rose E., 61
Walter F., 61
Lewis, Caleb, 114
Edwin E., 115
John R., 115
Lulu M., 115
Mary E., 114
Rhodes K., 114
Lillibridge, Albert W., 242
Alfred G., 458
Benjamin, 241
Bonnielyon, 458
Christopher, 458
Daniel, 241
Erroll C., 242
Gardiner, 241
Lydia A., 242
Thomas, 240
Thurston B., 240, 241
Lillie, Amos J., 489
Fred B., 491
Mary, 491
Mary A., 489
William P., 489, 491
Linton, Benjamin, 236
George, 236
Margaret, 236
London, Fabyan, 464
J. Hyman, 464
Joseph, 464
Lena, 464
Sarah, 464
Lord, Fannie, 38
Henry A., 38
James A., 37
James E., 37, 38
James L., 333
John W., 38
Joseph, 290
Judah, 333
Julia A., 291
Marie F., 333
Reginald L.,
(R. Lester), 333
Reuben, 290
Thomas, 290
William, 290
Loring, George, 44
George H., 43, 44
Isaac, 44
John, 43
Lillian, 44
Thomas, 43
William, 44
William, Capt., 44
Lovett, Charles E., 484
Donald J., 484
Dwight, 484
Leonard F., 484
Lucy E., 484
Lubchanskey, Max, 264
Mildred C., 264
Morris, 264
Luce, Cathcart, 380
Ervin J., 380
James V., 380
Myrtle, 380
Lyman, Albert G., 429
Eugene, 429
Gladys E., 276
Julia E., 429
Thomas A., 429
William P., 276
William W., 276
Lynch, Eleanor, 281
Michael, 281
Thomas J., 281
Timothy, 281

MacKenzie, Donald, 415
Elizabeth, 239
Hugh, 415
Jean G., 415
Nettie V., 415
Samuel S. B., 239
William, 239
McCall, Calvin H., 430
Cornelia L., 430
David H., 430
Edward H., 430
Edwin H., 430
Royce F., 430
McCarthy, Annie, 245
Bartholomew J., 245
Jeremiah, 245
McDonald, Adelaide A., 224
Alice A., 224
Barbara, 224
Donald, 224
John W., 224
Ruth W., 224
Sarah E., 224
William, 224
McGinley, Arthur B., 128
Evelyn, 127
John, 127, 128
John, Capt., 127
John Jr., 127
Lawrence J., 128
Morgan, 128
Stephen E., Rev., 128
Thomas S., 128
Winthrop E., Dr., 127, 128
McGuigan, Clara M., Dr., 124, 125
James A., Dr., 125
John L., Dr., 125
McKenna, George R., 211
Julia, 212
Patrick, 211
McNicol, Alexander, 307
Andrew, 307
Archibald, 307
Bernice, 308
Mary, 307
William M., 307
Machett, Annette V., 338
John, 337
Robert I., Capt., 337
Macready, John J., 58
Mary, 58
Morris, 58
Madden, George F., 277
George P., 276, 277
Hugh, 277
James J., 277
Mary E., 277
Mahan, Alfred W., 379
Andrew, 378
Bryan F., 378
Margaret, 379
Nora, 379
Mahoney, Carrie, 431
Cornelius, 431
Jeremiah J., 431
Main, Calvin R., 450
Calvin R., Dr., 438, 439
Daniel H., 451
Dwight W., 259
Ezekiel, 438
Gertrude, 439
Jeremiah, 438
John L., 439, 450
Leeds, 450
Nettie M., 259
Oscar H., 259
Phebe A., 450
Samuel L., 451
Sarah H., 450
Thomas, 438
William L., 438, 450
William L. (2), 450
Maine, Abbie M., 209
Amasa M., 159
Austin A., 248
Avery A., 248
Betsey A., 159
Carroll C., 209
Charles E., Dr., 343
Charles O., Dr., 342
Chester S., 208
Crawford R., 343
Eva A., 249

Ezekiel, 208
Harriet M., 131
Hattie M., 343
Isaac, 131, 158
Isaac (2), 159
Jabis, 342
Jeremiah, 342
John, 342
John S., 208
Jonathan, 342
Phebe S., 343
Prentice, 158
Sidney O., 342
Simeon, 158
Thomas, 342
Thurman P., Dr., 131, 159
Malloy, Frank H., 319
James, 319
Madeline, 319
Manning, Ann E., 168
Arad R., 340
E. Melville, 340
Edmund N., 433
Edward, 340
Elon R., 433
Fanny, 168
Francis M., 168
Frederick F., 340, 485
George, 340
Grace, 340
Harriet C., 168
Hezekiah, 167
John L., 168
Lillian E., 433
Luther, Dr., 167
Mason, Dr., 167
Maud, 168
Nathaniel, 433
Samuel, 167
Vera H., 485
William, 167
William E., 340, 485
Maples, Josie L., 205
Judson A., 205
Louis H., 205
Marcoux, Adelard, 275
John, 275
Joseph, 275
Joseph A., 275
Josephine, 275
Marion, Delia, 459
F. O., 459
Isaac, 459
Joseph, 459
Leon P., 459
Markoff, Kopland K., Dr., 334
Lazar, 334
Sarah, 334
Marquardt, Celia, 325
Charles A., 325
George, 325
Marshall, Andrew, 3
Benjamin T., Dr., 3
Laura A., 3
Martin, Anderson (4), 446
Anderson O., Jr., 410
Anderson O., 409, 445
Andre, 66
Anna S., 446
Annie L., 410
Charles W., 446
Emma, 410
Ernest L., 446
George E., 445, 446
Haywood C., 410
Jean B., 66
John W., 410
Margaret M., 67
Ralph E., 410
William, 409
William C., 445
Marvin, Elisha, 297
Joseph, 297
Julia N., 298
Reynold, 297
William, Hon., 297, 298
William J., 298
Mastroddi, Anna, 282
John, 282
Rose, 282
Vincent, 282
Mattern, August M., 485
Daniel, 485
Frederick, 485
John, 485
Julius, 485
Katherine, 485
Maxson, Charles L., 264
David, 48
George W., 264
John, 47
Mabel, 265
Maria, 49
Paul, 48
Richard, 47
Silas, 47, 48
Silas, Jr., 49
William E., 48, 49
Meister, Almon R., 406
Charlotte, 406
John, 406
Melcer, Grace A., 367
Ralph H., 367
William, 367
Melvin, Blanche C., 239
Clarence S., 239
Erving T., 239
Thomas, 238
William, 238
William R., 239
Miller, Abraham, 493
Albert, 324
Albert B., 323
Charles D., 323
Charles E., 324
Charles W., 323
Chester, 324
Clayton G., 418, 419
Elmer E., 227, 228
Everett A., 228
Frank, 324
George, 418
George B., 418
Hannah S., 419
Hattie, 323
Israel, 493
John, 324
Margaret, 324
Oliver S., 227
Rose, 493
Ruth E., 228
Sarah E., 228
Mills, Annah M., 408
George A., 408
Miner, Annie E. (Ethel), 164
Charles, 164
Christopher, 164
Elias, 164, 282
Ephraim, 164
Erastus D., 164, 282
Fanny F., 164
Fanny M., 164
George W., 430
Henry, 164
Herman E., 163, 164
James, 164
Jane, 282
Lodowick, 164
Mary A., 430
Palmer W., 430
Thomas, 164
William, 164
Moran, John A., 405
Mary E., 405
Walter P., 405
Morgan, Charles F., 172
Charles F., Jr., 172
Edward G., 403
James, 403
James, Capt., 403
John A., Capt., 403
Minda, 172
Nicholas, 403
Sarah, 404
Youngs, 403
Morin, Adelard, 487
Alma, 487
Henry, 487
Pierre, 487
Morse, George, 439, 440
Harry J., 439, 440
May M., 440
Mousley, Daisy, 197
Frank C., 197
Hattie E., 198
Louis H., 197

Moxley, Francis G., 280
George W., 280
Herbert V., 279, 280
Joseph, 279
Mary E., 280
Samuel, 279
William, 279
Mullen, Joseph M., 330
Martin E., Dr., 330
Mary E., 330
Müller, August, 202
August O., 202
Elizabeth, 202
Frank, 202
Henry A., 202
Munz, Charlotte A., 425
Jacob, 425
John J., 425
Murphey, George O., 369
Lillian G., 370
Oscar F., 369
Murphy, Alice M., 394
Cornelius, 393
Elizabeth N., 394
Isabelle A., 394
John H., 453
Mary A., 453
Wallin T., 453
William P., 394

Nash, Arthur N., 210, 211
Nathan E., 210
Nettie H., 211
Newbury, Adelaide I., 492
Christopher G., 492
Edwina D., 492
Horace M., 492
Newman, Daniel, 218
John, 488
John H., 218
Leona, 488
Margaret A., 218
Thomas, 488
Nielson, Christian, 479
Frederick, 479
Helma G., 479
Noble, John H., 337
Robert H., 337
Ruth, 337
Norton, Atta B., 272
Clarence H., 271, 272
Daniel I., 272
David, 271
Edward H., 272
Samuel S., 271
Noyes, Byron, 488
Elsie, 488
George, 488
John D. (1), 488
John D. (2), 488
William, 488
William P., 488

Oat, Jane M., 47
Lewis A., 47
William H., 47
O'Brien, Catherine, 258
Daniel, 258
Edward N., 489
Elizabeth, 186
Gretchen, 244
James E., Rev., 258
John T., 489
Mary J., 489
Terence V., 244
William, 186
William T., Rev., 186
Oldread, Ethel, 376
Robert, 375
Walter A., 375
Olsen, Hulda, 284
Ole, 283
Torres, 283, 284
Osgood, Artemas, 77
Hugh H., Hon., 76, 77
Mary R., 78
Osten,, Frank, 394
James M., 394
Sarah, 394
Ostman, Frederick, 260
Frederick J., 260
Mabel B., 260
Otis, Amos T. (A. Thatcher), 388, 389
Amos T., Jr., 388
Josephine, 389
Robert, 389
Pahlberg, Alfred T., 470
Charlotte E., 470
Jacob A., 469
John E., 469
Mary L., 469
Palmer, Abel, 159
Adelaide R., 424
Alden, Maj., 247
Caius C., 159, 160
Cecil [illegible], 160
Charles B., 101, 196
Cora H., 387
Ellen, [illegible]
Emma J., 196
Eugene, 247
Fannie E., 196
Frank E., 399, 424
George, 159, 423
George B., 101, 379
George D., 101, 379
Gershom, 159, 423
Gideon, 423
Helen G., 399
Henry R., 246, 247
Joseph, Dr., 159
Katherine J., 101
Mary A., 379
Mary C., 160
Mary P., 160
Nancy L., 247
Peleg, 196
Randall W., 423, 424
Reuben, 423
Simeon, 196
Sophia, 387
Walter, 159, 247, 423
Warren W., 387
William, 101, 379
William H., 399, 423
William W., 387
Paquette, Albert E., 263, 264
Corrinne, 264
Paul, 264
Park, Agnes, 256
Amos, 257
Parker, Ebenezer F., 122
Fannie T., 123
John, 122
John F., 122, 123
Joseph, 122
Mary H., 358
Mary M., 358
Myra F., 123
Nelson, 358
Richard S., 357
Robert, 122
Timothy, Capt., 122
William, 357
Paton, George, 426
Mary B., 426
Robert, 426
Payne, Anna B., 203
Charles W., Serg., 108
Jeannie C., 109
John W., Rev., 203
Morris B., Maj., 108
Wallace H., 203
Peabody, Annie, 418
Austin, 434
Charles H., 428, 434
Charles W., 434
Elmer, 434
George W., 418
Hadley L., 418
Joseph, 428, 434
Joseph, Jr., 434
Josephine, 428
Leslie L., 418
Marietta, 434
Raymond A., 428
Thomas, 418
Peck, Carlos C., 330
Daniel M., 474, 475
Eugene B., 330
George, 474
Harriett E., 474
Henry G., 382
Lizzie M., 383
Mabel L., 383
Mary, 330

Mary E., 206
Olmstead, 475
Richard E., 330
Seth L., 382
Vilette M., 383
William E., 205
William E., Jr., 205, 206

Peckham, Anna E., 328
Charles H., Rev., 55
Charles S., 472
Charlotte E., 472
Edward H., 55
Everett S., 472
Grace G., 55
Howard C., 328
Ivy B., 328
Jennie, 55
John O. (1), 328
John O. (2), 328
Joseph T., 328
Mary, 472
Robert M., 328
Stephen, 472
Peloquinn, Charles, 259
Joseph C., 259
Mary, 259
Pendleton, Blanche, 330
Claudius V., 329
Claudius V., Jr., 329
Perkins, Albert W., 119
Charles, 187
Charles A., 467
Charles C., 119
Clement I., 187
Emerson, 188
Fannie C., 467
Frank C., 467
Hattie S., 120
John, 467
Jonathan, 187
Josiah, 187
Julia A., 467
Mary, 188
Phineas, 119
Samuel, 467
Servillian, 119
Perry, Charles E., 377
Katherine, 377
Lawrence W., 377
Peterson, Henrietta L., 282
Stavros F., 282
Phillips, Charles E., 453
Charles H., 452
Evelyn, 453
Mabel H., 453
Ralph, 452
Pierce, Benjamin B., 80
Moses, 80
Susan, 80
Pitcher, Charles L., 209
David, 209
David W., 209, 210
Edna, 210
Elmer E., 10
George E., 9
George W., 9
Lyman, 209
Marian S., 10
Potter, Bertha I., 423
Caleb, 422
David, 422
Elisha, 422
Incom, 422
John, 422, 423
Nathaniel, 422
Paul B., 423
William, 422
Pratte, Louis, 204
Louis I., Dr., 204
Mary N., 205
Prentice, Alice M., 327
Amos, 71
Amos W., Hon., 70, 71
Charles W., 326, 327
Eleazer, 71
Ephraim, 326, 327
Hannah E., 72
Harry E., 326, 327
John, 71
Joseph, 71
Leonard C., 327
Mary, 327
Samuel, 71
Thomas, 71
Thomas, Capt., 71, 326
Prentis, Benjamin, Capt., 249
Eldredge P., 249
Olive, 249
Samuel M., 249
Prince, Emma, 132
Samuel, 132
Samuel V (S. Victor), Hon., 132, 133
Pullen, Annie L., 22
Benedict C., 22
Frank H., 22
Weston, 22
Weston C., 22
Purdy, Alexander M., Dr., 26
Alva B., Rev., 26
Carrie, 26
John, 26

Quinlan, John C., 200
Nellie M., 200
Patrick L., 200
Quinley, Augusta A., 299
David C., Capt., 298
David T., 298
Quinn, Annie, 384
James A., 384
John, 57
John F. X., Rev., 57
John J., 384
Maria, 57
Michael, 384
Race, A. Rockwell, 490
Frederick H., 490
Frederick H., Jr., 490
Henry A., 490
Jeannette T., 490
Rainville, Elizabeth, 328
Frederic E., Dr., 328
Paul, 328
Rathbun (Rathbone), Arthur E., 298
Carlotta, 392
Elijah, 391, 400, 401
Everett E., 298
Frederick, 391
Harriet E., 298
Henry A., 298
James W., 391
Jerome B., 298
John, 400
Mary E., 401
Richard, 401
Samuel, 400, 401
Samuel, Capt., 391, 400, 401
Samuel O., Capt., 400, 401
Stella, 392
William H., 391
William O., 400, 401
Ravenell, Anna, 402
Exeverie J., Jr., 402
Joseph, 402
Raymond, Charles L., 292
Edward I., 292
Georgette, 293
Levi Q., 292
May E., 293
Millie, 292
Thaddeus K., 292
Redden, Coleman, 215
Mary C., 215
Michael M., 214
William M., 214
Reeves, Ida L., 56
Peter, 56
Stephen H., 56
Reynolds, Charles H., 460
Clarence O., 460
Emma A., 460
Mary E., 254
Orville A., 460
Thomas W., 254
William F., 254
Rice, Austin D., 459
David A., 458, 459
Flora, 459
James, 458
James H., 459
John, 459
Mary D., 459
Thomas, 459
William, 459
Richards, Herbert A., 246
Iva M., 246

John H., 246
Richmond, Dwight B., 454
Edmund, 454
Edward, 295
Ernest A., 296
Harold A., 296
Henry A., 295, 296
John, 295
John H., 296
John M., 295
Juliette, 296
Lucy E., 296
Mary D., 296
Rose, 454
Roy B., 455
Stephen, 295
William R., 296
Riel, Ambrose, 473
Etienne, 473
Mary, 473
Neol, 473
Ring, Charles B., 455
David, 455
Joseph F., 455
M Bernard, 455
Mary, 455
Mary B. P., 455
Michael B., 455
Rioux, Ellen, 235
Francis, 235
Thomas A., 235
Rist, Albert A., 479
Ella M., 479
Isaac S., 479
Rivers, Joseph, 237
Joseph, Jr., 237
Marie, 237
Robinson, Catherine V., 338
Frances R., 147
George, 338
Harold T., 147
Joseph, 338
Joseph, Dr., 338
Mary H., 338
Thomas A., 147
Thomas B., 147
Rodier, Emma, 256
Ernest O., 256
Oliver, 256
Rodman, Fred A., 426
Frederick M., 426
Mary E., 426
Rogers, David, Dr., 87
Elford P., 308
Henry A., 4, 5
James, 87
John, 87
Jonathan, 4
Minnie E., 308
Samuel, 308
Samuel, Jr., 308
Susie B., 5
Sybil, 308
Uriah, Dr., 87
Rohmeling, Frederick, 469
Frederick, Jr., 468, 469
Jeanette, 469
Roode, Carrie E., 135
Frances, 134
Francis M., 135
Joseph, 134
Joseph, Jr., 134
Minnie, 135
Solomon, 134
Rose, Adam, 467
Bessie R., 468
Charles H., 467
Earl N., 468
John H., 467, 468
Roy, Arthur, 240
Arthur, Jr., 240
George, 240
John, 240
Mary, 240
Royall, Nathaniel B., 461
Ralph, 461
Rozycki, Anna, 494
Joseph, 494
Martin, 494
Rubin, Esaak, 492
Esther, 493
Hyman, 492
Russell, Albert E., 487
Benjamin F., 301
Claude C., 301
Ellen, 301
Elmer W., 487
Ernest C., 301
Frank W., 301
Lester W., 487
Mahlon L., 487
Marion C., 301
Mattie, 487

Santacroce, Frank, 484
James, 484
Mary, 484
Saxton, Alice D., 51
Charles A., 51
Eleanor S., 52
Lewis J. (L. Henry), 50
Louis H., 51
Minnie E., 51
Sarah, 51
Schröder, Henry C., 280
Jochiam, 280
John H. W., 280
Louisa R., 280
Maria W., 280
Wilhelmina D., 280
Scott, Abbey J., 303
Frank P., 382
George H., 303
Henkle S., 303
Malcolm Mac F., 302
Margaret, 382
William F., 382
Sellas, Alexandra, 479
James, 480
John K., 479
Peter, 479
Shalett, Fannie, 331
Haddie, 331
Harry M., 331
Jacob, 331
Moses, 331
Shandeor, Frank, 494
Peter J., 494
Sarah, 494
Shannon, Catherine F., 316
Ella C., 316
James B., 316
John H. (J. Henry), 317
Katherine F., 316
Mary G., 316
Patrick, 316
Thomas I., Dr., 316
Shea, Abbie E., 254
James H., Sr., 254
Timothy, 254
Shedd, Abby P., 352
Arthur E., 352
Frances, 352
George V., 351
Mary E., 352
Varnum A., 351
Sheffield, Amos, 45, 334
Edmund, 45
Harriett P., 46
John, Rev., 46, 334
Lucius T. (L. Tracy), 46
Lucius T., Jr., 46
Margaret D., 334
Mary J., 46
Nathaniel L., 334
Nathaniel L., Jr., 334
Washington K.(W.Kyle), 46
Washington W., Dr., 46
Silva, Anthony, 455
Hattie M., 455
John C., 455
Sinay, Albert J., Dr., 338, 339
Alexander, 338
Bessie T., 339
Sisk, Frank A., 433
Julia, 434
Thomas, 433
Thomas H., 433
Smiddy, Charles, 275
Johana, 275
Nellie, 275
William, 275
Smith, Annie, 66
Bertram G., 478

Bessie A., 372
Charles H., 231
Denison, 65
Dwight E., 478
Edith I., 478
Edmund B., 350
Elisha, 350
Elisha (2), 350
Ella, 350
Ella L., 350
F. Russell, 157
Florence, 157
Frank H., 156
Frank R., 190
Frederick M., 65
Frederick M., Jr., 66
Harriet, 372
Henrietta I., 190
Henry A., 372
Henry H., 66
James, 372
Jeannette F., 267
John B., 217
John O., 156
Leslie E., 478
Lillian M., 217
Lyman, 372
Lyman B., 372
Lyman E., 372
Marcella A., 214
Martha M., 157
Mary E., 232
Nathan, 65
Nathan D., 65
Nathan H., 66
Nehemiah, 65
Nehemiah, Rev., 65, 350
Olive A., 478
Oliver, 65
Oliver R., 231
Prentice P., 156
Reuben P., 267
Richard B., 66
Robert M., 217
Sarah, 350
Tryon, 213
Willard F., 213
William, 478
William W., 267
Soule, Edith, 155
Harriet A., 155
Ivory H., 155
Martha P., 155
William, Dr., 155
William O., 155
Sparks, Alfred, 278
George E., 278
Gertrude J., 278
Spencer, Charles E., 468
Edna, 468
Frank W., 468
Henry, 424
Henry J., 424
Lena C., 424
Spicer, Anna M., 11
Edmund, Capt., 11
Edward, 10
Frank, 12
John, 10, 11
John S. (J. Sands), 10, 11
John W., 12
Joseph E., 12
Peter, 10
Stanton, Amy L., 67
Elizabeth S., 315
Frances L., 67
George H., 67
Georgie C., 67
Howard L., 67
John, 314
John G., Dr., 314
Kathrine K., 67
Starr, Charles H., 404
Domenick, 113
Frederick A., 113
George E., 219
Harold H., 365
Hattie, 114
Henry L., 404
Lafayette H., 404
Lafayette W., 404
Marion G., 220
Richard M., 220
Roland G., 220
Rose, 404
Vine W., 404
Willard W., 404
William S., 219
Stebbins, Alfred L., 409
Henry D., 409
Mabel A., 409
William H., 409
Sterling, Gilbert B., 376
James A., 376
John R., 376
John R., Jr., 376
Minnie A., 376
Simon S., 376
Stevens, Clarence E., 337
Isabel, 336
John C., 336
Roswell C., 336
William, 336
Steward, Franklin W., 401
Livy, 401
Mary, 402
Willis G., 401
Stewart, Lyman, 466
Mary A., 466
Matilda J., 257
Maud, 466
Owen L., 466
Samuel E., 257
Samuel E., Jr., 257
Stoddard, Albert, 395
Amy J., 395
Anna, 395
Artis Z., 228
Bessie A., 395
Edgar C., 258
Ichabod, 228
James A., 395
James B., 258
Jessica S., 258
Sarah F., 258
Seymour A., 228
Stephen D., 395
Stephen M., 395
Stoll, Charles F., 262
Charles R., 262
Louisa, 262
Stone, George H., 271
George W., 271
Ruth, 271
Sullivan, Daniel, 450
Eileen K., 279
Elizabeth, 279
Eugene R., 175
James T., 175
Jeremiah J., 278, 279
Jerome J., 279
John P., 278
John S., 174, 175
Lucy A., 175
Marion E., 279
Mary R., 175
Michael L., 175
Michael O., 174
Patrick J., 175
Rose, 449
Sussler, David, Dr., 207, 208
Frank, 207
Viola, 207
Swain, Frances M., 273
George W., 273
Orrin L., 273
Swan, Amos C., 97
Charles, 97
Coddington B., 97
Coddington W., 97
Edna M., 98
Jennie P., 97
John, 97
LeRoy A., Lieut., 98
Richard, 97
Robert, 97
William, 97
Sweeney, Bridget, 244
James, 244
John, 244
John J., 361
Julia A., 361
Patrick F., 361
Sweet, Benoni, 198
Charles, Dr., 198
Charles, Jr., 198

Constant, 374
Ellen M., 375
Herbert W., 198
James, 198
James O., 374
Katherine, 198
Swinney, Belinda R., 301
Ethan E., 300
Herbert M., 300

Tanner, Abel, 35
Abel P., 35
Emma B., 36
Tarrant, Mary, 347
Nicholas, 347
Richard L., 347
Taylor, Frederick N., 362, 363
Hannah M., 364
John B., 363
John C., Dr., 363
Nelson, 363
William, 362
Tefft, Elmer, 284
Luther C., 284
Mabel, 284
Terry, David, 491
David K., 491
Frank B., 491
Susan A., 491
Tetreault, George H., 412, 413
Joseph, 413
Marie, 413
Thompson, Aaron, 169
Albert, 169
Benjamin, 169
Charles A., 492
Clarence G., Dr., 361
Clarence W., 263
Clifford B., 169
Edwin L., 388
Ellen, 361
Eugene W., 263
Everett C., 492
George, 361
George, Dr., 388
Hartwell G., Dr., 388
Helen G., 388
James, 388
John, 388
Laura A., 492
Marcia S., 170
Mary, 388
Milton, 388
Minnie F., 263
Throop, Henry H., 428
Mary S., 428
Sands W., 428
Thumm, Bertha, 233
Frederick G., 233
Gustave, 233
Tingley, Ethel F., 33
John H., 32
William H., 32
Witter K., Dr., 31, 32
Tinker, Amy E., 265
Bertha, 349
Carrie J., 349
Charles B., 265, 349
Matthew A., 265, 348
Matthew A. (2), 348
Ruth, 349
Stanley, 349
William, 348
William R., 349
Tirrell, Agnes H., 58
Eben, Rev., 58
Henry A., 58
Tooker, Mary J., 373
Meritt E., 372
William B., 372
Tracy, Ada R., 413
Almond, 413
Andrew, 99
Bertha, 100
Freeman, 99
Jeremiah, 99
Jesse, 99
John H., 99
John R., 99
Mabel A., 413
Oliver R., 413
Rose, 100
Thomas, 99
Thomas, Lieut., 99
Trail, Esther, 306
M. Henry, 306
Marcus, 306
Ruth R., 306
Stanley R., 306
Tripp, Arthur D., 324, 325
Henry D., 325
John, 324
Martha B., 325
Peregrine, 324
Troland, Roberta, 131
Thomas E., Capt., 130
Thomas H., 130
Trumbull, Daniel L., 82
David, 81, 84
John, 81, 84
John M., 81
Jonathan, 81, 82
Jonathan, Jr., 83
Jonathan G. W., 81
Joseph, 81, 82
Tucker, Edgar J., 486
Ezekiel J., 486
Laura V., 486
Leroy, 486
Louise, 486
Turnbill, Anna, 460
David J., 459, 460
William, 460
Turner, Charles G., 182
Giles, 182
Ianthe, 183
Twist, Carrie V., 254
Charles J., 253
Charles S., 253
Utley, Albert T., 277
John C., 277
Mary J., 277

Van Hoff, Frink, 437
Frink, Jr., 437
Frink G., 437
Harry E., 437
Leonora B., 437
William, 437
William A., 437
Vaughn, A. N. H., 375
Rena E., 375
Veal, Ruth E., 178
William J., 177
William T., Dr., 177
Vignot, Alfred, 132
Ellen, 132
Henry H., 132
Vining, Albert L., 415
Frank A., 415
Frank L., 415
Jennie E., 415
Pearly H., 415

Wade, Abby, 491
James L., 491
Jared, 491
Willis, 491
Walbridge, Leander, 225
Lenora M., 225
Richard E., 225
William E., 225
William S., 225
Walker, Anna J., 418
Frank B., 418
Ward, Albert A., 465
Edith F., 465
Harrison H., 465
John P., 465
Paul A., 465
Thomas H., 465
Waterman, Andrew, 27
Andrew, Capt., 27
Elisha, 27
Elisha, Lieut., 27
Ella M., 28
Robert, 27
Thomas, 27
Waters, Henry M., 154
Louis F., 154
Milo R., 154
Myra A., 155
Rachael, 154
Watson, Charles H., 299
George W., 299
Herbert, 396
Herbert C., 396
J. Lewis, 299
Jeffery, 396
John, 299
John W., 299
Marian, 299

Mary E., 396
Walter, 396
William R., 299
Weaver, Ella, 411
Melger, 411
William, 411
Wellington, George, 463
Joseph W., 463
Mary W., 463
Wells, Angeline, 21
Charles A., 21
Charles F., 21
David A., Hon., 95
Ellen A., 96
Foster P., 21
Mary S., 96
Welte, Annie E., 356
Carl M., 354, 355
Emil, 354
Emma M., 354, 355
West, Edwin, 267
Edwin E., 267
Ella, 268
Herbert, 268
Sarah A., 267
William, 267
Wetmore, Margaret E., 219
Thomas T., 219
Thomas T., Jr., 218
Whaley, Emma B., 315
Laura R., 315
William, 315
Wheeler, Albert L., 389
Amos B., 353
Arthur G., 181
Arthur G. (2), 181
Caroline, 262
Carrie, 150
Carrie M., 150
Charles H., 294, 352, 353
Charles H., Jr., 353
Clara P., 353
Donald B., 181
Eleazer, 353
Emma L., 353
Fernando, 181, 367, 368
Florence, 302
Frances M., 9
Frank S., 353
George A., 181
Grace D., 9
Hiram W., 148
Horace N., 294
Isaac, 181, 293, 368
John G., 293, 294
Jonathan, 293
Joseph, 181, 368
Josie E., 369
Lester, 293
Lucy A., 9
Marian M., 150
Mary, 181
Mary H., 389
Mary M., 262
Mary S., 181
Minnie A., 353
Nelson F., 181
Nelson H., 181, 368
Noyes D., 262
Percy A., 302
Ralph C., 148, 149
Ralph C., Jr., 150
Richard, 8, 148, 181, 293, 368
Richard A., 8
Sadie, 295
Samuel, 181, 368
Silas, 148
Silas B., 148, 149
Thomas, 8, 148, 181, 293, 367
Thomas E., 262
Vivian P., 369
William, 293
William A., 302
William E., 294
William E., Jr., 294
William F., 389
William U., 302
Whitman, Bessie M., 374
Clarence D., 373
Hugh R., 373, 374
Wight, Clara L., 459
Howard J., 459
Howard M., 459
Wilbur, Ida M., 188
James T., 188
Ralph C., 188
Robert A., 188
Thomas, 188
Wilcox, Abram, 3
Archibald A., 393
Augusta L., 452
Byron E., 452
Calvin, 386
Calvin E., 386
Denison E., 64
Elias, 451
Elias, Capt., 64
Elnathan M., 64
Emily M., 4
Erroll K., 4
Frank, 164
Frank A., 4
George S., 451
George W., 64
Gladys I., 64
Harold A., 64
Horace G., 451
James G., 393
Jesse, 451
Jesse H., 64
Jesse R., 386
John, Maj., 3
Lowell J., 4
Lynton G., 393
Mabel, 4
Mary E., 164
Mattie R., 386
Mina B., 64
Moses H., 64
Nellie, 393
Rosa S., 386
Ruth R., 452
Sidney B., 393
Susan R., 4
Thomas, 386
Walter E., 64
William A., 451, 452
William B., 3
Williams, Charles M., 364
Ephraim M., 364
Hazel, 364
Henry, 364
Julian LaP., 364
Leonard F., 445
Mabel C., 445
Robert, 364
Roger, 364
William, 445
Wilson, James, 265
Jennie S., 265
John H., 265
Winship, Bessie, 122
Ernest O., Dr., 121
John F., 121
Wolfe, Bessie, 226
Charles H., Capt., 226
Thomas E., Capt., 226
Woodmansee, Eunice C., 163
James, 163
Mary P., 163
Roswell P., 163
Worth, Joseph C., 137
Joseph C., Jr., 137
Olive, 137

Yerrington, Alice, 469
Catherine, 395
Charles E., 394
Edgar E., 394
Edwin F., 394, 469
Erastus W., 394
George R., 394
James B., 394
John F., 394, 469
York, Courtland B., 270
James, 270
Lena S., 271
William, 270
William, Jr., 270
Young, Alexander, 185
Charles, 354
Elizabeth C., 185
James M., 185
James M., Jr., 185
John B., 185
Marion L., 185
Phillipena T. F., 354